# Directory of Financial Aids for Women 2007-2009

# RSP FINANCIAL AID DIRECTORIES
# OF INTEREST TO WOMEN

### College Student's Guide to Merit and Other No-Need Funding, 2007-2009
Selected as one of the "Outstanding Titles of the Year" by *Choice,* this directory describes 1,300 no-need funding opportunities for college students. 464 pages. ISBN 1-58841-166-4. $32.50, plus $6 shipping.

### Directory of Financial Aids for Women, 2007-2009
More than 1,500 funding programs set aside for women are described in this biennial directory, which *School Library Journal* calls "the cream of the crop." 560 pages. ISBN 1-58841-167-2. $45, plus $6 shipping.

### Financial Aid for African Americans, 2006-2008
More than 1,300 scholarships, fellowships, grants, and internships open to African Americans are described in this award-winning directory. 538 pages. ISBN 1-58841-133-8. $40, plus $6 shipping.

### Financial Aid for Asian Americans, 2006-2008
This is the source to use if you are looking for financial aid for Asian Americans; nearly 1,000 funding opportunities are described. 356 pages. ISBN 1-58841-134-6. $37.50, plus $6 shipping.

### Financial Aid for Hispanic Americans, 2006-2008
Nearly 1,300 funding programs open to Americans of Mexican, Puerto Rican, Central American, or other Latin American heritage are described here. 492 pages. ISBN 1-58841-135-4. $40, plus $6 shipping.

### Financial Aid for Native Americans, 2006-2008
Detailed information is provided on 1,300 funding opportunities open to American Indians, Native Alaskans, and Native Pacific Islanders. 526 pages. ISBN 1-58841-136-2. $42.50, plus $6 shipping.

### Financial Aid for Research and Creative Activities Abroad, 2006-2008
Described here are more than 1,000 scholarships, fellowships, grants, etc. available to support research, professional, or creative activities abroad. 388 pages. ISBN 1-58841-107-9. $45, plus $6 shipping.

### Financial Aid for Study and Training Abroad, 2006-2008
This directory, which *Children's Bookwatch* calls "invaluable," describes nearly 1,000 financial aid opportunities available to support study abroad. 354 pages. ISBN 1-58841-094-3. $39.50, plus $6 shipping.

### Financial Aid for the Disabled and Their Families, 2006-2008
Named one of the "Best Reference Books of the Year" by *Library Journal,* this directory describes in detail more than 1,200 funding opportunities. 502 pages. ISBN 1-58841-148-6. $40, plus $6 shipping.

### Financial Aid for Veterans, Military Personnel, and Their Dependents, 2006-2008
According to *Reference Book Review,* this directory (with its 1,100 entries) is "the most comprehensive guide available on the subject." 443 pages. ISBN 1-58841-143-5. $40, plus $6 shipping.

### High School Senior's Guide to Merit and Other No-Need Funding, 2007-2009
Here's your guide to 1,100 funding programs that *never* look at income level when making awards to college-bound high school seniors. 436 pages. ISBN 1-58841-165-6. $29.95, plus $6 shipping.

### How to Pay for Your Degree in Education & Related Fields, 2006-2008
Here's hundreds of funding opportunities to support undergraduate and graduate students preparing for a career in teaching, guidance, etc. 290 pages. ISBN 1-58841-146-X. $30, plus $6 shipping.

### Money for Christian College Students, 2007-2009
This is the only directory to describe nearly 800 funding opportunities available to support Christian students working on an undergraduate or graduate degree (secular or religious). 238 pages. ISBN 1-58841-169-9. $30, plus $6 shipping.

### Money for Graduate Students in the Social & Behavioral Sciences, 2007-2009
Described here are the 1,100 biggest and best funding opportunities available to students working on a graduate degree in the social or behavioral sciences. 332 pages. ISBN 1-58841-173-7. $42.50, plus $6 shipping.

### RSP Funding for Nursing Students, 2006-2008
You'll find 900 scholarships, fellowships, loans, grants, and awards here that can be used for study, research, professional, or other nursing activities. 290 pages. ISBN 1-58841-157-5. $30, plus $6 shipping.

# Directory of Financial Aids for Women 2007-2009

**Gail Ann Schlachter**
**R. David Weber**

A List of: Scholarships, Fellowships, Loans, Grants, Awards, and Internships Available Primarily or Exclusively for Women

**Reference Service Press**
El Dorado Hills, California

**Library of Congress Cataloging in Publication Data**

Schlachter, Gail A.
    Directory of financial aids for women, 2007-2009
    Includes indexes.
    1. Women—United States—Scholarships, fellowships, etc.—Directories. 2. Grants-in-aid—United States—Directories. 3. Credit—United States—Directories. I. Title.
LB2338.5342 2110        378'.30'2573
ISBN 10: 1588411672
ISBN 13: 9781588411679
ISSN 0732-5215


10 9 8 7 6 5 4 3 2 1

**Reference Service Press (RSP)** began in 1977 with a single financial aid publication *(The Directory of Financial Aids for Women)* and now specializes in the development of financial aid resources in multiple formats, including books, large print books, disks, CD-ROMs, print-on-demand reports, eBooks, and online sources. Long recognized as a leader in the field, RSP has been called by the *Simba Report on Directory Publishing* "a true success in the world of independent directory publishers." Both Kaplan Educational Centers and Military.com have hailed RSP as "the leading authority on scholarships."

**Reference Service Press**
**El Dorado Hills Business Park**
**5000 Windplay Drive, Suite 4**
**El Dorado Hills, CA 95762-9319**
    **(916) 939-9620**
    **Fax: (916) 939-9626**
    **E-mail: info@rspfunding.com**
**Visit our web site: www.rspfunding.com**


Manufactured in the United States of America

Price: $45.00, plus $6 shipping.

**ACADEMIC INSTITUTIONS, LIBRARIES, ORGANIZATIONS AND OTHER QUANTITY BUYERS:**
Discounts on this book are available for bulk purchases. Write or call for information on our discount programs.

# Contents

# Introduction

## HOW THE DIRECTORY HAS GROWN IN THE PAST THIRTY YEARS

In 1977 and 1978, while we were furiously researching, writing, editing, and updating entries for the very first edition of the *Directory of Financial Aids for Women,* major events were occurring that would have a lasting effect on the role of women in American society:

- The first National Women's Conference was held in Houston, Texas, attended by 20,000 women who passed the landmark National Plan of Action.

- The National Coalition Against Domestic Violence was established.

- The Air Force graduated its first women pilots.

- Congress passed the Pregnancy Discrimination Act, prohibiting discrimination against pregnant women in all areas of employment.

- Congress allocated $5 million to the Department of Labor to set up centers for displaced homemakers.

- The Philadelphia Mint began stamping the Susan B. Anthony dollar.

- Dianne Feinstein became the first female mayor of San Francisco, replacing the assassinated George Moscone.

- Margaret Thatcher was chosen to become Britain's first female prime minister.

- Hanna Gray was named president of the University of Chicago, becoming the first woman to lead a major America university.

But, from our point of view, the most significant development occurred in the field of higher education. In 1978, for the first time ever, more women than men entered American colleges and universities. We knew these women would face many challenges, particularly financial ones. Numerous studies had shown that, historically, when women competed again men for college aid, they were notably unsuccessful. We believed we could help to level this funding playing field by compiling the first-ever listing of financial aid opportunities open primarily or exclusively to women. And, so, the *Directory of Financial Aids for Women* was launched. Finally, women could find out about the hundreds of funding opportunities that were available just for them!

We were right. The directory did make a difference. Orders poured in. Women wrote to us about their successes. The book was featured in numerous magazines, television shows, bibliographic guides, and reviewing sources. It became clear to us at Reference Service Press that there was an continuing need for this type of compilation. So, in 1980, we made a commitment to collect, organize, and disseminate—on an on-going basis—the most current and accurate information available on all types of funding opportunities open to women.

To accomplish this goal over the years, we have had to become sophisticated information sleuths, tracking down all possible leads, identifying even the slightest changes to existing programs, finding new sources of funding opportunities for women, and constantly expanding and updating the electronic database used to prepare each new biennial edition of the *Directory of Financial Aids for Women.* The results have been dramatic, especially when the first (1978) edition is compared, side-by-side, to this issue (2007-2009). In the past quarter century, the directory has tripled in size, growing from a modest 300 programs (200 pages) to the staggering 1,511 opportunities described in the 2007-2009 edition's more than 500 pages. Access to the information has advanced significantly as well, going beyond the simple program title listing in the first edition (with basic subject, geographic, and sponsor indexes) to a user-friendly grouping of records by program type (scholarships, fellowships, etc.) and six detailed and sub-divided indexes in the latest edition, making it possible to search the information by all current, variant, and former program titles; every sponsor and administering organization; each location where an applicant must live; every place where the money can be spent; hundreds of specific subject fields; and month-by-month deadline dates.

Even the physical appearance of the two editions is strikingly different. In 1978, we laboriously photocopied program information, cut and pasted the draft, and then produced the final "camera-ready" version on an IBM Selectric typewriter. If you look carefully in the first edition, you'll be able to see where we used White-Out and correction tape! In contrast, the entries in the 2007-2009 edition have been carefully selected from our database of 27,000 unique funding records, extensively reviewed electronically by editors in geographically-dispersed locations, formatted using a layout and font chosen specifically for maximum utility, and produced simultaneously in both book and eBook versions.

One thing that hasn't changed during the past 30 years, however, is our passionate commitment to making a difference. Little did we realize, when we first published the *Directory of Financial Aids for Women* in 1978, that we had taken the initial steps on what would become a life-long search for unique funding opportunities available specifically to special needs groups. And though our focus has broadened beyond women and our output has expanded beyond books, we have never lost sight of the fact that financial need is not just one of our publishing interests. It is and will be our only business. Perhaps that's why *The Simba Report on Directory Publishing* called Reference Service Press "a true success in the world of independent directory publishers" and why both Kaplan Educational Centers and Military.com have hailed the company as "the leading authority on scholarships."

## THE PURPOSE OF THE 2007-2009 EDITION

Currently, billions of dollars in financial aid are available primarily or exclusively for women. In fact, more money is available today than ever before. This funding is open to applicants at any level (high school through postdoctoral and professional) for study, research, travel, training, career development, or innovative effort. While numerous directories have been prepared to identify and describe general financial aid programs (those open to both men and women), they have never covered more than a small portion of the programs designed primarily or exclusively for women. As a result, many advisors, librarians, scholars, researchers, and students have not been aware of the impressive array of financial aid programs established with women in mind. Now, with the 2007-2009 edition of the *Directory of Financial Aids for Women,* up-to-date and comprehensive information is available in a single source about the special resources set aside for women.

The unique value of the *Directory* has been highly praised by the reviewers. Here are just some of the rave reviews:

- "The title is a must-purchase guide." —*American Reference Books Annual*

- "Nobody does a better job...a great resource and highly recommended."
  —*College Spotlight*

- "The only current source of information on financial aid specifically for
  women...an essential and reasonably priced purchase." —*Reference Books
  Bulletin*

- "The quintessential acquisition for public libraries of all sizes...feminists, homemakers, and women everywhere will welcome this book, since it is so well-done and simple to use." —*Small Press*

- "The variety of programs is amazing...an essential purchase...has become the standard source for information on scholarships, fellowships, loans, grants, awards, and internships available primarily to women." —*Library Journal*

Previous editions of the directory were selected as the "cream of the crop" in *School Library Journal's* "Reference Round-Up;" were included in *Recommended Reference Books for Small and Medium-sized Libraries and Media Centers;* were featured in *Glamour, Good Housekeeping, New Woman,* and *Teen* magazines; and were selected as the "Best of the Best" in education and career information print materials by members of the National Education and Information Center Advisory Committee. In the view of The Grantsmanship Center, "No organization interested in serving women should be without this directory!"

## THE EXTENT OF UPDATING IN THE 2007-2009 EDITION

The preparation of each new edition of the *Directory of Financial Aids for Women* involves extensive updating and revision. To insure that the information included in the *Directory* is both reliable and current, the editors at Reference Service Press 1) review and update all women-related programs currently in our funding database and 2) search exhaustively for new program leads in a variety of sources, including printed directories, news reports, journals, newsletters, house organs, annual reports, and sites on the Internet. Since all program descriptions included in the *Directory* are written directly from information supplied by the sponsoring organization in print or online (no information is ever taken from secondary sources), we send up to four data collection letters (followed by up to three telephone inquiries, if necessary) to each sponsor identified in this process. Despite our best efforts, however, some sponsoring organizations still failed to respond and, as a result, their programs are not included in the *Directory.*

The 2007-2009 edition of the *Directory* completely revises and updates the earlier biennial edition. Programs that have ceased operations have been dropped. Similarly, programs that have broadened their focus to include men have also been removed from the listing. Profiles of continuing programs have been rewritten to reflect operations in 2007-2009; more than 85 percent of the continuing programs reported substantive changes in their locations, requirements (particularly application deadline), benefits, or eligibility requirements since 2005. In addition, more than 700 new entries have been added to the program section of the *Directory.* The resulting listing describes more than 1,500 scholarships, fellowships, loans, grants, awards, and internships open primarily or exclusively to women.

## SCOPE OF THE DIRECTORY

The 2007-2009 edition of the *Directory of Financial Aids for Women* identifies billions of dollars available for study, research, creative activities, past accomplishments, future projects, professional development, and work experience. The listings cover every major subject area, are sponsored by more than 900 different private and public agencies and organizations, and are open to women at any level—from high school through postdoctorate and professional. This approach is unique. No other single source provides this type of comprehensive and current coverage of funding opportunities available primarily or exclusively to women.

In addition to its comprehensive coverage, the *Directory of Financial Aids for Women* offers several other unique features. Covered here are hundreds of funding opportunities not listed in any other source. Unlike other funding directories, which generally follow a straight alphabetical arrangement, this one groups entries by type (e.g., scholarships, loans, internships), making it easy to search for appropriate programs. The same convenience is offered in the indexes, where title, organization, geographic, subject, and deadline date entries are each subdivided by type of program. Finally, we have tried to anticipate all the ways you might wish to search for funding. The volume is organized so you can identify programs not only by type, but by specific subject, sponsoring organization, program title, residency requirements, where the money can be spent, and even deadline date. Plus, we've included all the information you'll need to decide if a program is right for you: purpose, eligibility requirements, financial data, duration, special features, limitations, number awarded, and application date. You even get fax numbers, toll-free numbers, e-mail addresses, and web sites (when available), along with complete contact information.

## THE ARRANGEMENT OF THE DIRECTORY

The *Directory* is divided into two sections: 1) a descriptive list of financial aid programs available primarily or exclusively for women and 2) a set of six indexes.

**Financial Aid Programs Designed Primarily or Exclusively for Women.** The first section of the *Directory* describes 1,511 financial aid programs designed primarily or exclusively for women. These programs are sponsored by government agencies, professional organizations, corporations, sororities and fraternities, foundations, religious groups, educational associations, and military/veterans organizations. They are open to women at any level (high school through postdoctoral) for study, research, travel, training, career development, personal needs, or creative activities. All areas of the sciences, social sciences, and humanities are covered in the awards listed. The focus is on programs tenable in the United States that are open to women who are U.S. citizens or permanent residents.

Entries in this section are grouped in the following six categories to facilitate your search for a specific kind of financial assistance (e.g., a scholarship for undergraduate courses, a grant for independent research, an award for outstanding literary achievement):

*Scholarships:* Programs that support studies at the undergraduate level in the United States. Usually no return of service or repayment is required. For information on funding for research on the undergraduate level, see the Grants category below.

*Fellowships:* Programs that support studies at the graduate or postgraduate level in the United States. Usually no return of service or repayment is required. For information on funding for research on the graduate, postgraduate, or postdoctoral levels, see the Grants category below.

*Loans:* Programs that provide money that eventually must be repaid—in cash or in service and with or without interest. Forgivable loans (along with scholarship/loans and loans-for-service) are also described in this section of the *Directory*.

*Grants:* Programs that provide funds to support women's innovative efforts, travel, projects, creative activities, or research on any level (from undergraduate to postdoctorate, professional, or other).

*Awards:* Competitions, prizes, and honoraria granted in recognition of women's personal accomplishments, professional contributions, or public service. Prizes received solely as the result of entering contests are excluded.

*Internships:* Work experience programs for women undergraduates, graduate students, and recent graduates. Only salaried positions are described.

Programs that supply more than one type of assistance are listed in all relevant subsections. For example, both undergraduate and graduate students may apply for the Agnes Missirian Scholarship, so the program is described in both the scholarship and the fellowship subsections.

Entries in each subsection appear alphabetically by program title. Each program entry has been designed to provide a concise profile that, as the sample on page 7 illustrates, includes information (when available) on program title, organization address and telephone number (including toll-free and fax numbers), e-mail address, web site, purpose, eligibility, remuneration, duration, special features, limitations, number of awards, and application deadline.

The information reported for each of the programs in this section was taken from Internet sites or supplied in response to questionnaires distributed through the first quarter of 2007. While the listing is intended to cover women-related programs as comprehensively as possible, some sponsoring organi-

## SAMPLE ENTRY

(1) **[241]**

(2) **HONEYWELL INTERNATIONAL SCHOLARSHIPS**

(3) Society of Women Engineers
230 East Ohio Street, Suite 400
Chicago, IL 60611-3265
(312) 596-5223          Toll-free: (877) SWE-INFO
Fax: (312) 644-8557
E-mail: scholarshipapplication@swe.org
Web: www.swe.org/scholarships

(4) **Summary** To provide financial assistance to women interested in studying specified fields of engineering in college.

(5) **Eligibility** This program is open to women who are graduating high school seniors or rising college sophomores or juniors. Applicants must be enrolled or planning to enroll full time at an ABET-accredited 4-year college or university and majoring in computer science or aerospace, architectural, chemical, computer, electrical, industrial, manufacturing, materials, or mechanical engineering. Along with their application, they must submit a 1-page essay on why they want to be an engineer or computer scientist, how they believe they will make a difference as an engineer or computer scientist, and what influenced them to study engineering or computer science. U.S. citizenship is required. Financial need is considered in the selection process.

(6) **Financial data** The stipend is $5,000.

(7) **Duration** 1 year.

(8) **Additional information** This program is sponsored by Honeywell International Inc.

(9) **Number awarded** 5 each year: 3 to high school seniors and 2 to college sophomores and juniors.

(10) **Deadline** January of each year for current college students; May of each year for high school seniors.

## DEFINITION

(1) **Entry number:** Consecutive number assigned to the references and used to index the entry.

(2) **Program title:** Title of the scholarship, fellowship, loan, grant, award, or internship.

(3) **Sponsoring organization:** Name, address, and telephone number, toll-free number, fax number, e-mail address, and/or web site (when information was supplied) for organization sponsoring the program.

(4) **Summary:** Identifies the major program requirements; read the rest of the entry for additional detail.

(5) **Eligibility:** Qualifications required of applicants, plus information on application procedure and selection process.

(6) **Financial data:** Financial details of the program, including fixed sum, average amount, or range of funds offered, expenses for which funds may and may not be applied, and cash-related benefits supplied (e.g., room and board).

(7) **Duration:** Period for which support is provided; renewal prospects.

(8) **Additional information:** Any unusual (generally nonmonetary) benefits, features, restrictions, or limitations associated with the program.

(9) **Number of awards:** Total number of recipients each year or other specified period.

(10) **Deadline:** The month by which applications must be submitted.

zations did not respond to the research inquiry and, consequently, are not included in this edition of the *Directory.*

The focus of the *Directory* is on noninstitution-specific programs open primarily or exclusively to women. Excluded from this listing are:

*Programs that are open equally to men and women:* Only funding opportunities set aside specifically for women are included here.

*Awards for which American citizens would be ineligible:* Programs open only to nationals from other countries, or to organizations (in the United States or any other country) rather than to individuals, are not covered.

*Awards tenable only outside the United States:* Since there are comprehensive and up-to-date directories that describe all available funding for study and research abroad (see the list of Reference Service Press titles opposite the directory's title page), only programs that fund activities for women in the United States are covered here.

*Programs that offer small monetary awards:* The emphasis here is on programs that offer significant compensation. If the maximum a scholarship, fellowship, loan, grant, or internship offers is not at least $500 per year, it is not included in this listing.

*Programs open to residents in a restricted geographic location:* In general, programs are excluded if they are open only to the residents of a limited geographic area (anything below the state level). To get information on these geographically restrictive programs, contact Reference Service Press directly. We have the details on thousands of these in our main database.

*Programs administered by individual academic institutions solely for their own students:* The directory identifies "portable" programs—ones that can be used at any number of schools. Financial aid administered by individual schools specifically for their currently-enrolled students is not covered. Write directly to the schools you are considering to get information on their offerings.

**Indexes.** The *Directory's* six indexes will facilitate your search for appropriate financial aid opportunities. Program Title, Sponsoring Organization, Residency, Tenability, Subject, and Calendar Indexes each follow a word-by-word alphabetical arrangement and pinpoint the entry numbers that you should check.

*Program Title Index.* If you know the name of a particular funding program and want to find out where it is covered in the *Directory,* use the Program Title Index. Here, program titles are arranged alphabetically, word by word. To assist you in your search, every program is listed by all its known names, former names, and abbreviations. Since one program can be listed in several subsections (e.g., a program providing assistance to both undergraduate and graduate students is described in both the scholarships and the fellowships subsections), each entry number in the index has been coded to indicate program type (e.g., "F" = Fellowships; "A" = Awards). By using this coding system, you can avoid duplicate entries and turn directly to the programs that match your financial interests.

*Sponsoring Organization Index.* This index makes it easy to identify agencies that offer funding primarily or exclusively to women. More than 900 organizations are listed alphabetically, word by word. As in the Program Title Index, we've used a code to help you determine which organizations offer scholarships, fellowships, loans, grants, awards, and/or internships.

*Residency Index.* Some programs listed in this book are restricted to women in a particular state or region. Others are open to women wherever they live. This index helps you identify programs available only to residents in your area as well as programs that have no residency requirements. Further, to assist you in your search, we've also indicated the type of funding offered to residents in each of the areas listed in the index.

*Tenability Index.* This index identifies the geographic locations where the funding described in the *Directory* may be used. Index entries (city, county, state, province, region, country, continent) are arranged alphabetically (word by word) and subdivided by program type. Use this index when you are looking for money to support your activities in a particular geographic area.

**Subject Index.** This index allows you to identify the subject focus of each of the financial aid opportunities described in the *Directory*. More than 250 different subject terms are listed. Extensive "see" and "see also" references, as well as type-of-program subdivisions, will help you in your search for appropriate funding opportunities.

**Calendar Index.** Since most financial aid programs have specific deadline dates, some may have closed by the time you begin to look for funding. You can use the Calendar Index to determine which programs are still open. This index is arranged by program type (e.g., scholarship, loan, internship) and subdivided by month during which the deadline falls. Filing dates can and quite often do vary from year to year; consequently, this index should be used only as a guide for deadlines beyond 2009.

## HOW TO USE THE DIRECTORY

**To Locate Programs Offering a Particular Type of Assistance.** If you are looking for programs offering a particular type of financial aid (e.g., a scholarship for undergraduate courses, a grant for independent research, an award for outstanding literary achievement), turn first to the definitions of these program types on page 6 in the Introduction and then browse through the entries in each of the appropriate categories in the first section of the *Directory*. Keep in mind that more than one of these subsections may contain funding leads for you. For example, if you are a graduate student looking for money to help you pay for the educational and research costs associated with your master's degree, you will not want to overlook the opportunities described in the fellowships, loans, grants, and even awards subsections. Note: since programs with multiple purposes are listed in every appropriate location, each subsection functions as a self-contained entity. In fact, you can browse through any of the sections or subsections in the *Directory* without first consulting an index.

**To Locate a Particular Women's Financial Aid Program.** If you know both the name of a particular financial aid program and the type of assistance offered by the program (scholarship, fellowship, grant, etc.), then go directly to the appropriate category in the first section of the *Directory,* where you'll find the program profiles arranged alphabetically by title. But be careful: program titles can be misleading. The Mildred Richards Taylor Memorial Scholarship is available only to graduate students and therefore is listed in the fellowship not the scholarship subsection. The Anne Peel Hopkins Grant turns out to be a scholarship, the Amy Lutz Rechel Award is really a grant, and the Ruth H. Bufton Scholarship is, in fact, a fellowship. So, if you are looking for a specific program and do not find it in the subsection you have checked, be sure to refer to the Program Title Index to see if it is covered elsewhere in the *Directory*. To save time, always check the Program Title Index first if you know the name of a specific award but are not sure under which category it has been listed. Since we index each program by all its known names or abbreviations, you'll also be able to track down a program there when you only know its popular rather than official name.

**To Locate Programs Sponsored by a Particular Organization.** The Sponsoring Organization Index makes it easy to identify agencies that provide financial assistance to women or to target specific financial aid programs for women offered by a particular organization. Each entry number in the index is coded to indicate type of funding, to help you identify appropriate entries.

**To Browse Quickly Through the Listings.** Turn to the type of funding that interests you (scholarships, fellowships, awards, etc.) and read the "Summary" field in each entry. In seconds, you'll know if this is an opportunity that you might want to pursue. If it is, be sure to read the rest of the information in the entry, to see if you are able to meet all of the program requirements before contacting the sponsor for an application form.

**To Locate Funding Open to Women from or Tenable in a Particular Geographic Location.**
The Residency Index identifies financial aid programs open to women in a particular geographic location. The Tenability Index shows where the money can be spent. In both indexes, "see" and "see also"

references are used liberally, and index entries for a particular geographic area are subdivided by type of program (scholarships, fellowships, loans, grants, awards, and internships) to help you identify the funding that's right for you. When using these indexes, always check the listings under the term "United States," since the programs indexed there have no geographic restrictions and can be used in any area.

**To Locate Financial Aid for Women in a Particular Subject Area.** Turn to the Subject Index first if you are interested in identifying financial aid programs for women in a particular subject area (more than 250 different subject fields are listed there). To facilitate your search, the type of funding offered (scholarships, fellowships, loans, grants, awards, or internships) is also clearly identified. Extensive cross-references are provided. As part of your search, be sure to check the listings in the index under the heading "General Programs;" those programs provide funding in any subject area (although they may be restricted in other ways).

**To Locate Financial Aid Programs for Women by Deadline Date.** If you are working with specific time constraints and want to weed out the financial aid programs whose filing dates you won't be able to meet, turn first to the Calendar Index and check the program references listed under the appropriate program type and month. Remember, not all sponsoring organizations supplied deadline information, so not all programs are listed in this index. To identify every relevant financial aid program, regardless of filing date, read through all the entries in each of the program subsections (scholarships, fellowships, etc.) that apply.

**To Locate Financial Aid Programs Open to Both Men and Women.** Only programs designed with women in mind are listed in this publication. There are thousands of other programs that are open equally to men and women. To identify these programs, use the publications listed on the page opposite's this directory's Table of Contents, talk to your local librarian, check with your financial aid office on campus, or use a computerized scholarship or grant search service.

## PLANS TO UPDATE THE DIRECTORY

This volume, covering 2007-2009, is the fourteenth edition of the *Directory of Financial Aids for Women.* The next biennial edition will cover the years 2009-2011 and will be released in the first half of 2009.

## OTHER RELATED PUBLICATIONS

In addition to the *Directory of Financial Aids for Women,* Reference Service Press publishes dozens of other titles dealing with fundseeking, including the *High School Senior's Guide to Merit and Other No-Need Funding; Money for Chrsitan College Students; How to Pay for Your Degree in Education; Financial Aid for the Disabled and Their Families; Financial Aid for Study and Training Abroad;* and *Financial Aid for Veterans, Military Personnel, and Their Dependents.* Since each of these titles focuses on a separate population group, there is little duplication in the listings. In fact, fewer than ten percent of the programs described in *Directory of Financial Aids for Women* can be found in any of the other Reference Service Press directories. For more information on Reference Service Press's publications, write to the company at 5000 Windplay Drive, Suite 4, El Dorado Hills, CA 95762-9319, call us at (916) 939-9620, fax us at (916) 939-9626, send us an e-mail at info@rspfunding.com, or visit us on the web: www.rspfunding.com.

## ACKNOWLEDGEMENTS

A debt of gratitude is owed all the organizations that contributed information to the 2007-2009 edition of the *Directory of Financial Aids for Women.* Their generous cooperation has helped to make this publication the most current and comprehensive survey of awards.

# ABOUT THE AUTHORS

**Dr. Gail Ann Schlachter** has worked for more than three decades as a library administrator, a library educator, and an administrator of library-related publishing companies. Among the reference books to her credit are the biennially-issued *College Student's Guide to Merit and Other No-Need Funding* (named by *Choice* as one of the outstanding reference titles of the year) and two award-winning bibliographic guides: *Minorities and Women: A Guide to Reference Literature in the Social Sciences* (which also was chosen as an "Outstanding Reference Book of the Year" by *Choice)* and *Reference Sources in Library and Information Services* (which won the first Knowledge Industry Publications "Award for Library Literature"). She was the reference book review editor for *RQ* (now *Reference and User Services Quarterly)* for 10 years, is a past president of the American Library Association's Reference and User Services Association, is the former editor of the *Reference and User Services Association Quarterly,* and is currently serving her fourth term on the American Library Association's governing Council. In recognition of her outstanding contributions to reference service, Dr. Schlachter has been awarded both the Isadore Gilbert Mudge Citation and the Louis Shores/Oryx Press Award.

**Dr. R. David Weber** has been teaching economics and history at Los Angeles Harbor College (Wilmington, California) since 1975. He is the author of a number of critically-acclaimed reference works, including *Dissertations in Urban History* and the three-volume *Energy Information Guide.* With Dr. Schlachter, he has edited Reference Service Press's award-winning *Financial Aid for the Disabled and Their Families* and dozens of other distinguished financial aid titles, including *Money for Graduate Students in the Social & Behavioral Sciences* and *Financial Aid for Hispanic Americans.*

# Financial Aid Programs Primarily or Exclusively for Women

- Scholarships
- Fellowships
- Loans
- Grants
- Awards
- Internships

# Scholarships

Described here are 659 programs designed primarily or exclusively for women that are available to fund studies on the undergraduate level in the United States. Usually no return of service or repayment is required. Note: other funding opportunities for undergraduate women are also described in the Loans, Grants, Awards, and Internships subsections. So, if you are looking for a particular program and don't find it here, be sure to check the Program Title Index to see if it is covered elsewhere in the *Directory.*

## [1]
## AAIA DISPLACED HOMEMAKER SCHOLARSHIPS

Association on American Indian Affairs, Inc.
Attn: Director of Scholarship Programs
966 Hungerford Drive, Suite 12-B
Rockville, MD 20850
(240) 314-7155      Fax: (240) 314-7159
E-mail: lw.aaia@verizon.net
Web: www.indian-affairs.org/scholarships.htm

**Summary** To provide financial assistance to Native American displaced homemakers who are trying to complete their college education.

**Eligibility** This program is open to full-time college students who are Native Americans and have special needs because of family responsibilities. Examples of displaced homemakers include students who are attending college for the first time at the age of 40 because they have put off higher education to raise their children, students who are entering or returning to college after their children enter elementary school, and men or women who have been divorced and had to leave college to care for children and are now returning. Applicants must submit documentation of financial need, a Certificate of Indian Blood showing at least one-quarter Indian blood, proof of tribal enrollment, an essay on their educational goals and family responsibilities, 2 letters of recommendation, and their most recent transcript.

**Financial data** The stipend is $1,500. Awards are intended to assist recipients with child care, transportation, and some basic living expenses as well as educational costs.

**Duration** Up to 3 years.

**Number awarded** Varies each year.

**Deadline** July of each year.

## [2]
## ADA I. PRESSMAN SCHOLARSHIP

Society of Women Engineers
230 East Ohio Street, Suite 400
Chicago, IL 60611-3265
(312) 596-5223      Toll-free: (877) SWE-INFO
Fax: (312) 644-8557
E-mail: scholarshipapplication@swe.org
Web: www.swe.org/scholarships

**Summary** To provide financial assistance to women working on an undergraduate or graduate degree in engineering or computer science.

**Eligibility** This program is open to women who will be sophomores, juniors, seniors, or graduate students at ABET-accredited colleges and universities. Applicants must be majoring in computer science or engineering and have a GPA of 3.0 or higher. Along with their application, they must submit a 1-page essay on why they want to be an engineer or computer scientist, how they believe they will make a difference as an engineer or computer scientist, and what influenced them to study engineering or computer science. U.S. citizenship is required. Selection is based on merit.

**Financial data** The stipend is $5,000.

**Duration** 1 year.

**Number awarded** 1 each year.

**Deadline** January of each year.

## [3]
## ADOBE SYSTEMS COMPUTER SCIENCE SCHOLARSHIPS

Society of Women Engineers
230 East Ohio Street, Suite 400
Chicago, IL 60611-3265
(312) 596-5223      Toll-free: (877) SWE-INFO
Fax: (312) 644-8557
E-mail: scholarshipapplication@swe.org
Web: www.swe.org/scholarships

**Summary** To provide financial assistance to upper-division women majoring in computer science.

**Eligibility** This program is open to women entering their junior or senior year at an ABET-accredited college or university. Applicants must be majoring in computer science and have a GPA of 3.0 or higher. Along with their application, they must submit a 1-page essay on why they want to be a computer scientist, how they believe they will make a difference as a computer scientist, and what influenced them to study computer science. Preference is given to students attending selected schools; for a list, contact the sponsor. Selection is based on merit.

**Financial data** Stipends are $2,000 or $1,500.

**Duration** 1 year.

**Additional information** This program, established in 2000, is sponsored by Adobe Systems Incorporated.

**Number awarded** 2 each year: 1 at $2,000 and 1 at $1,500.

**Deadline** January of each year.

## [4]
## ADVANCING WOMEN IN ACCOUNTING SCHOLARSHIP

Illinois CPA Society
Attn: CPA Endowment Fund of Illinois
550 West Jackson, Suite 900
Chicago, Il 60661-5716
(312) 993-0407, ext. 293
Toll-free: (800) 993-0407 (within IL)
Fax: (312) 993-9954
Web: www.icpas.org/icpas/endowment/programs.asp

**Summary** To provide financial assistance to women students in Illinois undertaking their fifth year of course work to complete the educational requirements to sit for the C.P.A. examination in Illinois.

**Eligibility** This program is open to female residents of Illinois who have completed 4 years of study at a college or university in the state and wish to take a fifth year of study to meet the 150-hour requirement. Applicants must be planning to sit for the C.P.A. examination in Illinois within 3 years of the application date. They must have at least a 3.0 GPA and be able to demonstrate financial need or special circumstances; the society is especially interested in assisting students who, because of limited options or opportunities, may not have alternative means of support. U.S. citizenship or permanent resident status is required. Selection is based on academic achievement and financial need.

**Financial data** The maximum stipend is $4,000.

**Duration** 1 year (fifth year for accounting students planning to become a C.P.A.).

**Additional information** This program was established by the Women's Executive Committee of the Illinois CPA Society. The scholarship does not cover the cost of C.P.A. examination review courses. Recipients may not receive a full graduate assistantship, fellowship, or scholarship from a college or university, participate in a full-tuition reimbursement cooperative education or internship program, or participate in an employee full-tuition reimbursement program during the scholarship period.

**Number awarded** 1 or more each year.

**Deadline** November of each year.

## [5]
## AEROSPACE ILLINOIS SPACE GRANT CONSORTIUM PROGRAM

Aerospace Illinois Space Grant Consortium
c/o University of Illinois at Urbana-Champaign
Department of Aeronautical and Astronomical
   Engineering
308 Talbot Lab
104 South Wright Street
Urbana, IL 61801-2935
(217) 244-8048        Fax: (217) 244-0720
E-mail: dejeffer@uiuc.edu
Web: www.ae.uiuc.edu/ISGC

**Summary** To provide financial support to faculty, staff, and students (particularly women, minorities, and persons with disabilities) at Aerospace Illinois member institutions who are interested in pursuing space-related academic activities.

**Eligibility** Aerospace Illinois has established 4 program elements: 1) undergraduate/high school teaching and research, to attract undergraduates and secondary school students to aerospace science and engineering; 2) training in graduate research, through research experiences focused on aerospace science and engineering; 3) outreach and public service, to employ the region's extensive existing public educational information networks and outreach programs to attract the highest quality student populations, especially underrepresented minorities, women, and persons with disabilities; and 4) fellowships with industry, to add substantially to the national aerospace science and engineering pool. Aerospace Illinois is a component of the U.S. National Aeronautics and Space Administration which encourages applications from women, minorities, and persons with disabilities.

**Financial data** Awards depend on the availability of funds and the nature of the proposal.

**Duration** Depends on the program.

**Additional information** Aerospace Illinois includes 4 member institutions: the University of Illinois at Urbana-Champaign (UIUC), the University of Chicago (UC), Illinois Institute of Technology (IIT), and Northwestern University (NU). It also includes 3 affiliate institutions: Southern Illinois University (SIU), Western Illinois University (WIU), and the University of Illinois at Chicago. This program is funded by NASA.

**Number awarded** Varies each year.

## [6]
## AGENDA FOR DELAWARE WOMEN TRAILBLAZER SCHOLARSHIPS

Delaware Higher Education Commission
Carvel State Office Building
820 North French Street
Wilmington, DE 19801
(302) 577-3240       Toll-free: (800) 292-7935
Fax: (302) 577-6765    E-mail: dhec@doe.k12.de.us
Web: www.doe.state.de.us/high-ed/agenda.htm

**Summary** To provide financial assistance for undergraduate studies to women in Delaware.

**Eligibility** This program is open to women who are Delaware residents planning to enroll in a public or private nonprofit college in Delaware as an undergraduate student in the coming year. Applicants must have a cumulative GPA of 2.5 or higher. Selection is based on financial need (50%) and community and school activities, vision, participation, and leadership (50%).

**Financial data** The stipend is $2,500 per year.

**Duration** 1 year; may be renewed.

**Number awarded** 1 or more each year.

**Deadline** April of each year.

## [7]
## AGNES C. ALLEN MEMORIAL SCHOLARSHIP

Pennsylvania Masonic Youth Foundation
Attn: Educational Endowment Fund
1244 Bainbridge Road
Elizabethtown, PA 17022-9423
(717) 367-1536    Toll-free: (800) 266-8424 (within PA)
Fax: (717) 367-0616    E-mail: pyf@pagrandlodge.org
Web: www.pagrandlodge.org/pyf/scholar/index.html

**Summary** To provide financial assistance for college to members of Rainbow Girls in Pennsylvania.

**Eligibility** This program is open to active Pennsylvania Rainbow Girls in good standing. Applicants must have completed at least 1 year at an accredited college, university, or nursing school.

**Financial data** The stipend depends on the availability of funds.

**Duration** 1 year; may be renewed.

**Additional information** Information is also available from Eva Gresko, RD #3, Box 102, Huntington, PA 16652-8703, (814) 658-3774.

**Number awarded** 1 each year.

**Deadline** Requests for applications must be submitted by January of each year. Completed applications are due by the end of February.

## [8]
## AGNES MISSIRIAN SCHOLARSHIP

Armenian International Women's Association
65 Main Street, Room 3A
Watertown, MA 02472
(617) 926-0171       E-mail: aiwainc@aol.com
Web: www.aiwa-net.org/scholarshipinfo.html

**Summary** To provide financial assistance to Armenian women upper-division and graduate students.

**Eligibility** This program is open to full-time women students of Armenian descent attending an accredited college or university. Applicants must be full-time juniors, seniors, or graduate students with a GPA of 3.2 or higher. They must submit an essay, up to 500 words, describing their planned academic program, their career goals, and the reasons why they believe they should be awarded this scholarship. Selection is based on financial need and merit.

**Financial data** The stipend is $2,000.

**Duration** 1 year.

**Number awarded** 1 or more each year.

**Deadline** April of each year.

## [9]
## AGNES MORRIS EDUCATION SCHOLARSHIP

Louisiana Federation of Business and Professional
Women's Clubs, Inc.
c/o Linda Burns
1424 Evangeline Road
Glenmora, LA 71433
(318) 748-7603     E-mail: lbrns760@wmconnect.com
Web: www.bpwlouisiana.org/files/index.php?id=15

**Summary** To provide financial assistance for college to mature women in Louisiana.

**Eligibility** This program is open to women who are 25 years of age or older and members of the Louisiana Federation of Business and Professional Women's Clubs (BPW/LA) and a BPW local organization in Louisiana. Applicants must be enrolled at or entering an accredited university, college, technical school, or program of course work for licensed or career advancement. Along with their application, they must submit transcripts from their high school and any institution of higher education they have attended, entrance examination scores, 3 letters of recommendation, and a 250-word statement on why they want this scholarship and their plans for using it. Financial need is not considered in the selection process.

**Financial data** The stipend is $1,000 per year.

**Duration** 2 years, provided the recipient remains enrolled full time with a GPA of 2.5 or higher.

**Additional information** This program originated as the Agnes Morris Educational Loan Fund.

**Number awarded** 1 or more each year.

**Deadline** January of each year.

## [10]
## AIR FORCE OFFICERS' WIVES' CLUB OF WASHINGTON, D.C. CONTINUING EDUCATION SCHOLARSHIPS FOR NON-MILITARY AIR FORCE SPOUSES

Air Force Officers' Wives' Club of Washington, D.C.
Attn: AFOWC Scholarship Committee
50 Theisen Street
Bolling Air Force Base
Washington, DC 20032-5411

**Summary** To provide financial assistance for undergraduate or graduate studies to the non-military spouses of Air Force members in the Washington, D.C. area.

**Eligibility** This program is open to the non-military spouses of Air Force members residing in the Washington,

D.C. metropolitan area in the following categories: active duty, retired, MIA/POW, or deceased. Spouses whose Air Force sponsor is assigned remote from the area or reassigned during the current school year are also eligible if they remained behind to continue education. Applicants must be enrolled or planning to enroll as an undergraduate or graduate student. Along with their application, they must submit a 500-word essay on their experiences, interests, goals, and how being an Air Force spouse has affected their life. Selection is based on academic and citizenship achievements; financial need is not considered.

**Financial data** A stipend is awarded (amount not specified). Funds may be used only for payment of tuition or academic fees.

**Duration** 1 year.

**Number awarded** Varies each year.

**Deadline** February of each year.

## [11]
## AIR FORCE SPOUSE SCHOLARSHIPS

Air Force Association
Attn: Member Services
1501 Lee Highway
Arlington, VA 22209-1198
(703) 247-5800          Toll-free: (800) 727-3337
Fax: (703) 247-5853      E-mail: AFAStaff@afa.org
Web: www.afa.org/aef/aid/spouse.asp

**Summary** To provide financial assistance for undergraduate or graduate study to spouses of Air Force members.

**Eligibility** This program is open to spouses of Air Force active duty, Air National Guard, or Air Force Reserve members. Spouses who are themselves military members or in ROTC are not eligible. Applicants must have a GPA of 3.5 or higher in college (or high school if entering college for the first time) and be able to provide proof of acceptance into an accredited undergraduate or graduate degree program. They must submit a 2-page essay on their academic and career goals, the motivation that led them to that decision, and how Air Force and other local community activities in which they are involved will enhance their goals. Selection is based on the essay and 2 letters of recommendation.

**Financial data** The stipend is $1,000 per year; funds are sent to the recipients' schools to be used for any reasonable cost related to working on a degree.

**Duration** 1 year; nonrenewable.

**Additional information** This program was established in 1995.

**Number awarded** 30 each year.

**Deadline** April of each year.

## [12]
## AIR PRODUCTS AND CHEMICALS SCHOLARSHIP FOR DIVERSITY IN ENGINEERING

Association of Independent Colleges and Universities
of Pennsylvania
101 North Front Street
Harrisburg, PA 17101-1405
(717) 232-8649                    Fax: (717) 233-8574
E-mail: info@aicup.org
Web: www.aicup.org

**Summary**  To provide financial assistance to women and minority students at member institutions of the Association of Independent Colleges and Universities of Pennsylvania (AICUP) who are majoring in designated fields of engineering.

**Eligibility**  This program is open to full-time undergraduate students at designated AICUP colleges and universities who are women and/or members of the following minority groups: American Indians, Alaska Natives, Asians, Blacks/African Americans, Hispanics/Latinos, Native Hawaiians, or Pacific Islanders. Applicants must be juniors majoring in chemical or mechanical engineering with a GPA of 2.7 or higher. Along with their application, they must submit an essay on their characteristics, accomplishments, primary interests, plans, and goals, and what sets them apart.

**Financial data**  The stipend is $7,500 per year.

**Duration**  1 year; may be renewed 1 additional year if the recipient maintains appropriate academic standards.

**Additional information**  This program, sponsored by Air Products and Chemicals, Inc., is available at the following AICUP colleges and universities: Bucknell University, Carnegie Mellon University, Drexel University, Gannon University, Geneva College, Grove City College, Lafayette College, Lehigh University, Messiah College, Swarthmore College, Villanova University, Widener University, and Wilkes University.

**Number awarded**  2 each year.

**Deadline**  April of each year.

## [13]
## AIRBUS LEADERSHIP GRANT

Women in Aviation, International
Attn: Scholarships
Morningstar Airport
3647 State Route 503 South
West Alexandria, OH 45381
(937) 558-7655                    Fax: (937) 839-4645
E-mail: scholarships@wai.org
Web: www.wai.org/education/scholarships.cfm

**Summary**  To provide financial assistance for college to members of Women in Aviation, International (WAI).

**Eligibility**  This program is open to WAI members who are college sophomores or higher working on a degree in an aviation-related field. Applicants must have earned a GPA of 3.0 or higher and be able to demonstrate leadership potential. They must submit a 500-word essay addressing their career aspirations and how they have exhibited leadership skills, 3 letters of recommendation, a resume, copies of all aviation and medical certificates, and the last 3 pages of their pilot logbook, if applicable. Selection is based on

achievements, attitude toward self and others, commitment to success, dedication to career, financial need, motivation, reliability, responsibility, and teamwork.

**Financial data**  The stipend is $5,000 per year.

**Duration**  1 year.

**Additional information**  WAI is a nonprofit professional organization dedicated to encouraging women to consider an aviation career, providing educational outreach activities, and providing networking opportunities to women active in the industry.

**Number awarded**  Varies each year; recently, 2 of these scholarships were awarded.

**Deadline**  November of each year.

## [14]
## AIRCRAFT ELECTRONICS ASSOCIATION AVIATION MAINTENANCE SCHOLARSHIP

Women in Aviation, International
Attn: Scholarships
Morningstar Airport
3647 State Route 503 South
West Alexandria, OH 45381
(937) 558-7655                    Fax: (937) 839-4645
E-mail: scholarships@wai.org
Web: www.wai.org/education/scholarships.cfm

**Summary**  To provide financial assistance to members of Women in Aviation, International (WAI) who are studying aircraft maintenance.

**Eligibility**  This program is open to WAI members who are seeking a degree in the aviation maintenance field at an accredited college or technical school. Preference is given to avionics majors. Applicants must have a GPA of 2.75 or higher. Selection is based on achievements, attitude toward self and others, commitment to success, dedication to career, financial need, motivation, reliability, responsibility, and teamwork.

**Financial data**  The stipend is $1,500.

**Duration**  1 year.

**Additional information**  WAI is a nonprofit professional organization dedicated to encouraging women to consider an aviation career, providing educational outreach activities, and providing networking opportunities to women active in the industry. This program is sponsored by the Aircraft Electronics Association (AEA).

**Number awarded**  1 each year.

**Deadline**  November of each year.

## [15]
## AL NEUHARTH FREE SPIRIT SCHOLARSHIP AND CONFERENCE PROGRAM

Freedom Forum
Attn: Al Neuharth Free Spirit Scholarship and
Conference Program
1101 Wilson Boulevard
Arlington, VA 22209
(703) 284-2814                    Fax: (703) 284-3529
E-mail: freespirit@freedomforum.org
Web: www.freedomforum.org/freespirit

**Summary**  To provide financial assistance for college to high school journalists who demonstrate a "free spirit."

**Eligibility** This program is open to high school seniors who are active in high school journalism. Applicants must be planning to attend college to prepare for a career in journalism. They must demonstrate qualities of a "free spirit" in their academic or personal life. A "free spirit" is defined as "a risk-taker, a visionary, an innovative leader, an entrepreneur, or a courageous achiever who accomplishes great things beyond his or her normal circumstances." Along with their application, they must submit 2 essays of 500 words each: 1) explaining why they want to prepare for a career in journalism, and 2) describing their specific qualities as a free spirit and their experiences and/or struggles that make them a free spirit. Men and women are judged separately. U.S. citizenship or permanent resident status is required.

**Financial data** The stipend is $50,000 or $1,000.

**Duration** 1 year.

**Additional information** Recipients are invited to Washington in March to receive their awards and participate in a journalism conference. All travel expenses are paid. This program began in 1999.

**Number awarded** 102 each year: a male and a female from each state and the District of Columbia. The recipients include 100 who receive $1,000 scholarships and 2 (a male and a female) who receive $50,000 scholarships.

**Deadline** October of each year.

## [16]
## ALABAMA G.I. DEPENDENTS' SCHOLARSHIP PROGRAM

Alabama Department of Veterans Affairs
770 Washington Avenue, Suite 530
P.O. Box 1509
Montgomery, AL 36102-1509
(334) 242-5077          Fax: (334) 242-5102
E-mail: willie.moore@va.state.al.us
Web: www.va.state.al.us/scholarship.htm

**Summary** To provide educational benefits to the dependents of disabled, deceased, and other Alabama veterans.

**Eligibility** Eligible are spouses, children, stepchildren, and unremarried widow(er)s of veterans who served honorably for 90 days or more and 1) are currently rated as 20% or more service-connected disabled or were so rated at time of death; 2) were a former prisoner of war; 3) have been declared missing in action; 4) died as the result of a service-connected disability; or 5) died while on active military duty in the line of duty. The veteran must have been a permanent civilian resident of Alabama for at least 1 year prior to entering active military service; veterans who were not Alabama residents at the time of entering active military service may also qualify if they have a 100% disability and were permanent residents of Alabama for at least 5 years prior to filing the application for this program or prior to death, if deceased. Children and stepchildren must be under the age of 26, but spouses and unremarried widow(er)s may be any age.

**Financial data** Eligible dependents may attend any state-supported Alabama institution of higher learning or enroll in a prescribed course of study at any Alabama state-supported trade school without payment of any tuition, book fees, or laboratory charges.

**Duration** This is an entitlement program for 4 years of full-time undergraduate or graduate study or part-time equiva-

lent. Spouses and unremarried widow(er)s whose veteran spouse is rated between 20% and 90% disabled, or 100% disabled but not permanently so, may attend only 2 standard academic years.

**Additional information** Benefits for children, spouses, and unremarried widow(er)s are available in addition to federal government benefits. Assistance is not provided for noncredit courses, placement testing, GED preparation, continuing educational courses, pre-technical courses, or state board examinations.

**Number awarded** Varies each year.

**Deadline** Applications may be submitted at any time.

## [17]
## ALASKA FREE TUITION FOR SPOUSES AND DEPENDENTS OF ARMED SERVICES MEMBERS

Department of Military and Veterans Affairs
Attn: Office of Veterans Affairs
P.O. Box 5800
Fort Richardson, AK 99505-5800
(907) 428-6016          Fax: (907) 428-6019
E-mail: jerry_beale@ak-prepared.com
Web: www.ak-prepared.com

**Summary** To provide financial assistance for college to dependents and spouses in Alaska of service members who died or were declared prisoners of war or missing in action.

**Eligibility** Eligible for this benefit are the spouses and dependent children of Alaska residents who died in the line of duty, died of injuries sustained in the line of duty, or were listed by the Department of Defense as a prisoner of war or missing in action. Applicants must be in good standing at a state-supported educational institution in Alaska.

**Financial data** Those eligible may attend any state-supported educational institution in Alaska without payment of tuition or fees.

**Duration** 1 year; may be renewed.

**Additional information** Information is available from the financial aid office of state-supported universities in Alaska.

**Number awarded** Varies each year.

## [18]
## ALBERT A. MARKS SCHOLARSHIP FOR TEACHER EDUCATION

Miss America Pageant
Attn: Scholarship Department
Two Miss America Way, Suite 1000
Atlantic City, NJ 08401
(609) 345-7571, ext. 27          Toll-free: (800) 282-MISS
Fax: (609) 347-6079          E-mail: info@missamerica.org
Web: www.missamerica.org

**Summary** To provide financial assistance to women who are working on a degree in education and who, in the past, competed at some level in the Miss America competition.

**Eligibility** This program is open to women who are working on an undergraduate, master's, or higher degree in education and who competed at the local, state, or national level in a Miss America competition during the current or any subsequent year. Applicants must be preparing for a career as a classroom teacher, special area teacher (e.g., art, physical education, music), school counselor, school psychologist, school nurse, or school administrator. They must submit an essay, up to 500 words, on the factors that influenced them to enter the field of education, what they consider to be the major issues facing education today, and what they would do to strengthen and improve our educational system. Selection is based on GPA, class rank, extracurricular activities, financial need, and level of participation within the system.

**Financial data**   The stipend is $5,000.

**Duration**   1 year; renewable.

**Additional information**   This scholarship was established in 1997.

**Number awarded**   Varies each year; recently, 2 of these scholarships were awarded.

**Deadline**   June of each year.

## [19]
## ALBERTA E. CROWE STAR OF TOMORROW AWARD

United States Bowling Congress
Attn: SMART Program
5301 South 76th Street
Greendale, WI 53129-1192
(414) 423-3343   Toll-free: (800) 514-BOWL, ext. 3343
Fax: (414) 421-3014          E-mail: smart@bowl.com
Web: www.bowl.com/scholarships/main.aspx

**Summary**   To provide financial assistance for college to outstanding women bowlers.

**Eligibility**   This program is open to women amateur bowlers who are current members in good standing of the United States Bowling Congress (USBC) or USBC Youth and competitors in events sanctioned by those organizations. Applicants must be high school or college students younger than 22 years of age, have a GPA of 2.5 or higher, and have a bowling average of 175 or greater. They may not have competed in a professional bowling tournament. Along with their application, they must submit an essay, up to 500 words, on how this scholarship will influence their bowling, academic, and personal goals. Selection is based on bowling performances on local, regional, state, and national levels; academic achievement; and extracurricular involvement.

**Financial data**   The stipend is $1,500 per year.

**Duration**   1 year; may be renewed for 3 additional years.

**Number awarded**   1 each year.

**Deadline**   September of each year.

## [20]
## ALEXANDRA APOSTOLIDES SONENFELD SCHOLARSHIP

Daughters of Penelope
Attn: Daughters of Penelope Foundation, Inc.
1909 Q Street, N.W., Suite 500
Washington, DC 20009-1007
(202) 234-9741          Fax: (202) 483-6983
E-mail: daughters@ahepa.org
Web: www.ahepa.org

**Summary**   To provide financial assistance for college to women of Greek descent.

**Eligibility**   This program is open to women who have been members of the Daughters or Penelope or the Maids of

Athena for at least 2 years, or whose parents or grandparents have been members of the Daughters of Penelope or the Order of Ahepa for at least 2 years. Applicants must be 1) high school seniors or recent high school graduates applying to a college, university, or accredited technical school, or 2) current undergraduates at the college level. They must have taken the SAT or ACT (or Canadian, Greek, or Cypriot equivalent) and must write an essay (in English) about their educational and vocational goals. Selection is based on academic merit and financial need.

**Financial data**   The stipend is $1,500 per year.

**Duration**   1 year; nonrenewable.

**Additional information**   Information is also available from Helen Santire, National Scholarship Chair, P.O. Box 19709, Houston, TX 77242-9709, (713) 468-6531, E-mail: helensantire@duchesne.org.

**Number awarded**   1 each year.

**Deadline**   May of each year.

## [21]
## ALPHA EPSILON PHI FOUNDATION SCHOLARSHIPS

Alpha Epsilon Phi
Attn: AEPhi Foundation
11 Lake Avenue Extension, Suite 1A
Danbury, CT 06811
(203) 748-0029          Fax: (203) 748-0039
E-mail: aephifoundation@aephi.org
Web: www.aephi.org

**Summary**   To provide financial assistance for undergraduate or graduate education to Alpha Epsilon Phi members or alumnae.

**Eligibility**   Current members or alumnae of the sorority are eligible to apply if they need financial assistance to pursue or continue studies at the undergraduate or graduate level. Selection is based on scholastic standing, university citizenship, activities in the sorority, and financial need.

**Financial data**   Stipends range from $1,000 to $2,000 per year.

**Duration**   1 year; may be renewed.

**Additional information**   This program includes the following named scholarships: the Judith Resnik Memorial Scholarship, the Anne Klauber Berson Memorial Scholarship, the Edith Hirsch Miller Memorial Scholarship (preference given to Jewish applicants), the Irma Loeb Cohen Scholarship (for students who are attending Ohio State University or Cleveland State University or who are residents of Ohio), the Ruth Rosenbaum Goldfeder Memorial Scholarship (preference given to residents of Los Angeles or Colorado), the Alpha Iota Scholarship (preference given to residents of Minnesota), the Constance Bauman Abraham Scholarship, and the Shonnette Meyer Kahn Scholarship (preference given to students at Ohio State University or Tulane University). Recipients must be willing to remain active in the sorority and live in the sorority house (if any) for the entire year the scholarship covers.

**Number awarded**   Several each year.

**Deadline**   April of each year.

## [22]
## ALPHA KAPPA ALPHA ENDOWMENT SCHOLARSHIPS

Alpha Kappa Alpha Sorority, Inc.
Attn: Educational Advancement Foundation
5656 South Stony Island Avenue
Chicago, IL 60637
(773) 947-0026          Toll-free: (800) 653-6528
Fax: (773) 947-0277          E-mail: akaeaf@aol.com
Web: www.akaeaf.org/scholarships.htm

**Summary**  To provide financial assistance for college to students (especially African American women) who meet designated requirements.

**Eligibility**  The sponsor is a traditionally African American women's sorority. Scholarships are offered through this program to undergraduate students, particularly African American women; Each of these scholarships includes specific requirements established by the donor of the endowment that supports it; for further information, contact the sponsor.

**Financial data**  Award amounts are determined by the availability of funds from the endowment. Most stipends average $1,000 per year.

**Duration**  1 year or longer.

**Number awarded**  Varies each year; recently, 16 of these scholarships were awarded.

**Deadline**  January of each year.

## [23]
## ALPHA KAPPA ALPHA FINANCIAL NEED SCHOLARSHIPS

Alpha Kappa Alpha Sorority, Inc.
Attn: Educational Advancement Foundation
5656 South Stony Island Avenue
Chicago, IL 60637
(773) 947-0026          Toll-free: (800) 653-6528
Fax: (773) 947-0277          E-mail: akaeaf@aol.com
Web: www.akaeaf.org/scholarships.htm

**Summary**  To provide financial assistance to undergraduate and graduate students (especially African American women) who demonstrate financial need.

**Eligibility**  This program is sponsored by an African American sorority and is open to undergraduate or graduate students who have completed at least 1 year in an accredited degree-granting institution or a work-in-progress program in a noninstitutional setting, are planning to continue their program of education, and can demonstrate unmet financial need. Applicants must have a GPA of 2.5 or higher.

**Financial data**  Awards range from $750 to $1,500 per year.

**Duration**  1 year; nonrenewable.

**Number awarded**  Varies each year. Recently, 38 of these scholarships were awarded: 26 to undergraduates and 12 to graduate students.

**Deadline**  January of each year.

## [24]
## ALPHA KAPPA ALPHA MERIT SCHOLARSHIPS

Alpha Kappa Alpha Sorority, Inc.
Attn: Educational Advancement Foundation
5656 South Stony Island Avenue
Chicago, IL 60637
(773) 947-0026          Toll-free: (800) 653-6528
Fax: (773) 947-0277          E-mail: akaeaf@aol.com
Web: www.akaeaf.org/scholarships.htm

**Summary**  To provide financial assistance to undergraduate and graduate students (especially African American women) who have excelled academically.

**Eligibility**  This program, sponsored by an African American womenÖs sorority, is open to undergraduate and graduate students who have completed at least 1 year in an accredited degree-granting institution and are planning to continue their program of education. Applicants must have demonstrated exceptional academic achievement (GPA of 3.0 or higher) and present evidence of leadership through community service and involvement.

**Financial data**  The stipend is $1,000 per year.

**Duration**  1 year; nonrenewable.

**Number awarded**  Varies each year. Recently, 27 of these scholarships were awarded: 20 to undergraduates and 7 to graduate students.

**Deadline**  January of each year.

## [25]
## ALPHA KAPPA/JEAN HALL SCHOLARSHIP

Epsilon Sigma Alpha
Attn: ESA Foundation Assistant Scholarship Director
P.O. Box 270517
Fort Collins, CO 80527
(970) 223-2824          Fax: (970) 223-4456
Web: www.esaintl.com/esaf

**Summary**  To provide financial assistance for college to women in Michigan.

**Eligibility**  This program is open to women residents of Michigan who are either 1) graduating high school seniors in the top 25% of their class or with minimum scores of 20 on the ACT or an equivalent score on the SAT, or 2) students already enrolled in college in Michigan with a GPA of 3.0 or higher. Students enrolled for training in a technical school or returning to school after an absence are also eligible. Applicants must be planning to attend at a college or university in Michigan. There are no restrictions on the major chosen. Selection is based on character (20%), leadership (20%), service (20%), financial need (20%), and scholastic ability (20%).

**Financial data**  The stipend is $500.

**Duration**  1 year; may be renewed.

**Additional information**  Epsilon Sigma Alpha (ESA) is a women's service organization. Information is also available from Lynn Hughes, Scholarship Director, 324 N.E. Mead, Grants Pass, OR 97526, (541) 476-4617, E-mail: orcycler@vsisp.net. Alpha Kappa chapter #4401 of ESA established this scholarship in 1997. Completed applications must be submitted to the ESA State Counselor who verifies the information before forwarding them to the scholarship director. Recipients must attend college in Michigan. A $5 processing fee is required.

**Number awarded** 1 each year.
**Deadline** January of each year.

## [26]
## ALPHA OMICRON PI SCHOLARSHIPS

Alpha Omicron Pi Foundation
Attn: Scholarship Committee
5390 Virginia Way
P.O. Box 395
Brentwood, TN 37024-0395
(615) 370-0920                    Fax: (615) 370-4424
E-mail: foundation@alphaomicronpi.org
Web: www.aoiifoundation.org

**Summary** To provide financial assistance for college or graduate school to collegiate and alumnae members of Alpha Omicron Pi.

**Eligibility** This program is open to collegiate members of Alpha Omicron Pi who wish to continue their undergraduate education and alumnae members who wish to work on a graduate degree. Applicants must submit 50-word essays on the following topics: 1) the circumstances that have created their need for this scholarship, and 2) their immediate and long-term life objectives. Selection is based on academic excellence, dedication to serving the community and Alpha Omicron Pi, and financial need.

**Financial data** A stipend is awarded (amount not specified).

**Duration** 1 year.

**Additional information** This program was established in 1962. Undergraduate recipients must enroll full time, but graduate recipients may enroll part time.

**Number awarded** Varies each year.

**Deadline** February of each year.

## [27]
## ALPHA TAU CHAPTER SCHOLARSHIP

Alpha Omicron Pi Foundation
Attn: Scholarship Committee
5390 Virginia Way
P.O. Box 395
Brentwood, TN 37024-0395
(615) 370-0920                    Fax: (615) 370-4424
E-mail: foundation@alphaomicronpi.org
Web: www.aoiifoundation.org

**Summary** To provide financial assistance for college or graduate school to collegiate and alumnae members of Alpha Omicron Pi.

**Eligibility** This program is open to collegiate members of Alpha Omicron Pi who wish to continue their undergraduate education and alumnae members who wish to work on a graduate degree. Applicants must submit 50-word essays on the following topics: 1) the circumstances that have created their need for this scholarship, and 2) their immediate and long-term life objectives. Selection is based on academic excellence, dedication to serving the community and Alpha Omicron Pi, and financial need. Preference is given to legacies.

**Financial data** A stipend is awarded (amount not specified).

**Duration** 1 year.

**Additional information** Undergraduate recipients must enroll full time, but graduate recipients may enroll part time.

**Number awarded** 1 each year.

**Deadline** February of each year.

## [28]
## ALPHA ZETA UNDERGRADUATE MEMBER ASSISTANCE GRANT IN MEMORY OF KAY ROH

Alpha Chi Omega Foundation
Attn: Foundation Programs Coordinator
5939 Castle Creek Parkway North Drive
Indianapolis, IN 46250-4343
(317) 579-5050, ext. 262        Fax: (317) 579-5051
E-mail: foundation@alphachiomega.org
Web: www.alphachiomega.org

**Summary** To provide funding to members of Alpha Chi Omega sorority with ties to Missouri who need assistance to remain enrolled in college.

**Eligibility** This program is open to members of the sorority at the undergraduate level who live or attend school in Missouri. Applicants must be seeking funding to remain enrolled as a full-time student and a participant in their collegiate chapter.

**Financial data** The grant is $1,500.

**Duration** 1 year.

**Number awarded** 1 each year.

**Deadline** Applications may be submitted at any time.

## [29]
## AMELIA EARHART MEMORIAL SCHOLARSHIPS

Ninety-Nines, Inc.
4300 Amelia Earhart Road
Oklahoma City, OK 73159
(405) 685-7969               Toll-free: (800) 994-1929
Fax: (405) 685-7985          E-mail: ihq99s@cs.com
Web: www.ninety-nines.org/aemsf.html

**Summary** To provide financial support to members of the Ninety-Nines (an organization of women pilots) who are interested in advanced flight training or academic study related to aviation.

**Eligibility** This program is open to women who have been members of the organization for at least 1 year. Applicants must be interested in 1 of the following 4 types of scholarships: 1) flight training, to complete an advanced pilot certificate or rating or pilot training course; 2) jet type rating, to complete type rating certification in any jet; 3) technical certification, to complete an aviation or aerospace technical training or certification course; or 4) academic, to work on an associate, bachelor's, master's, or doctoral degree in such fields as aerospace engineering, aviation technology, aviation business management, air traffic management, or professional pilot. They must submit their application to their Ninety-Nines scholarship chair, who forwards it to the appropriate Amelia Earhart Scholarship Trustee. Applicants for flight training scholarships must be a current pilot with the appropriate medical certification and approaching the flight time requirement for the rating or certificate. Applicants for jet type rating scholarships must be a current airline transport pilot with a first-class medical certificate and at least 100 hours of multi-engine flight time or combined multi-engine and turbine time. Applicants for academic scholarships must be currently enrolled; associate or bachelor's degree students must have a GPA of 3.0 or higher. Financial need is considered in the selection process.

**Financial data** Flight training, jet type rating, and technical certification scholarships provide payment of all costs to complete the appropriate rating or certificate. Academic scholarships provide a stipend of up to $5,000 per year.

**Duration** Support is provided until completion of the rating, certificate, or degree.

**Additional information** This program was established in 1941. It includes the following endowed scholarships: the Jane Zieber Kelley Memorial Scholarship of the Aeons (established in 1979), the Gerda Ruhnke Memorial Flight Instructor Scholarship (established in 1988), the Geraldine Mickelsen Memorial Scholarship (established in 1993), the Alice Hammond Memorial Scholarship (established in 1995), the Lydiellen M. Hagan Memorial Scholarship (established in 1997), the Katherine A. Menges Brick Scholarship (established in 1998), the Betty DeWitt Witmer Scholarship (established in 1999), the Virginia S. Richardson Memorial Scholarship (established in 2000), the Darlene Sanders Memorial Scholarship (established in 2000), the Milton and Bonnie Seymour Memorial Scholarship (established in 2000), the Marion Barnick Memorial Scholarship (established in 2001), the Evelyn Bryan Johnson Memorial Scholarship (established in 2002), and the Mary Kelley Memorial Scholarship (established in 2003).

**Number awarded** Varies each year; recently, 13 of these scholarships were awarded.

**Deadline** Applications must be submitted to the chapter scholarship chair by November of each year; they must forward the applications from their chapter to the designated trustee by January of each year.

## [30]
## AMERICAN ASSOCIATION OF JAPANESE UNIVERSITY WOMEN SCHOLARSHIP PROGRAM

American Association of Japanese University Women
c/o Akiko Agishi, Scholarship Committee Co-Chair
Creative International, Inc.
3127 Nicholas Canyon Road
Los Angeles, CA 90046
E-mail: scholarship@aajuw.org
Web: www.aajuw.org/Scholarship.htm

**Summary** To provide financial assistance to female students currently enrolled in upper-division or graduate classes in California.

**Eligibility** This program is open to female students enrolled in accredited colleges or universities in California. They must have junior, senior, or graduate standing. Applicants must be a contributor to U.S.-Japan relations, cultural exchanges, and leadership development in the areas of their designated field of study. To apply, they must submit a current resume, an official transcript of the past 2 years of college work, 2 letters of recommendation, and an essay (up to 2 pages in English or 1,200 characters in Japanese) on either 1) what they hope to accomplish in their field of study to develop leadership and role model qualities, or 2) thoughts on how their field of study can contribute to U.S.-Japan relations and benefit international relations.

**Financial data** The stipend is $1,500.

**Duration** 1 year.

**Additional information** The association was founded in 1970 to promote the education of women as well as to contribute to U.S.-Japan relations, cultural exchanges, and leadership development.

**Number awarded** 2 or 3 each year.

**Deadline** October of each year.

## [31]
## AMERICAN LEGION AUXILIARY EMERGENCY FUND

American Legion Auxiliary
777 North Meridian Street, Third Floor
Indianapolis, IN 46204-1189
(317) 955-3845                     Fax: (317) 955-3884
E-mail: alahq@legion-aux.org
Web: www.legion-aux.org

**Summary** To provide funding to members of the American Legion Auxiliary who are facing temporary emergency needs.

**Eligibility** This program is open to members of the American Legion Auxiliary who have maintained their membership for the immediate past 2 consecutive years and have paid their dues for the current year. Applicants must need emergency assistance for the following purposes: 1) food, shelter, and utilities during a time of financial crisis; 2) food and shelter for victims of weather-related emergencies and natural disasters; or 3) educational training for members who, because of changes in their life such as death of a spouse, divorce, or separation, have become the main source of support for their family. They must have exhausted all other sources of financial assistance, including funds and/or services available through the local Post and/or Unit, appropriate community welfare agencies, or state and federal financial aid for education. Grants are not available to settle already existing or accumulated debts, handle catastrophic illness, resettle disaster victims, or other similar problems.

**Financial data** The maximum grant is $2,400. Payments may be made directly to the member or to the mortgage company or utility. Educational grants may be paid directly to the educational institution.

**Duration** Grants are expended over no more than 3 months.

**Additional information** This program was established in 1969. In 1981, it was expanded to include the Displaced Homemaker Fund (although that title is no longer used).

**Number awarded** Varies each year.

**Deadline** Applications may be submitted at any time.

## [32]
## AMERICAN METEOROLOGICAL SOCIETY UNDERGRADUATE SCHOLARSHIPS

American Meteorological Society
Attn: Fellowship/Scholarship Program
45 Beacon Street
Boston, MA 02108-3693
(617) 227-2426, ext. 246          Fax: (617) 742-8718
E-mail: scholar@ametsoc.org
Web: www.ametsoc.org

**Summary**  To provide financial assistance to undergraduates (particularly women, minorities, and persons with disabilities) majoring in meteorology or an aspect of atmospheric sciences.

**Eligibility**  This program is open to full-time students entering their final year of undergraduate study and majoring in meteorology or an aspect of the atmospheric or related oceanic and hydrologic sciences. Applicants must intend to make atmospheric or related sciences their career. They must be U.S. citizens or permanent residents enrolled at a U.S. institution and have a cumulative GPA of 3.25 or higher. Along with their application, they must submit 200-word essays on 1) their most important achievements that qualify them for this scholarship, and 2) their career goals in the atmospheric or related oceanic or hydrologic fields. Selection is based on academic excellence and achievement; financial need is not considered. The sponsor specifically encourages applications from women, minorities, and students with disabilities who are traditionally underrepresented in the atmospheric and related oceanic sciences.

**Financial data**  Stipends range from $700 to $5,000 per year.

**Duration**  1 year.

**Additional information**  This program includes the following named scholarships: the Howard H. Hanks, Jr. Scholarship in Meteorology ($700), the AMS 75th Anniversary Endowed Scholarship ($2,000), the Om and Saraswati (Sara) Bahethi Scholarship ($2,000), the Howard T. Orville Endowed Scholarship in Meteorology ($5,000), the George S. Benton Scholarship ($3,500), the Carl W. Kreitzberg Endowed Scholarship ($2,000), the Dr. Pedro Grau Undergraduate Scholarship ($2,500), the Guillermo Salazar Rodriguez Scholarship ($2,500), the John R. Hope Endowed Scholarship in Atmospheric Science ($2,500), the Richard and Helen Hagemeyer Scholarship ($3,000), the Paros-Digiquartz Scholarship ($2,500) and the Werner A. Baum Endowed Scholarship ($5,000). Requests for an application must be accompanied by a self-addressed stamped envelope.

**Number awarded**  Varies each year; recently, 15 of these scholarships were awarded.

**Deadline**  February of each year.

## [33]
## AMERICAN MILITARY SPOUSE EDUCATION FOUNDATION SCHOLARSHIPS

American Military Spouse Education Foundation
9912 Great Oaks Way
Fairfax, VA 22030
(703) 591-8444          Fax: (703) 591-8333
E-mail: garybottorff@aol.com
Web: www.americanmilitaryspouse.org

**Summary**  To provide financial assistance for undergraduate study to spouses of military personnel.

**Eligibility**  This program is open to spouses of U.S. uniformed military service members (active-duty, Reserve, National Guard, and retired). Applicants must be enrolled in an undergraduate degree program. Spouses who are also uniformed military service members are ineligible. Within each category of military service (active-duty, Reserve, National Guard, retired), applicants with the lowest rank receive the highest priority. Ties are broken by date of rank. Special consideration is given to spouses whose military member was 1) killed while serving on active duty, or 2) wounded while serving on active duty and has received a disability rating of 50% or higher.

**Financial data**  Stipends range up to $3,000 per year.

**Duration**  1 year; may be renewed.

**Number awarded**  Varies each year.

**Deadline**  Applications may be submitted at any time.

## [34]
## AMERICAN NEWS WOMEN'S CLUB SCHOLARSHIPS

American News Women's Club
1607 22nd Street, N.W.
Washington, DC 20008
(202) 332-6770          Fax: (202) 265-6092
E-mail: anwclub@covad.net
Web: www.anwc.org/scholarships.html

**Summary**  To provide financial assistance to women working on a degree in journalism at designated universities in the Washington, D.C. area.

**Eligibility**  This program is open to women majoring in journalism at the following institutions: American University, Gallaudet University, George Washington University, Howard University, and University of Maryland. Applicants may be undergraduates or graduate students.

**Financial data**  A stipend is awarded (amount not specified).

**Duration**  1 year.

**Additional information**  This program began in 1975.

**Number awarded**  Varies each year; recently, 4 of these scholarships were awarded.

## [35]
## AMERICAN POLISH ENGINEERING SCHOLARSHIP

American Polish Engineering Association
c/o Dr. Barbara R. Koscierzynski
53657 Kristin Court
Shelby Township, MI 48316-2239
Web: www.apea.us

**Summary** To provide financial assistance to high school seniors of Polish origin who plan to study engineering in college.

**Eligibility** This program is open to high school seniors who are of Polish origin or descent. Applicants must have a GPA of 3.0 or higher and plans to attend a college or university with an accredited engineering-related program. They must be available for an interview with the sponsor's scholarship committee. Women and men applicants are judged separately.

**Financial data** The stipend is $1,000.

**Duration** 1 year.

**Number awarded** 2 each year: 1 to a woman and 1 to a man.

**Deadline** March of each year.

## [36]
## AMERICAN SOCIETY OF WOMEN ACCOUNTANTS UNDERGRADUATE SCHOLARSHIPS

American Society of Women Accountants
Attn: Educational Foundation
8405 Greensboro Drive, Suite 800
McLean, VA 22102
(703) 506-3265          Toll-free: (800) 326-2163
Fax: (703) 506-3266     E-mail: aswa@aswa.org
Web: www.aswa.org

**Summary** To provide financial assistance to undergraduate women interested in preparing for a career in accounting or finance.

**Eligibility** This program is open to women who are entering their third, fourth, or fifth year of undergraduate study at a college, university, or professional school of accounting. Applicants must have completed at least 60 semester hours with a declared major in accounting or finance. Selection is based on leadership, character, communication skills, scholastic average, and financial need. Membership in the American Society of Women Accountants (ASWA) is not required. Applications must be submitted to a local ASWA chapter.

**Financial data** The stipends range from $1,500 to $4,500 each.

**Duration** 1 year; recipients may reapply.

**Number awarded** Varies each year: recently, 8 of these scholarships were available, with a total value of $14,000.

**Deadline** Local chapters must submit their candidates to the national office by February of each year.

## [37]
## AMERICAN SOCIETY OF WOMEN ACCOUNTANTS 2-YEAR COLLEGE SCHOLARSHIPS

American Society of Women Accountants
Attn: Educational Foundation
8405 Greensboro Drive, Suite 800
McLean, VA 22102
(703) 506-3265          Toll-free: (800) 326-2163
Fax: (703) 506-3266     E-mail: aswa@aswa.org
Web: www.aswa.org

**Summary** To provide financial assistance to women working on an associate degree in accounting or finance.

**Eligibility** This program is open to women who are entering their second year of an associate degree program at a community or other 2-year college. Applicants must have completed at least 15 semester hours or the equivalent. They must be majoring in accounting or finance and have a GPA of 3.0 or higher. Selection is based on leadership, character, communication skills, scholastic average, and financial need. Membership in the American Society of Women Accountants (ASWA) is not required. Applications must be submitted to a local ASWA chapter.

**Financial data** The stipends range from $1,500 to $4,500 each.

**Duration** 1 year.

**Number awarded** Varies each year.

**Deadline** Local chapters must submit their candidates to the national office by February of each year.

## [38]
## AMERICA'S JUNIOR MISS SCHOLARSHIPS

America's Junior Miss
Attn: Foundation Administrator
751 Government Street
P.O. Box 2786
Mobile, AL 36652
(251) 438-3621          Fax: (251) 431-0063
TDD: (800) 256-5435     E-mail: foundation@ajm.org
Web: www.ajm.org

**Summary** To recognize and reward, with college scholarships, female high school seniors who enter the America's Junior Miss competition.

**Eligibility** This competition is open to girls who are seniors in high school. Contestants first enter local competitions, from which winners advance to the state level. The winner in each state is invited to the national competition, held in Mobile, Alabama in June of each year. Prior to the contestants' arrival for the national competition, the judges evaluate their high school academic records for the scholastics score (20% of the overall score). At the competition, girls are given scores on the basis of their personality, maturity, and ability to express themselves in an interview (25% of overall score); their performing arts talent presented on stage in front of an audience (25% of overall score); their fitness as demonstrated during a choreographed aerobic routine (15% of overall score); and their self-expression, demeanor, sense of style, and speaking ability (15% of overall score). The girls with the highest scores in the categories of talent, scholastics, fitness, and self-expression receive awards. Overall scores are used for selection of 8 finalists, from whom the winner and 2 runners-up are selected. Girls also submit a scrapbook, a daily journal, and essays on their community service, "Be Your Best Self," and "My Town." All of those are also evaluated for selection of awardees.

**Financial data** In a recent national competition, the winner received a $50,000 scholarship, first runner-up $15,000, second runner-up $10,000, and each other finalist $3,500. Other awards included $1,500 for the Community Service Essay Award and $1,000 each for the Spirit of Junior Miss Award, talent awards, scholastic awards, fitness awards, self-expression awards, "Be Your Best Self" Essay Awards, Scrapbook Awards, Daily Journal Award, and "My Town" Award. A total of $121,000 was awarded. Other scholarships are presented in state and local competitions.

**Duration** The competition is held annually.

**Additional information** This program was established in 1958 and closed in 2005. In 2006, it was reopened. National sponsors include Tyson Foods, SeaWorld, Busch Gardens, the Mitchell Company, the City of Mobile (Alabama), and Mobile County.

**Number awarded** Recently, awards included 1 winner, 1 first runner-up, 1 second runner up, 5 other finalists, 1 Community Service Essay Award, 1 Spirit of Junior Miss Award, 5 talent awards, 5 scholastic awards, 5 fitness awards, 5 self-expressions awards, 3 "Be Your Best Self" Essay Awards, 1 Scrapbook Award, 1 Daily Journal Award, and 1 "My Town" Award. Because each competitor could receive multiple awards, a total of 21 girls received awards.

**Deadline** Deadlines vary in different parts of the country.

## [39]
## AMERICA'S NATIONAL TEEN-AGER SCHOLARSHIP PROGRAM

> National Teen-Ager Scholarship Foundation
> Attn: Cheryl Snow
> 808 Deer Crossing Court
> Nashville, TN 37220
> (615) 370-4338        Toll-free: (866) NAT-TEEN
> Fax: (615) 377-0223      E-mail: telwar@comcast.net
> Web: www.nationalteen.com

**Summary** To recognize (locally and nationally) the scholastic and leadership achievements of America's teenage girls and to provide cash, tuition scholarships, and awards to the participants.

**Eligibility** Girls who are 12 to 15 years of age are eligible to enter the Miss Junior National Teenager competition and girls who are 16 to 18 may enter the Miss National Teenager competition. Entrants must have no children and never have been married. Selection is based on academic excellence (15%), school and community involvement (15%), social and conversational skills in an interview (30%), poise and personality in an evening gown (15%), personal expression (15%), and response to an on-stage question (10%). There is no swimsuit competition.

**Financial data** Miss National Teenager receives approximately $40,000 in cash, trips, and prizes, including a $10,000 college scholarship. Miss Junior National Teenager receives approximately $35,000 in cash, trips, and prizes, including a $5,000 college scholarship. In addition, a number of academic institutions offer scholarships to state or national winners.

**Duration** The contest is held annually.

**Additional information** The contest began in 1971, to recognize the leadership achievements of America's teenagers and to provide travel, entertainment, and scholarships for their college education. The application fee is $25.

**Deadline** Deadline dates vary. Check with the sponsors of your local and state pageant.

## [40]
## AMS FRESHMAN UNDERGRADUATE SCHOLARSHIPS

> American Meteorological Society
> Attn: Fellowship/Scholarship Coordinator
> 45 Beacon Street
> Boston, MA 02108-3693
> (617) 227-2426, ext. 246      Fax: (617) 742-8718
> E-mail: scholar@ametsoc.org
> Web: www.ametsoc.org

**Summary** To provide financial assistance to high school seniors planning to attend college to prepare for a career in the atmospheric and related oceanic and hydrologic sciences.

**Eligibility** This program is open to high school seniors entering their freshman year of college to work on a bachelor's degree in the atmospheric or related oceanic or hydrologic sciences. Applicants must be U.S. citizens or permanent residents planning to enroll full time. Along with their application, they must submit a 500-word essay on how they believe their college education, and what they learn in the atmospheric and related sciences, will help them to serve society during their professional career. Selection is based on performance in high school, including academic records, recommendations, scores from a national examination, and the essay. Financial need is not considered. The sponsor specifically encourages applications from women, minorities, and students with disabilities who are traditionally underrepresented in the atmospheric and related oceanic sciences.

**Financial data** The stipend is $2,500 per academic year.

**Duration** 1 year; may be renewed for the second year of college study.

**Additional information** Requests for an application must be accompanied by a self-addressed stamped envelope.

**Number awarded** Varies each year; recently, 14 of these scholarships were awarded.

**Deadline** February of each year.

## [41]
## AMVETS LADIES AUXILIARY CAREER START SCHOLARSHIPS

> AMVETS Ladies Auxiliary
> Attn: National Scholarship Officer
> 4647 Forbes Boulevard
> Lanham, MD 20706-4380
> (301) 459-6255
> Web: amvetsaux.org/programs.htm

**Summary** To provide financial assistance for college to members of the AMVETS Ladies Auxiliary who are interested in reentering the workforce.

**Eligibility** This program is open to current members who are interested in expanding, updating, and/or reentering the workforce. Applicants must have completed at least 1 semester of study at an accredited technical school, business school, college, or university. They must submit an essay, 200 to 500 words in length, on their past and future career and educational objectives. Selection is based on financial need (35%), academic record (25%), the essay (25%), and 3 letters of reference (15%).

**Financial data** The stipend is $500.

**Duration** 1 year.

**Number awarded** Up to 3 each year.

**Deadline** May of each year.

## [42]
## AMVETS NATIONAL LADIES AUXILIARY SCHOLARSHIPS

AMVETS Ladies Auxiliary
Attn: National Scholarship Officer
4647 Forbes Boulevard
Lanham, MD 20706-4380
(301) 459-6255                Fax: (301) 459-5403
E-mail: auxiliary@amvets.org
Web: amvetsaux.org/programs.htm

**Summary** To provide financial assistance to members and certain dependents of members of AMVETS Auxiliary who are already enrolled in college.

**Eligibility** Applicants must belong to AMVETS Auxiliary or be the child or grandchild of a member. They must be in at least the second year of undergraduate study at an accredited college or university. Applications must include 3 letters of recommendation and an essay (from 200 to 500 words) about their past accomplishments, career and educational goals, and objectives for the future. Selection is based on the letters of reference (15%), academic record (25%), the essay (25%), and financial need (35%).

**Financial data** Scholarships are $1,000 or $750 each.

**Duration** 1 year.

**Number awarded** Up to 7 each year: 2 at $1,000 and 5 at $750.

**Deadline** May of each year.

## [43]
## ANITA BORG SCHOLARSHIPS

Google Inc.
Attn: Scholarships
1600 Amphitheatre Parkway
Mountain View, CA 94043-8303
(650) 623-4000                Fax: (650) 618-1499
E-mail: anitaborgscholars@google.com
Web: www.google.com/anitaborg

**Summary** To provide financial assistance to women working on a bachelor's or graduate degree in a computer-related field.

**Eligibility** This program is open to women who are entering their senior year of undergraduate study or are enrolled in a graduate program in computer science, computer engineering, or a related field. Applicants must be full-time students at a university in the United States with a GPA of 3.5 or higher. They must submit essays of 400 to 600 words on

1) a significant technical project on which they have worked; 2) examples of their leadership abilities; 3) what they would do if someone gave them the funding and resources for a 3- to 12-month project to investigate a technical topic of their choice; and 4) what they would do if someone gave them $1,000 to plan an event or project to benefit women in technical fields. Selection is based on academic background and demonstrated leadership.

**Financial data** The stipend is $10,000.

**Duration** 1 year.

**Additional information** These scholarships were first offered in 2004.

**Number awarded** Varies each year. Recently, 4 of these scholarships were awarded: 1 to an undergraduate, 2 to master's degree candidates, and 1 to a doctoral candidate.

**Deadline** January of each year.

## [44]
## ANN ARBOR AWC SCHOLARSHIP FOR WOMEN IN COMPUTING

Association for Women in Computing-Ann Arbor
    Chapter
Attn: Scholarship
P.O. Box 1864
Ann Arbor, MI 48106-1864
E-mail: awc@hvcn.org
Web: www.awc-aa.org/gala/scholarship.php

**Summary** To provide financial assistance to women undergraduates working on a degree in a computer- or technology-related field at institutions in Michigan.

**Eligibility** This program is open to undergraduate women enrolled at institutions of higher education in Michigan. Applicants must be U.S. citizens or permanent residents preparing for a career in a field related to computers or technology. They must have at least 2 semesters of course work remaining. As part of the application, they must answer the following 3 questions: 1) "Why are you excited about working with computers and information technology?" 2) "Describe your most fulfilling computer-related project or experience;" and 3) "Identify a current trend in technology and describe how it might evolve over the next ten years." Based on those essays, awards are presented to applicants who demonstrate motivation, passion, thoughtfulness, creativity, skillful communication, and participation in the computing community. Financial need is not considered.

**Financial data** A stipend is awarded (amount not specified).

**Duration** 1 year.

**Number awarded** 1 or more each year.

**Deadline** March of each year.

## [45]
## ANNA GEAR JUNIOR SCHOLARSHIP

American Legion Auxiliary
Department of Virginia
Attn: Education Chair
1708 Commonwealth Avenue
Richmond, VA 23230
(804) 355-6410       Fax: (804) 353-1940

**Summary** To provide financial assistance for college to junior members of the American Legion Auxiliary in Virginia.

**Eligibility** This program is open to seniors at accredited high schools in Virginia. Applicants must have held junior membership in the American Legion Auxiliary for the 3 previous years. They must have completed at least 30 hours of volunteer service within their community and submit a 500-word article on "The Value of Volunteering in the Community."

**Financial data** The stipend is $1,000.

**Duration** 1 year.

**Number awarded** 1 each year.

**Deadline** March of each year.

## [46]
## ANNE MAUREEN WHITNEY BARROW MEMORIAL SCHOLARSHIP

Society of Women Engineers
230 East Ohio Street, Suite 400
Chicago, IL 60611-3265
(312) 596-5223       Toll-free: (877) SWE-INFO
Fax: (312) 644-8557
E-mail: scholarshipapplication@swe.org
Web: www.swe.org/scholarships

**Summary** To provide financial assistance to women interested in studying engineering or engineering technology in college.

**Eligibility** This program is open to women who are enrolled or planning to enroll full time at an ABET-accredited 4-year college or university. Applicants must have a GPA of 3.0 or higher and be planning to major in engineering or engineering technology. Along with their application, they must submit a 1-page essay on why they want to be an engineer, how they believe they will make a difference as an engineer, and what influenced them to study engineering. Selection is based on merit.

**Financial data** The stipend is $5,000.

**Duration** 1 year; may be renewed for 3 additional years.

**Additional information** This program was established in 1992.

**Number awarded** 1 every 4 years.

**Deadline** May of the years in which it is offered.

## [47]
## ANNE PEEL HOPKINS GRANT

Alpha Chi Omega Foundation
Attn: Foundation Programs Coordinator
5939 Castle Creek Parkway North Drive
Indianapolis, IN 46250-4343
(317) 579-5050, ext. 262       Fax: (317) 579-5051
E-mail: foundation@alphachiomega.org
Web: www.alphachiomega.org

**Summary** To provide financial assistance to undergraduate or alumnae members of Alpha Chi Omega who are interested in working on a degree in education.

**Eligibility** This program is open to undergraduate and graduate members of Alpha Chi Omega who are enrolled full time. Preference is given to education majors. Selection is based on academic achievement, chapter involvement, campus and community involvement, and financial need.

**Financial data** The stipend is $500.

**Duration** 1 year.

**Number awarded** 1 each year.

**Deadline** March of each year.

## [48]
## AOWCGWA SCHOLARSHIP PROGRAM

Army Officers' Wives' Club of the Greater Washington
   Area
c/o Sandy Oujiri, Scholarship Committee Chair
7753 Jewelweed Court
Springfield, VA 22152
E-mail: aowcgwascScholarship@fmthriftshop.org
Web: www.fmthriftshop.org/scholarshippage.html

**Summary** To provide financial assistance for college to the children and spouses of U.S. Army personnel and veterans in the Washington, D.C. metropolitan area.

**Eligibility** This program is open to 1) high school seniors who are children of Army personnel, 2) college students under 22 years of age who are children of Army personnel; and 3) spouses of Army personnel. High school seniors and spouses must reside with their sponsor in the Washington metropolitan area; the sponsor of college students must reside in that area. Sponsors may be active-duty, retired, or deceased, and officer or enlisted. Applicants must submit a 500-word statement on their personal ambitions and goals; a list of extracurricular activities, honors, church activities, community service, and employment; an official transcript that includes (for high school seniors) their SAT or ACT scores; and a letter of recommendation. Students who plan to attend a service academy or receive another full scholarship are not eligible. Selection is based on scholastic merit and community involvement; financial need is not considered.

**Financial data** The stipend is at least $2,000.

**Duration** 1 year.

**Additional information** The Washington metropolitan area is defined to include the Virginia cities of Alexandria, Fairfax, Falls Church, Manassas, and Manassas Park; the Virginia counties of Arlington, Fairfax, Fauquier, Loudoun, Prince William, and Stafford; the Maryland counties of Calvert, Charles, Frederick, Montgomery, and Prince George's; and the District of Columbia. This program is supported in part by the First Command Educational Foundation.

**Number awarded** 1 or more each year.

**Deadline** March of each year.

## [49]
## APPRAISAL INSTITUTE MINORITIES AND WOMEN EDUCATIONAL SCHOLARSHIP PROGRAM

Appraisal Institute
Attn: Minorities and Women Scholarship Fund
550 West Van Buren Street, Suite 1000
Chicago, IL 60607
(312) 335-4191                    Fax: (312) 335-4196
E-mail: wwoodburn@appraisalinstitute.org
Web: www.appraisalinstitute.org

**Summary** To provide financial assistance to women and minority undergraduate students majoring in real estate or allied fields.

**Eligibility** This program is open to members of groups underrepresented in the real estate appraisal profession. Those groups include women, American Indians, Alaska Natives, Asians, Black or African Americans, Hispanics or Latinos, and Native Hawaiians or other Pacific Islanders. Applicants must be full- or part-time students enrolled in real estate courses within a degree-granting college, university, or junior college. They must submit evidence of demonstrated financial need and a GPA of 2.5 or higher. U.S. citizenship is required.

**Financial data** The stipend is $1,000 per year. Funds are paid directly to the recipient's institution to be used for tuition and fees.

**Duration** 1 year.

**Number awarded** At least 1 each year.

**Deadline** April of each year.

## [50]
## ARFORA UNDERGRADUATE SCHOLARSHIP FOR WOMEN

Romanian Orthodox Episcopate of America
Attn: Scholarship Committee
1920 King James Parkway, Apartment 18
Westlake, OH 44145-3466
E-mail: roeasolia@aol.com
Web: www.roea.org/schol/schol-arfora.htm

**Summary** To provide financial assistance to women who are members of a parish of the Romanian Orthodox Episcopate of America and currently enrolled in college.

**Eligibility** Applicants must be women, voting members of a parish of the Romanian Orthodox Episcopate of America, and currently enrolled in college (at the sophomore or higher level). As part of the application process, students must submit a formal letter describing their personal goals, projected use of the degree, church and community involvement, and honors and awards.

**Financial data** The stipend is $500.

**Duration** 1 year.

**Additional information** The first scholarship was awarded in 1994. This program is offered by the Association of Romanian Orthodox Ladies Auxiliaries (ARFORA).

**Number awarded** 2 each year.

**Deadline** April of each year.

## [51]
## ARIZONA BPW FOUNDATION ANNUAL SCHOLARSHIPS

Arizona Business and Professional Women's Foundation
Attn: Administrator
P.O. Box 521
Clifton, AZ 85533
(928) 687-1300              E-mail: vcpage@aznex.net
Web: www.arizonabpwfoundation.com

**Summary** To provide financial assistance to women in Arizona who are attending or interested in attending a community college in the state.

**Eligibility** This program is open to women, at least 20 years of age, who are attending a community college in Arizona. Applicants must fall into 1 of the following categories: women who have been out of the workforce and wish to upgrade their skills; women with no previous experience in the workforce who are seeking a marketable skill, and women who are currently employed who are interested in career advancement or change. Along with their application, they must submit 2 letters of recommendation, a statement of financial need (latest income tax return must be provided), a career goal statement, and their most recent transcript (when available). Selection is based on financial need, field of study, and possibility of success.

**Financial data** The stipend is $1,000 per year.

**Duration** 1 year; renewable for up to 3 consecutive semesters if the recipient maintains a GPA of 2.0 or higher.

**Additional information** In addition to the general scholarship, there are 3 named endowments: Dr. Dorine Chancellor (established in 1990 and open to students at any community college in Arizona, although 1 is set aside specifically for a student at Eastern Arizona College), Lynda Crowell (established in 1999 and open to students at community colleges in Maricopa County), and Muriel Lothrop-Ely (established in 2006 and open to students at any community college in Arizona).

**Number awarded** Several each year.

**Deadline** February of each year.

## [52]
## ARIZONA NETWORK OF EXECUTIVE WOMEN IN HOSPITALITY SCHOLARSHIP AWARDS

Network of Executive Women in Hospitality-Arizona Chapter
Attn: Marie May, Director of Scholarship and Education
P.O. Box 7546
Phoenix, AZ 85011-7546
Toll-free: (800) 593-NEWH         Fax: (800) 693-NEWH
E-mail: marie.may@bestwestern.com
Web: www.newh.org/newh/scholarshippacket.php

**Summary** To provide financial assistance to women in Arizona and New Mexico who wish to work on a college degree in a hospitality-related field.

**Eligibility** This program is open to women who have completed half the requirements for a degree or certification program at a vocational school or college in Arizona or New Mexico. Applicants must have a GPA of 3.0 or higher and a career objective in the hospitality or food service industries (e.g., hotel and restaurant management, culinary, food service, architecture, design). Selection is based on financial need and academic accomplishments.

**Financial data** The stipend is $1,000 per year.

**Duration** 1 year.

**Number awarded** Varies each year; recently, 2 of these scholarships were awarded.

**Deadline** April of each year.

## [53]
## ARIZONA NON-TRADITIONAL EDUCATION FOR WOMEN SCHOLARSHIPS

Arizona Business and Professional Women's
    Foundation
Attn: Administrator
P.O. Box 521
Clifton, AZ 85533
(928) 687-1300            E-mail: vcpage@aznex.net
Web: www.arizonabpwfoundation.com

**Summary** To provide financial assistance to reentry women in Arizona who are interested in entering nontraditional fields.

**Eligibility** This program is open to women with Arizona residency who are reentering the workforce or changing careers in order to establish self-sufficiency. Applicants must be preparing for a career in an occupational field in which women constitute less than 25% of those employed. They should be enrolled in, accepted to, or making application to a school in Arizona that provides training in nontraditional employment, or be currently employed in a nontraditional field and taking career-related training. Along with their application, they must submit 2 letters of recommendation, a statement of financial need (latest income tax return must be provided), a career goal statement, and their most recent transcript (when available). Selection is based on financial need, field of study, and possibility of success.

**Financial data** The stipend is $1,000.

**Duration** 1 year.

**Number awarded** 1 or more each year.

**Deadline** February of each year.

## [54]
## ARKANSAS MISSING IN ACTION/KILLED IN ACTION DEPENDENTS' SCHOLARSHIP PROGRAM

Arkansas Department of Higher Education
Attn: Financial Aid Division
114 East Capitol Avenue
Little Rock, AR 72201-3818
(501) 371-2050            Toll-free: (800) 54-STUDY
Fax: (501) 371-2001    E-mail: finaid@adhe.arknet.edu
Web: www.arkansashighered.com/miakia.html

**Summary** To provide financial assistance for educational purposes to dependents of Arkansas veterans who were killed in action or became POWs or MIAs after January 1, 1960.

**Eligibility** This program is open to the natural children, adopted children, stepchildren, and spouses of Arkansas residents who became a prisoner of war, killed in action, missing in action, or killed on ordnance delivery after January 1, 1960. Applicants may be working or planning to work

on 1) an undergraduate degree in Arkansas or 2) a graduate or professional degree in Arkansas if their undergraduate degree was not received in Arkansas. Applicants need not be current Arkansas residents, but their parents or spouses must have been an Arkansas resident at the time of entering military service or at the time they were declared a prisoner of war, killed in action, or missing in action.

**Financial data** The program pays for tuition, general registration fees, special course fees, activity fees, room and board (if provided in campus facilities), and other charges associated with earning a degree or certificate.

**Duration** 1 year; undergraduates may obtain renewal as long as they make satisfactory progress toward a baccalaureate degree; graduate students may obtain renewal as long as they maintain a minimum GPA of 2.5 and make satisfactory progress toward a degree.

**Additional information** Return or reported death of the veteran will not alter benefits. Applications must be submitted to the financial aid director at an Arkansas state-supported institution of higher education or state-supported technical/vocational school.

**Number awarded** Varies each year; recently, 4 of these scholarships were awarded.

**Deadline** July of each year for the fall term; November of each year for the spring term; April of each year for summer term I; June of each year for summer term II.

## [55]
## ARKANSAS STATE FARM SCHOLAR-ATHLETE PROGRAM

Arkansas Activities Association
3920 Richards Road
North Little Rock, AR 72117
(501) 955-2500            Fax: (501) 955-2600
Web: www.ahsaa.org

**Summary** To provide financial assistance for college to high school seniors in Arkansas who have participated in athletics.

**Eligibility** This program is open to seniors graduating from high schools in Arkansas who have a GPA of 3.5 or higher and scores of at least 21 on the ACT or an equivalent score on the SAT. Boys must have participated in the following sports: football, basketball, baseball, track and field, or other sports; girls must have participated in volleyball, basketball, softball, track and field, or other sports. Applicants must submit an essay on the reasons they believe they qualify for this scholarship and why they want to receive it. Selection is based on the essay, academic achievement, citizenship in school and in the community, leadership traits, and participation in other school activities.

**Financial data** The stipend is $500.

**Duration** 1 year; nonrenewable.

**Additional information** This program is sponsored by State Farm Insurance Companies and its Arkansas agents.

**Number awarded** 10 each year: 1 boy in each of the 5 qualifying sports and 1 girl in each of the 5 qualifying sports.

**Deadline** April of each year.

## [56]
## ARLENE DAVIS SCHOLARSHIP

Delta Zeta Sorority
Attn: Foundation Coordinator
202 East Church Street
Oxford, OH 45056
(513) 523-7597    E-mail: DZFoundation@dzshq.com
Web: www.deltazeta.org

**Summary**  To provide financial assistance for continued undergraduate study to members of Delta Zeta Sorority.

**Eligibility**  This program is open to members of the sorority who have a GPA of 3.0 or higher. Applicants should be entering their sophomore or junior year and working on a degree closely related to aviation. They must submit an official transcript, a statement of their career goals, information on their service to the sorority, documentation of campus activities and/or community involvement, and a list of academic honors. Financial need is also considered in the selection process.

**Financial data**  The stipend ranges from $900 to $1,100, depending on the availability of funds.

**Duration**  1 year; nonrenewable.

**Number awarded**  1 each year.

**Deadline**  February of each year.

## [57]
## ARMY AVIATION ASSOCIATION OF AMERICA SCHOLARSHIPS

Army Aviation Association of America Scholarship
   Foundation
Attn: AAAA Scholarship Foundation
755 Main Street, Suite 4D
Monroe, CT 06468-2830
(203) 268-2450               Fax: (203) 268-5870
E-mail: aaaa@quad-a.org
Web: www.quad-a.org/scholarship.htm

**Summary**  To provide financial aid for undergraduate or graduate study to members of the Army Aviation Association of America (AAAA) and their relatives.

**Eligibility**  This program is open to AAAA members and their spouses, unmarried siblings, unmarried children, and unmarried grandchildren. Applicants must be enrolled or accepted for enrollment as an undergraduate or graduate student at an accredited college or university. Graduate students must include a 250-word essay on their life experiences, work history, and aspirations. Some scholarships are specifically reserved for enlisted, warrant officer, company grade, and Department of the Army civilian members. Selection is based on academic merit and personal achievement.

**Financial data**  Stipends range from $1,000 to $4,000.

**Duration**  Scholarships may be for 1 year, 2 years, or 4 years.

**Number awarded**  Varies each year; since the program began in 1963, the foundation has awarded more than $2.2 million to more than 1,300 qualified applicants.

**Deadline**  April of each year.

## [58]
## ARTHUR DEHARDT MEMORIAL SCHOLARSHIP

American Legion Press Club of New Jersey
c/o Jack W. Kuepfer, Scholarship Chairman
68 Merrill Road
Clifton, NJ 07012-1622
(973) 473-5176

**Summary**  To provide financial assistance to the children or grandchildren of New Jersey members of the American Legion or Auxiliary who are interested in studying communications in college.

**Eligibility**  To be eligible to apply for this scholarship, applicants must meet 1 of the following qualifications: 1) child or grandchild of a current card holding member of the American Legion or American Legion Auxiliary; 2) child or grandchild of deceased member of either organization who was in good standing at the time of death; 3) member of the Sons of the American Legion or Auxiliary Juniors; or 4) graduate of either American Legion Jersey Boys State or the Auxiliary Girls State Program. All applicants must be residents of New Jersey and freshmen entering a 4-year college to work toward a degree related to the field of communications, including public relations, journalism, computer graphics, or other fields accepted by the scholarship committee. Applicants must include an essay of not less than 500 words on why they chose their particular major course of study. Boys and girls are judged separately.

**Financial data**  The stipend is $500.

**Duration**  1 year.

**Additional information**  Applications must be accompanied by a stamped self-addressed envelope.

**Number awarded**  2 each year: 1 to a boy and 1 to a girl.

**Deadline**  June of each year.

## [59]
## ASCE MAINE SECTION SCHOLARSHIP

American Society of Civil Engineers-Maine Section
c/o Leslie L. Corrow, Scholarship Chair
Kleinschmidt Associates
75 Main Street
P.O. Box 576
Pittsfield, ME 04967
(207) 487-3328

**Summary**  To provide financial assistance to high school seniors in Maine (particularly women and minorities) who are interested in studying civil engineering in college.

**Eligibility**  This program is open to graduating high school seniors who are Maine residents and who intend to study civil engineering in college. Women and minorities are especially encouraged to apply. Applicants must submit a 200-word statement describing why they have chosen civil engineering as a career and what they hope to accomplish by being a civil engineer. Selection is based on the statement, academic performance, extracurricular activities, and letters of recommendation.

**Financial data**  The stipend is $2,000.

**Duration**  1 year; nonrenewable.

**Number awarded**  1 each year.

**Deadline**  January of each year.

## [60]
## ASSOCIATION FOR WOMEN GEOSCIENTISTS MINORITY SCHOLARSHIP

Association for Women Geoscientists
Attn: AWG Foundation
P.O. Box 30645
Lincoln, NE 68503-0645
E-mail: minorityscholarship@awg.org
Web: www.awg.org/eas/minority.html

**Summary** To provide financial assistance to minority women who are interested in working on an undergraduate degree in the geosciences.

**Eligibility** This program is open to women who are African American, Hispanic, or Native American (including Eskimo, Hawaiian, Samoan, or American Indian). Applicants must be full-time students working on, or planning to work on, an undergraduate degree in the geosciences (including geology, geophysics, geochemistry, hydrology, meteorology, physical oceanography, planetary geology, or earth science education). They must submit a 500-word essay on why they have chosen to major in the geosciences and their career goals, 2 letters of recommendation, high school and/or college transcripts, and SAT or ACT scores. Financial need is not considered in the selection process.

**Financial data** A total of $5,000 is available for this program each year.

**Duration** 1 year; may be renewed.

**Additional information** This program, first offered in 2004, is supported by ExxonMobil Foundation.

**Number awarded** 1 or more each year.

**Deadline** May of each year.

## [61]
## ASSOCIATION FOR WOMEN IN ARCHITECTURE SCHOLARSHIPS

Association for Women in Architecture
Attn: Scholarship Chair
22815 Frampton Avenue
Torrance, CA 90501-5034
(310) 534-8466         Fax: (310) 257-6885
E-mail: scholarship@awa-la.org
Web: www.awa-la.org/scholarships.php

**Summary** To provide financial assistance to women undergraduates in California who are interested in careers in architecture.

**Eligibility** Eligible to apply are women students who have completed at least 1 full year of study in any of the following fields: architecture; civil, structural, mechanical, or electrical engineering as related to architecture; landscape architecture; urban and land planning; interior design; architectural rendering and illustration; or environmental design. They must be residents of California or attending school in California. Interviews are required for semifinalists. Selection is based on grades, a personal statement, financial need, recommendations, and the quality and organization of materials submitted.

**Financial data** Stipends are $2,500, $1,500, or $1,000.

**Duration** 1 year.

**Number awarded** 3 each year: 1 at $2,500, 1 at $1,500, and 1 at $1,000.

**Deadline** April of each year.

## [62]
## ASSOCIATION FOR WOMEN IN SCIENCE COLLEGE SCHOLARSHIPS

Association for Women in Science
Attn: AWIS Educational Foundation
1200 New York Avenue, N.W., Suite 650
Washington, DC 20005
(202) 326-8940      Toll-free: (866) 657-AWIS
Fax: (202) 326-8960      E-mail: awisedfd@awis.org
Web: www.awis.org/careers/edfoundation.html

**Summary** To provide financial assistance to female high school seniors interested in studying engineering or designated sciences in college.

**Eligibility** This program is open to women who are high school seniors and U.S. citizens interested in a career in research and/or teaching. Applicants must have a GPA of 3.75 or higher and at least 25 on the ACT or 1200 on the SAT (mathematics and critical writing). They must plan to study astronomy, biology, chemistry, computer and information science, engineering, geoscience, mathematics, physics, or psychology in college. Along with their application, they must submit an essay on the following: 1) their scientific interests and career aspirations in research and/or teaching; 2) what led to their interest in science and the role of special mentors, if relevant; 3) key lessons they have learned during any research or teaching experiences they have had; 4) any social, economic, academic, or other barriers they have faced and how they overcame them; and 5) why they undertook community service or volunteer activities and key lessons they learned. Financial need is not considered.

**Financial data** The stipend is $1,000. Citations of merit are $300 and recognition awards are $100.

**Duration** 1 year.

**Additional information** This program, established in 1999, includes the Gail Naughton Undergraduate Award and the Helen Davies Award. Information is also available from Barbara Filner, President, AWIS Educational Foundation, 7008 Richard Drive, Bethesda, MD 20817-4838.

**Number awarded** 2 to 5 scholarships are awarded each year. The number of citations of merit and recognition awards varies.

**Deadline** January of each year.

## [63]
## ASSOCIATION FOR WOMEN IN SPORTS MEDIA SCHOLARSHIP/INTERNSHIP PROGRAM

Association for Women in Sports Media
c/o Rachel Cohen, Scholarship Coordinator
Dallas Morning News
P.O. Box 655237
Dallas, TX 75265
(979) 450-0146      E-mail: rcohen@dallasnews.com
Web: www.awsmonline.org/scholarship.htm

**Summary** To provide financial assistance and work experience to women undergraduate and graduate students who are interested in preparing for a career in sportswriting.

**Eligibility** This program is open to women who are enrolled in college or graduate school full time and plan to prepare for a career in sportswriting, sports copy editing, sports broadcasting, or sports public relations. Applicants must submit a 1-page essay describing their most memorable experience in sports or sports media, a 1-page resume highlighting their journalism experience, 2 letters of recommendation, up to 5 samples of their work, and a $15 application fee.

**Financial data** Awardees receive a paid summer internship, a $1,000 scholarship for the next year of college or graduate school, $300 toward travel expenses to attend the annual convention of the Association for Women in Sports Media, waived convention fees, and free lodging at the host hotel. Copy editing interns receive an additional $1,000 scholarship from the Associated Press Sports Editors.

**Duration** 1 year; nonrenewable.

**Additional information** Organizations that have hosted interns in the past include *Arizona Republic, Cleveland Plain Dealer, Colorado Springs Gazette, Detroit News,* ESPN, *Fort Worth Star-Telegram, Miami Herald, Newark Star-Ledger, Newsday,* Nike, *Sports Illustrated, St. Petersburg Times,* United States Olympic Committee, and USA Track & Field.

**Number awarded** Varies each year.

**Deadline** October of each year.

## [64]
## ASSOCIATION FOR WOMEN JOURNALISTS SCHOLARSHIPS FOR WOMEN

Association for Women Journalists
Attn: AWJ Grant
P.O. Box 2199
Fort Worth, TX 76113
(817) 685-3876
E-mail: jessamybrown@star-telegram.com
Web: www.awjdfw.org/scholarships_awards.html

**Summary** To provide financial assistance to women studying journalism at a college or university in Texas.

**Eligibility** This program is open to full-time juniors and seniors at colleges and universities in Texas. Applicants must be majoring in print, broadcast, or photojournalism and have a GPA of 2.5 or higher in their major. They must submit 3 samples of their print or broadcast work or photographs, a letter of recommendation from an instructor or adviser, a statement of professional goals and how the scholarship will help, and a statement of financial need (if that is to be considered).

**Financial data** The stipend is $1,000. Funds are paid directly to the college or university to be applied to tuition.

**Duration** 1 year.

**Number awarded** Up to 4 each year.

**Deadline** March of each year.

## [65]
## ATLANTA BRANCH AAUW SCHOLARSHIPS

American Association of University Women-Atlanta
Branch
Attn: Scholarship Committee
1795 Riverside Road
Roswell, GA 30076
(770) 998-2444
Web: www.aauwatlanta.org/AAUW/scholarship.htm

**Summary** To provide financial assistance to mature women from Georgia who are working on an undergraduate degree at a college or university in the Atlanta area.

**Eligibility** This program is open to female residents of Georgia who are at least 30 years of age. Applicants must be enrolled as juniors or seniors at a college or university in the Atlanta area and working on an undergraduate degree. They must be seeking funds for supplemental expenses (e.g., childcare, transportation, books); tuition funds must be covered from other sources. Along with their application, they must submit a short explanation of their background, goals, and academic interests. U.S. citizenship is required.

**Financial data** A stipend is awarded (amount not specified).

**Duration** 1 year.

**Number awarded** 1 or more each year.

**Deadline** April of each year.

## [66]
## ATLANTA NETWORK OF EXECUTIVE WOMEN IN HOSPITALITY SCHOLARSHIP AWARDS

Network of Executive Women in Hospitality-Atlanta
Chapter
Attn: Ansley Franke, Director of Scholarship and
Education
2283 Pembrook Place, N.E.
Atlanta, GA 30324
Toll-free: (800) 593-NEWH     Fax: (800) 693-NEWH
E-mail: afranke@aigroupdesign.com
Web: www.newh.org/newh/scholarshippacket.php

**Summary** To provide financial assistance to women in designated southern states interested in preparing for a career in the hospitality industry.

**Eligibility** This program is open to women who have completed half the requirements for a degree or certification program at a vocational school or college in Georgia, Kentucky, South Carolina, or Tennessee. Applicants must have a GPA of 3.0 or higher and a career objective in the hospitality or food service industries (e.g., hotel and restaurant management, culinary, food service, architecture, design). Selection is based on financial need and academic accomplishments.

**Financial data** The stipend depends on the availability of funds and the need of the recipient.

**Duration** 1 year.

**Number awarded** Varies each year.

**Deadline** March of each year.

## [67]
## AUXILIARY SCHOLARSHIP

National Society of Professional Engineers
Attn: Education Services
1420 King Street
Alexandria, VA 22314-2794
(703) 684-2833     Fax: (703) 836-4875
E-mail: jiglesias@nspe.org
Web: www.nspe.org/scholarships/sc1-hs.asp

**Summary** To provide financial assistance for college to women who are high school seniors and are interested in preparing for a career in engineering.

**Eligibility** This program is open to women who are high school seniors planning to study engineering in an EAC-ABET accredited college program. Applicants must have a GPA of 3.5 or higher, verbal SAT score of 600 or higher, and math SAT score of 700 or higher (or English ACT score of 29 or higher and math ACT score of 29 or higher). They must submit an essay (up to 500 words) on their interest in engineering, their major area of study and area of specialization, and the occupation they propose to pursue after graduation. Selection is based on GPA (20 points), the essay (20 points), extracurricular activities, including work experience and volunteer activities (25 points), financial need (5 points), SAT/ACT scores (20 points), and the composite application (10 points). U.S. citizenship is required.

**Financial data** The award is $1,000 per year; funds are paid directly to the recipient's institution.

**Duration** 4 years.

**Additional information** Recipients may attend any college or university, as long as the engineering curriculum is accredited by EAC-ABET.

**Number awarded** 1 each year.

**Deadline** November of each year.

## [68]
## B. JUNE WEST RECRUITMENT GRANT

Delta Kappa Gamma Society International-Theta State
   Organization
c/o Pat Graff, Committee on Professional Affairs Chair
8101 Krim N.E.
Albuquerque, NM 87109-5223
E-mail: pgraff@aol.com
Web: www.deltakappagamma.org/NM

**Summary** To provide financial assistance to women in New Mexico who are interested in preparing for a career as a teacher.

**Eligibility** This program is open to women residents of New Mexico who are 1) graduating high school seniors planning to go into education; 2) college students majoring in education; or 3) teachers needing educational assistance. Applicants must submit a list of activities in which they are involved, 3 letters of recommendation, a list of achievements and awards, and a statement of their educational goal and how this grant would be of assistance to them. Financial need is not considered in the selection process.

**Financial data** A stipend is awarded (amount not specified).

**Duration** 1 year.

**Number awarded** 1 or more each year.

**Deadline** February of each year.

## [69]
## BARBARA ALICE MOWER MEMORIAL SCHOLARSHIP

Barbara Alice Mower Memorial Scholarship Committee
c/o Nancy A. Mower
1536 Kamole Street
Honolulu, HI 96821-1424
(808) 373-2901

**Summary** To provide financial assistance to female residents of Hawaii who are interested in women's studies and

are attending college on the undergraduate or graduate level in the United States or abroad.

**Eligibility** This program is open to female residents of Hawaii who are at least juniors in college, are interested in and committed to women's studies, and have worked or studied in the field. Selection is based on interest in studying about and commitment to helping women, previous work and/or study in that area, previous academic performance, character, personality, and future plans to help women (particularly women in Hawaii). If there are several applicants who meet all these criteria, then financial need may be taken into consideration.

**Financial data** The stipend ranges from $1,000 to $3,500.

**Duration** 1 year; may be renewed.

**Additional information** Recipients may use the scholarship at universities in Hawaii, on the mainland, or in foreign countries. They must focus on women's studies or topics that relate to women in school.

**Number awarded** 1 or more each year.

**Deadline** April of each year.

## [70]
## BARBARA MCBRIDE SCHOLARSHIP

Society of Exploration Geophysicists
Attn: SEG Foundation
8801 South Yale, Suite 500
P.O. Box 702740
Tulsa, OK 74170-2740
(918) 497-5513            Fax: (918) 497-5557
E-mail: scholarships@seg.org
Web: seg.org

**Summary** To provide financial assistance to women undergraduate and graduate students who are interested in the field of applied geophysics.

**Eligibility** This program is open to women who are 1) high school students planning to enter college in the fall, or 2) undergraduate or graduate students whose grades are above average. Applicants must intend to work on a degree directed toward a career in applied geophysics or a closely-related field. Along with their application, they must submit a 150-word essay on how they plan to use geophysics in their future. Financial need is not considered in the selection process.

**Financial data** The stipend ranges from $1,000 to $3,000 per year.

**Duration** 1 academic year; may be renewable, based on scholastic standing, availability of funds, and continuance of a course of study leading to a career in applied geophysics.

**Number awarded** 1 each year.

**Deadline** January of each year.

## [71]
## BARNUM FESTIVAL FOUNDATION/JENNY LIND COMPETITION FOR SOPRANOS

Barnum Festival Foundation
Attn: Director
1070 Main Street
Bridgeport, CT 06604
(203) 367-8495          Toll-free: (866) 867-8495
E-mail: office@barnumfestival.com
Web: www.barnumfestival.com

**Summary** To recognize and reward (with scholarships and a concert trip to Sweden) outstanding young female singers who have not yet reached professional status.

**Eligibility** Applicants must be sopranos between the ages of 20 and 30 who have not yet attained professional status and who are residents and citizens of the United States. Past finalists may reapply, but former first-place winners and mezzo-sopranos are not eligible. The preliminary audition for 16 contestants chosen on the basis of audio tapes is held at the Barnum Festival in Bridgeport, Connecticut every April. From this audition, 6 finalists are chosen. Final selection of the winner is based on technique, musicianship, diction, interpretation, and stage presence.

**Financial data** The winner of the competition is presented with a $2,000 scholarship award to further her musical education at a recognized voice training school, academy, or college or with a recognized voice teacher or coach. She is featured in a concert in June with the Swedish Jenny Lind at a locale in Connecticut, and is sent to Sweden with her Swedish counterpart to perform in concerts for 2 weeks in July and August. The runner-up receives a $500 scholarship.

**Duration** The competition is held annually.

**Additional information** The winner of this competition serves as the American Jenny Lind, a 20th-century counterpart of the Swedish Nightingale brought to the United States for a successful concert tour in 1850 by P.T. Barnum. There is a $35 application fee.

**Number awarded** 2 each year: 1 winner and 1 runner-up.

**Deadline** March of each year.

## [72]
## BASF AGRICULTURAL PRODUCTS SCHOLARSHIPS

National FFA Organization
Attn: Scholarship Office
6060 FFA Drive
P.O. Box 68960
Indianapolis, IN 46268-0960
(317) 802-4321          Fax: (317) 802-5321
E-mail: scholarships@ffa.org
Web: www.ffa.org/programs/scholarships/index.html

**Summary** To provide financial assistance to women and minority FFA members who are interested in studying specified agribusiness fields in college.

**Eligibility** This program is open to members who are either graduating high school seniors planning to enroll in college or students already enrolled in college. Applicants must 1) be interested in working full time on a 4-year degree in agricultural marketing, merchandising, or sales; 2) be women or members of a minority group; 3) have a GPA of 3.0 or higher; 4) have participated in community service; and 5) be able to demonstrate strong leadership skills and financial need. Selection is based on academic achievement (10 points for GPA, 10 points for SAT or ACT score, 10 points for class rank), leadership in FFA activities (30 points), leadership in community activities (10 points), and participation in the Supervised Agricultural Experience (SAE) program (30 points). U.S. citizenship is required.

**Financial data** The stipend is $1,000. Funds are paid directly to the recipient.

**Duration** 1 year; nonrenewable.

**Additional information** Funding for these scholarships is provided by BASF Agricultural Products.

**Number awarded** 7 each year.

**Deadline** February of each year.

## [73]
## BASIC MIDWIFERY SCHOLARSHIPS

American College of Nurse-Midwives
Attn: ACNM Foundation, Inc.
8403 Coleville Road, Suite 1550
Silver Spring, MD 20915
(240) 485-1850          Fax: (240) 485-1818
Web: www.midwife.org

**Summary** To provide financial assistance for midwifery education to student members of the American College of Nurse-Midwives (ACNM).

**Eligibility** This program is open to ACNM members who are currently enrolled in an accredited basic midwife education program and have successfully completed 1 academic or clinical semester/quarter or clinical module. Applicants must submit a 150-word essay on their midwifery career plans and a 100-word essay on their intended future participation in the local, regional, and/or national activities of the ACNM. Selection is based on leadership potential, financial need, academic history, and potential for future professional contribution to the organization.

**Financial data** The stipend is $3,000.

**Duration** 1 year.

**Additional information** This program includes the following named scholarships: the A.C.N.M. Foundation Memorial Scholarship, the TUMS Calcium for Life Scholarship (presented by GlaxoSmithKline), the Edith B. Wonnell CNM Scholarship, and the Margaret Edmundson Scholarship.

**Number awarded** Varies each year; recently, 4 of these scholarships were awarded.

**Deadline** March of each year.

## [74]
## BECHTEL FOUNDATION SCHOLARSHIP

Society of Women Engineers
230 East Ohio Street, Suite 400
Chicago, IL 60611-3265
(312) 596-5223          Toll-free: (877) SWE-INFO
Fax: (312) 644-8557
E-mail: scholarshipapplication@swe.org
Web: www.swe.org/scholarships

**Summary** To provide financial assistance to undergraduate women who are members of the Society of Women Engineers and majoring in engineering.

**Eligibility**   This program is open to women who are entering their sophomore, junior, or senior year at an ABET-accredited college or university. Applicants must be studying computer science or architectural, civil, electrical, environmental, or mechanical engineering with a GPA of 3.0 or higher. Along with their application, they must submit a 1-page essay on why they want to be an engineer, how they believe they will make a difference as an engineer, and what influenced them to study engineering. Only members of the society are considered for this award. Selection is based on merit.

**Financial data**   The stipend is $1,400.

**Duration**   1 year.

**Additional information**   This program, established in 2000, is sponsored by Bechtel Foundation.

**Number awarded**   2 each year.

**Deadline**   January of each year.

## [75]
## BERNICE F. ELLIOTT MEMORIAL SCHOLARSHIP

Baptist Convention of New Mexico
Attn: Missions Education and Women's Ministry
    Department
5325 Wyoming Boulevard, N.E.
P.O. Box 94485
Albuquerque, NM 87199-4485
(505) 924-2333            Toll-free: (800) 898-8544
Fax: (505) 924-2320       E-mail: cpeek@bcnm.com
Web: www.bcnm.com

**Summary**   To provide financial assistance for college or seminary to women who are Southern Baptists from New Mexico.

**Eligibility**   This program is open to women college and seminary students who are members of churches affiliated with the Baptist Convention of New Mexico. Preference is given to applicants who are committed to full-time Christian service, have a background in the Woman's Missionary Union, and can demonstrate financial need.

**Financial data**   A stipend is awarded (amount not specified).

**Duration**   1 year; may be renewed.

**Number awarded**   1 or more each year.

**Deadline**   April of each year.

## [76]
## BERNICE MURRAY SCHOLARSHIP

Vermont Student Assistance Corporation
Attn: Scholarship Programs
10 East Allen Street
P.O. Box 2000
Winooski, VT 05404-2601
(802) 654-3798            Toll-free: (888) 253-4819
Fax: (802) 654-3765       TDD: (802) 654-3766
TDD: (800) 281-3341 (within VT)
E-mail: info@vsac.org
Web: www.vsac.org

**Summary**   To provide financial assistance for child care to single parents in Vermont who wish to improve their education or skills.

**Eligibility**   Applicants must be Vermont residents, single parents with primary custody of at least 1 child 12 years of age or younger, able to demonstrate financial need, and enrolled in a full- or part-time degree program at an approved postsecondary school. They must have a plan to further their education, and they must provide information on the annual cost of the child care services needed. Also required are up to 3 letters of recommendation, a 100-word essay (describing how furthering their education will upgrade their employment skills), and documentation of financial need.

**Financial data**   The maximum stipend is $2,000; funds must be used to pay for child care services while the recipient attends an approved postsecondary institution.

**Duration**   1 year; recipients may reapply.

**Additional information**   This program is sponsored by U.S. Senator James Jeffords and the Federal Executives' Association.

**Number awarded**   1 or more each year.

**Deadline**   May of each year.

## [77]
## BERTHA LAMME MEMORIAL SCHOLARSHIP

Society of Women Engineers
230 East Ohio Street, Suite 400
Chicago, IL 60611-3265
(312) 596-5223            Toll-free: (877) SWE-INFO
Fax: (312) 644-8557
E-mail: scholarshipapplication@swe.org
Web: www.swe.org/scholarships

**Summary**   To provide financial assistance to women who will be entering college as freshmen and are interested in studying electrical engineering.

**Eligibility**   This program is open to women who are entering college as freshmen with a GPA of 3.5 or higher. Applicants must be U.S. citizens planning to enroll full time at an ABET-accredited 4-year college or university and major in electrical engineering. Along with their application, they must submit a 1-page essay on why they want to be an engineer, how they believe they will make a difference as an engineer, and what influenced them to study engineering. Selection is based on merit.

**Financial data**   The stipend is $1,200.

**Duration**   1 year.

**Number awarded**   1 each year.

**Deadline**   May of each year.

## [78]
## BEST FRIENDS COLLEGE SCHOLARSHIP FUND

Best Friends Foundation
5335 Wisconsin Avenue, N.W., Suite 440
Washington, DC 20015
(202) 478-9677            Fax: (202) 478-9678
E-mail: ebennett@bestfriendsfoundation.org
Web: www.bestfriendsfoundation.org

**Summary**   To provide financial assistance for college to girls who have been members of the Best Friends organization in selected cities.

**Eligibility** This program is open to girls who are high school seniors at schools that participate in the Best Friends program. Applicants must have participated in Best Friends for at least 6 years before high school graduation. Selection is based on enthusiasm and overall commitment to Best Friends and its messages, demonstrated leadership, academic aptitude and performance, and courage in overcoming personal adversity.

**Financial data** A stipend is awarded (amount not specified).

**Duration** 1 year.

**Additional information** This program began in 1996.

**Number awarded** Varies each year; since the program was established, it has awarded more than $500,000 in scholarships.

## [79]
## BETA CHI CHAPTER OF ESA SCHOLARSHIP

Epsilon Sigma Alpha
Attn: ESA Foundation Assistant Scholarship Director
P.O. Box 270517
Fort Collins, CO 80527
(970) 223-2824             Fax: (970) 223-4456
Web: www.esaintl.com/esaf

**Summary** To provide financial assistance for continuing education to women from Oklahoma.

**Eligibility** Women residents of Oklahoma returning to school to acquire new job skills or update present skills are eligible. Selection is based on character (10%), leadership (10%), service (5%), financial need (50%), and scholastic ability (25%).

**Financial data** The stipend is $500.

**Duration** 1 year; nonrenewable.

**Additional information** Epsilon Sigma Alpha (ESA) is a women's service organization. Information is also available from Lynn Hughes, Scholarship Director, 324 N.E. Mead, Grants Pass, OR 97526, (541) 476-4617. Completed applications must be submitted to the ESA State Counselor who verifies the information before forwarding them to the scholarship director. A $5 processing fee is required.

**Number awarded** 1 each year.

**Deadline** January of each year.

## [80]
## BETTER CHANCE SCHOLARSHIP

Associates of Vietnam Veterans of America
Attn: Scholarship Program
8605 Cameron Street, Suite 400
Silver Spring, MD 20910
Toll-free: (800) VVA-1316
Web: www.avva.org/better_chance.htm

**Summary** To provide financial assistance for college to members of Vietnam Veterans of American (VVA) and Associates of Vietnam Veterans of America (AVVA), their families, and the families of Vietnam veterans killed or missing in action.

**Eligibility** This program is open to members of VVA and AVVA; their spouses, children, and grandchildren; and the spouses, children, and grandchildren of a Vietnam veteran killed in action (KIA) or missing in action (MIA). Especially

encouraged to apply are average students who are not eligible for academic scholarships but who can demonstrate financial need. Applicants must submit essays on their long-term goals, work experience, organizations or activities, and community service.

**Financial data** Stipends are $1,000, $750, or $500.

**Duration** 1 year.

**Additional information** This program was established in 1998.

**Number awarded** 3 each year: 1 at $1,000, 1 at $750, and 1 at $500.

**Deadline** May of each year.

## [81]
## BETTY HANSEN CONTINUING EDUCATION GRANTS

Danish Sisterhood of America
Attn: Lizette Burtis, Scholarship Chair
3020 Santa Juanita Court
Santa Rosa, CA 95405-8219
(707) 539-1884             E-mail: lburtis@sbcglobal.net
Web: www.danishsisterhood.org/rschol.asp

**Summary** To provide financial assistance for continuing education to members and children of members of the Danish Sisterhood of America.

**Eligibility** This program is open to sisterhood members who are in good standing with a sponsoring lodge and to the children of members who have belonged for at least 1 year. Applicants must be enrolled as less than full-time students at an accredited college or university in a course, workshop, seminar, or language class relating to Danish culture or heritage. No minimum GPA is required.

**Financial data** The stipend is $500.

**Duration** 1 year; recipients may reapply after a 1-year waiting period from the time of their award.

**Number awarded** Up to 10 each year.

**Deadline** January or August of each year.

## [82]
## BETTY HANSEN NATIONAL SCHOLARSHIPS

Danish Sisterhood of America
Attn: Lizette Burtis, Scholarship Chair
3020 Santa Juanita Court
Santa Rosa, CA 95405-8219
(707) 539-1884             E-mail: lburtis@sbcglobal.net
Web: www.danishsisterhood.org/rschol.asp

**Summary** To provide financial assistance for educational purposes in the United States or Denmark to members or relatives of members of the Danish Sisterhood of America.

**Eligibility** This program is open to members or the family of members of the sisterhood who are interested in attending an accredited 4-year college or university as a full-time undergraduate or graduate student. Members must have belonged to the sisterhood for at least 1 year. Selection is based on academic excellence (at least a 2.5 GPA). Upon written request, the scholarship may be used for study in Denmark.

**Financial data** The stipend is $1,000.

**Duration** 1 year; nonrenewable.

**Number awarded** Up to 8 each year.

**Deadline** February of each year.

## [83]
## BETTY MCKERN SCHOLARSHIP

Association for Iron & Steel Technology-Midwest
Chapter
c/o Michael Heaney, Education Chair
Mittal Steel USA-East Chicago
3001 Dickey Road
East Chicago, IN 46312
(219) 391-2026
Web: www.aist.org

**Summary** To provide financial assistance to female dependents of members of the Midwest Chapter of the Association for Iron & Steel Technology (AIST) who plan to study engineering in college.

**Eligibility** This program is open to female dependents of members of the AIST Midwest Chapter who are graduating high school seniors or currently enrolled in the first, second, or third year at an accredited college or university. Applicants must be studying or planning to study engineering on a full-time basis. Along with their application, they must submit a letter of recommendation, a current transcript, and a 1- to 2-page essay describing their objectives for college and career. Selection is based on merit.

**Financial data** The stipend is $2,500.

**Duration** 1 year.

**Additional information** The AIST was formed in 2004 by the merger of the Iron and Steel Society (ISS) and the Association of Iron and Steel Engineers (AISE). The Midwest Chapter replaced the former AISE Chicago Section in northern Illinois and northwestern Indiana and also includes the states of Wisconsin, Minnesota, Iowa, Nebraska, South Dakota, and North Dakota.

**Number awarded** 1 each year.

**Deadline** May of each year.

## [84]
## BETTY RENDEL SCHOLARSHIPS

National Federation of Republican Women
Attn: Scholarships and Internships
124 North Alfred Street
Alexandria, VA 22314-3011
(703) 548-9688              Fax: (703) 548-9836
E-mail: mail@nfrw.org
Web: www.nfrw.org/programs/scholarships.htm

**Summary** To provide financial assistance to undergraduate Republican women who are majoring in political science, government, or economics.

**Eligibility** This program is open to women who have completed at least 2 years of college. Applicants must be majoring in political science, government, or economics. Along with their application, they must submit 3 letters of recommendation, an official transcript, a 1-page essay on why they should be considered for the scholarship, and a 1-page essay on career goals. Optionally, a photograph may be supplied. Applications must be submitted to the Republican federation president in the applicant's state. Each president chooses 1 application from her state to submit for scholar-

ship consideration. Financial need is not a factor in the selection process. U.S. citizenship is required.

**Financial data** The stipend is $1,000.

**Duration** 1 year; nonrenewable.

**Additional information** This program was established in 1995.

**Number awarded** 3 each year.

**Deadline** Applications must be submitted to the state federation president by May of each year.

## [85]
## B.J. HARROD SCHOLARSHIPS

Society of Women Engineers
230 East Ohio Street, Suite 400
Chicago, IL 60611-3265
(312) 596-5223              Toll-free: (877) SWE-INFO
Fax: (312) 644-8557
E-mail: scholarshipapplication@swe.org
Web: www.swe.org/scholarships

**Summary** To provide financial assistance to women who will be entering college as freshmen and are interested in studying engineering or computer science.

**Eligibility** This program is open to women who are entering college as freshmen with a GPA of 3.5 or higher. Applicants must be planning to enroll full time at an ABET-accredited 4-year college or university and major in computer science or engineering. Along with their application, they must submit a 1-page essay on why they want to be an engineer or computer scientist, how they believe they will make a difference as an engineer or computer scientist, and what influenced them to study engineering or computer science. Selection is based on merit.

**Financial data** The stipend is $2,000.

**Duration** 1 year.

**Additional information** This program was established in 1999.

**Number awarded** 2 each year.

**Deadline** May of each year.

## [86]
## B.K. KRENZER REENTRY SCHOLARSHIP

Society of Women Engineers
230 East Ohio Street, Suite 400
Chicago, IL 60611-3265
(312) 596-5223              Toll-free: (877) SWE-INFO
Fax: (312) 644-8557
E-mail: scholarshipapplication@swe.org
Web: www.swe.org/scholarships

**Summary** To provide financial assistance to women interested in returning to college or graduate school to study engineering or computer science.

**Eligibility** This program is open to women who are planning to enroll at an ABET-accredited 4-year college or university. Applicants must have been out of the engineering workforce and school for at least 2 years and must be planning to return as an undergraduate or graduate student to major in computer science or engineering. Along with their application, they must submit a 1-page essay on why they want to be an engineer or computer scientist, how they believe they will make a difference as an engineer or computer scientist, and what influenced them to study engineering or computer science. Selection is based on merit. Preference is given to engineers who already have a degree and are planning to reenter the engineering workforce after a period of temporary retirement.

**Financial data**  The stipend is $2,000.

**Duration**  1 year.

**Additional information**  This program was established in 1996.

**Number awarded**  1 each year.

**Deadline**  January of each year.

## [87]
## BOB GLAHN SCHOLARSHIP IN STATISTICAL METEOROLOGY

American Meteorological Society
Attn: Fellowship/Scholarship Program
45 Beacon Street
Boston, MA 02108-3693
(617) 227-2426, ext. 246          Fax: (617) 742-8718
E-mail: scholar@ametsoc.org
Web: www.ametsoc.org

**Summary**  To provide financial assistance to undergraduates (particularly women, minorities, and persons with disabilities) majoring in meteorology or an aspect of atmospheric sciences with an interest in statistical meteorology.

**Eligibility**  This program is open to full-time students entering their final year of undergraduate study and majoring in meteorology or an aspect of the atmospheric or related oceanic and hydrologic sciences. Applicants must intend to make atmospheric or related sciences their career, with preference given to students who have demonstrated a strong interest in statistical meteorology. They must be U.S. citizens or permanent residents enrolled at a U.S. institution and have a cumulative GPA of 3.25 or higher. Along with their application, they must submit 200-word essays on 1) their studies in statistics and their career plans for the future, and 2) their career plans in the statistical meteorology field. Selection is based on academic excellence and achievement; financial need is also considered. The sponsor specifically encourages applications from women, minorities, and students with disabilities who are traditionally underrepresented in the atmospheric and related oceanic sciences.

**Financial data**  The stipend is $2,500 per year.

**Duration**  1 year.

**Additional information**  Requests for an application must be accompanied by a self-addressed stamped envelope.

**Number awarded**  1 each year.

**Deadline**  February of each year.

## [88]
## BOBBI MCCALLUM MEMORIAL SCHOLARSHIP

Seattle Post-Intelligencer
Attn: Assistant Managing Editor
101 Elliott Avenue West
Seattle, WA 98119-4220
(206) 448-8316          E-mail: janetgrimley@seattlepi.com
Web: www.seattlepi.com

**Summary**  To provide financial assistance to women college students in Washington who are interested in preparing for a career in journalism.

**Eligibility**  This program is open to women journalism majors entering their junior or senior year at a university in the state of Washington. Graduating community college students transferring to a 4-year school are also eligible. Applicants must submit 5 examples of news writing (published or unpublished); a general resume of their college experiences, including a transcript; 2 letters of recommendation; and documentation of financial need. Selection is based on need, talent, and motivation to prepare for a career in print journalism.

**Financial data**  The stipend is $1,000.

**Duration**  The scholarship is offered annually.

**Additional information**  This scholarship was established in 1970 by the late Dr. Walter Scott Brown in memory of Bobbi McCallum, a prizewinning reporter and columnist for the *Seattle Post-Intelligencer* who died in 1969 at age 25 while a patient of Dr. Brown. The scholarship is administered by the newspaper and the Seattle Foundation.

**Number awarded**  1 each year.

**Deadline**  March of each year.

## [89]
## BOBBY SOX HIGH SCHOOL SENIOR SCHOLARSHIP PROGRAM

Bobby Sox Softball
Attn: Scholarship
P.O. Box 5880
Buena Park, CA 90622-5880
(714) 522-1234          Fax: (714) 522-6548
Web: www.bobbysoxsoftball.org/scholar.html

**Summary**  To provide financial assistance for college to high school seniors who have participated in Bobby Sox Softball.

**Eligibility**  This program is open to girls graduating from high school with a GPA of 2.0 or higher. Applicants must have participated in Bobby Sox Softball for at least 5 seasons. They must submit an essay on "The Value of Participation in Bobby Sox Softball." Selection is based on the essay (60 points), academic excellence (20 points), and 3 letters of recommendation regarding participation in Bobby Sox Softball, participation in other extracurricular activities, and academic accomplishments (20 points).

**Financial data**  Stipends range from $100 to $2,500.

**Duration**  1 year.

**Number awarded**  Varies each year; recently, 44 of these scholarships were awarded.

**Deadline**  April of each year.

## [90]
## BOEING COMPANY CAREER ENHANCEMENT SCHOLARSHIP

Women in Aviation, International
Attn: Scholarships
Morningstar Airport
3647 State Route 503 South
West Alexandria, OH 45381
(937) 558-7655          Fax: (937) 839-4645
E-mail: scholarships@wai.org
Web: www.wai.org/education/scholarships.cfm

**Summary** To provide financial assistance to members of Women in Aviation, International (WAI) who are active in aerospace and need financial support to advance their career.

**Eligibility** This program is open to WAI members who wish to advance their career in the aerospace industry in the fields of engineering, technology development, or management. Applicants may be 1) full-time or part-time employees working in the aerospace industry or a related field, or 2) students working on an aviation-related degree who are at least juniors and have a GPA of 2.5 or higher. They must submit an essay that addresses their career aspirations and goals, in addition to an application form, 3 letters of recommendation, a resume, copies of all aviation and medical certificates, and the last 3 pages of their pilot logbook, if applicable. Selection is based on achievements, attitude toward self and others, commitment to success, dedication to career, financial need, motivation, reliability, responsibility, and teamwork.

**Financial data** A stipend is awarded (amount not specified).

**Duration** 1 year.

**Additional information** WAI is a nonprofit professional organization dedicated to encouraging women to consider an aviation career, providing educational outreach activities, and providing networking opportunities to women active in the industry.

**Number awarded** 1 each year.

**Deadline** November of each year.

## [91]
## BOSTON AFFILIATE AWSCPA SCHOLARSHIP

American Woman's Society of Certified Public
    Accountants-Boston Affiliate
c/o Andrea Costantino
Oxford Bioscience Partners
222 Berkeley Street, Suite 1650
Boston, MA 02116
(617) 357-7474        E-mail: acostantino@oxbio.com
Web: www.awscpa.org/frameset.php?cf=awards.htm

**Summary** To provide financial assistance to women who are working on an undergraduate or graduate degree in accounting at a college or university in New England.

**Eligibility** This program is open to women who are attending a college in New England and majoring in accounting. Applicants must have completed at least 12 semester hours of accounting or tax courses and have a cumulative GPA of 3.0 or higher. They must be planning to graduate between May of next year and May of the following year or, for the 15-month graduate program, before Sep-

tember of the current year. Along with their application, they must submit a brief essay on why they feel they would be a good choice for this award. Selection is based on that essay, academic achievement, work experience, extracurricular activities, scholastic honors, career plans, and financial need.

**Financial data** The stipend is $1,000.

**Duration** 1 year.

**Number awarded** 2 each year.

**Deadline** September of each year.

## [92]
## BOWFIN MEMORIAL CONTINUING EDUCATION SCHOLARSHIPS

Pacific Fleet Submarine Memorial Association
c/o USS Bowfin Submarine Museum and Park
11 Arizona Memorial Drive
Honolulu, HI 96818
(808) 423-1341          Fax: (808) 422-5201
E-mail: info@bowfin.org
Web: www.bowfin.org

**Summary** To provide financial assistance for continuing education to former or current Submarine Force personnel and their spouses who live in Hawaii.

**Eligibility** This program is open to active-duty and retired submarine force personnel, their spouses, and the spouses of deceased submarine force personnel. Applicants must be entering college, returning to college, or training for entry into the workforce. They must live in Hawaii and attend school in Hawaii. Selection is based on academic performance, community involvement, motivation, goals, and financial need.

**Financial data** Stipends range from $500 to $2,500 per year.

**Duration** 1 year; may be renewed upon annual reapplication.

**Additional information** This program was established in 1985 to honor the 3,505 submariners and 52 submarines lost during World War II.

**Number awarded** Varies each year; recently, 14 of these scholarships were awarded.

**Deadline** February of each year.

## [93]
## BPW/MAINE CAREER ADVANCEMENT SCHOLARSHIP

BPW/Maine Futurama Foundation
c/o Nancy Wadman, Scholarship Chair
478 Surry Road
Ellsworth, ME 04605
Web: www.bpwmaine.org

**Summary** To provide financial assistance for college to reentry women in Maine.

**Eligibility** This program is open to women. Applicants must be at least 30 years of age, Maine residents, able to document financial need, and continuing in or returning to a program of higher education or training. Selection is based on academic standing (20%), financial need (40%), savings or good reason for none (5%), realistic goals (25%), and other, such as parental assistance, siblings' educational status, letters of recommendation (10%).

**Financial data** The stipend is $1,200.

**Duration** 1 year.

**Additional information** The BPW/Maine Futurama Foundation was established in 1987 by the Maine Federation of Business and Professional Women's Clubs. Recipients may attend school on either a full-time or part-time basis.

**Number awarded** 1 each year.

**Deadline** April of each year.

## [94]
## BPW/MAINE CONTINUING EDUCATION SCHOLARSHIP

BPW/Maine Futurama Foundation
c/o Nancy Wadman, Scholarship Chair
478 Surry Road
Ellsworth, ME 04605
Web: www.bpwmaine.org

**Summary** To provide financial assistance to women who are residents of Maine and currently enrolled in college.

**Eligibility** Applicants must be women and residents of Maine. They must be currently enrolled in college and able to document financial need. Selection is based on academic standing (20%), financial need (40%), savings or good reason for none (5%), realistic goals (25%), and other, such as parental assistance, siblings' educational status, letters of recommendation (10%).

**Financial data** The stipend is $1,200.

**Duration** 1 year.

**Additional information** The BPW/Maine Futurama Foundation was established in 1987 by the Maine Federation of Business and Professional Women's Clubs.

**Number awarded** 1 each year.

**Deadline** April of each year.

## [95]
## BPW/NC FOUNDATION SCHOLARSHIP

North Carolina Federation of Business and Professional Women's Organizations, Inc.
Attn: BPW/NC Foundation
P.O. Box 276
Carrboro, NC 27510
Web: www.bpwnc.org/Foundation/foundation_nc.htm

**Summary** To provide financial assistance to women attending North Carolina colleges, community colleges, or graduate schools.

**Eligibility** This program is open to women who are currently enrolled in a community college, 4-year college, or graduate school in North Carolina. Applicants must be endorsed by a local BPW unit. Along with their application, they must submit a 1-page statement that summarizes their career goals, previous honors, or community activities and justifies their need for this scholarship.

**Financial data** The stipend is at least $500. Funds are paid directly to the recipient's school.

**Duration** 1 year; recipients may reapply.

**Additional information** This program was established in 1996. Information is also available from Patricia Ann McMurray, 510 Canna Place, Aberdeen, NC 28315.

**Number awarded** 1 each year.

**Deadline** April of each year.

## [96]
## BRADFORD GRANT-IN-AID

Delta Kappa Gamma Society International-Delta State Organization
c/o Karen Evans, Scholarship Committee Chair
1301 Melvin Drive
Festus, MO 63028-1087
(636) 937-5534          E-mail: evans@jcn1.com
Web: www.deltakappagamma-mo.org

**Summary** To provide financial assistance to upper-division women residents of Missouri who are relatives of members of Delta Kappa Gamma Society International and interested in preparing for a career in education.

**Eligibility** This program is open to residents of Missouri who are preparing for a career in education through a teacher preparation program as a second-semester junior or first-semester senior. Applicants must be a relative (e.g., daughter, granddaughter, niece, sister) of a member of Delta Kappa Gamma (an honorary society of women educators). Financial need is not considered in the selection process.

**Financial data** The stipend is $500.

**Duration** 1 year.

**Number awarded** Up to 2 each year.

**Deadline** February of each year.

## [97]
## BRIAN PEARSON MEMORIAL SCHOLARSHIPS

Iowa Sports Foundation
Attn: Scholarship
1421 South Bell Avenue, Suite 104
P.O. Box 2350
Ames, IA 50010
Toll-free: (888) 777-8881
E-mail: info@iowagames.org
Web: www.iowagames.org/Awards.aspx

**Summary** To provide financial assistance for college to high school students who participate in the Iowa Games.

**Eligibility** This program is open to students currently enrolled as juniors at high schools in Iowa. Applicants must have participated in events of the Iowa Sports Foundation. Along with the application, they must submit a 2-page essay describing their educational goals, examples of good character, citizenship, role modeling, and career aspirations. Males and females are judged separately.

**Financial data** The stipend is $1,000. Funds are held in deposit until the recipient graduates from high school and enrolls in college.

**Duration** 1 year.

**Additional information** This program is sponsored by Pioneer Hi-Bred International, Inc. and the Iowa Games. The Iowa Sports Foundation conducts the Iowa Games, a series of competitions involving 55 sports events held during both winter and summer.

**Number awarded** 2 each year: 1 female and 1 male.

**Deadline** May of each year.

## [98]
## BUENA M. CHESSHIR MEMORIAL WOMEN'S EDUCATIONAL SCHOLARSHIP

Business and Professional Women of Virginia
Attn: Virginia BPW Foundation
P.O. Box 4842
McLean, VA 22103-4842
Web: www.bpwva.org/scholarships.shtml

**Summary** To provide financial assistance to mature women in Virginia who are interested in upgrading their skills or education at a college, law school, or medical school in the state.

**Eligibility** This program is open to women who are residents of Virginia, U.S. citizens, and at least 25 years of age. Applicants must have been accepted into an accredited program or course of study at a Virginia institution, have a definite plan to use their training to improve their chances for upward mobility in the workforce, and be graduating within 2 years. Undergraduate applicants may be majoring in any field, but doctoral students must be working on a degree in law or medicine. Selection is based on academic achievement, demonstrated financial need, and defined career goals.

**Financial data** Stipends range from $100 to $1,000 per year; funds may be used for tuition, fees, books, transportation, living expenses, and dependent care.

**Duration** Recipients must complete their course of study within 2 years.

**Number awarded** 1 or more each year.

**Deadline** March of each year.

## [99]
## BUSINESS AND PROFESSIONAL WOMEN OF IOWA FOUNDATION EDUCATIONAL SCHOLARSHIP

Business and Professional Women of Iowa Foundation
c/o Debbie Floyd, President
4541 Woodland Avenue, Unit 6
West Des Moines, IA 50266-1754
(515) 225-4064

**Summary** To provide financial assistance for college to nontraditional students who reside in Iowa.

**Eligibility** Applicants must be Iowa residents (although they may be currently attending school in another state) who have completed at least 1 year of education beyond high school. They must be nontraditional students who 1) have been out of the workforce and need additional education to go back to work or 2) completed high school 5 or more years ago and now want to restart their college education. Along with their application, they must submit 3 letters of reference. Financial need is considered in the selection process.

**Financial data** The stipend is $500. Funds are sent directly to the recipient's school.

**Duration** 1 year.

**Additional information** Recipients may attend school in any state.

**Number awarded** 1 or more each year.

**Deadline** March of each year.

## [100]
## BUSINESS AND PROFESSIONAL WOMEN'S FOUNDATION OF MARYLAND SCHOLARSHIP

Maryland Federation of Business and Professional
  Women's Clubs, Inc.
c/o Pat Schroeder, Scholarship Chair
354 Driftwood Lane
Solomons, MD 20688
(410) 326-0167                Toll-free: (877) INFO-BPW
E-mail: patsc@csmd.edu
Web: www.bpwmaryland.org/scholarships.html

**Summary** To provide financial assistance for college to mature women in Maryland.

**Eligibility** This program is open to women who are at least 25 years of age and who are interested in working on undergraduate studies to upgrade their skills for career advancement, to train for a new career field, or to reenter the job market. Applicants must be residents of Maryland or, if a resident of another state, a member of the Maryland Federation of Business and Professional Women's Clubs. They must have been accepted into an accredited program or course of study at a Maryland academic institution and be able to demonstrate critical financial need.

**Financial data** The stipend is $1,000 per year.

**Duration** 1 year.

**Number awarded** 1 or more each year.

**Deadline** June of each year.

## [101]
## CADY MCDONNELL MEMORIAL SCHOLARSHIP

American Congress on Surveying and Mapping
Attn: Scholarships
6 Montgomery Village Avenue, Suite 403
Gaithersburg, MD 20879
(240) 632-9716, ext. 113        Fax: (240) 632-1321
E-mail: pat.canfield@acsm.net
Web: www.acsm.net/scholar.html

**Summary** To provide financial assistance for undergraduate study in surveying to women members of the American Congress on Surveying and Mapping (ACSM) from designated western states.

**Eligibility** This program is open to women ACSM members who are enrolled at a 2-year or 4-year college or university. Applicants must be residents of Alaska, Arizona, California, Colorado, Hawaii, Idaho, Montana, Nevada, New Mexico, Oregon, Utah, Washington, or Wyoming. They must be majoring in surveying or a closely-related program (e.g., geomatics, surveying engineering). Along with their application, they must submit a statement describing their educational program, future plans for study or research, and why the award is merited. Selection is based on that statement (30%), academic record (30%), letters of recommendation (20%), and professional activities (20%); if 2 or more applicants are judged equal based on those criteria, financial need may be considered.

**Financial data** The stipend is $1,000.

**Duration** 1 year.

**Number awarded**  1 each year.

**Deadline**  October of each year.

## [102]
## CALGON TAKE ME AWAY TO COLLEGE SCHOLARSHIPS

Coty US LLC
One Park Avenue, Fifth Floor
New York, NY 10016
(212) 479-4300                    Fax: (212) 479-4399
Web: www.takemeaway.com

**Summary**  To recognize and reward, with college scholarships, women who are graduating high school seniors or already enrolled in college and provide excellent answers to online essay questions.

**Eligibility**  This competition is open to women residents of the United States who are 18 years of age or older. Applicants must be enrolled or planning to enroll as a full-time undergraduate student at a 4-year U.S. college or university and have a GPA of 3.0 or higher. They must submit online answers (up to 900 characters) to questions that change annually; recently, applicants were invited to write on 1) how stepping outside their comfort zone to try something new has taken them on an unexpected path and changed their life; and 2) a childhood event that they feel has most shaped who they are and what they believe in. Those short answers are judged on the basis of originality, quality of expression, and accordance with standard rules of English grammar, mechanics, and spelling. Financial need is not considered. The 35 finalists are then invited to submit a short essay on a specified topic, transcripts, a list of extracurricular activities, and other documents as part of an application packet to be provided. Scholarship America ranks the finalists on the basis of merit, exclusive of the essays. Maddenmedia selects the winner on the basis of that ranking and the essays.

**Financial data**  First place is a $5,000 scholarship, second a $2,000 scholarship, third a $1,000 scholarship, and runners-up $500 scholarships.

**Duration**  The competition is held annually.

**Additional information**  This annual competition began in 1999. Information is also available from Scholarship America, One Scholarship Way, P.O. Box 297, St. Peter, MN 56082, (507) 931-1682, (800) 537-4180, Fax: (507) 931-9168, E-mail: smsinfo@csfa.org, and from Maddenmedia, 1650 East Fort Lowell Road, Suite 100, Tucson, AZ 85719.

**Number awarded**  9 each year: 1 first place, 1 second, 1 third, and 6 runners-up.

**Deadline**  February of each year.

## [103]
## CALIFORNIA FEE WAIVER PROGRAM FOR DEPENDENTS OF TOTALLY DISABLED VETERANS

California Department of Veterans Affairs
Attn: Division of Veterans Services
1227 O Street, Room 101
Sacramento, CA 95814
(916) 503-8397   Toll-free: (800) 952-LOAN (within CA)
Fax: (916) 653-2563              TDD: (800) 324-5966
E-mail: ruckergl@cdva.ca.gov
Web: www.cdva.ca.gov/service/feewaiver.asp

**Summary**  To provide financial assistance for college to dependents of disabled and other California veterans.

**Eligibility**  Eligible for this program are spouses (including registered domestic partners), children, and unremarried widow(er)s of veterans who are currently totally service-connected disabled (or are being compensated for a service-connected disability at a rate of 100%) or who died of a service-connected cause or disability. The veteran parent must have served during a qualifying war period and must have been discharged or released from military service under honorable conditions. The child cannot be over 27 years of age (extended to 30 if the student was in the military); there are no age limitations for spouses or surviving spouses. This program does not have an income limit. Dependents in college are not eligible if they are qualified to receive educational benefits from the U.S. Department of Veterans Affairs. Applicants must be attending or planning to attend a community college, branch of the California State University system, or campus of the University of California.

**Financial data**  Full-time college students receive a waiver of tuition and registration fees at any publicly-supported community or state college or university in California.

**Duration**  Children of eligible veterans may receive postsecondary benefits until the needed training is completed or until the dependent reaches 27 years of age (extended to 30 if the dependent serves in the armed forces). Widow(er)s and spouses are limited to a maximum of 48 months' full-time training or the equivalent in part-time training.

**Number awarded**  Varies each year.

## [104]
## CALIFORNIA INTERSCHOLASTIC FEDERATION SCHOLAR-ATHLETE OF THE YEAR

California Interscholastic Federation
Attn: State Office
1320 Harbor Bay Parkway, Suite 140
Alameda, CA 94502-6578
(510) 521-4447                    Fax: (510) 521-4449
E-mail: info@cifstate.org
Web: www.cifstate.org

**Summary**  To provide financial assistance to college-bound high school seniors in California who have participated in athletics.

**Eligibility**  This program is open to high school seniors in California who have an unweighted cumulative GPA of 3.7 or higher and have demonstrated superior athletic ability in at least 2 years of varsity play within California. Students must submit an application to their principal or counselor and an essay, up to 500 words, on how they display character in their athletic and academic efforts. They may include examples of meaningful behavior in their high school experience, lessons learned about the importance of character in their life, and opportunities that coaches, cheerleaders, athletes, and fans have to promote character in interscholastic athletics. Based on those essays, school officials nominate students for these scholarships. Males and females are judged separately.

**Financial data** The stipend is $2,000.

**Duration** 1 year; nonrenewable.

**Number awarded** 2 each year: 1 for a female and 1 for a male.

**Deadline** Students must submit their application and essay to their counselor or principal by mid-February of each year. School officials forward the packets to the state office by the end of March.

## [105]
## CALIFORNIA JOB'S DAUGHTERS SCHOLARSHIPS

International Order of Job's Daughters-Grand Guardian
    Council of California
Attn: Patricia Mosier, Grand Secretary
303 West Lincoln, Suite 210
Anaheim, CA 92805-2928
(714) 535-4575            Fax: (714) 991-6798
E-mail: GrSecCAiojd@aol.com
Web: www.caiojd.org

**Summary** To provide financial assistance for college to members of the International Order of Job's Daughters in California.

**Eligibility** This program is open to members of Job's Daughters in good standing, active or majority, in California. An applicant must submit 1) a transcript of 7 completed semesters if she is still in high school or of all completed course work if she is already in college; 2) a letter of recommendation signed by all members of her Executive Bethel Guardian Council; 3) a letter of recommendation from her high school principal, dean, counselor, or instructor, or, if in college, her college counselor; and 4) a letter describing her educational plans and goals. Transcripts account for 75% of the selection criteria.

**Financial data** Stipends range from $200 to $1,800.

**Duration** 1 year; nonrenewable.

**Additional information** The applicant with the highest score receives the Elise Bonneville Daskam Memorial Scholarship. The applicant with the second highest score receives the Harold Aggesen Grand Bethel Memorial Scholarship.

**Number awarded** Varies each year. Recently, 38 of these scholarships were awarded: 1 at $1,800, 1 at $1,500, 3 at $1,250, 1 at $1,200, 1 at $1,000, 11 at $900, 1 at $800, 14 at $500, 1 at $300, and 4 at $200.

**Deadline** March of each year.

## [106]
## CALIFORNIA LEGION AUXILIARY PAST DEPARTMENT PRESIDENT'S JUNIOR SCHOLARSHIP

American Legion Auxiliary
Attn: Department of California
Veterans War Memorial Building
401 Van Ness Avenue, Room 113
San Francisco, CA 94102-4586
(415) 861-5092            Fax: (415) 861-8365
E-mail: calegionaux@calegionaux.org
Web: www.calegionaux.org/scholarships.html

**Summary** To provide financial assistance for college to the daughters of California veterans who are active in the American Legion Junior Auxiliary.

**Eligibility** This program is open to the daughters, granddaughters, and great-granddaughters of veterans who served in World War I, World War II, Korea, Vietnam, Grenada/Lebanon, Panama, or Desert Shield/Desert Storm. Applicants must be in their senior year at an accredited high school, must have been members of the Junior Auxiliary for at least 3 consecutive years, and must be residents of California (if eligibility for Junior Auxiliary membership is by a current member of the American Legion or Auxiliary in California, the applicant may reside elsewhere). Selection is based on scholastic merit (20%); active participation in Junior Auxiliary (15%); record of service or volunteerism within the applicant's community, school, and/or unit (35%); a brief description of the applicant's desire to pursue a higher education (15%); and 3 letters of reference (15%).

**Financial data** The stipend depends on the availability of funds but ranges from $300 to $1,000.

**Duration** 1 year.

**Additional information** The recipient must attend college in California.

**Number awarded** 1 each year.

**Deadline** April of each year.

## [107]
## CALIFORNIA P.E.O. SCHOLARSHIPS

P.E.O. Foundation-California State Chapter
c/o Liz Wetzel
1887 Rim Rock Canyon Road
Laguna Beach, CA 92651
(949) 376-1568            E-mail: elwglw@cox.net

**Summary** To provide financial assistance to women in California whose undergraduate or graduate education has been interrupted.

**Eligibility** This program is open to female residents of California who have completed 4 years of high school (or the equivalent), are enrolled at or accepted by an accredited college, university, vocational school, or graduate school, and have an excellent academic record. Selection is based on financial need, character, academic ability, and school and community activities.

**Financial data** Stipends range from $200 to $4,000.

**Duration** 1 year; may be renewed for up to 3 additional years.

**Additional information** This program includes the following named scholarships: the Barbara Furse Mackey Scholarship (for women whose education has been interrupted); the Beverly Dye Anderson Scholarship (for the fields of teaching or health care); the Marjorie M. McDonald P.E.O. Scholarship (for women who are continuing their education after a long hiatus from school); the Ora Keck Scholarship (for women who are preparing for a career in music or the fine arts); the Phyllis J. Van Deventer Scholarship (for women who are preparing for a career in music performance or music education); the Stella May Nau Scholarship (for women who are interested in reentering the job market); the Linda Jones Memorial Fine Arts Scholarship (for women studying fine arts); the Polly Thompson Memorial Music Scholarship (for women studying music); the Ruby W. Henry Scholarship; the Jean W. Gratiot Scholarship; the Pearl Prime Scholarship; and the Helen D. Thompson Memorial Scholarship.

**Number awarded** Varies each year; recently, 18 of these scholarships were awarded.

**Deadline** February of each year.

## [108]
## CALIFORNIA REAL ESTATE ENDOWMENT FUND SCHOLARSHIP PROGRAM

California Community Colleges
Attn: Student Financial Assistance Programs
1102 Q Street
Sacramento, CA 95814-6511
(916) 324-0925          E-mail: rquintan@cccco.edu
Web: www.cccco.edu

**Summary** To provide financial assistance to disadvantaged California community college students who are studying real estate.

**Eligibility** This program is open to students at community colleges in California who are majoring in real estate or (if their college does not offer a real estate major) business administration with a concentration in real estate. Applicants must have completed at least a 3-unit college course in real estate with a grade of "C" or better and must be enrolled in at least 6 semester units of real estate for the semester of the scholarship. Students must meet 1 of the following financial need criteria: 1) have completed the Free Application for Federal Student Aid (FAFSA) and been determined by their college to have financial need; 2) come from a family with an income less than $13,965 for 1 person, $18,735 for 2 persons, $23,505 for 3 persons, $28,275 for 4 persons, or an additional $4,770 for each additional family member; or 3) come from a family with an income less than $50,000 and be from a disadvantaged group (have low economic status and/or have been denied opportunities in society for reasons of gender, race, ethnicity, economics, language, education, physical disabilities, or other mitigating factors). Scholarships are awarded on a first-come, first-served basis.

**Financial data** Awards up to $400 per semester ($800 per year) are available.

**Duration** 1 semester; may be renewed if the student remains enrolled in at least 6 units of real estate with a GPA of 2.0 or higher.

**Additional information** Students apply to their community college, not to the sponsoring organization.

**Number awarded** From 35 to 55 each year; approximately $30,000 per year is available for this program.

**Deadline** March of each year.

## [109]
## CALIFORNIA SPIRIT OF YOUTH SCHOLARSHIP FOR JUNIOR MEMBERS

American Legion Auxiliary
Attn: Department of California
Veterans War Memorial Building
401 Van Ness Avenue, Room 113
San Francisco, CA 94102-4586
(415) 861-5092          Fax: (415) 861-8365
E-mail: calegionaux@calegionaux.org
Web: www.calegionaux.org/scholarships.html

**Summary** To provide financial assistance for college to California residents who are American Legion Junior Auxiliary members.

**Eligibility** Applicants for this scholarship must be high school seniors who are junior members of the Auxiliary and have been members for at least 3 years; selection is based on scholarship, character, Americanism, leadership, and financial need. The winner competes for the national American Legion Auxiliary Spirit of Youth Scholarship. If the California winner is not awarded the national scholarship, then she receives this departmental scholarship.

**Financial data** The stipend is $500.

**Duration** 1 year.

**Additional information** The recipient must attend college in California.

**Number awarded** 1 each year.

**Deadline** March of each year.

## [110]
## CAREER ADVANCEMENT SCHOLARSHIPS

Business and Professional Women's Foundation
Attn: Scholarship Program
301 ACT Drive
P.O. Box 4030
Iowa City, IA 52243-4030
Toll-free: (800) 525-3729
E-mail: bpwfoundation@act.org
Web: www.bpwfoundation.org

**Summary** To provide financial assistance for college or graduate school to mature women who are employed or seeking employment in selected fields.

**Eligibility** This program is open to women who are at least 25 years of age, citizens of the United States, within 2 years of completing their course of study, officially accepted into an accredited program or course of study at an American institution (including those in American Samoa, Puerto Rico, and the Virgin Islands), able to demonstrate critical financial need, and planning to use the desired training to improve their chances for advancement, train for a new career field, or enter/reenter the job market. Applicants must be interested in working on an associate degree, bachelor's degree, master's degree, certificate program for a person with a degree (e.g., teacher's certificate), or certificate program that does not require a degree (e.g., nurse practitioner). Along with their application, they must submit a 1-page essay on their specific, short-term goals and how the proposed training and award will help them accomplish their goals and make a difference in their professional career. Study for a doctoral-level or terminal degree (e.g., Ph.D., M.D., D.D.S., D.V.M., J.D.) is not eligible.

**Financial data** Stipends range from $1,000 to $2,500 per year.

**Duration** 1 year; recipients may reapply.

**Additional information** The scholarship may be used to support part-time study as well as academic or vocational/paraprofessional/office skills training. The program was established in 1969. Scholarships cannot be used to pay for classes already in progress. The program does not cover study at the doctoral level, correspondence courses, postdoctoral studies, or studies in foreign countries. Training must be completed within 24 months.

**Number awarded** Varies each year; recently, 75 of these scholarships were awarded.

**Deadline** April of each year.

## [111]
## CAROLYN WEATHERFORD SCHOLARSHIP FUND

Woman's Missionary Union
Attn: WMU Foundation
100 Missionary Ridge
P.O. Box 11346
Birmingham, AL 35202-1346
(205) 408-5525        Toll-free: (877) 482-4483
Fax: (205) 408-5508
E-mail: wmufoundation@wmu.org
Web: www.wmufoundation.com/scholar_scholar.asp

**Summary** To provide an opportunity for women to prepare for service to the Woman's Missionary Union (WMU).

**Eligibility** This program is open to women who are members of the Baptist Church and are interested in 1) field work experience as interns or in women's missionary work in the United States; or 2) service in women's missionary work in the United States). Applicants must arrange for 3 letters of endorsement, from a recent professor, a state or associational WMU official, and a recent pastor. Selection is based on current active involvement in WMU, previous activity in WMU, plans for long-term involvement in WMU and/or home missions, academic strength, leadership skills, and personal and professional characteristics.

**Financial data** A stipend is awarded (amount not specified).

**Duration** 1 year.

**Additional information** This fund was begun by Woman's Mission Union, Auxiliary to Southern Baptist Convention, in appreciation for the executive director of WMU during its centennial year. Recipients must attend a Southern Baptist seminary or divinity school.

**Number awarded** 1 or more each year.

**Deadline** February of each year.

## [112]
## CATERPILLAR SCHOLARSHIPS

Society of Women Engineers
230 East Ohio Street, Suite 400
Chicago, IL 60611-3265
(312) 596-5223        Toll-free: (877) SWE-INFO
Fax: (312) 644-8557
E-mail: scholarshipapplication@swe.org
Web: www.swe.org/scholarships

**Summary** To provide financial assistance to women from selected states who are attending college or graduate school to study engineering or computer science.

**Eligibility** This program is open to women who are enrolled at an ABET-accredited 4-year college or university. Applicants must be U.S. citizens majoring in computer science or engineering as an undergraduate or graduate student. They must have a GPA of 2.8 or higher and be residents of the sponsor's region C (Arkansas, Louisiana, Mississippi, and Texas); D (Alabama, Florida, Georgia, Puerto Rico, North Carolina, South Carolina, Tennessee, and the U.S. Virgin Islands); H (Illinois, Indiana, Iowa, Michigan, Minnesota, North Dakota, South Dakota, and Wisconsin); or I (Colorado, Kansas, Missouri, Nebraska, Oklahoma, and Wyoming). Along with their application, they must submit a 1-page essay on why they want to be an engineer or computer scientist, how they believe they will make a difference as an engineer or computer scientist, and what influenced them to study engineering or computer science. Selection is based on merit.

**Financial data** The stipend is $2,400.

**Duration** 1 year.

**Additional information** This program is sponsored by Caterpillar, Inc.

**Number awarded** 3 each year.

**Deadline** January of each year.

## [113]
## CENTRAL NEW MEXICO SECTION SWE PIONEER SCHOLARSHIPS

Society of Women Engineers
230 East Ohio Street, Suite 400
Chicago, IL 60611-3265
(312) 596-5223        Toll-free: (877) SWE-INFO
Fax: (312) 644-8557
E-mail: scholarshipapplication@swe.org
Web: www.swe.org/scholarships

**Summary** To provide financial assistance to women interested in working on a degree in engineering or computer science at a college or university in New Mexico.

**Eligibility** This program is open to women who are enrolled in a program in engineering or computer science at an ABET-accredited college, university, or 4-year engineering technology program in New Mexico. Applicants may be entering their sophomore, junior, or senior year, or they may be returning to school after an absence of at least 2 years. Along with their application, they must submit a 1-page essay on why they want to be an engineer or computer scientist, how they believe they will make a difference as an engineer or computer scientist, and what influenced them to study engineering or computer science. Membership in the Society of Women Engineers (SWE) is required. Selection is based on merit.

**Financial data** The stipend is $1,000.

**Duration** 1 year; may be renewed up to 3 additional years.

**Additional information** This program was established in 2005.

**Number awarded** 2 each year: 1 to a sophomore, junior, or senior and 1 to a reentry student.

**Deadline** May of each year.

## [114]
## CHAPPIE HALL MEMORIAL SCHOLARSHIP PROGRAM

101st Airborne Division Association
2703 Michigan Avenue
P.O. Box 929
Fort Campbell, KY 42223-0929
(270) 439-0445          Fax: (270) 439-6645
E-mail: assn101abn@aol.com
Web: www.screamingeagle.org

**Summary** To provide financial assistance for college to the spouses, children, and grandchildren of members of the 101st Airborne Division Association.

**Eligibility** Eligible to apply for these scholarships are individuals who maintained a GPA of 2.0 or higher during the preceding school year and whose parent, grandparent, or spouse is (or, if deceased, was) a regular (not associate) member of the 101st Airborne Division. Selection is based on career objectives, academic record, and financial need.

**Financial data** The amount awarded varies, depending upon the needs of the recipient and the funds available.

**Number awarded** At least 1 each year.

**Deadline** May of each year.

## [115]
## CHERYL A. RUGGIERO SCHOLARSHIP

Rhode Island Society of Certified Public Accountants
45 Royal Little Drive
Providence, RI 02904
(401) 331-5720          Fax: (401) 454-5780
E-mail: rchurch@riscpa.org
Web: www.riscpa.org/student.php

**Summary** To provide financial assistance to female college students in Rhode Island who are majoring in accounting.

**Eligibility** This program is open to female students at Rhode Island colleges and universities who have expressed an interest in public accounting during their undergraduate years. Applicants must be U.S. citizens who have a GPA of 3.0 or higher. They are not required to be residents of Rhode Island. Selection is based on demonstrated potential to become a valued member of the public accounting profession. Finalists are interviewed.

**Financial data** The stipend is at least $1,000.

**Duration** 1 year.

**Additional information** This program was established in 2006.

**Number awarded** 1 each year.

**Deadline** March of each year.

## [116]
## CHERYL HENNESY SCHOLARSHIP

National FFA Organization
Attn: Scholarship Office
6060 FFA Drive
P.O. Box 68960
Indianapolis, IN 46268-0960
(317) 802-4321          Fax: (317) 802-5321
E-mail: scholarships@ffa.org
Web: www.ffa.org/programs/scholarships/index.html

**Summary** To provide financial assistance for college to female FFA members from Kentucky, Georgia, or Tennessee.

**Eligibility** This program is open to female members who are graduating high school seniors planning to enroll full time in college. Applicants must be residents of Kentucky, Georgia, or Tennessee interested in working on a 2- or 4-year degree in any area of study. They must demonstrate financial need and personal motivation. Selection is based on academic achievement (10 points for GPA, 10 points for SAT or ACT score, 10 points for class rank), leadership in FFA activities (30 points), leadership in community activities (10 points), and participation in the Supervised Agricultural Experience (SAE) program (30 points). U.S. citizenship is required.

**Financial data** The stipend is $1,250 per year.

**Duration** 1 year; may be renewed up to 3 additional years if the recipient maintains a GPA of 2.0 or higher.

**Number awarded** 1 or more each year.

**Deadline** February of each year.

## [117]
## CHEVRON CORPORATION SCHOLARSHIPS

Society of Women Engineers
230 East Ohio Street, Suite 400
Chicago, IL 60611-3265
(312) 596-5223          Toll-free: (877) SWE-INFO
Fax: (312) 644-8557
E-mail: scholarshipapplication@swe.org
Web: www.swe.org/scholarships

**Summary** To provide financial assistance to undergraduate women who are members of the Society of Women Engineers (SWE) and majoring in designated engineering specialties.

**Eligibility** This program is open to women who are entering their sophomore or junior year at an ABET-accredited 4-year college or university. Applicants must be majoring in computer science or chemical, civil, computer, mechanical, or petroleum engineering and have a GPA of 3.0 or higher. Along with their application, they must submit a 1-page essay on why they want to be an engineer or computer scientist, how they believe they will make a difference as an engineer or computer scientist, and what influenced them to study engineering or computer science. Selection is based on merit. Only members of the society are considered for this award.

**Financial data** The stipend is $2,000. The award includes a travel grant for the recipient to attend the SWE national conference.

**Duration** 1 year.

**Additional information** This program, established in 1991, is sponsored by Chevron Corporation.

**Number awarded** 8 each year.

**Deadline** January of each year.

## [118]
## CHICAGO ALUMNAE PANHELLENIC SCHOLARSHIP

National Panhellenic Conference
Attn: NPC Foundation
3500 DePauw Boulevard, Suite 1079
Indianapolis, IN 46268
(317) 876-7802                    Fax: (317) 876-7904
E-mail: npcfoundation@npcwomen.org
Web: www.npcwomen.org

**Summary** To provide financial assistance to sorority women from Illinois.

**Eligibility** This program is open to women who are either attending a college or university in Illinois or graduates of an Illinois high school attending a college or university in another state. Applicants must be members of a sorority and able to demonstrate financial need.

**Financial data** The stipend is $500.

**Duration** 1 year.

**Additional information** This program is sponsored by the Chicago Alumnae Panhellenic.

**Number awarded** 1 each year.

**Deadline** March of each year.

## [119]
## CHICAGO NETWORK OF EXECUTIVE WOMEN IN HOSPITALITY SCHOLARSHIP AWARDS

Network of Executive Women in Hospitality-Chicago
    Chapter
Attn: Lucy Coughlin, Director of Scholarship and
    Education
Looney and Associates
162 West Hubbard Street, Suite 302
Chicago, IL 60610
(312) 329-0464                    Toll-free: (800) 593-NEWH
Fax: (800) 693-NEWH
E-mail: lucyc@looney-associates.com
Web: www.newh.org/newh/scholarshippacket.php

**Summary** To provide financial assistance to undergraduate and graduate women working on a degree in hospitality in midwestern states.

**Eligibility** This program is open to women who have completed half of an accredited hospitality-related undergraduate or graduate program in Illinois, Indiana, Michigan, or Ohio. Applicants must have a GPA of 3.0 or higher and a career objective in the hospitality or food service industries (e.g., hotel and restaurant management, culinary, architecture, design). Selection is based on financial need and academic accomplishments.

**Financial data** The stipend depends on the availability of funds and the need of the recipient.

**Number awarded** 1 or more each year.

**Deadline** September of each year.

## [120]
## CITRUS DISTRICT 2 SCHOLARSHIPS

Daughters of Penelope-District 2
c/o Sophie Caras
6511 Lake Clark Drive
Palm Beach, FL 33406
(561) 582-9619                    E-mail: sophieh@adelphia.net
Web: www.ahepad2.org

**Summary** To provide financial assistance for college or graduate school to women who are residents of Florida or the Bahamas and members of organizations affiliated with the American Hellenic Educational Progressive Association (AHEPA).

**Eligibility** This program is open to women who are residents of Citrus District 2 (Florida and the Bahamas) and high school seniors, undergraduates, or graduate students with a high school or college GPA of 3.0 or higher. Applicants must have been a member of the Maids of Athena for at least 2 years or have an immediate family member who has belonged to the Daughters of Penelope or Order of Ahepa for at least 2 years. They must submit a personal essay of 200 to 500 words to give the selection committee a sense of their goals and personal effort. Selection is based on merit.

**Financial data** A stipend is awarded (amount not specified).

**Duration** 1 year; may be renewed.

**Additional information** This program includes the Past District Governors/Julie P. Microutsicos Scholarship, awarded to the runner-up.

**Number awarded** 2 each year.

**Deadline** May of each year.

## [121]
## COLLEEN CONLEY MEMORIAL SCHOLARSHIP

Society of Women Engineers-Central New Mexico
    Section
c/o Leslie Phinney, Scholarship Chair
Sandia National Laboratories
P.O. Box 5800, MS 1310
Albuquerque, NM 87185-1310
(505) 845-8484                    Fax: (505) 845-8620
E-mail: lmphinn@sandia.gov
Web: www.swecnm.org/scholarship.html

**Summary** To provide financial assistance to female high school seniors in New Mexico who are interested in studying science or engineering in college.

**Eligibility** This program is open to women graduating from high schools in New Mexico with a GPA of 3.0 or higher. Applicants must be interested in majoring in science, engineering technology, or engineering in college. Preference is given to students who are the first person in their immediate family within their generation to attend college.

**Financial data** The stipend is $1,000 per year.

**Duration** 1 year; may be renewed up to 3 additional years as long as the recipient remains enrolled at least half time, makes minimum progress toward a degree, and maintains a GPA of 2.5 or higher.

**Additional information** This program is administered by the New Mexico Engineering Foundation, P.O. Box 3828, Albuquerque, NM 87190-3828, (505) 213-0887, E-mail: nmef@swcp.com.

**Number awarded** 1 each year.

**Deadline** March of each year.

## [122]
## COLONEL HAROLD M. BEARDSLEE MEMORIAL SCHOLARSHIP AWARDS

Army Engineer Association
P.O. Box 30260
Alexandria, VA 22310-8260
(703) 428-7084          Fax: (703) 428-6043
E-mail: DCOps@armyengineer.com
Web: www.armyengineer.com/Scholarships.htm

**Summary** To provide financial assistance for college to children and spouses of members of the Army Engineer Association (AEA).

**Eligibility** This program is open to spouses and children of AEA members. Applicants must be attending or planning to attend a college or university as a full-time student. They must submit an essay on their reasons for seeking this award. Selection is based on the essay, scholastic aptitude, and letters of recommendation.

**Financial data** The stipend is $1,000.

**Duration** 1 year; nonrenewable.

**Number awarded** 5 each year. At least 1 scholarship is awarded to a graduating high school senior who is the child of an active-duty or civilian AEA member; at least 1 is awarded to a graduating high school senior who is the child of an Army Reserve or Army National Guard AEA member; at least 1 is awarded to a child or spouse of an AEA member who is entering the second, third, or fourth year of a baccalaureate degree program.

**Deadline** April of each year.

## [123]
## COLORADO BPW EDUCATION FOUNDATION SCHOLARSHIPS

Colorado Federation of Business and Professional Women
Attn: Colorado BPW Education Foundation
P.O. Box 1189
Boulder, CO 80306
(303) 443-2573          Fax: (720) 564-0397
E-mail: office@cbpwef.org
Web: www.cbpwef.org/Scholarships.aspx

**Summary** To provide financial assistance for college to mature women residing in Colorado.

**Eligibility** This program is open to women 25 years of age and older who are enrolled at an accredited Colorado college, university, or vocational school. Applicants must be U.S. citizens who have resided in Colorado for at least 12 months. They must have a GPA of 3.0 or higher. Along with their application, they must submit a copy of their most recent high school or college transcript, proof of Colorado residency and U.S. citizenship, a statement of their educa-

tional and career goals, 2 letters of recommendation, and documentation of financial need.

**Financial data** Stipends range from $250 to $1,000. Funds are to be used for tuition, fees, or books.

**Duration** 1 semester; recipients may reapply.

**Number awarded** Varies each year; recently, 22 of these scholarships, worth $18,050, were awarded.

**Deadline** January or August of each year.

## [124]
## COLORADO LEGION AUXILIARY DEPARTMENT PRESIDENT'S SCHOLARSHIP FOR JUNIOR AUXILIARY MEMBERS

American Legion Auxiliary
Attn: Department of Colorado
7465 East First Avenue, Suite D
Denver, CO 80230
(303) 367-5388          E-mail: ala@coloradolegion.org

**Summary** To provide financial assistance for college to junior members of the American Legion Auxiliary in Colorado.

**Eligibility** This program is open to seniors at high schools in Colorado who have been junior members of the auxiliary for the past 3 years. Applicants must be Colorado residents planning to attend college in the state. As part of the application process, they must submit a 1,000-word essay on the topic, "My Obligations as an American." Selection is based on character (20%), Americanism (20%), leadership (20%), scholarship (20%), and financial need (20%).

**Financial data** The stipend is $500.

**Duration** 1 year; nonrenewable.

**Number awarded** 1 each year.

**Deadline** March of each year.

## [125]
## COLORADO LEGION AUXILIARY PAST PRESIDENT'S PARLEY NURSE'S SCHOLARSHIP

American Legion Auxiliary
Attn: Department of Colorado
7465 East First Avenue, Suite D
Denver, CO 80230
(303) 367-5388          E-mail: ala@coloradolegion.org

**Summary** To provide financial assistance to wartime veterans and their descendants in Colorado who are interested in preparing for a career in nursing.

**Eligibility** This program is open to 1) daughters, spouses, granddaughters, and great-granddaughters of veterans, and 2) veterans who served in the armed forces during eligibility dates for membership in the American Legion. Applicants must be Colorado residents who have been accepted by an accredited school of nursing in the state. As part of the application process, they must submit a 500-word essay on the topic, "Americanism." Selection is based on scholastic ability (25%), financial need (25%), references (13%), a 500-word essay on Americanism (25%), and dedication to chosen field (12%).

**Financial data** The amount of the award depends on the availability of funds.

**Duration** 1 year; nonrenewable.

**Number awarded** Varies each year, depending on the availability of funds.

**Deadline** April of each year.

## [126]
## COLUMBIA CREW MEMORIAL UNDERGRADUATE SCHOLARSHIPS

Texas Space Grant Consortium
Attn: Administrative Assistant
3925 West Braker Lane, Suite 200
Austin, TX 78759
(512) 471-3583            Toll-free: (800) 248-8742
Fax: (512) 471-3585
E-mail: scholarships@tsgc.utexas.edu
Web: www.tsgc.utexas.edu/grants

**Summary** To provide financial assistance to upper-division and medical students in Texas (particularly women, minority and disabled students) who are working on degrees in the space science and engineering.

**Eligibility** Applicants must be U.S. citizens, eligible for financial assistance, and registered for full-time study at a participating college or university. They must be a sophomore at a 2-year institution, a junior or senior at a 4-year institution, or a first- or second-year student at a medical school. Supported fields of study have included aerospace engineering, biology, chemical engineering, chemistry, electrical engineering, geology, industrial engineering, mathematics, mechanical engineering, and physics. The program encourages participation by members of groups underrepresented in science and engineering (persons with disabilities, women, African Americans, Hispanic Americans, Native Americans, and Pacific Islanders). Selection is based on excellence in academics, participation in space education projects, participation in research projects, and exhibited leadership qualities.

**Financial data** The stipend is $1,000.

**Duration** 1 year; nonrenewable.

**Additional information** In 2003, the Texas Space Grant Consortium renamed its undergraduate scholarship program in honor of the 7 Space Shuttle Columbia astronauts. The participating universities are Baylor University, Lamar University, Prairie View A&M University, Rice University, San Jacinto College, Southern Methodist University, Sul Ross State University, Texas A&M University (including Kingsville and Corpus Christi campuses), Texas Christian University, Texas Southern University, Texas Tech University, Trinity University, University of Houston (including Clear Lake and Downtown campuses), University of Texas at Arlington, University of Texas at Austin, University of Texas at Dallas, University of Texas at El Paso, University of Texas at San Antonio, and University of Texas/Pan American. This program is funded by the National Aeronautics and Space Administration (NASA).

**Number awarded** Varies each year; recently, 29 of these scholarships were awarded.

**Deadline** March of each year.

## [127]
## COLUMBIA MEMORIAL SCHOLARSHIP

Nebraska Space Grant Consortium
c/o University of Nebraska at Omaha
Allwine Hall 422
6001 Dodge Street
Omaha, NE 68182-0589
(402) 554-3772
Toll-free: (800) 858-8648, ext. 4-3772 (within NE)
Fax: (402) 554-3781       E-mail: nasa@unomaha.edu
Web: www.unomaha.edu

**Summary** To provide financial assistance to undergraduate and graduate students (particularly women, minority and disabled students) majoring in science at institutions that are members of the Nebraska Space Grant Consortium.

**Eligibility** This program is open to undergraduate and graduate students at schools that are members of the Nebraska Space Grant Consortium. Applicants must submit an essay that describes their scientific research track, past or ongoing research, career goals, and how the scientific research track they are pursuing will be helpful in their career. This program is sponsored by the U.S. National Aeronautics and Space Administration (NASA), which strongly encourages women, minorities, and students with disabilities to apply. U.S. citizenship is required.

**Financial data** A stipend is awarded (amount not specified).

**Duration** 1 year.

**Additional information** This program was established in 2003 to honor the Columbia astronauts, especially Creighton University graduate Lt. Col. Michael Anderson. The following schools are members of the Nebraska Space Grant Consortium: University of Nebraska at Omaha, University of Nebraska at Lincoln, University of Nebraska at Kearney, University of Nebraska Medical Center, Creighton University, Western Nebraska Community College, Chadron State College, College of St. Mary, Metropolitan Community College, Grace University, Hastings College, Little Priest Tribal College, and Nebraska Indian Community College.

**Deadline** April of each year.

## [128]
## CONNECTICUT FEDERATION OF BUSINESS AND PROFESSIONAL WOMEN'S CLUBS EDUCATION SCHOLARSHIPS

Connecticut Federation of Business and Professional Women's Clubs, Inc.
Attn: President
P.O. Box 72
Plainfield, CT 06374-0072
(860) 486-3117          Fax: (860) 486-3127
E-mail: shelleym@maverick.facil.uconn.edu
Web: www.bpwct.org

**Summary** To provide financial assistance for college to reentry women in Connecticut.

**Eligibility** This program is open to women in Connecticut who are returning to school to prepare for a career or to upgrade their skills. Applicants must be at least 25 years of age and U.S. citizens. They must submit a 250-word essay on why they need this scholarship. Financial need is considered in the selection process.

**Financial data** The stipend is $500.

**Duration** 1 year.

**Additional information** These scholarships do not cover correspondence schools, doctoral studies, or postdoctoral training.

**Number awarded** 4 each year (1 for each district in the state).

**Deadline** March of each year.

## [129]
## CONSTANCE L. LLOYD SCHOLARSHIP

American College of Medical Practice Executives
Attn: ACMPE Scholarship Fund Inc.
104 Inverness Terrace East
Englewood, CO 80112-5306
(303) 799-1111, ext. 232    Toll-free: (877) ASK-MGMA
Fax: (303) 643-4439        E-mail: acmpe@mgma.com
Web: www.mgma.com/academics/scholar.cfm

**Summary** To provide financial assistance to undergraduate or graduate women in Georgia who are working on a degree in health care or health care administration.

**Eligibility** This program is open to women enrolled at the undergraduate or graduate level at an accredited college or university in Georgia who are working on either an administrative or clinically-related degree in the health care field. Students working on a degree in medicine, physical therapy, nursing, or other clinically-related professions are not eligible. Applicants must submit a letter describing their career goals and objectives relevant to medical practice management; a resume; 3 reference letters commenting on their performance, character, potential to succeed, and need for scholarship support; and either documentation indicating acceptance into an undergraduate or graduate program or academic transcripts indicating undergraduate or graduate work completed to date.

**Financial data** The stipend is $2,500. Funds are paid directly to the recipient's college or university.

**Duration** 1 year.

**Additional information** This program, established in 1993, is managed by Scholarship Program Administrators, Inc. 1201 Eighth Avenue South, P.O. Box 23737, Nashville, TN 27202-3737, (615) 320-3149, (800) 310-4053, Fax: (615) 320-3151, E-mail: info@spaprog.com.

**Number awarded** 1 each year.

**Deadline** April of each year.

## [130]
## CPO SCHOLARSHIP FUND

Senior Enlisted Academy Alumni Association
Attn: CPO Scholarship Fund
1269 Elliot Avenue
Newport, RI 02841-1525
E-mail: john@seaaa.org
Web: www.cposf.org

**Summary** To provide financial assistance for college to the dependents of Navy Chief Petty Officers (CPOs).

**Eligibility** This program is open to the spouses and children (natural born, adopted, or step) of active, Reserve, retired, and deceased Navy CPOs. Applicants must be high school graduates or seniors planning to graduate and must intend to enter their first year of college or university with the goal of obtaining an associate, bachelor's, or graduate degree. Members of the armed services are not eligible. Scholarships are awarded in 5 categories: 1) active duty East coast (stationed east of or at Great Lakes, Illinois); 2) active duty West coast (stationed west of Great Lakes, Illinois); 3) active duty stationed outside the continental United States; 4) Reserve; and 5) retired and deceased. Applicants must submit an essay of 250 to 300 words on "How my education will help society." Selection is based on the essay, honors and awards received during high school, extracurricular activities, community activities, and employment experience.

**Financial data** The amount of the stipend depends on the availability of funds; awards are sent directly to the recipient's school.

**Duration** 1 year.

**Additional information** Information is also available from Duane Bushey, Chief Executive Officer, CPOSF, 1034 Creamer Road, Norfolk, VA 23503.

**Number awarded** 10 each year: 2 in each of the categories.

**Deadline** March of each year.

## [131]
## CYNTHIA HUNT-LINES SCHOLARSHIP

Minnesota Nurses Association
Attn: Minnesota Nurses Association Foundation
1625 Energy Park Drive
St. Paul, MN 55108
(651) 646-4807            Toll-free: (800) 536-4662
Fax: (651) 647-5301 E-mail: mnnurses@mnnurses.org
Web: www.mnnurses.org

**Summary** To provide financial assistance to members of the Minnesota Nurses Association (MNA) and the Minnesota Student Nurses Association (MSNA) who are single parents and interested in working on a baccalaureate or master's degree in nursing.

**Eligibility** This program is open to MNA and MSNA members who are enrolled or entering a baccalaureate or master's program in nursing in Minnesota or North Dakota. Applicants must be single parents, at least 21 years of age, with at least 1 dependent. Along with their application, they must submit: a current transcript; a short essay describing their interest in nursing, their long-range career goals, and how their continuing education will have an impact on the profession of nursing in Minnesota; a description of their financial need; and 2 letters of support.

**Financial data** The stipend is $2,000 per year.

**Duration** 1 year; may be renewed.

**Number awarded** 1 each year.

**Deadline** May of each year.

## [132]
## DAGMAR JEPPESON GRANT-IN-AID

Delta Kappa Gamma Society International-Alpha Rho
    State Organization
c/o Carol Moody
564 Burgundy Circle
Medford, OR 97504
(541) 773-2982          E-mail: cmoody55@hotmail.com
Web: www.deltakappagamma.org

**Summary** To provide financial assistance to women
upper-division students in Oregon who are interested in
preparing for a career in elementary education.

**Eligibility** This program is open to residents of Oregon
who are at least juniors in college and interested in preparing for a career in elementary education. Applicants may not
be members of Delta Kappa Gamma (an honorary society
of women educators), but they must be sponsored by a
local chapter of the society. Along with their application,
they must submit a summary of their education from high
school through the present, high school and college activities and achievements, community service, employment
history, career goals, and financial need.

**Financial data** A stipend is awarded (amount not specified).

**Duration** 1 year.

**Additional information** Recipients may not accept a
scholarship from the Alpha Rho state organization and from
Delta Kappa Gamma International in the same year.

**Number awarded** 1 or more each year.

**Deadline** February of each year.

## [133]
## DAIMLERCHRYSLER CORPORATION FUND SCHOLARSHIP

Society of Women Engineers
230 East Ohio Street, Suite 400
Chicago, IL 60611-3265
(312) 596-5223              Toll-free: (877) SWE-INFO
Fax: (312) 644-8557
E-mail: scholarshipapplication@swe.org
Web: www.swe.org/scholarships

**Summary** To provide financial assistance to undergraduate women majoring in designated engineering specialties.

**Eligibility** This program is open to women who are entering their sophomore year at an ABET-accredited 4-year college or university. Applicants must be majoring in electrical
or mechanical engineering and have a GPA of 3.0 or higher.
Along with their application, they must submit a 1-page
essay on why they want to be an engineer, how they believe
they will make a difference as an engineer, and what influenced them to study engineering. Selection is based on
merit.

**Financial data** The stipend is $2,000.

**Duration** 1 year; may be renewed for up to 2 additional
years.

**Additional information** This program, established in
1997, is sponsored by DaimlerChrysler Corporation.

**Number awarded** 1 each year.

**Deadline** January of each year.

## [134]
## DALLAS NETWORK OF EXECUTIVE WOMEN IN HOSPITALITY SCHOLARSHIP AWARDS

Network of Executive Women in Hospitality-Dallas
    Chapter
Attn: Tracy Herrin, Director of Scholarship and
    Education
P.O. Box 701542
Dallas, TX 75370-1542
Toll-free: (800) 593-NEWH          Fax: (800) 693-NEWH
E-mail: tracy.herrin@ulstercarpets.com
Web: www.newh.org/newh/scholarshippacket.php

**Summary** To provide financial assistance to women in
Kansas, Missouri, Oklahoma, and northern Texas interested
in preparing for a career in the hospitality industry.

**Eligibility** This program is open to women who have completed half the requirements for a degree or certification
program at a vocational school or college in Kansas, Missouri, Oklahoma, or northern Texas. Applicants must have
a GPA of 3.0 or higher and a career objective in the hospitality or food service industries (e.g., hotel and restaurant management, culinary, food service, architecture, design).
Selection is based on financial need and academic accomplishments.

**Financial data** The stipend is $2,500.

**Duration** 1 year.

**Number awarded** 1 or more each year.

**Deadline** March of each year.

## [135]
## DASSAULT FALCON JET CORPORATION SCHOLARSHIP

Women in Aviation, International
Attn: Scholarships
Morningstar Airport
3647 State Route 503 South
West Alexandria, OH 45381
(937) 558-7655              Fax: (937) 839-4645
E-mail: scholarships@wai.org
Web: www.wai.org/education/scholarships.cfm

**Summary** To provide financial assistance to women who
are working on an undergraduate or graduate degree in a
field related to aviation.

**Eligibility** This program is open to women who are working on an undergraduate or graduate degree in an aviation-
related field. Applicants must be U.S. citizens, fluent in
English, and have a GPA of 3.0 or higher. They must submit
a 1-page essay describing their current status, what they
hope to achieve with a degree in aviation, and their aspirations in the field. Selection is based on the essay, achievements, attitude toward self and others, commitment to success, dedication to career, financial need, motivation, reliability, responsibility, and teamwork.

**Financial data** The stipend is $1,000.

**Duration** 1 year.

**Additional information** WAI is a nonprofit professional
organization dedicated to encouraging women to consider
an aviation career. This program is sponsored by Dassault
Falcon Jet Corporation.

**Number awarded** 1 each year.

**Deadline** November of each year.

## [136]
## DAUGHTERS OF AMERICAN AGRICULTURE SCHOLARSHIP

American Agri-Women
c/o Peggy Clark
2274 East Lytle Five Points Road
Dayton, OH 45458
E-mail: aawrc@americanagriwomen.org
Web: www.americanagriwomen.org/scholarships.htm

**Summary** To provide financial assistance for college to women involved in an aspect of agriculture.

**Eligibility** This program is open to women and their daughters who farm, ranch, or are involved in agribusiness or other agricultural activities. Applicants must be between 18 and 23 years of age and be interested in working on a degree in agricultural leadership, communications, technology, economics, rural sociology, medicine, or other courses directly related to agriculture and the needs of agricultural communities. Selection is based on financial need, knowledge of or work experience in agriculture, GPA, and test scores.

**Financial data** The stipend is $500.

**Duration** 1 year; nonrenewable.

**Number awarded** 1 each year.

**Deadline** May of each year.

## [137]
## DAUGHTERS OF PENELOPE PAST GRAND PRESIDENT'S SCHOLARSHIP

Daughters of Penelope
Attn: Daughters of Penelope Foundation, Inc.
1909 Q Street, N.W., Suite 500
Washington, DC 20009-1007
(202) 234-9741                Fax: (202) 483-6983
E-mail: daughters@ahepa.org
Web: www.ahepa.org

**Summary** To provide financial assistance for college to women of Greek descent.

**Eligibility** This program is open to women who have been members of the Daughters of Penelope or the Maids of Athena for at least 2 years, or whose parents or grandparents have been members of the Daughters of Penelope or the Order of Ahepa for at least 2 years. Applicants must be 1) high school seniors or recent high school graduates applying to a college, university, or accredited technical school, or 2) current undergraduates at the college level. They must have taken the SAT or ACT (or Canadian, Greek, or Cypriot equivalent) and must write an essay (in English) about their educational and vocational goals. Selection is based on academic merit and financial need.

**Financial data** The stipend is $1,500 per year.

**Duration** 1 year; nonrenewable.

**Additional information** Information is also available from Helen Santire, National Scholarship Chair, P.O. Box 19709, Houston, TX 77242-9709, (713) 468-6531, E-mail: helensantire@duchesne.org.

**Number awarded** 1 each year.

**Deadline** May of each year.

## [138]
## DAUGHTERS OF PENELOPE UNDERGRADUATE SCHOLARSHIPS

Daughters of Penelope
Attn: Daughters of Penelope Foundation, Inc.
1909 Q Street, N.W., Suite 500
Washington, DC 20009-1007
(202) 234-9741                Fax: (202) 483-6983
E-mail: daughters@ahepa.org
Web: www.ahepa.org

**Summary** To provide financial assistance for college to women of Greek descent.

**Eligibility** This program is open to women who have been members of the Daughters of Penelope or the Maids of Athena for at least 2 years, or whose parents or grandparents have been members of the Daughters of Penelope or the Order of Ahepa for at least 2 years. Applicants must be 1) high school seniors or recent high school graduates applying to a college, university, or accredited technical school, or 2) current undergraduates at the college level. They must have taken the SAT or ACT (or Canadian, Greek, or Cypriot equivalent) and must write an essay (in English) about their educational and vocational goals. Selection is based on academic merit only.

**Financial data** Stipends are $1,500 or $1,000 per year.

**Duration** 1 year; nonrenewable.

**Additional information** This program includes the following endowed awards: the Daughters of Penelope Past Grand Presidents' Memorial Scholarship, the Kottis Family Scholarship, the Mary M. Verges Scholarship, the Joanne V. Hologgitas, Ph.D. Scholarship, the Eos #1 Mother Lodge Chapter Scholarship, and the Paula J. Alexander Memorial Scholarship. Information is also available from Helen Santire, National Scholarship Chair, P.O. Box 19709, Houston, TX 77242-9709, (713) 468-6531.

**Number awarded** Varies each year. Recently, 9 of these scholarships were awarded: 1 at $1,500 and 8 at $1,000.

**Deadline** May of each year.

## [139]
## DAUGHTERS OF THE CINCINNATI SCHOLARSHIP PROGRAM

Daughters of the Cincinnati
Attn: Scholarship Administrator
122 East 58th Street
New York, NY 10022
(212) 319-6915
Web: fdncenter.org/grantmaker/cincinnati

**Summary** To provide financial assistance for college to high school seniors who are the daughters of active-duty, deceased, or retired military officers.

**Eligibility** This program is open to high school seniors who are the daughters of career commissioned officers of the regular Army, Navy, Air Force, Coast Guard, or Marine Corps on active duty, deceased, or retired. Applicants must submit an official school transcript, SAT or ACT scores, a letter of recommendation, and documentation of financial need.

**Financial data** Scholarship amounts vary but generally range from $1,000 to $3,000 per year. Funds are paid directly to the college of the student's choice.

**Duration** Scholarships are awarded annually and may be renewed up to 3 additional years while recipients are studying at an accredited college and are in good standing.

**Additional information** Scholarships are tenable at the college of the recipient's choice. This program was originally established in 1906.

**Number awarded** Approximately 12 each year.

**Deadline** March of each year.

## [140]
## DEAN WEESE SCHOLARSHIP

University Interscholastic League
Attn: Texas Interscholastic League Foundation
1701 Manor Road
P.O. Box 8028
Austin, TX 78713-8028
(512) 232-4937          Fax: (512) 471-5908
E-mail: bbaxendale@mail.utexas.edu
Web: www.uil.utexas.edu/tilf/scholarships.html

**Summary** To provide financial assistance to students who participate in programs of the Texas Interscholastic League Foundation (TILF) and have competed in girls' high school varsity basketball.

**Eligibility** This program is open to students who have competed in girlsÖ high school varsity basketball and meet the 5 basic requirements of the TILF: 1) graduate from high school during the current year and begin college or university in Texas by the following fall; 2) enroll full time and maintain a GPA of 2.5 or higher during the first semester; 3) compete in a University Interscholastic League (UIL) academic state meet contest in accounting, calculator applications, computer applications, computer science, current issues and events, debate (cross-examination and Lincoln-Douglas), journalism (editorial writing, feature writing, headline writing, and news writing), literary criticism, mathematics, number sense, 1-act play, ready writing, science, social studies, speech (prose interpretation, poetry interpretation, informative speaking, and persuasive speaking), or spelling and vocabulary; 4) submit high school transcripts that include SAT and/or ACT scores; and 5) submit parents' latest income tax returns.

**Financial data** The stipend is $1,000 per year.

**Duration** 1 year; nonrenewable.

**Additional information** This program is sponsored by Whataburger Inc. and Southwest Shootout Inc.

**Number awarded** 1 each year.

**Deadline** May of each year.

## [141]
## DEGENRING SCHOLARSHIP FUND

American Baptist Women of New Jersey
36-10 Garden View Terrace
East Windsor, NJ 08520
Web: www.abwminnj.org/custom.html

**Summary** To provide financial assistance to Baptist women in New Jersey who are interested in attending college to prepare for a career in Christian service.

**Eligibility** This program is open to Baptist women in New Jersey who are interested in pursuing a postsecondary degree and preparing for a career involving Christian work.

They must have been members of an American Baptist church in New Jersey for at least 5 years. Selection is based on financial need and career goals.

**Financial data** The amount awarded varies, depending upon the need of the recipient and her career goals in Christian work.

**Duration** 1 year.

**Number awarded** 1 or more each year.

**Deadline** February of each year.

## [142]
## DELAWARE BPW FOUNDATION SCHOLARSHIPS

Business and Professional Women's Foundation of
   Delaware, Inc.
P.O. Box 58
Dover, DE 19903
(302) 629-0267          Toll-free: (800) BPW-DELA
E-mail: info@bpwdelaware.org
Web: www.bpwdelaware.org/foundations.htm

**Summary** To provide financial assistance for college to female high school seniors in Delaware.

**Eligibility** This program is open to women graduating from high schools in Delaware and planning to attend an accredited college or university. Applicants must submit documentation of financial need, a statement of their objectives for their chosen field, their hopes and plans for their future, a letter from a current teacher or employer who has known them for at least 1 year, and a character reference from a nonrelated person who has known them for at least 3 years.

**Financial data** The stipend is $600.

**Duration** 1 year.

**Additional information** This program includes the following named scholarships: the Whelimina Miller Scholarship, the Wilmington BPW Scholarship, the Lillian Halse-Hanf Scholarship, and the Fleetwood-Phillips-Reihm Scholarship. Information is also available from Diana Young, BPW Foundation of Delaware CEO, 12075 Whiteville Road, Laurel, DE 19956, (302) 875-3917.

**Number awarded** 4 each year.

**Deadline** April of each year.

## [143]
## DELAYED EDUCATION SCHOLARSHIP FOR WOMEN

American Nuclear Society
Attn: Scholarship Coordinator
555 North Kensington Avenue
La Grange Park, IL 60526-5592
(708) 352-6611          Fax: (708) 352-0499
E-mail: outreach@ans.org
Web: www.ans.org/honors/scholarships

**Summary** To encourage mature women whose formal studies in nuclear science or nuclear engineering have been delayed or interrupted.

**Eligibility** Applicants must be mature women who have experienced at least a 1-year delay or interruption of their undergraduate studies and are returning to school to work on an undergraduate or graduate degree in nuclear science or nuclear engineering. They must be U.S. citizens or permanent residents, have proven academic ability, and be able to demonstrate financial need.

**Financial data**  The stipend is $4,000. Funds may be used by the student to cover any bona fide education costs, including tuition, books, room, and board.

**Duration**  1 year; nonrenewable.

**Number awarded**  1 each year.

**Deadline**  January of each year.

## [144]
## DELL SCHOLARSHIPS

Society of Women Engineers
230 East Ohio Street, Suite 400
Chicago, IL 60611-3265
(312) 596-5223                Toll-free: (877) SWE-INFO
Fax: (312) 644-8557
E-mail: scholarshipapplication@swe.org
Web: www.swe.org/scholarships

**Summary**  To provide financial assistance to upper-division women majoring in computer science or designated engineering specialties.

**Eligibility**  This program is open to women who are entering their junior or senior year at an ABET-accredited college or university. Applicants must be majoring in computer science or electrical, computer, or mechanical engineering and have a GPA of 3.0 or higher. Along with their application, they must submit a 1-page essay on why they want to be an engineer or computer scientist, how they believe they will make a difference as an engineer or computer scientist, and what influenced them to study engineering or computer science. Financial need is considered in the selection process.

**Financial data**  The stipend is $2,250.

**Duration**  1 year.

**Additional information**  This program, established in 1999, is sponsored by Dell Inc.

**Number awarded**  2 each year.

**Deadline**  January of each year.

## [145]
## DELLA VAN DEUREN MEMORIAL SCHOLARSHIPS

American Legion Auxiliary
Department of Wisconsin
Attn: Department Secretary/Treasurer
2930 American Legion Drive
P.O. Box 140
Portage, WI 53901-0140
(608) 745-0124                Toll-free: (866) 664-3863
Fax: (608) 745-1947
E-mail: alawi@amlegionauxwi.org
Web: www.amlegionauxwi.org

**Summary**  To provide financial assistance for college to Wisconsin residents who are members or children of members of the American Legion Auxiliary.

**Eligibility**  This program is open to members and children of members of the American Legion Auxiliary. Applicants must be high school seniors or graduates with a GPA of 3.2 or higher and be able to demonstrate financial need. They must be Wisconsin residents, although they are not required to attend school in the state. Along with their application,

they must submit a 300-word essay on "Education-An Investment in the Future."

**Financial data**  The stipend is $1,000.

**Duration**  1 year; nonrenewable.

**Additional information**  Information is also available from the Education Chair, Renae Allen, 206 West Fremont Street, Darien, WI 53114-1540, (262) 724-5059.

**Number awarded**  2 each year.

**Deadline**  March of each year.

## [146]
## DELTA AIR LINES AIRCRAFT MAINTENANCE TECHNOLOGY SCHOLARSHIPS

Women in Aviation, International
Attn: Scholarships
Morningstar Airport
3647 State Route 503 South
West Alexandria, OH 45381
(937) 558-7655                Fax: (937) 839-4645
E-mail: scholarships@wai.org
Web: www.wai.org/education/scholarships.cfm

**Summary**  To provide financial assistance to members of Women in Aviation, International (WAI) who are interested in a career in aviation maintenance.

**Eligibility**  This program is open to WAI members who are full-time students with at least 2 semesters of study remaining. Applicants must be preparing for an aviation maintenance technician license (A&P) or a degree in aviation maintenance technology with a cumulative GPA of 3.0 or higher. U.S. citizenship or permanent resident status is required. As part of the selection process, applicants must submit an essay of 500 to 1,000 words that addresses such topics as who or what influenced them to prepare for a career in aviation maintenance technology, their greatest life challenge, their greatest strength and strongest characteristic, their most memorable academic experience, and why they are the best candidate for this scholarship. In addition to the essay, selection is based on achievements, attitude toward self and others, commitment to success, dedication to career, financial need, motivation, reliability, responsibility, and teamwork.

**Financial data**  The stipend is $5,000.

**Duration**  1 year.

**Additional information**  WAI is a nonprofit professional organization dedicated to encouraging women to consider an aviation career, providing educational outreach activities, and providing networking opportunities to women active in the industry. This program is sponsored by Delta Air Lines. In addition to the scholarship, recipients are reimbursed for up to $1,000 in travel and lodging expenses to attend the WAIs annual conference.

**Number awarded**  1 each year.

**Deadline**  November of each year.

## [147]
## DELTA AIR LINES AVIATION MAINTENANCE MANAGEMENT/AVIATION BUSINESS MANAGEMENT SCHOLARSHIPS

Women in Aviation, International
Attn: Scholarships
Morningstar Airport
3647 State Route 503 South
West Alexandria, OH 45381
(937) 558-7655                    Fax: (937) 839-4645
E-mail: scholarships@wai.org
Web: www.wai.org/education/scholarships.cfm

**Summary** To provide financial assistance to members of Women in Aviation, International (WAI) who are interested in a career in aviation management.

**Eligibility** This program is open to WAI members who are full-time students with at least 2 semesters of study remaining. Applicants must be working on an associate or baccalaureate degree in aviation maintenance management or aviation business management with a cumulative GPA of 3.0 or higher. U.S. citizenship or permanent resident status is required. As part of the selection process, applicants must submit an essay of 500 to 1,000 words that addresses such topics as who or what influenced them to prepare for a career in aviation maintenance management or aviation business management, their greatest strength and strongest characteristic, their most memorable academic experience, their greatest life challenge and how has it enriched their life, and why are they the best candidate for this scholarship. In addition to the essay, selection is based on achievements, attitude toward self and others, commitment to success, dedication to career, financial need, motivation, reliability, responsibility, and teamwork.

**Financial data** The stipend is $5,000.

**Duration** 1 year.

**Additional information** WAI is a nonprofit professional organization dedicated to encouraging women to consider an aviation career, providing educational outreach activities, and providing networking opportunities to women active in the industry. This program is sponsored by Delta Air Lines. In addition to the scholarship, recipients are reimbursed for up to $1,000 in travel and lodging expenses to attend the WAI annual conference.

**Number awarded** 1 each year.

**Deadline** November of each year.

## [148]
## DELTA AIR LINES ENGINEERING SCHOLARSHIPS

Women in Aviation, International
Attn: Scholarships
Morningstar Airport
3647 State Route 503 South
West Alexandria, OH 45381
(937) 558-7655                    Fax: (937) 839-4645
E-mail: scholarships@wai.org
Web: www.wai.org/education/scholarships.cfm

**Summary** To provide financial assistance to members of Women in Aviation, International (WAI) who are studying engineering in college.

**Eligibility** This program is open to WAI members who are full-time juniors or seniors with at least 2 semesters of study remaining. Applicants must be working on a baccalaureate degree in aerospace, aeronautical, electrical, or mechanical engineering with a cumulative GPA of 3.0 or higher. U.S. citizenship is required. As part of the selection process, applicants must submit an essay of 500 to 1,000 words that addresses such questions as who or what influenced them to prepare for a career in engineering, their greatest strength and strongest characteristic, their most memorable academic experience, their greatest life challenge and how has it enriched their life, and why are they the best candidate for this scholarship. In addition to the essay, selection is based on achievements, attitude toward self and others, commitment to success, dedication to career, financial need, motivation, reliability, responsibility, and teamwork.

**Financial data** The stipend is $5,000.

**Duration** 1 year.

**Additional information** WAI is a nonprofit professional organization dedicated to encouraging women to consider an aviation career, providing educational outreach activities, and providing networking opportunities to women active in the industry. This program is sponsored by Delta Air Lines. In addition to the scholarship, recipients are reimbursed for up to $1,000 in travel and lodging expenses to attend the WAI annual conference.

**Number awarded** 1 each year.

**Deadline** November of each year.

## [149]
## DELTA DELTA DELTA UNRESTRICTED UNDERGRADUATE SCHOLARSHIPS

Delta Delta Delta
Attn: Tri Delta Foundation
2331 Brookhollow Plaza Drive
P.O. Box 5987
Arlington, TX 76005-5987
(817) 633-8001                    Fax: (817) 652-0212
E-mail: foundation@trideltaeo.org
Web: www.tridelta.org

**Summary** To provide financial assistance for undergraduate study to women students who are members of Delta Delta Delta.

**Eligibility** This program is open to undergraduate women, majoring in any field, who are current members of the sorority. Applicants must be entering their junior or senior year and planning to remain enrolled full time. Selection is based on academic achievement, past and present involvement in the sorority, community and campus involvement, and financial need.

**Financial data** The stipends range from $500 to $1,500. Funds are sent directly to the financial aid office of the recipient's college or university.

**Duration** 1 year.

**Additional information** This program, originally established in 1942, includes the following named scholarships: the Zoe Gore Perrin Scholarship, the Luella Atkins Key Scholarship, the Sarah Shinn Marshall Scholarship, the Martin Sisters Scholarship, and the Masters of Design Scholarship.

**Number awarded** Multiple awards are presented each year.

**Deadline** February of each year.

## [150]
## DELTA GAMMA SCHOLARSHIPS

Delta Gamma Foundation
Attn: Director of Scholarships, Fellowships and Loans
3250 Riverside Drive
P.O. Box 21397
Columbus, OH 43221-0397
(614) 481-8169                    Fax: (614) 481-0133
E-mail: DGScholarships07@aol.com
Web: www.deltagamma.org

**Summary** To provide financial assistance for college to members of Delta Gamma sorority who have made a significant contribution to both their chapter and their campus.

**Eligibility** This program is open to initiated members of a collegiate chapter of Delta Gamma in the United States or Canada who have completed 3 semesters or 4 quarters of their college course and have maintained a GPA of 3.0 or higher. Applicants must submit a 1- to 2-page essay in which they introduce themselves, including their career goals, their reasons for applying for this scholarship, and the impact Delta Gamma has had on their life. Selection is based on scholastic excellence and participation in chapter, campus, and community leadership activities.

**Financial data** The stipend is $1,000. Funds are sent directly to the university or college to be used for tuition, books, laboratory fees, room, and board. They may not be used for sorority dues, house fees, or other chapter expenses.

**Duration** 1 year.

**Additional information** This program includes several special endowment scholarships that give preference to members of specified chapters. Information is also available from Betty Plaggemeier, P.O. Box 1492, Cypress, TX 77410-1492, (281) 370-2863. Recipients are expected to remain active participating members of their collegiate chapter throughout the following academic year.

**Number awarded** Varies each year; recently, 132 of these scholarships were awarded.

**Deadline** February of each year.

## [151]
## DELTA PHI EPSILON SCHOLARSHIPS

Delta Phi Epsilon Educational Foundation
16A Worthington Drive
Maryland Heights, MO 63043
(314) 275-2626                    Fax: (314) 275-2655
E-mail: info@dphie.org
Web: www.dphie.org/foundation/scholars.htm

**Summary** To provide financial assistance for college or graduate school to Delta Phi Epsilon Sorority members, alumnae, and relatives.

**Eligibility** This program is open to undergraduate Delta Phi Epsilon sorority sisters (not pledges) and alumnae who are returning to college or graduate school. Sons and daughters of Delta Phi Epsilon members or alumnae are

also eligible for some of the programs. Selection is based on service and involvement, academics, and financial need.

**Financial data** The amount awarded varies, depending upon the specific scholarship awarded and/or the needs of the recipient.

**Duration** 1 year or longer, depending upon the scholarship awarded.

**Additional information** There are several funds within the foundation, including the Rita E. Rosser Scholarship, the San Francisco Bay Area Alumnae Scholarship, the Delta Kappa-Barbara Gold Fund, the Phi Lambda-Kim Bates Memorial Fund, the Pollack Scholarship, the Eve Effron Robin Founders Scholarship, and the Yetta Greene Memorial Scholarship.

**Number awarded** Varies each year; recently, 5 of these scholarships were awarded.

**Deadline** April of each year.

## [152]
## DENSLOW SCHOLARSHIP

Alpha Chi Omega Foundation
Attn: Foundation Programs Coordinator
5939 Castle Creek Parkway North Drive
Indianapolis, IN 46250-4343
(317) 579-5050, ext. 262          Fax: (317) 579-5051
E-mail: foundation@alphachiomega.org
Web: www.alphachiomega.org

**Summary** To provide financial assistance for college to undergraduate members of Alpha Chi Omega.

**Eligibility** This program is open to women full-time college students who are members of Alpha Chi Omega. Applicants may be at any undergraduate level. Selection is based on academic achievement, chapter involvement, campus and community service, and financial need.

**Financial data** A stipend is awarded (amount not specified).

**Duration** 1 year.

**Number awarded** 1 each year.

**Deadline** March of each year.

## [153]
## DENVER BRANCH AAUW SCHOLARSHIPS

American Association of University Women-Denver
   Branch
Attn: Valerie Yarbrough, President
P.O. Box 100373
Denver, CO 80250-0373
(303) 757-6062                    E-mail: valreey@msn.com
Web: www.coaauc.org/denver/more.htm

**Summary** To provide financial assistance to female residents of Colorado who are attending specified colleges and universities in the Denver area.

**Eligibility** This program is open to female residents of Colorado who are working on a certificate or degree at Community College of Denver, University of Denver's Women's College, Metropolitan State College of Denver, University of Colorado at Denver, or Regis University. Applicants must have completed at least 30 credit hours with a GPA of 2.75 or higher. Along with their application, they must submit an essay on their educational and career goals and financial need.

**Financial data** The stipend is $500.

**Duration** 1 year.

**Number awarded** 1 or more each year.

**Deadline** March of each year.

## [154]
## DENVER CHAPTER ASWA SCHOLARSHIPS

American Society of Women Accountants-Denver Chapter
c/o Nicolette Rounds, Scholarship Trustee
3773 Cherry Creek Drive North, Suite 575
Denver, CO 80209
(303) 377-4282        E-mail: roundscpa@qwest.net
Web: www.aswadenver.org/scholarshipinfo.html

**Summary** To provide financial assistance to women working on a degree in accounting at a college or university in Colorado.

**Eligibility** This program is open to women who have completed at least 60 semester hours toward a degree in accounting with a GPA of 3.0 or higher. Applicants must be attending a college or university in Colorado. Membership in the American Society of Women Accountants (ASWA) is not required. Selection is based on academic achievement, extracurricular activities and honors, a statement of career goals and objectives, 3 letters of recommendation, and financial need.

**Financial data** A total of $7,000 in scholarships is awarded each year.

**Duration** 1 year.

**Number awarded** Several each year.

**Deadline** June of each year.

## [155]
## DESGC UNDERGRADUATE TUITION SCHOLARSHIPS

Delaware Space Grant Consortium
c/o University of Delaware
Bartol Research Institute
106 Sharp Lab
Newark, DE 19716
(302) 831-1094        Fax: (302) 831-1843
E-mail: desgc@bartol.udel.edu
Web: www.delspace.org

**Summary** To provide financial support to undergraduate students (particularly women, minority and disabled students) in Delaware and Pennsylvania involved in space-related studies.

**Eligibility** This program is open to undergraduate students in aerospace engineering and space science-related fields studying at institutions belonging to the Delaware Valley Space Grant College (DVSGC) Consortium. U.S. citizenship is required. As a component of the U.S. National Aeronautics and Space Administration (NASA) Space Grant program, this program encourages applications from women, minorities, and persons with disabilities.

**Financial data** This program provides tuition assistance up to $4,000 per year.

**Duration** 1 year; may be renewed.

**Additional information** This program, established in 1996, is funded by NASA. Members of the consortium include Delaware State University (Dover, Delaware), Delaware Technical and Community College (Dover, Georgetown, Newark, and Wilmington, Delaware), Franklin and Marshall College (Lancaster, Pennsylvania), Gettysburg College (Gettysburg, Pennsylvania), Lehigh University (Bethlehem, Pennsylvania), Swarthmore College (Swarthmore, Pennsylvania), University of Delaware (Newark, Delaware), Villanova University (Villanova, Pennsylvania), and Wilmington College (New Castle, Delaware).

**Number awarded** Varies each year; recently, 8 of these scholarships were awarded.

**Deadline** February of each year.

## [156]
## DINAH SHORE SCHOLARSHIP

Ladies Professional Golf Association
Attn: LPGA Foundation
100 International Golf Drive
Daytona Beach, FL 32124-1092
(386) 274-6200        Fax: (386) 274-1099
E-mail: foundation.scholarships@lpga.com
Web: www.lpga.com/content_1.aspx?mid=6&pid=55

**Summary** To provide financial assistance for college to female graduating high school seniors who played golf in high school.

**Eligibility** This program is open to female high school seniors who have a GPA of 3.2 or higher. Applicants must have played in at least 50% of their high school golf team's scheduled events or have played golf "regularly" for the past 2 years. They must be planning to attend a college or university in the continental United States but not to play collegiate golf. Along with their application, they must submit a letter that describes how golf has been an integral part of their lives and includes their personal and professional goals, chosen discipline of study, and how this scholarship will be of assistance. Financial need is not considered in the selection process.

**Financial data** The stipend is $3,000.

**Duration** 1 year.

**Number awarded** 1 each year.

**Deadline** June of each year.

## [157]
## DOLORES E. FISHER AWARD

Mel Fisher Maritime Heritage Society and Museum
Attn: Curator, Department of Education
200 Greene Street
Key West, FL 33040
(305) 294-2633        Fax: (305) 294-5671
Web: www.melfisher.org/deoaward.htm

**Summary** To recognize and reward, with funding for college or graduate school, women who submit outstanding essays on the oceans.

**Eligibility** This competition is open to women between 16 and 30 years of age. Candidates must submit a 1,000-word essay on how they hope to make a difference in the world through their passion for the oceans, their career goals, and how this award will help them achieve those goals. They must also include 3 letters of recommendation and a brief statement on the personality characteristic they value most in themselves and why. If they are currently enrolled in school, they must identify their program, but school enrollment is not required.

**Financial data** The award is $1,000.

**Duration** The award is presented annually.

**Number awarded** 1 each year.

**Deadline** March of each year.

## [158]
## DOMINIQUE LISA PANDOLFO SCHOLARSHIP

Community Foundation of New Jersey
Attn: Scholarship Services
Knox Hill Road
P.O. Box 338
Morristown, NJ 07963-0338
(973) 267-5533, ext. 35  Toll-free: (800) 659-5533
Fax: (973) 267-2903  E-mail: fkrueger@cfnj.org
Web: www.cfnj.org

**Summary** To provide financial assistance for college to women who demonstrate outstanding scholarship, character, personality, and leadership qualities.

**Eligibility** This program is open to graduating female high school seniors who have already been accepted at a postsecondary educational institution. Applicants may not necessary be the top student in their class, but they must have shown outstanding potential, merit, and/or improvement. Selection is based primarily on financial need, but academic performance, extracurricular activities, and work experience are also considered.

**Financial data** The stipend is $1,000 per year. Funds are made payable jointly to the recipient and her educational institution.

**Duration** 4 years, provided the recipient maintains a GPA of 2.8 or higher.

**Additional information** This program was established after September 11, 2001 to honor a student who was killed in the attack on the World Trade Center.

**Number awarded** 1 each year.

**Deadline** April of each year.

## [159]
## DOROTHY CAMPBELL MEMORIAL SCHOLARSHIP

Oregon Student Assistance Commission
Attn: Grants and Scholarships Division
1500 Valley River Drive, Suite 100
Eugene, OR 97401-2146
(541) 687-7395  Toll-free: (800) 452-8807, ext. 7395
Fax: (541) 687-7419
E-mail: awardinfo@mercury.osac.state.or.us
Web: www.osac.state.or.us

**Summary** To provide financial assistance for college to women in Oregon who are interested in golf.

**Eligibility** This program is open to residents of Oregon who are U.S. citizens or permanent residents. Applicants must be female high school seniors or graduates with a cumulative GPA of 2.75 or higher and a strong continuing interest in golf. They must be or planning to be full-time stu-

dents at an Oregon 4-year college. Along with their application, they must submit a 1-page essay on the contribution that golf has made to their development. Financial need must be demonstrated.

**Financial data** The stipend is at least $1,500.

**Duration** 1 year; may be renewed up to 3 additional years.

**Additional information** This program is administered by the Oregon Student Assistance Commission (OSAC) with funds provided by the Oregon Community Foundation, 1221 S.W. Yamhill, Suite 100, Portland, OR 97205, (503) 227-6846, Fax: (503) 274-7771.

**Number awarded** Varies each year; recently, 2 of these scholarships were awarded.

**Deadline** February of each year.

## [160]
## DOROTHY COOKE WHINERY MUSIC BUSINESS/TECHNOLOGY SCHOLARSHIP

Sigma Alpha Iota Philanthropies, Inc.
One Tunnel Road
Asheville, NC 28805
(828) 251-0606  Fax: (828) 251-0644
E-mail: philonline@sai-national.org
Web: www.sai-national.org/phil/philmustech.html

**Summary** To provide financial assistance to members of Sigma Alpha Iota (an organization of women musicians) working on a degree in music, business, or technology.

**Eligibility** This program is open to members of the organization entering their junior or senior year of college. Applicants must be working on a degree in the field of music business or music technology, including music marketing, music business administration, entertainment industry, commercial music, recording and production, music management, or other related fields. They must have a GPA of 3.0 or higher. Along with their application, they must submit a statement of purpose that includes their career goals.

**Financial data** The stipend is $2,000.

**Duration** 1 year.

**Additional information** This program was established in 2003. There is a $25 nonrefundable application fee.

**Number awarded** 1 each year.

**Deadline** March of each year.

## [161]
## DOROTHY E. SCHOELZEL MEMORIAL SCHOLARSHIP

General Federation of Women's Clubs of Connecticut
c/o Hamden Women's Club
Antoinette Antonucci, Co-President
26 Country Way
Wallingford, CT 06492
(203) 265-9407  E-mail: gfwcct@yahoo.com
Web: www.gfwcct.org

**Summary** To provide financial assistance to women in Connecticut who are working on an undergraduate or graduate degree in education.

**Eligibility** This program is open to female residents of Connecticut who have completed at least 3 years of college.

Applicants must have a GPA of 3.0 or higher and be working on a bachelor's or master's degree in education.

**Financial data** The stipend is $1,000.

**Duration** 1 year.

**Number awarded** 1 each year.

**Deadline** February of each year.

## [162]
## DOROTHY L. WELLER PEO SCHOLARSHIP

P.E.O. Foundation-California State Chapter
c/o Sara Gustavson, Scholarship Committee Chair
1835 Newport Boulevard, A109
PMB 26
Costa Mesa, CA 92627
(626) 286-2792          E-mail: ghcoyle@aol.com
Web: www.peocalifornia.org/dlw.html

**Summary** To provide financial assistance for law school or paralegal studies to women in California.

**Eligibility** This program is open to women residents of California who have been admitted to an accredited law school or a licensed paralegal school. Applicants must have completed 4 years of high school and be able to demonstrate excellence in academic ability, character, integrity, and school activities. Financial need is also considered in the selection process.

**Financial data** Stipends range from $2,000 to $2,500.

**Duration** 1 year.

**Number awarded** Varies each year; recently, 9 of these scholarships were awarded.

**Deadline** February of each year.

## [163]
## DOROTHY LEMKE HOWARTH SCHOLARSHIPS

Society of Women Engineers
230 East Ohio Street, Suite 400
Chicago, IL 60611-3265
(312) 596-5223          Toll-free: (877) SWE-INFO
Fax: (312) 644-8557
E-mail: scholarshipapplication@swe.org
Web: www.swe.org/scholarships

**Summary** To provide financial assistance to lower-division women majoring in computer science or engineering.

**Eligibility** This program is open to women who are entering their sophomore year at a 4-year ABET-accredited college or university. Applicants must be U.S. citizens majoring in computer science or engineering and have a GPA of 3.0 or higher. Along with their application, they must submit a 1-page essay on why they want to be an engineer or computer scientist, how they believe they will make a difference as an engineer or computer scientist, and what influenced them to study engineering or computer science. Selection is based on merit.

**Financial data** The stipend is $2,000.

**Duration** 1 year.

**Additional information** This program was established in 1991.

**Number awarded** 5 each year.

**Deadline** January of each year.

## [164]
## DOROTHY M. & EARL S. HOFFMAN SCHOLARSHIPS

Society of Women Engineers
230 East Ohio Street, Suite 400
Chicago, IL 60611-3265
(312) 596-5223          Toll-free: (877) SWE-INFO
Fax: (312) 644-8557
E-mail: scholarshipapplication@swe.org
Web: www.swe.org
Web: www.swe.org/scholarships

**Summary** To provide financial assistance to women who will be entering college as freshmen and are interested in studying engineering or computer science.

**Eligibility** This program is open to women who are entering college as freshmen with a GPA of 3.5 or higher. Applicants must be planning to enroll full time at an ABET-accredited 4-year college or university and major in computer science or engineering. Along with their application, they must submit a 1-page essay on why they want to be an engineer or computer scientist, how they believe they will make a difference as an engineer or computer scientist, and what influenced them to study engineering or computer science. Selection is based on merit. Preference is given to students at Bucknell University and Rensselaer Polytechnic Institute.

**Financial data** The stipend is $3,000 per year.

**Duration** 1 year; may be renewed for up to 3 additional years.

**Additional information** This program was established in 1999.

**Number awarded** 7 each year.

**Deadline** May of each year.

## [165]
## DOROTHY P. MORRIS SCHOLARSHIP

Society of Women Engineers
230 East Ohio Street, Suite 400
Chicago, IL 60611-3265
(312) 596-5223          Toll-free: (877) SWE-INFO
Fax: (312) 644-8557
E-mail: scholarshipapplication@swe.org
Web: www.swe.org/scholarships

**Summary** To provide financial assistance to undergraduate women majoring in computer science or engineering.

**Eligibility** This program is open to women who are entering their sophomore, junior, or senior year at a 4-year ABET-accredited college or university. Applicants must be U.S. citizens majoring in computer science or engineering and have a GPA of 3.0 or higher. Along with their application, they must submit a 1-page essay on why they want to be an engineer or computer scientist, how they believe they will make a difference as an engineer or computer scientist, and what influenced them to study engineering or computer science. Selection is based on merit.

**Financial data** The stipend is $1,000.

**Duration** 1 year.

**Number awarded** 1 each year.

**Deadline** January of each year.

## [166]
## DR. BERTHA BEAZLEY MEMORIAL ENDOWED SCHOLARSHIP

Indiana Business and Professional Women's
　　Foundation, Inc.
P.O. Box 33
Knightstown, IN 46148-0033
(765) 345-9812　　　　　　　Fax: (765) 345-9812
E-mail: bpwin@msn.com
Web: www.indianabpwfoundation.org

**Summary**  To provide financial assistance to women in Indiana who are enrolled as upper-division undergraduates in a medical field.

**Eligibility**  This program is open to women who have been an Indiana resident for at least 1 year. Applicants must be entering their junior or senior year of a 4-year undergraduate program in a medical field. Along with their application, they must submit 1) a statement (up to 200 words) on their career goals and how their education relates to those goals, and 2) documentation of financial need. Preference is given to students attending an Indiana college or university.

**Financial data**  A stipend is awarded (amount not specified). Funds are paid directly to the recipient's school.

**Duration**  1 year; recipients may reapply.

**Number awarded**  1 each year.

**Deadline**  February of each year.

## [167]
## DR. DOROTHY WEITZNER KORNBLUTT SCHOLARSHIP FUND

Connecticut Association of Optometrists
342 North Main Street
West Hartford, CT 06117
(860) 586-7508　　　　　　　Fax: (860) 586-7550
E-mail: info@cao.org
Web: www.cao.org

**Summary**  To provide financial assistance to female undergraduates who are enrolled in accredited colleges of optometry.

**Eligibility**  Applicants must be female students enrolled in accredited colleges of optometry in the United States. Preference is given to residents of Fairfield County, Connecticut, the state of Connecticut, and New England, in that order. Selection is based on scholarship, character, and financial need.

**Financial data**  The stipend ranges from $300 to $900 per year. The exact amount depends upon the recipient's scholastic performance and financial need.

**Duration**  1 year; may be renewed.

**Additional information**  Information is also available from Clinton McLean, O.D., Vision Center Ltd., 880 Bridgeport Avenue, Shelton, CT 06484-4661, (203) 929-4030, Fax: (203) 929-9662, E-mail: cmclean@networksynergy.net.

**Number awarded**  1 each year.

**Deadline**  June of each year.

## [168]
## DR. JULIANNE MALVEAUX SCHOLARSHIP

National Association of Negro Business and
　　Professional Women's Clubs
Attn: Scholarship Committee
1806 New Hampshire Avenue, N.W.
Washington, DC 20009-3206
(202) 483-4206　　　　　　　Fax: (202) 462-7253
E-mail: info@nanbpwc.org
Web: www.nanbpwc.org/ScholarshipApplications.asp

**Summary**  To provide financial assistance to African American women studying journalism, economics, or a related field in college.

**Eligibility**  This program is open to African American women enrolled in an accredited college or university as a sophomore or junior. Applicants must have a GPA of 3.0 or higher and be majoring in journalism, economics, or a related field. Along with their application, they must submit an essay, up to 1,000 words in length, on their career plans and their relevance to the theme of the program, "Black Women's Hands Can Rock the World."

**Financial data**  The stipend is $1,000.

**Duration**  1 year.

**Number awarded**  1 or more each year.

**Deadline**  April of each year.

## [169]
## DUPONT COMPANY SCHOLARSHIPS

Society of Women Engineers
230 East Ohio Street, Suite 400
Chicago, IL 60611-3265
(312) 596-5223　　　　　　　Toll-free: (877) SWE-INFO
Fax: (312) 644-8557
E-mail: scholarshipapplication@swe.org
Web: www.swe.org/scholarships

**Summary**  To provide financial assistance to women interested in studying chemical or mechanical engineering at a college or university in the East.

**Eligibility**  This program is open to women entering their sophomore, junior, or senior year as a full-time student at an ABET-accredited 4-year college or university in an eastern state. Applicants must have a GPA of 3.0 or higher and be planning to major in chemical or mechanical engineering. Along with their application, they must submit a 1-page essay on why they want to be an engineer, how they believe they will make a difference as an engineer, and what influenced them to study engineering. Selection is based on merit.

**Financial data**  The stipend is $2,000 per year.

**Duration**  1 year.

**Additional information**  This program, established in 2000, is sponsored by E.I. duPont de Nemours and Company.

**Number awarded**  2 each year.

**Deadline**  January of each year.

## [170]
## DWIGHT MOSLEY SCHOLARSHIPS

United States Tennis Association
Attn: USTA Tennis & Education Foundation
70 West Road Oak Lane
White Plains, NY 10604
(914) 696-7223                 E-mail: eliezer@usta.com
Web: www.usta.com

**Summary** To provide financial assistance for college to high school seniors from diverse ethnic backgrounds who have participated in an organized community tennis program.

**Eligibility** This program is open to high school seniors from diverse ethnic backgrounds who have excelled academically, demonstrated achievements in leadership, and participated extensively in an organized community tennis program. Applicants must be planning to enroll as a full-time undergraduate student at a 4-year college or university. They must have a GPA of 3.0 or higher and be able to demonstrate financial need and sportsmanship. Along with their application, they must submit an essay about themselves and how their participation in a tennis program has impacted their lives. Males and females are considered separately.

**Financial data** The stipend is $2,500 per year. Funds are paid directly to the recipient's college or university.

**Duration** 4 years.

**Number awarded** 2 each year: 1 male and 1 female.

**Deadline** February of each year.

## [171]
## E. JEAN MEYERS SCHOLARSHIP

American Woman's Society of Certified Public
    Accountants-South Florida Affiliate
c/o Sharon Lassar
Florida International University
Ryder Business Building 239-B
Miami, FL 33199
(305) 348-2582                 Fax: (305) 348-2914
E-mail: lassars@fiu.edu
Web: www.awscpa.org/southflorida

**Summary** To provide financial assistance to women who are working on an undergraduate degree in accounting at a college or university in south Florida.

**Eligibility** This program is open to women who are entering their fourth or fifth year of an accounting degree program at a college or university in south Florida. U.S. citizenship or permanent resident status is required. Selection is based on academic achievement, financial need, and community involvement.

**Financial data** The stipend is $1,000.

**Duration** 1 year.

**Number awarded** 1 each year.

**Deadline** March of each year.

## [172]
## E. WAYNE COOLEY SCHOLARSHIP AWARD

Iowa Girls' High School Athletic Union
Attn: Scholarships
2900 Grand Avenue
P.O. Box 10348
Des Moines, IA 50306-0348
(515) 288-9741                 Fax: (515) 284-1969
E-mail: jasoneslinger@ighsau.org
Web: www.ighsau.org/aspx/cooley_award.aspx

**Summary** To provide financial assistance to female high school seniors in Iowa who have participated in athletics and plan to attend college in the state.

**Eligibility** This program is open to females graduating from high schools in Iowa who have a GPA of 3.75 or higher. Applicants must 1) have earned a varsity letter in at least 2 different sports, 2) be a first team all-conference selection, and/or 3) have participated in a state tournament in at least 1 sport. They must be planning to attend a college or university in Iowa. Each high school in the state may nominate 1 student. Selection is based on academic achievements, athletic accomplishments, non-sports extracurricular activities, and community involvement.

**Financial data** The stipend is $3,750 per year.

**Duration** 4 years, provided the recipient maintains at least a 2.5 GPA while enrolled in college.

**Number awarded** 1 each year.

**Deadline** December of each year.

## [173]
## ELECTRONICS FOR IMAGING SCHOLARSHIPS

Society of Women Engineers
230 East Ohio Street, Suite 400
Chicago, IL 60611-3265
(312) 596-5223                 Toll-free: (877) SWE-INFO
Fax: (312) 644-8557
E-mail: scholarshipapplication@swe.org
Web: www.swe.org/scholarships

**Summary** To provide financial assistance to women working on an undergraduate or graduate degree in engineering or computer science.

**Eligibility** This program is open to women who will be sophomores, juniors, seniors, or graduate students at ABET-accredited colleges and universities. Applicants must be majoring in computer science or engineering and have a GPA of 3.0 or higher. Along with their application, they must submit a 1-page essay on why they want to be an engineer or computer scientist, how they believe they will make a difference as an engineer or computer scientist, and what influenced them to study engineering or computer science. Selection is based on merit. Preference is given to students at designated colleges and universities; for a list, contact the sponsor.

**Financial data** The stipend is $4,000.

**Duration** 1 year.

**Additional information** This program, established in 2001, is sponsored by Electronics for Imaging, Inc.

**Number awarded** 4 each year.

**Deadline** January of each year.

## [174]
## ELINOR GLENN SCHOLARSHIPS
Service Employees International Union
Attn: Education Department
1313 L Street, N.W.
Washington, DC 20005
(202) 898-3326          Toll-free: (800) 424-8592
Fax: (202) 898-3348      TDD: (202) 898-3481
Web: www.seiu.org

**Summary** To provide financial assistance to women members of the Service Employees International Union (SEIU) who wish to attend college during the summer.

**Eligibility** This program is open to women members of SEIU local unions, including stewards, committee members, officers, and member activists. International and local staff members are not eligible. Applicants must have demonstrated a committed level of activity in the local union, have plans for bringing information back to the local, have the support of their local union president, and be able to cover their own transportation, lost work time, and incidental costs. They must be interested in attending 1 of 4 specified summer programs for union women.

**Financial data** Scholarships cover the cost of tuition, room, and board.

**Duration** Summer months.

**Additional information** Recently, the programs were held at the University of Arkansas in Little Rock, Arkansas, Cornell University in Ithaca, New York, Lewis and Clark College in Portland, Oregon, and Michigan State University in East Lansing, Michigan.

**Number awarded** 20 each year: 5 for each of the 4 programs.

**Deadline** April of each year.

## [175]
## ELIZABETH AHLEMEYER QUICK/GAMMA PHI BETA SCHOLARSHIP
National Panhellenic Conference
Attn: NPC Foundation
3500 DePauw Boulevard, Suite 1079
Indianapolis, IN 46268
(317) 876-7802          Fax: (317) 876-7904
E-mail: npcfoundation@npcwomen.org
Web: www.npcwomen.org

**Summary** To provide financial assistance to undergraduate women who are members of Greek-letter societies.

**Eligibility** This program is open to women enrolled full time as juniors or seniors at colleges and universities in the United States. Applicants must have a GPA of 3.0 or higher and be able to demonstrate financial need. They must be nominated by their college Panhellenic and have demonstrated outstanding service to that organization. Selection is based on campus, chapter, and community service; financial need; academic standing; and nomination by the applicant's college Panhellenic.

**Financial data** The stipend is $2,000.

**Duration** 1 year.

**Number awarded** 1 each year.

**Deadline** January of each year.

## [176]
## ELIZABETH BANTA MUELLER SCHOLARSHIPS
Kappa Delta Sorority
Attn: Foundation Manager
3205 Players Lane
Memphis, TN 38125
(901) 748-1897          Toll-free: (800) 536-1897
Fax: (901) 748-0949
E-mail: kappadelta@kappadelta.org
Web: www.kappadelta.org

**Summary** To provide financial assistance to members of Kappa Delta Sorority who are majoring in speech communications.

**Eligibility** This program is open to undergraduate members of Kappa Delta Sorority. Applicants must submit a personal statement giving their reasons for applying for this scholarship, an official undergraduate transcript, and 2 letters of recommendation. They must be majoring in speech communications. Selection is based on academic excellence, service to the chapter and university, service to the community, personal objectives and goals, potential, recommendations, and financial need.

**Financial data** The stipend is $2,000 per year. Funds may be used only for tuition, fees, and books, not for room and board.

**Duration** 1 year; may be renewed.

**Number awarded** 3 each year (including 1 open to a member with any major).

**Deadline** January of each year.

## [177]
## ELIZABETH CARMICHAEL ORMAN MEMORIAL SCHOLARSHIP
Chi Omega Fraternity
Attn: Chi Omega Foundation
3395 Players Club Parkway
Memphis, TN 38125
(901) 748-8600          Fax: (901) 748-8686
E-mail: foundation@chiomega.com
Web: ww2.chiomega.com/everyday/scholarship

**Summary** To provide financial assistance to women who are members of Chi Omega Fraternity entering their senior year of college.

**Eligibility** This program is open to women who are members of Chi Omega Fraternity enrolled in their junior year. Applicants must submit an essay, up to 200 words in length, on 1) why they want or need this scholarship, and 2) why they feel they are particularly qualified for a scholarship designed to honor Elizabeth Carmichael Orman. Selection is based on the essay; academic achievement; aptitude; contributions and service to Chi Omega, the university, and the community; professional and personal goals; and financial need.

**Financial data** The stipend is $1,000.

**Duration** 1 year.

**Additional information** This program was established in 1980.

**Number awarded** 5 each year.

**Deadline** February of each year.

## [178]
## ELIZABETH GARDE NATIONAL SCHOLARSHIP

Danish Sisterhood of America
Attn: Lizette Burtis, Scholarship Chair
3020 Santa Juanita Court
Santa Rosa, CA 95405-8219
(707) 539-1884        E-mail: lburtis@sbcglobal.net
Web: www.danishsisterhood.org/rschol.asp

**Summary**   To provide financial assistance for nursing or medical education to members or relatives of members of the Danish Sisterhood of America.

**Eligibility**   This program is open to members or the family of members of the sisterhood who have been members for at least 1 year. Applicants must be working on an undergraduate or graduate degree in the nursing or medical profession. They must have a GPA of 3.0 or higher.

**Financial data**   The stipend is $850.

**Duration**   1 year; nonrenewable.

**Number awarded**   1 each year.

**Deadline**   February of each year.

## [179]
## ELIZABETH MCLEAN MEMORIAL SCHOLARSHIP

Society of Women Engineers
230 East Ohio Street, Suite 400
Chicago, IL 60611-3265
(312) 596-5223        Toll-free: (877) SWE-INFO
Fax: (312) 644-8557
E-mail: scholarshipapplication@swe.org
Web: www.swe.org/scholarships

**Summary**   To provide financial assistance to undergraduate women majoring in civil engineering.

**Eligibility**   This program is open to women who are entering their sophomore year at an ABET-accredited 4-year college or university. Applicants must be majoring in civil engineering and have a GPA of 3.0 or higher. Along with their application, they must submit a 1-page essay on why they want to be an engineer, how they believe they will make a difference as an engineer, and what influenced them to study engineering. Selection is based on merit.

**Financial data**   The stipend is $1,000.

**Duration**   1 year.

**Number awarded**   1 each year.

**Deadline**   January of each year.

## [180]
## ELIZABETH WARE SCHOLARSHIP

Arkansas Business and Professional Women
c/o Cari Griffith White
Jonesboro Regional Chamber of Commerce
P.O. Box 789
Jonesboro, AR 72403
(870) 932-6691        Fax: (870) 933-5758
Web: www.arkansasbpw.org/scholarships.htm

**Summary**   To provide financial assistance to female residents of Arkansas who are completing their college education.

**Eligibility**   This program is open to women who are Arkansas residents attending an accredited college or university.

Applicants must be completing their college education and have a GPA as set forth by their institution. Along with their application, they must submit a statement covering their goals, choice of major, and reasons why the grant is needed.

**Financial data**   A stipend is awarded (amount not specified).

**Duration**   1 year.

**Additional information**   This program was established in 1995.

**Number awarded**   1 or more each year.

**Deadline**   March of each year.

## [181]
## ELKS NATIONAL FOUNDATION "MOST VALUABLE STUDENT" SCHOLARSHIP AWARD

Elks National Foundation
Attn: Scholarship Department
2750 North Lakeview Avenue
Chicago, IL 60614-2256
(773) 755-4732        Fax: (773) 755-4729
E-mail: scholarship@elks.org
Web: www.elks.org/enf/scholars/mvs.cfm

**Summary**   To provide financial assistance to outstanding high school seniors who can demonstrate financial need and are interested in attending college.

**Eligibility**   This program is open to graduating high school students (or the equivalent) who are U.S. citizens and residents within the jurisdiction of the B.P.O. Elks of the U.S.A. Applicants must be planning to work on a 4-year degree on a full-time basis at a college or university within the United States. They must submit an official form furnished by the Elks National Foundation (no photocopies); these are available at local Elks Lodges. Applications must be filed with the scholarship chair, Exalted Ruler, or secretary of the Elks Lodge in whose jurisdiction the applicant resides. Applications are reviewed by Lodge and District scholarship committees and then judged by the scholarship committee of the State Elks Association for inclusion in the state's quota of entries in the national competition. On the national level, selection is based on financial need (195 points), leadership (350 points), scholarship (450 points), and accompanying exhibits (5 points). Male and female students compete separately.

**Financial data**   First place is $15,000 per year; second place is $10,000 per year; third place is $5,000 per year; fourth place is $1,000 per year. More than $2.2 million is distributed through this program each year.

**Duration**   4 years.

**Additional information**   In addition to this program, established in 1931, many Elks State Associations and/or Lodges also offer scholarships. Applications must be submitted to an Elks Lodge in your community.

**Number awarded**   500 each year: 2 first awards (1 male and 1 female), 2 second awards (1 male and 1 female), 2 third awards (1 male and 1 female), and 494 fourth awards (247 males and 247 females).

**Deadline**   January of each year.

## [182]
### ELOISE CAMPBELL MEMORIAL SCHOLARSHIPS

United Daughters of the Confederacy
Attn: Education Director
328 North Boulevard
Richmond, VA 23220-4057
(804) 355-1636                    Fax: (804) 353-1396
E-mail: hqudc@rcn.com
Web: www.hqudc.org/scholarships/scholarships.html

**Summary** To provide financial assistance for college to women, particularly in selected areas of Arkansas or Texas, who are lineal descendants of Confederate veterans.

**Eligibility** Eligible to apply for these scholarships are lineal descendants of worthy Confederates or collateral descendants who are members of the Children of the Confederacy or the United Daughters of the Confederacy. Applicants must be female and have at least a 3.0 GPA in high school. Preference is given to candidates from Bowie County, Texas and Miller County, Arkansas. Applications must be accompanied by a family financial report and certified proof of the Confederate military record of 1 ancestor, with the company and regiment in which he served.

**Financial data** The amount of the scholarship depends on the availability of funds.

**Duration** 1 year; may be renewed for up to 3 additional years.

**Additional information** Information is also available from Mrs. Robert C. Kraus, Second Vice President General, 239 Deerfield Lane, Franklin, NC 28734-0112. Members of the same family may not hold scholarships simultaneously, and only 1 application per family will be accepted within any 1 year. Requests for applications must be accompanied by a self-addressed stamped envelope.

**Number awarded** 1 each year.

**Deadline** March of each year.

## [183]
### ELSIE G. RIDDICK SCHOLARSHIP

North Carolina Federation of Business and Professional
    Women's Organizations, Inc.
Attn: BPW/NC Foundation
P.O. Box 276
Carrboro, NC 27510
Web: www.bpwnc.org/Foundation/foundation_nc.htm

**Summary** To provide financial assistance to women attending North Carolina colleges, community colleges, or graduate schools.

**Eligibility** This program is open to women who are currently enrolled in a community college, 4-year college, or graduate school in North Carolina. Applicants must be endorsed by a local BPW unit. Along with their application, they must submit a 1-page statement that summarizes their career goals, previous honors, or community activities and justifies their need for this scholarship.

**Financial data** The stipend is at least $500. Funds are paid directly to the recipient's school.

**Duration** 1 year; recipients may reapply.

**Additional information** This program was established in 1925 as a loan fund. Since 1972 it has been administered as a scholarship program. Information is also available from

Patricia Ann McMurray, 510 Canna Place, Aberdeen, NC 28315.

**Number awarded** 1 each year.

**Deadline** April of each year.

## [184]
### ERMA METZ BROWN SCHOLARSHIP

Kappa Delta Sorority
Attn: Foundation Manager
3205 Players Lane
Memphis, TN 38125
(901) 748-1897                    Toll-free: (800) 536-1897
Fax: (901) 748-0949
E-mail: kappadelta@kappadelta.org
Web: www.kappadelta.org

**Summary** To provide financial assistance to members of Kappa Delta Sorority who are majoring in elementary education.

**Eligibility** This program is open to undergraduate members of Kappa Delta Sorority. Applicants must submit a personal statement giving their reasons for applying for this scholarship, an official undergraduate transcript, and 2 letters of recommendation. They must be majoring in elementary education. Selection is based on academic excellence, service to the chapter and university, service to the community, personal objectives and goals, potential, recommendations, and financial need.

**Financial data** The stipend is $2,000 per year. Funds may be used only for tuition, fees, and books, not for room and board.

**Duration** 1 year; may be renewed.

**Additional information** This program was established in 2005.

**Number awarded** 1 each year.

**Deadline** January of each year.

## [185]
### ETHAN AND ALLAN MURPHY ENDOWED MEMORIAL SCHOLARSHIP

American Meteorological Society
Attn: Fellowship/Scholarship Program
45 Beacon Street
Boston, MA 02108-3693
(617) 227-2426, ext. 246          Fax: (617) 742-8718
E-mail: scholar@ametsoc.org
Web: www.ametsoc.org

**Summary** To provide financial assistance to undergraduates (especially women, minorities, and persons with disabilities) majoring in meteorology or an aspect of atmospheric sciences with an interest in weather forecasting.

**Eligibility** This program is open to full-time students entering their final year of undergraduate study and majoring in meteorology or an aspect of the atmospheric or related oceanic and hydrologic sciences. Applicants must intend to make atmospheric or related sciences their career and be able to demonstrate, through curricular or extracurricular activities, an interest in weather forecasting or in the value and utilization of forecasts. They must be U.S. citizens or permanent residents enrolled at a U.S. institution and have a cumulative GPA of 3.25 or higher. Along with their application, they must submit 200-word essays on 1) their most important achievements that qualify them for this scholarship, and 2) their career goals in the atmospheric or related oceanic or hydrologic fields. Selection is based on academic excellence and achievement; financial need is not considered. The sponsor specifically encourages applications from women, minorities, and students with disabilities who are traditionally underrepresented in the atmospheric and related oceanic sciences.

**Financial data**   The stipend is $2,000 per year.

**Duration**   1 year.

**Additional information**   Requests for an application must be accompanied by a self-addressed stamped envelope.

**Number awarded**   1 each year.

**Deadline**   February of each year.

## [186]
## ETHEL O. GARDNER PEO SCHOLARSHIP

P.E.O. Foundation-California State Chapter
c/o Candy Northrop, Scholarship Committee Chair
15 Hidden Valley Road
Monrovia, CA 91016-1601
(626) 358-8966          E-mail: northfam@adelphia.net
Web: www.peocalifornia.org/eog.html

**Summary**   To provide financial assistance to women who are upper-division and graduate students in California.

**Eligibility**   This program is open to women residents of California who have completed at least 2 years of college. Applicants must be enrolled as full-time undergraduate or graduate students. Selection is based on financial need, character, and a record of academic and extracurricular activities achievement.

**Financial data**   Stipends range from $500 to $1,500.

**Duration**   1 year.

**Number awarded**   Varies each year; recently, 51 of these scholarships were awarded.

**Deadline**   February of each year.

## [187]
## EUGENIA VELLNER FISCHER AWARD FOR THE PERFORMING ARTS

Miss America Pageant
Attn: Scholarship Department
Two Miss America Way, Suite 1000
Atlantic City, NJ 08401
(609) 345-7571, ext. 27      Toll-free: (800) 282-MISS
Fax: (609) 347-6079     E-mail: info@missamerica.org
Web: www.missamerica.org/scholarships/eugenia.asp

**Summary**   To provide financial assistance to women who are working on an undergraduate or graduate degree in the performing arts and who, in the past, competed at some level in the Miss America competition.

**Eligibility**   This program is open to women who are working on an undergraduate, master's, or higher degree in the performing arts and who competed at the local, state, or national level in a Miss America competition within the past 10 years. Applicants may be studying dance, instrumental, monologue, or vocal. They must submit an essay, up to 500 words, on the factors that influenced their decision to enter

the field of performing arts, what they consider to be their major strengths in the field, and how they plan to use their degree in the field. Selection is based on GPA, class rank, extracurricular activities, financial need, and level of participation within the system.

**Financial data**   The stipend is $2,000.

**Duration**   1 year; renewable.

**Additional information**   This scholarship was established in 1999.

**Number awarded**   1 or more each year.

**Deadline**   June of each year.

## [188]
## EVE KRAFT EDUCATION AND COLLEGE SCHOLARSHIPS

United States Tennis Association
Attn: USTA Tennis & Education Foundation
70 West Road Oak Lane
White Plains, NY 10604
(914) 696-7223           E-mail: eliezer@usta.com
Web: www.usta.com

**Summary**   To provide financial assistance for college to high school seniors who have participated in an organized community tennis program.

**Eligibility**   This program is open to high school seniors who have excelled academically, demonstrated achievements in leadership, and participated extensively in an organized community tennis program. Applicants must be planning to enroll as a full-time undergraduate student at a 4-year college or university. They must be able to demonstrate financial need. Along with their application, they must submit an essay about themselves and how their participation in a tennis program has impacted their lives. Males and females are considered separately.

**Financial data**   The stipend is $2,500. Funds are paid directly to the recipient's college or university.

**Duration**   1 year; nonrenewable.

**Number awarded**   2 each year: 1 male and 1 female.

**Deadline**   February of each year.

## [189]
## EXELON SCHOLARSHIPS

Society of Women Engineers
230 East Ohio Street, Suite 400
Chicago, IL 60611-3265
(312) 596-5223           Toll-free: (877) SWE-INFO
Fax: (312) 644-8557
E-mail: scholarshipapplication@swe.org
Web: www.swe.org/scholarships

**Summary**   To provide financial assistance to women who will be entering college as freshmen and are interested in studying engineering or computer science.

**Eligibility**   This program is open to women who are entering college as freshmen with a GPA of 3.5 or higher. Applicants must be planning to enroll full time at an ABET-accredited 4-year college or university and major in computer science or engineering. Along with their application, they must submit a 1-page essay on why they want to be an engineer or computer scientist, how they believe they will make a difference as an engineer or computer scientist, and what influenced them to study engineering or computer science. Selection is based on merit.

**Financial data** The stipend is $1,000.

**Duration** 1 year.

**Additional information** This program is sponsored by Exelon Corporation, parent of ComEd and PECO, the electric utilities for northern Illinois and southeastern Pennsylvania, respectively.

**Number awarded** 5 each year.

**Deadline** May of each year.

## [190]
## EXEMPTION FROM TUITION FEES FOR DEPENDENTS OF KENTUCKY VETERANS

Kentucky Department of Veterans Affairs
Attn: Division of Field Operations
545 South Third Street, Room 123
Louisville, KY 40202
(502) 595-4447 Toll-free: (800) 928-4012 (within KY)
Fax: (502) 595-4448
Web: www.kdva.net/tuitionwaiver.htm

**Summary** To provide financial assistance for undergraduate or graduate studies to the children or unremarried widow(er)s of deceased Kentucky veterans.

**Eligibility** This program is open to the children, stepchildren, adopted children, and unremarried widow(er)s of veterans who were residents of Kentucky when they entered military service or joined the Kentucky National Guard. The qualifying veteran must have been killed in action during a wartime period or died as a result of a service-connected disability incurred during a wartime period. Applicants must be attending or planning to attend a state-supported college or university in Kentucky to work on an undergraduate or graduate degree.

**Financial data** Eligible dependents and survivors are exempt from tuition and matriculation fees at any state-supported institution of higher education in Kentucky.

**Duration** There are no age or time limits on the waiver.

**Number awarded** Varies each year.

## [191]
## FARM BUREAU INSURANCE-VHSL ACHIEVEMENT AWARDS

Virginia High School League
1642 State Farm Boulevard
Charlottesville, VA 22911
(434) 977-8475 Fax: (434) 977-5943
Web: www.vfbinsurance.com/VHSL/VHSLAbout.asp

**Summary** To provide financial assistance for college to high school seniors who have participated in activities of the Virginia High School League (VHSL).

**Eligibility** This program is open to college-bound seniors graduating from high schools that are members of the VHSL. Applicants must have participated in 1 or more VHSL athletic activities (baseball, basketball, cheer, cross country, field hockey, football, golf, gymnastics, soccer, softball, swimming, tennis, indoor and outdoor track, volleyball, wrestling) and/or academic activities (student publications, creative writing, theater, forensics, debate, scholastic bowl). They must have a GPA of 3.0 or higher. Each school may

nominate up to 4 students: 1 female athlete, 1 male athlete, 1 academic participant, and 1 courageous achievement candidate. The courageous achievement category is reserved for students who have overcome serious obstacles to make significant contributions to athletic and/or academic activities. The obstacles may include a serious illness, injury, or disability; a challenging social or home situation; or another extraordinary situation where the student has displayed tremendous courage against overwhelming odds. Along with their application, students must submit a 500-word essay describing how extracurricular activities have enhanced their educational experience. Candidates are judged separately in the 3 VHSL groups (A, AA, and AAA). Selection is based on the essay; involvement in other school-sponsored activities; involvement in activities outside of school; and 2 letters of support.

**Financial data** The stipend is $1,000.

**Duration** 1 year.

**Additional information** This program, which began in 1992, is supported by Farm Bureau Insurance. The courageous achievement category, designated the Andrew Mullins Courageous Achievement Award, was added in 2002.

**Number awarded** 10 each year. For each of the 3 groups (A, AA, and AAA), 1 female athlete, 1 male athlete, and 1 academic participant are selected. In addition, 1 courageous achievement candidate is selected statewide.

**Deadline** March of each year.

## [192]
## FHSAA ACADEMIC ALL-STATE AWARDS

Florida High School Athletic Association
1801 N.W. 80th Boulevard
Gainesville, FL 32606
(352) 372-9551 Toll-free: (800) 461-7895
Fax: (352) 373-1528
Web: www.fhsaa.org

**Summary** To provide financial assistance for college to student-athletes in Florida who have excelled in academics and athletics.

**Eligibility** This program is open to college-bound seniors graduating from high schools in Florida. Candidates must have a cumulative unweighted GPA of 3.5 or higher and have earned a varsity letter in at least 2 different sports during each of their junior and senior years. Boys and girls are judged separately.

**Financial data** Each honoree receives a $500 award. From among those honorees, the Scholar-Athletes of the Year receive an additional $2,500 scholarship.

**Duration** The awards are presented annually.

**Number awarded** 24 honorees (12 boys and 12 girls) are selected each year. From among those, 2 Scholar-Athletes of the Year (1 boy and 1 girl) are selected each year.

## [193]
## FINANCIAL WOMEN INTERNATIONAL OF HAWAII SCHOLARSHIP

Hawai'i Community Foundation
Attn: Scholarship Department
1164 Bishop Street, Suite 800
Honolulu, HI 96813
(808) 566-5570          Toll-free: (888) 731-3863
Fax: (808) 521-6286
E-mail: scholarships@hcf-hawaii.org
Web: www.hawaiicommunityfoundation.org

**Summary**  To provide financial assistance to women in Hawaii who are studying business on the upper-division or graduate school level.

**Eligibility**  This program is open to female residents of Hawaii who are majoring in business or a business-related field as a junior, senior, or graduate student. Applicants must be able to demonstrate academic achievement (GPA of 3.5 or higher), good moral character, and financial need. Along with their application, they must submit a short statement indicating their reasons for attending college, their planned course of study, and their career goals.

**Financial data**  The amounts of the awards depend on the availability of funds and the need of the recipient; recently, the stipend was $500.

**Duration**  1 year.

**Additional information**  This program was established in 1998.

**Number awarded**  Varies each year; recently, 1 of these scholarships was awarded.

**Deadline**  February of each year.

## [194]
## FIRST LIEUTENANT MICHAEL L. LEWIS, JR. MEMORIAL FUND SCHOLARSHIP

American Legion Auxiliary
Attn: Department of New York
112 State Street, Suite 1310
Albany, NY 12207
(518) 463-1162          Toll-free: (800) 421-6348
Fax: (518) 449-5406
E-mail: alanyhdqtrs@worldnet.att.net
Web: www.deptny.org/Scholarships.htm

**Summary**  To provide financial assistance for college to members of the American Legion Auxiliary in New York.

**Eligibility**  This program is open to 1) junior members of the New York Department of the American Legion Auxiliary who are high school seniors or graduates younger than 20 years of age; and 2) senior members who are continuing their education to further their studies or update their job skills. Applicants must submit a 200-word essay on "Why a college education is important to me," or "Why I want to continue my post high school education in a business or trade school." Selection is based on character (25%), Americanism (25%), leadership (25%), and scholarship (25%).

**Financial data**  The stipend is $1,000.

**Duration**  1 year.

**Number awarded**  2 each year: 1 to a junior member and 1 to a senior member. If no senior members apply, both scholarships are awarded to junior members.

**Deadline**  March of each year.

## [195]
## FLAMING ARROW CHAPTER SCHOLARSHIPS

American Business Women's Association-Flaming Arrow Chapter
Attn: Education Committee
P.O. Box 20124
Billings, MT 59101-0124
E-mail: mysasygirl@netzero.com
Web: www.abwaflamingarrow.org

**Summary**  To provide financial assistance to women attending college in Montana.

**Eligibility**  This program is open to women who are attending or planning to attend an institution of higher education in Montana. Applicants must be able to demonstrate financial need and good academic standing. Both traditional and nontraditional students are eligible.

**Financial data**  The stipend is $1,000.

**Duration**  1 year.

**Additional information**  Recipients must be present at the sponsorÖs Business Associate Night in June.

**Number awarded**  2 each year: 1 to a traditional student and 1 to a nontraditional student.

## [196]
## FLEET RESERVE ASSOCIATION SCHOLARSHIP

Fleet Reserve Association
Attn: Scholarship Administrator
125 North West Street
Alexandria, VA 22314-2754
(703) 683-1400          Toll-free: (800) 372-1924
Fax: (703) 549-6610          E-mail: fra@fra.org
Web: www.fra.org

**Summary**  To provide financial assistance for undergraduate or graduate studies to members of the Fleet Reserve Association (FRA) and their spouses, children, and grandchildren.

**Eligibility**  This program is open to members of the FRA and their dependent children, grandchildren, and spouses. The children, grandchildren, and spouses of deceased FRA members are also eligible. Selection is based on financial need, scholastic standing, character, and leadership qualities.

**Financial data**  The stipend is $5,000 per year.

**Duration**  1 year; may be renewed.

**Additional information**  Membership in the FRA is restricted to active-duty, retired, and Reserve members of the Navy, Marines, and Coast Guard.

**Number awarded**  6 each year.

**Deadline**  April of each year.

**[197]**
## FLORENCE A. COOK RECRUITMENT GRANTS

Delta Kappa Gamma Society International-Lambda
State Organization
c/o Inge Buchberger, Chair, Professional Affairs
Committee
1998 Fay's Lane
Sugar Grove, IL 60554-9771
(630) 466-1288          E-mail: iedfb@hotmail.com
Web: www.deltakappagamma.org

**Summary** To provide financial assistance to female high school seniors in Illinois who are interested in studying education in college.

**Eligibility** This program is open to women residents of Illinois who are high school seniors planning to enter the field of education. Each chapter of the sponsoring organization in Illinois may nominate 1 student for this scholarship. Nominees must be U.S. citizens who rank in the top 25% of their graduating class. They must submit an essay on their desired contribution to the education profession. Selection is based on the essay, academic excellence, leadership qualities, participation in school activities, contribution to the community and church, and letters of recommendation.

**Financial data** The stipend is $1,000.

**Duration** 1 year.

**Additional information** The sponsor is an honorary society of women educators.

**Number awarded** 4 each year.

**Deadline** January of each year.

**[198]**
## FLORENCE ALLEN SCHOLARSHIPS FOR OHIO WOMEN

Ohio Federation of Business and Professional Women
c/o Holly S. Goodyear
2500 Granger Road
Medina, OH 44256-8602
(330) 725-3333          E-mail: BPWOHIOFAEF@aol.com
Web: www.bpwohio.org

**Summary** To provide financial assistance for college to women from Ohio.

**Eligibility** This program is open to women who have graduated or will graduate from a high school in Ohio. Applicants must be enrolled or planning to enroll full time at a 4-year college or university. Along with their application, they must submit an essay describing their career plans and goals. Selection is based on that essay; academic, employment, and/or volunteer record; and financial need. Special consideration is given to members of the Ohio Federation of Business and Professional Women (BPW/Ohio) and/or applicants endorsed by a BPW/Ohio local organization. U.S. citizenship is required.

**Financial data** A stipend is awarded (amount not specified).

**Duration** 1 year.

**Number awarded** 1 or more each year.

**Deadline** March of each year.

**[199]**
## FLORENCE STAIGER LONN EDUCATIONAL FUND GRANTS

Alpha Chi Omega Foundation
Attn: Foundation Programs Coordinator
5939 Castle Creek Parkway, North Drive
Indianapolis, IN 46250-4343
(317) 579-5050, ext. 262          Fax: (317) 579-5051
E-mail: foundation@alphachiomega.org
Web: www.alphachiomega.org

**Summary** To provide financial assistance to qualified members of Alpha Chi Omega who are in need of funding to complete their college education or graduate studies.

**Eligibility** This program is open to undergraduate and graduate students who are initiated members of the sorority, in need of financial assistance to complete their degree, and enrolled full time in an accredited college or university. Applicants must include a statement outlining their reasons for applying for the funds, the amount requested, when they want to receive the funds, their career goals, and their participation in the sorority.

**Financial data** The grant depends on the need of the recipient.

**Duration** 1 year.

**Number awarded** Varies each year; recently, 9 of these grants were awarded.

**Deadline** Applications may be submitted at any time.

**[200]**
## FLORIDA BOARD OF ACCOUNTANCY MINORITY SCHOLARSHIPS

Florida Board of Accountancy
240 N.W. 76th Drive, Suite A
Gainesville, FL 32607
(850) 487-1395          Fax: (352) 333-2508
Web: www.state.fl.us

**Summary** To provide financial assistance for Florida residents who are gender or racial minorities and entering the fifth year of an accounting program.

**Eligibility** This program is open to Florida residents who have completed at least 120 credit hours at a college or university in the state. Applicants must be planning to remain in school for the fifth year required to sit for the C.P.A. examination. They must be members of an ethnic, gender, or racial minority group. Selection is based on scholastic ability and performance and financial need.

**Financial data** The stipend is $3,000 per semester.

**Duration** 1 semester; may be renewed 1 additional semester.

**Number awarded** Varies each year; a total of $100,000 is available for this program annually.

**Deadline** May of each year.

## [201]
## FLORIDA LEGION AUXILIARY MEMORIAL SCHOLARSHIP

American Legion Auxiliary
Attn: Department of Florida
1912 Lee Road
P.O. Box 547917
Orlando, FL 32854-7917
(407) 293-7411                    Fax: (407) 299-6522
E-mail: alaflorida@aol.com

**Summary**  To provide financial assistance for college to members and female dependents of members of the Florida American Legion Auxiliary.

**Eligibility**  Applicants must be members of the Florida Auxiliary or daughters or granddaughters of members who have at least 3 years of continuous membership. They must be sponsored by their local units, be Florida residents, and be attending Florida schools. Selection is based on academic record and financial need.

**Financial data**  The stipends are up to $1,000 for a 4-year university or up to $500 for a junior college or technical-vocational school. All funds are paid directly to the institution.

**Duration**  1 year; may be renewed if the recipient needs further financial assistance and has maintained at least a 2.5 GPA.

**Additional information**  Recipients must attend a Florida college, university, or technical school. All awards are for full-time study and are to be used for 2 semesters of the school year.

**Number awarded**  Varies each year, depending on the availability of funds.

**Deadline**  December of each year.

## [202]
## FORCE RECON ASSOCIATION SCHOLARSHIPS

Force Recon Association
P.O. Box 783
Angels Camp, CA 95222
E-mail: commchief@forcerecon.com
Web: www.forcerecon.com

**Summary**  To provide financial assistance for college to members of the Force Recon Association and their dependents.

**Eligibility**  This program is open to members of the Force Recon Association and family members of a relative who served both in the U.S. Marine Corps and was or is assigned to a Force Reconnaissance Company. The relative must be either an active or deceased member of the Force Recon Association. Family members include wives and widows, sons and daughters (including adopted and stepchildren), grandchildren, and great-grandchildren. Applicants may be pursuing scholastic, vocational, or technical education. Along with their application, they must submit a personal statement on why they desire this scholarship, their proposed course of study, their progress in their current course of study, and their long-range career goals. Selection is based on academic achievement, letters of recommendation, demonstrated character, and the written statements.

**Financial data**  A stipend is awarded (amount not specified).

**Duration**  1 year; may be renewed.

**Additional information**  Information is also available from the Scholarship Committee Chair, Dr. Wayne M. Lingenfelter, 2992 Calle Gaucho, San Clemente, CA 92673.

**Number awarded**  1 or more each year.

**Deadline**  Applications must be received at least 2 weeks prior to the annual meeting of the Force Recon Association.

## [203]
## FORD MOTOR COMPANY ASSE SCHOLARSHIPS

American Society of Safety Engineers
Attn: ASSE Foundation
1800 East Oakton Street
Des Plaines, IL 60018
(847) 768-3435                    Fax: (847) 768-3434
E-mail: agabanski@asse.org
Web: www.asse.org/foundation

**Summary**  To provide financial assistance to female undergraduate and graduate student members of the American Society of Safety Engineers (ASSE).

**Eligibility**  This program is open to female ASSE student members who are working on an undergraduate or graduate degree in occupational safety, health, and environment or a closely-related field (e.g., industrial or environmental engineering, environmental science, industrial hygiene, occupational health nursing). Undergraduates must be full-time students who have completed at least 60 semester hours with a GPA of 3.0 or higher. Graduate students must also be enrolled full time, have completed at least 9 semester hours with a GPA of 3.5 or higher, and have had a GPA of 3.0 or higher as an undergraduate. Along with their application, they must submit 2 essays of 300 words or less: 1) why they are seeking a degree in occupational safety and health or a closely-related field, a brief description of their current activities, and how those relate to their career goals and objectives; and 2) why they should be awarded this scholarship (including career goals and financial need).

**Financial data**  The stipend is $3,450.

**Duration**  1 year; nonrenewable.

**Additional information**  This program is supported by the Ford Motor Company.

**Number awarded**  4 each year.

**Deadline**  November of each year.

## [204]
## FORD MOTOR COMPANY SWE SCHOLARSHIPS

Society of Women Engineers
230 East Ohio Street, Suite 400
Chicago, IL 60611-3265
(312) 596-5223                    Toll-free: (877) SWE-INFO
Fax: (312) 644-8557
E-mail: scholarshipapplication@swe.org
Web: www.swe.org/scholarships

**Summary**  To provide financial assistance to lower-division women majoring in designated engineering specialties.

**Eligibility**  This program is open to women who are entering their sophomore or junior year at a 4-year ABET-accredited college or university. Applicants must be majoring in automotive, electrical, industrial, manufacturing, or mechanical engineering and have a GPA of 3.5 or higher. Along with their application, they must submit a 1-page essay on why they want to be an engineer, how they believe they will make a difference as an engineer, and what influenced them to study engineering. Selection is based on merit and leadership potential.

**Financial data** The stipend is $1,000.

**Duration** 1 year.

**Additional information** This program, established in 2002, is sponsored by the Ford Motor Company.

**Number awarded** 2 each year: 1 for a sophomore and 1 for a junior.

**Deadline** January of each year.

## [205]
## FORD OPPORTUNITY PROGRAM SCHOLARSHIP

Oregon Student Assistance Commission
Attn: Ford Family Foundation Scholarship Office
1700 Valley River Drive, Suite 400
Eugene, OR 97401
(541) 485-6211          Toll-free: (877) 864-2872
E-mail: fordscholarships@tfff.org
Web: www.osac.state.or.us/ford_opportunity.html

**Summary** To provide financial assistance to Oregon residents who are single parents working on a college degree.

**Eligibility** This program is open to residents of Oregon who are U.S. citizens or permanent residents. Applicants must be single heads of household with custody of a dependent child or children. They must have a cumulative high school or college GPA of 3.0 or higher or a GED score of 2650 or higher, and they must be planning to earn a 4-year degree at an Oregon college. Selection is based on community service, work ethic, personal initiative, and financial need.

**Financial data** This program provides up to 90% of a recipient's unmet financial need; recently, stipends averaged $11,261.

**Duration** 1 year; may be renewed for up to 3 additional years.

**Additional information** This program, funded by the Ford Family Foundation, began in 1996.

**Number awarded** 50 each year.

**Deadline** February of each year.

## [206]
## FUTURAMA FOUNDATION CAREER ADVANCEMENT SCHOLARSHIP

Maine Federation of Business and Professional Women
Attn: Futurama Foundation
c/o Jeanne L. Hammond, President
RR 1, Box 1610
Albion, ME 04910-9719
(207) 437-2325          E-mail: jlhammon@colby.edu
Web: www.bpwmaine.org/Scholarship.htm

**Summary** To provide financial assistance to Maine women over 30 years of age who are continuing a program of higher education.

**Eligibility** This program is open to women who are older than 30 years of age and residents of Maine. Applicants must be continuing in, or returning to, an accredited pro-

gram of higher education or job-related training, either full or part time. They must be able to demonstrate financial need.

**Financial data** The stipend is $1,200.

**Duration** 1 year.

**Additional information** Information is also available from Nancy Wadman, Scholarship Chair, BPW Maine Futurama Foundation, 478 Surry Road, Ellsworth, ME 04605.

**Number awarded** 1 or more each year.

**Deadline** March of each year.

## [207]
## GAT WINGS TO THE FUTURE MANAGEMENT SCHOLARSHIP

Women in Aviation, International
Attn: Scholarships
Morningstar Airport
3647 State Route 503 South
West Alexandria, OH 45381
(937) 558-7655          Fax: (937) 839-4645
E-mail: scholarships@wai.org
Web: www.wai.org/education/scholarships.cfm

**Summary** To provide financial assistance to members of Women in Aviation, International (WAI) who are interested in a career in aviation management.

**Eligibility** This program is open to WAI members who are enrolled in an aviation management or aviation business program at an accredited college or university. Applicants must be full-time students with a GPA of 3.0 or higher and interested in preparing for an aviation management career. Selection is based on achievements, attitude toward self and others, commitment to success, dedication to career, financial need, motivation, reliability, responsibility, and teamwork.

**Financial data** The stipend is $2,500.

**Duration** 1 year.

**Additional information** WAI is a nonprofit professional organization dedicated to encouraging women to consider an aviation career, providing educational outreach activities, and providing networking opportunities to women active in the industry. This program is sponsored by GAT Airline Ground Support. In addition to the scholarship, recipients are reimbursed for travel and lodging expenses to attend the WAI annual conference.

**Number awarded** 1 each year.

**Deadline** November of each year.

## [208]
## GENERAL ELECTRIC FOUNDATION SCHOLARSHIPS

Society of Women Engineers
230 East Ohio Street, Suite 400
Chicago, IL 60611-3265
(312) 596-5223          Toll-free: (877) SWE-INFO
Fax: (312) 644-8557
E-mail: scholarshipapplication@swe.org
Web: www.swe.org/scholarships

**Summary** To provide financial assistance to women who

will be entering college as freshmen and are interested in studying engineering or computer science.

**Eligibility**   This program is open to women who are entering college as freshmen with a GPA of 3.5 or higher. Applicants must be U.S. citizens planning to enroll full time at an ABET-accredited 4-year college or university and major in computer science or engineering. Along with their application, they must submit a 1-page essay on why they want to be an engineer or computer scientist, how they believe they will make a difference as an engineer or computer scientist, and what influenced them to study engineering or computer science. Selection is based on merit.

**Financial data**   The stipend is $1,250 per year. Also provided is $500 for the recipient to attend the sponsor's annual convention.

**Duration**   1 year; may be renewed up to 3 additional years.

**Additional information**   This program, established in 1975, is sponsored by the GE Foundation.

**Number awarded**   3 each year.

**Deadline**   May of each year.

## [209]
## GENERAL ELECTRIC WOMEN'S NETWORK SCHOLARSHIPS

Society of Women Engineers
230 East Ohio Street, Suite 400
Chicago, IL 60611-3265
(312) 596-5223          Toll-free: (877) SWE-INFO
Fax: (312) 644-8557
E-mail: scholarshipapplication@swe.org
Web: www.swe.org/scholarships

**Summary**   To provide financial assistance to undergraduate women majoring in computer science or engineering.

**Eligibility**   This program is open to women who are entering their sophomore, junior, or senior year at a 4-year ABET-accredited college or university. Applicants must be U.S. citizens majoring in computer science or engineering and have a GPA of 3.0 or higher. Along with their application, they must submit a 1-page essay on why they want to be an engineer or computer scientist, how they believe they will make a difference as an engineer or computer scientist, and what influenced them to study engineering or computer science. Selection is based on merit. Preference is given to students attending selected schools; for a list, contact the sponsor.

**Financial data**   The stipend is $2,425.

**Duration**   1 year.

**Additional information**   This program, established in 2002, is sponsored by the General Electric Women's Network of the General Electric Company.

**Number awarded**   13 each year.

**Deadline**   January of each year.

## [210]
## GENERAL EMMETT PAIGE SCHOLARSHIPS

Armed Forces Communications and Electronics
   Association
Attn: AFCEA Educational Foundation
4400 Fair Lakes Court
Fairfax, VA 22033-3899
(703) 631-6149     Toll-free: (800) 336-4583, ext. 6149
Fax: (703) 631-4693     E-mail: scholarship@afcea.org
Web: www.afcea.org

**Summary**   To provide funding to veterans, military personnel, and their family members who are majoring in specified scientific fields in college.

**Eligibility**   This program is open to veterans, persons on active duty in the uniformed military services, and their spouses or dependents who are currently enrolled full time in an accredited 4-year college or university in the United States. Graduating high school seniors are not eligible, but veterans entering college as freshmen may apply. Spouses or dependents must be sophomores or juniors. Applicants must be U.S. citizens, be of good moral character, have demonstrated academic excellence, be motivated to complete a college education, and be working toward a degree in engineering (aerospace, chemical, computer, or electrical), mathematics, physics, or computer science with a GPA of 3.4 or higher. They must provide a copy of Discharge Form DD214, Certificate of Service, or facsimile of their current Department of Defense or Coast Guard Identification Card.

**Financial data**   The stipend is $2,000.

**Duration**   1 year; may be renewed.

**Number awarded**   Varies each year; recently, 11 of these scholarships were awarded.

**Deadline**   February of each year.

## [211]
## GENERAL HENRY H. ARNOLD EDUCATION GRANT PROGRAM

Air Force Aid Society
Attn: Education Assistance Department
241 18th Street South, Suite 202
Arlington, VA 22202-3409
(703) 607-3072, ext. 51          Toll-free: (800) 429-9475
Web: www.afas.org

**Summary**   To provide financial assistance for college to dependents of active-duty, retired, or deceased Air Force personnel.

**Eligibility**   This program is open to 1) dependent children of Air Force personnel who are either active duty, Reservists on extended active duty, retired due to length of active-duty service or disability, or deceased while on active duty or in retired status; 2) spouses of active-duty Air Force members and Reservists on extended active duty; and 3) surviving spouses of Air Force members who died while on active duty or in retired status. Applicants must be enrolled or planning to enroll as full-time undergraduate students in an accredited college, university, or vocational/trade school. Spouses must be attending school within the 48 contiguous states. Selection is based on family income and education costs.

**Financial data**   The stipend is $1,500.

**Duration** 1 year; may be renewed if the recipient maintains a GPA of 2.0 or higher.

**Additional information** Since this program was established in the 1988-89 academic year, it has awarded more than 70,000 grants.

**Number awarded** Varies each year.

**Deadline** April of each year.

## [212]
## GENERAL MOTORS FOUNDATION UNDERGRADUATE SCHOLARSHIPS

Society of Women Engineers
230 East Ohio Street, Suite 400
Chicago, IL 60611-3265
(312) 596-5223          Toll-free: (877) SWE-INFO
Fax: (312) 644-8557
E-mail: scholarshipapplication@swe.org
Web: www.swe.org/scholarships

**Summary** To provide financial assistance to upper-division women majoring in designated engineering specialties.

**Eligibility** This program is open to women who are entering their junior year at a designated ABET-accredited college or university. Applicants must be majoring in automotive, chemical, electrical, industrial, manufacturing, materials, or mechanical engineering and have a GPA of 3.5 or higher. Along with their application, they must submit a 1-page essay on why they want to be an engineer, how they believe they will make a difference as an engineer, and what influenced them to study engineering. Selection is based on merit.

**Financial data** The stipend is $1,225 per year. Also provided is a $500 travel grant for the recipient to attend the society's national convention and student conference.

**Duration** 1 year; may be renewed for 1 additional year.

**Additional information** This program, established in 1991, is sponsored by the General Motors Foundation. Recipients must attend a designated college or university. For a list, contact the sponsor.

**Number awarded** 2 each year.

**Deadline** January of each year.

## [213]
## GENEVA THORNBERG UNDERGRADUATE SCHOLARSHIP

Delta Zeta Sorority
Attn: Foundation Coordinator
202 East Church Street
Oxford, OH 45056
(513) 523-7597      E-mail: DZFoundation@dzshq.com
Web: www.deltazeta.org

**Summary** To provide financial assistance for continued undergraduate study to members of Delta Zeta Sorority.

**Eligibility** This program is open to members of the sorority who have a GPA of 3.0 or higher. Applicants must submit an official transcript, a statement of their career goals, information on their service to the sorority, documentation of campus activities and/or community involvement, and a list of academic honors. Financial need is also considered in the selection process.

**Financial data** The stipend ranges from $900 to $1,100, depending on the availability of funds.

**Duration** 1 year; nonrenewable.

**Number awarded** 1 each year.

**Deadline** February of each year.

## [214]
## GEORGIA AFFILIATE AWSCPA SCHOLARSHIP

American Woman's Society of Certified Public
    Accountants-Georgia Affiliate
c/o Amy Knowles-Jones, President
Internal Audit Department
222 Piedmont Avenue, N.E.
Atlanta, GA 30308-3306
(404) 653-1242              Fax: (404) 653-1575
E-mail: aknowles-jones@oxfordinc.com
Web: www.awscpa.org/frameset.php?cf=awards.htm

**Summary** To provide financial assistance to women who are working on an undergraduate degree in accounting at a college or university in Georgia.

**Eligibility** This program is open to women who are enrolled in a Georgia college or university. Applicants must have completed or be currently enrolled in a course in intermediate accounting II.

**Financial data** The stipend is $1,000.

**Duration** 1 year.

**Number awarded** 1 each year.

## [215]
## GEORGIA LEGION AUXILIARY PAST PRESIDENT PARLEY NURSING SCHOLARSHIP

American Legion Auxiliary
Attn: Department of Georgia
3035 Mt. Zion Road
Stockbridge, GA 30281-4101
(678) 289-8446          E-mail: amlegaux@bellsouth.net

**Summary** To provide financial assistance to daughters of veterans in Georgia who are interested in preparing for a career in nursing.

**Eligibility** This program is open to George residents who are 1) interested in nursing education and 2) the daughters of veterans. Applicants must be sponsored by a local unit of the American Legion Auxiliary. Selection is based on a statement explaining why they want to become a nurse and why they need a scholarship, a transcript of all high school or college grades, and 4 letters of recommendation (1 from a high school principal or superintendent, 1 from the sponsoring American Legion Auxiliary local unit, and 2 from other responsible people).

**Financial data** The amount of the award depends on the availability of funds.

**Number awarded** Varies, depending upon funds available.

**Deadline** May of each year.

**[216]**

## GEORGIA SPACE GRANT CONSORTIUM FELLOWSHIPS

Georgia Space Grant Consortium
c/o Georgia Institute of Technology
Aerospace Engineering
Paul Weber Space Science and Technology Building,
    Room 210
Atlanta, GA 30332-0150
(404) 894-0521                          Fax: (404) 894-9313
E-mail: wanda.pierson@aerospace.gatech.edu
Web: www.ae.gatech.edu

**Summary**   To provide financial assistance for the study of space-related fields to undergraduate and graduate students (particularly women, minority and disabled students) at member institutions of the Georgia Space Grant Consortium (GSGC).

**Eligibility**   This program is open to U.S. citizens who are undergraduate and graduate students at member institutions of the GSGC. Applicants must be working on a degree in mathematics, science, engineering, computer science, or a technical discipline related to space. Selection is based on transcripts, 3 letters of reference, and an essay of 100 to 500 words on the applicant's professional interests and objectives and their relationship to the field of aerospace. Awards are provided as part of the Space Grant program of the U.S. National Aeronautics and Space Administration (NASA), which encourages participation by women, minorities, and people with disabilities.

**Financial data**   A stipend is awarded (amount not specified).

**Additional information**   Institutions that are members of the GSGC include Albany State University, Clark Atlanta University, Columbus State University, Fort Valley State University, Georgia Institute of Technology, Georgia State University, Kennesaw State University, Mercer University, Morehouse College, Spelman College, State University of West Georgia, and the University of Georgia. This program is funded by NASA.

**Number awarded**   1 each year.

**[217]**

## GIFT FOR LIFE SCHOLARSHIPS

United States Bowling Congress
Attn: SMART Program
5301 South 76th Street
Greendale, WI 53129-1192
(414) 423-3343   Toll-free: (800) 514-BOWL, ext. 3343
Fax: (414) 421-3014            E-mail: smart@bowl.com
Web: www.bowl.com/scholarships/main.aspx

**Summary**   To provide financial assistance for college to members of the United State Bowling Congress (USBC) who demonstrate a financial hardship.

**Eligibility**   This program is open to USBC members who are high school students (grades 9-12) and who have not yet competed in a professional bowling tournament. Applicants must be able to demonstrate a financial hardship, defined as residing in a household where the number of children, the income level of their parents, and possible extenuating circumstances make obtaining a college education financially unlikely. They must submit an essay, up to 500 words, explaining how their financial situation could hinder or stop them from achieving their educational goals. Other factors considered in the selection process include GPA (2.0 or higher required), scholastic honors, extracurricular activities, and bowling activities. Applications from males and females are evaluated separately. In honor of the heroes of September 11, 2001, 2 scholarships are reserved for a son and a daughter of fire/police/emergency rescue personnel.

**Financial data**   The stipend is $1,000.

**Duration**   Scholarships are presented annually. Students may apply each year they are eligible and may win 1 scholarship each year before their high school graduation.

**Number awarded**   12 each year: 6 specifically for females and 6 for males. That total includes 2 awards reserved for children (1 daughter and 1 son) of fire/police/emergency rescue department employees.

**Deadline**   March of each year.

**[218]**

## GILDA MURRAY SCHOLARSHIPS

Texas Federation of Business and Professional
    Women's Clubs, Inc.
Attn: TFBPW Foundation
803 Forest Ridge Drive, Suite 207
Bedford, TX 76022
(817) 283-0862                          Fax: (817) 283-0872
E-mail: bpwtx@swbell.net
Web: www.bpwtx.org/foundation.asp

**Summary**   To provide financial assistance to members of the Business and Professional Women's Association in Texas (BPW/Texas) who are interested in career advancement.

**Eligibility**   This program is open to members of BPW/Texas who are interested in pursuing the education or training necessary to prepare for employment or to advance in a business or profession. Applicants must be at least 25 years old and have a record of active participation in the association.

**Financial data**   The stipend is $500 per year; funds must be used for tuition and/or required materials (e.g., books) to an accredited college, university, technology institution, or other training.

**Duration**   1 year; may be renewed.

**Additional information**   This program was established in 1998.

**Number awarded**   1 or more each year.

**Deadline**   March of each year.

**[219]**

## GIRL SCOUT ACHIEVEMENT AWARD

American Legion Auxiliary
777 North Meridian Street, Third Floor
Indianapolis, IN 46204-1189
(317) 955-3845                          Fax: (317) 955-3884
E-mail: alahq@legion-aux.org
Web: www.legion-aux.org

**Summary**   To provide financial assistance for college to members of the Girl Scouts.

**Eligibility**   Candidates must belong to the Girl Scouts; have received the Gold Award; be an active member of a religious institution (and have received the appropriate religious emblem); have demonstrated practical citizenship in her religious institution, school, Scouting, and community; and submit at least 4 letters of recommendation, with 1 letter required from each of the following group leaders: religious institution, school, community, and Scouting. Candidates must be nominated at the local level; those selected at the state level compete at the national level.

**Financial data** The stipend is $1,000.

**Duration** 1 year; the award must be utilized within 1 year of high school graduation.

**Additional information** The scholarship must be used to attend an accredited school in the United States.

**Number awarded** 1 each year.

**Deadline** Local nominations must be submitted no later than February of each year.

## [220]
## GLADYS ANDERSON EMERSON SCHOLARSHIP

Iota Sigma Pi
c/o National Director for Student Awards, Kathryn A.
   Thomasson
University of North Dakota, Department of Chemistry
P.O. Box 9024
Grand Forks, ND 58202-9024
(701) 777-3199                     Fax: (701) 777-2331
E-mail: kthomasson@chem.und.edu
Web: www.iotasigmapi.info

**Summary** To provide financial assistance to women undergraduates who have achieved excellence in the study of chemistry or biochemistry.

**Eligibility** The nominee must be a female chemistry or biochemistry student who has attained at least junior standing but has at least 1 semester of work to complete. Both the nominator and the nominee must be members of Iota Sigma Pi, although students who are not members but wish to apply for the scholarship may be made members by National Council action. Selection is based on transcripts; a list of all academic honors and professional memberships; a short essay by the nominee describing herself, her goals in chemistry, any hobbies or talents, and her financial need; and letters of recommendation.

**Financial data** The stipend is $2,000.

**Duration** 1 year.

**Additional information** This scholarship was first awarded in 1987.

**Number awarded** 1 each year.

**Deadline** February of each year.

## [221]
## GLADYS C. ANDERSON MEMORIAL SCHOLARSHIP

American Foundation for the Blind
Attn: Scholarship Committee
11 Penn Plaza, Suite 300
New York, NY 10001
(212) 502-7661                Toll-free: (800) AFB-LINE
Fax: (212) 502-7771           TDD: (212) 502-7662
E-mail: afbinfo@afb.net
Web: www.afb.org/scholarships.asp

**Summary** To provide financial assistance to legally blind undergraduate or graduate women who are studying religious or classical music.

**Eligibility** This program is open to legally blind women who are U.S. citizens and have been accepted in an accredited undergraduate or graduate program in religious or classical music. Along with their application, they must submit an essay that includes the field of study they are pursuing and why they have chosen it; their educational and personal goals; their work experience; any extracurricular activities with which they have been involved, including those in school, religious organizations, and the community; and how they intend to use scholarship monies that may be awarded. They must also submit a sample performance tape (a voice or instrumental selection).

**Financial data** The stipend is $1,000.

**Duration** 1 academic year.

**Number awarded** 1 each year.

**Deadline** April of each year.

## [222]
## GLADYS L. MERSEREAU GRANTS-IN-AID

Delta Kappa Gamma Society International-Pi State
   Organization
c/o Andrea H. Morris
105 Ashland Place, Apartment 4D
Brooklyn, NY 11201
E-mail: abunnymorris@msn.com
Web: www.deltakappagamma.org/NY/awards.html

**Summary** To provide financial assistance to women in New York whose education was interrupted and who now need help to become teachers.

**Eligibility** This program is open to women in New York who are interested in completing teacher certification requirements but whose education has been interrupted. Along with their application, they must submit a statement on their educational philosophy, documentation of their financial need, and 3 letters of recommendation (including at least 1 from a member of the sponsoring organization). Members of that organization are not eligible.

**Financial data** The amounts of the grants depend on the availability of funds.

**Duration** 1 year.

**Additional information** This program was established in 1975.

**Number awarded** Varies each year; recently, 5 of these grants were awarded.

**Deadline** January of each year.

## [223]
## GOLDMAN, SACHS SCHOLARSHIPS

Society of Women Engineers
230 East Ohio Street, Suite 400
Chicago, IL 60611-3265
(312) 596-5223          Toll-free: (877) SWE-INFO
Fax: (312) 644-8557
E-mail: scholarshipapplication@swe.org
Web: www.swe.org/scholarships

**Summary** To provide financial assistance to upper-division women who are members of the Society of Women Engineers and majoring in designated engineering specialties.

**Eligibility** This program is open to women who are entering their junior or senior year at an ABET-accredited 4-year college or university. Applicants must be studying computer science or electrical or computer engineering with a GPA of 3.2 or higher. Along with their application, they must submit a 1-page essay on why they want to be an engineer or computer scientist, how they believe they will make a difference as an engineer or computer scientist, and what influenced them to study engineering or computer science. Selection is based on merit.

**Financial data** The stipend is $2,000.

**Duration** 1 year.

**Additional information** This program is sponsored by Goldman, Sachs & Company.

**Number awarded** 4 each year.

**Deadline** January of each year.

## [224]
## GOLF ASSOCIATION OF MICHIGAN SCHOLARSHIPS

Golf Association of Michigan
Attn: Junior Golf
24116 Research Drive
Farmington Hills, MI 48335
(248) 478-9242          Fax: (248) 478-5536
Web: www.gam.org/memberbenefits.asp?ID=16

**Summary** To provide financial assistance to high school seniors in Michigan who have participated in golf activities.

**Eligibility** This program is open to seniors graduating from high schools in Michigan with a GPA of 3.0 or higher. Applicants must have played in a junior tournament sponsored by the Golf Association of Michigan. They must be planning to attend college in the fall following high school graduation. Along with their application, they must submit an essay on why they deserve the award. Females and males are considered separately.

**Financial data** The stipend is $2,000.

**Duration** 1 year.

**Number awarded** 2 each year: 1 female and 1 male.

**Deadline** July of each year.

## [225]
## GRACE HARRINGTON WILSON SCHOLARSHIP

American Mensa Education and Research Foundation
1229 Corporate Drive West
Arlington, TX 76006-6103
(817) 607-0060          Toll-free: (800) 66-MENSA
Fax: (817) 649-5232
E-mail: info@mensafoundation.org
Web: www.mensafoundation.org

**Summary** To provide financial assistance for undergraduate or graduate study to women majoring in journalism.

**Eligibility** This program is open to women enrolled or planning to enroll in an undergraduate or graduate degree program in journalism at an accredited American institution of postsecondary education. Membership in Mensa is not required, but applicants must be U.S. citizens or permanent residents. Selection is based on a 550-word essay that describes the applicant's career, vocational, or academic goals.

**Financial data** The stipend is $600.

**Duration** 1 year; nonrenewable.

**Additional information** Applications are only available through the advertising efforts of participating Mensa local groups.

**Number awarded** 1 each year.

**Deadline** January of each year.

## [226]
## GRAND GUARDIAN COUNCIL OF PENNSYLVANIA SCHOLARSHIPS

Pennsylvania Masonic Youth Foundation
Attn: Educational Endowment Fund
1244 Bainbridge Road
Elizabethtown, PA 17022-9423
(717) 367-1536     Toll-free: (800) 266-8424 (within PA)
Fax: (717) 367-0616     E-mail: pyf@pagrandlodge.org
Web: www.pagrandlodge.org/pyf/scholar/index.html

**Summary** To provide financial assistance for college to members of Job's Daughters in Pennsylvania.

**Eligibility** This program is open to Pennsylvania Job's Daughters and unmarried majority members who are younger than 30 years of age and are in good standing in their Bethels. Applicants must be high school seniors, high school graduates, or current college students enrolled or planning to enroll in a higher education program as a full-time student. Selection is based on Bethel and other Job's Daughters activities.

**Financial data** The stipend depends on the availability of funds.

**Duration** 1 year.

**Additional information** Information is also available from Deborah Phillips, Scholarship Committee Chair, 2267 Sand Hill Road, Hershey, PA 17033, E-mail: info@paiojd.org.

**Number awarded** 1 or more each year.

**Deadline** April of each year.

## [227]
## GRANDMA MOSES SCHOLARSHIP

Western Art Association
Attn: Foundation
13730 Loumont Street
Whittier, CA 90601

**Summary** To provide financial assistance for art school to female high school seniors whose art demonstrates a "congruence with the art of Grandma Moses."

**Eligibility** This program is open to female graduating high school seniors. Applicants must be planning to study art in a college, university, or specialized school of art. Preference is given to applicants from the western United States. Candidates must submit samples of their artwork; selection is based on the extent to which their work "manifests a congruence with the work of the famed folk artist, Grandma Moses." Financial need is not considered.

**Financial data** The stipend is $3,000 per year.

**Duration** 1 year; may be renewed up to 3 additional years.

**Additional information** Requests for applications should be accompanied by a self-addressed stamped envelope, the student's e-mail address, and the source where they found the scholarship information.

**Number awarded** 1 each year.

**Deadline** March of each year.

## [228]
## GREATER NEW YORK NETWORK OF EXECUTIVE WOMEN IN HOSPITALITY SCHOLARSHIP AWARDS

Network of Executive Women in Hospitality-Greater
  New York Chapter
Attn: Sue Gould, Director of Scholarship and Education
386 Park Avenue, South, Suite 2015
New York, NY 10016
(212) 695-5700          Toll-free: (800) 593-NEWH
Fax: (800) 693-NEWH     E-mail: sgould@lgd-inc.com
Web: www.newh.org/newh/scholarshippacket.php

**Summary** To provide financial assistance to women in designated northeastern states interested in preparing for a career in the hospitality industry.

**Eligibility** This program is open to women who have completed half the requirements for a degree or certification program at a vocational school or college in Connecticut, Maine, Massachusetts, New Hampshire, New Jersey, New York, Rhode Island, or Vermont. Applicants must have a GPA of 3.0 or higher and a career objective in the hospitality or food service industries (e.g., hotel and restaurant management, culinary, food service, architecture, design). Selection is based on financial need and academic accomplishments.

**Financial data** The stipend depends on the availability of funds and the need of the recipient.

**Duration** 1 year.

**Number awarded** Varies each year.

**Deadline** March of each year.

## [229]
## GROTTO/JOB'S DAUGHTERS SCHOLARSHIP

International Order of Job's Daughters
Supreme Guardian Council Headquarters
Attn: Executive Manager
233 West Sixth Street
Papillion, NE 68046-2177
(402) 592-7987          Fax: (402) 592-2177
E-mail: sgc@iojd.org
Web: www.iojd.org

**Summary** To provide financial assistance to members of Job's Daughters who are working on an undergraduate or graduate degree in a dental field.

**Eligibility** This program is open to high school seniors and graduates; students in early graduation programs; junior college, technical, and vocational students; and college and graduate students. Applicants must be Job's Daughters in good standing in their Bethels; unmarried majority members under 30 years of age are also eligible. They must be working on a degree in a dental field, preferably with some training in the field of disabilities. Selection is based on scholastic standing, Job's Daughters activities, the applicant's self-help plan, recommendation by the Executive Bethel Guardian Council, faculty recommendations, achievements outside Job's Daughters, and financial need.

**Financial data** The stipend is $1,500.

**Duration** 1 year.

**Additional information** Information is also available from Barbara Hill, Education Scholarships Committee Chair, 337 Illinois Street, Pekin, IL 61554, (309) 346-5564.

**Number awarded** 1 or more each year.

**Deadline** April of each year.

## [230]
## GUIDANT FOUNDATION SCHOLARSHIPS

Society of Women Engineers
230 East Ohio Street, Suite 400
Chicago, IL 60611-3265
(312) 596-5223          Toll-free: (877) SWE-INFO
Fax: (312) 644-8557
E-mail: scholarshipapplication@swe.org
Web: www.swe.org/scholarships

**Summary** To provide financial assistance to upper-division women majoring in computer science or designated engineering specialties.

**Eligibility** This program is open to women who are entering their senior year at a designated ABET-accredited college or university. Applicants must be majoring in computer science or chemical, computer, electrical, industrial, manufacturing, materials, or mechanical engineering and have a GPA of 3.5 or higher. Along with their application, they must submit a 1-page essay on why they want to be an engineer or computer scientist, how they believe they will make a difference as an engineer or computer scientist, and what influenced them to study engineering or computer science. Selection is based on merit.

**Financial data** The stipend is $5,000.

**Duration** 1 year.

**Additional information** This program, established in 2004, is supported by Guidant Foundation. For a list of the designated colleges and universities, contact the sponsor.

**Number awarded** 2 each year.

**Deadline** January of each year.

## [231]
## HAL CONNOLLY SCHOLAR-ATHLETE AWARD

California Governor's Committee on Employment of
   People with Disabilities
Employment Development Department
Attn: Scholar-Athlete Awards Program
800 Capitol Mall, MIC 41
Sacramento, CA 95814
(916) 654-8055         Toll-free: (800) 695-0350
Fax: (916) 654-9821       TTY: (916) 654-9820
E-mail: rnagle@edd.ca.gov
Web: www.disabilityemployment.org/yp_hal_con.htm

**Summary** To provide financial assistance to disabled high school seniors in California who have participated in athletics.

**Eligibility** Applicants must be high school seniors with disabilities, no more than 19 years of age on January 1 of the year of application, who have competed in California high school athletics at a varsity or equivalent level and possess academic and athletic records that demonstrate leadership and accomplishment. They must have completed high school with a GPA of 2.8 or better and plan to attend an accredited college or university in California, but they do not have to intend to participate formally in collegiate athletic activities. Selection is based on cumulative GPA (15%), cumulative GPA as it relates to the nature of the student's disability (15%), athletic accomplishments as they relate to the student's disability (30%), an essay on "How Sports Participation Has Affected My Life at School and in the Community As a Person with a Disability" (25%), and overall personal achievement (15%). The top finalists may be interviewed before selections are made. Male and female students compete separately.

**Financial data** The stipend is $1,000, contingent upon the winners' acceptance at an accredited California college or university. Funds may be used for tuition, books, supplies, and other educational expenses. Exceptions are granted to students who choose to attend schools out of state primarily to accommodate their disability.

**Duration** Awards are granted annually.

**Number awarded** Up to 6 each year: 3 are set aside for females and 3 for males.

**Deadline** January of each year.

## [232]
## HANNAH KEENAN SCHOLARSHIPS

Alpha Chi Omega Foundation
Attn: Foundation Programs Coordinator
5939 Castle Creek Parkway North Drive
Indianapolis, IN 46250-4343
(317) 579-5050, ext. 262       Fax: (317) 579-5051
E-mail: foundation@alphachiomega.org
Web: www.alphachiomega.org

**Summary** To provide financial assistance for college to undergraduate members of Alpha Chi Omega.

**Eligibility** This program is open to women attending college full time who are members of Alpha Chi Omega. Applicants must have junior or senior standing. Selection is based on academic achievement, chapter involvement, campus and community service, and financial need.

**Financial data** The stipend is $1,240.

**Duration** 1 year.

**Number awarded** 5 each year.

**Deadline** March of each year.

## [233]
## HANSCOM OFFICERS' SPOUSES' CLUB SCHOLARSHIPS

Hanscom Officers' Spouses' Club
Attn: Scholarship Chair
P.O. Box 557
Bedford, MA 01730
(781) 275-1251   E-mail: scholarship@hanscomosc.org
Web: www.hanscomosc.org

**Summary** To provide financial assistance for college to spouses and children of military personnel and veterans in New England.

**Eligibility** This program is open to high school seniors and spouses living in New England who are dependents of active-duty, retired, or deceased military members of any branch of service. Also eligible are dependents of military recruiters working in the New York area and students living elsewhere but whose military sponsor is stationed at Hanscom Air Force Base. Applicants must demonstrate responsibility, leadership, scholastics, citizenship, and diversity of interest. They must have a valid military identification card and be working on or planning to work on a bachelor's or associate degree. Along with their application, they must submit a 2-page essay on their educational goals, how their educational experience will help prepare them to pursue future goals, and how they intend to apply their education to better their community. The Chief of Staff Award is presented to the highest-ranked high school applicant. The Carmen Schipper Memorial Award is presented to the highest-ranked spouse applicant. The Scott Corey Scholarship is awarded to another spouse applicant.

**Financial data** Stipends range from $1,200 to $4,000.

**Duration** 1 year; nonrenewable.

**Additional information** The Paul Revere Chapter of the Air Force Association sponsors the Chief of Staff Award. Other sponsors include the Armed Forces Communications and Electronics Association, Boeing Company, First Command Educational Foundation, Association of Old Crows, Air Force Sergeants Association, Company Grade Officer's

Council, and Patriot Senior Noncommissioned Officer's Council.

**Number awarded** Varies each year; recently, 17 of these scholarships were awarded.

**Deadline** March of each year.

## [234]
## HAZEL HEFFNER BECCHINA AWARD

National Federation of Music Clubs
1336 North Delaware Street
Indianapolis, IN 46202-2481
(317) 638-4003          Fax: (317) 638-0503
E-mail: info@nfmc-music.org
Web: www.nfmc-music.org

**Summary** To recognize and reward outstanding young singers who are members of the National Federation of Music Clubs (NFMC).

**Eligibility** This award is presented to singers between 18 and 26 years of age. Men and women are judged separately. Membership in the federation and U.S. citizenship are required. Candidates for the NFMC Biennial Student Audition Awards competition are automatically considered for this award; no separate application is necessary.

**Financial data** The prize is $1,500. Funds must be used for continued study.

**Duration** The competition is held biennially, in odd-numbered years.

**Additional information** Applications and further information on these awards are available from Mrs. Robert Carroll, 17583 North 1090 East Road, Pontiac, IL 61764-9801, E-mail: scarroll@frontiernet.net; information on all federation scholarships and awards is available from Chair, Competitions and Awards Board, Dr. George R. Keck, 421 Cherry Street, Arkadelphia, AR 71923-5116, E-mail: keckg@obu.edu. The entry fee is $30.

**Number awarded** 2 every other year: 1 to a woman and 1 to a man.

**Deadline** January of odd-numbered years.

## [235]
## HEALTH RESEARCH AND EDUCATIONAL TRUST SCHOLARSHIPS

New Jersey Hospital Association
Attn: Health Research and Educational Trust
760 Alexander Road
P.O. Box 1
Princeton, NJ 08543-0001
(609) 275-4224          Fax: (609) 452-8097
Web: www.njha.com/hret/scholarship.aspx

**Summary** To provide financial assistance to New Jersey residents (particularly women and minorities) working on an undergraduate or graduate degree in a health-related field.

**Eligibility** This program is open to residents of New Jersey enrolled in an upper-division or graduate program in hospital or health care administration, public administration, nursing, or other allied health profession. Applicants must have a GPA of 3.0 or higher and be able to demonstrate financial need. Along with their application, they must submit a 2-page essay (on which 50% of the selection is based)

describing their academic plans for the future. Women and minorities are especially encouraged to apply.

**Financial data** The stipend is $2,000.

**Duration** 1 year.

**Additional information** This program began in 1983.

**Number awarded** Varies each year; recently, 2 of these scholarships were awarded.

**Deadline** July of each year.

## [236]
## HELEN AND ARNOLD BARBEN SCHOLARSHIP

Daughters of the American Revolution-New York State
   Organization
c/o Layla Voll
311 West 21st Street
New York, NY 10011
E-mail: Layla_Voll@hotmail.com
Web: www.nydar.org/education/barben.html

**Summary** To provide financial assistance for college to female high school seniors in New York.

**Eligibility** This program is open to women graduating from high schools in New York who plan to attend an accredited 4-year college or university in the state. Applicants must have been born in the United States. Selection is based on merit, including achievement in high school and the community and personal and academic interests.

**Financial data** The stipend is $500 per year.

**Duration** 4 years, provided the recipient maintains a GPA of 3.0 or higher.

**Number awarded** 1 each year.

**Deadline** January of each year.

## [237]
## HELEN COPELAND SCHOLARSHIP FOR FEMALES

United States Association of Blind Athletes
Attn: Scholarship Committee
33 North Institute Street
Colorado Springs, CO 80903
(719) 630-0422          Fax: (719) 630-0616
E-mail: usaba@usa.net
Web: www.usaba.org

**Summary** To provide financial assistance for undergraduate or graduate study to female members of the United States Association for Blind Athletes (USABA).

**Eligibility** This program is open to legally blind females who have participated in USABA activities for the past year and are current members. Applicants must have been admitted to an academic, vocational, technical, professional, or certification program at the postsecondary level. Selection is based on demonstrated academic record, involvement in extracurricular and civic activities, academic goals and objectives, and USABA involvement at various levels.

**Financial data** The stipend is $500.

**Number awarded** 1 each year.

**Deadline** August of each year.

## [238]
## HELPING HANDS OF WSC ENDOWMENT SCHOLARSHIP

Epsilon Sigma Alpha
Attn: ESA Foundation Assistant Scholarship Director
P.O. Box 270517
Fort Collins, CO 80527
(970) 223-2824    Fax: (970) 223-4456
Web: www.esaintl.com/esaf

**Summary** To provide financial assistance for college to women members of Epsilon Sigma Alpha (ESA) from Australia or selected U.S. western states.

**Eligibility** This program is open to women ESA members from Alaska, Arizona, Australia, California, Oregon, and Washington. Applicants must be either 1) graduating high school seniors in the top 25% of their class or with minimum scores of 20 on the ACT or an equivalent score on the SAT, or 2) students already in college with a GPA of 3.0 or higher. Students enrolled for training in a technical school or returning to school after an absence are also eligible. They may be planning to major in any field at a college or university in any state. Selection is based on character (20%), leadership (20%), service (20%), financial need (20%), and scholastic ability (20%).

**Financial data** The stipend is $500.

**Duration** 1 year; nonrenewable.

**Additional information** Epsilon Sigma Alpha (ESA) is a women's service organization. Information is also available from Lynn Hughes, Scholarship Director, 324 N.E. Mead, Grants Pass, OR 97526, (541) 476-4617. Completed applications must be submitted to the ESA State Counselor who verifies the information before forwarding them to the scholarship director. A $5 processing fee is required.

**Number awarded** 1 each year.

**Deadline** January of each year.

## [239]
## HERMINE DALKOWITZ TOBOLOWSKY SCHOLARSHIP

Texas Federation of Business and Professional
   Women's Clubs, Inc.
Attn: TFBPW Foundation
803 Forest Ridge Drive, Suite 207
Bedford, TX 76022
(817) 283-0862    Fax: (817) 283-0872
E-mail: bpwtx@swbell.net
Web: www.bpwtx.org/foundation.asp

**Summary** To provide financial assistance to women in Texas who are preparing to enter selected professions.

**Eligibility** This program is open to women in Texas who are interested in attending school to prepare for a career in law, public service, government, political science, or women's history. Applicants must have completed at least 2 semesters of study at an accredited college or university in Texas, have a GPA of 3.0 or higher, and be U.S. citizens. Selection is based on academic achievement and financial need.

**Financial data** A stipend is awarded (amount not specified).

**Duration** 1 year.

**Additional information** This program was established in 1995.

**Number awarded** 1 or more each year.

**Deadline** April of each year.

## [240]
## HERMIONE GRANT CALHOUN SCHOLARSHIPS

National Federation of the Blind
c/o Peggy Elliott, Scholarship Committee Chair
805 Fifth Avenue
Grinnell, IA 50112
(641) 236-3366
Web: www.nfb.org/sch_intro.htm

**Summary** To provide financial assistance to female blind students interested in working on an undergraduate or graduate degree.

**Eligibility** This program is open to legally blind women who are working on or planning to work full time on an undergraduate or graduate degree. Selection is based on academic excellence, service to the community, and financial need.

**Financial data** The stipend is $3,000.

**Duration** 1 year; recipients may resubmit applications up to 2 additional years.

**Additional information** Scholarships are awarded at the federation convention in July. Recipients attend the convention at federation expense; that funding is in addition to the scholarship grant.

**Number awarded** 1 each year.

**Deadline** March of each year.

## [241]
## HONEYWELL INTERNATIONAL SCHOLARSHIPS

Society of Women Engineers
230 East Ohio Street, Suite 400
Chicago, IL 60611-3265
(312) 596-5223    Toll-free: (877) SWE-INFO
Fax: (312) 644-8557
E-mail: scholarshipapplication@swe.org
Web: www.swe.org/scholarships

**Summary** To provide financial assistance to women interested in studying specified fields of engineering in college.

**Eligibility** This program is open to women who are graduating high school seniors or rising college sophomores or juniors. Applicants must be enrolled or planning to enroll full time at an ABET-accredited 4-year college or university and majoring in computer science or aerospace, architectural, chemical, computer, electrical, industrial, manufacturing, materials, or mechanical engineering. Along with their application, they must submit a 1-page essay on why they want to be an engineer or computer scientist, how they believe they will make a difference as an engineer or computer scientist, and what influenced them to study engineering or computer science. U.S. citizenship is required. Financial need is considered in the selection process.

**Financial data** The stipend is $5,000.

**Duration** 1 year.

**Additional information** This program is sponsored by Honeywell International Inc.

**Number awarded** 5 each year: 3 to high school seniors and 2 to college sophomores and juniors.

**Deadline** January of each year for current college students; May of each year for high school seniors.

## [242]
## HONOLULU ALUMNAE PANHELLENIC ASSOCIATION COLLEGIATE SCHOLARSHIPS

Honolulu Alumnae Panhellenic Association
Attn: Scholarship and Recruitment Chair
P.O. Box 11962
Honolulu, HI 96828-0962
(808) 284-1290          E-mail: sdilbeck@netscape.net
Web: www.greekhawaii.com

**Summary** To provide financial assistance to female college student from Hawaii who are members of a National Panhellenic Conference (NPC) sorority.

**Eligibility** This program is open to women who are initiated and active members of an NPC-affiliated sorority at a college or university where they are working on an undergraduate degree. Their permanent home address or college address must be in Hawaii. Along with their application, they must submit 1) a brief essay stating why they would like the scholarship, their plans, and the part they feel sorority membership has played in their lives; 2) a list of all school, sorority, and community activities and offices; and 3) letters of recommendation from a professor, sorority officer, and another person in the community. Financial need is not considered in the selection process.

**Financial data** A stipend is awarded (amount not specified).

**Duration** 1 year.

**Number awarded** 1 or more each year.

**Deadline** February of each year.

## [243]
## HONOLULU ALUMNAE PANHELLENIC ASSOCIATION HIGH SCHOOL SCHOLARSHIPS

Honolulu Alumnae Panhellenic Association
Attn: Scholarship and Recruitment Chair
P.O. Box 11962
Honolulu, HI 96828-0962
(808) 284-1290          E-mail: sdilbeck@netscape.net
Web: www.greekhawaii.com

**Summary** To provide financial assistance to female high school seniors in Hawaii who are interested in going to a college with National Panhellenic Conference (NPC) sororities on campus.

**Eligibility** This program is open to females graduating from high schools in Hawaii. Applicants must be interested in attending 1 of the more than 500 colleges and universities with NPC sororities. Along with their application, they must submit 1) a brief essay stating why they would like the scholarship, what they hope to get out of their college experience, and the part they feel sorority membership could play in their college years; 2) SAT and/or ACT scores; 3) a list of all class and school offices, other offices and responsibilities, school and athletic activities, extracurricular and community activities, honors, and awards; and 4) letters of recommendation from their high school senior counselor

and another person in the community. Financial need is also considered in the selection process, but the program gives priority to well-rounded students who have balanced scholastics with school and/or community activities. Interviews are included.

**Financial data** A stipend is awarded (amount not specified).

**Duration** 1 year.

**Number awarded** 1 or more each year.

**Deadline** February of each year.

## [244]
## HOPPER MEMORIAL SCHOLARSHIPS

Society of Women Engineers
230 East Ohio Street, Suite 400
Chicago, IL 60611-3265
(312) 596-5223          Toll-free: (877) SWE-INFO
Fax: (312) 644-8557
E-mail: scholarshipapplication@swe.org
Web: www.swe.org/scholarships

**Summary** To provide financial assistance to women who will be entering college as freshmen and are interested in studying engineering or computer science.

**Eligibility** This program is open to women who are entering college as freshmen with a GPA of 3.5 or higher. Applicants must be U.S. citizens planning to enroll full time at an ABET-accredited 4-year college or university and major in computer science or engineering. Along with their application, they must submit a 1-page essay on why they want to be an engineer or computer scientist, how they believe they will make a difference as an engineer or computer scientist, and what influenced them to study engineering or computer science. Selection is based on merit. Preference is given to students in computer-related engineering.

**Financial data** The stipend is $1,500.

**Duration** 1 year.

**Additional information** This program, established in 1992, is named for the "mother of computerized data automation in the naval service."

**Number awarded** 5 each year.

**Deadline** May of each year.

## [245]
## HOUSTON NETWORK OF EXECUTIVE WOMEN IN HOSPITALITY SCHOLARSHIP AWARDS

Network of Executive Women in Hospitality-Houston
   Chapter
Attn: Tiffany Gehlbach, Director of Scholarship and
   Education
P.O. Box 22090
Houston, TX 77227-2090
Toll-free: (800) 593-NEWH          Fax: (800) 693-NEWH
E-mail: t.gehlbach@tri-kes.com
Web: www.newh.org/newh/scholarshippacket.php

**Summary** To provide financial assistance to women in Arkansas, Louisiana, and southern Texas interested in preparing for a career in the hospitality industry.

**Eligibility** This program is open to women who have completed half the requirements for a degree or certification program at a vocational school or college in Arkansas, Louisiana, or southern Texas. Applicants must have a GPA of 3.0 or higher and a career objective in the hospitality or food service industries (e.g., hotel and restaurant management, culinary, food service, architecture, design). Selection is based on financial need and academic accomplishments.

**Financial data** The stipend depends on the availability of funds and the need of the recipient.

**Duration** 1 year.

**Number awarded** Varies each year; recently, 5 of these scholarships were awarded.

## [246]
## H.S. AND ANGELINE LEWIS SCHOLARSHIPS

American Legion Auxiliary
Department of Wisconsin
Attn: Department Secretary/Treasurer
2930 American Legion Drive
P.O. Box 140
Portage, WI 53901-0140
(608) 745-0124          Toll-free: (866) 664-3863
Fax: (608) 745-1947
E-mail: alawi@amlegionauxwi.org
Web: www.amlegionauxwi.org

**Summary** To provide financial assistance for undergraduate or graduate study to Wisconsin residents who are related to veterans or members of the American Legion Auxiliary.

**Eligibility** This program is open to the children, wives, and widows of veterans who are high school seniors or graduates with a GPA of 3.2 or higher. Granddaughters as well as great-granddaughters of veterans are eligible if they are members of the American Legion Auxiliary. Applicants must be able to demonstrate financial need, be interested in working on an undergraduate or graduate degree, and be residents of Wisconsin. They do not need to attend a college in the state. Along with their application, they must submit a 300-word essay on "Education-An Investment in the Future."

**Financial data** The stipend is $1,000.

**Duration** 1 year; nonrenewable.

**Additional information** Information is also available from the Education Chair, Renae Allen, 206 West Fremont Street, Darien, WI 53114-1540, (262) 724-5059.

**Number awarded** 6 each year: 1 to a graduate student and 5 to undergraduates.

**Deadline** March of each year.

## [247]
## HUMBLE ARTESIAN CHAPTER OUTRIGHT GRANTS

American Business Women's Association-Humble
    Artesian Chapter
c/o Stacey Jameson, Education Committee
19906 Bishops Gate Lane
Humble, TX 77338
(281) 804-0186          E-mail: sjameson1@verizon.net
Web: www.abwahumble.org/ships.htm

**Summary** To provide financial assistance to women who have completed at least the sophomore year of college.

**Eligibility** This program is open to all women who are U.S. citizens. Applicants must have completed at least the sophomore year of college with a GPA of 2.5 or higher.

**Financial data** The stipend is $1,200.

**Duration** 1 year.

**Number awarded** 1 each year.

**Deadline** April of each year.

## [248]
## HUNTSVILLE CHAPTER ASWA SCHOLARSHIPS

American Society of Women Accountants-Huntsville
    Chapter
c/o Joyce Skinner, Scholarship Committee Chair
P.O. Box 1561
Huntsville, AL 35807
(256) 603-1752          Fax: (601) 252-7776
E-mail: melissa.butler@us.pwc.com
Web: www.birminghamaswa.org

**Summary** To provide financial assistance to women working on an undergraduate or graduate degree in accounting at a college or university in Alabama.

**Eligibility** This program is open to women working full or part time on a bachelor's or master's degree in accounting at a college, university, or professional school of accounting in Alabama. Applicants must have completed at least 60 semester hours. They are not required to be members of the American Society of Women Accountants (ASWA). Along with their application, they must submit a 75-word essay on how they plan to incorporate into their strategic career goals the sponsor's philosophy of achieving balance among life priorities, including career, personal development, family, friendships, and community and societal needs. Selection is based on that essay, academic record, extracurricular activities and honors, employment history, a statement of career goals and objectives, and financial need.

**Financial data** The stipend is $500.

**Duration** 1 year.

**Number awarded** 1 or more each year.

**Deadline** March of each year.

## [249]
## HVTO WOMAN OF DISTINCTION AWARD

Electronic Document Systems Foundation
Attn: EDSF Scholarship Awards
608 Silver Spur Road, Suite 280
Rolling Hills Estates, CA 90274-3616
(310) 265-5510          Fax: (310) 265-5588
E-mail: jmowlds@edsf.org
Web: www.edsf.org/scholarships.cfm

**Summary** To provide financial assistance to women working on an undergraduate or graduate degree in a field related to the high volume transaction output (HVTO) industry.

**Eligibility** This program is open to female undergraduate and graduate students who are working on a degree in a field related to the HVTO industry, including information technology, graphic arts, or business. Applicants must be enrolled full time at a technical school, trade school, community college, university, college, or graduate school in the United States with a GPA of 3.0 or higher. Along with their application, they must submit a statement of their career goals in the field of document communications, an essay on a topic related to their view of the future of the document management and production industry, a list of current professional and college extracurricular activities and achievements, college transcripts, samples of their creative work, and 2 letters of recommendation. Financial need is not considered.

**Financial data** The stipend is $5,000.

**Duration** 1 year.

**Additional information** This program is sponsored by COPI/OutputLinks.

**Number awarded** 1 each year.

**Deadline** May of each year.

## [250]
## IBM CORPORATION SWE SCHOLARSHIPS

Society of Women Engineers
230 East Ohio Street, Suite 400
Chicago, IL 60611-3265
(312) 596-5223          Toll-free: (877) SWE-INFO
Fax: (312) 644-8557
E-mail: scholarshipapplication@swe.org
Web: www.swe.org/scholarships

**Summary** To provide financial assistance to lower-division women majoring in designated engineering specialties.

**Eligibility** This program is open to women who are entering their sophomore or junior year at a 4-year ABET-accredited college or university. Applicants must be majoring in computer science or electrical or computer engineering and have a GPA of 3.4 or higher. They must be U.S. citizens or authorized to work in the United States. Along with their application, they must submit a 1-page essay on why they want to be an engineer or computer scientist, how they believe they will make a difference as an engineer or computer scientist, and what influenced them to study engineering or computer science. Selection is based on merit.

**Financial data** The stipend is $1,000.

**Duration** 1 year.

**Additional information** This program is sponsored by the IBM Corporation.

**Number awarded** 4 each year.

**Deadline** January of each year.

## [251]
## IDA M. POPE MEMORIAL TRUST SCHOLARSHIPS

Hawai'i Community Foundation
Attn: Scholarship Department
1164 Bishop Street, Suite 800
Honolulu, HI 96813
(808) 566-5570          Toll-free: (888) 731-3863
Fax: (808) 521-6286
E-mail: scholarships@hcf-hawaii.org
Web: www.hawaiicommunityfoundation.org

**Summary** To provide financial assistance to Native Hawaiian women who are interested in working on an undergraduate or graduate degree.

**Eligibility** This program is open to female residents of Hawaii who are Native Hawaiian, defined as a descendant of the aboriginal inhabitants of the Hawaiian islands prior to 1778. Applicants must be enrolled in an accredited associate, bachelor's, or graduate degree program. They must be able to demonstrate academic achievement (GPA of 3.0 or higher), good moral character, and financial need. Along with their application, they must submit a short statement indicating their reasons for attending college, their planned course of study, and their career goals.

**Financial data** The amounts of the awards depend on the availability of funds and the need of the recipient; recently, stipends averaged $1,000.

**Duration** 1 year; may be renewed.

**Number awarded** Varies each year; recently, 60 of these scholarships were awarded.

**Deadline** February of each year.

## [252]
## IDA V. HOLLAND MISSIONARY SCHOLARSHIP

San Antonio Area Foundation
110 Broadway, Suite 230
San Antonio, TX 78205
(210) 225-2243          Fax: (210) 225-1980
E-mail: info@saafdn.org
Web: www.saafdn.org

**Summary** To provide financial assistance to women and others in Texas who are interested in preparing for a religious career.

**Eligibility** Applicants for this scholarship must be interested in attending Moody Bible Institute in Chicago or another seminary of equal standing to prepare for missionary work, ministry, or Christian education. They must be between 18 and 24 years of age. Preference is given to women and to residents of Bexar County, Texas.

**Financial data** The stipend is $1,500 per year.

**Duration** 1 year; may be renewed.

**Additional information** This program was established in 1973.

**Number awarded** 1 each year.

**Deadline** October of each year.

## [253]
## IDAHO SPACE GRANT CONSORTIUM SCHOLARSHIP PROGRAM

Idaho Space Grant Consortium
c/o University of Idaho
College of Engineering
P.O. Box 441011
Moscow, ID 83844-1011
(208) 885-6438          Fax: (208) 885-1399
E-mail: isgc@uidaho.edu
Web: isgc.uidaho.edu

**Summary** To provide financial assistance for study in space-related fields to undergraduate students (especially women, minorities, and persons with disabilities) at institutions belonging to the Idaho Space Grant Consortium (ISGC).

**Eligibility** This program is open to full-time undergraduate students at ISGC member institutions. Applicants must be majoring in engineering, mathematics, science, or science/math education and have a cumulative GPA of 3.0 or higher. They should be planning to work on a 4-year degree in a space-related field. Along with their application, they must submit a 500-word essay on their future career and educational goals and why they believe the U.S. National Aeronautics and Space Administration (NASA) should support their education. U.S. citizenship is required. As a component of the NASA Space Grant program, the ISGC encourages participation by women, underrepresented minorities, and persons with disabilities.

**Financial data** The stipend is up to $1,000 per year. Funds are to be used to pay for registration at colleges in the consortium.

**Duration** 1 year; may be renewed.

**Additional information** Members of the consortium include Albertson College of Idaho, Boise State University, College of Southern Idaho, Idaho State University, Lewis Clark State College, North Idaho College, Northwest Nazarene College, Brigham Young University of Idaho, and the University of Idaho. This program is funded by NASA.

**Number awarded** Varies each year; recently, 24 of these scholarships were awarded.

**Deadline** February of each year.

## [254]
## ILLINOIS MIA/POW SCHOLARSHIP

Illinois Department of Veterans' Affairs
833 South Spring Street
P.O. Box 19432
Springfield, IL 62794-9432
(217) 782-6641     Toll-free: (800) 437-9824 (within IL)
Fax: (217) 524-0344          TDD: (217) 524-4645
E-mail: webmail@dva.state.il.us
Web: www.state.il.us/agency/dva

**Summary** To provide financial assistance for 1) the undergraduate education of Illinois dependents of disabled or deceased veterans or those listed as prisoners of war or missing in action, and 2) the rehabilitation or education of disabled dependents of those veterans.

**Eligibility** This program is open to the spouses, natural children, legally adopted children, or stepchildren of a veteran or service member who 1) has been declared by the U.S. Department of Defense or the U.S. Department of Veterans Affairs to be permanently disabled from service-connected causes with 100% disability, deceased as the result of a service-connected disability, a prisoner of war, or missing in action, and 2) at the time of entering service was an Illinois resident or was an Illinois resident within 6 months of entering such service. Special support is available for dependents who are disabled.

**Financial data** An eligible dependent is entitled to full payment of tuition and certain fees at any Illinois state-supported college, university, or community college. In lieu of that benefit, an eligible dependent who has a physical, mental, or developmental disability is entitled to receive a grant to be used to cover the cost of treating the disability at 1 or more appropriate therapeutic, rehabilitative, or educational facilities. For disabled dependents, the total benefit cannot exceed the cost equivalent of 4 calendar years of full-time enrollment, including summer terms, at the University of Illinois.

**Duration** This scholarship may be used for a period equivalent to 4 calendar years, including summer terms. Dependents have 12 years from the initial term of study to complete the equivalent of 4 calendar years. Disabled dependents who elect to use the grant for rehabilitative purposes may do so as long as the total benefit does not exceed the cost equivalent of 4 calendar years of full-time enrollment at the University of Illinois.

**Additional information** An eligible child must begin using the scholarship prior to his or her 26th birthday. An eligible spouse must begin using the scholarship prior to 10 years from the effective date of eligibility (e.g., prior to August 12, 1989 or 10 years from date of disability or death).

**Number awarded** Varies each year.

## [255]
## INDIANA BPW WOMEN IN TRANSITION SCHOLARSHIP

Indiana Business and Professional Women's
    Foundation, Inc.
P.O. Box 33
Knightstown, IN 46148-0033
(765) 345-9812          Fax: (765) 345-9812
E-mail: bpwin@msn.com
Web: www.indianabpwfoundation.org

**Summary** To provide financial assistance for college to mature women in Indiana.

**Eligibility** This program is open to women who are 30 years of age or older and have been an Indiana resident for at least 1 year. Applicants must be reentering the workforce, be changing careers, or be a displaced worker. They must have applied to a postsecondary institution for at least part-time attendance. Along with their application, they must submit 1) a statement (up to 200 words) on their career goals and how their education relates to those goals, and 2) documentation of financial need.

**Financial data** A stipend is awarded (amount not specified). Funds are paid directly to the recipient's school.

**Duration** 1 year; recipients may reapply.

**Number awarded** 2 each year.

**Deadline** February of each year.

## [256]
## INDIANA BPW WORKING WOMAN SCHOLARSHIP

Indiana Business and Professional Women's
    Foundation, Inc.
P.O. Box 33
Knightstown, IN 46148-0033
(765) 345-9812          Fax: (765) 345-9812
E-mail: bpwin@msn.com
Web: www.indianabpwfoundation.org

**Summary** To provide financial assistance for college to women in Indiana who are also working at least part time.

**Eligibility** This program is open to women who are 25 years of age or older and have been an Indiana resident for at least 1 year. Applicants must be employed at least 20 hours per week and must have applied to or be attending a postsecondary institution on at least a part-time basis. Along with their application, they must submit 1) a statement (up to 200 words) on their career goals and how their education relates to those goals, and 2) documentation of financial need.

**Financial data** A stipend is awarded (amount not specified). Funds are paid directly to the recipient's school.

**Duration** 1 year; recipients may reapply.

**Number awarded** 2 each year.

**Deadline** February of each year.

## [257]
## INDIANA EXTENSION HOMEMAKERS ASSOCIATION CAREER ADVANCEMENT SCHOLARSHIPS

Indiana Extension Homemakers Association
c/o Rosalind Richey, Past President
1813 North 650 West
New Castle, IN 47362
(765) 533-6612
Web: www.ieha-families.org/resources.cfm

**Summary** To provide financial assistance for college to homemakers in Indiana.

**Eligibility** This program is open to homemakers who are 25 years of age or older and residents of Indiana. Applicants must be working or accepted to work on an undergraduate degree. Along with their application, they must submit 2 character reference letters, a transcript, documentation of financial need, and a biographical statement that includes educational background, financial need, volunteer or community service activities, and other pertinent information. The program includes scholarships reserved for members of the Indiana Extension Homemakers Association (IEHA) and for students working on a degree in the medical profession. Selection is based on financial need (40%), willingness to self-help (20%), potential success in chosen field (20%), volunteer and community experience (10%), references (5%), and neatness of application (5%).

**Financial data** The stipend is $500.

**Duration** 1 year; recipients may reapply.

**Number awarded** 8 each year: 1 Eleanor Arnold Award for an IEHA member, 1 Ann Hancock Award for a student working on a degree in the medical profession, and 6 others.

**Deadline** March of each year.

## [258]
## INDIANA LEGION AUXILIARY PAST PRESIDENTS PARLEY NURSING SCHOLARSHIP

American Legion Auxiliary
Attn: Department of Indiana
777 North Meridian Street, Room 107
Indianapolis, IN 46204
(317) 630-1390        Fax: (317) 630-1277
E-mail: liford@indy.net

**Summary** To provide financial assistance for nursing education to daughters and other female descendants of American Legion Auxiliary members in Indiana.

**Eligibility** This program is open to daughters, granddaughters, and great-granddaughters of American Legion Auxiliary members (living or deceased). Applicants must be Indiana residents and attending or planning to attend an Indiana institution of higher education. If qualified, they must also be auxiliary members. Selection is based on academic record, interest in the nursing profession, and financial need.

**Financial data** The stipend is $500, which is given to the recipient at the time she enters school.

**Duration** 2 years.

**Additional information** Requests for applications must be accompanied by a self-addressed stamped envelope.

**Number awarded** 1 or more each year.

**Deadline** March of each year.

## [259]
## INTERNATIONAL COMMUNICATIONS INDUSTRIES FOUNDATION AV SCHOLARSHIPS

InfoComm International
Attn: International Communications Industries
     Foundation
11242 Waples Mill Road, Suite 200
Fairfax, VA 22030
(703) 273-7200        Toll-free: (800) 659-7469
Fax: (703) 278-8082    E-mail: dwilbert@infocomm.org
Web: www.infocomm.org/Foundation/Scholarships

**Summary** To provide financial assistance to high school seniors and college students (particularly women and minorities) who are interested in preparing for a career in the audiovisual (AV) industry.

**Eligibility** This program is open to high school seniors and students already enrolled in college. Applicants must have a GPA of 2.75 or higher and be majoring or planning to major in audiovisual subjects, including audio, visual, electronics, telecommunications, technical aspects of the theater, data networking, software development, or information technology. Students in other programs, such as journalism, may be eligible if they can demonstrate a relationship to career goals in the AV industry. Along with their application, they must submit essays on why they are applying for this scholarship, why they are interested in the audiovisual industry, and their professional plans following graduation. Minority and women candidates are especially encouraged to apply. Selection is based on the essays, presentation of the application, GPA, work experience, and letters of recommendation.

**Financial data** The stipend is $1,200.

**Duration** 1 year.

**Additional information** InfoComm International, formerly the International Communications Industries Association, established the International Communications Industries Foundation (ICIF) to manage its charitable and educational activities.

**Number awarded** Varies each year; recently, 29 of these scholarships were awarded.

**Deadline** April of each year.

## [260]
## IOWA PORK QUEEN CONTEST

Iowa Pork Producers Association
Attn: Iowa Pork Youth Team
1636 N.W. 114th Street
P.O. Box 71009
Cliva, IA 50325
(515) 225-7675          Toll-free: (800) 372-7675
Fax: (515) 225-0563     E-mail: info@iowapork.org
Web: www.iowapork.org/ipyt/pork_queen.html

**Summary** To provide financial assistance for college to high school seniors in Iowa who are selected to assist the Iowa Pork Producers Association in its promotional and educational activities.

**Eligibility** This program is open to high school seniors in Iowa who are involved in the pork industry or whose parents are involved in the pork industry, preferably as members of the Iowa Pork Producers Association. Applicants must first be selected as County Pork Queen or County Pork Princess for their county, They participate in a competition at the annual Iowa Pork Congress where they are judged on the basis of a 10-minute personal interview (20 points), a 3- to 5-minute speech on the pork industry (20 points), a 2- to 3-minute media interview (25 points), a personal presentation (20 points), a biography (5 points), and a skill-a-thon that tests their knowledge of the pork industry (10 points). The highest-ranked applicant is selected as the Iowa Pork Queen and the second as the Iowa Pork Princess.

**Financial data** The Iowa Pork Queen receives a $2,000 scholarship and the Iowa Pork Princess receives a $1,000 scholarship.

**Duration** 1 year.

**Additional information** During their year as Iowa Pork Queen and Iowa Pork Princess, the winners serve as ambassadors for the Iowa Pork Producers Association by assisting with such activities as the Iowa State Fair, World Pork Expo, Pork Youth Conference, and consumer events throughout Iowa. This program began in 1960.

**Number awarded** 2 each year.

**Deadline** November of each year.

## [261]
## IOWA SPACE GRANT SCHOLARSHIP PROGRAM

Iowa Space Grant Consortium
Attn: Director
Iowa State University
2271 Howe Hall, Room 2365
Ames, IA 50011-2271
(515) 294-3106          Toll-free: (800) 854-1667
Fax: (515) 294-3361     E-mail: isgc@iastate.edu
Web: www.ia.spacegrant.org

**Summary** To provide financial assistance to undergraduate and graduate students (especially women, minorities, and persons with disabilities) majoring in science, technology, engineering, or mathematics (STEM) disciplines at member institutions of the Iowa Space Grant Consortium (ISGC).

**Eligibility** This program is open to U.S. citizens enrolled full time as undergraduate or graduate students at ISGC member institutions. Applicants must be majoring in a STEM discipline of interest to the National Aeronautics and Space Administration. They must be interested in working on the space research program at their institution. Students from underrepresented groups (women, minorities, and persons with disabilities) are especially encouraged to apply.

**Financial data** The stipend is $6,000.

**Duration** 1 year.

**Additional information** Member institutions of ISGC, and their base programs, include Drake University (molecular biology and space life sciences), Iowa State University (the Spacecraft Systems and Operations Laboratory), the University of Iowa (the Operator Performance Laboratory), and the University of Northern Iowa (student research program on Iowa's lakes and wetlands). Funding for this program is provided by NASA.

**Number awarded** Approximately 16 each year.

**Deadline** March of each year.

## [262]
## IRENE S. MUIR AWARD

National Federation of Music Clubs
1336 North Delaware Street
Indianapolis, IN 46202-2481
(317) 638-4003          Fax: (317) 638-0503
E-mail: info@nfmc-music.org
Web: www.nfmc-music.org

**Summary** To recognize and reward outstanding young singers who are members of the National Federation of Music Clubs (NFMC).

**Eligibility** This award is presented to singers between 18 and 26 years of age. Men and women are judged separately. Membership in the federation and U.S. citizenship are required. Candidates for the NFMC Biennial Student Audition Awards competition are automatically considered for this award; no separate application is necessary.

**Financial data** The prize is $1,000. Funds must be used for continued study.

**Duration** The competition is held biennially, in odd-numbered years.

**Additional information** Applications and further information on these awards are available from Mrs. Robert Carroll, 17583 North 1090 East Road, Pontiac, IL 61764-9801, E-mail: scarroll@frontiernet.net; information on all federation scholarships and awards is available from Chair, Competitions and Awards Board, Dr. George R. Keck, 421 Cherry Street, Arkadelphia, AR 71923-5116, E-mail: keckg@obu.edu. The entry fee is $30.

**Number awarded** 2 every other year: 1 to a woman and 1 to a man.

**Deadline** January of odd-numbered years.

## [263]
## ISABELLA M. GILLEN MEMORIAL SCHOLARSHIP

Aviation Boatswain's Mates Association
P.O. Box 1106
Lakehurst, NJ 08733
E-mail: Scholarship@abma-usn.org
Web: www.abma-usn.org/scholarship.htm

**Summary** To provide financial assistance for college to the spouses and other dependents of paid-up members of the Aviation Boatswains Mates Association (ABMA).

**Eligibility** Applicants must be dependents whose sponsor has been an active, dues-paying member of the ABMA for at least 2 years. They must prepare a statement describing their vocational or professional goals and relating how their past, present, and future activities make the accomplishment of those goals probable. Other submissions include transcripts, SAT or ACT scores, letters of recommendation, and copies of awards in scholarship, leadership, athletics, dramatics, community service, or other activities. Selection is based on financial need, character, leadership, and academic achievement.

**Financial data** The stipend is $2,500 per year.

**Duration** 1 year; may be renewed.

**Additional information** This program was established in 1976. Membership in ABMA is open to all U.S. Navy personnel (active, retired, discharged, or separated) who hold or held the rating of aviation boatswains mate. Information is also available from the Scholarship Chair Lanny Vines, 144 CR 1515, Alba, TX 75410.

**Number awarded** Varies each year.

**Deadline** May of each year.

## [264]
## IVY M. PARKER MEMORIAL SCHOLARSHIP

Society of Women Engineers
230 East Ohio Street, Suite 400
Chicago, IL 60611-3265
(312) 596-5223          Toll-free: (877) SWE-INFO
Fax: (312) 644-8557
E-mail: scholarshipapplication@swe.org
Web: www.swe.org/scholarships

**Summary** To provide financial assistance to upper-division women majoring in computer science or engineering.

**Eligibility** This program is open to women who are entering their junior or senior year at an ABET-accredited college or university. Applicants must be majoring in computer science or engineering and have a GPA of 3.0 or higher. Along with their application, they must submit a 1-page essay on why they want to be an engineer or computer scientist, how they believe they will make a difference as an engineer or computer scientist, and what influenced them to study engineering or computer science. Financial need is considered in the selection process.

**Financial data** The stipend is $2,500.

**Duration** 1 year.

**Additional information** This program was established in 1986.

**Number awarded** 1 each year.

**Deadline** January of each year.

## [265]
## JAIME HORN MEMORIAL SOFTBALL SCHOLARSHIP

Babe Ruth League, Inc.
1770 Brunswick Pike
P.O. Box 5000
Trenton, NJ 08638
(609) 695-1434          Fax: (609) 695-2505
E-mail: info@baberuthleague.org
Web: www.baberuthleague.org/scholarship.html

**Summary** To provide financial assistance for college to high school senior girls who played Babe Ruth League softball.

**Eligibility** This program is open to graduating high school senior girls who played Babe Ruth League softball previously. Applicants must be planning to attend college. Along with their application, they must submit a 100-word essay on how playing Babe Ruth softball has affected their life. Financial need is not considered in the selection process.

**Financial data** The stipend is $1,000.

**Duration** 1 year.

**Number awarded** 1 each year.

**Deadline** June of each year.

## [266]
## JAMES J. WYCHOR SCHOLARSHIPS

Minnesota Broadcasters Association
Attn: Scholarship Program
3033 Excelsior Boulevard, Suite 301
Minneapolis, MN 55416
(612) 926-8123          Toll-free: (800) 245-5838
Fax: (612) 926-9761
E-mail: meischen@minnesotabroadcasters.com
Web: www.minnesotabroadcasters.com

**Summary** To provide financial assistance to Minnesota residents interested in studying broadcasting in college.

**Eligibility** This program is open to residents of Minnesota who are accepted or enrolled at an accredited postsecondary institution offering a broadcast-related curriculum. Applicants must have a high school or college GPA of 2.5 or higher and must submit a 200-word essay on why they wish to prepare for a career in broadcasting or electronic media. Employment in the broadcasting industry is not required, but students who are employed must include a letter from their general manager describing the duties they have performed as a radio or television station employee and evaluating their potential for success in the industry. Financial need is not considered in the selection process. Some of the scholarships are awarded only to minority and women candidates.

**Financial data** The stipend is $1,500.

**Duration** 1 year; recipients who are college seniors may reapply for an additional 1-year renewal.

**Number awarded** 10 each year, distributed as follows: 3 within the 7-county metro area, 5 allocated geographically throughout the state (northeast, northwest, central, southeast, southwest), and 2 reserved specifically for women and minority applicants.

**Deadline** May of each year.

## [267]
## JANE M. KLAUSMAN WOMEN IN BUSINESS SCHOLARSHIPS

Zonta International
Attn: Foundation
557 West Randolph Street
Chicago, IL 60661-2202
(312) 930-5848          Fax: (312) 930-0951
E-mail: Zontafdtn@Zonta.org
Web: www.zonta.org

**Summary** To provide financial assistance to women working on an undergraduate degree in business.

**Eligibility** This program is open to women who are entering the third or fourth year of a business-related undergraduate degree program at a college or university anywhere in the world. Applicants first enter at the club level, and then advance to district and international levels. Along with their application, they must submit a 500-word essay that describes their academic and professional goals, the relevance on their program to the business field, and how this scholarship will assist them in reaching their goals. Selection is based on that essay, academic record, demonstrated intent to complete a program in business, achievement in business-related subjects, and 2 letters of recommendation.

**Financial data** Each winner at the U.S. district level receives a small scholarship; the international winners receive a $5,000 scholarship.

**Duration** 1 year.

**Additional information** This program was established in 1997.

**Number awarded** Several U.S. district winners and 6 international winners are selected each year.

**Deadline** Clubs set their own deadlines but must submit their winners to the district governor by May of each year.

## [268]
## JANE RING/SUE RING-JARVI GIRLS'/WOMEN'S HOCKEY SCHOLARSHIP

Saint Paul Foundation
Attn: Program Officer
600 Fifth Street Center
55 Fifth Street East
St. Paul, MN 55101-1797
(651) 325-4236          Toll-free: (800) 875-6167
Fax: (651) 224-8123
E-mail: trh@saintpaulfoundation.org
Web: www.saintpaulfoundation.org/scholarships

**Summary** To provide financial assistance for college to female high school seniors in Minnesota who have played hockey in high school.

**Eligibility** This program is open to women hockey players graduating from high school in Minnesota. Applicants must have a GPA of 3.0 or higher and be planning to attend an accredited 4-year college or university. Along with their application, they must submit a 2-page personal statement describing how hockey has affected their life, the contributions they have made to hockey in high school, and what role they expect hockey to play in their future. Selection is based on athletic and academic achievement, character, leadership ability, ambition to succeed, and evidence of present and future useful citizenship.

**Financial data** The stipend is $2,000.

**Duration** 1 year; nonrenewable.

**Additional information** This program was established in 1996.

**Number awarded** 2 each year.

**Deadline** April of each year.

## [269]
## JANET H. GRISWOLD SCHOLARSHIPS

P.E.O. Foundation-California State Chapter
c/o Patty Colligan, Scholarship Committee Chair
529 Shell Drive
Redding, CA 96003
(530) 247-7044          E-mail: pattyinrdng@hotmail.com
Web: www.peocalifornia.org/jhg.html

**Summary** To provide financial assistance to women from California who are working on an undergraduate or graduate degree in education.

**Eligibility** This program is open to female residents of California who are studying education at the undergraduate or graduate level. Applicants must be able to demonstrate financial need, character, and a record of academic and extracurricular activities achievement.

**Financial data** Stipends range from $500 to $1,100.

**Duration** 1 year.

**Number awarded** Varies each year; recently, 7 of these scholarships were awarded.

**Deadline** February of each year.

## [270]
## JANIE CREE BOSE ANDERSON SCHOLARSHIPS

Kentucky Woman's Missionary Union
Attn: Scholarships
13420 Eastpoint Centre Drive
P.O. Box 436569
Louisville, KY 40253-6569
(502) 489-3534    Toll-free: (866) 489-3534 (within KY)
Fax: (502) 489-3566          E-mail: kywmu@kybaptist.org
Web: www.kywmu.org/scholars.htm

**Summary** To provide financial assistance to women Baptists from Kentucky who are attending college or seminary to prepare for Christian service.

**Eligibility** This program is open to women who are active members of churches affiliated with the Kentucky Baptist Convention or the General Association of Baptists in Kentucky. Applicants must be attending an accredited college, university, or seminary as a full-time student. They must have a GPA of 2.7 or higher and be preparing for Christian service.

**Financial data** Stipends range from $250 to $750.

**Duration** 1 year.

**Number awarded** 1 or more each year.

**Deadline** January of each year.

## [271]
## JAZZ PERFORMANCE AWARDS

Sigma Alpha Iota Philanthropies, Inc.
One Tunnel Road
Asheville, NC 28805
(828) 251-0606                    Fax: (828) 251-0644
E-mail: philonline@sai-national.org
Web: www.sai-national.org/phil/philsch3.html

**Summary**  To provide financial assistance to members of Sigma Alpha Iota (an organization of women musicians) who are interested in working on an undergraduate or graduate degree in jazz performance.

**Eligibility**  This program is open to members of the organization who are enrolled in an undergraduate or graduate degree program in jazz performance or studies. Applicants must be younger than 32 years of age. Along with their application, they must submit a CD recording of a performance "set" of 30 to 45 minutes.

**Financial data**  Stipends are $2,000 for the winner or $1,500 for the runner-up.

**Duration**  1 year.

**Additional information**  There is a $25 nonrefundable application fee.

**Number awarded**  2 every 3 years.

**Deadline**  March of the year of the awards (2009, 2012, etc.).

## [272]
## JAZZ STUDIES SCHOLARSHIP

Sigma Alpha Iota Philanthropies, Inc.
One Tunnel Road
Asheville, NC 28805
(828) 251-0606                    Fax: (828) 251-0644
E-mail: philonline@sai-national.org
Web: www.sai-national.org/phil/philsch1.html

**Summary**  To provide financial assistance to members of Sigma Alpha Iota (an organization of women musicians) who are interested in working on an undergraduate degree in jazz studies.

**Eligibility**  This program is open to members of the organization who are enrolled in a university jazz studies program. Applicants must submit a 500-word essay on their career plans and professional goals in jazz studies and why they feel they are deserving of this scholarship.

**Financial data**  The stipend is $1,500.

**Duration**  1 year.

**Additional information**  There is a $25 nonrefundable application fee.

**Number awarded**  1 each year.

**Deadline**  March of each year.

## [273]
## JEAN FITZGERALD SCHOLARSHIP

Hawai'i Community Foundation
Attn: Scholarship Department
1164 Bishop Street, Suite 800
Honolulu, HI 96813
(808) 566-5570                Toll-free: (888) 731-3863
Fax: (808) 521-6286
E-mail: scholarships@hcf-hawaii.org
Web: www.hawaiicommunityfoundation.org

**Summary**  To provide financial assistance to women tennis players in Hawaii who are just beginning college.

**Eligibility**  This program is open to female Hawaiian residents who are active tennis players entering their freshman year in college as full-time students. Preference may be given to members of the Hawai'i Pacific Section of the United States Tennis Association (USTA). Applicants must be able to demonstrate academic achievement (GPA of 2.7 or higher), good moral character, and financial need. Along with their application, they must submit a short statement indicating their reasons for attending college, their planned course of study, and their career goals.

**Financial data**  The amounts of the awards depend on the availability of funds and the need of the recipient; recently, the stipend was $7,000.

**Duration**  1 year.

**Additional information**  Recipients may attend college in Hawaii or on the mainland.

**Number awarded**  Varies each year; recently, 1 of these scholarships was awarded.

**Deadline**  February of each year.

## [274]
## JEAN TUCKER STRADLEY SCHOLARSHIP

Kappa Delta Sorority
Attn: Foundation Manager
3205 Players Lane
Memphis, TN 38125
(901) 748-1897                Toll-free: (800) 536-1897
Fax: (901) 748-0949
E-mail: kappadelta@kappadelta.org
Web: www.kappadelta.org

**Summary**  To provide financial assistance to members of Kappa Delta Sorority who are majoring in elementary education.

**Eligibility**  This program is open to undergraduate members of Kappa Delta Sorority. Applicants must submit a personal statement giving their reasons for applying for this scholarship, an official undergraduate transcript, and 2 letters of recommendation. They must be majoring in elementary education. Selection is based on academic excellence, service to the chapter and university, service to the community, personal objectives and goals, potential, recommendations, and financial need.

**Financial data**  The stipend is $2,000 per year. Funds may be used only for tuition, fees, and books, not for room and board.

**Duration**  1 year; may be renewed.

**Number awarded**  1 each year.

**Deadline**  January of each year.

## [275]
## JEANNETTE RANKIN AWARD

Jeannette Rankin Foundation, Inc.
P.O. Box 6653
Athens, GA 30604-6653
(706) 208-1211              Fax: (706) 548-0202
E-mail: info@rankinfoundation.org
Web: www.rankinfoundation.org

**Summary**  To provide financial assistance for college to women who are 35 years or older.

**Eligibility**  Women who are 35 years of age or older are eligible to apply for this scholarship if they are in financial need and have clear educational goals. They must be U.S. citizens and enrolled in a certified program of technical/vocational training or undergraduate education.

**Financial data**  The stipend is $2,000.

**Duration**  1 year; nonrenewable.

**Additional information**  This program began in 1978. Awards are not given to students enrolled in graduate courses or working on a second undergraduate degree.

**Number awarded**  Varies each year; recently, 45 of these scholarships were awarded.

**Deadline**  February of each year.

## [276]
## JESSICA POWELL LOFTIS SCHOLARSHIP FOR ACTEENS

Woman's Missionary Union
Attn: WMU Foundation
100 Missionary Ridge
P.O. Box 11346
Birmingham, AL 35202-1346
(205) 408-5525              Toll-free: (877) 482-4483
Fax: (205) 408-5508
E-mail: wmufoundation@wmu.org
Web: www.wmufoundation.com/scholar_scholar.asp

**Summary**  To provide financial assistance for college or other activities to female high school seniors who have been active in the Southern Baptist Convention's Acteens (Academic/Events/Training).

**Eligibility**  This program is open to female high school seniors who are members of a Baptist church and active in Acteens. Applicants must 1) be planning to attend college and have completed *Quest for Vision* in the MissionsQuest program or StudiAct; 2) have been an Acteen for at least 1 year and be planning to attend an Acteens event; or 3) be an Acteens leader who is pursuing academic or leadership training to lead an Acteens group. Along with their application, they must submit an essay listing their major accomplishments and missions activities.

**Financial data**  A stipend is awarded (amount not specified).

**Duration**  1 year.

**Additional information**  This program was established in 1995 by Woman's Missionary Union, an Auxiliary to Southern Baptist Convention.

**Number awarded**  1 or more each year.

**Deadline**  February of each year.

## [277]
## JESSIE FANYO PAYNE GRANT

Alpha Chi Omega Foundation
Attn: Foundation Programs Coordinator
5939 Castle Creek Parkway North Drive
Indianapolis, IN 46250-4343
(317) 579-5050, ext. 262        Fax: (317) 579-5051
E-mail: foundation@alphachiomega.org
Web: www.alphachiomega.org

**Summary**  To provide financial assistance to undergraduate or alumnae members of Alpha Chi Omega who are interested in working on a degree in communications.

**Eligibility**  This program is open to junior, senior, and graduate members of Alpha Chi Omega who are full-time students in the field of communications with an emphasis on journalism and public relations. Selection is based on academic achievement, chapter involvement, campus and community involvement, and financial need.

**Financial data**  The stipend is $500.

**Duration**  1 year.

**Number awarded**  1 each year.

**Deadline**  March of each year.

## [278]
## JILL S. TIETJEN SCHOLARSHIP

Society of Women Engineers
230 East Ohio Street, Suite 400
Chicago, IL 60611-3265
(312) 596-5223              Toll-free: (877) SWE-INFO
Fax: (312) 644-8557
E-mail: scholarshipapplication@swe.org
Web: www.swe.org/scholarships

**Summary**  To provide financial assistance to women working on an undergraduate or graduate degree in engineering or computer science.

**Eligibility**  This program is open to women who will be sophomores, juniors, seniors, or graduate students at ABET-accredited colleges and universities. Applicants must be U.S. citizens majoring in computer science or engineering and have a GPA of 3.0 or higher. Along with their application, they must submit a 1-page essay on why they want to be an engineer or computer scientist, how they believe they will make a difference as an engineer or computer scientist, and what influenced them to study engineering or computer science. Selection is based on merit.

**Financial data**  The stipend is $1,000.

**Duration**  1 year.

**Number awarded**  1 each year.

**Deadline**  January of each year.

## [279]
## JOB'S DAUGHTERS SUPREME GUARDIAN COUNCIL SCHOLARSHIPS

International Order of Job's Daughters
Supreme Guardian Council Headquarters
Attn: Executive Manager
233 West Sixth Street
Papillion, NE 68046-2177
(402) 592-7987          Fax: (402) 592-2177
E-mail: sgc@iojd.org
Web: www.iojd.org

**Summary** To provide financial assistance for college or graduate school to members of Job's Daughters.

**Eligibility** This program is open to high school seniors and graduates; students in early graduation programs; junior college, technical, and vocational students; and college and graduate students. Applicants must be Job's Daughters in good standing in their Bethels; unmarried majority members under 30 years of age are also eligible. Selection is based on scholastic standing, Job's Daughters activities, the applicant's self-help plan, recommendation by the Executive Bethel Guardian Council, faculty recommendations, achievements outside Job's Daughters, and financial need.

**Financial data** The stipend is $750.

**Duration** 1 year; may be renewed 1 additional year.

**Additional information** Information is also available from Barbara Hill, Education Scholarships Committee Chair, 337 Illinois Street, Pekin, IL 61554, (309) 346-5564.

**Number awarded** Varies each year.

**Deadline** April of each year.

## [280]
## JOHN F. KENNEDY SCHOLARSHIP

Massachusetts Democratic Party
Attn: Executive Director
56 Roland Street, North Lobby, Suite 203
Boston, MA 02129
(617) 776-2676          Fax: (617) 776-2579
E-mail: Susan.Thompson@massdems.org
Web: www.massdems.org/involved/internship.htm

**Summary** To provide financial assistance for college to Massachusetts residents, with preference given to registered Democrats.

**Eligibility** This program is open to Massachusetts residents who are entering their third or fourth year of study at a college or university anywhere in the United States. Applicants must be majoring in political science, government, or history. They must be able to demonstrate a serious commitment to the study of American politics and be qualified to receive financial aid (as certified by their financial aid officer). Males and females compete separately. Preference is given to registered Democrats who have a GPA of 3.0 or higher. Finalists may be interviewed in Boston.

**Financial data** The stipend is $1,500.

**Duration** 1 year.

**Number awarded** 2 each year: 1 is set aside specifically for a female and 1 for a male.

**Deadline** April of each year.

## [281]
## JOHN W. MCDEVITT (FOURTH DEGREE) SCHOLARSHIPS

Knights of Columbus
Attn: Department of Scholarships
P.O. Box 1670
New Haven, CT 06507-0901
(203) 752-4332          Fax: (203) 772-2696
E-mail: info@kofc.org
Web: www.kofc.org

**Summary** To provide financial assistance to entering freshmen at Catholic colleges and universities who have ties to the Knights of Columbus.

**Eligibility** Eligible are students entering their freshman year in a program leading to a baccalaureate degree at a Catholic college or university in the United States; applicants must be members in good standing of the Knights of Columbus, or the wife, widow, son, or daughter of a current member or of a deceased member who was in good standing at the time of death. Selection is based on secondary school record, class rank, and aptitude test scores.

**Financial data** The stipend is $1,500 per year.

**Duration** 1 year; may be renewed up to 3 additional years upon evidence of satisfactory academic performance.

**Number awarded** Approximately 36 each year.

**Deadline** February of each year.

## [282]
## JUDGE HAZEL PALMER GENERAL SCHOLARSHIP

Missouri Business and Professional Women's
    Foundation, Inc.
P.O. Box 338
Carthage, MO 64836-0338
Web: bpwmo.org/files/index.php?id=14

**Summary** To provide financial assistance to members of the Missouri Federation of Business and Professional Women (BPW Missouri) who are interested in working on a college degree leading to public service.

**Eligibility** This program is open to BPW Missouri members who have been accepted into an accredited program or course of study to work on a degree leading to public service. Along with their application, they must submit brief statements on the following: achievements and/or specific recognitions in their field of endeavor; professional and/or civic affiliations; present and long-range career goals; how they plan to participate in and contribute to their community upon completion of their program of study; why they feel they would make a good recipient; and any special circumstances that may have influenced their ability to continue or complete their education. They must also demonstrate financial need and U.S. citizenship.

**Financial data** A stipend is awarded (amount not specified).

**Duration** 1 year.

**Additional information** Information is also available from Mary Kay Pace, Scholarship Committee Chair, 1503 Paradise Valley Drive, High Ridge, MO 63049, (636) 677-2951.

**Number awarded** 1 each year.

**Deadline** January of each year.

## [283]
## JUDGE WILLIAM F. COOPER SCHOLARSHIP

Center for Scholarship Administration, Inc.
Attn: Wachovia Accounts
4320-G Wade Hampton Boulevard
Taylors, SC 29687
Toll-free: (866) 608-0001
E-mail: wachoviascholars@bellsouth.net
Web: www.wachoviascholars.com/wscholarships.php

**Summary** To provide financial assistance for college to female high school seniors in Georgia, especially residents of Chatham County.

**Eligibility** This program is open to female seniors graduating from high schools in Georgia. Preference is given to residents of Chatham County. Applicants must be planning to enroll at an accredited college or university to study any field except law, theology, or medicine. They must be able to demonstrate financial need. Along with their application, they must submit a 1-page essay on their strengths and their most important achievements in their school and community, including hobbies, interests, sports, volunteer work, employment, future plans, and career goals. Selection is based on academic achievement, potential to succeed in their chosen educational field, and financial need.

**Financial data** A stipend is awarded (amount not specified).

**Duration** 1 year; may be renewed up to 3 additional years or until completion of a bachelor's degree, whichever is earlier.

**Number awarded** 1 or more each year.

**Deadline** March of each year.

## [284]
## JUDITH MCMANUS PRICE SCHOLARSHIPS

American Planning Association
Attn: Leadership Affairs Associate
122 South Michigan Avenue, Suite 1600
Chicago, IL 60603-6107
(312) 431-9100         Fax: (312) 431-9985
E-mail: fellowship@planning.org
Web: www.planning.org/institutions/scholarship.htm

**Summary** To provide financial assistance to women and underrepresented minority students enrolled in undergraduate or graduate degree programs at recognized planning schools.

**Eligibility** This program is open to undergraduate and graduate students in urban and regional planning who are women or members of the following minority groups: African American, Hispanic American, or Native American. Applicants must be citizens of the United States and able to document financial need. They must intend to work as practicing planners in the public sector. Along with their application, they must submit a 2- to 5-page personal statement describing how their education will be applied to career goals and why they chose planning as a career path. Selection is based (in order of importance) on 1) commitment to planning as reflected in the personal statement and resume; 2) academic achievement and/or improvement during the past 2 years; 3) letters of recommendation; 4) financial need; and 5) professional presentation.

**Financial data** Stipends range from $2,000 to $4,000 per year. The money may be applied to tuition and living expenses only. Payment is made to the recipient's university and divided by terms in the school year.

**Duration** 1 year; recipients may reapply.

**Additional information** This program was established in 2004.

**Number awarded** Varies each year; recently, 3 of these scholarships were awarded.

**Deadline** April of each year.

## [285]
## JUDITH RESNIK MEMORIAL SCHOLARSHIP

Society of Women Engineers
230 East Ohio Street, Suite 400
Chicago, IL 60611-3265
(312) 596-5223         Toll-free: (877) SWE-INFO
Fax: (312) 644-8557
E-mail: scholarshipapplication@swe.org
Web: www.swe.org/scholarships

**Summary** To provide financial assistance to undergraduate women who are members of the Society of Women Engineers and majoring in designated engineering specialties.

**Eligibility** This program is open to women who are entering their sophomore, junior, or senior year at an ABET-accredited 4-year college or university. Applicants must be studying aerospace, aeronautical, or astronautical engineering with a GPA of 3.0 or higher. Along with their application, they must submit a 1-page essay on why they want to be an engineer, how they believe they will make a difference as an engineer, and what influenced them to study engineering. Only members of the society are considered for this award. Selection is based on merit.

**Financial data** The stipend is $2,500.

**Duration** 1 year.

**Additional information** This award was established in 1988 to honor society member Judith Resnik, who was killed aboard the Challenger space shuttle.

**Number awarded** 1 each year.

**Deadline** January of each year.

## [286]
## JULIA H. DODDS JUNIOR GIRL'S AWARD

Illinois Women's Golf Association
c/o Marlene Miller
351 Birkdale Road
Lake Bluff, IL 60044
(847) 234-2154         E-mail: mememiller@aol.com
Web: www.iwga.org

**Summary** To provide financial assistance for college to women in Illinois who have participated in golf.

**Eligibility** This program is open to female high school seniors in Illinois who have played in the Illinois Women's Golf Association (IWGA) State Junior Tournament. Nominations may be submitted by anyone with knowledge of qualified girls. Nominees must arrange for 2 letters of recommendation, 1 from their high school golf coach and 1 from a teacher or principal at their high school. Selection is based on character, scholarship, leadership, sportsmanship, and love for the game of golf.

**Financial data** The stipend is $1,000. Funds are paid directly to the recipient's college.

**Duration** 1 year.

**Additional information** This scholarship was first awarded in 1992.

**Number awarded** 1 each year.

**Deadline** April of each year.

## [287]
## JUNIOR GIRLS SCHOLARSHIPS

Ladies Auxiliary to the Veterans of Foreign Wars
c/o National Headquarters
406 West 34th Street
Kansas City, MO 64111
(816) 561-8655, ext 19          Fax: (816) 931-4753
E-mail: info@ladiesauxvfw.com
Web: www.ladiesauxvfw.com

**Summary** To provide financial assistance for college to outstanding members of a Junior Girls Unit of the Ladies Auxiliary to the Veterans of Foreign Wars.

**Eligibility** Applicants must have been active members of a unit for 1 year, have held an office in the unit, and be between 13 and 16 years of age. Previous winners are not eligible, although former applicants who did not receive scholarships may reapply. Selection is based on participation in the Junior Girls Unit, community activities, school activities, and scholastic aptitude.

**Financial data** The first-place winner receives a $10,000 scholarship; the second-place winner receives a $5,000 scholarship. Funds are paid directly to the college of the recipient's choice. In addition, $100 is awarded to each Junior Girl who is selected as the department winner and entered in the national competition.

**Duration** 1 year.

**Additional information** The first-place winner must attend the Ladies Auxiliary National Convention and participate in the American Academy of Achievement's Salute to Excellence.

**Number awarded** 2 each year.

**Deadline** March of each year.

## [288]
## KA'IULANI HOME FOR GIRLS TRUST SCHOLARSHIP

Hawai'i Community Foundation
Attn: Scholarship Department
1164 Bishop Street, Suite 800
Honolulu, HI 96813
(808) 566-5570          Toll-free: (888) 731-3863
Fax: (808) 521-6286
E-mail: scholarships@hcf-hawaii.org
Web: www.hawaiicommunityfoundation.org

**Summary** To provide financial assistance for college to women of Hawaiian ancestry.

**Eligibility** This program is open to women of native Hawaiian ancestry who are entering their freshman or sophomore year of college. Applicants must demonstrate academic achievement (GPA of 3.0 or higher), good moral char-

acter, and financial need. In addition to filling out the standard application form, they must write a short statement indicating their reasons for attending.

**Financial data** The amounts of the awards depend on the availability of funds and the need of the recipient; recently, stipends averaged $670.

**Duration** 1 year; may be renewed.

**Additional information** Awards are tenable either in Hawaii or on the mainland. The fund was established in 1963 when the Ka'iulani Home for Girls, formerly used to provide boarding home facilities for young women of Hawaiian ancestry, was demolished and the property sold.

**Number awarded** Varies each year; recently, 237 of these scholarships were awarded.

**Deadline** February of each year.

## [289]
## KANSAS AFRICAN AMERICAN LEGISLATIVE CAUCUS SCHOLARSHIPS

Kansas African American Legislative Caucus
c/o Dale M. Dennis
State Department of Education
120 East Tenth Street
Topeka, KS 66612

**Summary** To provide financial assistance African American college students in Kansas who are interested in a career in politics.

**Eligibility** This program is open to residents of Kansas of African American ethnic background who are attending a college or university in the state. Applicants must have a GPA of 2.6 or higher. Selection is based on academic achievement, leadership ability, and community involvement. Preference is given to students majoring in communications or political science. Males and females are judged separately.

**Financial data** The stipend is $1,000.

**Duration** 1 year.

**Additional information** This program is funded by past and present African American members of the Kansas Legislature.

**Number awarded** 2 each year: 1 female and 1 male.

**Deadline** March of each year.

## [290]
## KANSAS SPACE GRANT CONSORTIUM PROGRAM

Kansas Space Grant Consortium
c/o University of Kansas
Learned Hall
1530 West 15th
Lawrence, KS 66045-7609
(785) 864-7401          Fax: (785) 864-3361
E-mail: ksgc@nasainkansas.org
Web: nasainkansas.org

**Summary** To provide funding for space-related activities to students and faculty (particularly women, minorities, and persons with disabilities) at member institutions of the Kansas Space Grant Consortium.

**Eligibility** This program is open to faculty and students at member institutions. Support is provided for undergraduate research scholarships, graduate research assistant-ships, undergraduate and graduate student participation in activities sponsored by the U.S. National Aeronautics and Space Administration (NASA), faculty participation in NASA research projects, and other activities in fields of interest to NASA. The consortium is a component of NASA's Space Grant program, which encourages participation by women, underrepresented minorities, and persons with disabilities.

**Financial data** Each participating institution determines the amounts of its awards.

**Additional information** The member institutions of the consortium are Emporia State University, Fort Hayes State University, Haskell Indian Nations University, Kansas State University, Pittsburgh State University, University of Kansas, and Wichita State University. Funding for this program is provided by NASA.

**Number awarded** Varies each year.

**Deadline** Each participating institution establishes its own deadlines.

## [291]
## KAPPA ALPHA THETA FOUNDERS' MEMORIAL SCHOLARSHIPS

Kappa Alpha Theta
Attn: Foundation
8740 Founders Road
Indianapolis, IN 46268-1337
(317) 876-1870, ext. 119
Toll-free: (888) 526-1870, ext. 119
Fax: (317) 876-1925
E-mail: cthoennes@kappaalphatheta.org
Web: www.kappaalphatheta.org

**Summary** To provide financial assistance for undergraduate study in the United States or abroad to members of Kappa Alpha Theta (the first Greek letter fraternity for women).

**Eligibility** This program is open to members of Kappa Alpha Theta who are enrolled full time as juniors at a college or university in Canada or the United States. Applicants must submit an official transcript, a resume, 3 letters of reference, and a 1-page statement describing their goals and ambitions and how being a member of Kappa Alpha Theta has impacted their life. Selection is based on 4 categories: academic achievement, participation in Kappa Alpha Theta activities, participation in campus and/or community activities, and references. Financial need is not considered.

**Financial data** The stipend is $8,000 per year.

**Duration** 1 year. Recipients may apply for an alumnae scholarship, but they may receive a maximum lifetime amount of $20,000 from the foundation.

**Additional information** Recipients may study abroad, provided they do so as part of a program leading to a degree from an institution in the United States or Canada. This program consists of the following named scholarships: the Bettie Locke Hamilton Memorial Scholarship, the Alice Allen Brant Memorial Scholarship, the Bettie Tipton Lindsey Memorial Scholarship, and the Hannah Fitch Shaw Memorial Scholarship.

**Number awarded** 4 each year.

**Deadline** January of each year.

## [292]
## KAPPA ALPHA THETA UNDERGRADUATE SCHOLARSHIPS

Kappa Alpha Theta
Attn: Foundation
8740 Founders Road
Indianapolis, IN 46268-1337
(317) 876-1870, ext. 119
Toll-free: (888) 526-1870, ext. 119
Fax: (317) 876-1925
E-mail: cthoennes@kappaalphatheta.org
Web: www.kappaalphatheta.org

**Summary** To provide financial assistance for college in the United States or abroad to members of Kappa Alpha Theta (the first Greek letter fraternity for women).

**Eligibility** This program is open to members of Kappa Alpha Theta who are enrolled full time at a college or university in Canada or the United States. Applicants must submit an official transcript, a resume, and 2 letters of reference. Selection is based on 4 categories: academic achievement, participation in Kappa Alpha Theta activities, participation in campus and/or community activities, and references. Financial need is not considered.

**Financial data** Stipends range from $1,000 to $7,100. Recently, the average was $2.700.

**Duration** 1 year. Recipients may reapply, but they may receive a maximum lifetime amount of $20,000 from the foundation.

**Additional information** Recipients may study abroad, provided they do so as part of a program leading to a degree from an institution in the United States or Canada.

**Number awarded** Varies each year; recently, 70 of these scholarships were awarded.

**Deadline** January of each year.

## [293]
## KAPPA DELTA MAGAZINE AGENCY SCHOLARSHIP

Kappa Delta Sorority
Attn: Foundation Manager
3205 Players Lane
Memphis, TN 38125
(901) 748-1897          Toll-free: (800) 536-1897
Fax: (901) 748-0949
E-mail: kappadelta@kappadelta.org
Web: www.kappadelta.org

**Summary** To provide financial assistance to members of Kappa Delta Sorority who are majoring in business.

**Eligibility** This program is open to undergraduate members of Kappa Delta Sorority. Applicants must submit a personal statement giving their reasons for applying for this scholarship, an official undergraduate transcript, and 2 letters of recommendation. They must be majoring in business, including accounting, finance, and marketing. Selection is based on academic excellence, service to the chapter and university, service to the community, personal objectives and goals, potential, recommendations, and financial need.

**Financial data** The stipend is $2,000 per year. Funds may be used only for tuition, fees, and books, not for room and board.

**Duration** 1 year; may be renewed.

**Additional information** This program is sponsored by the sorority's magazine agency and by QSP/Reader's Digest.

**Number awarded** 1 each year.

**Deadline** January of each year.

## [294]
## KAPPA DELTA SORORITY UNDERGRADUATE SCHOLARSHIPS

Kappa Delta Sorority
Attn: Foundation Manager
3205 Players Lane
Memphis, TN 38125
(901) 748-1897          Toll-free: (800) 536-1897
Fax: (901) 748-0949
E-mail: kappadelta@kappadelta.org
Web: www.kappadelta.org

**Summary** To provide financial assistance to members of Kappa Delta Sorority who are interested in continuing their undergraduate education.

**Eligibility** This program is open to undergraduate members of Kappa Delta Sorority. Applicants must submit a personal statement giving their reasons for applying for this scholarship, an official undergraduate transcript, and 2 letters of recommendation. Most scholarships are available to all undergraduate members, but some restrict the field of study and others are limited to members at specified chapters. Selection is based on academic excellence, service to the chapter and university, service to the community, personal objectives and goals, potential, recommendations, and financial need.

**Financial data** Stipends range from $500 to $4,000 per year. Funds may be used only for tuition, fees, and books, not for room and board.

**Duration** 1 year; may be renewed.

**Additional information** This program includes the following named scholarships that have no additional restrictions: the Kappa Delta Founders' Scholarships, the Grayce Chase Scholarship, the Grace Follmer Scholarship, the M. Amanda Gordon Scholarships, the Marilyn Mock Scholarship, the Dorothy Ramage Scholarship, the Margaret Budd Haemer Scholarship, the Muriel Johnstone Scholarships, the Ernestine L. Newman Scholarship, and the Pam Barton Staples Scholarship.

**Number awarded** Varies each year. Recently, the sorority awarded a total of 35 scholarships: 4 at $4,000, 23 at $2,000, 3 at $1,000, and 5 at $500.

**Deadline** January of each year.

## [295]
## KAPPA KAPPA GAMMA UNDERGRADUATE SCHOLARSHIPS

Kappa Kappa Gamma Foundation
530 East Town Street
P.O. Box 38
Columbus, OH 43216-0038
(614) 228-6515          Toll-free: (866) KKG-1870
Fax: (614) 228-7809          E-mail: kkghq@kappa.org
Web: www.kappakappagamma.org

**Summary** To provide financial assistance for college to members of Kappa Kappa Gamma.

**Eligibility** This program is open to members of Kappa Kappa Gamma who are enrolled full time and have a GPA of 3.0 or higher for each academic term. Applicants must be initiated members; associate members are not eligible. Along with their application, they must submit a personal essay or letter describing their educational and career goals and financial need. Selection is based on merit, academic achievement, participation in sorority activities, and financial need.

**Financial data** A stipend is awarded (amount not specified).

**Duration** 1 year.

**Number awarded** Varies each year; in a recent biennium, the foundation awarded a total of $936,681 in undergraduate and graduate scholarships.

**Deadline** January of each year.

## [296]
## KAREN B. LEWIS CAREER EDUCATION SCHOLARSHIP

Business and Professional Women of Virginia
Attn: Virginia BPW Foundation
P.O. Box 4842
McLean, VA 22103-4842
Web: www.bpwva.org/scholarships.shtml

**Summary** To provide financial assistance to girls and women pursuing postsecondary job-oriented career education (in business, trade, or industrial occupations) in Virginia.

**Eligibility** This program is open to women who are at least 18 years of age; are U.S. citizens and Virginia residents; have been accepted into an accredited training program in Virginia; have a definite plan to use their education in a business, trade, or industrial occupation; and are able to demonstrate financial need. They may not be pursuing education leading to a bachelor's or higher degree.

**Financial data** Stipends range from $100 to $1,000 per year; funds may be used for tuition, fees, books, transportation, living expenses, and dependent care.

**Duration** Funds must be used within 12 months. Prior recipients may reapply, but they are not given priority.

**Number awarded** At least 1 is awarded each year.

**Deadline** March of each year.

## [297]
## KAREN TUCKER CENTENNIAL SCHOLARSHIP

Alpha Omicron Pi Foundation
Attn: Scholarship Committee
5390 Virginia Way
P.O. Box 395
Brentwood, TN 37024-0395
(615) 370-0920                    Fax: (615) 370-4424
E-mail: foundation@alphaomicronpi.org
Web: www.aoiifoundation.org

**Summary**  To provide financial assistance for college or graduate school to collegiate and alumnae members of Alpha Omicron Pi.

**Eligibility**  This program is open to collegiate members of Alpha Omicron Pi who wish to continue their undergraduate education and alumnae members who wish to work on a graduate degree. Applicants must submit 50-word essays on the following topics: 1) the circumstances that have created their need for this scholarship, and 2) their immediate and long-term life objectives. Selection is based on academic excellence, dedication to serving the community and Alpha Omicron Pi, and financial need.

**Financial data**  A stipend is awarded (amount not specified).

**Duration**  1 year.

**Additional information**  Undergraduate recipients must enroll full time, but graduate recipients may enroll part time.

**Number awarded**  1 each year.

**Deadline**  February of each year.

## [298]
## KATHRYN M. DAUGHERTY SCHOLARSHIP FOR EDUCATION MAJORS

Maryland Federation of Business and Professional
   Women's Clubs, Inc.
c/o Pat Schroeder, Scholarship Chair
354 Driftwood Lane
Solomons, MD 20688
(410) 326-0167                    Toll-free: (877) INFO-BPW
E-mail: patsc@csmd.edu
Web: www.bpwmaryland.org/scholarships.html

**Summary**  To provide financial assistance to women in Maryland who are majoring in education.

**Eligibility**  This program is open to women residents of Maryland who are majoring in education at an academic institution in the state, with preference given to majors in elementary education. Applicants must be registered full time and entering their sophomore year in college. They must be able to demonstrate critical financial need. Graduate study, correspondence courses, and non-degree programs are not eligible.

**Financial data**  The stipend is $1,000 for the sophomore year and $250 per year for the junior and senior years.

**Duration**  1 year; may be renewed for 2 additional years, provided the recipient maintains a GPA of 3.0 or higher and enrollment in an education program.

**Number awarded**  1 or more each year.

**Deadline**  June of each year.

## [299]
## KATHY LOUDAT MUSIC SCHOLARSHIP

New Mexico Baptist Foundation
5325 Wyoming Boulevard, N.E.
P.O. Box 16560
Albuquerque, NM 87191-6560
(505) 332-3777                    Toll-free: (877) 841-3777
Fax: (505) 332-2777        E-mail: foundation@nmbf.com
Web: www.bcnm.com

**Summary**  To provide financial assistance to female members of Southern Baptist churches in New Mexico who are preparing for a career in church music.

**Eligibility**  This program is open to full-time female college, university, and seminary students who are preparing for a career in church music. Applicants must have a GPA of 3.0 or higher and be able to demonstrate financial need. They must be members of Southern Baptist churches in New Mexico or former members in good standing with the Southern Baptist Convention.

**Financial data**  A stipend is awarded (amount not specified).

**Duration**  1 year.

**Number awarded**  1 or more each year.

**Deadline**  April of each year.

## [300]
## KENTUCKY SPACE GRANT CONSORTIUM UNDERGRADUATE SCHOLARSHIPS

Kentucky Space Grant Consortium
c/o Western Kentucky University
Department of Physics and Astronomy, TCCW 246
1906 College Heights Boulevard 11077
Bowling Green, KY 42101-1077
(270) 745-4156                    Fax: (270) 745-4255
E-mail: Richard.Hackney@wku.edu
Web: www.wku.edu/KSGC

**Summary**  To provide financial assistance to undergraduate students (particularly women, minority, and disabled students) at member institutions of the Kentucky Space Grant Consortium (KSGC) interested in pursuing education and research in space-related fields.

**Eligibility**  This program is open to undergraduate students at member institutions of the KSGC. Applicants must be enrolled in a baccalaureate degree program in a space-related field or teaching specialization. As part of the program, a faculty member must agree to serve as a mentor on a research project. U.S. citizenship is required. Selection is based on academic qualifications of the applicant, quality of the proposed research program and its relevance to space-related science and technology, and applicant's motivation for a space-related career as expressed in an essay on interests and goals. Applications are especially encouraged from women, members of other underrepresented groups (including minorities and people with disabilities), and students involved in projects of the U.S. National Aeronautics and Space Administration (NASA), such as NASA EPSCoR and SHARP.

**Financial data**  The grant is $5,000, including a stipend of $4,500 and an additional $500 to support the student's mentored research project. Matching grants of at least $4,000 are required. Preference is given to applicants from schools that agree to waive tuition for the scholar as part of the program.

**Duration** 1 year; may be renewed depending on the quality of the student's research and satisfactory performance in the program of study as evidenced by grades, presentation of research results, and evaluation of progress by the mentor.

**Additional information** This program is funded by NASA. The KSGC member institutions are Bellarmine University, Centre College, Eastern Kentucky University, Kentucky State University, Morehead State University, Murray State University, Northern Kentucky University, Thomas More College, Transylvania University, University of Kentucky, University of Louisville, and Western Kentucky University.

**Number awarded** Varies each year.

**Deadline** February of each year.

## [301]
## KENTUCKY VETERANS TUITION WAIVER PROGRAM

Kentucky Department of Veterans Affairs
Attn: Division of Field Operations
545 South Third Street, Room 123
Louisville, KY 40202
(502) 595-4447    Toll-free: (800) 928-4012 (within KY)
Fax: (502) 595-4448
Web: www.kdva.net/tuitionwaiver.htm

**Summary** To provide financial assistance for college to the children, spouses, or unremarried widow(er)s of disabled or deceased Kentucky veterans.

**Eligibility** This program is open to the children, stepchildren, spouses, and unremarried widow(er)s of veterans who are residents of Kentucky (or were residents at the time of their death). The qualifying veteran must meet 1 of the following conditions: 1) died on active duty (regardless of wartime service); 2) died as a result of a service-connected disability (regardless of wartime service); 3) has a 100% service-connected disability; or 4) was a prisoner of war or declared missing in action. The military service may have been as a member of the U.S. armed forces, the Kentucky National Guard, or a Reserve component; service in the Guard or Reserves must have been on state active duty, active duty for training, inactive duty training, or active duty with the U.S. armed forces. Children of veterans must be under 23 years of age; no age limit applies to spouses or unremarried widow(er)s. All applicants must be attending or planning to attend a 2-year, 4-year, or vocational technical school operated and funded by the Kentucky Department of Education.

**Financial data** Eligible dependents and survivors are exempt from tuition and matriculation fees at any state-supported institution of higher education in Kentucky.

**Duration** Tuition is waived until the recipient completes 36 months of training, receives a college degree, or (in the case of children of veterans) reaches 23 years of age, whichever comes first. Spouses and unremarried widow(er)s are not subject to the age limitation.

**Number awarded** Varies each year.

## [302]
## KIRSTEN R. LORENTZEN AWARD

Association for Women in Science
Attn: AWIS Educational Foundation
1200 New York Avenue, N.W., Suite 650
Washington, DC 20005
(202) 326-8940          Toll-free: (866) 657-AWIS
Fax: (202) 326-8960       E-mail: awisedfd@awis.org
Web: www.awis.org/careers/edfoundation.html

**Summary** To provide financial assistance to women undergraduates majoring in physics or geoscience.

**Eligibility** This program is open to women who are sophomores or juniors in college and U.S. citizens. Applicants must be studying physics (including space physics and geophysics) or geoscience. They must demonstrate excellence in their studies as well as outdoor activities, service, sports, music or other non-academic pursuits, or a record of overcoming significant obstacles. Along with their application, they must submit a 2- to 3-page essay on 1) their academic interests and plans, including class work and any relevant research, teaching, or outreach activities; 2) their career goals; 3) the non-academic pursuits that are most important to them; and 4) any significant barriers they have faced and how they overcame them. Financial need is not considered.

**Financial data** The stipend is $1,000.

**Duration** 1 year.

**Additional information** This program was established in 2004. Information is also available from Barbara Filner, President, AWIS Educational Foundation, 7008 Richard Drive, Bethesda, MD 20817-4838.

**Number awarded** 1 each year.

**Deadline** January of each year.

## [303]
## KITTREDGE CODDINGTON MEMORIAL SCHOLARSHIP

Vermont Student Assistance Corporation
Attn: Scholarship Programs
10 East Allen Street
P.O. Box 2000
Winooski, VT 05404-2601
(802) 654-3798          Toll-free: (888) 253-4819
Fax: (802) 654-3765       TDD: (802) 654-3766
TDD: (800) 281-3341 (within VT)
E-mail: info@vsac.org
Web: www.vsac.org

**Summary** To provide financial assistance to high school seniors in Vermont who are interested in working on a degree in business.

**Eligibility** This scholarship is available to the residents of Vermont who are seniors in high school. Applicants must be planning to work on a 2-year or 4-year degree in business or a related field at a postsecondary institution in Vermont. Males and females compete separately. Selection is based on required essays and letters of recommendation.

**Financial data** The stipend is $500.

**Duration** 1 year; nonrenewable.

**Additional information** This program was established by the Vermont Chamber of Commerce in 1989.

**Number awarded** 2 each year: 1 is set aside for a female and 1 for a male.
**Deadline** April of each year.

## [304]
## KRAUSE CORPORATION SCHOLARSHIPS

National FFA Organization
Attn: Scholarship Office
6060 FFA Drive
P.O. Box 68960
Indianapolis, IN 46268-0960
(317) 802-4321          Fax: (317) 802-5321
E-mail: scholarships@ffa.org
Web: www.ffa.org/programs/scholarships/index.html

**Summary** To provide financial assistance to female FFA members interested in studying agronomy and plant and soil science at selected universities.

**Eligibility** This program is open to female members who are graduating high school seniors or currently-enrolled college students. Applicants must be enrolled or planning to enroll at University of Illinois, Kansas State University, Purdue University, Ohio State University, or Cornell University. Their major must be agronomy or plant or soil science. They must have work-related experience and an interest in managing a farm. At least 50% of their family income must come from production agriculture. Selection is based on academic achievement (10 points for GPA, 10 points for SAT or ACT score, 10 points for class rank), leadership in FFA activities (30 points), leadership in community activities (10 points), and participation in the Supervised Agricultural Experience (SAE) program (30 points). Financial need is also considered. U.S. citizenship is required.

**Financial data** The stipend is $2,500 per year. Funds are paid directly to the recipient.

**Duration** 1 year; nonrenewable.

**Additional information** This program is sponsored by Krause Corporation.

**Number awarded** 2 each year.

**Deadline** February of each year.

## [305]
## LA FRA SCHOLARSHIP

Ladies Auxiliary of the Fleet Reserve Association
Attn: Scholarship Administrator
125 North West Street
Alexandria, VA 22314-2754
(703) 683-1400          Toll-free: (800) 372-1924
Fax: (703) 549-6610          E-mail: fra@fra.org
Web: www.fra.org

**Summary** To provide financial assistance for college to the daughters and granddaughters of naval personnel.

**Eligibility** Eligible to apply for these scholarships are the daughters and granddaughters of Navy, Marine, Coast Guard, active Fleet Reserve, Fleet Marine Corps Reserve, and Coast Guard Reserve personnel on active duty, retired with pay, or deceased while on active duty or retired with pay. Selection is based on financial need, academic proficiency, and character. Preference is given to dependents of members of the Fleet Reserve Association and the Ladies

Auxiliary of the Fleet Reserve Association, if other factors are equal.

**Financial data** The stipend is $2,500.

**Duration** 1 year; may be renewed.

**Number awarded** 1 each year.

**Deadline** April of each year.

## [306]
## LAS VEGAS NETWORK OF EXECUTIVE WOMEN IN HOSPITALITY SCHOLARSHIP AWARDS

Network of Executive Women in Hospitality-Las Vegas Chapter
Attn: Sue Flamming, Scholarship Chair
P.O. Box 15563
Las Vegas, NV 89114
Toll-free: (800) 593-NEWH          Fax: (800) 693-NEWH
E-mail: suef@graphicencounter.com
Web: www.newh.org/newh/scholarshippacket.php

**Summary** To provide financial assistance to undergraduate and graduate women in Nevada and Utah who are working on a degree in hospitality.

**Eligibility** This program is open to women who have completed half of an accredited hospitality-related undergraduate or graduate program in Nevada or Utah. Applicants must have a GPA of 3.0 or higher and a career objective in the hospitality or food service industries (e.g., hotel and restaurant management, culinary, architecture, design). Selection is based on financial need and academic accomplishments.

**Financial data** The stipend depends on the availability of funds and the need of the recipient.

**Number awarded** 1 or more each year.

**Deadline** March of each year.

## [307]
## LASPACE MINORITY RESEARCH SCHOLARS PROGRAM

Louisiana Space Consortium
c/o Louisiana State University
Department of Physics and Astronomy
371 Nicholson Hall
Baton Rouge, LA 70803-4001
(225) 578-8697          Fax: (225) 578-1222
E-mail: laspace@lsu.edu
Web: laspace.lsu.edu/scholarships.html

**Summary** To provide financial assistance for study in science, technology, engineering, or mathematics (STEM) to undergraduates from underrepresented groups at colleges and universities that are members or affiliates of the Louisiana Space Consortium (LaSPACE).

**Eligibility** This program is open to U.S. citizens who are members of groups underrepresented in STEM disciplines (women, African Americans, Native Americans, Native Pacific Islanders, Mexican Americans, Puerto Ricans, Alaska Natives, and persons with disabilities). Applicants must be enrolled full time at an LaSPACE member or affiliated institution in a space or aerospace STEM discipline with a GPA of 2.25 or higher. They may not have received a TOPS award from the state of Louisiana or an equivalent scholarship. Selection is based on STEM and aerospace relevance of the student's planned program, including research participation; support of LaSPACE research, education, and workforce development objectives; and applicant's need, including post-hurricane related needs, if applicable.

**Financial data** The stipend is $4,000 .

**Duration** 1 year. Recipients may reapply.

**Additional information** The LaSPACE member institutions are Louisiana State University, Louisiana Tech University, Loyola University, McNeese State University, Nicholls State University, Northwestern State University of Louisiana, Southeastern Louisiana University, Southern University and A&M College, Southern University in New Orleans, Tulane University, University of New Orleans, University of Louisiana at Lafayette, University of Louisiana at Monroe, and Xavier University of Louisiana. The affiliated institutions are Dillard University, Grambling State University, and Southern University at Shreveport. This program was established in 2005. Funding is provided by the National Aeronautics and Space Administration (NASA).

**Number awarded** Approximately 10 each year.

**Deadline** Applications may be submitted at any time.

## [308]
## LATINA LEADERSHIP NETWORK STUDENT SCHOLARSHIPS

Latina Leadership Network
c/o Maria E. Ramirez, Vice President North
Ohlone College Counseling Department
43600 Mission Boulevard
Fremont, CA 94539-0390
(510) 659-6126
Web: www.latina-leadership-network.org/awards.php

**Summary** To provide financial assistance to Latina students attending community colleges in California.

**Eligibility** This program is open to Latina students (one parent fully Latino or each parent half Latino) enrolled at community colleges in California. Applicants must have completed at least 24 units of college work with a GPA of 2.0 or higher. Along with their application, they must submit a 1-page essay on the impact of their college experience on their personal life, what they expect to be doing 5 years from now, and their personal commitment to Latina leadership. Selection is based on the essay, academic achievement, community involvement, and 2 letters of recommendation.

**Financial data** The stipend is $500.

**Duration** 1 year.

**Number awarded** 5 each year.

**Deadline** February of each year.

## [309]
## LAVONNE HEGHINIAN SCHOLARSHIP

Delta Zeta Sorority
Attn: Foundation Coordinator
202 East Church Street
Oxford, OH 45056
(513) 523-7597    E-mail: DZFoundation@dzshq.com
Web: www.deltazeta.org

**Summary** To provide financial assistance for continued undergraduate study to members of Delta Zeta Sorority.

**Eligibility** This program is open to members of the sorority who have a GPA of 3.0 or higher. Applicants must submit an official transcript, a statement of their career goals, information on their service to the sorority, documentation of campus activities and/or community involvement, and a list of academic honors. Financial need is also considered in the selection process. Preference is given to applicants from southern California.

**Financial data** The stipend ranges from $900 to $1,100, depending on the availability of funds.

**Duration** 1 year; nonrenewable.

**Number awarded** 1 each year.

**Deadline** February of each year.

## [310]
## LELA MURPHY SCHOLARSHIP

American Legion Auxiliary
Attn: Department of Missouri
600 Ellis Boulevard
Jefferson City, MO 65101-2204
(573) 636-9133    Fax: (573) 635-3467
E-mail: dptmoala@socket.net

**Summary** To provide financial assistance for college to the granddaughters and great-granddaughters of members of the American Legion Auxiliary in Missouri.

**Eligibility** This program is open to residents of Missouri who are graduating from high school and planning to attend a college or university. Applicants must be the granddaughter or great-granddaughter of a living or deceased member of the American Legion Auxiliary.

**Financial data** The stipend is $500.

**Duration** 1 year.

**Number awarded** 1 each year.

**Deadline** March of each year.

## [311]
## LEROY CALLENDAR AWARDS

National Society of Black Engineers
Attn: Pre-College Initiative
1454 Duke Street
Alexandria, VA 22314
(703) 549-2207, ext. 204    Fax: (703) 683-5312
E-mail: pci@nsbe.org
Web: www.nsbe.org

**Summary** To provide financial assistance for college to high school students who are junior members of the National Society of Black Engineers (NSBE).

**Eligibility** This program is open to junior members of the society who are in grades 9-12 at a high school in the NSBE region that is hosting the annual convention. Selection is based on academic achievement, extracurricular activities, and community involvement. Males and females are judged separately.

**Financial data**   The stipend is $500.

**Duration**   1 year.

**Number awarded**   2 each year: 1 female and 1 male.

**Deadline**   January of each year.

## [312]
## LESLIE WICKFIELD SCHOLARSHIP

Aero Club of New England
Attn: Education Committee
Civil Air Terminal
200 Hanscom Drive, Suite 322
Bedford, MA 01730
(617) 277-0100            Fax: (617) 232-7571
E-mail: scholarships@acone.org
Web: www.acone.org/scholarship/overview.html

**Summary**   To provide financial assistance for flight school to women in New England who intend to pursue a professional aviation career.

**Eligibility**   This program is open to women in New England who are interested in attending a flight school in the region. Applicants must intend to pursue a professional aviation career, have a current Airman Certificate, have a current Medical Certificate, have accumulated 160 hours total flight time, be at least 16 years of age, be a U.S. citizen, have a current Biennial Flight Review, and be able to demonstrate financial need. Along with their application, they must submit academic transcripts, a personal letter giving their reasons for selecting a professional aviation career path and describing their aviation-related activities, a financial statement, 2 letters of recommendation, and their flight time record. Selection is based on ability to meet the planned aviation goals (as shown by recommendations and academic records), participation in aviation activities (as described in the personal letter and recommendations), and financial need.

**Financial data**   A stipend is awarded (amount not specified).

**Duration**   1 year.

**Additional information**   This program was established in 1999.

**Number awarded**   1 each year.

**Deadline**   March of each year.

## [313]
## LETA ANDREWS SCHOLARSHIP

University Interscholastic League
Attn: Texas Interscholastic League Foundation
1701 Manor Road
P.O. Box 8028
Austin, TX 78713-8028
(512) 232-4937            Fax: (512) 471-5908
E-mail: bbaxendale@mail.utexas.edu
Web: www.uil.utexas.edu/tilf/scholarships.html

**Summary**   To provide financial assistance to students who participate in programs of the Texas Interscholastic

League Foundation (TILF) and have competed in girls' high school varsity basketball.

**Eligibility**   This program is open to students who have competed in girlsÖ high school varsity basketball and meet the 5 basic requirements of the TILF: 1) graduate from high school during the current year and begin college in Texas by the following fall; 2) enroll full time and maintain a GPA of 2.5 or higher during the first semester; 3) compete in a University Interscholastic League (UIL) academic state meet contest in accounting, calculator applications, computer applications, computer science, current issues and events, debate (cross-examination and Lincoln-Douglas), journalism (editorial writing, feature writing, headline writing, and news writing), literary criticism, mathematics, number sense, 1-act play, ready writing, science, social studies, speech (prose interpretation, poetry interpretation, informative speaking, and persuasive speaking), or spelling and vocabulary; 4) submit high school transcripts that include SAT and/or ACT scores; and 5) submit parents' latest income tax returns.

**Financial data**   The stipend is $1,000 per year.

**Duration**   1 year; nonrenewable.

**Additional information**   This program is sponsored by Whataburger Inc. and Southwest Shootout Inc.

**Number awarded**   1 each year.

**Deadline**   May of each year.

## [314]
## LILLIAN MOLLER GILBRETH SCHOLARSHIP

Society of Women Engineers
230 East Ohio Street, Suite 400
Chicago, IL 60611-3265
(312) 596-5223            Toll-free: (877) SWE-INFO
Fax: (312) 644-8557
E-mail: scholarshipapplication@swe.org
Web: www.swe.org/scholarships

**Summary**   To provide financial assistance to upper-division women majoring in computer science or engineering.

**Eligibility**   This program is open to women who are entering their junior or senior year at an ABET-accredited college or university. Applicants must be majoring in computer science or engineering and have a GPA of 3.0 or higher. Along with their application, they must submit a 1-page essay on why they want to be an engineer or computer scientist, how they believe they will make a difference as an engineer or computer scientist, and what influenced them to study engineering or computer science. Selection is based on merit.

**Financial data**   The stipend is $6,000 per year.

**Duration**   1 year; may be renewed.

**Additional information**   This program was established in 1958.

**Number awarded**   1 each year.

**Deadline**   January of each year.

## [315]
## LILLIE LOIS FORD SCHOLARSHIPS

American Legion
Attn: Department of Missouri
P.O. Box 179
Jefferson City, MO 65102-0179
(573) 893-2353　　　　Toll-free: (800) 846-9023
Fax: (573) 893-2980　E-mail: info@missourilegion.org
Web: www.missourilegion.org

**Summary** To provide financial assistance for college to descendants of Missouri veterans who have participated in specified American Legion programs.

**Eligibility** This program is open to the unmarried children, grandchildren, and great-grandchildren under 21 years of age of honorably-discharged Missouri veterans who served at least 90 days on active duty. Applicants must have attended a complete session of Missouri Boys State, Girls State, or Cadet Patrol Academy. They must be enrolled or planning to enroll at an accredited college or university as a full-time student. Financial need is considered in the selection process. Girls and boys compete separately.

**Financial data** The stipend is $1,000.

**Duration** 1 year (the first year of college).

**Additional information** Information is also available from the Education and Scholarship Committee Chairman, John Doane, (417) 924-8186.

**Number awarded** 2 each year: 1 is set aside specifically for a girl who attended Missouri Girls State or Missouri Cadet Patrol Academy and 1 for a boy who attended Missouri Boys State or Missouri Cadet Patrol Academy.

**Deadline** April of each year.

## [316]
## LINCOLN COMMUNITY FOUNDATION MEDICAL RESEARCH SCHOLARSHIP

Lincoln Community Foundation
215 Centennial Mall South, Suite 100
Lincoln, NE 68508
(402) 474-2345　　　　Fax: (402) 476-8532
E-mail: lcf@lcf.org
Web: www.lcf.org

**Summary** To provide financial assistance to residents of Nebraska (especially women) who are interested in working on an advanced degree in a medical field.

**Eligibility** This program is open to residents of Nebraska who are working on an advanced degree in a medical field (nursing students may apply as undergraduates). Applicants must submit an essay explaining their progress toward completing their education, why they have chosen to prepare for a career in a medical field, and their future career goals once they complete their degree. Preference is given to 1) female applicants; 2) students preparing for careers as physicians and nurses; and 3) applicants who demonstrate financial need.

**Financial data** Stipends provided by the foundation generally range from $500 to $2,000.

**Duration** 1 year; may be renewed.

**Number awarded** 1 or more each year.

**Deadline** May of each year.

## [317]
## LINDY CALLAHAN SCHOLAR ATHLETE

Mississippi High School Activities Association
P.O. Box 127
Clinton, MS 39060
(601) 924-6400　　　　Fax: (601) 924-1725
E-mail: mhsaa@netdoor.com
Web: www.misshsaa.com

**Summary** To provide financial assistance for college to graduating high school scholar-athletes in Mississippi.

**Eligibility** This program is open to seniors graduating from high schools that belong to the Mississippi High School Activities Association. Applicants must be scholar-athletes. Males and females compete separately.

**Financial data** The award is $1,000.

**Duration** These are 1-time awards.

**Number awarded** 16 each year: 1 female and 1 male graduating high school senior in each of the association's 8 districts.

**Deadline** February of each year.

## [318]
## LINLY HEFLIN SCHOLARSHIP

Linly Heflin Unit
c/o Mrs. Beff King, Scholarship Committee Co-Chair
13 Office Park Circle, Suite 8
Birmingham, AL 35223
(205) 870-4192

**Summary** To provide financial assistance to women attending colleges and universities in Alabama.

**Eligibility** This program is open to female residents of Alabama attending accredited 4-year colleges in the state. Applicants must have an ACT score of 22 or higher. U.S. citizenship is required. Selection is based on academic proficiency and financial need.

**Financial data** The stipend is $2,500 per year.

**Duration** 1 year; may be renewed until completion of an undergraduate degree, provided the recipient continues to demonstrate financial need and maintains a GPA of 2.5 or higher.

**Number awarded** A limited number of these scholarships are awarded each year.

**Deadline** January of each year.

## [319]
## LISA MARIE WHALEN MEMORIAL SCHOLARSHIP

Delta Gamma Foundation
Attn: Director of Scholarships, Fellowships and Loans
3250 Riverside Drive
P.O. Box 21397
Columbus, OH 43221-0397
(614) 481-8169　　　　Fax: (614) 481-0133
E-mail: DGScholarships07@aol.com
Web: www.deltagamma.org

**Summary** To provide financial assistance for college to members of Delta Gamma sorority, especially those interested in alcohol/drug education.

**Eligibility** This program is open to initiated members of a collegiate chapter of Delta Gamma in the United States or Canada who have completed 3 semesters or 5 quarters of their college course and have maintained a GPA of 3.0 or higher. Applicants must submit a 1- to 2-page essay in which they introduce themselves, including their career goals, their reasons for applying for this scholarship, and the impact Delta Gamma has had on their life. Selection is based on scholastic excellence and participation in chapter, campus, and community leadership activities. Preference is given to candidates who have been effective in alcohol and/or drug education.

**Financial data** The stipend is $1,000. Funds are sent directly to the university or college to be used for tuition, books, laboratory fees, room, and board. They may not be used for sorority dues, house fees, or other chapter expenses.

**Duration** 1 year.

**Additional information** Information is also available from Betty Plaggemeier, P.O. Box 1492, Cypress, TX 77410-1492, (281) 370-2863.

**Number awarded** 1 each year.

**Deadline** February of each year.

## [320]
## LISA SECHRIST MEMORIAL FOUNDATION SCHOLARSHIP

Lisa Sechrist Memorial Foundation
Attn: Kim Mackmin, Scholarship Selection Committee
Brookfield Homes
8500 Executive Park Avenue, Suite 300
Fairfax, VA 22031
Web: www.lisasechrist.com/scholarship.html

**Summary** To provide financial assistance for college to female high school seniors from Virginia who come from disadvantaged backgrounds.

**Eligibility** This program is open to women graduating from high schools in Virginia who come from a disadvantaged background. Applicants should be able to demonstrate membership in honor societies, participation in sports or other extracurricular activities, citizenship and service within the community, and/or leadership skills within the school or community. Selection is based on merit, integrity, academic potential, and financial need.

**Financial data** The stipend is $2,500 per year.

**Duration** 4 years, provided the recipient maintains a GPA of 2.5 or higher.

**Number awarded** 1 each year.

**Deadline** March of each year.

## [321]
## LOCKHEED MARTIN AERONAUTICS COMPANY SCHOLARSHIPS

Society of Women Engineers
230 East Ohio Street, Suite 400
Chicago, IL 60611-3265
(312) 596-5223          Toll-free: (877) SWE-INFO
Fax: (312) 644-8557
E-mail: scholarshipapplication@swe.org
Web: www.swe.org/scholarships

**Summary** To provide financial assistance to upper-division women majoring in designated engineering specialties.

**Eligibility** This program is open to women who are entering their junior year at an ABET-accredited 4-year college or university. Applicants must be majoring in electrical or mechanical engineering and have a GPA of 3.5 or higher. Along with their application, they must submit a 1-page essay on why they want to be an engineer, how they believe they will make a difference as an engineer, and what influenced them to study engineering. Selection is based on merit.

**Financial data** The stipend is $1,000.

**Duration** 1 year.

**Additional information** This program, established in 1996, is supported by Lockheed Martin Aeronautics Company.

**Number awarded** 2 each year: 1 to a student in electrical engineering and 1 to a student in mechanical engineering.

**Deadline** January of each year.

## [322]
## LOCKHEED MARTIN FOUNDATION SCHOLARSHIPS

Society of Women Engineers
230 East Ohio Street, Suite 400
Chicago, IL 60611-3265
(312) 596-5223          Toll-free: (877) SWE-INFO
Fax: (312) 644-8557
E-mail: scholarshipapplication@swe.org
Web: www.swe.org/scholarships

**Summary** To provide financial assistance to women who will be entering college as freshmen and are interested in studying engineering or computer science.

**Eligibility** This program is open to women who are entering college as freshmen with a GPA of 3.5 or higher. Applicants must be planning to enroll full time at an ABET-accredited 4-year college or university and major in computer science or engineering. Along with their application, they must submit a 1-page essay on why they want to be an engineer or computer scientist, how they believe they will make a difference as an engineer or computer scientist, and what influenced them to study engineering or computer science. Selection is based on merit.

**Financial data** The stipend is $3,000. Also provided is $500 for the recipient to attend the sponsor's annual convention.

**Duration** 1 year.

**Additional information** This program, established in 1996, is supported by Lockheed Martin Foundation.

**Number awarded** 2 each year.

**Deadline** May of each year.

## [323]
## L'OREAL/FAMILY CIRCLE CUP "PERSONAL BEST" SCHOLARSHIP

Family Circle Cup
c/o Family Circle Tennis Center
161 Seven Farms Drive
Charleston, SC 29492
(843) 856-7900          Toll-free: (800) 677-2293
Web: www.familycirclecup.com

**Summary** To provide financial assistance for college to female high school seniors in North Carolina, South Carolina, and Georgia.

**Eligibility** This program is open to women graduating from high schools in North Carolina, South Carolina, and Georgia. Applicants must be planning to enroll full time at an accredited 2-year or 4-year college or university. They must have a GPA of 2.0 or higher and be able to demonstrate that they have made a difference in the lives of others through role modeling, community involvement and services, volunteer experiences, athletics, and extracurricular activities.

**Financial data** The stipend is $2,500.

**Duration** 1 year.

**Additional information** This program was established in 1998. Winners and their families are also invited to attend the Family Circle Cup tennis championship on Daniel Island in Charleston, South Carolina with hotel and travel expenses provided.

**Number awarded** 3 each year: 1 from each of the eligible states.

**Deadline** February of each year.

## [324]
## LOREN W. CROW MEMORIAL SCHOLARSHIP

American Meteorological Society
Attn: Fellowship/Scholarship Program
45 Beacon Street
Boston, MA 02108-3693
(617) 227-2426, ext. 246          Fax: (617) 742-8718
E-mail: scholar@ametsoc.org
Web: www.ametsoc.org

**Summary** To provide financial assistance to undergraduates (particularly women, minorities, and persons with disabilities) majoring in meteorology or an aspect of atmospheric sciences with an interest in applied meteorology.

**Eligibility** This program is open to full-time students entering their final year of undergraduate study and majoring in meteorology or an aspect of the atmospheric or related oceanic and hydrologic sciences. Applicants must intend to make atmospheric or related sciences their career, with preference given to students who have demonstrated a strong interest in applied meteorology. They must be U.S. citizens or permanent residents enrolled at a U.S. institution and have a cumulative GPA of 3.25 or higher. Along with their application, they must submit 200-word essays on 1) their most important achievements that qualify them for this scholarship, and 2) their career goals in the atmospheric or related oceanic or hydrologic fields. Selection is based on academic excellence and achievement; financial need is not considered. The sponsor specifically encourages applications from women, minorities, and students with disabilities who are traditionally underrepresented in the atmospheric and related oceanic sciences.

**Financial data** The stipend is $2,000 per year.

**Duration** 1 year.

**Additional information** Requests for an application must be accompanied by a self-addressed stamped envelope.

**Number awarded** 1 each year.

**Deadline** February of each year.

## [325]
## LOUISE MORITZ MOLITORIS LEADERSHIP AWARD

Women's Transportation Seminar
Attn: National Headquarters
1701 K Street, N.W., Suite 800
Washington, DC 20006
(202) 955-5085          Fax: (202) 955-5088
E-mail: wts@wtsinternational.org
Web: www.wtsinternational.org

**Summary** To provide financial assistance to undergraduate women interested in a career in transportation.

**Eligibility** This program is open to women who are working on an undergraduate degree in transportation or a transportation-related field (e.g., transportation engineering, planning, finance, or logistics). Applicants must have a GPA of 3.0 or higher. Along with their application, they must submit a 500-word statement about their career goals after graduation and why they think they should receive the scholarship award; their statement should specifically address the issue of leadership. Applications must be submitted first to a local chapter; the chapters forward selected applications for consideration on the national level. Minority candidates are encouraged to apply. Selection is based on transportation involvement and goals, job skills, academic record, and leadership potential; financial need is not considered.

**Financial data** The stipend is $3,000.

**Duration** 1 year.

**Additional information** Local chapters may also award additional funding to winners for their area.

**Number awarded** 1 each year.

**Deadline** Applications must be submitted by November to a local WTS chapter.

## [326]
## LOUISIANA STATE FARM SCHOLARSHIP PROGRAM

Louisiana High School Athletic Association
Attn: Commissioner
8075 Jefferson Highway
Baton Rouge, LA 70809-7675
(225) 925-0100          Fax: (225) 925-5901
E-mail: lhsaa@lhsaa.org
Web: www.lhsaa.org/Scholarships.htm

**Summary** To provide financial assistance for college to student-athletes in Louisiana.

**Eligibility** This program is open to student-athletes who are seniors graduating from high schools in Louisiana with a GPA of 3.5 or higher for their first 7 semesters. Applicants must be planning to attend a college or university and be nominated by their principal. They must have participated in 1 of the following 8 sports: girls' volleyball, girls' basketball, girls' softball, girls' track and field, boys' football, boys' basketball, boys' baseball, or boys' track and field. Selection is based on leadership traits, citizenship in school and community, participation in non-athletic school activities and organizations, and non-athletic school honors.

**Financial data** The stipend is $500.

**Duration** 1 year.

**Additional information** This program is sponsored by State Farm Insurance Companies and its Louisiana agents.

**Number awarded** 8 each year: 1 for a participant in each of the qualifying sports.

**Deadline** May of each year.

## [327]
## LOUISIANA VETERANS STATE AID PROGRAM

Louisiana Department of Veterans Affairs
1885 Wooddale Boulevard, Room 1013
P.O. Box 94095, Capitol Station
Baton Rouge, LA 70804-9095
(225) 922-0500          Fax: (225) 922-0511
E-mail: dperkins@vetaffairs.com
Web: www.vetaffairs.com

**Summary** To provide financial assistance for college to children and surviving spouses of certain disabled or deceased Louisiana veterans.

**Eligibility** Eligible under this program are children (between 16 and 25 years of age) of veterans who served during World War I, World War II, the Korean war, or the Vietnam conflict and either died or sustained a disability rated as 90% or more by the U.S. Department of Veterans Affairs. Deceased veterans must have resided in Louisiana for at least 12 months prior to entry into service. Living disabled veterans must have resided in Louisiana for at least 24 months prior to the child's admission into the program. Also eligible are surviving spouses (of any age) of veterans who had been residents of Louisiana for at least 1 year preceding entry into service and who died in war service in the line of duty or from an established wartime service-connected disability subsequently.

**Financial data** Eligible persons accepted as full-time students at Louisiana state-supported colleges, universities, trade schools, or vocational/technical schools will be admitted free and are exempt from payment of all tuition, laboratory, athletic, medical, and other special fees. Free registration does not cover books, supplies, room and board, or fees assessed by the student body on themselves (such as yearbooks and weekly papers).

**Duration** Tuition, fee exemption, and possible payment of cash subsistence allowance are provided for a maximum of 4 school years to be completed in not more than 5 years from date of original entry.

**Additional information** Attendance must be on a full-time basis. Surviving spouses must remain unmarried and must take advantage of the benefit within 10 years after eligibility is established.

**Number awarded** Varies each year.

**Deadline** Applications must be received no later than 3 months prior to the beginning of a semester.

## [328]
## LUCILE B. KAUFMAN WOMEN'S SCHOLARSHIPS

Society of Manufacturing Engineers
Attn: SME Education Foundation
One SME Drive
P.O. Box 930
Dearborn, MI 48121-0930
(313) 425-3300      Toll-free: (800) 733-4763, ext. 3300
Fax: (313) 425-3411      E-mail: foundation@sme.org
Web: www.sme.org

**Summary** To provide financial assistance to undergraduate women enrolled in a degree program in manufacturing engineering or manufacturing engineering technology.

**Eligibility** Applicants must be female students attending a degree-granting institution in North America on a full-time basis and preparing for a career in manufacturing engineering. They must have completed at least 30 units in a manufacturing engineering or manufacturing engineering technology curriculum with a GPA of 3.0 or higher. Along with their application, they must submit a 300-word essay that covers their career and educational objectives, how this scholarship will help them attain those objectives, and why they want to enter this field. Financial need is not considered in the selection process.

**Financial data** The stipend is $1,500.

**Duration** 1 year; may be renewed.

**Number awarded** 1 or 2 each year.

**Deadline** January of each year.

## [329]
## LYDIA I. PICKUP MEMORIAL SCHOLARSHIP

Society of Women Engineers
230 East Ohio Street, Suite 400
Chicago, IL 60611-3265
(312) 596-5223          Toll-free: (877) SWE-INFO
Fax: (312) 644-8557
E-mail: scholarshipapplication@swe.org
Web: www.swe.org/scholarships

**Summary** To provide financial assistance to women working on an undergraduate or graduate degree in engineering or computer science.

**Eligibility** This program is open to women who will be sophomores, juniors, seniors, or graduate students at ABET-accredited colleges and universities. Applicants must be majoring in computer science or engineering and have a GPA of 3.0 or higher. Along with their application, they must submit a 1-page essay on why they want to be an engineer or computer scientist, how they believe they will make a difference as an engineer or computer scientist, and what influenced them to study engineering or computer science. Preference is given to graduate student. Selection is based on merit.

**Financial data** The stipend is $2,000.

**Duration** 1 year.

**Additional information** This program was established in 2001.

**Number awarded** 1 each year.
**Deadline** January of each year.

## [330]
## M. JOSEPHINE O'NEAL ARTS AWARD

Delta Kappa Gamma Society International-Lambda
State Organization
c/o Betty W. Carbol
920 Buena Road
Lake Forest, IL 60045-2927
Web: www.deltakappagamma.org/IL

**Summary** To provide financial assistance to women residents of Illinois who are studying an arts-related field in college.

**Eligibility** This program is open to women residents of Illinois who are in or approaching junior standing at an accredited college or university or in the sophomore year at an accredited community college. Applicants must be majoring in 1 or more areas of the arts, including music, visual arts, dance, theater, and the literary arts. Along with their application, they must submit 1) evidence of the quality and extent of accomplishment in the arts, such as programs of performances, catalogs, articles from the media, published reviews of their work, listings of awards and prizes, or other recognition; 2) samples of their work on 35mm slides, videotapes, or audio tapes; 3) college transcripts; 4) letters of recommendation; and 5) a personal essay on their family, personal interests, awards, achievements, goals (short- and long-term), and philosophy. Selection is based on the essay, letters of recommendation, academic background, and evidence from all sources of potential for contribution to society.

**Financial data** The stipend ranges up to $6,000.

**Duration** 1 year.

**Additional information** The sponsor is an honorary society of women educators.

**Number awarded** 1 each year.

**Deadline** January of each year.

## [331]
## MAIDS OF ATHENA SCHOLARSHIPS

Maids of Athena
1909 Q Street, N.W., Suite 500
Washington, DC 20009-1007
(202) 232-6300                    Fax: (202) 232-2140
Web: www.ahepa.org

**Summary** To provide financial assistance for undergraduate and graduate education to women of Greek descent.

**Eligibility** This program is open to women who are members of the Maids of Athena. Applicants may be a graduating high school senior, an undergraduate student, or a graduate student. Selection is based on academic merit, financial need, and participation in the organization.

**Financial data** The stipend is $1,000.

**Duration** 1 year.

**Additional information** Membership in Maids of Athena is open to unmarried women between 14 and 24 years of age who are of Greek descent from either parent.

**Number awarded** 3 each year: 1 each to a graduating high school senior, undergraduate student, and graduate student.

## [332]
## MAINE BPW CONTINUING EDUCATION SCHOLARSHIP

Maine Federation of Business and Professional Women
Attn: Futurama Foundation
c/o Jeanne L. Hammond, President
RR 1, Box 1610
Albion, ME 04910-9719
(207) 437-2325              E-mail: jlhammon@colby.edu
Web: www.bpwmaine.org/Scholarship.htm

**Summary** To provide financial assistance for college to women in Maine.

**Eligibility** This program is open to women who are residents of Maine. Applicants must be continuing in an accredited program of higher education or job-related training, either full or part time. They must be able to demonstrate financial need.

**Financial data** The stipend is $1,200.

**Duration** 1 year.

**Additional information** Information is also available from Nancy Wadman, Scholarship Chair, BPW Maine Futurama Foundation, 478 Surry Road, Ellsworth, ME 04605.

**Number awarded** 1 or more each year.

**Deadline** March of each year.

## [333]
## MAINE MEDIA WOMEN SCHOLARSHIP

Maine Media Women
c/o Carol Jaeger
P.O. Box 175
Round Pond, ME 04564-0175
(207) 529-5304
Web: www.mainemediawomen.org/scholarships.html

**Summary** To provide financial assistance to women in Maine who are interested in working on an undergraduate or graduate degree in communications.

**Eligibility** This program is open to women of any age who are residents of Maine, will be enrolled in a related college program in the fall, and are interested in preparing for or furthering a career in a media-related area. Their field of study may be art, photography, design and marketing, creative writing, desktop publishing, photojournalism, videography, or communications. Along with their application, they must submit a 1-page essay on their career goals, why they have chosen communications as their field, and how they plan to reach their goals. Selection is based on the essay; academic record; experience, such as internships, volunteering, or part-time work, with the mass media, advertising, or public relations; academic, extracurricular, and public service activities that demonstrate commitment to a career in mass communications; and financial need.

**Financial data** The stipend is $700.

**Duration** 1 year.

**Additional information** Information is also available from Jude Stone, Scholarship Committee Chair, 9 Sanborns Grove Road, Bridgton, ME 04009.

**Number awarded** 1 each year.

**Deadline** March of each year.

## [334]
## MAINE VETERANS DEPENDENTS EDUCATIONAL BENEFITS

Bureau of Veterans' Services
117 State House Station
Augusta, ME 04333-0117
(207) 626-4464　　Toll-free: (800) 345-0116 (within ME)
Fax: (207) 626-4471　　E-mail: mainebvs@maine.gov
Web: www.mainebvs.org/benefits.htm

**Summary** To provide financial assistance for undergraduate or graduate education to dependents of disabled and other Maine veterans.

**Eligibility** Applicants for these benefits must be children (high school seniors or graduates under 25 years of age), non-divorced spouses, or unremarried widow(er)s of veterans who meet 1 or more of the following requirements: 1) living and determined to have a total permanent disability resulting from a service-connected cause; 2) killed in action; 3) died from a service-connected disability; 4) died while totally and permanently disabled due to a service-connected disability but whose death was not related to the service-connected disability; or 5) a member of the armed forces on active duty who has been listed for more than 90 days as missing in action, captured, forcibly detained, or interned in the line of duty by a foreign government or power. The veteran parent must have been a resident of Maine at the time of entry into service or a resident of Maine for 5 years preceding application for these benefits. Children may be seeking no higher than a bachelor's degree. Spouses, widows, and widowers may work on an advanced degree if they already have a bachelor's degree at the time of enrollment into this program.

**Financial data** Recipients are entitled to free tuition at institutions of higher education supported by the state of Maine.

**Duration** Benefits extend for a maximum of 8 semesters. Recipients have 6 consecutive academic years to complete their education.

**Additional information** College preparatory schooling and correspondence courses do not qualify under this program.

**Number awarded** Varies each year.

## [335]
## MAKING A DIFFERENCE SCHOLARSHIP

Royal Neighbors of America
Attn: Fraternal Services
230 16th Street
Rock Island, IL 61201-8645
(309) 788-4561　　　　　　　Toll-free: (800) 627-4762
E-mail: contact@royalneighbors.org
Web: www.royalneighbors.org

**Summary** To provide financial assistance for college to women members of the Royal Neighbors of America who graduate in the top quarter of their high school class.

**Eligibility** These scholarships are provided to students in the top quarter of their senior class with highest national test scores, immediately upon graduation from high school. Applicants must have a qualifying Royal Neighbors beneficial certificate and a record of volunteerism and have been members of the society for at least 2 years.

**Financial data** The stipend is $2,000 per year.

**Duration** 4 years.

**Number awarded** 10 each year.

**Deadline** December of each year.

## [336]
## MARA CRAWFORD PERSONAL DEVELOPMENT SCHOLARSHIP

Kansas Federation of Business & Professional
　　Women's Clubs, Inc.
Attn: Kansas BPW Educational Foundation
c/o Diane Smith, Executive Secretary
10418 Haskins
Lenexa, KS 66215-2162
E-mail: desmith@fcbankonline.com
Web: www.bpwkansas.org

**Summary** To provide financial assistance to women in Kansas who are already in the workforce but are interested in pursuing additional education.

**Eligibility** This program is open to women residents of Kansas who graduated from high school more than 5 years previously and are already in the workforce. Applicants may be seeking a degree in any field of study and may be attending a 2-year, 4-year, vocational, or technological program. They must submit 1) documentation of financial need, and 2) a 3-page personal biography in which they express their career goals, the direction they want to take in the future, their proposed field of study, their reason for selecting that field, the institutions they plan to attend and why, their circumstances for reentering school (if a factor), and what makes them uniquely qualified for this scholarship. Applications must be submitted through a local unit of the sponsor.

**Financial data** A stipend is awarded (amount not specified).

**Duration** 1 year.

**Number awarded** 1 or more each year.

**Deadline** December of each year.

## [337]
## MARIAN MCKEE SMITH–ROSALIE MCKINNEY JACKSON SCHOLARSHIPS

Alpha Chi Omega Foundation
Attn: Foundation Programs Coordinator
5939 Castle Creek Parkway North Drive
Indianapolis, IN 46250-4343
(317) 579-5050, ext. 262　　　　Fax: (317) 579-5051
E-mail: foundation@alphachiomega.org
Web: www.alphachiomega.org

**Summary** To provide financial assistance for college to Alpha Chi Omega members.

**Eligibility** This program is open to full-time junior or senior college women who are members of the sorority.

Selection is based on academic achievement, chapter and campus activity, and leadership.

**Financial data** The stipend is $1,550.

**Duration** 1 year.

**Number awarded** 2 each year.

**Deadline** March of each year.

## [338]
## MARILYNN SMITH SCHOLARSHIP

Ladies Professional Golf Association
Attn: LPGA Foundation
100 International Golf Drive
Daytona Beach, FL 32124-1092
(386) 274-6200                    Fax: (386) 274-1099
E-mail: foundation.scholarships@lpga.com
Web: www.lpga.com/content_1.aspx?mid=6&pid=55

**Summary** To provide financial assistance to female graduating high school seniors who played golf in high school and plan to major in education or business in college.

**Eligibility** This program is open to female high school seniors who have a GPA of 3.2 or higher. Applicants must have played in at least 50% of their high school golf team's scheduled events or have played golf "regularly" for the past 2 years. They must be planning to attend a college or university in the continental United States, major in business or education, and play collegiate golf. Along with their application, they must submit a letter that describes how golf has been an integral part of their lives and includes their personal and professional goals, their chosen discipline of study, and how this scholarship will be of assistance. Financial need is not considered in the selection process.

**Financial data** The stipend is $3,000.

**Duration** 1 year.

**Number awarded** 1 each year.

**Deadline** June of each year.

## [339]
## MARINE CORPS COUNTERINTELLIGENCE ASSOCIATION SCHOLARSHIPS

Marine Corps Counterintelligence Association
c/o Samuel L. Moyer
3125 Palmdale Drive
Oldsmar, FL 34677
E-mail: scholarship@mccia.org
Web: www.mccia.org

**Summary** To provide financial assistance for college to dependents of members of the Marine Corps Counterintelligence Association (MCCIA).

**Eligibility** This program is open to children, grandchildren, and spouses of 1) current MCCIA members; 2) deceased Marines who were MCCIA members at the time of death; and 3) counterintelligence Marines who lost their lives in the line of duty (whether they were a member of MCCIA or not). Spouses of deceased Marines must also be MCCIA Auxiliary members. Applicants must be enrolled or planning to enroll as a full-time undergraduate student at an accredited college or university. Along with their application, they must submit a 1-page essay on a topic of their choice, letters of recommendation, SAT or ACT scores, transcripts, copies of awards and other honors, and evi-

dence of acceptance at a college or university. Financial need is not considered.

**Financial data** Stipends are $1,000 or $500. Funds must be used to help pay for tuition, books, fees, and materials; they may not be used for personal or living expenses.

**Duration** 1 year; may be renewed up to 3 additional years (need not be consecutive).

**Number awarded** Varies each year; recently, 5 of these scholarships, at $1,000 each, were awarded.

**Deadline** June of each year.

## [340]
## MARION DAY MULLINS SCHOLARSHIP

Kappa Delta Sorority
Attn: Foundation Manager
3205 Players Lane
Memphis, TN 38125
(901) 748-1897                    Toll-free: (800) 536-1897
Fax: (901) 748-0949
E-mail: kappadelta@kappadelta.org
Web: www.kappadelta.org

**Summary** To provide financial assistance to members of Kappa Delta Sorority who are majoring in business.

**Eligibility** This program is open to undergraduate members of Kappa Delta Sorority. Applicants must submit a personal statement giving their reasons for applying for this scholarship, an official undergraduate transcript, and 2 letters of recommendation. They must be majoring in business, including accounting, economics, finance, and marketing. Selection is based on academic excellence, service to the chapter and university, service to the community, personal objectives and goals, potential, recommendations, and financial need.

**Financial data** The stipend is $1,000 per year. Funds may be used only for tuition, fees, and books, not for room and board.

**Duration** 1 year; may be renewed.

**Number awarded** 1 each year.

**Deadline** January of each year.

## [341]
## MARK J. SCHROEDER ENDOWED SCHOLARSHIP IN METEOROLOGY

American Meteorological Society
Attn: Fellowship/Scholarship Program
45 Beacon Street
Boston, MA 02108-3693
(617) 227-2426, ext. 246                    Fax: (617) 742-8718
E-mail: scholar@ametsoc.org
Web: www.ametsoc.org

**Summary** To provide financial assistance to undergraduate students (particularly women, minority, and disabled students) majoring in meteorology or some aspect of atmospheric sciences who demonstrate financial need.

**Eligibility** This program is open to full-time students entering their final year of undergraduate study and majoring in meteorology or an aspect of the atmospheric or related oceanic and hydrologic sciences. Applicants must intend to make atmospheric or related sciences their career. They must be U.S. citizens or permanent residents enrolled at a U.S. institution and have a cumulative GPA of 3.25 or higher. Along with their application, they must submit 200-word essays on 1) their most important achievements that qualify them for this scholarship, and 2) their career goals in the atmospheric or related oceanic or hydrologic fields. Selection is based on academic achievement and financial need. The sponsor specifically encourages applications from women, minorities, and students with disabilities who are traditionally underrepresented in the atmospheric and related oceanic sciences.

**Financial data**  The stipend is $5,000.

**Duration**  1 year.

**Additional information**  This scholarship was established in 1995. Requests for an application must be accompanied by a self-addressed stamped envelope.

**Number awarded**  1 each year.

**Deadline**  February of each year.

## [342]
## MARTHA AND DON ROMEO SCHOLARSHIPS

Nebraska Association of Fair Managers
c/o Stan Brodine
15095 39th Road
Kearney, NE 68845-0666
(308) 234-9449
Web: www.nefairs.org

**Summary**  To provide financial assistance for college to members of 4-H in Nebraska who have participated in county or state fairs.

**Eligibility**  This program is open to seniors graduating from high schools in Nebraska who are members of 4-H. Applicants must have exhibited a project in a county fair or at the state fair within the last 4 years. They must have a GPA of 2.5 or higher and be planning to attend a 2-year or 4-year college or university as a full-time student. Along with their application, they must submit a 250-word essay on how their experience in 4-H will help them achieve their future goals. Selection is based on experiences in 4-H projects and activities (60%), citizenship and community service (25%), and future goals (15%). Financial need is not considered. Separate awards are made to males and females.

**Financial data**  The stipend is $500.

**Duration**  1 year.

**Number awarded**  2 each year: 1 to a male and 1 to a female.

**Deadline**  Applications must be submitted to the 4-H award committee in each local county extension office by November of each year.

## [343]
## MARTHA STICKLAND SCHOLARSHIP

Epsilon Sigma Alpha
Attn: ESA Foundation Assistant Scholarship Director
P.O. Box 270517
Fort Collins, CO 80527
(970) 223-2824                    Fax: (970) 223-4456
Web: www.esaintl.com/esaf

**Summary**  To provide financial assistance for college to women from Florida who are seeking retraining.

**Eligibility**  This program is open to women who are current or former residents of Florida returning to college. Applicants must be seeking to 1) receive retraining due to company downsizing or 2) reenter the workforce. Selection is based on character (10%), leadership (20%), service (10%), financial need (30%), and scholastic ability (30%).

**Financial data**  The stipend is $537.

**Duration**  1 year; may be renewed.

**Additional information**  Epsilon Sigma Alpha (ESA) is a women's service organization. Information is also available from Lynn Hughes, Scholarship Director, 324 N.E. Mead, Grants Pass, OR 97526, (541) 476-4617. This scholarship was first awarded in 1999. Completed applications must be submitted to the ESA State Counselor who verifies the information before forwarding them to the scholarship director. A $5 processing fee is required.

**Number awarded**  1 each year.

**Deadline**  January of each year.

## [344]
## MARY BARRETT MARSHALL SCHOLARSHIP

American Legion Auxiliary
Attn: Department of Kentucky
105 North Public Square
P.O. Box 189
Greensburg, KY 42743-1530
(270) 932-7533                    Fax: (270) 932-7672
E-mail: secretarykyala@aol.com

**Summary**  To provide financial assistance for college to female dependents of veterans in Kentucky.

**Eligibility**  This program is open to the daughters, wives, sisters, widows, granddaughters, or great-granddaughters of veterans eligible for membership in the American Legion who are high school seniors or graduates and 5-year residents of Kentucky. Applicants must be planning to attend a college or university in Kentucky.

**Financial data**  The stipend is $500. The funds may be used for tuition, registration fees, laboratory fees, and books, but not for room and board.

**Duration**  1 year.

**Additional information**  Further information is also available from Chair, Velma Greenleaf, 1448 Leafdale Road, Hodgenville, KY 42748-9379, (270) 358-3341. Requests for applications must be accompanied by a self-addressed stamped envelope.

**Number awarded**  1 each year.

**Deadline**  March of each year.

## [345]
## MARY CRAIG SCHOLARSHIP FOR WOMEN IN TRANSITION

American Society of Women Accountants-Billings Big Sky Chapter
c/o Cherie Curry, Scholarship Chair
P.O. Box 20593
Billings, MT 59104

**Summary**  To provide financial assistance to women in Montana who are returning to school to work on an undergraduate degree in accounting.

**Eligibility** This program is open to women in Montana who are incoming freshmen, currently enrolled, or returning to school with sufficient credits to qualify for freshman status. Applicants must be women who are single, divorced, or widowed and have become the sole source of support for themselves and their family. They must wish to work on a degree in accounting as a means to gainful employment. Selection is based on commitment to the goal of working on a degree in accounting, including evidence of continued commitment after receiving this award; aptitude for accounting and business; clear evidence that the candidate has established goals and a plan for achieving those goals, both personal and professional; and financial need.

**Financial data** The stipend is $1,500.

**Duration** 1 year.

**Number awarded** 1 each year.

**Deadline** February of each year.

## [346]
## MARY CRAIG SCHOLARSHIP FUND

American Society of Women Accountants-Billings Big
    Sky Chapter
c/o Cherie Curry, Scholarship Chair
P.O. Box 20593
Billings, MT 59104

**Summary** To provide financial assistance to women working on a bachelor's or master's degree in accounting at a college or university in Montana.

**Eligibility** This program is open to women working on a bachelor's or master's degree in accounting at an accredited Montana college, university, or professional school of accounting. Applicants must have completed at least 60 semester hours. Selection is based on career goals, communication skills, GPA, personal circumstances, and financial need. Membership in the American Society of Women Accountants (ASWA) is not required.

**Financial data** The stipend is $1,500.

**Duration** 1 year.

**Number awarded** 1 each year.

**Deadline** February of each year.

## [347]
## MARY FRANCES GUILBERT MARIANI–BIGLER CONTINUING EDUCATION GRANT

Alpha Chi Omega Foundation
Attn: Foundation Programs Coordinator
5939 Castle Creek Parkway North Drive
Indianapolis, IN 46250-4343
(317) 579-5050, ext. 262        Fax: (317) 579-5051
E-mail: foundation@alphachiomega.org
Web: www.alphachiomega.org

**Summary** To provide financial assistance for college to reentry women who are members of Alpha Chi Omega.

**Eligibility** Members of Alpha Chi Omega who are 30 years of age or older are eligible to apply for this support if they are in need of financial assistance to resume their education due to changing demands in their lives.

**Financial data** Up to $3,000 in awards is available each year.

**Duration** 1 year.

**Number awarded** Varies each year; recently, 2 of these grants were awarded.

**Deadline** Applications may be submitted at any time.

## [348]
## MARY LOU HENTGES SCHOLARSHIP

National Federation of the Blind of Missouri
c/o Gary Wunder, President
3910 Tropical Lane
Columbia, MO 65202-6205
(573) 874-1774        Toll-free: (888) 604-1774
E-mail: info@nfbmo.org
Web: www.nfbmo.org

**Summary** To provide financial assistance for undergraduate or graduate study to blind female students in Missouri.

**Eligibility** This program is open to legally blind women residents of Missouri who are working on or planning to work on an undergraduate or graduate degree. Preference is given to applicants working on a degree in a field related to the home or to children.

**Financial data** The maximum stipend is $500.

**Duration** 1 year.

**Additional information** Additional information is also available from Chair, Achievement Awards Committee, Sheila Koenig, 634 South National, Apartment 303, Springfield, MO 65804, (417) 869-1078.

**Number awarded** 1 each year.

**Deadline** February of each year.

## [349]
## MARY MACON MCGUIRE EDUCATIONAL GRANT

Virginia Federation of Women's Clubs
Attn: Scholarships/Fellowships/Loan Committee
513 Forest Avenue
P.O. Box 8750
Richmond, VA 23226
(804) 288-3724        Toll-free: (800) 699-8392
Fax: (804) 288-0341
E-mail: h.vfwcofgfwc@verizon.net
Web: www.gfwcvirginia.org

**Summary** To provide financial assistance to women heads of households in Virginia who have returned to school.

**Eligibility** This program is open to women residents of Virginia who are heads of households. Applicants must be currently enrolled in a course of study (vocational or academic) at an accredited Virginia school. They must have returned to school to upgrade their education and employment skills in order to better provide for their families. Selection is based on 3 letters of recommendation (1 of a general nature, 2 from recent professors, teachers, counselors, or advisors); a resume of educational and employment history, financial circumstances, and community activities; and an essay that outlines the financial need for the grant as well as the reasons for entering the field of study selected.

**Financial data** The stipend is $5,000. Funds are paid directly to the student.

**Duration** 1 year.

**Additional information** This program began in 1929 as a loan fund. It was converted to its current form in 2000.

**Number awarded** 1 each year.

**Deadline** March of each year.

## [350]
## MARY PAOLOZZI MEMBER'S SCHOLARSHIP

Navy Wives Club of America
P.O. Box 54022
Millington, TN 38053-6022
Toll-free: (866) 511-NWCA
E-mail: nwca@navywivesclubsofamerica.org
Web: www.navywivesclubsofamerica.org

**Summary** To provide financial assistance for undergraduate or graduate study to members of the Navy Wives' Club of America (NWCA).

**Eligibility** This program is open to NWCA members who can demonstrate financial need. Applicants must be 1) a high school graduate or senior planning to attend college full time next year; 2) currently enrolled in an undergraduate program and planning to continue as a full-time undergraduate; 3) a college graduate or senior planning to be a full-time graduate student next year; and 4) a high school graduate or GED recipient planning to attend vocational or business school next year.

**Financial data** Stipends range from $500 to $1,000 each year (depending upon the donations from the NWCA chapters).

**Duration** 1 year.

**Additional information** Information is also available from Denise Johnson, NWCA National President, 534 Madrona Street, Chula Vista, CA 91910. Membership in the NWCA is open to spouses of enlisted personnel serving in the Navy, Marine Corps, Coast Guard, and the active Reserve units of those services; spouses of enlisted personnel who have been honorable discharged, retired, or transferred to the Fleet Reserve on completion of duty; and widows of enlisted personnel in those services.

**Number awarded** 1 or more each year.

**Deadline** May of each year.

## [351]
## MARY RUBIN AND BENJAMIN M. RUBIN SCHOLARSHIP FUND

Central Scholarship Bureau
Pomona Square
1700 Reisterstown Road, Suite 220
Baltimore, MD 21208-2903
(410) 415-5558                    Fax: (410) 415-5501
E-mail: info@centralsb.org
Web: www.centralsb.org/html/rubin.htm

**Summary** To provide financial assistance for college to women in Maryland.

**Eligibility** This program is open to women residents of Maryland who have a GPA of 3.0 or higher. Applicants must have been out of high school for at least 12 months and must meet specified financial guidelines. For dependent applicants, combined adjusted gross income of parents must be less than $50,000 with an additional $7,500 for each dependent; for married applicants, combined household adjusted gross income must be less than $50,000 with an additional $7,500 for each dependent; for single applicants,

maximum adjusted gross income is $30,000 with an additional $10,000 for each dependent. Selection is based on academic achievement, extracurricular activities, and financial need.

**Financial data** Stipends range from $500 to $2,500 per year. Funds may be used to pay tuition only.

**Duration** 1 year. May be renewed up to 4 additional years. Renewal applicants who maintain a GPA of 3.0 or higher are given preference over new applicants.

**Additional information** This nonsectarian fund, established in 1988, is administered by the Central Scholarship Bureau for the Jewish Community Federation of Baltimore.

**Deadline** February of each year.

## [352]
## MARY V. MUNGER MEMORIAL SCHOLARSHIP

Society of Women Engineers
230 East Ohio Street, Suite 400
Chicago, IL 60611-3265
(312) 596-5223                    Toll-free: (877) SWE-INFO
Fax: (312) 644-8557
E-mail: scholarshipapplication@swe.org
Web: www.swe.org/scholarships

**Summary** To provide financial assistance to undergraduate women majoring in computer science or engineering.

**Eligibility** This program is open to women who are entering their sophomore, junior, or senior year at a 4-year ABET-accredited college or university. Applicants must be majoring in computer science or engineering and have a GPA of 3.0 or higher. Along with their application, they must submit a 1-page essay on why they want to be an engineer or computer scientist, how they believe they will make a difference as an engineer or computer scientist, and what influenced them to study engineering or computer science. Selection is based on merit.

**Financial data** The stipend is $4,000.

**Duration** 1 year.

**Number awarded** 1 each year.

**Deadline** January of each year.

## [353]
## MARYLAND LEGION AUXILIARY CHILDREN AND YOUTH FUND SCHOLARSHIP

American Legion Auxiliary
Attn: Department of Maryland
1589 Sulphur Spring Road, Suite 105
Baltimore, MD 21227
(410) 242-9519                    Fax: (410) 242-9553
E-mail: anna@alamd.org

**Summary** To provide financial assistance for college to the daughters of veterans who are Maryland residents and wish to study arts, sciences, business, public administration, education, or a medical field.

**Eligibility** Eligible for this scholarship are Maryland senior high girls with veteran parents who wish to study arts, sciences, business, public administration, education, or a medical field other than nursing at a college or university in the state. Preference is given to children of members of the American Legion or American Legion Auxiliary. Selection is based on character (30%), Americanism (20%), leadership (10%), scholarship (20%), and financial need (20%).

**Financial data** The stipend is $2,000.

**Duration** 1 year; may be renewed up to 3 additional years.

**Number awarded** 1 each year.

**Deadline** April of each year.

## [354]
## MARYLAND LEGION AUXILIARY PAST PRESIDENTS' PARLEY NURSING SCHOLARSHIP

American Legion Auxiliary
Attn: Department of Maryland
1589 Sulphur Spring Road, Suite 105
Baltimore, MD 21227
(410) 242-9519          Fax: (410) 242-9553
E-mail: anna@alamd.org

**Summary** To provide financial assistance for nursing education to the female descendants of Maryland veterans.

**Eligibility** This program is open to Maryland residents who are the daughters, granddaughters, great-granddaughters, step-daughters, step-granddaughters, or step-great-granddaughters of ex-servicewomen (or of ex-servicemen, if there are no qualified descendants of ex-servicewomen). Applicants must be interested in becoming a registered nurse and be able to show financial need. They must submit a 300-word essay on the topic "What a Nursing Career Means to Me."

**Financial data** The stipend is $2,000. Funds are sent directly to the recipient's school.

**Duration** 1 year; may be renewed for up to 3 additional years if the recipient remains enrolled full time.

**Number awarded** 1 each year.

**Deadline** April of each year.

## [355]
## MARYLAND SPACE SCHOLARS PROGRAM

Maryland Space Grant Consortium
c/o Johns Hopkins University
203 Bloomberg Center for Physics and Astronomy
3400 North Charles Street
Baltimore, MD 21218-2686
(410) 516-7351          Fax: (410) 516-4109
E-mail: info@mdspacegrant.org
Web: www.mdspacegrant.org/scholars_about.html

**Summary** To provide financial assistance to undergraduate students (particularly women, minority, and disabled students) who are interested in studying space-related fields at selected universities in Maryland that are members of the Maryland Space Grant Consortium.

**Eligibility** This program is open to residents of Maryland and graduates of Maryland high schools who are enrolled full time at a member institution. Applicants must be interested in preparing for a career in mathematics, science, engineering, technology, or a space-related field. They must be majoring in a relevant field, including (but not limited to) astronomy, the biological and life sciences, chemistry, computer science, engineering, geological sciences, or physics. U.S. citizenship is required. Along with their application, they must submit an essay of 200 to 500 words on how this

scholarship will help them meet their educational and financial goals. This program is a component of the U.S. National Aeronautics and Space Administration (NASA) Space Grant program, which encourages participation by women, underrepresented minorities, and persons with disabilities.

**Financial data** Scholars receive partial payment of tuition at the participating university they attend.

**Duration** 1 year; may be renewed if the recipient maintains a GPA of 3.0 or higher.

**Additional information** The participating universities are Hagerstown Community College, Johns Hopkins University, Morgan State University, Towson University, the University of Maryland at College Park, and Washington College. Funding for this program is provided by NASA.

**Number awarded** Varies each year; recently 16 of these scholarships were awarded (2 at Johns Hopkins University, 5 at Morgan State University, 2 at Hagerstown Community College, 2 at Towson University, and 5 at the University of Maryland at College Park).

**Deadline** August of each year.

## [356]
## MASSACHUSETTS EDUCATIONAL ASSISTANCE FUND

Massachusetts Federation of Business and
    Professional Women's Clubs, Inc.
c/o Patricia Stowell, President
University of Massachusetts
530 Goodell Building
140 Hicks Way
Amherst, MA 01003-9333
(413) 545-0721          E-mail: pstowell@resgs.umass.edu
Web: www.bpwma.org/MEAF.html

**Summary** To provide financial assistance to members of the Massachusetts Federation of Business and Professional Women's Clubs (BPW/MA) who are interested in additional training to improve their marketability and professional opportunities.

**Eligibility** Applicants must have been members of the BPW/MA for at least 24 months. They must be seeking funding for 1 or more of the following activities: refresher courses, seminars in advanced theory and training in connection with their current position, courses that will lead to a new career, courses to fulfill certification requirements, upgrading of present skills, acquisition of a degree to keep their current position or to be eligible for promotion, or any other activity in connection with education or upgrading of skills that will lead to advancement. Financial need is considered in the selection process.

**Financial data** The maximum stipend is $500.

**Duration** A period of 2 consecutive years must elapse before a grantee may reapply.

**Number awarded** Varies each year.

**[357]**
## MASSACHUSETTS YOUTH SOCCER STUDENT-ATHLETE SCHOLARSHIPS

Mass Youth Soccer
2444 Old Union Turnpike
Lancaster, MA 01523
(978) 466-8812          Toll-free: (800) 852-8111
Fax: (978) 466-8817
Web: www.mayouthsoccer.org

**Summary**  To provide financial assistance for college to high school seniors in Massachusetts who have been involved in soccer.

**Eligibility**  This program is open to college-bound seniors graduating from high schools in Massachusetts who have been registered players with Mass Youth Soccer for at least the past 2 years. Applicants must submit a 500-word essay on their soccer career thus far and what they have learned that they will be able to apply to their future endeavors. Selection is based on the essay, extracurricular activities, volunteer and community service work, academic awards, and athletic awards. Financial need is not considered. Males and females are considered separately.

**Financial data**  The stipend is $1,000.

**Duration**  1 year.

**Number awarded**  2 each year: 1 male and 1 female.

**Deadline**  March of each year.

**[358]**
## MASWE SCHOLARSHIP

Society of Women Engineers
230 East Ohio Street, Suite 400
Chicago, IL 60611-3265
(312) 596-5223          Toll-free: (877) SWE-INFO
Fax: (312) 644-8557
E-mail: scholarshipapplication@swe.org
Web: www.swe.org/scholarships

**Summary**  To provide financial assistance to undergraduate women majoring in computer science or engineering.

**Eligibility**  This program is open to women who are entering their sophomore, junior, or senior year at a 4-year ABET-accredited college or university. Applicants must be majoring in computer science or engineering and have a GPA of 3.0 or higher. Along with their application, they must submit a 1-page essay on why they want to be an engineer or computer scientist, how they believe they will make a difference as an engineer or computer scientist, and what influenced them to study engineering or computer science. Financial need is considered in the selection process.

**Financial data**  The stipend is $2,000.

**Duration**  1 year.

**Additional information**  These scholarships were established by the Men's Auxiliary of the Society of Women Engineers (MASWE) in 1971 and are continued through a fund established by the organization when it disbanded in 1976 (effective with the opening of Society of Women Engineer's membership to men).

**Number awarded**  4 each year.

**Deadline**  January of each year.

**[359]**
## MENTOR GRAPHICS SCHOLARSHIPS

Oregon Student Assistance Commission
Attn: Grants and Scholarships Division
1500 Valley River Drive, Suite 100
Eugene, OR 97401-2146
(541) 687-7395          Toll-free: (800) 452-8807, ext. 7395
Fax: (541) 687-7419
E-mail: awardinfo@mercury.osac.state.or.us
Web: www.osac.state.or.us

**Summary**  To provide financial assistance to Oregon residents (particularly women and minorities) who are working on a college degree in computer science or engineering.

**Eligibility**  This program is open to residents of Oregon who are U.S. citizens or permanent residents. Applicants must be full-time students in their junior or senior year of college and majoring in electrical engineering or computer science/engineering. Preference is given to female, African American, Native American, or Hispanic applicants. Financial need must be demonstrated.

**Financial data**  The stipend is at least $2,000.

**Duration**  1 year.

**Number awarded**  Varies each year; recently, 4 of these scholarships were awarded.

**Deadline**  February of each year.

**[360]**
## MERIDITH THOMS MEMORIAL SCHOLARSHIPS

Society of Women Engineers
230 East Ohio Street, Suite 400
Chicago, IL 60611-3265
(312) 596-5223          Toll-free: (877) SWE-INFO
Fax: (312) 644-8557
E-mail: scholarshipapplication@swe.org
Web: www.swe.org/scholarships

**Summary**  To provide financial assistance to undergraduate women majoring in computer science or engineering.

**Eligibility**  This program is open to women who are entering their sophomore, junior, or senior year at a 4-year ABET-accredited college or university. Applicants must be majoring in computer science or engineering and have a GPA of 3.0 or higher. Along with their application, they must submit a 1-page essay on why they want to be an engineer or computer scientist, how they believe they will make a difference as an engineer or computer scientist, and what influenced them to study engineering or computer science. Selection is based on merit.

**Financial data**  The stipend is $2,000.

**Duration**  1 year.

**Additional information**  This program was established in 2001.

**Number awarded**  6 each year.

**Deadline**  January of each year.

## [361]
## MHSAA SCHOLAR-ATHLETE AWARDS

Michigan High School Athletic Association
1661 Ramblewood Drive
East Lansing, MI 48823-7392
(517) 332-5046                    Fax: (517) 332-4071
E-mail: afrushour@mhsaa.com
Web: www.mhsaa.com/recognition/sahome.htm

**Summary** To provide financial assistance for college to seniors who have participated in athletics at high schools that are members of the Michigan High School Athletic Association (MHSAA).

**Eligibility** This program is open to seniors graduating from high schools that are members of the MHSAA. Applicants must be planning to attend an accredited college, university, or trade school and have a GPA of 3.5 or higher. They must have won a varsity letter in 1 of the following 28 sports in which post-season tournaments are sponsored by MHSAA: baseball, boys' and girls' basketball, boys' and girls' bowling, girls' competitive cheer, boys' and girls' cross country, football, boys' and girls' golf, girls' gymnastics, ice hockey, boys' and girls' lacrosse, boys' and girls' soccer, softball, boys' and girls' skiing, boys' and girls' swimming and diving, boys' and girls' tennis, boys' and girls' track and field, girls' volleyball, and wrestling. Along with their application, they must submit a 500-word essay on the importance of sportsmanship in educational athletics. Selection is based on the essay, involvement in other school-sponsored activities, involvement in activities outside of school, and 2 letters of recommendation.

**Financial data** The stipend is $1,000.

**Duration** 1 year; nonrenewable.

**Additional information** This program is sponsored by Farm Bureau Insurance.

**Number awarded** 32 each year: 12 from Class A schools (6 boys and 6 girls), 8 from Class B schools (4 boys and 4 girls), 6 from Class C schools (3 boys and 3 girls), 4 from Class D schools (2 boys and 2 girls), and 2 selected at large to minority students.

**Deadline** Students must submit applications to their school by November of each year. The number of nominations each school may submit depends on the size of the school; Class A schools may nominate 6 boys and 6 girls, Class B schools may nominate 4 boys and 4 girls, Class C schools may nominate 3 boys and 3 girls, and Class D schools may nominate 2 boys and 2 girls.

## [362]
## MICHAEL AXE/FIRST STATE ORTHOPAEDICS SCHOLARSHIPS

Delaware Women's Alliance for Sport and Fitness
c/o Evelyn Campbell, Scholarship Committee Chair
Howard High School of Technology
401 East 12th Street
Wilmington, DE 19801
(302) 571-5422          E-mail: scholarships@dwasf.org
Web: wwww.dwasf.org/scholarships.html

**Summary** To provide financial assistance to female graduating high school seniors in Delaware who have significantly contributed to sports at the varsity level.

**Eligibility** This program is open to female high school seniors in Delaware who have a GPA of 3.0 or higher and have participated in at least 1 varsity sport. Applicants must submit 1) a student profile describing their sports participation, school activities, community activities, and career objectives; 2) a short paragraph describing why they feel they are deserving of this scholarship; and 3) 3 letters of recommendation. Financial need is not considered in the selection process.

**Financial data** The stipend ranges from $500 to $1,000.

**Duration** 1 year.

**Number awarded** 2 each year: 1 to a student from north of the canal and 1 to a student from south of the canal.

**Deadline** April of each year.

## [363]
## MICHAEL BAKER CORPORATION SCHOLARSHIP PROGRAM FOR DIVERSITY IN ENGINEERING

Association of Independent Colleges and Universities
    of Pennsylvania
101 North Front Street
Harrisburg, PA 17101-1405
(717) 232-8649                    Fax: (717) 233-8574
E-mail: info@aicup.org
Web: www.aicup.org

**Summary** To provide financial assistance to women and minority students at member institutions of the Association of Independent Colleges and Universities of Pennsylvania (AICUP) who are majoring in designated fields of engineering.

**Eligibility** This program is open to full-time undergraduate students at designated AICUP colleges and universities who are women and/or members of the following minority groups: American Indians, Alaska Natives, Asians, Blacks/African Americans, Hispanics/Latinos, Native Hawaiians, or Pacific Islanders. Applicants must be juniors majoring in architectural, civil, or environmental engineering with a GPA of 3.0 or higher. Along with their application, they must submit an essay on what they believe will be the greatest challenge facing the engineering profession over the next decade, and why.

**Financial data** The stipend is $1,000 per year.

**Duration** 1 year; may be renewed 1 additional year if the recipient maintains appropriate academic standards.

**Additional information** This program, sponsored by the Michael Baker Corporation, is available at the following AICUP colleges and universities: Bucknell University, Carnegie Mellon University, Drexel University, Gannon University, Geneva College, Grove City College, Lafayette College, Lehigh University, Messiah College, Swarthmore College, Villanova University, Widener University, and Wilkes University.

**Number awarded** 1 each year.

**Deadline** April of each year.

## [364]
## MICHIGAN LEGION AUXILIARY MEDICAL CAREER SCHOLARSHIP

American Legion Auxiliary
Attn: Department of Michigan
212 North Verlinden Street
Lansing, MI 48915
(517) 371-4720                    Fax: (517) 371-2401
E-mail: michalaux@voyager.net
Web: www.michalaux.org/Scholarships.htm

**Summary** To provide financial assistance for college to Michigan veterans' dependents and descendants who are interested in preparing for careers in nursing, physical therapy, or respiratory therapy.

**Eligibility** This program is open to the daughters, granddaughters, great-granddaughters, sons, grandsons, great-grandsons, wives, and widows of honorably-discharged or deceased veterans of World War I, World War II, Korea, Vietnam, Grenada, Lebanon, Panama, or the Persian Gulf. They must be in the top quarter of their class, in financial need, and residents of Michigan at the time of application and for 1 year preceding the date of the award. Applicants must be willing to train as a registered nurse, licensed practical nurse, physical therapist, or respiratory therapist at a school in Michigan.

**Financial data** The stipend is $500.

**Duration** 1 year.

**Additional information** Information is also available from Jacklyn Skinner, 339 Tulip Drive, Schoolcraft, MI 49087. The grant, paid directly to the recipient's school, may be used for tuition, room and board, fees, books, and supplies for the first year of study at a Michigan school of nursing, physical therapy, or respiratory therapy.

**Number awarded** 3 each year: 1 each for nursing, physical therapy, and respiratory therapy.

**Deadline** March of each year.

## [365]
## MICHIGAN LEGION AUXILIARY MEMORIAL SCHOLARSHIP

American Legion Auxiliary
Attn: Department of Michigan
212 North Verlinden Street
Lansing, MI 48915
(517) 371-4720                    Fax: (517) 371-2401
E-mail: michalaux@voyager.net
Web: www.michalaux.org/Scholarships.htm

**Summary** To provide financial assistance for college to wartime veterans' female descendants who are Michigan residents.

**Eligibility** This program is open to the daughters, granddaughters, and great-granddaughters of honorably-discharged or deceased veterans of World War I, World War II, Korea, Vietnam, Grenada, Lebanon, Panama, or the Persian Gulf who are between 16 and 21 years of age. Applicants must be residents of Michigan at the time of application and for 1 year preceding the date of the award. Selection is based on financial need and scholastic standing.

**Financial data** The stipend is $500. The grant, payable in 2 installments of $250 each, may be used for tuition, room and board, fees, books, or supplies necessary for study at

any school, college, or other educational institution in Michigan. Funds are sent directly to the financial aid office of the school.

**Duration** 1 year; may be renewed 1 additional year.

**Additional information** Information is also available from Reina Svacha, 16371 Forest Way, Macomb, MI 48042-2352.

**Number awarded** Varies each year.

**Deadline** March of each year.

## [366]
## MICROSOFT CORPORATION SCHOLARSHIPS

Society of Women Engineers
230 East Ohio Street, Suite 400
Chicago, IL 60611-3265
(312) 596-5223                    Toll-free: (877) SWE-INFO
Fax: (312) 644-8557
E-mail: scholarshipapplication@swe.org
Web: www.swe.org/scholarships

**Summary** To provide financial assistance to women working on an undergraduate or graduate degree in computer engineering or computer science.

**Eligibility** This program is open to women who will be sophomores, juniors, seniors, or first year master's degree students at ABET-accredited colleges and universities. Applicants must be majoring in computer science or engineering and have a GPA of 3.5 or higher. Along with their application, they must submit a 1-page essay on why they want to be an engineer or computer scientist, how they believe they will make a difference as an engineer or computer scientist, and what influenced them to study engineering or computer science. Selection is based on merit.

**Financial data** The stipend is $2,500.

**Duration** 1 year.

**Additional information** This program, established in 1994, is sponsored by Microsoft Corporation.

**Number awarded** 2 each year.

**Deadline** January of each year.

## [367]
## MICROSOFT NATIONAL SCHOLARSHIPS

Microsoft Corporation
Attn: National Minority Technical Scholarship
One Microsoft Way
Redmond, WA 98052-8303
(425) 882-8080                    TTY: (800) 892-9811
E-mail: scholars@microsoft.com
Web: www.microsoft.com/college/ss_overview.mspx

**Summary** To provide financial assistance and summer work experience to undergraduate students, especially members of underrepresented groups, interested in preparing for a career in computer science or other related technical fields.

**Eligibility** This program is open to students who are enrolled full time and making satisfactory progress toward an undergraduate degree in computer science, computer engineering, or a related technical discipline (such as electrical engineering, mathematics, or physics) with a demonstrated interest in computer science. Applicants must be enrolled at a 4-year college or university in the United

States, Canada, or Mexico. They must have a GPA of 3.0 or higher. Although all students who meet the eligibility criteria may apply, a large majority of scholarships are awarded to women, underrepresented minorities (African Americans, Hispanics, and Native Americans), and students with disabilities. Along with their application, students must submit an essay that describes the following 4 items: 1) how they demonstrate their passion for technology outside the classroom; 2) the toughest technical problem they have worked on, how they addressed the problem, their role in reaching the outcome if it was team-based, and the final outcome; 3) a situation that demonstrates initiative and their willingness to go above and beyond; and 4) how they are currently funding their college education.

**Financial data** Scholarships cover 100% of the tuition as posted by the financial aid office of the university or college the recipient designates. Scholarships are made through that school and are not transferable to other academic institutions. Funds may be used for tuition only and may not be used for other costs on the recipient's bursar bill, such as room and board.

**Duration** 1 year.

**Additional information** Selected recipients are offered a paid summer internship where they will have a chance to develop Microsoft products.

**Number awarded** Varies; a total of $540,000 is available for this program each year.

**Deadline** January of each year.

## [368]
## MIKE KABANICA SCHOLARSHIPS

Wisconsin Youth Soccer Association
Attn: Scholarships
10201 West Lincoln Avenue, Suite 207
West Allis, WI 53227
(414) 328-WYSA          Toll-free: (888) 328-WYSA
Fax: (414) 328-8008     E-mail: info@wiyouthsoccer.net
Web: www.wiyouthsoccer.com/scholarship.html

**Summary** To provide financial assistance for college to high school seniors in Wisconsin who have played soccer.

**Eligibility** This program is open to college-bound seniors graduating from high schools in Wisconsin who have participated in the Wisconsin Youth Soccer Association and other soccer activities in the state. Applicants must submit 1) a paragraph detailing their team honors (high school and club) and any difficulties they have had with penalties, suspensions, or other challenges; 2) a list of their school activities and organizations; 3) a list of community activities and organizations; 4) a paragraph detailing their involvement in community service; 5) a brief narrative on their greatest moment in soccer; 6) a brief narrative on a person who influenced them and how; and 7) a statement of their future career plans. Financial need is not considered in the selection process. Male and female players are considered separately.

**Financial data** The stipend is $500.

**Duration** 1 year.

**Number awarded** 6 each year: 3 females and 3 males.

**Deadline** February of each year.

## [369]
## MIKE NASH MEMORIAL SCHOLARSHIP FUND

Vietnam Veterans of America
Attn: Mike Nash Scholarship Program
8605 Cameron Street, Suite 400
Silver Spring, MD 20910-3710
(301) 585-4000          Toll-free: (800) VVA-1316
E-mail: finance@vva.org
Web: www.vva.org/Scholarship/index.htm

**Summary** To provide financial assistance for college to members of Vietnam Veterans of America (VVA), their families, and the families of other Vietnam veterans.

**Eligibility** This program is open to 1) members of VVA; 2) the spouses, children, stepchildren, and grandchildren of VVA members; and 3) the spouses, children, stepchildren, and grandchildren of MIA, KIA, or deceased Vietnam veterans. Applicants must be enrolled or planning to enroll at least half time at an accredited college, university, or technical institution. Along with their application, they must submit high school or college transcripts; SAT, ACT, or other recognized test scores; a letter of recommendation from a VVA state council, chapter, or national; 2 letters of recommendation; a letter describing their current educational goals and objectives, individual accomplishments, and any other personal information that may assist in the selection process; and documentation of financial need.

**Financial data** The stipend is $1,000 per year.

**Duration** 1 year; may be renewed for up to 3 additional years.

**Additional information** This program was established in 1991 and given its current name in 1997.

**Number awarded** Varies each year; recently, 9 of these scholarships were awarded.

**Deadline** June of each year.

## [370]
## MIKE SHINN DISTINGUISHED MEMBER OF THE YEAR AWARDS

National Society of Black Engineers
Attn: Programs Department
1454 Duke Street
Alexandria, VA 22314
(703) 549-2207, ext. 249          Fax: (703) 683-5312
E-mail: scholarships@nsbe.org
Web: www.nsbe.org/programs/schol_mshinn.php

**Summary** To provide financial assistance to members of the National Society of Black Engineers (NSBE) who are working on a degree in engineering.

**Eligibility** This program is open to members of the society who are undergraduate or graduate engineering students. Applicants must have a GPA of 3.5 or higher. Selection is based on an essay; academic achievement; service to the society at the chapter, regional, and/or national level; and other professional, campus, and community activities. The male and female applicants for the NSBE Fellows Scholarship Program who are judged most outstanding receive these awards.

**Financial data** The stipend is $7,500. Travel, hotel accommodations, and registration to the national convention are also provided.

**Duration** 1 year.

**Number awarded** 2 each year: 1 male and 1 female.
**Deadline** January of each year.

## [371]
## MIKE WARTER COLLEGE SCHOLARSHIP

Minnesota Youth Soccer Association
Attn: Scholarship Fund
11577 Encore Circle
Minnetonka, MN 55343
(952) 933-2384                    Fax: (952) 933-2627
E-mail: mysa@mnyouthsoccer.org
Web: www.mnyouthsoccer.org

**Summary** To provide financial assistance for college to high school seniors in Minnesota who have been active in soccer.

**Eligibility** This program is open to seniors graduating from high schools in Minnesota who plan to attend an accredited college, university, or community college. Applicants must be registered in a club affiliated with the Minnesota Youth Soccer Association. Males and females are considered separately in the selection process.

**Financial data** The stipend is $500.

**Duration** 1 year.

**Number awarded** 2 each year: 1 male and 1 female.

**Deadline** April of each year.

## [372]
## MILDRED A. BUTLER CAREER DEVELOPMENT AWARDS

Business and Professional Women/New Jersey
1977 North Olden Avenue Extension
PMB 624
Ewing, NJ 08618
(908) 218-0994                    Fax: (908) 252-2020
E-mail: BPWNJ@bpwnj.org
Web: www.bpwnj.org

**Summary** To provide financial assistance for further education to mature women in New Jersey.

**Eligibility** This program is open to women in New Jersey who are 25 years of age or older. Applicants must be seeking funding to advance their careers, reenter the workforce, or make a career change.

**Financial data** The stipend is $500.

**Duration** 1 year.

**Additional information** Information is also available from Jeanne Jameson, 155 Highland Lakes Road, Highland Lakes, NJ 07422, (973) 992-6970. Requests for applications must be accompanied by a self-addressed stamped envelope.

**Number awarded** Varies each year.

**Deadline** March of each year.

## [373]
## MILDRED SORENSEN NATIONAL SCHOLARSHIP

Danish Sisterhood of America
Attn: Lizette Burtis, Scholarship Chair
3020 Santa Juanita Court
Santa Rosa, CA 95405-8219
(707) 539-1884          E-mail: lburtis@sbcglobal.net
Web: www.danishsisterhood.org/rschol.asp

**Summary** To provide financial assistance for technical or vocational education to members or relatives of members of the Danish Sisterhood of America.

**Eligibility** Members or the family of members of the sisterhood are eligible to apply if they are full-time students enrolled in a technical/vocational program leading to a certificate, diploma, or associate degree. Members must have belonged to the sisterhood for at least 1 year. Selection is based on academic excellence (at least a 2.5 GPA).

**Financial data** The stipend is $750.

**Duration** 1 year; nonrenewable.

**Number awarded** 2 each year.

**Deadline** February of each year.

## [374]
## MILITARY ORDER OF THE PURPLE HEART SCHOLARSHIP PROGRAM

Military Order of the Purple Heart
Attn: Scholarships
5413-B Backlick Road
Springfield, VA 22151-3960
(703) 642-5360                    Fax: (703) 642-2054
E-mail: info@purpleheart.org
Web: www.purpleheart.org/scholar.html

**Summary** To provide financial assistance for college or graduate school to spouses and children of members of the Military Order of the Purple Heart.

**Eligibility** This program is open to children (natural, step-, and adopted), grandchildren, great-grandchildren and spouses of veterans who are members in good standing of the order or who received the Purple Heart. Applicants must be U.S. citizens, graduating seniors or graduates of an accredited high school, enrolled or accepted for enrollment in a full-time program of study in a college, trade school, or graduate school with a GPA of 3.5 or higher. Selection is based on merit; financial need is not considered in the selection process.

**Financial data** The stipend is $1,750 per year.

**Duration** 1 year; may be renewed up to 3 additional years.

**Number awarded** Varies each year; recently, 28 of these scholarships were awarded.

**Deadline** March of each year.

**[375]**
## MILITARY TUITION WAIVER DURING ASSIGNMENT AFTER TEXAS

Texas Higher Education Coordinating Board
Attn: Grants and Special Programs
1200 East Anderson Lane
P.O. Box 12788, Capitol Station
Austin, TX 78711-2788
(512) 427-6101                    Toll-free: (800) 242-3062
Fax: (512) 427-6127
E-mail: grantinfo@thecb.state.tx.us
Web: www.collegefortexans.com

**Summary** To provide educational assistance to the spouses and children of Texas military personnel assigned elsewhere.

**Eligibility** This program is open to the spouses and dependent children of members of the U.S. armed forces or commissioned officers of the Public Health Service who remain in Texas when the member is reassigned to duty outside of the state. The spouse or dependent child must reside continuously in Texas. Applicants must be attending or planning to attend a Texas public college or university.

**Financial data** Eligible students are entitled to pay tuition and fees at the resident rate at publicly-supported colleges and universities in Texas.

**Duration** The waiver remains in effect for the duration of the member's first assignment outside of Texas.

**Additional information** This program became effective in September, 2003.

**Number awarded** Varies each year.

**[376]**
## MILLIE GONZALEZ MEMORIAL SCHOLARSHIPS

Factor Support Network Pharmacy
Attn: Scholarship Committee
900 Avenida Acaso, Suite A
Camarillo, CA 93012-8749
(805) 388-9336                    Toll-free: (877) FSN-4-YOU
Fax: (805) 482-6324
E-mail: Scholarships@FactorSupport.com
Web: www.factorsupport.com/scholarships.htm

**Summary** To provide financial assistance to women with hemophilia.

**Eligibility** This program is open to women with bleeding disorders who are entering or attending a college, university, juniors college, or vocational school. Applicants must submit 3 short essays: 1) their career goals; 2) how hemophilia or von Willebrand disease has affected their life; and 3) how they are educating themselves, their family, and their community about hemophilia and/or von Willebrand disease. Selection is based on academic goals, volunteer work, school activities, other pertinent experience and achievements, and financial need.

**Financial data** The stipend is $1,000. Funds are paid directly to the recipient.

**Duration** 1 year.

**Number awarded** 5 each year.

**Deadline** April of each year.

**[377]**
## MINNESOTA BUSINESS AND PROFESSIONAL WOMEN'S FOUNDATION SCHOLARSHIPS

Minnesota State Federation of Business and
    Professional Women's Clubs, Inc.
Attn: Minnesota Business and Professional Women's
    Foundation
3432 Denmark Avenue
PMB 167
Eagan, MN 55123
E-mail: MinnesotaBPW_Foundation@hotmail.com
Web: www.bpwmn.org/bpw_mn_foundation.htm

**Summary** To provide financial assistance for higher education or professional certification to members of the Minnesota State Federation of Business and Professional Women's Clubs (BPW/MN).

**Eligibility** This program is open to BPW/MN members who are 25 years of age or older. Applicants must have been officially accepted into a program or course of study at an accredited academic institution in Minnesota. They must be U.S. citizens and able to demonstrate financial need. Along with their application, they must submit a 200-word autobiography and a 500-word essay discussing their specific short-term goals and how the proposed training will help them to accomplish those goals and make a difference in their professional career.

**Financial data** The stipend is $500. Funds must be used for tuition and mandatory academic fees.

**Duration** The scholarship must be used within 1 year.

**Number awarded** Several each year.

**[378]**
## MINNESOTA CHAPTER WTS SCHOLARSHIPS

Women's Transportation Seminar-Minnesota Chapter
c/o Jessica Overmohle, Director
URS Corporation
700 Third Street South
Minneapolis, MN 55415-1199
(612) 373-6404                    Fax: (612) 370-1378
E-mail: Jessica_Overmohle@URSCorp.com
Web: www.wtsinternational.org

**Summary** To provide financial assistance to women working on an undergraduate or graduate degree in a transportation-related field at colleges and universities in Minnesota.

**Eligibility** This program is open to women currently enrolled in a undergraduate or graduate degree program at a college or university in Minnesota. Applicants must be preparing for a career in transportation or a transportation-related field and be majoring in such fields as transportation engineering, planning, finance, or logistics. They must have a GPA of 3.0 or higher. Along with their application, they must submit a 750-word statement on their career goals after graduation and why they think they should receive this award. Selection is based on transportation goals, academic record, and transportation-related activities or job skills.

**Financial data** The stipend is $2,000.

**Duration** 1 year.

**Additional information** Winners are also nominated for scholarships offered by the national organization of the Women's Transportation Seminar.

**Number awarded** 2 each year: 1 undergraduate and 1 graduate student.

**Deadline** November of each year.

## [379]
## MINNESOTA CHILD CARE GRANT PROGRAM

Minnesota Higher Education Services Office
1450 Energy Park Drive, Suite 350
St. Paul, MN 55108-5227
(651) 642-0567       Toll-free: (800) 657-3866
Fax: (651) 642-0675       TTY: (800) 627-3529
E-mail: info@heso.state.mn.us
Web: www.mheso.state.mn.us

**Summary** To provide financial assistance for child care to students in Minnesota who are not receiving Minnesota Family Investment Program (MFIP) benefits.

**Eligibility** Minnesota residents who are working on an undergraduate degree or vocational certificate in the state and who have children age 12 and under (14 and under if disabled) may receive this assistance to help pay child care expenses. Recipients must demonstrate financial need but must not be receiving MFIP benefits. U.S. citizenship or permanent resident status is required.

**Financial data** The amount of the assistance depends on the income of applicant and spouse, number of day care hours necessary to cover education and work obligations, student's enrollment status, and number of eligible children in applicant's family. The maximum available is $2,200 per eligible child per academic year.

**Duration** 1 year; may be renewed as long as the recipient remains enrolled on at least a half-time basis in an undergraduate program.

**Additional information** Assistance may cover up to 40 hours per week per eligible child.

**Number awarded** Varies each year. Recently, a total of $1.1 million was provided for this program.

## [380]
## MINNESOTA LEGION AUXILIARY PAST PRESIDENTS PARLEY HEALTH CARE SCHOLARSHIP

American Legion Auxiliary
Attn: Department of Minnesota
State Veterans Service Building
20 West 12th Street, Room 314
St. Paul, MN 55155-2069
(651) 224-7634       Toll-free: (888) 217-9598
Fax: (651) 224-5243     E-mail: deptoffice@mnala.org
Web: www.mnala.org/ala/scholarship.asp

**Summary** To provide financial assistance for education in health care fields to members of the American Legion Auxiliary in Minnesota.

**Eligibility** Applicants must be residents of Minnesota, have been members of the American Legion Auxiliary for at least 3 years, have a GPA of 2.0 or higher, and intend to study in Minnesota. Their proposed major may be in any phase of health care, including nursing assistant, registered nursing, licensed practical nurse, X-ray or other technician, physical or other therapist, dental hygienist, and dental assistant.

**Financial data** The stipend is $750. Funds are sent directly to the recipient's school after satisfactory completion of the first quarter.

**Duration** 1 year.

**Additional information** These scholarships are tenable only in Minnesota.

**Number awarded** Up to 3 each year.

**Deadline** March of each year.

## [381]
## MINNESOTA SPACE GRANT CONSORTIUM SCHOLARSHIPS AND FELLOWSHIPS

Minnesota Space Grant Consortium
c/o University of Minnesota
Department of Aerospace Engineering and Mechanics
107 Akerman Hall
110 Union Street S.E.
Minneapolis, MN 55455
(612) 626-9295       Fax: (612) 626-1558
E-mail: mnsgc@aem.umn.edu
Web: www.aem.umn.edu/msgc/Scholarships/sf.shtml

**Summary** To provide financial assistance for space-related studies to undergraduate and graduate students in Minnesota, especially women, minorities, and persons with disabilities.

**Eligibility** This program is open to full-time graduate and undergraduate students at institutions that are affiliates of the Minnesota Space Grant Consortium. U.S. citizenship and a GPA of 3.2 or higher are required. Eligible fields of study include the physical sciences (astronomy, astrophysics, chemistry, computer science, mathematics, physics, planetary geoscience, and planetary science), life sciences (biology, biochemistry, botany, health science/nutrition, medicine, molecular/cellular biology, and zoology), social sciences (anthropology, architecture, art, economics, education, history, philosophy, political science/public policy, and psychology), earth sciences (atmospheric science, climatology/meteorology, environmental science, geography, geology, geophysics, and oceanography), and engineering (agricultural, aeronautical, aerospace, architectural, bioengineering, chemical, civil, computer, electrical, electronic, environmental, industrial, materials science, mechanical, mining, nuclear, petroleum, engineering science, and engineering mechanics). The Minnesota Space Grant Consortium is a component of the U.S. National Aeronautics and Space Administration (NASA) Space Grant program, which encourages participation by women, underrepresented minorities, and persons with disabilities.

**Financial data** This program awards approximately $125,000 in undergraduate scholarships and graduate fellowships each year. The amounts of the awards are set by each of the participating institutions, which augment funding from this program with institutional resources.

**Duration** 1 year; renewable.

**Additional information** This program is funded by NASA. The member institutions are: Augsburg College, Bethel College, Bemidji State University, College of St. Catherine, Carleton College, Concordia College, Fond du

Lac Community College, Itasca Community College, Leech Lake Tribal College, Macalaster College, Normandale Community College, Southwest State University, University of Minnesota at Duluth, University of Minnesota at Twin Cities, and University of St. Thomas.

**Number awarded** 8 to 12 undergraduate scholarships and 2 to 3 graduate fellowships are awarded each year.

**Deadline** March of each year.

## [382]
## MINNESOTA STATE HIGH SCHOOL LEAGUE TRIPLE "A" AWARDS

Minnesota State High School League
2100 Freeway Boulevard
Brooklyn Center, MN 55430-1735
(763) 560-2262
Web: www.mshsl.org

**Summary** To provide financial assistance for college to high school seniors in Minnesota who excel in the Triple "A" activities: academics, arts, and athletics.

**Eligibility** This program is open to college-bound seniors graduating from high schools in Minnesota. Each school may nominate 2 students, a female and a male. Selection of state winners is based on academic performance; involvement in athletic programs sponsored by the Minnesota State High School League (badminton, baseball, basketball, cross country running, football, golf, gymnastics, hockey, lacrosse, skiing, soccer, softball, swimming and diving, synchronized swimming, tennis, track, volleyball, wrestling, and adapted soccer, bowling, floor hockey, and softball); involvement in League-sponsored fine arts activities (state, section, sub-section, school, or community-sponsored activities in instrumental or vocal music, drama, debate, or speech); and involvement in other school and community activities. Nominees must have a GPA of 3.0 or higher and be in compliance with the League's Student Code of Conduct. They must submit a 250-word essay on what they plan to do after high school and how their participation in athletics and fine arts activities has prepared them to achieve that goal. Students from Class A and Class AA schools are judged separately, as are females and males.

**Financial data** The stipend is $1,000 per year.

**Duration** 4 years.

**Number awarded** 4 each year: a female and a male from each of the 2 classes of schools.

**Deadline** January of each year.

## [383]
## MINNESOTA VETERANS' DEPENDENTS ASSISTANCE PROGRAM

Minnesota Higher Education Services Office
1450 Energy Park Drive, Suite 350
St. Paul, MN 55108-5227
(651) 642-0567          Toll-free: (800) 657-3866
Fax: (651) 642-0675      TTY: (800) 627-3529
E-mail: info@heso.state.mn.us
Web: www.mheso.state.mn.us

**Summary** To provide financial assistance for college to the dependents of Minnesota veterans and military personnel listed as POWs or MIAs.

**Eligibility** Eligible for this assistance are 1) spouses of a prisoner of war or person missing in action, or 2) children born before or during the period of time the parent served as a POW or was declared MIA, or 3) children legally adopted or in the legal custody of a parent prior to and during the time the parent served as a POW or was declared to be MIA. Veteran parents must have been residents of Minnesota at the time of entry into service or at the time declared to be a POW or MIA, which must have occurred after August 1, 1958.

**Financial data** Students who attend private postsecondary institutions receive up to $250 per year for tuition and fees. Students who attend a Minnesota public postsecondary institution are exempt from tuition charges.

**Duration** Assistance continues until the student completes a bachelor's degree or receives a certificate of completion.

**Number awarded** Varies each year.

## [384]
## MINNESOTA WOMEN'S GOLF ASSOCIATION SCHOLARSHIP

Minnesota Women's Golf Association
Attn: MWGA Charitable Foundation
6550 York Avenue South, Suite 211
Edina, MN 55435-2333
(952) 927-4643, ext. 11          Fax: (952) 927-9642
E-mail: paula@mwga-online.org
Web: www.mwga-online.org/new/foundation.cfm

**Summary** To provide financial assistance for college to female high school seniors in Minnesota who are interested in golf.

**Eligibility** This program is open to women who are graduating seniors at high schools in Minnesota planning to attend a 4-year college or university. Applicants must have an interest or involvement in the sport of golf, although skill or excellence in the game is not considered in the selection process. They must have a GPA of 3.0 or higher and be able to demonstrate financial need.

**Financial data** The stipend is $2,000 per year.

**Duration** 1 year; may be renewed up to 3 additional years.

**Number awarded** Varies each year; recently, 3 of these scholarships were awarded.

**Deadline** March of each year.

## [385]
## MISS AMERICA COMPETITION AWARDS

Miss America Pageant
Attn: Scholarship Department
Two Miss America Way, Suite 1000
Atlantic City, NJ 08401
(609) 345-7571, ext. 27          Toll-free: (800) 282-MISS
Fax: (609) 347-6079      E-mail: info@missamerica.org
Web: www.missamerica.org

**Summary** To provide educational scholarships to participants in the Miss America Pageant on local, state, and national levels.

**Eligibility** To enter an official Miss America Preliminary Pageant, candidates must meet certain basic requirements and agree to abide by all the rules of the local, state, and national Miss America Pageants. Among the qualifications required are that the applicant be female, between the ages of 17 and 24, a resident of the town or state in which they first compete, in good health, of good moral character, and a citizen of the United States. A complete list of all eligibility requirements is available from each local and state pageant. In addition to the general scholarship awards, participants are also considered for a number of special awards: the Bernie Wayne Performing Arts Award is presented to the contestant with the highest talent score among those women with performing arts as a stated ambition; the Charles and Theresa Brown Scholarships are presented to Miss America, the 4 runners-up, Miss Alaska, Miss Hawaii, Miss Illinois, and Miss Ohio; and the Quality of Life Awards are presented to the 3 contestants who demonstrate the most outstanding commitment to enhancing the quality of life for others through volunteerism and community service.

**Financial data**  More than $45 million in cash and tuition assistance is awarded annually at the local, state, and national Miss America Pageants. At the national level, a total of $455,000 is awarded: Miss America receives $30,000 in scholarship money, the first runner-up $20,000, second runner-up $15,000, third runner-up $10,000, fourth runner-up $8,000, finalists $7,000 each, and national contestants $3,000 each. Other awards include those for the preliminary talent winners at $2,000 each, the preliminary lifestyle and fitness in swimsuit winners at $1,000 each, and the non-finalist talent winners at $1,000 each. Of the special awards presented to national contestants, the Bernie Wayne Performing Arts Award is $2,500; the Charles and Theresa Brown Scholarships are $2,500 each; and the Quality of Life Awards are $3,000 for the winner, $3,000 for first runner-up, and $1,000 for second runner-up.

**Duration**  The pageants are held every year.

**Additional information**  The Miss America Pageant has been awarding scholarships since 1945. Scholarships are to be used for tuition, room, board, supplies, and other college expenses. Use of the scholarships must begin within 4 years from the date of the award (5 years if the recipient is Miss America), unless a reasonable extension is requested and granted. Training under the scholarship should be continuous and completed within 10 years from the date the scholarship is activated; otherwise, the balance of the scholarship may be canceled without further notice.

**Number awarded**  At the national level, 52 contestants (1 from each state, the District of Columbia, and the Virgin Islands) share the awards.

**Deadline**  Varies, depending upon the date of local pageants leading to the state and national finals.

## [386]
## MISS CHEERLEADER OF AMERICA SCHOLARSHIPS

Miss Cheerleader of America
Attn: Program Director
P.O. Box 667
Taylor, MI 48180
(734) 946-1200                    Fax: (734) 946-1204
E-mail: misscheerleaderofamerica@yahoo.com
Web: www.misscheerleaderofamerica.com

**Summary**  To recognize and reward, with college scholarships, women who are high school cheerleaders.

**Eligibility**  This program is open to female high school cheerleaders in grades 9 through 12. Girls who are interested apply to participate in a pageant in their home state. Based on their applications, finalists are invited to their state pageant, where they participate in an evening gown demonstration and an interview. The program is not a beauty, bathing suit, cheer skill, or talent competition. Judges attempt to select "the all-American girl, who normally would not even think about being in a pageant."

**Financial data**  Prizes are generally scholarships of $1,000 for first place, $750 for second, and $500 for third.

**Duration**  The competition is held annually.

**Number awarded**  Varies each year; normally, 3 prizes are awarded in each state in which a pageant is held.

## [387]
## MISS INDIAN USA SCHOLARSHIP PROGRAM

American Indian Heritage Foundation
P.O. Box 6301
Falls Church, VA 22040
(703) 532-1921        E-mail: MissIndianUSA@indians.org
Web: www.indians.org

**Summary**  To recognize and reward the most beautiful and talented Indian women.

**Eligibility**  American Indian women between the ages of 18 and 26 are eligible to enter this national contest if they are high school graduates and have never been married, cohabited with the opposite sex, been pregnant, or had children. U.S. citizenship is required. Selection is based on public appearance (20%), a traditional interview (15%), a contemporary interview (15%), beauty of spirit (15%), a cultural presentation (10%), scholastic achievement (10%), a platform question (10%), and a finalist question (5%).

**Financial data**  Miss Indian USA receives an academic scholarship of $4,000 plus a cash grant of $6,500, a wardrobe allowance of $2,000, appearance fees of $3,000, a professional photo shoot worth $500, gifts worth more than $4,000, honoring gifts worth more than $2,000, promotional materials worth more than $2,000, and travel to Washington, D.C. with a value of approximately $2,000; the total value of the prize is more than $26,000. Members of her court receive scholarships of $2,000 for the first runner-up, $1,500 for the second runner-up, $1,000 for the third runner-up, and $500 for the fourth runner-up.

**Duration**  This competition is held annually.

**Additional information**  The program involves a week-long competition in the Washington, D.C. metropolitan area that includes seminars, interviews, cultural presentations, and many public appearances. The application fee is $100 if submitted prior to mid-April or $200 if submitted later. In addition, a candidate fee of $750 is required.

**Number awarded** 1 winner and 4 runners-up are selected each year.

**Deadline** May of each year.

## [388]
## MISS JOB'S DAUGHTER OF PENNSYLVANIA PAGEANT SCHOLARSHIP

Pennsylvania Masonic Youth Foundation
Attn: Educational Endowment Fund
1244 Bainbridge Road
Elizabethtown, PA 17022-9423
(717) 367-1536    Toll-free: (800) 266-8424 (within PA)
Fax: (717) 367-0616    E-mail: pyf@pagrandlodge.org
Web: www.pagrandlodge.org/pyf/scholar/index.html

**Summary** To provide financial assistance for college to members of Job's Daughters in Pennsylvania.

**Eligibility** This program is open to Pennsylvania Job's Daughters and unmarried majority members who are younger than 30 years of age and are in good standing in their Bethels. Applicants must be high school seniors, high school graduates, or current college students enrolled or planning to enroll in a higher education program as a full-time student. Selection is based on Bethel and other Job's Daughters activities.

**Financial data** The stipend depends on the availability of funds.

**Duration** 1 year.

**Additional information** Funding for this program is provided through the proceeds of the Miss Job's Daughter of Pennsylvania Scholarship Pageant. Information is also available from Deborah Phillips, Scholarship Committee Chair, 2267 Sand Hill Road, Hershey, PA 17033, E-mail: info@paiojd.org.

**Number awarded** 1 each year.

**Deadline** April of each year.

## [389]
## MISS LATINA WORLD

Dawn Rochele Productions
6150 West El Dorado Parkway, Suite 160-120
McKinney, TX 75070
(206) 666-DAWN    E-mail: info@misslatina.com
Web: www.misslatina.com

**Summary** To recognize and reward young Latina women, with college scholarships and other funds, who compete in a national beauty pageant.

**Eligibility** This program is open to women between 18 and 35 years of age who are at least 25% Hispanic. Applicants may be single, married, or divorced, and they may have children. They appear in a nationally-televised pageant where selection is based one third on an interview, one third on swimsuit appearances, and one third on evening gown appearances. Height and weight are not factors, but contestants should be proportionate. Pageant experience and fluency in Spanish are not required.

**Financial data** Each year, prizes include scholarships, gifts, a cruise to the Bahamas, a trip to Las Vegas, a model-

ing contract, and use of an apartment in Miami. The total value is more than $25,000.

**Duration** The pageant is held annually.

**Number awarded** 1 winner and 4 runners-up are selected each year.

## [390]
## MISS STATE SCHOLAR AWARDS

Miss America Pageant
Attn: Scholarship Department
Two Miss America Way, Suite 1000
Atlantic City, NJ 08401
(609) 345-7571, ext. 27    Toll-free: (800) 282-MISS
Fax: (609) 347-6079    E-mail: info@missamerica.org
Web: www.missamerica.org

**Summary** To recognize and reward, with college scholarships, women who participate in the Miss America Pageant at the state level and demonstrate academic excellence.

**Eligibility** This competition is open to women who compete at the state level of the Miss America Pageant. Selection is based on academic excellence (grades, course content, and academic standing of the institution).

**Financial data** The stipend is $1,000.

**Duration** 1 year.

**Additional information** This program, established in 1998, is administered by Scholarship America, One Scholarship Way, P.O. Box 297, St. Peter, MN 56082, (507) 931-1682, (800) 537-4180, Fax: (507) 931-9168.

**Number awarded** Up to 52 each year: 1 for each of the states, the District of Columbia, and the Virgin Islands.

**Deadline** Varies, depending upon the date of local pageants leading to the state finals.

## [391]
## MISS TEEN AMERICA

Continental Miss Teen America Scholarship Program, Inc.
Attn: CEO/President
P.O. Box 330
Middletown, CT 06457
(860) 346-2200    Fax: (860) 346-2201
E-mail: rfenmore@missteenamerica.com
Web: www.missteenamerica.com

**Summary** To recognize and reward, with college scholarships and other prizes, teen-aged women who participate in a talent and beauty competition.

**Eligibility** This competition is open to women between 14 and 18 years of age who have never been to college, been married, or given birth to a child. Applicants must first apply for state or metropolitan area competitions by submitting a 1-page essay on why they want to represent their state. At the national level, winners participate in talent, modeling, and photogenic competitions. Selection is based on a personal interview with judges (20%), talent or spokesmodel presentation (20%), physical fitness, in recommended swimsuit (20%). a formal eveningwear presentation (10%), a 30-second commercial or public service announcement about their state (10%), the photogenic competition (10%), and modeling (10%).

**Financial data** Cash scholarships, for use at an accredited college or university, are $5,000 for Miss Teen America, $2,500 for the first alternate, $2,000 for the second alternate, $1,500 for the third alternate, and $1,000 for the fourth alternate. All winners, including those at the state level, receive scholarships for use at Nova Southeastern University and many other prizes and awards.

**Duration** The competition is held annually.

**Additional information** All participants are required to pay a total sponsorship fee of $1,050, including a deposit of $75 to accompany the application. They are also required to sell $400 worth of ads for the national program.

**Number awarded** 5 winners receive national scholarships each year.

## [392]
## MISS TEEN USA

Miss Universe Organization
1370 Avenue of the Americas, 16th Floor
New York, NY 10019
(212) 373-4999        Fax: (212) 315-5378
E-mail: MissUPR@missuniverse.com
Web: www.missteenusa.com

**Summary** To recognize and reward beautiful and talented women between 15 and 19 years of age in the United States.

**Eligibility** Some cities and all states have preliminary pageants. The winner of the city pageant goes on to compete in the state pageant for her home city. A delegate may also enter a state pageant without having won a city title. One delegate from each of the 50 states and the District of Columbia is selected to compete in the pageant. Participants must be between 15 and 19 years of age. They must never have been married or pregnant. Selection is based on beauty, intelligence, and ability to handle an interview.

**Financial data** Miss Teen USA receives cash and prizes worth more than $150,000. Recently, that included a $45,000 scholarship to the School for Film and Television, a Preciosa trophy worth $3,500, a crystal chandelier from Preciosa worth $5,000, a $2,500 pre-paid VISA BUXX card, a $2,000 cash prize and complimentary UV-Free Tanning for the year of her reign from Mystic Tan, a pearl tiara worth $12,000 from Mikimoto, a fashion footwear wardrobe from Nina Footwear, a swimwear wardrobe from Pink Sands Swim, a 5-day/4 night trip for 2 anywhere American Airlines flies in the continental United States or Caribbean, a pajama wardrobe by Jamatex worth $500, a 1-year salary, a luxury apartment while in New York City, a personal appearance wardrobe, a modeling portfolio, and other services and training. Other prizes included $3,000 for first runner-up, $2,000 for second runner-up, $1,000 for third and fourth runners-up, and $500 for semifinalists. In addition, the delegate selected by the television audience as Miss Photogenic and the delegate selected by her peers as Miss Congeniality each received $1,000 cash prizes and a commemorative Preciosa crystal trophy worth $3,500.

**Duration** The national pageant is held annually, usually at the end of the summer.

**Additional information** The competition began in 1983.

**Number awarded** 1 national winner each year.

**Deadline** June of each year.

## [393]
## MISS USA

Miss Universe Organization
1370 Avenue of the Americas, 16th Floor
New York, NY 10019
(212) 373-4999        Fax: (212) 315-5378
E-mail: MissUPR@missuniverse.com
Web: www.missusa.com

**Summary** To identify and reward the most beautiful women selected in a competition among women from each state.

**Eligibility** This program is open to women between 18 and 27 years of age who have never been married or pregnant. Entrants are first selected in state competitions, and then 51 women (1 from each state and the District of Columbia) compete in the Miss USA Pageant. Selection of the winner is based on interviews by pageant judges (on successes, talents, goals, and ambitions), a swimsuit competition (with swimsuit styles provided by the pageant), and an evening gown competition (with gowns chosen by the competitors). The Photogenic Award is presented to the delegate voted on and selected by the television audience, and the Congeniality Award is presented to the delegate selected by her sister delegates as the most charismatic and inspirational.

**Financial data** Miss USA receives cash and prizes that recently included a 2-year scholarship valued at $60,000 from The School for Film and Television, a pearl tiara worth $17,500 from Mikimoto, a cash prize of $3,000 and a shoe wardrobe from Steve Madden, a cash prize of $5,000 and a year supply of Covergirl cosmetics, a 1-year salary, a luxury apartment while in New York City, a personal appearance wardrobe from Tadashi Fashions, a modeling portfolio, and other services and training. Other prizes included $3,000 for first runner-up, $2,000 for second runner-up, $1,000 for third and fourth runners-up, and $500 for semifinalists. In addition, the delegate selected by the television audience as Miss Photogenic and the delegate selected by her peers as Miss Congeniality each received $1,000 cash prizes.

**Duration** The national pageant is held annually, in February or March.

**Additional information** This pageant began in 1952. Miss USA competes for additional prizes in the Miss Universe Pageant.

**Number awarded** 1 each year.

**Deadline** January of each year.

## [394]
## MISSISSIPPI SPACE GRANT CONSORTIUM SCHOLARSHIPS AND FELLOWSHIPS

Mississippi Space Grant Consortium
c/o University of Mississippi
217 Vardaman Hall
P.O. Box 1848
University, MS 38677-1848
(662) 915-1187        Fax: (662) 915-3927
E-mail: mschaff@olemiss.edu
Web: www.olemiss.edu/programs/nasa

**Summary** To provide funding to undergraduate and graduate students (particularly women, minority, and disabled students) for space-related activities at colleges and universities that are members of the Mississippi Space Grant Consortium.

**Eligibility** This program is open to undergraduate and graduate students at member institutions of the Mississippi consortium. Each participating college or university establishes its own program and criteria for admission, but all activities are in engineering, mathematics, and science fields of interest to the U.S. National Aeronautics and Space Administration (NASA). U.S. citizenship is required. The consortium is a component of NASA's Space Grant program, which encourages participation by women, underrepresented minorities, and persons with disabilities.

**Financial data** Each participating institution establishes the amounts of the awards. Recently, the average undergraduate award was $1,308 and the average graduate award was $2,975. A total of $96,350 was awarded.

**Additional information** Consortium members include Alcorn State University, Coahoma Community College, Delta State University, Hinds Community College (Utica Campus), Itawamba Community College, Jackson State University, Meridian Community College, Mississippi Delta Community College, Mississippi Gulf Coast Community College, Mississippi State University, Mississippi University for Women, Mississippi Valley State University, Northeast Mississippi Community College, Pearl River Community College, the University of Mississippi, and the University of Southern Mississippi. This program is funded by NASA.

**Number awarded** Varies each year; recently, a total of 47 students received support through this program.

## [395]
## MISSOURI GENERAL BPW SCHOLARSHIPS

Missouri Business and Professional Women's
   Foundation, Inc.
P.O. Box 338
Carthage, MO 64836-0338
Web: bpwmo.org/files/index.php?id=14

**Summary** To provide financial assistance for college to women in Missouri.

**Eligibility** This program is open to women in Missouri who have been accepted into an accredited program or course of study to upgrade their skills and/or complete education for career advancement. Along with their application, they must submit brief statements on the following: their achievements and/or specific recognitions in their field of endeavor; professional and/or civic affiliations; present and long-range career goals; how they plan to participate in and contribute to their community upon completion of their program of study; why they feel they would make a good recipient; and any special circumstances that may have influenced their ability to continue or complete their education. They must also demonstrate financial need and U.S. citizenship.

**Financial data** A stipend is awarded (amount not specified).

**Duration** 1 year.

**Additional information** Information is also available from Mary Kay Pace, Scholarship Committee Chair, 1503 Paradise Valley Drive, High Ridge, MO 63049, (636) 677-2951.

**Number awarded** Varies each year; recently, 3 of these scholarships were awarded.

**Deadline** January of each year.

## [396]
## MISSOURI VIETNAM VETERANS SURVIVOR GRANT PROGRAM

Missouri Department of Higher Education
Attn: Student Financial Assistance
3515 Amazonas Drive
Jefferson City, MO 65109-5717
(573) 526-7958      Toll-free: (800) 473-6757
Fax: (573) 751-6635     E-mail: info@dhe.mo.gov
Web: www.dhe.mo.gov/hsstudentsvietnamvet.shtml

**Summary** To provide financial assistance for college to survivors of certain deceased Missouri Vietnam veterans.

**Eligibility** This program is open to surviving spouses and children of veterans who served in the military in Vietnam or the war zone in southeast Asia, who were residents of Missouri when first entering military service and at the time of death, whose death was attributed to or caused by exposure to toxic chemicals during the Vietnam conflict, and who served in the Vietnam theater between 1961 and 1972. Applicants must be Missouri residents enrolled in a program leading to a certificate, associate degree, or baccalaureate degree at an approved postsecondary institution in the state. Students working on a degree or certificate in theology or divinity are not eligible. U.S. citizenship or permanent resident status is required.

**Financial data** The maximum annual grant is the lesser of 1) the actual tuition charged at the school where the recipient is enrolled, or 2) the amount of tuition charged to a Missouri undergraduate resident enrolled full time in the same class level and in the same academic major as an applicant at the Missouri public 4-year regional institutions.

**Duration** 1 semester; may be renewed until the recipient has obtained a baccalaureate degree or has completed 150 semester credit hours, whichever comes first.

**Additional information** Awards are not available for summer study.

**Number awarded** Varies each year.

## [397]
## MISSOURI WOMEN'S GOLF EDUCATION ASSOCIATION SCHOLARSHIPS

Missouri Women's Golf Association
c/o Virginia Halpern, Membership Director
24 Picardy Hill Drive
Chesterfield, MO 63017
E-mail: vchalpern@charter.net
Web: www.mowomensga.org/scholarship.html

**Summary** To provide financial assistance for college to female high school seniors in Missouri who have been involved in golf.

**Eligibility** This program is open to females graduating from high schools in Missouri or Johnson County, Kansas. Applicants must submit a copy of their high school transcript and a brief account of their golf achievements. Financial need is not considered in the selection process.

**Financial data** A stipend is awarded (amount not specified).

**Duration** 1 year; nonrenewable.

**Additional information** This program includes the Susan E. Shepherd Memorial Scholarship, funded by the Shepherd Foundation of St. Louis, and the Mary Jane Landreth Scholarship, established in 2006.

**Number awarded** Varies each year; recently, 5 of these scholarships were awarded.

## [398]
## MODINE MANUFACTURING COLLEGE-TO-WORK PROGRAM

Wisconsin Foundation for Independent Colleges, Inc.
Attn: College-to-Work Program
735 North Water Street, Suite 600
Milwaukee, WI 53202-4100
(414) 273-5980        Fax: (414) 273-5995
E-mail: wfic@wficweb.org
Web: www.wficweb.org/work.html

**Summary** To provide financial assistance and work experience to students (particularly women and minorities) who are majoring in fields related to business at member institutions of the Wisconsin Foundation for Independent Colleges (WFIC).

**Eligibility** This program is open to full-time juniors and seniors at WFIC member colleges or universities. Women and minorities are especially encouraged to apply. Applicants must be preparing for or considering a career in business, finance, or marketing and have a GPA of 3.0 or higher. They must be interested in an internship at Modine Manufacturing Company in Racine, Wisconsin. Along with their application, they must submit a 1-page essay that includes why they are applying for the internship, why they have selected their major and what interests them about it, why they are attending their chosen college or university, and their future career objectives.

**Financial data** The stipend is $1,500 for the scholarship; the internship is paid hourly.

**Duration** 1 year for the scholarship; 10 weeks for the internship.

**Additional information** The WFIC member schools are Alverno College, Beloit College, Cardinal Stritch University, Carroll College, Carthage College, Concordia University of Wisconsin, Edgewood College, Lakeland College, Lawrence University, Marian College, Marquette University, Milwaukee Institute of Art & Design, Milwaukee School of Engineering, Mount Mary College, Northland College, Ripon College, St. Norbert College, Silver Lake College, Viterbo University, and Wisconsin Lutheran College. This program is sponsored by Modine Manufacturing Company.

**Number awarded** 1 each year.

**Deadline** February of each year.

## [399]
## MONTANA DEPENDENTS OF PRISONERS OF WAR FEE WAIVER

Montana Guaranteed Student Loan Program
2500 Broadway
P.O. Box 203101
Helena, MT 59620-3101
(406) 444-0638        Toll-free: (800) 537-7508
Fax: (406) 444-1869
E-mail: scholar@mgslp.state.mt.us
Web: www.mgslp.state.mt.us

**Summary** To provide financial assistance for college to dependents of veterans and military personnel declared missing in action or prisoners of war in southeast Asia.

**Eligibility** To be eligible for this fee waiver, students must be the spouses or children of residents of Montana who, while serving in southeast Asia after January 1, 1961 either in the armed forces or as a civilian, have been declared missing in action or prisoner of war. Financial need is considered.

**Financial data** Students eligible for this benefit are entitled to attend any unit of the Montana University System without payment of undergraduate registration or incidental fees.

**Duration** Undergraduate students are eligible for continued fee waivers as long as they maintain reasonable academic progress as full-time students.

**Number awarded** Varies each year.

## [400]
## MONTANA SPACE GRANT CONSORTIUM UNDERGRADUATE SCHOLARSHIPS

Montana Space Grant Consortium
c/o Montana State University
416 Cobleigh Hall
P.O. Box 173835
Bozeman, MT 59717-3835
(406) 994-4223        Fax: (406) 994-4452
E-mail: msgc@montana.edu
Web: spacegrant.montana.edu

**Summary** To provide financial assistance to students in Montana (particularly women, minority, and disabled students) who are interested in working on an undergraduate degree in the space sciences and/or engineering.

**Eligibility** This program is open to full-time undergraduate students at member institutions of the Montana Space Grant Consortium (MSGC) majoring in fields related to space sciences and engineering. Those fields include, but are not limited to, astronomy, biological and life sciences, chemical engineering, chemistry, civil engineering, computer sciences, electrical engineering, geological sciences, mathematics, mechanical engineering, and physics. Priority is given to students who have been involved in aerospace-related research. U.S. citizenship is required. The MSGC is a component of the U.S. National Aeronautics and Space Administration (NASA) Space Grant program, which encourages participation by women, underrepresented minorities, and persons with disabilities.

**Financial data** The stipend is $1,000 per year.

**Duration** 1 year; may be renewed.

**Additional information** The MSGC member institutions are Blackfeet Community College, Carroll College, Chief Dull Knife College, Fort Belknap College, Fort Peck Community College, Little Big Horn College, Montana State University at Billings, Montana State University at Bozeman, Montana State University Northern, Montana Tech, Rocky Mountain College, Salish Kootenai College, Stone Child College, University of Great Falls, University of Montana, and University of Montana Western. Funding for this program is provided by NASA.

**Number awarded** Varies each year; recently, 23 of these scholarships were awarded.

**Deadline** March of each year.

## [401]
## MONTANA STATE WOMEN'S GOLF ASSOCIATION SCHOLARSHIPS

Montana State Women's Golf Association
c/o Carla Berg, Executive Secretary/Director
P.O. Box 52
Sidney, MT 59270
(406) 488-5135          E-mail: carla@mswga.org
Web: www.mswga.org/applications.html

**Summary** To provide financial assistance for college to women golfers in Montana.

**Eligibility** This program is open to female residents of Montana who are entering their freshman year of college. Applicants must have been involved with golf sometime (on a high school team or in a junior program), although they are not required to be participating presently. They must submit information on their high school golf playing record, amateur playing record, leadership positions, activities and organizations, community and volunteer service, and honors and awards. They must also submit a brief essay on their career aspirations and how they hope to achieve those life goals. Neither financial need nor skill in golf are considered in the selection process.

**Financial data** The stipend is $500.

**Duration** 1 year.

**Additional information** This scholarship was first awarded in 1990.

**Number awarded** 1 or more each year.

**Deadline** March of each year.

## [402]
## MSCPA WOMEN IN ACCOUNTING SCHOLARSHIP

Massachusetts Society of Certified Public Accountants
Attn: MSCPA Educational Foundation
105 Chauncy Street, Tenth Floor
Boston, MA 02111
(617) 556-4000          Toll-free: (800) 392-6145
Fax: (617) 556-4126
E-mail: biannoni@MSCPAonline.org
Web: www.cpatrack.com

**Summary** To provide financial assistance to women from Massachusetts working on an undergraduate degree in accounting at a college or university in the state.

**Eligibility** This program is open to female Massachusetts residents enrolled at a college or university in the state.

Applicants must have completed the first semester of their junior year and be able to demonstrate financial need, academic excellence, and an intention to prepare for a career as a certified public accountant at a firm in Massachusetts.

**Financial data** The stipend is $2,500.

**Duration** 1 year.

**Additional information** This program is sponsored by the Women's Golf Committee of the Massachusetts Society of Certified Public Accountants (MSCPA).

**Number awarded** 1 or more each year.

**Deadline** April of each year.

## [403]
## MUSEMECHE SCHOLARSHIP PROGRAM

Louisiana High School Athletic Association
Attn: Commissioner
8075 Jefferson Highway
Baton Rouge, LA 70809-7675
(225) 925-0100          Fax: (225) 925-5901
E-mail: lhsaa@lhsaa.org
Web: www.lhsaa.org/Scholarships.htm

**Summary** To provide financial assistance to student-athletes in Louisiana who plan to attend college in the state.

**Eligibility** This program is open to student-athletes who are seniors graduating from high schools in Louisiana. Applicants must be planning to attend a college or university in the state. They must be nominated by their principal. Females and males are considered separately. Selection is based primarily on financial need.

**Financial data** The stipend is $500.

**Duration** 1 year.

**Additional information** This program is sponsored by Musemeche Photography.

**Number awarded** 4 each year: 2 for females and 2 for males.

**Deadline** April of each year.

## [404]
## MUSIC THERAPY SCHOLARSHIP

Sigma Alpha Iota Philanthropies, Inc.
One Tunnel Road
Asheville, NC 28805
(828) 251-0606          Fax: (828) 251-0644
E-mail: philonline@sai-national.org
Web: www.sai-national.org/phil/philsch1.html

**Summary** To provide financial assistance to members of Sigma Alpha Iota (an organization of women musicians) who are interested in working on an undergraduate or graduate degree in music therapy.

**Eligibility** Members of the organization may apply for these scholarships if they wish to study music therapy at the undergraduate or graduate level. Applicants must submit an essay that includes their personal definition of music therapy, their career plans and professional goals as a music therapist, and why they feel they are deserving of this scholarship. Selection is based on music therapy skills, musicianship, fraternity service, community service, leadership, self-reliance, and dedication to the field of music therapy as a career.

**Financial data** The stipend is $1,000.

**Duration** 1 year.

**Additional information** There is a $25 nonrefundable application fee.

**Number awarded** 1 each year.

**Deadline** March of each year.

## [405]
## NAHB WOMEN'S COUNCIL STRATEGIES FOR SUCCESS SCHOLARSHIP

National Housing Endowment
1201 15th Street, N.W.
Washington, DC 20005
(202) 266-8483    Toll-free: (800) 368-5242, ext. 8483
Fax: (202) 266-8177    E-mail: nhe@nahb.com
Web: www.nationalhousingendowment.com

**Summary** To provide financial assistance to undergraduate students, especially women, interested in preparing for a career in the building industry.

**Eligibility** This program is open to high school seniors and current undergraduates who are enrolled or planning to enroll full time at a 2- or 4-year college or university or vocational program. Applicants must be working on or planning to work on a degree in a housing-related program, such as construction management, building, construction technology, civil engineering, architecture, or a trade specialty. They must have at least a 2.5 GPA in all courses and at least a 3.0 GPA in core curriculum classes. Preference is given to 1) women; 2) applicants who would be unable to afford college without financial assistance; and 3) students who are current members (or will be members in the upcoming semester) of a student chapter of the National Association of Home Builders (NAHB). Along with their application, they must submit an essay on their reasons for becoming a professional in the housing industry and their career goals. Selection is based on financial need, career goals, academic achievement, employment history, extracurricular activities, and letters of recommendation.

**Financial data** The stipend is $2,000. Funds are made payable to the recipient and sent to the recipient's school.

**Duration** 1 year; may be renewed.

**Additional information** The National Housing Endowment is the philanthropic arm of the National Association of Home Builders (NAHB). Its women's council established this scholarship in 2001.

**Number awarded** Varies each year; recently, 2 of these scholarships were awarded.

**Deadline** March of each year.

## [406]
## NANCY REAGAN PATHFINDER SCHOLARSHIPS

National Federation of Republican Women
Attn: Scholarships and Internships
124 North Alfred Street
Alexandria, VA 22314-3011
(703) 548-9688    Fax: (703) 548-9836
E-mail: mail@nfrw.org
Web: www.nfrw.org/programs/scholarships.htm

**Summary** To provide financial assistance for college or graduate school to Republican women.

**Eligibility** This program is open to women currently enrolled as college sophomores, juniors, seniors, or master's degree students. Recent high school graduates and first-year college women are not eligible. Applicants must submit 3 letters of recommendation, an official transcript, a 1-page essay on why they should be considered for the scholarship, and a 1-page essay on career goals. Optionally, a photograph may be supplied. Applications must be submitted to the Republican federation president in the applicant's state. Each president chooses 1 application from her state to submit for scholarship consideration. Financial need is not a factor in the selection process. U.S. citizenship is required.

**Financial data** The stipend is $2,500.

**Duration** 1 year; nonrenewable.

**Additional information** This program, established in 1985, is also known as the National Pathfinder Scholarship.

**Number awarded** 3 each year.

**Deadline** Applications must be submitted to the state federation president by May of each year.

## [407]
## NANNIE W. NORFLEET SCHOLARSHIP

American Legion Auxiliary
Attn: Department of North Carolina
P.O. Box 25726
Raleigh, NC 27611-5726
(919) 832-4051    Fax: (919) 832-1888
E-mail: ala_nc@bellsouth.net

**Summary** To provide financial assistance for college to members of the American Legion Auxiliary in North Carolina and their children and grandchildren.

**Eligibility** This program is open to North Carolina residents who are either adult members of the American Legion Auxiliary or high school seniors (with preference to the children and grandchildren of members). Applicants must be able to demonstrate financial need.

**Financial data** The stipend is $2,000 per year.

**Duration** 1 year.

**Number awarded** 1 each year.

**Deadline** March of each year.

## [408]
## NAOMI BERBER MEMORIAL SCHOLARSHIP

Print and Graphics Scholarship Foundation
Attn: Scholarship Competition
200 Deer Run Road
Sewickley, PA 15143-2600
(412) 259-1740    Toll-free: (800) 910-GATF
Fax: (412) 741-2311    E-mail: pgsf@piagatf.org
Web: www.gain.net

**Summary** To provide financial assistance for college to women who want to prepare for a career in the printing or publishing industry.

**Eligibility** This program is open to females who are high school seniors or already in college. They must be interested in preparing for a career in publishing or printing while in college. This is a merit-based program; financial need is not considered.

**Financial data** The stipend ranges from $1,000 to $1,500, depending upon the funds available each year.

**Duration** 1 year; may be renewed for up to 3 additional years.

**Additional information** This program is named for Naomi Berber, the first woman elected to the Graphic Arts Technical Foundation Society of Fellows. Recipients must attend school on a full-time basis.

**Number awarded** 1 or more each year.

**Deadline** February of each year for high school seniors; March of each year for students already in college.

## [409]
### NATASHA MATSON FIFE SCHOLARSHIP

Kansas Women's Golf Association
c/o Phyllis Fast, Scholarship Chair
3006 S.E. Skylark Drive
Topeka, KS 66605
(785) 266-8033        E-mail: phast@networksplus.net
Web: www.kwga.org/scholarship.htm

**Summary** To provide financial assistance for college to women in Kansas who have participated in activities of the Kansas Women's Golf Association (KWGA).

**Eligibility** This program is open to women in Kansas who are graduating or have graduated from a high school in the state. Applicants must have participated in at least 1 KWGA Junior Girls Championship or State Amateur Championship. They must be planning to attend an accredited collegiate institution in the following academic year. Eligibility is not limited to junior golfers. Along with their application, they must submit information on the number of years they have played golf; their handicap index; the KWGA amateur and junior championships and years in which they have participated; an essay of more than 100 words on why they play golf and the benefits they have gained from golf; their golf accomplishments; participation in other high school and/or community activities; a copy of their high school transcript (including name of school, year of graduation, and GPA); and 3 letters of recommendation.

**Financial data** A stipend is awarded (amount not specified). Funds are paid directly to the recipient's collegiate institution.

**Duration** 1 year; nonrenewable.

**Number awarded** 1 or more each year.

**Deadline** March of each year.

## [410]
### NATHALIE A. PRICE MEMORIAL SCHOLARSHIP

Ocean State Women's Golf Association
P.O. Box 597
Portsmouth, RI 02871-0597
(401) 683-6301        E-mail: oswgari@aol.com
Web: www.oswga.org

**Summary** To provide financial assistance for college to women in Rhode Island who have played golf.

**Eligibility** This program is open to women in Rhode Island who are graduating high school seniors or current college students. Applicants must have been active in golf, as a member of the Ocean State Women's Golf Association (OSWGA), as a member of another association, or on their

school golf team. Along with their application, they must submit a transcript, a list of their citizenship and community service activities, and letters of recommendation. Financial need is not considered.

**Financial data** A stipend is awarded (amount not specified).

**Duration** 1 year; may be renewed.

**Additional information** This scholarship was first awarded in 1996.

**Number awarded** Varies each year; recently, 8 of these scholarships were awarded.

**Deadline** June of each year.

## [411]
### NATIONAL ASSOCIATION OF WOMEN IN CONSTRUCTION VERMONT SCHOLARSHIP

Vermont Student Assistance Corporation
Attn: Scholarship Programs
10 East Allen Street
P.O. Box 2000
Winooski, VT 05404-2601
(802) 654-3798        Toll-free: (888) 253-4819
Fax: (802) 654-3765        TDD: (802) 654-3766
TDD: (800) 281-3341 (within VT)
E-mail: info@vsac.org
Web: www.vsac.org

**Summary** To provide financial assistance for college to women in Vermont who are interested in preparing for a career in the construction industry.

**Eligibility** This program is open to women residents of Vermont who are graduating high school seniors or current college students. Applicants must be interested in working on an academic, vocational, technical, or advanced training program in a field related to construction. Selection is based on academic achievement, a letter of recommendation, required essays, and financial need.

**Financial data** The stipend is $500.

**Duration** 1 year; nonrenewable.

**Number awarded** 1 each year.

**Deadline** March of each year.

## [412]
### NATIONAL CITY/KHSAA SWEET 16 SCHOLARSHIPS

Kentucky High School Athletic Association
2280 Executive Drive
Lexington, KY 40505
(859) 299-5472        Fax: (859) 293-5999
E-mail: general@khsaa.org
Web: www.khsaa.org

**Summary** To provide financial assistance for college to student-athletes in Kentucky high schools.

**Eligibility** This program is open to high school seniors in Kentucky who have participated in athletics or cheerleading. The awards are presented in conjunction with the state basketball tournament, but all student-athletes, not just basketball players, are eligible. Students must be nominated by a school representative. Letters of nomination must explain why the student is an exemplary leader and should receive the scholarship. Selection is based on academic achievement, leadership, citizenship, and sportsmanship. Men and women are judged separately.

**Financial data**   The stipend is $1,000.

**Duration**   1 year; nonrenewable.

**Additional information**   This program is sponsored by National City Bank.

**Number awarded**   32 each year: 1 female and 1 male in each of 16 regions in Kentucky.

**Deadline**   February of each year.

## [413]
## NATIONAL COMMUNITY SERVICE SCHOLARSHIP

Miss America Pageant
Attn: Scholarship Department
Two Miss America Way, Suite 1000
Atlantic City, NJ 08401
(609) 345-7571, ext. 27       Toll-free: (800) 282-MISS
Fax: (609) 347-6079       E-mail: info@missamerica.org
Web: www.missamerica.org

**Summary**   To recognize and reward, with college scholarships, women who participate in the Miss America Pageant at the state level and demonstrate outstanding community service.

**Eligibility**   This program is open to women who compete at the state level of the Miss America Pageant but do not win their state title. Selection is based on excellence of community service.

**Financial data**   The stipend is $5,000.

**Duration**   1 year.

**Additional information**   This program was established in 1994.

**Number awarded**   1 each year.

**Deadline**   Varies, depending upon the date of local pageants leading to the state finals.

## [414]
## NATIONAL LATINA ALLIANCE SCHOLARSHIPS

National Latina Alliance
633 West Fifth Street, Suite 1150
Los Angeles, CA 90071
(323) 980-7992   E-mail: info@nationallatinaalliance.org
Web: www.nationallatinaalliance.org/ScholProg.htm

**Summary**   To provide financial assistance for college or other career education to Latinas.

**Eligibility**   This program is open to Latinas who are 1) graduating high school seniors; 2) currently enrolled in a college or university; 3) returning to school after an absence of at least 2 years; or 4) preparing for a non-traditional career (e.g., chef, artist, entrepreneur, nurse). Applicants must have a GPA of 2.5 or higher and be able to document financial need. They must submit a 1-page essay on the question, "As a Latina, what do you think is important for the success of the community?" Reentry applicants must also provide a 1-page essay discussing their reason for withdrawing from school. Non-traditional career students must provide documentation regarding their career.

**Financial data**   Stipends range from $500 to $1,000, depending on the need of the recipient.

**Duration**   1 year.

**Additional information**   Information is also available from Gloria Michel, Education Committee Chair, c/o Guerra & Associates, 1100 South Flower Street, Suite 2100, Los Angeles, CA 90015.

**Number awarded**   Varies each year; recently, 17 of these scholarships were awarded.

**Deadline**   March of each year.

## [415]
## NATIONAL SORORITY OF PHI DELTA KAPPA SCHOLARSHIPS

National Sorority of Phi Delta Kappa, Inc.
Attn: Perpetual Scholarship Foundation
8233 South King Drive
Chicago, IL 60619
(773) 783-7379       Fax: (773) 783-7354
E-mail: info@sororitynpdk.org
Web: www.sororitynpdk.org/scholarships.html

**Summary**   To provide financial assistance to African American high school seniors interested in studying education in college.

**Eligibility**   This program is open to African American high school seniors who are interested in working on a 4-year college degree in education. Men and women compete separately. Financial need is considered in the selection process.

**Financial data**   The stipend is $1,250 per year.

**Duration**   4 years, provided the recipient maintains a GPA of 3.0 or higher and a major in education.

**Additional information**   The sponsor was founded in 1923 as an organization of female African American educators.

**Number awarded**   10 each year: 1 male and 1 female in each of the organization's 5 regions.

**Deadline**   Applications must be submitted to a local chapter of the organization by January of each year.

## [416]
## NATIVE AMERICAN WOMEN'S HEALTH EDUCATION RESOURCE CENTER SCHOLARSHIPS

Native American Women's Health Education Resource
   Center
P.O. Box 572
Lake Andes, SD 57356-0572
(605) 487-7072       Fax: (605) 487-7964
Web: www.nativeshop.org/nawherc.html

**Summary**   To provide financial assistance to American Indian women currently enrolled in college.

**Eligibility**   This program is open to American Indian women who are currently enrolled in college and need financial assistance.

**Financial data**   The stipend is either $300 or $500 per semester.

**Duration**   The stipends are offered each semester.

**Additional information**   The Native American Women's Health Education Resource Center is a project of the Native American Community Board.

**Number awarded** 2 per semester.

**Deadline** March of each year.

## [417]
## NAVY/MARINE CORPS/COAST GUARD ENLISTED DEPENDENT SPOUSE SCHOLARSHIP

Navy Wives Club of America
P.O. Box 54022
Millington, TN 38053-6022
Toll-free: (866) 511-NWCA
E-mail: nwca@navywivesclubsofamerica.org
Web: www.navywivesclubsofamerica.org

**Summary** To provide financial assistance for undergraduate or graduate study to spouses of naval personnel.

**Eligibility** This program is open to the spouses of active-duty Navy, Marine Corps, or Coast Guard members who can demonstrate financial need. Applicants must be 1) a high school graduate or senior planning to attend college full time next year; 2) currently enrolled in an undergraduate program and planning to continue as a full-time undergraduate; 3) a college graduate or senior planning to be a full-time graduate student next year; and 4) a high school graduate or GED recipient planning to attend vocational or business school next year.

**Financial data** The stipends range from $500 to $1,000 each year (depending upon the donations from chapters of the Navy Wives Club of America).

**Duration** 1 year.

**Additional information** Information is also available from NWCA National Vice President, Winnie Rednour, 39743 Clements Way, Murrieta, GA 92563-4021.

**Number awarded** 1 or more each year.

**Deadline** May of each year.

## [418]
## NCAIAW SCHOLARSHIP

North Carolina Alliance for Athletics, Health, Physical
    Education, Recreation and Dance
Attn: Executive Director
P.O. Box 27751
Raleigh, NC 27611
Toll-free: (888) 840-6500        Fax: (919) 833-7700
E-mail: ncaahperd@ncaahperd.org
Web: www.ncaahperd.org/awards/scholarships.htm

**Summary** To provide financial assistance to women who are college seniors involved in sports at an institution that is a member of the former North Carolina Association of Intercollegiate Athletics for Women (NCAIAW).

**Eligibility** This program is open to women who have been a participant on 1 or more varsity athletic teams either as a player or in the support role of manager, trainer, etc. Applicants must be attending 1 of the following former NCAIAW colleges or universities in North Carolina: Appalachian State, Belmont Abbey, Bennett, Campbell, Davidson, Duke, East Carolina, Gardner-Webb, High Point, Mars Hill, Meredith, North Carolina A&T, North Carolina State, Pembroke State, Salem, University of North Carolina at Ashville, University of North Carolina at Chapel Hill, University of North Carolina at Charlotte, University of North Carolina at Wilmington, Wake Forest, or Western Carolina. They must

be college seniors at the time of application, be able to demonstrate high standards of scholarship, and show evidence of leadership potential (as indicated by participation in school and community activities).

**Financial data** The stipend is $1,000. Funds are sent to the recipient's school.

**Duration** 1 year.

**Additional information** This scholarship was established in 1983.

**Number awarded** 1 each year.

**Deadline** June of each year.

## [419]
## NCCE SCHOLARSHIPS

National Commission for Cooperative Education
360 Huntington Avenue, 384 CP
Boston, MA 02115-5096
(617) 373-3770                Fax: (617) 373-3463
E-mail: ncce@co-op.edu
Web: www.co-op.edu/scholarships.htm

**Summary** To provide financial assistance to students (particularly women and minorities) who are participating in cooperative education projects at designated colleges and universities.

**Eligibility** This program is open to high school seniors and community college transfer students entering 1 of the 10 partner colleges and universities. Applicants must be planning to participate in college cooperative education. They must have a GPA of 3.5 or higher. Along with their application, they must submit a 1-page essay describing why they have chosen to enter a college cooperative education program. Applications are especially encouraged from minorities, women, and students interested in science, mathematics, engineering, and technology. Selection is based on merit; financial need is not considered.

**Financial data** The stipend is $5,000.

**Duration** 1 year.

**Additional information** The schools currently participating in this program are Antioch College (Yellow Springs, Ohio), Drexel University (Philadelphia, Pennsylvania), Johnson & Wales University (Providence, Rhode Island; Charleston, South Carolina; Norfolk, Virginia; North Miami, Florida; Denver, Colorado; and Charlotte, North Carolina), Kettering University (Flint, Michigan), C.W. Post Campus of Long Island University (Brookville, New York), Northeastern University (Boston, Massachusetts), Pace University (New York, New York; White Plains, New York; and Pleasantville, New York), Rochester Institute of Technology (Rochester, New York), University of Cincinnati (Cincinnati, Ohio), and University of Toledo (Toledo, Ohio). Applications must be sent directly to the college or university.

**Number awarded** 113 each year: 5 at Antioch, 15 at Drexel, 15 at Johnson & Wales, 15 at Kettering, 8 at C.W. Post Campus of LIU, 15 at Northeastern, 10 at Pace, 10 at Rochester Tech, 10 at Cincinnati, and 10 at Toledo.

**Deadline** February of each year for Antioch, Johnson & Wales, C.W. Post Campus of LIU, Northeastern, and Rochester Tech; March of each year for Drexel, Kettering, Pace, Cincinnati, and Toledo.

## [420]
## NEBRASKA ELKS PAST EXALTED RULER'S SCHOLARSHIP

Nebraska Elks Association
c/o Melvin Nespor, Scholarship Committee
P.O. Box 14
Endicott, NE 68350
E-mail: mnespor@beatricene.com

**Summary** To provide financial assistance for college to high school seniors in Nebraska who demonstrate financial need.

**Eligibility** This program is open to seniors graduating from high schools in Nebraska. Applicants may be planning to attend any type of postsecondary school: beauty school, community college, trade school, 2-year college, or 4-year college or university. Selection is based primarily on financial need. Each Nebraska Elks Lodge can submit 1 application from a boy and 1 from a girl; boys and girls compete separately.

**Financial data** For both boys and girls, stipends are $800 for first place, $600 for second place, and $400 for third place.

**Duration** 1 year.

**Number awarded** 6 each year: 3 specifically for girls and 3 for boys.

**Deadline** January of each year.

## [421]
## NEBRASKA RURAL COMMUNITY SCHOOLS ASSOCIATION SCHOLARSHIPS

Nebraska Rural Community Schools Association
P.O. Box 22529
Lincoln, NE 68542
(402) 499-6756                    Fax: (402) 423-4961
E-mail: nrcsa@neb.rr.com
Web: www.nrcsa.net

**Summary** To provide financial assistance to students at high schools that are members of the Nebraska Rural Community Schools Association (NRCSA) who are interested in majoring in education or related fields in college.

**Eligibility** This program is open to seniors graduating from high schools holding current membership in NRCSA. Each school may submit 2 applications: 1 from a male and 1 from a female. Applicants must be planning to attend college in Nebraska and major in education or a related field to become a teacher, counselor, or media specialist. They must have a GPA of 3.5 or higher and scores of at least 22 on the ACT or 1020 on the mathematics and critical reasoning components of the SAT. Along with their application, they must submit a 300-word statement on why they deserve this scholarship, including their goals. Selection is based on that statement, academic achievement, leadership, character, initiative, involvement in school and community activities, and financial need. Males and females are considered separately.

**Financial data** The stipend is $750.

**Duration** 1 year; may be renewed.

**Additional information** This program is offered through the Lincoln Community Foundation. Information is also available from the foundation at 215 Centennial Mall South,

Suite 100, Lincoln, NE 68508, (402) 474-2345, Fax: (402) 476-8532, E-mail: lcf@lcf.org.

**Number awarded** 6 each year: 3 to females and 3 to males.

**Deadline** February of each year.

## [422]
## NEBRASKA SPACE GRANT STATEWIDE SCHOLARSHIP COMPETITION

Nebraska Space Grant Consortium
c/o University of Nebraska at Omaha
Allwine Hall 422
6001 Dodge Street
Omaha, NE 68182-0406
(402) 554-3772
Toll-free: (800) 858-8648, ext. 4-3772 (within NE)
Fax: (402) 554-3781          E-mail: nasa@unomaha.edu
Web: nasa.unomaha.edu/Funding/funding.php

**Summary** To provide financial assistance to undergraduate and graduate students (particularly women, minority, and disabled students) at member institutions of the Nebraska Space Grant Consortium.

**Eligibility** This program is open to undergraduate and graduate students at schools that are members of the Nebraska Space Grant Consortium. Students in all academic disciplines are eligible. This program is sponsored by the U.S. National Aeronautics and Space Administration (NASA), which strongly encourages women, minorities, and students with disabilities to apply. U.S. citizenship is required. Financial need is not considered in the selection process.

**Financial data** A stipend is awarded (amount not specified).

**Duration** 1 year.

**Additional information** The following schools are members of the Nebraska Space Grant Consortium: University of Nebraska at Omaha, University of Nebraska at Lincoln, University of Nebraska at Kearney, University of Nebraska Medical Center, Creighton University, Western Nebraska Community College, Chadron State College, College of St. Mary, Metropolitan Community College, Grace University, Hastings College, Little Priest Tribal College, and Nebraska Indian Community College.

**Number awarded** At least 2 students from each institution are supported each year.

**Deadline** April of each year.

## [423]
## NEBRASKA WAIVER OF TUITION FOR VETERANS' DEPENDENTS

Department of Veterans' Affairs
State Office Building
301 Centennial Mall South, Sixth Floor
P.O. Box 95083
Lincoln, NE 68509-5083
(402) 471-2458                    Fax: (402) 471-2491
E-mail: dparker@notes.state.ne.us
Web: www.vets.state.ne.us

**Summary** To provide financial assistance for college to

dependents of deceased and disabled veterans and military personnel in Nebraska.

**Eligibility** Eligible are spouses, widow(er)s, and children who are residents of Nebraska and whose parent, stepparent, or spouse was a member of the U.S. armed forces and 1) died of a service-connected disability; 2) died subsequent to discharge as a result of injury or illness sustained while in service; 3) is permanently and totally disabled as a result of military service; or 4) is classified as missing in action or as a prisoner of war during armed hostilities after August 4, 1964. Applicants must be attending or planning to attend a branch of the University of Nebraska, a state college, or a community college in Nebraska.

**Financial data** Tuition is waived at public institutions in Nebraska.

**Duration** The waiver is valid for 1 degree, diploma, or certificate from a community college and 1 baccalaureate degree.

**Additional information** Applications may be submitted through 1 of the recognized veterans' organizations or any county service officer.

**Number awarded** Varies each year; recently, 302 of these grants were awarded.

## [424]
## NETWORK OF EXECUTIVE WOMEN SCHOLARSHIP

Network of Executive Women
Attn: Scholarship Program
Accenture/Avanade
161 North Clark Street, 37th Floor
Chicago, IL 60601
(312) 373-5683 Fax: (312) 726-4704
E-mail: ngranger@newonline.org
Web: www.newonline.org/scholarships.cfm

**Summary** To provide financial assistance to upper-division and graduate student women preparing for a career in the consumer products and retail industry.

**Eligibility** This program is open to women enrolled full time as juniors, seniors, or graduate students in a retail, food, or consumer packaged goods related program at a U.S. college or university. Applicants must have a GPA of 3.0 or higher. Along with their application, they must submit a 1-page essay explaining why they merit this scholarship and outlining their food, retail, consumer packaged goods industry interests. Selection is based on that essay, a current resume, a transcript, and 2 letters of recommendation; financial need is not considered.

**Financial data** A stipend is awarded (amount not specified).

**Duration** 1 year.

**Number awarded** 1 or more each year.

**Deadline** February of each year.

## [425]
## NEVADA SPACE GRANT CONSORTIUM UNDERGRADUATE SCHOLARSHIP PROGRAM

Nevada Space Grant Consortium
c/o University of Nevada at Reno
Mackay School of Mines Building, Room 308
MS 168
Reno, NV 89557
(775) 784-6261 Fax: (775) 327-2235
E-mail: nvsg@mines.unr.edu
Web: www.unr.edu/spacegrant

**Summary** To provide financial assistance for space-related study to undergraduate students (particularly women, minority, and disabled students) at institutions that are members of the University and Community College System of Nevada (UCCSN) and participate in the Nevada Space Grant Consortium (NSGC).

**Eligibility** This program is open to undergraduate students at UCCSN member institutions. Applicants must be working on a degree in an aerospace-related field, including any science, mathematics, engineering, or technology discipline that is concerned with or likely to improve the understanding, assessment, development, and utilization of space. They must be U.S. citizens and enrolled full time. This program is part of the Space Grant program of the U.S. National Aeronautics and Space Administration (NASA), which encourages participation by members of underrepresented groups (African Americans, Hispanics, American Indians, Pacific Islanders, people with physical disabilities, and women of all races). Selection is based on the academic qualifications of the applicant, the quality of a career goal statement, and an assessment of the applicant's motivation for an aerospace career.

**Financial data** The stipend is $2,500 per year. Funds may be used for tuition or registration fees. Funds may not be regarded as payment for research work or any other work.

**Duration** 1 year; may be renewed.

**Additional information** Funding for this program is provided by NASA.

**Number awarded** Varies each year; recently, 13 of these awards were granted.

**Deadline** March of each year.

## [426]
## NEVADA WOMEN'S FUND SCHOLARSHIPS

Nevada Women's Fund
770 Smithridge Drive, Suite 300
Reno, NV 89502
(775) 786-2335 Fax: (775) 786-8152
E-mail: info@nevadawomensfund.org
Web: www.nevadawomensfund.org/Scholarships.html

**Summary** To provide funding to women in Nevada who are interested in working on an undergraduate or graduate degree.

**Eligibility** This program is open to women who are working on or planning to work on academic study or vocational training on the undergraduate or graduate level. Preference is given to northern Nevada residents and those attending northern Nevada institutions. Selection is based on academic achievement, financial need, work experience, community involvement, other life experiences, family responsibilities, and the applicant's plan after completing study. Women of all ages are eligible. An interview may be required.

**Financial data** Stipends range from $300 to $5,000 per year. Recently, a total of $185,330 was awarded.

**Duration** 1 year; may be renewed.

**Additional information** This program includes a large number of named scholarships.

**Number awarded** Varies each year. Recently 118 of these scholarships were awarded.

**Deadline** February of each year.

## [427]
## NEW HAMPSHIRE CHARTER CHAPTER SCHOLARSHIPS

American Business Women's Association-New
    Hampshire Charter Chapter
c/o Kathleen Emond, Education Committee Chair
100 Gilman Street
Nashua, NH 03060
E-mail: info@abwanh.com
Web: www.abwanh.com

**Summary** To provide financial assistance to women in New Hampshire who are interested in attending a community college or vocational/technical school in the state.

**Eligibility** This program is open to female residents of New Hampshire who are attending or have been accepted at a licensed or accredited vocational/technical school or community college in the state. Applicants must be entering the second year of study and have a GPA of 3.0 or higher. They must be U.S. citizens.

**Financial data** The stipend is $1,000.

**Duration** 1 year.

**Number awarded** 2 each year.

**Deadline** March of each year.

## [428]
## NEW HAMPSHIRE WOMEN'S GOLF ASSOCIATION SCHOLARSHIPS

New Hampshire Women's Golf Association
c/o Pat Pierson
P.O. Box 2201
Dover, NH 03821-2210
E-mail: nhwga@usga.org
Web: www.nhwga.org

**Summary** To provide financial assistance for college to members of the New Hampshire Women's Golf Association (NHWGA) and their families.

**Eligibility** This program is open to residents of New Hampshire who are enrolled or planning to enroll as a full-time undergraduate student at an accredited college or university. Applicants must be members or relatives of members of the NHWGA. Along with their application, they must submit an essay about their plans for the future and how they intend to use their education. Selection is based on the essay, GPA, and financial need.

**Financial data** Stipends are approximately $500.

**Duration** 1 year; may be renewed up to 3 additional years.

**Number awarded** Varies each year; recently, 20 of these scholarships were awarded.

**Deadline** July of each year.

## [429]
## NEW HORIZONS SCHOLARSHIPS

Royal Neighbors of America
Attn: Fraternal Services
230 16th Street
Rock Island, IL 61201-8645
(309) 788-4561        Toll-free: (800) 627-4762
E-mail: contact@royalneighbors.org
Web: www.royalneighbors.org

**Summary** To provide financial assistance for college to women members of the Royal Neighbors of America who don't fall into the usual college age range.

**Eligibility** This program is open to women members of the society who who don't fall into the usual college age range. Applicants must be at least 35 years of age. They may be attending college, junior college, or vocational school on either a part-time or full-time basis.

**Financial data** Stipends range up to $5,000 per year.

**Duration** 1 year.

**Number awarded** 5 each year.

**Deadline** December of each year.

## [430]
## NEW JERSEY COALITION ON WOMEN AND DISABILITIES SCHOLARSHIP

New Jersey Coalition on Women and Disabilities
c/o Dorothy McDowell, President
67 Bay View Drive
Brick, NJ 08723-7449
(732) 255-2733        E-mail: DorMcD@aol.com

**Summary** To provide financial assistance for college to women with disabilities in New Jersey.

**Eligibility** This program is open to women with a diagnosed disability who are attending an accredited New Jersey college, university, or vocational/technical school. Applicants must submit proof of current enrollment in good standing.

**Financial data** The stipend is $1,000.

**Duration** 1 year.

**Additional information** This program was established in 1999.

**Number awarded** Up to 5 each year.

## [431]
## NEW JERSEY SCHOLARSHIP

Society of Women Engineers
230 East Ohio Street, Suite 400
Chicago, IL 60611-3265
(312) 596-5223        Toll-free: (877) SWE-INFO
Fax: (312) 644-8557
E-mail: scholarshipapplication@swe.org
Web: www.swe.org
Web: www.swe.org/scholarships

**Summary** To provide financial assistance to women from

New Jersey who will be entering college as freshmen and are interested in studying engineering or computer science.

**Eligibility** This program is open to women who are entering college as freshmen with a GPA of 3.5 or higher. Applicants must be residents of New Jersey planning to enroll full time at an ABET-accredited 4-year college or university and major in computer science or engineering. Along with their application, they must submit a 1-page essay on why they want to be an engineer or computer scientist, how they believe they will make a difference as an engineer or computer scientist, and what influenced them to study engineering or computer science. Selection is based on merit.

**Financial data** The stipend is $1,500.

**Duration** 1 year.

**Additional information** This program was established in 1998 by the New Jersey Section of the Society of Women Engineers (SWE).

**Number awarded** 1 each year.

**Deadline** May of each year.

## [432]
## NEW JERSEY SCHOOLWOMEN'S CLUB SCHOLARSHIPS

New Jersey Schoolwomen's Club
c/o Judy Jordan
67 Spray Way
Lavallette, NJ 08735

**Summary** To provide financial assistance for college to female high school seniors in New Jersey who intend to prepare for a career in education.

**Eligibility** This program is open to women graduating from high schools in New Jersey. Applicants must be planning to attend a 4-year college or university to prepare for a career in the field of education. They must have an academic average of "C+" or higher and a combined SAT mathematics and critical reading score of at least 950. Selection is based on academic achievement, community involvement, and extracurricular activities.

**Financial data** The stipend is $1,000.

**Duration** 1 year.

**Additional information** This program includes the Patricia Barber Scholarship and the Jeanette Hodge Scholarship.

**Number awarded** 2 each year.

**Deadline** February of each year.

## [433]
## NEW JERSEY STATE ELKS HANDICAPPED CHILDREN'S SCHOLARSHIP

New Jersey State Elks
Attn: Handicapped Children's Committee
665 Rahway Avenue
P.O. Box 1596
Woodbridge, NJ 07095-1596
(732) 326-1300          E-mail: info@njelks.org
Web: www.njelks.org

**Summary** To provide financial assistance for college to high school seniors in New Jersey who have a disability.

**Eligibility** This program is open to seniors graduating from high schools in New Jersey who have a disability. Selection is based on academic standing, general worthiness, and financial need. Boys and girls are judged separately.

**Financial data** The stipend is $2,500 per year. Funds are paid directly to the recipient's college or university.

**Duration** 4 years.

**Number awarded** 2 each year: 1 to a boy and 1 to a girl.

**Deadline** April of each year.

## [434]
## NEW JERSEY UTILITIES ASSOCIATION SCHOLARSHIPS

New Jersey Utilities Association
50 West State Street, Suite 1117
Trenton, NJ 08608
(609) 392-1000          Fax: (609) 396-4231
Web: www.njua.org

**Summary** To provide financial assistance to minority, female, and disabled high school seniors in New Jersey interested in majoring in selected subjects in college.

**Eligibility** Eligible to apply for this scholarship are women, minorities (Black, Hispanic, American Indian/Alaska Native, or Asian American/Pacific Islander), and persons with disabilities who are high school seniors in New Jersey. They must be able to demonstrate financial need, be planning to enroll on a full-time basis at an institute of higher education, and be planning to work on a bachelor's degree in engineering, environmental science, chemistry, biology, business administration, or accounting. Children of employees of any New Jersey Utilities Association-member company are ineligible. Selection is based on overall academic excellence and demonstrated financial need.

**Financial data** The stipend is $1,500 per year.

**Duration** 4 years.

**Number awarded** 2 each year.

**Deadline** March of each year.

## [435]
## NEW MEXICO ELKS ASSOCIATION CHARITABLE AND BENEVOLENT TRUST SCHOLARSHIPS

New Mexico Elks Association
Attn: Charitable and Benevolent Trust Commission
c/o Jim Larrabbee, Scholarship Committee
302 Ciniza Court
Gallup, NM 87301
Fax: (505) 863-3821
E-mail: JimLarrabee@cnetco.com
Web: www.nmelks.org

**Summary** To provide financial assistance for college to high school seniors in New Mexico.

**Eligibility** Applicants must be seniors graduating from a high school in New Mexico. They must have exhibited outstanding scholastic and leadership ability, including extracurricular and civic activities. High school class rank, GPA, and standardized test scores must be validated by a school official. An endorsement from the local Elks Lodge is required. Financial need is also considered in the selection process. Some awards are designated for females and some for males.

**Financial data** Stipends are either $2,000 or $1,000 per year.

**Duration** 1 or 4 years.

**Additional information** Recipients may attend any level of academic institution and may major in any field. This program includes the following named awards: the Charles Mahr Memorial Scholarship, the Evelyn Boney Memorial Scholarships, the Howard Medlin Memorial Scholarship, and the Robert E. Boney Memorial Scholarship.

**Number awarded** 14 each year: 1 at $2,000 per year for 4 years to the top female applicant, 1 at $2,000 per year for 4 years to the top male applicant, 6 at $2,000 for 1 year, and 6 at $1,000 for 1 year.

**Deadline** March of each year.

## [436]
## NMSGC PARTNER SCHOLARSHIPS

New Mexico Space Grant Consortium
c/o New Mexico State University
Sugerman Space Grant Building
3050 Knox Street
MSC SG, Box 30001
Las Cruces, NM 88003-0001
(505) 646-6414                    Fax: (505) 646-7791
E-mail: nmsgc@pathfinder.nmsu.edu
Web: spacegrant.nmsu.edu

**Summary** To provide financial assistance to undergraduate and graduate students (especially women, minority, and disabled students) who are interested in working on a degree in space-related fields at institutions that are members of the New Mexico Space Grant Consortium (NMSGC).

**Eligibility** This program is open to full-time undergraduate and graduate students at NMSGC institutions who are working on a degree in a field relevant to the mission of the U.S. National Aeronautics and Space Administration (NASA). Each institution determines the details of the program on its campus. The NMSGC is a component of the NASA Space Grant program, which encourages participation by groups underrepresented in science, technology, engineering and mathematics: women, minorities, and persons with disabilities.

**Financial data** Stipends are established by the partner institutions, but are approximately $2,000 for undergraduates or $4,000 for graduate students.

**Duration** 1 year. Some institutions permit renewals for 1 additional year.

**Additional information** The NMSGC institutional members are: New Mexico State University, New Mexico Institute of Mining and Technology, University of New Mexico, Doña Ana Branch Community College, and San Juan Community College. This program is funded by NASA. Fields of study currently accepted at New Mexico State university include those in the arts and sciences (astronomy, biology, chemistry, computer science, earth science, mathematics, or physics), engineering (chemical, civil, computer, electrical, industrial, mechanical, surveying, or engineering technology), agriculture and home economics (agronomy, animal and range sciences, entomology, fishery and wildlife sciences, horticulture, plant pathology, and weed science),

or education (elementary or secondary science). Projects at New Mexico Institute of Mining and Technology focus on image processing and meteorology. The University of New Mexico supports students in aerospace science, space power and propulsion, and aerospace engineering. Programs at the community colleges are designed for students working on a degree in computer technology with a related space science application.

**Number awarded** Varies each year.

**Deadline** Each institution sets its own deadlines.

## [437]
## NON COMMISSIONED OFFICERS ASSOCIATION SCHOLARSHIP FUND

Non Commissioned Officers Association of the United
   States of America
Attn: Scholarship Administrator
10635 IH 35 North
P.O. Box 33610
San Antonio, TX 78265-3610
(210) 653-6161                    Toll-free: (800) 662-2620
E-mail: membsvc@ncoausa.org
Web: www.ncoausa.org

**Summary** To provide financial assistance for college to spouses and children of members of the Non Commissioned Officers Association.

**Eligibility** This program is open to spouses and children (under 25 years of age) of members of the association. Children must submit 2 letters of recommendation from teachers, a personal recommendation from an adult who is not a relative, a handwritten autobiography, a certified transcript of high school or college grades, ACT or SAT scores, and a composition on Americanism. Spouses must submit a copy of their high school diploma or GED equivalent; a certified transcript of all college courses completed (if any); a certificate of completion for any other courses or training; a brief biographical background statement; and a letter of intent that includes a description of their proposed course of study for a degree, plans for completion of a degree, and a paragraph on "What a College Degree Means to Me." Financial need is not normally considered in the selection process and no applicant will be rejected because of a lack of need, but in some cases of extreme need it may be used as a factor. Each year, 2 special awards are presented: the Mary Barraco Scholarship to the student submitting the best essay on Americanism, and the William T. Green Scholarship to the student with the best high school academic record.

**Financial data** The scholarship stipend is $900 and the special awards are $1,000; funds are paid directly to the designated school to be used for the recipient's room and board, tuition, library fees, textbooks, and related instructional material.

**Duration** 1 year; may be renewed if the student maintains a GPA of 3.0 or higher and carries at least 15 hours.

**Additional information** Spouses who receive a grant must apply for membership in 1 of the NCOA membership categories (regular, associate, veteran, or auxiliary).

**Number awarded** 15 each year: 9 scholarships to children of members, 4 scholarships to spouses of members, and 2 special awards.

**Deadline** March of each year.

## [438]
### NORMA L. MOORE ENDOWMENT SCHOLARSHIP
Epsilon Sigma Alpha
Attn: ESA Foundation Assistant Scholarship Director
P.O. Box 270517
Fort Collins, CO 80527
(970) 223-2824          Fax: (970) 223-4456
Web: www.esaintl.com/esaf

**Summary** To provide financial assistance for college to women from Oklahoma.

**Eligibility** This program is open to women from Oklahoma who are either 1) graduating high school seniors in the top 25% of their class or with minimum scores of 20 on the ACT or an equivalent score on the SAT, or 2) students already in college with a GPA of 3.0 or higher. Students enrolled for training in a technical school or returning to school after an absence are also eligible. Applicants may be planning to major in any field at a college or university in any state. Selection is based on character (10%), leadership (10%), service (5%), financial need (50%), and scholastic ability (25%).

**Financial data** The stipend is $500.

**Duration** 1 year; nonrenewable.

**Additional information** Epsilon Sigma Alpha (ESA) is a women's service organization. Information is also available from Lynn Hughes, Scholarship Director, 324 N.E. Mead, Grants Pass, OR 97526, (541) 476-4617, E-mail: orcycler@vsisp.net. This scholarship was first awarded in 1998. Completed applications must be submitted to the ESA State Counselor who verifies the information before forwarding them to the scholarship director. A $5 processing fee is required.

**Number awarded** 1 each year.

**Deadline** January of each year.

## [439]
### NORMA ROSS WALTER SCHOLARSHIP PROGRAM
Willa Cather Pioneer Memorial and Educational
   Foundation
Attn: Scholarship Program
413 North Webster
Red Cloud, NE 68970
(402) 746-2653          Fax: (402) 746-2652
Web: www.willacather.org/scholarship.htm

**Summary** To provide financial assistance to female graduates of Nebraska high schools who are or will be majoring in English at an accredited college or university.

**Eligibility** This program is open to women who have graduated or plan to graduate from a Nebraska high school and enter a college or university as a first-year student. Applicants must plan to continue their education as English majors (journalism is not acceptable). Along with their application, they must submit a 1,500-word essay on several of the short stories or a novel written by Willa Cather. Selection is based on intellectual promise, creativity, and character.

**Financial data** The stipend is $1,000.

**Duration** 1 year; nonrenewable.

**Number awarded** 1 each year.

**Deadline** January of each year.

## [440]
### NORTH CAROLINA SPACE GRANT CONSORTIUM UNDERGRADUATE SCHOLARSHIPS
North Carolina Space Grant Consortium
c/o North Carolina State University
Mechanical and Aerospace Engineering
1009 Capability Drive, Suite 210
Box 7515
Raleigh, NC 27695-7515
(919) 515-4240          Fax: (919) 515-5934
E-mail: scholarships@ncspacegrant.org
Web: www.ncspacegrant.org

**Summary** To provide funding to undergraduate students (particularly women, minority, and disabled students) at institutions affiliated with the North Carolina Space Grant Consortium (NCSGC) interested in major in space-related fields.

**Eligibility** This program is open to full-time undergraduate students at institutions affiliated with the NCSGC who are freshmen, sophomores, or recent transfers from a community or junior college. Applicants must be working on a degree in a science, technology, engineering, or mathematics (STEM) discipline of interest to the U.S. National Aeronautics and Space Administration (NASA). Selection is based on the student's academic achievement, a letter of recommendation, and exhibited leadership qualities. U.S. citizenship is required. A primary goal of this program is the recruitment and retention of underrepresented minorities, women, and persons with disabilities into space-related fields.

**Financial data** The stipend is $1,000 per year.

**Duration** 1 year; may be renewed 1 additional year.

**Additional information** The affiliated institutions are North Carolina State University, North Carolina A&T State University, Duke University, North Carolina Central University, the University of North Carolina at Charlotte, the University of North Carolina at Chapel Hill, the University of North Carolina at Pembroke, and Winston-Salem State University. This program is funded by NASA.

**Number awarded** Varies each year.

**Deadline** March of each year.

## [441]
### NORTH CENTRAL NETWORK OF EXECUTIVE WOMEN IN HOSPITALITY SCHOLARSHIP AWARDS
Network of Executive Women in Hospitality-North
   Central Chapter
Attn: Kate Koskey, Director of Scholarship and
   Education
P.O. Box 80242
Minneapolis, MN 55408
Toll-free: (800) 593-NEWH          Fax: (800) 693-NEWH
E-mail: kkoskey@hilineinc.com
Web: www.newh.org/newh/scholarshippacket.php

**Summary** To provide financial assistance to women in north central states who wish to work on a college degree in a hospitality-related field.

**Eligibility** This program is open to women who have completed half the requirements for a degree or certification program at a vocational school or college in Iowa, Minnesota, North Dakota, South Dakota, or Wisconsin. Applicants must have a GPA of 3.0 or higher and a career objective in the hospitality or food service industries (e.g., hotel and restaurant management, culinary, food service, architecture, design). Selection is based on financial need and academic accomplishments.

**Financial data**  A stipend is awarded (amount not specified).

**Duration**  1 year.

**Number awarded**  1 or more each year.

## [442]
## NORTH DAKOTA EDUCATIONAL ASSISTANCE FOR DEPENDENTS OF VETERANS

Department of Veterans Affairs
1411 32nd Street South
P.O. Box 9003
Fargo, ND 58106-9003
(701) 239-7165                    Toll-free: (866) 634-8387
Fax: (701) 239-7166
Web: www.state.nd.us/veterans/benefits/waiver.html

**Summary**  To provide financial assistance for college to the spouses, widow(er)s, and children of disabled and other North Dakota veterans and military personnel.

**Eligibility**  This program is open to the spouses, widow(er)s, and dependent children of veterans who are totally disabled as a result of service-connected causes, or who were killed in action, or who have died as a result of wounds or service-connected disabilities, or who were identified as prisoners of war or missing in action. Veteran parents must have been born in and lived in North Dakota until entrance into the armed forces (or must have resided in the state for at least 6 months prior to entrance into military service) and must have served during wartime.

**Financial data**  Eligible dependents receive free tuition and are exempt from fees at any state-supported institution of higher education, technical school, or vocational school in North Dakota.

**Duration**  Up to 36 months or 8 academic semesters.

**Number awarded**  Varies each year.

## [443]
## NORTH DAKOTA SPACE GRANT PROGRAM SCHOLARSHIPS

North Dakota Space Grant Program
c/o University of North Dakota
Department of Space Studies
Clifford Hall, Fifth Floor
P.O. Box 9008
Grand Forks, ND 58202-9008
(701) 777-4856                    Toll-free: (800) 828-4274
Fax: (701) 777-3711              E-mail: bieri@space.edu
Web: www.space.edu/spacegrant/fellowships.html

**Summary**  To provide financial assistance for space-related study to undergraduates (particularly women, minorities, and students with disabilities) at tribal and public 2- or 4-year institutions of higher education in North Dakota.

**Eligibility**  This program is open to undergraduate students at tribal and public 2- and 4-year institutions of higher education in North Dakota. Applicants must be working on

a degree in a field of mathematics, science, or engineering that is relevant to the interests of the U.S. National Aeronautics and Space Administration (NASA). They must have a GPA of 3.0 or higher. A goal of the program is to encourage members of underrepresented groups (women, minorities, and persons with disabilities) to enter mathematics, science, or engineering fields of study. Students at the University of North Dakota and at North Dakota State University are not eligible. Selection is based on academic excellence and relevance of the student's disciplines and interests to mathematics, science, or engineering.

**Financial data**  Stipends are $500 at 2-year public and tribal colleges or $750 at 4-year public state universities.

**Additional information**  This program is funded by NASA.

**Number awarded**  3 scholarships are awarded each year at each participating college and university.

**Deadline**  January of each year.

## [444]
## NORTHROP GRUMMAN SCHOLARSHIPS

Society of Women Engineers
230 East Ohio Street, Suite 400
Chicago, IL 60611-3265
(312) 596-5223                    Toll-free: (877) SWE-INFO
Fax: (312) 644-8557
E-mail: scholarshipapplication@swe.org
Web: www.swe.org/scholarships

**Summary**  To provide financial assistance to female high school seniors interested in studying specified fields of engineering in college.

**Eligibility**  This program is open to women who are graduating high school seniors planning to enroll full time at an ABET-accredited 4-year college or university. Applicants must have a GPA of 3.0 or higher and be planning to major in computer science or aerospace, chemical, computer, electrical, industrial, manufacturing, or mechanical engineering. Along with their application, they must submit a 1-page essay on why they want to be an engineer or computer scientist, how they believe they will make a difference as an engineer or computer scientist, and what influenced them to study engineering or computer science. Selection is based on merit.

**Financial data**  The stipend is $5,000.

**Duration**  1 year.

**Additional information**  This program, established in 1983, is sponsored by Northrup Grumman.

**Number awarded**  3 each year.

**Deadline**  May of each year.

## [445]
## NORTHWEST NETWORK OF EXECUTIVE WOMEN IN HOSPITALITY SCHOLARSHIP AWARDS

Network of Executive Women in Hospitality-Northwest Chapter
Attn: My Nguyen, Director of Scholarship and Education
NB Design Group
1932 First Avenue, Suite 926
Seattle, WA 98125
(206) 441-7754                    Toll-free: (800) 593-NEWH
Fax: (800) 693-NEWH  E-mail: my@nbdesigngroup.net
Web: www.newh.org/newh/scholarshippacket.php

**Summary** To provide financial assistance to women in northwestern states who wish to work on a college degree in a hospitality-related field.

**Eligibility** This program is open to women who have completed half the requirements for a degree or certification program at a vocational school or college in Alaska, Idaho, Montana, Oregon, or Washington. Applicants must have a GPA of 3.0 or higher and a career objective in the hospitality or food service industries (e.g., hotel and restaurant management, culinary, food service, architecture, design). Selection is based on financial need and academic accomplishments.

**Financial data** The stipend is $1,000.

**Duration** 1 year.

**Number awarded** Up to 3 each year.

**Deadline** April of each year.

## [446]
## NORTHWEST WOMEN IN EDUCATIONAL ADMINISTRATION SCHOLARSHIP

Confederation of Oregon School Administrators
Attn: COSA Foundation
707 13th Street, S.E., Suite 100
Salem, OR 97301-4035
(503) 581-3141                    Fax: (503) 581-9840
E-mail: nancy@oasc.org
Web: www.cosa.k12.or.us

**Summary** To provide financial assistance to women who are high school seniors in Oregon and interested in preparing for a teaching career at a community college, college, or university in the state.

**Eligibility** This program is open to women who are graduating from high schools in Oregon. Applicants should be interested in attending a community college, college, or university in the state to major in education. They must have been active in community and school affairs, have a GPA of 3.5 or higher, and enroll in the fall term after graduating from high school. Along with their application, they must submit a 1-page autobiography (that states personal goals), the name of the school they plan to attend, and the endorsement of a member of the Confederation of Oregon School Administrators (COSA). Financial need is not considered in the selection process.

**Financial data** The stipend is $1,000. Funds are paid directly to the recipient.

**Duration** 1 year; nonrenewable.

**Additional information** This program is offered through Northwest Women in Educational Administration.

**Number awarded** 1 each year.

**Deadline** February of each year.

## [447]
## NPC FOUNDATION REGIONAL SCHOLARSHIPS

National Panhellenic Conference
Attn: NPC Foundation
3500 DePauw Boulevard, Suite 1079
Indianapolis, IN 46268
(317) 876-7802                    Fax: (317) 876-7904
E-mail: npcfoundation@npcwomen.org
Web: www.npcwomen.org

**Summary** To provide financial assistance to undergraduate women who are members of Greek-letter societies.

**Eligibility** This program is open to Greek-affiliated women at colleges and universities in the United States. Applicants must provide information on their university committees, activities, and honors received; Panhellenic offices, committees, and honors received; chapter offices, committees, and honors received; and financial need. Scholarships are presented to students in each of 4 regions of the country.

**Financial data** The stipend is $1,000.

**Duration** 1 year.

**Additional information** This program includes the Mid-American Greek Council Association Scholarship, the Northeast Greek Leadership Association Scholarship, the Southeastern Panhellenic Conference Scholarship, and the Western Regional Greek Association Scholarship, awarded respectively in the 4 regions. In addition, the Alpha Phi/Betty Mullins Jones Scholarship is awarded to the highest-ranked applicant from all regions.

**Number awarded** 5 each year.

**Deadline** January of each year.

## [448]
## NSBE/SHPE/SWE MEMBERS SCHOLARSHIP

Morgan Stanley
c/o Joyce Arencibia, IT College Recruiting
750 Seventh Avenue, 30th Floor
New York, NY 10019
(212) 762-4000
E-mail: diversityrecruiting@morganstanley.com
Web: www.morganstanley.com

**Summary** To provide financial assistance and work experience to members of the National Society of Black Engineers (NSBE), Society of Hispanic Professional Engineers (SHPE), and Society of Women Engineers (SWE) who are working on an undergraduate degree in computer science or engineering.

**Eligibility** This program is open to active members of NSBE, SHPE, and SWE who are enrolled in their sophomore or junior year of college (or the third or fourth year of a 5-year program). Applicants must be enrolled full time and have a GPA of 3.0 or higher. They must be willing to commit to a paid summer internship in the Morgan Stanley Information Technology Division. All majors and disciplines are eligible, but preference is given to students preparing for a career in computer science or engineering. Along with their application, they must submit 1-page essays on 1) why they are applying for this scholarship and why they should be selected as a recipient; 2) a technical project on which they worked, either through a university course or previous work experience, their role in the project, and how they contributed to the end result; and 3) a software, hardware, or new innovative application of existing technology that they would create if they could and the impact it would have. Financial need is not considered in the selection process.

**Financial data** Students who receive a scholarship as juniors (or fourth-year students in a 5-year program) receive $10,000 for their final year of college. Students who receive a scholarship as sophomores (or third-year students in a 5-year program) receive $5,000 for their junior year (or fourth year of a 5-year program).

**Duration** 1 year; may be renewed for the final year for students who receive a scholarship as sophomores (or third-year students in a 5-year program).

**Additional information** The program includes a paid summer internship in the Morgan Stanley Information Technology Division during the summer following the time of application.

**Number awarded** 1 or more each year.

**Deadline** February of each year.

## [449]
## NSPS FORUM FOR EQUAL OPPORTUNITY SCHOLARSHIP/MARY FEINDT SCHOLARSHIP

American Congress on Surveying and Mapping
Attn: Scholarships
6 Montgomery Village Avenue, Suite 403
Gaithersburg, MD 20879
(240) 632-9716, ext. 113        Fax: (240) 632-1321
E-mail: pat.canfield@acsm.net
Web: www.acsm.net/scholar.html

**Summary** To provide financial assistance to female members of the American Congress on Surveying and Mapping (ACSM) who are working on an undergraduate degree in surveying.

**Eligibility** This program is open to female ACSM members who are enrolled at a 4-year college or university. Applicants must be majoring in a surveying or mapping program. Along with their application, they must submit a statement describing their educational program, future plans for study or research, and why the award is merited. Selection is based on that statement (30%), academic record (30%), letters of recommendation (20%), and professional activities (20%); if 2 or more applicants are judged equal based on those criteria, financial need may be considered.

**Financial data** The stipend is $1,000.

**Duration** 1 year.

**Additional information** Funding for these scholarships is provided by Forum for Equal Opportunity of the National Society of Professional Surveyors (NSPS).

**Number awarded** 1 each year.

**Deadline** October of each year.

## [450]
## NYWICI FOUNDATION SCHOLARSHIPS

New York Women in Communications, Inc.
Attn: NYWICI Foundation
355 Lexington Avenue, 15th Floor
New York, NY 10017-6603
(212) 297-2133        Fax: (212) 370-9047
E-mail: nywicipr@nywici.org
Web: www.nywici.org/foundation.scholarships.html

**Summary** To provide financial assistance for college or graduate school to female residents of designated eastern states who are interested in preparing for a career in the communications profession.

**Eligibility** This program is open to females who are 1) seniors graduating from high schools in New York, New Jersey, Connecticut, or Pennsylvania; 2) undergraduate students who are permanent residents of New York, New Jersey, Connecticut, or Pennsylvania; and 3) graduate students who are permanent residents of New York, New Jersey, Connecticut, or Pennsylvania. Applicants must be majoring in a communications-related field (advertising, broadcasting, communications, journalism, marketing, new media, or public relations) and have a GPA of 3.2 or higher. Along with their application, they must submit a resume that includes school and extracurricular activities, significant achievements, academic honors and awards, and community service work; a personal essay of 300 to 500 words describing how events in their lives have inspired them to achieve success and overcome difficulty in the face of any financial and/or other obstacles; 2 letters of recommendation; and an official transcript. Selection is based on academic record, need, demonstrated leadership, participation in school and community activities, honors, work experience, goals and aspirations, and unusual personal and/or family circumstances.

**Financial data** The maximum stipend is $10,000.

**Duration** 1 year; recipients may reapply.

**Number awarded** Varies each year; recently, 18 of these scholarships were awarded.

**Deadline** January of each year.

## [451]
## OHIO HOME ECONOMISTS IN HOME AND COMMUNITY SCHOLARSHIP

Ohio Association of Family and Consumer Sciences
c/o Donna Green, Scholarship Chair
OSU Extension
2900 South Columbus Avenue
Sandusky, OH 44870
E-mail: green.308@osu.edu
Web: oafcs.org/students.htm

**Summary** To provide financial assistance to Ohio homemakers who are returning to school to complete a bachelor's degree or pursue graduate study in family and consumer sciences.

**Eligibility** This program is open to Ohio homemakers who are returning to school to study family and consumer sciences at the undergraduate or graduate level. Applicants must be members of both the American Association of Family and Consumer Sciences and the Ohio Association of Family and Consumer Sciences. They must submit a statement that includes their goals and career plans in family and consumer science, background and interests, participation and leadership in professional and/or community organizations, community service, ability to support their educational costs, and how their education is currently being financed.

**Financial data**   The stipend is $500.

**Duration**   1 year.

**Number awarded**   1 each year.

**Deadline**   January of each year.

## [452]
## OHIO LEGION AUXILIARY PAST PRESIDENTS' PARLEY SCHOLARSHIPS

American Legion Auxiliary
Attn: Department of Ohio
1100 Brandywine Boulevard, Building D
P.O. Box 2760
Zanesville, OH 43702-2760
(740) 452-8245                          Fax: (740) 452-2620
E-mail: ala_pam@rrohio.com

**Summary**   To provide financial assistance for nursing or medical education to Ohio residents who are dependents or descendants of veterans.

**Eligibility**   The wives, children, stepchildren, grandchildren, adopted children, or great-grandchildren of veterans may apply for this scholarship if they are interested in education in nursing or a medical field, are sponsored by a unit of the American Legion Auxiliary, and are residents of Ohio. The qualifying veteran must be disabled, deceased, or in financial need. Selection is based on character, scholastic standing, qualifications for the nursing profession, and financial need.

**Financial data**   Scholarships are either $750 or $300. Funds are paid directly to the recipients upon proof of enrollment.

**Duration**   1 year.

**Number awarded**   Varies each year; recently, 17 of these scholarships were awarded (2 at $750 and 15 at $300).

**Deadline**   May of each year.

## [453]
## OHIO LEGION SCHOLARSHIPS

American Legion
Attn: Department of Ohio
60 Big Run Road
P.O. Box 8007
Delaware, OH 43015
(740) 362-7478                          Fax: (740) 362-1429
E-mail: ohlegion@iwaynet.net
Web: www.ohioamericanlegion.org/scholars.htm

**Summary**   To provide financial assistance for college to Ohio Legionnaires, their spouses, and their descendants.

**Eligibility**   Eligible to apply for these scholarships are residents of Ohio who are Legionnaires, direct descendants of living or deceased Legionnaires, and surviving spouses or children of deceased U.S. military personnel who died on active duty or of injuries received on active duty. All applicants must be attending or planning to attend colleges, universities, or other approved postsecondary schools in Ohio.

Selection is based on academic achievement as measured by course grades, scholastic test scores, difficulty of curriculum, participation in outside activities, and the judging committee's general impression.

**Financial data**   Stipends are at least $2,000.

**Duration**   1 year.

**Number awarded**   Varies each year; recently, 18 of these scholarships were awarded.

**Deadline**   April of each year.

## [454]
## OHIO PART-TIME STUDENT INSTRUCTIONAL GRANT PROGRAM

Ohio Board of Regents
Attn: State Grants and Scholarships
57 East Main Street, Fourth Floor
P.O. Box 182452
Columbus, OH 43218-2452
(614) 466-7420                          Toll-free: (888) 833-1133
Fax: (614) 752-5903
E-mail: bmetheney@regents.state.oh.us
Web: www.regents.state.oh.us/sgs/parttimegrant.htm

**Summary**   To provide financial assistance for part-time undergraduate education to students in Ohio.

**Eligibility**   To be eligible for these scholarships, students must be Ohio residents who are attending or planning to attend public, private, and proprietary colleges and universities in Ohio and take fewer than 12 credit hours per term. Financial need must be demonstrated. Special consideration is given to single heads of household and displaced homemakers. Participating schools select the recipients.

**Financial data**   Participating schools determine the amount of each award, based on guidelines set by the Board of Regents and the need of the recipient. Grants may not exceed the actual cost of attendance.

**Duration**   1 year; may be renewed up to 3 additional years.

**Additional information**   This program was established in 1993.

**Number awarded**   Varies each year; recently, 28,349 students received these grants.

**Deadline**   Each participating college or university sets its own deadline.

## [455]
## OHIO SPACE GRANT CONSORTIUM COMMUNITY COLLEGE SCHOLARSHIP

Ohio Space Grant Consortium
c/o Ohio Aerospace Institute
22800 Cedar Point Road
Cleveland, OH 44142
(440) 962-3032                          Toll-free: (800) 828-OSGC
Fax: (440) 962-3057                     E-mail: osgc@oai.org
Web: www.osgc.org/Scholarship.html

**Summary**   To provide financial assistance to students (particularly women, minority, and disabled students) at selected community colleges in Ohio who are interested in continuing their studies at a 4-year university in the state that is a member of the Ohio Space Grant Consortium (OSGC).

**Eligibility** This program is open to U.S. citizens who are students at designated community colleges in Ohio, normally enrolled full time in their freshman year (although applications are accepted from part-time students demonstrating academic merit and from students at any stage of their college career). Applicants must be enrolled in a program that includes course work related to an understanding of or interest in technological fields supporting aerospace, e.g. associate degrees related to mathematics, science, and such advanced technology fields as engineering, computers, electronics, and industrial technology. They must also have a GPA of 3.0 or higher and plans to continue their education in a 4-year program at an OSGC-member university. Along with their application, they must submit college transcripts, 2 letters of recommendation, and a brief resume of their education, significant accomplishments, work experience, educational and professional goals, and any other relevant information. Women, underrepresented minorities, and persons with disabilities are particularly encouraged to apply.

**Financial data** The stipend is $1,000.

**Duration** 1 year; nonrenewable.

**Additional information** These scholarships are funded through the National Space Grant College and Fellowship Program administered by the National Aeronautics and Space Administration (NASA), with matching funds provided by the member colleges, the Ohio Aerospace Institute, and private industry. The participating institutions include Columbus State Community College, Cuyahoga Community College, Lorain County Community College, Owens Community College, Lakeland Community College, and Terra Community College. OSGC member institutions include the Air Force Institute of Technology, University of Akron, Case Western Reserve University, Central State University, University of Cincinnati, Cleveland State University, University of Dayton, Ohio State University, Ohio University, University of Toledo, Wilberforce University, and Wright State University.

**Number awarded** 2 each year.

**Deadline** October of each year.

## [456]
## OHIO SPACE GRANT CONSORTIUM JUNIOR SCHOLARSHIPS

Ohio Space Grant Consortium
c/o Ohio Aerospace Institute
22800 Cedar Point Road
Cleveland, OH 44142
(440) 962-3032　　　　Toll-free: (800) 828-OSGC
Fax: (440) 962-3057　　　E-mail: osgc@oai.org
Web: www.osgc.org/Scholarship.html

**Summary** To provide financial assistance to students in their junior year at selected universities in Ohio (particularly women, minority, and disabled students) who wish to work on a bachelor's degree in an aerospace-related field.

**Eligibility** These scholarships are available to U.S. citizens who expect to complete within 2 years the requirements for a bachelor of science degree in an aerospace-related discipline (aeronautical engineering, aerospace engineering, astronomy, biology, chemical engineering, chemistry, civil engineering, computer engineering and science, control engineering, electrical engineering, engineer-

ing mechanics, geography, geology, industrial engineering, manufacturing engineering, materials science and engineering, mathematics, mechanical engineering, petroleum engineering, physics, and systems engineering). Applicants must be attending a member university of the Ohio Space Grant Consortium (OSGC) or another participating university. They must propose and initiate a research project on campus under the guidance of a faculty member. Along with their application, they must submit a 1-page personal objective statement that discusses their career goals and anticipated benefits to be derived from this program. Women, underrepresented minorities, and persons with disabilities are particularly encouraged to apply.

**Financial data** The stipend is $2,000.

**Duration** 1 year; recipients may apply for a senior scholarship if they maintain satisfactory academic performance and good progress on their research project.

**Additional information** These scholarships are funded through the National Space Grant College and Fellowship Program administered by the National Aeronautics and Space Administration (NASA), with matching funds provided by the member universities, the Ohio Aerospace Institute, and private industry. The OSGC member universities include the University of Akron, Case Western Reserve University, Central State University, University of Cincinnati, Cleveland State University, University of Dayton, Ohio State University, Ohio University, University of Toledo, Wilberforce University, and Wright State University. Other participating universities are Cedarville University, Marietta College (petroleum engineering), Miami University (manufacturing engineering), Ohio Northern University (mechanical engineering), and Youngstown State University (mechanical and industrial engineering). Recipients are required to attend the annual spring research symposium sponsored by the OSGC and present a poster on their research project.

**Number awarded** Varies each year; recently, 20 of these scholarships were awarded.

**Deadline** February of each year.

## [457]
## OKLAHOMA NASA SPACE GRANT CONSORTIUM SCHOLARSHIPS

Oklahoma NASA Space Grant Consortium
c/o University of Oklahoma
Ditmars House, Suite 9
1623 Cross Center Drive
Norman, OK 73069
(405) 325-6559　　　　　　Fax: (405) 325-5537
E-mail: vduca@ou.edu
Web: www.okspacegrant.ou.edu

**Summary** To provide financial assistance to upper-division students (particularly women, minority, and disabled students) at member institutions of the Oklahoma NASA Space Grant Consortium who are enrolled in aerospace-related studies.

**Eligibility** This program is open to juniors and seniors at member institutions of the Oklahoma NASA Space Grant Consortium (OSGC). Applicants must be majoring in science, mathematics, engineering, technology, geography, or other aeronautics or space-related disciplines. They must have a GPA of 2.5 or higher. U.S. citizenship is required. The OSGC is a component of the U.S. National Aeronautics and

Space Administration (NASA) Space Grant program, which encourages participation by women, underrepresented minorities, and persons with disabilities.

**Financial data** Stipends range from $500 to $1,000.

**Duration** 1 year.

**Additional information** Members of OSGC are Oklahoma State University, the University of Oklahoma, Cameron University, Langston University. Cameron University, East Central University, Southeastern Oklahoma State University, Southern Nazarene University, and Southwestern Oklahoma State University. This program is funded by NASA.

**Number awarded** Approximately 40 each year.

**Deadline** December of each year.

## [458]
## OLGA CHRISTENSEN NATIONAL SCHOLARSHIP

Danish Sisterhood of America
Attn: Lizette Burtis, Scholarship Chair
3020 Santa Juanita Court
Santa Rosa, CA 95405-8219
(707) 539-1884          E-mail: lburtis@sbcglobal.net
Web: www.danishsisterhood.org/rschol.asp

**Summary** To provide financial assistance for educational purposes to members or relatives of members of the Danish Sisterhood of America.

**Eligibility** Members or the family of members of the sisterhood are eligible to apply if they are full-time students enrolled in a technical school or associate degree program. Members must have belonged to the sisterhood for at least 1 year. Selection is based on academic excellence (at least a 2.5 GPA).

**Financial data** The stipend is $500.

**Duration** 1 year; nonrenewable.

**Number awarded** 2 each year.

**Deadline** February of each year.

## [459]
## OLIVE LYNN SALEMBIER SCHOLARSHIP

Society of Women Engineers
230 East Ohio Street, Suite 400
Chicago, IL 60611-3265
(312) 596-5223          Toll-free: (877) SWE-INFO
Fax: (312) 644-8557
E-mail: scholarshipapplication@swe.org
Web: www.swe.org/scholarships

**Summary** To provide financial assistance to women interested in returning to college or graduate school to study engineering or computer science.

**Eligibility** This program is open to women who are planning to enroll at an ABET-accredited 4-year college or university. Applicants must have been out of the engineering workforce and school for at least 2 years and must be planning to return as an undergraduate or graduate student to major in computer science or engineering. Along with their application, they must submit a 1-page essay on why they want to be an engineer or computer scientist, how they believe they will make a difference as an engineer or computer scientist, and what influenced them to study engineering or computer science. Selection is based on merit.

**Financial data** The award is $2,000.

**Duration** 1 year.

**Additional information** This program was established in 1979.

**Number awarded** 1 each year.

**Deadline** May of each year.

## [460]
## OLIVE WHITMAN MEMORIAL SCHOLARSHIP

Daughters of the American Revolution-New York State Organization
c/o Layla Voll
311 West 21st Street
New York, NY 10011
E-mail: Layla_Voll@hotmail.com
Web: www.nydar.org/education/whitman.html

**Summary** To provide financial assistance for college to Native American women in New York.

**Eligibility** This program is open to women who are at least 50% Native American and graduating seniors at high schools in New York. Applicants must be planning to attend an accredited 4-year college or university in the state.

**Financial data** The stipend is $2,000.

**Duration** 1 year.

**Number awarded** 1 each year.

**Deadline** January of each year.

## [461]
## OLIVER AND ESTHER R. HOWARD SCHOLARSHIP

Fleet Reserve Association
Attn: Scholarship Administrator
125 North West Street
Alexandria, VA 22314-2754
(703) 683-1400          Toll-free: (800) 372-1924
Fax: (703) 549-6610          E-mail: fra@fra.org
Web: www.fra.org

**Summary** To provide financial assistance for undergraduate education to children of members of the Fleet Reserve Association or its Ladies Auxiliary.

**Eligibility** Applicants for these scholarships must be dependent children of members of the association or its ladies auxiliary (in good standing as of April 1 of the year of the award), or of members in good standing at the time of death. They must be interested in working on an undergraduate degree. Awards alternate annually between female dependents (in even-numbered years) and male dependents (in odd-numbered years). Selection is based on financial need, scholastic standing, character, and leadership qualities.

**Financial data** The amount awarded varies, depending upon the needs of the recipient and the funds available.

**Duration** 1 year; may be renewed.

**Additional information** Membership in the Fleet Reserve Association is restricted to active-duty, retired, and Reserve members of the Navy, Marine Corps, and Coast Guard.

**Number awarded** 1 each year.

**Deadline** April of each year.

## [462]
## OPERATING ENGINEERS LOCAL 3 ACADEMIC SCHOLARSHIPS

International Union of Operating Engineers, Local 3
Attn: Recording-Corresponding Secretary
1620 South Loop Road
Alameda, CA 94502-7090
(510) 748-7400                    Fax: (510) 748-7401
Web: www.oe3.org

**Summary**   To provide financial assistance for undergraduate education to the children of members of Operating Engineers Local 3.

**Eligibility**   This program is open to children, stepchildren, and foster children of members in good standing (the jurisdiction covers northern California, northern Nevada, Utah, and Hawaii). Applicants must be high school seniors planning to enroll at an accredited college or university in the United States. They must have a GPA of 3.0 or higher. Along with their application, they must submit a 250-word essay on why they believe unions are good for America and how unions affect their lives. Males and females compete separately.

**Financial data**   For the first year of college, each winner receives $3,000 and each runner-up receives $2,000. For subsequent years, the stipend is $1,000 per year for all recipients.

**Duration**   1 year; may be renewed for up to 3 additional years.

**Number awarded**   4 each year: 2 winners (1 female and 1 male) and 2 runners-up (1 female and 1 male).

**Deadline**   March of each year.

## [463]
## OPPORTUNITY SCHOLARSHIPS FOR LUTHERAN LAYWOMEN

Women of the Evangelical Lutheran Church in America
Attn: Scholarships
8765 West Higgins Road
Chicago, IL 60631-4189
(773) 380-2730     Toll-free: (800) 638-3522, ext. 2730
Fax: (773) 380-2419      E-mail: womenelca@elca.org
Web: www.womenoftheelca.org

**Summary**   To provide financial assistance to lay women who are members of Evangelical Lutheran Church of America (ELCA) congregations and who wish to take classes on the undergraduate, graduate, professional, or vocational school level.

**Eligibility**   These scholarships are aimed at ELCA lay women who are at least 21 years of age and have experienced an interruption of at least 2 years in their education since high school. Applicants must have been admitted to an educational institution to prepare for a career in other than a church-certified profession. They may be working on an undergraduate, graduate, professional, or vocational school degree. U.S. citizenship is required.

**Financial data**   The amounts of the awards depend on the availability of funds.

**Duration**   Up to 2 years.

**Additional information**   These scholarships are supported by several endowment funds: the Cronk Memorial Fund, the First Triennial Board Scholarship Fund, the General Scholarship Fund, the Mehring Fund, the Paepke Scholarship Fund, the Piero/Wade/Wade Fund, and the Edwin/Edna Robeck Estate.

**Number awarded**   Varies each year, depending upon the funds available.

**Deadline**   February of each year.

## [464]
## OPTIMIST INTERNATIONAL ORATORICAL CONTEST

Optimist International
Attn: Programs Department
4494 Lindell Boulevard
St. Louis, MO 63108
(314) 371-6000     Toll-free: (800) 500-8130, ext. 235
Fax: (314) 371-6009     E-mail: programs@optimist.org
Web: www.optimist.org

**Summary**   To recognize and reward outstanding orators at the high school or younger level.

**Eligibility**   All students in public, private, or parochial elementary, junior high, and senior high schools in the United States, Canada, or the Caribbean who are under 16 years of age may enter. All contestants must prepare their own orations of 4 to 5 minutes, but they may receive advice and make minor changes or improvements in the oration at any time. Each year a different subject is selected for the orations; a recent topic was "My Future is Bright because..." The orations may be delivered in a language other than English if that language is an official language of the country in which the sponsoring club is located. Selection is based on poise (20 points), content of speech (35 points), delivery and presentation (35 points), and overall effectiveness (10 points). Competition is first conducted at the level of individual clubs, with winners advancing to zone and then district competitions. At the discretion of the district, boys may compete against boys and girls against girls in separate contests.

**Financial data**   Each district awards either 2 scholarships of $1,500 (1 for a boy and 1 for a girl) or (if the district chooses to have a combined gender contest) a first-place scholarship of $1,500, a second-place scholarship of $1,000, and a third-place scholarship of $500.

**Duration**   The competition is held annually.

**Additional information**   This competition was first held in 1928. Nearly 2,000 Optimist International local clubs participate in the program each year. Entry information is available only from local Optimist Clubs.

**Number awarded**   Each year, more than $150,000 is awarded in scholarships.

**Deadline**   Each local club sets its own deadline. The district deadline is the end of June.

## [465]
## ORDER OF THE AMARANTH IN PENNSYLVANIA SCHOLARSHIP PROGRAM

Pennsylvania Masonic Youth Foundation
Attn: Educational Endowment Fund
1244 Bainbridge Road
Elizabethtown, PA 17022-9423
(717) 367-1536   Toll-free: (800) 266-8424 (within PA)
Fax: (717) 367-0616   E-mail: pyf@pagrandlodge.org
Web: www.pagrandlodge.org/pyf/scholar/index.html

**Summary** To provide financial assistance for college to women in Pennsylvania who have a connection to Masonry.

**Eligibility** This program is open to 1) daughters and granddaughters of members of the Order of the Amaranth in Pennsylvania, and 2) active Pennsylvania Rainbow Girls and Job's Daughters. Applicants must be between 18 and 21 years of age, high school graduates, and enrolled in an institution of higher learning.

**Financial data** The stipend depends on the availability of funds.

**Duration** 1 year.

**Additional information** Information is also available from Barbara Ullrich, 6945 Torresdale Avenue, Philadelphia, PA 19135-1931, (215) 332-5515.

**Number awarded** 1 or more each year.

**Deadline** June of each year.

## [466]
## OREGON LEGION AUXILIARY DEPARTMENT NURSES SCHOLARSHIP

American Legion Auxiliary
Attn: Department of Oregon
30450 S.W. Parkway Avenue
P.O. Box 1730
Wilsonville, OR 97070-1730
(503) 682-3162   Fax: (503) 685-5008
E-mail: pcalhoun@pcez.com

**Summary** To provide financial assistance for nursing education to the wives, widows, and children of Oregon veterans.

**Eligibility** Eligible for these scholarships are the wives of veterans with disabilities, the widows of deceased veterans, and the sons and daughters of veterans who are Oregon residents. Applicants must have been accepted by an accredited hospital or university school of nursing in Oregon. Selection is based on ability, aptitude, character, determination, seriousness of purpose, and financial need.

**Financial data** The stipend is $1,500.

**Duration** 1 year; may be renewed.

**Number awarded** 1 each year.

**Deadline** May of each year.

## [467]
## OREGON LEGION AUXILIARY DEPARTMENT SCHOLARSHIPS

American Legion Auxiliary
Attn: Department of Oregon
30450 S.W. Parkway Avenue
P.O. Box 1730
Wilsonville, OR 97070-1730
(503) 682-3162   Fax: (503) 685-5008
E-mail: pcalhoun@pcez.com

**Summary** To provide financial assistance for college to the dependents of Oregon veterans.

**Eligibility** This program is open to Oregon residents who are children or wives of disabled veterans or widows of veterans. Applicants must be interested in obtaining education beyond the high school level. Selection is based on ability, aptitude, character, seriousness of purpose, and financial need.

**Financial data** The stipend is $1,000. It must be used for college, university, business school, vocational school, or any other accredited postsecondary school in the state of Oregon.

**Duration** The awards are offered each year. They are nonrenewable.

**Number awarded** 3 each year; 1 of these is to be used for vocational or business school.

**Deadline** March of each year.

## [468]
## OREGON LEGION AUXILIARY DEPARTMENT SPIRIT OF YOUTH SCHOLARSHIP

American Legion Auxiliary
Attn: Department of Oregon
30450 S.W. Parkway Avenue
P.O. Box 1730
Wilsonville, OR 97070-1730
(503) 682-3162   Fax: (503) 685-5008
E-mail: pcalhoun@pcez.com

**Summary** To provide financial assistance for college to junior members of the American Legion Auxiliary in Oregon.

**Eligibility** Applicants for this scholarship must be Oregon residents who are junior members of the Auxiliary and have been members for at least 3 years. They must be children (including stepchildren), grandchildren, or great-grandchildren of veterans and in their senior year of high school.

**Financial data** The stipend is $1,000.

**Duration** 1 year; nonrenewable.

**Additional information** The scholarship may be used at the college of the recipient's choice.

**Number awarded** 1 each year.

**Deadline** March of each year.

## [469]
## OREGON SPACE GRANT UNDERGRADUATE SCHOLARSHIP PROGRAM

Oregon NASA Space Grant Consortium
c/o Oregon State University
92 Kerr Administration Building
Corvallis, OR 97331-2103
(541) 737-2414          Fax: (541) 737-9946
E-mail: spacegrant@oregonstate.edu
Web: www.oregonspacegrant.orst.edu

**Summary**  To provide financial assistance for study in space-related fields to undergraduate students (particularly women, minority, and disabled students) at colleges and universities that are members of the Oregon Space Grant Consortium (OSGC).

**Eligibility**  This program is open to U.S. citizens enrolled full time at OSGC member institutions. Applicants must be working on 1) a baccalaureate degree in a science, technology, engineering, or mathematics (STEM) field (including mathematics or science education) related to the mission of the U.S. National Aeronautics and Space Administration (NASA); or 2) an associate degree in applied science and planning to transfer to a 4-year institution to complete a baccalaureate in the same fields. Along with their application, they must submit a letter of intent of 250 to 300 words on their career goals as they relate to NASA and how this scholarship will contribute to those goals. Selection is based on scholastic achievement, aerospace-related career goals, and 2 letters of recommendation. Applications are especially encouraged from members of underrepresented groups (women, minorities, and people with disabilities).

**Financial data**  The stipend is $2,000.

**Duration**  1 year.

**Additional information**  Institutions that are members of OSG include Oregon State University, Portland State University, the University of Oregon, Southern Oregon University, Eastern Oregon University, Western Oregon University, George Fox University, Lane Community College, Linfield College, Portland Community College, and Oregon Institute of Technology. This program is funded by NASA.

**Number awarded**  Varies each year.

**Deadline**  January of each year.

## [470]
## PATRICIA CREED SCHOLARSHIP

Connecticut Women's Golf Association
c/o Deborah Boynton, Scholarship Committee
52 Mountain Spring Road
Farmington, CT 06032
(860) 674-1195          E-mail: scholarships@cwga.org
Web: www.cwga.org/JUNIORS/juniorhome.htm

**Summary**  To provide financial assistance for college to women high school seniors from Connecticut who are golfers.

**Eligibility**  This program is open to female high school seniors who are residents of Connecticut planning to attend a college or university in the state. Applicants must be active golfers with a handicap. Along with their application, they must submit a 200-word essay on how golf has made an impact on their life. Selection is based on character, academic achievement, interest in golf, and financial need.

**Financial data**  A stipend is awarded (amount not specified).

**Duration**  1 year.

**Additional information**  This program was established in 1997.

**Number awarded**  2 each year.

**Deadline**  April of each year.

## [471]
## PENELOPE HANSHAW SCHOLARSHIP

Association for Women Geoscientists
Attn: AWG Foundation
P.O. Box 30645
Lincoln, NE 68503-0645
E-mail: awgscholarship@yahoo.com
Web: www.awg.org/members/po_scholarships.html

**Summary**  To provide financial assistance for undergraduate or graduate study in the geosciences to women in the Potomac Bay region.

**Eligibility**  This program is open to women who are currently enrolled as full-time undergraduate or graduate geoscience majors at an accredited, degree-granting college or university in Delaware, the District of Columbia, Maryland, Virginia, or West Virginia. Applicants must have a GPA of 3.0 or higher. Selection is based on the applicant's awareness of the importance of community outreach, geoscience or earth science education activities, and potential for career and leadership success as a future geoscience professional.

**Financial data**  The stipend is $500. The recipient also is granted a 1-year membership in the Association for Women Geoscientists (AWG).

**Duration**  1 year.

**Additional information**  This program is sponsored by the AWG Potomac Area Chapter. Information is also available from Laurel M. Bybell, U.S. Geological Survey, 926 National Center, Reston, VA 20192.

**Number awarded**  1 each year.

**Deadline**  April of each year.

## [472]
## PENNSYLVANIA BUSINESS AND PROFESSIONAL WOMEN SCHOLARSHIP

Pennsylvania Federation of Business and Professional Women's Clubs, Inc.
Attn: Dorothy Hammond, Education and Service Funds Chair
308 Twin Bridges Road
Charleroi, PA 15022
(724) 489-0873          E-mail: info@bpwpa.org
Web: www.bpwpa.org

**Summary**  To provide financial assistance for continuing education to women in Pennsylvania.

**Eligibility**  This program is open to women in Pennsylvania who have been accepted into an accredited educational institution. Applicants must be able to demonstrate financial need. They must submit an essay that discusses their specific short-term career goals, how the proposed training will help them to accomplish those goals, and how those apply to their long-range career goals. The essay should include a summary of the following topics: individual goals, educational goals, and issues that are important to working women in today's world.

**Financial data** A stipend is awarded (amount not specified).

**Number awarded** Varies each year.

**Deadline** June of each year for programs beginning in September; October of each year for programs beginning in January.

## [473]
## PENNSYLVANIA RAINBOW NURSING SCHOLARSHIP

Pennsylvania Masonic Youth Foundation
Attn: Educational Endowment Fund
1244 Bainbridge Road
Elizabethtown, PA 17022-9423
(717) 367-1536    Toll-free: (800) 266-8424 (within PA)
Fax: (717) 367-0616    E-mail: pyf@pagrandlodge.org
Web: www.pagrandlodge.org/pyf/scholar/index.html

**Summary** To provide financial assistance for nursing school to members of Rainbow Girls in Pennsylvania.

**Eligibility** This program is open to active Pennsylvania Rainbow Girls in good standing. Applicants must have completed at least 1 year in an accredited nursing school.

**Financial data** The stipend depends on the availability of funds.

**Duration** 1 year; may be renewed.

**Additional information** Information is also available from Eva Gresko, RD #3, Box 102, Huntington, PA 16652-8703, (814) 658-3774.

**Number awarded** Varies each year, depending on the availability of funds.

**Deadline** Requests for applications must be submitted by January of each year. Completed applications are due by the end of February.

## [474]
## PENNSYLVANIA RAINBOW SCHOLARSHIP

Pennsylvania Masonic Youth Foundation
Attn: Educational Endowment Fund
1244 Bainbridge Road
Elizabethtown, PA 17022-9423
(717) 367-1536    Toll-free: (800) 266-8424 (within PA)
Fax: (717) 367-0616    E-mail: pyf@pagrandlodge.org
Web: www.pagrandlodge.org/pyf/scholar/index.html

**Summary** To provide financial assistance for college to members of Rainbow Girls in Pennsylvania.

**Eligibility** This program is open to active Pennsylvania Rainbow Girls in good standing. Applicants must have completed at least 1 year in an accredited college, university, or nursing school.

**Financial data** The stipend depends on the availability of funds.

**Duration** 1 year; may be renewed.

**Additional information** Information is also available from Eva Gresko, RD #3, Box 102, Huntington, PA 16652-8703, (814) 658-3774.

**Number awarded** Varies each year, depending on the availability of funds.

**Deadline** Requests for applications must be submitted by January of each year. Completed applications are due by the end of February.

## [475]
## PENNSYLVANIA SPACE GRANT CONSORTIUM SCHOLARSHIPS

Pennsylvania Space Grant Consortium
c/o Pennsylvania State University
2217 Earth-Engineering Sciences Building
University Park, PA 16802
(814) 863-7687    Fax: (814) 863-8286
E-mail: spacegrant@psu.edu
Web: www.psu.edu/spacegrant/highered/scholar.html

**Summary** To provide financial assistance for space-related study to undergraduate students (particularly women, minority, and disabled students) at universities affiliated with the Pennsylvania Space Grant Consortium.

**Eligibility** This program is open to full-time undergraduate students at participating universities. Applicants must be studying a field that does, or can, promote a strategic enterprise of the U.S. National Aeronautics and Space Administration (NASA): aerospace technology, earth science, human exploration and development of space, biological and physical research, or space science. U.S. citizenship is required. Students from underrepresented groups (women, minorities, rural populations, and those with disabilities) are especially encouraged to apply.

**Financial data** The stipend is set by each participating university. At Pennsylvania State University, for instance, it is $4,000 per year.

**Duration** 1 year.

**Additional information** Participating institutions include California University of Pennsylvania, Carnegie Mellon University, Clarion University, Lincoln University, Pennsylvania State University, University of Pittsburgh, Susquehanna University, Lincoln University, Temple University, West Chester University, and Pennsylvania State University at Abington. At Pennsylvania State University, the award is designated the Sylvia Stein Memorial Space Grant Scholarship. This program is sponsored by the U.S. National Aeronautics and Space Administration (NASA).

**Number awarded** Varies each year.

**Deadline** Each participating university sets its own deadline.

## [476]
## PENNSYLVANIA STATE COUNCIL OF AUXILIARIES GRANT

Pennsylvania Society of Professional Engineers
Attn: Pennsylvania Engineering Foundation
908 North Second Street
Harrisburg, PA 17102
(717) 441-6051    Fax: (717) 236-2046
E-mail: pspeinfo@pspe.org
Web: www.pspe.org/scholarships.shtml

**Summary** To provide financial assistance to female Pennsylvania high school seniors who are interested in studying engineering at a college or university in the state.

**Eligibility** This program is open to females graduating from high schools in Pennsylvania. Applicants must be planning to enroll in an engineering program at an ABET-accredited college or university in the state. They must have a GPA of 3.6 or higher and excellent scores on the SAT. U.S. citizenship in required. Interviews are included in the selection process.

**Financial data** The stipend is $1,000.

**Duration** 1 year; nonrenewable.

**Additional information** Scholarships are awarded by 22 local chapters of the Pennsylvania Engineering Foundation (PEF) in the state. Applications are available from the sponsor, but they must be submitted to the local chapter where the student lives. Students who live in counties with no local chairperson may submit their applications directly to the PEF. This program is sponsored by the Pennsylvania State Council of Auxiliaries (PSCA).

**Number awarded** 1 each year.

**Deadline** Each local chapter sets its own deadline. Students who submit their application to the state PEF office must do so by April of each year.

## [477]
## PENTAGON ASSISTANCE FUND

Navy-Marine Corps Relief Society
Attn: Education Division
875 North Randolph Street, Suite 225
Arlington, VA 22203-1977
(703) 696-4960                    Fax: (703) 696-0144
E-mail: education@hq.nmcrs.org
Web: www.nmcrs.org/child-dec.html

**Summary** To provide financial assistance for college to the children and spouses of deceased military personnel who died at the Pentagon on September 11, 2001.

**Eligibility** Eligible for this assistance are the children and spouses of deceased military personnel who died at the Pentagon as a result of the terrorist attack of September 11, 2001. The families of Marines whose aircraft crashed in Pakistan and Afghanistan in mid-January 2002 are also eligible.

**Financial data** The amount of assistance varies; funds may be used for any purpose, including tuition, fees, books, room, or board at a college or university offering a 2-year or 4-year course of study or at a vocational training school.

**Duration** Up to 4 years.

**Number awarded** Varies each year.

**Deadline** Applications may be submitted at any time.

## [478]
## P.E.O. PROGRAM FOR CONTINUING EDUCATION

P.E.O. Sisterhood
Attn: Executive Office
3700 Grand Avenue
Des Moines, IA 50312-2899
(515) 255-3153                    Fax: (515) 255-3820
Web: www.peointernational.org

**Summary** To provide financial assistance to mature women interested in resuming or continuing their education.

**Eligibility** This program is open to mature women who are citizens of the United States or Canada and have experienced an interruption in their education that has lasted at least 24 consecutive months during their adult life. Applicants are frequently single parents who must acquire marketable skills to support their families. They must be within 2 years of completing an academic or technical course of study. Applicants must be sponsored by a local P.E.O. chapter. Students enrolled in a doctoral degree program are not eligible.

**Financial data** The maximum award is $2,000.

**Duration** 1 year; nonrenewable.

**Additional information** This program was established in 1973 by the Women's Philanthropic Educational Organization (P.E.O.).

**Number awarded** Varies each year; recently, 1,467 of these grants were awarded, including 365 for the full amount of $2,000.

**Deadline** Applications may be submitted at any time.

## [479]
## PEPPY MOLDOVAN MEMORIAL AWARD

Illinois Society of Professional Engineers
Attn: ISPE Foundation, Inc.
600 South Second Street, Suite 403
Springfield, IL 62704
(217) 544-7424                    Fax: (217) 528-6545
E-mail: info@IllinoisEngineer.com
Web: www.ilspe.com/StudentsAndYouth.asp

**Summary** To provide financial assistance to women from selected colleges in Illinois who are planning to work on an engineering degree.

**Eligibility** This program is open to women currently enrolled as sophomore engineering students at the following institutions: Illinois Central College, Kaskaskia Community College, Rend Lake Community College, Bradley University, Southern Illinois University (SIU) at Carbondale, Southern Illinois University (SIU) at Edwardsville, or the University of Illinois at Urbana-Champaign (UIUC). Applicants must have been accepted for enrollment in an ABET-accredited engineering program at SIU Carbondale, SIU Edwardsville, or UIUC. Along with their application, they must submit a 500-word essay on their interest in engineering, their major area of study and specialization, the occupation they propose to pursue after graduation, their long-term goals, and how they hope to achieve those. Selection is based on the essay, transcripts, work experience, extracurricular activities, honors and scholarships, and 2 letters of reference.

**Financial data** The stipend is $1,000 per year.

**Duration** 1 year.
**Number awarded** 1 each year.
**Deadline** January of each year.

## [480]
## PEPSI USBC YOUTH BOWLING CHAMPIONSHIPS
United States Bowling Congress
Attn: Pepsi-Cola Youth Bowling Event Manager
5301 South 76th Street
Greendale, WI 53129-1192
(414) 423-3442 Toll-free: (800) 514-BOWL, ext. 3442
Fax: (414) 421-3014
E-mail: maureen.vicena@bowl.com
Web: www.bowl.com

**Summary** To recognize and reward (with college scholarships) members of the United States Bowling Congress (USBC) who achieve high scores in an international competition.

**Eligibility** This competition is open to USBC members in the United States, Puerto Rico, U.S. military zones, and Canada. Applicants enter in 1 of 6 categories: 11 and under boys' handicap, 12 and above boys' handicap, 12 and above boys' scratch, 11 and under girls' handicap, 12 and above girls' handicap, and 12 and above girls' scratch. Based on their bowling scores in state and zone competitions, the top bowlers in the 12 and above boys' and girls' handicap categories advance to the international finals. Also advancing to the international finals are the state and zone winners in the 12 and above boys' and girls' scratch categories who are also USBC Junior Gold members (boys must have an average of 175 or above, girls must have an average of 165 or above). All selected finalists (more than 200 qualify each year), are then assigned to Division I or Division II for the international competition, held annually at a site in the United States; assignment is based on their adjusted score from year-end averages and state and zone competitions. Bowlers whose scores are in the top half are assigned to Division I and bowlers whose scores are in the bottom half are assigned to Division II. Scholarships are awarded solely on the basis of bowling performance in the international finals.

**Financial data** At the international finals, the top finishers in each division receive scholarships of $2,000, $1,500, $1,000, and $500, respectively.

**Duration** The competition is held annually.

**Additional information** This competition is sponsored by the Pepsi-Cola Company and conducted by the USBC. More than $300,000 is scholarships is awarded at state and zone competitions for all 6 categories. USBC also awards a $400 stipend to each competitor at the international finals (Canadian athletes are not eligible for the stipend and competitors from U.S. military bases must pay for their own transportation to the United States); the stipend is intended to assist with the cost of travel, meals, and housing.

**Number awarded** Each year, 16 scholarships are awarded: 8 are set aside for girls (4 in each division) and 8 for boys (4 in each division).

**Deadline** Qualifying tournaments are held in bowling centers from October through February of each year. Center and section qualifying takes place in March and April. State and zone competitions take place through the end of May. The national finals are held in July.

## [481]
## PHI CHI THETA SCHOLARSHIPS
Phi Chi Theta
Attn: Foundation
1508 East Beltline Road, Suite 104
Carrollton, TX 75006
(972) 245-7202 E-mail: PCTEdScholarship@aol.com
Web: www.phichitheta.org

**Summary** To provide financial assistance to members of Phi Chi Theta (an honorary society for women in business-related fields) who are working on a degree in business administration or economics.

**Eligibility** This program is open to members who have completed at least 1 semester or 2 quarters of full-time study in business administration or economics. Applicants must be enrolled at an approved college or university in the United States in a bachelor's, master's, or doctoral degree program. Along with their application, they must submit an essay on where they see themselves in 3 and 5 years and a statement of career goals and philosophy. Selection is based on the essay and statement, Phi Chi Theta achievements and contributions; scholastic achievement; school and community achievements and activities; a faculty letter of recommendation; and a Phi Chi Theta member letter of recommendation.

**Financial data** The stipend is $1,000 or $500.

**Duration** 1 year.

**Additional information** Phi Chi Theta is a national honorary society for women in business administration and economics. Information is also available from Mary Ellen Lewis, 1886 South Poplar Street, Denver, CO 80224-2272, (303) 757-2535. This program includes the following named awards: the Anna E. Hall Memorial Scholarship (established in 1989), the Helen D. Snow Memorial Scholarship, the Irene Meyer Memorial Scholarship, the Lester F. Richardson Memorial Scholarship (established in 2005), and the Naomi L. Satterfield Scholarship (established in 2001).

**Number awarded** Varies each year. Recently, 4 of these scholarships were awarded: 1 at $1,000 and 3 at $500.

**Deadline** April of each year.

## [482]
## PHIPPS MEMORIAL SCHOLARSHIP
General Federation of Women's Clubs of Connecticut
c/o Hamden Women's Club
Antoinette Antonucci, Co-President
26 Country Way
Wallingford, CT 06492
(203) 265-9407 E-mail: gfwcct@yahoo.com
Web: www.gfwcct.org

**Summary** To provide financial assistance to women in Connecticut who are working on an undergraduate or graduate degree in education.

**Eligibility** This program is open to female residents of Connecticut who have completed at least 2 years of college. Applicants must have a GPA of 3.0 or higher and be working on a bachelor's or master's degree in education.

**Financial data** The stipend is $1,000.

**Duration** 1 year.

**Number awarded** 1 each year.

**Deadline** February of each year.

## [483]
## PHOENIX SECTION SCHOLARSHIP

Society of Women Engineers
230 East Ohio Street, Suite 400
Chicago, IL 60611-3265
(312) 596-5223          Toll-free: (877) SWE-INFO
Fax: (312) 644-8557
E-mail: scholarshipapplication@swe.org
Web: www.swe.org
Web: www.swe.org/scholarships

**Summary**   To provide financial assistance to women from Arizona who will be entering college as freshmen and are interested in studying engineering or computer science.

**Eligibility**   This program is open to women who are entering college as freshmen with a GPA of 3.5 or higher. Applicants must be residents of Arizona or attending school in the state and planning to enroll full time at an ABET-accredited 4-year college or university and major in computer science or engineering. Along with their application, they must submit a 1-page essay on why they want to be an engineer or computer scientist, how they believe they will make a difference as an engineer or computer scientist, and what influenced them to study engineering or computer science. Selection is based on merit.

**Financial data**   The stipend is $1,000.

**Duration**   1 year.

**Additional information**   This program was established in 2001 by the Phoenix Section of the Society of Women Engineers (SWE).

**Number awarded**   2 each year.

**Deadline**   May of each year.

## [484]
## PHYLLIS SANDERS SCHOLARSHIP

Missouri Business and Professional Women's
   Foundation, Inc.
P.O. Box 338
Carthage, MO 64836-0338
Web: bpwmo.org/files/index.php?id=14

**Summary**   To provide financial assistance for college to members of the Missouri Federation of Business and Professional Women (BPW Missouri).

**Eligibility**   This program is open to BPW Missouri members who have been accepted into an accredited program or course of study to upgrade their skills and/or complete education for career advancement. Along with their application, they must submit brief statements on the following: their achievements and/or specific recognitions in their field of endeavor; professional and/or civic affiliations; present and long-range career goals; how they plan to participate in and contribute to their community upon completion of their program of study; why they feel they would make a good recipient; and any special circumstances that may have influenced their ability to continue or complete their education. They must also demonstrate financial need and U.S. citizenship.

**Financial data**   A stipend is awarded (amount not specified).

**Duration**   1 year.

**Additional information**   Information is also available from Mary Kay Pace, Scholarship Committee Chair, 1503

Paradise Valley Drive, High Ridge, MO 63049, (636) 677-2951.

**Number awarded**   Varies each year; recently, 2 of these scholarships were awarded.

**Deadline**   January of each year.

## [485]
## PI BETA PHI HOLIDAY SCHOLARSHIPS

Pi Beta Phi
Attn: Pi Beta Phi Foundation
1154 Town and Country Commons Drive
Town and Country, MO 63017
(636) 256-0680          Fax: (636) 256-8124
E-mail: fndn@pibetaphi.org
Web: www.pibetaphifoundation.org

**Summary**   To provide financial assistance to members of Pi Beta Phi who are working on an undergraduate degree.

**Eligibility**   This program is open to women who are officially enrolled at a college or university where there is a Pi Beta Phi chapter. They must be active members in good standing in the sorority and have a GPA of 3.0 or higher (70% or higher for Canadian members). Selection is based on financial need, academic record, and service to the sorority, campus, and community.

**Financial data**   The stipend is $1,000 per year.

**Duration**   1 year.

**Additional information**   This program, established in 1995, is funded by members and staff of the foundation who contribute to it in lieu of sending holiday greetings to each other.

**Number awarded**   Varies each year; recently, 10 of these scholarships were awarded.

**Deadline**   January of each year.

## [486]
## PI BETA PHI UNDERGRADUATE SCHOLARSHIPS

Pi Beta Phi
Attn: Pi Beta Phi Foundation
1154 Town and Country Commons Drive
Town and Country, MO 63017
Fax: (636) 256-8124          Fax: (636) 256-8124
E-mail: fndn@pibetaphi.org
Web: www.pibetaphifoundation.org

**Summary**   To provide financial assistance for college to members of Pi Beta Phi.

**Eligibility**   This program is open to women who are officially enrolled at a college or university where there is a Pi Beta Phi chapter. They must be active members in good standing in the sorority and have a GPA of 3.0 or higher (70% or higher for Canadian members). Selection is based on financial need, academic record, and service to the sorority, campus, and community.

**Financial data**   A stipend is awarded (amount not specified). Recently, the average stipend for all scholarships awarded by this sponsor was $1,630.

**Duration**   1 year.

**Additional information**   This program includes the following named scholarships: Friendship Fund Scholarships, Arizona Alpha Scholarship (first preference given to members of that chapter), Joyce Wherritt Bowers Scholarship (for juniors with a GPA of 3.6 or higher), Judy Boucher Chamberlain Art Scholarship (restricted to Illinois Theta art majors), Frances Hall Comly Scholarship (first preference given to members from Illinois, Michigan, or Wisconsin), Dallas Alumnae Club/Ann Dudgeon Phy Scholarship (first preference for members from Dallas), Marcia Hart Foster/D.C. Alpha Scholarship, Frances H. Hofacre Scholarship (restricted to members of Minnesota Alpha chapter), Holiday Scholarships, Harriet Rutherford Johnstone Scholarship, Kansas Alpha Scholarship (restricted to members of that chapter who have financial need), Kansas Alpha 4.0 Awards (restricted to members of that chapter who have a 4.0 GPA), Jo Marie Lilly Scholarship (first preference to residents of Texas), Betty Blades Lofton Scholarship (first preference given to members of Indiana Gamma chapter), Louisiana Alpha Triple M Scholarship (first preference given to members from Louisiana), Adele Collins Mason Scholarship (first preference given to members from southern California), Hannah Mervine Miles Scholarship (restricted to members of Pennsylvania Beta chapter), Annette Mitchell Mills Scholarship (first preference given to a member of Alabama Alpha chapter), Sarah Ruth Mullis Scholarship, (preference given to pharmacy students), New York Zeta Scholarship (first preference given to members of a New York chapter), New York Alpha Scholarship (restricted to members of that chapter), Ohio Beta Scholarship (first preference for members of that chapter), Oklahoma Alpha Scholarship (first preference given to members of that chapter), Oklahoma Beta Scholarship (first preference given to members of that chapter), Ruth Trinkle Read Scholarship (first preference given to members of Kansas Beta chapter), Jo Ann Minor Roderick Scholarship, Ruth Barrett Smith Scholarship, Jane Porter Warmack Scholarship (first preference given to chapter officers), Carol Inge Warren Scholarship (first preference given to members of North Carolina Beta chapter), and Johnanna Zournas Scholarship (restricted to members of Texas Gamma chapter). Recipients must use the funds during the immediately succeeding academic year and must be willing to write a brief report of their academic progress at the end of the school year.

**Number awarded** Varies each year. Recently, 65 of these scholarships were awarded, including 29 named scholarships, 14 Friendship Fund Scholarships, 10 Holiday Scholarships, and 12 general undergraduate scholarships.

**Deadline** January of each year.

## [487]
## PI STATE NATIVE AMERICAN GRANTS-IN-AID
Delta Kappa Gamma Society International-Pi State Organization
c/o Patricia Hershberger, Native American Grants Committee
35 Frost Lane
Cornwall, NY 12518
E-mail: pbhersh@aol.com
Web: www.deltakappagamma.org/NY/awards.html

**Summary** To provide funding to Native American women from New York who plan to work in education or another service field.

**Eligibility** This program is open to Native American women from New York who are attending a 2-year or 4-year college in the state. Applicants must be planning to work in education or another service field, but preference is given to those majoring in education. Both undergraduate and graduate students are eligible.

**Financial data** The grant is $500 per semester ($1,000 per year). Funds may be used for any career-related purpose, including purchase of textbooks.

**Duration** 1 semester; may be renewed for a total of 5 years and a total of $5,000 over a recipient's lifetime.

**Number awarded** Varies each year; recently, 3 of these grants were awarded.

## [488]
## P.O. PISTILLI SCHOLARSHIPS
Design Automation Conference
c/o Cherrice Traver
Union College
ECE Department
Schenectady, NY 12308
(518) 388-6326                    Fax: (518) 388-6789
E-mail: traverc@union.edu
Web: doc.union.edu/acsee.html

**Summary** To provide financial assistance to female, minority, or disabled high school seniors who are interested in preparing for a career in computer science or electrical engineering.

**Eligibility** Eligible to apply are "underrepresented" high school seniors: women, African Americans, Hispanic Americans, Native Americans, and persons with disabilities. Applicants must be interested in preparing for a career in electrical engineering, computer engineering, or computer science. They must have at least a 3.0 GPA, have demonstrated high achievements in math and science courses, and be able to demonstrate significant financial need. U.S. citizenship is not required, but applicants must be U.S. residents when they apply and must plan to attend an accredited U.S. college or university. They must submit a completed application form, 3 letters of recommendation, official transcripts, ACT/SAT and/or PSAT scores, a personal statement outlining future goals, a copy of their latest income tax return, and a copy of the FAFSA form they submitted.

**Financial data** Stipends are $4,000 per year. Awards are paid each year in 2 equal installments.

**Duration** 1 year; renewable for up to 4 additional years.

**Additional information** This program is funded by the Design Automation Conference and the IEEE Circuits and System Society. It is directed by the Association for Computing Machinery's Special Interest Group on Design Automation.

**Number awarded** 2 to 7 each year.

**Deadline** January of each year.

## [489]
## PORTLAND WOMEN'S CLUB SCHOLARSHIP

Oregon Student Assistance Commission
Attn: Grants and Scholarships Division
1500 Valley River Drive, Suite 100
Eugene, OR 97401-2146
(541) 687-7395     Toll-free: (800) 452-8807, ext. 7395
Fax: (541) 687-7419
E-mail: awardinfo@mercury.osac.state.or.us
Web: www.osac.state.or.us

**Summary**  To provide financial assistance to college students, preferably women, who graduated from a high school in Oregon.

**Eligibility**  This program is open to graduates of high schools in Oregon who had a cumulative high school GPA of 3.0 or higher. Preference is given to women.

**Financial data**  The stipend is at least $1,500 per year.

**Duration**  1 year; may be renewed if the recipient shows satisfactory academic progress and continued financial need.

**Number awarded**  Varies each year; recently, 5 of these scholarships were awarded.

**Deadline**  February of each year.

## [490]
## POSSIBLE WOMAN FOUNDATION INTERNATIONAL SCHOLARSHIP

Possible Woman Enterprises
Attn: Possible Woman Foundation International
3475 Oak Valley Road, Suite 3040
P.O. Box 78851
Atlanta, GA 30357
Fax: (404) 869-7202
E-mail: linda@possiblewomanfoundation.org
Web: www.possiblewomanfoundation.org/Home.htm

**Summary**  To provide financial assistance for college or graduate school to women of all ages.

**Eligibility**  This program is open to women who are returning to school after a hiatus, changing careers, seeking advancement in their career or work life, or stay-at-home mothers entering the work place and in need of additional education or training. Applicants must be at least 25 years of age and at any level of education (high school graduate, some college, 4-year college graduate, graduate school, doctoral). Along with their application, they must submit a 2-page essay on the topic, "How Having the Opportunity for Beginning or Continuing My Academic Education Will Positively Impact My Life." Selection is based on the essay, career and life goals, leadership and participation in community activities, honors and awards received, and financial need.

**Financial data**  The stipend ranges from $3,000 to $5,000.

**Duration**  1 year; nonrenewable.

**Additional information**  Information is also available from Stacie Shelby, P.O. Box 117740, Carrollton, TX 75011-7740, Fax: (817) 497-2497.

**Number awarded**  Varies each year; recently, 6 of these scholarships were awarded.

**Deadline**  February of each year.

## [491]
## PRISCILLA MAXWELL ENDICOTT SCHOLARSHIPS

Connecticut Women's Golf Association
c/o Deborah Boynton, Scholarship Committee
52 Mountain Spring Road
Farmington, CT 06032
(860) 674-1195          E-mail: scholarships@cwga.org
Web: www.cwga.org/JUNIORS/juniorhome.htm

**Summary**  To provide financial assistance for college to women golfers from Connecticut.

**Eligibility**  This program is open to high school seniors and college students who are residents of Connecticut attending or planning to attend a 4-year college or university. Applicants must be active women golfers with a handicap. Along with their application, they must submit a 200-word essay on how golf has made an impact on their life. Selection is based on participation in golf programs, academic achievement and financial need.

**Financial data**  The maximum stipend is $1,000 per year.

**Duration**  Up to 4 years.

**Additional information**  This program was established in 1977.

**Number awarded**  5 each year.

**Deadline**  April of each year.

## [492]
## PROFESSIONAL GOLF MANAGEMENT DIVERSITY SCHOLARSHIP

Professional Golfers' Association of America
Attn: PGA Foundation
100 Avenue of the Champions
Palm Beach Gardens, FL 33418
Toll-free: (888) 532-6661
Web: www.pgafoundation.com/scholarships.cfm

**Summary**  To provide financial assistance to women and minorities interested in attending a designated college or university to prepare for a career as a golf professional.

**Eligibility**  This program is open to women and minorities interested in becoming a licensed PGA Professional. Applicants must be interested in attending 1 of 18 colleges and universities that offer the Professional Golf Management (PGM) curriculum sanctioned by the PGA.

**Financial data**  The stipend is $3,000 per year.

**Duration**  1 year; may be renewed.

**Additional information**  This program began in 1993. Programs are offered at Arizona State University (Mesa, Arizona), Campbell University (Buies Creek, North Carolina), Clemson University (Clemson, South Carolina), Coastal Carolina University (Conway, South Carolina), Eastern Kentucky University (Richmond, Kentucky), Ferris State University (Big Rapids, Michigan), Florida Gulf Coast University (Fort Myers, Florida), Florida State University (Tallahassee, Florida), Methodist College (Fayetteville, North Carolina), Mississippi State University (Mississippi State, Mississippi), New Mexico State University (Las Cruces, New Mexico), North Carolina State University (Raleigh, North Carolina), Pennsylvania State University (University Park, Pennsylvania), Sam Houston University (Huntsville, Texas), University of Colorado (Colorado Springs, Colorado), University of

Idaho (Moscow, Idaho), University of Nebraska (Lincoln, Nebraska), and University of Nevada (Las Vegas, Nevada).

**Number awarded** 1 or more each year.

## [493]
## PROJECT RED FLAG ACADEMIC SCHOLARSHIP FOR WOMEN WITH BLEEDING DISORDERS

National Hemophilia Foundation
Attn: Department of Finance, Administration & MIS
116 West 32nd Street, 11th Floor
New York, NY 10001-3212
(212) 328-3700     Toll-free: (800) 42-HANDI, ext. 3700
Fax: (212) 328-3777     E-mail: info@hemophilia.org
Web: www.hemophilia.org

**Summary** To provide financial assistance for college or graduate school to women who have a bleeding disorder.

**Eligibility** This program is open to women who are entering or already enrolled in an undergraduate or graduate program at a university, college, or accredited vocational school. Applicants must have von Willebrand disease, hemophilia or other clotting factor deficiency, or carrier status. Along with their application, they must submit a 250-word essay that describes their educational and future career plans, including how they intend to use their education to enhance the bleeding disorders community. Financial need is not considered in the selection process.

**Financial data** The stipend is $2,500.

**Duration** 1 year.

**Additional information** The program was established in 2005.

**Number awarded** 2 each year.

**Deadline** May of each year.

## [494]
## PUGET SOUND CHAPTER LOUISE MORITZ MOLITORIS LEADERSHIP AWARD FOR UNDERGRADUATES

Women's Transportation Seminar-Puget Sound Chapter
c/o Kristin Overleese, Scholarship Chair
City of Shoreline, Capital Projects Manager
17544 Midvale Avenue North
Shoreline, WA 98133-4821
(206) 546-1700                    Fax: (206) 546-2200
TDD: (206) 546-0457
Web: www.wtsinternational.org/puget_sound

**Summary** To provide financial assistance to women undergraduate students from Washington working on a degree related to transportation.

**Eligibility** This program is open to women who are residents of Washington, studying at a college in the state, or working as an intern in the state. Applicants must be currently enrolled in an undergraduate degree program in a transportation-related field, such as engineering, planning, finance, or logistics. They must have a GPA of 3.0 or higher and plans to prepare for a career in a transportation-related field. Minority candidates are encouraged to apply. Along with their application, they must submit a 500-word statement about their career goals after graduation and why they think they should receive this scholarship award; the statement should specifically address the issue of leadership.

Selection is based on that statement, academic record, leadership potential, and transportation-related activities or job skills. Financial need is not considered.

**Financial data** The stipend is $1,500.

**Duration** 1 year.

**Additional information** The winner is also nominated for scholarships offered by the national organization of the Women's Transportation Seminar.

**Number awarded** 1 each year.

**Deadline** October of each year.

## [495]
## PYRAMID AWARD FOR MARKETING AND PUBLIC RELATIONS

Miss America Pageant
Attn: Scholarship Department
Two Miss America Way, Suite 1000
Atlantic City, NJ 08401
(609) 345-7571, ext. 27          Toll-free: (800) 282-MISS
Fax: (609) 347-6079        E-mail: info@missamerica.org
Web: www.missamerica.org

**Summary** To provide financial assistance to women who are working on an undergraduate or graduate degree in marketing or public relations and who, in the past, competed at some level in the Miss America competition.

**Eligibility** This program is open to women who are working on an undergraduate, master's, or higher degree in marketing or public relations and who competed at the local, state, or national level in a Miss America competition within the past 10 years. Selection is based on GPA, class rank, extracurricular activities, financial need, and level of participation within the system.

**Financial data** The stipend is $2,500.

**Duration** 1 year; renewable.

**Additional information** This scholarship was established in 2004.

**Number awarded** Varies each year; recently, 2 of these scholarships were awarded.

**Deadline** June of each year.

## [496]
## RACHEL E. LEMIEUX YOUTH SCHOLARSHIP

BPW/Maine Futurama Foundation
c/o Nancy Wadman, Scholarship Chair
478 Surry Road
Ellsworth, ME 04605
Web: www.bpwmaine.org

**Summary** To provide financial assistance for college to female high school seniors in Maine.

**Eligibility** This program is open to female high school seniors in Maine who have been accepted at an accredited college or university. Applicants must be able to document financial need. Selection is based on academic standing (20%), financial need (40%), savings or good reason for none (5%), realistic goals (25%), and other factors, such as parental assistance, siblings' educational status, and letters of recommendation (10%).

**Financial data** The stipend is $1,200.

**Duration** 1 year.

**Additional information** The BPW/Maine Futurama Foundation was established in 1987 by the Maine Federation of Business and Professional Women's Clubs.

**Number awarded** 1 each year.

**Deadline** April of each year.

## [497]
## RACHEL E. LEMIEUX YOUTH SCHOLARSHIP

Maine Federation of Business and Professional Women
Attn: Futurama Foundation
c/o Jeanne L. Hammond, President
RR 1, Box 1610
Albion, ME 04910-9719
(207) 437-2325          E-mail: jlhammon@colby.edu
Web: www.bpwmaine.org/Scholarship.htm

**Summary** To provide financial assistance for college to female high school seniors in Maine.

**Eligibility** This program is open to women who are seniors graduating from high schools in Maine. Applicants must be planning to attend an accredited college or university. They must be able to demonstrate financial need.

**Financial data** The stipend is $1,200.

**Duration** 1 year.

**Additional information** Information is also available from Nancy Wadman, Scholarship Chair, BPW Maine Futurama Foundation, 478 Surry Road, Ellsworth, ME 04605.

**Number awarded** 1 or more each year.

**Deadline** March of each year.

## [498]
## REAM'S FOOD STORES SCHOLARSHIPS

Utah Sports Hall of Fame Foundation
Attn: Scholarship Chair
10182 South Cornerstone
South Jordan, UT 84095
(801) 253-7361

**Summary** To recognize and reward outstanding high school seniors in Utah who have been involved in athletics and are interested in attending college in the state.

**Eligibility** Each high school in Utah may nominate 1 boy and 1 girl who are graduating this year. Nominees must be planning to attend college in the state. Selection is based on academic record, personal character, financial need, leadership qualities, and involvement in athletic activities, including football, basketball, cross country, volleyball, tennis, track and field, soccer, rodeo, baseball, swimming, wrestling, officiating, community recreation, or intramural sports.

**Financial data** The stipend is $2,000. Funds are paid to the recipient's institution.

**Duration** 1 year; nonrenewable.

**Additional information** Additional information is also available from Berdean Jarman, 873 West 1200 North, Orem, UT 84057, (801) 225-3352. Formerly, the sponsoring organization was known as the Old Time Athletes Association. Recipients must attend an academic institution in Utah.

**Number awarded** 6 each year: 3 to boys and 3 to girls.

**Deadline** March of each year.

## [499]
## RECOGNITION SCHOLARSHIPS

Zeta Tau Alpha Foundation, Inc.
Attn: Director of Foundation Administration
3450 Founders Road
Indianapolis, IN 46268
(317) 872-0540          Fax: (317) 876-3948
E-mail: zetataualpha@zetataualpha.org
Web: www.zetataualpha.org

**Summary** To provide financial assistance for college to women who are members of Zeta Tau Alpha.

**Eligibility** This program is open to undergraduate women who are enrolled at a 4-year college or university and student members of the school's Zeta Tau Alpha chapter. These scholarships have been established with endowment monies and annual gifts in memory or honor of a member of the sorority. Selection is based on academic achievement (GPA of 2.75 or higher), involvement in campus and community activities, recommendations, current class status, and financial need.

**Financial data** The stipend is $1,300.

**Duration** 1 year; renewable.

**Number awarded** Varies each year. Annually, the foundation provides nearly $150,000 in scholarships and fellowships for undergraduate and graduate study.

**Deadline** March of each year.

## [500]
## RED RIVER VALLEY FIGHTER PILOTS ASSOCIATION SCHOLARSHIP GRANT PROGRAM

Red River Valley Association Foundation
P.O. Box 1916
Harrisonburg, VA 22801
(540) 442-7782          Fax: (540) 443-3105
E-mail: afbridger@aol.com
Web: www.river-rats.org

**Summary** To provide financial assistance for college or graduate school to the spouses and children of selected service personnel and members of the Red River Valley Fighter Pilots Association.

**Eligibility** This program is open to the spouses and children of 1) service members missing in action (MIA) or killed in action (KIA) in armed conflicts by U.S. forces since August 1964, including those lost in the World Trade Center or Pentagon on September 11, 2001; 2) surviving dependents of U.S. military aircrew members killed in a noncombat aircraft accident in which they were performing aircrew duties; and 3) current members of the association and deceased members who were in good standing at the time of their death. Applicants must be interested in attending an accredited college or university to work on an undergraduate or graduate degree. Selection is based on demonstrated academic achievement, college entrance examination scores, financial need, and accomplishments in school, church, civic, and social activities.

**Financial data** The amount awarded varies, depending upon the need of the recipient. Recently, undergraduate stipends have ranged from $500 to $3,500 and averaged $1,725; graduate stipends have ranged from $500 to $2,000 and averaged $1,670. Funds are paid directly to the recipient's institution and are to be used for tuition, fees, books, and room and board for full-time students.

**Duration** 1 year.

**Additional information** This program was established in 1970, out of concern for the families of aircrews (known as "River Rats") who were killed or missing in action in the Red River Valley of North Vietnam. Information is also available from Herm Davis, 16728 Frontenac Terrace, Rockville, MD 20855, (301) 548-9423.

**Number awarded** Varies each year; since this program was established, it has awarded more than 900 scholarships worth nearly $1,500,000.

**Deadline** May of each year.

## [501]
## REDI-TAG CORPORATION SCHOLARSHIP

American Health Information Management Association
Attn: Foundation of Research and Education
233 North Michigan Avenue, Suite 2150
Chicago, IL 60601-5806
(312) 233-1131                    Fax: (312) 233-1431
E-mail: fore@ahima.org
Web: www.ahima.org/fore/student/programs.asp

**Summary** To provide financial assistance to members of the American Health Information Management Association (AHIMA) who are single parents interested in working on an undergraduate or graduate degree in health information administration or technology.

**Eligibility** This program is open to AHIMA members who are single parents enrolled in a health information administration or health information technology program accredited by the Commission on Accreditation of Allied Health Education Programs. Applicants must be working on an undergraduate or graduate degree on at least a half-time basis and have a GPA of 3.0 or higher. U.S. citizenship is required. Selection is based on (in order of importance) GPA and academic achievement, volunteer and work experience, commitment to the health information management profession, suitability to the health information management profession, quality and suitability of references provided, and clarity of application.

**Financial data** The stipend ranges from $1,000 to $5,000.

**Duration** 1 year; nonrenewable.

**Additional information** Funding for this program is provided by the Redi-Tag Corporation.

**Number awarded** 1 each year.

**Deadline** April of each year.

## [502]
## REED AND GLORIA PENNINGTON SCHOLARSHIP

Kappa Delta Sorority
Attn: Foundation Manager
3205 Players Lane
Memphis, TN 38125
(901) 748-1897                    Toll-free: (800) 536-1897
Fax: (901) 748-0949
E-mail: kappadelta@kappadelta.org
Web: www.kappadelta.org

**Summary** To provide financial assistance to members of Kappa Delta Sorority who are majoring in journalism or communications.

**Eligibility** This program is open to undergraduate members of Kappa Delta Sorority. Applicants must submit a personal statement giving their reasons for applying for this scholarship, an official undergraduate transcript, and 2 letters of recommendation. They must be majoring in journalism or communications. Selection is based on academic excellence, service to the chapter and university, service to the community, personal objectives and goals, potential, recommendations, and financial need.

**Financial data** The stipend is $2,000 per year. Funds may be used only for tuition, fees, and books, not for room and board.

**Duration** 1 year; may be renewed.

**Number awarded** 1 each year.

**Deadline** January of each year.

## [503]
## RHODE ISLAND COMMISSION ON WOMEN/FREDA H. GOLDMAN EDUCATION AWARDS

Rhode Island Foundation
Attn: Scholarship Coordinator
One Union Station
Providence, RI 02903
(401) 274-4564                    Fax: (401) 331-8085
E-mail: libbym@rifoundation.org
Web: www.rifoundation.org

**Summary** To provide financial assistance to women in Rhode Island who are working on a degree or job training beyond high school.

**Eligibility** This program is open to women in Rhode Island who are 1) preparing for a nontraditional job or career through an educational program; 2) returning to the labor market and in need of training to sharpen their skills; 3) seeking skills to improve their job status; 4) ex-offenders wishing to undertake vocational or career education and training; or 5) displaced homemakers and single mothers wishing to further their education. Applicants must be enrolled or registered in an educational or job skills training program and be able to demonstrate financial need. Preference is given to highly motivated, self-supporting, low-income women who are completing their first undergraduate degree or certificate program. As part of the selection process, applicants must submit an essay (up to 300 words) in which they explain their reasons for returning to school, how they chose their intended career or job training, how this scholarship can help them achieve their goals, and specifically how the money will be used.

**Financial data** Stipends range from $300 to $600.

**Duration** 1 year; may be renewed.

**Additional information** This program, established in 1983 and transferred to the foundation in 1997, is supported by the Rhode Island Commission on Women.

**Number awarded** 2 each year.

**Deadline** June of each year.

## [504]
## RHODE ISLAND SPACE GRANT UNDERGRADUATE SCHOLARSHIP PROGRAM

Rhode Island Space Grant
c/o Brown University
Lincoln Field Building
Box 1846
Providence, RI 02912-1846
(401) 863-2889          Fax: (401) 863-1292
E-mail: RISpaceGrant@brown.edu
Web: www.planetary.brown.edu/RI_Space_Grant

**Summary** To provide financial assistance to undergraduate students (particularly women, minority, and disabled students) at institutions that are members of the Rhode Island Space Grant Consortium (RISGC) who are interested in a career in a space-related field of science, mathematics, or engineering.

**Eligibility** This program is open to undergraduate students beyond their freshman year at RISGC-member universities. Applicants must be studying in science, mathematics, or engineering fields of interest to the National Aeronautics and Space Administration (NASA). U.S. citizenship is required. The sponsor is a component of NASA's Space Grant program, which encourages participation by women, underrepresented minorities, and persons with disabilities.

**Financial data** The stipend is $4,000.

**Duration** 1 year.

**Additional information** Members of the RISGC are Bryant College, Community College of Rhode Island, Providence College, Roger Williams University, Rhode Island College, Rhode Island School of Design, Salve Regina University, University of Rhode Island, and Wheaton College. This program is funded by NASA. Scholars are designated as research scholars (who are required to devote up to 4 hours per week to outreach activities in science education for K-12 children and teachers through Rhode Island), outreach scholars (who are required to devote up to 8 hours per week to outreach activities), or "Science En Español" scholars (who are required to devote up to 8 hours per week to curriculum support for K-12 children and teachers throughout Rhode Island).

**Number awarded** Varies each year; recently, 9 of these scholarships were awarded.

**Deadline** February of each year.

## [505]
## RHODE ISLAND WOMEN'S GOLF ASSOCIATION SCHOLARSHIPS

Rhode Island Women's Golf Association
c/o Pat Davitt
17 Oak Manor Drive
Barrington, RI 02806
(401) 245-4959          E-mail: pdavitt@lincolnschool.org
Web: www.riwga.org/scholarships.htm

**Summary** To provide financial assistance for college to women golfers from Rhode Island.

**Eligibility** This program is open to women who have participated in the program of the Rhode Island Women's Golf Association. Applicants must be high school seniors or current undergraduates. They must submit information on their community service experiences; special recognition received at school (e.g., athletic, academic, clubs); financial need; and involvement with golf.

**Financial data** A stipend is awarded (amount not specified).

**Duration** 1 year.

**Additional information** This program began in 1981.

**Number awarded** Varies each year; recently, 17 of these scholarships were awarded.

**Deadline** May of each year.

## [506]
## RICHARD J. PHELPS SCHOLAR-ATHLETE PROGRAM

Boston Globe
135 Morrissey Boulevard
P.O. Box 2378
Boston, MA 02107-2378
(617) 929-2000
Web: www.boston.com

**Summary** To provide financial assistance for college to outstanding scholar-athletes from Massachusetts.

**Eligibility** This program is open to seniors graduating from high schools in Massachusetts who are nominated by their principals. Selection is based on academic and athletic excellence. Females and males are evaluated separately.

**Financial data** The stipend is $2,000 per year.

**Duration** 1 year.

**Additional information** This program was established in 1991 as an adjunct to the *Boston Globe's* All-Scholastic sports teams.

**Number awarded** 14 each year: 1 female and 1 male from each district of the Massachusetts Interscholastic Athletic Association (MIAA).

**Deadline** April of each year.

## [507]
## RITA LEVINE MEMORIAL SCHOLARSHIP

American Mensa Education and Research Foundation
1229 Corporate Drive West
Arlington, TX 76006-6103
(817) 607-0060 Toll-free: (800) 66-MENSA
Fax: (817) 649-5232
E-mail: info@mensafoundation.org
Web: www.mensafoundation.org

**Summary** To provide financial assistance for undergraduate or graduate study to women returning to school after an absence of at least 7 years.

**Eligibility** This program is open to women students who are enrolled or will enroll in an undergraduate or graduate degree program at an accredited American institution of postsecondary education after an absence of 7 or more years. Membership in Mensa is not required, but applicants must be U.S. citizens or permanent residents. Selection is based on a 550-word essay that describes the applicant's career, vocational, or academic goals.

**Financial data** The stipend is $600.

**Duration** 1 year; nonrenewable.

**Additional information** Applications are only available through the advertising efforts of participating Mensa local groups.

**Number awarded** 1 each year.

**Deadline** January of each year.

## [508]
## R.L. GILLETTE SCHOLARSHIPS

American Foundation for the Blind
Attn: Scholarship Committee
11 Penn Plaza, Suite 300
New York, NY 10001
(212) 502-7661 Toll-free: (800) AFB-LINE
Fax: (212) 502-7771 TDD: (212) 502-7662
E-mail: afbinfo@afb.net
Web: www.afb.org/scholarships.asp

**Summary** To provide financial assistance to legally blind undergraduate women who are studying literature or music.

**Eligibility** This program is open to women who are legally blind, U.S. citizens, and enrolled in a 4-year baccalaureate degree program in literature or music. Along with their application, they must submit an essay that includes the field of study they are pursuing and why they have chosen it; their educational and personal goals; their work experience; any extracurricular activities with which they have been involved, including those in school, religious organizations, and the community; and how they intend to use scholarship monies that may be awarded. They must also submit a sample performance tape (not to exceed 30 minutes) or a creative writing sample.

**Financial data** The stipend is $1,000.

**Duration** 1 academic year.

**Number awarded** 2 each year.

**Deadline** April of each year.

## [509]
## ROBERT SMILEY SCHOLARSHIP

Iowa Girls' High School Athletic Union
Attn: Scholarships
2900 Grand Avenue
P.O. Box 10348
Des Moines, IA 50306-0348
(515) 288-9741 Fax: (515) 284-1969
E-mail: lisa@ighsau.org
Web: www.ighsau.org

**Summary** To provide financial assistance to female high school seniors in Iowa who have participated in athletics and plan to attend college in the state.

**Eligibility** This program is open to females graduating from high schools in Iowa who have lettered in 1 varsity sport sponsored by the Iowa Girls' High School Athletic Union (IGHSAU) each year of high school and have a GPA of 2.5 or higher. Applicants must be planning to attend a college or university in Iowa. Each high school in the state may nominate 1 student. Selection is based on academic achievements, athletic accomplishments, non-sports extracurricular activities, and community involvement.

**Financial data** The stipend is $1,000.

**Duration** 1 year.

**Number awarded** 1 each year.

**Deadline** March of each year.

## [510]
## ROCKWELL AUTOMATION SCHOLARSHIPS

Society of Women Engineers
230 East Ohio Street, Suite 400
Chicago, IL 60611-3265
(312) 596-5223 Toll-free: (877) SWE-INFO
Fax: (312) 644-8557
E-mail: scholarshipapplication@swe.org
Web: www.swe.org/scholarships

**Summary** To provide financial assistance to upper-division women majoring in computer science or selected engineering specialties at specified colleges and universities.

**Eligibility** This program is open to women who are entering their junior year at a designated ABET-accredited college or university. Applicants must be majoring in computer science or computer, electrical, industrial, mechanical, or software engineering and have at GPA of 3.0 or higher. Along with their application, they must submit a 1-page essay on why they want to be an engineer, how they believe they will make a difference as an engineer, and what influenced them to study engineering. Selection is based on merit and leadership potential. Preference is given to members of underrepresented minority groups.

**Financial data** The stipend is $2,500.

**Duration** 1 year.

**Additional information** This program, established in 1991, is supported by Rockwell Automation, Inc. Recipients must attend a designated college or university. For a list, contact the sponsor.

**Number awarded** 2 each year.

**Deadline** January of each year.

## [511]
## ROCKY MOUNTAIN NASA SPACE GRANT CONSORTIUM UNDERGRADUATE SCHOLARSHIPS

Rocky Mountain NASA Space Grant Consortium
c/o Utah State University
EL Building, Room 302
Logan, UT 84322-4140
(435) 797-3666                    Fax: (435) 797-3382
E-mail: spacegrant@cc.usu.edu
Web: spacegrant.usu.edu

**Summary**  To provide financial support to undergraduate students (particularly women, minority, and disabled students) at designated universities in Utah or Colorado who are working on a degree in fields of interest to the National Aeronautics and Space Administration (NASA).

**Eligibility**  This program is open to undergraduate students at member institutions of the Rocky Mountain NASA Space Grant Consortium who are studying engineering, science, medicine, or technology. U.S. citizenship is required. Selection is based on academic performance to date and potential for the future, with emphasis on space-related research interests. This program is part of the NASA Space Grant program, which encourages participation by women, underrepresented minorities, and persons with disabilities.

**Financial data**  The amount of the awards depends on the availability of funds.

**Duration**  1 year.

**Additional information**  Members of the consortium are Utah State University, the University of Utah, Brigham Young University, Dixie State College, Salt Lake Community College, Shoshone-Bannock School, Snow College, Southern Utah University, the University of Denver, and Weber State University. This program is funded by NASA.

**Number awarded**  Varies each year.

**Deadline**  June of each year.

## [512]
## ROCKY MOUNTAIN NETWORK OF EXECUTIVE WOMEN IN HOSPITALITY SCHOLARSHIP AWARDS

Network of Executive Women in Hospitality-Rocky
    Mountain Chapter
Attn: Katie Toth-Siers, Director of Scholarship and
    Education
12503 Bradford Drive
Parker, CO 80134
Toll-free: (800) 593-NEWH        Fax: (800) 693-NEWH
E-mail: k.tothsiers@tri-kes.com
Web: www.newh.org/newh/scholarshippacket.php

**Summary**  To provide financial assistance to women in the Rocky Mountain region who wish to work on a college degree in a hospitality-related field.

**Eligibility**  This program is open to women who have completed half the requirements for a degree or certification program at a vocational school or college in Colorado, Nebraska, or Wyoming. Applicants must have a GPA of 3.0 or higher and a career objective in the hospitality or food service industries (e.g., hotel and restaurant management, culinary, food service, architecture, design). Selection is based on financial need and academic accomplishments.

**Financial data**  A stipend is awarded (amount not specified).

**Duration**  1 year.

**Number awarded**  1 or more each year.

**Deadline**  April of each year.

## [513]
## RODGER AND RHEA WEAVER ENDOWMENT SCHOLARSHIP

Epsilon Sigma Alpha
Attn: ESA Foundation Assistant Scholarship Director
P.O. Box 270517
Fort Collins, CO 80527
(970) 223-2824                    Fax: (970) 223-4456
Web: www.esaintl.com/esaf

**Summary**  To provide financial assistance to women interested in acquiring new job skills or updating present skills.

**Eligibility**  This program is open to women older than 25 years of age who are returning to school to acquire new job skills or update present skills. Selection is based on character (20%), leadership (20%), service (20%), financial need (20%), and scholastic ability (20%).

**Financial data**  The stipend is $500.

**Duration**  1 year; nonrenewable.

**Additional information**  Epsilon Sigma Alpha (ESA) is a women's service organization. Information is also available from Lynn Hughes, Scholarship Director, 324 N.E. Mead, Grants Pass, OR 97526, (541) 476-4617, E-mail: orcycler@vsisp.net. Completed applications must be submitted to the ESA State Counselor who verifies the information before forwarding them to the scholarship director. A $5 processing fee is required.

**Number awarded**  1 each year.

**Deadline**  January of each year.

## [514]
## ROLLIE HOPGOOD FUTURE TEACHERS SCHOLARSHIP

AFT Michigan
Attn: Scholarship Committee
2661 East Jefferson Avenue
Detroit, MI 48207
(313) 393-2200                    Toll-free: (800) MFT-8868
Fax: (313) 393-2236
Web: aftmichigan.org/members/scholarships.html

**Summary**  To provide financial assistance to high school seniors in Michigan who are interested in becoming a teacher.

**Eligibility**  This program is open to seniors graduating from high schools that are represented by AFT Michigan. Applicants must submit a 500-word essay in which they explain why they want to become a teacher and why they should be considered for this scholarship. Selection is based on the essay, GPA, extracurricular activities, community-related activities, and financial need. Female and male applicants compete separately.

**Financial data**  The stipend is $1,000.

**Duration**  1 year.

**Additional information** AFT Michigan was formerly the Michigan Federation of Teachers & School Related Personnel. Recipients must enroll as full-time students.

**Number awarded** 2 each year: 1 female and 1 male.

**Deadline** April of each year.

## [515]
## ROSE MCGILL FUND EMERGENCY ASSISTANCE GRANTS

Kappa Kappa Gamma Foundation
530 East Town Street
P.O. Box 38
Columbus, OH 43216-0038
(614) 228-6515          Toll-free: (866) KKG-1870
Fax: (614) 228-7809      E-mail: kkghq@kappa.org
Web: www.kappakappagamma.org

**Summary** To provide emergency grants of money to Kappa Kappa Gamma members in need.

**Eligibility** Upper-division students who are Kappa Kappa Gamma members and face sudden financial emergency are eligible to apply. Applicants must be in good standing and be making a contribution to their chapter and campus.

**Financial data** Grants range from $500 to $1,000.

**Additional information** The Rose McGill Fund was established in 1922 to provide confidential aid to Kappa Kappa Gamma members. Applicants must be recommended by the Kappa Kappa Gamma Advisory Board. Associate members are not eligible for assistance. Recipients must remain in school the term following the term of the grant. Requests for applications must be accompanied by a self-addressed stamped envelope and chapter membership identification. All awards granted are held in confidence.

**Number awarded** Varies each year; in a recent biennium, the Rose McGill program provided $760,762 in support.

**Deadline** Applications are accepted at any time.

## [516]
## R.O.S.E. SCHOLARSHIPS

R.O.S.E. Fund
175 Federal Street, Suite 455
Boston, MA 02110
(617) 482-5400          Toll-free: (800) 253-6425
Fax: (617) 482-3443      E-mail: info@rosefund.org
Web: www.rosefund.org/programs/scholarship.asp

**Summary** To provide financial assistance to women who have been victims of violence and are working on an undergraduate degree in New England.

**Eligibility** This program is open to women who have completed at least 1 full year of undergraduate study at a college or university in New England. Candidates must be survivors who have broken the cycle of domestic violence. They must be nominated by another person; self-nominations are not accepted. The nominator must provide the nominee's biography and other relevant background information; a description of why the nominee is deserving of this scholarship; a description of the nominee's accomplishments, including volunteer work, extracurricular activities, and other honors and awards; a copy of the nominee's high school diploma or GED certificate; if the nominee is in

the second or subsequent semester of college, transcripts from the prior semester; 3 written references; and documentation of financial need. The nominees must submit an essay of 1 to 2 pages on why they are deserving of this scholarship.

**Financial data** The maximum stipend is $10,000 per year.

**Duration** 1 year; may be renewed. Recipients who maintain a GPA of 2.5 or higher are given preference for renewable scholarships.

**Additional information** The sponsoring organization, which stands for Regaining One's Self-Esteem, established this scholarship program in 1998. It also sponsors scholarships at the University of Massachusetts.

**Number awarded** 1 or more each year.

**Deadline** June of each year for fall semester; December of each year for spring semester.

## [517]
## RURAL MUTUAL INSURANCE COMPANY SCHOLARSHIPS

Wisconsin Towns Association
Attn: Scholarship Program
W7686 County Road MMM
Shawano, WI 54166-6086
(715) 526-3157          Fax: (715) 524-3917
E-mail: wtastaff@wisctowns.com
Web: www.wisctowns.com

**Summary** To provide financial assistance for college to high seniors in Wisconsin who submit outstanding essays on town government in the state.

**Eligibility** This program is open to seniors graduating from high schools in Wisconsin who plan to attend a college, university, or vocational/technical institute in the state. Applicants must live in a town or village that has insurance from Rural Mutual Insurance Company for its municipal government. Along with their application, they must submit an essay of 500 to 1,000 words on the topic, "What about the history of town government has made town government effective in Wisconsin." Selection is based primarily on the essay's originality and subject matter in relationship to the topic. Boys and girls are judged separately.

**Financial data** The stipend is $1,000.

**Duration** 1 year.

**Additional information** This program is supported by Rural Mutual Insurance Company, 1241 John Q. Hammons Drive, Suite 200, P.O. Box 5555, Madison, WI 53705-0555.

**Number awarded** 2 each year: 1 to a boy and 1 to a girl.

**Deadline** May of each year.

## [518]
## RUTH BILLOW MEMORIAL EDUCATION FUND

Delta Gamma Foundation
Attn: Director, Service for Sight
3250 Riverside Drive
P.O. Box 21397
Columbus, OH 43221-0397
(614) 481-8169                    Fax: (614) 481-0133
E-mail: freeman14@comcast.net
Web: www.deltagamma.org

**Summary**  To provide financial assistance to members of Delta Gamma sorority who are visually impaired or preparing for a career in working with the visually impaired.

**Eligibility**  This program is open to undergraduate and graduate members of the sorority who are either 1) blind or visually impaired or 2) pursuing professional training in areas related to working with persons who are blind or visually impaired or in sight preservation. Applicants must be pursuing a program of postsecondary education in the United States or Canada.

**Financial data**  The stipend is $1,000 for undergraduates or $2,500 for graduate students.

**Duration**  1 year or more.

**Number awarded**  2 each year: 1 to an undergraduate and 1 to a graduate student.

**Deadline**  Applications may be submitted at any time.

## [519]
## RUTH E. BLACK SCHOLARSHIP FUND

American Association of University Women-Honolulu
   Branch
Attn: Scholarship Committee
1802 Keeaumoku Street
Honolulu, HI 96822
(808) 537-4702                    Fax: (808) 537-4702*51
E-mail: aauwhnb@att.net

**Summary**  To provide financial assistance to undergraduate women in Hawaii.

**Eligibility**  Eligible to apply are women who are residents of Hawaii and are currently enrolled in an accredited college, university, or vocational/technical institute in the state. Selection is based on academic record after at least 2 semesters of college or university study, career plans, personal involvement in school and community activities, and financial need. First-time applicants receive priority. U.S. citizenship is required.

**Financial data**  The amount awarded varies, depending upon the needs of the recipient. Generally, individual awards range from $500 to $1,000.

**Duration**  1 year.

**Additional information**  This program was established in 1969 and given its current name in 1975.

**Number awarded**  Varies each year; recently, 5 of these scholarships were awarded.

**Deadline**  February of each year.

## [520]
## RUTH MU-LAN CHU AND JAMES S.C. CHAO SCHOLARSHIP

US Pan Asian American Chamber of Commerce
Attn: Scholarship Coordinator
1329 18th Street, N.W.
Washington, DC 20036
(202) 296-5221                    Fax: (202) 296-5225
E-mail: administrator@uspaacc.com
Web: www.uspaacc.com

**Summary**  To provide financial assistance for college to female Asian American high school seniors who demonstrate financial need.

**Eligibility**  This program is open to female high school seniors of Asian heritage who are U.S. citizens or permanent residents. Applicants must be planning to enroll full time at an accredited postsecondary educational institution in the United States. Along with their application, they must submit a 500-word essay on "Why I need this scholarship." Selection is based on academic excellence (GPA of 3.5 or higher), community service involvement, and financial need.

**Financial data**  The maximum stipend is $5,000. Funds are paid directly to the recipient's college or university.

**Duration**  1 year.

**Additional information**  This program was established in 2000. Funding is not provided for correspondence courses, Internet courses, or study in a country other than the United States.

**Number awarded**  1 each year.

**Deadline**  February of each year.

## [521]
## S. EVELYN LEWIS MEMORIAL SCHOLARSHIP IN MEDICAL HEALTH SCIENCES

Zeta Phi Beta Sorority, Inc.
Attn: National Education Foundation
1734 New Hampshire Avenue, N.W.
Washington, DC 20009
(202) 387-3103                    Fax: (202) 232-4593
E-mail: scholarship@ZPhiBNEF.org
Web: www.zphib1920.org/nef

**Summary**  To provide financial assistance to women interested in studying medicine or health sciences on the undergraduate or graduate school level.

**Eligibility**  This program is open to women enrolled in a program on the undergraduate or graduate school level leading to a degree in medicine or health sciences. Proof of enrollment is required. Applicants need not be members of Zeta Phi Beta Sorority. They must submit 3 letters of recommendation, high school or university transcripts, a 150-word essay on their educational and professional goals, and information on financial need.

**Financial data**  The stipend ranges from $500 to $1,000. Funds are paid directly to the college or university.

**Duration**  1 academic year.

**Additional information**  Information is also available from Cheryl Williams, National Second Vice President, 6322 Bocage Drive, Shreveport, LA 71119. Recipients must attend school on a full-time basis. No awards are made just for summer study.

**Number awarded**  1 or more each year.

**Deadline** January of each year.

## [522]
## SALLY TOMPKINS NURSING AND APPLIED HEALTH SCIENCES SCHOLARSHIP

United Daughters of the Confederacy-Virginia Division
c/o Suzie Snyder, Education Committee Chair
8440 Bradshaw Road
Salem, VA 24153-2246
(540) 384-6884          E-mail: Suzienotes@aol.com
Web: users.erols.com/va-udc/scholarships.html

**Summary** To provide financial assistance for college to women who are Confederate descendants from Virginia and working on a degree in nursing.

**Eligibility** This program is open to women residents of Virginia interested in working on a degree in nursing. Applicants must be 1) lineal descendants of Confederates, or 2) collateral descendants and also members of the Children of the Confederacy or the United Daughters of the Confederacy. They must submit proof of the Confederate military record of at least 1 ancestor, with the company and regiment in which he served. They must also submit a personal letter pledging to make the best possible use of the scholarship; describing their health, social, family, religious, and fraternal connections within the community; and reflecting on what a Southern heritage means to them (using the term "War Between the States" in lieu of "Civil War"). They must have a GPA of 3.0 or higher and be able to demonstrate financial need.

**Financial data** The amount of the stipend depends on the availability of funds. Payment is made directly to the college or university the recipient attends.

**Duration** 1 year; may be renewed up to 3 additional years if the recipient maintains a GPA of 3.0 or higher.

**Additional information** Information is also available from Mrs. George W. Bryson, 10103 Rixeyville Road, Culpeper, VA 22701-4422, E-mail: brysdale@aol.com.

**Number awarded** This scholarship is offered whenever a prior recipient graduates or is no longer eligible.

**Deadline** May of the years in which a scholarship is available.

## [523]
## SARAH E. HUNEYCUTT SCHOLARSHIP

Florida Women's State Golf Association
Attn: Executive Director
8875 Hidden River Parkway, Suite 110
Tampa, FL 33637
(813) 864-2130          Fax: (813) 864-2129
E-mail: info@fwsga.org
Web: www.fwsga.org/juniors

**Summary** To provide financial assistance for college to women in Florida who have an interest in golf.

**Eligibility** This program is open to females in Florida who have an interest in golf but are not skilled enough to qualify for an athletic scholarship. Applicants must have a need for financial assistance. They must have a GPA of 3.0 or higher and be attending or planning to attend a junior college, college, university, or technical school in Florida.

**Financial data** Stipends range from $1,000 to $2,000. Funds are paid directly to the recipient's school.

**Duration** 1 year.

**Additional information** This program was established in 1994.

**Number awarded** Varies each year; recently, 7 of these scholarships were awarded.

**Deadline** March of each year.

## [524]
## SCHOLARSHIPS FOR WOMEN RESIDENTS OF THE STATE OF DELAWARE

American Association of University Women-Wilmington Branch
Attn: Scholarship Committee
1800 Fairfax Boulevard
Wilmington, DE 19803-3106
(302) 428-0939          Fax: (775) 890-9043
E-mail: aauwwilm@magpage.com
Web: www.aauwwilmington.org/procedure.html

**Summary** To provide financial assistance for college or graduate school to women residents of Delaware.

**Eligibility** This program is open to women who are residents of Delaware and U.S. citizens working on a baccalaureate or graduate degree at an accredited college or university. High school graduates may be from any Delaware county; high school seniors must be graduating from a public or private high school in New Castle County. Selection is based on scholastic standing, contributions to school and community, results of standardized testing, and financial need. An interview is required.

**Financial data** A stipend is awarded (amount not specified).

**Duration** 1 year.

**Number awarded** Varies each year; recently, 17 of these scholarships, worth $55,000, were awarded.

**Deadline** February of each year.

## [525]
## SCHUYLER S. PYLE SCHOLARSHIP

Fleet Reserve Association
Attn: Scholarship Administrator
125 North West Street
Alexandria, VA 22314-2754
(703) 683-1400          Toll-free: (800) 372-1924
Fax: (703) 549-6610          E-mail: fra@fra.org
Web: www.fra.org

**Summary** To provide financial assistance for undergraduate or graduate education to members of the Fleet Reserve Association (FRA) who are current or former naval personnel and their spouses and children.

**Eligibility** Applicants for these scholarships must be dependent children or spouses of members of the association in good standing as of April 1 of the year of the award or at the time of death. FRA members are also eligible. Selection is based on financial need, academic standing, character, and leadership qualities.

**Financial data** The stipend is $5,000 per year.

**Duration** 1 year; may be renewed.

**Additional information** Membership in the FRA is restricted to active-duty, retired, and Reserve members of the Navy, Marine Corps, and Coast Guard.

**Number awarded** 1 each year.

**Deadline** April of each year.

## [526]
## SCOTTS COMPANY SCHOLARS PROGRAM

Golf Course Superintendents Association of America
Attn: Environmental Institute for Golf
1421 Research Park Drive
Lawrence, KS 66049-3859
(785) 832-4424    Toll-free: (800) 472-7878, ext. 4424
Fax: (785) 832-3673    E-mail: ahoward@gcsaa.org
Web: www.gcsaa.org

**Summary** To provide financial assistance and summer work experience to high school seniors and college students, particularly those from diverse backgrounds, who are preparing for a career in golf management.

**Eligibility** This program is open to high school seniors and college students (freshmen, sophomores, and juniors) who are interested in preparing for a career in golf management (the "green industry"). Applicants should come from diverse ethnic, cultural, and socioeconomic backgrounds, defined to include women, minorities, and people with disabilities. Selection is based on cultural diversity, academic achievement, extracurricular activities, leadership, employment potential, essay responses, and letters of recommendation. Financial need is not considered. Finalists are selected for summer internships and then compete for scholarships.

**Financial data** The finalists receive a $500 award to supplement their summer internship income. Scholarship stipends are $2,500.

**Duration** 1 year.

**Additional information** The program is funded by a permanent endowment established by Scotts Company. Finalists are responsible for securing their own internships.

**Number awarded** 5 finalists, of whom 2 receive scholarships, are selected each year.

**Deadline** February of each year.

## [527]
## SEATTLE CHAPTER ASWA SCHOLARSHIPS

American Society of Women Accountants-Seattle
  Chapter
c/o Anne Macnab
800 Fifth Avenue, Suite 101
PMB 237
Seattle, WA 98104-3191
(206) 467-8645  E-mail: scholarship@aswaseattle.com
Web: www.aswaseattle.com/scholarships.htm

**Summary** To provide financial assistance to female students working on a bachelor's or master's degree in accounting at a college or university in Washington.

**Eligibility** This program is open to women working part time or full time on an associate, bachelor's, or master's degree in accounting at a college or university in Washington. Applicants must have completed at least 30 semester hours and have maintained a GPA of at least 2.5 overall and

3.0 in accounting. Membership in the American Society of Women Accountants (ASWA) is not required. Selection is based on career goals, communication skills, GPA, personal circumstances, and financial need.

**Financial data** The amounts of the awards vary. Recently, a total of $12,000 was available for this program. Funds are paid directly to the recipient's school.

**Duration** 1 year.

**Number awarded** April of each year.

**Deadline** Varies each year; recently, 3 of these scholarships were awarded.

## [528]
## SECOND WIND SCHOLARSHIP PROGRAM

Independent Colleges of Indiana
101 West Ohio Street, Suite 440
Indianapolis, IN 46204-1970
(317) 236-6090        Fax: (317) 236-6086
Web: www.icindiana.org

**Summary** To provide financial assistance to minority women entering their junior year as a mathematics or science major at a member institution of Independent Colleges of Indiana (ICI).

**Eligibility** This program is open to women entering their junior year at ICI member institutions and working on an undergraduate degree in mathematics or science. Applicants must be members of a minority group, defined as African American or Black, Latino or Hispanic, Native American or Alaskan Native, or Asian American or Asian (including Indian subcontinent). They must have confronted serious economic challenges that present barriers to graduation and degree attainment. Along with their application, they must submit a 1-page essay that covers why they believe they deserve this award, their educational and/or career goals, their interest in and commitment to science and mathematics, and any additional factors that they believe should be considered in evaluating their application.

**Financial data** The stipend is $5,000 per year.

**Duration** 1 year (the junior year of college); may be renewed for the senior year.

**Additional information** This program is sponsored by the Charlotte R. Schmidlapp Fund. ICI member institutions include Ancilla College, Anderson University, Bethel College, Butler University, Calumet College of St. Joseph, DePauw University, Earlham College, Franklin College, Goshen College, Grace College and Seminary, Hanover College, Holy Cross College, Huntington University, Indiana Tech, Indiana Wesleyan University, Manchester College, Marian College, Martin University, Oakland City University, Rose-Hulman Institute of Technology, Saint Joseph's College, Saint Mary's College, Saint Mary-of-the-Woods College, Taylor University (Fort Wayne and Upland campuses), Tri-State University, University of Evansville, University of Indianapolis, University of Notre Dame, University of Saint Francis, Valparaiso University, and Wabash College.

**Number awarded** 1 or more each year.

**Deadline** June of each year.

## [529]
## SEHAR SALEHA AHMAD AND ABRAHIM EKRAMULLAH ZAFAR FOUNDATION SCHOLARSHIP

Oregon Student Assistance Commission
Attn: Grants and Scholarships Division
1500 Valley River Drive, Suite 100
Eugene, OR 97401-2146
(541) 687-7395    Toll-free: (800) 452-8807, ext. 7395
Fax: (541) 687-7419
E-mail: awardinfo@mercury.osac.state.or.us
Web: www.osac.state.or.us

**Summary** To provide financial assistance to high school seniors in Oregon who are interested in studying English in college.

**Eligibility** This program is open to graduating high school seniors in Oregon who have a GPA of 3.5 or higher. Applicants must be planning to major in English in college. Preference is given to women.

**Financial data** The stipend is at least $500.

**Duration** 1 year; may be renewed if the recipient shows satisfactory academic progress and continued financial need.

**Number awarded** 1 or more each year.

**Deadline** February of each year.

## [530]
## SHARON D. BANKS MEMORIAL UNDERGRADUATE SCHOLARSHIP

Women's Transportation Seminar
Attn: National Headquarters
1701 K Street, N.W., Suite 800
Washington, DC 20006
(202) 955-5085                Fax: (202) 955-5088
E-mail: wts@wtsinternational.org
Web: www.wtsinternational.org

**Summary** To provide financial assistance to undergraduate women interested in a career in transportation.

**Eligibility** This program is open to women who are working on an undergraduate degree in transportation or a transportation-related field (e.g., transportation engineering, planning, finance, or logistics). Applicants must have a GPA of 3.0 or higher and be interested in a career in transportation. Along with their application, they must submit a 500-word statement about their career goals after graduation and why they think they should receive the scholarship award. Applications must be submitted first to a local chapter; the chapters forward selected applications for consideration on the national level. Minority candidates are encouraged to apply. Selection is based on transportation involvement and goals, job skills, and academic record; financial need is not considered.

**Financial data** The stipend is $3,000.

**Duration** 1 year.

**Additional information** This program was established in 1992. Local chapters may also award additional funding to winners in their area.

**Number awarded** 1 each year.

**Deadline** Applications must be submitted by November to a local WTS chapter.

## [531]
## SHARON D. BANKS/PUGET SOUND CHAPTER MEMORIAL UNDERGRADUATE SCHOLARSHIP

Women's Transportation Seminar-Puget Sound Chapter
c/o Kristin Overleese, Scholarship Chair
City of Shoreline, Capital Projects Manager
17544 Midvale Avenue North
Shoreline, WA 98133-4821
(206) 546-1700                Fax: (206) 546-2200
TDD: (206) 546-0457
Web: www.wtsinternational.org/puget_sound

**Summary** To provide financial assistance to women undergraduate students from Washington working on a degree related to transportation.

**Eligibility** This program is open to women who are residents of Washington, studying at a college in the state, or working as an intern in the state. Applicants must be currently enrolled in an undergraduate degree program in a transportation-related field, such as engineering, planning, finance, or logistics. They must have a GPA of 3.0 or higher and plans to prepare for a career in a transportation-related field. Minority candidates are encouraged to apply. Along with their application, they must submit a 500-word statement about their career goals after graduation and why they think they should receive this scholarship award. Selection is based on that statement, academic record, and transportation-related activities or job skills. Financial need is not considered.

**Financial data** The stipend is $1,500.

**Duration** 1 year.

**Additional information** The winner is also nominated for scholarships offered by the national organization of the Women's Transportation Seminar.

**Number awarded** 1 each year.

**Deadline** October of each year.

## [532]
## SHAWN MARGARET DONNELLEY SCHOLARSHIP

Alpha Chi Omega Foundation
Attn: Foundation Programs Coordinator
5939 Castle Creek Parkway North Drive
Indianapolis, IN 46250-4343
(317) 579-5050, ext. 262        Fax: (317) 579-5051
E-mail: foundation@alphachiomega.org
Web: www.alphachiomega.org

**Summary** To provide financial assistance for college or graduate school to undergraduate or graduate members of Alpha Chi Omega.

**Eligibility** This program is open to undergraduate and graduate members of Alpha Chi Omega. Preference is given to applicants affiliated with Zeta Psi Chapter (Loyola University of New Orleans). If there are no qualified applicants from that chapter, the grant is then opened to all undergraduate and graduate members of the sorority. Selection is based on academic achievement, chapter involvement, community and campus involvement, and financial need.

**Financial data** The stipend is $500.

**Duration** 1 year.

**Number awarded** 1 each year.

**Deadline** March of each year.

## [533]
## SIEMENS CORPORATION SCHOLARSHIPS

Society of Women Engineers
230 East Ohio Street, Suite 400
Chicago, IL 60611-3265
(312) 596-5223       Toll-free: (877) SWE-INFO
Fax: (312) 644-8557
E-mail: scholarshipapplication@swe.org
Web: www.swe.org/scholarships

**Summary** To provide financial assistance to female high school seniors interested in studying specified fields of engineering in college.

**Eligibility** This program is open to women who are graduating high school seniors planning to enroll full time at an ABET-accredited 4-year college or university. Applicants must have a GPA of 3.0 or higher and be planning to major in computer science or electrical, industrial, or manufacturing engineering. Along with their application, they must submit a 1-page essay on why they want to be an engineer or computer scientist, how they believe they will make a difference as an engineer or computer scientist, and what influenced them to study engineering or computer science. Selection is based on merit.

**Financial data** The stipend is $2,500.

**Duration** 1 year.

**Additional information** This program is sponsored by Siemens Corporation.

**Number awarded** 2 each year.

**Deadline** May of each year.

## [534]
## SIGMA ALPHA IOTA REGIONAL SUMMER MUSIC SCHOLARSHIPS

Sigma Alpha Iota Philanthropies, Inc.
One Tunnel Road
Asheville, NC 28805
(828) 251-0606       Fax: (828) 251-0644
E-mail: philonline@sai-national.org
Web: www.sai-national.org/phil/philsumr.html

**Summary** To provide financial assistance for summer study in music, in the United States or abroad, to members of Sigma Alpha Iota (an organization of women musicians).

**Eligibility** Undergraduate and graduate student members of the organization may apply if they are planning to study at a summer music program in the United States or abroad. Applicants must submit a complete resume (including musical studies and activities, academic GPA, community service record, and record of participation in Sigma Alpha Iota), supporting materials (recital and concert programs, reviews, repertoire list, etc.), a statement of why they chose this program and how it will aid their musical growth, a full brochure of information on the program (including cost and payment due dates), a copy of the completed summer school application and acceptance letter (when available), and a letter of recommendation from their major teacher.

**Financial data** The stipend is $1,000.

**Duration** Summer months.

**Additional information** Applications must be accompanied by a nonrefundable fee of $25.

**Number awarded** 5 each year: 1 from each region of Sigma Alpha Iota.

**Deadline** March of each year.

## [535]
## SIGMA ALPHA IOTA SPECIAL NEEDS SCHOLARSHIP

Sigma Alpha Iota Philanthropies, Inc.
One Tunnel Road
Asheville, NC 28805
(828) 251-0606       Fax: (828) 251-0644
E-mail: philonline@sai-national.org
Web: www.sai-national.org/phil/philsch1.html

**Summary** To provide financial assistance for college or graduate school to members of Sigma Alpha Iota (an organization of women musicians) who have a disability and are working on a degree in music.

**Eligibility** This program is open to members of the organization who have a sensory or physical impairment. Applicants must be enrolled in a graduate or undergraduate degree program in music. Performance majors must submit a video or DVD of their work; non-performance majors must submit evidence of work in their area of specialization, such as composition, musicology, or research.

**Financial data** The stipend is $1,000.

**Duration** 1 year.

**Additional information** There is a $25 nonrefundable application fee.

**Number awarded** 1 each year.

**Deadline** March of each year.

## [536]
## SIGMA ALPHA IOTA UNDERGRADUATE SCHOLARSHIPS

Sigma Alpha Iota Philanthropies, Inc.
One Tunnel Road
Asheville, NC 28805
(828) 251-0606       Fax: (828) 251-0644
E-mail: philonline@sai-national.org
Web: www.sai-national.org/phil/philsch1.html

**Summary** To provide financial assistance for college to members of Sigma Alpha Iota (an organization of women musicians).

**Eligibility** This program is open to members of the organization in the first 3 years of undergraduate study. Candidates must be nominated by their chapter and their chapter adviser must submit a letter of recommendation. Selection is based on financial need, musical ability, scholarship, potential leadership, and contribution to campus and community life.

**Financial data** Stipends are $2,000 or $1,500.

**Duration** 1 year.

**Number awarded** 15 each year: 3 at $2,000 and 12 at $1,500.

**Deadline** March of each year.

## [537]
## SIGN OF THE ARROW MELISSA SCHOLARSHIP

Pi Beta Phi
Attn: Pi Beta Phi Foundation
1154 Town and Country Commons Drive
Town and Country, MO 63017
(636) 256-0680          Fax: (636) 256-8124
E-mail: fndn@pibetaphi.org
Web: www.pibetaphifoundation.org

**Summary** To provide financial assistance to members of Pi Beta Phi who are working on an undergraduate degree.

**Eligibility** This program is open to women who are officially enrolled at a college or university where there is a Pi Beta Phi chapter. They must be active members in good standing in the sorority and entering their senior year as a full-time student with a GPA of 3.1 or higher. Applicants must commit to 1) continue a program of community service for the year the scholarship is applicable; 2) promote and inspire others to community service; and 3) write a reflective piece summarizing community service efforts during the award year. Financial need is not considered.

**Financial data** Stipends up to $10,000 are available.

**Duration** 1 year.

**Additional information** This scholarship was first awarded in 2001.

**Number awarded** 1 each year.

**Deadline** January of each year.

## [538]
## SISTER ELIZABETH CANDON SCHOLARSHIP

Vermont Student Assistance Corporation
Attn: Scholarship Programs
10 East Allen Street
P.O. Box 2000
Winooski, VT 05404-2601
(802) 654-3798          Toll-free: (888) 253-4819
Fax: (802) 654-3765          TDD: (802) 654-3766
TDD: (800) 281-3341 (within VT)
E-mail: info@vsac.org
Web: www.vsac.org

**Summary** To provide financial assistance for college to single parent mothers in Vermont.

**Eligibility** This program is open to women residents of Vermont who are single parents with primary custody of at least 1 child 12 years of age or younger. Applicants must be enrolled at least half time in an accredited undergraduate degree program. Selection is based on financial need, a letter of recommendation, and required essays.

**Financial data** The stipend is $1,000 per year.

**Duration** 1 year; may be renewed up to 3 additional years.

**Number awarded** 1 each year.

**Deadline** June of each year.

## [539]
## SISTER THOMAS MORE BERTELS SCHOLARSHIP

American Agri-Women
c/o Peggy Clark
2274 East Lytle Five Points Road
Dayton, OH 45458
E-mail: aawrc@americanagriwomen.org
Web: www.americanagriwomen.org/scholarships.htm

**Summary** To provide financial assistance for college to women involved in agriculture.

**Eligibility** This program is open to women and their daughters who farm, ranch, or are involved in agribusiness or other agricultural activities. Applicants must be 24 years of age or older and be interested in working on a degree in agricultural leadership, communications, technology, economics, rural sociology, medicine, or other courses directly related to agriculture and the needs of agricultural communities. Selection is based on financial need, knowledge of or work experience in agriculture, GPA, and test scores.

**Financial data** The stipend is $500.

**Duration** 1 year; nonrenewable.

**Number awarded** 1 each year.

**Deadline** May of each year.

## [540]
## SLOVENIAN WOMEN'S UNION OF AMERICA CONTINUING EDUCATION AWARDS

Slovenian Women's Union of America
Attn: Scholarship Program
52 Oakridge Drive
Marquette, MI 49855
(906) 249-4288          E-mail: mturvey@aol.com
Web: www.swua.org/scholarships

**Summary** To provide financial assistance to members of the Slovenian Women's Union of America (SWUA) who are returning to college.

**Eligibility** This program is open to students returning to college on a full- or part-time basis after an absence. Applicants must have held paid membership in the SWUA for at least 3 years. Along with their application, they must submit a resume, statement of financial need, and letter of recommendation from their SWUA branch president or secretary.

**Financial data** The stipend is $500 per year.

**Duration** 1 year.

**Number awarded** 1 each year.

**Deadline** February of each year.

**[541]**

## SLOVENIAN WOMEN'S UNION OF AMERICA SCHOLARSHIPS

Slovenian Women's Union of America
Attn: Scholarship Program
52 Oakridge Drive
Marquette, MI 49855
(906) 249-4288                    E-mail: mturvey@aol.com
Web: www.swua.org/scholarships

**Summary** To provide financial assistance for college to members of the Slovenian Women's Union of America (SWUA).

**Eligibility** This program is open to graduating high school seniors and full-time students at colleges, universities, and technical schools. Applicants must have held paid membership in the SWUA for at least 3 years. Along with their application, they must submit a brief autobiography that includes their educational and personal goals. Selection is based on that essay; academic achievement; school, church, and community involvement; and financial need.

**Financial data** Stipends are $2,000 or $1,000 per year.

**Duration** 1 year.

**Number awarded** Varies each year. Recently, 6 of these scholarships were awarded: 2 at $2,000 and 4 at $1,000.

**Deadline** February of each year.

**[542]**

## SOCIETY OF DAUGHTERS OF THE UNITED STATES ARMY SCHOLARSHIPS

Society of Daughters of the United States Army
c/o Mary P. Maroney,
Chair, Memorial and Scholarship Funds
11804 Grey Birch Place
Reston, VA 20191-4223

**Summary** To provide financial assistance for college to daughters and granddaughters of active, retired, or deceased career Army warrant and commissioned officers.

**Eligibility** This program is open to the daughters, adopted daughters, stepdaughters, or granddaughters of career commissioned officers or warrant officers of the U.S. Army (active, regular, or Reserve) who 1) are currently on active duty, 2) retired after 20 years of active duty or were medically retired, or 3) died while on active duty or after retiring from active duty with 20 or more years of service. Applicants must have at least a 3.0 GPA and be studying or planning to study at the undergraduate level. Selection is based on depth of character, leadership, seriousness of purpose, academic achievement, and financial need.

**Financial data** Scholarships, to a maximum of $1,000, are paid directly to the college or school for tuition, laboratory fees, books, or other expenses.

**Duration** 1 year; may be renewed up to 4 additional years if the recipient maintains at least a 3.0 GPA.

**Additional information** Recipients may attend any accredited college, professional, or vocational school. This program includes named scholarships from the following funds: the Colonel Hayden W. Wagner Memorial Fund, the Eugenia Bradford Roberts Memorial Fund, the Daughters of the U.S. Army Scholarship Fund, the Gladys K. and John K. Simpson Scholarship Fund, and the Margaret M. Prickett

Scholarship Fund. Requests for applications must be accompanied by a self-addressed stamped envelope.

**Number awarded** Varies each year.

**Deadline** February of each year.

**[543]**

## SOUTH CAROLINA LEGION AUXILIARY GIFT SCHOLARSHIPS

American Legion Auxiliary
Attn: Department of South Carolina
132 Pickens Street
Columbia, SC 29205-2903
(803) 799-6695                    Fax: (803) 799-7907
E-mail: aux@aldsc.org

**Summary** To provide financial assistance for college to South Carolina senior and junior members of the American Legion Auxiliary.

**Eligibility** This program is open to South Carolina residents who have been senior or junior members of the American Legion Auxiliary for at least 3 consecutive years.

**Financial data** The stipend is $500.

**Duration** 1 year.

**Number awarded** 2 each year.

**Deadline** April of each year.

**[544]**

## SOUTH CAROLINA SPACE GRANT CONSORTIUM PRE-SERVICE TEACHER SCHOLARSHIPS

South Carolina Space Grant Consortium
c/o College of Charleston
Department of Geology and Environmental Sciences
66 George Street
Charleston, SC 29424
(843) 953-5463                    Fax: (843) 953-5446
E-mail: scozzarot@cofc.edu
Web: www.cofc.edu/~scsgrant/scholar/overview.html

**Summary** To provide financial assistance to upper-division and graduate students in South Carolina (particularly women, minority, and disabled students) who are preparing for a career as a science and mathematics teacher.

**Eligibility** This program is open to juniors, seniors, and graduate students at member institutions of the South Carolina Space Grant Consortium. Applicants must be working on a teaching certificate in science, mathematics, or engineering. Their areas of interest may include, but are not limited to, the basic sciences, astronomy, science education, planetary science, environmental studies, or engineering. U.S. citizenship is required. Selection is based on academic qualifications of the applicant; 2 letters of recommendation; a description of past activities, current interests, and future plans concerning a space science or aerospace-related field; a sample lesson plan using curriculum materials available from the U.S. National Aeronautics and Space Administration (NASA); and faculty sponsorship. Women, minorities, and persons with disabilities are encouraged to apply.

**Financial data** The stipend is $2,000. Funds may be used for such expenses as 1) partial payment of tuition; 2) travel and registration for attending science and mathematics education workshops or conferences for the purpose of professional development; 3) purchase of supplies for student teaching activities; or 4) other supportive activities that lead to successful professional development and graduation as an educator in South Carolina.

**Duration** 1 year.

**Additional information** Members of the consortium are Benedict College, The Citadel, College of Charleston, Clemson University, Coastal Carolina University, Furman University, University of South Carolina, Wofford College, South Carolina State University, The Medical University of South Carolina, and University of the Virgin Islands. This program is funded by NASA.

**Number awarded** Varies each year.

**Deadline** January of each year.

## [545]
## SOUTH DAKOTA FREE TUITION FOR DEPENDENTS OF PRISONERS OR MISSING IN ACTION

South Dakota Board of Regents
Attn: Scholarship Committee
306 East Capitol Avenue, Suite 200
Pierre, SD 57501-2545
(605) 773-3455                    Fax: (605) 773-2422
E-mail: info@ris.sdbor.edu
Web: www.sdbor.edu

**Summary** To provide free tuition at South Dakota public colleges and universities to dependents of prisoners of war (POWs) and persons missing in action (MIAs).

**Eligibility** This program is open to residents of South Dakota who are the spouses or children of POWs or of MIAs. Applicants may not be eligible for equal or greater benefits from any federal financial assistance program.

**Financial data** Eligible dependents are entitled to attend any South Dakota state-supported institution of higher education or state-supported technical or vocational school free of tuition and mandatory fees.

**Duration** 8 semesters or 12 quarters of either full- or part-time study.

**Additional information** Recipients must attend a state-supported school in South Dakota.

**Number awarded** Varies each year.

## [546]
## SOUTH DAKOTA SPACE GRANT CONSORTIUM GRADUATE FELLOWSHIPS AND UNDERGRADUATE SCHOLARSHIPS

South Dakota Space Grant Consortium
Attn: Deputy Director and Outreach Coordinator
South Dakota School of Mines and Technology
Mineral Industries Building, Room 228
501 East St. Joseph Street
Rapid City, SD 57701-3995
(605) 394-1975                    Fax: (605) 394-5360
E-mail: Thomas.Durkin@sdsmt.edu
Web: www.sdsmt.edu/space

**Summary** To provide funding to undergraduate and graduate students (particularly women, minority, and disabled students) for space-related activities in South Dakota.

**Eligibility** This program is open to undergraduate and graduate students at member and affiliated institutions of the South Dakota Space Grant Consortium. Applicants must be interested in 1) earth- and space-science related educational and research projects in fields relevant to the goals of the U.S. National Aeronautics and Space Administration (NASA); or 2) eventual employment with NASA or in a NASA-related career field in science, technology, engineering, and mathematics (STEM) education. Activities may include student research and educational efforts in remote sensing, GIS, global and regional geoscience, environmental science, and K-12 educational outreach; exposure to NASA-relevant projects; and internship experiences at various NASA centers and the Earth Resources Observation and Science (EROS) Center in Sioux Falls. U.S. citizenship is required. Women, members of underrepresented groups (African Americans, Hispanics, Pacific Islanders, Asian Americans, Native Americans, and persons with disabilities), and Tribal College students are specifically encouraged to apply. Selection is based on academic qualifications of the application (preference is given to students with a GPA of 3.0 or higher), quality of the application and its career goal statement, and assessment of the applicant's motivation toward an earth science, aerospace, or engineering career or research.

**Financial data** Stipends range from $1,000 to $7,500.

**Duration** 1 academic year, semester, or summer.

**Additional information** Member institutions include South Dakota School of Mines and Technology, South Dakota State University, and Augustana College. Educational affiliates include Black Hills State University, the University of South Dakota, Dakota State University, Lower Brule Community College, Oglala Lakota College, Sinte Gleska University, and Lake Area Technical Institute.

**Number awarded** Varies each year. Approximately $70,000 is available for this program annually.

**Deadline** January of each year.

## [547]
## SOUTH FLORIDA NETWORK OF EXECUTIVE WOMEN IN HOSPITALITY SCHOLARSHIP AWARDS

Network of Executive Women in Hospitality-South
    Florida Chapter
Attn: Lorraine Bragg, Director of Scholarship and
    Education
Sequeira & Gavarrete Architects
811 Ponce de Leon Boulevard
Coral Gables, FL 33134
(305) 441-1556                    Toll-free: (800) 593-NEWH
Fax: (800) 693-NEWH
E-mail: lbragg@s-garchitects.com
Web: www.newh.org/newh/scholarshippacket.php

**Summary** To provide financial assistance to women in Alabama and south Florida who wish to work on a college degree in a hospitality-related field.

**Eligibility** This program is open to women who have completed half the requirements for a degree or certification program at a vocational school or college in south Florida or Alabama. Applicants must have a GPA of 3.0 or higher and a career objective in the hospitality or food service industries (e.g., hotel and restaurant management, culinary, food service, architecture, design). Selection is based on financial need and academic accomplishments.

**Financial data** The stipend is $2,000.
**Duration** 1 year.
**Number awarded** 1 or more each year.
**Deadline** March of each year.

## [548]
## SOUTHERN CALIFORNIA CHAPTER SCHOLARSHIP

Society of Satellite Professionals International
Attn: Scholarship Program
New York Information Technology Center
55 Broad Street, 14th Floor
New York, NY 10004
(212) 809-5199　　　　Fax: (212) 825-0075
E-mail: sspi@sspi.org
Web: www.sspi.org

**Summary** To provide financial assistance to minority and female members of the Society of Satellite Professionals (SSPI) from any state who are attending college or graduate school in designated southern California counties and majoring in satellite-related disciplines.

**Eligibility** This program is open to SSPI members who are high school seniors, college undergraduates, or graduate students majoring or planning to major in fields related to satellite technologies, policies, or applications. Fields of study in the past have included broadcasting, business, distance learning, energy, government, imaging, meteorology, navigation, remote sensing, space law, and telecommunications. Applicants must be women or students of color with a GPA of 3.2 or higher. They must be attending or planning to attend schools in Los Angeles, Orange, San Diego, Santa Barbara, or Ventura counties in California. Selection is based on academic and leadership achievement; commitment to pursue educational and career opportunities in the satellite industry or a field making direct use of satellite technology; potential for significant contribution to that industry; and a scientific, engineering, research, business, or creative submission. Financial need is not considered.

**Financial data** The stipend is $5,000.
**Duration** 1 year.
**Number awarded** 1 each year.
**Deadline** Preliminary applications must be submitted by February of each year.

## [549]
## SOUTHERN COUNTIES NETWORK OF EXECUTIVE WOMEN IN HOSPITALITY SCHOLARSHIP AWARDS

Network of Executive Women in Hospitality-Southern
　　Counties Chapter
Attn: Director of Scholarship and Education
7668 El Camino Real, Suite 104-470
Carlsbad, CA 92009
Toll-free: (800) 593-NEWH　　Fax: (800) 693-NEWH
E-mail: mark@huntsingerassociates.com
Web: www.newh.org/newh/scholarshippacket.php

**Summary** To provide financial assistance to women in Hawaii and southern California interested in preparing for a career in the hospitality industry.

**Eligibility** This program is open to women who have completed half the requirements for a degree or certification program at a vocational school or college in California from Orange County south or in Hawaii. Applicants must have a GPA of 3.0 or higher and a career objective in the hospitality or food service industries (e.g., hotel and restaurant management, culinary, food service, architecture, design). Selection is based on financial need and academic accomplishments.

**Financial data** The stipend depends on the availability of funds and the need of the recipient.
**Duration** 1 year.
**Number awarded** Varies each year.
**Deadline** March of each year.

## [550]
## SPIRIT OF YOUTH SCHOLARSHIP FOR JUNIOR MEMBERS

American Legion Auxiliary
777 North Meridian Street, Third Floor
Indianapolis, IN 46204-1189
(317) 955-3845　　　　Fax: (317) 955-3884
E-mail: alahq@legion-aux.org
Web: www.legion-aux.org

**Summary** To provide financial assistance for college to junior members of the American Legion Auxiliary.

**Eligibility** Applicants for this scholarship must have been junior members of the Auxiliary for at least the past 3 years. They must be seniors at an accredited high school in the United States and have earned a GPA of 3.0 or higher. Each unit of the Auxiliary may select a candidate for application to the department level, and each department submits a candidate for the national award. Nominees must submit a 1,000-word essay on a topic that changes annually; a recent topic was "My Vision of Freedom." Selection is based on character and leadership (30%), the essay (30%) and academic record (40%).

**Financial data** The scholarship is $1,000 per year, to be used at an accredited institution of higher learning or a professional or technical school that awards a certificate upon completion of an accredited course.
**Duration** 4 years.
**Additional information** Applications are available from the president of the candidate's own unit or from the secretary or education chair of the department. The awardees must enroll for a minimum of 12 semester hours of work or its equivalent.
**Number awarded** 5 each year: 1 in each division of the American Legion Auxiliary.
**Deadline** Applications must be submitted to the unit president by March of each year.

## [551]
## SPORTQUEST ALL-AMERICAN SCHOLARSHIPS FOR FEMALES

Athletes of Good News
Attn: SportQuest All-American Program
6425 N.W. Cache Road, Suites 217 and 218
P.O. Box 6272
Lawton, OK 73506
(580) 536-9524          Fax: (580) 536-7495
E-mail: allamerican@aogn.org
Web: www.aogn.org

**Summary** To provide financial assistance for college to outstanding female Christian high school athletes.

**Eligibility** This program is open to female high school sophomores, juniors, and seniors who believe in the Lord Jesus Christ as their personal Lord and Savior and attend a church regularly. Nominees must be 1 of the top 3 Christian athletes in their school and have an overall GPA of 3.0 or higher. They must be able to demonstrate an active Christian influence in school and community. Selection is based on GPA, athletic accomplishments, church and community involvement, essays, and references.

**Financial data** The award is a $1,000 scholarship for the winner and a $500 scholarship for the runner-up.

**Duration** 1 year.

**Number awarded** 2 each year: 1 winner and 1 runner-up.

**Deadline** November of each year.

## [552]
## SPORTSMANSHIP RECOGNITION PROGRAM SCHOLARSHIP

Kentucky High School Athletic Association
2280 Executive Drive
Lexington, KY 40505
(859) 299-5472          Fax: (859) 293-5999
E-mail: general@khsaa.org
Web: www.khsaa.org

**Summary** To recognize and reward, with college scholarships, outstanding student-athletes (including cheerleaders) in Kentucky high schools.

**Eligibility** This program is open to high school seniors in Kentucky who have participated in athletics or cheerleading. Applicants must have at least a 2.5 GPA, 3 letters of recommendation from coaches and administrators illustrating the student's traits of good sportsmanship, demonstrated leadership within the school and the community, and a 2-page response to a case study developed for each competition. They must be planning to attend a college or university in Kentucky. A male and a female are recognized from each school in the state. They are chosen on the basis of these traits: playing the game by the rules; treating game officials and others with due respect, shaking hands with opponents, taking victory and defeat without undue emotionalism, controlling their tempers, being positive with officials and others who criticize them, cooperating with officials and others, being positive with opponents, letting student and adult audiences know that inappropriate behavior reflects poorly on the team, and serving as a role model for future student-athletes. These students are awarded a certificate and are entered into a regional competition. Males and females continue to compete separately. The regional winners are given a plaque and are considered for the Sportsmanship Recognition Program Scholarship. Selection is based on GPA, recommendations, leadership roles and honors, and the case study essay.

**Financial data** The stipend is $3,000.

**Duration** 1 year.

**Additional information** This program, instituted in 1997, is currently sponsored by First Corbin Financial Corporation.

**Number awarded** 2 each year: 1 for a female and 1 for a male.

**Deadline** Applications must be submitted to the school's athletic director in March.

## [553]
## STATE COMMUNITY SERVICE SCHOLARSHIPS

Miss America Pageant
Attn: Scholarship Department
Two Miss America Way, Suite 1000
Atlantic City, NJ 08401
(609) 345-7571, ext. 27     Toll-free: (800) 282-MISS
Fax: (609) 347-6079     E-mail: info@missamerica.org
Web: www.missamerica.org

**Summary** To recognize and reward, with college scholarships, women who participate in the Miss America Pageant at the state level and demonstrate outstanding community service.

**Eligibility** This competition is open to women who compete at the state level of the Miss America Pageant. Applicants must demonstrate that they have fulfilled a legitimate need in their community through the creation, development, and/or participation in a community service project. Selection is based on excellence of community service.

**Financial data** The stipend is $1,000.

**Duration** 1 year.

**Additional information** This program, established in 1998, is administered by Scholarship America, One Scholarship Way, P.O. Box 297, St. Peter, MN 56082, (507) 931-1682, (800) 537-4180, Fax: (507) 931-9168.

**Number awarded** Up to 52 each year: 1 for each of the states, the District of Columbia, and the Virgin Islands.

**Deadline** Varies, depending upon the date of local pageants leading to the state finals.

## [554]
## STEPHEN BUFTON MEMORIAL EDUCATION FUND GRANTS

American Business Women's Association
Attn: Stephen Bufton Memorial Educational Fund
9100 Ward Parkway
P.O. Box 8728
Kansas City, MO 64114-0728
(816) 361-6621          Toll-free: (800) 228-0007
Fax: (816) 361-4991     E-mail: abwa@abwahq.org
Web: www.abwahq.org/ProfDev.asp

**Summary** To provide financial assistance to women undergraduate and graduate students who are sponsored by a chapter of the American Business Women's Association (ABWA).

**Eligibility** This program is open to women who are at least sophomores at an accredited college or university. Applicants must be working on an undergraduate or graduate degree and have a GPA of 2.5 or higher. They are not required to be ABWA members, but they must be sponsored by an ABWA chapter that has contributed to the fund in the previous chapter year. U.S. citizenship is required.

**Financial data** The maximum grant is $1,200. Funds are paid directly to the recipient's institution to be used only for tuition, books, and fees.

**Duration** 1 year. Grants are not automatically renewed, but recipients may reapply.

**Additional information** This program was established in 1953. The ABWA does not provide the names and addresses of local chapters; it recommends that applicants check with their local Chamber of Commerce, library, or university to see if any chapter has registered a contact's name and number.

**Number awarded** Varies each year; since the inception of this program, it has awarded more than $14 million to more than 14,000 students.

**Deadline** May of each year.

## [555]
## STRATTON/TIPTON SCHOLARSHIP FOR ADULT RETURNING STUDENTS

Kentucky Association of Vocational Education Special
    Needs Personnel
c/o Donna Ledden
Boone County High School
7056 Burlington Pike
Florence, KY 41042
(859) 282-5655    E-mail: dledden1@boone.k12.ky.us
Web: www.kavesnp.org/scholar.htm

**Summary** To provide financial assistance to students with special needs enrolled at a college or university in Kentucky.

**Eligibility** This program is open to adults in Kentucky who are studying for 1) an associate degree or certificate/diploma through the Kentucky Community and Technical College System (KCTCS), or 2) an associate or bachelor's degree from a Kentucky college or university. Applicants must meet the definition of a special needs student: persons with disabilities, educationally and economically disadvantaged people, foster children, individuals preparing for nontraditional employment, single parents (including single pregnant women), displaced homemakers, individuals with limited English language proficiency, individuals in a correctional institution, and individuals with other barriers to educational achievement. They must have earned a GPA of 2.5 or higher in their most recently completed semester of course work at a KCTCS institution or a Kentucky college or university. Selection is based on academic achievement, letters of reference, and career potential.

**Financial data** The stipend is $500.

**Duration** 1 year; nonrenewable.

**Number awarded** 1 each year.

**Deadline** March of each year.

## [556]
## STRATTON/TIPTON SCHOLARSHIP FOR HIGH SCHOOL SENIORS

Kentucky Association of Vocational Education Special
    Needs Personnel
c/o Donna Ledden
Boone County High School
7056 Burlington Pike
Florence, KY 41042
(859) 282-5655    E-mail: dledden1@boone.k12.ky.us
Web: www.kavesnp.org/scholar.htm

**Summary** To provide financial assistance for college to high school seniors with special needs in Kentucky.

**Eligibility** This program is open to seniors at high schools in Kentucky who are planning to 1) enroll in a certificate/diploma program or associate degree program at an institution that is part of the Kentucky Community and Technical College System (KCTCS), or 2) work on an associate or bachelor's degree at a college or university. Applicants must meet the definition of a special needs student: persons with disabilities, educationally and economically disadvantaged people, foster children, individuals preparing for nontraditional employment, single parents (including single pregnant women), displaced homemakers, individuals with limited English language proficiency, individuals in a correctional institution, and individuals with other barriers to educational achievement. They must have a cumulative GPA of 2.5 or higher for grades 9-12. Selection is based on academic achievement, letters of reference, and career potential.

**Financial data** The stipend is $500.

**Duration** 1 year; nonrenewable.

**Number awarded** 1 each year.

**Deadline** March of each year.

## [557]
## SUNSHINE CHAPTER NETWORK OF EXECUTIVE WOMEN IN HOSPITALITY SCHOLARSHIP AWARDS

Network of Executive Women in Hospitality-Sunshine
    Chapter
Attn: Eric Taylor, Director of Scholarship and Education
L2 Studios, Inc.
55 East Jackson Street
Orlando, FL 32801
(407) 648-8888        Toll-free: (800) 593-NEWH
Fax: (800) 693-NEWH    E-mail: etaylor@l2studios.com
Web: www.newh.org/newh/scholarshippacket.php

**Summary** To provide financial assistance to women in Mississippi and central and northern Florida who wish to work on a college degree in a hospitality-related field.

**Eligibility** This program is open to women who have completed half the requirements for a degree or certification program at a vocational school or college in central and northern Florida or Mississippi. Applicants must have a GPA of 3.0 or higher and a career objective in the hospitality or food service industries (e.g., hotel and restaurant management, culinary, food service, architecture, design). Selection is based on financial need and academic accomplishments.

**Financial data** The stipend is $2,000.

**Duration** 1 year.

**Number awarded** Varies each year; recently, 3 of these scholarships were awarded.

## [558]
## SURVIVORS' AND DEPENDENTS' EDUCATIONAL ASSISTANCE PROGRAM

Department of Veterans Affairs
810 Vermont Avenue, N.W.
Washington, DC 20420
(202) 418-4343          Toll-free: (888) GI-BILL1
Web: www.gibill.va.gov

**Summary** To provide financial assistance for undergraduate or graduate study to children and spouses of deceased and disabled veterans, MIAs, and POWs.

**Eligibility** Eligible for this assistance are spouses and children of 1) veterans who died or are permanently and totally disabled as the result of active service in the armed forces; 2) veterans who died from any cause while rated permanently and totally disabled from a service-connected disability; 3) servicemembers listed for more than 90 days as currently missing in action or captured in the line of duty by a hostile force; and 4) servicemembers listed for more than 90 days as presently detained or interned by a foreign government or power. Children must be between 18 and 26 years of age, although extensions may be granted. Spouses and children over 14 years of age with physical or mental disabilities are also eligible.

**Financial data** Monthly stipends from this program for study at an academic institution are $827 for full time, $621 for three-quarter time, or $413 for half-time. For farm cooperative work, the monthly stipends are $667 for full-time, $500 for three-quarter time, or $334 for half-time. For an apprenticeship or on-the-job training, the monthly stipend is $650 for the first 6 months, $507 for the second 6 months, $366 for the third 6 months, and $151 for the remainder of the program.

**Duration** Up to 45 months (or the equivalent in part-time training). Spouses must complete their training within 10 years of the date they are first found eligible.

**Additional information** Benefits may be used to work on associate, bachelor, or graduate degrees at colleges and universities, including independent study, cooperative training, and study abroad programs. Courses leading to a certificate or diploma from business, technical, or vocational schools may also be taken. Other eligible programs include apprenticeships, on-job training programs, farm cooperative courses, correspondence courses (for spouses only), secondary school programs (for recipients who are not high school graduates), tutorial assistance, remedial deficiency and refresher training, or work-study (for recipients who are enrolled at least three-quarter time). Eligible children who are handicapped by a physical or mental disability that prevents pursuit of an educational program may receive special restorative training that includes language retraining, lip reading, auditory training, Braille reading and writing, and similar programs. Eligible spouses and children over 14 years of age who are handicapped by a physical or mental disability that prevents pursuit of an educational program may receive specialized vocational training that includes specialized courses, alone or in combination with other courses, leading to a vocational objective that is suitable for the person and required by reason of physical or mental handicap. Ineligible courses include bartending or personality development courses; correspondence courses by dependent or surviving children; non-accredited independent study courses; any course given by radio; self-improvement courses, such as reading, speaking, woodworking, basic seamanship, and English as a second language; audited courses; any course that is avocational or recreational in character; courses not leading to an educational, professional, or vocational objective; courses taken and successfully completed previously; courses taken by a federal government employee and paid for under the Government Employees' Training Act; and courses taken while in receipt of benefits for the same program from the Office of Workers' Compensation Programs.

**Number awarded** Varies each year.

**Deadline** Applications may be submitted at any time.

## [559]
## SUSAN EKDALE MEMORIAL SCHOLARSHIP

Association for Women Geoscientists
Attn: AWG Foundation
P.O. Box 30645
Lincoln, NE 68503-0645
E-mail: awgscholarship@yahoo.com
Web: www.awg.org/eas/ekdale.html

**Summary** To provide financial assistance for a summer field camp to women majoring in geoscience at a college or university in Utah.

**Eligibility** This program is open to women majoring in geoscience at a college or university in Utah who must attend a summer field camp as part of their graduation requirements. Women geoscience students from Utah attending college in other states are also eligible. Applicants must submit a 1- to 2-page essay in which they describe their personal and academic highlights, their plans for applying their geoscience education to their future work or education, their reasons for applying for the scholarship, and what they, as women, can contribute to the geosciences. Selection is based on merit and need.

**Financial data** The stipend is $1,500. Funds must be used to help pay field camp expenses.

**Duration** Summer months.

**Additional information** This program is sponsored by the Salt Lake chapter of the Association for Women Geoscientists. Information is also available from the Ekdale Scholarship Co-chair, Janae Wallace Boyer, P.O. Box 58691, Salt Lake City, UT 84158-0691, (801) 537-3387, E-mail: janaewallace@utah.gov.

**Number awarded** 1 each year.

**Deadline** March of each year.

## [560]
## SUSAN MISZKOWICZ MEMORIAL SCHOLARSHIP

Society of Women Engineers
230 East Ohio Street, Suite 400
Chicago, IL 60611-3265
(312) 596-5223                    Toll-free: (877) SWE-INFO
Fax: (312) 644-8557
E-mail: scholarshipapplication@swe.org
Web: www.swe.org/scholarships

**Summary**  To provide financial assistance to undergraduate women majoring in computer science or engineering.

**Eligibility**  This program is open to women who are entering their sophomore, junior, or senior year at a 4-year ABET-accredited college or university. Applicants must be majoring in computer science or engineering and have a GPA of 3.0 or higher. Along with their application, they must submit a 1-page essay on why they want to be an engineer or computer scientist, how they believe they will make a difference as an engineer or computer scientist, and what influenced them to study engineering or computer science. Selection is based on merit.

**Financial data**  The stipend is $1,000.

**Duration**  1 year.

**Additional information**  This program was established in 2002 to honor a member of the Society of Women Engineers who was killed in the New York World Trade Center on September 11, 2001.

**Number awarded**  1 each year.

**Deadline**  January of each year.

## [561]
## SUSIE HOLMES MEMORIAL SCHOLARSHIP

International Order of Job's Daughters
Supreme Guardian Council Headquarters
Attn: Executive Manager
233 West Sixth Street
Papillion, NE 68046-2177
(402) 592-7987                    Fax: (402) 592-2177
E-mail: sgc@iojd.org
Web: www.iojd.org

**Summary**  To provide financial assistance for college to members of Job's Daughters.

**Eligibility**  This program is open to high school graduates who are members of Job's Daughters. Applicants must be able to demonstrate dedicated, continuous, and joyful service to Job's Daughters; regular attendance at Supreme and/or Grand Sessions; participation in competitions at Supreme and/or Grand Sessions; friendship and impartiality in their Bethel; good character and integrity; and a GPA of 2.5 or higher.

**Financial data**  The stipend is $1,000.

**Duration**  1 year.

**Additional information**  Information is also available from Barbara Hill, Education Scholarships Committee Chair, 337 Illinois Street, Pekin, IL 61554, (309) 346-5564.

**Number awarded**  Varies each year; recently, 3 of these scholarships were awarded.

**Deadline**  April of each year.

## [562]
## SWE PAST PRESIDENTS SCHOLARSHIPS

Society of Women Engineers
230 East Ohio Street, Suite 400
Chicago, IL 60611-3265
(312) 596-5223                    Toll-free: (877) SWE-INFO
Fax: (312) 644-8557
E-mail: scholarshipapplication@swe.org
Web: www.swe.org/scholarships

**Summary**  To provide financial assistance to women working on an undergraduate or graduate degree in engineering or computer science.

**Eligibility**  This program is open to women who will be sophomores, juniors, seniors, or graduate students at ABET-accredited colleges and universities. Applicants must be U.S. citizens majoring in computer science or engineering and have a GPA of 3.0 or higher. Along with their application, they must submit a 1-page essay on why they want to be an engineer or computer scientist, how they believe they will make a difference as an engineer or computer scientist, and what influenced them to study engineering or computer science. Selection is based on merit.

**Financial data**  The stipend is $1,500.

**Duration**  1 year.

**Additional information**  This program was established in 1999 by an anonymous donor to honor the commitment and accomplishments of past presidents of the Society of Women Engineers (SWE).

**Number awarded**  2 each year.

**Deadline**  January of each year.

## [563]
## SWE/ADC COMMUNICATIONS AND FOUNDATION SCHOLARSHIP

Society of Women Engineers
230 East Ohio Street, Suite 400
Chicago, IL 60611-3265
(312) 596-5223                    Toll-free: (877) SWE-INFO
Fax: (312) 644-8557
E-mail: scholarshipapplication@swe.org
Web: www.swe.org/scholarships

**Summary**  To provide financial assistance to upper-division women who are members of the Society of Women Engineers and majoring in engineering.

**Eligibility**  This program is open to women who are entering their junior or senior year at an ABET-accredited college or university. Applicants must be studying computer science or electrical or computer engineering with a GPA of 3.0 or higher. They must be U.S. citizens and members of the society. Along with their application, they must submit a 1-page essay on why they want to be an engineer or computer scientist, how they believe they will make a difference as an engineer or computer scientist, and what influenced them to study engineering or computer science. Selection is based on merit.

**Financial data**  The stipend is $2,250.

**Duration**  1 year.

**Additional information**  This program is sponsored by the ADC Foundation.

**Number awarded**  4 each year.

**Deadline**  January of each year.

## [564]
## SWEET 16 MAGAZINE SCHOLARSHIP CONTEST

Guideposts
Attn: Sweet 16 Magazine Scholarship Contest
16 East 34th Street
New York, NY 10016
(212) 251-8100          Toll-free: (800) 932-2145
Fax: (212) 684-0679
E-mail: scholarship@sweet16mag.com
Web: www.guidepostsmag.com

**Summary** To recognize and reward, with college scholarships, middle and high school girls who submit outstanding spiritual stories.

**Eligibility** This competition is open to girls between 13 and 18 years of age. Applicants must submit a true, first-person story about a memorable or life-changing experience they have had. Manuscripts must be written in English and be no more than 1,200 words.

**Financial data** Prizes, in the form of scholarships to accredited 4-year colleges or universities of the recipients' choice, are $16,000 for first, $10,000 for second, $5,000 for third, and $2,500 for fourth. Honorable mentions are cash prizes of $500.

**Duration** The competition is held annually. Scholarships must be used within 5 years of high school graduation.

**Additional information** This competition was formerly known as the Guideposts Young Writers Contest. Manuscripts will not be returned unless accompanied by a self-addressed stamped envelope.

**Number awarded** 16 each year: 4 scholarships and 12 honorable mentions.

**Deadline** October of each year.

## [565]
## TALBOTS WOMEN'S SCHOLARSHIP FUND

Talbots Charitable Foundation
c/o Scholarship America
Scholarship Management Services
One Scholarship Way
P.O. Box 297
St. Peter, MN 56082
(507) 931-1682          Toll-free: (800) 537-4180
Fax: (507) 931-9168     E-mail: smsinfo@csfa.org
Web: www1.talbots.com/about/scholar/scholar.asp

**Summary** To provide financial assistance to women returning to college after an absence of at least 10 years.

**Eligibility** This program is open to women who earned their high school diploma or GED at least 10 years ago and are now seeking a degree from an accredited 2- or 4-year college, university, or vocational/technical school. (Eligibility for the $10,000 scholarships is limited to women working on a bachelor's degree at a 4-year college or university.) Applicants must have at least 2 full-time semesters remaining to complete their undergraduate degree. Along with their application, they must submit an essay on their plans as they relate to their educational and career objectives and long-term goals. Selection is based on the essay, academic record, leadership and participation in community activities, honors, work experience, an outside appraisal, and financial need.

**Financial data** Stipends are either $10,000 or $1,000. Checks are mailed to the recipient's home address and are made payable jointly to the student and the school.

**Duration** 1 year; nonrenewable.

**Additional information** This program was established in 1997. Applications are available at Talbots' stores in the United States. The program is administered by Scholarship Management Services, a department of Scholarship America. Only the first 1,000 eligible applications received are processed.

**Number awarded** 55 each year: 5 at $10,000 and 50 at $1,000.

**Deadline** December of each year.

## [566]
## TEACHER EDUCATION SCHOLARSHIP PROGRAM OF THE ALABAMA SPACE GRANT CONSORTIUM

Alabama Space Grant Consortium
c/o University of Alabama in Huntsville
Materials Science Building, Room 205
Huntsville, AL 35899
(256) 824-6800          Fax: (256) 824-6061
E-mail: reasonj@uah.edu
Web: www.uah.edu/ASGC

**Summary** To provide financial assistance to undergraduate students (particularly women and minority students) at universities participating in the Alabama Space Grant Consortium who wish to prepare for a career as a teacher of science or mathematics.

**Eligibility** This program is open to students enrolled in or accepted for enrollment as full-time undergraduates at universities in Alabama participating in the consortium. Applicants must intend to enter the teacher certification program and teach in a pre-college setting. Priority is given to those majoring in science, mathematics, or earth, space, or environmental sciences. Applicants should have a GPA of 3.0 or higher and must be U.S. citizens. Members of underrepresented groups in science and mathematics (women and minorities) are especially encouraged to apply. Along with their application, they must submit a 1- to 2-page statement on the reasons for their desire to enter the teaching profession, specifically the fields of science or mathematics education.

**Financial data** The stipend is $1,000 per year.

**Duration** 1 year; nonrenewable.

**Additional information** The member universities are University of Alabama in Huntsville, Alabama A&M University, University of Alabama, University of Alabama at Birmingham, University of South Alabama, Tuskegee University, and Auburn University. Funding for this program is provided by NASA.

**Number awarded** Varies each year; recently, 10 of these scholarships were awarded.

**Deadline** February of each year.

## [567]
## TEEN LATINA WORLD

Dawn Rochele Productions
6150 West El Dorado Parkway, Suite 160-120
McKinney, TX 75070
(206) 666-DAWN          E-mail: info@misslatina.com
Web: www.misslatina.com

**Summary** To recognize and reward teen-aged Latina women, with college scholarships and other awards, who compete in a national beauty pageant.

**Eligibility** This program is open to women between 13 and 17 years of age who are at least 25% Hispanic. Applicants must be single and they may not have children. They appear in a nationally-televised pageant where selection is based one third on an interview, one third on swimsuit appearances, and one third on evening gown appearances. Height and weight are not factors, but contestants should be proportionate. Pageant experience and fluency in Spanish are not required.

**Financial data** Each year, prizes include scholarships, gifts, a cruise to the Bahamas, a trip to Las Vegas, a modeling contract, and use of an apartment in Miami. The total value is more than $25,000.

**Duration** The pageant is held annually.

**Number awarded** 1 winner and 4 runners-up are selected each year.

## [568]
## TESA SCHOLARSHIP PROGRAM

Texas Elks State Association
c/o Rod Trailkill, Scholarship Chair
2441 Liberty Avenue
Beaumont, TX 77702
E-mail: txelks@gvec.net
Web: texaselks.org/Youth%20Activities.htm

**Summary** To provide financial assistance for college to high school seniors in Texas who are not at the top of their class.

**Eligibility** This program is open to seniors at high schools in Texas who are not in the top 5% of their class. Candidates are nominated by their high school counselors; up to 3 boys and 3 girls may be nominated per school. Nominees must be U.S. citizens, residents of Texas, and planning to attend an accredited junior college, college, or university in Texas as a full-time student. The names of these nominees are submitted to the local lodge; each lodge then selects 1 boy and 1 girl and submits their applications to the state scholarship chair. Those students must submit a 300-word statement on their professional goals and how their past, present, and future activities make attainment of those goals probable. Females and males compete separately. Final selection at the state level is based on leadership and extracurricular activities (200 points), character (200 points), scholarship (300 points), and financial need (300 points).

**Financial data** The stipend is $1,250 per year.

**Duration** 4 years.

**Number awarded** 6 each year: 3 boys and 3 girls.

**Deadline** School nominations must be submitted to the local lodges by March of each year.

## [569]
## TEXAS STATE FIRE FIGHTERS COLLEGE SCHOLARSHIP FUND

Texas State Association of Fire Fighters
Attn: Texas State Fire Fighters Emergency Relief and
    College Scholarship Fund
627 Radam Lane
Austin, TX 78745-1121
(512) 326-5050          Fax: (512) 326-5040
Web: www.tsaff.org

**Summary** To provide financial assistance for college to dependent children of certified Texas fire fighters.

**Eligibility** This program is open to dependents under 24 years of age of current, retired, or deceased certified fire fighters in Texas. Applicants must be first-time college students enrolled full time at an accredited institution. Along with their application, they must submit a brief essay about their life and school years. Financial need is considered in the selection process. Males and females compete separately for scholarships.

**Financial data** The stipend is at least $500 for the first 2 terms or semesters of college (a total of $1,000). Funds are paid directly to the recipient's school.

**Duration** Freshman year.

**Additional information** This fund was established in 1997.

**Number awarded** At least 2 each year: 1 is set aside specifically for a female and 1 for a male. If additional funds are available, the program may award additional scholarships to equal numbers of female and male applicants.

**Deadline** April of each year.

## [570]
## TEXAS WAIVERS OF NONRESIDENT TUITION FOR MILITARY PERSONNEL AND THEIR DEPENDENTS

Texas Higher Education Coordinating Board
Attn: Grants and Special Programs
1200 East Anderson Lane
P.O. Box 12788, Capitol Station
Austin, TX 78711-2788
(512) 427-6101          Toll-free: (800) 242-3062
Fax: (512) 427-6127
E-mail: grantinfo@thecb.state.tx.us
Web: www.collegefortexans.com

**Summary** To exempt military personnel stationed in Texas and their dependents from the payment of nonresident tuition at public institutions of higher education in the state.

**Eligibility** Eligible for these waivers are members of the U.S. armed forces and commissioned officers of the Public Health Service from states other than Texas, their spouses, and dependent children. Applicants must be assigned to Texas and attending or planning to attend a public college or university in the state.

**Financial data** Although persons eligible under this program are classified as nonresidents, they are entitled to pay the resident tuition at Texas institutions of higher education, regardless of their length of residence in Texas.

**Duration** 1 year; may be renewed.

**Number awarded** Varies each year; recently, 10,333 students received these waivers.

## [571]
## TEXAS WAIVERS OF NONRESIDENT TUITION FOR MILITARY SURVIVORS

Texas Higher Education Coordinating Board
Attn: Grants and Special Programs
1200 East Anderson Lane
P.O. Box 12788, Capitol Station
Austin, TX 78711-2788
(512) 427-6101          Toll-free: (800) 242-3062
Fax: (512) 427-6127
E-mail: grantinfo@thecb.state.tx.us
Web: www.collegefortexans.com

**Summary** To provide a partial tuition exemption to the surviving spouses and dependent children of deceased military personnel who move to Texas following the service member's death.

**Eligibility** Eligible for these waivers are the surviving spouses and dependent children of members of the U.S. armed forces and commissioned officers of the Public Health Service who died while in service. Applicants must move to Texas within 60 days of the date of the death of the service member. They must be attending or planning to attend a public college or university in the state. Children are eligible even if the surviving parent does not accompany them to Texas.

**Financial data** Although persons eligible under this program are still classified as nonresidents, they are entitled to pay the resident tuition at Texas institutions of higher education on an immediate basis.

**Duration** 1 year.

**Additional information** This program became effective in 2003.

**Number awarded** Varies each year.

## [572]
## TEXAS WAIVERS OF NONRESIDENT TUITION FOR VETERANS AND THEIR DEPENDENTS

Texas Higher Education Coordinating Board
Attn: Grants and Special Programs
1200 East Anderson Lane
P.O. Box 12788, Capitol Station
Austin, TX 78711-2788
(512) 427-6101          Toll-free: (800) 242-3062
Fax: (512) 427-6127
E-mail: grantinfo@thecb.state.tx.us
Web: www.collegefortexans.com

**Summary** To exempt veterans who move to Texas and their dependents from the payment of nonresident tuition at public institutions of higher education in the state.

**Eligibility** Eligible for these waivers are former members of the U.S. armed forces and commissioned officers of the Public Health Service who are retired or have been honorably discharged, their spouses, and dependent children. Applicants must have moved to Texas upon separation from the service and be attending or planning to attend a public college or university in the state. They must have indicated an intent to become a Texas resident by registering to vote

and doing 1 of the following: owning real property in Texas, registering an automobile in Texas, or executing a will indicating that they are a resident of the state.

**Financial data** Although persons eligible under this program are still classified as nonresidents, they are entitled to pay the resident tuition at Texas institutions of higher education on an immediate basis.

**Duration** 1 year.

**Number awarded** Varies each year.

## [573]
## THADDEUS COLSON AND ISABELLE SAALWAECHTER FITZPATRICK MEMORIAL SCHOLARSHIP

Community Foundation of Louisville
Attn: Director of Grants
Waterfront Plaza, Suite 1110
325 West Main Street
Louisville, KY 40202-4251
(502) 585-4649, ext. 1005          Fax: (502) 587-7484
E-mail: info@cflouisville.org
Web: www.cflouisville.org

**Summary** To provide financial assistance to women studying fields related to the environment at colleges and universities in Kentucky.

**Eligibility** This program is open to female residents of Kentucky who are entering their sophomore, junior, or senior year at a 4-year public college or university in the state. Applicants must be majoring in an environmentally related program (e.g., agriculture, biology, horticulture, environmental studies, environmental engineering). They must be enrolled full time with a GPA of 3.0 or higher. Along with their application, they must submit a 200-word essay describing their interest, leadership, volunteer efforts, and work experience in the environmental field; their future plans and goals in the environmental field; and what they hope to accomplish with their college degree. Financial need is also considered in the selection process.

**Financial data** The stipend is $2,000. Funds are paid directly to the college or university.

**Duration** 1 year; nonrenewable.

**Number awarded** 1 each year.

**Deadline** February of each year.

## [574]
## THEODORE AND MARY JANE RICH MEMORIAL SCHOLARSHIPS

Slovak Catholic Sokol
Attn: Membership Memorial Scholarship Fund
205 Madison Street
P.O. Box 899
Passaic, NJ 07055-0899
(973) 777-2605          Toll-free: (800) 886-7656
Fax: (973) 779-8245
E-mail: life@slovakcatholicsokol.org
Web: www.slovakcatholicsokol.org

**Summary** To provide financial assistance for college or graduate school to members of the Slovak Catholic Sokol.

**Eligibility** This program is open to members of the Slovak Catholic Sokol who have completed at least 1 semester of college and are currently enrolled full time as an undergraduate or graduate student at an accredited college, university, or professional school. Applicants must have been a member for at least 5 years, have at least $3,000 permanent life insurance coverage, and have at least 1 parent who is a member and is of Slovak ancestry. They must be majoring in a medical program. Males and females compete for scholarships separately.

**Financial data** The stipend is $2,500 per year.

**Duration** 1 year; may be renewed 1 additional year.

**Additional information** Slovak Catholic Sokol was founded as a fraternal benefit society in 1905. It is licensed to operate in the following states: Connecticut, Illinois, Indiana, Massachusetts, Michigan, New Jersey, New York, Ohio, Pennsylvania, and Wisconsin. This program was established in 2003.

**Number awarded** 2 each year: 1 for a male and 1 for a female.

**Deadline** March of each year.

## [575]
## TRAMPOLINE AND TUMBLING SCHOLARSHIP PROGRAM

USA Gymnastics
Attn: Trampoline and Tumbling Program
1309 Tahoka Road
P.O. Box 306
Brownfield, TX 79316
(806) 637-8670                    Fax: (806) 637-9046
E-mail: ktyler@usa-gymnastics.org
Web: www.usa-gymnastics.org/tt/about-tt.html

**Summary** To provide financial assistance for college to gymnasts who participate in trampoline and tumbling activities.

**Eligibility** This program is open to high school seniors and currently-enrolled college students who are registered athletes, training and competing with USA Gymnastics trampoline and tumbling. Applicants must be enrolled or planning to enroll full or part time at an accredited college or university. They must have a GPA of 2.5 or higher. Along with their application, they must submit information on their athletic accomplishments, athletic goals for the current and next 5 years, academic goals, probable career goals, how a scholarship would contribute to their goals, honors and activities, and financial need.

**Financial data** The size of the scholarship varies, depending upon the funds raised throughout the year in support of the program. Funds must be used for college or postsecondary educational expenses.

**Duration** 1 year.

**Number awarded** Varies each year; recently, 11 of these scholarships, with a value of $23,000, were awarded.

**Deadline** May of each year.

## [576]
## TRANSPORTATION FELLOWSHIP PROGRAM

North Central Texas Council of Governments
Attn: Transportation Department
616 Six Flags Drive, Centerpoint Two
P.O. Box 5888
Arlington, TX 76005-5888
(817) 695-9242                    Fax: (817) 640-7806
Web: www.nctcog.org/trans/admin/fellowship

**Summary** To provide financial assistance to ethnic minorities, women, and economically disadvantaged persons who are interested in obtaining an undergraduate or graduate degree and work experience in a transportation-related field in Texas.

**Eligibility** This program is open to ethnic minorities (African Americans, Hispanics, American Indians, Alaskan Natives, Asians, and Pacific Islanders), women, and those who are economically disadvantaged. Only U.S. citizens or permanent residents may apply. They must attend or be willing to attend a college or university within the 16-county north central Texas region as an undergraduate or graduate student. Applicants must have a GPA of 2.5 or higher. They may be enrolled full or part time, but they must be majoring in a designated transportation-related field: transportation planning, transportation or civil engineering, urban and regional planning, transportation/environmental sciences, transportation law, urban or spatial geography, logistics, geographic information systems, or transportation management. Selection is based on financial need, interest in a professional career in transportation, and ability to complete the program.

**Financial data** The stipend is $2,000.

**Duration** 1 year; may be renewed if the recipient maintains a GPA of 3.0 or higher.

**Additional information** These fellowships are financed by the Federal Highway Administration, Federal Transit Administration, and Texas Department of Transportation, in conjunction with local governments in north central Texas. An important part of the fellowship is an internship with a local agency (city or county), school, or transportation agency.

**Deadline** March of each year.

## [577]
## TREWA SCHOLARSHIPS

Texas Electric Cooperatives, Inc.
Attn: Vice President of Member Services
2550 South IH-35
Austin, TX 78704
(512) 454-0311                    E-mail: twortham@texas-ec.org
Web: www.texas-ec.org

**Summary** To provide financial assistance for college to members and children of members of the Texas Rural Electric Women's Association (TREWA).

**Eligibility** Eligible are current members of the association, their children, and the grandchildren. Applicants may be enrolled or planning to enroll in an accredited college, university, junior or community college, trade/technical school, or business school of their choice to work on a degree, certificate, diploma, or license. Grades received in high school are not the deciding factor in the selection process; leadership qualities, career focus, energy awareness, a 250-word essay on the applicant's plans and goals, and general knowledge of the rural electric problem are considered.

**Financial data** The stipend is $1,000. Funds are paid directly to the recipient's institution, half at the beginning of the first semester and half upon verification of completion of the first semester with passing grades.

**Duration** 1 year; nonrenewable.

**Additional information** This scholarship is sponsored by TREWA and administered by Texas Electric Cooperatives, Inc. Membership in TREWA is open to rural electric employees, directors, and co-op members. The organization is run by women, but men are also eligible to join.

**Number awarded** Varies each year; recently, 7 of these scholarships were awarded.

**Deadline** April of each year.

## [578]
## TULSA AREA COUNCIL ENDOWMENT SCHOLARSHIP

Epsilon Sigma Alpha
Attn: ESA Foundation Assistant Scholarship Director
P.O. Box 270517
Fort Collins, CO 80527
(970) 223-2824          Fax: (970) 223-4456
Web: www.esaintl.com/esaf

**Summary** To provide financial assistance for college to women in Oklahoma.

**Eligibility** This program is open to women residents of Oklahoma who are either 1) graduating high school seniors in the top 25% of their class or with minimum scores of 20 on the ACT or 950 on the SAT, or 2) students already enrolled in college in Oklahoma with a GPA of 3.0 or higher. Students enrolled for training in a technical school or returning to school after an absence are also eligible. Selection is based on character (10%), leadership (20%), service (10%), financial need (30%), and scholastic ability (30%).

**Financial data** The stipend is $500.

**Duration** 1 year; may be renewed.

**Additional information** Epsilon Sigma Alpha (ESA) is a women's service organization. Information is also available from Lynn Hughes, Scholarship Director, 324 N.E. Mead, Grants Pass, OR 97526, (541) 476-4617. This scholarship was first awarded in 2003. Completed applications must be submitted to the ESA State Counselor who verifies the information before forwarding them to the scholarship director. Recipients must attend college in Oklahoma. A $5 processing fee is required.

**Number awarded** 1 each year.

**Deadline** January of each year.

## [579]
## TWEET COLEMAN AVIATION SCHOLARSHIP

American Association of University Women-Honolulu Branch
Attn: Scholarship Committee
1802 Keeaumoku Street
Honolulu, HI 96822
(808) 537-4702          Fax: (808) 537-4702*51
E-mail: aauwhnb@att.net

**Summary** To provide financial assistance to women in Hawaii who are interested in a career in aviation.

**Eligibility** This program is open to women who are residents of Hawaii and either college graduates or attending an accredited college in the state. Applicants must be able to pass a First Class FAA medical examination. As part of their application, they must include a 2-page statement on "Why I Want to be a Pilot." Selection is based on the merit of the applicant and a personal interview.

**Financial data** The amount awarded varies.

**Duration** 1 year.

**Additional information** This scholarship was first awarded in 1990.

**Number awarded** Varies; at least 1 each year.

**Deadline** September of each year.

## [580]
## UNDERGRADUATE SCHOLARSHIP PROGRAM OF THE ALABAMA SPACE GRANT CONSORTIUM

Alabama Space Grant Consortium
c/o University of Alabama in Huntsville
Materials Science Building, Room 205
Huntsville, AL 35899
(256) 824-6800          Fax: (256) 824-6061
E-mail: reasonj@uah.edu
Web: www.uah.edu/ASGC

**Summary** To provide financial assistance to undergraduates (particularly women, minorities, and students with disabilities) who are studying space-related subjects at universities participating in the Alabama Space Grant Consortium (ASGC).

**Eligibility** This program is open to full-time students entering their junior or senior year at universities participating in the ASGC. Applicants must be studying in a field related to space, including the physical, natural, and biological sciences; engineering, education; economics; business; sociology; behavioral sciences; computer science; communications; law; international affairs; and public administration. They must be U.S. citizens and have a GPA of 3.0 or higher. Individuals from underrepresented groups (African Americans, Hispanic, American Indians, Pacific Islanders, Asian Americans, and women) are especially encouraged to apply. Interested students should submit a completed application with a career goal statement, personal references, a brief resume, and transcripts. Selection is based on 1) academic qualifications, 2) quality of the career goal statement, and 3) assessment of the applicant's motivation for a career in aerospace.

**Financial data** The stipend is $1,000 per year.

**Duration** 1 year; may be renewed 1 additional year.

**Additional information** The member universities are University of Alabama in Huntsville, Alabama A&M University, University of Alabama, University of Alabama at Birmingham, University of South Alabama, Tuskegee University, and Auburn University. Funding for this program is provided by NASA.

**Number awarded** Varies each year; recently, 32 of these scholarships were awarded.

**Deadline** February of each year.

## [581]
## UNITED PARCEL SERVICE SCHOLARSHIP FOR FEMALE STUDENTS

Institute of Industrial Engineers
Attn: Scholarship Coordinator
3577 Parkway Lane, Suite 200
Norcross, GA 30092
(770) 449-0461, ext. 105     Toll-free: (800) 494-0460
Fax: (770) 263-8532     E-mail: bcameron@iienet.org
Web: www.iienet.org

**Summary** To provide financial assistance to female undergraduates who are studying industrial engineering at a school in the United States, Canada, or Mexico.

**Eligibility** Eligible to be nominated are female undergraduate students enrolled at any school in the United States and its territories, Canada, or Mexico, provided the school's engineering program is accredited by an agency recognized by the Institute of Industrial Engineers (IIE) and the student is pursuing a full-time course of study in industrial engineering with a GPA of at least 3.4. Nominees must have at least 5 full quarters or 3 full semesters remaining until graduation. Students may not apply directly for these awards; they must be nominated by the head of their industrial engineering department. Nominees must be IIE members. Selection is based on scholastic ability, character, leadership, potential service to the industrial engineering profession, and need for financial assistance.

**Financial data** The stipend is $4,000.

**Duration** 1 year.

**Additional information** Funding for this program is provided by the UPS Foundation.

**Number awarded** 1 each year.

**Deadline** November of each year.

## [582]
## USBC JUNIOR GOLD CHAMPIONSHIPS

United States Bowling Congress
Attn: Junior Gold Program
5301 South 76th Street
Greendale, WI 53129-1192
(414) 423-3171     Toll-free: (800) 514-BOWL, ext. 3171
Fax: (414) 421-3014
E-mail: USBCjuniorgold@bowl.com
Web: www.bowl.com/bowl/yaba

**Summary** To recognize and reward, with college scholarships, United States Bowling Congress (USBC) Junior Gold program members who achieve high scores in a national competition.

**Eligibility** This program is open to USBC members who qualify for the Junior Gold program by maintaining a bowling average score of 165 for girls or 175 for boys, based on at least 21 games. Competitions for Junior Gold members are held throughout the season at bowling centers and in bowling leagues in the United States. Each approved competition may enter its top 10% of scorers in the Junior Gold Championships, held annually at a site in the United States. In addition, USBC Junior Gold members who participate in the Pepsi USBC Youth Bowling Championship in the girls' and boys' 12 and over scratch categories and achieve high scores in state and zone competitions are eligible to advance to the national tournament of this program. They compete in separate divisions for boys and girls. Scholarships are awarded solely on the basis of bowling performance in the national tournament.

**Financial data** Scholarships depend on the availability of funding provided by sponsors. Recently, more than $50,000 in scholarships was awarded. Another $15,000 in scholarships was awarded to Junior Gold participants who qualified for the national tournament through the Pepsi competition. That includes $3,000 for first, $2,000 for second, $1,500 for third, and $1,000 for fourth for boys and girls.

**Duration** The competition is held annually.

**Additional information** This competition was first held in 1998. The sponsoring league or center must pay a fee of $150 for each participant who advances to the national tournament.

**Number awarded** Varies each year. Recently, a total of 1,458 spots were available at the national tournament and scholarships were provided to approximately 10% of the competitors. For bowlers from the Pepsi competition, 4 girls and 4 boys win scholarships.

**Deadline** Applications must by submitted by May of each year. The national finals are held in July.

## [583]
## USBC YOUTH LEADERS OF THE YEAR AWARDS

United States Bowling Congress
Attn: SMART Program
5301 South 76th Street
Greendale, WI 53129-1192
(414) 423-3223     Toll-free: (800) 514-BOWL, ext. 3223
Fax: (414) 421-3014     E-mail: smart@bowl.com
Web: www.bowl.com/scholarships/main.aspx

**Summary** To recognize and reward, with college scholarships, outstanding young bowlers.

**Eligibility** These awards are presented to participants in the Youth Leader program of the United States Bowling Congress (USBC) who are 18 years of age or older. Males and females are considered in separate competitions. Selection is based on exemplary Youth Leader activities and contributions to the sport of bowling.

**Financial data** The awards consist of $1,500 college scholarships.

**Duration** The awards are presented annually.

**Additional information** Awardees also serve for 2 years on the USBC Board of Directors.

**Number awarded** 2 each year: 1 for a female and 1 for a male.

**Deadline** Nominations must be submitted by January of each year.

## [584]
## USO DESERT STORM EDUCATION FUND

USO World Headquarters
Attn: Scholarship Program
Washington Navy Yard, Building 198
901 M Street, S.E.
Washington, DC 20374
(202) 610-5700                    Fax: (202) 610-5699
Web: www.desert-storm.com/soldiers/uso.html

**Summary**  To provide financial assistance for academic or vocational education to spouses and children of military personnel who died in the Persian Gulf War.

**Eligibility**  This program is open to the spouses and children of armed service personnel killed, either through accidental causes or in combat, during Operations Desert Shield and Desert Storm. Department of Defense guidelines will be used to determine those service personnel who were taking part in either of these operations at the time of their deaths. This is an entitlement program; neither financial need nor academic achievement are factors in allocating support from the fund. All eligible candidates are contacted directly.

**Financial data**  It is the purpose of the fund to provide as much financial support as possible to all eligible persons. To this end, USO will distribute all of the funds to the eligible persons in equal amounts.

**Duration**  This will be a 1-time distribution of these funds.

**Number awarded**  All eligible survivors will receive funding.

## [585]
## USS LAKE CHAMPLAIN (CG-57) SCHOLARSHIP FUND

USS Lake Champlain Foundation
c/o Captain R.K. Martin, USN (ret)
P.O. Box 233
Keeseville, NY 12944
(518) 834-7660
Web: www.usslakechamplainfoundation.com

**Summary**  To provide financial assistance for college to naval personnel who are (or have been) attached to the USS Lake Champlain and to their dependents.

**Eligibility**  Eligible to apply are 1) past and present crew members of the USS Lake Champlain; 2) spouses and dependent children of officers and enlisted personnel currently serving aboard the USS Lake Champlain; and 3) spouses and dependent children of officers and enlisted personnel on active duty, retired with pay, or deceased who were previously assigned to the USS Lake Champlain since commissioning on August 12, 1988. Applicants must submit an essay on their career objectives, why they are interested in that career, and how furthering their education will lead to their accomplishing their career objective. Selection is based on that essay, financial need, high school and/or college transcripts, 2 letters of recommendation, extracurricular activities and awards, and work experience.

**Financial data**  Stipends range from $100 to $1,000. Scholarships greater than $250 are paid in 2 installments: 1 at the beginning of the fall semester and 1 at the beginning of the second semester upon verification of satisfactory completion of the first semester and continued enrollment. Funds are paid directly to the academic institution.

**Duration**  1 year.

**Number awarded**  Varies each year. Recently, 11 of these scholarships were awarded: 5 at $1,000, 3 at $250, and 3 at $100.

**Deadline**  May of each year.

## [586]
## USS STARK MEMORIAL SCHOLARSHIP FUND

Navy-Marine Corps Relief Society
Attn: Education Division
875 North Randolph Street, Suite 225
Arlington, VA 22203-1977
(703) 696-4960                    Fax: (703) 696-0144
E-mail: education@hq.nmcrs.org
Web: www.nmcrs.org/child-dec.html

**Summary**  To provide financial assistance for college to the spouses and children of deceased crewmembers of the USS Stark (FFG 31).

**Eligibility**  Eligible for this assistance are the spouses and children of crewmembers of the USS Stark (FFG 31) who died as a result of the missile attack on the ship in the Persian Gulf on May 17, 1987.

**Financial data**  The amount of assistance varies; funds may be used for any purpose, including tuition, fees, books, room, or board at a college or university offering a 2-year or 4-year course of study or at a vocational training school.

**Duration**  Up to 4 years.

**Number awarded**  Varies each year.

**Deadline**  February of each year.

## [587]
## UTAH AFFILIATE AWSCPA SCHOLARSHIP

American Woman's Society of Certified Public
    Accountants-Utah Affiliate
c/o Jodi Nichols
1008 North Omni Circle
Salt Lake City, UT 85750
(801) 378-5036            E-mail: jodinichols@attbi.com
Web: www.awscpa.org/frameset.php?cf=awards.htm

**Summary**  To provide financial assistance to women who are majoring in accounting at a college or university in Utah.

**Eligibility**  This program is open to women who are majoring in accounting at a college or university in Utah.

**Financial data**  A stipend is awarded (amount not specified).

**Duration**  1 year.

**Number awarded**  1 or more each year.

## [588]
## UTAH ELKS ASSOCIATION SCHOLARSHIP PROGRAM

Utah Elks Association
c/o Jim Fugua, Scholarship Chair
Provo Lodge 849
1000 South University Avenue
P.O. Box 83
Provo, UT 84603
(801) 373-0849
Web: www.utahelks.org

**Summary**  To provide financial assistance for college to high school seniors in Utah.

**Eligibility**  This program is open to seniors graduating from high schools in Utah. Applicants must submit a 500-word essay on their career and life goals and their plan to achieve those. Selection is based on that essay, academic achievement, community service, honors and awards, leadership, and financial need. U.S. citizenship is required. Females and males compete separately.

**Financial data**  Stipends are $4,000, $800, or $700.

**Duration**  1 year.

**Number awarded**  Varies each year, recently, the program awarded 4 scholarships (2 to males and 2 to females) at $4,000, 16 (8 to males and 8 to females) at $800, and 16 (8 to males and 8 to females) at $700.

**Deadline**  January of each year.

## [589]
## VADM ROBERT L. WALTERS SCHOLARSHIP

Surface Navy Association
2550 Huntington Avenue, Suite 202
Alexandria, VA 22303
(703) 960-6800          Toll-free: (800) NAVY-SNA
Fax: (703) 960-6807      E-mail: navysna@aol.com
Web: www.navysna.org/awards/index.html

**Summary**  To provide financial assistance for college or graduate school to members of the Surface Navy Association (SNA) and their dependents.

**Eligibility**  This program is open to SNA members and their children, stepchildren, wards, and spouses. The SNA member must 1) be in the second or subsequent consecutive year of membership; 2) be serving, retired, or honorably discharged; 3) be a Surface Warfare Officer or Enlisted Surface Warfare Specialist; and 4) have served for at least 3 years on a surface ship of the U.S. Navy or Coast Guard. Applicants must be studying or planning to study at an accredited undergraduate or graduate institution. Along with their application, they must submit a 200-word essay about themselves; a list of their extracurricular activities, community service activities, academic honors and/or positions of leadership that represent their interests, with an estimate of the amount of time involved with each activity; and 3 letters of reference. High school seniors should also include a transcript of high school grades and a copy of ACT or SAT scores. Applicants who are on active duty or drilling Reservists should also include a letter from their commanding officer commenting on their military service and leadership potential, a transcript of grades from their most recent 4 semesters of school, a copy of their ACT or SAT scores if available, and an indication of whether they have applied for or are enrolled in the Enlisted Commissioning Program. Applicants who are not high school seniors, active duty, or drilling Reservists should also include a transcript of the grades from their most recent 4 semesters of school and a copy of ACT or SAT test scores (unless they are currently attending a college or university). Selection is based on demonstrated leadership, community service, academic achievement, and commitment to pursuing higher educational objectives.

**Financial data**  The stipend is $2,000 per year.

**Duration**  4 years, provided the recipient maintains a GPA of 3.0 or higher.

**Number awarded**  Varies each year.

**Deadline**  January of each year.

## [590]
## VANESSA RUDLOFF SCHOLARSHIP PROGRAM

Texas Women in Law Enforcement
Attn: Scholarship Awards Chair
P.O. Box 925185
Houston, TX 77292-5185
E-mail: mem4204@aol.com
Web: www.acob.com/twle/scholar_award.html

**Summary**  To provide financial assistance for college to members of the Texas Women in Law Enforcement (TWLE) and their relatives.

**Eligibility**  Members of TWLE must have been active for the past 2 years, must be currently in good standing with their department, must submit a 1-page essay stating why they deserve the scholarship, and must be majoring in criminal justice or a related field. Relatives of TWLE members must be the spouse, child, brother, sister, niece, nephew, or grandchild of the member; must be in the top 25% of their graduating class; must have a GPA of 3.0 or higher; must score at least 21 on the ACT (or the equivalent on the SAT); must submit 2 letters of recommendation; and must submit a 1-page essay stating why they deserve the scholarship. For these relatives, the sponsor must have been an active member of TWLE for the past 2 years.

**Financial data**  The stipend is $1,000.

**Duration**  1 year.

**Number awarded**  At least 4 each year.

**Deadline**  March of each year.

## [591]
## VERMONT ARMED SERVICES SCHOLARSHIPS

Office of the Adjutant General
789 Vermont National Guard Road
Colchester, VT 05446-3099
(802) 338-3450
Web: www.vtguard.com

**Summary**  To provide financial assistance for college to the children and spouses of deceased members of the armed services in Vermont.

**Eligibility**  This program is open to the children and spouses of 1) members of the Vermont National Guard who have been killed since 1955 or who since January 1, 2001 have died while on active or inactive duty; 2) members in good standing of the active Reserve forces of the United States who since January 1, 2001 have died while on active or inactive duty and who were Vermont residents at the time of death; and 3) members of the active armed forces of the United States who since January 1, 2001 have died while on active duty and who, at the time of death, were Vermont residents, nonresident members of the Vermont National Guard mobilized to active duty, or nonresident active Reserve force members of a Vermont-based Reserve unit mobilized to active duty. Applicants must be residents of Vermont and attending or planning to attend a Vermont public university, college, or technical institute.

**Financial data** Full tuition, in excess of any funds the student receives as a federal Pell Grant, is paid at Vermont public institutions.

**Duration** 1 year; may be renewed until completion of 130 academic credits.

**Number awarded** Varies each year.

## [592]
## VERMONT SPACE GRANT UNDERGRADUATE SCHOLARSHIPS

Vermont Space Grant Consortium
c/o University of Vermont
College of Engineering and Mathematics
Votey Building, Room 209
12 Colchester Avenue
Burlington, VT 05405-0156
(802) 656-1429    Fax: (802) 656-1102
E-mail: zeno@cems.uvm.edu
Web: www.vtspacegrant.org/vtscholarship.htm

**Summary** To provide financial assistance for undergraduate study in space-related fields to students in Vermont, particularly women, minority, and disabled students.

**Eligibility** This program is open to Vermont residents who are 1) enrolled in an undergraduate degree program at a Vermont institution of higher education with a GPA of 3.0 or higher or 2) seniors graduating from a high school in Vermont. Applicants must be planning to pursue a professional career that has direct relevance to the U.S. aerospace industry and the goal of the National Aeronautics and Space Administration (NASA) in such fields as astronomy, biology, engineering, mathematics, physics, and other basic sciences (including earth sciences and medicine). They must submit an essay, up to 3 pages in length, on their career plans and the relationship of those plans to areas of interest to NASA. U.S. citizenship is required. Selection is based on academic standing, letters of recommendation, and the essay. The Vermont Space Grant Consortium (VSGC) is a component of the NASA Space Grant program, which encourages participation by women, underrepresented minorities, and persons with disabilities.

**Financial data** The stipend is $1,500 per year.

**Duration** 1 year; may be renewed upon reapplication.

**Additional information** This program is funded by NASA. Participating institutions are the College of Engineering and Mathematics at the University of Vermont, St. Michael's College, Norwich University, Vermont Technical College, the Vermont State Mathematics Coalition, and Burlington Aviation Technology School/Burlington Technical Center.

**Number awarded** Varies each year; recently, 8 of these scholarships were awarded.

**Deadline** April of each year.

## [593]
## VICE ADMIRAL E.P. TRAVERS SCHOLARSHIP

Navy-Marine Corps Relief Society
Attn: Education Division
875 North Randolph Street, Suite 225
Arlington, VA 22203-1977
(703) 696-4960    Fax: (703) 696-0144
E-mail: education@hq.nmcrs.org
Web: www.nmcrs.org/travers.html

**Summary** To provide financial assistance for college to the dependents of Navy and Marine Corps personnel.

**Eligibility** This program is open to the dependent children of active-duty and retired Navy and Marine Corps personnel and the spouses of active-duty Navy and Marine Corps personnel. Applicants must have a cumulative GPA of 2.0 or higher and must demonstrate financial need. They must be enrolled or planning to enroll as a full-time undergraduate student at an accredited college, university, or vocational/technical school.

**Financial data** The stipend is $2,000 per year.

**Duration** 1 year; may be renewed up to 3 additional years as long as the recipient maintains a GPA of 2.0 or higher and the parent remains on active duty in the Navy or Marines.

**Number awarded** Up to 500 each year.

**Deadline** February of each year.

## [594]
## VII CORPS DESERT STORM VETERANS ASSOCIATION SCHOLARSHIP

VII Corps Desert Storm Veterans Association
Attn: Scholarship Committee
Army Historical Foundation
2425 Wilson Boulevard
Arlington, VA 22201
(703) 604-6565    E-mail: viicorpsdsva@aol.com
Web: www.desertstormvets.org

**Summary** To provide financial assistance for college to students who served, or are the spouses or other family members of individuals who served, with VII Corps in Operations Desert Shield, Desert Storm, or related activities.

**Eligibility** Applicants must have served, or be a family member of those who served, with VII Corps in Operations Desert Shield/Desert Storm, Provide Comfort, or 1 of the support base activities. Scholarships are limited to students entering or enrolled in accredited technical institutions (trade or specialty), 2-year colleges, and 4-year colleges or universities. Awards will not be made to individuals receiving military academy appointments or full 4-year scholarships. Letters of recommendation and a transcript are required. Selection is not based solely on academic standing; consideration is also given to extracurricular activities and other self-development skills and abilities obtained through on-the-job training or correspondence courses. Priority is given to survivors of VII Corps soldiers who died during Operations Desert Shield/Desert Storm or Provide Comfort, veterans who are also members of the VII Corps Desert Storm Veterans Association, and family members of veterans who are also members of the VII Corps Desert Storm Veterans Association.

**Financial data** The stipend is $5,000 per year. Funds are paid to the recipients upon proof of admission or registration at an accredited institution, college, or university.

**Duration** 1 year; recipients may reapply.

**Additional information** This program began in 1998.

**Number awarded** 3 each year.

**Deadline** January of each year.

## [595]
## VIRGINIA ARMY/AIR NATIONAL GUARD ENLISTED ASSOCIATION SCHOLARSHIP

Virginia Army/Air National Guard Enlisted Association
Attn: Executive Secretary
2503 Ravenwood Avenue, N.W.
Roanoke, VA 24012-3245
(540) 366-5133                    Fax: (540) 362-4417
E-mail: sfcjj@aol.com
Web: www.staunton.com

**Summary** To provide financial assistance for college to members of the Virginia Army/Air National Guard Enlisted Association (VaA/ANGEA) and to members of their families.

**Eligibility** This program is open to 1) enlisted soldiers or enlisted airmen currently serving as a member of the Virginia National Guard (VNG) who are also a member of the VaA/ANGEA; 2) retired enlisted soldiers or retired enlisted airmen of the VNG who are also a member of the VaA/ANGEA; 3) spouses of current enlisted soldiers or enlisted airmen of the VNG who are also a member of the VaA/ANGEA; 4) spouses of retired enlisted soldiers or retired enlisted airmen of the VNG who are also a member of the VaA/ANGEA; and 5) dependents of current or retired enlisted soldiers or airmen of the VNG (a copy of the dependency decree may be required) who are also members of the VaA/ANGEA. Applicants must submit a copy of their school transcript (high school or college), a statement of their desire to continue their education and their need for assistance, 3 letters of recommendation, a letter of academic reference, and a photocopy of their VaA/ANGEA membership card. Selection is based on academics (15 points), personal statement (15 points), letters of recommendation (16 points), school involvement (15 points), community involvement (15 points), responsibility (15 points), and financial need (9 points).

**Financial data** Generally, stipends are either $1,000 or $500.

**Duration** 1 year; recipients may reapply.

**Additional information** Recipients may attend school on either a part-time or full-time basis. Information is also available from CMS Charles P. Smith, 10163 Tunstall Road, New Kent, VA 23124.

**Number awarded** Generally, 2 scholarships at $1,000 and 4 scholarships at $500 are awarded each year.

**Deadline** February of each year.

## [596]
## VIRGINIA D. HENRY SCHOLARSHIP

National Society of Professional Engineers
Attn: Education Services
1420 King Street
Alexandria, VA 22314-2794
(703) 684-2833                    Fax: (703) 836-4875
E-mail: jiglesias@nspe.org
Web: www.nspe.org/scholarships/sc1-hs.asp

**Summary** To provide financial assistance for college to women who are high school seniors and interested in preparing for a career in engineering.

**Eligibility** This program is open to women who are high school seniors planning to study engineering in an EAC-ABET accredited college program. Applicants must have earned a GPA of 3.5 or higher, verbal SAT score of 600 or higher, and math SAT score of 700 or higher (or English ACT score of 29 or higher and math ACT score of 29 or higher). They must submit an essay (up to 500 words) on their interest in engineering, their major area of study and area of specialization, and the occupation they propose to pursue after graduation. Selection is based on GPA (20 points), the essay (20 points), extracurricular activities, including work experience and volunteer activities (25 points), financial need (5 points), SAT/ACT scores (20 points), and the composite application (10 points). U.S. citizenship is required.

**Financial data** The stipend is $1,000 per year; funds are paid directly to the institution.

**Duration** 1 year.

**Additional information** Recipients may attend any college or university, as long as the engineering curriculum is accredited by EAC-ABET.

**Number awarded** 1 each year.

**Deadline** November of each year.

## [597]
## VIRGINIA GOLF FOUNDATION SCHOLARSHIP PROGRAM

Virginia State Golf Association
Attn: Virginia Golf Foundation, Inc.
600 Founders Bridge Boulevard
Midlothian, VA 23113
(804) 378-2300, ext. 11              Fax: (804) 378-8216
E-mail: info@vsga.org
Web: www.vsga.org/article.asp?ID=4857

**Summary** To provide financial assistance for college to young Virginians who have an interest in golf.

**Eligibility** This program is open to high school seniors in Virginia who are interested in golf and wish to attend a college or university in the state. Applicants must submit an essay of 500 words or less on how golf has influenced their life, the role it will play in their future plans, why they are applying for this scholarship, and their career plans following graduation. Selection is based on the essay, interest in golf (excellence and ability are not considered), academic achievement, citizenship, character, and financial need. Applications must be made on behalf of the candidate by a member club of the Virginia State Golf Association (VSGA). Some scholarships are reserved for students working on degrees in turfgrass management at Virginia Polytechnic Institute and State University.

**Financial data** Stipends range from $750 to $5,000. Funds may be used only for tuition, room, and other approved educational expenses.

**Duration** The program includes 4-year scholarships and 1-year merit awards.

**Additional information** This program was established in 1984. Since then, more than 530 students have received more than $1.29 million in scholarships.

**Number awarded** Varies each year. Recently, 30 of these scholarships were awarded: 2 at $5,000 (the Spencer-Wilkinson Award for a woman and the C. Dan Keffer Award for a man), 5 at $3,500, 3 at $3,000, 2 at $2,500, 3 at $2,000 (including the David A. King Merit Award and the Red Speigle Award reserved for a golfer from the Peninsula area), 11 at $1,000, and 4 at $750 for turfgrass management students at Virginia Tech. The 26 golf scholarships included 13 for 4 years and 13 merit awards for 1 year.

**Deadline** February of each year.

## [598]
## VIRGINIA NETWORK OF EXECUTIVE WOMEN IN HOSPITALITY SCHOLARSHIP AWARDS

Network of Executive Women in Hospitality-Virginia
  Chapter
Attn: Linda Mansy, Director of Scholarship and
  Education
McIntyre-Mansy Associates
5901 Mount Eagle Drive, Suite 1204
Richmond, VA 23220-4003
Toll-free: (800) 593-NEWH          Fax: (800) 693-NEWH
E-mail: lindajoe2@verizon.net
Web: www.newh.org/newh/scholarshippacket.php

**Summary** To provide financial assistance to women in Virginia, North Carolina, and West Virginia who wish to work on a college degree in a hospitality-related field.

**Eligibility** This program is open to women who have completed half the requirements for a degree or certification program at a vocational school or college in Virginia, North Carolina, or West Virginia. Applicants must have a GPA of 3.0 or higher and a career objective in the hospitality or food service industries (e.g., hotel and restaurant management, culinary, food service, architecture, design). Selection is based on financial need and academic accomplishments.

**Financial data** The stipend is $1,500.

**Duration** 1 year.

**Number awarded** Varies each year; recently, 2 of these scholarships were awarded.

**Deadline** September of each year.

## [599]
## VIRGINIA SPACE GRANT COMMUNITY COLLEGE SCHOLARSHIP PROGRAM

Virginia Space Grant Consortium
Attn: Fellowship Coordinator
Old Dominion University Peninsula Center
600 Butler Farm Road
Hampton, VA 23666
(757) 766-5210                    Fax: (757) 766-5205
E-mail: vsgc@odu.edu
Web: www.vsgc.odu.edu/Menu3_1_1.htm

**Summary** To provide financial assistance to students (particularly women, minority, and disabled students) who are interested in pursuing space-related studies at community colleges in Virginia.

**Eligibility** This program is open to students currently enrolled in a Virginia community college who are U.S. citizens and have completed at least the first semester of their program with a GPA of 3.0 or higher. Awards are generally made to full-time students, but part-time students demonstrating academic merit are also eligible. Applicants can be enrolled in any program that includes course work related to an understanding of or interest in technological fields supporting aerospace; that includes (but is not limited to) computers, electronics, engineering, or industrial technology. Since a particular goal of the program is to increase the participation of underrepresented minorities, women, and persons with disabilities in aerospace-related, high technology careers, the sponsor especially encourages applications from those students.

**Financial data** The maximum stipend is $1,500.

**Duration** 1 year; nonrenewable.

**Additional information** This program is funded by the U.S. National Aeronautics and Space Administration (NASA).

**Number awarded** Approximately 10 each year.

**Deadline** February of each year.

## [600]
## VIRGINIA SPACE GRANT TEACHER EDUCATION SCHOLARSHIP PROGRAM

Virginia Space Grant Consortium
Attn: Fellowship Coordinator
Old Dominion University Peninsula Center
600 Butler Farm Road
Hampton, VA 23666
(757) 766-5210                    Fax: (757) 766-5205
E-mail: vsgc@odu.edu
Web: www.vsgc.odu.edu/Menu3_1_1.htm

**Summary** To provide financial assistance for college or graduate school to students in Virginia (particularly women, minority, and disabled students) who are planning a career as science, mathematics, or technology educators.

**Eligibility** This program is open to full-time undergraduate students at the Virginia Space Grant Consortium (VSGC) colleges and universities in a track that will qualify them to teach in a pre-college setting. Priority is given to those majoring in technology education, mathematics, or science, particularly earth, space, or environmental science. Applicants may apply while seniors in high school or sophomores in a community college, with the award contingent on their enrollment at a VSGC college and entrance into a teacher certification program. They must submit a statement of academic goals and plan of study, explaining their reasons for desiring to enter the teaching profession, specifically the fields of science, mathematics, or technology education. Students currently enrolled in a VSGC college can apply when they declare their intent to enter the teacher certification program. Students enrolled in a master's of education degree program leading to teacher certification in approved fields are also eligible to apply. Applicants must be U.S. citizens with a GPA of 3.0 or higher. Since an important purpose of this program is to increase the participation of underrepresented minorities, women, and persons with disabilities in science, mathematics, and technology education, the VSGC especially encourages applications from those students.

**Financial data**  The maximum stipend is $1,000.

**Duration**  1 year; nonrenewable.

**Additional information**  The VSGC institutions are College of William and Mary, Hampton University, Old Dominion University, the University of Virginia, and Virginia Polytechnic Institute and State University. This program is funded by the U.S. National Aeronautics and Space Administration (NASA).

**Number awarded**  Approximately 10 each year.

**Deadline**  February of each year.

## [601]
## WACHOVIA CITIZENSHIP AWARDS

Virginia High School League
1642 State Farm Boulevard
Charlottesville, VA 22911
(434) 977-8475                    Fax: (434) 977-5943
Web: www.vhsl.org

**Summary**  To provide financial assistance for college to high school seniors who have participated in activities of the Virginia High School League (VHSL).

**Eligibility**  This program is open to college-bound seniors graduating from high schools that are members of the VHSL. Applicants must have participated in 1 or more of the following VHSL activities: baseball, basketball, cheer, creative writing, cross country, debate, drama, field hockey, football, forensics, golf, gymnastics, lacrosse, leaders conference, magazines, newspapers/newsmagazines, scholastic bowl, soccer, softball, sportsmanship summit/committee, swimming and diving, tennis, track (indoor and outdoor), volleyball, wrestling, or yearbook. They must submit an essay (from 500 to 1,000 words) on what they have done that meets a definition of citizenship and how others have benefited. Each school may nominate 1 female and 1 male. Candidates are judged separately in the 3 VHSL groups (A, AA, and AAA). Selection is based on the essay; contributions to family, school, and community; promotion of good citizenship and sportsmanship; and 2 letters of support.

**Financial data**  The stipend is $1,000.

**Duration**  1 year.

**Additional information**  This program is supported by Wachovia Bank.

**Number awarded**  6 each year: a female and a male in each of the 3 VHSL groups.

**Deadline**  March of each year.

## [602]
## WAIVERS OF NONRESIDENT TUITION FOR DEPENDENTS OF MILITARY PERSONNEL MOVING TO TEXAS

Texas Higher Education Coordinating Board
Attn: Grants and Special Programs
1200 East Anderson Lane
P.O. Box 12788, Capitol Station
Austin, TX 78711-2788
(512) 427-6101                    Toll-free: (800) 242-3062
Fax: (512) 427-6127
E-mail: grantinfo@thecb.state.tx.us
Web: www.collegefortexans.com

**Summary**  To exempt dependents of military personnel who move to Texas from the payment of nonresident tuition at public institutions of higher education in the state.

**Eligibility**  Eligible for these waivers are the spouses and dependent children of members of the U.S. armed forces and commissioned officers of the Public Health Service who move to Texas while the service member remains assigned to another state. Applicants must be attending or planning to attend a public college or university in the state. They must indicate their intent to become a Texas resident. For dependent children to qualify, the spouse must also move to Texas.

**Financial data**  Although persons eligible under this program are still classified as nonresidents, they are entitled to pay the resident tuition at Texas institutions of higher education on an immediate basis.

**Duration**  1 year.

**Additional information**  This program became effective in September 2003.

**Number awarded**  Varies each year.

## [603]
## WAIVERS OF NONRESIDENT TUITION FOR DEPENDENTS OF MILITARY PERSONNEL WHO PREVIOUSLY LIVED IN TEXAS

Texas Higher Education Coordinating Board
Attn: Grants and Special Programs
1200 East Anderson Lane
P.O. Box 12788, Capitol Station
Austin, TX 78711-2788
(512) 427-6101                    Toll-free: (800) 242-3062
Fax: (512) 427-6127
E-mail: grantinfo@thecb.state.tx.us
Web: www.collegefortexans.com

**Summary**  To provide a partial tuition exemption to the spouses and dependent children of military personnel who are Texas residents but are not assigned to duty in the state.

**Eligibility**  Eligible for these waivers are the spouses and dependent children of members of the U.S. armed forces who are not assigned to duty in Texas but have previously resided in the state for at least 6 months. Service members must verify that they remain Texas residents by designating Texas as their place of legal residence for income tax purposes, registering to vote in the state, and doing 1 of the following: owning real property in Texas, registering an automobile in Texas, or executing a will indicating that they are a resident of the state. The spouse or dependent child must be attending or planning to attend a Texas public college or university.

**Financial data** Although persons eligible under this program are classified as nonresidents, they are entitled to pay the resident tuition at Texas institutions of higher education, regardless of their length of residence in Texas.

**Duration** 1 year.

**Number awarded** Varies each year.

## [604]
## WALDO AND ALICE AYER MUSIC SCHOLARSHIP
Waldo and Alice Ayer Charitable Trust
c/o Citizens Bank New Hampshire
875 Elm Street
Manchester, NH 03101-2104
(603) 634-7719

**Summary** To provide financial assistance to New Hampshire residents (particularly women) who are interested in majoring in music or music education in college.

**Eligibility** This program is open to New Hampshire residents who are interested in attending college to become professional musicians or music teachers. Applicants must have a GPA of 2.5 or higher and be able to demonstrate financial need. Preference is given to women applicants.

**Financial data** A stipend is awarded (amount not specified).

**Duration** 1 year.

**Number awarded** 1 or more each year.

**Deadline** May of each year.

## [605]
## WALTER REED SMITH SCHOLARSHIP PROGRAM
United Daughters of the Confederacy
Attn: Education Director
328 North Boulevard
Richmond, VA 23220-4057
(804) 355-1636          Fax: (804) 353-1396
E-mail: hqudc@rcn.com
Web: www.hqudc.org/scholarships/scholarships.html

**Summary** To provide financial assistance to mature women who are lineal descendants of Confederate veterans and plan to major in selected fields in college.

**Eligibility** Eligible to apply for these scholarships are women over the age of 30 who are lineal descendants of worthy Confederates or collateral descendants and members of the Children of the Confederacy or the United Daughters of the Confederacy. Applicants must intend to study business administration, computer science, home economics, nutrition, or nursing. They must submit certified proof of the Confederate record of 1 ancestor, with the company and regiment in which he served, and must have had at least a 3.0 GPA in high school.

**Financial data** The amount of this scholarship depends on the availability of funds.

**Duration** 1 year; may be renewed.

**Additional information** Information is also available from Mrs. Robert C. Kraus, Second Vice President General, 239 Deerfield Lane, Franklin, NC 28734-0112. Members of the same family may not hold scholarships simultaneously, and only 1 application per family will be accepted within any 1 year. All requests for applications must be accompanied by a self-addressed stamped envelope.

**Number awarded** 1 each year.

**Deadline** March of each year.

## [606]
## WASHINGTON BUSINESS AND PROFESSIONAL WOMEN'S FOUNDATION EDUCATIONAL SCHOLARSHIP
Washington Business and Professional Women's Foundation
Attn: Madeleine Cooper, Scholarship Committee Chair
100 North 60111 Avenue, Number 15
Yakima, WA 98908
Web: www.bpwwa.com/files/index.php?id=14

**Summary** To provide financial assistance to women from Washington working on an undergraduate or graduate degree.

**Eligibility** This program is open to women from Washington who are enrolled or planning to enroll in a vocational/technical school, community college, or 4-year college or university. Applicants must be working on an associate, bachelor's, master's, or doctoral degree. Along with their application, they must submit a 300-word essay on their specific short-term goals and how the proposed training will help them accomplish those goals and make a difference in their professional career. Financial need is considered in the selection process.

**Financial data** Stipends range from $500 to $1,000.

**Duration** 1 year.

**Additional information** This program was established in 1992.

**Number awarded** Varies each year. Since the program was established, it has awarded 112 scholarships.

**Deadline** March of each year.

## [607]
## WASHINGTON DC AREA CHAPTER SCHOLARSHIP
Association for Women in Communications-Washington DC Area Chapter
Attn: Frappa Stout, Vice President of Student Affairs
USA Weekend
7950 Jones Branch Drive
McLean, VA 22108-0001
Toll-free: (800) 487-2956          Fax: (703) 854-2122
E-mail: fstout@usaweekend.com
Web: www.awcdc.net/scholar_app.shtml

**Summary** To provide financial assistance to women who are working on undergraduate degrees in a communications-related field at universities in the Washington, D.C. area.

**Eligibility** This program is open to female sophomores and juniors attending a Washington, D.C. area university or college studying advertising, communications, graphic arts, journalism, marketing, public relations, or a related field. Applicants must have an overall GPA of 3.0 or higher and work experience in communications or a related field. They must be active in extracurricular activities, including family obligations, volunteer work, clubs, and organizations, and their involvement must show versatility and commitment. Along with their application, they must submit a 500-word essay on how their present communications-related activities will contribute to the achievement of their career goals. Selection is based on that essay, at least 2 letters of recommendation, academic achievement, and communications activities; financial need is not considered.

**Financial data**    The stipend is $1,000.

**Duration**    1 year.

**Number awarded**    1 each year.

**Deadline**    March of each year.

## [608]
## WASHINGTON DC METROPOLITAN NETWORK OF EXECUTIVE WOMEN IN HOSPITALITY SCHOLARSHIP AWARDS

Network of Executive Women in Hospitality-Washington
   DC Metropolitan Chapter
Attn: Bill Wildes, Director of Scholarship and Education
Marriott International, Inc.
10400 Fernwood Drive, Department 70/100.06
Washington, DC 20058
Toll-free: (800) 593-NEWH        Fax: (800) 693-NEWH
E-mail: bill.wildes@marriott.com
Web: www.newh.org

**Summary**    To provide financial assistance to women in the Washington, D.C. area interested in preparing for a career in the hospitality industry.

**Eligibility**    This program is open to women who have completed half the requirements for a degree or certification program at a vocational school or college in the District of Columbia, Delaware, Maryland, or Pennsylvania. Applicants must have a GPA of 3.0 or higher and a career objective in the hospitality or food service industries (e.g., hotel and restaurant management, culinary, food service, architecture, design). Selection is based on financial need and academic accomplishments.

**Financial data**    Stipends are $4,000 or $2,000.

**Duration**    1 year.

**Number awarded**    6 each year: 1 at $4,000 and 5 at $2,000.

**Deadline**    March of each year.

## [609]
## WASHINGTON NASA SPACE GRANT CONSORTIUM UNDERGRADUATE SCHOLARSHIPS

Washington NASA Space Grant Consortium
c/o University of Washington
Johnson Hall, Room 141
Box 351310
Seattle, WA 98195-1310
(206) 543-1943            Toll-free: (800) 659-1943
Fax: (206) 543-0179    E-mail: nasa@u.washington.edu
Web: www.waspacegrant.org/undergr.html

**Summary**    To provide funding for college to students in Washington (particularly women, minority, and disabled students) who wish to study science, engineering, or mathematics with an emphasis on space.

**Eligibility**    This program is open to residents of Washington who are attending or planning to attend designated institutions that are members of the Washington NASA Space Grant Consortium. Applicants must be interested in majoring in space-related aspects of science, engineering, or mathematics. U.S. citizenship is required. The program values diversity and strongly encourages women and minorities to apply.

**Financial data**    Stipends vary at participating institutions, but range from $1,000 to $5,000.

**Duration**    1 year; may be renewed.

**Additional information**    This program is funded by the U.S. National Aeronautics and Space Administration (NASA). Members of the consortium that offer undergraduate scholarships are Northwest Indian College, Seattle Central Community College, University of Washington, and Washington State University.

**Number awarded**    Varies each year.

**Deadline**    Each participating institution sets its own deadline.

## [610]
## WASHINGTON STATE CHAPTER WAI SCHOLARSHIP

Women in Aviation, International
Attn: Scholarships
Morningstar Airport
3647 State Route 503 South
West Alexandria, OH 45381
(937) 558-7655            Fax: (937) 839-4645
E-mail: scholarships@wai.org
Web: www.wai.org/education/scholarships.cfm

**Summary**    To provide financial assistance to members of Women in Aviation, International (WAI) from Washington who are studying aviation in college.

**Eligibility**    This program is open to WAI members who are residents of Washington and members of the state WAI chapter. Applicants must be enrolled in school to prepare for a career in aviation (including, but not limited to, pilot, mechanic, avionics technician, engineer, meteorologist, dispatcher, flight attendant, air traffic controller, or airport manager). If they plan a career as a pilot, they must have a private pilot's license. Selection is based on merit and commitment to chosen career in aviation. If they are enrolled in a program that issues grades, the selection process also includes GPA. Preference is given to applicants who have already made steps toward their chosen aviation career. An interview may be conducted at the WAI conference or at a location in Washington.

**Financial data** The stipend is $1,000. Funds are paid directly to an accredited program to be used for tuition, books, specific training, or housing.

**Duration** Funds must be used within 1 year of receipt.

**Additional information** WAI is a nonprofit professional organization dedicated to encouraging women to consider an aviation career, providing educational outreach activities, and providing networking opportunities to women active in the industry.

**Number awarded** 1 each year.

**Deadline** November of each year.

## [611]
## WASHINGTON WOMEN IN NEED EDUCATIONAL GRANTS

Washington Women in Need
1849 114th Avenue, N.E.
Bellevue, WA 98004
(425) 451-8838     Toll-free: (888) 440-WWIN
Fax: (425) 451-8845
E-mail: wwininfo@wawomeninneed.org
Web: www.wawomeninneed.org

**Summary** To provide financial assistance for college to low-income women in the state of Washington.

**Eligibility** Applicants must be low-income women who are at least 18 years of age and residing in the state of Washington. They must first apply for assistance from Washington Women in Need; then, as clients, they may submit an application for an educational grant. Any field of study is eligible, at any level of degree or vocational certification through a bachelor's degree, including GED completion and college transfer.

**Financial data** Funds are available for tuition and books while attending an accredited educational institution in the state.

**Duration** 1 year; renewal is possible if the recipient maintains a GPA of 2.5 or higher.

**Number awarded** Varies each year.

## [612]
## WASHINGTON ZONTA CLUB SCHOLARSHIPS

Zonta Club of Washington, D.C.
c/o Yvonne Boggan, President
350 Chaplin Street, S.E.
Washington, DC 20019-4261
(202) 575-4808
Web: www.zontawashingtondc.org

**Summary** To provide financial assistance to women undergraduates attending universities in the Washington, D.C. area.

**Eligibility** This program is open to women undergraduates who are attending universities in the Washington, D.C. area. Selection is based on financial need and scholastic achievement.

**Financial data** The amount awarded varies, recently, stipends averaged $4,875.

**Duration** 1 year.

**Number awarded** Varies each year; recently, 4 of these scholarships were awarded.

**Deadline** December of each year.

## [613]
## WICHITA CHAPTER ASWA SCHOLARSHIPS

American Society of Women Accountants-Wichita Chapter
c/o Vonda Wilson, Scholarship Chair
417 North Topeka
Wichita, KS 67202
Web: www.wichitaaswa.org

**Summary** To provide financial assistance to female undergraduate and graduate students working on a degree in accounting at a college or university in Kansas.

**Eligibility** This program is open to female part- and full-time students working on a bachelor's or master's degree in accounting at a college or university in Kansas. Applicants must have completed at least 60 semester hours. They are not required to be a member of the American Society of Women Accountants (ASWA). Along with their application, they must submit a 100-word essay on how they plan to incorporate into their strategic career goals the sponsor's philosophy of achieving balance among life priorities, including career, personal development, family, friendships, and community and societal needs. Selection is based on that essay, academic record, extracurricular activities and honors, letters of recommendation, and financial need.

**Financial data** The stipend is $1,000 or $500.

**Duration** 1 year.

**Additional information** The highest-ranked recipient is entered into the national competition for scholarships that range from $1,500 to $4,500.

**Number awarded** Varies each year. Recently, 3 of these scholarships were awarded: 1 at $1,000 and 2 at $500.

**Deadline** February of each year.

## [614]
## WILLIAM BRIDGE SCHOLARSHIP

Ninety-Nines, Inc.-Eastern New England Chapter
c/o Katharine Barr
278 Elm Street
North Reading, MA 01864-2526

**Summary** To provide financial assistance to female residents of New England who are interested in preparing for a career in aviation.

**Eligibility** Eligible to apply are high school seniors or beyond who are female, hold a private pilot license, and reside or study in 1 of the following states: Maine, New Hampshire, Rhode Island, Vermont, Massachusetts, or Connecticut. They must be planning a career in aviation and need financial assistance to pursue appropriate education or flight training. Criteria for selecting recipients include: aviation activities, science fair projects, aviation employment, recommendations, academic record, aviation goals, and financial need.

**Financial data** The stipend is $1,000. Funds may be applied to academic tuition, technical school, or flight training.

**Duration** 1 year.

**Number awarded** 1 each year.

**Deadline** January of each year.

## [615]
## WILLIAM J. POLISSINO MEMORIAL SCHOLARSHIP

Pennsylvania Masonic Youth Foundation
Attn: Educational Endowment Fund
1244 Bainbridge Road
Elizabethtown, PA 17022-9423
(717) 367-1536    Toll-free: (800) 266-8424 (within PA)
Fax: (717) 367-0616    E-mail: pyf@pagrandlodge.org
Web: www.pagrandlodge.org/pyf/scholar/index.html

**Summary** To provide financial assistance for college to members of Rainbow Girls in Pennsylvania.

**Eligibility** This program is open to active Pennsylvania Rainbow Girls in good standing. Applicants must have completed at least 1 year in an accredited college, university, or nursing school.

**Financial data** The stipend depends on the availability of funds.

**Duration** 1 year; may be renewed.

**Additional information** Information is also available from Eva Gresko, RD #3, Box 102, Huntington, PA 16652-8703, (814) 658-3774.

**Number awarded** 1 each year.

**Deadline** Requests for applications must be submitted by January of each year. Completed applications are due by the end of February.

## [616]
## WILLIAM RUCKER GREENWOOD SCHOLARSHIP

Association for Women Geoscientists
Attn: AWG Foundation
P.O. Box 30645
Lincoln, NE 68503-0645
E-mail: awgscholarship@yahoo.com
Web: www.awg.org/members/po_scholarships.html

**Summary** To provide financial assistance to minority women working on an undergraduate or graduate degree in the geosciences in the Potomac Bay region.

**Eligibility** This program is open to minority women who are currently enrolled as full-time undergraduate or graduate geoscience majors in an accredited, degree-granting college or university in Delaware, the District of Columbia, Maryland, Virginia, or West Virginia. Selection is based on the applicant's 1) participation in geoscience or earth science educational activities, and 2) potential for leadership as a future geoscience professional.

**Financial data** The stipend is $1,000. The recipient also is granted a 1-year membership in the Association for Women Geoscientists (AWG).

**Duration** 1 year.

**Additional information** This program is sponsored by the AWG Potomac Area Chapter. Information is also avail-

able from Laurel M. Bybell, U.S. Geological Survey, 926 National Center, Reston, VA 20192.

**Number awarded** 1 each year.

**Deadline** April of each year.

## [617]
## WILMA H. WRIGHT MEMORIAL SCHOLARSHIP

Delta Gamma Foundation
Attn: Director of Scholarships, Fellowships and Loans
3250 Riverside Drive
P.O. Box 21397
Columbus, OH 43221-0397
(614) 481-8169                    Fax: (614) 481-0133
E-mail: DGScholarships07@aol.com
Web: www.deltagamma.org

**Summary** To provide financial assistance to members of Delta Gamma sorority who are visually impaired or preparing for a career working with the visually impaired.

**Eligibility** This program is open to initiated members of a collegiate chapter of Delta Gamma in the United States or Canada who have completed 3 semesters or 5 quarters of their college course and have maintained a GPA of 3.0 or higher. Applicants must submit a 1- to 2-page essay in which they introduce themselves, including their career goals, their reasons for applying for this scholarship, and the impact Delta Gamma has had on their life. Selection is based on scholastic excellence and participation in chapter, campus, and community leadership activities. Preference is given to candidates who are either 1) blind or visually impaired or 2) pursuing professional training in areas related to working with persons who are blind or visually impaired.

**Financial data** The stipend is $1,000. Funds are sent directly to the recipient's university or college to be used for tuition, books, laboratory fees, room, and board. They may not be used for sorority dues, house fees, or other chapter expenses.

**Duration** 1 year.

**Additional information** Information is also available from Betty Plaggemeier, P.O. Box 1492, Cypress, TX 77410-1492, (281) 370-2863.

**Number awarded** 1 each year.

**Deadline** February of each year.

## [618]
## WINGS OVER AMERICA SCHOLARSHIPS

Wings Over America Scholarship Foundation
1551 Dillingham Boulevard
Norfolk, VA 23511
E-mail: info@wingsoveramerica.us
Web: www.wingsoveramerica.us

**Summary** To provide financial assistance for college to dependents of naval aviators.

**Eligibility** This program is open to dependent children and spouses of naval air command personnel. Applicants must be planning to continue their education. Selection is based on academic merit, community service, and financial need.

**Financial data** A stipend is awarded (amount not specified).

**Duration** 1 year.

**Additional information** This foundation was established as Wings Over the Atlantic in 1986 and began awarding scholarships in 2000.

**Number awarded** Varies each year; recently, 31 of these scholarships were awarded.

## [619]
## WISCONSIN FEDERATION OF BUSINESS AND PROFESSIONAL WOMEN SCHOLARSHIP

Community Foundation for the Fox Valley Region, Inc.
Attn: Scholarships
4455 West Lawrence Street
P.O. Box 563
Appleton, WI 54912-0563
(920) 830-1290              Fax: (920) 830-1293
E-mail: cffvr@cffoxvalley.org
Web: www.cffoxvalley.org/scholarship_fundslist.html

**Summary** To provide financial assistance to mature women in Wisconsin who are working on an undergraduate or graduate degree.

**Eligibility** This program is open to Wisconsin women who are 25 years of age or older. Applicants must be attending a technical college or an accredited 2-year or 4-year college or university to work on an undergraduate or graduate degree. They must submit a personal statement of their reasons for working on a degree in their chosen field, including their special professional interests, goals, and purposes within that field.

**Financial data** The stipend is $500.

**Duration** 1 year.

**Additional information** This program is sponsored by the Wisconsin Business and Professional Women's Foundation Fund, 1067 Oak Street, Neenah, WI 54956, (262) 352-4617.

**Number awarded** 1 or more each year.

**Deadline** February of each year.

## [620]
## WISCONSIN JOB RETRAINING GRANTS

Wisconsin Department of Veterans Affairs
30 West Mifflin Street
P.O. Box 7843
Madison, WI 53707-7843
(608) 266-1311              Toll-free: (800) WIS-VETS
Fax: (608) 267-0403
E-mail: wdvaweb@dva.state.wi.us
Web: dva.state.wi.us/Ben_retraininggrants.asp

**Summary** To provide funds to recently unemployed Wisconsin veterans or their families who need financial assistance while being retrained for employment.

**Eligibility** This program is open to current residents of Wisconsin who 1) were residents of the state when they entered or reentered active duty in the U.S. armed forces, or 2) have moved to the state and have been residents for any consecutive 12-month period after entry or reentry into service. Applicants must have served on active duty for at least 2 continuous years or for at least 90 days during specified wartime periods. Unremarried spouses and minor or dependent children of deceased veterans who would have been eligible for the grant if they were living today may also

be eligible. The applicant must, within the year prior to the date of application, have become unemployed (involuntarily laid off or discharged, not due to willful misconduct) or underemployed (experienced an involuntary reduction of income). Underemployed applicants must have current annual income from employment that does not exceed federal poverty guidelines. All applicants must be retraining at accredited schools in Wisconsin or in a structured on-the-job program. Course work toward a college degree does not qualify. Training does not have to be full time, but the program must be completed within 2 years and must reasonably be expected to lead to employment.

**Financial data** The maximum grant is $3,000 per year; the actual amount varies, depending upon the amount of the applicant's unmet need. In addition to books, fees, and tuition, the funds may be used for living expenses.

**Duration** 1 year; may be renewed 1 additional year.

**Number awarded** Varies each year.

**Deadline** Applications may be submitted at any time.

## [621]
## WISCONSIN LEGION AUXILIARY HEALTH CAREER AWARDS

American Legion Auxiliary
Department of Wisconsin
Attn: Department Secretary/Treasurer
2930 American Legion Drive
P.O. Box 140
Portage, WI 53901-0140
(608) 745-0124              Toll-free: (866) 664-3863
Fax: (608) 745-1947
E-mail: alawi@amlegionauxwi.org
Web: www.amlegionauxwi.org

**Summary** To provide financial assistance for health-related education to the children and spouses of veterans in Wisconsin.

**Eligibility** This program is open to the children, wives, and widows of veterans who are entering a hospital, university, or technical school to prepare for a health-related career. Grandchildren and great-grandchildren of veterans are eligible if they are members of the American Legion Auxiliary. Applicants must have a GPA of 3.2 or higher and be in need of financial assistance. They must be residents of Wisconsin, although they do not need to attend school in the state. Along with their application, they must submit a 300-page essay on "The Importance of Health Careers Today."

**Financial data** The stipend is $750.

**Duration** 1 year; nonrenewable.

**Additional information** Information is also available from the Education Chair, Renae Allen, 206 West Fremont Street, Darien, WI 53114-1540, (262) 724-5059.

**Number awarded** 2 each year.

**Deadline** March of each year.

## [622]
## WISCONSIN LEGION AUXILIARY MERIT AND MEMORIAL SCHOLARSHIPS

American Legion Auxiliary
Department of Wisconsin
Attn: Department Secretary/Treasurer
2930 American Legion Drive
P.O. Box 140
Portage, WI 53901-0140
(608) 745-0124                    Toll-free: (866) 664-3863
Fax: (608) 745-1947
E-mail: alawi@amlegionauxwi.org
Web: www.amlegionauxwi.org

**Summary** To provide financial assistance for college to Wisconsin residents who are the children or spouses of veterans.

**Eligibility** This program is open to the children, wives, and widows of veterans who are high school seniors or graduates with a GPA of 3.2 or higher. Grandchildren and great-grandchildren of veterans are eligible if they are members of the American Legion Auxiliary. Applicants must be able to demonstrate financial need and be residents of Wisconsin, although they do not need to attend college in the state. Along with their application, they must submit a 300-word essay on "Education-An Investment in the Future."

**Financial data** The stipend is $1,000.

**Duration** 1 year; nonrenewable.

**Additional information** Information is also available from the Education Chair, Renae Allen, 206 West Fremont Street, Darien, WI 53114-1540, (262) 724-5059 This program includes the following named scholarships: the Harriet Hass Scholarship, the Adalin Macauley Scholarship, the Eleanor Smith Scholarship, the Pearl Behrend Scholarship, and the Barbara Kranig Scholarship.

**Number awarded** 6 each year.

**Deadline** March of each year.

## [623]
## WISCONSIN LEGION AUXILIARY REGISTERED NURSE DEGREE SCHOLARSHIP

American Legion Auxiliary
Department of Wisconsin
Attn: Department Secretary/Treasurer
2930 American Legion Drive
P.O. Box 140
Portage, WI 53901-0140
(608) 745-0124                    Toll-free: (866) 664-3863
Fax: (608) 745-1947
E-mail: alawi@amlegionauxwi.org
Web: www.amlegionauxwi.org

**Summary** To provide financial assistance for nursing education to the dependents of Wisconsin veterans.

**Eligibility** This program is open to the wives, widows, and children of Wisconsin veterans who are enrolled or have been accepted in an accredited school of nursing. Grandchildren and great-grandchildren of veterans are also eligible if they are American Legion Auxiliary members. All applicants must have a GPA of 3.2 or higher and be in financial need. They must be Wisconsin residents, but they do not need to attend school in the state. Along with their applica-

tion, they must submit a 300-word essay on "The Need for Trained Nurses Today."

**Financial data** The stipend is $750.

**Duration** 1 year.

**Additional information** Information is also available from the Education Chair, Renae Allen, 206 West Fremont Street, Darien, WI 53114-1540, (262) 724-5059. Recipients must attend an accredited hospital or university R.N. program.

**Number awarded** 2 each year.

**Deadline** March of each year.

## [624]
## WISCONSIN LEGION AUXILIARY STATE PRESIDENT'S SCHOLARSHIP

American Legion Auxiliary
Department of Wisconsin
Attn: Department Secretary/Treasurer
2930 American Legion Drive
P.O. Box 140
Portage, WI 53901-0140
(608) 745-0124                    Toll-free: (866) 664-3863
Fax: (608) 745-1947
E-mail: alawi@amlegionauxwi.org
Web: www.amlegionauxwi.org

**Summary** To provide financial assistance for college to members or the children of members of the American Legion Auxiliary in Wisconsin.

**Eligibility** Eligible are the members or children of members of the American Legion Auxiliary who are in need of financial aid to continue their education and are high school seniors or graduates with a GPA of 3.2 or higher. Applicants must be Wisconsin residents, but they are not required to attend college in the state. Along with their application, they must submit a 300-word essay on "Education-An Investment in the Future."

**Financial data** The stipend is $1,000.

**Duration** 1 year.

**Additional information** Information is also available from the Education Chair, Renae Allen, 206 West Fremont Street, Darien, WI 53114-1540, (262) 724-5059.

**Number awarded** 3 each year.

**Deadline** March of each year.

## [625]
## WISCONSIN SPACE GRANT CONSORTIUM UNDERGRADUATE SCHOLARSHIPS

Wisconsin Space Grant Consortium
c/o University of Wisconsin at Green Bay
Department of Natural and Applied Sciences
2420 Nicolet Drive
Green Bay, WI 54311-7001
(920) 465-2108                    Fax: (920) 465-2376
E-mail: wsgc@uwgb.edu
Web: www.uwgb.edu/wsgc/students/us.asp

**Summary** To provide financial assistance to undergraduate students at colleges and universities participating in the Wisconsin Space Grant Consortium (WSGC).

**Eligibility** This program is open to undergraduate students enrolled at universities participating in the WSGC.

Applicants must be U.S. citizens; be working full time on a bachelor's degree in space science, aerospace, or interdisciplinary space studies (including, but not limited to, engineering, the sciences, architecture, law, business, nursing, and medicine); and have a GPA of 3.0 or higher. The consortium especially encourages applications from underrepresented minorities, women, and students with disabilities. Selection is based on academic performance and space-related promise.

**Financial data**  Stipends up to $1,500 per year are available.

**Duration**  1 academic year.

**Additional information**  Funding for this program is provided by the U.S. National Aeronautics and Space Administration (NASA). The schools participating in the consortium include the University of Wisconsin campuses at Fox Valley, Green Bay, La Crosse, Madison, Milwaukee, Oshkosh, Parkside, Superior, and Whitewater; Alverno College; Marquette University; College of the Menominee Nation; Carroll College; Lawrence University; Milwaukee School of Engineering; Ripon College; Medical College of Wisconsin; Western Wisconsin Technical College; and Wisconsin Lutheran College.

**Number awarded**  Varies each year; recently, 26 of these scholarships were awarded.

**Deadline**  February of each year.

## [626]
## WISCONSIN TOWNS ASSOCIATION SCHOLARSHIPS

Wisconsin Towns Association
Attn: Scholarship Program
W7686 County Road MMM
Shawano, WI 54166-6086
(715) 526-3157                    Fax: (715) 524-3917
E-mail: wtastaff@wisctowns.com
Web: www.wisctowns.com

**Summary**  To provide financial assistance for college to high school seniors in Wisconsin who submit outstanding essays on town government in the state.

**Eligibility**  This program is open to seniors graduating from high schools in Wisconsin who plan to attend a college, university, or vocational/technical institute in the state. Applicants must submit an essay of 500 to 1,000 words on the topic, "What about the history of town government has made town government effective in Wisconsin." Selection is based primarily on the essay's originality and subject matter in relationship to the topic. Boys and girls are judged separately.

**Financial data**  The stipend is $750.

**Duration**  1 year.

**Additional information**  This program is supported by Rural Mutual Insurance Company, 1241 John Q. Hammons Drive, Suite 200, P.O. Box 5555, Madison, WI 53705-0555.

**Number awarded**  4 each year: 2 to boys and 2 to girls.

**Deadline**  May of each year.

## [627]
## WISCONSIN WOMEN IN GOVERNMENT, INC.

Wisconsin Women in Government Scholars Program
Attn: Scholarship Committee
P.O. Box 2543
Madison, WI 53701
(608) 848-2321
E-mail: info@WiscWomeninGovernment.org
Web: www.WiscWomeninGovernment.org

**Summary**  To provide financial assistance to women in Wisconsin interested in attending a college or university in the state to prepare for a career in public service.

**Eligibility**  This program is open to women in Wisconsin who are enrolled full or part time at an institution that is a member of the University of Wisconsin system, the Wisconsin Technical College System, or a private college in the state. Applicants must have a GPA of 2.75 or higher and be able to demonstrate financial need. They must possess leadership potential, initiative, and excellent communication skills and have an interest in public service, government, and the political process. Juniors and seniors must have declared a major. Selection is based on leadership, demonstrated ability to handle responsibility, initiative, communication skills, academic achievement, community involvement, and commitment to public service.

**Financial data**  The stipend is $2,500 per year. Funds may be used for tuition, school supplies, child care, or to reduce loan burden.

**Duration**  1 year; may be renewed.

**Number awarded**  6 each year.

**Deadline**  April of each year.

## [628]
## WOMEN IN AVIATION, INTERNATIONAL ACHIEVEMENT AWARDS

Women in Aviation, International
Attn: Scholarships
Morningstar Airport
3647 State Route 503 South
West Alexandria, OH 45381
(937) 558-7655                    Fax: (937) 839-4645
E-mail: scholarships@wai.org
Web: www.wai.org/education/scholarships.cfm

**Summary**  To provide financial assistance to members of Women in Aviation, International (WAI) who are working on a college degree or other training in the aviation field.

**Eligibility**  This program is open to WAI members who are attending a college or university on a full-time basis, and preparing for a career in aviation or a related field. Also eligible are women who are not in college but are interested in an aviation topic, such as attending space camp, working on a private pilot license, or pursuing another aviation objective. All applicants should submit a 500-word essay on their background and goals, 3 letters of recommendation, a resume, copies of all aviation and medical certificates, and the last 3 pages of their pilot logbook, if applicable. Selection is based on achievements, attitude toward self and others, commitment to success, dedication to career, financial need, motivation, reliability, responsibility, and teamwork.

**Financial data**  The stipend is $750.

**Duration** 1 year.

**Additional information** WAI is a nonprofit professional organization dedicated to encouraging women to consider an aviation career, providing educational outreach activities, and providing networking opportunities to women active in the industry.

**Number awarded** 2 each year: 1 college scholarship and 1 non-college scholarship.

**Deadline** November of each year.

## [629]
## WOMEN IN CORPORATE AVIATION CAREER SCHOLARSHIP

Women in Aviation, International
Attn: Scholarships
Morningstar Airport
3647 State Route 503 South
West Alexandria, OH 45381
(937) 558-7655                    Fax: (937) 839-4645
E-mail: scholarships@wai.org
Web: www.wai.org/education/scholarships.cfm

**Summary** To provide financial assistance to members of Women in Aviation, International (WAI) who are interested in career development activities in corporate aviation.

**Eligibility** This program is open to WAI members interested in continued pursuit of a career in any job classification in corporate or business aviation. Applicants must be interested in participating in the NBAA Professional Development Program (PDP) courses, flight training, dispatcher training, upgrades in aviation education, or similar activities. General business course work is ineligible. Applicants should be actively working toward their goal and be able to show financial need.

**Financial data** The stipend is $1,000.

**Additional information** WAI is a nonprofit professional organization dedicated to encouraging women to consider an aviation career, providing educational outreach activities, and providing networking opportunities to women active in the industry.

**Number awarded** 1 each year.

**Deadline** November of each year.

## [630]
## WOMEN IN NEED SCHOLARSHIPS

Educational Foundation for Women in Accounting
Attn: Foundation Administrator
P.O. Box 1925
Southeastern, PA 19399-1925
(610) 407-9229                    Fax: (610) 644-3713
E-mail: info@efwa.org
Web: www.efwa.org/witwin.htm

**Summary** To provide financial support to currently-enrolled women accounting students who are the sole source of support for themselves and their families.

**Eligibility** This program is open to women who, either through divorce or death of a spouse, have become the sole source of support for themselves and their family. They must wish to work on a degree in accounting as a means to gainful employment. Women who are single parents as a result of other circumstances are also considered. Appli-

cants should be in their third, fourth, or fifth year of study. Selection is based on aptitude for accounting, commitment to the goal of working on a degree in accounting (including evidence of continued commitment after receiving this award), clear evidence that the candidate has established goals and a plan for achieving those goals, and financial need.

**Financial data** The stipend is $2,000 per year.

**Duration** 1 year; may be renewed 1 additional year if the recipient completes at least 12 hours each semester.

**Number awarded** 1 each year.

**Deadline** April of each year.

## [631]
## WOMEN IN SCIENCE AND TECHNOLOGY SCHOLARSHIP

Business and Professional Women of Virginia
Attn: Virginia BPW Foundation
P.O. Box 4842
McLean, VA 22103-4842
Web: www.bpwva.org/scholarships.shtml

**Summary** To provide financial assistance to women in Virginia who are interested in working on a bachelor's or advanced degree in science or technology.

**Eligibility** This program is open to women who are at least 18 years of age, U.S. citizens, Virginia residents, accepted at or currently studying at a Virginia college or university, and working on a bachelor's, master's, or doctoral degree in 1 of the following fields: actuarial science, biology, bioengineering, chemistry, computer science, dentistry, engineering, mathematics, medicine, physics, or a similar scientific or technical field. Applicants must have a definite plan to use their education in a scientific or technical profession. They must be able to demonstrate financial need.

**Financial data** Stipends range from $500 to $1,000 per year, depending on the need of the recipient; funds may be used for tuition, fees, books, transportation, living expenses, and dependent care.

**Duration** 1 year; recipients may reapply (but prior recipients are not given priority).

**Additional information** Recipients must complete their studies within 2 years.

**Number awarded** At least 1 each year.

**Deadline** March of each year.

## [632]
## WOMEN IN SPORTS DAY SCHOLARSHIPS

Delaware Women's Alliance for Sport and Fitness
c/o Evelyn Campbell, Scholarship Committee Chair
Howard High School of Technology
401 East 12th Street
Wilmington, DE 19801
(302) 571-5422           E-mail: scholarships@dwasf.org
Web: wwww.dwasf.org/scholarships.html

**Summary** To provide financial assistance to female graduating high school seniors in Delaware who have significantly contributed to sports at the varsity level.

**Eligibility** This program is open to female high school seniors in Delaware who have a GPA of 3.0 or higher and have participated in at least 1 varsity sport. Applicants must submit 1) a student profile describing their sports participation, school activities, community activities, and career objectives; 2) a short paragraph describing why they feel they are deserving of this scholarship; and 3) 3 letters of recommendation. Financial need is not considered in the selection process.

**Financial data**   The stipend ranges from $500 to $1,000.

**Duration**   1 year.

**Number awarded**   Several each year.

**Deadline**   April of each year.

## [633]
## WOMEN IN TECHNOLOGY SCHOLARSHIP

Morgan Stanley
c/o Joyce Arencibia, IT College Recruiting
750 Seventh Avenue, 30th Floor
New York, NY 10019
(212) 762-4000
E-mail: diversityrecruiting@morganstanley.com
Web: www.morganstanley.com

**Summary**   To provide financial assistance and work experience to women who are working on an undergraduate degree in computer science or engineering.

**Eligibility**   This program is open to women who are enrolled in their sophomore or junior year of college (or the third or fourth year of a 5-year program). Applicants must be enrolled full time and have a GPA of 3.0 or higher. They must be willing to commit to a paid summer internship in the Morgan Stanley Information Technology Division. All majors and disciplines are eligible, but preference is given to students preparing for a career in computer science or engineering. Along with their application, they must submit 1-page essays on 1) why they are applying for this scholarship and why they should be selected as a recipient; 2) a technical project on which they worked, either through a university course or previous work experience, their role in the project, and how they contributed to the end result; and 3) a software, hardware, or new innovative application of existing technology that they would create if they could and the impact it would have. Financial need is not considered in the selection process.

**Financial data**   Students who receive a scholarship as juniors (or fourth-year students in a 5-year program) receive $10,000 for their final year of college. Students who receive a scholarship as sophomores (or third-year students in a 5-year program) receive $5,000 for their junior year (or fourth year of a 5-year program).

**Duration**   1 year; may be renewed for the final year for students who receive a scholarship as sophomores (or third-year students in a 5-year program).

**Additional information**   The program includes a paid summer internship in the Morgan Stanley Information Technology Division in the summer following the time of application.

**Number awarded**   1 or more each year.

**Deadline**   February of each year.

## [634]
## WOMEN IN TRANSITION ACCOUNTING SCHOLARSHIP

Educational Foundation for Women in Accounting
Attn: Foundation Administrator
P.O. Box 1925
Southeastern, PA 19399-1925
(610) 407-9229                    Fax: (610) 644-3713
E-mail: info@efwa.org
Web: www.efwa.org/witwin.htm

**Summary**   To provide financial support to women who have become the sole support of their family and wish to begin work on an undergraduate accounting degree.

**Eligibility**   This program is open to women who, either through divorce of death of a spouse, have become the sole source of support for themselves and their family. They must wish to work on a degree in accounting as a means to gainful employment. Women who are single parents as a result of other circumstances are also considered. Applicants should be incoming or current freshmen, or they may be returning to school with sufficient credits to qualify for freshman status. Selection is based on aptitude for accounting, commitment to the goal of working on a degree in accounting (including evidence of continued commitment after receiving this award), clear evidence that the candidate has established goals and a plan for achieving those goals, and financial need.

**Financial data**   The stipend is $4,000 per year.

**Duration**   1 year; may be renewed 3 additional years if the recipient completes at least 12 hours each semester.

**Additional information**   This program, established in 1990, was formerly called the Displaced Homemaker's Scholarship.

**Number awarded**   1 each year.

**Deadline**   April of each year.

## [635]
## WOMEN MILITARY AVIATORS MEMORIAL SCHOLARSHIP

Women in Aviation, International
Attn: Scholarships
Morningstar Airport
3647 State Route 503 South
West Alexandria, OH 45381
(937) 558-7655                    Fax: (937) 839-4645
E-mail: scholarships@wai.org
Web: www.wai.org/education/scholarships.cfm

**Summary**   To provide financial assistance to members of Women in Aviation, International (WAI) who are interested in flight training or academic study.

**Eligibility**   This program is open to WAI members who are 1) academic students interested in a program of study at an accredited institution or school; or 2) flight students interested in training for an FAA private pilot rating. Applicants. must submit an application form, 3 letters of recommendation, a 500-word essay on their aviation dream and how they hope to use this scholarship to achieve it, a resume, and copies of all aviation and medical certificates. Selection is based on the applicant's ambition to further women in aviation, demonstrated persistence and determination, financial need, ability to complete training, and ability to bring honor to the women of Women Military Aviators, Inc. (WMA).

**Financial data** The stipend is $2,500.

**Duration** Recipients must be able to complete training within 1 year.

**Additional information** WAI is a nonprofit professional organization dedicated to encouraging women to consider an aviation career, providing educational outreach activities, and providing networking opportunities to women active in the industry. WMA established this program in 2005 to honor the women aviators who are serving or have served in Iraq and Afghanistan.

**Number awarded** 1 each year.

**Deadline** November of each year.

## [636]
## WOMEN WHO MADE A DIFFERENCE SCHOLARSHIPS

Arizona Business and Professional Women's
    Foundation
Attn: Administrator
P.O. Box 521
Clifton, AZ 85533
(928) 687-1300          E-mail: vcpage@aznex.net
Web: www.arizonabpwfoundation.com

**Summary** To provide financial assistance to women in Arizona who are attending or interested in attending a community college or university in the state.

**Eligibility** This program is open to women, at least 20 years of age, who are attending a community college or university in Arizona. Applicants must fall into 1 of the following categories: women who have been out of the workforce and wish to upgrade their skills; women with no previous experience in the workforce who are seeking a marketable skill, and women who are currently employed who are interested in career advancement or change. Along with their application, they must submit 2 letters of recommendation, a statement of financial need (latest income tax return must be provided), a career goal statement, and their most recent transcript (when available). Preference is given to members of Arizona Business and Professional Women.

**Financial data** The stipend is $1,000.

**Duration** 1 year.

**Additional information** This program was established in 1992 with proceeds from the book, *Women Who Made a Difference.* It was originally limited to BPW members only, but is now open to all students.

**Number awarded** 1 or more each year.

**Deadline** February of each year.

## [637]
## WOMEN@MICROSOFT HOPPERS SCHOLARSHIP

Fargo-Moorhead Area Foundation
Attn: Gifts and Grants Specialist
502 First Avenue North, Suite 202
Fargo, ND 58102-4804
(701) 234-0756     E-mail: wendy@areafoundation.org
Web: www.areafoundation.org/page27556.cfm

**Summary** To provide financial assistance to women who

are interested in studying computer science at a college or university in Minnesota or the Dakotas.

**Eligibility** This program is open to women who are accepted or enrolled in a college or university in Minnesota, North Dakota, or South Dakota. Applicants must be undergraduates with a declared major of either computer science or a related computer science discipline and a GPA of 3.0 or higher. Along with their application, they must submit essays, up to 500 words each, on 2 of the following topics: 1) What do you see as the computer industry's primary shortcomings? If you were a leader in the technical world today, in what direction would you guide technology and why? 2) Why have you chosen a degree in the discipline you are currently pursuing? 3) Describe a coding, class, or work project related to your field of study that you significantly contributed towards; describe your contribution and what impact this project had on you or others. Along with the essays, selection is based on extracurricular activities, awards and honors, community service, work experience, letters of recommendation, and transcripts.

**Financial data** The stipend is $1,500.

**Duration** 1 year.

**Additional information** This program was established in 1990 as part of an effort to make Microsoft a great place for women. In addition to scholarships, other Hoppers committees deal with outreach, technical women, mentoring, career development, and diversity. The program is named for Grace Hopper, a computer science pioneer.

**Number awarded** 1 each year.

**Deadline** March of each year.

## [638]
## WOMEN'S ALABAMA GOLF ASSOCIATION SCHOLARSHIPS

Women's Alabama Golf Association
1025 Montgomery Highway, Suite 210
Birmingham, AL 35216
E-mail: info@womensalabamagolf.com
Web: womensalabamagolf.com/Scholarships.asp

**Summary** To provide financial assistance for college to women in Alabama who can demonstrate an interest in golf.

**Eligibility** This program is open to women graduating from high schools in Alabama who are planning to attend a college or university in the state. Applicants must be able to demonstrate an interest in the game of golf and financial need. They must have an ACT score of 22 or higher. Along with their application, they must submit a 200-word statement on why a college education is important to them. Selection is based on academic excellence, citizenship, sportsmanship, community involvement, and financial need.

**Financial data** The stipend is $2,000 per year.

**Duration** 1 year; may be renewed if the recipient maintains a GPA of 2.4 or higher during her freshman year and 2.8 or higher during subsequent years.

**Additional information** This program, established in 1993, includes the Stone Hodo Scholarship and the Ann Samford Upchurch Scholarship. Information is also available from Mrs. H.E. Watlington, 3309 Sommerville Drive, Montgomery, AL 36111, (334) 264-6102.

**Number awarded** 1 each year.

**Deadline** March of each year.

## [639]
## WOMEN'S BASKETBALL COACHES ASSOCIATION SCHOLARSHIP AWARDS

Women's Basketball Coaches Association
Attn: Manager of Awards
4646 Lawrenceville Highway
Lilburn, GA 30047-3620
(770) 279-8027, ext. 102        Fax: (770) 279-6290
E-mail: alowe@wbca.org
Web: www.wbca.org/WBCAScholarAward.asp

**Summary** To provide financial assistance for undergraduate or graduate study to women's basketball players.

**Eligibility** This program is open to women's basketball players who are competing in any of the 4 intercollegiate divisions (NCAA Divisions I, II, and III, and NAIA). Applicants must be interested in completing an undergraduate degree or beginning work on an advanced degree. They must be nominated by a member of the Women's Basketball Coaches Association (WBCA). Selection is based on sportsmanship, commitment to excellence as a student-athlete, honesty, ethical behavior, courage, and dedication to purpose.

**Financial data** The stipend is $1,000 per year.

**Duration** 1 year.

**Number awarded** 2 each year.

## [640]
## WOMEN'S BUSINESS ALLIANCE SCHOLARSHIP PROGRAM

Choice Hotels International
Attn: Foundation
10750 Columbia Pike
Silver Spring, MD 20901
(301) 592-6258
Web: www.choicehotels.com

**Summary** To provide financial assistance to women interested in preparing for a career in the hospitality industry.

**Eligibility** This program is open to female high school seniors, undergraduates, and graduate students. Applicants must be U.S. citizens or permanent residents interested in preparing for a career in the hospitality industry. They must submit an essay of 500 words or less on their experience or interest in the hospitality industry and how it relates to their career goals, including any community service experience that has impacted their career goals or their interest in the industry. Financial need is not considered in the selection process.

**Financial data** The stipend is $2,000.

**Duration** 1 year; recipients may reapply.

**Number awarded** 2 or more each year.

**Deadline** January or July of each year.

## [641]
## WOMEN'S ENVIRONMENTAL COUNCIL SCHOLARSHIPS

Women's Environmental Council
Attn: Scholarship Chair
P.O. Box 36
Solano Beach, CA 92075
E-mail: C2CEnvironmental@aol.com
Web: www.wecweb.org

**Summary** To provide financial assistance to women from any state working on an undergraduate or graduate degree in an environmental field at colleges and universities in southern California.

**Eligibility** This program is open to female undergraduate and graduate students at colleges and universities in Los Angeles, Orange, and San Diego counties in California. Applicants must be studying such environmental fields as architecture, biology, chemistry, environmental science, ecology, engineering, forestry, geology, or urban planning. They must have a GPA of 3.0 or higher. Along with their application, they must submit a personal statement that includes a description of their environmental commitment and activities, how they became interested in environmental issues, and how they plan to apply the knowledge they gain through the use of this scholarship to improve environmental conditions and pursue their environmental professional and personal goals. Selection is based on that statement (50%); personal incentive, volunteerism, and extracurricular activities (20%); grades and course work (20%); and a letter of references (10%).

**Financial data** The stipend is $1,300. Recipients are also given a 1-year membership in the Women's Environmental Council (WEC).

**Duration** 1 year.

**Additional information** The WEC, founded in 1993, currently has chapters in Los Angeles, Orange County, and San Diego. Recipients are expected to attend the WEC annual meeting in the spring to receive their awards.

**Number awarded** Varies each year; recently, 6 of these scholarships were awarded.

**Deadline** January of each year.

## [642]
## WOMEN'S GOLF ASSOCIATION OF MASSACHUSETTS JUNIOR SCHOLAR PROGRAM

Women's Golf Association of Massachusetts, Inc.
Attn: WGAM Junior Scholarship Fund, Inc.
William F. Connell Golf House & Museum
300 Arnold Palmer Boulevard
Norton, MA 02766
(774) 430-9010        Fax: (774) 430-9011
E-mail: info@wgam.org
Web: www.wgam.org/Junior/jrschol.htm

**Summary** To provide financial assistance for college to women golfers from Massachusetts.

**Eligibility** This program is open to junior girl golfers who have participated in the Women's Golf Association of Massachusetts (WGAM) junior golf program. Applicants must be attending or planning to attend a college or university. Selection is based on high school academic record and performance, leadership qualities, community and civic involvement, character, personality, and extent of participation in the WGAM junior golf program. Financial need may determine the size of the stipend, but it is not considered in the selection process. An interview is required.

**Financial data**   A stipend is awarded (amount not specified).

**Duration**   1 year; may be renewed.

**Additional information**   This program was established in 1985.

**Number awarded**   Varies each year; recently, 8 of these scholarships were awarded.

**Deadline**   May of each year.

## [643]
## WOMEN'S JEWELRY ASSOCIATION SCHOLARSHIP

Women's Jewelry Association
Attn: Scholarship Committee
373 B Route 46 West, Building E, Suite 215
Fairfield, NJ 07004
(973) 575-7190                    Fax: (973) 575-1445
E-mail: info@womensjewelry.org
Web: www.womensjewelry.org/scholarships.html

**Summary**   To provide financial assistance for college to women who are interested in careers in jewelry.

**Eligibility**   Women who are enrolled in a jewelry-related curriculum at an institution of higher learning located anywhere in the United States are eligible to apply. Eligible fields of study range from design to gemological analysis and include metalsmithing, finance, business, and marketing. Applicants must submit 2 letters of recommendation, a short essay explaining why they wish to prepare for a career in jewelry/toolmaking and their aspirations for the future, 3 slides showing examples of their work, and a list of 3 courses related to jewelry that have been most important to them. Financial need is considered in the selection process.

**Financial data**   Stipends range from $500 to $5,000 per year.

**Duration**   1 year.

**Additional information**   This program includes the June Herman Scholarship of $5,000, awarded for the first time in 2001.

**Number awarded**   Varies each year. Recently, 12 of these scholarships were awarded: 1 at $5,000, 2 at $3,000, 1 at $2,500, 1 at $1,500 and 7 at $1,000.

**Deadline**   April of each year.

## [644]
## WOMEN'S OPPORTUNITY AWARDS PROGRAM

Soroptimist International of the Americas
Attn: Program Department
1709 Spruce Street
Philadelphia, PA 19103-6103
(215) 893-9000                    Fax: (215) 893-5200
E-mail: siahq@soroptimist.org
Web: www.soroptimist.org

**Summary**   To provide financial assistance to women reentering the job market to upgrade their employment status through education.

**Eligibility**   This program is open to mature women who are the heads of their households with financial responsibility for their family. Applicants must have been accepted to a vocational/skills training program or an undergraduate degree program. They must reside in 1 of the 19 countries or territories that are part of Soroptimist International of the Americas. Along with their application, they must submit 1) a 300-word description of their career goals and how their education and/or skills training support those goals; 2) a 750-word essay on the economic and personal hardships they have faced and their plans to gain additional skills, training, and education; and 3) documentation of financial need.

**Financial data**   Awards are $10,000, $5,000, or $3,000.

**Duration**   The awards are issued each year and are nonrenewable.

**Additional information**   This program, established in 1972, was formerly known as the Training Awards Program. The awards may not be used for graduate study or international travel. Applications are to be processed through the local Soroptimist club. Countries that are part of Soroptimist International of the Americas include Argentina, Bolivia, Brazil, Canada, Chile, Costa Rica, Ecuador, Guam, Japan, Republic of Korea, Mexico, Panama, Paraguay, Peru, Philippines, Puerto Rico, Taiwan, United States, and Venezuela.

**Number awarded**   In each of the 28 regions, the winner receives an award of $5,000; most regions grant additional $3,000 awards. From among the regional winners, 3 receive an additional award of $10,000 from Soroptimist International of the Americas. Since the program was established, it has awarded approximately $15 million in scholarships to more than 22,500 women.

**Deadline**   Applications must be submitted to local clubs by November of each year.

## [645]
## WOMEN'S OVERSEAS SERVICE LEAGUE SCHOLARSHIPS FOR WOMEN

Women's Overseas Service League
P.O. Box 7124
Washington, DC 20044-7124
E-mail: chabgood@world-net.net
Web: www.wosl.org/scholarships.htm

**Summary**   To provide financial assistance for college to women who are committed to a military or other public service career.

**Eligibility**   This program is open to women who are committed to a military or other public service career. Applicants must have completed at least 12 semester or 18 quarter hours of postsecondary study with at a GPA of 2.5 or higher. They must be working on an academic degree (the program may be professional or technical in nature) and must agree to enroll for at least 6 semester or 9 quarter hours of study each academic period. Along with their application, they must submit an official transcript, a 1-page essay on their career goals, 3 current letters of reference, and a brief statement describing sources of financial support and the need for scholarship assistance. They must also provide information on their educational background, employment experience, civic and volunteer activities, and expected degree completion date.

**Financial data** Stipends range from $500 to $1,000 per year.

**Duration** 1 year; may be renewed 1 additional year.

**Additional information** The Women's Overseas Service League is a national organization of women who have served overseas in or with the armed forces.

**Deadline** February of each year.

## [646]
## WOMEN'S SECOND CHANCE COLLEGE SCHOLARSHIP

Community Foundation of Louisville
Attn: Director of Grants
Waterfront Plaza, Suite 1110
325 West Main Street
Louisville, KY 40202-4251
(502) 585-4649, ext. 1005          Fax: (502) 587-7484
E-mail: info@cflouisville.org
Web: www.cflouisville.org

**Summary** To provide financial assistance for college to mature female residents of Kentucky and southern Indiana.

**Eligibility** This program is open to women between 25 and 40 years of age who reside in Kentucky or the Indiana counties of Clark, Crawford, Floyd, Harrison, Scott, or Washington. Applicants must have a high school diploma or GED certificate and may have some college credits. They must commit to attend a participating college or university and complete a baccalaureate degree within an agreed upon period of time. Selection is based on financial need and desire to learn.

**Financial data** The stipend is at least $500 per year.

**Duration** 1 year; renewable until completion of a baccalaureate degree if the recipient maintains a GPA of 2.5 or higher.

**Number awarded** 1 or more each year.

**Deadline** February of each year.

## [647]
## WOMEN'S SOUTHERN GOLF ASSOCIATION SCHOLARSHIP

Women's Southern Golf Association
c/o Martha Lang
2075 Knollwood Place
Birmingham, AL 34242
(205) 995-6671
E-mail: scholarship@womens-southerngolfassociation.org
Web: www.womens-southerngolfassociation.org

**Summary** To provide financial assistance for college to women golfers in the southern states.

**Eligibility** This program is open to amateur female golfers who are residents of the 1 of the 15 southern states (Alabama, Arkansas, Florida, Georgia, Kentucky, Louisiana, Maryland, Mississippi, North Carolina, Oklahoma, South Carolina, Tennessee, Texas, Virginia, and West Virginia) or the District of Columbia. Applicants must be graduating high school seniors planning to work on an undergraduate degree at an accredited institution of higher learning. Along with their application, they must submit a 200-word essay on why a college education is important to them. Selection

is based on academic excellence, citizenship, sportsmanship, and financial need.

**Financial data** The stipend is $3,000 per year. Funds are paid directly to the recipient's college.

**Duration** 1 year; may be renewed up to 3 additional years if the recipient maintains a GPA of 3.0 or higher.

**Additional information** This scholarship was first awarded in 1973.

**Number awarded** 1 each year.

**Deadline** May of each year.

## [648]
## WOMEN'S TRANSPORTATION SEMINAR CHAPTER OF COLORADO ANNUAL SCHOLARSHIPS

Women's Transportation Seminar-Colorado Chapter
c/o Chris Proud, Scholarship Chair
CH2M Hill
9193 South Jamaica Street, South Building
Englewood, CO 80112
(720) 286-5702          Fax: (720) 286-9732
E-mail: Chris.Proud@ch2m.com
Web: www.wtsinternational.org

**Summary** To provide financial assistance to female undergraduate and graduate students in Colorado and Wyoming preparing for a career in transportation.

**Eligibility** This program is open to women at colleges and universities in Colorado and Wyoming who are working on a bachelor's or graduate degree in a field related to transportation. Those fields may include engineering (civil, electrical, or mechanical), urban planning, finance, aviation, transit, or railways. Applicants must submit an essay on their career goals after graduation and why they should receive this scholarship. Minorities are especially encouraged to apply.

**Financial data** Undergraduate stipends are $1,000 or $800. Graduate stipends are $1,200.

**Duration** 1 year.

**Additional information** Winners are also nominated for scholarships offered by the national organization of the Women's Transportation Seminar.

**Number awarded** 3 each year: 2 to undergraduates and 1 to a graduate student.

**Deadline** November of each year.

## [649]
## WOMEN'S WESTERN GOLF FOUNDATION SCHOLARSHIP

Women's Western Golf Foundation
c/o Mrs. Richard Willis
393 Ramsay Road
Deerfield, IL 60015
Web: www.wwga.org/scholarship_info.htm

**Summary** To provide undergraduate scholarships to high school senior girls who are interested in the sport of golf.

**Eligibility** Applicants must be high school senior girls who intend to graduate in the year they submit their application. They must meet entrance requirements of, and plan to enroll at, an accredited college or university. Selection is based on academic achievement, financial need, excellence of character, and involvement with the sport of golf. Skill or excellence in the game is not a criterion.

**Financial data** The stipend is $2,000 per year. The funds are to be used to pay for room, board, tuition, and other university fees or charges.

**Duration** 1 year; may be renewed up to 3 additional years if the recipient maintains a GPA of 3.0 or higher.

**Number awarded** 15 each year.

**Deadline** February of each year.

## [650]
## WPS RESOURCES FOUNDATION BUSINESS AND TECHNOLOGY SCHOLARSHIPS

Wisconsin Public Service Corporation
Attn: WPS Resources Foundation, Inc.
c/o Scholarship Assessment Service
P.O. Box 5189
Appleton, WI 54912-5189
(920) 832-8322
Web: www.wpsr.com/community/minoritybus.asp

**Summary** To provide financial assistance to women and minority upper-division students who are majoring in business or engineering at universities in selected states.

**Eligibility** This program is open to women and African American, Native American, Asian American, and Hispanic students who are enrolled full time as a junior or senior with a GPA of 2.8 or higher. Applicants must be attending a college or university in Illinois, Indiana, Iowa, Michigan, Minnesota, or Wisconsin. They must be majoring in business or engineering (chemical, civil, computer, electrical, environmental, industrial, or mechanical). Along with their application, they must submit a 500-word essay on renewable energy, future generation, or competitive markets.

**Financial data** The stipend is $1,500.

**Duration** 1 year; may be renewed if the recipient remains in good academic standing.

**Number awarded** Varies each year; recently, 15 of these scholarships were awarded.

**Deadline** January of each year.

## [651]
## WTS PUGET SOUND CHAPTER SCHOLARSHIP

Women's Transportation Seminar-Puget Sound Chapter
c/o Kristin Overleese, Scholarship Chair
City of Shoreline, Capital Projects Manager
17544 Midvale Avenue North
Shoreline, WA 98133-4821
(206) 546-1700          Fax: (206) 546-2200
TDD: (206) 546-0457
Web: www.wtsinternational.org/puget_sound

**Summary** To provide financial assistance to women undergraduate and graduate students from Washington who are working on a degree related to transportation and have financial need.

**Eligibility** This program is open to women who are residents of Washington, studying at a college in the state, or working as an intern in the state. Applicants must be currently enrolled in an undergraduate or graduate degree program in a transportation-related field, such as engineering, planning, finance, or logistics. They must have a GPA of 3.0

or higher and plans to prepare for a career in a transportation-related field. Minority candidates are encouraged to apply. Along with their application, they must submit a 500-word statement about their career goals after graduation, their financial need, and why they think they should receive this scholarship award. Selection is based on transportation goals, academic record, transportation-related activities or job skills, and financial need.

**Financial data** The stipend is $1,500.

**Duration** 1 year.

**Additional information** The winner is also nominated for scholarships offered by the national organization of the Women's Transportation Seminar.

**Number awarded** 1 each year.

**Deadline** October of each year.

## [652]
## WYOMING EDUCATION BENEFITS FOR NATIONAL GUARD FAMILY MEMBERS

Wyoming Veterans' Commission
Wyoming Army National Guard Armory
5905 CY Avenue, Room 101
Casper, WY 82604
(307) 265-7372    Toll-free: (800) 833-5987 (within WY)
Fax: (307) 265-7392          E-mail: wvac@bresnan.net

**Summary** To provide financial assistance for college to dependents of deceased and disabled members of the Wyoming National Guard.

**Eligibility** This program is open to children and spouses of Wyoming National Guard members who have died or sustained permanent total disability from duty as a Guard member while on state active duty or another authorized training duty. Applicants must be attending or planning to attend the University of Wyoming or a junior college or vocational training institution in the state.

**Financial data** Payment of tuition and fees is provided by this program.

**Additional information** Applications may be obtained from the institution the applicant is attending or planning to attend.

**Number awarded** Varies each year.

**Deadline** Applications may be submitted at any time, but they should be received 2 or 3 weeks before the beginning of the semester.

## [653]
## YOUNG LADIES' RADIO LEAGUE SCHOLARSHIP

Foundation for Amateur Radio, Inc.
Attn: Scholarship Committee
P.O. Box 831
Riverdale, MD 20738
E-mail: aa3of@arrl.net
Web: www.amateurradio-far.org/scholarships.php

**Summary** To provide funding to licensed radio amateurs (especially women) who are interested in earning a bachelor's or graduate degree in the United States.

**Eligibility** Applicants must have at least an FCC Technician Class or equivalent foreign authorization and intend to work on a bachelor's or graduate degree in the United

States. There are no restrictions on the course of study or residency location. Preference is given to female applicants.

**Financial data** The stipend is $1,500.

**Duration** 1 year.

**Additional information** This program is sponsored by the Young Ladies' Radio League. It includes the following named scholarships: the Ethel Smith-K4LMB Memorial Scholarship and the Mary Lou Brown-NM7N Memorial Scholarship. Recipients must attend an accredited school (university, college, or technical institute) on a full-time basis.

**Number awarded** 2 each year.

**Deadline** Requests for applications must be submitted by April of each year.

## [654]
## YOUTH-PAC SCHOLARSHIP FUND

Alpha Kappa Alpha Sorority, Inc.
Attn: Educational Advancement Foundation
5656 South Stony Island Avenue
Chicago, IL 60637
(773) 947-0026          Toll-free: (800) 653-6528
Fax: (773) 947-0277          E-mail: akaeaf@aol.com
Web: www.akaeaf.org/scholarships.htm

**Summary** To provide financial assistance for college to members of Alpha Kappa Alpha sorority.

**Eligibility** This program is open to members of the organization, a traditionally African American women's sorority. Applicants must 1) have a GPA of 3.0 or higher, 2) be at least sophomores, 3) have demonstrated exceptional community service and involvement, 4) submit 2 letters of recommendation, and 5) submit a statement (up to 250 words) on their aspirations, goals, and community involvement.

**Financial data** Award amounts are determined by the availability of funds. Recently, a total of $10,000 was available for this program.

**Duration** 1 year; nonrenewable.

**Additional information** This program, the Youth Partners Accessing Capital, is administered by undergraduate members of Alpha Kappa Alpha.

**Number awarded** At least 2 each year.

**Deadline** January of each year.

## [655]
## ZAROUHI Y. GETSOYAN SCHOLARSHIP

Armenian International Women's Association
65 Main Street, Room 3A
Watertown, MA 02472
(617) 926-0171          E-mail: aiwainc@aol.com
Web: www.aiwa-net.org/scholarshipinfo.html

**Summary** To provide financial assistance to Armenian women who are upper-division and graduate students.

**Eligibility** This program is open to full-time women students of Armenian descent attending an accredited college or university. Applicants must be full-time juniors, seniors, or graduate students with a GPA of 3.2 or higher. They must submit an essay, up to 500 words, describing their planned academic program, their career goals, and the reasons why they believe they should be awarded this scholarship. Selection is based on financial need and merit.

**Financial data** The stipend is $500.

**Duration** 1 year.

**Number awarded** 1 or more each year.

**Deadline** April of each year.

## [656]
## ZETA STATE GRANT-IN-AID

Delta Kappa Gamma Society International-Zeta State
    Organization
Attn: Professional Affairs Committee
875 William Boulevard, Apartment 305
Ridgeland, MS 39157
Web: www.deltakappagamma.org/MS

**Summary** To provide financial assistance to female college seniors in Mississippi who are preparing for a career in education.

**Eligibility** This program is open to female residents of Mississippi who are attending a college or university in the state. Applicants must be entering their senior year and have demonstrated an aptitude for and desire to prepare for a career in the field of education. Along with their application, they must submit 3 letters of recommendation (including 1 from a chapter president of Delta Kappa Gamma) and a short essay on their reasons for choosing education as their profession. Financial need is not considered in the selection process.

**Financial data** The stipend is $500.

**Duration** 1 year.

**Number awarded** 1 each year.

**Deadline** January of each year.

## [657]
## ZETA TAU ALPHA ACHIEVEMENT SCHOLARSHIPS

Zeta Tau Alpha Foundation, Inc.
Attn: Director of Foundation Administration
3450 Founders Road
Indianapolis, IN 46268
(317) 872-0540          Fax: (317) 876-3948
E-mail: zetataualpha@zetataualpha.org
Web: www.zetataualpha.org

**Summary** To provide financial assistance for college to women who are members of Zeta Tau Alpha.

**Eligibility** This program is open to undergraduate women who are enrolled at a 4-year college or university and student members of the school's Zeta Tau Alpha chapter. Applicants must demonstrate leadership qualities within their chapter or in campus activities while maintaining a high scholastic average. Selection is based on academic achievement (GPA of 2.75 or higher), involvement in campus and community activities, recommendations, current class status, and financial need.

**Financial data** The stipend is at least $1,000.

**Duration** 1 year; renewable.

**Number awarded** Varies each year. Annually, the foundation provides nearly $150,000 in scholarships and fellowships for undergraduate and graduate study.

**Deadline** March of each year.

## [658]
## ZETA TAU ALPHA ENDOWED SCHOLARSHIPS

Zeta Tau Alpha Foundation, Inc.
Attn: Director of Foundation Administration
3450 Founders Road
Indianapolis, IN 46268
(317) 872-0540          Fax: (317) 876-3948
E-mail: zetataualpha@zetataualpha.org
Web: www.zetataualpha.org

**Summary** To provide financial assistance to undergraduate women who are members of Zeta Tau Alpha.

**Eligibility** This program is open to undergraduate women who are enrolled at a 4-year college or university and student members of the school's Zeta Tau Alpha chapter. These scholarships have been established for specific chapters, with preference for the award going to a member of that particular chapter. Selection is based on academic achievement (GPA of 2.75 or higher), involvement in campus and community activities, recommendations, current class status, and financial need.

**Financial data** The stipend is at least $1,000.

**Duration** 1 year; renewable.

**Number awarded** Varies each year. Annually, the foundation provides nearly $150,000 in scholarships and fellowships for undergraduate and graduate study.

**Deadline** March of each year.

## [659]
## ZOE CAVALARIS OUTSTANDING FEMALE ATHLETE AWARD

Daughters of Penelope
1909 Q Street, N.W., Suite 500
Washington, DC 20009-1007
(202) 234-9741          Fax: (202) 483-6983
E-mail: daughters@ahepa.org
Web: www.ahepa.org

**Summary** To recognize and reward, with a college scholarship, women of Greek descent who demonstrate excellence in high school or college athletics.

**Eligibility** This award is presented to a young women of Hellenic descent who has unusually high quality athletic ability and a record of accomplishment in any sport or any series of sports. Nominees must be outstanding high school or college amateur female athletes recognized for their accomplishments during their high school and/or college years. Along with a letter of nomination from a sponsoring chapter of Daughters of Penelope, they must submit documentation of their current overall GPA, academic honors, other honors, extracurricular activities (other than sports), church and/or community activities, and special achievements (other than sports).

**Financial data** The award includes a $500 college scholarship, an engraved plaque, and public recognition through Daughters of Penelope events and publications.

**Duration** The award is presented annually.

**Additional information** Information is also available from Kiki Sekles, Athletics Chair, 2035 Streamwood Lane, Sterling Heights, MI 48310-7816, (586) 979-8359, E-mail: ksekles@wowway.com.

**Number awarded** 1 each year.

**Deadline** May of each year.

# Fellowships

Described here are 334 programs designed primarily or exclusively for women that are available to fund studies on the graduate or postgraduate levels in United States. Usually no return of service or repayment is required. Note: other funding opportunities for graduate and postgraduate women are also described in the Loans, Grants, Awards, and Internships subsections. So, if you are looking for a particular program and don't find it here, be sure to check the Program Title Index to see if it is covered elsewhere in the *Directory.*

## [660]
## AAUW CAREER DEVELOPMENT GRANTS

American Association of University Women
Attn: AAUW Educational Foundation
301 ACT Drive, Department 60
P.O. Box 4030
Iowa City, IA 52243-4030
(319) 337-1716          Fax: (319) 337-1204
E-mail: aauw@act.org
Web: www.aauw.org

**Summary** To provide financial assistance to women who are seeking career advancement, career change, or reentry into the workforce.

**Eligibility** This program is open to women who are U.S. citizens or permanent residents, have earned a bachelor's degree, received their most recent degree more than 4 years ago, and plan to work toward a master's degree, second bachelor's degree, or specialized training in technical or professional fields. Applicants must be planning to undertake course work at an accredited 2- or 4-year college or university (or a technical school that is licensed, accredited, or approved by the U.S. Department of Education). Special consideration is given to qualified members of the American Association of University Women (AAUW), women of color, women working on their first advanced degree, and women working on degrees in nontraditional fields. Doctoral students and candidates eligible for other AAUW fellowship programs may not apply for these grants. Selection is based on demonstrated commitment to education and equity for women and girls, reason for seeking a higher education or technical training, degree, potential for success in chosen field, documentation of opportunities in chosen field, feasibility of study plans and proposed time schedule, validity of proposed budget and budget narrative (including sufficient outside support), and quality of written proposal.

**Financial data** Grants range from $2,000 to $8,000. The funds are to be used for tuition, fees, books, supplies, local transportation, and dependent care.

**Duration** 1 year, beginning in July; nonrenewable.

**Additional information** The filing fee is $25 for AAUW members or $35 for nonmembers.

**Number awarded** Varies each year; recently, 34 of these grants were awarded.

**Deadline** December of each year.

## [661]
## ABWA PRESIDENT'S SCHOLARSHIP

American Business Women's Association
Attn: Stephen Bufton Memorial Educational Fund
9100 Ward Parkway
P.O. Box 8728
Kansas City, MO 64114-0728
(816) 361-6621          Toll-free: (800) 228-0007
Fax: (816) 361-4991     E-mail: abwa@abwahq.org
Web: www.abwahq.org/ProfDev.asp

**Summary** To provide financial assistance to women graduate students who are working on a degree in a specified field.

**Eligibility** This program is open to women who are working on a graduate degree and have a cumulative GPA of 2.5 or higher. Applicants are not required to be members of the American Business Women's Association, but they must be sponsored by an ABWA chapter that has contributed to the fund in the previous chapter year. Each year, the trustees designate an academic discipline for which the scholarship will be presented that year; recently, eligibility was limited to women working on a graduate degree in systems or computer engineering. U.S. citizenship is required.

**Financial data** The stipend is $3,000. Funds are paid directly to the recipient's institution to be used only for tuition, books, and fees.

**Duration** 1 year.

**Additional information** This program was created in 1969 as part of ABWA's Stephen Bufton Memorial Education Fund. The ABWA does not provide the names and addresses of local chapters; it recommends that applicants check with their local Chamber of Commerce, library, or university to see if any chapter has registered a contact's name and number.

**Number awarded** 1 each year.

**Deadline** May of each year.

## [662]
## ACNM FOUNDATION FELLOWSHIP FOR GRADUATE EDUCATION

American College of Nurse-Midwives
Attn: ACNM Foundation, Inc.
8403 Coleville Road, Suite 1550
Silver Spring, MD 20915
(240) 485-1850          Fax: (240) 485-1818
Web: www.midwife.org

**Summary** To provide financial assistance for midwifery education to graduate student members of the American College of Nurse-Midwives (ACNM).

**Eligibility** This program is open to ACNM members who are currently enrolled in a doctoral or postdoctoral midwife education program. Applicants must be a certified nurse midwife (CNM) or a certified midwife (CM). Along with their application, they must submit a curriculum vitae; a sample of up to 30 pages of scholarly work; and brief essays on their 5-year academic career plans, intended use of the fellowship money, and intended future participation in the local, regional, and/or national activities of ACNM or other activities that contribute to midwifery research, education, or practice.

**Financial data** A stipend is awarded (amount not specified).

**Duration** 1 year.

**Additional information** This program was established in 1997 with a grant from Ortho-McNeil Pharmaceutical Corporation.

**Number awarded** 1 each year.

**Deadline** March of each year.

## [663]
## ADA I. PRESSMAN SCHOLARSHIP

Society of Women Engineers
230 East Ohio Street, Suite 400
Chicago, IL 60611-3265
(312) 596-5223                    Toll-free: (877) SWE-INFO
Fax: (312) 644-8557
E-mail: scholarshipapplication@swe.org
Web: www.swe.org/scholarships

**Summary** To provide financial assistance to women working on an undergraduate or graduate degree in engineering or computer science.

**Eligibility** This program is open to women who will be sophomores, juniors, seniors, or graduate students at ABET-accredited colleges and universities. Applicants must be majoring in computer science or engineering and have a GPA of 3.0 or higher. Along with their application, they must submit a 1-page essay on why they want to be an engineer or computer scientist, how they believe they will make a difference as an engineer or computer scientist, and what influenced them to study engineering or computer science. U.S. citizenship is required. Selection is based on merit.

**Financial data** The stipend is $5,000.

**Duration** 1 year.

**Number awarded** 1 each year.

**Deadline** January of each year.

## [664]
## ADVANCED POSTDOCTORAL FELLOWSHIPS IN DIABETES RESEARCH

Juvenile Diabetes Research Foundation
Attn: Grant Administrator
120 Wall Street, 19th Floor
New York, NY 10005-4001
(212) 479-7572                    Toll-free: (800) 533-CURE
Fax: (212) 785-9595              E-mail: info@jdrf.org
Web: www.jdrf.org/index.cfm?page_id=103207

**Summary** To provide advanced research training to scientists (particularly women, minorities, and persons with disabilities) who are beginning their professional careers and are interested in conducting research on the causes, treatment, prevention, or cure of diabetes or its complications.

**Eligibility** This program is open to postdoctorates who show extraordinary promise for a career in diabetes research. Applicants must have received their first doctoral degree (M.D., Ph.D., D.M.D., or D.V.M.) within the past 5 years and should have completed 1 to 3 years of postdoctoral training. They may not have a faculty appointment. There are no citizenship requirements. Applications are encouraged from women, members of minority groups underrepresented in the sciences, and people with disabilities. The proposed research training may be conducted at foreign and domestic, for-profit and nonprofit, and public and private institutions, including universities, colleges, hospitals, laboratories, units of state and local government, and eligible agencies of the federal government. Selection is based on the applicant's previous experience and academic record; the caliber of the proposed research; the quality of the mentor, training program, and environment;

and the applicant's potential to obtain an independent research position in the future. Fellows who obtain a faculty position at any time during the term of the fellowship may apply for a transition award for support during their first year as a faculty member.

**Financial data** The total award is $90,000 per year, including salary that depends on number of years of experience, ranging from $35,568 for zero up to $51,036 for 7 or more years of experience. In the first year only, funds in excess of the grant may be used for travel to scientific meetings (up to $2,000), journal subscriptions, books, training courses, laboratory supplies, equipment, or purchase of a personal computer (up to $2,000). Indirect costs are not allowed. Fellows who receive a faculty position and are granted a transition award of up to $110,000 for 1 year, including up to 10% in indirect costs.

**Duration** Up to 3 years.

**Deadline** January or July of each year.

## [665]
## AEROSPACE ILLINOIS SPACE GRANT CONSORTIUM PROGRAM

Aerospace Illinois Space Grant Consortium
c/o University of Illinois at Urbana-Champaign
Department of Aeronautical and Astronomical
  Engineering
308 Talbot Lab
104 South Wright Street
Urbana, IL 61801-2935
(217) 244-8048                    Fax: (217) 244-0720
E-mail: dejeffer@uiuc.edu
Web: www.ae.uiuc.edu/ISGC

**Summary** To provide financial support to faculty, staff, and students (particularly women, minorities, and persons with disabilities) at Aerospace Illinois member institutions who are interested in pursuing space-related academic activities.

**Eligibility** Aerospace Illinois has established 4 program elements: 1) undergraduate/high school teaching and research, to attract undergraduates and secondary school students to aerospace science and engineering; 2) training in graduate research, through research experiences focused on aerospace science and engineering; 3) outreach and public service, to employ the region's extensive existing public educational information networks and outreach programs to attract the highest quality student populations, especially underrepresented minorities, women, and persons with disabilities; and 4) fellowships with industry, to add substantially to the national aerospace science and engineering pool. Aerospace Illinois is a component of the U.S. National Aeronautics and Space Administration which encourages applications from women, minorities, and persons with disabilities.

**Financial data** Awards depend on the availability of funds and the nature of the proposal.

**Duration** Depends on the program.

**Additional information** Aerospace Illinois includes 4 member institutions: the University of Illinois at Urbana-Champaign (UIUC), the University of Chicago (UC), Illinois Institute of Technology (IIT), and Northwestern University (NU). It also includes 3 affiliate institutions: Southern Illinois University (SIU), Western Illinois University (WIU), and the

University of Illinois at Chicago. This program is funded by NASA.

**Number awarded** Varies each year.

## [666]
## AGA FELLOWSHIP/FACULTY TRANSITION AWARDS

Foundation for Digestive Health and Nutrition
Attn: Research Awards Program
4930 Del Ray Avenue
Bethesda, MD 20814-2512
(301) 222-4012                    Fax: (301) 652-3890
E-mail: info@fdhn.org
Web: www.fdhn.org/html/awards/elect_app.html

**Summary** To provide funding to physicians for research training in an area of gastrointestinal, liver function, or related diseases.

**Eligibility** This program is open to trainee members of the American Gastroenterological Association (AGA) who are M.D.s or M.D./Ph.D.s currently holding a gastroenterology-related fellowship at an accredited North American institution. Applicants must be committed to an academic career; have completed 2 years of research training at the start of this award; be sponsored by an AGA member who directs a gastroenterology-related unit that is engaged in research training in a North American medical school, affiliated teaching hospital, or research institute; and be cosponsored by the director of a basic research laboratory (or other comparable laboratory) who is committed to the training and development of the applicant. Minorities and women investigators are strongly encouraged to apply. Selection is based on novelty, feasibility, and significance of the proposal; attributes of the candidate; record and commitment of the sponsors; and the institutional and laboratory environment.

**Financial data** The stipend is $40,000 per year. Funds are to be used as salary support for the recipient. Indirect costs are not allowed.

**Duration** 2 years.

**Additional information** This award is administered by the Foundation for Digestive Health and Nutrition (FDHN) and sponsored by the AGA. Finalists for the award are interviewed. Although the host institution may supplement the award, the applicant may not concurrently have a similar training award or grant from another organization. All publications coming from work funded by this program must acknowledge the support of the award.

**Number awarded** Up to 4 each year.

**Deadline** September of each year.

## [667]
## AGNES MISSIRIAN SCHOLARSHIP

Armenian International Women's Association
65 Main Street, Room 3A
Watertown, MA 02472
(617) 926-0171                    E-mail: aiwainc@aol.com
Web: www.aiwa-net.org/scholarshipinfo.html

**Summary** To provide financial assistance to Armenian women upper-division and graduate students.

**Eligibility** This program is open to full-time women students of Armenian descent attending an accredited college or university. Applicants must be full-time juniors, seniors, or graduate students with a GPA of 3.2 or higher. They must submit an essay, up to 500 words, describing their planned academic program, their career goals, and the reasons why they believe they should be awarded this scholarship. Selection is based on financial need and merit.

**Financial data** The stipend is $2,000.

**Duration** 1 year.

**Number awarded** 1 or more each year.

**Deadline** April of each year.

## [668]
## AHRQ MENTORED CLINICAL SCIENTIST DEVELOPMENT AWARD

Agency for Healthcare Research and Quality
Attn: Office of Extramural Research, Education and
    Priority Populations
540 Gaither Road
Rockville, MD 20850
(301) 427-1449                    E-mail: training@ahrq.gov
Web: www.ahrq.gov

**Summary** To provide funding to postdoctorates (particularly women, minorities, and persons with disabilities) interested in obtaining additional research training to enable them to become independent investigators in health services research.

**Eligibility** This program is open to U.S. citizens or permanent residents who have received a clinical doctoral degree (M.D., D.O., D.C., O.D., D.D.S., Pharm.D., or doctorally-prepared nurses). Applicants must have identified a mentor with extensive research experience and be willing to spend at least 75% of full-time professional effort conducting research and developing a research career to improve the outcomes, effectiveness, quality, access to, and cost and utilization of health care services. Special attention is paid to applications that focus on developing the careers of investigators who will study minority, child, and older adult health services research; some awards are made specifically to applications that foster the research careers of investigators studying those populations. Awards are also made specifically to individual investigators from predominantly minority institutions. Applications are especially encouraged from women, minorities, and individuals with disabilities.

**Financial data** Grants provide salary up to $75,000 annually, plus associated fringe benefits. Also available are up to $25,000 per year for research development support (tuition, fees, and books related to career development; research expenses, such as supplies, equipment, and technical personnel; travel to research meetings or training; and statistical services, including personnel and computer time) and reimbursement of indirect costs at 8% of modified total direct costs.

**Duration** 3 to 5 years.

**Additional information** Recipients must spend at least 75% of full-time professional effort conducting research and developing a research career.

**Number awarded** Varies each year.

**Deadline** January, May, or September of each year.

## [669]
## AIR FORCE OFFICERS' WIVES' CLUB OF WASHINGTON, D.C. CONTINUING EDUCATION SCHOLARSHIPS FOR NON-MILITARY AIR FORCE SPOUSES

Air Force Officers' Wives' Club of Washington, D.C.
Attn: AFOWC Scholarship Committee
50 Theisen Street
Bolling Air Force Base
Washington, DC 20032-5411

**Summary** To provide financial assistance for undergraduate or graduate studies to the non-military spouses of Air Force members in the Washington, D.C. area.

**Eligibility** This program is open to the non-military spouses of Air Force members residing in the Washington, D.C. metropolitan area in the following categories: active duty, retired, MIA/POW, or deceased. Spouses whose Air Force sponsor is assigned remote from the area or reassigned during the current school year are also eligible if they remained behind to continue education. Applicants must be enrolled or planning to enroll as an undergraduate or graduate student. Along with their application, they must submit a 500-word essay on their experiences, interests, goals, and how being an Air Force spouse has affected their life. Selection is based on academic and citizenship achievements; financial need is not considered.

**Financial data** A stipend is awarded (amount not specified). Funds may be used only for payment of tuition or academic fees.

**Duration** 1 year.

**Number awarded** Varies each year.

**Deadline** February of each year.

## [670]
## AIR FORCE SPOUSE SCHOLARSHIPS

Air Force Association
Attn: Member Services
1501 Lee Highway
Arlington, VA 22209-1198
(703) 247-5800                    Toll-free: (800) 727-3337
Fax: (703) 247-5853              E-mail: AFAStaff@afa.org
Web: www.afa.org/aef/aid/spouse.asp

**Summary** To provide financial assistance for undergraduate or graduate study to spouses of Air Force members.

**Eligibility** This program is open to spouses of Air Force active duty, Air National Guard, or Air Force Reserve members. Spouses who are themselves military members or in ROTC are not eligible. Applicants must have a GPA of 3.5 or higher in college (or high school if entering college for the first time) and be able to provide proof of acceptance into an accredited undergraduate or graduate degree program. They must submit a 2-page essay on their academic and career goals, the motivation that led them to that decision, and how Air Force and other local community activities in which they are involved will enhance their goals. Selection is based on the essay and 2 letters of recommendation.

**Financial data** The stipend is $1,000 per year; funds are sent to the recipients' schools to be used for any reasonable cost related to working on a degree.

**Duration** 1 year; nonrenewable.

**Additional information** This program was established in 1995.

**Number awarded** 30 each year.

**Deadline** April of each year.

## [671]
## ALABAMA G.I. DEPENDENTS' SCHOLARSHIP PROGRAM

Alabama Department of Veterans Affairs
770 Washington Avenue, Suite 530
P.O. Box 1509
Montgomery, AL 36102-1509
(334) 242-5077                    Fax: (334) 242-5102
E-mail: willie.moore@va.state.al.us
Web: www.va.state.al.us/scholarship.htm

**Summary** To provide educational benefits to the dependents of disabled, deceased, and other Alabama veterans.

**Eligibility** Eligible are spouses, children, stepchildren, and unremarried widow(er)s of veterans who served honorably for 90 days or more and 1) are currently rated as 20% or more service-connected disabled or were so rated at time of death; 2) were a former prisoner of war; 3) have been declared missing in action; 4) died as the result of a service-connected disability; or 5) died while on active military duty in the line of duty. The veteran must have been a permanent civilian resident of Alabama for at least 1 year prior to entering active military service; veterans who were not Alabama residents at the time of entering active military service may also qualify if they have a 100% disability and were permanent residents of Alabama for at least 5 years prior to filing the application for this program or prior to death, if deceased. Children and stepchildren must be under the age of 26, but spouses and unremarried widow(er)s may be any age.

**Financial data** Eligible dependents may attend any state-supported Alabama institution of higher learning or enroll in a prescribed course of study at any Alabama state-supported trade school without payment of any tuition, book fees, or laboratory charges.

**Duration** This is an entitlement program for 4 years of full-time undergraduate or graduate study or part-time equivalent. Spouses and unremarried widow(er)s whose veteran spouse is rated between 20% and 90% disabled, or 100% disabled but not permanently so, may attend only 2 standard academic years.

**Additional information** Benefits for children, spouses, and unremarried widow(er)s are available in addition to federal government benefits. Assistance is not provided for noncredit courses, placement testing, GED preparation, continuing educational courses, pre-technical courses, or state board examinations.

**Number awarded** Varies each year.

**Deadline** Applications may be submitted at any time.

## [672]
## ALABAMA SPACE GRANT CONSORTIUM GRADUATE FELLOWSHIP PROGRAM

Alabama Space Grant Consortium
c/o University of Alabama in Huntsville
Materials Science Building, Room 205
Huntsville, AL 35899
(256) 824-6800                     Fax: (256) 824-6061
E-mail: reasonj@uah.edu
Web: www.uah.edu/ASGC

**Summary** To provide financial assistance for graduate study or research related to the space sciences at universities participating in the Alabama Space Grant Consortium.

**Eligibility** This program is open to full-time graduate students enrolled at universities participating in the consortium. Applicants must be studying in a field related to space, including the physical, natural, and biological sciences; engineering; education; economics; business; sociology; behavioral sciences; computer science; communications; law; international affairs; and public administration. They must 1) present a proposed research plan related to space that includes an extramural experience at a field center of the National Aeronautics and Space Administration (NASA); 2) propose a multidisciplinary plan and course of study; 3) plan to be involved in consortium outreach activities; and 4) intend to prepare for a career in line with NASA's aerospace, science, and technology programs. U.S. citizenship is required. Individuals from underrepresented groups (African Americans, Hispanics, American Indians, Pacific Islanders, Asian Americans, and women) are especially encouraged to apply. Interested students should submit a completed application form, a description of the proposed research or study program, a schedule, a budget, a list of references, a vitae, and undergraduate and graduate transcripts. Selection is based on 1) academic qualifications, 2) quality of the proposed research program or plan of study and its relevance to the aerospace science and technology program of NASA, 3) quality of the proposed interdisciplinary approach, 4) merit of the proposed utilization of a NASA center to carry out the objectives of the program, 5) prospects for completing the project within the allotted time, and 6) applicant's motivation for a career in aerospace.

**Financial data** The annual award includes $16,000 for a student stipend and up to $6,000 for a tuition/student research allowance.

**Duration** 12 months; may be renewed up to 24 additional months.

**Additional information** The member universities are University of Alabama in Huntsville, Alabama A&M University, University of Alabama, University of Alabama in Birmingham, University of South Alabama, Tuskegee University, and Auburn University. Funding for this program is provided by NASA.

**Number awarded** Varies each year; recently, 12 of these fellowships were awarded.

**Deadline** February of each year.

## [673]
## ALABAMA WMU SCHOLARSHIPS

Alabama Baptist Convention
Attn: Woman's Missionary Union
2001 East South Boulevard
P.O. Box 11870
Montgomery, AL 36111-0870
(334) 288-2460                     Toll-free: (800) 264-1225
Fax: (334) 288-2693              E-mail: hickslcp@aol.com
Web: www.alawoman.com

**Summary** To provide financial assistance to women from Alabama who are attending a Southern Baptist seminary or divinity school.

**Eligibility** This program is open to women residents of Alabama and the daughters of Southern Baptist missionaries serving in or from Alabama. Applicants must be enrolled full time in a graduate program at a Southern Baptist seminary or divinity school as preparation to enter a Southern Baptist church-related vocation. Selection is based on involvement in church and Woman's Missionary Union (WMU) activities, plans to enter a Southern Baptist church-related vocation, and financial need.

**Financial data** The stipend depends on the availability of funds and the number of applicants.

**Duration** 1 year; may be renewed.

**Number awarded** Varies each year; recently, 10 of these scholarships were awarded.

**Deadline** April of each year.

## [674]
## ALBERT A. MARKS SCHOLARSHIP FOR TEACHER EDUCATION

Miss America Pageant
Attn: Scholarship Department
Two Miss America Way, Suite 1000
Atlantic City, NJ 08401
(609) 345-7571, ext. 27          Toll-free: (800) 282-MISS
Fax: (609) 347-6079         E-mail: info@missamerica.org
Web: www.missamerica.org

**Summary** To provide financial assistance to women who are working on a degree in education and who, in the past, competed at some level in the Miss America competition.

**Eligibility** This program is open to women who are working on an undergraduate, master's, or higher degree in education and who competed at the local, state, or national level in a Miss America competition during the current or any subsequent year. Applicants must be preparing for a career as a classroom teacher, special area teacher (e.g., art, physical education, music), school counselor, school psychologist, school nurse, or school administrator. They must submit an essay, up to 500 words, on the factors that influenced them to enter the field of education, what they consider to be the major issues facing education today, and what they would do to strengthen and improve our educational system. Selection is based on GPA, class rank, extracurricular activities, financial need, and level of participation within the system.

**Financial data** The stipend is $5,000.

**Duration** 1 year; renewable.

**Additional information** This scholarship was established in 1997.

**Number awarded** Varies each year; recently, 2 of these scholarships were awarded.

**Deadline** June of each year.

## [675]
## ALPHA CHI OMEGA FOUNDERS FELLOWSHIP

Alpha Chi Omega Foundation
Attn: Foundation Programs Coordinator
5939 Castle Creek Parkway North Drive
Indianapolis, IN 46250-4343
(317) 579-5050, ext. 262        Fax: (317) 579-5051
E-mail: foundation@alphachiomega.org
Web: www.alphachiomega.org

**Summary** To provide financial assistance to graduating Alpha Chi Omega members who are interested in studying on the graduate school level.

**Eligibility** This program is open to women college seniors or graduates who are members of the sorority. Applicants must be interested in attending graduate school. They may study any field. Financial need is considered in the selection process.

**Financial data** The stipend is $2,000.

**Duration** 1 year.

**Number awarded** 1 each year.

**Deadline** Applications may be submitted at any time.

## [676]
## ALPHA EPSILON IOTA SCHOLARSHIP FUND

Alpha Epsilon Iota
c/o McDonald Financial Group
Attn: Key Trust Financial Services
Mail code OH-01-27-1614
P.O. Box 89464
Cleveland, OH 44101-6464
Toll-free: (800) 999-9658

**Summary** To provide financial assistance to women enrolled or accepted at an accredited school or college of medicine in the United States.

**Eligibility** Applicants must be candidates for degrees in accredited schools or colleges of medicine or osteopathy in the United States. Only women may apply. Selection is based on scholastic merit, work experience, scholarly publication, research experience, and financial need (last year's income cannot exceed $15,000 and assets cannot exceed $10,000). Race, age, religion, political affiliation, or national origin are not considered in awarding the fellowships. Priority is given to applicants in their first year of medical school. An interview may be required.

**Financial data** Awards range from $3,000 to $4,000 each year. Funds may be used for tuition-related fees, books, materials, food, clothing, housing, transportation, medical and dental expenses, insurance, and child care.

**Duration** 1 year; renewal is possible.

**Number awarded** 2 each year.

**Deadline** April of each year.

## [677]
## ALPHA EPSILON PHI FOUNDATION SCHOLARSHIPS

Alpha Epsilon Phi
Attn: AEPhi Foundation
11 Lake Avenue Extension, Suite 1A
Danbury, CT 06811
(203) 748-0029        Fax: (203) 748-0039
E-mail: aephifoundation@aephi.org
Web: www.aephi.org

**Summary** To provide financial assistance for undergraduate or graduate education to Alpha Epsilon Phi members or alumnae.

**Eligibility** Current members or alumnae of the sorority are eligible to apply if they need financial assistance to pursue or continue studies at the undergraduate or graduate level. Selection is based on scholastic standing, university citizenship, activities in the sorority, and financial need.

**Financial data** Stipends range from $1,000 to $2,000 per year.

**Duration** 1 year; may be renewed.

**Additional information** This program includes the following named scholarships: the Judith Resnik Memorial Scholarship, the Anne Klauber Berson Memorial Scholarship, the Edith Hirsch Miller Memorial Scholarship (preference given to Jewish applicants), the Irma Loeb Cohen Scholarship (for students who are attending Ohio State University or Cleveland State University or who are residents of Ohio), the Ruth Rosenbaum Goldfeder Memorial Scholarship (preference given to residents of Los Angeles or Colorado), the Alpha Iota Scholarship (preference given to residents of Minnesota), the Constance Bauman Abraham Scholarship, and the Shonnette Meyer Kahn Scholarship (preference given to students at Ohio State University or Tulane University). Recipients must be willing to remain active in the sorority and live in the sorority house (if any) for the entire year the scholarship covers.

**Number awarded** Several each year.

**Deadline** April of each year.

## [678]
## ALPHA KAPPA ALPHA FINANCIAL NEED SCHOLARSHIPS

Alpha Kappa Alpha Sorority, Inc.
Attn: Educational Advancement Foundation
5656 South Stony Island Avenue
Chicago, IL 60637
(773) 947-0026        Toll-free: (800) 653-6528
Fax: (773) 947-0277        E-mail: akaeaf@aol.com
Web: www.akaeaf.org/scholarships.htm

**Summary** To provide financial assistance to undergraduate and graduate students (especially African American women) who demonstrate financial need.

**Eligibility** This program is sponsored by an African American sorority and is open to undergraduate or graduate students who have completed at least 1 year in an accredited degree-granting institution or a work-in-progress program in a noninstitutional setting, are planning to continue their program of education, and can demonstrate unmet financial need. Applicants must have a GPA of 2.5 or higher.

**Financial data** Awards range from $750 to $1,500 per year.

**Duration** 1 year; nonrenewable.

**Number awarded** Varies each year. Recently, 38 of these scholarships were awarded: 26 to undergraduates and 12 to graduate students.

**Deadline** January of each year.

## [679]
## ALPHA KAPPA ALPHA MERIT SCHOLARSHIPS

Alpha Kappa Alpha Sorority, Inc.
Attn: Educational Advancement Foundation
5656 South Stony Island Avenue
Chicago, IL 60637
(773) 947-0026          Toll-free: (800) 653-6528
Fax: (773) 947-0277      E-mail: akaeaf@aol.com
Web: www.akaeaf.org/scholarships.htm

**Summary** To provide financial assistance to undergraduate and graduate students (especially African American women) who have excelled academically.

**Eligibility** This program, sponsored by an African American womenÖs sorority, is open to undergraduate and graduate students who have completed at least 1 year in an accredited degree-granting institution and are planning to continue their program of education. Applicants must have demonstrated exceptional academic achievement (GPA of 3.0 or higher) and present evidence of leadership through community service and involvement.

**Financial data** The stipend is $1,000 per year.

**Duration** 1 year; nonrenewable.

**Number awarded** Varies each year. Recently, 27 of these scholarships were awarded: 20 to undergraduates and 7 to graduate students.

**Deadline** January of each year.

## [680]
## ALPHA OMICRON PI SCHOLARSHIPS

Alpha Omicron Pi Foundation
Attn: Scholarship Committee
5390 Virginia Way
P.O. Box 395
Brentwood, TN 37024-0395
(615) 370-0920          Fax: (615) 370-4424
E-mail: foundation@alphaomicronpi.org
Web: www.aoiifoundation.org

**Summary** To provide financial assistance for college or graduate school to collegiate and alumnae members of Alpha Omicron Pi.

**Eligibility** This program is open to collegiate members of Alpha Omicron Pi who wish to continue their undergraduate education and alumnae members who wish to work on a graduate degree. Applicants must submit 50-word essays on the following topics: 1) the circumstances that have created their need for this scholarship, and 2) their immediate and long-term life objectives. Selection is based on academic excellence, dedication to serving the community and Alpha Omicron Pi, and financial need.

**Financial data** A stipend is awarded (amount not specified).

**Duration** 1 year.

**Additional information** This program was established in 1962. Undergraduate recipients must enroll full time, but graduate recipients may enroll part time.

**Number awarded** Varies each year.

**Deadline** February of each year.

## [681]
## ALPHA TAU CHAPTER SCHOLARSHIP

Alpha Omicron Pi Foundation
Attn: Scholarship Committee
5390 Virginia Way
P.O. Box 395
Brentwood, TN 37024-0395
(615) 370-0920          Fax: (615) 370-4424
E-mail: foundation@alphaomicronpi.org
Web: www.aoiifoundation.org

**Summary** To provide financial assistance for college or graduate school to collegiate and alumnae members of Alpha Omicron Pi.

**Eligibility** This program is open to collegiate members of Alpha Omicron Pi who wish to continue their undergraduate education and alumnae members who wish to work on a graduate degree. Applicants must submit 50-word essays on the following topics: 1) the circumstances that have created their need for this scholarship, and 2) their immediate and long-term life objectives. Selection is based on academic excellence, dedication to serving the community and Alpha Omicron Pi, and financial need. Preference is given to legacies.

**Financial data** A stipend is awarded (amount not specified).

**Duration** 1 year.

**Additional information** Undergraduate recipients must enroll full time, but graduate recipients may enroll part time.

**Number awarded** 1 each year.

**Deadline** February of each year.

## [682]
## ALPHA THETA STATE SCHOLARSHIP AWARDS

Delta Kappa Gamma Society International-Alpha Theta State Organization
c/o Nyla Adamson, Scholarship Chair
1901 Vintage Woods Court
Salt Lake City, UT 84117
Web: www.deltakappagamma.org

**Summary** To provide funding to members of Delta Kappa Gamma Society International in Utah who are interested in pursuing graduate education.

**Eligibility** This program is open to residents of Utah who have been members of Delta Kappa Gamma (an honorary society of women educators) for at least 3 years. Applicants must be engaged in graduate work leading to an advanced degree or a special certificate at an accredited institution of higher learning. Selection is based on involvement and service to Delta Kappa Gamma, leadership, and professional promise. Recipients of Delta Kappa Gamma international scholarships are not eligible.

**Financial data** The amount of the scholarship depends on the need of the recipient and the availability of funds.

**Duration** 1 year.

**Additional information** Recipients are expected to remain members for at least 3 years following completion of the proposed program.

**Number awarded** Varies each year.

**Deadline** May of each year.

## [683]
## AMELIA EARHART FELLOWSHIP AWARDS

Zonta International
Attn: Foundation
557 West Randolph Street
Chicago, IL 60661-2202
(312) 930-5848                    Fax: (312) 930-0951
E-mail: Zontafdtn@Zonta.org
Web: www.zonta.org

**Summary** To provide financial assistance to women interested in graduate study in scientific or engineering areas related to aerospace.

**Eligibility** This program is open to women who have a bachelor's degree in an area of science or engineering related to aerospace. Applicants must be registered in an accredited Ph.D. program at a recognized institution of higher learning and be able to provide evidence of a well-defined research and development program. They may be citizens of any country and studying in any country. Along with their application, they must submit a 500-word statement on their academic research program, their professional goals, and the relevance of their research program to aerospace-related sciences or engineering.

**Financial data** The stipend is $6,000, paid in 2 installments. Funds may be used for tuition, books, and fees.

**Duration** 1 year; renewable.

**Additional information** The fellowship may be used at any institution offering accredited courses in the applicant's field of study in the United States or abroad. Fellows may receive financial assistance from other programs. This program, established in 1938, is named for Amelia Earhart, famed air pioneer and Zontian, who disappeared over the Pacific in 1937. Graduate school acceptance is mandatory for application. Progress reports should be submitted at the end of each semester.

**Number awarded** Varies each year, depending upon the number of qualified applicants. Currently, approximately 35 fellowships are awarded annually.

**Deadline** November of each year.

## [684]
## AMELIA EARHART MEMORIAL SCHOLARSHIPS

Ninety-Nines, Inc.
4300 Amelia Earhart Road
Oklahoma City, OK 73159
(405) 685-7969                    Toll-free: (800) 994-1929
Fax: (405) 685-7985              E-mail: ihq99s@cs.com
Web: www.ninety-nines.org/aemsf.html

**Summary** To provide financial support to members of the Ninety-Nines (an organization of women pilots) who are interested in advanced flight training or academic study related to aviation.

**Eligibility** This program is open to women who have been members of the organization for at least 1 year. Applicants

must be interested in 1 of the following 4 types of scholarships: 1) flight training, to complete an advanced pilot certificate or rating or pilot training course; 2) jet type rating, to complete type rating certification in any jet; 3) technical certification, to complete an aviation or aerospace technical training or certification course; or 4) academic, to work on an associate, bachelor's, master's, or doctoral degree in such fields as aerospace engineering, aviation technology, aviation business management, air traffic management, or professional pilot. They must submit their application to their Ninety-Nines scholarship chair, who forwards it to the appropriate Amelia Earhart Scholarship Trustee. Applicants for flight training scholarships must be a current pilot with the appropriate medical certification and approaching the flight time requirement for the rating or certificate. Applicants for jet type rating scholarships must be a current airline transport pilot with a first-class medical certificate and at least 100 hours of multi-engine flight time or combined multi-engine and turbine time. Applicants for academic scholarships must be currently enrolled; associate or bachelor's degree students must have a GPA of 3.0 or higher. Financial need is considered in the selection process.

**Financial data** Flight training, jet type rating, and technical certification scholarships provide payment of all costs to complete the appropriate rating or certificate. Academic scholarships provide a stipend of up to $5,000 per year.

**Duration** Support is provided until completion of the rating, certificate, or degree.

**Additional information** This program was established in 1941. It includes the following endowed scholarships: the Jane Zieber Kelley Memorial Scholarship of the Aeons (established in 1979), the Gerda Ruhnke Memorial Flight Instructor Scholarship (established in 1988), the Geraldine Mickelsen Memorial Scholarship (established in 1993), the Alice Hammond Memorial Scholarship (established in 1995), the Lydiellen M. Hagan Memorial Scholarship (established in 1997), the Katherine A. Menges Brick Scholarship (established in 1998), the Betty DeWitt Witmer Scholarship (established in 1999), the Virginia S. Richardson Memorial Scholarship (established in 2000), the Darlene Sanders Memorial Scholarship (established in 2000), the Milton and Bonnie Seymour Memorial Scholarship (established in 2000), the Marion Barnick Memorial Scholarship (established in 2001), the Evelyn Bryan Johnson Memorial Scholarship (established in 2002), and the Mary Kelley Memorial Scholarship (established in 2003).

**Number awarded** Varies each year; recently, 13 of these scholarships were awarded.

**Deadline** Applications must be submitted to the chapter scholarship chair by November of each year; they must forward the applications from their chapter to the designated trustee by January of each year.

## [685]
## AMERICAN ASSOCIATION OF JAPANESE UNIVERSITY WOMEN SCHOLARSHIP PROGRAM

American Association of Japanese University Women
c/o Akiko Agishi, Scholarship Committee Co-Chair
Creative International, Inc.
3127 Nicholas Canyon Road
Los Angeles, CA 90046
E-mail: scholarship@aajuw.org
Web: www.aajuw.org/Scholarship.htm

**Summary**  To provide financial assistance to female students currently enrolled in upper-division or graduate classes in California.

**Eligibility**  This program is open to female students enrolled in accredited colleges or universities in California. They must have junior, senior, or graduate standing. Applicants must be a contributor to U.S.-Japan relations, cultural exchanges, and leadership development in the areas of their designated field of study. To apply, they must submit a current resume, an official transcript of the past 2 years of college work, 2 letters of recommendation, and an essay (up to 2 pages in English or 1,200 characters in Japanese) on either 1) what they hope to accomplish in their field of study to develop leadership and role model qualities, or 2) thoughts on how their field of study can contribute to U.S.-Japan relations and benefit international relations.

**Financial data**  The stipend is $1,500.

**Duration**  1 year.

**Additional information**  The association was founded in 1970 to promote the education of women as well as to contribute to U.S.-Japan relations, cultural exchanges, and leadership development.

**Number awarded**  2 or 3 each year.

**Deadline**  October of each year.

## [686]
## AMERICAN ASSOCIATION OF OBSTETRICIANS AND GYNECOLOGISTS FOUNDATION SCHOLARSHIPS

American Association of Obstetricians and
   Gynecologists Foundation
Attn: Administrative Director
409 12th Street, S.W.
Washington, DC 20024-2188
(202) 863-1649                    Fax: (202) 554-0453
E-mail: clarkins@acog.org
Web: www.agosonline.org/aaogf.asp

**Summary**  To provide funding to physicians (particularly women and minorities) who are interested in a program of research training in obstetrics and gynecology.

**Eligibility**  Applicants must have an M.D. degree and be eligible for the certification process of the American Board of Obstetrics and Gynecology (ABOG). They must document departmental planning for a significant research training experience to be conducted by 1 or more faculty mentors. There is no formal application form, but departments must supply a description of the candidate's qualifications, including a curriculum vitae, bibliography, prior training, past research experience, and evidence of completion of residency training in obstetrics and gynecology; a comprehensive description of the proposed training program; a description of departmental resources appropriate to the training; a list of other research grants, training grants, or scholarships previously or currently held by the applicant; and a budget. Applicants for the scholarship co-sponsored by ABOG must verify that 90% of their time and effort will be dedicated to the research training and conduct of research. Applicants for the scholarship co-sponsored by the Society for Maternal-Fetal Medicine (SMFM) must also have completed MFM subspecialty training or be in the second or third year of an ABOG-approved MFM training program at the time of applying. Candidates for that scholarship must also be members or associate members of the SMFM. Preference for both awards is given to training in areas currently underrepresented in obstetrics and gynecology. A personal interview may be requested. Priority is given to individuals who have not previously received extramural funding for research training. Women and minority candidates are strongly encouraged to apply. Selection is based on the scholarly, clinical, and research qualifications of the candidate; evidence of the candidate's commitment to an investigative career in academic obstetrics and gynecology in the United States or Canada; qualifications of the sponsoring department and mentor; and quality of the research project.

**Financial data**  The grant is $100,000 per year, of which at least $5,000 but not more than $15,000 must be used for employee benefits. In addition, sufficient funds to support travel to the annual fellows' retreat must be set aside. The balance of the funds may be used for salary, technical support, and supplies. The grant co-sponsored by the SMFM must be matched by an institutional commitment of at least $30,000 per year.

**Duration**  1 year; may be renewed for 2 additional years, based on satisfactory progress of the scholar.

**Additional information**  Scholars must devote at least 75% of their effort to the program of research training.

**Number awarded**  2 each year: 1 co-sponsored by ABOG and 1 co-sponsored by SMFM.

**Deadline**  August of each year.

## [687]
## AMERICAN NEWS WOMEN'S CLUB SCHOLARSHIPS

American News Women's Club
1607 22nd Street, N.W.
Washington, DC 20008
(202) 332-6770                    Fax: (202) 265-6092
E-mail: anwclub@covad.net
Web: www.anwc.org/scholarships.html

**Summary**  To provide financial assistance to women working on a degree in journalism at designated universities in the Washington, D.C. area.

**Eligibility**  This program is open to women majoring in journalism at the following institutions: American University, Gallaudet University, George Washington University, Howard University, and University of Maryland. Applicants may be undergraduates or graduate students.

**Financial data**  A stipend is awarded (amount not specified).

**Duration**  1 year.

**Additional information**  This program began in 1975.

**Number awarded** Varies each year; recently, 4 of these scholarships were awarded.

## [688]
## AMERICAN WOMAN'S SOCIETY OF CERTIFIED PUBLIC ACCOUNTANTS NATIONAL SCHOLARSHIP

American Woman's Society of Certified Public
   Accountants
Attn: Executive Director
136 South Keowee Street
Dayton, OH 45402
(937) 222-1872      Toll-free: (800) AWSCPA-1
Fax: (937) 222-5794     E-mail: info@awscpa.org
Web: www.awscpa.org/frameset.php?cf=awards.htm

**Summary** To provide funding to women interested in taking a review course to prepare for the C.P.A. examination.

**Eligibility** This program is open to women who are entering college seniors, fifth-year students, graduate students, or recent graduates and eligible to take a C.P.A. review course within 1 year. Applicants must have a GPA of 3.0 or higher in accounting and overall. U.S. citizenship or permanent resident status is required. Along with their application, they must submit an essay up to 1,000 words, explaining why they have chosen the field of accounting, how networking or mentoring can be beneficial to their professional development, why they deserve the scholarship, and any special circumstances they believe should be considered. Selection is based on the essay, academic achievement, extracurricular activities, scholastic honors, work experience, and financial need.

**Financial data** The grant is worth approximately $2,200. Funds are paid directly to a recognized C.P.A. review provider.

**Duration** Grants are presented annually.

**Number awarded** 1 or more each year.

**Deadline** March of each year.

## [689]
## ANITA BORG SCHOLARSHIPS

Google Inc.
Attn: Scholarships
1600 Amphitheatre Parkway
Mountain View, CA 94043-8303
(650) 623-4000      Fax: (650) 618-1499
E-mail: anitaborgscholars@google.com
Web: www.google.com/anitaborg

**Summary** To provide financial assistance to women working on a bachelor's or graduate degree in a computer-related field.

**Eligibility** This program is open to women who are entering their senior year of undergraduate study or are enrolled in a graduate program in computer science, computer engineering, or a related field. Applicants must be full-time students at a university in the United States with a GPA of 3.5 or higher. They must submit essays of 400 to 600 words on 1) a significant technical project on which they have worked; 2) examples of their leadership abilities; 3) what they would do if someone gave them the funding and resources for a 3- to 12-month project to investigate a technical topic of their choice; and 4) what they would do if someone gave them $1,000 to plan an event or project to benefit women in technical fields. Selection is based on academic background and demonstrated leadership.

**Financial data** The stipend is $10,000.

**Duration** 1 year.

**Additional information** These scholarships were first offered in 2004.

**Number awarded** Varies each year. Recently, 4 of these scholarships were awarded: 1 to an undergraduate, 2 to master's degree candidates, and 1 to a doctoral candidate.

**Deadline** January of each year.

## [690]
## ANN E. DICKERSON SCHOLARSHIPS

Christian Church (Disciples of Christ)
Attn: Higher Education and Leadership Ministries
11477 Olde Cabin Road, Suite 310
St. Louis, MO 6314-7130
(314) 991-3000      Fax: (314) 991-2957
E-mail: helm@helmdisciples.org
Web: www.helmdisciples.org/aid/dickerson.htm

**Summary** To provide financial assistance to women members of the Christian Church (Disciples of Christ) who are working on a Ph.D. degree in religion.

**Eligibility** This program is open to women working on a Ph.D. degree in religion. Applicants must members of the Christian Church (Disciples of Christ). Along with their application, they must submit a 300-word essay describing their vocational goals, academic interests, and how they envision being of service to the church.

**Financial data** The stipend is $2,000.

**Duration** 1 year.

**Number awarded** 3 each year.

**Deadline** April of each year.

## [691]
## ANNE PEEL HOPKINS GRANT

Alpha Chi Omega Foundation
Attn: Foundation Programs Coordinator
5939 Castle Creek Parkway North Drive
Indianapolis, IN 46250-4343
(317) 579-5050, ext. 262      Fax: (317) 579-5051
E-mail: foundation@alphachiomega.org
Web: www.alphachiomega.org

**Summary** To provide financial assistance to undergraduate or alumnae members of Alpha Chi Omega who are interested in working on a degree in education.

**Eligibility** This program is open to undergraduate and graduate members of Alpha Chi Omega who are enrolled full time. Preference is given to education majors. Selection is based on academic achievement, chapter involvement, campus and community involvement, and financial need.

**Financial data** The stipend is $500.

**Duration** 1 year.

**Number awarded** 1 each year.

**Deadline** March of each year.

## [692]
## ARFORA–MARTHA GAVRILA SCHOLARSHIP FOR WOMEN

Romanian Orthodox Episcopate of America
Attn: Scholarship Committee
1920 King James Parkway, Apartment 18
Westlake, OH 44145-3466
E-mail: roeasolia@aol.com
Web: www.roea.org/schol/schol-gavrila.htm

**Summary** To provide financial assistance to women who are members of a parish of the Romanian Orthodox Episcopate of America and interested in working on a graduate degree.

**Eligibility** Applicants must be women, voting members of a parish of the Romanian Orthodox Episcopate of America, graduates of an accredited university or college, and accepted by a graduate school. As part of the application process, students must submit a formal letter describing their personal goals, projected use of the degree, church and community involvement, and honors and awards.

**Financial data** The stipend is $1,000.

**Duration** 1 year.

**Additional information** The first scholarship was awarded in 1985. This program is offered by the Association of Romanian Orthodox Ladies Auxiliaries (ARFORA).

**Number awarded** 1 each year.

**Deadline** April of each year.

## [693]
## ARIZONA NON-TRADITIONAL EDUCATION FOR WOMEN SCHOLARSHIPS

Arizona Business and Professional Women's
    Foundation
Attn: Administrator
P.O. Box 521
Clifton, AZ 85533
(928) 687-1300          E-mail: vcpage@aznex.net
Web: www.arizonabpwfoundation.com

**Summary** To provide financial assistance to reentry women in Arizona who are interested in entering nontraditional fields.

**Eligibility** This program is open to women with Arizona residency who are reentering the workforce or changing careers in order to establish self-sufficiency. Applicants must be preparing for a career in an occupational field in which women constitute less than 25% of those employed. They should be enrolled in, accepted to, or making application to a school in Arizona that provides training in nontraditional employment, or be currently employed in a nontraditional field and taking career-related training. Along with their application, they must submit 2 letters of recommendation, a statement of financial need (latest income tax return must be provided), a career goal statement, and their most recent transcript (when available). Selection is based on financial need, field of study, and possibility of success.

**Financial data** The stipend is $1,000.

**Duration** 1 year.

**Number awarded** 1 or more each year.

**Deadline** February of each year.

## [694]
## ARKANSAS MISSING IN ACTION/KILLED IN ACTION DEPENDENTS' SCHOLARSHIP PROGRAM

Arkansas Department of Higher Education
Attn: Financial Aid Division
114 East Capitol Avenue
Little Rock, AR 72201-3818
(501) 371-2050          Toll-free: (800) 54-STUDY
Fax: (501) 371-2001     E-mail: finaid@adhe.arknet.edu
Web: www.arkansashighered.com/miakia.html

**Summary** To provide financial assistance for educational purposes to dependents of Arkansas veterans who were killed in action or became POWs or MIAs after January 1, 1960.

**Eligibility** This program is open to the natural children, adopted children, stepchildren, and spouses of Arkansas residents who became a prisoner of war, killed in action, missing in action, or killed on ordnance delivery after January 1, 1960. Applicants may be working or planning to work on 1) an undergraduate degree in Arkansas or 2) a graduate or professional degree in Arkansas if their undergraduate degree was not received in Arkansas. Applicants need not be current Arkansas residents, but their parents or spouses must have been an Arkansas resident at the time of entering military service or at the time they were declared a prisoner of war, killed in action, or missing in action.

**Financial data** The program pays for tuition, general registration fees, special course fees, activity fees, room and board (if provided in campus facilities), and other charges associated with earning a degree or certificate.

**Duration** 1 year; undergraduates may obtain renewal as long as they make satisfactory progress toward a baccalaureate degree; graduate students may obtain renewal as long as they maintain a minimum GPA of 2.5 and make satisfactory progress toward a degree.

**Additional information** Return or reported death of the veteran will not alter benefits. Applications must be submitted to the financial aid director at an Arkansas state-supported institution of higher education or state-supported technical/vocational school.

**Number awarded** Varies each year; recently, 4 of these scholarships were awarded.

**Deadline** July of each year for the fall term; November of each year for the spring term; April of each year for summer term I; June of each year for summer term II.

## [695]
## ARMY AVIATION ASSOCIATION OF AMERICA SCHOLARSHIPS

Army Aviation Association of America Scholarship
    Foundation
Attn: AAAA Scholarship Foundation
755 Main Street, Suite 4D
Monroe, CT 06468-2830
(203) 268-2450          Fax: (203) 268-5870
E-mail: aaaa@quad-a.org
Web: www.quad-a.org/scholarship.htm

**Summary** To provide financial aid for undergraduate or graduate study to members of the Army Aviation Association of America (AAAA) and their relatives.

**Eligibility** This program is open to AAAA members and their spouses, unmarried siblings, unmarried children, and unmarried grandchildren. Applicants must be enrolled or accepted for enrollment as an undergraduate or graduate student at an accredited college or university. Graduate students must include a 250-word essay on their life experiences, work history, and aspirations. Some scholarships are specifically reserved for enlisted, warrant officer, company grade, and Department of the Army civilian members. Selection is based on academic merit and personal achievement.

**Financial data** Stipends range from $1,000 to $4,000.

**Duration** Scholarships may be for 1 year, 2 years, or 4 years.

**Number awarded** Varies each year; since the program began in 1963, the foundation has awarded more than $2.2 million to more than 1,300 qualified applicants.

**Deadline** April of each year.

## [696]
## ARNE ADMINISTRATIVE LEADERSHIP SCHOLARSHIP

Women of the Evangelical Lutheran Church in America
Attn: Scholarships
8765 West Higgins Road
Chicago, IL 60631-4189
(773) 380-2730     Toll-free: (800) 638-3522, ext. 2730
Fax: (773) 380-2419     E-mail: womenelca@elca.org
Web: www.womenoftheelca.org

**Summary** To provide financial assistance to women members of congregations of the Evangelical Lutheran Church of America (ELCA) who wish to train for administrative positions.

**Eligibility** This program is open to women members of the ELCA who have completed a bachelor's degree or its equivalent and have taken some academic or professional courses since completing that degree. Applicants must have been admitted to an academic institution to work on an administrative degree, certification, or continuing education. U.S. citizenship is required.

**Financial data** The maximum amount awarded is $1,000.

**Duration** Up to 2 years.

**Number awarded** Varies each year.

**Deadline** February of each year.

## [697]
## ART SCHOLARSHIPS FOR MATURE WOMEN

National League of American Pen Women
1300 17th Street, N.W.
Washington, DC 20036-1973
(202) 785-1997                    Fax: (202) 452-8868
E-mail: nlapw1@verizon.net
Web: www.americanpenwomen.org

**Summary** To provide financial assistance for education to mature women artists.

**Eligibility** Women artists or photographers who are 35 years of age or older are eligible to apply if neither they nor members of their immediate family are members of the league. They must submit 3 color prints (4 by 6 inches or larger) of any media (oil, water color, original works on paper, acrylic, or sculpture) or 3 color or black-and-white prints (8 by 10 inches) of photographic works.

**Financial data** The award is $1,000. Funds are to be used for education.

**Duration** The award is granted biennially.

**Additional information** This award is offered in memory of Helen Trueheart Cox. An entry fee of $8 and a self-addressed stamped envelope must accompany each application.

**Number awarded** 1 each even-numbered year.

**Deadline** January of even-numbered years.

## [698]
## ASME GRADUATE TEACHING FELLOWSHIP

ASME International
Attn: Coordinator, Educational Operations
Three Park Avenue
New York, NY 10016-5990
(212) 591-8131                    Toll-free: (800) THE-ASME
Fax: (212) 591-7143     E-mail: OluwanifiseK@asme.org
Web: www.asme.org

**Summary** To provide funding to members of the American Society of Mechanical Engineers (ASME), particularly women and minorities, who are working on a doctorate in mechanical engineering.

**Eligibility** This program is open to U.S. citizens or permanent residents who have an undergraduate degree from an ABET-accredited program, belong to the society as a student member, are currently employed as a teaching assistant, and are working on a Ph.D. in mechanical engineering. Along with their application, they must submit a statement about their interest in a faculty career. Applications from women and minorities are particularly encouraged.

**Financial data** Fellowship stipends are $5,000 per year.

**Duration** Up to 2 years.

**Additional information** Recipients must teach at least 1 lecture course.

**Number awarded** Up to 4 each year.

**Deadline** November of each year.

## [699]
## ASSOCIATION FOR WOMEN IN SPORTS MEDIA SCHOLARSHIP/INTERNSHIP PROGRAM

Association for Women in Sports Media
c/o Rachel Cohen, Scholarship Coordinator
Dallas Morning News
P.O. Box 655237
Dallas, TX 75265
(979) 450-0146          E-mail: rcohen@dallasnews.com
Web: www.awsmonline.org/scholarship.htm

**Summary** To provide financial assistance and work experience to women undergraduate and graduate students who are interested in preparing for a career in sportswriting.

**Eligibility** This program is open to women who are enrolled in college or graduate school full time and plan to prepare for a career in sportswriting, sports copy editing, sports broadcasting, or sports public relations. Applicants must submit a 1-page essay describing their most memorable experience in sports or sports media, a 1-page resume highlighting their journalism experience, 2 letters of recommendation, up to 5 samples of their work, and a $15 application fee.

**Financial data**  Awardees receive a paid summer internship, a $1,000 scholarship for the next year of college or graduate school, $300 toward travel expenses to attend the annual convention of the Association for Women in Sports Media, waived convention fees, and free lodging at the host hotel. Copy editing interns receive an additional $1,000 scholarship from the Associated Press Sports Editors.

**Duration**  1 year; nonrenewable.

**Additional information**  Organizations that have hosted interns in the past include *Arizona Republic, Cleveland Plain Dealer, Colorado Springs Gazette, Detroit News*, ESPN, *Fort Worth Star-Telegram, Miami Herald, Newark Star-Ledger, Newsday*, Nike, *Sports Illustrated, St. Petersburg Times*, United States Olympic Committee, and USA Track & Field.

**Number awarded**  Varies each year.

**Deadline**  October of each year.

## [700]
## AT&T LABORATORIES FELLOWSHIP PROGRAM

AT&T Laboratories
Attn: Fellowship Administrator
180 Park Avenue, Room C103
P.O. Box 971
Florham Park, NJ 07932-0971
(973) 360-8109                    Fax: (973) 360-8881
E-mail: recruiting@research.att.com
Web: www.research.att.com/academic/alfp.html

**Summary**  To provide financial assistance and work experience to underrepresented minority and women students who are working on a doctoral degree in computer and communications-related fields.

**Eligibility**  This program is open to minorities underrepresented in the sciences (Blacks, Hispanics, and Native Americans) and to women. Applicants must be U.S. citizens or permanent residents beginning full-time Ph.D. study in disciplines relevant to the business of AT&T; currently, those include communications, computer science, electrical engineering, human computer interaction, industrial engineering, information science, mathematics, operations research, and statistics. Along with their application, they must submit a personal statement on why they are enrolled in their present academic program and how they intend to use their technical training, official transcripts, 3 academic references, and GRE scores. Selection is based on potential for success in scientific research.

**Financial data**  This program covers all educational expenses during the school year, including tuition, books, fees, and approved travel expenses; educational expenses for summer study or university research; a stipend for living expenses of $2,380 per month (paid for 10 months of the year); and support for attending approved scientific conferences.

**Duration**  1 year; may be renewed for up to 2 additional years, as long as the fellow continues making satisfactory progress toward the Ph.D.

**Additional information**  The AT&T Laboratories Fellowship Program (ALFP) provides a mentor who is a staff member at AT&T Labs as well as a summer research internship within AT&T Laboratories during the first summer. The ALFP

replaces the Graduate Research Program for Women (GRPW) and the Cooperative Research Fellowship Program (CRFP) run by the former AT&T Bell Laboratories. If recipients accept other support, the tuition payment and stipend received from that fellowship will replace that provided by this program. The other provisions of this fellowship will remain in force and the stipend will be replaced by an annual grant of $2,000.

**Number awarded**  Approximately 8 each year.

**Deadline**  January of each year.

## [701]
## BAPTIST WOMEN IN MINISTRY OF NORTH CAROLINA STUDENT SCHOLARSHIPS

Baptist Women in Ministry of North Carolina
Attn: Karen Metcalf, Convenor
Trinity Baptist Church
4815 Six Forks Road
Raleigh, NC 27609
(919) 787-3740          E-mail: childmin@tbcraleigh.com
Web: www.bwimnc.com/Scholarships.htm

**Summary**  To provide financial assistance to women ministerial students enrolled at North Carolina Baptist institutions.

**Eligibility**  This program is open to women working on a graduate degree in theological education at North Carolina Baptist institutions. Applicants must be able to demonstrate a clear call and commitment to vocational Christian ministry, academic excellence, leadership skills, and expressed support of inclusiveness in all dimensions of life.

**Financial data**  The stipend is $1,000.

**Duration**  1 year.

**Additional information**  The eligible schools include Duke Divinity School, Campbell University Divinity School, M. Christopher White School of Divinity at Gardner-Webb University, and the Wake Forest University Divinity School.

**Number awarded**  4 each year: 1 at each of the eligible schools.

## [702]
## BARBARA ALICE MOWER MEMORIAL SCHOLARSHIP

Barbara Alice Mower Memorial Scholarship Committee
c/o Nancy A. Mower
1536 Kamole Street
Honolulu, HI 96821-1424
(808) 373-2901

**Summary**  To provide financial assistance to female residents of Hawaii who are interested in women's studies and are attending college on the undergraduate or graduate level in the United States or abroad.

**Eligibility**  This program is open to female residents of Hawaii who are at least juniors in college, are interested in and committed to women's studies, and have worked or studied in the field. Selection is based on interest in studying about and commitment to helping women, previous work and/or study in that area, previous academic performance, character, personality, and future plans to help women (particularly women in Hawaii). If there are several applicants who meet all these criteria, then financial need may be taken into consideration.

**Financial data** The stipend ranges from $1,000 to $3,500.

**Duration** 1 year; may be renewed.

**Additional information** Recipients may use the scholarship at universities in Hawaii, on the mainland, or in foreign countries. They must focus on women's studies or topics that relate to women in school.

**Number awarded** 1 or more each year.

**Deadline** April of each year.

## [703]
## BARBARA MCBRIDE SCHOLARSHIP

Society of Exploration Geophysicists
Attn: SEG Foundation
8801 South Yale, Suite 500
P.O. Box 702740
Tulsa, OK 74170-2740
(918) 497-5513          Fax: (918) 497-5557
E-mail: scholarships@seg.org
Web: seg.org

**Summary** To provide financial assistance to women undergraduate and graduate students who are interested in the field of applied geophysics.

**Eligibility** This program is open to women who are 1) high school students planning to enter college in the fall, or 2) undergraduate or graduate students whose grades are above average. Applicants must intend to work on a degree directed toward a career in applied geophysics or a closely-related field. Along with their application, they must submit a 150-word essay on how they plan to use geophysics in their future. Financial need is not considered in the selection process.

**Financial data** The stipend ranges from $1,000 to $3,000 per year.

**Duration** 1 academic year; may be renewable, based on scholastic standing, availability of funds, and continuance of a course of study leading to a career in applied geophysics.

**Number awarded** 1 each year.

**Deadline** January of each year.

## [704]
## BASIC MIDWIFERY SCHOLARSHIPS

American College of Nurse-Midwives
Attn: ACNM Foundation, Inc.
8403 Coleville Road, Suite 1550
Silver Spring, MD 20915
(240) 485-1850          Fax: (240) 485-1818
Web: www.midwife.org

**Summary** To provide financial assistance for midwifery education to student members of the American College of Nurse-Midwives (ACNM).

**Eligibility** This program is open to ACNM members who are currently enrolled in an accredited basic midwife education program and have successfully completed 1 academic or clinical semester/quarter or clinical module. Applicants must submit a 150-word essay on their midwifery career plans and a 100-word essay on their intended future participation in the local, regional, and/or national activities of the

ACNM. Selection is based on leadership potential, financial need, academic history, and potential for future professional contribution to the organization.

**Financial data** The stipend is $3,000.

**Duration** 1 year.

**Additional information** This program includes the following named scholarships: the A.C.N.M. Foundation Memorial Scholarship, the TUMS Calcium for Life Scholarship (presented by GlaxoSmithKline), the Edith B. Wonnell CNM Scholarship, and the Margaret Edmundson Scholarship.

**Number awarded** Varies each year; recently, 4 of these scholarships were awarded.

**Deadline** March of each year.

## [705]
## BEHAVIORAL SCIENCES POSTDOCTORAL FELLOWSHIPS IN EPILEPSY

Epilepsy Foundation
Attn: Research Department
8301 Professional Place
Landover, MD 20785-2237
(301) 459-3700          Toll-free: (800) EFA-1000
Fax: (301) 577-2684        TDD: (800) 332-2070
E-mail: grants@efa.org
Web: www.epilepsyfoundation.org

**Summary** To provide funding to postdoctorates in the behavioral sciences (particularly women, minorities, and persons with disabilities) who wish to pursue research training in an area related to epilepsy.

**Eligibility** Individuals who have received their doctoral degree in a behavioral science field by the time the fellowship begins and desire additional postdoctoral research experience in epilepsy may apply. Academic faculty holding the rank of instructor or above are not eligible, nor are graduate or medical students, medical residents, permanent government employees, or employees of private industry. Appropriate fields of study in the behavioral sciences include sociology, social work, anthropology, nursing, economics, and others relevant to epilepsy research and practice. Because these fellowships are designed as training opportunities, the quality of the training plans and environment are considered in the selection process. Other selection criteria include the scientific quality of the proposed research, a statement regarding the relevance of the research to epilepsy, the applicant's qualifications, the preceptor's qualifications, adequacy of the facility, and related epilepsy programs at the institution. Applications from women, members of minority groups, and people with disabilities are especially encouraged. U.S. citizenship is not required, but the research must be conducted in the United States.

**Financial data** Grants up to $40,000 per year are available.

**Duration** 1 year.

**Number awarded** Varies each year; recently, 1 of these fellowships was awarded.

**Deadline** February of each year.

## [706]
## BERNADINE JOHNSON MARSHALL-MARTHA BELLE SCHOLARSHIPS

Association of Black Women Lawyers of New Jersey, Inc.
P.O. Box 22524
Trenton, NJ 08607
E-mail: abwlnj@yahoo.com
Web: www.abwlnj.org

**Summary** To provide financial assistance to African American women law students from New Jersey.

**Eligibility** This program is open to African American women who are residents of New Jersey and currently enrolled in their first, second, or third year at an accredited law school. Selection is based on a writing sample, community service, and financial need.

**Financial data** The stipend is $1,500.

**Duration** 1 year.

**Additional information** Information is also available from the scholarship committee chair, Mylyn K. Alexander, (201) 967-4622.

**Number awarded** At least 3 each year.

**Deadline** February of each year.

## [707]
## BERNICE F. ELLIOTT MEMORIAL SCHOLARSHIP

Baptist Convention of New Mexico
Attn: Missions Education and Women's Ministry Department
5325 Wyoming Boulevard, N.E.
P.O. Box 94485
Albuquerque, NM 87199-4485
(505) 924-2333          Toll-free: (800) 898-8544
Fax: (505) 924-2320      E-mail: cpeek@bcnm.com
Web: www.bcnm.com

**Summary** To provide financial assistance for college or seminary to women who are Southern Baptists from New Mexico.

**Eligibility** This program is open to women college and seminary students who are members of churches affiliated with the Baptist Convention of New Mexico. Preference is given to applicants who are committed to full-time Christian service, have a background in the Woman's Missionary Union, and can demonstrate financial need.

**Financial data** A stipend is awarded (amount not specified).

**Duration** 1 year; may be renewed.

**Number awarded** 1 or more each year.

**Deadline** April of each year.

## [708]
## BETTY HANSEN NATIONAL SCHOLARSHIPS

Danish Sisterhood of America
Attn: Lizette Burtis, Scholarship Chair
3020 Santa Juanita Court
Santa Rosa, CA 95405-8219
(707) 539-1884          E-mail: lburtis@sbcglobal.net
Web: www.danishsisterhood.org/rschol.asp

**Summary** To provide financial assistance for educational purposes in the United States or Denmark to members or relatives of members of the Danish Sisterhood of America.

**Eligibility** This program is open to members or the family of members of the sisterhood who are interested in attending an accredited 4-year college or university as a full-time undergraduate or graduate student. Members must have belonged to the sisterhood for at least 1 year. Selection is based on academic excellence (at least a 2.5 GPA). Upon written request, the scholarship may be used for study in Denmark.

**Financial data** The stipend is $1,000.

**Duration** 1 year; nonrenewable.

**Number awarded** Up to 8 each year.

**Deadline** February of each year.

## [709]
## BIG FIVE SCHOLARSHIP

Daughters of Penelope
Attn: Daughters of Penelope Foundation, Inc.
1909 Q Street, N.W., Suite 500
Washington, DC 20009-1007
(202) 234-9741          Fax: (202) 483-6983
E-mail: daughters@ahepa.org
Web: www.ahepa.org

**Summary** To provide financial assistance for graduate study to women of Greek descent.

**Eligibility** This program is open to women who have been members of the Daughters of Penelope or the Maids of Athena for at least 2 years, or whose parents or grandparents have been members of the Daughters of Penelope or the Order of Ahepa for at least 2 years. Applicants must be accepted or currently enrolled for a minimum of 9 units per academic year in an M.A., M.S., M.B.A., J.D., Ph.D., D.D.S., M.D., or other university graduate degree program. They must have taken the GRE or other entrance examination (or Canadian, Greek, or Cypriot equivalent) and must write an essay (in English) about their educational and vocational goals. Selection is based on academic merit.

**Financial data** The stipend is $1,000 per year.

**Duration** 1 year; nonrenewable.

**Additional information** Information is also available from Helen Santire, National Scholarship Chair, P.O. Box 19709, Houston, TX 77242-9709, (713) 468-6531.

**Number awarded** 1 each year.

**Deadline** May of each year.

## [710]
## BISHOP CHARLES P. GRECO GRADUATE FELLOWSHIPS

Knights of Columbus
Attn: Committee on Fellowships
P.O. Box 1670
New Haven, CT 06507-0901
(203) 752-4332                    Fax: (203) 772-2696
E-mail: info@kofc.org
Web: www.kofc.org

**Summary**  To provide financial assistance to members of the Knights of Columbus and their families who are interested in working on a graduate degree to prepare for a career as a teacher of mentally retarded children.

**Eligibility**  This program is open to members as well as to their wives, sons, and daughters and to the widows and children of deceased members. Applicants must be working full time on a master's degree to prepare for a career as a teacher of mentally retarded children. They must be at the beginning of their graduate program. Special consideration is given to applicants who select a Catholic graduate school.

**Financial data**  The stipend is $500 per semester, payable to the university.

**Duration**  1 semester; may be renewed for up to 3 additional semesters.

**Additional information**  This program was established in 1973.

**Deadline**  April of each year.

## [711]
## BISHOP FRANK MURPHY SCHOLARSHIP FOR WOMEN IN MINISTRY

Women's Ordination Conference
Attn: Scholarship Committee
P.O. Box 2693
Fairfax, VA 22031-0693
(703) 352-1006
E-mail: nvazquez@womensordination.org
Web: www.womensordination.org

**Summary**  To provide financial assistance to members of the Women's Ordination Conference (WOC) who are working on a graduate degree to prepare for Catholic ministry.

**Eligibility**  This program is open to women who are members or become members of the WOC. Applicants must be enrolled or accepted in a graduate program at a seminary or a diocesan certificate program preparing for Catholic ministry. They must submit a letter of recommendation from a mentor who can testify to their commitment to WOC's goals, a personal statement of how their future ministry supports WOC's mission, a resume or curriculum vitae, and proof of enrollment.

**Financial data**  The stipend is $1,000. Funds must be used for educational expenses.

**Duration**  1 year.

**Additional information**  The WOC is an organization "working locally and nationally in collaboration with the worldwide movement for women's ordination." In pursuit of its goals, it "works for justice and equality for women in our church; strives to eliminate all forms of domination and discrimination in the Catholic church; advocates inclusive church structures; supports and affirms women's talents, gifts and calls to ministry." Recipients are required to submit a report at the end of the grant period explaining how the award impacted their study and growth.

**Number awarded**  2 or more each year.

**Deadline**  January of each year.

## [712]
## B.K. KRENZER REENTRY SCHOLARSHIP

Society of Women Engineers
230 East Ohio Street, Suite 400
Chicago, IL 60611-3265
(312) 596-5223                    Toll-free: (877) SWE-INFO
Fax: (312) 644-8557
E-mail: scholarshipapplication@swe.org
Web: www.swe.org/scholarships

**Summary**  To provide financial assistance to women interested in returning to college or graduate school to study engineering or computer science.

**Eligibility**  This program is open to women who are planning to enroll at an ABET-accredited 4-year college or university. Applicants must have been out of the engineering workforce and school for at least 2 years and must be planning to return as an undergraduate or graduate student to major in computer science or engineering. Along with their application, they must submit a 1-page essay on why they want to be an engineer or computer scientist, how they believe they will make a difference as an engineer or computer scientist, and what influenced them to study engineering or computer science. Selection is based on merit. Preference is given to engineers who already have a degree and are planning to reenter the engineering workforce after a period of temporary retirement.

**Financial data**  The stipend is $2,000.

**Duration**  1 year.

**Additional information**  This program was established in 1996.

**Number awarded**  1 each year.

**Deadline**  January of each year.

## [713]
## BOEING COMPANY CAREER ENHANCEMENT SCHOLARSHIP

Women in Aviation, International
Attn: Scholarships
Morningstar Airport
3647 State Route 503 South
West Alexandria, OH 45381
(937) 558-7655                    Fax: (937) 839-4645
E-mail: scholarships@wai.org
Web: www.wai.org/education/scholarships.cfm

**Summary**  To provide financial assistance to members of Women in Aviation, International (WAI) who are active in aerospace and need financial support to advance their career.

**Eligibility**  This program is open to WAI members who wish to advance their career in the aerospace industry in the fields of engineering, technology development, or management. Applicants may be 1) full-time or part-time employees working in the aerospace industry or a related field, or 2) students working on an aviation-related degree who are at least juniors and have a GPA of 2.5 or higher. They must submit an essay that addresses their career aspirations and goals, in addition to an application form, 3 letters of recommendation, a resume, copies of all aviation and medical certificates, and the last 3 pages of their pilot logbook, if applicable. Selection is based on achievements, attitude toward self and others, commitment to success, dedication to career, financial need, motivation, reliability, responsibility, and teamwork.

**Financial data** A stipend is awarded (amount not specified).

**Duration** 1 year.

**Additional information** WAI is a nonprofit professional organization dedicated to encouraging women to consider an aviation career, providing educational outreach activities, and providing networking opportunities to women active in the industry.

**Number awarded** 1 each year.

**Deadline** November of each year.

## [714]
## BOSTON AFFILIATE AWSCPA SCHOLARSHIP

American Woman's Society of Certified Public
   Accountants-Boston Affiliate
c/o Andrea Costantino
Oxford Bioscience Partners
222 Berkeley Street, Suite 1650
Boston, MA 02116
(617) 357-7474        E-mail: acostantino@oxbio.com
Web: www.awscpa.org/frameset.php?cf=awards.htm

**Summary** To provide financial assistance to women who are working on an undergraduate or graduate degree in accounting at a college or university in New England.

**Eligibility** This program is open to women who are attending a college in New England and majoring in accounting. Applicants must have completed at least 12 semester hours of accounting or tax courses and have a cumulative GPA of 3.0 or higher. They must be planning to graduate between May of next year and May of the following year or, for the 15-month graduate program, before September of the current year. Along with their application, they must submit a brief essay on why they feel they would be a good choice for this award. Selection is based on that essay, academic achievement, work experience, extracurricular activities, scholastic honors, career plans, and financial need.

**Financial data** The stipend is $1,000.

**Duration** 1 year.

**Number awarded** 2 each year.

**Deadline** September of each year.

## [715]
## BPW/NC FOUNDATION SCHOLARSHIP

North Carolina Federation of Business and Professional
   Women's Organizations, Inc.
Attn: BPW/NC Foundation
P.O. Box 276
Carrboro, NC 27510
Web: www.bpwnc.org/Foundation/foundation_nc.htm

**Summary** To provide financial assistance to women attending North Carolina colleges, community colleges, or graduate schools.

**Eligibility** This program is open to women who are currently enrolled in a community college, 4-year college, or graduate school in North Carolina. Applicants must be endorsed by a local BPW unit. Along with their application, they must submit a 1-page statement that summarizes their career goals, previous honors, or community activities and justifies their need for this scholarship.

**Financial data** The stipend is at least $500. Funds are paid directly to the recipient's school.

**Duration** 1 year; recipients may reapply.

**Additional information** This program was established in 1996. Information is also available from Patricia Ann McMurray, 510 Canna Place, Aberdeen, NC 28315.

**Number awarded** 1 each year.

**Deadline** April of each year.

## [716]
## BUENA M. CHESSHIR MEMORIAL WOMEN'S EDUCATIONAL SCHOLARSHIP

Business and Professional Women of Virginia
Attn: Virginia BPW Foundation
P.O. Box 4842
McLean, VA 22103-4842
Web: www.bpwva.org/scholarships.shtml

**Summary** To provide financial assistance to mature women in Virginia who are interested in upgrading their skills or education at a college, law school, or medical school in the state.

**Eligibility** This program is open to women who are residents of Virginia, U.S. citizens, and at least 25 years of age. Applicants must have been accepted into an accredited program or course of study at a Virginia institution, have a definite plan to use their training to improve their chances for upward mobility in the workforce, and be graduating within 2 years. Undergraduate applicants may be majoring in any field, but doctoral students must be working on a degree in law or medicine. Selection is based on academic achievement, demonstrated financial need, and defined career goals.

**Financial data** Stipends range from $100 to $1,000 per year; funds may be used for tuition, fees, books, transportation, living expenses, and dependent care.

**Duration** Recipients must complete their course of study within 2 years.

**Number awarded** 1 or more each year.

**Deadline** March of each year.

## [717]
## CAA PROFESSIONAL DEVELOPMENT FELLOWSHIPS

College Art Association of America
Attn: Fellowship Program
275 Seventh Avenue
New York, NY 10001-6798
(212) 691-1051, ext. 242    Fax: (212) 627-2381
E-mail: fellowship@collegeart.org
Web: www.collegeart.org/fellowships

**Summary** To provide financial assistance to graduate students from socially and economically diverse backgrounds who are completing an advanced degree in art history or the visual arts.

**Eligibility** This program is open to candidates for an M.F.A. degree in the visual arts or a Ph.D. in art history. Applicants must have been underrepresented in the field because of their race, religion, gender, age, national origin, sexual orientation, disability, or financial status. They must be U.S. citizens or permanent residents who can demonstrate financial need and an expected completion of their degree in the year following application.

**Financial data** The stipend is $5,000.

**Duration** 1 year: the final year of the degree program.

**Additional information** In addition to providing a stipend for the terminal year of their degree program, the College Art Association (CAA) helps fellows search for employment at a museum, art center, college, or university. Upon securing a position, CAA provides a $10,000 subsidy to the employer as part of the fellow's salary. Participating organizations must match this 2:1. In addition to administrative and/or teaching responsibilities, all fellows' positions must include a curatorial or public service component. Salary or stipend, position description, and term of employment will vary and are determined in consultation with individual fellows and their potential employers. This program began in 1993. Funding for the M.F.A. program in the visual arts is provided by the National Endowment for the Arts. Funding for the Ph.D. program in art history is provided by the National Endowment for the Humanities.

**Number awarded** Varies each year. Recently, 4 of these fellowships were awarded: 2 to M.F.A. candidates in the visual arts and 2 to Ph.D. candidates in art history.

**Deadline** January of each year.

## [718]
## CALIFORNIA P.E.O. SCHOLARSHIPS

P.E.O. Foundation-California State Chapter
c/o Liz Wetzel
1887 Rim Rock Canyon Road
Laguna Beach, CA 92651
(949) 376-1568    E-mail: elwglw@cox.net

**Summary** To provide financial assistance to women in California whose undergraduate or graduate education has been interrupted.

**Eligibility** This program is open to female residents of California who have completed 4 years of high school (or the equivalent), are enrolled at or accepted by an accredited college, university, vocational school, or graduate school, and have an excellent academic record. Selection is based on financial need, character, academic ability, and school and community activities.

**Financial data** Stipends range from $200 to $4,000.

**Duration** 1 year; may be renewed for up to 3 additional years.

**Additional information** This program includes the following named scholarships: the Barbara Furse Mackey Scholarship (for women whose education has been interrupted); the Beverly Dye Anderson Scholarship (for the fields of teaching or health care); the Marjorie M. McDonald P.E.O. Scholarship (for women who are continuing their education after a long hiatus from school); the Ora Keck Scholarship (for women who are preparing for a career in music or the fine arts); the Phyllis J. Van Deventer Scholarship (for women who are preparing for a career in music performance or music education); the Stella May Nau Scholarship (for women who are interested in reentering the job market); the Linda Jones Memorial Fine Arts Scholarship (for women studying fine arts); the Polly Thompson Memorial Music Scholarship (for women studying music); the Ruby W. Henry Scholarship; the Jean W. Gratiot Scholarship; the Pearl Prime Scholarship; and the Helen D. Thompson Memorial Scholarship.

**Number awarded** Varies each year; recently, 18 of these scholarships were awarded.

**Deadline** February of each year.

## [719]
## CALIFORNIA SPACE GRANT CONSORTIUM GRADUATE RESEARCH FELLOWSHIPS

California Space Grant Consortium
c/o University of California at San Diego
Chemistry Research Building, Room 319
9500 Gilman Drive, Department 0524
La Jolla, CA 92093-0524
(858) 822-1597    Fax: (858) 534-7840
E-mail: spacegrant@ucsd.edu
Web: calspace.ucsd.edu/casgc/grad_fellowships.html

**Summary** To provide financial assistance for graduate study and research in space-related science, engineering, or technology at institutions that are affiliates of the California Space Grant Consortium (CaSGC).

**Eligibility** This program is open to graduate students in space-related science, engineering, and technology at CaSGC affiliates. Each participating institution encourages aerospace science and engineering graduate students, particularly underrepresented ethnic or gender groups, to apply. U.S. citizenship is required.

**Financial data** Each campus sets its own stipend.

**Duration** 1 year.

**Additional information** CaSGC affiliates include the University of California campuses at Berkeley, Davis, Irvine, Los Angeles, Riverside, San Diego, Santa Barbara, and Santa Cruz; the California State University campuses at Long Beach, Los Angeles, Sacramento, San Bernardino, San Diego, and San Luis Obispo; Santa Clara University; Stanford University; and the University of Southern California. This program is funded by the U.S. National Aeronautics and Space Administration (NASA). Award recipients are encouraged to mentor within the campus minority engineering and science programs and in the Space Grant Outreach programs.

**Number awarded** Varies each year. A total of $100,000 is available for these fellowships each year.

**Deadline** Each of the participating institutions sets its own deadline.

## [720]
## CAREER ADVANCEMENT SCHOLARSHIPS

Business and Professional Women's Foundation
Attn: Scholarship Program
301 ACT Drive
P.O. Box 4030
Iowa City, IA 52243-4030
Toll-free: (800) 525-3729
E-mail: bpwfoundation@act.org
Web: www.bpwfoundation.org

**Summary** To provide financial assistance for college or graduate school to mature women who are employed or seeking employment in selected fields.

**Eligibility** This program is open to women who are at least 25 years of age, citizens of the United States, within 2 years of completing their course of study, officially accepted into an accredited program or course of study at an American institution (including those in American Samoa, Puerto Rico, and the Virgin Islands), able to demonstrate critical financial need, and planning to use the desired training to improve their chances for advancement, train for a new career field, or enter/reenter the job market. Applicants must be interested in working on an associate degree, bachelor's degree, master's degree, certificate program for a person with a degree (e.g., teacher's certificate), or certificate program that does not require a degree (e.g., nurse practitioner). Along with their application, they must submit a 1-page essay on their specific, short-term goals and how the proposed training and award will help them accomplish their goals and make a difference in their professional career. Study for a doctoral-level or terminal degree (e.g., Ph.D., M.D., D.D.S., D.V.M., J.D.) is not eligible.

**Financial data** Stipends range from $1,000 to $2,500 per year.

**Duration** 1 year; recipients may reapply.

**Additional information** The scholarship may be used to support part-time study as well as academic or vocational/paraprofessional/office skills training. The program was established in 1969. Scholarships cannot be used to pay for classes already in progress. The program does not cover study at the doctoral level, correspondence courses, postdoctoral studies, or studies in foreign countries. Training must be completed within 24 months.

**Number awarded** Varies each year; recently, 75 of these scholarships were awarded.

**Deadline** April of each year.

## [721]
## CAREER AWARDS AT THE SCIENTIFIC INTERFACE

Burroughs Wellcome Fund
21 T.W. Alexander Drive, Suite 100
P.O. Box 13901
Research Triangle Park, NC 27709-3901
(919) 991-5100                    Fax: (919) 991-5160
E-mail: info@bwfund.org
Web: www.bwfund.org

**Summary** To provide funding to postdoctorates (particularly women and minorities) in the physical and computational sciences who are interested in pursuing research training in the biomedical sciences.

**Eligibility** Applicants must have a Ph.D. degree in the fields of mathematics, physics, chemistry (physical, theoretical, or computational), computer science, statistics, or engineering. They must have completed at least 6 but not more than 48 months of postdoctoral training and must not hold or have accepted a faculty appointment as an assistant professor at the time of application. Degree-granting institutions in the United States and Canada, including their medical schools, graduate schools, and all affiliated hospitals and research institutes, may nominate up to 2 candidates for the award. Institutions are encouraged to nominate women and members of underrepresented minority groups. If they nominate at least 1 African American, Hispanic, or Native American postdoctorate, they may nominate up to 3 total candidates. The research proposal must address questions in an area of biomedical science, including any combination of experiment, computation, mathematical modeling, statistical analysis, or computer simulation. Nominees must be citizens or permanent residents of the United States or Canada. Selection is based on the depth and rigor of training in a scientific discipline other than biology, importance of biological questions identified in the proposal and innovation in the approaches chosen to answer them, interdisciplinary nature of the research plan, potential of the candidate to establish a successful independent research career, and quality of proposed collaborations.

**Financial data** In the first year of postdoctoral support, the salary is $44,000, the research allowance is $31,000, and the administrative fee is $5,000; in the second year of postdoctoral support, the salary is $47,000, the research allowance is $8,000, and the administrative fee is $5,000; in the first year of faculty support, the maximum salary support is $45,000, the research allowance is $65,000, and the administrative fee is $10,000; in the second year of faculty support, the maximum salary support is $49,000, the research allowance is $61,000, and the administrative fee is $10,000; in the third year of faculty support, the maximum salary support is $54,000, the research allowance is $56,000, and the administrative fee is $10,000. The maximum total grant is $500,000. During the first year of the faculty period, at least 50% of the starting salary must be provided by the institution. If an institution's salary scale for either the postdoctoral or faculty position exceeds the amounts provided by the award, then the institution must supplement the awardee's salary. For awardees in the United States, the administrative fee is intended to cover the cost of medical insurance and other benefits. For awardees in Canada, the fee is to be used as a contribution to the employer's benefit plan.

**Duration** 5 years: up to 2 years for advanced postdoctoral training and the first 3 years of a faculty appointment.

**Additional information** Awardees are required to devote at least 80% of their time to research-related activities.

**Number awarded** Varies each year; recently, 12 of these grants were awarded.

**Deadline** April of each year.

## [722]
## CAROLYN WEATHERFORD SCHOLARSHIP FUND

Woman's Missionary Union
Attn: WMU Foundation
100 Missionary Ridge
P.O. Box 11346
Birmingham, AL 35202-1346
(205) 408-5525          Toll-free: (877) 482-4483
Fax: (205) 408-5508
E-mail: wmufoundation@wmu.org
Web: www.wmufoundation.com/scholar_scholar.asp

**Summary** To provide an opportunity for women to prepare for service to the Woman's Missionary Union (WMU).

**Eligibility** This program is open to women who are members of the Baptist Church and are interested in 1) field work experience as interns or in women's missionary work in the United States; or 2) service in women's missionary work in the United States). Applicants must arrange for 3 letters of endorsement, from a recent professor, a state or associational WMU official, and a recent pastor. Selection is based on current active involvement in WMU, previous activity in WMU, plans for long-term involvement in WMU and/or home missions, academic strength, leadership skills, and personal and professional characteristics.

**Financial data** A stipend is awarded (amount not specified).

**Duration** 1 year.

**Additional information** This fund was begun by Woman's Mission Union, Auxiliary to Southern Baptist Convention, in appreciation for the executive director of WMU during its centennial year. Recipients must attend a Southern Baptist seminary or divinity school.

**Number awarded** 1 or more each year.

**Deadline** February of each year.

## [723]
## CATERPILLAR SCHOLARSHIPS

Society of Women Engineers
230 East Ohio Street, Suite 400
Chicago, IL 60611-3265
(312) 596-5223          Toll-free: (877) SWE-INFO
Fax: (312) 644-8557
E-mail: scholarshipapplication@swe.org
Web: www.swe.org/scholarships

**Summary** To provide financial assistance to women from selected states who are attending college or graduate school to study engineering or computer science.

**Eligibility** This program is open to women who are enrolled at an ABET-accredited 4-year college or university. Applicants must be U.S. citizens majoring in computer science or engineering as an undergraduate or graduate student. They must have a GPA of 2.8 or higher and be resi-

dents of the sponsor's region C (Arkansas, Louisiana, Mississippi, and Texas); D (Alabama, Florida, Georgia, Puerto Rico, North Carolina, South Carolina, Tennessee, and the U.S. Virgin Islands); H (Illinois, Indiana, Iowa, Michigan, Minnesota, North Dakota, South Dakota, and Wisconsin); or I (Colorado, Kansas, Missouri, Nebraska, Oklahoma, and Wyoming). Along with their application, they must submit a 1-page essay on why they want to be an engineer or computer scientist, how they believe they will make a difference as an engineer or computer scientist, and what influenced them to study engineering or computer science. Selection is based on merit.

**Financial data** The stipend is $2,400.

**Duration** 1 year.

**Additional information** This program is sponsored by Caterpillar, Inc.

**Number awarded** 3 each year.

**Deadline** January of each year.

## [724]
## CELIA M. HOWARD FELLOWSHIP

Illinois Federation of Business and Professional Women's Clubs
Attn: Chair, Howard Fellowship Fund Committee
50 Old Ottawa Road
Danville, IL 61834
(217) 442-3686
E-mail: info@celiamhowardfellowship.org
Web: www.celiamhowardfellowship.org

**Summary** To provide funding to women in Illinois who are interested in working on a graduate degree in specified fields at eligible universities.

**Eligibility** This program is open to Illinois women who are U.S. citizens; have been Illinois residents for at least the past 2 years; have earned a bachelor's degree with at least 12 hours of undergraduate work in economics, history, and/or political science; and have a GPA of 3.0 of higher. A personal interview may be required. Applicants must be planning to study for a masterÖs degree in administration of justice at Southern Illinois University at Carbondale, a J.D. degree at the University of Illinois College of Law at Urbana-Champaign, a masterÖs degree in diplomacy at the Fletcher School of Law and Diplomacy in Medford, Massachusetts, a masterÖs degree in management at the Northwestern University J.L. Kellogg Graduate School of Management in Evanston, Illinois, or a masterÖs degree in international management at the American Graduate School of International Management in Glendale, Arizona. Selection is based on financial need, previous graduate study, practical business experience in government, and leadership experience.

**Financial data** The amount awarded varies, from $500 to $10,000 per year. Funds are paid directly to the recipient's school.

**Duration** 1 year; renewable.

**Additional information** This program was established in 1948.

**Number awarded** 1 or more each year.

**Deadline** October of each year.

## [725]
### CHARLES T. STONER LAW SCHOLARSHIP AWARD

Women's Basketball Coaches Association
Attn: Manager of Awards
4646 Lawrenceville Highway
Lilburn, GA 30047-3620
(770) 279-8027, ext. 102          Fax: (770) 279-6290
E-mail: alowe@wbca.org
Web: www.wbca.org/StonerAward.asp

**Summary** To provide financial assistance for law school to women's basketball players.

**Eligibility** This program is open to women's college basketball players who are seniors planning to attend law school. Applicants must be nominated by a member of the Women's Basketball Coaches Association (WBCA). Selection is based on a letter of recommendation, academic major and GPA, basketball statistics for all 4 years of college, academic and athletic honors, and campus activities.

**Financial data** The stipend is $1,000 per year.

**Duration** 1 year.

**Additional information** This program began in 2001.

**Number awarded** 1 each year.

## [726]
### CHI OMEGA FOUNDATION ALUMNAE EDUCATIONAL GRANTS

Chi Omega Fraternity
Attn: Chi Omega Foundation
3395 Players Club Parkway
Memphis, TN 38125
(901) 748-8600          Fax: (901) 748-8686
E-mail: foundation@chiomega.com
Web: ww2.chiomega.com/everyday/scholarship

**Summary** To provide financial assistance for graduate school to women who are members of Chi Omega Fraternity and have been out of college for a period of time.

**Eligibility** This program is open to women over 24 years of age who are alumnae members of Chi Omega Fraternity. Applicants must have experienced an interruption in their education but now be planning to enter graduate school as a full- or part-time student for career qualification or advancement. Selection is based on academic achievement, aptitude, service to Chi Omega, contributions to the university and community, and financial need.

**Financial data** The stipend is $1,000.

**Duration** 1 year.

**Additional information** This program was established in 1997.

**Number awarded** 10 each year.

**Deadline** January of each year.

## [727]
### CHICAGO NETWORK OF EXECUTIVE WOMEN IN HOSPITALITY SCHOLARSHIP AWARDS

Network of Executive Women in Hospitality-Chicago Chapter
Attn: Lucy Coughlin, Director of Scholarship and Education
Looney and Associates
162 West Hubbard Street, Suite 302
Chicago, IL 60610
(312) 329-0464          Toll-free: (800) 593-NEWH
Fax: (800) 693-NEWH
E-mail: lucyc@looney-associates.com
Web: www.newh.org/newh/scholarshippacket.php

**Summary** To provide financial assistance to undergraduate and graduate women working on a degree in hospitality in midwestern states.

**Eligibility** This program is open to women who have completed half of an accredited hospitality-related undergraduate or graduate program in Illinois, Indiana, Michigan, or Ohio. Applicants must have a GPA of 3.0 or higher and a career objective in the hospitality or food service industries (e.g., hotel and restaurant management, culinary, architecture, design). Selection is based on financial need and academic accomplishments.

**Financial data** The stipend depends on the availability of funds and the need of the recipient.

**Number awarded** 1 or more each year.

**Deadline** September of each year.

## [728]
### CIRCLE KEY GRANTS OF THE ROSE MCGILL FUND

Kappa Kappa Gamma Foundation
530 East Town Street
P.O. Box 38
Columbus, OH 43216-0038
(614) 228-6515          Toll-free: (866) KKG-1870
Fax: (614) 228-7809          E-mail: kkghq@kappa.org
Web: www.kappakappagamma.org

**Summary** To assist alumna members of Kappa Kappa Gamma who wish to pursue additional education.

**Eligibility** This program is open to Kappa Kappa Gamma alumnae needing financial assistance for part-time educational programs related to career opportunities. The grants are awarded on the basis of need, merit, and individual goals for study.

**Financial data** The amount awarded varies, depending upon the circumstances and the money available. Generally, awards do not exceed $750 each.

**Additional information** The Rose McGill fund was established in 1922 to provide confidential aid to Kappa Kappa Gamma members. These funds are to be used to continue, not to start, a course of study. Requests for applications must be accompanied by a self-addressed stamped envelope and chapter membership identification.

**Number awarded** Varies each year; in a recent biennium, Rose McGill programs provided $760,762 in support.

**Deadline** Applications are accepted throughout the year.

**[729]**
## CITRUS DISTRICT 2 SCHOLARSHIPS

Daughters of Penelope-District 2
c/o Sophie Caras
6511 Lake Clark Drive
Palm Beach, FL 33406
(561) 582-9619          E-mail: sophieh@adelphia.net
Web: www.ahepad2.org

**Summary**   To provide financial assistance for college or graduate school to women who are residents of Florida or the Bahamas and members of organizations affiliated with the American Hellenic Educational Progressive Association (AHEPA).

**Eligibility**   This program is open to women who are residents of Citrus District 2 (Florida and the Bahamas) and high school seniors, undergraduates, or graduate students with a high school or college GPA of 3.0 or higher. Applicants must have been a member of the Maids of Athena for at least 2 years or have an immediate family member who has belonged to the Daughters of Penelope or Order of Ahepa for at least 2 years. They must submit a personal essay of 200 to 500 words to give the selection committee a sense of their goals and personal effort. Selection is based on merit.

**Financial data**   A stipend is awarded (amount not specified).

**Duration**   1 year; may be renewed.

**Additional information**   This program includes the Past District Governors/Julie P. Microutsicos Scholarship, awarded to the runner-up.

**Number awarded**   2 each year.

**Deadline**   May of each year.

**[730]**
## CLARE BOOTHE LUCE PROGRAM SCHOLARSHIP

Society of Women Engineers
230 East Ohio Street, Suite 400
Chicago, IL 60611-3265
(312) 596-5223          Toll-free: (877) SWE-INFO
Fax: (312) 644-8557
E-mail: scholarshipapplication@swe.org
Web: www.swe.org/scholarships

**Summary**   To provide financial assistance to graduate women majoring in science, mathematics, or engineering.

**Eligibility**   This program is open to women working on a graduate degree in the sciences, mathematics, or engineering. Applicants must have a GPA of 3.0 or higher. Along with their application, they must submit a 1-page essay on why they want to be an engineer or scientist, how they believe they will make a difference as an engineer or scientist, and what influenced them to study engineering or science. Selection is based on merit. Preference is given to applicants expressing a career interest in academia.

**Financial data**   The stipend is $10,000.

**Duration**   1 year.

**Additional information**   This program was established in 2004.

**Number awarded**   1 each year.

**Deadline**   January of each year.

**[731]**
## CLAUDIA STEELE BAKER GRADUATE FELLOWSHIPS

Alpha Chi Omega Foundation
Attn: Foundation Programs Coordinator
5939 Castle Creek Parkway North Drive
Indianapolis, IN 46250-4343
(317) 579-5050, ext. 262          Fax: (317) 579-5051
E-mail: foundation@alphachiomega.org
Web: www.alphachiomega.org

**Summary**   To provide financial assistance to Alpha Chi Omega members who are interested in studying social services in graduate school.

**Eligibility**   Women college seniors and graduates who are members of the sorority are eligible to apply if they have majored in a social service field, are committed to peace and understanding, and plan to attend graduate school. Selection is based on campus, community, and chapter service.

**Financial data**   The stipend is $1,500.

**Duration**   1 year.

**Number awarded**   1 each year.

**Deadline**   March of each year.

**[732]**
## COLUMBIA CREW MEMORIAL UNDERGRADUATE SCHOLARSHIPS

Texas Space Grant Consortium
Attn: Administrative Assistant
3925 West Braker Lane, Suite 200
Austin, TX 78759
(512) 471-3583          Toll-free: (800) 248-8742
Fax: (512) 471-3585
E-mail: scholarships@tsgc.utexas.edu
Web: www.tsgc.utexas.edu/grants

**Summary**   To provide financial assistance to upper-division and medical students in Texas (particularly women, minority and disabled students) who are working on degrees in the space science and engineering.

**Eligibility**   Applicants must be U.S. citizens, eligible for financial assistance, and registered for full-time study at a participating college or university. They must be a sophomore at a 2-year institution, a junior or senior at a 4-year institution, or a first- or second-year student at a medical school. Supported fields of study have included aerospace engineering, biology, chemical engineering, chemistry, electrical engineering, geology, industrial engineering, mathematics, mechanical engineering, and physics. The program encourages participation by members of groups underrepresented in science and engineering (persons with disabilities, women, African Americans, Hispanic Americans, Native Americans, and Pacific Islanders). Selection is based on excellence in academics, participation in space education projects, participation in research projects, and exhibited leadership qualities.

**Financial data**   The stipend is $1,000.

**Duration**   1 year; nonrenewable.

**Additional information**   In 2003, the Texas Space Grant Consortium renamed its undergraduate scholarship program in honor of the 7 Space Shuttle Columbia astronauts. The participating universities are Baylor University, Lamar

University, Prairie View A&M University, Rice University, San Jacinto College, Southern Methodist University, Sul Ross State University, Texas A&M University (including Kingsville and Corpus Christi campuses), Texas Christian University, Texas Southern University, Texas Tech University, Trinity University, University of Houston (including Clear Lake and Downtown campuses), University of Texas at Arlington, University of Texas at Austin, University of Texas at Dallas, University of Texas at El Paso, University of Texas at San Antonio, and University of Texas/Pan American. This program is funded by the National Aeronautics and Space Administration (NASA).

**Number awarded** Varies each year; recently, 29 of these scholarships were awarded.

**Deadline** March of each year.

## [733]
## COLUMBIA MEMORIAL SCHOLARSHIP

Nebraska Space Grant Consortium
c/o University of Nebraska at Omaha
Allwine Hall 422
6001 Dodge Street
Omaha, NE 68182-0589
(402) 554-3772
Toll-free: (800) 858-8648, ext. 4-3772 (within NE)
Fax: (402) 554-3781    E-mail: nasa@unomaha.edu
Web: www.unomaha.edu

**Summary** To provide financial assistance to undergraduate and graduate students (particularly women, minority and disabled students) majoring in science at institutions that are members of the Nebraska Space Grant Consortium.

**Eligibility** This program is open to undergraduate and graduate students at schools that are members of the Nebraska Space Grant Consortium. Applicants must submit an essay that describes their scientific research track, past or ongoing research, career goals, and how the scientific research track they are pursuing will be helpful in their career. This program is sponsored by the U.S. National Aeronautics and Space Administration (NASA), which strongly encourages women, minorities, and students with disabilities to apply. U.S. citizenship is required.

**Financial data** A stipend is awarded (amount not specified).

**Duration** 1 year.

**Additional information** This program was established in 2003 to honor the Columbia astronauts, especially Creighton University graduate Lt. Col. Michael Anderson. The following schools are members of the Nebraska Space Grant Consortium: University of Nebraska at Omaha, University of Nebraska at Lincoln, University of Nebraska at Kearney, University of Nebraska Medical Center, Creighton University, Western Nebraska Community College, Chadron State College, College of St. Mary, Metropolitan Community College, Grace University, Hastings College, Little Priest Tribal College, and Nebraska Indian Community College.

**Deadline** April of each year.

## [734]
## CONDUCTING SCHOLARSHIP FOR GRADUATE STUDENTS

Sigma Alpha Iota Philanthropies, Inc.
One Tunnel Road
Asheville, NC 28805
(828) 251-0606    Fax: (828) 251-0644
E-mail: philonline@sai-national.org
Web: www.sai-national.org/phil/philsch1.html

**Summary** To provide financial assistance to members of Sigma Alpha Iota (an organization of women musicians) working on a degree in conducting.

**Eligibility** Members of the organization may apply for these scholarships if they are currently enrolled in a graduate degree program with an emphasis on conducting. Applicants must include a videotape of a performance they conducted.

**Financial data** The stipend is $2,500.

**Duration** 1 year.

**Additional information** There is a $25 nonrefundable application fee.

**Number awarded** 1 each year.

**Deadline** March of each year.

## [735]
## CONGRESSIONAL FELLOWSHIPS ON WOMEN AND PUBLIC POLICY

Women's Research and Education Institute
Attn: Education and Training Programs
3300 North Fairfax Drive, Suite 218
Arlington, VA 22201
(703) 812-7990    Fax: (703) 812-0687
E-mail: wrei@wrei.org
Web: www.wrei.org

**Summary** To provide tuition assistance and an opportunity to work as a legislative aide on policy issues affecting women to female graduate students and young professionals.

**Eligibility** This program is open to women who are currently enrolled in a master's or doctoral program at an accredited institution in the United States or who have completed such a program within the past 18 months. Students should have completed at least 9 hours of graduate course work or the equivalent and have a demonstrated interest in research or political activity relating to women's social and political status. Applicants of diverse age, race, religions, sexual orientation, experience, and academic field are encouraged to apply. They must be articulate and adaptable and have strong writing skills; they may come from diverse traditional or nontraditional academic backgrounds. Selection is based on academic competence, as well as demonstrated interest and skills in the public policy process. Interviews are required of semifinalists.

**Financial data** Fellows receive a stipend of $1,300 per month, $500 for health insurance, and up to $1,500 for reimbursement of 3 hours of tuition at their home institutions.

**Duration** 8 months, from January through August; nonrenewable.

**Additional information** Fellows are assigned to Congressional or committee offices to work for at least 30 hours per week as a legislative assistant monitoring, researching, and providing information on policy issues affecting women.

**Number awarded**  6 to 10 each year.

**Deadline**  May of each year.

## [736]
## CONSTANCE L. LLOYD SCHOLARSHIP

American College of Medical Practice Executives
Attn: ACMPE Scholarship Fund Inc.
104 Inverness Terrace East
Englewood, CO 80112-5306
(303) 799-1111, ext. 232    Toll-free: (877) ASK-MGMA
Fax: (303) 643-4439        E-mail: acmpe@mgma.com
Web: www.mgma.com/academics/scholar.cfm

**Summary**  To provide financial assistance to undergraduate or graduate women in Georgia who are working on a degree in health care or health care administration.

**Eligibility**  This program is open to women enrolled at the undergraduate or graduate level at an accredited college or university in Georgia who are working on either an administrative or clinically-related degree in the health care field. Students working on a degree in medicine, physical therapy, nursing, or other clinically-related professions are not eligible. Applicants must submit a letter describing their career goals and objectives relevant to medical practice management; a resume; 3 reference letters commenting on their performance, character, potential to succeed, and need for scholarship support; and either documentation indicating acceptance into an undergraduate or graduate program or academic transcripts indicating undergraduate or graduate work completed to date.

**Financial data**  The stipend is $2,500. Funds are paid directly to the recipient's college or university.

**Duration**  1 year.

**Additional information**  This program, established in 1993, is managed by Scholarship Program Administrators, Inc. 1201 Eighth Avenue South, P.O. Box 23737, Nashville, TN 27202-3737, (615) 320-3149, (800) 310-4053, Fax: (615) 320-3151, E-mail: info@spaprog.com.

**Number awarded**  1 each year.

**Deadline**  April of each year.

## [737]
## CYNTHIA HUNT-LINES SCHOLARSHIP

Minnesota Nurses Association
Attn: Minnesota Nurses Association Foundation
1625 Energy Park Drive
St. Paul, MN 55108
(651) 646-4807            Toll-free: (800) 536-4662
Fax: (651) 647-5301  E-mail: mnnurses@mnnurses.org
Web: www.mnnurses.org

**Summary**  To provide financial assistance to members of the Minnesota Nurses Association (MNA) and the Minnesota Student Nurses Association (MSNA) who are single parents and interested in working on a baccalaureate or master's degree in nursing.

**Eligibility**  This program is open to MNA and MSNA members who are enrolled or entering a baccalaureate or master's program in nursing in Minnesota or North Dakota. Applicants must be single parents, at least 21 years of age,

with at least 1 dependent. Along with their application, they must submit: a current transcript; a short essay describing their interest in nursing, their long-range career goals, and how their continuing education will have an impact on the profession of nursing in Minnesota; a description of their financial need; and 2 letters of support.

**Financial data**  The stipend is $2,000 per year.

**Duration**  1 year; may be renewed.

**Number awarded**  1 each year.

**Deadline**  May of each year.

## [738]
## C200 SCHOLAR AWARDS

Committee of 200
Attn: C200 Foundation
980 North Michigan Avenue, Suite 1575
Chicago, IL 60611
(312) 255-0296, ext. 108        Fax: (312) 255-0789
E-mail: slombardi@c200.org
Web: www.c200.org/external/foundation/scholars.asp

**Summary**  To provide financial assistance to women working on an M.B.A. degree at universities that host outreach seminars conducted by the Committee of 200 (C200).

**Eligibility**  Twice each year, C200 co-sponsors 1-day outreach seminars for women M.B.A. students. Seminars rotate among the outstanding business schools in the country. These scholarships are available to first-year women students at each of the schools where a seminar is held. The schools select finalists on the basis of work experience, GPA, recommendations, and essays. Members of C200 interview the finalists and select the winners.

**Financial data**  The stipend is $25,000.

**Duration**  1 year.

**Additional information**  Scholars also receive an internship at a C200 member's company.

**Number awarded**  2 each year.

## [739]
## DASSAULT FALCON JET CORPORATION SCHOLARSHIP

Women in Aviation, International
Attn: Scholarships
Morningstar Airport
3647 State Route 503 South
West Alexandria, OH 45381
(937) 558-7655            Fax: (937) 839-4645
E-mail: scholarships@wai.org
Web: www.wai.org/education/scholarships.cfm

**Summary**  To provide financial assistance to women who are working on an undergraduate or graduate degree in a field related to aviation.

**Eligibility**  This program is open to women who are working on an undergraduate or graduate degree in an aviation-related field. Applicants must be U.S. citizens, fluent in English, and have a GPA of 3.0 or higher. They must submit a 1-page essay describing their current status, what they hope to achieve with a degree in aviation, and their aspirations in the field. Selection is based on the essay, achievements, attitude toward self and others, commitment to success, dedication to career, financial need, motivation, reliability, responsibility, and teamwork.

**Financial data** The stipend is $1,000.

**Duration** 1 year.

**Additional information** WAI is a nonprofit professional organization dedicated to encouraging women to consider an aviation career. This program is sponsored by Dassault Falcon Jet Corporation.

**Number awarded** 1 each year.

**Deadline** November of each year.

## [740]
## DELAYED EDUCATION SCHOLARSHIP FOR WOMEN

American Nuclear Society
Attn: Scholarship Coordinator
555 North Kensington Avenue
La Grange Park, IL 60526-5592
(708) 352-6611          Fax: (708) 352-0499
E-mail: outreach@ans.org
Web: www.ans.org/honors/scholarships

**Summary** To encourage mature women whose formal studies in nuclear science or nuclear engineering have been delayed or interrupted.

**Eligibility** Applicants must be mature women who have experienced at least a 1-year delay or interruption of their undergraduate studies and are returning to school to work on an undergraduate or graduate degree in nuclear science or nuclear engineering. They must be U.S. citizens or permanent residents, have proven academic ability, and be able to demonstrate financial need.

**Financial data** The stipend is $4,000. Funds may be used by the student to cover any bona fide education costs, including tuition, books, room, and board.

**Duration** 1 year; nonrenewable.

**Number awarded** 1 each year.

**Deadline** January of each year.

## [741]
## DELTA DELTA DELTA UNRESTRICTED GRADUATE SCHOLARSHIPS

Delta Delta Delta
Attn: Tri Delta Foundation
2331 Brookhollow Plaza Drive
P.O. Box 5987
Arlington, TX 76005-5987
(817) 633-8001          Fax: (817) 652-0212
E-mail: foundation@trideltaeo.org
Web: www.tridelta.org

**Summary** To provide financial assistance for graduate study to women students who are members of Delta Delta Delta.

**Eligibility** This program is open to members of the sorority who are entering or already engaged in graduate study. Applicants must submit a personal statement outlining their educational and vocational goals, 2 academic recommendations, a Tri Delta recommendation, academic transcripts, and documentation of financial need. Selection is based on academic merit, chapter and campus activities, and community activities.

**Financial data** The stipend is $3,000.

**Duration** 1 year.

**Additional information** This program, originally established in 1938, includes the following named awards: the Mary Margaret Hafter Fellowship, the Luella Akins Key Graduate Scholarship, the Second Century Graduate Scholarship, the Margaret Stafford Memorial Scholarship, and the Sarah Shinn Marshall Graduate Scholarship.

**Number awarded** 5 each year.

**Deadline** February of each year.

## [742]
## DELTA GAMMA FELLOWSHIPS

Delta Gamma Foundation
Attn: Director of Scholarships, Fellowships and Loans
3250 Riverside Drive
P.O. Box 21397
Columbus, OH 43221-0397
(614) 481-8169          Fax: (614) 481-0133
E-mail: dgfoundation@deltagamma.org
Web: www.deltagamma.org

**Summary** To provide financial assistance to members of Delta Gamma sorority who are interested in working on a graduate degree.

**Eligibility** This program is open to dues-paying members of Delta Gamma who are currently enrolled in graduate school or will have completed their undergraduate work by June 30 of the year in which the fellowship is granted and will begin graduate study in the following fall. Applicants must submit a 1- to 2-page essay in which they introduce themselves, including their career goals, their reasons for applying, and the impact Delta Gamma has had upon their life. Selection is based on scholastic excellence, contributions to their chosen field, past and current Delta Gamma activities, and campus and community involvement.

**Financial data** The stipend is $2,500.

**Duration** 1 year.

**Additional information** The fellowship is tenable at an accredited university in the United States or Canada. Graduate study may be pursued in any field.

**Number awarded** Varies each year; recently, 36 of these fellowships were awarded.

**Deadline** March of each year.

## [743]
## DELTA KAPPA GAMMA SCHOLARSHIP PROGRAM

Delta Kappa Gamma Society International
416 West 12th Street
P.O. Box 1589
Austin, TX 78767-1589
(512) 478-5748          Toll-free: (888) 762-4685
Fax: (512) 478-3961
E-mail: scholarships@deltakappagamma.org
Web: www.deltakappagamma.org

**Summary** To provide financial assistance to members of Delta Kappa Gamma Society International interested in graduate study or research.

**Eligibility** Applicants must have been members in good standing of the Delta Kappa Gamma Society International (an honorary society of women educators) for at least 3 years, have completed a master's degree or equivalent, and have been accepted and enrolled in a graduate program at a nationally accredited institution of higher education, preferably working on a doctoral degree. Selection is based on active participation and demonstrated leadership in Delta Kappa Gamma, excellence in scholarship, and service to the community.

**Financial data**  The stipend is $5,000.

**Duration**  1 year.

**Additional information**  Delta Kappa Gamma Society International has 170,000 members in 13 countries and is the largest organization of its kind. This program includes the following named awards: the Marjorie Jeanne Allen Scholarship, the Mamie Sue Bastian Scholarship, the Annie Webb Blanton Scholarship, the Blanton Centennial Scholarship, the A. Margaret Boyd Scholarship, the Edna McGuire Boyd Scholarship, the Eula Lee Carter Scholarship, the Delta Kappa Gamma Founders Scholarship, the Delta Kappa Gamma Golden Anniversary Scholarship, the Delta Kappa Gamma 60th Anniversary Scholarship, the Delta Kappa Gamma 70th Anniversary Scholarship, the Zora Ellis Scholarship, the Emma Giles Scholarship, the Carolyn Guss Scholarship, the Ola B. Hiller Scholarship, the Eunah Temple Holden Scholarship, the Berneta Minkwitz Scholarship, the Lois and Marguerite Morse Scholarship, the Catherine Nutterville Scholarship, the Alida W. Parker Scholarship, the J. Maria Pierce Scholarship, the Emma Reinhart Scholarship, the Norma Bristow Salter Scholarship, the Mary Katherine Shoup Scholarship, the Maycie K. Southall Scholarship, the M. Margaret Stroh Scholarship, the Letti P. Trefz Scholarship, and the Mary Frances White Scholarship. Recipients must remain active members of Delta Kappa Gamma, work full time on the study or research outlined in their applications, submit reports requested by the society, and acknowledge assistance of the society in any publication that results from data gathered while the award was being used.

**Number awarded**  28 each year.

**Deadline**  January of each year.

## [744]
## DELTA PHI EPSILON SCHOLARSHIPS

Delta Phi Epsilon Educational Foundation
16A Worthington Drive
Maryland Heights, MO 63043
(314) 275-2626                    Fax: (314) 275-2655
E-mail: info@dphie.org
Web: www.dphie.org/foundation/scholars.htm

**Summary**  To provide financial assistance for college or graduate school to Delta Phi Epsilon Sorority members, alumnae, and relatives.

**Eligibility**  This program is open to undergraduate Delta Phi Epsilon sorority sisters (not pledges) and alumnae who are returning to college or graduate school. Sons and daughters of Delta Phi Epsilon members or alumnae are also eligible for some of the programs. Selection is based on service and involvement, academics, and financial need.

**Financial data**  The amount awarded varies, depending upon the specific scholarship awarded and/or the needs of the recipient.

**Duration**  1 year or longer, depending upon the scholarship awarded.

**Additional information**  There are several funds within the foundation, including the Rita E. Rosser Scholarship, the San Francisco Bay Area Alumnae Scholarship, the Delta Kappa-Barbara Gold Fund, the Phi Lambda-Kim Bates Memorial Fund, the Pollack Scholarship, the Eve Effron Robin Founders Scholarship, and the Yetta Greene Memorial Scholarship.

**Number awarded**  Varies each year; recently, 5 of these scholarships were awarded.

**Deadline**  April of each year.

## [745]
## DENISE GAUDREAU AWARD FOR EXCELLENCE IN QUATERNARY STUDIES

American Quaternary Association
c/o Eric Grimm, President
Illinois State Museum Research and Collections Center
1011 East Ash Street
Springfield, IL 62703
(217) 785-4846                    Fax: (217) 785-2857
E-mail: president@amqua.org
Web: www.amqua.org/about/awards

**Summary**  To support the early career development of women graduate students in quaternary studies.

**Eligibility**  This program is open to female scientists in any field of quaternary studies who are within 2 years of completing a doctoral degree. Applicants must not have completed their dissertation research. The application should include a curriculum vitae, a summary of research interests, copies of graduate transcripts, and the names of 2 referees. Selection is based on scientific accomplishments, promise, and demonstration of original thinking. Emphasis is placed on the quality and carefulness of the work, rather than simply on quantity.

**Financial data**  The award is $500.

**Duration**  The award is presented biennially, in even-numbered years.

**Additional information**  This award was established in 1993.

**Number awarded**  1 every other year.

**Deadline**  February of even-numbered years.

## [746]
## DOLORES E. FISHER AWARD

Mel Fisher Maritime Heritage Society and Museum
Attn: Curator, Department of Education
200 Greene Street
Key West, FL 33040
(305) 294-2633                    Fax: (305) 294-5671
Web: www.melfisher.org/deoaward.htm

**Summary**  To recognize and reward, with funding for college or graduate school, women who submit outstanding essays on the oceans.

**Eligibility**  This competition is open to women between 16 and 30 years of age. Candidates must submit a 1,000-word essay on how they hope to make a difference in the world through their passion for the oceans, their career goals, and how this award will help them achieve those goals. They must also include 3 letters of recommendation and a brief statement on the personality characteristic they value most in themselves and why. If they are currently enrolled in school, they must identify their program, but school enrollment is not required.

**Financial data** The award is $1,000.

**Duration** The award is presented annually.

**Number awarded** 1 each year.

**Deadline** March of each year.

## [747]
### DORIS B. ORMAN, '25, FELLOWSHIP
Gallaudet University Alumni Association
Attn: Graduate Fellowship Fund Committee
Peikoff Alumni House
Gallaudet University
800 Florida Avenue, N.E.
Washington, DC 20002-3695
(202) 651-5060          Fax: (202) 651-5062
TTY: (202) 651-5061
E-mail: alumni.relations@gallaudet.edu
Web: www.gallaudet.edu

**Summary** To provide financial assistance to deaf women who wish to work on a graduate degree at universities for people who hear normally.

**Eligibility** This program is open to deaf or hard of hearing women graduates of Gallaudet University or other accredited academic institutions who have been accepted for graduate study at colleges or universities for people who hear normally. Applicants must be working on a doctorate or other terminal degree. They must have a particular interest in the arts, the humanities, and community leadership. Financial need is considered in the selection process.

**Financial data** The amount awarded varies, depending upon the needs of the recipient and the availability of funds.

**Duration** 1 year; may be renewed.

**Additional information** This program is 1 of 11 designated funds within the Graduate Fellowship Fund of the Gallaudet University Alumni Association. Recipients must carry a full-time semester load.

**Number awarded** Up to 1 each year.

**Deadline** April of each year.

## [748]
### DOROTHEA BUCK FELLOWSHIP
Virginia Federation of Women's Clubs
Attn: Scholarship/Fellowship Committee
513 Forest Avenue
P.O. Box 8750
Richmond, VA 23226
(804) 288-3724          Toll-free: (800) 699-8392
Fax: (804) 288-0341
E-mail: h.vfwcofgfwc@verizon.net
Web: www.gfwcvirginia.org

**Summary** To provide financial assistance to women from the United States and Latin American countries who are working on a graduate degree in specified fields at universities in Virginia.

**Eligibility** This program is open to women graduate students from the United States and Latin America who are enrolled at a Virginia college or university. Applicants must be studying international law, international finance, international business, international studies, Spanish, or Portuguese. Selection is based on academic record; moral character, personality, and adaptability; 3 recommendations of a general nature and 2 recommendations from recent professors; a resume of educational, employment, and community service history; and a 2,000-word essay on reasons for pursuing this course of study and this fellowship.

**Financial data** The stipend is $5,000. Funds are paid to the college or university the recipient attends.

**Duration** 1 year.

**Number awarded** 1 each year.

**Deadline** March of each year.

## [749]
### DOROTHY E. SCHOELZEL MEMORIAL SCHOLARSHIP
General Federation of Women's Clubs of Connecticut
c/o Hamden Women's Club
Antoinette Antonucci, Co-President
26 Country Way
Wallingford, CT 06492
(203) 265-9407          E-mail: gfwcct@yahoo.com
Web: www.gfwcct.org

**Summary** To provide financial assistance to women in Connecticut who are working on an undergraduate or graduate degree in education.

**Eligibility** This program is open to female residents of Connecticut who have completed at least 3 years of college. Applicants must have a GPA of 3.0 or higher and be working on a bachelor's or master's degree in education.

**Financial data** The stipend is $1,000.

**Duration** 1 year.

**Number awarded** 1 each year.

**Deadline** February of each year.

## [750]
### DOROTHY HARRIS ENDOWED SCHOLARSHIP
Women's Sports Foundation
Attn: Award and Grant Programs Manager
Eisenhower Park
1899 Hempstead Turnpike, Suite 400
East Meadow, NY 11554-1000
(516) 542-4700          Toll-free: (800) 227-3988
Fax: (516) 542-4716
E-mail: info@womenssportsfoundation.org
Web: www.womenssportsfoundation.org

**Summary** To provide financial support to female graduate students in fields related to athletics.

**Eligibility** This program is open to women who will be enrolled in a full-time course of study at an accredited graduate school in physical education, sports management, sports psychology, or sports sociology. U.S. citizenship or legal resident status is required. Applicants must submit brief essays on their career goals, how those goals will impact girls and women in sports and fitness, how they will participate in creating opportunities for girls and women in sports and fitness, and how sports participation has influenced their lives. Financial need is considered in the selection process.

**Financial data**   The stipend is $1,500.

**Duration**   1 year; may be renewed if the recipient maintains a GPA of 3.0 or higher.

**Number awarded**   Up to 3 each year.

**Deadline**   December of each year.

## [751]
## DOROTHY L. WELLER PEO SCHOLARSHIP

P.E.O. Foundation-California State Chapter
c/o Sara Gustavson, Scholarship Committee Chair
1835 Newport Boulevard, A109
PMB 26
Costa Mesa, CA 92627
(626) 286-2792              E-mail: ghcoyle@aol.com
Web: www.peocalifornia.org/dlw.html

**Summary**   To provide financial assistance for law school or paralegal studies to women in California.

**Eligibility**   This program is open to women residents of California who have been admitted to an accredited law school or a licensed paralegal school. Applicants must have completed 4 years of high school and be able to demonstrate excellence in academic ability, character, integrity, and school activities. Financial need is also considered in the selection process.

**Financial data**   Stipends range from $2,000 to $2,500.

**Duration**   1 year.

**Number awarded**   Varies each year; recently, 9 of these scholarships were awarded.

**Deadline**   February of each year.

## [752]
## DR. AND MRS. DAVID B. ALLMAN MEDICAL SCHOLARSHIPS

Miss America Pageant
Attn: Scholarship Department
Two Miss America Way, Suite 1000
Atlantic City, NJ 08401
(609) 345-7571, ext. 27        Toll-free: (800) 282-MISS
Fax: (609) 347-6079      E-mail: info@missamerica.org
Web: www.missamerica.org

**Summary**   To provide financial assistance to medical students who have competed or are competing in the Miss America contest at any level.

**Eligibility**   This program is open to women who have competed in the Miss America competition at least once, at any level of competition, within the past 10 years. Applicants do not have to apply during the year they competed; they may apply any year following as long as they are attending or accepted by a medical school and plan to become a medical doctor. They must submit an essay, up to 500 words, on why they wish to become a medical doctor and how this scholarship can help them attain that goal. Selection is based on GPA, class rank, MCAT score, extracurricular activities, financial need, and level of participation within the system.

**Financial data**   Stipends are $2,100 or $1,500.

**Duration**   1 year.

**Additional information**   This scholarship was established in 1974.

**Number awarded**   Varies each year. Recently, 4 of these scholarships were awarded: 2 at $2,100 and 2 at $1,500.

**Deadline**   June of each year.

## [753]
## DR. LAUREL SALTON CLARK MEMORIAL GRADUATE FELLOWSHIP

Wisconsin Space Grant Consortium
c/o University of Wisconsin at Green Bay
Department of Natural and Applied Sciences
2420 Nicolet Drive
Green Bay, WI 54311-7001
(920) 465-2108              Fax: (920) 465-2376
E-mail: wsgc@uwgb.edu
Web: www.uwgb.edu/wsgc/students/clark.asp

**Summary**   To provide financial assistance to graduate students (especially women, minority, and disabled students) at member institutions of the Wisconsin Space Grant Consortium (WSGC) who are working on a degree in environmental or life sciences.

**Eligibility**   This program is open to graduate students enrolled at colleges and universities participating in the WSGC. Applicants must be U.S. citizens, be enrolled full time in a master's or Ph.D. program, and have a GPA of 3.0 or higher. They must be working on a degree in environmental or life sciences with a research or engineering design component related to space or aerospace. The consortium especially encourages applications from underrepresented minorities, women, persons with disabilities, and those pursuing interdisciplinary aerospace studies. Selection is based on the applicant's 1) broad, balanced set of interests and pursuits outside the field of science; and 2) leadership and ongoing commitment to improving the human condition.

**Financial data**   The stipend is $5,000.

**Duration**   1 academic year.

**Additional information**   This program was established in 2004 to honor a Wisconsin resident who lost her life aboard Space Shuttle Columbia. Funding is provided by the U.S. National Aeronautics and Space Administration (NASA). The schools participating in the consortium include the University of Wisconsin campuses at Fox Valley, Green Bay, La Crosse, Madison, Milwaukee, Oshkosh, Parkside, Superior, and Whitewater; Alverno College; Marquette University; College of the Menominee Nation; Carroll College; Lawrence University; Milwaukee School of Engineering; Ripon College; Medical College of Wisconsin; Western Wisconsin Technical College; and Wisconsin Lutheran College.

**Number awarded**   1 each year.

**Deadline**   March of each year.

## [754]
## DR. MARIE E. ZAKRZEWSKI MEDICAL SCHOLARSHIP

Kosciuszko Foundation
Attn: Educational Programs
15 East 65th Street
New York, NY 10021-6595
(212) 734-2130, ext. 210          Fax: (212) 628-4552
E-mail: addy@thekf.org
Web: www.thekf.org/EDScholarships_US_MZMS.html

**Summary** To provide financial assistance to women of Polish ancestry studying medicine.

**Eligibility** This program is open to young women of Polish ancestry entering their first, second, or third year of study at an accredited medical school in the United States. Applicants must be U.S. citizens or permanent residents of Polish descent and have a GPA of 3.0 or higher. First preference is given to residents of Massachusetts or former presentees of the Federation Kosciuszko Foundation Ball. If no candidates from the first preference group apply, qualified residents of New England are considered. Selection is based on academic excellence; the applicant's academic achievements, interests, and motivation; the applicant's interest in Polish subjects or involvement in the Polish American community; and financial need.

**Financial data** The stipend is $3,500.

**Duration** 1 year; nonrenewable.

**Additional information** This program is funded by the Massachusetts Federation of Polish Women's Clubs but administered by the Kosciuszko Foundation. There is a nonrefundable application fee of $25.

**Number awarded** 1 each year.

**Deadline** January of each year.

## [755]
## DR. PRENTICE GAUTT POSTGRADUATE SCHOLARSHIPS

Big 12 Conference
2201 Stemmons Freeway, 28th Floor
Dallas, TX 75207
(214) 742-1212          Fax: (214) 753-0145
Web: www.big12sports.com

**Summary** To provide financial assistance for graduate school to student athletes who complete their undergraduate study at a Big 12 university.

**Eligibility** This program is open to students graduating from a Big 12 university who have participated in at least 2 years of intercollegiate athletics. Applicants must have a GPA of 3.5 or higher and be planning to enroll in a program of professional or graduate study. Male and female athletes are considered separately.

**Financial data** The stipend is $6,900.

**Duration** 1 year.

**Additional information** This program began with the inception of the league in 1996-97. Members of the Big 12 include Baylor, Colorado, Iowa State, Kansas, Kansas State, Missouri, Nebraska, Oklahoma, Oklahoma State, Texas, Texas A&M, and Texas Tech. Recipients must graduate from their Big 12 university within 15 months of their selection for this scholarship and must enroll in a graduate or professional school within 2 years of graduation.

**Number awarded** 24 each year: 2 (1 male and 1 female) at each member institution.

## [756]
## DRI LAW STUDENT DIVERSITY SCHOLARSHIP

DRI-The Voice of the Defense Bar
Attn: Diversity Scholarship Committee
150 North Michigan Avenue, Suite 300
Chicago, IL 60601
(312) 795-1101          Fax: (312) 795-0747
E-mail: dri@dri.org
Web: www.dri.org

**Summary** To provide financial assistance to minority and women law students.

**Eligibility** This program is open to students entering their second year of law school who are African American, Hispanic, Asian, Pan Asian, Native American, or female. Applicants must submit an essay, up to 1,000 words, on the topic "With the Continuing Decline in the Number of Civil Trials, What Methods Can Defense Lawyers Adopt to Preserve the Civil Jury System?" Selection is based on that essay, demonstrated academic excellence, service to the profession, service to the community, and service to the cause of diversity. Students affiliated with the Association of Trial Lawyers of America as members, student members, or employees are not eligible. Finalists are invited to participate in personal interviews.

**Financial data** The stipend is $10,000 per year.

**Duration** 1 year.

**Additional information** This program was established in 2004.

**Number awarded** 2 each year.

**Deadline** July of each year.

## [757]
## DURNING SISTERS FELLOWSHIP

Delta Delta Delta
Attn: Tri Delta Foundation
2331 Brookhollow Plaza Drive
P.O. Box 5987
Arlington, TX 76005-5987
(817) 633-8001          Fax: (817) 652-0212
E-mail: foundation@trideltaeo.org
Web: www.tridelta.org

**Summary** To provide financial assistance for graduate study to unmarried women students who are members of Delta Delta Delta.

**Eligibility** This program is open to members of the sorority who have completed at least 12 hours of graduate study. Applicants must be unmarried. Along with their application, they must submit a personal statement outlining their educational and vocational goals, 2 academic recommendations, a Tri Delta recommendation, academic transcripts, and documentation of financial need. Selection is based on academic merit, chapter and campus activities, and community activities.

**Financial data** The stipend is $3,000.

**Duration** 1 year.

**Number awarded** 1 each year.

**Deadline** February of each year.

**[758]**
## EARLY CAREER PATIENT-ORIENTED DIABETES RESEARCH AWARD

Juvenile Diabetes Research Foundation
Attn: Grant Administrator
120 Wall Street, 19th Floor
New York, NY 10005-4001
(212) 479-7572          Toll-free: (800) 533-CURE
Fax: (212) 785-9595            E-mail: info@jdrf.org
Web: www.jdrf.org/index.cfm?page_id=103207

**Summary**  To provide funding to physician scientists (particularly women, minorities, and persons with disabilities) interested in pursuing a program of clinical diabetes-related research training.

**Eligibility**  This program is open to investigators in diabetes-related research who have an M.D. or M.D./Ph.D. degree and a faculty appointment at the late training or assistant professor level. Applicants must be sponsored by an investigator who is affiliated full time with an accredited institution, who pursues patient-oriented clinical research, and who agrees to supervise the applicant's training. There are no citizenship requirements. Applications are encouraged from women, members of minority groups underrepresented in the sciences, and people with disabilities. Areas of relevant research can include: mechanisms of human disease, therapeutic interventions, clinical trials, and the development of new technologies. The proposed research may be conducted at foreign and domestic, for-profit and non-profit, and public and private institutions, including universities, colleges, hospitals, laboratories, units of state and local government, and eligible agencies of the federal government.

**Financial data**  The total award may be up to $150,000 each year, up to $75,000 of which may be requested for research (including a technician, supplies, equipment, and travel). The salary request must be consistent with the established salary structure of the applicant's institution. Equipment purchases in years other than the first must be strongly justified. Indirect costs may not exceed 10%.

**Duration**  The award is for 5 years.

**Deadline**  January or July of each year.

**[759]**
## EDITH HUNTINGTON ANDERSON SCHOLARSHIP

Alpha Omicron Pi Foundation
Attn: Scholarship Committee
5390 Virginia Way
P.O. Box 395
Brentwood, TN 37024-0395
(615) 370-0920               Fax: (615) 370-4424
E-mail: foundation@alphaomicronpi.org
Web: www.aoiifoundation.org

**Summary**  To provide financial assistance to alumnae members of Alpha Omicron Pi who are interested in preparing for a medical career.

**Eligibility**  This program is open to alumnae members of Alpha Omicron Pi who have a bachelor's degree and are preparing for a career in medicine or a medical-related field. Applicants must submit 50-word essays on the following topics: 1) the circumstances that have created their need for this scholarship, and 2) their immediate and long-term life objectives. Selection is based primarily on academic

excellence and personal attributes and attitudes, although financial need may also be considered.

**Financial data**  A stipend is awarded (amount not specified).

**Duration**  1 year.

**Number awarded**  1 each odd-numbered year.

**Deadline**  February of each odd-numbered year.

**[760]**
## EDITH SEVILLE COALE SCHOLARSHIPS

Zonta Club of Washington, D.C.
c/o Yvonne Boggan, President
350 Chaplin Street, S.E.
Washington, DC 20019-4261
(202) 575-4808
Web: www.zontawashingtondc.org

**Summary**  To provide financial assistance to Protestant women in the Washington, D.C. area who have completed the first year of medical school.

**Eligibility**  Protestant women who are in the second, third, or fourth year of medical school in the Washington, D.C. area are eligible to apply. Selection is based on financial need and scholastic achievement.

**Financial data**  The amount awarded varies; recently, stipends averaged $8,500.

**Duration**  1 year.

**Additional information**  The trust fund contains limited funds. Awards are not made for the first year of medical school. Preference is given to women students nominated by medical school faculty members.

**Number awarded**  Varies each year; recently, 4 of these scholarships were awarded.

**Deadline**  December of each year.

**[761]**
## ELA FOUNDATION SCHOLARSHIPS

Ethel Louise Armstrong Foundation
Attn: Executive Director
2460 North Lake Avenue
PMB 128
Altadena, CA 91001
(626) 398-8840               Fax: (626) 398-8843
E-mail: executivedirector@ela.org
Web: www.ela.org/scholarships/scholarships.html

**Summary**  To provide financial assistance for graduate school to women with disabilities.

**Eligibility**  This program is open to women with disabilities who are currently enrolled in or actively applying to a graduate program at an accredited college or university in the United States. Applicants must be active in a local, state, or national disability organization, either in person or electronically, that is providing services or advocacy for people with disabilities. Along with their application, they must submit a 1,000-word essay on "How I will change the face of disability on the planet." Selection is based on academic and leadership merit.

**Financial data**  The stipend ranges from $500 to $2,000 per year.

**Duration**  1 year.

**Additional information** The sponsoring foundation was founded in 1994 by Margaret Staton, who was disabled by a spinal cord tumor at 2 years of age. Recipients must agree to 1) network with the sponsor's board of directors and current and alumni scholarship recipients, and 2) update the sponsor on their progress in their academic and working career.

**Number awarded** Varies each year; recently, 4 of these scholarships were awarded.

**Deadline** May of each year.

## [762]
## ELAINE OSBORNE JACOBSON AWARD FOR WOMEN WORKING IN HEALTH CARE LAW

Roscoe Pound Institute
Attn: Membership and Education Coordinator
1054 31st Street, N.W., Suite 260
Washington, DC 20007
Fax: (202) 342-0298 E-mail: pound@roscoepound.org
Web: www.roscoepound.org

**Summary** To provide financial assistance to women who are interested in preparing for a career in health care law.

**Eligibility** This program is open to women currently enrolled in an accredited North American law school. Candidates are selected if they, through their law school academic and clinical work and other related activities, demonstrate their aptitude for and a long-term commitment to a legal career of advocacy on behalf of the health care needs of children, women, the elderly, or the disabled. Only nominations are accepted (multiple nominations per school are accepted); candidates may not apply directly. Nominees must submit a 1-page statement on their view of the civil justice system as a means of achieving a safe society.

**Financial data** The award is $3,000 and an all-expense paid trip to the Pound Law School Award Reception (attendance is required).

**Duration** 1 year.

**Additional information** This award was established in 1991.

**Number awarded** 1 each year.

**Deadline** February of each year.

## [763]
## ELECTRONICS FOR IMAGING SCHOLARSHIPS

Society of Women Engineers
230 East Ohio Street, Suite 400
Chicago, IL 60611-3265
(312) 596-5223 Toll-free: (877) SWE-INFO
Fax: (312) 644-8557
E-mail: scholarshipapplication@swe.org
Web: www.swe.org/scholarships

**Summary** To provide financial assistance to women working on an undergraduate or graduate degree in engineering or computer science.

**Eligibility** This program is open to women who will be sophomores, juniors, seniors, or graduate students at ABET-accredited colleges and universities. Applicants must be majoring in computer science or engineering and have a GPA of 3.0 or higher. Along with their application, they must submit a 1-page essay on why they want to be an engineer or computer scientist, how they believe they will make a difference as an engineer or computer scientist, and what influenced them to study engineering or computer science. Selection is based on merit. Preference is given to students at designated colleges and universities; for a list, contact the sponsor.

**Financial data** The stipend is $4,000.

**Duration** 1 year.

**Additional information** This program, established in 2001, is sponsored by Electronics for Imaging, Inc.

**Number awarded** 4 each year.

**Deadline** January of each year.

## [764]
## ELIZABETH FURBER FELLOWSHIP

American Indian Graduate Center
Attn: Executive Director
4520 Montgomery Boulevard, N.E., Suite 1-B
Albuquerque, NM 87109-1291
(505) 881-4584 Toll-free: (800) 628-1920
Fax: (505) 884-0427 E-mail: aigc@aigc.com
Web: www.aigc.com

**Summary** To provide financial assistance to Native American women interested in working on a graduate degree in the arts.

**Eligibility** This program is open to women who are either enrolled members of U.S. federally-recognized American Indian tribes and Alaska Native groups or otherwise able to document one-fourth degree federally-recognized Indian blood. Applicants must be enrolled full time in a master's, doctoral, or professional degree program at an accredited college or university in the United States. They must be studying creative fine arts, visual arts, crafts, music, performing, dance, literary arts, or creative writing and poetry. Selection is based on academic achievement, financial need, and an essay on the meaning of their graduate education to the Indian community.

**Financial data** A stipend is awarded (amount not specified).

**Duration** 1 year; may be renewed.

**Additional information** The application fee is $15. Since this a supplemental program, applicants must apply in a timely manner for federal financial aid and campus-based aid at the college they are attending to be considered for this program. Failure to apply will disqualify an applicant.

**Number awarded** 1 or more each year.

**Deadline** May of each year.

## [765]
## ELIZABETH GARDE NATIONAL SCHOLARSHIP

Danish Sisterhood of America
Attn: Lizette Burtis, Scholarship Chair
3020 Santa Juanita Court
Santa Rosa, CA 95405-8219
(707) 539-1884 E-mail: lburtis@sbcglobal.net
Web: www.danishsisterhood.org/rschol.asp

**Summary** To provide financial assistance for nursing or medical education to members or relatives of members of the Danish Sisterhood of America.

**Eligibility** This program is open to members or the family of members of the sisterhood who have been members for at least 1 year. Applicants must be working on an undergraduate or graduate degree in the nursing or medical profession. They must have a GPA of 3.0 or higher.

**Financial data** The stipend is $850.

**Duration** 1 year; nonrenewable.

**Number awarded** 1 each year.

**Deadline** February of each year.

## [766]
## ELLEN CUSHING SCHOLARSHIPS

American Baptist Churches USA
National Ministries
Attn: Office of Financial Aid for Studies
P.O. Box 851
Valley Forge, PA 19482-0851
(610) 768-2067   Toll-free: (800) ABC-3USA, ext. 2067
Fax: (610) 768-2453
E-mail: Financialaid.Web@abc-usa.org
Web: www.nationalministries.org

**Summary** To provide financial assistance to Baptist women interested in working on a graduate degree.

**Eligibility** This program is open to female Baptists in graduate programs planning to enter a church-related or human service vocation. Applicants must be U.S. citizens who have been a member of a church affiliated with American Baptist Churches USA for at least 1 year. M.Div. and D.Min. students are not eligible. Preference is given to students active in their school, church, or region.

**Financial data** A stipend is awarded (amount not specified).

**Duration** 1 year.

**Number awarded** Up to 3 each year.

**Deadline** May of each year.

## [767]
## ELOISE COLLINS SCHOLARSHIP

Epsilon Sigma Alpha
Attn: ESA Foundation Assistant Scholarship Director
P.O. Box 270517
Fort Collins, CO 80527
(970) 223-2824                    Fax: (970) 223-4456
Web: www.esaintl.com/esaf

**Summary** To provide financial assistance for medical school to women from Louisiana.

**Eligibility** This program is open to women who are residents of Louisiana working on a degree in the field of medicine. Selection is based on character (10%), leadership (10%), service (5%), financial need (50%), and scholastic ability (25%).

**Financial data** The stipend is $500.

**Duration** 1 year; may be renewed.

**Additional information** Epsilon Sigma Alpha (ESA) is a women's service organization. Information is also available from Lynn Hughes, Scholarship Director, 324 N.E. Mead, Grants Pass, OR 97526, (541) 476-4617. Completed applications must be submitted to the ESA State Counselor who verifies the information before forwarding them to the scholarship director. A $5 processing fee is required.

**Number awarded** 1 each year.

**Deadline** January of each year.

## [768]
## ELSIE G. RIDDICK SCHOLARSHIP

North Carolina Federation of Business and Professional
    Women's Organizations, Inc.
Attn: BPW/NC Foundation
P.O. Box 276
Carrboro, NC 27510
Web: www.bpwnc.org/Foundation/foundation_nc.htm

**Summary** To provide financial assistance to women attending North Carolina colleges, community colleges, or graduate schools.

**Eligibility** This program is open to women who are currently enrolled in a community college, 4-year college, or graduate school in North Carolina. Applicants must be endorsed by a local BPW unit. Along with their application, they must submit a 1-page statement that summarizes their career goals, previous honors, or community activities and justifies their need for this scholarship.

**Financial data** The stipend is at least $500. Funds are paid directly to the recipient's school.

**Duration** 1 year; recipients may reapply.

**Additional information** This program was established in 1925 as a loan fund. Since 1972 it has been administered as a scholarship program. Information is also available from Patricia Ann McMurray, 510 Canna Place, Aberdeen, NC 28315.

**Number awarded** 1 each year.

**Deadline** April of each year.

## [769]
## ETHEL O. GARDNER PEO SCHOLARSHIP

P.E.O. Foundation-California State Chapter
c/o Candy Northrop, Scholarship Committee Chair
15 Hidden Valley Road
Monrovia, CA 91016-1601
(626) 358-8966            E-mail: northfam@adelphia.net
Web: www.peocalifornia.org/eog.html

**Summary** To provide financial assistance to women who are upper-division and graduate students in California.

**Eligibility** This program is open to women residents of California who have completed at least 2 years of college. Applicants must be enrolled as full-time undergraduate or graduate students. Selection is based on financial need, character, and a record of academic and extracurricular activities achievement.

**Financial data** Stipends range from $500 to $1,500.

**Duration** 1 year.

**Number awarded** Varies each year; recently, 51 of these scholarships were awarded.

**Deadline** February of each year.

## [770]
## EUGENIA VELLNER FISCHER AWARD FOR THE PERFORMING ARTS

Miss America Pageant
Attn: Scholarship Department
Two Miss America Way, Suite 1000
Atlantic City, NJ 08401
(609) 345-7571, ext. 27        Toll-free: (800) 282-MISS
Fax: (609) 347-6079        E-mail: info@missamerica.org
Web: www.missamerica.org/scholarships/eugenia.asp

**Summary**  To provide financial assistance to women who are working on an undergraduate or graduate degree in the performing arts and who, in the past, competed at some level in the Miss America competition.

**Eligibility**  This program is open to women who are working on an undergraduate, master's, or higher degree in the performing arts and who competed at the local, state, or national level in a Miss America competition within the past 10 years. Applicants may be studying dance, instrumental, monologue, or vocal. They must submit an essay, up to 500 words, on the factors that influenced their decision to enter the field of performing arts, what they consider to be their major strengths in the field, and how they plan to use their degree in the field. Selection is based on GPA, class rank, extracurricular activities, financial need, and level of participation within the system.

**Financial data**  The stipend is $2,000.

**Duration**  1 year; renewable.

**Additional information**  This scholarship was established in 1999.

**Number awarded**  1 or more each year.

**Deadline**  June of each year.

## [771]
## EULA MAE HENDERSON SCHOLARSHIPS

Baptist General Convention of Texas
Attn: Woman's Missionary Union of Texas
333 North Washington, Suite 160
Dallas, TX 75246-1716
(214) 828-5150        Toll-free: (888) 968-6389
E-mail: wmutx@bgct.org
Web: www.bgct.org

**Summary**  To provide financial assistance to women members of Baptist churches in Texas who are preparing for a career in ministry at a Texas Baptist institution.

**Eligibility**  This program is open to women who are active members of Baptist churches in Texas. Applicants must be full-time students in at least their second semester of graduate work in preparation for a career in vocational Christian ministry through the International Mission Board, the North American Mission Board, or the Woman's Missionary Union (all of the Southern Baptist Convention). They must be able to document a GPA of 3.0 or higher, "sound moral character," and financial need. Preference is given to applicants who have been involved in missions organizations on the local church, associational, or state level.

**Financial data**  The stipend is $500 per semester ($1,000 per year).

**Duration**  1 semester; may be renewed up to 4 additional semesters if the recipient continues to meet the requirements.

**Additional information**  This program was established in 1986. The eligible schools include 1) Southwestern Baptist Theological Seminary; 2) a Texas Baptist theological school, including (but not limited to) George W. Truett Seminary at Baylor University and Logsdon School of Theology at Hardin-Simmons University; and 3) Baylor University's School of Social Work, provided the student is also taking theological courses pursuant to a career in missions or missions education.

**Number awarded**  Varies each year; recently, 3 of these scholarships were awarded.

**Deadline**  February of each year.

## [772]
## EXEMPTION FROM TUITION FEES FOR DEPENDENTS OF KENTUCKY VETERANS

Kentucky Department of Veterans Affairs
Attn: Division of Field Operations
545 South Third Street, Room 123
Louisville, KY 40202
(502) 595-4447        Toll-free: (800) 928-4012 (within KY)
Fax: (502) 595-4448
Web: www.kdva.net/tuitionwaiver.htm

**Summary**  To provide financial assistance for undergraduate or graduate studies to the children or unremarried widow(er)s of deceased Kentucky veterans.

**Eligibility**  This program is open to the children, stepchildren, adopted children, and unremarried widow(er)s of veterans who were residents of Kentucky when they entered military service or joined the Kentucky National Guard. The qualifying veteran must have been killed in action during a wartime period or died as a result of a service-connected disability incurred during a wartime period. Applicants must be attending or planning to attend a state-supported college or university in Kentucky to work on an undergraduate or graduate degree.

**Financial data**  Eligible dependents and survivors are exempt from tuition and matriculation fees at any state-supported institution of higher education in Kentucky.

**Duration**  There are no age or time limits on the waiver.

**Number awarded**  Varies each year.

## [773]
## FACULTY EARLY CAREER DEVELOPMENT PROGRAM

National Science Foundation
Directorate for Education and Human Resources
Attn: Senior Staff Associate for Cross Directorate Programs
4201 Wilson Boulevard, Room 805
Arlington, VA 22230
(703) 292-8600        TDD: (800) 281-8749
Web: www.nsf.gov

**Summary**  To provide support for science and engineering research to outstanding new faculty (especially women, minorities, and persons with disabilities) who intend to develop academic careers involving both research and education.

**Eligibility**  This program, identified as the CAREER program, is open to faculty members who meet all of the following requirements: 1) be employed in a tenure-track (or equivalent) position at an institution in the United States, its territories or possessions, or the Commonwealth of Puerto Rico that awards degrees in a field supported by the National Science Foundation (NSF) or that is a nonprofit, non-degree granting organization such as a museum, observatory, or research laboratory; 2) have a doctoral degree in a field of science or engineering supported by NSF: 3) not have competed more than 3 times in this program; 4) be untenured; and 5) not be a current or former recipient of a Presidential Early Career Award for Scientists and Engineers (PECASE) or CAREER award. Applicants must be U.S. citizens, nationals, or permanent residents. They must submit a career development plan that indicates a description of the proposed research project, including preliminary supporting data if appropriate, specific objectives, methods, and procedures to be used, and expected significance of the results; a description of the proposed educational activities, including plans to evaluate their impact; a description of how the research and educational activities are integrated with each other; and results of prior NSF support, if applicable. Proposals from women, underrepresented minorities, and persons with disabilities are especially encouraged.

**Financial data** The total grant is $400,000 (or $500,000 for the Directorate of Biological Sciences) over the full period of the award.

**Duration** 5 years.

**Additional information** This program is operated by various disciplinary divisions within the NSF; for a list of the participating divisions and their telephone numbers, contact the sponsor. Outstanding recipients of these grants are nominated for the NSF component of the PECASE awards, which are awarded to 20 recipients of these grants as an honorary award.

**Number awarded** 300 to 400 each year. Approximately $85 million is budgeted to support this program annually.

**Deadline** July of each year.

## [774]
## FINANCIAL WOMEN INTERNATIONAL OF HAWAII SCHOLARSHIP

Hawai'i Community Foundation
Attn: Scholarship Department
1164 Bishop Street, Suite 800
Honolulu, HI 96813
(808) 566-5570        Toll-free: (888) 731-3863
Fax: (808) 521-6286
E-mail: scholarships@hcf-hawaii.org
Web: www.hawaiicommunityfoundation.org

**Summary** To provide financial assistance to women in Hawaii who are studying business on the upper-division or graduate school level.

**Eligibility** This program is open to female residents of Hawaii who are majoring in business or a business-related field as a junior, senior, or graduate student. Applicants must be able to demonstrate academic achievement (GPA of 3.5 or higher), good moral character, and financial need. Along with their application, they must submit a short statement indicating their reasons for attending college, their planned course of study, and their career goals.

**Financial data** The amounts of the awards depend on the availability of funds and the need of the recipient; recently, the stipend was $500.

**Duration** 1 year.

**Additional information** This program was established in 1998.

**Number awarded** Varies each year; recently, 1 of these scholarships was awarded.

**Deadline** February of each year.

## [775]
## FLEET RESERVE ASSOCIATION SCHOLARSHIP

Fleet Reserve Association
Attn: Scholarship Administrator
125 North West Street
Alexandria, VA 22314-2754
(703) 683-1400        Toll-free: (800) 372-1924
Fax: (703) 549-6610        E-mail: fra@fra.org
Web: www.fra.org

**Summary** To provide financial assistance for undergraduate or graduate studies to members of the Fleet Reserve Association (FRA) and their spouses, children, and grandchildren.

**Eligibility** This program is open to members of the FRA and their dependent children, grandchildren, and spouses. The children, grandchildren, and spouses of deceased FRA members are also eligible. Selection is based on financial need, scholastic standing, character, and leadership qualities.

**Financial data** The stipend is $5,000 per year.

**Duration** 1 year; may be renewed.

**Additional information** Membership in the FRA is restricted to active-duty, retired, and Reserve members of the Navy, Marines, and Coast Guard.

**Number awarded** 6 each year.

**Deadline** April of each year.

## [776]
## FLORENCE STAIGER LONN EDUCATIONAL FUND GRANTS

Alpha Chi Omega Foundation
Attn: Foundation Programs Coordinator
5939 Castle Creek Parkway, North Drive
Indianapolis, IN 46250-4343
(317) 579-5050, ext. 262        Fax: (317) 579-5051
E-mail: foundation@alphachiomega.org
Web: www.alphachiomega.org

**Summary** To provide financial assistance to qualified members of Alpha Chi Omega who are in need of funding to complete their college education or graduate studies.

**Eligibility** This program is open to undergraduate and graduate students who are initiated members of the sorority, in need of financial assistance to complete their degree, and enrolled full time in an accredited college or university. Applicants must include a statement outlining their reasons for applying for the funds, the amount requested, when they want to receive the funds, their career goals, and their participation in the sorority.

**Financial data** The grant depends on the need of the recipient.

**Duration** 1 year.

**Number awarded** Varies each year; recently, 9 of these grants were awarded.

**Deadline** Applications may be submitted at any time.

## [777]
## FLORIDA SPACE GRANT CONSORTIUM FELLOWSHIP PROGRAM

Florida Space Grant Consortium
c/o Center for Space Education
Building M6-306, Room 7010
Mail Stop: FSGC
Kennedy Space Center, FL 32899
(321) 452-4301                    Fax: (321) 449-0739
E-mail: fsgc@mail.ucf.edu
Web: fsgc.engr.ucf.edu

**Summary** To provide financial assistance to graduate students (particularly women, minority, and disabled students) in space studies at universities participating in the Florida Space Grant Consortium (FSGC).

**Eligibility** Eligible to be nominated for this program are U.S. citizens who are enrolled full time in master's or doctoral programs at universities participating in the consortium. Nominees must be enrolled in a space-related field of study, broadly defined to include aeronautics, astronautics, remote sensing, atmospheric sciences, and other fundamental sciences and technologies relying on and/or directly impacting space technological resources. Included within that definition are space science; earth observing science; space life sciences; space medicine; space policy, law, and engineering; astronomy and astrophysics; space facilities and applications; and space education. The nomineeÖs undergraduate GPA should be at least 3.5. The program particularly solicits nominations of women, minorities, and students with disabilities.

**Financial data** The maximum stipend is $20,000 per year for doctoral candidates or $12,000 per year for master's degree students.

**Duration** 1 year; may be renewed up to 2 additional years for doctoral candidates or 1 additional year for master's degree students, provided the recipient maintains a GPA of 3.5 or higher.

**Additional information** This program is funded by the U.S. National Aeronautics and Space Administration (NASA). The consortium member universities are Bethune-Cookman College, Eckerd College, Embry-Riddle Aeronautical University, Florida A&M University, Florida Atlantic University, Florida Community Colleges, Florida Gulf Coast University, Florida Institute of Technology, Florida International University, Florida Southern College, Florida State University, University of Central Florida, University of Florida, University of Miami, University of North Florida, University of South Florida, and University of West Florida.

**Number awarded** 2 each year: 1 master's degree student and 1 doctoral candidate.

**Deadline** Notices of intent must be submitted by January of each year. Completed proposals are due in March.

## [778]
## FOCUS PROFESSIONS GROUP FELLOWSHIPS

American Association of University Women
Attn: AAUW Educational Foundation
301 ACT Drive, Department 60
P.O. Box 4030
Iowa City, IA 52243-4030
(319) 337-1716                    Fax: (319) 337-1204
E-mail: aauw@act.org
Web: www.aauw.org

**Summary** To aid women of color who are in their final year of graduate training in the fields of business administration, law, or medicine.

**Eligibility** This program is open to women of color who are entering their final year of graduate study in these historically underrepresented fields: business administration (M.B.A., E.M.B.A.), law (J.D.), or medicine (M.D., D.O.). Women in medical programs may apply for either their third or final year of study. U.S. citizenship or permanent resident status is required. Special consideration is given 1) to applicants who demonstrate their intent to enter professional practice in disciplines in which women are underrepresented, to serve underserved populations and communities, or to pursue public interest areas; and 2) to applicants who are nontraditional students. Selection is based on professional promise and personal attributes (50%), academic excellence and related academic success indicators (40%), and financial need (10%).

**Financial data** Stipends range from $5,000 to $12,000 for the academic year.

**Duration** 1 academic year, beginning in September.

**Additional information** The filing fee is $35.

**Number awarded** Varies each year.

**Deadline** January of each year.

## [779]
## FORD MOTOR COMPANY ASSE SCHOLARSHIPS

American Society of Safety Engineers
Attn: ASSE Foundation
1800 East Oakton Street
Des Plaines, IL 60018
(847) 768-3435                    Fax: (847) 768-3434
E-mail: agabanski@asse.org
Web: www.asse.org/foundation

**Summary** To provide financial assistance to female undergraduate and graduate student members of the American Society of Safety Engineers (ASSE).

**Eligibility** This program is open to female ASSE student members who are working on an undergraduate or graduate degree in occupational safety, health, and environment or a closely-related field (e.g., industrial or environmental engineering, environmental science, industrial hygiene, occupational health nursing). Undergraduates must be full-time students who have completed at least 60 semester hours with a GPA of 3.0 or higher. Graduate students must also be enrolled full time, have completed at least 9 semester hours with a GPA of 3.5 or higher, and have had a GPA of 3.0 or higher as an undergraduate. Along with their application, they must submit 2 essays of 300 words or less: 1) why they are seeking a degree in occupational safety and health or a closely-related field, a brief description of their current activities, and how those relate to their career goals and objectives; and 2) why they should be awarded this scholarship (including career goals and financial need).

**Financial data**   The stipend is $3,450.

**Duration**   1 year; nonrenewable.

**Additional information**   This program is supported by the Ford Motor Company.

**Number awarded**   4 each year.

**Deadline**   November of each year.

## [780]
## GENERAL MOTORS FOUNDATION GRADUATE SCHOLARSHIP

Society of Women Engineers
230 East Ohio Street, Suite 400
Chicago, IL 60611-3265
(312) 596-5223                    Toll-free: (877) SWE-INFO
Fax: (312) 644-8557
E-mail: scholarshipapplication@swe.org
Web: www.swe.org/scholarships

**Summary**   To provide financial assistance to graduate women working on a degree in designated engineering specialties.

**Eligibility**   This program is open to women who are enrolled in graduate school at a designated ABET-accredited college or university. Applicants must be studying automotive, chemical, electrical, industrial, manufacturing, materials, or mechanical engineering and have a GPA of 3.5 or higher. Along with their application, they must submit a 1-page essay on why they want to be an engineer, how they believe they will make a difference as an engineer, and what influenced them to study engineering. Selection is based on merit.

**Financial data**   The stipend is $1,325.

**Duration**   1 year.

**Additional information**   This program, established in 1991, is sponsored by the General Motors Foundation. Recipients must attend a designated college or university. For a list, contact the sponsor.

**Number awarded**   1 each year.

**Deadline**   January of each year.

## [781]
## GEORGE BAUER CONTINUING EDUCATION SCHOLARSHIP

Wisconsin Library Association
Attn: Scholarship Committee
5250 East Terrace Drive, Suite A1
Madison, WI 53718-8345
(608) 245-3640                    Fax: (608) 245-3646
E-mail: wla@scls.lib.wi.us
Web: www.wla.lib.wi.us/scholarships/lccce.htm

**Summary**   To provide funding to librarians in Wisconsin (particularly women, minorities, and persons with disabilities) who are interested in attending a continuing education program.

**Eligibility**   This program is open to librarians who are currently employed in a library and information agency in Wisconsin. Applicants must be planning to attend a continuing education program in any state. Along with their application,

they must submit 1) a benefits essay on the knowledge, information, or benefits they will share from the continuing education program with other Wisconsin librarians and information professionals; and 2) a career essay of 250 words or less on why they are seeking this scholarship support and what it will mean to them. Racial and ethnic minorities, women, and persons with disabilities are specifically encouraged to apply and may identify themselves as such.

**Financial data**   The stipend is $500.

**Duration**   The award is presented annually.

**Number awarded**   1 each year.

**Deadline**   February of each year.

## [782]
## GEORGIA ASSOCIATION FOR WOMEN LAWYERS SCHOLARSHIPS

Georgia Association for Women Lawyers
Attn: GAWL Foundation, Inc.
3855 Spalding Bluff Drive
Norcross, GA 30092
(770) 446-1517                    Fax: (770) 446-7721
E-mail: info@gawl.org
Web: www.gawl.org

**Summary**   To provide financial assistance to women enrolled at law schools in Georgia.

**Eligibility**   This program is open to women entering the second or third year at a law school in Georgia. Applicants must submit a 200-word statement describing their career objectives and expectations with respect to the practice of law. Selection is based on involvement in programs that affect and/or promote the advancement of women in the profession and in the community, participation in community outreach activities and/or philanthropic endeavors, demonstrated leadership ability, commitment to the legal profession, and academic achievement.

**Financial data**   The stipend is generally $2,000.

**Duration**   1 year.

**Additional information**   Information is also available from Cheryl B. Legare, Seyfarth Shaw LLP, 1545 Peachtree Street, N.E., Suite 700, Atlanta, GA 30309, (404) 881-5438, E-mail: clegare@seyfarth.com.

**Number awarded**   2 to 4 each year.

**Deadline**   February of each year.

## [783]
## GEORGIA SPACE GRANT CONSORTIUM FELLOWSHIPS

Georgia Space Grant Consortium
c/o Georgia Institute of Technology
Aerospace Engineering
Paul Weber Space Science and Technology Building,
    Room 210
Atlanta, GA 30332-0150
(404) 894-0521                    Fax: (404) 894-9313
E-mail: wanda.pierson@aerospace.gatech.edu
Web: www.ae.gatech.edu

**Summary**   To provide financial assistance for the study of space-related fields to undergraduate and graduate students (particularly women, minority and disabled students) at member institutions of the Georgia Space Grant Consortium (GSGC).

**Eligibility** This program is open to U.S. citizens who are undergraduate and graduate students at member institutions of the GSGC. Applicants must be working on a degree in mathematics, science, engineering, computer science, or a technical discipline related to space. Selection is based on transcripts, 3 letters of reference, and an essay of 100 to 500 words on the applicant's professional interests and objectives and their relationship to the field of aerospace. Awards are provided as part of the Space Grant program of the U.S. National Aeronautics and Space Administration (NASA), which encourages participation by women, minorities, and people with disabilities.

**Financial data** A stipend is awarded (amount not specified).

**Additional information** Institutions that are members of the GSGC include Albany State University, Clark Atlanta University, Columbus State University, Fort Valley State University, Georgia Institute of Technology, Georgia State University, Kennesaw State University, Mercer University, Morehouse College, Spelman College, State University of West Georgia, and the University of Georgia. This program is funded by NASA.

**Number awarded** 1 each year.

## [784]
## GERTRUDE M. COX SCHOLARSHIP IN STATISTICS

American Statistical Association
Attn: Executive Secretary
732 North Washington Street
Alexandria, VA 22314-1943
(703) 684-1221, ext. 134      Toll-free: (888) 231-3473
Fax: (703) 684-6456           E-mail: awards@amstat.org
Web: www.amstat.org

**Summary** To provide funding to women who wish to earn a graduate degree in order to enter statistically-oriented professions.

**Eligibility** Women who are either citizens or permanent residents of the United States or Canada are eligible to apply if they are admitted to full-time study in a graduate statistical program. Women in or entering the early stages of graduate training are especially encouraged to apply. Selection is based on academic record, employment history, references, and a personal statement of interests.

**Financial data** The stipend is $1,000.

**Duration** 1 year.

**Additional information** This program was established in 1989.

**Number awarded** 3 each year.

**Deadline** March of each year.

## [785]
## GILDA MURRAY SCHOLARSHIPS

Texas Federation of Business and Professional
   Women's Clubs, Inc.
Attn: TFBPW Foundation
803 Forest Ridge Drive, Suite 207
Bedford, TX 76022
(817) 283-0862               Fax: (817) 283-0872
E-mail: bpwtx@swbell.net
Web: www.bpwtx.org/foundation.asp

**Summary** To provide financial assistance to members of the Business and Professional Women's Association in Texas (BPW/Texas) who are interested in career advancement.

**Eligibility** This program is open to members of BPW/Texas who are interested in pursuing the education or training necessary to prepare for employment or to advance in a business or profession. Applicants must be at least 25 years old and have a record of active participation in the association.

**Financial data** The stipend is $500 per year; funds must be used for tuition and/or required materials (e.g., books) to an accredited college, university, technology institution, or other training.

**Duration** 1 year; may be renewed.

**Additional information** This program was established in 1998.

**Number awarded** 1 or more each year.

**Deadline** March of each year.

## [786]
## GLADYS C. ANDERSON MEMORIAL SCHOLARSHIP

American Foundation for the Blind
Attn: Scholarship Committee
11 Penn Plaza, Suite 300
New York, NY 10001
(212) 502-7661               Toll-free: (800) AFB-LINE
Fax: (212) 502-7771          TDD: (212) 502-7662
E-mail: afbinfo@afb.net
Web: www.afb.org/scholarships.asp

**Summary** To provide financial assistance to legally blind undergraduate or graduate women who are studying religious or classical music.

**Eligibility** This program is open to legally blind women who are U.S. citizens and have been accepted in an accredited undergraduate or graduate program in religious or classical music. Along with their application, they must submit an essay that includes the field of study they are pursuing and why they have chosen it; their educational and personal goals; their work experience; any extracurricular activities with which they have been involved, including those in school, religious organizations, and the community; and how they intend to use scholarship monies that may be awarded. They must also submit a sample performance tape (a voice or instrumental selection).

**Financial data** The stipend is $1,000.

**Duration** 1 academic year.

**Number awarded** 1 each year.

**Deadline** April of each year.

## [787]
## GLENN F. GLEZEN SCHOLARSHIP

Fleet Reserve Association
Attn: Scholarship Administrator
125 North West Street
Alexandria, VA 22314-2754
(703) 683-1400　　　　Toll-free: (800) 372-1924
Fax: (703) 549-6610　　　E-mail: fra@fra.org
Web: www.fra.org

**Summary** To provide financial assistance for graduate education to members of the Fleet Reserve Association (FRA) and their spouses, children, and grandchildren.

**Eligibility** This program is open to the dependent children, grandchildren, and spouses of members of the association in good standing as of April 1 of the year of the award or at the time of death. FRA members are also eligible. Applicants should be enrolled in a graduate program. Selection is based on financial need, academic standing, character, and leadership qualities.

**Financial data** The stipend is $5,000 per year.

**Duration** 1 year; may be renewed.

**Additional information** Membership in the FRA is restricted to active-duty, retired, and Reserve members of the Navy, Marine Corps, and Coast Guard. This program was established in 2001.

**Number awarded** 1 each year.

**Deadline** April of each year.

## [788]
## GLORIA HOEGH MEMORIAL SCHOLARSHIP FOR THE EDUCATION OF RURAL LIBRARIANS

Wisconsin Library Association
Attn: Scholarship Committee
5250 East Terrace Drive, Suite A1
Madison, WI 53718-8345
(608) 245-3640　　　　Fax: (608) 245-3646
E-mail: wla@scls.lib.wi.us
Web: www.wla.lib.wi.us/scholarships/rural.htm

**Summary** To provide funding to librarians (particularly women, minorities, and persons with disabilities) in rural areas of Wisconsin who are interested in attending a continuing education program.

**Eligibility** This program is open to librarians who are currently employed in a Wisconsin community with a population of 5,000 or less or who work with library employees in those communities. Applicants must be planning to attend a workshop, conference, or continuing education program in any state. Along with their application, they must submit an essay that explains what this scholarship would mean to them; the knowledge, information, or benefits they will acquire from this continuing education program that they can share with other rural Wisconsin library staff and information professionals; how they will share this information; and how the scholarship will help them reach their career goals. Selection is based on need and desire for the scholarship (as shown in the essay), employment responsibilities; and potential to contribute to rural librarianship. Racial and ethnic minorities, women, and persons with disabilities are specifically encouraged to apply and may identify themselves as such.

**Financial data** The stipend is $600.

**Duration** The award is presented annually.

**Number awarded** 1 each year.

**Deadline** July of each year.

## [789]
## GLORINE TUOHEY MEMORIAL SCHOLARSHIP

American Business Women's Association
Attn: Stephen Bufton Memorial Educational Fund
9100 Ward Parkway
P.O. Box 8728
Kansas City, MO 64114-0728
(816) 361-6621　　　　Toll-free: (800) 228-0007
Fax: (816) 361-4991　　　E-mail: abwa@abwahq.org
Web: www.abwahq.org/ProfDev.asp

**Summary** To provide financial assistance to women graduate students who are working on a degree in a specified field.

**Eligibility** This program is open to women who are working on a graduate degree and have a cumulative GPA of 2.5 or higher. Applicants are not required to be members of the American Business Women's Association, but they must be sponsored by an ABWA chapter that has contributed to the fund in the previous chapter year. Annually, the trustees designate an academic discipline for which the scholarship will be presented that year; recently, eligibility was limited to women working on a doctoral degree in pharmacy. U.S. citizenship is required.

**Financial data** The stipend is $3,000. Funds are paid directly to the recipient's institution to be used only for tuition, books, and fees.

**Duration** 1 year.

**Additional information** This program was created in 1997 as part of ABWA's Stephen Bufton Memorial Education Fund. The ABWA does not provide the names and addresses of local chapters; it recommends that applicants check with their local Chamber of Commerce, library, or university to see if any chapter has registered a contact's name and number.

**Number awarded** 1 each year.

**Deadline** May of each year.

## [790]
## GRACE HARRINGTON WILSON SCHOLARSHIP

American Mensa Education and Research Foundation
1229 Corporate Drive West
Arlington, TX 76006-6103
(817) 607-0060　　　　Toll-free: (800) 66-MENSA
Fax: (817) 649-5232
E-mail: info@mensafoundation.org
Web: www.mensafoundation.org

**Summary** To provide financial assistance for undergraduate or graduate study to women majoring in journalism.

**Eligibility** This program is open to women enrolled or planning to enroll in an undergraduate or graduate degree program in journalism at an accredited American institution of postsecondary education. Membership in Mensa is not required, but applicants must be U.S. citizens or permanent residents. Selection is based on a 550-word essay that describes the applicant's career, vocational, or academic goals.

**Financial data** The stipend is $600.

**Duration** 1 year; nonrenewable.

**Additional information** Applications are only available through the advertising efforts of participating Mensa local groups.

**Number awarded** 1 each year.

**Deadline** January of each year.

## [791]
## GRACE LEGENDRE FELLOWSHIP FOR ADVANCED GRADUATE STUDY

Business and Professional Women's Clubs of New York State
Attn: Cynthia B. Gillmore, GLG Fellowship Chair
P.O. Box 200
Johnstown, NY 12095-0200
(518) 762-8483                    Fax: (518) 762-2279
E-mail: CyndyG@aol.com
Web: www.gracelegendre.org

**Summary** To provide financial assistance to women in New York who wish to continue their education on the graduate level.

**Eligibility** This program is open to women who are permanent residents of New York state and citizens of the United States, have a bachelor's degree, and are currently registered full time or have completed 1 year in an advanced graduate degree program at a recognized college or university in New York. Applicants must show evidence of scholastic ability and need for financial assistance. They should be within 2 years of completing their degree.

**Financial data** The stipend is $1,000.

**Duration** 1 year; recipients may reapply.

**Additional information** This program was established in 1969. Requests for applications must be accompanied by a self-addressed stamped envelope.

**Number awarded** Varies each year; recently, 4 of these fellowships were awarded.

**Deadline** February of each year.

## [792]
## GROTTO/JOB'S DAUGHTERS SCHOLARSHIP

International Order of Job's Daughters
Supreme Guardian Council Headquarters
Attn: Executive Manager
233 West Sixth Street
Papillion, NE 68046-2177
(402) 592-7987                    Fax: (402) 592-2177
E-mail: sgc@iojd.org
Web: www.iojd.org

**Summary** To provide financial assistance to members of Job's Daughters who are working on an undergraduate or graduate degree in a dental field.

**Eligibility** This program is open to high school seniors and graduates; students in early graduation programs; junior college, technical, and vocational students; and college and graduate students. Applicants must be Job's Daughters in good standing in their Bethels; unmarried majority members under 30 years of age are also eligible. They must be working on a degree in a dental field, preferably with some training in the field of disabilities. Selection

is based on scholastic standing, Job's Daughters activities, the applicant's self-help plan, recommendation by the Executive Bethel Guardian Council, faculty recommendations, achievements outside Job's Daughters, and financial need.

**Financial data** The stipend is $1,500.

**Duration** 1 year.

**Additional information** Information is also available from Barbara Hill, Education Scholarships Committee Chair, 337 Illinois Street, Pekin, IL 61554, (309) 346-5564.

**Number awarded** 1 or more each year.

**Deadline** April of each year.

## [793]
## HARRIETT G. JENKINS PREDOCTORAL FELLOWSHIP PROGRAM

United Negro College Fund Special Programs Corporation
2750 Prosperity Avenue, Suite 600
Fairfax, VA 22031
(703) 205-7656                    Toll-free: (800) 231-9155
Fax: (703) 205-7645          E-mail: hgjfellows@uncfsp.org
Web: www.uncfsp.org/divstJPFP.aspx

**Summary** To provide financial assistance to women, minorities, and people with disabilities working on a graduate degree in a field of interest to the National Aeronautics and Space Administration (NASA).

**Eligibility** This program is open to members of groups underrepresented in mathematics, science, technology, and engineering, including women, minorities, and people with disabilities. Applicants must be full-time graduate students in a program leading to a master's or doctoral degree in a NASA-related discipline (aeronautics, aerospace engineering, astronomy, atmospheric science, bioengineering, biology, chemistry, computer science, earth sciences, engineering, environmental sciences, life sciences, materials sciences, mathematics, meteorology, neuroscience, physics, or robotics). They must be U.S. citizens with a GPA of 3.0 or higher. Priority is given to 1) applicants who have previously participated in NASA undergraduate programs; 2) applicants who have received their undergraduate degree from minority institutions; and 3) undergraduate minority, women, and disabled applicants from majority institutions.

**Financial data** The stipend is $22,000 per year for doctoral fellows or $16,000 for master's degree students. The tuition offset is at least $8,500. Fellows who are also selected for a mini research award at a NASA Center or the Jet Propulsion Laboratory receive an additional grant of $3,000 to $7,000.

**Duration** 3 years.

**Additional information** This program, established in 2001, is funded by NASA and administered by the United Negro College Fund Special Programs Corporation. Fellows may also compete for a mini research award to engage in a NASA research experience that is closely aligned with the research conducted at the fellow's institution. The participating NASA facilities are Ames Research Center (Moffett Field, California), Jet Propulsion Laboratory (Pasadena, California), Dryden Flight Research Center (Edwards, California), Johnson Space Center (Houston, Texas), Stennis Space Center (Stennis Space Center, Mississippi), Marshall

Space Flight Center (Marshall Space Flight Center, Alabama), Glenn Research Center (Cleveland, Ohio), Kennedy Space Center (Kennedy Space Center, Florida), Langley Research Center (Hampton, Virginia), and Goddard Space Flight Center (Greenbelt, Maryland).

**Number awarded**  Up to 20 each year.

**Deadline**  January of each year.

## [794]
## HEALTH RESEARCH AND EDUCATIONAL TRUST SCHOLARSHIPS

New Jersey Hospital Association
Attn: Health Research and Educational Trust
760 Alexander Road
P.O. Box 1
Princeton, NJ 08543-0001
(609) 275-4224                    Fax: (609) 452-8097
Web: www.njha.com/hret/scholarship.aspx

**Summary**  To provide financial assistance to New Jersey residents (particularly women and minorities) working on an undergraduate or graduate degree in a health-related field.

**Eligibility**  This program is open to residents of New Jersey enrolled in an upper-division or graduate program in hospital or health care administration, public administration, nursing, or other allied health profession. Applicants must have a GPA of 3.0 or higher and be able to demonstrate financial need. Along with their application, they must submit a 2-page essay (on which 50% of the selection is based) describing their academic plans for the future. Women and minorities are especially encouraged to apply.

**Financial data**  The stipend is $2,000.

**Duration**  1 year.

**Additional information**  This program began in 1983.

**Number awarded**  Varies each year; recently, 2 of these scholarships were awarded.

**Deadline**  July of each year.

## [795]
## HELEN COPELAND SCHOLARSHIP FOR FEMALES

United States Association of Blind Athletes
Attn: Scholarship Committee
33 North Institute Street
Colorado Springs, CO 80903
(719) 630-0422                    Fax: (719) 630-0616
E-mail: usaba@usa.net
Web: www.usaba.org

**Summary**  To provide financial assistance for undergraduate or graduate study to female members of the United States Association for Blind Athletes (USABA).

**Eligibility**  This program is open to legally blind females who have participated in USABA activities for the past year and are current members. Applicants must have been admitted to an academic, vocational, technical, professional, or certification program at the postsecondary level. Selection is based on demonstrated academic record, involvement in extracurricular and civic activities, academic goals and objectives, and USABA involvement at various levels.

**Financial data**  The stipend is $500.

**Number awarded**  1 each year.

**Deadline**  August of each year.

## [796]
## HELENE M. OVERLY MEMORIAL GRADUATE SCHOLARSHIP

Women's Transportation Seminar
Attn: National Headquarters
1701 K Street, N.W., Suite 800
Washington, DC 20006
(202) 955-5085                    Fax: (202) 955-5088
E-mail: wts@wtsinternational.org
Web: www.wtsinternational.org

**Summary**  To provide financial assistance to women graduate students interested in preparing for a career in transportation.

**Eligibility**  This program is open to women who are enrolled in a graduate degree program in a transportation-related field (e.g., transportation engineering, planning, finance, or logistics). Applicants must have at least a 3.0 GPA and be interested in a career in transportation. Along with their application, they must submit a 750-word statement about their career goals after graduation and why they think they should receive the scholarship award. Applications must be submitted first to a local chapter; the chapters forward selected applications for consideration on the national level. Minority women are particularly encouraged to apply. Selection is based on transportation involvement and goals, job skills, and academic record.

**Financial data**  The stipend is $6,000.

**Duration**  1 year.

**Additional information**  This program was established in 1981. Local chapters may also award additional funding to winners for their area.

**Number awarded**  1 each year.

**Deadline**  Applications must be submitted by November to a local WTS chapter.

## [797]
## HERMINE DALKOWITZ TOBOLOWSKY SCHOLARSHIP

Texas Federation of Business and Professional
    Women's Clubs, Inc.
Attn: TFBPW Foundation
803 Forest Ridge Drive, Suite 207
Bedford, TX 76022
(817) 283-0862                    Fax: (817) 283-0872
E-mail: bpwtx@swbell.net
Web: www.bpwtx.org/foundation.asp

**Summary**  To provide financial assistance to women in Texas who are preparing to enter selected professions.

**Eligibility**  This program is open to women in Texas who are interested in attending school to prepare for a career in law, public service, government, political science, or women's history. Applicants must have completed at least 2 semesters of study at an accredited college or university in Texas, have a GPA of 3.0 or higher, and be U.S. citizens. Selection is based on academic achievement and financial need.

**Financial data** A stipend is awarded (amount not specified).

**Duration** 1 year.

**Additional information** This program was established in 1995.

**Number awarded** 1 or more each year.

**Deadline** April of each year.

## [798]
## HERMIONE GRANT CALHOUN SCHOLARSHIPS

National Federation of the Blind
c/o Peggy Elliott, Scholarship Committee Chair
805 Fifth Avenue
Grinnell, IA 50112
(641) 236-3366
Web: www.nfb.org/sch_intro.htm

**Summary** To provide financial assistance to female blind students interested in working on an undergraduate or graduate degree.

**Eligibility** This program is open to legally blind women who are working on or planning to work full time on an undergraduate or graduate degree. Selection is based on academic excellence, service to the community, and financial need.

**Financial data** The stipend is $3,000.

**Duration** 1 year; recipients may resubmit applications up to 2 additional years.

**Additional information** Scholarships are awarded at the federation convention in July. Recipients attend the convention at federation expense; that funding is in addition to the scholarship grant.

**Number awarded** 1 each year.

**Deadline** March of each year.

## [799]
## HILARY A. BUFTON JR. SCHOLARSHIP

American Business Women's Association
Attn: Stephen Bufton Memorial Educational Fund
9100 Ward Parkway
P.O. Box 8728
Kansas City, MO 64114-0728
(816) 361-6621          Toll-free: (800) 228-0007
Fax: (816) 361-4991          E-mail: abwa@abwahq.org
Web: www.abwahq.org/ProfDev.asp

**Summary** To provide financial assistance to women graduate students who are working on a degree in a specified field.

**Eligibility** This program is open to women who are working on a graduate degree and have a cumulative GPA of 2.5 or higher. Applicants are not required to be members of the American Business Women's Association, but they must be sponsored by an ABWA chapter that has contributed to the fund in the previous chapter year. Annually, the trustees designate an academic discipline for which the scholarship will be presented that year; recently, eligibility was limited to women working on a graduate degree in entrepreneurship. U.S. citizenship is required.

**Financial data** The stipend is $10,000. Funds are paid directly to the recipient's institution to be used only for tuition, books, and fees.

**Duration** 1 year.

**Additional information** This program was created in 1986 as part of ABWA's Stephen Bufton Memorial Education Fund. The ABWA does not provide the names and addresses of local chapters; it recommends that applicants check with their local Chamber of Commerce, library, or university to see if any chapter has registered a contact's name and number.

**Number awarded** 1 each year.

**Deadline** May of each year.

## [800]
## HOLLY A. CORNELL SCHOLARSHIP

American Water Works Association
Attn: Scholarship Coordinator
6666 West Quincy Avenue
Denver, CO 80235-3098
(303) 794-7711          Toll-free: (800) 926-7337
Fax: (303) 347-0804          E-mail: swheeler@awwa.org
Web: www.awwa.org/About/scholars

**Summary** To provide financial assistance to outstanding minority and female students interested in pursuing advanced training in the field of water supply and treatment.

**Eligibility** Minority and female students who anticipate completing the requirements for a master's degree in engineering no sooner than December of the following year are eligible. Students who have been accepted into graduate school but have not yet begun graduate study are encouraged to apply. Recipients of the Larson Aquatic Research Support (LARS) M.S. Scholarship are not eligible for this program. Selection is based on the quality of the applicant's academic record and the potential to provide leadership in the field of water supply and treatment.

**Financial data** The stipend is $5,000.

**Duration** 1 year.

**Additional information** Funding for this program comes from the consulting firm CH2M Hill. The association reserves the right not to make an award for any year in which an outstanding candidate is not identified.

**Number awarded** 1 each year.

**Deadline** January of each year.

## [801]
## HONORABLE HARRISON W. EWING FELLOWSHIPS

Alpha Chi Omega Foundation
Attn: Foundation Programs Coordinator
5939 Castle Creek Parkway North Drive
Indianapolis, IN 46250-4343
(317) 579-5050, ext. 262          Fax: (317) 579-5051
E-mail: foundation@alphachiomega.org
Web: www.alphachiomega.org

**Summary** To provide financial assistance to graduating Alpha Chi Omega members who are interested in attending law school.

**Eligibility** Women college seniors or college graduates who are members of the sorority are eligible to apply if they are interested in attending law school. Selection is based on academic achievement, chapter involvement, campus and community service, and financial need.

**Financial data**   The stipend is $1,400.
**Duration**   1 year.
**Number awarded**   5 each year.
**Deadline**   March of each year.

## [802]
## HOWARD & HOWARD AWARD

Women Lawyers Association of Michigan Foundation
3300 Penobscot Building
645 Griswold
Detroit, MI 48226
(313) 256-9833                E-mail: dvanhoek@sado.org
Web: www.wlamfoundation.org/where.html#3

**Summary**   To provide financial assistance to women enrolled at law schools in Michigan.

**Eligibility**   This program is open to women enrolled full or part time at accredited law schools in Michigan. Applicants must be able to demonstrate 1) leadership capabilities; 2) community service in such areas as family law, child advocacy, or domestic violence; or 3) potential for advancing the position of women in society. Along with their application, they must submit law school transcripts, a detailed letter of interest explaining how they meet the award criteria, a resume, and up to 3 letters of recommendation.

**Financial data**   The stipend is $2,500.

**Duration**   1 year.

**Additional information**   The accredited law schools are the University of Michigan Law School, Wayne State University Law School, University of Detroit Mercy School of Law, Thomas M. Cooley Law School, and Michigan State University-Detroit College of Law.

**Number awarded**   1 each year.

**Deadline**   October of each year.

## [803]
## HOWARD HUGHES MEDICAL INSTITUTE RESEARCH TRAINING FELLOWSHIPS FOR MEDICAL STUDENTS

Howard Hughes Medical Institute
Attn: Office of Grants and Special Programs
4000 Jones Bridge Road
Chevy Chase, MD 20815-6789
(301) 215-8889     Toll-free: (800) 448-4882, ext. 8889
Fax: (301) 215-8888        E-mail: fellows@hhmi.org
Web: www.hhmi.org

**Summary**   To provide financial assistance to medical students (particularly women, minority, and disabled students) interested in pursuing research training.

**Eligibility**   Applicants must be enrolled in a medical school in the United States, although they may be citizens of any country. They must describe a proposed research project to be conducted at an academic or nonprofit research institution in the United States, other than a facility of the National Institutes of Health in Bethesda, Maryland. Research proposals should reflect the interests of the Howard Hughes Medical Institute (HHMI), especially in biochemistry, bioinformatics, biomedical engineering, biophysics, biostatistics, cell biology, developmental biology, epidemiology, genetics, immunology, mathematical and computational biology, microbiology, molecular biology, neuro-

science, pharmacology, physiology, structural biology, or virology. Applications from women and minorities underrepresented in the sciences (Blacks, Hispanics, American Indians, Native Alaskans, and Native Pacific Islanders) are especially encouraged. Students enrolled in M.D./Ph.D., Ph.D., or Sc.D. programs and those who have completed a Ph.D. or Sc.D. in a laboratory-based science are not eligible. Selection is based on the applicant's ability and promise for a research career as a physician-scientist and the quality of training that will be provided.

**Financial data**   Fellows receive a stipend of $25,000 per year; their institution receives an institutional allowance of $5,500 and a research allowance of $5,500.

**Duration**   1 year.

**Additional information**   This program complements the HHMI-NIH Research Scholars Program; students may not apply to both programs in the same year.

**Number awarded**   Up to 60 each year.

**Deadline**   January of each year.

## [804]
## H.S. AND ANGELINE LEWIS SCHOLARSHIPS

American Legion Auxiliary
Department of Wisconsin
Attn: Department Secretary/Treasurer
2930 American Legion Drive
P.O. Box 140
Portage, WI 53901-0140
(608) 745-0124                Toll-free: (866) 664-3863
Fax: (608) 745-1947
E-mail: alawi@amlegionauxwi.org
Web: www.amlegionauxwi.org

**Summary**   To provide financial assistance for undergraduate or graduate study to Wisconsin residents who are related to veterans or members of the American Legion Auxiliary.

**Eligibility**   This program is open to the children, wives, and widows of veterans who are high school seniors or graduates with a GPA of 3.2 or higher. Granddaughters as well as great-granddaughters of veterans are eligible if they are members of the American Legion Auxiliary. Applicants must be able to demonstrate financial need, be interested in working on an undergraduate or graduate degree, and be residents of Wisconsin. They do not need to attend a college in the state. Along with their application, they must submit a 300-word essay on "Education-An Investment in the Future."

**Financial data**   The stipend is $1,000.

**Duration**   1 year; nonrenewable.

**Additional information**   Information is also available from the Education Chair, Renae Allen, 206 West Fremont Street, Darien, WI 53114-1540, (262) 724-5059.

**Number awarded**   6 each year: 1 to a graduate student and 5 to undergraduates.

**Deadline**   March of each year.

## [805]
## HUNTSVILLE CHAPTER ASWA SCHOLARSHIPS

American Society of Women Accountants-Huntsville
   Chapter
c/o Joyce Skinner, Scholarship Committee Chair
P.O. Box 1561
Huntsville, AL 35807
(256) 603-1752                    Fax: (601) 252-7776
E-mail: melissa.butler@us.pwc.com
Web: www.birminghamaswa.org

**Summary** To provide financial assistance to women working on an undergraduate or graduate degree in accounting at a college or university in Alabama.

**Eligibility** This program is open to women working full or part time on a bachelor's or master's degree in accounting at a college, university, or professional school of accounting in Alabama. Applicants must have completed at least 60 semester hours. They are not required to be members of the American Society of Women Accountants (ASWA). Along with their application, they must submit a 75-word essay on how they plan to incorporate into their strategic career goals the sponsor's philosophy of achieving balance among life priorities, including career, personal development, family, friendships, and community and societal needs. Selection is based on that essay, academic record, extracurricular activities and honors, employment history, a statement of career goals and objectives, and financial need.

**Financial data** The stipend is $500.

**Duration** 1 year.

**Number awarded** 1 or more each year.

**Deadline** March of each year.

## [806]
## HVTO WOMAN OF DISTINCTION AWARD

Electronic Document Systems Foundation
Attn: EDSF Scholarship Awards
608 Silver Spur Road, Suite 280
Rolling Hills Estates, CA 90274-3616
(310) 265-5510                    Fax: (310) 265-5588
E-mail: jmowlds@edsf.org
Web: www.edsf.org/scholarships.cfm

**Summary** To provide financial assistance to women working on an undergraduate or graduate degree in a field related to the high volume transaction output (HVTO) industry.

**Eligibility** This program is open to female undergraduate and graduate students who are working on a degree in a field related to the HVTO industry, including information technology, graphic arts, or business. Applicants must be enrolled full time at a technical school, trade school, community college, university, college, or graduate school in the United States with a GPA of 3.0 or higher. Along with their application, they must submit a statement of their career goals in the field of document communications, an essay on a topic related to their view of the future of the document management and production industry, a list of current professional and college extracurricular activities and achievements, college transcripts, samples of their creative work, and 2 letters of recommendation. Financial need is not considered.

**Financial data** The stipend is $5,000.

**Duration** 1 year.

**Additional information** This program is sponsored by COPI/OutputLinks.

**Number awarded** 1 each year.

**Deadline** May of each year.

## [807]
## IADES FELLOWSHIP AWARD

International Alumnae of Delta Epsilon Sorority
Attn: Fellowship Award Committee
9406 Steeple Court
Laurel, MD 20723
(301) 490-5076              E-mail: Fellowship@iades.org
Web: www.iades.org

**Summary** To provide financial assistance to deaf women who are working on a graduate degree.

**Eligibility** Eligible to apply are deaf women who have completed 12 or more units in a doctoral-level program with a GPA of 3.0 or more. They need not be members of Delta Epsilon. Along with their application, they must submit official transcripts, a recent copy of their audiogram, and 2 letters of recommendation.

**Financial data** The stipend is $1,200.

**Duration** 1 year.

**Additional information** This program, established in 1989, is also known as the Betty G. Miller Fellowship Award. Information is also available from Virginia Borgaard, 2453 Bear Den Road, Frederick, MD 21701-9321.

**Number awarded** 1 or more each year.

**Deadline** August of each year.

## [808]
## IDA M. POPE MEMORIAL TRUST SCHOLARSHIPS

Hawai'i Community Foundation
Attn: Scholarship Department
1164 Bishop Street, Suite 800
Honolulu, HI 96813
(808) 566-5570              Toll-free: (888) 731-3863
Fax: (808) 521-6286
E-mail: scholarships@hcf-hawaii.org
Web: www.hawaiicommunityfoundation.org

**Summary** To provide financial assistance to Native Hawaiian women who are interested in working on an undergraduate or graduate degree.

**Eligibility** This program is open to female residents of Hawaii who are Native Hawaiian, defined as a descendant of the aboriginal inhabitants of the Hawaiian islands prior to 1778. Applicants must be enrolled in an accredited associate, bachelor's, or graduate degree program. They must be able to demonstrate academic achievement (GPA of 3.0 or higher), good moral character, and financial need. Along with their application, they must submit a short statement indicating their reasons for attending college, their planned course of study, and their career goals.

**Financial data** The amounts of the awards depend on the availability of funds and the need of the recipient; recently, stipends averaged $1,000.

**Duration** 1 year; may be renewed.

**Number awarded** Varies each year; recently, 60 of these scholarships were awarded.

**Deadline** February of each year.

## [809]
## IDA V. HOLLAND MISSIONARY SCHOLARSHIP

San Antonio Area Foundation
110 Broadway, Suite 230
San Antonio, TX 78205
(210) 225-2243                      Fax: (210) 225-1980
E-mail: info@saafdn.org
Web: www.saafdn.org

**Summary** To provide financial assistance to women and others in Texas who are interested in preparing for a religious career.

**Eligibility** Applicants for this scholarship must be interested in attending Moody Bible Institute in Chicago or another seminary of equal standing to prepare for missionary work, ministry, or Christian education. They must be between 18 and 24 years of age. Preference is given to women and to residents of Bexar County, Texas.

**Financial data** The stipend is $1,500 per year.

**Duration** 1 year; may be renewed.

**Additional information** This program was established in 1973.

**Number awarded** 1 each year.

**Deadline** October of each year.

## [810]
## INDUSTRY/GOVERNMENT GRADUATE FELLOWSHIPS

American Meteorological Society
Attn: Fellowship/Scholarship Coordinator
45 Beacon Street
Boston, MA 02108-3693
(617) 227-2426, ext. 246          Fax: (617) 742-8718
E-mail: scholar@ametsoc.org
Web: www.ametsoc.org

**Summary** To encourage students (particularly women, minority, and disabled students) who are entering their first year of graduate school to work on an advanced degree in the atmospheric and related oceanic and hydrologic sciences.

**Eligibility** This program is open to students entering their first year of graduate study who wish to pursue advanced degrees in the atmospheric or related oceanic or hydrologic sciences. Applicants must be U.S. citizens or permanent residents and have a GPA of 3.25 or higher. Along with their application, they must submit 200-word essays on 1) their most important achievements that qualify them for this scholarship, and 2) their career goals in the atmospheric or related oceanic or hydrologic fields. Selection is based on academic record as an undergraduate. The sponsor specifically encourages applications from women, minorities, and students with disabilities who are traditionally underrepresented in the atmospheric and related oceanic sciences.

**Financial data** The stipend is $22,000 per academic year.

**Duration** 9 months.

**Additional information** This program was initiated in 1991. It is funded by high-technology firms and government

agencies. Requests for an application must be accompanied by a self-addressed stamped envelope.

**Number awarded** Varies each year; recently, 17 of these scholarships were awarded.

**Deadline** February of each year.

## [811]
## IRENE AND DAISY MACGREGOR MEMORIAL SCHOLARSHIP

National Society Daughters of the American Revolution
Attn: Committee Services Office, Scholarships
1776 D Street, N.W.
Washington, DC 20006-5303
(202) 628-1776
Web: www.dar.org/natsociety/edout_scholar.cfm

**Summary** To provide financial assistance for medical or psychiatric nursing study.

**Eligibility** This program is open to outstanding students who have been accepted into or are pursuing an approved program of graduate psychiatric nursing or medicine. Applicants must be U.S. citizens and attend an accredited medical school, college, or university in the United States. They must obtain a letter of sponsorship from a local Daughters of the American Revolution (DAR) chapter. Preference is given to women applicants if they are "equally qualified." Selection is based on academic excellence, commitment to the field of study, and financial need.

**Financial data** The stipend is $5,000.

**Duration** 1 year; may be renewed for up to 3 additional years.

**Additional information** Requests for applications must be accompanied by a self-addressed stamped envelope.

**Number awarded** 1 or more each year.

**Deadline** April of each year.

## [812]
## J. FRANCES ALLEN SCHOLARSHIP AWARD

American Fisheries Society
Attn: Scholarship Committee
5410 Grosvenor Lane, Suite 110
Bethesda, MD 20814-2199
(301) 897-8616                      Fax: (301) 897-8096
E-mail: main@fisheries.org
Web: www.fisheries.org

**Summary** To provide financial assistance for doctoral studies to female members of the American Fisheries Society (AFS).

**Eligibility** This program is open to women Ph.D. students who are AFS members. Applicants must be studying a branch of fisheries science, including but not limited to aquatic biology, engineering, fish culture, limnology, oceanography, or sociology. Selection is based on research promise, scientific merit, and academic achievement.

**Financial data** The stipend is $2,500, paid directly to the student. Funds may be used for any aspect of doctoral education, including tuition, textbooks, equipment, travel, or living expenses.

**Duration** 1 year; nonrenewable.

**Additional information** This program was established in 1986.

**Number awarded** 1 each year.

**Deadline** March of each year.

## [813]
### JANET H. GRISWOLD SCHOLARSHIPS

P.E.O. Foundation-California State Chapter
c/o Patty Colligan, Scholarship Committee Chair
529 Shell Drive
Redding, CA 96003
(530) 247-7044        E-mail: pattyinrdng@hotmail.com
Web: www.peocalifornia.org/jhg.html

**Summary** To provide financial assistance to women from California who are working on an undergraduate or graduate degree in education.

**Eligibility** This program is open to female residents of California who are studying education at the undergraduate or graduate level. Applicants must be able to demonstrate financial need, character, and a record of academic and extracurricular activities achievement.

**Financial data** Stipends range from $500 to $1,100.

**Duration** 1 year.

**Number awarded** Varies each year; recently, 7 of these scholarships were awarded.

**Deadline** February of each year.

## [814]
### JANIE CREE BOSE ANDERSON SCHOLARSHIPS

Kentucky Woman's Missionary Union
Attn: Scholarships
13420 Eastpoint Centre Drive
P.O. Box 436569
Louisville, KY 40253-6569
(502) 489-3534    Toll-free: (866) 489-3534 (within KY)
Fax: (502) 489-3566      E-mail: kywmu@kybaptist.org
Web: www.kywmu.org/scholars.htm

**Summary** To provide financial assistance to women Baptists from Kentucky who are attending college or seminary to prepare for Christian service.

**Eligibility** This program is open to women who are active members of churches affiliated with the Kentucky Baptist Convention or the General Association of Baptists in Kentucky. Applicants must be attending an accredited college, university, or seminary as a full-time student. They must have a GPA of 2.7 or higher and be preparing for Christian service.

**Financial data** Stipends range from $250 to $750.

**Duration** 1 year.

**Number awarded** 1 or more each year.

**Deadline** January of each year.

## [815]
### JAZZ PERFORMANCE AWARDS

Sigma Alpha Iota Philanthropies, Inc.
One Tunnel Road
Asheville, NC 28805
(828) 251-0606          Fax: (828) 251-0644
E-mail: philonline@sai-national.org
Web: www.sai-national.org/phil/philsch3.html

**Summary** To provide financial assistance to members of Sigma Alpha Iota (an organization of women musicians) who are interested in working on an undergraduate or graduate degree in jazz performance.

**Eligibility** This program is open to members of the organization who are enrolled in an undergraduate or graduate degree program in jazz performance or studies. Applicants must be younger than 32 years of age. Along with their application, they must submit a CD recording of a performance "set" of 30 to 45 minutes.

**Financial data** Stipends are $2,000 for the winner or $1,500 for the runner-up.

**Duration** 1 year.

**Additional information** There is a $25 nonrefundable application fee.

**Number awarded** 2 every 3 years.

**Deadline** March of the year of the awards (2009, 2012, etc.).

## [816]
### JESSIE FANYO PAYNE GRANT

Alpha Chi Omega Foundation
Attn: Foundation Programs Coordinator
5939 Castle Creek Parkway North Drive
Indianapolis, IN 46250-4343
(317) 579-5050, ext. 262          Fax: (317) 579-5051
E-mail: foundation@alphachiomega.org
Web: www.alphachiomega.org

**Summary** To provide financial assistance to undergraduate or alumnae members of Alpha Chi Omega who are interested in working on a degree in communications.

**Eligibility** This program is open to junior, senior, and graduate members of Alpha Chi Omega who are full-time students in the field of communications with an emphasis on journalism and public relations. Selection is based on academic achievement, chapter involvement, campus and community involvement, and financial need.

**Financial data** The stipend is $500.

**Duration** 1 year.

**Number awarded** 1 each year.

**Deadline** March of each year.

## [817]
## JILL S. TIETJEN SCHOLARSHIP

Society of Women Engineers
230 East Ohio Street, Suite 400
Chicago, IL 60611-3265
(312) 596-5223          Toll-free: (877) SWE-INFO
Fax: (312) 644-8557
E-mail: scholarshipapplication@swe.org
Web: www.swe.org/scholarships

**Summary**  To provide financial assistance to women working on an undergraduate or graduate degree in engineering or computer science.

**Eligibility**  This program is open to women who will be sophomores, juniors, seniors, or graduate students at ABET-accredited colleges and universities. Applicants must be U.S. citizens majoring in computer science or engineering and have a GPA of 3.0 or higher. Along with their application, they must submit a 1-page essay on why they want to be an engineer or computer scientist, how they believe they will make a difference as an engineer or computer scientist, and what influenced them to study engineering or computer science. Selection is based on merit.

**Financial data**  The stipend is $1,000.

**Duration**  1 year.

**Number awarded**  1 each year.

**Deadline**  January of each year.

## [818]
## JOB'S DAUGHTERS SUPREME GUARDIAN COUNCIL SCHOLARSHIPS

International Order of Job's Daughters
Supreme Guardian Council Headquarters
Attn: Executive Manager
233 West Sixth Street
Papillion, NE 68046-2177
(402) 592-7987          Fax: (402) 592-2177
E-mail: sgc@iojd.org
Web: www.iojd.org

**Summary**  To provide financial assistance for college or graduate school to members of Job's Daughters.

**Eligibility**  This program is open to high school seniors and graduates; students in early graduation programs; junior college, technical, and vocational students; and college and graduate students. Applicants must be Job's Daughters in good standing in their Bethels; unmarried majority members under 30 years of age are also eligible. Selection is based on scholastic standing, Job's Daughters activities, the applicant's self-help plan, recommendation by the Executive Bethel Guardian Council, faculty recommendations, achievements outside Job's Daughters, and financial need.

**Financial data**  The stipend is $750.

**Duration**  1 year; may be renewed 1 additional year.

**Additional information**  Information is also available from Barbara Hill, Education Scholarships Committee Chair, 337 Illinois Street, Pekin, IL 61554, (309) 346-5564.

**Number awarded**  Varies each year.

**Deadline**  April of each year.

## [819]
## JOHN RAINER FELLOWSHIPS

American Indian Graduate Center
Attn: Executive Director
4520 Montgomery Boulevard, N.E., Suite 1-B
Albuquerque, NM 87109-1291
(505) 881-4584          Toll-free: (800) 628-1920
Fax: (505) 884-0427          E-mail: aigc@aigc.com
Web: www.aigc.com

**Summary**  To provide financial assistance to Native American graduate students.

**Eligibility**  This program is open to enrolled members of U.S. federally-recognized American Indian tribes and Alaska Native groups and other students who can document one-fourth degree federally-recognized Indian blood. Applicants must be enrolled full time in a master's, doctoral, or professional degree program at an accredited college or university in the United States. Selection is based on academic achievement, financial need, and an essay on the meaning of their graduate education to the Indian community. Males and females are considered in separate selection processes.

**Financial data**  The stipend is $1,000.

**Duration**  1 year; may be renewed.

**Additional information**  The application fee is $15. Since this a supplemental program, applicants must apply in a timely manner for federal financial aid and campus-based aid at the college they are attending to be considered for this program. Failure to apply will disqualify an applicant.

**Number awarded**  2 each year: 1 for a female and 1 for a male.

**Deadline**  May of each year.

## [820]
## JOSEPH R. BARANSKI EMERITUS SCHOLARSHIP

Fleet Reserve Association
Attn: Scholarship Administrator
125 North West Street
Alexandria, VA 22314-2754
(703) 683-1400          Toll-free: (800) 372-1924
Fax: (703) 549-6610          E-mail: fra@fra.org
Web: www.fra.org

**Summary**  To provide financial assistance for graduate education to members of the Fleet Reserve Association (FRA) and their spouses, children, and grandchildren.

**Eligibility**  This program is open to the dependent children, grandchildren, and spouses of members of the association in good standing as of April 1 of the year of the award or at the time of death. FRA members are also eligible. Applicants must be enrolled in a graduate program. Selection is based on financial need, academic standing, character, and leadership qualities.

**Financial data**  The stipend is $5,000.

**Duration**  1 year; may be renewed.

**Additional information**  Membership in the FRA is restricted to active-duty, retired, and Reserve members of the Navy, Marine Corps, and Coast Guard. This program was established in 2001.

**Number awarded**  1 each year.

**Deadline**  April of each year.

## [821]
### JUDGE JUDY M. WEST SCHOLARSHIP

Northern Kentucky Bar Association
130 Dudley Road, Suite 190
Edgewood, KY 41017
(859) 781-1300                    Fax: (859) 781-1277
E-mail: christine@nkybar.com
Web: www.nkybar.com

**Summary** To provide financial assistance to outstanding women law students who are residents of Kentucky.

**Eligibility** Applicants must be female law students who are residents of Kentucky and entering their last year of school. Special consideration is given to nontraditional or returning students. To apply, women must submit a completed application, a cover letter or resume, and a recent photograph. Selection is based on academic record and other personal characteristics.

**Financial data** The stipend is $1,000.

**Duration** The stipend is offered annually.

**Additional information** This scholarship was established in 1991 to honor the first woman appellate judge in Kentucky.

**Number awarded** 1 each year.

## [822]
### JUDITH MCMANUS PRICE SCHOLARSHIPS

American Planning Association
Attn: Leadership Affairs Associate
122 South Michigan Avenue, Suite 1600
Chicago, IL 60603-6107
(312) 431-9100                    Fax: (312) 431-9985
E-mail: fellowship@planning.org
Web: www.planning.org/institutions/scholarship.htm

**Summary** To provide financial assistance to women and underrepresented minority students enrolled in undergraduate or graduate degree programs at recognized planning schools.

**Eligibility** This program is open to undergraduate and graduate students in urban and regional planning who are women or members of the following minority groups: African American, Hispanic American, or Native American. Applicants must be citizens of the United States and able to document financial need. They must intend to work as practicing planners in the public sector. Along with their application, they must submit a 2- to 5-page personal statement describing how their education will be applied to career goals and why they chose planning as a career path. Selection is based (in order of importance) on 1) commitment to planning as reflected in the personal statement and resume; 2) academic achievement and/or improvement during the past 2 years; 3) letters of recommendation; 4) financial need; and 5) professional presentation.

**Financial data** Stipends range from $2,000 to $4,000 per year. The money may be applied to tuition and living expenses only. Payment is made to the recipient's university and divided by terms in the school year.

**Duration** 1 year; recipients may reapply.

**Additional information** This program was established in 2004.

**Number awarded** Varies each year; recently, 3 of these scholarships were awarded.

**Deadline** April of each year.

## [823]
### KAILASH, MONA, AND ANILA JAIN SCHOLARSHIP

Kappa Delta Sorority
Attn: Foundation Manager
3205 Players Lane
Memphis, TN 38125
(901) 748-1897                    Toll-free: (800) 536-1897
Fax: (901) 748-0949
E-mail: kappadelta@kappadelta.org
Web: www.kappadelta.org

**Summary** To provide financial assistance to members of Kappa Delta Sorority who are working on a graduate degree in health care.

**Eligibility** This program is open to graduate members of Kappa Delta Sorority. Applicants must submit a personal statement giving their reasons for applying for this scholarship, official undergraduate and graduate transcripts, and 2 letters of recommendation. They must be working on a graduate degree in a field related to health care. Selection is based on academic excellence; service to the chapter, alumnae association, or national Kappa Delta; service to the campus and community; personal objectives and goals; potential; recommendations; and financial need.

**Financial data** The stipend is $2,000 per year. Funds may be used only for tuition, fees, and books, not for room and board.

**Duration** 1 year; may be renewed.

**Additional information** This program was established in 2001.

**Number awarded** 1 each year.

**Deadline** January of each year.

## [824]
### KANSAS SPACE GRANT CONSORTIUM PROGRAM

Kansas Space Grant Consortium
c/o University of Kansas
Learned Hall
1530 West 15th
Lawrence, KS 66045-7609
(785) 864-7401                    Fax: (785) 864-3361
E-mail: ksgc@nasainkansas.org
Web: nasainkansas.org

**Summary** To provide funding for space-related activities to students and faculty (particularly women, minorities, and persons with disabilities) at member institutions of the Kansas Space Grant Consortium.

**Eligibility** This program is open to faculty and students at member institutions. Support is provided for undergraduate research scholarships, graduate research assistantships, undergraduate and graduate student participation in activities sponsored by the U.S. National Aeronautics and Space Administration (NASA), faculty participation in NASA research projects, and other activities in fields of interest to NASA. The consortium is a component of NASA's Space Grant program, which encourages participation by women, underrepresented minorities, and persons with disabilities.

**Financial data** Each participating institution determines the amounts of its awards.

**Additional information** The member institutions of the consortium are Emporia State University, Fort Hayes State University, Haskell Indian Nations University, Kansas State University, Pittsburgh State University, University of Kansas, and Wichita State University. Funding for this program is provided by NASA.

**Number awarded** Varies each year.

**Deadline** Each participating institution establishes its own deadlines.

## [825]
## KAPPA ALPHA THETA ALUMNAE SCHOLARSHIPS

Kappa Alpha Theta
Attn: Foundation
8740 Founders Road
Indianapolis, IN 46268-1337
(317) 876-1870, ext. 119
Toll-free: (888) 526-1870, ext. 119
Fax: (317) 876-1925
E-mail: cthoennes@kappaalphatheta.org
Web: www.kappaalphatheta.org

**Summary** To provide financial assistance to members of Kappa Alpha Theta (the first Greek letter fraternity for women) who are pursuing advanced degrees in North America or abroad.

**Eligibility** This program is open to members of Kappa Alpha Theta who are enrolled as graduate students at a university in Canada or the United States. Applicants must submit an official transcript, a resume, and 2 letters of reference. Selection is based on 4 categories: academic achievement, participation in Kappa Alpha Theta activities, participation in campus and/or community activities, and references. Financial need is not considered.

**Financial data** Stipends range from $1,000 to $10,000. Recently, the average was $4,760.

**Duration** 1 year. Recipients may reapply, but they may not receive a maximum lifetime amount of more than $20,000 from the foundation.

**Additional information** Recipients may study abroad, provided they do so as part of a program leading to a degree from an institution in the United States or Canada. This program has a number of named scholarships, including the Betty B. and James B. Lambert Graduate Scholarships.

**Number awarded** Varies each year; recently, 67 of these scholarships were awarded, including 27 Betty B. and James B. Lambert Graduate Scholarships.

**Deadline** January of each year.

## [826]
## KAPPA DELTA SORORITY GRADUATE SCHOLARSHIPS

Kappa Delta Sorority
Attn: Foundation Manager
3205 Players Lane
Memphis, TN 38125
(901) 748-1897     Toll-free: (800) 536-1897
Fax: (901) 748-0949
E-mail: kappadelta@kappadelta.org
Web: www.kappadelta.org

**Summary** To provide financial assistance to members of Kappa Delta Sorority who are interested in continuing their education at the graduate level.

**Eligibility** This program is open to graduate members of Kappa Delta Sorority. Applicants must submit a personal statement giving their reasons for applying for this scholarship, official undergraduate and graduate transcripts, and 2 letters of recommendation. Most scholarships are available to all graduate members, but some have additional restrictions. Selection is based on academic excellence; service to the chapter, alumnae association, or national Kappa Delta; service to the campus and community; personal objectives and goals; potential; recommendations; and financial need.

**Financial data** Stipends are range from $1,000 to $5,000 per year. Funds may be used only for tuition, fees, and books, not for room and board.

**Duration** 1 year; may be renewed.

**Additional information** This program includes the following named scholarships that have no additional restrictions: the Dorothea B. Cavin Scholarship, the Helen A. Snyder Scholarship, the Minnie Mae Prescott Scholarship, the Muriel Johnstone Scholarship, the Herff Jones Graduate Scholarship, and the Alumna Grant for Continuing Education.

**Number awarded** Varies each year. Recently, the sorority awarded a total of 10 graduate scholarships: 1 at $5,000, 7 at $2,000, 1 at $1,500, and 1 at $1,000.

**Deadline** January of each year.

## [827]
## KAPPA KAPPA GAMMA GRADUATE FELLOWSHIP AWARDS

Kappa Kappa Gamma Foundation
530 East Town Street
P.O. Box 38
Columbus, OH 43216-0038
(614) 228-6515     Toll-free: (866) KKG-1870
Fax: (614) 228-7809     E-mail: kkghq@kappa.org
Web: www.kappakappagamma.org

**Summary** To provide financial assistance for graduate school to members of Kappa Kappa Gamma.

**Eligibility** This program is open to members of Kappa Kappa Gamma who are full-time graduate students with a GPA of 3.0 or higher. Applicants must be initiated members who were in good standing as undergraduates. Along with their application, they must submit a personal essay or letter describing their educational and career goals and financial need. Selection is based on merit, academic achievement, participation in sorority activities, and financial need.

**Financial data** A stipend is awarded (amount not specified).

**Duration** 1 year; nonrenewable.

**Number awarded** Varies each year; in a recent biennium, the foundation awarded a total of $936,681 in undergraduate and graduate scholarships.

**Deadline** January of each year.

## [828]
## KAREN TUCKER CENTENNIAL SCHOLARSHIP

Alpha Omicron Pi Foundation
Attn: Scholarship Committee
5390 Virginia Way
P.O. Box 395
Brentwood, TN 37024-0395
(615) 370-0920                    Fax: (615) 370-4424
E-mail: foundation@alphaomicronpi.org
Web: www.aoiifoundation.org

**Summary** To provide financial assistance for college or graduate school to collegiate and alumnae members of Alpha Omicron Pi.

**Eligibility** This program is open to collegiate members of Alpha Omicron Pi who wish to continue their undergraduate education and alumnae members who wish to work on a graduate degree. Applicants must submit 50-word essays on the following topics: 1) the circumstances that have created their need for this scholarship, and 2) their immediate and long-term life objectives. Selection is based on academic excellence, dedication to serving the community and Alpha Omicron Pi, and financial need.

**Financial data** A stipend is awarded (amount not specified).

**Duration** 1 year.

**Additional information** Undergraduate recipients must enroll full time, but graduate recipients may enroll part time.

**Number awarded** 1 each year.

**Deadline** February of each year.

## [829]
## KATHERINE J. SCHUTZE MEMORIAL SCHOLARSHIP

Christian Church (Disciples of Christ)
Attn: Division of Homeland Ministries
130 East Washington Street
P.O. Box 1986
Indianapolis, IN 46206-1986
(317) 713-2672                    Toll-free: (888) DHM-2631
Fax: (317) 635-4426    E-mail: mail@dhm.disciples.org
Web: www.homelandministries.org

**Summary** To provide funding to female seminary students affiliated with the Christian Church (Disciples of Christ).

**Eligibility** This program is open to women seminary students who are members of the Christian Church (Disciples of Christ). Applicants must plan to prepare for the ordained ministry, have at least a "C+" GPA, provide evidence of financial need, be enrolled full time in an accredited school or seminary, provide a transcript of academic work, and be under the care of a regional Commission on the Ministry or in the process of coming under care.

**Financial data** A stipend is awarded (amount not specified).

**Duration** 1 year; may be renewed.

**Number awarded** 1 or more each year.

**Deadline** March of each year.

## [830]
## KENTUCKY SPACE GRANT CONSORTIUM GRADUATE FELLOWSHIPS

Kentucky Space Grant Consortium
c/o Western Kentucky University
Department of Physics and Astronomy, TCCW 246
1906 College Heights Boulevard 11077
Bowling Green, KY 42101-1077
(270) 745-4156                    Fax: (270) 745-4255
E-mail: Richard.Hackney@wku.edu
Web: www.wku.edu/KSGC

**Summary** To provide financial assistance for study and research in space-related fields to graduate students in Kentucky, particularly women, minority, and disabled students.

**Eligibility** This program is open to graduate students at member institutions of the Kentucky Space Grant Consortium (KSGC). Applicants must be enrolled in a graduate degree program in a space-related field or teaching specialization. As part of the program, a faculty member must agree to serve as a mentor on a research project. U.S. citizenship is required. Selection is based on the academic qualifications of the applicant, quality of the proposed research program and its relevance to space-related science and technology, and applicant's motivation for a space-related career as expressed in an essay on interests and goals. Applications are especially encouraged from women, members of other underrepresented groups (including minorities and people with disabilities), and students involved in projects of the U.S. National Aeronautics and Space Administration (NASA), such as NASA EPSCoR and SHARP.

**Financial data** The stipend is $16,000 per year, with an additional $2,000 for use in support of the student's mentored research project. Matching grants of at least $12,000 are required. Preference is given to applicants from schools that agree to waive tuition for the fellow as part of the program.

**Duration** 1 year; may be renewed, depending on the quality of the student's research and satisfactory grades, presentation of research results, and evaluation of progress by the mentor.

**Additional information** This program is funded by NASA. The KSGC member institutions are Bellarmine University, Centre College, Eastern Kentucky University, Kentucky State University, Morehead State University, Murray State University, Northern Kentucky University, Thomas More College, Transylvania University, University of Kentucky, University of Louisville, and Western Kentucky University.

**Number awarded** Varies each year.

**Deadline** February of each year.

## [831]
## LAS VEGAS NETWORK OF EXECUTIVE WOMEN IN HOSPITALITY SCHOLARSHIP AWARDS

Network of Executive Women in Hospitality-Las Vegas
   Chapter
Attn: Sue Flamming, Scholarship Chair
P.O. Box 15563
Las Vegas, NV 89114
Toll-free: (800) 593-NEWH          Fax: (800) 693-NEWH
E-mail: suef@graphicencounter.com
Web: www.newh.org/newh/scholarshippacket.php

**Summary**  To provide financial assistance to undergraduate and graduate women in Nevada and Utah who are working on a degree in hospitality.

**Eligibility**  This program is open to women who have completed half of an accredited hospitality-related undergraduate or graduate program in Nevada or Utah. Applicants must have a GPA of 3.0 or higher and a career objective in the hospitality or food service industries (e.g., hotel and restaurant management, culinary, architecture, design). Selection is based on financial need and academic accomplishments.

**Financial data**  The stipend depends on the availability of funds and the need of the recipient.

**Number awarded**  1 or more each year.

**Deadline**  March of each year.


## [832]
## LASPACE GRADUATE FELLOWSHIPS

Louisiana Space Consortium
c/o Louisiana State University
Department of Physics and Astronomy
371 Nicholson Hall
Baton Rouge, LA 70803-4001
(225) 578-8697                     Fax: (225) 578-1222
E-mail: laspace@lsu.edu
Web: laspace.lsu.edu/fellowships.html

**Summary**  To provide financial assistance to students (particularly women, minority, and disabled students) who are working on a graduate degree in an aerospace-related discipline at a college or university belonging to the Louisiana Space Consortium (LaSPACE).

**Eligibility**  This program is open to U.S. citizens working on a master's or doctoral degree in a space- or aerospace-related field as a full-time student at 1 of the LaSPACE member schools. Applicants should have a GPA of 3.0 or higher and a GRE score in excess of 900 (including 500 on the quantitative). Members of groups underrepresented in science, mathematics, and engineering (women, minorities, and persons with disabilities) are strongly encouraged to apply. Selection is based on scholastic accomplishment, research experience and productivity, leadership and recognitions, intellectual abilities and character, and relevance of the proposed graduate work to space and aerospace fields or programs.

**Financial data**  The stipend is $17,500 per year for students working on a master's degree or $20,000 per year for students working on a doctorate.

**Duration**  1 year; renewable for up to 2 additional years for master's degree students and up to 4 additional years for Ph.D. students.

**Additional information**  Fellows work with an established aerospace researcher at 1 of the LaSPACE member institutions: Dillard University, Grambling State University, Louisiana State University, Louisiana Tech University, Loyola University, McNeese State University, Nicholls State University, Northwestern State University of Louisiana, Southeastern Louisiana University, Southern University and A&M College, Southern University in New Orleans, Southern University at Shreveport, Tulane University, University of New Orleans, University of Louisiana at Lafayette, University of Louisiana at Monroe, and Xavier University of Louisiana. Funding for this program is provided by the U.S. National Aeronautics and Space Administration (NASA). Fellows are expected to describe the work in a yearly written report and in seminars presented to various audiences.

**Number awarded**  2 to 4 each year.

**Deadline**  October of each year.


## [833]
## LAURELS FUND SCHOLARSHIPS

Educational Foundation for Women in Accounting
Attn: Foundation Administrator
P.O. Box 1925
Southeastern, PA 19399-1925
(610) 407-9229                     Fax: (610) 644-3713
E-mail: info@efwa.org
Web: www.efwa.org/laurels.htm

**Summary**  To provide financial support to women doctoral students in accounting.

**Eligibility**  This program is open to women who are working on a Ph.D. degree in accounting and have completed their comprehensive examinations. Selection is based on academic achievement in course work and research activities, employment record, professional activities, scholarships and other academic honors, volunteer work in which the applicant has made significant or long-term commitments, a 2-page statement of personal and career goals and objectives, and financial need.

**Financial data**  Stipends range from $1,000 to $5,000 per year.

**Duration**  1 year; may be renewed up to 3 additional years.

**Additional information**  This program was established in 1978.

**Number awarded**  Varies each year. A total of $20,000 is available for this program each year.

**Deadline**  April of each year.


## [834]
## LEONARD C. HORN AWARD FOR LEGAL STUDIES

Miss America Pageant
Attn: Scholarship Department
Two Miss America Way, Suite 1000
Atlantic City, NJ 08401
(609) 345-7571, ext. 27          Toll-free: (800) 282-MISS
Fax: (609) 347-6079      E-mail: info@missamerica.org
Web: www.missamerica.org

**Summary**  To provide financial assistance to women who

are working on a degree in law and who, in the past, competed at some level in the Miss America competition.

**Eligibility** This program is open to women who are working on a law degree and who competed at the local, state, or national level in a Miss America competition within the past 10 years. Applicants must submit an essay, up to 500 words, on why they wish to become a lawyer and how this scholarship will help them to achieve their goal. Selection is based on GPA, class rank, LSAT score, extracurricular activities, financial need, and level of participation within the system.

**Financial data** The stipend is $10,000 per year.

**Duration** 1 year; renewable.

**Additional information** This scholarship was established in 1998.

**Number awarded** 1 each year.

**Deadline** June of each year.

## [835]
## LINCOLN COMMUNITY FOUNDATION MEDICAL RESEARCH SCHOLARSHIP

Lincoln Community Foundation
215 Centennial Mall South, Suite 100
Lincoln, NE 68508
(402) 474-2345          Fax: (402) 476-8532
E-mail: lcf@lcf.org
Web: www.lcf.org

**Summary** To provide financial assistance to residents of Nebraska (especially women) who are interested in working on an advanced degree in a medical field.

**Eligibility** This program is open to residents of Nebraska who are working on an advanced degree in a medical field (nursing students may apply as undergraduates). Applicants must submit an essay explaining their progress toward completing their education, why they have chosen to prepare for a career in a medical field, and their future career goals once they complete their degree. Preference is given to 1) female applicants; 2) students preparing for careers as physicians and nurses; and 3) applicants who demonstrate financial need.

**Financial data** Stipends provided by the foundation generally range from $500 to $2,000.

**Duration** 1 year; may be renewed.

**Number awarded** 1 or more each year.

**Deadline** May of each year.

## [836]
## LINDA J. MURPHY SCHOLARSHIPS

Women Lawyers' Association of Greater St. Louis
c/o Helen Paulson
P.O. Box 1428
St. Louis, MO 63188
(314) 454-6767          E-mail: wlastl@yahoo.com
Web: www.wlastl.org/scholarship.html

**Summary** To provide financial assistance to women attending law school in Missouri.

**Eligibility** This program is open to women attending law school in Missouri on a part-time or full-time basis. Selection is based on grades, history of public service, desire to

continue public service, commitment to equal access to the law, and financial need.

**Financial data** Stipends range from $1,000 to $6,000.

**Duration** 1 year.

**Additional information** This program started in 1996.

**Number awarded** 3 each year.

**Deadline** March of each year.

## [837]
## LOIS SHAFER SCHOLARSHIP

Women in Aviation, International
Attn: Scholarships
Morningstar Airport
3647 State Route 503 South
West Alexandria, OH 45381
(937) 558-7655          Fax: (937) 839-4645
E-mail: scholarships@wai.org
Web: www.wai.org/education/scholarships.cfm

**Summary** To provide financial assistance to members of Women in Aviation, International (WAI) who are pursuing a career as a corporate pilot and currently working on a commercial rating.

**Eligibility** This program is open to WAI members working on a commercial pilot certificate as well as preparing for a career in commercial aviation. Applicants must submit a 500-word essay that addresses their career aspirations and goals, 3 letters of recommendation, a resume, copies of all aviation and medical certificates, and the last 3 pages of their pilot logbook, if applicable. Selection is based on achievements, attitude toward self and others, commitment to success, dedication to career, financial need, motivation, reliability, responsibility, and teamwork.

**Financial data** The stipend is $2,500.

**Duration** 1 year.

**Additional information** WAI is a nonprofit professional organization dedicated to encouraging women to consider an aviation career, providing educational outreach activities, and providing networking opportunities to women active in the industry.

**Number awarded** 1 each year.

**Deadline** November of each year.

## [838]
## LYDIA I. PICKUP MEMORIAL SCHOLARSHIP

Society of Women Engineers
230 East Ohio Street, Suite 400
Chicago, IL 60611-3265
(312) 596-5223          Toll-free: (877) SWE-INFO
Fax: (312) 644-8557
E-mail: scholarshipapplication@swe.org
Web: www.swe.org/scholarships

**Summary** To provide financial assistance to women working on an undergraduate or graduate degree in engineering or computer science.

**Eligibility** This program is open to women who will be sophomores, juniors, seniors, or graduate students at ABET-accredited colleges and universities. Applicants must be majoring in computer science or engineering and have a GPA of 3.0 or higher. Along with their application, they must submit a 1-page essay on why they want to be an engineer or computer scientist, how they believe they will make a difference as an engineer or computer scientist, and what influenced them to study engineering or computer science. Preference is given to graduate student. Selection is based on merit.

**Financial data**   The stipend is $2,000.

**Duration**   1 year.

**Additional information**   This program was established in 2001.

**Number awarded**   1 each year.

**Deadline**   January of each year.

## [839]
## M.A. CARTLAND SHACKFORD MEDICAL FELLOWSHIP

Wellesley College
Center for Work and Service
Attn: Secretary to the Committee on Extramural
   Graduate Fellowships and Scholarships
106 Central Street
Wellesley, MA 02181-8203
(781) 283-3525                    Fax: (781) 283-3674
E-mail: cws-fellowships@wellesley.edu
Web: www.wellesley.edu/CWS/alumnae/wellfs.html

**Summary**   To provide financial assistance to women for graduate study in the medical fields.

**Eligibility**   Women who have graduated from an American academic institution and are interested in general medical practice (but not psychiatry) may apply.

**Financial data**   The fellowship of at least $10,500 is tenable at any institution of the recipient's choice.

**Duration**   1 year.

**Additional information**   The recipient must pursue full-time graduate study.

**Number awarded**   1 each year.

**Deadline**   January of each year.

## [840]
## MABEL BIEVER MUSIC EDUCATION SCHOLARSHIP FOR GRADUATE STUDENTS

Sigma Alpha Iota Philanthropies, Inc.
One Tunnel Road
Asheville, NC 28805
(828) 251-0606                    Fax: (828) 251-0644
E-mail: philonline@sai-national.org
Web: www.sai-national.org/phil/philsch1.html

**Summary**   To provide financial assistance for graduate study in music education to members of Sigma Alpha Iota (an organization of women musicians).

**Eligibility**   This program is open to alumnae members of the organization who have completed an undergraduate degree in music education and are currently enrolled in a program leading to a graduate degree in that field. Candidates should have had at least 1 year of teaching experience. Applications must include a taped performance audition or a videotape demonstrating effectiveness as a teacher.

**Financial data**   The stipend is $1,500 per year.

**Duration**   1 year.

**Additional information**   This program is sponsored by the Oak Park Alumnae Chapter of Sigma Alpha Iota. Further information is also available from Donna Budil, 385 Desplaines Avenue, Riverside, IL 60546, (708) 442-1979, E-mail: musicladydb@yahoo.com. There is a $25 nonrefundable application fee.

**Number awarded**   1 each year.

**Deadline**   March of each year.

## [841]
## MAIDS OF ATHENA SCHOLARSHIPS

Maids of Athena
1909 Q Street, N.W., Suite 500
Washington, DC 20009-1007
(202) 232-6300                    Fax: (202) 232-2140
Web: www.ahepa.org

**Summary**   To provide financial assistance for undergraduate and graduate education to women of Greek descent.

**Eligibility**   This program is open to women who are members of the Maids of Athena. Applicants may be a graduating high school senior, an undergraduate student, or a graduate student. Selection is based on academic merit, financial need, and participation in the organization.

**Financial data**   The stipend is $1,000.

**Duration**   1 year.

**Additional information**   Membership in Maids of Athena is open to unmarried women between 14 and 24 years of age who are of Greek descent from either parent.

**Number awarded**   3 each year: 1 each to a graduating high school senior, undergraduate student, and graduate student.

## [842]
## MAINE MEDIA WOMEN SCHOLARSHIP

Maine Media Women
c/o Carol Jaeger
P.O. Box 175
Round Pond, ME 04564-0175
(207) 529-5304
Web: www.mainemediawomen.org/scholarships.html

**Summary**   To provide financial assistance to women in Maine who are interested in working on an undergraduate or graduate degree in communications.

**Eligibility**   This program is open to women of any age who are residents of Maine, will be enrolled in a related college program in the fall, and are interested in preparing for or furthering a career in a media-related area. Their field of study may be art, photography, design and marketing, creative writing, desktop publishing, photojournalism, videography, or communications. Along with their application, they must submit a 1-page essay on their career goals, why they have chosen communications as their field, and how they plan to reach their goals. Selection is based on the essay; academic record; experience, such as internships, volunteering, or part-time work, with the mass media, advertising, or public relations; academic, extracurricular, and public service activities that demonstrate commitment to a career in mass communications; and financial need.

**Financial data**   The stipend is $700.

**Duration**   1 year.

Additional information Information is also available from Jude Stone, Scholarship Committee Chair, 9 Sanborns Grove Road, Bridgton, ME 04009.

**Number awarded** 1 each year.

**Deadline** March of each year.

## [843]
## MAINE VETERANS DEPENDENTS EDUCATIONAL BENEFITS

Bureau of Veterans' Services
117 State House Station
Augusta, ME 04333-0117
(207) 626-4464    Toll-free: (800) 345-0116 (within ME)
Fax: (207) 626-4471    E-mail: mainebvs@maine.gov
Web: www.mainebvs.org/benefits.htm

**Summary** To provide financial assistance for undergraduate or graduate education to dependents of disabled and other Maine veterans.

**Eligibility** Applicants for these benefits must be children (high school seniors or graduates under 25 years of age), non-divorced spouses, or unremarried widow(er)s of veterans who meet 1 or more of the following requirements: 1) living and determined to have a total permanent disability resulting from a service-connected cause; 2) killed in action; 3) died from a service-connected disability; 4) died while totally and permanently disabled due to a service-connected disability but whose death was not related to the service-connected disability; or 5) a member of the armed forces on active duty who has been listed for more than 90 days as missing in action, captured, forcibly detained, or interned in the line of duty by a foreign government or power. The veteran parent must have been a resident of Maine at the time of entry into service or a resident of Maine for 5 years preceding application for these benefits. Children may be seeking no higher than a bachelor's degree. Spouses, widows, and widowers may work on an advanced degree if they already have a bachelor's degree at the time of enrollment into this program.

**Financial data** Recipients are entitled to free tuition at institutions of higher education supported by the state of Maine.

**Duration** Benefits extend for a maximum of 8 semesters. Recipients have 6 consecutive academic years to complete their education.

**Additional information** College preparatory schooling and correspondence courses do not qualify under this program.

**Number awarded** Varies each year.

## [844]
## MARIAN J. WETTRICK CHARITABLE FOUNDATION MEDICAL SCHOLARSHIPS

Marian J. Wettrick Charitable Foundation
c/o Citizens Trust Company
10 North Main Street
P.O. Box 229
Coudersport, PA 16915-0229
(814) 274-9150    Toll-free: (800) 921-9150
Fax: (814) 274-0401    E-mail: ctc.info@citztrust.com
Web: www.CitizensTrustCompany.com

**Summary** To provide financial assistance to women who graduated from a college in Pennsylvania and are interested in attending a medical school in the state.

**Eligibility** This program is open to women who graduated from a college or university in Pennsylvania with a recognized pre-medical major. They must be interested in attending a medical school in the state. Priority is given to applicants who are interested in practicing medicine at Charles Cole Medical Center in Coudersport (although this is not a binding requirement). A personal interview may be required. Financial need is considered in the selection process.

**Financial data** Stipends range up to $10,000 per year.

**Duration** 1 year; may be renewed.

**Number awarded** Up to 6 each year.

**Deadline** May of each year.

## [845]
## MARILYNNE GRABOYS WOOL SCHOLARSHIP

Rhode Island Foundation
Attn: Scholarship Coordinator
One Union Station
Providence, RI 02903
(401) 274-4564    Fax: (401) 331-8085
E-mail: libbym@rifoundation.org
Web: www.rifoundation.org

**Summary** To provide financial assistance to women residents of Rhode Island who are interested in studying law.

**Eligibility** This program is open to women residents of Rhode Island who are planning to enroll or are registered in an accredited law school. Applicants must be able to demonstrate financial need. Along with their application, they must submit an essay (up to 300 words) on the impact they would like to have on the legal field.

**Financial data** The stipend is $2,000.

**Duration** 1 year; nonrenewable.

**Number awarded** 1 each year.

**Deadline** June of each year.

## [846]
## MARY CRAIG SCHOLARSHIP FUND

American Society of Women Accountants-Billings Big Sky Chapter
c/o Cherie Curry, Scholarship Chair
P.O. Box 20593
Billings, MT 59104

**Summary** To provide financial assistance to women working on a bachelor's or master's degree in accounting at a college or university in Montana.

**Eligibility** This program is open to women working on a bachelor's or master's degree in accounting at an accredited Montana college, university, or professional school of accounting. Applicants must have completed at least 60 semester hours. Selection is based on career goals, communication skills, GPA, personal circumstances, and financial need. Membership in the American Society of Women Accountants (ASWA) is not required.

**Financial data** The stipend is $1,500.

**Duration** 1 year.

**Number awarded** 1 each year.

**Deadline** February of each year.

## [847]
## MARY LOU HENTGES SCHOLARSHIP

National Federation of the Blind of Missouri
c/o Gary Wunder, President
3910 Tropical Lane
Columbia, MO 65202-6205
(573) 874-1774                 Toll-free: (888) 604-1774
E-mail: info@nfbmo.org
Web: www.nfbmo.org

**Summary** To provide financial assistance for undergraduate or graduate study to blind female students in Missouri.

**Eligibility** This program is open to legally blind women residents of Missouri who are working on or planning to work on an undergraduate or graduate degree. Preference is given to applicants working on a degree in a field related to the home or to children.

**Financial data** The maximum stipend is $500.

**Duration** 1 year.

**Additional information** Additional information is also available from Chair, Achievement Awards Committee, Sheila Koenig, 634 South National, Apartment 303, Springfield, MO 65804, (417) 869-1078.

**Number awarded** 1 each year.

**Deadline** February of each year.

## [848]
## MARY LOUISE ROLLER PANHELLENIC SCHOLARSHIPS

North American Interfraternal Foundation.
Attn: Executive Director
10023 Cedar Point Drive
Carmel, IN 46032
(317) 848-7829                 Fax: (317) 571-9686
E-mail: nancyfrick@nif-inc.net
Web: www.nif-inc.net/scholarships/mary_louise_roller

**Summary** To provide financial assistance to graduating college senior women who have been members of a sorority and plan to attend graduate school.

**Eligibility** This program is open to undergraduate women who plan to attend graduate school the following fall. Each college Panhellenic council may nominate 1 member. Nominees must have displayed outstanding service to their local college Panhellenic during their undergraduate years. They must include an essay, up to 500 words, on how they have benefited from their Panhellenic experiences.

**Financial data** The stipend is $1,000 per year.

**Duration** 1 year.

**Number awarded** 2 each year.

**Deadline** May of each year.

## [849]
## MARY LOVE COLLINS MEMORIAL SCHOLARSHIP

Chi Omega Fraternity
Attn: Chi Omega Foundation
3395 Players Club Parkway
Memphis, TN 38125
(901) 748-8600                 Fax: (901) 748-8686
E-mail: foundation@chiomega.com
Web: ww2.chiomega.com/everyday/scholarship

**Summary** To provide financial assistance to women who are members of Chi Omega Fraternity entering graduate school.

**Eligibility** This program is open to women who are members of Chi Omega Fraternity planning to enter graduate school as a full-time student. Applicants must submit an essay, from 200 to 500 words in length, on 1) why they want to pursue graduate study, 2) what they hope to gain from it, and 3) why they feel they are particularly qualified for a scholarship designed to honor Mary Love Collins. Selection is based on the essay; academic achievement; aptitude; contributions and service to Chi Omega, the university, and the community; and professional and personal goals.

**Financial data** The stipend is $2,850.

**Duration** 1 year.

**Additional information** This program was established in 1972.

**Number awarded** 6 each year.

**Deadline** February of each year.

## [850]
## MARY MCEWEN SCHIMKE SCHOLARSHIP

Wellesley College
Center for Work and Service
Attn: Secretary to the Committee on Extramural
    Graduate Fellowships and Scholarships
106 Central Street
Wellesley, MA 02181-8203
(781) 283-3525                 Fax: (781) 283-3674
E-mail: cws-fellowships@wellesley.edu
Web: www.wellesley.edu/CWS/alumnae/wellfs.html

**Summary** To provide financial assistance to women working on a graduate degree who need relief from household or child care responsibilities.

**Eligibility** Women who have graduated from an American academic institution, are over 30 years of age, are currently engaged in graduate study in literature and/or history (preference is given to American studies), and need relief from household or child care responsibilities while pursuing graduate studies may apply. The award is made on the basis of scholarly ability and financial need.

**Financial data** The fellowship awards range up to $1,500 and are tenable at the institution of the recipient's choice.

**Deadline** January of each year.

## [851]
### MARY MURPHY GRADUATE SCHOLARSHIP

Delta Sigma Theta Sorority, Inc.-Century City Alumnae Chapter
Attn: Scholarship Committee
P.O. Box 90956
Los Angeles, CA 90009
(213) 243-0594          E-mail: centurycitydst@yahoo.com
Web: www.centurycitydst.org/programs.html

**Summary** To provide financial assistance to African American women interested in working on a graduate degree.

**Eligibility** This program is designed to support women who have a bachelor's degree from an accredited institution and are pursuing (or interested in pursuing) graduate study in any field. Members of Delta Sigma Theta Sorority are not eligible to apply. Candidates must have a reputation as a person of good character, a commitment to serving others in the African American community, and an outstanding academic record (at least a 3.0 GPA). Each applicant is requested to submit a completed application form, 3 letters of recommendation, an official transcript, verification of application or admission to a graduate program, and a statement describing career goals and service to the African American community. Financial need is considered in the selection process.

**Financial data** A stipend is awarded (amount not specified).

**Duration** 1 year; may be renewed.

**Number awarded** 1 each year.

**Deadline** March of each year.

## [852]
### MARY PAOLOZZI MEMBER'S SCHOLARSHIP

Navy Wives Club of America
P.O. Box 54022
Millington, TN 38053-6022
Toll-free: (866) 511-NWCA
E-mail: nwca@navywivesclubsofamerica.org
Web: www.navywivesclubsofamerica.org

**Summary** To provide financial assistance for undergraduate or graduate study to members of the Navy Wives' Club of America (NWCA).

**Eligibility** This program is open to NWCA members who can demonstrate financial need. Applicants must be 1) a high school graduate or senior planning to attend college full time next year; 2) currently enrolled in an undergraduate program and planning to continue as a full-time undergraduate; 3) a college graduate or senior planning to be a full-time graduate student next year; and 4) a high school graduate or GED recipient planning to attend vocational or business school next year.

**Financial data** Stipends range from $500 to $1,000 each year (depending upon the donations from the NWCA chapters).

**Duration** 1 year.

**Additional information** Information is also available from Denise Johnson, NWCA National President, 534 Madrona Street, Chula Vista, CA 91910. Membership in the NWCA is open to spouses of enlisted personnel serving in the Navy, Marine Corps, Coast Guard, and the active

Reserve units of those services; spouses of enlisted personnel who have been honorable discharged, retired, or transferred to the Fleet Reserve on completion of duty; and widows of enlisted personnel in those services.

**Number awarded** 1 or more each year.

**Deadline** May of each year.

## [853]
### MASSACHUSETTS SPACE GRANT CONSORTIUM GRADUATE FELLOWSHIPS

Massachusetts Space Grant Consortium
c/o Massachusetts Institute of Technology
Building 33, Room 208
77 Massachusetts Avenue
Cambridge, MA 02139
(617) 258-5546                    Fax: (617) 253-0823
E-mail: halaris@mit.edu
Web: www.mit.edu:8001/activities/masgc/phase1.html

**Summary** To provide funding to first-year graduate students (particularly women, minority, and disabled students) for space-related research or study at institutions in Massachusetts.

**Eligibility** This program is open to first-year graduate students at institutions that are members of the Massachusetts Space Grant Consortium (MASGC). Applicants must be pursuing research or study in space-related science or engineering fields. U.S. citizenship is required. Selection is based on academic achievement and interest in space science or space engineering. MASGC is a component of the U.S. National Aeronautics and Space Administration (NASA) Space Grant program, which encourages participation by women, underrepresented minorities, and persons with disabilities.

**Financial data** The fellowships provide full tuition plus a stipend.

**Duration** 1 academic year.

**Additional information** Graduate member institutions of the MASGC are Boston University, College of the Holy Cross, the Five College Astronomy Department, Franklin W. Olin College of Engineering, Harvard University, Massachusetts Institute of Technology, Tufts University, University of Massachusetts, Wellesley College, Williams College, the Woods Hole Marine Biological Laboratory, and Worcester Polytechnic Institute. This program is funded by NASA.

**Number awarded** Varies each year.

**Deadline** February of each year.

## [854]
### MCCONNEL FAMILY SCHOLARSHIP

Epsilon Sigma Alpha
Attn: ESA Foundation Assistant Scholarship Director
P.O. Box 270517
Fort Collins, CO 80527
(970) 223-2824                    Fax: (970) 223-4456
Web: www.esaintl.com/esaf

**Summary** To provide financial assistance to women interested in studying veterinary medicine.

**Eligibility** This program is open to young women interested in studying veterinary medicine. Selection is based on character (10%), leadership (20%), service (10%), financial need (30%), and scholastic ability (30%).

**Financial data**  The stipend is $1,000.

**Duration**  1 year; may be renewed.

**Additional information**  Epsilon Sigma Alpha (ESA) is a women's service organization. Information is also available from Lynn Hughes, Scholarship Director, 324 N.E. Mead, Grants Pass, OR 97526, (541) 476-4617. Completed applications must be submitted to the ESA State Counselor who verifies the information before forwarding them to the scholarship director. A $5 processing fee is required.

**Number awarded**  1 each year.

**Deadline**  January of each year.


## [855]
## MEMORIAL EDUCATION FELLOWSHIPS

General Federation of Women's Clubs of
    Massachusetts
Attn: Scholarship Chair
245 Dutton Road
P.O. Box 679
Sudbury, MA 01776-0679
(781) 444-9105                    E-mail: janeh@gis.net

**Summary**  To provide financial assistance to Massachusetts women interested in working on a graduate degree.

**Eligibility**  Applicants must be women college graduates who have resided in Massachusetts for at least 5 years, have applied for admission to an accredited graduate program, and are sponsored by a local federated women's club in Massachusetts. They must submit a personal statement of no more than 500 words addressing their professional goals and financial need. An interview is required. The areas of study to be supported change annually; recently, they were early childhood education and physical therapy.

**Financial data**  The stipend is $3,000. It is paid directly to the college or university for tuition only.

**Duration**  1 year; nonrenewable.

**Additional information**  Information is also available from Marianne Norman, (781) 665-0676.

**Number awarded**  2 each year.

**Deadline**  February of each year.


## [856]
## MICROSOFT CORPORATION SCHOLARSHIPS

Society of Women Engineers
230 East Ohio Street, Suite 400
Chicago, IL 60611-3265
(312) 596-5223                    Toll-free: (877) SWE-INFO
Fax: (312) 644-8557
E-mail: scholarshipapplication@swe.org
Web: www.swe.org/scholarships

**Summary**  To provide financial assistance to women working on an undergraduate or graduate degree in computer engineering or computer science.

**Eligibility**  This program is open to women who will be sophomores, juniors, seniors, or first year master's degree students at ABET-accredited colleges and universities. Applicants must be majoring in computer science or engineering and have a GPA of 3.5 or higher. Along with their application, they must submit a 1-page essay on why they want to be an engineer or computer scientist, how they believe they will make a difference as an engineer or computer scientist, and what influenced them to study engineering or computer science. Selection is based on merit.

**Financial data**  The stipend is $2,500.

**Duration**  1 year.

**Additional information**  This program, established in 1994, is sponsored by Microsoft Corporation.

**Number awarded**  2 each year.

**Deadline**  January of each year.


## [857]
## MIKE SHINN DISTINGUISHED MEMBER OF THE YEAR AWARDS

National Society of Black Engineers
Attn: Programs Department
1454 Duke Street
Alexandria, VA 22314
(703) 549-2207, ext. 249          Fax: (703) 683-5312
E-mail: scholarships@nsbe.org
Web: www.nsbe.org/programs/schol_mshinn.php

**Summary**  To provide financial assistance to members of the National Society of Black Engineers (NSBE) who are working on a degree in engineering.

**Eligibility**  This program is open to members of the society who are undergraduate or graduate engineering students. Applicants must have a GPA of 3.5 or higher. Selection is based on an essay; academic achievement; service to the society at the chapter, regional, and/or national level; and other professional, campus, and community activities. The male and female applicants for the NSBE Fellows Scholarship Program who are judged most outstanding receive these awards.

**Financial data**  The stipend is $7,500. Travel, hotel accommodations, and registration to the national convention are also provided.

**Duration**  1 year.

**Number awarded**  2 each year: 1 male and 1 female.

**Deadline**  January of each year.


## [858]
## MILDRED CATER BRADHAM SOCIAL WORK FELLOWSHIP

Zeta Phi Beta Sorority, Inc.
Attn: National Education Foundation
1734 New Hampshire Avenue, N.W.
Washington, DC 20009
(202) 387-3103                    Fax: (202) 232-4593
E-mail: scholarship@ZPhiBNEF.org
Web: www.zphib1920.org/nef

**Summary**  To provide financial assistance to members of Zeta Phi Beta Sorority who are interested in studying social work on the graduate level.

**Eligibility**  This program is open to members of Zeta Phi Beta who are interested in working on a graduate or professional degree in social work. Applicants must have shown scholarly distinction or unusual ability in their chosen profession. Applications must be accompanied by 3 letters of recommendation (1 from a professor, 1 from a minister or community leader, and 1 from the Zeta chapter advisor or

Basileus), university transcripts, a 150-word essay on the applicant's educational and professional goals, and information on financial need.

**Financial data** The stipend ranges from $500 to $1,000 per year; funds are paid directly to the college or university.

**Duration** 1 academic year; may be renewed.

**Additional information** Information is also available from Cheryl Williams, National Second Vice President, 6322 Bocage Drive, Shreveport, LA 71119.

**Number awarded** 1 each year.

**Deadline** January of each year.

## [859]
## MILDRED RICHARDS TAYLOR MEMORIAL SCHOLARSHIP

United Daughters of the Confederacy
Attn: Education Director
328 North Boulevard
Richmond, VA 23220-4057
(804) 355-1636      Fax: (804) 353-1396
E-mail: hqudc@rcn.com
Web: www.hqudc.org/scholarships/scholarships.html

**Summary** To provide financial assistance for graduate education in business to female lineal descendants of Confederate veterans.

**Eligibility** Eligible to apply for these scholarships are female lineal descendants of worthy Confederates or collateral descendants who are members of the Children of the Confederacy or the United Daughters of the Confederacy. Applicants must intend to study business or a business-related field at the graduate level and must submit certified proof of the Confederate record of 1 ancestor, with the company and regiment in which he served. They must have a GPA of 3.0 or higher.

**Financial data** The amount of this scholarship depends on the availability of funds.

**Duration** 1 year; may be renewed up to 2 additional years.

**Additional information** Information is also available from Mrs. Robert C. Kraus, Second Vice President General, 239 Deerfield Lane, Franklin, NC 28734-0112. Members of the same family may not hold scholarships simultaneously, and only 1 application per family will be accepted within any 1 year. All requests for applications must be accompanied by a self-addressed stamped envelope.

**Number awarded** 1 each year.

**Deadline** March of each year.

## [860]
## MILITARY ORDER OF THE PURPLE HEART SCHOLARSHIP PROGRAM

Military Order of the Purple Heart
Attn: Scholarships
5413-B Backlick Road
Springfield, VA 22151-3960
(703) 642-5360      Fax: (703) 642-2054
E-mail: info@purpleheart.org
Web: www.purpleheart.org/scholar.html

**Summary** To provide financial assistance for college or graduate school to spouses and children of members of the Military Order of the Purple Heart.

**Eligibility** This program is open to children (natural, step-, and adopted), grandchildren, great-grandchildren and spouses of veterans who are members in good standing of the order or who received the Purple Heart. Applicants must be U.S. citizens, graduating seniors or graduates of an accredited high school, enrolled or accepted for enrollment in a full-time program of study in a college, trade school, or graduate school with a GPA of 3.5 or higher. Selection is based on merit; financial need is not considered in the selection process.

**Financial data** The stipend is $1,750 per year.

**Duration** 1 year; may be renewed up to 3 additional years.

**Number awarded** Varies each year; recently, 28 of these scholarships were awarded.

**Deadline** March of each year.

## [861]
## MINNESOTA CHAPTER WTS SCHOLARSHIPS

Women's Transportation Seminar-Minnesota Chapter
c/o Jessica Overmohle, Director
URS Corporation
700 Third Street South
Minneapolis, MN 55415-1199
(612) 373-6404      Fax: (612) 370-1378
E-mail: Jessica_Overmohle@URSCorp.com
Web: www.wtsinternational.org

**Summary** To provide financial assistance to women working on an undergraduate or graduate degree in a transportation-related field at colleges and universities in Minnesota.

**Eligibility** This program is open to women currently enrolled in a undergraduate or graduate degree program at a college or university in Minnesota. Applicants must be preparing for a career in transportation or a transportation-related field and be majoring in such fields as transportation engineering, planning, finance, or logistics. They must have a GPA of 3.0 or higher. Along with their application, they must submit a 750-word statement on their career goals after graduation and why they think they should receive this award. Selection is based on transportation goals, academic record, and transportation-related activities or job skills.

**Financial data** The stipend is $2,000.

**Duration** 1 year.

**Additional information** Winners are also nominated for scholarships offered by the national organization of the Women's Transportation Seminar.

**Number awarded** 2 each year: 1 undergraduate and 1 graduate student.

**Deadline** November of each year.

## [862]
## MINNESOTA SPACE GRANT CONSORTIUM SCHOLARSHIPS AND FELLOWSHIPS

Minnesota Space Grant Consortium
c/o University of Minnesota
Department of Aerospace Engineering and Mechanics
107 Akerman Hall
110 Union Street S.E.
Minneapolis, MN 55455
(612) 626-9295                    Fax: (612) 626-1558
E-mail: mnsgc@aem.umn.edu
Web: www.aem.umn.edu/msgc/Scholarships/sf.shtml

**Summary** To provide financial assistance for space-related studies to undergraduate and graduate students in Minnesota, especially women, minorities, and persons with disabilities.

**Eligibility** This program is open to full-time graduate and undergraduate students at institutions that are affiliates of the Minnesota Space Grant Consortium. U.S. citizenship and a GPA of 3.2 or higher are required. Eligible fields of study include the physical sciences (astronomy, astrophysics, chemistry, computer science, mathematics, physics, planetary geoscience, and planetary science), life sciences (biology, biochemistry, botany, health science/nutrition, medicine, molecular/cellular biology, and zoology), social sciences (anthropology, architecture, art, economics, education, history, philosophy, political science/public policy, and psychology), earth sciences (atmospheric science, climatology/meteorology, environmental science, geography, geology, geophysics, and oceanography), and engineering (agricultural, aeronautical, aerospace, architectural, bioengineering, chemical, civil, computer, electrical, electronic, environmental, industrial, materials science, mechanical, mining, nuclear, petroleum, engineering science, and engineering mechanics). The Minnesota Space Grant Consortium is a component of the U.S. National Aeronautics and Space Administration (NASA) Space Grant program, which encourages participation by women, underrepresented minorities, and persons with disabilities.

**Financial data** This program awards approximately $125,000 in undergraduate scholarships and graduate fellowships each year. The amounts of the awards are set by each of the participating institutions, which augment funding from this program with institutional resources.

**Duration** 1 year; renewable.

**Additional information** This program is funded by NASA. The member institutions are: Augsburg College, Bethel College, Bemidji State University, College of St. Catherine, Carleton College, Concordia College, Fond du Lac Community College, Itasca Community College, Leech Lake Tribal College, Macalaster College, Normandale Community College, Southwest State University, University of Minnesota at Duluth, University of Minnesota at Twin Cities, and University of St. Thomas.

**Number awarded** 8 to 12 undergraduate scholarships and 2 to 3 graduate fellowships are awarded each year.

**Deadline** March of each year.

## [863]
## MINNIE L. MAFFETT FELLOWSHIPS

Texas Federation of Business and Professional
    Women's Foundation, Inc.
Attn: TFBPW Foundation
803 Forest Ridge Drive, Suite 207
Bedford, TX 76022
(817) 283-0862                    Fax: (817) 283-0872
E-mail: bpwtx@swbell.net
Web: www.bpwtx.org/foundation.asp

**Summary** To provide financial assistance to women in Texas interested in continuing their education or conducting research in a medical field.

**Eligibility** This program is open to 1) women graduates of Texas medical schools interested in postgraduate or research work; 2) women who have been awarded a Ph.D. degree from a Texas university and are doing research in a medical field; 3) women who need financial aid for the first year in establishing a family practice in a rural area of Texas with a population of less than 5,000; and 4) fourth-year women medical students for completion of an M.D. or O.D. degree in an accredited medical school in Texas.

**Financial data** The stipend recently was $1,500.

**Duration** 1 year; nonrenewable.

**Additional information** This program was established in 1948.

**Number awarded** Varies each year; recently, 3 of these fellowships were awarded.

**Deadline** January of each year.

## [864]
## MISSISSIPPI SPACE GRANT CONSORTIUM SCHOLARSHIPS AND FELLOWSHIPS

Mississippi Space Grant Consortium
c/o University of Mississippi
217 Vardaman Hall
P.O. Box 1848
University, MS 38677-1848
(662) 915-1187                    Fax: (662) 915-3927
E-mail: mschaff@olemiss.edu
Web: www.olemiss.edu/programs/nasa

**Summary** To provide funding to undergraduate and graduate students (particularly women, minority, and disabled students) for space-related activities at colleges and universities that are members of the Mississippi Space Grant Consortium.

**Eligibility** This program is open to undergraduate and graduate students at member institutions of the Mississippi consortium. Each participating college or university establishes its own program and criteria for admission, but all activities are in engineering, mathematics, and science fields of interest to the U.S. National Aeronautics and Space Administration (NASA). U.S. citizenship is required. The consortium is a component of NASA's Space Grant program, which encourages participation by women, underrepresented minorities, and persons with disabilities.

**Financial data** Each participating institution establishes the amounts of the awards. Recently, the average undergraduate award was $1,308 and the average graduate award was $2,975. A total of $96,350 was awarded.

**Additional information** Consortium members include Alcorn State University, Coahoma Community College, Delta State University, Hinds Community College (Utica Campus), Itawamba Community College, Jackson State University, Meridian Community College, Mississippi Delta Community College, Mississippi Gulf Coast Community College, Mississippi State University, Mississippi University for Women, Mississippi Valley State University, Northeast Mississippi Community College, Pearl River Community College, the University of Mississippi, and the University of Southern Mississippi. This program is funded by NASA.

**Number awarded** Varies each year; recently, a total of 47 students received support through this program.

## [865]
## MISSOURI SPACE GRANT CONSORTIUM GRADUATE FELLOWSHIPS

Missouri Space Grant Consortium
c/o University of Missouri at Rolla
226 Mechanical Engineering Building
1870 Miner Circle
Rolla, MO 65409-0050
(573) 341-4887              Fax: (573) 341-4607
E-mail: spaceg@umr.edu
Web: www.umr.edu/~spaceg

**Summary** To provide financial assistance to graduate students in Missouri (particularly women, minority, and disabled students) who are working on a degree in an aerospace field.

**Eligibility** This program is open to graduate students working on a degree in an aerospace field at member institutions of the Missouri Space Grant Consortium. Selection is based on academic records, GRE scores, letters of recommendation, and reasons for wanting to enter the program. U.S. citizenship is required. The Missouri Space Grant Consortium is a component of the U.S. National Aeronautics and Space Administration (NASA), which encourages participation by women, underrepresented minorities, and people with disabilities.

**Financial data** The maximum stipend is $13,000 per year.

**Duration** 1 year.

**Additional information** The consortium members are Southwest Missouri State University, University of Missouri at Columbia, University of Missouri at Rolla, University of Missouri at St. Louis, and Washington University. This program is funded by NASA.

**Number awarded** 7 each year.

## [866]
## MONTANA SPACE GRANT CONSORTIUM GRADUATE FELLOWSHIPS

Montana Space Grant Consortium
c/o Montana State University
416 Cobleigh Hall
P.O. Box 173835
Bozeman, MT 59717-3835
(406) 994-4223              Fax: (406) 994-4452
E-mail: msgc@montana.edu
Web: spacegrant.montana.edu

**Summary** To provide financial assistance to students (particularly women, minority, and disabled students) at institutions that are members of the Montana Space Grant Consortium (MSGC) who are interested in working on a graduate degree in the space sciences and/or engineering.

**Eligibility** This program is open to full-time graduate students at MSGC institutions working on degrees in fields related to space sciences and engineering; those fields include, but are not limited to, astronomy, biological and life sciences, chemical engineering, chemistry, civil engineering, computer sciences, electrical engineering, geological sciences, mathematics, mechanical engineering, and physics. Priority is given to students who have been involved in aerospace-related research. U.S. citizenship is required. The Montana Space Grant Consortium is a component of the U.S. National Aeronautics and Space Administration (NASA) Space Grant program, which encourages participation by women, underrepresented minorities, and persons with disabilities.

**Financial data** The fellowships provide payment of in-state tuition plus a stipend of $15,000 per year.

**Duration** 1 year; may be renewed.

**Additional information** MSGC members include Blackfeet Community College, Carroll College, Chief Dull Knife College, Fort Belknap College, Fort Peck Community College, Little Big Horn College, Montana State University at Billings, Montana State University at Bozeman, Montana State University Northern, Montana Tech, Rocky Mountain College, Salish Kootenai College, Stone Child College, University of Great Falls, University of Montana, and University of Montana Western. Funding for this program is provided by NASA.

**Number awarded** Varies each year; recently, 3 of these fellowships were awarded.

**Deadline** March of each year.

## [867]
## MUSIC SCHOLARSHIPS FOR MATURE WOMEN

National League of American Pen Women
1300 17th Street, N.W.
Washington, DC 20036-1973
(202) 785-1997              Fax: (202) 452-8868
E-mail: nlapw1@verizon.net
Web: www.americanpenwomen.org

**Summary** To provide financial assistance for education to mature women composers.

**Eligibility** Women composers who are 35 years of age or older are eligible to apply if they (or their immediate family) are not affiliated with the sponsor. They must submit 2 compositions that have not been publicly performed as part of their application. At least 1 of the scores should have been written in the past 5 years. The performance time for the scores must range between 10 and 25 minutes.

**Financial data** The award is $1,000. Funds are to be used for education.

**Duration** The award is granted biennially.

**Additional information** These awards are presented in honor of Grace Powers Hudson. An entry fee of $8 and a self-addressed stamped envelope must accompany each application.

**Number awarded** 1 each even-numbered year.

**Deadline** January of even-numbered years.

## [868]
## MUSIC THERAPY SCHOLARSHIP

Sigma Alpha Iota Philanthropies, Inc.
One Tunnel Road
Asheville, NC 28805
(828) 251-0606          Fax: (828) 251-0644
E-mail: philonline@sai-national.org
Web: www.sai-national.org/phil/philsch1.html

**Summary** To provide financial assistance to members of Sigma Alpha Iota (an organization of women musicians) who are interested in working on an undergraduate or graduate degree in music therapy.

**Eligibility** Members of the organization may apply for these scholarships if they wish to study music therapy at the undergraduate or graduate level. Applicants must submit an essay that includes their personal definition of music therapy, their career plans and professional goals as a music therapist, and why they feel they are deserving of this scholarship. Selection is based on music therapy skills, musicianship, fraternity service, community service, leadership, self-reliance, and dedication to the field of music therapy as a career.

**Financial data** The stipend is $1,000.

**Duration** 1 year.

**Additional information** There is a $25 nonrefundable application fee.

**Number awarded** 1 each year.

**Deadline** March of each year.

## [869]
## NANCY B. WOOLRIDGE MCGEE GRADUATE FELLOWSHIP

Zeta Phi Beta Sorority, Inc.
Attn: National Education Foundation
1734 New Hampshire Avenue, N.W.
Washington, DC 20009
(202) 387-3103          Fax: (202) 232-4593
E-mail: scholarship@ZPhiBNEF.org
Web: www.zphib1920.org/nef

**Summary** To provide financial assistance for graduate school to members of Zeta Phi Beta Sorority.

**Eligibility** This program is open to members of Zeta Phi Beta Sorority who are working on or are interested in working on a graduate or professional degree. Applicants must have shown scholarly distinction or unusual ability in their chosen profession. They must submit letters of recommendation (1 from a professor, 1 from a minister or community

leader, and 1 from the Zeta chapter advisor or Basileus), university transcripts, a 150-word essay on their educational and professional goals, and information on financial need.

**Financial data** The stipend ranges from $500 to $1,000 per year; funds are paid to the college or university.

**Duration** 1 academic year; may be renewed.

**Additional information** Information is also available from Cheryl Williams, National Second Vice President, 6322 Bocage Drive, Shreveport, LA 71119. The recipient must pursue full-time study.

**Number awarded** 1 each year.

**Deadline** January of each year.

## [870]
## NANCY REAGAN PATHFINDER SCHOLARSHIPS

National Federation of Republican Women
Attn: Scholarships and Internships
124 North Alfred Street
Alexandria, VA 22314-3011
(703) 548-9688          Fax: (703) 548-9836
E-mail: mail@nfrw.org
Web: www.nfrw.org/programs/scholarships.htm

**Summary** To provide financial assistance for college or graduate school to Republican women.

**Eligibility** This program is open to women currently enrolled as college sophomores, juniors, seniors, or master's degree students. Recent high school graduates and first-year college women are not eligible. Applicants must submit 3 letters of recommendation, an official transcript, a 1-page essay on why they should be considered for the scholarship, and a 1-page essay on career goals. Optionally, a photograph may be supplied. Applications must be submitted to the Republican federation president in the applicant's state. Each president chooses 1 application from her state to submit for scholarship consideration. Financial need is not a factor in the selection process. U.S. citizenship is required.

**Financial data** The stipend is $2,500.

**Duration** 1 year; nonrenewable.

**Additional information** This program, established in 1985, is also known as the National Pathfinder Scholarship.

**Number awarded** 3 each year.

**Deadline** Applications must be submitted to the state federation president by May of each year.

## [871]
## NASA-DESGC GRADUATE STUDENT FELLOWSHIPS

Delaware Space Grant Consortium
c/o University of Delaware
Bartol Research Institute
106 Sharp Lab
Newark, DE 19716
(302) 831-1094          Fax: (302) 831-1843
E-mail: desgc@bartol.udel.edu
Web: www.delspace.org/gradfellowdescription.htm

**Summary** To provide financial support to graduate students (particularly women, minority, and disabled students) in Delaware and Pennsylvania involved in space-related studies.

**Eligibility** This program is open to graduate students at member institutions of the Delaware Space Grant Consortium (DESGC) embarking on or involved in aerospace-related research, technology, or design. Fields of interest have included astronomy, chemical engineering, geography, marine studies, materials science, mechanical engineering, and physics. U.S. citizenship is required. The DESGC is a component of the U.S. National Aeronautics and Space Administration (NASA) Space Grant program, which encourages applications from women, minorities, and persons with disabilities.

**Financial data** This program covers tuition and provides stipends.

**Duration** 1 year; may be renewed.

**Additional information** This program, established in 1991, is funded by NASA. Members of the consortium include Delaware State University (Dover, Delaware), Delaware Technical and Community College (Dover, Georgetown, Newark, and Wilmington, Delaware), Franklin and Marshall College (Lancaster, Pennsylvania), Gettysburg College (Gettysburg, Pennsylvania), Lehigh University (Bethlehem, Pennsylvania), Swarthmore College (Swarthmore, Pennsylvania), University of Delaware (Newark, Delaware), Villanova University (Villanova, Pennsylvania), and Wilmington College (New Castle, Delaware).

**Number awarded** Varies each year; recently, 4 of these fellowships were awarded.

**Deadline** February of each year.

## [872]
## NATIONAL DEFENSE SCIENCE AND ENGINEERING GRADUATE FELLOWSHIP PROGRAM

American Society for Engineering Education
Attn: NDSEG Fellowship Program
1818 N Street, N.W., Suite 600
Washington, DC 20036-2479
(202) 331-3516                    Fax: (202) 265-8504
E-mail: ndseg@asee.org
Web: www.asee.org/ndseg

**Summary** To provide financial assistance to doctoral students (particularly women, minorities, and persons with disabilities) who are working on degrees in areas of science and engineering that are of military importance.

**Eligibility** Graduate students in the following specialties are eligible: aeronautical and astronautical engineering; biosciences, including toxicology; chemical engineering; chemistry; civil engineering; cognitive, neural, and behavioral sciences; computer and computational sciences; electrical engineering; geosciences, including terrain, water, and air; materials science and engineering; mathematics; mechanical engineering; naval architecture and ocean engineering; oceanography; and physics, including optics. Applicants must be U.S. citizens or nationals in the final year of undergraduate study or the first year of graduate study and planning to work on a doctoral degree in 1 of the indicated specialties. Applications are particularly encouraged from women, members of ethnic minority groups (American Indians, African Americans, Hispanics or Latinos, Native Hawaiians, Alaska Natives, Asians, and Pacific Islanders),

and persons with disabilities. Selection is based on all available evidence of ability, including academic records, letters of recommendation, and GRE scores.

**Financial data** The annual stipend is $30,500 for the first year, $31,000 for the second year; and $31,500 for the third year; the program also pays the recipient's institution full tuition and required fees (not to include room and board). An additional allowance may be considered for a student with a disability.

**Duration** 3 years, as long as satisfactory academic progress is maintained.

**Additional information** This program is sponsored by the Army Research Office, the Air Force Office of Scientific Research, and the Office of Naval Research. Recipients do not incur any military or other service obligation. They must attend school on a full-time basis.

**Number awarded** Approximately 180 each year.

**Deadline** January of each year.

## [873]
## NATIONAL PHYSICAL SCIENCE CONSORTIUM GRADUATE FELLOWSHIPS

National Physical Science Consortium
c/o University of Southern California
3716 South Hope Street, Suite 348
Los Angeles, CA 90007-4344
(213) 743-2409                    Toll-free: (800) 854-NPSC
Fax: (213) 743-2407             E-mail: npschq@npsc.org
Web: www.npsc.org

**Summary** To provide financial assistance and summer work experience to women and underrepresented minorities interested in working on a Ph.D. in designated science and engineering fields.

**Eligibility** This program is open to U.S. citizens who are seniors graduating from college with a GPA of 3.0 or higher, enrolled in the first year of a doctoral program, completing a terminal master's degree, or returning from the work force and holding no more than a master's degree. Students currently in the third or subsequent year of a Ph.D. program or who already have a doctoral degree in any field (Ph.D., M.D., J.D., Ed.D.) are ineligible. Applicants must be interested in working on a Ph.D. in the physical sciences or related fields of science or engineering. The program welcomes applications from all qualified students and continues to emphasize the recruitment of underrepresented minority (African American, Hispanic, Native American Indian, Eskimo, Aleut, and Pacific Islander) and women physical science and engineering students. Fellowships are provided to students at the 116 universities that are members of the consortium. Selection is based on academic standing (GPA), course work taken in preparation for graduate school, university and/or industry research experience, letters of recommendation, and GRE scores.

**Financial data** The fellowship pays tuition and fees plus an annual stipend of $16,000. It also provides on-site paid summer employment to enhance technical experience. The exact value of the fellowship depends on academic standing, summer employment, and graduate school attended; the total amount awarded generally exceeds $200,000.

**Duration** Support is initially provided for 2 or 3 years, depending on the employer-sponsor. If the fellow makes satisfactory progress and continues to meet the conditions of the award, support may continue for a total of up to 6 years or completion of the Ph.D., whichever comes first.

**Additional information** This program began in 1989. Tuition and fees are provided by the participating universities. Stipends and summer internships are provided by sponsoring organizations. Students must submit separate applications for internships, which may have additional eligibility requirements. Internships are currently available at Lawrence Livermore National Laboratory in Livermore, California (astronomy, chemistry, computer science, geology, materials science, mathematics, and physics); Los Alamos National Laboratory in Los Alamos, New Mexico (computer science, engineering, mathematics, and physics); National Security Agency in Fort Meade, Maryland (astronomy, chemistry, computer science, geology, materials science, mathematics, and physics); Sandia National Laboratory in Livermore, California (biology, chemistry, computer science, environmental science, geology, materials science, mathematics, and physics); and Sandia National Laboratory in Albuquerque, New Mexico (chemical engineering, chemistry, computer science, materials science, mathematics, mechanical engineering, and physics). Fellows must submit a separate application for dissertation support in the year prior to the beginning of their dissertation research program, but not until they can describe their intended research in general terms.

**Number awarded** Varies each year; recently, 11 of these fellowships were awarded.

**Deadline** November of each year.

## [874]
## NAVY/MARINE CORPS/COAST GUARD ENLISTED DEPENDENT SPOUSE SCHOLARSHIP

Navy Wives Club of America
P.O. Box 54022
Millington, TN 38053-6022
Toll-free: (866) 511-NWCA
E-mail: nwca@navywivesclubsofamerica.org
Web: www.navywivesclubsofamerica.org

**Summary** To provide financial assistance for undergraduate or graduate study to spouses of naval personnel.

**Eligibility** This program is open to the spouses of active-duty Navy, Marine Corps, or Coast Guard members who can demonstrate financial need. Applicants must be 1) a high school graduate or senior planning to attend college full time next year; 2) currently enrolled in an undergraduate program and planning to continue as a full-time undergraduate; 3) a college graduate or senior planning to be a full-time graduate student next year; and 4) a high school graduate or GED recipient planning to attend vocational or business school next year.

**Financial data** The stipends range from $500 to $1,000 each year (depending upon the donations from chapters of the Navy Wives Club of America).

**Duration** 1 year.

**Additional information** Information is also available from NWCA National Vice President, Winnie Rednour, 39743 Clements Way, Murrieta, GA 92563-4021.

**Number awarded** 1 or more each year.

**Deadline** May of each year.

## [875]
## NCAA POSTGRADUATE SCHOLARSHIP PROGRAM

National Collegiate Athletic Association
Attn: Leadership Advisory Board
700 West Washington Avenue
P.O. Box 6222
Indianapolis, IN 46206-6222
(317) 917-6650        Fax: (317) 917-6888
E-mail: tksmith@ncaa.org
Web: www.ncaa.org

**Summary** To provide financial support for graduate education to student-athletes.

**Eligibility** Eligible are student-athletes who have excelled academically and athletically and who are in their final year of intercollegiate athletics competition at member schools of the National Collegiate Athletic Association (NCAA). Candidates must be nominated by the faculty athletic representative or director of athletics and must have a GPA of 3.2 or higher. Nominees must be planning full- or part-time graduate study. For the fall term, scholarships are presented to athletes who participated in men's and women's cross country, men's football, men's and women's soccer, men's water polo, women's volleyball, women's field hockey, women's equestrian, and women's badminton. For the winter term, scholarships are presented to athletes who participated in men's and women's basketball, men's and women's fencing, men's and women's gymnastics, men's and women's ice hockey, men's and women's rifle, men's and women's skiing, men's and women's swimming and diving, men's and women's indoor track and field, men's wrestling, women's archery, women's bowling, women's squash, and women's team handball. For the spring term, scholarships are presented to athletes who participated in men's baseball, men's and women's golf, men's and women's lacrosse, women's rowing, women's softball, men's and women's tennis, men's volleyball, men's and women's outdoor track and field, women's water polo, and women's synchronized swimming. Financial need is not considered in the selection process.

**Financial data** The stipend is $7,500.

**Duration** These are 1-time, nonrenewable awards.

**Number awarded** 174 each year: 87 for women and 87 for men. Each term, 29 scholarships are awarded to men and 29 to women.

**Deadline** December of each year for fall sports; February of each year for winter sports; May of each year for spring sports.

## [876]
## NCAA WOMEN'S ENHANCEMENT POSTGRADUATE SCHOLARSHIP PROGRAM

National Collegiate Athletic Association
Attn: Office for Diversity and Inclusion
700 West Washington Avenue
P.O. Box 6222
Indianapolis, IN 46206-6222
(317) 917-6222        Fax: (317) 917-6888
E-mail: tksmith@ncaa.org
Web: www.ncaa.org

**Summary** To provide funding for women who are interested in working on a graduate degree in athletics.

**Eligibility** This program is open to women who have been accepted into a program at a National Collegiate Athletic Association (NCAA) member institution that will prepare them for a career in intercollegiate athletics (athletics administrator, coach, athletic trainer, or other career that provides a direct service to intercollegiate athletics). Applicants must be U.S. citizens, have performed with distinction as a student body member at their respective undergraduate institution, and be entering the first semester or term of full time postgraduate study. Selection is based on the applicant's involvement in extracurricular activities, course work, commitment to preparing for a career in intercollegiate athletics, and promise for success in that career. Financial need is not considered.

**Financial data** The stipend is $6,000; funds are paid to the college or university of the recipient's choice.

**Duration** 1 year; nonrenewable.

**Number awarded** 13 each year.

**Deadline** January of each year.

## [877]
## NEBRASKA SPACE GRANT STATEWIDE SCHOLARSHIP COMPETITION

Nebraska Space Grant Consortium
c/o University of Nebraska at Omaha
Allwine Hall 422
6001 Dodge Street
Omaha, NE 68182-0406
(402) 554-3772
Toll-free: (800) 858-8648, ext. 4-3772 (within NE)
Fax: (402) 554-3781      E-mail: nasa@unomaha.edu
Web: nasa.unomaha.edu/Funding/funding.php

**Summary** To provide financial assistance to undergraduate and graduate students (particularly women, minority, and disabled students) at member institutions of the Nebraska Space Grant Consortium.

**Eligibility** This program is open to undergraduate and graduate students at schools that are members of the Nebraska Space Grant Consortium. Students in all academic disciplines are eligible. This program is sponsored by the U.S. National Aeronautics and Space Administration (NASA), which strongly encourages women, minorities, and students with disabilities to apply. U.S. citizenship is required. Financial need is not considered in the selection process.

**Financial data** A stipend is awarded (amount not specified).

**Duration** 1 year.

**Additional information** The following schools are members of the Nebraska Space Grant Consortium: University of Nebraska at Omaha, University of Nebraska at Lincoln, University of Nebraska at Kearney, University of Nebraska Medical Center, Creighton University, Western Nebraska Community College, Chadron State College, College of St. Mary, Metropolitan Community College, Grace University, Hastings College, Little Priest Tribal College, and Nebraska Indian Community College.

**Number awarded** At least 2 students from each institution are supported each year.

**Deadline** April of each year.

## [878]
## NELLIE YEOH WHETTEN AWARD

American Vacuum Society
Attn: Scholarship Committee
120 Wall Street, 32nd Floor
New York, NY 10005-3993
(212) 248-0200                    Fax: (212) 248-0245
E-mail: angela@avs.org
Web: www.avs.org/inside.awards.aspx

**Summary** To provide financial assistance to women interested in studying vacuum science and technology on the graduate school level.

**Eligibility** This program is open to women of any nationality who are accepted at or enrolled in a graduate school in North America and studying vacuum science and technology. Applicants are normally expected not to graduate before the award selection. They must submit a description of their current research, including its goals and objectives, the scientific and/or technological reasons that motivate the work, their approach for achieving the goals, progress (if any), program plans, and impact the results might have in the advancement of the area of research. Selection is based on research and academic excellence.

**Financial data** The award consists of $1,500 in cash, a certificate, and reimbursed travel support to attend the society's international symposium.

**Duration** 1 year.

**Additional information** This award was established in 1989.

**Number awarded** 1 each year.

**Deadline** March of each year.

## [879]
## NESBITT MEDICAL STUDENT FOUNDATION SCHOLARSHIP

Nesbitt Medical Student Foundation
c/o National Bank & Trust Company of Sycamore
230 West State Street
Sycamore, IL 60178
(815) 895-2125, ext. 228

**Summary** To provide financial assistance to needy medical students (particularly women) residing in Illinois and to encourage their entry into general practice in the state.

**Eligibility** The applicant must be a U.S. citizen, a resident of Illinois, and either accepted for enrollment or a regular full-time student in good standing at an approved college of medicine. Applicants must be interested in entry into general practice either in DeKalb County or in any county in Illinois having a population of less than 50,000 residents. Preference is given to women, persons who are or have been residents of DeKalb County, and students already attending an approved medical school in Illinois. Financial need must be demonstrated.

**Financial data** The maximum stipend is $2,000 per year, depending upon the needs of the recipient.

**Duration** 1 academic year; renewable.

**Deadline** April of each year.

**[880]**
## NETWORK OF EXECUTIVE WOMEN SCHOLARSHIP

Network of Executive Women
Attn: Scholarship Program
Accenture/Avanade
161 North Clark Street, 37th Floor
Chicago, IL 60601
(312) 373-5683                    Fax: (312) 726-4704
E-mail: ngranger@newonline.org
Web: www.newonline.org/scholarships.cfm

**Summary** To provide financial assistance to upper-division and graduate student women preparing for a career in the consumer products and retail industry.

**Eligibility** This program is open to women enrolled full time as juniors, seniors, or graduate students in a retail, food, or consumer packaged goods related program at a U.S. college or university. Applicants must have a GPA of 3.0 or higher. Along with their application, they must submit a 1-page essay explaining why they merit this scholarship and outlining their food, retail, consumer packaged goods industry interests. Selection is based on that essay, a current resume, a transcript, and 2 letters of recommendation; financial need is not considered.

**Financial data** A stipend is awarded (amount not specified).

**Duration** 1 year.

**Number awarded** 1 or more each year.

**Deadline** February of each year.


**[881]**
## NEVADA SPACE GRANT CONSORTIUM GRADUATE FELLOWSHIP PROGRAM

Nevada Space Grant Consortium
c/o University of Nevada at Reno
Mackay School of Mines Building, Room 308
MS 168
Reno, NV 89557
(775) 784-6261                    Fax: (775) 327-2235
E-mail: nvsg@mines.unr.edu
Web: www.unr.edu/spacegrant

**Summary** To provide financial assistance for space-related study or research to graduate students (particularly women, minority, and disabled students) at institutions that are members of the University and Community College System of Nevada (UCCSN) and participate in the Nevada Space Grant Consortium (NSGC).

**Eligibility** This program is open to graduate students at UCCSN member institutions. Applicants must be working on a degree in an aerospace-related field (including engineering, mathematics, physical and life sciences, and technology) that will prepare them for a career in aerospace science, technology, and related fields. They must be U.S. citizens, be enrolled full time (or accepted for full-time study), present a proposed study or research plan related to aerospace, include in the research or activity plan an extramural experience at a field center of the U.S. National Aeronautics and Space Administration (NASA), plan to be involved in NSGC outreach activities, not receive other federal funds, and intend to prepare for a career in a field of interest to NASA. Members of underrepresented groups (African Amer-

icans, Hispanics, American Indians, Pacific Islanders, people with physical disabilities, and women of all races) who have an interest in aerospace fields are encouraged to apply. Selection is based on the academic qualifications of the applicant, the quality of the proposed research program or plan of study and its relevant to NASA's aerospace science and technology program, the quality of the approach to achieving the objectives of the proposed utilization of a NASA center in carrying out the objectives of the program, the prospects for completion of the project within the allotted time, and the applicant's motivation for an aerospace career.

**Financial data** The grant is $22,500, including $16,000 as a stipend for the student and $6,500 for tuition and a student research and travel allowance.

**Duration** 12 months; may be renewed up to 24 additional months.

**Additional information** Funding for this program is provided by NASA.

**Number awarded** Varies each year; recently, 3 of these awards were granted.

**Deadline** March of each year.


**[882]**
## NEVADA WOMEN'S FUND SCHOLARSHIPS

Nevada Women's Fund
770 Smithridge Drive, Suite 300
Reno, NV 89502
(775) 786-2335                    Fax: (775) 786-8152
E-mail: info@nevadawomensfund.org
Web: www.nevadawomensfund.org/Scholarships.html

**Summary** To provide funding to women in Nevada who are interested in working on an undergraduate or graduate degree.

**Eligibility** This program is open to women who are working on or planning to work on academic study or vocational training on the undergraduate or graduate level. Preference is given to northern Nevada residents and those attending northern Nevada institutions. Selection is based on academic achievement, financial need, work experience, community involvement, other life experiences, family responsibilities, and the applicant's plan after completing study. Women of all ages are eligible. An interview may be required.

**Financial data** Stipends range from $300 to $5,000 per year. Recently, a total of $185,330 was awarded.

**Duration** 1 year; may be renewed.

**Additional information** This program includes a large number of named scholarships.

**Number awarded** Varies each year. Recently 118 of these scholarships were awarded.

**Deadline** February of each year.

## [883]
## NEW HORIZONS MEMORIAL SCHOLARSHIP

Women in Aviation, International
Attn: Scholarships
Morningstar Airport
3647 State Route 503 South
West Alexandria, OH 45381
(937) 558-7655                    Fax: (937) 839-4645
E-mail: scholarships@wai.org
Web: www.wai.org/education/scholarships.cfm

**Summary**   To provide financial assistance to members of Women in Aviation, International (WAI), especially mature members, who are interested in completing a private pilot certificate.

**Eligibility**   This program is open to women who are WAI members and interested in completing a private pilot certificate in any aircraft type. Preference is given to applicants who are at least 35 years of age. They must submit an application form, 3 letters of recommendation, a 500-word essay on their aviation dream and how they hope to use this scholarship to achieve it, a resume, and copies of all aviation and medical certificates. Selection is based on achievements, attitude toward self and others, commitment to success, dedication to career, financial need, motivation, reliability, responsibility, and teamwork.

**Financial data**   The stipend is $1,000.

**Duration**   1 year.

**Additional information**   WAI is a nonprofit professional organization dedicated to encouraging women to consider an aviation career, providing educational outreach activities, and providing networking opportunities to women active in the industry.

**Number awarded**   1 each year.

**Deadline**   November of each year.

## [884]
## NEW MEXICO GRADUATE SCHOLARSHIP PROGRAM

New Mexico Higher Education Department
Attn: Financial Aid Director
1068 Cerrillos Road
P.O. Box 15910
Santa Fe, NM 87506-5910
(505) 476-6506                    Toll-free: (800) 279-9777
Fax: (505) 476-6511
E-mail: ofelia.morales@state.nm.us
Web: hed.state.nm.us/collegefinance/gradshol.asp

**Summary**   To provide financial assistance for graduate education to underrepresented groups in New Mexico.

**Eligibility**   Applicants for this program must be New Mexico residents who are members of underrepresented groups, particularly women and minorities. Preference is given to 1) students enrolled in business, engineering, computer science, mathematics, or agriculture and 2) American Indian students enrolled in any graduate program. All applicants must be U.S. citizens or permanent residents enrolled in graduate programs at public institutions of higher education in New Mexico.

**Financial data**   The maximum stipend is $7,500 per year.

**Duration**   1 year; may be renewed.

**Additional information**   Information is available from the dean of graduate studies at the participating New Mexico public institution. Recipients must serve 10 hours per week in an unpaid internship or assistantship.

**Number awarded**   Varies each year, depending on the availability of funds.

**Deadline**   Deadlines are established by the participating institutions.

## [885]
## NEW YORK SPACE GRANT CONSORTIUM GRADUATE FELLOWSHIPS

New York Space Grant Consortium
c/o Cornell University
517 Space Sciences Building
Ithaca, NY 14853-6801
(607) 255-2710                    Fax: (607) 255-1767
E-mail: spacegrant@astro.cornell.edu
Web: astro.cornell.edu/SpaceGrant/grads.html

**Summary**   To provide financial assistance for graduate study in space-related fields at designated universities in New York.

**Eligibility**   This program is open to graduate students at selected universities that belong to the New York Space Grant Consortium. Applicants must be studying space-related fields, including aerospace engineering, astronomy, electrical engineering, geological sciences, or mechanical engineering. U.S. citizenship is required. The New York Space Grant Consortium is a component of the U.S. National Aeronautics and Space Administration (NASA) Space Grant program, which encourages participation by women, underrepresented minorities, and persons with disabilities.

**Financial data**   Each participating institution establishes its own stipend level.

**Duration**   1 year.

**Additional information**   The participating universities are Cornell University, City College of the City University of New York, Clarkson University, Columbia University, SUNY Buffalo, Polytechnic University, and Rensselaer Polytechnic Institute. This program is funded by NASA.

**Number awarded**   Varies each year; recently, 16 of these fellowships were awarded.

## [886]
## NMSGC PARTNER SCHOLARSHIPS

New Mexico Space Grant Consortium
c/o New Mexico State University
Sugerman Space Grant Building
3050 Knox Street
MSC SG, Box 30001
Las Cruces, NM 88003-0001
(505) 646-6414                    Fax: (505) 646-7791
E-mail: nmsgc@pathfinder.nmsu.edu
Web: spacegrant.nmsu.edu

**Summary**   To provide financial assistance to undergraduate and graduate students (especially women, minority, and disabled students) who are interested in working on a degree in space-related fields at institutions that are members of the New Mexico Space Grant Consortium (NMSGC).

**Eligibility** This program is open to full-time undergraduate and graduate students at NMSGC institutions who are working on a degree in a field relevant to the mission of the U.S. National Aeronautics and Space Administration (NASA). Each institution determines the details of the program on its campus. The NMSGC is a component of the NASA Space Grant program, which encourages participation by groups underrepresented in science, technology, engineering and mathematics: women, minorities, and persons with disabilities.

**Financial data** Stipends are established by the partner institutions, but are approximately $2,000 for undergraduates or $4,000 for graduate students.

**Duration** 1 year. Some institutions permit renewals for 1 additional year.

**Additional information** The NMSGC institutional members are: New Mexico State University, New Mexico Institute of Mining and Technology, University of New Mexico, Doña Ana Branch Community College, and San Juan Community College. This program is funded by NASA. Fields of study currently accepted at New Mexico State university include those in the arts and sciences (astronomy, biology, chemistry, computer science, earth science, mathematics, or physics), engineering (chemical, civil, computer, electrical, industrial, mechanical, surveying, or engineering technology), agriculture and home economics (agronomy, animal and range sciences, entomology, fishery and wildlife sciences, horticulture, plant pathology, and weed science), or education (elementary or secondary science). Projects at New Mexico Institute of Mining and Technology focus on image processing and meteorology. The University of New Mexico supports students in aerospace science, space power and propulsion, and aerospace engineering. Programs at the community colleges are designed for students working on a degree in computer technology with a related space science application.

**Number awarded** Varies each year.

**Deadline** Each institution sets its own deadlines.

## [887]
## NORTHWESTERN REGION FELLOWSHIP AWARD

Soroptimist International of the Americas-Northwestern Region
c/o Kathy A. Wagoner
820 Quail Lane
Oak Harbor, WA 98277-3677

**Summary** To provide financial assistance for graduate study to women who reside in the Northwestern Region of Soroptimist International of the Americas.

**Eligibility** This program is open to women who reside in the Northwestern Region of Soroptimist International of the Americas. Applicants must be established in business or a profession and have a bachelor's or master's degree from an accredited university. They must present a plan of graduate study at an accredited college or university that leads to an advanced degree or enhanced standing or competence in their business or profession.

**Financial data** The stipend is $4,000.

**Duration** 1 year.

**Additional information** The Northwestern Region includes Alaska, designated counties in Idaho (Benewah,

Bonner, Boundary, Clearwater, Idaho, Kootenai, Latah, Lewis, Nez Perce, and Shoshone), Montana, Oregon (except Malheur County), and Washington.

**Number awarded** 1 each year.

**Deadline** The application must be submitted to the sponsoring Soroptimist Club by January of each year.

## [888]
## NSCA WOMEN'S SCHOLARSHIPS

National Strength and Conditioning Association
Attn: Grants and Scholarships
1885 Bob Johnson Drive
Colorado Springs, CO 80906
(719) 632-6722, ext. 105     Toll-free: (800) 815-6826
Fax: (719) 632-6367     E-mail: nsca@nsca-lift.org
Web: www.nsca-lift.org/Foundation

**Summary** To provide financial assistance to members of the National Strength and Conditioning Association (NSCA) who are women and interested in working on a graduate degree.

**Eligibility** This program is open to members who are women 17 years of age and older. Applicants must have been accepted into an accredited postsecondary institution to work on a graduate degree in the strength and conditioning field. They must submit a 500-word essay describing their course of study, career goals, and financial need.

**Financial data** The stipend is $1,000.

**Duration** 1 year.

**Additional information** The NSCA is a nonprofit organization of strength and conditioning professionals, including coaches, athletic trainers, physical therapists, educators, researchers, and physicians. This program was first offered in 2003.

**Number awarded** 2 each year.

**Deadline** March of each year.

## [889]
## NSF GRADUATE RESEARCH FELLOWSHIPS

National Science Foundation
Directorate for Education and Human Resources
Attn: Division of Graduate Education
4201 Wilson Boulevard, Room 907N
Arlington, VA 22230
(703) 331-3424     Toll-free: (866) NSF-GRFP
Fax: (703) 292-9048     E-mail: grfp@nsf.gov
Web: www.nsf.gov

**Summary** To provide financial assistance to graduate students, especially those who will increase diversity, interested in working on a master's or doctoral degree in fields supported by the National Science Foundation (NSF).

**Eligibility** This program is open to U.S. citizens, nationals, and permanent residents who wish to work on research-based master's or doctoral degrees in a field of science, technology, engineering, or mathematics (STEM) supported by NSF. Research in bioengineering is eligible if it involves 1) diagnosis or treatment-related goals that apply engineering principles to problems in biology and medicine while advancing engineering knowledge, or 2) aiding persons with disabilities. Other work in medical, dental, law, public health, or practice-oriented professional degree programs, or in joint science-professional degree programs, such as M.D./Ph.D. and J.D./Ph.D. programs, is not eligible. Other categories of ineligible support include 1) clinical, counseling, business, or management fields; 2) education (except science education); 3) history (except in history of science); 4) social work; 5) medical sciences or research with disease-related goals, including work on the etiology, diagnosis, or treatment of physical or mental disease, abnormality, or malfunction in human beings or animals; 6) research involving animal models of research with disease-related goals; and 7) testing of drugs or other procedures for disease-related goals. Applications normally should be submitted during the senior year in college or in the first year of graduate study; eligibility is limited to those who have completed no more than 12 months of graduate study since completion of a baccalaureate degree. Applicants who have already earned an advanced degree in science, engineering, or medicine (including an M.D., D.D.S., or D.V.M.) are ineligible. Selection is based on intellectual merit and broader impacts. Intellectual merit includes intellectual ability and other accepted requisites for scholarly scientific study, such as the ability to work as a member of a team as well as independently, to interpret and communicate research findings, and to plan and conduct research. The broader impacts criterion includes contributions that 1) effectively integrate research and education at all levels, infuse learning with the excitement of discovery, and assure that the findings and methods of research are communicated in a broad context and to a large audience; 2) encourage diversity, broaden opportunities, and enable the participation of all citizens (including women and men, underrepresented minorities, and persons with disabilities) in science and engineering; 3) enhance scientific and technical understanding; and 4) benefit society.

**Financial data** The stipend is $30,000 per year, plus a $10,500 cost-of-education allowance given to the recipient's institution. If a fellow affiliates with a foreign institution, tuition and fees are reimbursed to the fellow up to a maximum of $10,500 per tenure year and an additional international research travel allowance of $1,000 is provided.

**Duration** Up to 3 years, usable over a 5-year period.

**Additional information** Fellows may choose as their fellowship institution any appropriate nonprofit U.S. or foreign institution of higher education.

**Number awarded** Approximately 1,000 each year.

**Deadline** November of each year. Deadlines are staggered for life sciences; psychology and mathematical sciences; social sciences; chemistry, physics, and astronomy; engineering; and computer and information science and engineering (CISE) and geosciences.

## [890]
## NYWICI FOUNDATION SCHOLARSHIPS

New York Women in Communications, Inc.
Attn: NYWICI Foundation
355 Lexington Avenue, 15th Floor
New York, NY 10017-6603
(212) 297-2133          Fax: (212) 370-9047
E-mail: nywicipr@nywici.org
Web: www.nywici.org/foundation.scholarships.html

**Summary** To provide financial assistance for college or graduate school to female residents of designated eastern

states who are interested in preparing for a career in the communications profession.

**Eligibility** This program is open to females who are 1) seniors graduating from high schools in New York, New Jersey, Connecticut, or Pennsylvania; 2) undergraduate students who are permanent residents of New York, New Jersey, Connecticut, or Pennsylvania; and 3) graduate students who are permanent residents of New York, New Jersey, Connecticut, or Pennsylvania. Applicants must be majoring in a communications-related field (advertising, broadcasting, communications, journalism, marketing, new media, or public relations) and have a GPA of 3.2 or higher. Along with their application, they must submit a resume that includes school and extracurricular activities, significant achievements, academic honors and awards, and community service work; a personal essay of 300 to 500 words describing how events in their lives have inspired them to achieve success and overcome difficulty in the face of any financial and/or other obstacles; 2 letters of recommendation; and an official transcript. Selection is based on academic record, need, demonstrated leadership, participation in school and community activities, honors, work experience, goals and aspirations, and unusual personal and/or family circumstances.

**Financial data** The maximum stipend is $10,000.

**Duration** 1 year; recipients may reapply.

**Number awarded** Varies each year; recently, 18 of these scholarships were awarded.

**Deadline** January of each year.

## [891]
## OHIO HOME ECONOMISTS IN HOME AND COMMUNITY SCHOLARSHIP

Ohio Association of Family and Consumer Sciences
c/o Donna Green, Scholarship Chair
OSU Extension
2900 South Columbus Avenue
Sandusky, OH 44870
E-mail: green.308@osu.edu
Web: oafcs.org/students.htm

**Summary** To provide financial assistance to Ohio homemakers who are returning to school to complete a bachelor's degree or pursue graduate study in family and consumer sciences.

**Eligibility** This program is open to Ohio homemakers who are returning to school to study family and consumer sciences at the undergraduate or graduate level. Applicants must be members of both the American Association of Family and Consumer Sciences and the Ohio Association of Family and Consumer Sciences. They must submit a statement that includes their goals and career plans in family and consumer science, background and interests, participation and leadership in professional and/or community organizations, community service, ability to support their educational costs, and how their education is currently being financed.

**Financial data** The stipend is $500.

**Duration** 1 year.

**Number awarded** 1 each year.

**Deadline** January of each year.

## [892]
## OHIO SPACE GRANT CONSORTIUM DOCTORAL FELLOWSHIP

Ohio Space Grant Consortium
c/o Ohio Aerospace Institute
22800 Cedar Point Road
Cleveland, OH 44142
(440) 962-3032                     Toll-free: (800) 828-OSGC
Fax: (440) 962-3057                E-mail: osgc@oai.org
Web: www.osgc.org/Fellowship.html

**Summary**  To provide financial assistance to graduate students (particularly women, minority, and disabled students) working on a doctoral degree in an aerospace-related discipline at major universities in Ohio.

**Eligibility**  This program is open to U.S. citizens enrolled full time in a doctoral program in an aerospace-related discipline (aeronautical engineering, aerospace engineering, astronomy, biology, chemical engineering, chemistry, civil engineering, computer engineering and science, control engineering, electrical engineering, engineering mechanics, geology, industrial engineering, manufacturing engineering, materials science and engineering, mathematics, mechanical engineering, petroleum engineering, physics, and systems engineering) at a participating university in Ohio. Applicants must have completed a master's degree or 2 years of graduate study. Their proposed dissertation research area must be of technical interest and importance to work being done at NASA Glenn Research Center or another federal research center (such as the Air Force Research Laboratories). Women, underrepresented minorities, and persons with disabilities are particularly encouraged to apply. Selection is based on academic achievement, recommendations, research background, and the research project.

**Financial data**  The stipend is $20,000 per year plus tuition at the university attended.

**Duration**  Up to 3 years.

**Additional information**  These fellowships are funded through the National Space Grant College and Fellowship Program administered by the National Aeronautics and Space Administration (NASA), with matching funds provided by the member universities, the Ohio Aerospace Institute, and private industry. The participating universities include Air Force Institute of Technology, University of Akron, Case Western Reserve University, University of Cincinnati, Cleveland State University, University of Dayton, Ohio State University, Ohio University, University of Toledo, Wright State University, and Youngstown State University. Fellows are required to present their research at an annual symposium sponsored by the Ohio Space Grant Consortium (OSGC).

**Number awarded**  2 each year.

**Deadline**  February of each year.

## [893]
## OHIO SPACE GRANT CONSORTIUM MASTER'S FELLOWSHIP

Ohio Space Grant Consortium
c/o Ohio Aerospace Institute
22800 Cedar Point Road
Cleveland, OH 44142
(440) 962-3032                     Toll-free: (800) 828-OSGC
Fax: (440) 962-3057                E-mail: osgc@oai.org
Web: www.osgc.org/Fellowship.html

**Summary**  To provide financial assistance to graduate students (particularly women, minority, and disabled students) who wish to work on a master's degree in an aerospace-related discipline at designated universities in Ohio.

**Eligibility**  This program is open to U.S. citizens enrolled full time in a master's degree program in an aerospace-related discipline (aeronautical engineering, aerospace engineering, astronomy, biology, chemical engineering, chemistry, civil engineering, computer engineering and science, control engineering, electrical engineering, engineering mechanics, geology, industrial engineering, manufacturing engineering, materials science and engineering, mathematics, mechanical engineering, petroleum engineering, physics, and systems engineering) at a participating university in Ohio. Applicants must have selected a thesis option for their program with a thesis topic related to aerospace. Women, underrepresented minorities, and persons with disabilities are particularly encouraged to apply. Selection is based on academic achievement, recommendations, research background, and the research topic.

**Financial data**  The stipend is $16,000 per academic year plus tuition at the university attended.

**Duration**  Up to 18 months; may be renewed for an additional 12 months.

**Additional information**  These fellowships are funded through the National Space Grant College and Fellowship Program administered by the National Aeronautics and Space Administration (NASA), with matching funds provided by the member universities, the Ohio Aerospace Institute, and private industry. The participating universities include: Air Force Institute of Technology, University of Akron, Case Western Reserve University, University of Cincinnati, Cleveland State University, University of Dayton, Ohio State University, Ohio University, University of Toledo, Wright State University, and Youngstown State University. Fellows are required to present their research at an annual symposium sponsored by the Ohio Space Grant Consortium (OSGC).

**Number awarded**  4 each year.

**Deadline**  February of each year.

## [894]
### OKLAHOMA NASA SPACE GRANT CONSORTIUM FELLOWSHIPS

Oklahoma NASA Space Grant Consortium
c/o University of Oklahoma
Ditmars House, Suite 9
1623 Cross Center Drive
Norman, OK 73069
(405) 325-6559          Fax: (405) 325-5537
E-mail: vduca@ou.edu
Web: www.okspacegrant.ou.edu

**Summary** To provide financial assistance to graduate students (particularly women, minority, and disabled students) at member institutions of the Oklahoma NASA Space Grant Consortium who are enrolled in aerospace-related studies.

**Eligibility** This program is open to graduate students at member institutions of the Oklahoma NASA Space Grant Consortium (OSGC). Applicants must be majoring in science, mathematics, engineering, technology, geography, or other aeronautics or space-related disciplines. U.S. citizenship is required. The OSGC is a component of the U.S. National Aeronautics and Space Administration (NASA) Space Grant program, which encourages participation by women, underrepresented minorities, and persons with disabilities.

**Financial data** A stipend is awarded (amount not specified).

**Duration** 1 year.

**Additional information** Members of OSGC are Oklahoma State University, the University of Oklahoma, Cameron University, Langston University. Cameron University, East Central University, Southeastern Oklahoma State University, Southern Nazarene University, and Southwestern Oklahoma State University. This program is funded by NASA.

**Number awarded** Varies each year.

**Deadline** December of each year.

## [895]
### OLIVE LYNN SALEMBIER SCHOLARSHIP

Society of Women Engineers
230 East Ohio Street, Suite 400
Chicago, IL 60611-3265
(312) 596-5223          Toll-free: (877) SWE-INFO
Fax: (312) 644-8557
E-mail: scholarshipapplication@swe.org
Web: www.swe.org/scholarships

**Summary** To provide financial assistance to women interested in returning to college or graduate school to study engineering or computer science.

**Eligibility** This program is open to women who are planning to enroll at an ABET-accredited 4-year college or university. Applicants must have been out of the engineering workforce and school for at least 2 years and must be planning to return as an undergraduate or graduate student to major in computer science or engineering. Along with their application, they must submit a 1-page essay on why they want to be an engineer or computer scientist, how they believe they will make a difference as an engineer or computer scientist, and what influenced them to study engineering or computer science. Selection is based on merit.

**Financial data** The award is $2,000.

**Duration** 1 year.

**Additional information** This program was established in 1979.

**Number awarded** 1 each year.

**Deadline** May of each year.

## [896]
### OPPORTUNITY SCHOLARSHIPS FOR LUTHERAN LAYWOMEN

Women of the Evangelical Lutheran Church in America
Attn: Scholarships
8765 West Higgins Road
Chicago, IL 60631-4189
(773) 380-2730     Toll-free: (800) 638-3522, ext. 2730
Fax: (773) 380-2419     E-mail: womenelca@elca.org
Web: www.womenoftheelca.org

**Summary** To provide financial assistance to lay women who are members of Evangelical Lutheran Church of America (ELCA) congregations and who wish to take classes on the undergraduate, graduate, professional, or vocational school level.

**Eligibility** These scholarships are aimed at ELCA lay women who are at least 21 years of age and have experienced an interruption of at least 2 years in their education since high school. Applicants must have been admitted to an educational institution to prepare for a career in other than a church-certified profession. They may be working on an undergraduate, graduate, professional, or vocational school degree. U.S. citizenship is required.

**Financial data** The amounts of the awards depend on the availability of funds.

**Duration** Up to 2 years.

**Additional information** These scholarships are supported by several endowment funds: the Cronk Memorial Fund, the First Triennial Board Scholarship Fund, the General Scholarship Fund, the Mehring Fund, the Paepke Scholarship Fund, the Piero/Wade/Wade Fund, and the Edwin/Edna Robeck Estate.

**Number awarded** Varies each year, depending upon the funds available.

**Deadline** February of each year.

## [897]
### OREGON SPACE GRANT GRADUATE FELLOWSHIP PROGRAM

Oregon NASA Space Grant Consortium
c/o Oregon State University
92 Kerr Administration Building
Corvallis, OR 97331-2103
(541) 737-2414          Fax: (541) 737-9946
E-mail: spacegrant@oregonstate.edu
Web: www.oregonspacegrant.orst.edu

**Summary** To provide financial assistance for study in space-related fields to graduate students (particularly women, minority, and disabled students) at colleges and universities that are members of the Oregon Space Grant Consortium (OSGC).

**Eligibility** This program is open to U.S. citizens enrolled at OSGC member institutions. Applicants must be working on a graduate degree in a field related to the mission of the U.S. National Aeronautics and Space Administration (NASA), including engineering (chemical, electrical, industrial, mechanical, nuclear), space science, computer science, oceanography, atmospheric science, remote sensing, forest science, or other relevant biological, chemical, or physical science. Preference may be given to students who will be receiving an appointment as a graduate teaching and/or research assistant at their university. Selection is based on GRE scores, probability of completing a graduate degree, relevance of the student's proposed program of study to aerospace sciences, and letters of recommendation. Applications are especially encouraged from members of underrepresented groups (women, minorities, and people with disabilities).

**Financial data** The stipend is $6,000 per year.

**Duration** 3 years.

**Additional information** Institutions that are members of OSG include Oregon State University, Portland State University, the University of Oregon, Southern Oregon University, Eastern Oregon University, Western Oregon University, George Fox University, and Oregon Institute of Technology. This program is funded by NASA.

**Number awarded** Varies each year.

**Deadline** March of each year.

## [898]
## ORGANIC CHEMISTRY GRADUATE STUDENT FELLOWSHIPS

American Chemical Society
Division of Organic Chemistry
1155 16th Street, N.W.
Washington, DC 20036
(202) 872-4408          Toll-free: (800) 227-5558
E-mail: divisions@acs.org
Web: www.organicdivision.org/fellowships.html

**Summary** To provide financial assistance to advanced doctoral students (particularly women, minority, and disabled students) in organic chemistry.

**Eligibility** This program is open to students working toward a Ph.D. degree in organic chemistry who are entering the third or fourth year of graduate study. Applicants must submit 3 letters of recommendation, a resume, and a short essay on a research area of their choice. U.S. citizenship or permanent resident status is required. Selection is based primarily on evidence of research accomplishment. Applications from women and minorities are especially encouraged.

**Financial data** The stipend is $24,000. Fellows also receive travel support to present a poster of their work at the National Organic Symposium.

**Duration** 1 year.

**Additional information** This program was established in 1982. It includes the Emmanuil Troyansky Fellowship. Information is also available from Scott Rychnovsky, University of California at Irvine, School of Physical Sciences, 3038A FRH, Mail Code 2025, Irvine, CA 92697, (949) 824-8292, Fax: (949) 824-6369, E-mail: srychnov@uci.edu.

**Number awarded** Varies each year; recently, 14 of these fellowships were awarded.

**Deadline** May of each year.

## [899]
## PAULA DE MERIEUX RHEUMATOLOGY FELLOWSHIP AWARD

American College of Rheumatology
Attn: Research and Education Foundation
1800 Century Place, Suite 250
Atlanta, GA 30345
(404) 633-3777          Fax: (404) 633-1870
E-mail: ref@rheumatology.org
Web: www.rheumatology.org

**Summary** To provide funding to women and underrepresented minority interested in a program of training for a career providing clinical care to people affected by rheumatic diseases.

**Eligibility** This program is open to trainees at ACGME-accredited institutions. Applications must be submitted by the training program director at the institution who is responsible for selection and appointment of trainees. The program must train and prepare fellows to provide clinical care to those affected by rheumatic diseases. Trainees must be women or members of underrepresented minority groups, defined as Black Americans, Native Americans (Native Hawaiians, Alaska Natives, and American Indians), Mexican Americans, and Puerto Ricans, and U.S. citizens, nationals, or permanent residents. Selection is based on the institution's pass rate of rheumatology fellows, publication history of staff and previous fellows, current positions of previous fellows, and status of clinical faculty.

**Financial data** The grant is $25,000 per year, to be used as salary for the trainee. Other trainee costs (e.g., fees, health insurance, travel, attendance at scientific meetings) are to be incurred by the recipient's institutional program. Supplemental or additional support to offset the cost of living may be provided by the grantee institution.

**Duration** Up to 1 year.

**Additional information** This fellowship was first awarded in 2005.

**Number awarded** 1 each year.

**Deadline** July of each year.

## [900]
## PEGGY VATTER MEMORIAL SCHOLARSHIPS

Washington Science Teachers Association
c/o Patricia MacGowan, Washington MESA
University of Washington
P.O. Box 352181
Seattle, WA 98195-2181
(206) 543-0562          Fax: (206) 685-0666
E-mail: pmac@engr.washington.edu
Web: wsta.net/html

**Summary** To provide financial assistance to upper-division students and teachers in Washington interested in training in science education.

**Eligibility** This program is open to 1) juniors and seniors at colleges and universities in Washington who are working on certification in science education or in elementary education with an emphasis on science; and 2) certified teachers in Washington interested in improving their skills in providing equitable science education through professional development. In the student category, preference is given to African Americans, Hispanics, Native Americans, and women. Applicants must submit a 1-page essay on why they are applying for this scholarship.

**Financial data** The stipend is $1,500.

**Duration** 1 year; nonrenewable.

**Additional information** This program was established in 2003.

**Number awarded** At least 2 each year: 1 to a student and 1 to a certified teacher.

**Deadline** April of each year.

## [901]
## PENELOPE HANSHAW SCHOLARSHIP

Association for Women Geoscientists
Attn: AWG Foundation
P.O. Box 30645
Lincoln, NE 68503-0645
E-mail: awgscholarship@yahoo.com
Web: www.awg.org/members/po_scholarships.html

**Summary** To provide financial assistance for undergraduate or graduate study in the geosciences to women in the Potomac Bay region.

**Eligibility** This program is open to women who are currently enrolled as full-time undergraduate or graduate geoscience majors at an accredited, degree-granting college or university in Delaware, the District of Columbia, Maryland, Virginia, or West Virginia. Applicants must have a GPA of 3.0 or higher. Selection is based on the applicant's awareness of the importance of community outreach, geoscience or earth science education activities, and potential for career and leadership success as a future geoscience professional.

**Financial data** The stipend is $500. The recipient also is granted a 1-year membership in the Association for Women Geoscientists (AWG).

**Duration** 1 year.

**Additional information** This program is sponsored by the AWG Potomac Area Chapter. Information is also available from Laurel M. Bybell, U.S. Geological Survey, 926 National Center, Reston, VA 20192.

**Number awarded** 1 each year.

**Deadline** April of each year.

## [902]
## PENNSYLVANIA SPACE GRANT CONSORTIUM FELLOWSHIPS

Pennsylvania Space Grant Consortium
c/o Pennsylvania State University
2217 Earth-Engineering Sciences Building
University Park, PA 16802
(814) 863-7687     Fax: (814) 863-8286
E-mail: spacegrant@psu.edu
Web: www.psu.edu/spacegrant/highered/scholar.html

**Summary** To provide financial assistance for space-related study to graduate students (particularly women,

minority, and disabled students) at universities affiliated with the Pennsylvania Space Grant Consortium.

**Eligibility** This program is open to graduate students at participating universities. Applicants must be studying a field that does, or can, promote the understanding, assessment, and utilization of space, or a strategic enterprise of the U.S. National Aeronautics and Space Administration (NASA): aerospace technology, earth science, human exploration and development of space, biological and physical research, or space science. U.S. citizenship is required. Students from underrepresented groups (women, minorities, rural populations, and those with disabilities) are especially encouraged to apply.

**Financial data** The stipend is $5,000 per year.

**Duration** 2 years.

**Additional information** Participating institutions include Pennsylvania State University, Carnegie-Mellon University, Temple University, and the University of Pittsburgh. This program is sponsored by the U.S. National Aeronautics and Space Administration (NASA).

**Number awarded** Varies each year.

**Deadline** February of each year.

## [903]
## P.E.O. SCHOLAR AWARDS

P.E.O. Sisterhood
Attn: Executive Office
3700 Grand Avenue
Des Moines, IA 50312-2899
(515) 255-3153     Fax: (515) 255-3820
Web: www.peointernational.org

**Summary** To provide financial assistance for graduate studies to women in the United States or Canada.

**Eligibility** This program is open to women who are working on a graduate degree or research as full-time students at universities in the United States or Canada. Applicants must be within 2 years of achieving their educational goal but have least 1 full academic year remaining. They must be sponsored by a local P.E.O. chapter. Selection is based on academic excellence and achievement, career goals, recommendations, and potential of applicant to make a significant contribution to her field; financial need is not considered.

**Financial data** The stipend is $10,000.

**Duration** 1 year; nonrenewable.

**Additional information** This program was established in 1991 by the Women's Philanthropic Educational Organization (P.E.O.).

**Number awarded** 75 each year.

**Deadline** November of each year.

## [904]
## PHI CHI THETA SCHOLARSHIPS

Phi Chi Theta
Attn: Foundation
1508 East Beltline Road, Suite 104
Carrollton, TX 75006
(972) 245-7202　　E-mail: PCTEdScholarship@aol.com
Web: www.phichitheta.org

**Summary**　To provide financial assistance to members of Phi Chi Theta (an honorary society for women in business-related fields) who are working on a degree in business administration or economics.

**Eligibility**　This program is open to members who have completed at least 1 semester or 2 quarters of full-time study in business administration or economics. Applicants must be enrolled at an approved college or university in the United States in a bachelor's, master's, or doctoral degree program. Along with their application, they must submit an essay on where they see themselves in 3 and 5 years and a statement of career goals and philosophy. Selection is based on the essay and statement, Phi Chi Theta achievements and contributions; scholastic achievement; school and community achievements and activities; a faculty letter of recommendation; and a Phi Chi Theta member letter of recommendation.

**Financial data**　The stipend is $1,000 or $500.

**Duration**　1 year.

**Additional information**　Phi Chi Theta is a national honorary society for women in business administration and economics. Information is also available from Mary Ellen Lewis, 1886 South Poplar Street, Denver, CO 80224-2272, (303) 757-2535. This program includes the following named awards: the Anna E. Hall Memorial Scholarship (established in 1989), the Helen D. Snow Memorial Scholarship, the Irene Meyer Memorial Scholarship, the Lester F. Richardson Memorial Scholarship (established in 2005), and the Naomi L. Satterfield Scholarship (established in 2001).

**Number awarded**　Varies each year. Recently, 4 of these scholarships were awarded: 1 at $1,000 and 3 at $500.

**Deadline**　April of each year.

## [905]
## PHIPPS MEMORIAL SCHOLARSHIP

General Federation of Women's Clubs of Connecticut
c/o Hamden Women's Club
Antoinette Antonucci, Co-President
26 Country Way
Wallingford, CT 06492
(203) 265-9407　　E-mail: gfwcct@yahoo.com
Web: www.gfwcct.org

**Summary**　To provide financial assistance to women in Connecticut who are working on an undergraduate or graduate degree in education.

**Eligibility**　This program is open to female residents of Connecticut who have completed at least 2 years of college. Applicants must have a GPA of 3.0 or higher and be working on a bachelor's or master's degree in education.

**Financial data**　The stipend is $1,000.

**Duration**　1 year.

**Number awarded**　1 each year.

**Deadline**　February of each year.

## [906]
## PI BETA PHI GRADUATE FELLOWSHIPS

Pi Beta Phi
Attn: Pi Beta Phi Foundation
1154 Town and Country Commons Drive
Town and Country, MO 63017
(636) 256-0680　　　　　　　Fax: (636) 256-8124
E-mail: fndn@pibetaphi.org
Web: www.pibetaphifoundation.org

**Summary**　To provide financial assistance for graduate school to members of Pi Beta Phi.

**Eligibility**　This program is open to women who are dues-paying members in good standing of Pi Beta Phi (as a graduating senior or alumna) and graduated no more than 4 years previously. Applicants must be planning full-time graduate work at an accredited college, university, or technical professional school. They must have a GPA of 3.0 or higher for all undergraduate and graduate study. Selection is based on financial need, academic record, and service to the sorority, campus, and community.

**Financial data**　The stipend is $2,000 per year.

**Duration**　1 year.

**Additional information**　This program was established in 1909. It includes the Past Grand Presidents Memorial Graduate Fellowship, the Corrine Hammond Gray Graduate Fellowship, the Joanie Arnold Graduate Fellowship, and Friendship Fund Fellowships.

**Number awarded**　Varies each year; recently, 5 of these fellowships were awarded.

**Deadline**　January of each year.

## [907]
## PI STATE NATIVE AMERICAN GRANTS-IN-AID

Delta Kappa Gamma Society International-Pi State Organization
c/o Patricia Hershberger, Native American Grants Committee
35 Frost Lane
Cornwall, NY 12518
E-mail: pbhersh@aol.com
Web: www.deltakappagamma.org/NY/awards.html

**Summary**　To provide funding to Native American women from New York who plan to work in education or another service field.

**Eligibility**　This program is open to Native American women from New York who are attending a 2-year or 4-year college in the state. Applicants must be planning to work in education or another service field, but preference is given to those majoring in education. Both undergraduate and graduate students are eligible.

**Financial data**　The grant is $500 per semester ($1,000 per year). Funds may be used for any career-related purpose, including purchase of textbooks.

**Duration**　1 semester; may be renewed for a total of 5 years and a total of $5,000 over a recipient's lifetime.

**Number awarded**　Varies each year; recently, 3 of these grants were awarded.

## [908]
## POSSIBLE WOMAN FOUNDATION INTERNATIONAL SCHOLARSHIP

Possible Woman Enterprises
Attn: Possible Woman Foundation International
3475 Oak Valley Road, Suite 3040
P.O. Box 78851
Atlanta, GA 30357
Fax: (404) 869-7202
E-mail: linda@possiblewomanfoundation.org
Web: www.possiblewomanfoundation.org/Home.htm

**Summary** To provide financial assistance for college or graduate school to women of all ages.

**Eligibility** This program is open to women who are returning to school after a hiatus, changing careers, seeking advancement in their career or work life, or stay-at-home mothers entering the work place and in need of additional education or training. Applicants must be at least 25 years of age and at any level of education (high school graduate, some college, 4-year college graduate, graduate school, doctoral). Along with their application, they must submit a 2-page essay on the topic, "How Having the Opportunity for Beginning or Continuing My Academic Education Will Positively Impact My Life." Selection is based on the essay, career and life goals, leadership and participation in community activities, honors and awards received, and financial need.

**Financial data** The stipend ranges from $3,000 to $5,000.

**Duration** 1 year; nonrenewable.

**Additional information** Information is also available from Stacie Shelby, P.O. Box 117740, Carrollton, TX 75011-7740, Fax: (817) 497-2497.

**Number awarded** Varies each year; recently, 6 of these scholarships were awarded.

**Deadline** February of each year.

## [909]
## POSTDOCTORAL FELLOWSHIPS IN DIABETES RESEARCH

Juvenile Diabetes Research Foundation
Attn: Grant Administrator
120 Wall Street, 19th Floor
New York, NY 10005-4001
(212) 479-7572          Toll-free: (800) 533-CURE
Fax: (212) 785-9595          E-mail: info@jdrf.org
Web: www.jdrf.org/index.cfm?page_id=103207

**Summary** To provide research training to scientists (particularly women, minorities, and persons with disabilities) who are beginning their professional careers and are interested in participating in research training on the causes, treatment, prevention, or cure of diabetes or its complications.

**Eligibility** This program is open to postdoctorates who are interested in a career in Type 1 diabetes-relevant research. Applicants must have received their first doctoral (M.D., Ph.D., D.M.D., or D.V.M.) degree within the past 5 years and may not have a faculty appointment. There are no citizenship requirements. Applications are encouraged from women, members of minority groups underrepresented in the sciences, and people with disabilities. The proposed research training may be conducted at foreign and domestic, for-profit and nonprofit, and public and private institutions, including universities, colleges, hospitals, laboratories, units of state and local government, and eligible agencies of the federal government. Applicants must be sponsored by an investigator who is affiliated full time with an accredited institution and who agrees to supervise the applicant's training. Selection is based on the applicant's previous experience and academic record; the caliber of the proposed research; and the quality of the mentor, training program, and environment.

**Financial data** Stipends range from $36,996 to $46,992 (depending upon years of experience). In any case, the award may not exceed the salary the recipient is currently earning. Fellows also receive a research allowance of $5,500 per year.

**Duration** 1 year; may be renewed for up to 1 additional year.

**Additional information** Fellows must devote at least 80% of their effort to the fellowship project.

**Deadline** January or July of each year.

## [910]
## POSTDOCTORAL RESEARCH FELLOWSHIPS IN EPILEPSY

Epilepsy Foundation
Attn: Research Department
8301 Professional Place
Landover, MD 20785-2237
(301) 459-3700          Toll-free: (800) EFA-1000
Fax: (301) 577-2684          TDD: (800) 332-2070
E-mail: grants@efa.org
Web: www.epilepsyfoundation.org

**Summary** To provide funding for a program of postdoctoral training to academic physicians and scientists (particularly women, minorities, and persons with disabilities) committed to epilepsy research.

**Eligibility** Applicants must have a doctoral degree (M.D., Ph.D., or equivalent) and be a resident or postdoctoral fellow at a university, medical school, research institution, or medical center. They must be interested in participating in a training experience and research project that has potential significance for understanding the causes, treatment, or consequences of epilepsy. The program is geared toward applicants who will be trained in research in epilepsy rather than those who use epilepsy as a tool for research in other fields. Equal consideration is given to applicants interested in acquiring experience either in basic laboratory research or in the conduct of human clinical studies. Academic faculty holding the rank of instructor or higher are not eligible, nor are graduate or medical students, medical residents, permanent government employees, or employees of private industry. Applications from women, members of minority groups, and people with disabilities are especially encouraged. Selection is based on scientific quality of the proposed research, a statement regarding its relevance to epilepsy, the applicant's qualifications, the preceptor's qualifications, and the adequacy of facility and related epilepsy programs at the institution.

**Financial data** The grant is $40,000. No indirect costs are provided.

**Duration** 1 year.

**Additional information** Support for this program is provided by many individuals, families, and corporations, especially the American Epilepsy Society, Abbott Laboratories, Ortho-McNeil Pharmaceutical, and Pfizer Inc. The fellowship must be carried out at a facility in the United States where there is an ongoing epilepsy research program.

**Number awarded** Varies each year; recently, 13 of these fellowships were awarded.

**Deadline** August of each year.

## [911]
## PROCTER & GAMBLE SCHOLARSHIP

Franklin Pierce Law Center
Attn: Assistant Dean for Admissions
Two White Street
Concord, NH 03301
(603) 228-9217        E-mail: kmcdonald@piercelaw.edu
Web: www.piercelaw.edu/finan/06ProcGamble.pdf

**Summary** To provide an opportunity for law students, especially women and minorities, to study patent and intellectual property law as a visiting scholar at Franklin Pierce Law Center in Concord, New Hampshire.

**Eligibility** This program is open to full-time second- and third-year students at law schools in the United States and Canada. Applicants must be interested in a program of study in patent and intellectual property law at the center. They must have sufficient undergraduate scientific and/or technical education to be admitted to the patent bar, including work in biology, biochemistry, botany, electronics technology, engineering (all types, especially civil, computer, and industrial), food technology, general chemistry, marine technology, microbiology, molecular biology, organic chemistry, pharmacology, physics, and textile technology. Their home school must agree to apply a year's credits earned at another school toward the J.D. degree. Preference is given to members of groups underrepresented among lawyers practicing patent law, including women and minorities.

**Financial data** The stipend is $5,000. Scholars must pay the tuition charged either by the Franklin Pierce Law Center or their home school, whichever is less.

**Duration** 1 academic year.

**Additional information** This program is sponsored by the Procter & Gamble Company.

**Number awarded** 1 each year.

**Deadline** April of each year.

## [912]
## PROJECT RED FLAG ACADEMIC SCHOLARSHIP FOR WOMEN WITH BLEEDING DISORDERS

National Hemophilia Foundation
Attn: Department of Finance, Administration & MIS
116 West 32nd Street, 11th Floor
New York, NY 10001-3212
(212) 328-3700     Toll-free: (800) 42-HANDI, ext. 3700
Fax: (212) 328-3777        E-mail: info@hemophilia.org
Web: www.hemophilia.org

**Summary** To provide financial assistance for college or graduate school to women who have a bleeding disorder.

**Eligibility** This program is open to women who are entering or already enrolled in an undergraduate or graduate program at a university, college, or accredited vocational school. Applicants must have von Willebrand disease, hemophilia or other clotting factor deficiency, or carrier status. Along with their application, they must submit a 250-word essay that describes their educational and future career plans, including how they intend to use their education to enhance the bleeding disorders community. Financial need is not considered in the selection process.

**Financial data** The stipend is $2,500.

**Duration** 1 year.

**Additional information** The program was established in 2005.

**Number awarded** 2 each year.

**Deadline** May of each year.

## [913]
## PUGET SOUND CHAPTER HELENE M. OVERLY MEMORIAL SCHOLARSHIP

Women's Transportation Seminar-Puget Sound Chapter
c/o Kristin Overleese, Scholarship Chair
City of Shoreline, Capital Projects Manager
17544 Midvale Avenue North
Shoreline, WA 98133-4821
(206) 546-1700                    Fax: (206) 546-2200
TDD: (206) 546-0457
Web: www.wtsinternational.org/puget_sound

**Summary** To provide financial assistance to women from Washington working on a graduate degree related to transportation.

**Eligibility** This program is open to women who are residents of Washington, studying at a college in the state, or working as an intern in the state. Applicants must be currently enrolled in a graduate degree program in a transportation-related field, such as engineering, planning, finance, or logistics. They must have a GPA of 3.0 or higher and plans to prepare for a career in a transportation-related field. Minority candidates are encouraged to apply. Along with their application, they must submit a 750-word statement about their career goals after graduation and why they think they should receive this scholarship award. Selection is based on that statement, academic record, and transportation-related activities or job skills. Financial need is not considered.

**Financial data** The stipend is $1,700.

**Duration** 1 year.

**Additional information** The winner is also nominated for scholarships offered by the national organization of the Women's Transportation Seminar.

**Number awarded** 1 each year.

**Deadline** October of each year.

## [914]
## PYRAMID AWARD FOR MARKETING AND PUBLIC RELATIONS

Miss America Pageant
Attn: Scholarship Department
Two Miss America Way, Suite 1000
Atlantic City, NJ 08401
(609) 345-7571, ext. 27      Toll-free: (800) 282-MISS
Fax: (609) 347-6079      E-mail: info@missamerica.org
Web: www.missamerica.org

**Summary** To provide financial assistance to women who are working on an undergraduate or graduate degree in marketing or public relations and who, in the past, competed at some level in the Miss America competition.

**Eligibility** This program is open to women who are working on an undergraduate, master's, or higher degree in marketing or public relations and who competed at the local, state, or national level in a Miss America competition within the past 10 years. Selection is based on GPA, class rank, extracurricular activities, financial need, and level of participation within the system.

**Financial data** The stipend is $2,500.

**Duration** 1 year; renewable.

**Additional information** This scholarship was established in 2004.

**Number awarded** Varies each year; recently, 2 of these scholarships were awarded.

**Deadline** June of each year.

## [915]
## RACHEL ROYSTON PERMANENT SCHOLARSHIP

Delta Kappa Gamma Society International-Alpha Sigma
   State Organization
c/o Marilynn M. Russell
P.O. Box 99454
Lakewood, WA 98499-0454
(253) 584-0147      Fax: (253) 589-6813
E-mail: MarillynnR@aol.com
Web: www.deltakappagamma.org

**Summary** To provide financial assistance to women in Washington who are interested in working on a graduate degree in education.

**Eligibility** This program is open to women who are Washington residents doing graduate work at an approved institution of higher learning, pursuing either a master's or doctoral degree or working in a field of special interest. Selection is based, at least in part, on the importance of the project on which the candidate wishes to work (its significance to the field of education) and evidence of the candidate's ability to pursue it. A personal interview is required of all finalists. The applicant who has achieved the highest level of self-improvement and success in the area of educational scholarship receives the Margaret L. Harvin Award.

**Financial data** The amount of each award is set at the discretion of the foundation's board of trustees. Awards generally range from $500 to $2,000.

**Duration** Awards may be made for 1 quarter, semester, or academic year. A recipient may, upon fulfilling certain conditions, reapply for a second award.

**Additional information** This program became operational in 1967.

**Number awarded** Varies each year; recently, 6 of these scholarships, with a value of $10,000, were awarded. Since the program began, 285 scholarships worth $534,640 have been awarded.

**Deadline** November of each year.

## [916]
## RALPH W. SHRADER DIVERSITY SCHOLARSHIPS

Armed Forces Communications and Electronics
   Association
Attn: AFCEA Educational Foundation
4400 Fair Lakes Court
Fairfax, VA 22033-3899
(703) 631-6149      Toll-free: (800) 336-4583, ext. 6149
Fax: (703) 631-4693      E-mail: scholarship@afcea.org
Web: www.afcea.org

**Summary** To provide financial assistance to master's degree students in fields related to communications and electronics.

**Eligibility** This program is open to students working on a master's degree who are U.S. citizens attending an accredited college or university in the United States. Applicants must be enrolled full time and studying electronics, engineering (aerospace, chemical, electrical, computer, communications, or systems), physics, communications technology, mathematics, computer science or technology, or information management systems. At least 1 of these scholarships is set aside for a woman or a minority.

**Financial data** The stipend is $3,000. Funds are paid directly to the recipient.

**Duration** 1 year.

**Number awarded** 5 each year, at least 1 of which is for a woman or minority candidate.

**Deadline** January of each year.

## [917]
## RED RIVER VALLEY FIGHTER PILOTS ASSOCIATION SCHOLARSHIP GRANT PROGRAM

Red River Valley Association Foundation
P.O. Box 1916
Harrisonburg, VA 22801
(540) 442-7782      Fax: (540) 443-3105
E-mail: afbridger@aol.com
Web: www.river-rats.org

**Summary** To provide financial assistance for college or graduate school to the spouses and children of selected service personnel and members of the Red River Valley Fighter Pilots Association.

**Eligibility** This program is open to the spouses and children of 1) service members missing in action (MIA) or killed in action (KIA) in armed conflicts by U.S. forces since August 1964, including those lost in the World Trade Center or Pentagon on September 11, 2001; 2) surviving dependents of U.S. military aircrew members killed in a non-combat aircraft accident in which they were performing aircrew duties; and 3) current members of the association and deceased members who were in good standing at the time of their death. Applicants must be interested in attending an accredited college or university to work on an undergraduate or graduate degree. Selection is based on demonstrated academic achievement, college entrance examination scores, financial need, and accomplishments in school, church, civic, and social activities.

**Financial data** The amount awarded varies, depending upon the need of the recipient. Recently, undergraduate stipends have ranged from $500 to $3,500 and averaged $1,725; graduate stipends have ranged from $500 to $2,000 and averaged $1,670. Funds are paid directly to the recipient's institution and are to be used for tuition, fees, books, and room and board for full-time students.

**Duration** 1 year.

**Additional information** This program was established in 1970, out of concern for the families of aircrews (known as "River Rats") who were killed or missing in action in the Red River Valley of North Vietnam. Information is also available from Herm Davis, 16728 Frontenac Terrace, Rockville, MD 20855, (301) 548-9423.

**Number awarded** Varies each year; since this program was established, it has awarded more than 900 scholarships worth nearly $1,500,000.

**Deadline** May of each year.

## [918]
## REDI-TAG CORPORATION SCHOLARSHIP

American Health Information Management Association
Attn: Foundation of Research and Education
233 North Michigan Avenue, Suite 2150
Chicago, IL 60601-5806
(312) 233-1131                     Fax: (312) 233-1431
E-mail: fore@ahima.org
Web: www.ahima.org/fore/student/programs.asp

**Summary** To provide financial assistance to members of the American Health Information Management Association (AHIMA) who are single parents interested in working on an undergraduate or graduate degree in health information administration or technology.

**Eligibility** This program is open to AHIMA members who are single parents enrolled in a health information administration or health information technology program accredited by the Commission on Accreditation of Allied Health Education Programs. Applicants must be working on an undergraduate or graduate degree on at least a half-time basis and have a GPA of 3.0 or higher. U.S. citizenship is required. Selection is based on (in order of importance) GPA and academic achievement, volunteer and work experience, commitment to the health information management profession, suitability to the health information management profession, quality and suitability of references provided, and clarity of application.

**Financial data** The stipend ranges from $1,000 to $5,000.

**Duration** 1 year; nonrenewable.

**Additional information** Funding for this program is provided by the Redi-Tag Corporation.

**Number awarded** 1 each year.

**Deadline** April of each year.

## [919]
## RESEARCH AND TRAINING FELLOWSHIPS IN EPILEPSY FOR CLINICIANS

Epilepsy Foundation
Attn: Research Department
8301 Professional Place
Landover, MD 20785-2237
(301) 459-3700                     Toll-free: (800) EFA-1000
Fax: (301) 577-2684                TDD: (800) 332-2070
E-mail: clinical_postdocs@efa.org
Web: www.epilepsyfoundation.org

**Summary** To provide funding to clinically trained professionals (particularly women, minorities, and persons with disabilities) interested in gaining additional training in order to develop an epilepsy research program.

**Eligibility** Applicants must have an M.D., D.O., Ph.D., D.S., or equivalent degree and be a clinical or postdoctoral fellow at a university, medical school, or other appropriate research institution. Holders of other doctoral-level degrees (e.g., Pharm.D., D.S.N.) may also be eligible. Candidates must be interested in a program of research training that may include mechanisms of epilepsy, novel therapeutic approaches, clinical trials, development of new technologies, or behavioral and psychosocial impact of epilepsy. The training program may consist of both didactic training and a supervised research experience that is designed to develop the necessary knowledge and skills in the chosen area of research and foster the career goals of the candidate. Academic faculty holding the rank of instructor or higher are not eligible, nor are graduate or medical students, medical residents, permanent government employees, or employees of private industry. Applications from women, members of minority groups, and people with disabilities are especially encouraged. Selection is based on the quality of the proposed research training program, the applicant's qualifications, the preceptor's qualifications, and the adequacy of clinical training, research facilities, and other epilepsy-related programs at the institution.

**Financial data** The grant is $50,000 per year. No indirect costs are provided.

**Duration** Up to 2 years.

**Additional information** Support for this program is provided by many individuals, families, and corporations, especially the American Epilepsy Society, Abbott Laboratories, Ortho-McNeil Pharmaceutical, and Pfizer Inc. Grantees are expected to dedicate at least 50% of their time to research training and conducting research.

**Number awarded** Varies each year; recently, 5 of these fellowships were awarded.

**Deadline** October of each year.

## [920]
## RHODE ISLAND SPACE GRANT GRADUATE FELLOWSHIP PROGRAM

Rhode Island Space Grant
c/o Brown University
Lincoln Field Building
Box 1846
Providence, RI 02912-1846
(401) 863-2889                     Fax: (401) 863-1292
E-mail: RISpaceGrant@brown.edu
Web: www.planetary.brown.edu/RI_Space_Grant

**Summary** To provide financial assistance to graduate students (particularly women, minority, and disabled students) at institutions that are members of the Rhode Island Space Grant Consortium (RISGC) who wish to pursue studies and space-related research in science, mathematics, or engineering.

**Eligibility** This program is open to graduate students at RISGC-member universities. Applicants must be studying in science, mathematics, or engineering fields of interest to the National Aeronautics and Space Administration (NASA). U.S. citizenship is required. The sponsor is a component of NASA's Space Grant program, which encourages participation by women, underrepresented minorities, and persons with disabilities.

**Financial data** The stipend is $19,500 per year, plus payment of tuition and the health services fee.

**Duration** 1 year.

**Additional information** Members of the RISGC are Bryant College, Community College of Rhode Island, Providence College, Roger Williams University, Rhode Island College, Rhode Island School of Design, Salve Regina University, University of Rhode Island, and Wheaton College. This program is funded by NASA. Fellows are required to devote 75% of their time to their studies and research and 25% of their time to science education outreach activities organized and coordinated by Rhode Island Space Grant.

**Number awarded** Varies each year; recently, 3 of these fellowships were awarded.

**Deadline** February of each year.

## [921]
## RITA LEVINE MEMORIAL SCHOLARSHIP

American Mensa Education and Research Foundation
1229 Corporate Drive West
Arlington, TX 76006-6103
(817) 607-0060                     Toll-free: (800) 66-MENSA
Fax: (817) 649-5232
E-mail: info@mensafoundation.org
Web: www.mensafoundation.org

**Summary** To provide financial assistance for undergraduate or graduate study to women returning to school after an absence of at least 7 years.

**Eligibility** This program is open to women students who are enrolled or will enroll in an undergraduate or graduate degree program at an accredited American institution of postsecondary education after an absence of 7 or more years. Membership in Mensa is not required, but applicants must be U.S. citizens or permanent residents. Selection is based on a 550-word essay that describes the applicant's career, vocational, or academic goals.

**Financial data** The stipend is $600.

**Duration** 1 year; nonrenewable.

**Additional information** Applications are only available through the advertising efforts of participating Mensa local groups.

**Number awarded** 1 each year.

**Deadline** January of each year.

## [922]
## ROBERT W. NOLAN EMERITUS SCHOLARSHIP

Fleet Reserve Association
Attn: Scholarship Administrator
125 North West Street
Alexandria, VA 22314-2754
(703) 683-1400                    Toll-free: (800) 372-1924
Fax: (703) 549-6610               E-mail: fra@fra.org
Web: www.fra.org

**Summary** To provide financial assistance for graduate education to members of the Fleet Reserve Association (FRA) and their spouses, children, and grandchildren.

**Eligibility** This program is open to the dependent children, grandchildren, and spouses of members of the association in good standing as of April 1 of the year of the award or at the time of death. FRA members are also eligible. Preference is given to applicants enrolled in a graduate program. Selection is based on financial need, academic standing, character, and leadership qualities.

**Financial data** The stipend is $5,000 per year.

**Duration** 1 year; may be renewed.

**Additional information** Membership in the FRA is restricted to active-duty, retired, and Reserve members of the Navy, Marine Corps, and Coast Guard. This program was established in 2001.

**Number awarded** 1 each year.

**Deadline** April of each year.

## [923]
## ROBIN ROBERTS/WBCA SPORTS COMMUNICATION SCHOLARSHIP AWARD

Women's Basketball Coaches Association
Attn: Manager of Awards
4646 Lawrenceville Highway
Lilburn, GA 30047-3620
(770) 279-8027, ext. 102          Fax: (770) 279-6290
E-mail: alowe@wbca.org
Web: www.wbca.org/RobertsAward.asp

**Summary** To provide financial assistance for graduate study in sports communications to women's basketball players.

**Eligibility** This program is open to women's college basketball players who are seniors planning to work on a graduate degree in sports communication and journalism. Applicants must be nominated by a member of the Women's Basketball Coaches Association (WBCA). Selection is based on a letter of recommendation, academic major and GPA, basketball statistics for all 4 years of college, and campus activities.

**Financial data** The stipend is $5,000. That includes $4,500 paid directly to the recipient's institution and $500 for travel to and from the WBCA national convention.

**Duration**  1 year.

**Additional information**  This program began in 2001.

**Number awarded**  1 each year.

## [924]
## ROCKY MOUNTAIN NASA SPACE GRANT CONSORTIUM GRADUATE RESEARCH FELLOWSHIPS

Rocky Mountain NASA Space Grant Consortium
c/o Utah State University
EL Building, Room 302
Logan, UT 84322-4140
(435) 797-3666                     Fax: (435) 797-3382
E-mail: spacegrant@cc.usu.edu
Web: spacegrant.usu.edu

**Summary**  To provide financial support for research and study to graduate students (particularly women, minority, and disabled students) at designated universities in Utah or Colorado who are working on a degree in fields of interest to the National Aeronautics and Space Administration (NASA).

**Eligibility**  This program is open to graduate students at member institutions of the Rocky Mountain NASA Space Grant Consortium who are studying engineering, science, medicine, or technology. U.S. citizenship is required. Selection is based on academic performance to date and potential for the future, with emphasis on space-related research interests. This program is part of the NASA Space Grant program, which encourages participation by women, underrepresented minorities, and persons with disabilities.

**Financial data**  Stipends range from $500 to $1,200.

**Duration**  1 year.

**Additional information**  Members of the consortium are Utah State University, the University of Utah, Brigham Young University, Dixie State College, Salt Lake Community College, Shoshone-Bannock School, Snow College, Southern Utah University, the University of Denver, and Weber State University. This program is funded by NASA.

**Number awarded**  Varies each year; recently, 23 of these fellowships, worth $20,000, were awarded.

**Deadline**  June of each year.

## [925]
## RUTH BILLOW MEMORIAL EDUCATION FUND

Delta Gamma Foundation
Attn: Director, Service for Sight
3250 Riverside Drive
P.O. Box 21397
Columbus, OH 43221-0397
(614) 481-8169                     Fax: (614) 481-0133
E-mail: freeman14@comcast.net
Web: www.deltagamma.org

**Summary**  To provide financial assistance to members of Delta Gamma sorority who are visually impaired or preparing for a career in working with the visually impaired.

**Eligibility**  This program is open to undergraduate and graduate members of the sorority who are either 1) blind or visually impaired or 2) pursuing professional training in areas related to working with persons who are blind or visually impaired or in sight preservation. Applicants must be

pursuing a program of postsecondary education in the United States or Canada.

**Financial data**  The stipend is $1,000 for undergraduates or $2,500 for graduate students.

**Duration**  1 year or more.

**Number awarded**  2 each year: 1 to an undergraduate and 1 to a graduate student.

**Deadline**  Applications may be submitted at any time.

## [926]
## RUTH G. WHITE P.E.O. SCHOLARSHIP

P.E.O. Foundation-California State Chapter
c/o Daisy Baer, Scholarship Committee Chair
5332 Brookside Court
Pleasanton, CA 94588-3756
(925) 462-4720                     E-mail: daisybaer@aol.com
Web: www.peocalifornia.org/rgw.html

**Summary**  To provide financial assistance to women from California who are interested in working on a graduate degree in the medical field.

**Eligibility**  This program is open to women residents of California who have completed their first year of graduate work in the field of medicine. Applicants may be studying in any state. They must submit a personal narrative that describes their background, interests, scholastic achievements, extracurricular activities, service, talents, and goals. Selection is based on character, integrity, academic excellence, and financial need.

**Financial data**  Stipends range from $2,500 to $4,900.

**Duration**  1 year; recipients may reapply.

**Additional information**  This fund was established in 1957. Since then, the fund has awarded more than $700,000 to nearly 400 California women studying throughout the United States.

**Number awarded**  Varies each year; recently, 14 of these scholarships were awarded.

**Deadline**  February of each year.

## [927]
## RUTH H. BUFTON SCHOLARSHIP

American Business Women's Association
Attn: Stephen Bufton Memorial Educational Fund
9100 Ward Parkway
P.O. Box 8728
Kansas City, MO 64114-0728
(816) 361-6621                     Toll-free: (800) 228-0007
Fax: (816) 361-4991               E-mail: abwa@abwahq.org
Web: www.abwahq.org/ProfDev.asp

**Summary**  To provide financial assistance to women graduate students who are working on a degree in a specified field.

**Eligibility**  This program is open to women who are working on a graduate degree and have a cumulative GPA of 2.5 or higher. Applicants are not required to be members of the American Business Women's Association, but they must be sponsored by an ABWA chapter that has contributed to the fund in the previous chapter year. Annually, the trustees designate an academic discipline for which the scholarship will be presented that year. U.S. citizenship is required.

**Financial data** The stipend is $10,000. Funds are paid directly to the recipient's institution to be used only for tuition, books, and fees.

**Duration** 1 year.

**Additional information** This program was created in 1986 as part of ABWA's Stephen Bufton Memorial Education Fund. The ABWA does not provide the names and addresses of local chapters; it recommends that applicants check with their local Chamber of Commerce, library, or university to see if any chapter has registered a contact's name and number.

**Number awarded** 1 each year.

**Deadline** May of each year.

## [928]
## RUTH M. JOHNSON SCHOLARSHIP

Alpha Omicron Pi Foundation
Attn: Scholarship Committee
5390 Virginia Way
P.O. Box 395
Brentwood, TN 37024-0395
(615) 370-0920　　　　　Fax: (615) 370-4424
E-mail: foundation@alphaomicronpi.org
Web: www.aoiifoundation.org

**Summary** To provide financial assistance to alumnae members of Alpha Omicron Pi who are interested in preparing for a medical career.

**Eligibility** This program is open to alumnae members of Alpha Omicron Pi who wish to work on a medical degree or participate in a medical research program. Applicants must submit 50-word essays on the following topics: 1) the circumstances that have created their need for this scholarship, and 2) their immediate and long-term life objectives. Selection is based on academic excellence, dedication to serving the community and Alpha Omicron Pi, and financial need.

**Financial data** A stipend is awarded (amount not specified).

**Duration** 1 year.

**Number awarded** 1 each odd-numbered year.

**Deadline** February of each odd-numbered year.

## [929]
## RUTH SATTER MEMORIAL AWARD

Association for Women in Science
Attn: AWIS Educational Foundation
1200 New York Avenue, N.W., Suite 650
Washington, DC 20005
(202) 326-8940　　　　　Toll-free: (866) 657-AWIS
Fax: (202) 326-8960　　　　E-mail: awisedfd@awis.org
Web: www.awis.org/careers/edfoundation.html

**Summary** To provide financial assistance to reentry women interested in working on a doctoral degree in engineering or the sciences.

**Eligibility** Female students enrolled in any life science, physical science, social science, or engineering program leading to a Ph.D. degree are eligible to apply if they have had to interrupt their education for 3 or more years to raise a family. They may apply at any time in their Ph.D. program, including the first year. Foreign students are eligible if they

are enrolled in a U.S. institution of higher education. Selection is based on academic achievement, the importance of the research question addressed, the quality of the research, and the applicant's potential for future contributions to science or engineering.

**Financial data** The stipend is $1,000. Funds may be used for tuition, books, housing, research, travel and meeting registration, or publication costs.

**Duration** 1 year.

**Additional information** Information is also available from Barbara Filner, President, AWIS Educational Foundation, 7008 Richard Drive, Bethesda, MD 20817-4838.

**Number awarded** 1 each year.

**Deadline** January of each year.

## [930]
## S. EVELYN LEWIS MEMORIAL SCHOLARSHIP IN MEDICAL HEALTH SCIENCES

Zeta Phi Beta Sorority, Inc.
Attn: National Education Foundation
1734 New Hampshire Avenue, N.W.
Washington, DC 20009
(202) 387-3103　　　　　Fax: (202) 232-4593
E-mail: scholarship@ZPhiBNEF.org
Web: www.zphib1920.org/nef

**Summary** To provide financial assistance to women interested in studying medicine or health sciences on the undergraduate or graduate school level.

**Eligibility** This program is open to women enrolled in a program on the undergraduate or graduate school level leading to a degree in medicine or health sciences. Proof of enrollment is required. Applicants need not be members of Zeta Phi Beta Sorority. They must submit 3 letters of recommendation, high school or university transcripts, a 150-word essay on their educational and professional goals, and information on financial need.

**Financial data** The stipend ranges from $500 to $1,000. Funds are paid directly to the college or university.

**Duration** 1 academic year.

**Additional information** Information is also available from Cheryl Williams, National Second Vice President, 6322 Bocage Drive, Shreveport, LA 71119. Recipients must attend school on a full-time basis. No awards are made just for summer study.

**Number awarded** 1 or more each year.

**Deadline** January of each year.

## [931]
## SARAH BRADLEY TYSON MEMORIAL FELLOWSHIP FOR ADVANCED STUDY IN AGRICULTURE OR HORTICULTURE

Woman's National Farm and Garden Association, Inc.
P.O. Box 1175
Midland, MI 48641-1175
Web: www.wnfga.org/code/fellowships.htm

**Summary** To provide funding to women interested in advanced study in agriculture, horticulture, and allied subjects.

**Eligibility** The fellowship is open to women interested in working on an advanced degree in the fields of agriculture, horticulture, or allied subjects at educational institutions of recognized standing within the United States. Applicants must have several years of experience. There are no application forms. Interested women should send a letter of application that contains a description of their educational background, a plan of study, references, samples of publishable papers, and a health certificate.

**Financial data** The fellowship award is $1,000 and is tenable at an American institution of higher learning chosen by the candidate with the approval of the fellowship committee.

**Duration** 1 year.

**Additional information** Information is also available from Mrs. Edward E. Phillips, 83 Webster Road, Weston, MA 02493. Students who accept the fellowships must agree to devote themselves to the study outlined in their application and to submit any proposed change in their plan to the committee for approval. They must send the committee at least 2 reports on their work, 1 at the end of the first semester and another upon completion of the year's work.

**Number awarded** Varies each year.

**Deadline** April of each year.

## [932]
## SCHOLARSHIPS FOR WOMEN RESIDENTS OF THE STATE OF DELAWARE

American Association of University Women-Wilmington
   Branch
Attn: Scholarship Committee
1800 Fairfax Boulevard
Wilmington, DE 19803-3106
(302) 428-0939                          Fax: (775) 890-9043
E-mail: aauwwilm@magpage.com
Web: www.aauwwilmington.org/procedure.html

**Summary** To provide financial assistance for college or graduate school to women residents of Delaware.

**Eligibility** This program is open to women who are residents of Delaware and U.S. citizens working on a baccalaureate or graduate degree at an accredited college or university. High school graduates may be from any Delaware county; high school seniors must be graduating from a public or private high school in New Castle County. Selection is based on scholastic standing, contributions to school and community, results of standardized testing, and financial need. An interview is required.

**Financial data** A stipend is awarded (amount not specified).

**Duration** 1 year.

**Number awarded** Varies each year; recently, 17 of these scholarships, worth $55,000, were awarded.

**Deadline** February of each year.

## [933]
## SCHUYLER S. PYLE SCHOLARSHIP

Fleet Reserve Association
Attn: Scholarship Administrator
125 North West Street
Alexandria, VA 22314-2754
(703) 683-1400                     Toll-free: (800) 372-1924
Fax: (703) 549-6610                 E-mail: fra@fra.org
Web: www.fra.org

**Summary** To provide financial assistance for undergraduate or graduate education to members of the Fleet Reserve Association (FRA) who are current or former naval personnel and their spouses and children.

**Eligibility** Applicants for these scholarships must be dependent children or spouses of members of the association in good standing as of April 1 of the year of the award or at the time of death. FRA members are also eligible. Selection is based on financial need, academic standing, character, and leadership qualities.

**Financial data** The stipend is $5,000 per year.

**Duration** 1 year; may be renewed.

**Additional information** Membership in the FRA is restricted to active-duty, retired, and Reserve members of the Navy, Marine Corps, and Coast Guard.

**Number awarded** 1 each year.

**Deadline** April of each year.

## [934]
## SCIENCE AND TECHNOLOGY GROUP FELLOWSHIPS

American Association of University Women
Attn: AAUW Educational Foundation
301 ACT Drive, Department 60
P.O. Box 4030
Iowa City, IA 52243-4030
(319) 337-1716                        Fax: (319) 337-1204
E-mail: aauw@act.org
Web: www.aauw.org

**Summary** To aid women who are in the final year of their master's degree in the fields of architecture, computer science, information science, engineering, mathematics, or statistics.

**Eligibility** This program is open to women who are U.S. citizens or permanent residents and who intend to pursue their professional careers in the United States. Applicants must be working on a master's degree in architecture, computer science, information science, engineering, mathematics, or statistics. They must be students in an accredited American institution of higher learning and must be ready to begin the final year of their master's degree program in September of the award year. (Women in engineering master's programs are eligible to apply for either the first or final year of study.) Special consideration is given 1) to applicants who demonstrate their intent to enter professional practice in disciplines in which women are underrepresented, to serve underserved populations and communities, or to pursue public interest areas; and 2) to applicants who are nontraditional students. Selection is based on professional promise and personal attributes (50%), academic excellence and related academic success indicators (40%), and financial need (10%).

**Financial data** Stipends range from $5,000 to $12,000 for the academic year.

**Duration** 1 academic year, beginning in September.

**Additional information** The filing fee is $35.

**Number awarded** Varies each year.

**Deadline** January of each year.

## [935]
## SEATTLE CHAPTER ASWA SCHOLARSHIPS

American Society of Women Accountants-Seattle
   Chapter
c/o Anne Macnab
800 Fifth Avenue, Suite 101
PMB 237
Seattle, WA 98104-3191
(206) 467-8645  E-mail: scholarship@aswaseattle.com
Web: www.aswaseattle.com/scholarships.htm

**Summary** To provide financial assistance to female students working on a bachelor's or master's degree in accounting at a college or university in Washington.

**Eligibility** This program is open to women working part time or full time on an associate, bachelor's, or master's degree in accounting at a college or university in Washington. Applicants must have completed at least 30 semester hours and have maintained a GPA of at least 2.5 overall and 3.0 in accounting. Membership in the American Society of Women Accountants (ASWA) is not required. Selection is based on career goals, communication skills, GPA, personal circumstances, and financial need.

**Financial data** The amounts of the awards vary. Recently, a total of $12,000 was available for this program. Funds are paid directly to the recipient's school.

**Duration** 1 year.

**Number awarded** April of each year.

**Deadline** Varies each year; recently, 3 of these scholarships were awarded.

## [936]
## SEMICONDUCTOR RESEARCH CORPORATION MASTER'S SCHOLARSHIP PROGRAM

Semiconductor Research Corporation
Attn: Graduate Fellowship Program
Brighton Hall, Suite 120
P.O. Box 12053
Research Triangle Park, NC 27709-2053
(919) 941-9400          Fax: (919) 941-9450
E-mail: students@src.org
Web: www.src.org/member/about/aboutmas.asp

**Summary** To provide financial assistance to women and minorities interested in working on a master's degree in a field of microelectronics relevant to the interests of the Semiconductor Research Corporation (SRC).

**Eligibility** This program is open to women and members of underrepresented minority groups (African Americans, Hispanics, and Native Americans). Applicants must be U.S. citizens or permanent residents admitted to an SRC participating university to work on a master's degree in a field relevant to microelectronics under the guidance of an SRC-sponsored faculty member and under an SRC-funded contract. Selection is based on academic achievement.

**Financial data** The fellowship provides full tuition and fee support, a monthly stipend of $2,000, an annual grant of $2,000 to the university department with which the student recipient is associated, and travel expenses to the Graduate Fellowship Program Annual Conference.

**Duration** Up to 2 years.

**Additional information** This program was established in 1997 for underrepresented minorities and expanded to include women in 1999.

**Number awarded** Varies each year; recently 9 new scholars were appointed to this program.

**Deadline** February of each year.

## [937]
## SHAWN MARGARET DONNELLEY SCHOLARSHIP

Alpha Chi Omega Foundation
Attn: Foundation Programs Coordinator
5939 Castle Creek Parkway North Drive
Indianapolis, IN 46250-4343
(317) 579-5050, ext. 262          Fax: (317) 579-5051
E-mail: foundation@alphachiomega.org
Web: www.alphachiomega.org

**Summary** To provide financial assistance for college or graduate school to undergraduate or graduate members of Alpha Chi Omega.

**Eligibility** This program is open to undergraduate and graduate members of Alpha Chi Omega. Preference is given to applicants affiliated with Zeta Psi Chapter (Loyola University of New Orleans). If there are no qualified applicants from that chapter, the grant is then opened to all undergraduate and graduate members of the sorority. Selection is based on academic achievement, chapter involvement, community and campus involvement, and financial need.

**Financial data** The stipend is $500.

**Duration** 1 year.

**Number awarded** 1 each year.

**Deadline** March of each year.

## [938]
## SIGMA ALPHA IOTA GRADUATE PERFORMANCE AWARDS

Sigma Alpha Iota Philanthropies, Inc.
One Tunnel Road
Asheville, NC 28805
(828) 251-0606          Fax: (828) 251-0644
E-mail: philonline@sai-national.org
Web: www.sai-national.org/phil/philsch3.html

**Summary** To recognize and reward outstanding performances in vocal and instrumental categories by graduate student members of Sigma Alpha Iota (an organization of women musicians).

**Eligibility** This program is open to college and alumna members of the organization who are working on a graduate degree in the field of performance. Competitions are held in 4 categories: voice, piano and percussion, strings, and winds and brass.

**Financial data** Awards are $2,000 for first place or $1,500 for second place. Funds must be used for graduate study in the field of performance.

**Duration** The competition is held triennially.

**Additional information** The awards for piano and percussion and for woodwinds and brass are designated as the Mary Ann Starring Memorial Awards. The awards for strings are designated as the Dorothy E. Morris Memorial Awards. For vocalists, the award for first place is designated the Glad Robinson Youse Memorial Award and the award for second place is designated the Lucille Malish Memorial Award. There is a $25 nonrefundable application fee.

**Number awarded** 8 every 3 years: 1 first place and 1 second place in each of the 4 categories.

**Deadline** March of the year of the awards (2009, 2012, etc.).

## [939]
## SIGMA ALPHA IOTA REGIONAL SUMMER MUSIC SCHOLARSHIPS

Sigma Alpha Iota Philanthropies, Inc.
One Tunnel Road
Asheville, NC 28805
(828) 251-0606                          Fax: (828) 251-0644
E-mail: philonline@sai-national.org
Web: www.sai-national.org/phil/philsumr.html

**Summary** To provide financial assistance for summer study in music, in the United States or abroad, to members of Sigma Alpha Iota (an organization of women musicians).

**Eligibility** Undergraduate and graduate student members of the organization may apply if they are planning to study at a summer music program in the United States or abroad. Applicants must submit a complete resume (including musical studies and activities, academic GPA, community service record, and record of participation in Sigma Alpha Iota), supporting materials (recital and concert programs, reviews, repertoire list, etc.), a statement of why they chose this program and how it will aid their musical growth, a full brochure of information on the program (including cost and payment due dates), a copy of the completed summer school application and acceptance letter (when available), and a letter of recommendation from their major teacher.

**Financial data** The stipend is $1,000.

**Duration** Summer months.

**Additional information** Applications must be accompanied by a nonrefundable fee of $25.

**Number awarded** 5 each year: 1 from each region of Sigma Alpha Iota.

**Deadline** March of each year.

## [940]
## SIGMA ALPHA IOTA SPECIAL NEEDS SCHOLARSHIP

Sigma Alpha Iota Philanthropies, Inc.
One Tunnel Road
Asheville, NC 28805
(828) 251-0606                          Fax: (828) 251-0644
E-mail: philonline@sai-national.org
Web: www.sai-national.org/phil/philsch1.html

**Summary** To provide financial assistance for college or graduate school to members of Sigma Alpha Iota (an organization of women musicians) who have a disability and are working on a degree in music.

**Eligibility** This program is open to members of the organization who have a sensory or physical impairment. Applicants must be enrolled in a graduate or undergraduate degree program in music. Performance majors must submit a video or DVD of their work; non-performance majors must submit evidence of work in their area of specialization, such as composition, musicology, or research.

**Financial data** The stipend is $1,000.

**Duration** 1 year.

**Additional information** There is a $25 nonrefundable application fee.

**Number awarded** 1 each year.

**Deadline** March of each year.

## [941]
## SONJA STEFANADIS GRADUATE STUDENT FELLOWSHIP

Daughters of Penelope
Attn: Daughters of Penelope Foundation, Inc.
1909 Q Street, N.W., Suite 500
Washington, DC 20009-1007
(202) 234-9741                          Fax: (202) 483-6983
E-mail: daughters@ahepa.org
Web: www.ahepa.org

**Summary** To provide financial assistance for graduate study to women of Greek descent.

**Eligibility** This program is open to women who have been members of the Daughters of Penelope or the Maids of Athena for at least 2 years, or whose parents or grandparents have been members of the Daughters of Penelope or the Order of Ahepa for at least 2 years. Applicants must be accepted or currently enrolled in at least 9 units per academic year in an M.A., M.S., M.B.A., Ph.D., D.D.S., M.D., or other university graduate degree program. They must have taken the GRE or other entrance examination (or Canadian, Greek, or Cypriot equivalent) and must write an essay (in English) about their educational and vocational goals. Selection is based on academic merit.

**Financial data** The stipend is $1,000.

**Duration** 1 year; nonrenewable.

**Additional information** Information is also available from Helen Santire, National Scholarship Chair, P.O. Box 19709, Houston, TX 77242-9709, (713) 468-6531, E-mail: helensantire@duchesne.org.

**Number awarded** 1 each year.

**Deadline** May of each year.

## [942]
## SOUTH CAROLINA SPACE GRANT CONSORTIUM GRADUATE STUDENT RESEARCH PROGRAM FELLOWSHIPS

South Carolina Space Grant Consortium
c/o College of Charleston
Department of Geology and Environmental Sciences
66 George Street
Charleston, SC 29424
(843) 953-5463　　　　　　Fax: (843) 953-5446
E-mail: scozzarot@cofc.edu
Web: www.cofc.edu/~scsgrant/scholar/overview.html

**Summary** To provide financial assistance for space-related study to graduate students in South Carolina, particularly women, minority, and disabled students.

**Eligibility** This program is open to graduate students at member institutions of the South Carolina Space Grant Consortium (SCSGC). Applicants must be interested in working on a master's or doctoral degree in fields of science, mathematics, and engineering related to aerospace, space science, space applications, or space technology. U.S. citizenship is required. Selection is based on academic qualifications of the applicant, the ability of the student to accomplish the proposed research, the quality of the proposed research and its relevance to programs of the U.S. National Aeronautics and Space Administration (NASA), and proposed utilization of NASA center research facilities. Women, underrepresented minorities, and persons with disabilities are strongly urged to apply.

**Financial data** SCSGC awards $10,000, which must be matched 1:1 by the host institution. The student receives a stipend of $17,000 plus an allowance of $3,000 for research.

**Duration** 1 year.

**Additional information** Members of the consortium are Benedict College, The Citadel, College of Charleston, Clemson University, Coastal Carolina University, Furman University, University of South Carolina, Wofford College, South Carolina State University, The Medical University of South Carolina, and University of the Virgin Islands. This program is funded by NASA.

**Number awarded** Varies each year.

**Deadline** January of each year.

## [943]
## SOUTH CAROLINA SPACE GRANT CONSORTIUM PRE-SERVICE TEACHER SCHOLARSHIPS

South Carolina Space Grant Consortium
c/o College of Charleston
Department of Geology and Environmental Sciences
66 George Street
Charleston, SC 29424
(843) 953-5463　　　　　　Fax: (843) 953-5446
E-mail: scozzarot@cofc.edu
Web: www.cofc.edu/~scsgrant/scholar/overview.html

**Summary** To provide financial assistance to upper-division and graduate students in South Carolina (particularly women, minority, and disabled students) who are preparing for a career as a science and mathematics teacher.

**Eligibility** This program is open to juniors, seniors, and graduate students at member institutions of the South Carolina Space Grant Consortium. Applicants must be working on a teaching certificate in science, mathematics, or engineering. Their areas of interest may include, but are not limited to, the basic sciences, astronomy, science education, planetary science, environmental studies, or engineering. U.S. citizenship is required. Selection is based on academic qualifications of the applicant; 2 letters of recommendation; a description of past activities, current interests, and future plans concerning a space science or aerospace-related field; a sample lesson plan using curriculum materials available from the U.S. National Aeronautics and Space Administration (NASA); and faculty sponsorship. Women, minorities, and persons with disabilities are encouraged to apply.

**Financial data** The stipend is $2,000. Funds may be used for such expenses as 1) partial payment of tuition; 2) travel and registration for attending science and mathematics education workshops or conferences for the purpose of professional development; 3) purchase of supplies for student teaching activities; or 4) other supportive activities that lead to successful professional development and graduation as an educator in South Carolina.

**Duration** 1 year.

**Additional information** Members of the consortium are Benedict College, The Citadel, College of Charleston, Clemson University, Coastal Carolina University, Furman University, University of South Carolina, Wofford College, South Carolina State University, The Medical University of South Carolina, and University of the Virgin Islands. This program is funded by NASA.

**Number awarded** Varies each year.

**Deadline** January of each year.

## [944]
## SOUTH DAKOTA SPACE GRANT CONSORTIUM GRADUATE FELLOWSHIPS AND UNDERGRADUATE SCHOLARSHIPS

South Dakota Space Grant Consortium
Attn: Deputy Director and Outreach Coordinator
South Dakota School of Mines and Technology
Mineral Industries Building, Room 228
501 East St. Joseph Street
Rapid City, SD 57701-3995
(605) 394-1975　　　　　　Fax: (605) 394-5360
E-mail: Thomas.Durkin@sdsmt.edu
Web: www.sdsmt.edu/space

**Summary** To provide funding to undergraduate and graduate students (particularly women, minority, and disabled students) for space-related activities in South Dakota.

**Eligibility** This program is open to undergraduate and graduate students at member and affiliated institutions of the South Dakota Space Grant Consortium. Applicants must be interested in 1) earth- and space-science related educational and research projects in fields relevant to the goals of the U.S. National Aeronautics and Space Administration (NASA); or 2) eventual employment with NASA or in a NASA-related career field in science, technology, engineering, and mathematics (STEM) education. Activities may include student research and educational efforts in remote sensing, GIS, global and regional geoscience, environmental science, and K-12 educational outreach; exposure to NASA-relevant projects; and internship experiences at various NASA centers and the Earth Resources Observation and Science (EROS) Center in Sioux Falls. U.S. citizenship is required. Women, members of underrepresented groups (African Americans, Hispanics, Pacific Islanders, Asian Americans, Native Americans, and persons with disabilities), and Tribal College students are specifically encouraged to apply. Selection is based on academic qualifications of the application (preference is given to students with a GPA of 3.0 or higher), quality of the application and its career goal statement, and assessment of the applicant's motivation toward an earth science, aerospace, or engineering career or research.

**Financial data** Stipends range from $1,000 to $7,500.

**Duration** 1 academic year, semester, or summer.

**Additional information** Member institutions include South Dakota School of Mines and Technology, South Dakota State University, and Augustana College. Educational affiliates include Black Hills State University, the University of South Dakota, Dakota State University, Lower Brule Community College, Oglala Lakota College, Sinte Gleska University, and Lake Area Technical Institute.

**Number awarded** Varies each year. Approximately $70,000 is available for this program annually.

**Deadline** January of each year.

## [945]
## SOUTHEAST EUROPEAN LANGUAGE GRANTS TO INDIVIDUALS FOR SUMMER STUDY

American Council of Learned Societies
Attn: Office of Fellowships and Grants
633 Third Avenue, 8C
New York, NY 10017-6795
(212) 697-1505        Fax: (212) 949-8058
E-mail: grants@acls.org
Web: www.acls.org/seguide.htm

**Summary** To provide financial support to graduate students and others (particularly women and minorities) who are interested in studying southeastern European languages during the summer.

**Eligibility** Applicants must have completed at least a 4-year college degree. They must be interested in a program of training in the languages of southeastern Europe, including Albanian, Bosnian-Croatian-Serbian, Bulgarian, Macedonian, or Romanian. The language course may be at the beginning, intermediate, or advanced level. Normally, requests for beginning and intermediate level training should be for attendance at intensive courses offered by institutions in the United States; proposals for study at the advanced level are ordinarily for courses in southeastern Europe. Applications are particularly encouraged from women and members of minority groups.

**Financial data** Grants up to $2,500 are available.

**Duration** Summer months.

**Additional information** This program, reinstituted in 2002, is supported by the U.S. Department of State under the Research and Training for Eastern Europe and the Independent States of the Former Soviet Union Act of 1983 (Title VIII).

**Number awarded** Approximately 10 each year.

**Deadline** January of each year.

## [946]
## SOUTHERN CALIFORNIA CHAPTER SCHOLARSHIP

Society of Satellite Professionals International
Attn: Scholarship Program
New York Information Technology Center
55 Broad Street, 14th Floor
New York, NY 10004
(212) 809-5199        Fax: (212) 825-0075
E-mail: sspi@sspi.org
Web: www.sspi.org

**Summary** To provide financial assistance to minority and female members of the Society of Satellite Professionals (SSPI) from any state who are attending college or graduate school in designated southern California counties and majoring in satellite-related disciplines.

**Eligibility** This program is open to SSPI members who are high school seniors, college undergraduates, or graduate students majoring or planning to major in fields related to satellite technologies, policies, or applications. Fields of study in the past have included broadcasting, business, distance learning, energy, government, imaging, meteorology, navigation, remote sensing, space law, and telecommunications. Applicants must be women or students of color with a GPA of 3.2 or higher. They must be attending or planning to attend schools in Los Angeles, Orange, San Diego, Santa Barbara, or Ventura counties in California. Selection is based on academic and leadership achievement; commitment to pursue educational and career opportunities in the satellite industry or a field making direct use of satellite technology; potential for significant contribution to that industry; and a scientific, engineering, research, business, or creative submission. Financial need is not considered.

**Financial data** The stipend is $5,000.

**Duration** 1 year.

**Number awarded** 1 each year.

**Deadline** Preliminary applications must be submitted by February of each year.

## [947]
## STEPHEN BUFTON MEMORIAL EDUCATION FUND GRANTS

American Business Women's Association
Attn: Stephen Bufton Memorial Educational Fund
9100 Ward Parkway
P.O. Box 8728
Kansas City, MO 64114-0728
(816) 361-6621        Toll-free: (800) 228-0007
Fax: (816) 361-4991        E-mail: abwa@abwahq.org
Web: www.abwahq.org/ProfDev.asp

**Summary** To provide financial assistance to women undergraduate and graduate students who are sponsored by a chapter of the American Business Women's Association (ABWA).

**Eligibility** This program is open to women who are at least sophomores at an accredited college or university. Applicants must be working on an undergraduate or graduate degree and have a GPA of 2.5 or higher. They are not required to be ABWA members, but they must be sponsored by an ABWA chapter that has contributed to the fund in the previous chapter year. U.S. citizenship is required.

**Financial data** The maximum grant is $1,200. Funds are paid directly to the recipient's institution to be used only for tuition, books, and fees.

**Duration** 1 year. Grants are not automatically renewed, but recipients may reapply.

**Additional information** This program was established in 1953. The ABWA does not provide the names and addresses of local chapters; it recommends that applicants check with their local Chamber of Commerce, library, or university to see if any chapter has registered a contact's name and number.

**Number awarded** Varies each year; since the inception of this program, it has awarded more than $14 million to more than 14,000 students.

**Deadline** May of each year.

## [948]
## SURVIVORS' AND DEPENDENTS' EDUCATIONAL ASSISTANCE PROGRAM

Department of Veterans Affairs
810 Vermont Avenue, N.W.
Washington, DC 20420
(202) 418-4343          Toll-free: (888) GI-BILL1
Web: www.gibill.va.gov

**Summary** To provide financial assistance for undergraduate or graduate study to children and spouses of deceased and disabled veterans, MIAs, and POWs.

**Eligibility** Eligible for this assistance are spouses and children of 1) veterans who died or are permanently and totally disabled as the result of active service in the armed forces; 2) veterans who died from any cause while rated permanently and totally disabled from a service-connected disability; 3) servicemembers listed for more than 90 days as currently missing in action or captured in the line of duty by a hostile force; and 4) servicemembers listed for more than 90 days as presently detained or interned by a foreign government or power. Children must be between 18 and 26 years of age, although extensions may be granted. Spouses and children over 14 years of age with physical or mental disabilities are also eligible.

**Financial data** Monthly stipends from this program for study at an academic institution are $827 for full time, $621 for three-quarter time, or $413 for half-time. For farm cooperative work, the monthly stipends are $667 for full-time, $500 for three-quarter time, or $334 for half-time. For an apprenticeship or on-the-job training, the monthly stipend is $650 for the first 6 months, $507 for the second 6 months, $366 for the third 6 months, and $151 for the remainder of the program.

**Duration** Up to 45 months (or the equivalent in part-time training). Spouses must complete their training within 10 years of the date they are first found eligible.

**Additional information** Benefits may be used to work on associate, bachelor, or graduate degrees at colleges and universities, including independent study, cooperative training, and study abroad programs. Courses leading to a certificate or diploma from business, technical, or vocational schools may also be taken. Other eligible programs include apprenticeships, on-job training programs, farm cooperative courses, correspondence courses (for spouses only), secondary school programs (for recipients who are not high school graduates), tutorial assistance, remedial deficiency and refresher training, or work-study (for recipients who are enrolled at least three-quarter time). Eligible children who are handicapped by a physical or mental disability that prevents pursuit of an educational program may receive special restorative training that includes language retraining, lip reading, auditory training, Braille reading and writing, and similar programs. Eligible spouses and children over 14 years of age who are handicapped by a physical or mental disability that prevents pursuit of an educational program may receive specialized vocational training that includes specialized courses, alone or in combination with other courses, leading to a vocational objective that is suitable for the person and required by reason of physical or mental handicap. Ineligible courses include bartending or personality development courses; correspondence courses by dependent or surviving children; non-accredited independent study courses; any course given by radio; self-improvement courses, such as reading, speaking, woodworking, basic seamanship, and English as a second language; audited courses; any course that is avocational or recreational in character; courses not leading to an educational, professional, or vocational objective; courses taken and successfully completed previously; courses taken by a federal government employee and paid for under the Government Employees' Training Act; and courses taken while in receipt of benefits for the same program from the Office of Workers' Compensation Programs.

**Number awarded** Varies each year.

**Deadline** Applications may be submitted at any time.

## [949]
## SWE PAST PRESIDENTS SCHOLARSHIPS

Society of Women Engineers
230 East Ohio Street, Suite 400
Chicago, IL 60611-3265
(312) 596-5223          Toll-free: (877) SWE-INFO
Fax: (312) 644-8557
E-mail: scholarshipapplication@swe.org
Web: www.swe.org/scholarships

**Summary** To provide financial assistance to women working on an undergraduate or graduate degree in engineering or computer science.

**Eligibility** This program is open to women who will be sophomores, juniors, seniors, or graduate students at ABET-accredited colleges and universities. Applicants must be U.S. citizens majoring in computer science or engineering and have a GPA of 3.0 or higher. Along with their application, they must submit a 1-page essay on why they want to be an engineer or computer scientist, how they believe they will make a difference as an engineer or computer scientist, and what influenced them to study engineering or computer science. Selection is based on merit.

**Financial data** The stipend is $1,500.

**Duration** 1 year.

**Additional information** This program was established in 1999 by an anonymous donor to honor the commitment and accomplishments of past presidents of the Society of Women Engineers (SWE).

**Number awarded** 2 each year.

**Deadline** January of each year.

**[950]**

## SYNOD WOMEN'S ADVOCACY NETWORK THEOLOGICAL EDUCATION SCHOLARSHIP

Synod of Southern California and Hawaii
Attn: Synod Women's Advocacy Network
1501 Wilshire Boulevard
Los Angeles, CA 90017-2205
(213) 483-3840, ext. 201          Fax: (213) 483-4275
E-mail: nwafriyie@synod.org
Web: www.synod.org/SWAN/activ.html

**Summary**  To provide financial assistance to women in the Presbyterian Church (USA) Synod of Southern California and Hawaii who are preparing for a career as a pastor or other church vocation.

**Eligibility**  This program is open to women who have completed at least 1 semester in a seminary and are under care of a presbytery within the Synod of Southern California and Hawaii. Applicants must be interested in becoming a Presbyterian pastor or other church worker (e.g., commissioned lay pastor, certified Christian educator) and serving within the PC(USA). Along with their application, they must submit documentation of financial need, recommendations from the appropriate committee or session, a current transcript, and essays on their goals and objectives. Selection is based on academic ability, promise for ministry, and financial need.

**Financial data**  Stipends up to $600 are available.

**Duration**  1 year; may be renewed.

**Number awarded**  Varies each year.

**Deadline**  June of each year.

**[951]**

## TED SCRIPPS FELLOWSHIPS IN ENVIRONMENTAL JOURNALISM

University of Colorado at Boulder
Attn: Center for Environmental Journalism
1511 University Avenue
Campus Box 478
Boulder, CO 80309-0478
(303) 492-4114          E-mail: cej@colorado.edu
Web: www.colorado.edu/journalism/cej

**Summary**  To provide journalists (particularly women, minorities, and journalists with disabilities) with an opportunity to gain more knowledge about environmental issues at the University of Colorado at Boulder.

**Eligibility**  This program is open to full-time U.S. print and broadcast journalists who have at least 5 years' professional experience and have completed an undergraduate degree. Applicants may be general assignment reporters, editors, producers, environmental reporters, or full-time freelancers. Prior experience in covering the environment is not required. Professionals in such related fields as teaching, public relations, or advertising are not eligible. Applicants must be interested in a program at the university that includes classes, weekly seminars, and field trips. They also must engage in independent study expected to lead to a significant piece of journalistic work. Applications are especially encouraged from women, ethnic minorities, disabled persons, and veterans (particularly veterans of the Vietnam era).

**Financial data**  The program covers tuition and fees and pays a $44,000 stipend. Employers are strongly encouraged to continue benefits, including health insurance.

**Duration**  9 months.

**Additional information**  This program, established in 1992 at the University of Michigan and transferred to the University of Colorado in 1997, is supported by the Scripps Howard Foundation. This is a non-degree program. Fellows must obtain a leave of absence from their regular employment and must return to their job following the fellowship.

**Number awarded**  5 each year.

**Deadline**  February of each year.

**[952]**

## TEXAS SPACE GRANT CONSORTIUM GRADUATE FELLOWSHIPS

Texas Space Grant Consortium
Attn: Administrative Assistant
3925 West Braker Lane, Suite 200
Austin, TX 78759
(512) 471-3583          Toll-free: (800) 248-8742
Fax: (512) 471-3585
E-mail: fellowships@tsgc.utexas.edu
Web: www.tsgc.utexas.edu/grants

**Summary**  To provide financial assistance to graduate students (especially women, minority, and disabled students) at Texas universities working on degrees in the fields of space science and engineering.

**Eligibility**  Applicants must be U.S. citizens, eligible for financial assistance, and registered for full-time study in a graduate program at 1 of the participating universities. Students apply to their respective university representative; each representative then submits up to 3 candidates into the statewide selection process. Fields of study have included aerospace engineering, astronomy, computer science and engineering, electrical engineering, materials science and engineering, medicine, physics, and physiology. Applications from women and underrepresented students (persons with disabilities, African Americans, Hispanic Americans, Native Americans, and Pacific Islanders) are encouraged. Selection is based on academic excellence, interest in space, and recommendations from the applicant's university.

**Financial data**  The stipend is $5,000 per year, to be used to supplement half-time graduate support (or a fellowship) offered by the home institution.

**Duration**  1 year; may be renewed for up to a maximum of 3 years, provided the recipient spends no more than 2 of those years as a master's degree candidate.

**Additional information**  The participating universities are Baylor University, Lamar University, Prairie View A&M University, Rice University, San Jacinto College, Southern Methodist University, Sul Ross State University, Texas A&M University (including Kingsville and Corpus Christi campuses), Texas Christian University, Texas Southern University, Texas Tech University, Trinity University, University of Houston (including Clear Lake and Downtown campuses), University of Texas at Arlington, University of Texas at Austin, University of Texas at Dallas, University of Texas at El Paso, University of Texas at San Antonio, University of Texas Health Science Center at Houston, University of Texas Health Science Center at San Antonio, University of

Texas Medical Branch at Galveston, University of Texas/Pan American, and University of Texas Southwestern Medical Center. This program is funded by the National Aeronautics and Space Administration (NASA).

**Number awarded** Varies each year; recently, 18 of these fellowships were awarded.

**Deadline** February of each year.

## [953]
## TEXAS WAIVERS OF NONRESIDENT TUITION FOR MILITARY PERSONNEL AND THEIR DEPENDENTS

Texas Higher Education Coordinating Board
Attn: Grants and Special Programs
1200 East Anderson Lane
P.O. Box 12788, Capitol Station
Austin, TX 78711-2788
(512) 427-6101          Toll-free: (800) 242-3062
Fax: (512) 427-6127
E-mail: grantinfo@thecb.state.tx.us
Web: www.collegefortexans.com

**Summary** To exempt military personnel stationed in Texas and their dependents from the payment of nonresident tuition at public institutions of higher education in the state.

**Eligibility** Eligible for these waivers are members of the U.S. armed forces and commissioned officers of the Public Health Service from states other than Texas, their spouses, and dependent children. Applicants must be assigned to Texas and attending or planning to attend a public college or university in the state.

**Financial data** Although persons eligible under this program are classified as nonresidents, they are entitled to pay the resident tuition at Texas institutions of higher education, regardless of their length of residence in Texas.

**Duration** 1 year; may be renewed.

**Number awarded** Varies each year; recently, 10,333 students received these waivers.

## [954]
## TEXAS YOUNG LAWYERS ASSOCIATION MINORITY SCHOLARSHIP PROGRAM

Texas Young Lawyers Association
Attn: Minority Involvement Committee
1414 Colorado, Suite 502
P.O. Box 12487
Austin, TX 78711-2487
(512) 463-1463, ext. 6429
Toll-free: (800) 204-2222, ext. 6429
Fax: (512) 463-1503
Web: www.tyla.org/scholarships.html

**Summary** To provide financial assistance to women and minorities attending law school in Texas.

**Eligibility** This program is open to members of recognized minority groups, including but not limited to women, African Americans, Hispanics, Asian Americans, and Native Americans. Applicants must be attending an ABA-accredited law school in Texas. Selection is based on participation in extracurricular activities inside and outside law school and financial need.

**Financial data** The stipend is $1,000.

**Duration** 1 year.

**Number awarded** 1 at each accredited law school in Texas.

**Deadline** October of each year.

## [955]
## THEODORE AND MARY JANE RICH MEMORIAL SCHOLARSHIPS

Slovak Catholic Sokol
Attn: Membership Memorial Scholarship Fund
205 Madison Street
P.O. Box 899
Passaic, NJ 07055-0899
(973) 777-2605          Toll-free: (800) 886-7656
Fax: (973) 779-8245
E-mail: life@slovakcatholicsokol.org
Web: www.slovakcatholicsokol.org

**Summary** To provide financial assistance for college or graduate school to members of the Slovak Catholic Sokol.

**Eligibility** This program is open to members of the Slovak Catholic Sokol who have completed at least 1 semester of college and are currently enrolled full time as an undergraduate or graduate student at an accredited college, university, or professional school. Applicants must have been a member for at least 5 years, have at least $3,000 permanent life insurance coverage, and have at least 1 parent who is a member and is of Slovak ancestry. They must be majoring in a medical program. Males and females compete for scholarships separately.

**Financial data** The stipend is $2,500 per year.

**Duration** 1 year; may be renewed 1 additional year.

**Additional information** Slovak Catholic Sokol was founded as a fraternal benefit society in 1905. It is licensed to operate in the following states: Connecticut, Illinois, Indiana, Massachusetts, Michigan, New Jersey, New York, Ohio, Pennsylvania, and Wisconsin. This program was established in 2003.

**Number awarded** 2 each year: 1 for a male and 1 for a female.

**Deadline** March of each year.

## [956]
## THOMPSON SCHOLARSHIP FOR WOMEN IN SAFETY

American Society of Safety Engineers
Attn: ASSE Foundation
1800 East Oakton Street
Des Plaines, IL 60018
(847) 768-3435          Fax: (847) 768-3434
E-mail: agabanski@asse.org
Web: www.asse.org/foundation

**Summary** To provide financial assistance to women working on a graduate degree in safety-related fields.

**Eligibility** This program is open to women who are working on a graduate degree in safety engineering, safety management, occupational health nursing, occupational medicine, risk management, ergonomics, industrial hygiene, fire safety, environmental safety, environmental health, or another safety-related field. Applicants must be full-time students who have completed at least 9 semester hours with a GPA of 3.5 or higher. Their undergraduate GPA must have been 3.0 or higher. Along with their application, they must submit 2 essays of 300 words or less: 1) why they are seeking a degree in occupational safety and health or a closely-related field, a brief description of their current activities, and how those relate to their career goals and objectives; and 2) why they should be awarded this scholarship (including career goals and financial need).

**Financial data** The stipend is $1,000.

**Duration** 1 year; nonrenewable.

**Number awarded** 1 each year.

**Deadline** November of each year.

## [957]
## TRANSPORTATION FELLOWSHIP PROGRAM

North Central Texas Council of Governments
Attn: Transportation Department
616 Six Flags Drive, Centerpoint Two
P.O. Box 5888
Arlington, TX 76005-5888
(817) 695-9242                    Fax: (817) 640-7806
Web: www.nctcog.org/trans/admin/fellowship

**Summary** To provide financial assistance to ethnic minorities, women, and economically disadvantaged persons who are interested in obtaining an undergraduate or graduate degree and work experience in a transportation-related field in Texas.

**Eligibility** This program is open to ethnic minorities (African Americans, Hispanics, American Indians, Alaskan Natives, Asians, and Pacific Islanders), women, and those who are economically disadvantaged. Only U.S. citizens or permanent residents may apply. They must attend or be willing to attend a college or university within the 16-county north central Texas region as an undergraduate or graduate student. Applicants must have a GPA of 2.5 or higher. They may be enrolled full or part time, but they must be majoring in a designated transportation-related field: transportation planning, transportation or civil engineering, urban and regional planning, transportation/environmental sciences, transportation law, urban or spatial geography, logistics, geographic information systems, or transportation management. Selection is based on financial need, interest in a professional career in transportation, and ability to complete the program.

**Financial data** The stipend is $2,000.

**Duration** 1 year; may be renewed if the recipient maintains a GPA of 3.0 or higher.

**Additional information** These fellowships are financed by the Federal Highway Administration, Federal Transit Administration, and Texas Department of Transportation, in conjunction with local governments in north central Texas. An important part of the fellowship is an internship with a local agency (city or county), school, or transportation agency.

**Deadline** March of each year.

## [958]
## URBAN FELLOWSHIP PROGRAM

North Central Texas Council of Governments
Attn: Transportation Department
616 Six Flags Drive, Centerpoint Two
P.O. Box 5888
Arlington, TX 76005-5888
(817) 695-9103                    Fax: (817) 640-7806
Web: www.nctcog.org/edo/ufp.asp

**Summary** To provide financial assistance and work experience to ethnic minorities, women, and economically disadvantaged persons who are interested in obtaining a master's degree in Texas in preparation for a career in public management and/or planning.

**Eligibility** This program is open to ethnic minorities (African Americans, Hispanics, American Indians, Alaskan Natives, Asians, and Pacific Islanders), women, and those who are economically disadvantaged. Only U.S. citizens or permanent residents may apply. Applicants must be interested in obtaining a master's degree at a participating university in Texas as preparation for a career in public management and/or planning. Full-time enrollment is required. Selection is based on 1) financial need; 2) interest in, and commitment to, a professional career in urban management and/or planning; and 3) the ability to complete the academic and work placement responsibilities of the program.

**Financial data** The program provides up to $30,000 for tuition, books, professional memberships, and conferences, and a 20 hour-a-week internship.

**Duration** 1 year; may be renewed if the recipient maintains a GPA of 3.0 or higher.

**Additional information** This program was established in 1970. The fellowships are financed by the U.S. Department of Housing and Urban Development in conjunction with local governments in north central Texas (the Dallas/Fort Worth metropolitan area). Fellows are assigned to an internship in a local government unit in that area. Universities currently participating in the program are the University of North Texas, the University of Texas at Arlington, and the University of Texas at Dallas. Fellows are required to agree to make a good-faith effort to obtain employment in community-building fields for at least 2 consecutive years after graduation.

**Deadline** July of each year.

## [959]
## VADM ROBERT L. WALTERS SCHOLARSHIP

Surface Navy Association
2550 Huntington Avenue, Suite 202
Alexandria, VA 22303
(703) 960-6800                    Toll-free: (800) NAVY-SNA
Fax: (703) 960-6807                E-mail: navysna@aol.com
Web: www.navysna.org/awards/index.html

**Summary** To provide financial assistance for college or graduate school to members of the Surface Navy Association (SNA) and their dependents.

**Eligibility** This program is open to SNA members and their children, stepchildren, wards, and spouses. The SNA member must 1) be in the second or subsequent consecutive year of membership; 2) be serving, retired, or honorably discharged; 3) be a Surface Warfare Officer or Enlisted Surface Warfare Specialist; and 4) have served for at least 3 years on a surface ship of the U.S. Navy or Coast Guard. Applicants must be studying or planning to study at an accredited undergraduate or graduate institution. Along with their application, they must submit a 200-word essay about themselves; a list of their extracurricular activities, community service activities, academic honors and/or positions of leadership that represent their interests, with an estimate of the amount of time involved with each activity; and 3 letters of reference. High school seniors should also include a transcript of high school grades and a copy of ACT or SAT scores. Applicants who are on active duty or drilling Reservists should also include a letter from their commanding officer commenting on their military service and leadership potential, a transcript of grades from their most recent 4 semesters of school, a copy of their ACT or SAT scores if available, and an indication of whether they have applied for or are enrolled in the Enlisted Commissioning Program. Applicants who are not high school seniors, active duty, or drilling Reservists should also include a transcript of the grades from their most recent 4 semesters of school and a copy of ACT or SAT test scores (unless they are currently attending a college or university). Selection is based on demonstrated leadership, community service, academic achievement, and commitment to pursuing higher educational objectives.

**Financial data** The stipend is $2,000 per year.

**Duration** 4 years, provided the recipient maintains a GPA of 3.0 or higher.

**Number awarded** Varies each year.

**Deadline** January of each year.

## [960]
## VERNA ROSS ORNDORFF CAREER PERFORMANCE GRANT

Sigma Alpha Iota Philanthropies, Inc.
One Tunnel Road
Asheville, NC 28805
(828) 251-0606                    Fax: (828) 251-0644
E-mail: philonline@sai-national.org
Web: www.sai-national.org/phil/philsch1.html

**Summary** To provide funding for advanced study, coaching, or other activities directly related to the development of a musical career to members of Sigma Alpha Iota (an organization of women musicians).

**Eligibility** This program is open to members of the organization who are preparing for a concert career. Singers may not be older than 35 years of age and instrumentalists may not be older than 32. Applicants may not have professional management, but they must have had considerable performing experience outside the academic environment.

**Financial data** The grant is $5,000; funds must be used for advanced study, coaching, or other purposes directly related to the development of a professional performing career.

**Duration** 1 year.

**Additional information** The area supported rotates annually among piano, harpsichord, organ, and percussion (2008); and voice (2009); and strings, woodwinds, and brass (2010) There is a $35 nonrefundable application fee.

**Number awarded** 1 each year.

**Deadline** October of each year.

## [961]
## VIRGINIA A. POMEROY SCHOLARSHIPS

Association for Women Lawyers
Attn: AWL Foundation
3322 North 92nd Street
Milwaukee, WI 53222
(414) 778-0602                    E-mail: awlwi@yahoo.com
Web: www.wisbar.org/bars/awl

**Summary** To provide financial assistance to women who are attending law school in Wisconsin.

**Eligibility** This program is open to women law students in Wisconsin who have "exhibited academic excellence and outstanding service to the law school community and community at large."

**Financial data** The stipend varies; recently, awards averaged $2,500.

**Duration** 1 year.

**Additional information** This program was established in 1998.

**Number awarded** Varies each year; recently, 4 of these scholarships were awarded.

**Deadline** June of each year.

## [962]
## VIRGINIA SPACE GRANT TEACHER EDUCATION SCHOLARSHIP PROGRAM

Virginia Space Grant Consortium
Attn: Fellowship Coordinator
Old Dominion University Peninsula Center
600 Butler Farm Road
Hampton, VA 23666
(757) 766-5210                    Fax: (757) 766-5205
E-mail: vsgc@odu.edu
Web: www.vsgc.odu.edu/Menu3_1_1.htm

**Summary** To provide financial assistance for college or graduate school to students in Virginia (particularly women, minority, and disabled students) who are planning a career as science, mathematics, or technology educators.

**Eligibility** This program is open to full-time undergraduate students at the Virginia Space Grant Consortium (VSGC) colleges and universities in a track that will qualify them to teach in a pre-college setting. Priority is given to those majoring in technology education, mathematics, or science, particularly earth, space, or environmental science. Applicants may apply while seniors in high school or sophomores in a community college, with the award contingent on their enrollment at a VSGC college and entrance into a teacher certification program. They must submit a statement of academic goals and plan of study, explaining their reasons for desiring to enter the teaching profession, specifically the fields of science, mathematics, or technology education. Students currently enrolled in a VSGC college can apply when they declare their intent to enter the teacher certification program. Students enrolled in a master's of education degree program leading to teacher certification in approved fields are also eligible to apply. Applicants must be U.S. citizens with a GPA of 3.0 or higher. Since an important purpose of this program is to increase the participation of underrepresented minorities, women, and persons with disabilities in science, mathematics, and technology education, the VSGC especially encourages applications from those students.

**Financial data** The maximum stipend is $1,000.

**Duration** 1 year; nonrenewable.

**Additional information** The VSGC institutions are College of William and Mary, Hampton University, Old Dominion University, the University of Virginia, and Virginia Polytechnic Institute and State University. This program is funded by the U.S. National Aeronautics and Space Administration (NASA).

**Number awarded** Approximately 10 each year.

**Deadline** February of each year.

## [963]
## WALTER BYERS POSTGRADUATE SCHOLARSHIP PROGRAM

National Collegiate Athletic Association
Attn: Walter Byers Scholarship Committee Staff Liaison
700 West Washington Avenue
P.O. Box 6222
Indianapolis, IN 46206-6222
(317) 917-6477                    Fax: (317) 917-6888
Web: www1.ncaa.org

**Summary** To provide financial assistance for graduate education in any field to student-athletes with outstanding academic records.

**Eligibility** This program is open to student-athletes who are seniors or already enrolled in graduate school while completing their final year of athletics eligibility at a member institution of the National Collegiate Athletic Association (NCAA). Men and women compete for scholarships separately. Applicants must be planning to work full time on a graduate degree or postbaccalaureate professional degree. They must have a GPA of 3.5 or higher, have evidenced superior character and leadership, and have demonstrated that participation in athletics has been a positive influence on their personal and intellectual development. Candidates must be nominated by their institution's faculty athletic representative or chief academics officer. Financial need is not considered in the selection process.

**Financial data** The stipend is $21,500 per year.

**Duration** 2 years.

**Additional information** This program was established in 1988 in honor of the former executive director of the NCAA.

**Number awarded** 2 each year: 1 is set aside for a female and 1 for a male.

**Deadline** January of each year.

## [964]
## WASHINGTON BUSINESS AND PROFESSIONAL WOMEN'S FOUNDATION EDUCATIONAL SCHOLARSHIP

Washington Business and Professional Women's Foundation
Attn: Madeleine Cooper, Scholarship Committee Chair
100 North 60111 Avenue, Number 15
Yakima, WA 98908
Web: www.bpwwa.com/files/index.php?id=14

**Summary** To provide financial assistance to women from Washington working on an undergraduate or graduate degree.

**Eligibility** This program is open to women from Washington who are enrolled or planning to enroll in a vocational/technical school, community college, or 4-year college or university. Applicants must be working on an associate, bachelor's, master's, or doctoral degree. Along with their application, they must submit a 300-word essay on their specific short-term goals and how the proposed training will help them accomplish those goals and make a difference in their professional career. Financial need is considered in the selection process.

**Financial data** Stipends range from $500 to $1,000.

**Duration** 1 year.

**Additional information** This program was established in 1992.

**Number awarded** Varies each year. Since the program was established, it has awarded 112 scholarships.

**Deadline** March of each year.

## [965]
## WASHINGTON EPISCOPAL CHURCH WOMEN MEMORIAL SCHOLARSHIP FUND

Episcopal Diocese of Washington
Attn: Episcopal Church Women
Episcopal Church House
Mount St. Alban
Washington, DC 20016-5094
(202) 537-6530                    TDD: (800) 642-4427
Fax: (202) 364-6605              E-mail: ecw@edow.org
Web: www.edow.org/diocese/outreach/ecw.html

**Summary** To provide financial assistance for graduate school to women who are members of Episcopal churches in Washington, D.C.

**Eligibility** This program is open to women members of the Episcopal Church who have been a canonical member of the Diocese of Washington for at least 1 year prior to application. Priority is given to members who reside in the Diocese of Washington. Applicants must be enrolled in graduate or professional study and their course of study must be related to church work or activity in preparation for some pertinent field of Christian endeavor. Along with their application, they must submit a statement of purpose for working on a graduate degree and how they plan to use it, letters of recommendation (including 1 from their vicar or rector), financial information, and (if seeking ordination) a letter from their parish intern committee.

**Financial data** A stipend is awarded (amount not specified); funds are sent directly to the recipient's school.

**Duration** 1 year; may be renewed.

**Additional information** This program was established in 1925.

**Number awarded** 1 or more each year.

**Deadline** May of each year.

## [966]
## WATSON MIDWIVES OF COLOR SCHOLARSHIP

American College of Nurse-Midwives
Attn: ACNM Foundation, Inc.
8403 Coleville Road, Suite 1550
Silver Spring, MD 20915
(240) 485-1850                    Fax: (240) 485-1818
Web: www.midwife.org

**Summary** To provide financial assistance for midwifery education to students of color who belong to the American College of Nurse-Midwives (ACNM).

**Eligibility** This program is open to ACNM members of color who are currently enrolled in an accredited basic midwife education program and have successfully completed 1 academic or clinical semester/quarter or clinical module. Applicants must submit a 150-word essay on their midwifery career plans and a 100-word essay on their intended future participation in the local, regional, and/or national activities of the ACNM. Selection is based on leadership potential, financial need, academic history, and potential for future professional contribution to the organization.

**Financial data** The stipend is $3,000.

**Duration** 1 year.

**Number awarded** Varies each year; recently, 2 of these scholarships were awarded.

**Deadline** March of each year.

## [967]
## WBF SCHOLARSHIP AWARDS

Women's Bar Association of Illinois
Attn: Women's Bar Foundation
P.O. Box 641068
Chicago, IL 60664-1068
(312) 909-0391          E-mail: rkrimbel@sbcglobal.net
Web: www.womensbarfoundation.org/7.html

**Summary** To provide financial assistance to women attending law school in Illinois.

**Eligibility** This program is open to women enrolled at accredited law schools in Illinois.

**Financial data** Stipends vary; recently, they averaged $4,000.

**Duration** 1 year.

**Additional information** This program was established in 1966. It includes the Chief Justice Mary Ann G. McMorrow Scholarship, first presented in 2004, and the Esther Rothstein Scholarship, first awarded in 2002.

**Number awarded** Varies each year; recently, 11 of these scholarships were awarded.

## [968]
## WICHITA CHAPTER ASWA SCHOLARSHIPS

American Society of Women Accountants-Wichita Chapter
c/o Vonda Wilson, Scholarship Chair
417 North Topeka
Wichita, KS 67202
Web: www.wichitaaswa.org

**Summary** To provide financial assistance to female undergraduate and graduate students working on a degree in accounting at a college or university in Kansas.

**Eligibility** This program is open to female part- and full-time students working on a bachelor's or master's degree in accounting at a college or university in Kansas. Applicants must have completed at least 60 semester hours. They are not required to be a member of the American Society of Women Accountants (ASWA). Along with their application, they must submit a 100-word essay on how they plan to incorporate into their strategic career goals the sponsor's philosophy of achieving balance among life priorities, including career, personal development, family, friendships, and community and societal needs. Selection is based on that essay, academic record, extracurricular activities and honors, letters of recommendation, and financial need.

**Financial data** The stipend is $1,000 or $500.

**Duration** 1 year.

**Additional information** The highest-ranked recipient is entered into the national competition for scholarships that range from $1,500 to $4,500.

**Number awarded** Varies each year. Recently, 3 of these scholarships were awarded: 1 at $1,000 and 2 at $500.

**Deadline** February of each year.

## [969]
## WILHELM-FRANKOWSKI SCHOLARSHIP

American Medical Women's Association Foundation
Attn: AMWA Foundation
211 North Union Street, Suite 100
Alexandria, VA 22314
(703) 838-0500                    Fax: (703) 549-3864
E-mail: foundation@amwa-doc.org
Web: www.amwa-doc.org

**Summary** To provide financial assistance for medical education to members of the American Medical Women's Association (AMWA).

**Eligibility** Eligible for this scholarship are student members of the association attending an accredited U.S. medical or osteopathic medical school in their first, second, or third year. Selection is based on community service; work, research, and participation in women's health issues; participation in association activities; and participation in women-in-medicine or medical student groups other than this association.

**Financial data** The stipend is $4,000.

**Duration** 1 year.

**Additional information** This scholarship was first awarded in 1996.

**Number awarded** 1 each year.

**Deadline** April of each year.

[970]
## WILLIAM RUCKER GREENWOOD SCHOLARSHIP

Association for Women Geoscientists
Attn: AWG Foundation
P.O. Box 30645
Lincoln, NE 68503-0645
E-mail: awgscholarship@yahoo.com
Web: www.awg.org/members/po_scholarships.html

**Summary** To provide financial assistance to minority women working on an undergraduate or graduate degree in the geosciences in the Potomac Bay region.

**Eligibility** This program is open to minority women who are currently enrolled as full-time undergraduate or graduate geoscience majors in an accredited, degree-granting college or university in Delaware, the District of Columbia, Maryland, Virginia, or West Virginia. Selection is based on the applicant's 1) participation in geoscience or earth science educational activities, and 2) potential for leadership as a future geoscience professional.

**Financial data** The stipend is $1,000. The recipient also is granted a 1-year membership in the Association for Women Geoscientists (AWG).

**Duration** 1 year.

**Additional information** This program is sponsored by the AWG Potomac Area Chapter. Information is also available from Laurel M. Bybell, U.S. Geological Survey, 926 National Center, Reston, VA 20192.

**Number awarded** 1 each year.

**Deadline** April of each year.

[971]
## WILSON MEMORIAL EDUCATIONAL GRANTS

Arkansas Business and Professional Women
c/o Cari Griffith White
Jonesboro Regional Chamber of Commerce
P.O. Box 789
Jonesboro, AR 72403
(870) 932-6691                    Fax: (870) 933-5758
Web: www.arkansasbpw.org/scholarships.htm

**Summary** To provide financial assistance to female residents of Arkansas who are working on a graduate degree.

**Eligibility** This program is open to women who are Arkansas residents attending an accredited college or university. Applicants must be working on a master's or doctoral degree and have a GPA as set forth by their institution. Along with their application, they must submit a statement covering their goals, choice of major, and reasons why the grant is needed.

**Financial data** The stipend is $1,000.

**Duration** 1 year.

**Number awarded** 1 or more each year.

**Deadline** March of each year.

[972]
## WINIFRED HILL BOYD GRADUATE SCHOLARSHIP

Kappa Delta Sorority
Attn: Foundation Manager
3205 Players Lane
Memphis, TN 38125
(901) 748-1897                    Toll-free: (800) 536-1897
Fax: (901) 748-0949
E-mail: kappadelta@kappadelta.org
Web: www.kappadelta.org

**Summary** To provide financial assistance to members of Kappa Delta Sorority who are working on a graduate degree in science or mathematics.

**Eligibility** This program is open to graduate members of Kappa Delta Sorority. Applicants must submit a personal statement giving their reasons for applying for this scholarship, official undergraduate and graduate transcripts, and 2 letters of recommendation. They must be working on a graduate degree in science or mathematics. Selection is based on academic excellence; service to the chapter, alumnae association, or national Kappa Delta; service to the campus and community; personal objectives and goals; potential; recommendations; and financial need.

**Financial data** The stipend is $5,000 per year. Funds may be used only for tuition, fees, and books, not for room and board.

**Duration** 1 year; may be renewed.

**Additional information** This program was established in 2002.

**Number awarded** 1 each year.

**Deadline** January of each year.

[973]
## WISCONSIN FEDERATION OF BUSINESS AND PROFESSIONAL WOMEN SCHOLARSHIP

Community Foundation for the Fox Valley Region, Inc.
Attn: Scholarships
4455 West Lawrence Street
P.O. Box 563
Appleton, WI 54912-0563
(920) 830-1290                    Fax: (920) 830-1293
E-mail: cffvr@cffoxvalley.org
Web: www.cffoxvalley.org/scholarship_fundslist.html

**Summary** To provide financial assistance to mature women in Wisconsin who are working on an undergraduate or graduate degree.

**Eligibility** This program is open to Wisconsin women who are 25 years of age or older. Applicants must be attending a technical college or an accredited 2-year or 4-year college or university to work on an undergraduate or graduate degree. They must submit a personal statement of their reasons for working on a degree in their chosen field, including their special professional interests, goals, and purposes within that field.

**Financial data** The stipend is $500.

**Duration** 1 year.

**Additional information** This program is sponsored by the Wisconsin Business and Professional Women's Foundation Fund, 1067 Oak Street, Neenah, WI 54956, (262) 352-4617.

**Number awarded** 1 or more each year.

**Deadline** February of each year.

## [974]
## WISCONSIN JOB RETRAINING GRANTS

Wisconsin Department of Veterans Affairs
30 West Mifflin Street
P.O. Box 7843
Madison, WI 53707-7843
(608) 266-1311          Toll-free: (800) WIS-VETS
Fax: (608) 267-0403
E-mail: wdvaweb@dva.state.wi.us
Web: dva.state.wi.us/Ben_retraininggrants.asp

**Summary** To provide funds to recently unemployed Wisconsin veterans or their families who need financial assistance while being retrained for employment.

**Eligibility** This program is open to current residents of Wisconsin who 1) were residents of the state when they entered or reentered active duty in the U.S. armed forces, or 2) have moved to the state and have been residents for any consecutive 12-month period after entry or reentry into service. Applicants must have served on active duty for at least 2 continuous years or for at least 90 days during specified wartime periods. Unremarried spouses and minor or dependent children of deceased veterans who would have been eligible for the grant if they were living today may also be eligible. The applicant must, within the year prior to the date of application, have become unemployed (involuntarily laid off or discharged, not due to willful misconduct) or underemployed (experienced an involuntary reduction of income). Underemployed applicants must have current annual income from employment that does not exceed federal poverty guidelines. All applicants must be retraining at accredited schools in Wisconsin or in a structured on-the-job program. Course work toward a college degree does not qualify. Training does not have to be full time, but the program must be completed within 2 years and must reasonably be expected to lead to employment.

**Financial data** The maximum grant is $3,000 per year; the actual amount varies, depending upon the amount of the applicant's unmet need. In addition to books, fees, and tuition, the funds may be used for living expenses.

**Duration** 1 year; may be renewed 1 additional year.

**Number awarded** Varies each year.

**Deadline** Applications may be submitted at any time.

## [975]
## WISCONSIN LEGION AUXILIARY CHILD WELFARE SCHOLARSHIP

American Legion Auxiliary
Department of Wisconsin
Attn: Department Secretary/Treasurer
2930 American Legion Drive
P.O. Box 140
Portage, WI 53901-0140
(608) 745-0124          Toll-free: (866) 664-3863
Fax: (608) 745-1947
E-mail: alawi@amlegionauxwi.org
Web: www.amlegionauxwi.org

**Summary** To provide financial assistance for graduate training in special education to dependents and descendants of veterans in Wisconsin.

**Eligibility** This program is open to the children, wives, and widows of veterans who have a GPA of 3.2 or higher. Grandchildren and great-grandchildren of veterans are eligible if they are members of the American Legion Auxiliary. Applicants must be graduate students in some facet of special education and able to demonstrate financial need. They must be residents of Wisconsin, although they are not required to attend college in the state. If no graduate student in special education applies, the scholarship may be awarded to a student in education. Applicants must submit a 300-word essay on "Education-An Investment in the Future."

**Financial data** The stipend is $1,000.

**Duration** 1 year; nonrenewable.

**Additional information** Information is also available from the Education Chair, Renae Allen, 206 West Fremont Street, Darien, WI 53114-1540, (262) 724-5059.

**Number awarded** 1 each year.

**Deadline** March of each year.

## [976]
## WLAM FOUNDATION SCHOLARS

Women Lawyers Association of Michigan Foundation
3300 Penobscot Building
645 Griswold
Detroit, MI 48226
(313) 256-9833          E-mail: dvanhoek@sado.org
Web: www.wlamfoundation.org/where.html#3

**Summary** To provide financial assistance to women enrolled at law schools in Michigan.

**Eligibility** This program is open to women enrolled full or part time at accredited law schools in Michigan. Applicants must be able to demonstrate 1) leadership capabilities; 2) community service in such areas as family law, child advocacy, or domestic violence; or 3) potential for advancing the position of women in society. Along with their application, they must submit law school transcripts, a detailed letter of interest explaining how they meet the award criteria, a resume, and up to 3 letters of recommendation.

**Financial data** The stipend is $1,500.

**Duration** 1 year.

**Additional information** The accredited law schools are the University of Michigan Law School, Wayne State University Law School, University of Detroit Mercy School of Law, Thomas M. Cooley Law School, and Michigan State University-Detroit College of Law.

**Number awarded** 9 each year.

**Deadline** October of each year.

## [977]
## WOMEN IN AVIATION MANAGEMENT SCHOLARSHIP

Women in Aviation, International
Attn: Scholarships
Morningstar Airport
3647 State Route 503 South
West Alexandria, OH 45381
(937) 558-7655                    Fax: (937) 839-4645
E-mail: scholarships@wai.org
Web: www.wai.org/education/scholarships.cfm

**Summary** To provide financial assistance to members of Women in Aviation, International (WAI) who are in an aviation management field and interested in attending leadership-related courses or seminars.

**Eligibility** This program is open to WAI members in an aviation management field who have exemplified the traits of leadership, community spirit, and volunteerism. They must be interested in attending a leadership-related course or seminar or participating in some other means of advancing their managerial position. Applicants should include a cover letter describing their current job position as well as their community involvement and volunteer work, along with a 1-page resume.

**Financial data** The stipend is $1,000.

**Additional information** WAI is a nonprofit professional organization dedicated to encouraging women to consider an aviation career, providing educational outreach activities, and providing networking opportunities to women active in the industry.

**Number awarded** 1 each year.

**Deadline** November of each year.

## [978]
## WOMEN IN CORPORATE AVIATION CAREER SCHOLARSHIP

Women in Aviation, International
Attn: Scholarships
Morningstar Airport
3647 State Route 503 South
West Alexandria, OH 45381
(937) 558-7655                    Fax: (937) 839-4645
E-mail: scholarships@wai.org
Web: www.wai.org/education/scholarships.cfm

**Summary** To provide financial assistance to members of Women in Aviation, International (WAI) who are interested in career development activities in corporate aviation.

**Eligibility** This program is open to WAI members interested in continued pursuit of a career in any job classification in corporate or business aviation. Applicants must be interested in participating in the NBAA Professional Development Program (PDP) courses, flight training, dispatcher training, upgrades in aviation education, or similar activities. General business course work is ineligible. Applicants should be actively working toward their goal and be able to show financial need.

**Financial data** The stipend is $1,000.

**Additional information** WAI is a nonprofit professional organization dedicated to encouraging women to consider an aviation career, providing educational outreach activi-

ties, and providing networking opportunities to women active in the industry.

**Number awarded** 1 each year.

**Deadline** November of each year.

## [979]
## WOMEN IN SCIENCE AND TECHNOLOGY SCHOLARSHIP

Business and Professional Women of Virginia
Attn: Virginia BPW Foundation
P.O. Box 4842
McLean, VA 22103-4842
Web: www.bpwva.org/scholarships.shtml

**Summary** To provide financial assistance to women in Virginia who are interested in working on a bachelor's or advanced degree in science or technology.

**Eligibility** This program is open to women who are at least 18 years of age, U.S. citizens, Virginia residents, accepted at or currently studying at a Virginia college or university, and working on a bachelor's, master's, or doctoral degree in 1 of the following fields: actuarial science, biology, bioengineering, chemistry, computer science, dentistry, engineering, mathematics, medicine, physics, or a similar scientific or technical field. Applicants must have a definite plan to use their education in a scientific or technical profession. They must be able to demonstrate financial need.

**Financial data** Stipends range from $500 to $1,000 per year, depending on the need of the recipient; funds may be used for tuition, fees, books, transportation, living expenses, and dependent care.

**Duration** 1 year; recipients may reapply (but prior recipients are not given priority).

**Additional information** Recipients must complete their studies within 2 years.

**Number awarded** At least 1 each year.

**Deadline** March of each year.

## [980]
## WOMEN IN SCIENCE GRANTS OF DELTA GAMMA

Delta Gamma Foundation
Attn: Director of Scholarships, Fellowships and Loans
3250 Riverside Drive
P.O. Box 21397
Columbus, OH 43221-0397
(614) 481-8169                    Fax: (614) 481-0133
E-mail: dgfoundation@deltagamma.org
Web: www.deltagamma.org

**Summary** To provide financial assistance to members of Delta Gamma sorority who are interested in working on a graduate degree in science.

**Eligibility** This program is open to dues-paying members of Delta Gamma who are currently enrolled in graduate school or will have completed their undergraduate work by June 30 of the year in which the fellowship is granted and will begin graduate study in the following fall. Applicants must be interested in working on a degree in science. They must include a 1- to 2-page essay in which they introduce themselves, including their career goals, their reasons for applying, and the impact Delta Gamma has had upon their life. Selection is based on scholastic excellence, potential for achievement, and contribution to their chosen field, campus, community, and Delta Gamma.

**Financial data** The stipend is $2,500.

**Duration** 1 year.

**Additional information** The fellowship is tenable at any accredited university in the United States or Canada. Graduate study may be pursued in any field.

**Number awarded** 1 or more each year.

**Deadline** March of each year.

## [981]
## WOMEN MILITARY AVIATORS MEMORIAL SCHOLARSHIP

Women in Aviation, International
Attn: Scholarships
Morningstar Airport
3647 State Route 503 South
West Alexandria, OH 45381
(937) 558-7655             Fax: (937) 839-4645
E-mail: scholarships@wai.org
Web: www.wai.org/education/scholarships.cfm

**Summary** To provide financial assistance to members of Women in Aviation, International (WAI) who are interested in flight training or academic study.

**Eligibility** This program is open to WAI members who are 1) academic students interested in a program of study at an accredited institution or school; or 2) flight students interested in training for an FAA private pilot rating. Applicants. must submit an application form, 3 letters of recommendation, a 500-word essay on their aviation dream and how they hope to use this scholarship to achieve it, a resume, and copies of all aviation and medical certificates. Selection is based on the applicant's ambition to further women in aviation, demonstrated persistence and determination, financial need, ability to complete training, and ability to bring honor to the women of Women Military Aviators, Inc. (WMA).

**Financial data** The stipend is $2,500.

**Duration** Recipients must be able to complete training within 1 year.

**Additional information** WAI is a nonprofit professional organization dedicated to encouraging women to consider an aviation career, providing educational outreach activities, and providing networking opportunities to women active in the industry. WMA established this program in 2005 to honor the women aviators who are serving or have served in Iraq and Afghanistan.

**Number awarded** 1 each year.

**Deadline** November of each year.

## [982]
## WOMEN'S BASKETBALL COACHES ASSOCIATION SCHOLARSHIP AWARDS

Women's Basketball Coaches Association
Attn: Manager of Awards
4646 Lawrenceville Highway
Lilburn, GA 30047-3620
(770) 279-8027, ext. 102        Fax: (770) 279-6290
E-mail: alowe@wbca.org
Web: www.wbca.org/WBCAScholarAward.asp

**Summary** To provide financial assistance for undergraduate or graduate study to women's basketball players.

**Eligibility** This program is open to women's basketball players who are competing in any of the 4 intercollegiate divisions (NCAA Divisions I, II, and III, and NAIA). Applicants must be interested in completing an undergraduate degree or beginning work on an advanced degree. They must be nominated by a member of the Women's Basketball Coaches Association (WBCA). Selection is based on sportsmanship, commitment to excellence as a student-athlete, honesty, ethical behavior, courage, and dedication to purpose.

**Financial data** The stipend is $1,000 per year.

**Duration** 1 year.

**Number awarded** 2 each year.

## [983]
## WOMEN'S BUSINESS ALLIANCE SCHOLARSHIP PROGRAM

Choice Hotels International
Attn: Foundation
10750 Columbia Pike
Silver Spring, MD 20901
(301) 592-6258
Web: www.choicehotels.com

**Summary** To provide financial assistance to women interested in preparing for a career in the hospitality industry.

**Eligibility** This program is open to female high school seniors, undergraduates, and graduate students. Applicants must be U.S. citizens or permanent residents interested in preparing for a career in the hospitality industry. They must submit an essay of 500 words or less on their experience or interest in the hospitality industry and how it relates to their career goals, including any community service experience that has impacted their career goals or their interest in the industry. Financial need is not considered in the selection process.

**Financial data** The stipend is $2,000.

**Duration** 1 year; recipients may reapply.

**Number awarded** 2 or more each year.

**Deadline** January or July of each year.

## [984]
## WOMEN'S ENVIRONMENTAL COUNCIL SCHOLARSHIPS

Women's Environmental Council
Attn: Scholarship Chair
P.O. Box 36
Solano Beach, CA 92075
E-mail: C2CEnvironmental@aol.com
Web: www.wecweb.org

**Summary**  To provide financial assistance to women from any state working on an undergraduate or graduate degree in an environmental field at colleges and universities in southern California.

**Eligibility**  This program is open to female undergraduate and graduate students at colleges and universities in Los Angeles, Orange, and San Diego counties in California. Applicants must be studying such environmental fields as architecture, biology, chemistry, environmental science, ecology, engineering, forestry, geology, or urban planning. They must have a GPA of 3.0 or higher. Along with their application, they must submit a personal statement that includes a description of their environmental commitment and activities, how they became interested in environmental issues, and how they plan to apply the knowledge they gain through the use of this scholarship to improve environmental conditions and pursue their environmental professional and personal goals. Selection is based on that statement (50%); personal incentive, volunteerism, and extracurricular activities (20%); grades and course work (20%); and a letter of references (10%).

**Financial data**  The stipend is $1,300. Recipients are also given a 1-year membership in the Women's Environmental Council (WEC).

**Duration**  1 year.

**Additional information**  The WEC, founded in 1993, currently has chapters in Los Angeles, Orange County, and San Diego. Recipients are expected to attend the WEC annual meeting in the spring to receive their awards.

**Number awarded**  Varies each year; recently, 6 of these scholarships were awarded.

**Deadline**  January of each year.

## [985]
## WOMEN'S TRANSPORTATION SEMINAR CHAPTER OF COLORADO ANNUAL SCHOLARSHIPS

Women's Transportation Seminar-Colorado Chapter
c/o Chris Proud, Scholarship Chair
CH2M Hill
9193 South Jamaica Street, South Building
Englewood, CO 80112
(720) 286-5702                     Fax: (720) 286-9732
E-mail: Chris.Proud@ch2m.com
Web: www.wtsinternational.org

**Summary**  To provide financial assistance to female undergraduate and graduate students in Colorado and Wyoming preparing for a career in transportation.

**Eligibility**  This program is open to women at colleges and universities in Colorado and Wyoming who are working on a bachelor's or graduate degree in a field related to transportation. Those fields may include engineering (civil, elec-

trical, or mechanical), urban planning, finance, aviation, transit, or railways. Applicants must submit an essay on their career goals after graduation and why they should receive this scholarship. Minorities are especially encouraged to apply.

**Financial data**  Undergraduate stipends are $1,000 or $800. Graduate stipends are $1,200.

**Duration**  1 year.

**Additional information**  Winners are also nominated for scholarships offered by the national organization of the Women's Transportation Seminar.

**Number awarded**  3 each year: 2 to undergraduates and 1 to a graduate student.

**Deadline**  November of each year.

## [986]
## WRITING SCHOLARSHIPS FOR MATURE WOMEN

National League of American Pen Women
1300 17th Street, N.W.
Washington, DC 20036-1973
(202) 785-1997                     Fax: (202) 452-8868
E-mail: nlapw1@verizon.net
Web: www.americanpenwomen.org

**Summary**  To provide financial assistance for education to mature women writers.

**Eligibility**  Women writers who are 35 years of age or older are eligible to apply if they (or their immediate family) are not affiliated with the league. They must submit an article, short story (up to 4,000 words), editorial, drama, TV script, 3 poems, or first chapter of novel and 10-page outline.

**Financial data**  The award is $1,000. Funds are to be used for education.

**Duration**  The award is granted biennially.

**Additional information**  These scholarships are presented in memory of Dr. Adeline Hoffman. An entry fee of $8 and a self-addressed stamped envelope must accompany each application.

**Number awarded**  1 each even-numbered year.

**Deadline**  January of even-numbered years.

## [987]
## WTS PUGET SOUND CHAPTER SCHOLARSHIP

Women's Transportation Seminar-Puget Sound Chapter
c/o Kristin Overleese, Scholarship Chair
City of Shoreline, Capital Projects Manager
17544 Midvale Avenue North
Shoreline, WA 98133-4821
(206) 546-1700                     Fax: (206) 546-2200
TDD: (206) 546-0457
Web: www.wtsinternational.org/puget_sound

**Summary**  To provide financial assistance to women undergraduate and graduate students from Washington who are working on a degree related to transportation and have financial need.

**Eligibility**  This program is open to women who are residents of Washington, studying at a college in the state, or working as an intern in the state. Applicants must be currently enrolled in an undergraduate or graduate degree program in a transportation-related field, such as engineering, planning, finance, or logistics. They must have a GPA of 3.0 or higher and plans to prepare for a career in a transportation-related field. Minority candidates are encouraged to apply. Along with their application, they must submit a 500-word statement about their career goals after graduation, their financial need, and why they think they should receive this scholarship award. Selection is based on transportation goals, academic record, transportation-related activities or job skills, and financial need.

**Financial data** The stipend is $1,500.

**Duration** 1 year.

**Additional information** The winner is also nominated for scholarships offered by the national organization of the Women's Transportation Seminar.

**Number awarded** 1 each year.

**Deadline** October of each year.

## [988]
## YOUNG LADIES' RADIO LEAGUE SCHOLARSHIP

Foundation for Amateur Radio, Inc.
Attn: Scholarship Committee
P.O. Box 831
Riverdale, MD 20738
E-mail: aa3of@arrl.net
Web: www.amateurradio-far.org/scholarships.php

**Summary** To provide funding to licensed radio amateurs (especially women) who are interested in earning a bachelor's or graduate degree in the United States.

**Eligibility** Applicants must have at least an FCC Technician Class or equivalent foreign authorization and intend to work on a bachelor's or graduate degree in the United States. There are no restrictions on the course of study or residency location. Preference is given to female applicants.

**Financial data** The stipend is $1,500.

**Duration** 1 year.

**Additional information** This program is sponsored by the Young Ladies' Radio League. It includes the following named scholarships: the Ethel Smith-K4LMB Memorial Scholarship and the Mary Lou Brown-NM7N Memorial Scholarship. Recipients must attend an accredited school (university, college, or technical institute) on a full-time basis.

**Number awarded** 2 each year.

**Deadline** Requests for applications must be submitted by April of each year.

## [989]
## ZAROUHI Y. GETSOYAN SCHOLARSHIP

Armenian International Women's Association
65 Main Street, Room 3A
Watertown, MA 02472
(617) 926-0171          E-mail: aiwainc@aol.com
Web: www.aiwa-net.org/scholarshipinfo.html

**Summary** To provide financial assistance to Armenian women who are upper-division and graduate students.

**Eligibility** This program is open to full-time women students of Armenian descent attending an accredited college or university. Applicants must be full-time juniors, seniors, or graduate students with a GPA of 3.2 or higher. They must

submit an essay, up to 500 words, describing their planned academic program, their career goals, and the reasons why they believe they should be awarded this scholarship. Selection is based on financial need and merit.

**Financial data** The stipend is $500.

**Duration** 1 year.

**Number awarded** 1 or more each year.

**Deadline** April of each year.

## [990]
## ZETA PHI BETA GENERAL GRADUATE FELLOWSHIPS

Zeta Phi Beta Sorority, Inc.
Attn: National Education Foundation
1734 New Hampshire Avenue, N.W.
Washington, DC 20009
(202) 387-3103          Fax: (202) 232-4593
E-mail: scholarship@ZPhiBNEF.org
Web: www.zphib1920.org/nef

**Summary** To provide financial assistance to women who are working on a professional degree, master's degree, doctorate, or postdoctoral studies.

**Eligibility** Women graduate or postdoctoral students are eligible to apply if they have achieved distinction or shown promise of distinction in their chosen fields. Applicants need not be members of Zeta Phi Beta. They must submit 3 letters of recommendation, university transcripts, a 150-word essay on their educational and professional goals, and information on financial need.

**Financial data** The stipend ranges up to $2,500, paid directly to the recipient.

**Duration** 1 academic year; may be renewed.

**Additional information** Information is also available from Cheryl Williams, National Second Vice President, 6322 Bocage Drive, Shreveport, LA 71119.

**Deadline** January of each year.

## [991]
## ZETA STATE SCHOLARSHIP

Delta Kappa Gamma Society International-Zeta State Organization
Attn: Scholarship Committee
875 William Boulevard, Apartment 305
Ridgeland, MS 39157
Web: www.deltakappagamma.org/MS

**Summary** To provide financial assistance to members of Delta Kappa Gamma Society International in Mississippi who are interested in working on a graduate degree in education.

**Eligibility** This program is open to members of Delta Kappa Gamma (an honorary society of women educators) in Mississippi. Applicants must be currently employed as a teacher in the state. They must be planning to work on a graduate degree. Selection is based primarily on participation in society activities.

**Financial data** A stipend is awarded (amount not specified).

**Duration** 1 year.

**Additional information** This program includes the Amanda Lowther Scholarship.

**Number awarded** 1 or more each year.

**Deadline** January of each year.

## [992]
## ZETA TAU ALPHA FOUNDERS GRANTS

Zeta Tau Alpha Foundation, Inc.
Attn: Director of Foundation Administration
3450 Founders Road
Indianapolis, IN 46268
(317) 872-0540          Fax: (317) 876-3948
E-mail: zetataualpha@zetataualpha.org
Web: www.zetataualpha.org

**Summary** To provide financial assistance to graduate women who are alumnae of Zeta Tau Alpha.

**Eligibility** This program is open to graduate students who have been members of Zeta Tau Alpha. Applicants must be able to demonstrate leadership abilities, academic achievement, and financial need. Selection is based on academic achievement (GPA of 2.75 or higher), involvement in campus and community activities, recommendations, current class status, and financial need.

**Financial data** The stipend is $6,000.

**Duration** 1 year; renewable.

**Number awarded** 9 each year.

**Deadline** March of each year.

## [993]
## ZETA TAU ALPHA SERVICE SCHOLARSHIPS

Zeta Tau Alpha Foundation, Inc.
Attn: Director of Foundation Administration
3450 Founders Road
Indianapolis, IN 46268
(317) 872-0540          Fax: (317) 876-3948
E-mail: zetataualpha@zetataualpha.org
Web: www.zetataualpha.org

**Summary** To provide financial assistance for study in specified fields to women who are alumnae of Zeta Tau Alpha.

**Eligibility** This program is open to graduate students who have been members of Zeta Tau Alpha. Applicants must be studying special education, social work, or other health-related professions. Selection is based on academic achievement (GPA of 2.75 or higher), involvement in campus and community activities, recommendations, current class status, and financial need.

**Financial data** The stipend is at least $1,000.

**Duration** 1 year; renewable.

**Number awarded** Varies each year. Annually, the foundation provides nearly $150,000 in scholarships and fellowships for undergraduate and graduate study.

**Deadline** March of each year.

# Loans

Described here are 39 programs designed primarily or exclusively for women that provide money which must eventually be repaid—in cash or in service and with or without interest. If you are looking for a particular program and don't find it here, be sure to check the Program Title Index to see if it is covered elsewhere in the *Directory*.

## [994]
## AIR FORCE AID SOCIETY EMERGENCY FINANCIAL ASSISTANCE

Air Force Aid Society
Attn: Financial Assistance Department
241 18th Street South, Suite 202
Arlington, VA 22202-3409
(703) 607-3072, ext. 51    Toll-free: (800) 429-9475
Web: www.afas.org/body_financial.htm

**Summary** To provide loans and grants-in-aid to current and former Air Force personnel and their families who are facing emergency situations.

**Eligibility** This program is open to active-duty Air Force members and their dependents, retired Air Force personnel and their dependents, Air National Guard and Air Force Reserve personnel on extended duty over 30 days, and spouses and dependent age children of deceased Air Force personnel who died on active duty or in retired status. Applicants must be facing problems, usually for relatively short periods, that affect their job or the essential quality and dignity of life the Air Force wants for its people. Examples of such needs include basic living expenses (food, rent, utilities), medical care, dental care, funeral expenses, vehicle repairs, disasters, or pay/allotment problems. Funding is generally not provided if it merely postpones a long-term inability to exist on present pay and allowances, for non-essentials, for continuing long-term assistance commitments, or to replace funds due to garnishment.

**Financial data** Assistance is provided as an interest-free loan, a grant, or a combination of both.

**Number awarded** Varies each year.

**Deadline** Applications may be submitted at any time.

## [995]
## ALASKA STATE VETERANS INTEREST RATE PREFERENCE

Alaska Housing Finance Corporation
Attn: Communications Officer
4300 Boniface Parkway
P.O. Box 101020
Anchorage, AK 99510-1020
(907) 330-8447   Toll-free: (800) 478-AHFC (within AK)
Fax: (907) 338-9218
Web: www.ahfc.state.ak.us

**Summary** To provide Alaskan veterans and their spouses with lower interest rates on loans to purchase housing.

**Eligibility** This program is open to Alaska residents who served at least 90 days on active duty in the U.S. armed forces after April 6, 1917 and received an honorable discharge. Also eligible are 1) honorably-discharged members of the Alaska Army or Air National Guard who served at least 5 years; 2) honorably discharged Reservists who served at least 5 years; and 3) widows and widowers of qualified veterans. Members of the military currently serving on active duty are not eligible. Applicants must be proposing to purchase an owner-occupied single-family residence, condominium, unit within a PUD, duplex, triplex, fourplex, or Type I mobile home using Alaska's taxable, tax-exempt, taxable first-time home buyer, rural owner, or non-conforming programs. Their family income may not exceed specified limits that depend on location within the state and size of family.

**Financial data** Qualified veterans and widow(er)s receive a 1% rate reduction on the first $50,000 of the loan amount.

**Duration** Loans are for either 15 years or 30 years.

**Additional information** Recently, income limits ranged from $28,050 to $36,750 for families with 1 person, from $32,050 to $42,000 for families with 2 persons, from $36,050 to $47,250 for families with 3 persons, and from $40,100 to $52,500 for families with 4 or more persons.

**Number awarded** Varies each year.

## [996]
## ARMY AVIATION ASSOCIATION OF AMERICA LOAN PROGRAM

Army Aviation Association of America
Attn: AAAA Scholarship Foundation
755 Main Street, Suite 4D
Monroe, CT 06468-2830
(203) 268-2450    Fax: (203) 268-5870
E-mail: aaaa@quad-a.org
Web: www.quad-a.org/scholarship.htm

**Summary** To provide educational loans to members of the Army Aviation Association of America (AAAA) and their relatives.

**Eligibility** This program is open to AAAA members and their spouses, unmarried siblings, and unmarried children. Applicants must be enrolled or accepted for enrollment as an undergraduate or graduate student at an accredited college or university.

**Financial data** The maximum loan is $1,000 per year. All loans are interest free.

**Duration** Up to 4 years.

**Number awarded** Varies each year.

**Deadline** April of each year.

## [997]
## ARMY EMERGENCY RELIEF LOANS/GRANTS

Army Emergency Relief
200 Stovall Street
Alexandria, VA 22332-0600
(703) 428-0000    Toll-free: (866) 878-0000
Fax: (703) 325-7183    E-mail: aer@aerhq.org
Web: www.aerhq.org

**Summary** To provide loans and grants-in-aid to help with the emergency financial need of veterans, military personnel, and their dependents.

**Eligibility** Eligible to apply are active-duty soldiers (single or married) and their dependents, Army National Guard and Army Reserve soldiers on continuous active duty for more than 30 days and their dependents, soldiers retired from active duty for longevity or physical disability and their dependents, Army National Guard and Army Reserve soldiers who retired at age 60 and their dependents, and surviving spouses and orphans of soldiers who died while on active duty or after they retired. Applicants must be seeking assistance for such emergency needs as food, rent, and utilities; emergency transportation and vehicle repair; funeral expenses; medical and dental expenses; or personal needs when pay is delayed or stolen. Support is not available to help pay for nonessentials, finance ordinary leave or vacation, pay fines or legal expenses, help liquidate or consolidate debt, assist with house purchase or home improvements, cover bad checks, pay credit card bills, or help purchase, rent, or lease a vehicle.

**Financial data** Support is provided in the form of loans or grants (or a combination).

**Duration** Qualifying individuals can apply whenever they have a valid emergency need.

**Additional information** Since it was established in 1942, the organization has helped more than 2 million qualifying individuals with more than $882 million in financial assistance.

**Number awarded** Varies each year; recently, the organization helped 53,865 Army people with more than $41 million, including $29 million to active-duty soldiers and their families, $3.9 million to retired soldiers and their families, and $1.3 million to widow(er)s and orphans of deceased soldiers.

**Deadline** Applications may be submitted at any time.

## [998]
## CALIFORNIA JOB'S DAUGHTERS EDUCATIONAL LOAN FUND

International Order of Job's Daughters-Grand Guardian
    Council of California
Attn: Patricia Mosier, Grand Secretary
303 West Lincoln, Suite 210
Anaheim, CA 92805-2928
(714) 535-4575           Fax: (714) 991-6798
E-mail: GrSecCAiojd@aol.com
Web: www.caiojd.rg

**Summary** To provide loans for college to members of the International Order of Job's Daughters in California.

**Eligibility** This program is open to members of Job's Daughters in good standing, active or majority, in California. An applicant must submit a loan application signed by the Bethel Guardian of her Bethel, a promissory note signed by herself and her parents or 2 other responsible adults as cosigners, and verification of her enrollment in an approved educational institution.

**Financial data** Loans up to $750 per year are available. Repayment begins 5 years from the date of the note or 120 days after the applicant completes her education, whichever date occurs first.

**Duration** 1 year; may be renewed.

**Number awarded** Varies each year.

**Deadline** Applications may be submitted at any time, but they must be received at least 60 days but not more than 4 months prior to the date the loan is desired.

## [999]
## CALVET HOME IMPROVEMENT LOAN PROGRAM

California Department of Veterans Affairs
Attn: Division of Farm and Home Purchases
1227 O Street, Room 200
P.O. Box 942895
Sacramento, CA 94295-0001
(916) 653-2525  Toll-free: (800) 952-LOAN (within CA)
Fax: (916) 653-2401         TDD: (800) 324-5966
E-mail: Kenn.Capps@cdva.ca.gov
Web: www.cdva.ca.gov/calvet/improve.asp

**Summary** To enable current holders of CalVet Loans to obtain additional funding for home improvements.

**Eligibility** This program is open to active CalVet contract holders, including unremarried spouses of military personnel who died while on active duty or were designated a prisoner of war or missing in action. The basic CalVet contract must have at least 3 remaining months. Applicants must have a good payment record on the basic CalVet loan. Loans are available to improve the basic livability of the home or property; increase the energy efficiency of the home; perform general maintenance such as painting, reroofing, and general repairs; add living space; renovate baths, kitchens, plumbing and electrical systems; install or update heating or air conditioning systems; install insulation, weather stripping, or thermal windows; add a garage, fence, landscaping, flatwork, retaining wall, or septic system; or connect to public utilities with water, sewer, or electrical lines from the property line to the dwelling. Unacceptable are improvements for recreational or entertainment purposes (such as swimming pools, saunas, hot tubs, pool houses, cabanas, or tennis courts) and improvements to farm property for the purpose of increasing agricultural productivity.

**Financial data** Loans are available up to 90% of loan to value on "improved value," ranging from $15,000 (for veterans whose service was entirely during peacetime) to $50,000 (for veterans who service included at least 1 day during a qualifying wartime period, even though none of the service was in the theater of operations). A loan origination fee of 1.5% of the loan amount is charged. Recently, the interest rate was 5.15% or 5.5%, depending on the source of funding for the loans.

**Duration** The maximum loan term is 10 years for loans up to $15,000, 12 years for loans up to $20,000, and 15 years for loans up to $50,000.

**Number awarded** Varies each year.

**Deadline** Applications may be submitted at any time.

## [1000]
## CHAMBERLIN LOAN FUND

American Association of University Women-Buffalo
    Branch
Attn: Chamberlin Loan Fund
P.O. Box 397
Amherst, NY 14226-0397
(716) 885-2486    E-mail: chamberlinfund@yahoo.com
Web: www.aauw.buffalo.edu/edu.htm

**Summary** To provide educational loans to women from New York, working on an undergraduate or graduate degree.

**Eligibility** This program is open to women who have completed at least 1 year of college or are enrolled in a graduate or professional school. Women enrolled in a 2-year program must be planning to continue toward a baccalaureate degree. Students interested in foreign study must be enrolled in a credit-granting program recognized by their college or university. Preference is given to residents of western New York and students at Cornell University. Selection is based on financial need and potential to repay the loan. Personal interviews are required.

**Financial data** The maximum loan is $2,500 per year. Loans must be repaid within 4 years, but no interest is charged.

**Duration** 1 year; may be renewed.

**Additional information** This program was established in 1937.

**Number awarded** Varies each year.

**Deadline** May or November of each year.

## [1001]
## COUNT-ME-IN LOANS

Count-Me-In
240 Central Park, Suite 7H
New York, NY 10019
(212) 245-1236          Fax: (347) 438-3235
E-mail: info@count-me-in.org
Web: www.count-me-in.org

**Summary** To provide business loans to women.

**Eligibility** This program is open to women seeking to borrow money for business purposes. Applicants must be interested in borrowing money for working capital, purchase of inventory or equipment, marketing materials for a sales event, or any other purpose that helps the business generate cash. They may not be applying for loans for gambling, in-home day care, multi-level marketing ventures, or to purchase real estate. Priority is given to applications for businesses that already exist.

**Financial data** Small business loans range from $500 to $10,000, although first loans must be $5,000 or less. The interest rate ranges from 10 to 15%. Second loans range up to $10,000.

**Duration** Terms for the loan range from 6 months to 60 months, depending upon the amount of the loan. All first loans must be repaid in 18 months or less. Each time a loan is repaid in full, the recipient may borrow again.

**Additional information** If applicants are denied a loan, the sponsor provides some suggestions about what they can do to improve their ability to qualify in the future. The funds for these loans come from contributions women and men make to the web site; currently, the site has raised over $1 million from contributions that average $15 each. The application fee is $25.

**Number awarded** Varies each year; recently, 40 of these loans were issued.

**Deadline** Applications may be submitted at any time.

## [1002]
## DELTA GAMMA ALUMNAE STUDENT LOANS

Delta Gamma Foundation
Attn: Director of Scholarships, Fellowships and Loans
3250 Riverside Drive
P.O. Box 21397
Columbus, OH 43221-0397
(614) 481-8169          Fax: (614) 481-0133
E-mail: ernieh@deltagamma.org
Web: www.deltagamma.org/ed_loans.shtml

**Summary** To provide educational loans to alumnae of Delta Gamma sorority who are working on a graduate degree.

**Eligibility** Loans are available only to graduate students who are alumnae of the sorority. Applicants must submit a letter stating the intended purpose of the loan, indicating need and a willingness to accept the financial obligation of the loan; a statement regarding payment of Delta Gamma alumna dues; a completed application with a co-signer statement; an official transcript or proof of recent acceptance into a degree program; and 3 letters of recommendation, from 1) the president of the alumnae group or a Delta Gamma friend; 2) a recent employer, faculty member, or faculty adviser; and 3) a Delta Gamma friend who will always know the applicant's address.

**Financial data** Loans do not exceed $2,000 per year. Repayment must begin 3 months after graduation or leaving school and consists of 25 monthly payments of $80 each. If a payment delinquency occurs, interest at the rate of 6% is charged on the principal balance owed.

**Duration** 1 year. Borrowers may have only 1 loan at a time.

**Number awarded** Varies each year.

**Deadline** Applications may be submitted at any time.

## [1003]
## DELTA GAMMA COLLEGIATE STUDENT LOANS

Delta Gamma Foundation
Attn: Director of Scholarships, Fellowships and Loans
3250 Riverside Drive
P.O. Box 21397
Columbus, OH 43221-0397
(614) 481-8169          Fax: (614) 481-0133
E-mail: ernieh@deltagamma.org
Web: www.deltagamma.org/ed_loans.shtml

**Summary** To provide loans to current members of Delta Gamma sorority who need money to complete their college education.

**Eligibility** Loans are available only to upper-division women who are members of the sorority. Applicants must submit a letter stating the intended purpose of the loan, indicating need and a willingness to accept the financial obligation of the loan; a completed application with a co-signer statement; an official transcript; and 4 letters of recommendation from 1) the advisory team chair, 2) the chapter vice president for finance affirming membership in good standing, 3) a faculty member, and 4) a Delta Gamma friend who will always know the applicant's address.

**Financial data** Loans do not exceed $2,000 per year. Repayment must begin 3 months after graduation or departure from school and consists of 25 monthly payments of

$80 each. If a payment delinquency occurs, interest at the rate of 6% is charged on the principal balance owed.

**Duration** 1 year. Borrowers may have only 1 loan at a time.

**Number awarded** Varies each year.

**Deadline** Applications may be submitted at any time.

## [1004]
## DIRECT LOANS FOR SOCIALLY DISADVANTAGED FARMERS AND RANCHERS

Department of Agriculture
Farm Service Agency
Attn: Office of Minority and Socially Disadvantaged
    Farmers Assistance
1400 Independence Avenue, S.W.
Washington, DC 20250-0568
(202) 720-1584          Toll-free: (866) 538-2610
Fax: (202) 690-3432          Fax: (888) 211-7286
E-mail: msda@wdc.usda.gov
Web: www.fsa.usda.gov

**Summary** To lend money to eligible members of socially disadvantaged groups for the purchase or operation of family-size farms or ranches.

**Eligibility** For the purposes of this program, a "socially disadvantaged group" is 1 whose members "have been subjected to racial, ethnic, or gender prejudice because of their identity as members of a group without regard to their individual qualities." Those groups are women, African Americans, American Indians, Alaskan Natives, Hispanics, Asian Americans, and Pacific Islanders. Applicants may be seeking either farm ownership loans (to purchase or enlarge a farm or ranch, purchase easements or rights of way needed in the farm's operation, erect or improve buildings such as a dwelling or barn, promote soil and water conservation, or pay closing costs) or farm operating loans (to purchase livestock, poultry, farm and home equipment, feed, seed, fertilizer, chemicals, hail and other crop insurance, food, clothing, medical care, and hired labor). Loans are made to individuals, partnerships, joint operations, corporations, and cooperatives primarily and directly engaged in farming and ranching on family-size operations; a family-size farm is defined as a farm that a family can operate and manage itself. In addition to belonging to a "socially disadvantaged group," borrowers must have a satisfactory history of meeting credit obligations, have 3 years of experience in operating a farm or ranch for an ownership loan or 1 year's experience within the last 5 years for an operating loan, be a U.S. citizen or legal resident, possess the legal capacity to incur the obligations of a loan or credit sale, and be unable to obtain sufficient credit elsewhere at reasonable rates.

**Financial data** The maximum loan is $200,000. Interest rates are set periodically according to the federal government's cost of borrowing; recently, the rate for ownership loans was 5.5% and for operating loans it was 5.25%.

**Duration** Repayment terms are generally up to 40 years for ownership loans or 1 to 7 years for operating loans.

**Deadline** Applications may be submitted at any time.

## [1005]
## DISABLED AMERICAN VETERANS AUXILIARY NATIONAL EDUCATION LOAN FUND

Disabled American Veterans Auxiliary
Attn: National Education Loan Fund Director
3725 Alexandria Pike
Cold Spring, KY 41076
(606) 441-7300          Fax: (606) 442-2095
Web: www.dav.org/dava/index.html

**Summary** To provide loans for college to women who are members of the Disabled American Veterans Auxiliary or to their children or grandchildren.

**Eligibility** This loan fund is open to women who are paid life members of the auxiliary and to their children and grandchildren. Applicants must be enrolled full time in a college, university, or vocational school. They must demonstrate academic achievement and financial need.

**Financial data** A maximum of $2,000 per year is loaned, payable to the school. The loan is to be repaid within 7 years in installments of at least $100 per month. Repayment must begin upon graduation or leaving school. No interest is charged.

**Duration** The loan is renewable each year for up to 4 consecutive years, provided the student maintains full-time status and a GPA of 2.0 or higher.

**Number awarded** Varies; generally, 15 each year.

**Deadline** February of each year.

## [1006]
## DOT SHORT TERM LENDING PROGRAM

Department of Transportation
Attn: Office of Small and Disadvantaged Business
    Utilization
400 Seventh Street, S.W., S-40
Washington, DC 20590
(202) 366-2852     Toll-free: (800) 532-1169, ext. 65343
Fax: (202) 366-7538
Web: www.osdbuweb.dot.gov

**Summary** To loan short-term working capital for transportation-related projects to Disadvantaged Business Enterprises (DBE).

**Eligibility** This program is open to small businesses (as defined by the Small Business Administration) that are also either an 8(a) firm certified by the Small Business Administration or a DBE certified by the Department of Transportation (DOT). Owners of DBEs are either 1) women or 2) economically or socially disadvantaged individuals, defined as Black Americans; Hispanic Americans (Mexicans, Puerto Ricans, Cubans, Central or South Americans, or others of Spanish or Portuguese culture or origin); Native Americans (American Indians, Eskimos, Aleuts, and Native Hawaiians); Asia Pacific Americans (persons with origins from Japan, China, Taiwan, Macau, Hong Kong, Korea, Burma, Vietnam, Laos, Cambodia, Thailand, Malaysia, Indonesia, Brunei, the Philippines, Samoa, Guam, the Commonwealth of the Northern Mariana Islands, Fiji, Tonga, Kiribati, Juvalu, Nauru, Federated States of Micronesia, or the U.S. Trust Territories of the Pacific Islands); and subcontinent Asian Americans (persons with origins from India, Pakistan, Bhutan, the Maldives Islands, Nepal, Sri Lanka, and Bangladesh). Firms must possess a transportation-related contract which supports the application to finance accounts receivables.

**Financial data** The amount loaned varies, up to a maximum of $500,000; most loans have ranged from $100,00 to $200,000. Interest is charged at the current New York Prime Rate.

**Duration** Normally, loans must be repayable in 1 year; in exceptional cases, a 2-year loan may be approved.

**Additional information** This program is a public/private partnership, under which DOT provides up to 75% of the funding for each line-of-credit and 1 of 6 participating banks provides the balance of the financing and administers the line-of-credit. Currently, the 6 participating banks are Premier Bank of Denver, Continental National Bank of Miami, Harbor Bank of (Baltimore) Maryland, Adams National Bank of Washington, D.C., Lone Star National Bank of Pharr, Texas, and Seaway National Bank of Chicago.

**Number awarded** Varies each year; recently, 18 of these loans were approved, for a total of $7,642,213.

**Deadline** Applications may be submitted at any time.

## [1007]
## E.K. WISE LOAN PROGRAM

American Occupational Therapy Association
Attn: Membership Department
4720 Montgomery Lane
P.O. Box 31220
Bethesda, MD 20824-1220
(301) 652-2682     Toll-free: (800) 729-2682, ext. 2760
Fax: (301) 652-7711          TDD: (800) 377-8555
Web: www.aota.org/featured/area2/links/link23.asp

**Summary** To provide loans to women enrolled in advanced standing courses in occupational therapy.

**Eligibility** Applicants must be women who are U.S. citizens or permanent residents entering an entry-level master's program in occupational therapy or a post-professional master's curriculum in occupational therapy. They must plan to seek future employment in occupational therapy and must be members of the American Occupational Therapy Association throughout the period of the loan. U.S. citizenship or permanent resident status is required.

**Financial data** The maximum loan is $5,000. The loan must be repaid within 3 years after graduation or earlier should the recipient withdraw from the approved course of study before graduating.

**Duration** 1 year; this is a 1-time loan.

**Additional information** This fund was established in 1969.

**Number awarded** Up to 20 each year.

**Deadline** Applications may be submitted at any time.

## [1008]
## GILLETTE HAYDEN MEMORIAL FUND LOAN PROGRAM

American Association of Women Dentists
216 West Jackson Boulevard, Suite 625
Chicago, IL 60606
Toll-free: (800) 920-AAWD          Fax: (312) 750-1203
E-mail: info@aawd.org
Web: www.aawd.org

**Summary** To provide low-interest loans to promising women dental students.

**Eligibility** Eligible to apply are women dental students exhibiting financial need who are juniors, seniors, or graduate students. Selection is based on scholarship, need for assistance, and reasons for and amount of indebtedness already accumulated.

**Financial data** Loans are made up to $2,000. Interest at 8% begins 1 month after graduation. The note is due and payable 13 months after graduation.

**Number awarded** Varies, depending upon available funds; generally ranges from 2 to 6 each year.

**Deadline** July of each year.

## [1009]
## GUARANTEED LOANS FOR SOCIALLY DISADVANTAGED FARMERS AND RANCHERS

Department of Agriculture
Farm Service Agency
Attn: Office of Minority and Socially Disadvantaged
    Farmers Assistance
1400 Independence Avenue, S.W.
Washington, DC 20250-0568
(202) 720-1584          Toll-free: (866) 538-2610
Fax: (202) 690-3432          Fax: (888) 211-7286
E-mail: msda@wdc.usda.gov
Web: www.fsa.usda.gov

**Summary** To guarantee loans to eligible members of socially disadvantaged groups for the purchase or operation of family-size farms or ranches.

**Eligibility** For the purposes of this program, a "socially disadvantaged group" is 1 whose members "have been subjected to racial, ethnic, or gender prejudice because of their identity as members of a group without regard to their individual qualities." Those groups are women, African Americans, American Indians, Alaskan Natives, Hispanic Americans, Asian Americans, and Pacific Islanders. Applicants may be seeking guarantees of loans either for farm ownership (to purchase or enlarge a farm or ranch, purchase easements or rights of way needed in the farm's operation, erect or improve buildings such as a dwelling or barn, promote soil and water conservation, or pay closing costs) or farm operation (to purchase livestock, poultry, farm and home equipment, feed, seed, fertilizer, chemicals, hail and other crop insurance, food, clothing, medical care, and hired labor). Guarantees are provided on loans by lending institutions subject to federal or state supervision. Loans are made to individuals, partnerships, joint operations, corporations, and cooperatives primarily and directly engaged in farming and ranching on family-size operations; a family-size farm is defined as a farm that a family can operate and manage itself. In addition to belonging to a "socially disadvantaged group," borrowers must have an acceptable credit history, not have caused the Farm Service Agency (FSA) a loss by receiving debt forgiveness on more than 3 occasions, be the owner or tenant operator of a family farm, be a U.S. citizen or legal resident, possess the legal capacity to incur the obligations of a loan or credit sale, and be unable to obtain a loan without a guarantee.

**Financial data** The size of the loan is agreed upon by the borrower and the lender, but the maximum indebtedness in guaranteed loans of the Farm Service Agency (FSA) may not exceed $899,000. Interest rates can be fixed or variable, as agreed upon by the borrower and the lender, but they may not exceed the rate the lender charges its average farm customer. In most cases, FSA guarantees up to 90% of the loan principal and interest against loss. Guarantees up to 95% are available if 1) the purpose of the loan is to refinance direct FSA farm credit debt, or 2) the loan is made to a beginning farmer to participate in the beginning farmer down payment loan program or a qualifying state beginning farmer program.

**Duration** Repayment terms are generally up to 40 years for ownership loans or 1 to 7 years for operating loans.

**Deadline** Applications may be submitted at any time.

## [1010]
## HAZEL E. RITCHEY LOANS
Sigma Alpha Iota Philanthropies, Inc.
One Tunnel Road
Asheville, NC 28805
(828) 251-0606                    Fax: (828) 251-0644
E-mail: philonline@sai-national.org
Web: www.sai-national.org/phil/philhazl.html

**Summary** To provide loans for educational purposes to members of Sigma Alpha Iota (an organization of women musicians).

**Eligibility** Members of the organization may apply if they are enrolled as graduate or undergraduate students. They may be seeking funds to support education leading to an undergraduate or graduate degree in music, to purchase a new musical instrument, for study at a summer musical festival in the United States or abroad, or for special applied music lessons or coaching.

**Financial data** The maximum loans are $2,500. The interest rate is 5% and must be paid while the recipient is still in school. Repayment of principal begins immediately upon graduation and must be completed within 2 year.

**Duration** 1 year; may be renewed for 2 additional years while the recipient is in school and has begun payment of interest.

**Additional information** This program was established in 1927.

**Number awarded** Varies each year.

**Deadline** Applications may be submitted at any time.

## [1011]
## KAPPA ALPHA THETA STUDENT LOANS
Kappa Alpha Theta
Attn: Student Loan Fund
8740 Founders Road
Indianapolis, IN 46268-1337
(317) 876-1870, ext. 123
Toll-free: (888) 526-1870, ext. 123
Fax: (317) 876-1925
E-mail: myoung@kappaalphatheta.org
Web: www.kappaalphatheta.org

**Summary** To provide loans to members of Kappa Alpha Theta (the first Greek letter fraternity for women) who have encountered financial difficulties in the pursuit of their degrees.

**Eligibility** Loans are available to initiated undergraduate members of Kappa Alpha Theta in Canada and the United States who are experiencing financial difficulties in the pursuit of their university degrees. Preference is given to junior and senior members. Loans are granted on the basis of financial need, scholastic achievement, and contribution to the fraternity and the university.

**Financial data** Loans are granted up to a lifetime maximum of $2,500. The interest rate currently is 8%. The first interest payment is due 1 year from the date the loan is granted and again on that date until the loan is amortized and monthly interest and principal payments begin (generally 6 months after graduation).

**Number awarded** Varies each year.

**Deadline** January of each year.

## [1012]
## MARY BARRETT MARSHALL STUDENT LOAN FUND
American Legion Auxiliary
Attn: Department of Kentucky
105 North Public Square
P.O. Box 189
Greensburg, KY 42743-1530
(270) 932-7533                    Fax: (270) 932-7672
E-mail: secretarykyala@aol.com

**Summary** To provide loans to female dependents or descendants of veterans who need financial assistance to attend college in Kentucky.

**Eligibility** This program is open to the daughters, wives, sisters, widows, granddaughters, or great-granddaughters of veterans eligible for membership in the American Legion. Applicants must be high school graduates with financial need, 5-year residents of Kentucky, and planning to attend college in Kentucky.

**Financial data** Loans may be made up to $800 per year. Funds may be used for books, tuition, and laboratory fees, but not for room and board. Repayment begins after graduation or upon securing employment, with monthly payments of the principal but no interest for 5 years, after which interest is 6%.

**Duration** 1 year; renewable.

**Additional information** Further information is also available from Chair, Velma Greenleaf, 1448 Leafdale Road, Hodgenville, KY 42748-9379, (270) 358-3341.

**Number awarded** Varies each year.

## [1013]
## MEDICAL EDUCATION LOAN PROGRAM

American Medical Women's Association Foundation
Attn: AMWA Foundation
211 North Union Street, Suite 100
Alexandria, VA 22314
(703) 838-0500          Fax: (703) 549-3864
E-mail: foundation@amwa-doc.org
Web: www.amwa-doc.org

**Summary**   To provide loans to student members of the American Medical Women's Association.

**Eligibility**   Loans are available to women enrolled in medical or osteopathic medicine schools in their mid-first, second, or third year. Applicants must be student members of the association and U.S. citizens or permanent residents.

**Financial data**   Loans are either $2,500 or $5,000 per year; the maximum loan total during medical school is $5,000. Loans must be repaid in 3 annual installments, beginning 1 year after graduation. The interest rate is 5% and starts December following graduation.

**Duration**   Loans are available every year. If a recipient maintains a good GPA, application for additional loans will receive preferred attention.

**Number awarded**   Varies each year.

**Deadline**   April of each year.

## [1014]
## MISSISSIPPI VETERANS' MORTGAGE LOAN PROGRAM

Mississippi Veterans' Home Purchase Board
3466 Highway 80 East
P.O. Box 54111
Pearl, MS 39288-4411
(601) 576-4800          Fax: (601) 576-4812
E-mail: vhpbinfo@vhpb.state.ms.us
Web: www.vhpb.state.ms.us

**Summary**   To provide loans to veterans, their widow(er)s, and selected military personnel who are interested in purchasing or constructing a house in Mississippi.

**Eligibility**   This program is open to honorably-discharged veterans who were Mississippi residents prior to entering military service or have been residents for at least 2 consecutive years prior to applying for a loan. Reserve and National Guard personnel who currently serve and have at least 7 years of service are also eligible. Active-duty military personnel are eligible if they meet the residency requirements. The unmarried surviving spouse of an eligible veteran who died as a result of service or service-connected injuries also qualifies, as does the unremarried spouse of an eligible veteran who has not purchased a home since the veteran's death. Applicants must be planning to purchase an existing single family home in Mississippi or to construct a new home in the state. Farms, raw land, mobile homes, and condominiums do not qualify.

**Financial data**   This program provides low-interest mortgage loans in amounts up to $195,000. Interest rates are fixed and are generally 1 to 2 percentage points below market rates.

**Duration**   Available terms are 10, 15, 20, 25, and 30 years.

**Number awarded**   Varies each year.

**Deadline**   Applications may be submitted at any time.

## [1015]
## NATIONAL INSTITUTES OF HEALTH UNDERGRADUATE SCHOLARSHIP PROGRAM

National Institutes of Health
Attn: Office of Loan Repayment and Scholarship
2 Center Drive, Room 2E24
Bethesda, MD 20892-0230
Toll-free: (800) 528-7689          Fax: (301) 480-5481
TTY: (888) 352-3001          E-mail: ugsp@nih.gov
Web: ugsp.info.nih.gov

**Summary**   To provide loans-for-service for undergraduate education in the life sciences to students from disadvantaged backgrounds.

**Eligibility**   This program is open to U.S. citizens, nationals, and permanent residents who are enrolled or accepted for enrollment as full-time students at accredited institutions of higher education and committed to careers in biomedical, behavioral, and social science health-related research. Applicants must come from a family that meets federal standards of low income, currently defined as a family with an annual income below $18,620 for a 1-person family, ranging to below $63,140 for families of 8 or more. They must have a GPA of 3.5 or higher or be in the top 5% of their class. Selection is based on commitment to a career in biomedical, behavioral, or social science health-related research as an employee of the National Institutes of Health (NIH); academic achievements; recommendations and evaluations of skills, abilities, and goals; and relevant extracurricular activities. Applicants are ranked according to the following priorities: first, juniors and seniors who have completed 2 years of undergraduate course work including 4 core science courses in biology, chemistry, physics, and calculus; second, other undergraduates who have completed those 4 core science courses; third, freshmen and sophomores at accredited undergraduate institutions; and fourth, high school seniors who have been accepted for enrollment as full-time students at accredited undergraduate institutions. The sponsor especially encourages applications from underrepresented minorities, women, and individuals with disabilities.

**Financial data**   Stipends are available up to $20,000 per year, to be used for tuition, educational expenses (such as books and lab fees), and qualified living expenses while attending a college or university. Recipients incur a service obligation to work as an employee of the NIH in Bethesda, Maryland for 10 consecutive weeks (during the summer) during the sponsored year and, upon graduation, for 52 weeks for each academic year of scholarship support. The NIH 52-week employment obligation may be deferred if the recipient goes to graduate or medical school.

**Duration**   1 year; may be renewed for up to 3 additional years.

**Number awarded**   15 each year.

**Deadline**   February of each year.

## [1016]
## NEW MEXICO COMMUNITY DEVELOPMENT LOANS

New Mexico Community Development Loan Fund
423 Iron Street, S.W.
P.O. Box 705
Albuquerque, NM 87103
(505) 243-3196          Toll-free: (866) 873-6746
Fax: (505) 243-8803     E-mail: info@loanfund.org
Web: www.nmcdlf.org/loans.htm

**Summary**  To provide loans to businesses and nonprofit organizations in New Mexico and the Navajo Nation.

**Eligibility**  This program is open to owners of established businesses, individuals who want to start their own businesses, and nonprofit organizations. Applicants must be located in New Mexico or the Navajo Nation. Loans are available to new and existing small businesses for such needs as equipment, inventory, building renovations, and operating capital; loans to nonprofit organizations are available for such needs as bridge financing against awarded private and public contracts, capital improvements, and equipment. Particular emphasis is placed on helping low-income people, women, and minorities who are unable to access loans from banks or other traditional sources. Applicants must meet standard lending qualifications, such as credit history, collateral, and ability to repay the loan.

**Financial data**  The amount of the loan depends on the nature of the request and may be in excess of $20,000. Interest rates generally range from 8% to 10%.

**Duration**  Loan terms are generally from 1 to 7 years.

**Additional information**  The New Mexico Community Development Loan Fund was established in 1989 by the New Mexico Conference of Churches as a means to address poverty in New Mexico. Application fees are $50 for corporations or $25 for individuals and partnerships.

**Number awarded**  Varies each year.

## [1017]
## NEW MEXICO MINORITY DOCTORAL ASSISTANCE LOAN-FOR-SERVICE PROGRAM

New Mexico Higher Education Department
Attn: Financial Aid Director
1068 Cerrillos Road
P.O. Box 15910
Santa Fe, NM 87506-5910
(505) 476-6506          Toll-free: (800) 279-9777
Fax: (505) 476-6511
E-mail: ofelia.morales@state.nm.us
Web: hed.state.nm.us/collegefinance/minoritydoc.asp

**Summary**  To provide loans-for-service to women and underrepresented minorities who reside in New Mexico and are interested in working on a graduate degree in selected fields.

**Eligibility**  Eligible to apply for this program are women and ethnic minorities who have received a baccalaureate and/or master's degree from a state-supported 4-year higher education institution in New Mexico; wish to work on a doctoral degree at an eligible sponsoring New Mexico institution in mathematics, engineering, the physical or life sciences, or any other academic discipline in which ethnic minorities and women are demonstrably underrepresented in New Mexico colleges and universities; and are willing after obtaining their degree to teach at an institution of higher education in the state. Applicants must be U.S. citizens and New Mexico residents.

**Financial data**  This is a loan-for-service program in which the amount of the loan (up to $25,000 per year) may be wholly or partially forgiven upon completion of service as a college instructor in New Mexico.

**Duration**  1 year; may be renewed for up to 2 additional years for students who enter with a master's degree or up to 3 additional years for students who begin with a baccalaureate degree.

**Additional information**  Sponsoring institutions nominate candidates to the Commission on Higher Education for these awards. Recipients must agree to teach at the college/university level in New Mexico upon completion of their doctoral degree. If the sponsoring institution where the recipient completes the degree is unable to provide a tenure-track position, it must arrange placement at another alternate and mutually-acceptable New Mexico public postsecondary institution.

**Number awarded**  Up to 12 each year.

**Deadline**  March of each year.

## [1018]
## NORTH DAKOTA VETERANS' AID LOANS

Department of Veterans Affairs
1411 32nd Street South
P.O. Box 9003
Fargo, ND 58106-9003
(701) 239-7165          Toll-free: (866) 634-8387
Fax: (701) 239-7166
Web: www.state.nd.us/veterans/benefits/loan.html

**Summary**  To loan money to meet the emergency needs of North Dakota veterans and their unremarried surviving spouses.

**Eligibility**  This program is open to North Dakota veterans who served in peacetime, wartime, or the National Guard with active duty and received other than a dishonorable discharge. Surviving spouses of deceased veterans are also eligible if they have not remarried. Applicants must be facing a temporary and unexpected financial emergency, including dental work, education expenses for the applicant or dependents, emergency eyeglasses, first-time home buyer improvements, medical care, repair bills (in certain cases), temporary unemployment, expenses related to purchase of a primary family residence, or waiting for relief or assistance from other agencies.

**Financial data**  Veterans and surviving spouses may borrow up to $5,000 at 8% interest. If the loan is repaid within 2 years, half of the interest is refunded.

**Duration**  Loans may be granted for periods of 6 to 48 months.

**Number awarded**  Varies each year.

**Deadline**  Applications may be submitted at any time.

## [1019]
## OREGON VETERANS HOME LOAN PROGRAM

Oregon Department of Veterans' Affairs
Attn: Veterans' Home Loan Program
700 Summer Street N.E., Suite 150
Salem, OR 97310-1285
(503) 373-2070
Toll-free: (800) 828-8801, ext. 2267 (within OR)
Fax: (503) 373-2393          TDD: (503) 373-2217
E-mail: orvetshomeloans@odva.state.or.us
Web: www.odva.state.or.us

**Summary** To help disabled and other Oregon veterans or the surviving spouses of certain veterans buy homes.

**Eligibility** This program is open to veterans who served honorably on active duty for not less than 210 consecutive days (unless released earlier because of a service-connected disability). Applicants must either have entered military service prior to 1977 or served in a theater of operations for which a campaign or expeditionary ribbon or medal is authorized by the United States (including Grenada, Libya, Panama, Somalia, Haiti, El Salvador, the Persian Gulf, the Balkans, Kosovo, Afghanistan, or Iraq). They must be Oregon residents at the time of application for the loan. Spouses who are eligible must be Oregon residents who have not remarried and whose spouses either died while on active duty or are listed as prisoners of war or missing in action. The eligibility of a veteran ends 30 years after the last date of separation from service; the eligibility of a spouse expires 30 years after notification of the veteran's death, capture, or disappearance, or upon remarriage. Applicants must demonstrate sufficient income to make loan repayments and be good credit risks. Loans may be used only to finance owner-occupied, single-family residential housing for qualified eligible veterans or their spouses. The purchase of vacation homes, the refinancing of existing loans, or the purchase of income properties, such as farms and rentals, cannot be financed.

**Financial data** Insured loans are made up to 97% of the net appraised value on homes that are real property (to a current maximum of $359,650) or to 85% of the net appraised value on homes that are not real property. For farms that are real property, loans are made up to 90% of the net appraised value, to a maximum of $185,000. Interest rates vary and depend on the service record of the veteran and the amount of the origination fee. Recently, for veterans who entered military service prior to 1977, the rate was 4.99% with a 1.5% origination fee or 5.25% with a 1% origination fee. For veterans who earned a campaign medal or ribbon after 1977, the rate was 5.125% with a 1.5% origination fee or 5.25% with a 1% origination fee.

**Duration** The maximum loan term is 30 years and the minimum is 15 years. Normally, veterans may receive only 2 loans. If they are rated by the U.S. Department of Veterans Affairs or a branch of the U.S. armed forces as at least 50% disabled, they may assume more than 2 loans if they must acquire a different principal residence for compelling medical reasons, they are transferred by an employer for employment reasons, or their spouse is transferred by an employer for employment reasons and the spouse provides more than 50% of the household income.

**Additional information** Recipients must live on the property and use it as their primary home within 90 days after the loan has closed.

**Number awarded** Varies each year.

**Deadline** Applications may be submitted at any time.

## [1020]
## P.E.O. EDUCATIONAL LOAN FUND

P.E.O. Sisterhood
Attn: Executive Office
3700 Grand Avenue
Des Moines, IA 50312-2899
(515) 255-3153          Fax: (515) 255-3820
Web: www.peointernational.org

**Summary** To offer low-interest loans to women interested in pursuing educational activities beyond high school.

**Eligibility** Women from the United States or Canada who are interested in working on a college degree are eligible to apply. They must be sponsored by a local P.E.O. chapter and within 2 years (but not less than 4 months) of completing their educational goals.

**Financial data** The amount of the loan varies, depending upon the needs of the recipient, to a maximum of $9,000. Undergraduates may receive that maximum in 2 installments; full-time seniors and graduate, law, and medical students may receive the full amount in 1 installment. The loan must be repaid within 6 years at an interest rate of 2%.

**Duration** 1 year; renewable.

**Additional information** This program began in 1907; it is the oldest project of the international chapter of the Women's Philanthropic Educational Organization (P.E.O.).

**Number awarded** Varies each year; recently, nearly $9 million was available for loans.

**Deadline** Applications may be submitted at any time.

## [1021]
## SIGMA ALPHA IOTA FOUNDERS LOAN FUND

Sigma Alpha Iota Philanthropies, Inc.
One Tunnel Road
Asheville, NC 28805
(828) 251-0606          Fax: (828) 251-0644
E-mail: philonline@sai-national.org
Web: www.sai-national.org/phil/philfounders.html

**Summary** To provide loans to alumnae members of Sigma Alpha Iota (an organization of women musicians) who wish to continue their studies or undertake a musical project.

**Eligibility** Applicants are not required to be a member of an alumnae chapter or a full-time student, but they must be in good standing with the organization and have paid national dues. They must be seeking funding to pursue such projects as continuing studies in music, studies at a major summer music center, private applied music studies or coaching, purchase of a musical instrument, or other expenses for musical activities.

**Financial data** The maximum loans are $2,500. The interest rate is 5%. Repayment begins within 30 days of the date of the promissory note.

**Number awarded** Varies each year.

**Deadline** Applications may be submitted at any time.

## [1022]
## SOUTH DAKOTA EMERGENCY LOAN FUND FOR VETERANS AND THEIR DEPENDENTS

South Dakota Division of Veterans Affairs
Soldiers and Sailors Memorial Building
500 East Capitol Avenue
Pierre, SD 57501-5070
(605) 773-4981                     Fax: (605) 773-5380
E-mail: andy.gerlach@state.sd.us
Web: www.state.sd.us/military/VetAffairs/sdmva.htm

**Summary**   To provide loans for emergencies to veterans and their dependents in South Dakota.

**Eligibility**   This program is open to veterans and veterans' dependents who require financial relief for an emergency. The veteran must have served during specified qualifying wartime periods, been discharged honorably or under honorable conditions, and been a legal resident of South Dakota at the time of entry into service and for at least 1 year immediately prior to application.

**Financial data**   Interest-free loans up to $500 are available.

**Duration**   Loans must be repaid within 2 years.

**Number awarded**   Varies each year.

## [1023]
## TEXAS VETERANS HOME IMPROVEMENT PROGRAM

Texas Veterans Land Board
Stephen F. Austin Building
1700 North Congress Avenue, Room 700
P.O. Box 12873
Austin, TX 78711-2873
(512) 463-5060   Toll-free: (800) 252-VETS (within TX)
TDD: (512) 463-5330      E-mail: vlbinfo@glo.state.tx.us
Web: www.glo.state.tx.us/vlb/vhip/index.html

**Summary**   To assist Texas veterans, National Guard members, and unremarried surviving spouses who wish to maintain older homes but who cannot qualify for the high interest rates of conventional home improvement loans.

**Eligibility**   This program is open to 1) veterans who served for at least 90 consecutive days of active duty after September 16, 1940 in the Army, Navy, Air Force, Marines, Coast Guard, U.S. Public Health Service, or a Reserve component of those services; 2) members of the Texas National Guard or Reserves who have enlisted or received an appointment and have completed all Initial Active Duty for Training (IADT) requirements; and 3) veterans who served in the armed forces of the Republic of Vietnam (ARVN) between February 28, 1961 and May 7, 1975. Applicants may not have been dishonorably discharged and must have listed Texas as their home of record at the time of entry into the military or have been a resident of Texas for at least 1 year prior to filing an application. The unremarried surviving spouses of Texas veterans who are missing in action, died in the line of duty, or died from a service-connected cause may be eligible to participate in the program. Applicants must be interested in making alterations, repairs, and improvements to, or in connection with, their existing residence if, and only if, repairs will 1) substantially protect or improve the basic livability or energy efficiency of the property; 2) correct damage resulting from a natural disaster; or 3) correct conditions that are hazardous to health or safety. Examples of

eligible improvements include carpeting, fencing, room additions, patios, driveways, and garages. Examples of ineligible improvements include exterior spas, saunas, whirlpools, tree surgery, tennis courts, swimming pools, and barbecue pits. The home must be in Texas and the veteran's primary residence. In addition to single family dwellings, condominiums, duplexes, triplexes, and fourplexes are eligible as long as 1 of the units is the veteran's primary residence. Duplexes, triplexes, and fourplexes must be at least 5 years old. Modular or manufactured homes that are on a permanent foundation and are a part of the real estate may also be eligible. Interest rate incentives are available to Texas veterans who 1) entered the armed services before January 1, 1977 and have been discharged from active duty for less than 30 years; 2) have a service-connected disability of 50% or greater as verified by the U.S. Department of Veterans Affairs; or 3) agree to a loan with a term of 15 or fewer years.

**Financial data**   The maximum loan on a single family residence is $25,000. The maximum loan on a manufactured or modular home is $17,500. Loans over $10,000 are for 2 to 20 years; those for $10,000 or less are for 2 to 10 years. Interest rates recently were 5.40%. Interest rate reductions included 1.35 percentage points for qualified service era (prior to January 1, 1977) veterans, 0.35 percentage points for the Veterans with Disabilities program, and 0.25 percentage points for loans with a term of 15 or fewer years.

**Number awarded**   Varies each year.

**Deadline**   Applications may be submitted at any time.

## [1024]
## TEXAS VETERANS HOUSING ASSISTANCE PROGRAM

Texas Veterans Land Board
Stephen F. Austin Building
1700 North Congress Avenue, Room 700
P.O. Box 12873
Austin, TX 78711-2873
(512) 463-5060   Toll-free: (800) 252-VETS (within TX)
TDD: (512) 463-5330      E-mail: vlbinfo@glo.state.tx.us
Web: www.glo.state.tx.us/vlb/vhap/index.html

**Summary**   To provide low-interest loans to assist Texas veterans, National Guard members, and unremarried surviving spouses in purchasing their own homes.

**Eligibility**   This program is open to 1) veterans who served for at least 90 consecutive days of active duty after September 16, 1940 in the Army, Navy, Air Force, Marines, Coast Guard, U.S. Public Health Service, or a Reserve component of those services; 2) members of the Texas National Guard or Reserves who have enlisted or received an appointment and have completed all Initial Active Duty for Training (IADT) requirements; and 3) veterans who served in the armed forces of the Republic of Vietnam (ARVN) between February 28, 1961 and May 7, 1975. Applicants may not have been dishonorably discharged and must have listed Texas as their home of record at the time of entry into the military or have been a resident of Texas for at least 1 year prior to filing an application. The unremarried surviving spouses of Texas veterans who are missing in action, died in the line of duty, or died from a service-connected cause may be eligible to participate in the program. Applicants must be interested in purchasing a new or existing home, including a duplex, triplex, or fourplex if the structure is more than 5 years old, or a modular or manufactured home if it is on a permanent foundation and meets loan guidelines established by the Federal National Mortgage Association or the Federal Home Loan Mortgage Corporation and has an economic life of at least 30 years. Any home purchased with funds from this program must be the primary residence of the veteran for at least 3 years. Interest rate incentives are available to Texas veterans who 1) entered the armed services before January 1, 1977 and have been discharged from active duty for less than 30 years; 2) have a service-connected disability of 50% or greater as verified by the U.S. Department of Veterans Affairs; or 3) agree to a loan with a term of 15 or fewer years.

**Financial data** The maximum loan available through this program is $240,000. Loans for $45,000 or less may be requested directly from the Texas Veterans Land Board (VLB) and may cover up to 85% of the home's appraised value. Loans over $45,000 are originated through a VLB participating lender. The price of the home may exceed $200,000, but loans in excess of that amount must be a "2-note loan" made in conjunction with a conventional, FHA, or VA loan. No fees are charged on direct loans; loans available through a VLB-approved lender require an origination fee up to 1% and a participation fee up to 1%. Interest rates recently were 5.40%. Interest rate reductions included 1.35 percentage points for qualified service era (prior to January 1, 1977) veterans, 0.35 percentage points for the Veterans with Disabilities program, and 0.25 percentage points for loans with a term of 15 or fewer years.

**Duration** Loans are available with 15, 20, 25, or 30 year terms.

**Number awarded** Varies each year.

**Deadline** Applications may be submitted at any time.

## [1025]
## TEXAS VETERANS LAND PROGRAM

Texas Veterans Land Board
Stephen F. Austin Building
1700 North Congress Avenue, Room 700
P.O. Box 12873
Austin, TX 78711-2873
(512) 463-5060   Toll-free: (800) 252-VETS (within TX)
TDD: (512) 463-5330   E-mail: vlbinfo@glo.state.tx.us
Web: www.glo.state.tx.us/vlb/land/index.html

**Summary** To assist Texas veterans, National Guard members, and unremarried surviving spouses interested in purchasing land in Texas.

**Eligibility** This program is open to 1) veterans who served for at least 90 consecutive days of active duty after September 16, 1940 in the Army, Navy, Air Force, Marines, Coast Guard, U.S. Public Health Service, or a Reserve component of those services; 2) members of the Texas National Guard or Reserves who have enlisted or received an appointment and have completed all Initial Active Duty for Training (IADT) requirements. Applicants may not have been dishonorably discharged and must have listed Texas as their home of record at the time of entry into the military or have been a resident of Texas for at least 1 year prior to filing an application. The unremarried surviving spouses of Texas veterans who are missing in action, died in the line of duty, or died from a service-connected cause may be eligible to partici-

pate in the program. Applicants must be interested in purchasing land that contains at least 5 net acres within Texas, excluding public roadways and canals. It must have legal access to a public road, and such right-of-way must be the minimum width required by the county commissioners. Land must be officially surveyed and appraised.

**Financial data** The maximum investment by the Veterans Land Board (VLB) for a standard loan is $60,000, less a 5% down payment, for a net loan of $57,000. If the purchase price is greater than the VLB's commitment, the veteran must pay the difference to the VLB in cash. The VLB then purchases the land directly from the seller and resells the land to the veteran using a 30-year contract of sale and purchase. In addition to the down payment, the veteran must pay a closing fee of $325. The interest rate recently was 6.64%.

**Number awarded** Varies each year.

**Deadline** Applications may be submitted at any time.

## [1026]
## VA HOME LOAN GUARANTY BENEFITS

Department of Veterans Affairs
810 Vermont Avenue, N.W.
Washington, DC 20420
(202) 418-4343         Toll-free: (800) 827-1000
Web: www.va.gov

**Summary** To assist disabled and other veterans, certain military personnel, and their unremarried surviving spouses in the purchase of residences.

**Eligibility** This benefit is available to 1) veterans who served for specified periods of time and were discharged since September 16, 1940 under other than dishonorable conditions; 2) military personnel who have served at least 90 days; 3) members of the Reserves or National Guard who have completed at least 6 years of honorable service or were discharged because of a service-related disability; 4) unmarried spouses of veterans or Reservists who died on active duty or as a result of service-connected causes; 5) surviving spouses who remarry after attaining 57 years of age; 6) spouses of active-duty servicemembers who have been missing in action or a prisoner of war for at least 90 days; 7) U.S. citizens who served in the armed forces of a U.S. ally in World War II; and 8) members of organizations with recognized contributions to the U.S. World War II effort.

**Financial data** The Department of Veterans Affairs (VA) does not lend money; the actual loan must come from a commercial lender. The loan may be for any amount, and the VA will guarantee payment on loans for the purchase of homes, farm homes, condominium units, or refinancing of existing loans. The largest guaranty that VA can give is an amount equal to 25% of the Freddie Mac conforming loan limit for single family residences (currently $89,912). Lenders generally limit the maximum VA loan to 4 times the maximum VA guaranty (or $359,650). Interest rates vary with market conditions but are fixed for the life of the loan, which may be as long as 30 years and 32 days. No down payments are prescribed by VA. A funding fee must be paid to VA, although it may be included in the loan amount; the amount of the fee varies, depending on the type of loan and whether the borrower is a veteran or a Reservist, but ranges from 0.5% to 3% of the amount of the loan. The funding fee is waived for disabled veterans and unremarried surviving spouses of veterans who died as a result of service.

**Additional information** In addition to the purchase of a new home, VA Loans may be used to buy a residential condominium; to build a home; to repair, alter, or improve a home; to refinance an existing home loan; to buy a manufactured home with or without a lot; to buy and improve a manufactured home lot; to install a solar heating and/or cooling system or other weatherization improvements; to purchase and improve simultaneously a home with energy conserving measures; to refinance an existing VA loan to reduce the interest rate; or to refinance a manufactured home loan to acquire a lot. Mortgages guaranteed by VA usually offer an interest rate lower than conventional mortgage rates, require no down payment, provide a long repayment period, allow the VA to appraise the property and inspect it to ensure that it conforms to the plans and specifications, and permit early prepayment without premium or penalty. The VA does not have legal authority to act as an architect, supervise construction of the home, guarantee that the home is free of defects, or act as an attorney if the veteran encounters legal difficulties in buying or constructing a home. Veterans must certify that they intend to live in the home they are buying or building with a VA loan. Veterans who wish to refinance or improve a home must certify that they are actually in residence at the time of application.

**Number awarded** Varies each year.

**Deadline** Applications may be submitted at any time.

## [1027]
## VICE ADMIRAL E.P. TRAVERS LOAN PROGRAM

Navy-Marine Corps Relief Society
Attn: Education Division
875 North Randolph Street, Suite 225
Arlington, VA 22203-1977
(703) 696-4960      Fax: (703) 696-0144
E-mail: education@hq.nmcrs.org
Web: www.nmcrs.org/travers.html

**Summary** To provide interest-free loans for college to the dependents Navy and Marine Corps personnel.

**Eligibility** This program is open to the dependent children of active-duty and retired Navy and Marine Corps personnel and the spouses of active-duty Navy and Marine Corps personnel. Applicants must have a GPA of 2.0 or higher and be able to demonstrate financial need. They must be enrolled or planning to enroll as a full-time undergraduate student at an accredited college, university, or vocational/technical school.

**Financial data** The loan amount is determined on the basis of need, from $500 to $3,000 per academic year. No interest is charged on the money borrowed. The loan must be repaid within 24 months by allotment of pay, at a monthly rate of at least $50.

**Number awarded** Varies each year.

**Deadline** February of each year.

## [1028]
## VIRGINIA NURSE PRACTITIONER/NURSE MIDWIFE SCHOLARSHIP PROGRAM

Virginia Department of Health
Attn: Office of Health Policy and Planning
109 Governor Street, Suite 1016
P.O. Box 2448
Richmond, VA 23218
(804) 864-7433      Fax: (804) 864-7440
E-mail: Margie.Thomas@vdh.virginia.gov
Web: www.vdh.state.va.us

**Summary** To provide forgivable loans to nursing students in Virginia who are willing to work as nurse practitioners and/or midwives in the state following graduation.

**Eligibility** This program is open to residents of Virginia who are enrolled or accepted for enrollment full time at a nurse practitioner program in the state or a nurse midwifery program in Virginia or a nearby state. Applicants must have a cumulative GPA of at least 3.0 in undergraduate and/or graduate courses. Preference is given to 1) residents of designated medically underserved areas of Virginia; 2) students enrolled in family practice, obstetrics and gynecology, pediatric, adult health, and geriatric nurse practitioner programs; and 3) minority students. Selection is based on scholastic achievement, character, and stated commitment to postgraduate employment in a medically underserved area of Virginia.

**Financial data** The amount of the award depends on the availability of funds; recently, stipends were $5,000. Recipients must agree to serve in a designated medically underserved area of Virginia for a period of years equal to the number of years of scholarship support received. The required service must begin within 2 years of the recipient's graduation and must be in a facility that provides services to persons who are unable to pay for the service and that participates in all government-sponsored insurance programs designed to assure full access to medical care service for covered persons. If the recipient fails to complete the course of study, or pass the licensing examination, or provide the required service, all scholarship funds received must be repaid with interest.

**Duration** 1 year; may be renewed for 1 additional year.

**Number awarded** Varies each year; recently, 3 of these scholarships were awarded.

**Deadline** June of each year.

## [1029]
## VOCATIONAL AND TECHNICAL TRAINING STUDENT LOAN PROGRAM

Coast Guard Mutual Assistance
4200 Wilson Boulevard, Suite 610
Arlington, VA 22203-1804
(202) 493-6624      Toll-free: (800) 881-2462
Fax: (202) 493-6686
Web: www.cgmahq.org

**Summary** To provide loans to the members of Coast Guard Mutual Assistance (CGMA) and their spouses and dependent children who require assistance for vocational or technical training.

**Eligibility** This program is open to members of the organization, their spouses, and dependent children. Applicants should be seeking assistance to help pay the costs of non-college courses that provide the technical knowledge and skills needed for entry into a specific career field. Financial need must be demonstrated.

**Financial data** The maximum loan is $1,500.

**Additional information** CGMA membership is open to active-duty and retired members of the U.S. Coast Guard, civilian employees of the U.S. Coast Guard, U.S. Coast Guard Reserve members, U.S. Coast Guard Auxiliary members, Public Health Service officers serving with the U.S. Coast Guard, and family members of all of those.

**Number awarded** Varies each year.

**Deadline** Requests must be submitted within 30 days after the course begins.

## [1030]
## WISCONSIN HOME IMPROVEMENT LOAN PROGRAM

Wisconsin Department of Veterans Affairs
30 West Mifflin Street
P.O. Box 7843
Madison, WI 53707-7843
(608) 266-1311                Toll-free: (800) WIS-VETS
Fax: (608) 267-0403        E-mail: loans@dva.state.wi.us
Web: dva.state.wi.us/Ben_improvementloans.asp

**Summary** To provide low-interest loans to veterans and their families in Wisconsin to pay for improvements to their homes.

**Eligibility** This program is open to current residents of Wisconsin who 1) were residents of the state when they entered or reentered active duty in the U.S. armed forces, or 2) have moved to the state and have been residents for any consecutive 12-month period after entry or reentry into service. Applicants must have served on active duty for at least 2 continuous years or for at least 90 days during specified wartime periods. Also eligible are 1) members and former members of the National Guard and Reserves who have completed at least 6 years of continuous service under honorable conditions; 2) unremarried spouses of deceased veterans; and 3) dependent children under 26 years of age and attending school full time. Applicants may be planning to use the loan funds for additions, construction, repairs, or alterations of their principal residence. The loan also may be used for garage construction. The applicant must have at least 10% equity in the property to be improved.

**Financial data** Loans up to 90% of home equity are available if secured by a mortgage or up to $3,000 if secured with a guarantor. The interest rate varies. Recently, the rate was 5.0% on 5-year loans, 5.35% on 10-year loans, or 5.65% on 15-year loans. Funds may be used only for qualifying home improvements, not for personal property such as furniture or certain types of appliances.

**Duration** The minimum loan repayment term is 1 year and the maximum term is 15 years.

**Number awarded** Varies each year.

**Deadline** Applications may be submitted at any time.

## [1031]
## WISCONSIN VETERANS' PERSONAL LOAN PROGRAM

Wisconsin Department of Veterans Affairs
30 West Mifflin Street
P.O. Box 7843
Madison, WI 53707-7843
(608) 266-1311                Toll-free: (800) WIS-VETS
Fax: (608) 267-0403        E-mail: loans@dva.state.wi.us
Web: dva.state.wi.us/Ben_personalloans.asp

**Summary** To provide eligible Wisconsin veterans or their dependents with loans for any purpose, including education.

**Eligibility** This program is open to current residents of Wisconsin who 1) were residents of the state when they entered or reentered active duty in the U.S. armed forces, or 2) have moved to the state and have been residents for any consecutive 12-month period after entry or reentry into service. Applicants must have served on active duty for at least 2 continuous years or for at least 90 days during specified wartime periods. Also eligible are unremarried spouses of deceased veterans and dependent children (adult children must be under 26 years of age and attending school full time). A remarried spouse or parent of a veterans' child may qualify if the loan is used for the child's education. Applicants may borrow money for any purpose. They must meet basic credit and underwriting standards. Loans must be secured by a mortgage on the applicant's property or with a guarantor.

**Financial data** This program provides loans up to $25,000. The interest rate is 5% for 5-year loans secured by a mortgage, 7% for 10-year loans secured by a mortgage, or 6% for loans secured by a guarantor.

**Number awarded** Varies each year.

**Deadline** Applications may be submitted at any time.

## [1032]
## WISCONSIN VETERANS PRIMARY MORTGAGE LOAN PROGRAM

Wisconsin Department of Veterans Affairs
30 West Mifflin Street
P.O. Box 7843
Madison, WI 53707-7843
(608) 266-1311                Toll-free: (800) WIS-VETS
Fax: (608) 267-0403        E-mail: loans@dva.state.wi.us
Web: dva.state.wi.us/Ben_mortgageloans.asp

**Summary** To provide housing loans to Wisconsin veterans or their unremarried spouses or children who cannot obtain the necessary funds from other sources.

**Eligibility** This program is open to current residents of Wisconsin who 1) were residents of the state when they entered or reentered active duty in the U.S. armed forces, or 2) have moved to the state and have been residents for any consecutive 12-month period after entry or reentry into service. Applicants must have served on active duty for at least 2 continuous years or for at least 90 days during specified wartime periods. Also eligible are 1) dependent children and unremarried surviving spouses of eligible deceased veterans; and 2) members and former members of the National Guard and Reserves who have completed 6 years of continuous service under honorable conditions. Applicants must be seeking to borrow money for the purchase, or the purchase and improvement, of a single family home or condominium; construction of a new single family home; purchase of certain existing 2- to 4-unit owner occupied residences; or refinance of the balance due on existing mortgage loans used for purchase, construction, or improvement of a residence.

**Financial data**  The veteran or dependent may obtain a loan of up to 95% of the total cost of the property. The required down payment is 5% and the department pays the loan origination fees for veterans with a disability rating of 30% or more. Other attractive features include: no private mortgage insurance or loan guaranty, no discount points, no interest rate increase, and no prepayment penalty. The current interest rate is 5.99%.

**Duration**  Loan terms up to 30 years are available.

**Number awarded**  Varies each year.

**Deadline**  Applications may be submitted at any time.

# Grants

Described here are 248 programs that provide funds directly to women for innovative efforts, travel, projects, creative activities, or research on any level (from undergraduate to postdoctorate and professional). If you are looking for a particular program and don't find it here, be sure to check the Program Title Index to see if it is covered elsewhere in the *Directory*.

## [1033]
## AAUW LEGAL ADVOCACY FUND SUPPORT FOR SEX DISCRIMINATION LAWSUITS

American Association of University Women
Attn: Legal Advocacy Fund
1111 16th Street, N.W.
Washington, DC 20036-4873
(202) 785-7750          Toll-free: (800) 326-AAUW
Fax: (202) 872-8754      TDD: (202) 785-7777
E-mail: laf@aauw.org
Web: www.aauw.org/laf/cases/casesupp.cfm

**Summary** To provide funding to women in higher education who are involved in sex discrimination lawsuits.

**Eligibility** This program is open to women who are fighting sex discrimination in higher education with a lawsuit filed in state or federal court. Applicants must be seeking case support that involves direct financial aid, technical assistance, or fundraising support; assistance in litigation is not provided. Selection is based on the plaintiff's need for financial aid, the probability of success, and the potential significance of the case for women in higher education.

**Financial data** The amount of the award depends on the circumstances of the case.

**Duration** These are 1-time awards.

**Additional information** This program was established in 1981.

**Number awarded** Varies each year; since its establishment, this program has contributed more than $1.3 million to more than 100 cases.

**Deadline** April, August, or December of each year.

## [1034]
## AAUW SUMMER/SHORT-TERM RESEARCH PUBLICATION GRANTS

American Association of University Women
Attn: AAUW Educational Foundation
301 ACT Drive, Department 60
P.O. Box 4030
Iowa City, IA 52243-4030
(319) 337-1716          Fax: (319) 337-1204
E-mail: aauw@act.org
Web: www.aauw.org

**Summary** To provide summer fellowships to women scholars interested in conducting postdoctoral research.

**Eligibility** This program is open to women who are interested in preparing research manuscripts for publication (but not to undertake new research). Applicants may be tenure track, part-time, or temporary faculty or may be independent scholars or researchers, either new or established. They must have completed a doctoral or M.F.A. degree. U.S. citizenship or permanent resident status is required. Scholars with strong publishing records are discouraged from applying. Selection is based on scholarly excellence, quality of project design, originality of project, scholarly significance of project to discipline, feasibility of project and proposed schedule, qualifications of applicant, potential of applicant to make a significant contribution to field, applicant's commitment to women's issues in profession and community, applicant's teaching experience, and applicant's mentoring of other women.

**Financial data** The grant is $6,000. Funds may be used for stipends for recipient, clerical and technical support, research assistance related to verification (not basic research), supplies, and expenses. Grants do not cover travel, purchase of equipment, indirect costs, salary increase, or doctoral dissertation research or writing.

**Duration** 8 weeks during the summer.

**Additional information** The filing fee is $40.

**Number awarded** Varies each year; recently, 19 of these grants were awarded.

**Deadline** November of each year.

## [1035]
## ACADEMY OF NATURAL SCIENCES RESEARCH EXPERIENCES FOR UNDERGRADUATES FELLOWSHIPS

Academy of Natural Sciences of Philadelphia
Attn: REU Coordinator
1900 Benjamin Franklin Parkway
Philadelphia, PA 19103-1195
(215) 299-1000          Fax: (215) 299-1028
E-mail: reucoordinator@acnatsci.org
Web: www.acnatsci.org/research/reu.html

**Summary** To provide undergraduate students (particularly women, minority and disabled students) with an opportunity to conduct summer research in botany, entomology, ichthyology, malacology, ornithology, or paleontology at the Academy of Natural Sciences of Philadelphia.

**Eligibility** This program is open to U.S. citizens and permanent residents who are entering their sophomore, junior, or senior year at a college or university. Applicants must be interested in working on a research project under the mentorship of an academy scientist in systematics, natural history, evolutionary biology, and ecology. Their proposals should draw upon the academy's collections in botany, entomology, ichthyology, malacology, ornithology, and paleontology, as well as the library and archives. Applications are particularly encouraged from women, minorities, and students with disabilities.

**Financial data** The program provides travel to and from Philadelphia; housing; expenses for supplies, field trips, and research; and a stipend of $350 per week.

**Duration** 10 weeks, beginning in June.

**Number awarded** Varies each year.

**Deadline** February of each year.

## [1036]
## ACLS DIGITAL INNOVATION FELLOWSHIPS

American Council of Learned Societies
Attn: Office of Fellowships and Grants
633 Third Avenue, 8C
New York, NY 10017-6795
(212) 697-1505          Fax: (212) 949-8058
E-mail: grants@acls.org
Web: www.acls.org/difguide.htm

**Summary** To provide funding to scholars (particularly women and minorities) interested in conducting digitally-based research in the humanities and the humanities-related social sciences.

**Eligibility** This program is open to scholars who have a Ph.D. in all fields of the humanities and the humanistic social sciences. Applicants must be interested in conducting research projects that utilize digital technologies intensively and innovatively. Projects might include, but are not limited to, digital research archives, new media representations of extant data, innovative databases, and digital tools that further humanistic research. The program does not support creative works (e.g., novels or films), textbooks, straightforward translations, or purely pedagogical projects. U.S. citizenship or permanent resident status is required. Applications are particularly invited from women and members of minority groups. Selection is based on scholarly excellence (the intellectual ambitions of the project, its technological underpinnings, and how digital technologies add value to humanistic study), technical requirements for completing a successful research project, evidence of significant preliminary work already completed, the plan for development of the project, and the budget.

**Financial data** Fellows receive a stipend of $55,000 and up to $25,000 for project costs.

**Duration** 1 academic year.

**Additional information** This program, first available for the 2006-07 academic year, is supported by funding from the Andrew W. Mellon Foundation.

**Number awarded** Up to 5 each year.

**Deadline** September of each year.

## [1037]
## ACLS FELLOWSHIPS

American Council of Learned Societies
Attn: Office of Fellowships and Grants
633 Third Avenue, 8C
New York, NY 10017-6795
(212) 697-1505              Fax: (212) 949-8058
E-mail: grants@acls.org
Web: www.acls.org/felguide.htm

**Summary** To provide research funding to scholars (particularly women and minorities) in all disciplines of the humanities and the humanities-related social sciences.

**Eligibility** This program is open to scholars at all stages of their careers who received a Ph.D. degree at least 2 years previously. Established scholars who can demonstrate the equivalent of the Ph.D. in publications and professional experience may also qualify. Applicants must be U.S. citizens or permanent residents who have not had supported leave time for at least 3 years prior to the start of the proposed research. Appropriate fields of specialization include, but are not limited to, anthropology, archaeology, art and architectural history, economic history, film, geography, history, languages and literatures, legal studies, linguistics, musicology, philosophy, political science, psychology, religion, rhetoric and communication, sociology, and theater studies. Proposals in those fields of the social sciences are eligible only if they employ predominantly humanistic approaches (e.g., economic history, law and literature, political philosophy). Proposals in interdisciplinary and cross-disciplinary studies are welcome, as are proposals focused on any geographic region or on any cultural or linguistic group. Awards are available at 3 academic levels: full professor, associate professor, and assistant professor. Appli-

cations are particularly invited from women and members of minority groups.

**Financial data** The maximum grant is $60,000 for full professors and equivalent, $40,000 for associate professors and equivalent, or $30,000 for assistant professors and equivalent. Normally, fellowships are intended as salary replacement and may be held concurrently with other fellowships, grants, and sabbatical pay, up to an amount equal to the candidate's current academic year salary.

**Duration** 6 to 12 months.

**Additional information** This program is supported in part by funding from the Ford Foundation, the Andrew W. Mellon Foundation, the National Endowment for the Humanities, the William and Flora Hewlett Foundation, and the Rockefeller Foundation.

**Number awarded** Approximately 45 each year: 25 at the full professor level and 20 as the assistant and associate professor level.

**Deadline** September of each year.

## [1038]
## ACLS/SSRC/NEH INTERNATIONAL AND AREA STUDIES FELLOWSHIPS

American Council of Learned Societies
Attn: Office of Fellowships and Grants
633 Third Avenue, 8C
New York, NY 10017-6795
(212) 697-1505              Fax: (212) 949-8058
E-mail: grants@acls.org
Web: www.acls.org/felguide.htm

**Summary** To provide funding to postdoctoral scholars (particularly women and minorities) who are interested on conducting humanities-related research on the societies and cultures of Asia, Africa, the Near and Middle East, Latin America and the Caribbean, eastern Europe, and the former Soviet Union.

**Eligibility** This program is open to U.S. citizens and residents who have lived in the United States for at least 3 years. Applicants must have a Ph.D. degree and not have received supported research leave time for at least 3 years prior to the start of the proposed research. They must be interested in conducting humanities and humanities-related social science research on the societies and cultures of Asia, Africa, the Middle East, Latin America and the Caribbean, eastern Europe, or the former Soviet Union. Selection is based on the intellectual merit of the proposed research and the likelihood that it will produce significant and innovative scholarship. Applications are particularly invited from women and members of minority groups.

**Financial data** The maximum grant is $60,000 for full professors and equivalent, $40,000 for associate professors and equivalent, or $30,000 for assistant professors and equivalent. These fellowships may not be held concurrently with another major fellowship.

**Duration** 6 to 12 months.

**Additional information** This program is jointly supported by the American Council of Learned Societies (ACLS) and the Social Science Research Council (SSRC), with funding provided by the National Endowment for the Humanities (NEH).

**Number awarded** Approximately 10 each year.

**Deadline** September of each year.

## [1039]
## ADVANCED POSTDOCTORAL FELLOWSHIPS IN DIABETES RESEARCH

Juvenile Diabetes Research Foundation
Attn: Grant Administrator
120 Wall Street, 19th Floor
New York, NY 10005-4001
(212) 479-7572          Toll-free: (800) 533-CURE
Fax: (212) 785-9595          E-mail: info@jdrf.org
Web: www.jdrf.org/index.cfm?page_id=103207

**Summary** To provide advanced research training to scientists (particularly women, minorities, and persons with disabilities) who are beginning their professional careers and are interested in conducting research on the causes, treatment, prevention, or cure of diabetes or its complications.

**Eligibility** This program is open to postdoctorates who show extraordinary promise for a career in diabetes research. Applicants must have received their first doctoral degree (M.D., Ph.D., D.M.D., or D.V.M.) within the past 5 years and should have completed 1 to 3 years of postdoctoral training. They may not have a faculty appointment. There are no citizenship requirements. Applications are encouraged from women, members of minority groups underrepresented in the sciences, and people with disabilities. The proposed research training may be conducted at foreign and domestic, for-profit and nonprofit, and public and private institutions, including universities, colleges, hospitals, laboratories, units of state and local government, and eligible agencies of the federal government. Selection is based on the applicant's previous experience and academic record; the caliber of the proposed research; the quality of the mentor, training program, and environment; and the applicant's potential to obtain an independent research position in the future. Fellows who obtain a faculty position at any time during the term of the fellowship may apply for a transition award for support during their first year as a faculty member.

**Financial data** The total award is $90,000 per year, including salary that depends on number of years of experience, ranging from $35,568 for zero up to $51,036 for 7 or more years of experience. In the first year only, funds in excess of the grant may be used for travel to scientific meetings (up to $2,000), journal subscriptions, books, training courses, laboratory supplies, equipment, or purchase of a personal computer (up to $2,000). Indirect costs are not allowed. Fellows who receive a faculty position and are granted a transition award of up to $110,000 for 1 year, including up to 10% in indirect costs.

**Duration** Up to 3 years.

**Deadline** January or July of each year.

## [1040]
## AFRICAN AMERICAN STUDIES PROGRAM VISITING SCHOLARS

University of Houston
African American Studies Program
Attn: Visiting Scholars Program
315 Agnes Arnold Hall
Houston, TX 77204-3047
(713) 743-2813          Fax: (713) 743-2818
E-mail: jconyers@uh.edu
Web: www.class.uh.edu/aas/visiting_scholars.asp

**Summary** To provide support to junior scholars (particularly women, veterans, and persons with disabilities) who are interested in conducting research on the African American community while affiliated with the University of Houston's African American Studies Program.

**Eligibility** Applications are sought from junior scholars in social sciences, humanities, or African American studies who completed their Ph.D. within the past 6 years. They must be interested in conducting research on the African American community while affiliated with the University of Houston's African American Studies Program and in assuming a tenured or tenure-track position there after their residency as a Visiting Scholar is completed. Applicants proposing to conduct research on the African American community in Houston and the state of Texas are given priority. Interested applicants should submit a current curriculum vitae, a 2-page description of the proposed research, 3 letters of recommendation, and a syllabus of the undergraduate course to be taught. Minorities, women, veterans, and persons with disabilities are specifically encouraged to apply.

**Financial data** Visiting Scholars receive a salary appropriate to their rank.

**Duration** 1 academic year.

**Additional information** Visiting Scholars are assigned a research assistant, if needed, and are provided administrative support. Recipients must teach 1 class related to African American studies. They are required to be in residence at the university for the entire academic year and must make 2 presentations on their research. In addition, they must acknowledge the sponsor's support in any publication that results from their tenure at the university.

**Number awarded** At least 2 each year.

**Deadline** December of each year.

## [1041]
## AGA FELLOWSHIP/FACULTY TRANSITION AWARDS

Foundation for Digestive Health and Nutrition
Attn: Research Awards Program
4930 Del Ray Avenue
Bethesda, MD 20814-2512
(301) 222-4012          Fax: (301) 652-3890
E-mail: info@fdhn.org
Web: www.fdhn.org/html/awards/elect_app.html

**Summary** To provide funding to physicians for research training in an area of gastrointestinal, liver function, or related diseases.

**Eligibility** This program is open to trainee members of the American Gastroenterological Association (AGA) who are

M.D.s or M.D./Ph.D.s currently holding a gastroenterology-related fellowship at an accredited North American institution. Applicants must be committed to an academic career; have completed 2 years of research training at the start of this award; be sponsored by an AGA member who directs a gastroenterology-related unit that is engaged in research training in a North American medical school, affiliated teaching hospital, or research institute; and be cosponsored by the director of a basic research laboratory (or other comparable laboratory) who is committed to the training and development of the applicant. Minorities and women investigators are strongly encouraged to apply. Selection is based on novelty, feasibility, and significance of the proposal; attributes of the candidate; record and commitment of the sponsors; and the institutional and laboratory environment.

**Financial data** The stipend is $40,000 per year. Funds are to be used as salary support for the recipient. Indirect costs are not allowed.

**Duration** 2 years.

**Additional information** This award is administered by the Foundation for Digestive Health and Nutrition (FDHN) and sponsored by the AGA. Finalists for the award are interviewed. Although the host institution may supplement the award, the applicant may not concurrently have a similar training award or grant from another organization. All publications coming from work funded by this program must acknowledge the support of the award.

**Number awarded** Up to 4 each year.

**Deadline** September of each year.

## [1042]
## AGA FOUNDATION OUTCOMES RESEARCH AWARDS

Foundation for Digestive Health and Nutrition
Attn: Research Awards Program
4930 Del Ray Avenue
Bethesda, MD 20814-2512
(301) 222-4012                Fax: (301) 652-3890
E-mail: info@fdhn.org
Web: www.fdhn.org/html/awards/elect_app.html

**Summary** To provide funding to young investigators (particularly women and minorities) who are interested in conducting outcomes research related to gastroenterology or hepatology.

**Eligibility** Applicants must hold faculty positions at accredited North American academic institutions at the time of application. They should be early in their careers (established investigators are not eligible). Candidates with an M.D. degree must have completed clinical training within the past 5 years and those with a Ph.D. must have received their degree within the past 5 years. Membership in the American Gastroenterological Association (AGA) is required. Selection is based on feasibility, scientific and technical significance, merit, originality, the anticipated contribution of the proposed research, and the availability of adequate facilities, personnel, and resources. Priority for 2 of the grants is given for the study of acid-peptic disease. Women and minority investigators are strongly encouraged to apply.

**Financial data** The grant is $35,000. Funds are to be used for project costs, including salary, supplies, and equipment but excluding travel. Indirect costs are not allowed.

**Duration** 1 year.

**Additional information** This award is administered by the Foundation for Digestive Health and Nutrition (FDHN) and sponsored by the AGA. Funding is provided by TAP Pharmaceuticals, Inc.

**Number awarded** 4 each year.

**Deadline** September of each year.

## [1043]
## AGA PILOT RESEARCH AWARDS

Foundation for Digestive Health and Nutrition
Attn: Research Awards Program
4930 Del Ray Avenue
Bethesda, MD 20814-2512
(301) 222-4012                Fax: (301) 652-3890
E-mail: info@fdhn.org
Web: www.fdhn.org/html/awards/elect_app.html

**Summary** To provide funding to new or established investigators (particularly women and minorities) for pilot research projects in areas related to gastroenterology or hepatology.

**Eligibility** Applicants must have an M.D. or Ph.D. degree (or the equivalent) and a faculty position at an accredited North American institution. They may not hold grants for projects on a similar topic from other agencies. Individual membership in the American Gastroenterology Association (AGA) is required. The proposal must involve obtaining new data that can ultimately provide the basis of subsequent grant applications for more substantial funding and duration in gastroenterology- or hepatology-related areas. Women and minority investigators are strongly encouraged to apply. Selection is based on novelty, importance, feasibility, environment, commitment of the institution, and overall likelihood that the project will lead to more substantial grant applications.

**Financial data** The grant is $25,000 per year. Funds may be used for salary, supplies, or equipment. Indirect costs are not allowed.

**Duration** 1 year.

**Additional information** This award, formerly known as the Elsevier Research Initiative Award, is administered by the Foundation for Digestive Health and Nutrition and sponsored by the AGA.

**Number awarded** 1 or more each year.

**Deadline** January of each year.

## [1044]
## AGA RESEARCH SCHOLAR AWARDS

Foundation for Digestive Health and Nutrition
Attn: Research Awards Program
4930 Del Ray Avenue
Bethesda, MD 20814-2512
(301) 222-4012                Fax: (301) 652-3890
E-mail: info@fdhn.org
Web: www.fdhn.org/html/awards/elect_app.html

**Summary** To provide salary support for young investigators (particularly women and minorities) who are developing an independent career in an area of gastroenterology, hepatology, or related fields.

**Eligibility** Applicants must hold full-time faculty positions at North American universities or professional institutes at the time of application. They should be early in their careers (fellows and established investigators are not appropriate candidates). Candidates with an M.D. degree must have completed clinical training within the past 5 years and those with a Ph.D. must have received their degree within the past 5 years. Membership in the American Gastroenterological Association (AGA) is required. Selection is based on novelty, feasibility and significance of the proposal; attributes of the candidate, including potential for independence; evidence of institutional commitment; and the research environment. Special consideration is given to applications with a focus on nutrition or geriatrics. Women, minorities, and physician/scientist investigators are strongly encouraged to apply.

**Financial data** The grant is $75,000 per year. Funds are to be used for project costs, including salary, supplies, and equipment but excluding travel. Indirect costs are not allowed.

**Duration** 3 years.

**Additional information** This program is administered by the Foundation for Digestive Health and Nutrition (FDHN) and sponsored by the AGA. Funding is provided by TAP Pharmaceuticals, Inc., AstraZeneca Pharmaceuticals, L.P., Janssen Pharmaceutica Products, L.P., Johnson & Johnson/Merck Consumer Pharmaceuticals, Roche Pharmaceuticals, and Wyeth-Ayerst Laboratories. At least 70% of the recipient's research effort should relate to the gastrointestinal tract or liver. Recipients cannot hold or have held an R01, R29, K121, K08, VA Research Award, or any award with similar objectives from nonfederal sources.

**Number awarded** Varies each year. Recently, 6 of the awards were granted.

**Deadline** September of each year.

## [1045]
## AGA STUDENT RESEARCH FELLOWSHIP AWARDS

Foundation for Digestive Health and Nutrition
Attn: Research Awards Program
4930 Del Ray Avenue
Bethesda, MD 20814-2512
(301) 222-4012                    Fax: (301) 652-3890
E-mail: info@fdhn.org
Web: www.fdhn.org/html/awards/elect_app.html

**Summary** To provide funding for research on digestive diseases or nutrition to students at any level, particularly women and minority students.

**Eligibility** This program is open to high school, college, graduate, and medical students at accredited institutions in North America who are not yet engaged in thesis research. They must be interested in conducting research on digestive diseases or nutrition. Candidates must not hold similar salary support awards from other agencies (e.g., American Liver Foundation, Crohn's and Colitis Foundation). Women and underrepresented minority students are strongly encouraged to apply. Research must be conducted under the supervision of a preceptor who is a full-time faculty member at a North American institution, directing a research project in a gastroenterology-related area, and a member of the American Gastroenterological Association (AGA). Selection is based on novelty, feasibility, and significance of the proposal; attributes of the candidate; record of the preceptor; evidence of institutional commitment; and laboratory environment. Applicants are grouped and evaluated according to educational level.

**Financial data** Grants range from $2,000 to $3,000. No indirect costs are allowed. The award is paid directly to the student and is to be used as a stipend or for thesis research.

**Duration** At least 10 weeks. The work may take place at any time during the year.

**Additional information** In an effort to attract and encourage minorities, several of the awards are set aside specifically for underrepresented minority students, defined as African Americans, Mexican Americans, Mainland Puerto Ricans, and Native Americans (Alaskan Natives, American Indians, and Native Hawaiians). This award is administered by the Foundation for Digestive Health and Nutrition (FDHN) and sponsored by the AGA. Funds may not be used to support thesis research.

**Number awarded** Varies each year. Recently, 21 of these awards were granted, including several set aside specifically for underrepresented minorities (African Americans, American Indians, Alaska and Hawaiian Natives, Mexican Americans, and Mainland Puerto Ricans).

**Deadline** March of each year.

## [1046]
## AHRQ HEALTH SERVICES RESEARCH GRANTS

Agency for Healthcare Research and Quality
Attn: Division of Grants Management
540 Gaither Road
Rockville, MD 20850
(301) 427-1450                    Fax: (301) 427-1462
E-mail: JMetcalf@ahrq.gov
Web: www.ahrq.gov

**Summary** To provide funding to scholars (particularly women, minorities, and persons with disabilities) who are interested in conducting research that is designed to improve the outcomes, quality, cost, and utilization of health care services.

**Eligibility** This program is open to investigators at domestic and foreign, nonprofit, public and private organizations, including universities, clinics, units of state and local governments, nonprofit firms, and nonprofit foundations. Applicants must be proposing research in 1 of the priority areas of the Agency for Healthcare Research and Quality (AHRQ): 1) support improvements in health outcomes; 2) improve quality and patient safety; and 3) identify strategies to improve access, foster appropriate use, and reduce unnecessary expenditures. Research should also focus on population groups that are particularly vulnerable to impaired access to and suboptimal quality of care: low-income groups, racial and ethnic minority groups, women, children, the elderly, individuals with special health needs (such as individuals with disabilities and those who need chronic care and end-of-life health care), and individuals living in inner-city, rural, and frontier areas. The agency especially encourages women, members of minority groups, and persons with disabilities to apply as principal investigators.

**Financial data** The amount of the award depends on the nature of the proposal. Applications for more than $500,000 per year in direct costs must have prior approval from the agency before they will be accepted.

**Duration** Up to 2 years.

**Number awarded** Varies each year.

**Deadline** Applications may be submitted at any time.

## [1047]
## AHRQ INDEPENDENT SCIENTIST AWARD

Agency for Healthcare Research and Quality
Attn: Office of Extramural Research, Education and
    Priority Populations
540 Gaither Road
Rockville, MD 20850
(301) 427-1449          E-mail: training@ahrq.gov
Web: www.ahrq.gov

**Summary** To provide funding to newly independent scientists (particularly women, minorities, and persons with disabilities) who are interested in conducting research to improve the outcomes, effectiveness, quality, cost, and utilization of health care services.

**Eligibility** This program is open to U.S. citizens or permanent residents who have a clinical (e.g., M.D., D.O., D.D.S.) or research (e.g., Ph.D., Sc.D.) doctoral degree and are no more than 5 years beyond their latest research training experience. Applicants must be interested in conducting health services research designed to 1) support improvements in health outcomes at both the clinical and systems levels; 2) strengthen quality measurement and improvement, including the use of evidence-based practice information and tools; 3) identify strategies to improve access, foster appropriate use, and reduce unnecessary expenditures, including research on the organization, financing, and delivery of health care and the characteristics of primary care practices; 4) advance methodologies in health services research, especially cost-effectiveness analysis; and 5) focus on ethical issues across the spectrum of health care delivery. Special attention is paid to applications that focus on developing the careers of investigators who will study minority, child, and older adult health services research; some awards are made specifically to applications that foster the research careers of investigators studying those populations. Awards are also made specifically to individual investigators from predominantly minority institutions. Applications are especially encouraged from women, minorities, and individuals with disabilities.

**Financial data** Grants provide salary up to $75,000 annually, plus associated fringe benefits. Applicants may request additional funding to offset the cost of tuition, fees, books, and travel related to career development. Indirect costs are reimbursed at 8% of modified total direct costs.

**Duration** 3 to 5 years; nonrenewable.

**Additional information** At least 75% of the recipient's full-time professional effort must be devoted to the program and the remainder devoted to other research-related and/or teaching pursuits consistent with the objectives of the award.

**Number awarded** Varies each year.

## [1048]
## AHRQ MENTORED CLINICAL SCIENTIST DEVELOPMENT AWARD

Agency for Healthcare Research and Quality
Attn: Office of Extramural Research, Education and
    Priority Populations
540 Gaither Road
Rockville, MD 20850
(301) 427-1449          E-mail: training@ahrq.gov
Web: www.ahrq.gov

**Summary** To provide funding to postdoctorates (particularly women, minorities, and persons with disabilities) interested in obtaining additional research training to enable them to become independent investigators in health services research.

**Eligibility** This program is open to U.S. citizens or permanent residents who have received a clinical doctoral degree (M.D., D.O., D.C., O.D., D.D.S., Pharm.D., or doctorally-prepared nurses). Applicants must have identified a mentor with extensive research experience and be willing to spend at least 75% of full-time professional effort conducting research and developing a research career to improve the outcomes, effectiveness, quality, access to, and cost and utilization of health care services. Special attention is paid to applications that focus on developing the careers of investigators who will study minority, child, and older adult health services research; some awards are made specifically to applications that foster the research careers of investigators studying those populations. Awards are also made specifically to individual investigators from predominantly minority institutions. Applications are especially encouraged from women, minorities, and individuals with disabilities.

**Financial data** Grants provide salary up to $75,000 annually, plus associated fringe benefits. Also available are up to $25,000 per year for research development support (tuition, fees, and books related to career development; research expenses, such as supplies, equipment, and technical personnel; travel to research meetings or training; and statistical services, including personnel and computer time) and reimbursement of indirect costs at 8% of modified total direct costs.

**Duration** 3 to 5 years.

**Additional information** Recipients must spend at least 75% of full-time professional effort conducting research and developing a research career.

**Number awarded** Varies each year.

**Deadline** January, May, or September of each year.

## [1049]
## AHRQ SMALL RESEARCH GRANT PROGRAM

Agency for Healthcare Research and Quality
Attn: Division of Grants Management
540 Gaither Road
Rockville, MD 20850
(301) 427-1451          E-mail: mburr@ahrq.gov
Web: www.ahrq.gov

**Summary** To provide funding for small research projects designed to improve the quality, appropriateness, and effectiveness of health care services and access to those services.

**Eligibility** This program is open to investigators at domestic, nonprofit, public and private organizations, including universities, clinics, units of state and local governments, nonprofit firms, and nonprofit foundations. Applicants must be proposing projects for promoting improvements in clinical practice and in the organization, financing, and delivery of health care services. Proposals may be for research, evaluation, demonstrations, or pilot studies. The Agency for Healthcare Research and Quality (AHRQ) especially encourages women, members of minority racial and ethnic groups, and persons with disabilities to apply as principal investigators.

**Financial data** Total direct costs may not exceed $100,000.

**Duration** Up to 2 years.

**Additional information** Funding from this program may not be used for dissertation research.

**Number awarded** Varies each year.

**Deadline** March, July, or November of each year.

## [1050]
## ALABAMA SPACE GRANT CONSORTIUM GRADUATE FELLOWSHIP PROGRAM

Alabama Space Grant Consortium
c/o University of Alabama in Huntsville
Materials Science Building, Room 205
Huntsville, AL 35899
(256) 824-6800                    Fax: (256) 824-6061
E-mail: reasonj@uah.edu
Web: www.uah.edu/ASGC

**Summary** To provide financial assistance for graduate study or research related to the space sciences at universities participating in the Alabama Space Grant Consortium.

**Eligibility** This program is open to full-time graduate students enrolled at universities participating in the consortium. Applicants must be studying in a field related to space, including the physical, natural, and biological sciences; engineering; education; economics; business; sociology; behavioral sciences; computer science; communications; law; international affairs; and public administration. They must 1) present a proposed research plan related to space that includes an extramural experience at a field center of the National Aeronautics and Space Administration (NASA); 2) propose a multidisciplinary plan and course of study; 3) plan to be involved in consortium outreach activities; and 4) intend to prepare for a career in line with NASA's aerospace, science, and technology programs. U.S. citizenship is required. Individuals from underrepresented groups (African Americans, Hispanics, American Indians, Pacific Islanders, Asian Americans, and women) are especially encouraged to apply. Interested students should submit a completed application form, a description of the proposed research or study program, a schedule, a budget, a list of references, a vitae, and undergraduate and graduate transcripts. Selection is based on 1) academic qualifications, 2) quality of the proposed research program or plan of study and its relevance to the aerospace science and technology program of NASA, 3) quality of the proposed interdisciplinary approach, 4) merit of the proposed utilization of a NASA center to carry out the objectives of the program, 5) prospects for completing the project within the allotted time, and 6) applicant's motivation for a career in aerospace.

**Financial data** The annual award includes $16,000 for a student stipend and up to $6,000 for a tuition/student research allowance.

**Duration** 12 months; may be renewed up to 24 additional months.

**Additional information** The member universities are University of Alabama in Huntsville, Alabama A&M University, University of Alabama, University of Alabama in Birmingham, University of South Alabama, Tuskegee University, and Auburn University. Funding for this program is provided by NASA.

**Number awarded** Varies each year; recently, 12 of these fellowships were awarded.

**Deadline** February of each year.

## [1051]
## AMELIA EARHART RESEARCH SCHOLAR GRANT

Ninety-Nines, Inc.
Attn: Chair, Research Scholar Grants
4300 Amelia Earhart Road
Oklahoma City, OK 73159
(405) 685-7969                    Toll-free: (800) 994-1929
Fax: (405) 685-7985
E-mail: AEChair@ninety-nines.org
Web: www.ninety-nines.org/aemsf.html

**Summary** To provide funding to scholars interested in expanding knowledge about women in aviation and space.

**Eligibility** This program is open to scholars who are conducting research on the role of women in aviation and space. Disciplines may include, but are not limited to, biology, business administration, economics, ergonomics, history, human engineering, psychology, and sociology. Applicants may be seeking funding to be used in conjunction with other research activities, such as completion of requirements for an advanced degree or matching funds with other grants to support a program larger than either grant could sponsor independently.

**Financial data** The amount awarded varies; generally, the grant is at least $1,000.

**Duration** The grant is awarded periodically.

**Additional information** Information is also available from Dr. Jacqueline Boyd, 27 San Mateo Drive, P.O. Box 94, Angel Fire, NM 87710, (505) 377-3166, E-mail: AEChair@ninety-nines.org.

**Number awarded** 1 each granting period.

## [1052]
## AMERICAN ASSOCIATION OF OBSTETRICIANS AND GYNECOLOGISTS FOUNDATION SCHOLARSHIPS

American Association of Obstetricians and
    Gynecologists Foundation
Attn: Administrative Director
409 12th Street, S.W.
Washington, DC 20024-2188
(202) 863-1649                    Fax: (202) 554-0453
E-mail: clarkins@acog.org
Web: www.agosonline.org/aaogf.asp

**Summary** To provide funding to physicians (particularly women and minorities) who are interested in a program of research training in obstetrics and gynecology.

**Eligibility** Applicants must have an M.D. degree and be eligible for the certification process of the American Board of Obstetrics and Gynecology (ABOG). They must document departmental planning for a significant research training experience to be conducted by 1 or more faculty mentors. There is no formal application form, but departments must supply a description of the candidate's qualifications, including a curriculum vitae, bibliography, prior training, past research experience, and evidence of completion of residency training in obstetrics and gynecology; a comprehensive description of the proposed training program; a description of departmental resources appropriate to the training; a list of other research grants, training grants, or scholarships previously or currently held by the applicant; and a budget. Applicants for the scholarship co-sponsored by ABOG must verify that 90% of their time and effort will be dedicated to the research training and conduct of research. Applicants for the scholarship co-sponsored by the Society for Maternal-Fetal Medicine (SMFM) must also have completed MFM subspecialty training or be in the second or third year of an ABOG-approved MFM training program at the time of applying. Candidates for that scholarship must also be members or associate members of the SMFM. Preference for both awards is given to training in areas currently underrepresented in obstetrics and gynecology. A personal interview may be requested. Priority is given to individuals who have not previously received extramural funding for research training. Women and minority candidates are strongly encouraged to apply. Selection is based on the scholarly, clinical, and research qualifications of the candidate; evidence of the candidate's commitment to an investigative career in academic obstetrics and gynecology in the United States or Canada; qualifications of the sponsoring department and mentor; and quality of the research project.

**Financial data** The grant is $100,000 per year, of which at least $5,000 but not more than $15,000 must be used for employee benefits. In addition, sufficient funds to support travel to the annual fellows' retreat must be set aside. The balance of the funds may be used for salary, technical support, and supplies. The grant co-sponsored by the SMFM must be matched by an institutional commitment of at least $30,000 per year.

**Duration** 1 year; may be renewed for 2 additional years, based on satisfactory progress of the scholar.

**Additional information** Scholars must devote at least 75% of their effort to the program of research training.

**Number awarded** 2 each year: 1 co-sponsored by ABOG and 1 co-sponsored by SMFM.

**Deadline** August of each year.

## [1053]
## AMERICAN ASSOCIATION OF UNIVERSITY WOMEN DISSERTATION FELLOWSHIPS

American Association of University Women
Attn: AAUW Educational Foundation
301 ACT Drive, Department 60
P.O. Box 4030
Iowa City, IA 52243-4030
(319) 337-1716                    Fax: (319) 337-1204
E-mail: aauw@act.org
Web: www.aauw.org

**Summary** To provide funding to women in the final year of writing their dissertation.

**Eligibility** This program is open to U.S. citizens and permanent residents who are women and intend to pursue professional careers in the United States. They should have successfully completed all required course work for their doctorate, passed all preliminary examinations, and received written acceptance of their prospectus. Applicants may propose research in any field except engineering (the association offers Engineering Dissertation Fellowships as a separate program). Selection is based on scholarly excellence, quality of project design, originality of project, scholarly significance of project to discipline, feasibility of project and proposed schedule, qualifications of applicant, potential of applicant to make a significant contribution to field, applicant's commitment to women's issues in profession and community, and applicant's mentoring of other women.

**Financial data** The stipend is $20,000.

**Duration** 1 year, beginning in July.

**Additional information** The filing fee is $40. It is expected that the fellowship will be used for the final year of doctoral work and that the degree will be received at the end of the fellowship year. The fellowship is not intended to fund extended field research. The recipient should be prepared to devote full time to the dissertation during the fellowship year.

**Number awarded** Varies each year; recently, 48 of these fellowships were awarded.

**Deadline** November of each year.

## [1054]
## AMERICAN METEOROLOGICAL SOCIETY GRADUATE FELLOWSHIP IN THE HISTORY OF SCIENCE

American Meteorological Society
Attn: Fellowship/Scholarship Program
45 Beacon Street
Boston, MA 02108-3693
(617) 227-2426, ext. 246           Fax: (617) 742-8718
E-mail: scholar@ametsoc.org
Web: www.ametsoc.org

**Summary** To provide funding to graduate students (particularly women, minority, and disabled students) interested in conducting dissertation research on the history of meteorology.

**Eligibility** This program is open to graduate students who are planning to complete a dissertation on the history of the atmospheric or related oceanic or hydrologic sciences. Applicants must be U.S. citizens or permanent residents and working on a degree at a U.S. institution. Fellowships may be used to support research at a location away from the student's institution, provided the plan is approved by the student's thesis advisor. In such an instance, an effort is made to place the student into a mentoring relationship with a member of the society at an appropriate institution. The sponsor specifically encourages applications from women, minorities, and students with disabilities who are traditionally underrepresented in the atmospheric and related oceanic sciences.

**Financial data** The stipend is $15,000 per year.

**Duration** 1 year.

**Number awarded** 1 each year.

**Deadline** February of each year.

## [1055]
## AMY LUTZ RECHEL AWARD

Association for Women in Science
Attn: AWIS Educational Foundation
1200 New York Avenue, N.W., Suite 650
Washington, DC 20005
(202) 326-8940　　　　　Toll-free: (866) 657-AWIS
Fax: (202) 326-8960　　　E-mail: awisedfd@awis.org
Web: www.awis.org/careers/edfoundation.html

**Summary** To provide funding to women conducting doctoral research in plant biology.

**Eligibility** This program is open to women graduate students in the field of plant biology. Applicants must have passed their qualifying exam and be within 2 years of completing their Ph.D. Foreign students are eligible if they are enrolled in a U.S. institution of higher education. Selection is based on academic achievement, the importance of the research question addressed, the quality of the research, and the applicant's potential for future contributions to plant science.

**Financial data** The stipend is $1,000. Funds may be used for tuition, books, housing, research, travel and meeting registration, or publication costs.

**Duration** 1 year.

**Additional information** Information is also available from Barbara Filner, President, AWIS Educational Foundation, 7008 Richard Drive, Bethesda, MD 20817-4838.

**Number awarded** 1 each year.

**Deadline** January of each year.

## [1056]
## ANDREW W. MELLON FOUNDATION/ACLS DISSERTATION COMPLETION FELLOWSHIPS

American Council of Learned Societies
Attn: Office of Fellowships and Grants
633 Third Avenue, 8C
New York, NY 10017-6795
(212) 697-1505　　　　　Fax: (212) 949-8058
E-mail: grants@acls.org
Web: www.acls.org/ecfguide.htm

**Summary** To provide research funding to doctoral candidates (particularly women and minorities) in all disciplines of the humanities and the humanities-related social sciences who are ready to complete their dissertations.

**Eligibility** This program is open to doctoral candidates in a humanities or humanities-related social science discipline at a U.S. institution. Applicants must have completed all requirements for the Ph.D. except the dissertation. They may have completed no more than 6 years in the degree program. Research may be conducted at the home institution, abroad, or at another appropriate site. Appropriate fields of specialization include, but are not limited to, anthropology, archaeology, art and architectural history, economic history, film, geography, history, languages and literatures, legal studies, linguistics, musicology, philosophy, political science, psychology, religion, rhetoric and communication, sociology and theater studies. Proposals in those fields of the social sciences are eligible only if they employ predominantly humanistic approaches (e.g., economic history, law and literature, political philosophy). Proposals in interdisciplinary and cross-disciplinary studies are welcome, as are proposals focused on any geographic region or on any cultural or linguistic group. Applications are particularly invited from women and members of minority groups.

**Financial data** Grants provide a stipend of $25,000, funds for research costs up to $3,000, and university fees up to $5,000.

**Duration** 1 academic year. Grantees may accept this fellowship no later than their seventh year.

**Additional information** This program, which began in 2006, is supported by funding from the Andrew W. Mellon Foundation and administered by the American Council of Learned Societies (ACLS).

**Number awarded** 65 each year.

**Deadline** November of each year.

## [1057]
## ANN E. KAMMER MEMORIAL FELLOWSHIP FUND

Woods Hole Marine Biological Laboratory
Attn: Fellowship Coordinator
7 MBL Street
Woods Hole, MA 02543-1015
(508) 289-7340　　　　　Fax: (508) 457-1924
E-mail: fellows@mbl.edu
Web: www.mbl.edu

**Summary** To support women scientists who wish to conduct research at the Woods Hole Marine Biological Laboratory (MBL).

**Eligibility** This program is open to women scientists interested in conducting research at the MBL, with a preference given to those working in the neurosciences.

**Financial data** The award provides funds for summer research at the MBL. Recently, grants averaged approximately $1,500.

**Duration** Summer months.

**Number awarded** 1 each year.

**Deadline** January of each year.

## [1058]
## ANNALEY NAEGLE REDD STUDENT AWARD IN WOMEN'S HISTORY

Brigham Young University
Attn: Charles Redd Center for Western Studies
366 SWKT
Provo, UT 84602
(801) 422-4048     E-mail: redd_center@byu.edu
Web: fhss.byu.edu

**Summary** To provide funding to undergraduate and graduate students interested in conducting research on women in the Intermountain West.

**Eligibility** This program is open to undergraduate and graduate students who are interested in conducting a research project related to women in the American West. Applicants may be proposing any kind of project, including seminar papers, theses, or dissertations. Along with their application, they must submit 200-word statements on a description of the proposed research question, a summary of the project's relationship to the Intermountain West (Idaho, Montana, Nevada, Arizona, New Mexico, Utah, and Colorado), a description of the primary sources available and where they are located, a summary of the secondary literature available, a description of what makes this study unique, a summary of the planned use of the research, and a detailed budget.

**Financial data** The grant is $1,500. Funds may be used for research support (supplies, travel, etc.) but not for salary or capital equipment.

**Duration** Normally work is to be undertaken during the summer.

**Number awarded** 1 each year.

**Deadline** March of each year.

## [1059]
## ARKANSAS SPACE GRANT CONSORTIUM COLLABORATIVE RESEARCH GRANTS

Arkansas Space Grant Consortium
c/o University of Arkansas at Little Rock
Graduate Institute of Technology
2801 South University Avenue
Little Rock, AR 72204
(501) 569-8212     Fax: (501) 569-8039
E-mail: asgc@ualr.edu
Web: asgc.ualr.edu/spacegrant

**Summary** To provide funding to faculty (particularly women, minorities, and persons with disabilities) at member universities of the Arkansas Space Grant Consortium (ASGC) for research that involves collaboration with students and faculty at other institutions in Arkansas.

**Eligibility** This program is open to faculty at institutions that are members of the ASGC. Applicants must be seeking funding for research projects in fields of interest to the National Aeronautics and Space Administration (NASA), including astronomy, biochemistry, biology, chemistry, computer science, earth science, engineering, engineering technology, instrumentation, materials science, mathematics, physics, psychology, and space medicine. The inclusion of faculty and students at other Arkansas institutions of higher education is favorably considered; at least 1 faculty member and 1 student at 1 or more institutions must be funded. Inclusion of women, minorities, and people with disabilities is given special consideration.

**Financial data** The maximum grant is $15,000 per year. Requests for faculty stipends are considered for summer only and are limited to 6% of base salary from collaborative research funds.

**Duration** 1 year. May be renewed for a second year if the grantee submits a proposal for external funding by the end of the first year. May be renewed for a third year if the grantee submits a proposal to at least 2 sources of external funding by the end of the second year.

**Additional information** ASGC member institutions are Arkansas State University, University, Arkansas Tech University, Harding University, Henderson State University, Hendrix College, Lyon College, Ouachita Baptist University, University of Central Arkansas, University of Arkansas at Fayetteville, University of Arkansas at Little Rock, University of Arkansas at Montecito, University of Arkansas at Pine Bluff, University of Arkansas for Medical Sciences, and University of the Ozarks. This program is funded by NASA.

**Number awarded** Varies each year.

**Deadline** September of each year.

## [1060]
## ARKANSAS SPACE GRANT CONSORTIUM RESEARCH INFRASTRUCTURE GRANTS

Arkansas Space Grant Consortium
c/o University of Arkansas at Little Rock
Graduate Institute of Technology
2801 South University Avenue
Little Rock, AR 72204
(501) 569-8212     Fax: (501) 569-8039
E-mail: asgc@ualr.edu
Web: asgc.ualr.edu/spacegrant

**Summary** To provide research funding to faculty (particularly women, minorities, and persons with disabilities) at member universities of the Arkansas Space Grant Consortium (ASGC).

**Eligibility** This program is open to faculty at institutions that are members of the ASGC. Applicants must be seeking research starter grants for projects that seem likely to receive support from the U.S. National Aeronautics and Space Administration (NASA) and be willing to mentor student scholarship and fellowship research. Fields of study include astronomy, biochemistry, biology, chemistry, computer science, earth science, engineering, engineering technology, instrumentation, materials science, mathematics, physics, psychology, and space medicine. The consortium is a component of NASA's Space Grant program, which encourages participation by underrepresented minorities, women, and persons with disabilities.

**Financial data** The funding depends on the nature of the proposal.

**Duration** Up to 3 years.

**Additional information** ASGC member institutions are Arkansas State University, University, Arkansas Tech University, Harding University, Henderson State University, Hendrix College, Lyon College, Ouachita Baptist University, University of Central Arkansas, University of Arkansas at Fayetteville, University of Arkansas at Little Rock, University of Arkansas at Montecito, University of Arkansas at Pine Bluff, University of Arkansas for Medical Sciences, and University of the Ozarks. This program is funded by NASA.

**Number awarded** Varies each year; since this program began in 1990, it has awarded approximately 300 of these grants.

## [1061]
## ARKANSAS SPACE GRANT CONSORTIUM SCHOLARSHIPS AND FELLOWSHIPS

Arkansas Space Grant Consortium
c/o University of Arkansas at Little Rock
Graduate Institute of Technology
2801 South University Avenue
Little Rock, AR 72204
(501) 569-8212                          Fax: (501) 569-8039
E-mail: asgc@ualr.edu
Web: asgc.ualr.edu/spacegrant

**Summary** To provide funding to students (especially women, minority, and disabled students) at designated universities in Arkansas who are interested in working on a space-related research project.

**Eligibility** This program is open to undergraduate and graduate students at colleges and universities that participate in the Arkansas Space Grant Consortium (ASGC). Applicants must be interested in working with a faculty mentor on a specific research project. Fields of study include astronomy, biochemistry, biology, chemistry, computer science, earth science, engineering, engineering technology, instrumentation, materials science, mathematics, physics, psychology, and space medicine. Students must be U.S. citizens. The consortium is a component of NASA's Space Grant program, which encourages participation by underrepresented minorities, women, and persons with disabilities.

**Financial data** The funding depends on the nature of the proposal.

**Additional information** ASGC member institutions are Arkansas State University, Arkansas Tech University, Harding University, Henderson State University, Hendrix College, Lyon College, Ouachita Baptist University, University of Central Arkansas, University of Arkansas at Fayetteville, University of Arkansas at Little Rock, University of Arkansas at Montecito, University of Arkansas at Pine Bluff, University of Arkansas for Medical Sciences, and University of the Ozarks. This program is funded by NASA.

**Number awarded** Varies each year; since this program began in 1990, it has awarded nearly 400 undergraduate scholarships and 100 graduate fellowships.

## [1062]
## ART MEETS ACTIVISM GRANT PROGRAM

Kentucky Foundation for Women
Heyburn Building
332 West Broadway, Suite 1215-A
Louisville, KY 40202-2184
(502) 562-0045                     Toll-free: (866) 654-7564
Fax: (502) 561-0420                E-mail: info@kfw.org
Web: www.kfw.org/artact.html

**Summary** To support women and organizations in Kentucky wishing to promote positive social change through feminist expression in the arts.

**Eligibility** This program is open to women artists who have resided in Kentucky for at least 1 year and whose work is feminist in nature and is intentionally focused on social change outcomes. Nonprofit organizations are also eligible if their proposed project is artist driven. Applicants may be seeking funding for a range of artistic activities, including arts education programs focused on women or girls, community participation in the creation of new art forms, artist-centered projects involving non-traditional venues or new partnerships between artists and activists, and artist-centered projects with social change themes or contents. They must submit work samples (1 copy of a CD, DVD, videotape, audiocassette, or CD-ROM; 10 to 12 slides or photographs; 15 to 20 pages of fiction, nonfiction, poetry, or a play script). Selection is based on strength and originality of the artwork; explanation of the artist's commitment to feminism; clear understanding of the relationship between art and social change; explanation of the ways the proposed activities will benefit Kentucky women; clear, well thought-out work plans and detailed, realistic budget; and evidence of ability to complete the proposed activities.

**Financial data** Grants may range from $1,000 to $7,500, but most average between $3,000 and $5,000.

**Duration** Up to 1 year.

**Additional information** The foundation was established in 1985. It defines social change as eliminating societal barriers to women; neutralizing discrimination against women based on age, race, ethnicity, sexual orientation, physical ability, education, economic condition, and geographic origin; and producing actions, conditions, policies, attitudes, and behaviors that benefit women. Funding is not provided for business enterprises; for-profit organizations; tuition costs or living expenses while working toward a degree; endowment or capital campaigns; projects that do not focus on changing the lives of women in Kentucky; the promotion of religious doctrines; non-art related expenses, such as overdue bills or taxes; or work conducted by artists or programs residing or operating outside of Kentucky.

**Number awarded** Varies each year; recently, 28 of these grants were awarded. A total of $100,000 is available annually.

**Deadline** February of each year.

## [1063]
## ART-IN-EDUCATION RESIDENCY GRANTS

Women's Studio Workshop
722 Binnewater Lane
P.O. Box 489
Rosendale, NY 12472
(845) 658-9133                   Fax: (845) 658-9031
E-mail: info@wsworkshop.org
Web: www.wsworkshop.org

**Summary**  To provide a residency and financial support to women interested in producing a limited edition artist's book and working with young people.

**Eligibility**  This program is open to emerging artists who come from different regions of the country and/or diverse cultural backgrounds. Applicants must be interested in spending half their time involved with the design and production of a limited edition artist's book, and the other half working with young people in an arts-in-education program. For the artist's book project, they should include a 1-page description of the proposed project; specify the medium used to print the book, the number of pages, page size, and edition size (100 is preferred); and provide a structural dummy, a materials budget, and a resume.

**Financial data**  The program provides a stipend of $3,200, a $500 materials grant, travel costs (within the continental United States) and housing while in residence.

**Duration**  8 weeks (March and April with fifth-grade students or September and October with high school students).

**Number awarded**  2 each year.

**Deadline**  March of each year.

## [1064]
## ARTIST ENRICHMENT GRANT PROGRAM

Kentucky Foundation for Women
Heyburn Building
332 West Broadway, Suite 1215-A
Louisville, KY 40202-2184
(502) 562-0045                   Toll-free: (866) 654-7564
Fax: (502) 561-0420               E-mail: info@kfw.org
Web: www.kfw.org/artenr.html

**Summary**  To support women in Kentucky who wish to promote positive social change through feminist expression in the arts.

**Eligibility**  This program is open to women who have resided in Kentucky for at least 1 year and are artists at any stage in their career able to demonstrate potential in terms of quality of work and an understanding of the power of art for social change. Applicants must be seeking funding for continued development of a body of work, including professional development activities, exploration of new areas of work or techniques, or related creative activities. They must submit work samples (1 copy of a CD, DVD, videotape, audiocassette, or CD-ROM; 10 to 12 slides or photographs; 15 to 20 pages of fiction, nonfiction, poetry, or a play script). Selection is based on strength and originality of the artwork; explanation of the artist's commitment to feminism; clear understanding of the relationship between art and social change; explanation of ways the proposed activities will benefit the artist; a clear, well thought-out work plan with a detailed, realistic budget; and evidence of ability to complete successfully the proposed activities.

**Financial data**  Grants may range from $1,000 to $7,500, but most average between $3,000 and $5,000.

**Duration**  Up to 1 year.

**Additional information**  The foundation was established in 1985. It defines social change as eliminating societal barriers to women; neutralizing discrimination against women based on age, race, ethnicity, sexual orientation, physical ability, education, economic condition, and geographic origin; and producing actions, conditions, policies, attitudes, and behaviors that benefit women. Funding is not provided for business enterprises; for-profit organizations; tuition costs or living expenses while working toward a degree; endowment or capital campaigns; projects that do not focus on changing the lives of women in Kentucky; the promotion of religious doctrines; non-art related expenses, such as overdue bills or taxes; or work conducted by artists or programs residing or working outside of Kentucky.

**Number awarded**  Varies each year; recently, 29 of these grants were awarded. A total of $100,000 is available annually.

**Deadline**  August of each year.

## [1065]
## ARTISTS' BOOK RESIDENCY GRANTS

Women's Studio Workshop
722 Binnewater Lane
P.O. Box 489
Rosendale, NY 12472
(845) 658-9133                   Fax: (845) 658-9031
E-mail: info@wsworkshop.org
Web: www.wsworkshop.org

**Summary**  To provide financial assistance and a residency at the Women's Studio Workshop (WSW) to women book artists.

**Eligibility**  Female artists should submit proposals for new books that will have a press run of at least 100 copies. Applicants must provide a 1-paragraph description of the proposed project; specify the medium to be used to print the book, number of pages, page size, and edition size; and provide a structural dummy, a materials budget, a resume, and 6 to 10 slides of recent work. International artists are especially encouraged to apply.

**Financial data**  The program provides a stipend of $2,000 to $3,000, a $500 materials grant, and housing while in residence.

**Duration**  6 to 8 weeks.

**Additional information**  This program provides an opportunity for book artists to come and work in residency at WSW in Rosendale, New York. Selected artists are involved in all aspects of the design and production of their new books. The studio provides technical advice and, when possible, help with editing. Assistance with marketing is also available. No residencies are available during the summer.

**Number awarded**  Varies each year.

**Deadline**  November of each year.

## [1066]
## ASA/NSF/BLS FELLOWSHIP PROGRAM

American Statistical Association
Attn: Fellowship Program
732 North Washington Street
Alexandria, VA 22314-1943
(703) 684-1221                    Toll-free: (888) 231-3473
Fax: (703) 684-2037        E-mail: asainfo@amstat.org
Web: www.amstat.org/research_grants

**Summary**  To provide funding to senior researchers (particularly women and minorities) who are interested in conducting research in residence at the Bureau of Labor Statistics (BLS).

**Eligibility**  This program is open to scholars interested in conducting research in the broad field of labor economics and statistics that is of interest to the BLS. Applicants must be planning to work in residence, using BLS data and facilities, and interacting with BLS staff. They should have a recognized research record and considerable expertise in their area of proposed research. Selection is based on the applicability of the proposed research to BLS programs, the value of the proposed research to science, and the quality of the applicant's research record. Qualified women and members of minority groups are especially encouraged to apply.

**Financial data**  The stipends paid to senior research fellows are commensurate with their qualifications and experience. Fellows also receive fringe benefits and a travel allowance.

**Duration**  The usual term is 6 to 12 months, although the duration is flexible.

**Additional information**  Fellows are given an opportunity to conduct their research in residence and interact with staff. Funding for this program is provided by the National Science Foundation (NSF). Information is also available from the Bureau of Labor Statistics, Attn: Stephen Cohen, 2 Massachusetts Avenue, N.E., Suite 1950, Washington, DC 20212, (202) 691-7400, E-mail: Cohen.Steve@bls.gov.

**Number awarded**  Varies each year.

**Deadline**  December of each year.

## [1067]
## ASECS WOMEN'S CAUCUS EDITING AND TRANSLATION FELLOWSHIP

American Society for Eighteenth-Century Studies
c/o Wake Forest University
P.O. Box 7867
Winston-Salem, NC 27109
(336) 727-4694                    Fax: (336) 727-4697
E-mail: asecs@wfu.edu
Web: asecs.press.jhu.edu/awards.html

**Summary**  To provide funding to pre- and postdoctoral scholars working on an editing or translating project that deals with women's issues in the 18th century.

**Eligibility**  This program is open to members of the American Society for Eighteenth-Century Studies (ASECS) who are working on an editing or translating project. Applicants must have a Ph.D. or be an emeritae/i faculty who does not already have professional support for the project. The project must translate and/or edit works by women writers or works that significantly advance understanding of women's

experiences in the 18th century or offer a feminist analysis of an aspect of 18th-century culture and/or society.

**Financial data**  The grant is $1,000.

**Duration**  The grant is offered annually.

**Additional information**  This award offered by the Women's Caucus of the ASECS was first presented in 2004. The recipient is asked to submit a brief written report on the progress of the project 1 year after receiving the award and, wherever possible, will serve on the award committee in the following year.

**Number awarded**  1 each year.

**Deadline**  January of each year.

## [1068]
## ASPET INDIVIDUAL SUMMER UNDERGRADUATE RESEARCH FELLOWSHIPS

American Society for Pharmacology and Experimental
    Therapeutics
9650 Rockville Pike
Bethesda, MD 20814-3995
(301) 634-7060                    Fax: (301) 634-7061
E-mail: info@aspet.org
Web: www.aspet.org/public/surf/surf.htm

**Summary**  To provide funding to undergraduate students who are interested in participating in a summer research project at a laboratory affiliated with the American Society for Pharmacology and Experimental Therapeutics (ASPET).

**Eligibility**  This program is open to undergraduate students interested in working during the summer in the laboratory of a society member who must agree to act as a sponsor. Applications must be submitted jointly by the student and the sponsor, and they must include 1) a letter from the sponsor with a brief description of the proposed research, a statement of the qualifications of the student, the degree of independence the student will have, a description of complementary activities available to the student, and a description of how the student will report on the research results; 2) a letter from the student indicating the nature of his or her interest in the project and a description of future plans; 3) a copy of the sponsor's updated curriculum vitae; and 4) copies of all the student's undergraduate transcripts. Selection is based on the nature of the research opportunities provided, student and sponsor qualifications, and the likelihood the student will prepare for a career in pharmacology. Applications from women and underrepresented minorities are particularly encouraged.

**Financial data**  The stipend is $2,500. Funds are paid directly to the institution but may be used only for student stipends.

**Duration**  10 weeks during the summer.

**Additional information**  Some of these awards are funded through the Glenn E. Ullyot Fund; those recipients are designated as the Ullyot Fellows.

**Number awarded**  Varies each year; recently, 4 of these fellowships were awarded.

**Deadline**  February of each year.

## [1069]
## ASSOCIATION FOR WOMEN IN MATHEMATICS MENTORING TRAVEL GRANTS

Association for Women in Mathematics
11240 Waples Mill Road, Suite 200
Fairfax, VA 22030
(703) 934-0163					Fax: (703) 359-7562
E-mail: awm@math.umd.edu
Web: www.awm-math.org/travelgrants.html

**Summary** To provide funding to junior women postdoctorates in mathematics who wish to travel to develop a long-term working and mentoring relationship with a senior mathematician.

**Eligibility** This program is open to women holding a doctorate or with equivalent experience and with a work address in the United States. They must be untenured. The applicant's research may be in any field that is funded by the Division of Mathematical Sciences (DMS) of the National Science Foundation (NSF). The proposed travel must be to an institute or a department (in the United States or abroad) to do research with a senior mathematician so the applicant can establish her research program and eventually receive tenure.

**Financial data** These grants provide full or partial support for travel, subsistence, and other required expenses, to a maximum of $5,000.

**Duration** The proposed visit may last up to 1 month.

**Additional information** Funding for this program is provided by the Division of Mathematical Sciences of the NSF. For foreign travel, U.S. carriers must be used whenever possible.

**Number awarded** Up to 7 each year.

**Deadline** January of each year.


## [1070]
## AWARDS FOR RESEARCH IN ENGINEERING AND SCIENCE (ARES) PROGRAM

Montana Space Grant Consortium
c/o Montana State University
416 Cobleigh Hall
P.O. Box 173835
Bozeman, MT 59717-3835
(406) 994-4223					Fax: (406) 994-4452
E-mail: msgc@montana.edu
Web: spacegrant.montana.edu/Text/ARES.html

**Summary** To provide funding to undergraduate students in Montana (particularly women, minority, and disabled students) who are interested in working on a space-related science or engineering research project.

**Eligibility** This program is open to full-time undergraduate students at selected member institutions of the Montana Space Grant Consortium (MSGC) majoring in fields related to space sciences and engineering. Applicants must be interested in working on a research project as a team with a faculty mentor. Students must submit a 3- to 4-page proposal, including a project title, explanation of the problem to be studied, goals to be achieved, experimental approach, and references. The faculty member must write a supporting letter, describing how the student will contribute to the research project and indicating support for the proposal. U.S. citizenship is required. The MSGC is a component of

the U.S. National Aeronautics and Space Administration (NASA) Space Grant program, which encourages participation by women, underrepresented minorities, and persons with disabilities.

**Financial data** The grant is $500 per semester or $330 per quarter.

**Duration** 1 semester or quarter; may be renewed.

**Additional information** The MSGC member institutions are Blackfeet Community College, Carroll College, Chief Dull Knife College, Fort Belknap College, Fort Peck Community College, Little Big Horn College, Montana State University at Billings, Montana State University Northern, Rocky Mountain College, Salish Kootenai College, Stone Child College, University of Great Falls, and University of Montana Western. Funding for this program is provided by NASA.

**Number awarded** Varies each year.


## [1071]
## AWHONN NOVICE RESEARCHER AWARD

Association of Women's Health, Obstetric and Neonatal Nurses
Attn: Research Grants Program
2000 L Street, N.W., Suite 740
Washington, DC 20036
(202) 261-2431					Toll-free: (800) 673-8499
Fax: (202) 728-0575
E-mail: ResearchPrograms@awhonn.org
Web: www.awhonn.org

**Summary** To provide funding for small research projects to members of the Association of Women's Health, Obstetric and Neonatal Nurses (AWHONN).

**Eligibility** This program is open to members of the association who qualify as novice researchers. Applicants must be interested in beginning areas of study, investigating clinical issues, and/or launching a pilot study.

**Financial data** The grant is $5,000. Funds may not be used for indirect costs, tuition, computer hardware or printers, conference attendance, or salary for the principal investigator or other investigators.

**Duration** 1 year.

**Number awarded** 1 or more each year.

**Deadline** November of each year.


## [1072]
## BARBARA ROSENBLUM SCHOLARSHIP FOR THE STUDY OF WOMEN AND CANCER

Sociologists for Women in Society
Attn: Executive Officer
University of Rhode Island
Department of Sociology
Kingston, RI 02881
(401) 874-9510					Fax: (401) 874-2588
E-mail: jessicasherwood@mail.uri.edu
Web: www.socwomen.org

**Summary** To provide funding to women interested in conducting doctoral research on the social science aspects of women and cancer.

**Eligibility** This program is open to women doctoral students with a feminist orientation who are interested in studying breast cancer and its impact on women of color, lesbians, and other women from diverse social classes and cultural backgrounds. The research may be conducted in the areas of sociology, anthropology, psychology, or other social science fields concerned with women's experiences with breast cancer and the prevention of breast cancer. Priority is given to research that is not only useful academically but will have pragmatic and practical applications.

**Financial data** The grant is $1,500.

**Duration** 1 year.

**Additional information** This program was established in 1991. Further information is available from Jennie Kronenfeld, Arizona State University, P.O. Box 872101, Tempe, AZ 82587-2101, (480) 965-8053, Fax: (480) 965-0065.

**Number awarded** 1 every other year.

**Deadline** March of each even-numbered year.

## [1073]
## BEHAVIORAL SCIENCES POSTDOCTORAL FELLOWSHIPS IN EPILEPSY

Epilepsy Foundation
Attn: Research Department
8301 Professional Place
Landover, MD 20785-2237
(301) 459-3700          Toll-free: (800) EFA-1000
Fax: (301) 577-2684     TDD: (800) 332-2070
E-mail: grants@efa.org
Web: www.epilepsyfoundation.org

**Summary** To provide funding to postdoctorates in the behavioral sciences (particularly women, minorities, and persons with disabilities) who wish to pursue research training in an area related to epilepsy.

**Eligibility** Individuals who have received their doctoral degree in a behavioral science field by the time the fellowship begins and desire additional postdoctoral research experience in epilepsy may apply. Academic faculty holding the rank of instructor or above are not eligible, nor are graduate or medical students, medical residents, permanent government employees, or employees of private industry. Appropriate fields of study in the behavioral sciences include sociology, social work, anthropology, nursing, economics, and others relevant to epilepsy research and practice. Because these fellowships are designed as training opportunities, the quality of the training plans and environment are considered in the selection process. Other selection criteria include the scientific quality of the proposed research, a statement regarding the relevance of the research to epilepsy, the applicant's qualifications, the preceptor's qualifications, adequacy of the facility, and related epilepsy programs at the institution. Applications from women, members of minority groups, and people with disabilities are especially encouraged. U.S. citizenship is not required, but the research must be conducted in the United States.

**Financial data** Grants up to $40,000 per year are available.

**Duration** 1 year.

**Number awarded** Varies each year; recently, 1 of these fellowships was awarded.

**Deadline** February of each year.

## [1074]
## BEHAVIORAL SCIENCES STUDENT FELLOWSHIPS IN EPILEPSY

Epilepsy Foundation
Attn: Research Department
8301 Professional Place
Landover, MD 20785-2237
(301) 459-3700          Toll-free: (800) EFA-1000
Fax: (301) 577-2684     TDD: (800) 332-2070
E-mail: grants@efa.org
Web: www.epilepsyfoundation.org

**Summary** To provide funding to undergraduate and graduate students (particularly women, minority, and disabled students) interested in working on a summer research training project in a field relevant to epilepsy.

**Eligibility** This program is open to undergraduate and graduate students in a behavioral science program relevant to epilepsy research or clinical care, including, but not limited to, sociology, social work, psychology, anthropology, nursing, economics, vocational rehabilitation, counseling, and political science. Applicants must be interested in working on an epilepsy research project under the supervision of a qualified mentor. Because the program is designed as a training opportunity, the quality of the training plans and environment are considered in the selection process. Other selection criteria include the quality of the proposed project, the relevance of the proposed work to epilepsy, the applicant's interest in the field of epilepsy, the applicant's qualifications, and the mentor's qualifications, including his or her commitment to the student and the project. U.S. citizenship is not required, but the project must be conducted in the United States. Applications from women, members of minority groups, and people with disabilities are especially encouraged. The program is not intended for students working on a dissertation research project.

**Financial data** The grant is $3,000.

**Duration** 3 months during the summer.

**Additional information** This program is supported by the American Epilepsy Society, Abbott Laboratories, Ortho-McNeil Pharmaceutical Corporation, and Pfizer Inc.

**Number awarded** Varies each year; recently, 2 of these fellowships were awarded.

**Deadline** February of each year.

## [1075]
## BERKSHIRE CONFERENCE OF WOMEN HISTORIANS GRADUATE STUDENT FELLOWSHIP

Coordinating Council for Women in History
211 Marginal Way, Number 733
P.O. Box 9715
Portland, ME 04104-5015
Web: theccwh.org/berkwellsapp.htm

**Summary** To provide funding to women graduate students in history for completion of their doctoral dissertations.

**Eligibility** This program is open to women graduate students in history departments at U.S. institutions who are members of the Coordinating Council for Women in History (CCWH). Applicants must have passed to A.B.D. status. They may be specializing in any field of history.

**Financial data**  The grant is $500.

**Duration**  1 year.

**Additional information**  This program, established in 1991, is administered by the CCWH and the Berkshire Conference of Women Historians. The award is presented at the CCWH luncheon at the annual meeting of the American Historical Association, although the recipient does not need to be present to accept the award. Information is also available from Ann Le Bar, Eastern Washington University, Department of History, Patterson Hall 200, Cheney, WA 99004.

**Number awarded**  1 each year.

**Deadline**  August of each year.

## [1076]
## BUTCHER SCHOLAR AWARD

Autry National Center
Attn: Institute for the Study of the American West
4700 Western Heritage Way
Los Angeles, CA 90027-1462
(323) 667-2000                    Fax: (323) 660-5721
Web: www.autry-museum.org/butcher_scholar.php

**Summary**  To provide funding to scholars interested in conducting research on the history of women in the West at the Autry Museum of Western Heritage.

**Eligibility**  This program is open to scholars interested in conducting research projects that explore the relationships between the experiences, stories, and memories of women in the American West. Preference is given to projects that examine the interwoven aspects of myth and history, that speak to the diversity of women in the West, and that use historical themes to provide a greater understanding of contemporary issues. Each year, the sponsor selects a theme for this program that relates to a current museum initiative; recently, the theme was "Women and the Wild." Selection is based on the proposed project's relevance to the theme, description of the final product, originality and creativity of approach, and qualifications of the applicant to complete the proposed project successfully.

**Financial data**  The maximum grant is $5,000.

**Duration**  1 year.

**Additional information**  This program was established in 2001 by the Women of the West Museum, which has since merged with the Autry National Center. The museum works with the scholar to create and implement a community outreach component that enhances its public impact. In addition, the scholar is asked to make a presentation at the Autry Museum History Workshop.

**Number awarded**  1 each year.

**Deadline**  May of each year.

## [1077]
## BYRD FELLOWSHIP PROGRAM

Ohio State University
Byrd Polar Research Center
Attn: Fellowship Committee
Scott Hall Room 108
1090 Carmack Road
Columbus, OH 43210-1002
(614) 292-6531                    Fax: (614) 292-4697
Web: www-bprc.mps.ohio-state.edu

**Summary**  To provide funding to postdoctorates (particularly women, minorities, and persons with disabilities) who are interested in conducting research on the Arctic or Antarctic areas at Ohio State University.

**Eligibility**  This program is open to postdoctorates of superior academic background who are interested in pursuing advanced research on either Arctic or Antarctic problems at the Byrd Polar Research Center at Ohio State University. Applicants must have received their doctorates within the past 5 years. Each application should include a statement of general research interest, a description of the specific research to be conducting during the fellowship, and a curriculum vitae. Women, minorities, Vietnam-era veterans, disabled veterans, and individuals with disabilities are particularly encouraged to apply.

**Financial data**  The stipend is $35,000 per year; an allowance of $3,000 for research and travel is also provided.

**Duration**  18 months.

**Additional information**  This program was established by a major gift from the Byrd Foundation in memory of Rear Admiral Richard Evelyn Byrd and Marie Ames Byrd, his wife. Except for field work or other research activities requiring absence from campus, fellows are expected to be in residence at the university for the duration of the program.

**Deadline**  November of each year.

## [1078]
## CALDER SUMMER UNDERGRADUATE RESEARCH PROGRAM

Fordham University
Attn: Louis Calder Center Biological Field Station
53 Whippoorwill Road
P.O. Box 887
Armonk, NY 10504
(914) 273-3078, ext. 10                    Fax: (914) 273-2167
E-mail: REUatCalder@fordham.edu
Web: www.fordham.edu/calder_center

**Summary**  To provide an opportunity for undergraduates (particularly women and minorities) to pursue summer research activities in biology at Fordham University's Louis Calder Center Biological Field Station.

**Eligibility**  This program is open to undergraduates interested in conducting a summer research project of their own design at the center. Fields of interest must relate to the activities of staff who will serve as mentors on the projects; those include forest ecology, limnology, wildlife ecology, microbial ecology, Lyme disease, insect-plant interactions, evolutionary ecology, and the effects of urbanization on ecosystem processes. Applications from women and underrepresented minorities are especially encouraged.

**Financial data** The program provides a stipend of $4,800, housing on the site, and support for research supplies and local travel.

**Duration** 12 weeks during the summer.

**Additional information** This program has operated since 1967.

**Number awarded** Up to 12 each year.

**Deadline** February of each year.

## [1079]
## CALIFORNIA SPACE GRANT CONSORTIUM GRADUATE RESEARCH FELLOWSHIPS

California Space Grant Consortium
c/o University of California at San Diego
Chemistry Research Building, Room 319
9500 Gilman Drive, Department 0524
La Jolla, CA 92093-0524
(858) 822-1597                    Fax: (858) 534-7840
E-mail: spacegrant@ucsd.edu
Web: calspace.ucsd.edu/casgc/grad_fellowships.html

**Summary** To provide financial assistance for graduate study and research in space-related science, engineering, or technology at institutions that are affiliates of the California Space Grant Consortium (CaSGC).

**Eligibility** This program is open to graduate students in space-related science, engineering, and technology at CaSGC affiliates. Each participating institution encourages aerospace science and engineering graduate students, particularly underrepresented ethnic or gender groups, to apply. U.S. citizenship is required.

**Financial data** Each campus sets its own stipend.

**Duration** 1 year.

**Additional information** CaSGC affiliates include the University of California campuses at Berkeley, Davis, Irvine, Los Angeles, Riverside, San Diego, Santa Barbara, and Santa Cruz; the California State University campuses at Long Beach, Los Angeles, Sacramento, San Bernardino, San Diego, and San Luis Obispo; Santa Clara University; Stanford University; and the University of Southern California. This program is funded by the U.S. National Aeronautics and Space Administration (NASA). Award recipients are encouraged to mentor within the campus minority engineering and science programs and in the Space Grant Outreach programs.

**Number awarded** Varies each year. A total of $100,000 is available for these fellowships each year.

**Deadline** Each of the participating institutions sets its own deadline.

## [1080]
## CAREER AWARDS AT THE SCIENTIFIC INTERFACE

Burroughs Wellcome Fund
21 T.W. Alexander Drive, Suite 100
P.O. Box 13901
Research Triangle Park, NC 27709-3901
(919) 991-5100                    Fax: (919) 991-5160
E-mail: info@bwfund.org
Web: www.bwfund.org

**Summary** To provide funding to postdoctorates (particularly women and minorities) in the physical and computational sciences who are interested in pursuing research training in the biomedical sciences.

**Eligibility** Applicants must have a Ph.D. degree in the fields of mathematics, physics, chemistry (physical, theoretical, or computational), computer science, statistics, or engineering. They must have completed at least 6 but not more than 48 months of postdoctoral training and must not hold or have accepted a faculty appointment as an assistant professor at the time of application. Degree-granting institutions in the United States and Canada, including their medical schools, graduate schools, and all affiliated hospitals and research institutes, may nominate up to 2 candidates for the award. Institutions are encouraged to nominate women and members of underrepresented minority groups. If they nominate at least 1 African American, Hispanic, or Native American postdoctorate, they may nominate up to 3 total candidates. The research proposal must address questions in an area of biomedical science, including any combination of experiment, computation, mathematical modeling, statistical analysis, or computer simulation. Nominees must be citizens or permanent residents of the United States or Canada. Selection is based on the depth and rigor of training in a scientific discipline other than biology, importance of biological questions identified in the proposal and innovation in the approaches chosen to answer them, interdisciplinary nature of the research plan, potential of the candidate to establish a successful independent research career, and quality of proposed collaborations.

**Financial data** In the first year of postdoctoral support, the salary is $44,000, the research allowance is $31,000, and the administrative fee is $5,000; in the second year of postdoctoral support, the salary is $47,000, the research allowance is $8,000, and the administrative fee is $5,000; in the first year of faculty support, the maximum salary support is $45,000, the research allowance is $65,000, and the administrative fee is $10,000; in the second year of faculty support, the maximum salary support is $49,000, the research allowance is $61,000, and the administrative fee is $10,000; in the third year of faculty support, the maximum salary support is $54,000, the research allowance is $56,000, and the administrative fee is $10,000. The maximum total grant is $500,000. During the first year of the faculty period, at least 50% of the starting salary must be provided by the institution. If an institution's salary scale for either the postdoctoral or faculty position exceeds the amounts provided by the award, then the institution must supplement the awardee's salary. For awardees in the United States, the administrative fee is intended to cover the cost of medical insurance and other benefits. For awardees in Canada, the fee is to be used as a contribution to the employer's benefit plan.

**Duration** 5 years: up to 2 years for advanced postdoctoral training and the first 3 years of a faculty appointment.

**Additional information** Awardees are required to devote at least 80% of their time to research-related activities.

**Number awarded** Varies each year; recently, 12 of these grants were awarded.

**Deadline** April of each year.

## [1081]
## CAREER AWARDS FOR MEDICAL SCIENTISTS

Burroughs Wellcome Fund
21 T.W. Alexander Drive, Suite 100
P.O. Box 13901
Research Triangle Park, NC 27709-3901
(919) 991-5100                    Fax: (919) 991-5160
E-mail: info@bwfund.org
Web: www.bwfund.org/programs/CAMS/index.html

**Summary** To provide funding to biomedical scientists (particularly women and minorities) in the United States and Canada who require assistance to make the transition from postdoctoral training to faculty appointment.

**Eligibility** Applicants must have an M.D., D.D.S., D.V.M., or equivalent degree. They must be interested in a program of research training in the area of basic biomedical, disease-oriented, translational, or molecular, genetic, or pharmacological epidemiology research. Training must take place at a degree-granting institution in the United States or Canada. Each U.S. and Canadian institution may nominate up to 5 candidates; nomination of women and underrepresented minorities is especially encouraged. Following their postdoctoral training, awardees may accept a faculty position at a U.S. or Canadian institution.

**Financial data** For each year of postdoctoral support, the stipend is $65,000, the research allowance is $20,500, and the administrative fee is $9,500. For each year of faculty support, the stipend is $150,000, the research allowance is $3,000, and the administrative fee is $17,000. The maximum portion of the award that can be used during the postdoctoral period is $190,000 or $95,000 per year. The faculty portion of the award is $700,000 minus the portion used during the postdoctoral years.

**Duration** The awards provide up to 2 years of postdoctoral support and up to 3 years of support during the faculty appointment.

**Additional information** This program began in 1995 as Career Awards in the Biomedical Sciences (CABS). It was revised to its current format in 2006 as a result of the NIH K99/R00 Pathway to Independence program. As the CABS, the program provided more than $100 million in support to 241 U.S. and Canadian scientists. Awardees are required to devote at least 75% of their time to research-related activities.

**Number awarded** Varies each year: recently, 22 of these awards were granted.

**Deadline** September of each year.

## [1082]
## CAREER DEVELOPMENT AWARDS IN DIABETES RESEARCH

Juvenile Diabetes Research Foundation
Attn: Grant Administrator
120 Wall Street, 19th Floor
New York, NY 10005-4001
(212) 479-7572                    Toll-free: (800) 533-CURE
Fax: (212) 785-9595              E-mail: info@jdrf.org
Web: www.jdrf.org/index.cfm?page_id=103207

**Summary** To assist young scientists of any nationality (particularly women, minorities, and persons with disabilities) to develop into independent investigators in diabetes-related research.

**Eligibility** This program is open to postdoctorates early in their faculty careers who show promise as diabetes researchers. Applicants must have received their first doctoral (M.D., Ph.D., D.M.D., D.V.M., or equivalent) degree at least 3 but not more than 7 years previously. They may not have an academic position at the associate professor, professor, or equivalent level, but they must be a faculty member (instructor or assistant professor) at a university, health science center, or comparable institution with strong, well-established research and training programs. The proposed research must relate to Type 1 diabetes, but it may be basic or clinical. There are no citizenship requirements. Applications are encouraged from women, members of minority groups underrepresented in the sciences, and people with disabilities. The proposed research may be conducted at foreign and domestic, for-profit and nonprofit, and public and private institutions, including universities, colleges, hospitals, laboratories, units of state and local government, and eligible agencies of the federal government. Selection is based on the applicant's perceived ability and potential for a career in Type 1 diabetes research, the caliber of the proposed research, and the quality and commitment of the host institution.

**Financial data** The total award may be up to $150,000 each year. Indirect costs cannot exceed 10%.

**Duration** Up to 5 years.

**Additional information** Fellows must spend up to 75% of their time in research.

**Deadline** January or July of each year.

## [1083]
## CATHERINE PRELINGER AWARD

Coordinating Council for Women in History
211 Marginal Way, Number 733
P.O. Box 9715
Portland, ME 04104-5015
Web: theccwh.org/preapp.htm

**Summary** To provide funding to members of the Coordinating Council for Women in History (CCWH) for a project that focuses on women's roles in history.

**Eligibility** This program is open to members of CCWH whose academic path has not followed the traditional pattern of uninterrupted study. Applicants must hold either A.B.D. status or a Ph.D. and be engaged in scholarship that is historical in nature, although their degree may be in related fields. They must submit a description of a project they propose to undertake with this award, including the work they intend to complete, the schedule they have developed, they sources they intend to use, and the contribution the work will make to women in history.

**Financial data**  The grant is $20,000.

**Duration**  1 year.

**Additional information**  This program was established in 1998. Information is also available from Nupur Chaudhuri, 2210 Dorrington Street, Number 202, Houston, TX 77030.

**Number awarded**  1 each year.

**Deadline**  March of each year.

## [1084]
## CHARLES A. RYSKAMP RESEARCH FELLOWSHIPS

American Council of Learned Societies
Attn: Office of Fellowships and Grants
633 Third Avenue, 8C
New York, NY 10017-6795
(212) 697-1505          Fax: (212) 949-8058
E-mail: grants@acls.org
Web: www.acls.org/rysguide.htm

**Summary**  To provide research funding to advanced assistant professors (particularly women and minorities) in all disciplines of the humanities and the humanities-related social sciences.

**Eligibility**  This program is open to tenure-track faculty members at the advanced assistant professor level and untenured associate professors in the humanities and related social sciences. Applicants must have successfully completed their institution's last reappointment review before tenure review. They must have a Ph.D. or equivalent degree and be employed at an academic institution in the United States. Appropriate fields of specialization include, but are not limited to, anthropology, archaeology, art and architectural history, economic history, film, geography, history, languages and literatures, legal studies, linguistics, musicology, philosophy, political science, psychology, religion, rhetoric and communication, sociology, and theater studies. Proposals in the social sciences are eligible only if they employ predominantly humanistic approaches (e.g., law and literature, political philosophy). Proposals in interdisciplinary and cross-disciplinary studies are welcome, as are proposals focused on any geographic region or on any cultural or linguistic group. Applicants are encouraged to spend substantial periods of their leaves in residential interdisciplinary centers, research libraries, or other scholarly archives in the United States or abroad. Applications are particularly invited from women and members of minority groups.

**Financial data**  Fellows receive a stipend of $64,000, a fund of $2,500 for research and travel, and the possibility of an additional summer's support, if justified by a persuasive case.

**Duration**  1 academic year (9 months) plus an additional summer's research (2 months) if justified.

**Additional information**  This program, first available for the 2002-03 academic year, is supported by funding from the Andrew W. Mellon Foundation.

**Number awarded**  Up to 12 each year.

**Deadline**  September of each year.

## [1085]
## CHRYSALIS SCHOLARSHIP

Association for Women Geoscientists
Attn: AWG Foundation
P.O. Box 30645
Lincoln, NE 68503-0645
E-mail: chrysalis@awg.org
Web: www.awg.org/AWGFoundation/chrysalis.html

**Summary**  To provide assistance to women who have returned to graduate school to earn a degree in the geosciences and need funding to complete their thesis.

**Eligibility**  This program is open to women geoscience graduate students whose education has been interrupted for at least 1 year for personal or financial reasons. Applicants must submit a letter describing their background, expected graduation date, career objectives, community service, how the scholarship will be used, and nature and length of the interruption to their education.

**Financial data**  The stipend is $2,000. The funds may be used for typing, drafting, child care, or anything necessary to allow a degree candidate to finish her thesis and enter a geoscience profession.

**Duration**  1 year.

**Number awarded**  2 each year.

**Deadline**  February of each year.

## [1086]
## CLINICAL SCIENTIST AWARDS IN TRANSLATIONAL RESEARCH

Burroughs Wellcome Fund
21 T.W. Alexander Drive, Suite 100
P.O. Box 13901
Research Triangle Park, NC 27709-3901
(919) 991-5100          Fax: (919) 991-5160
E-mail: info@bwfund.org
Web: www.bwfund.org

**Summary**  To provide funding to physician/scientists in the United States and Canada (particularly women and minorities) who wish to conduct translational research on the 2-way transfer between basic research and patient care.

**Eligibility**  This program is open to established independent physician/scientists who are citizens or permanent residents of the United States or Canada affiliated with accredited degree-granting U.S. or Canadian medical schools. Applicants must be interested in conducting translational research, defined to involve studies in the following areas: 1) etiology, pathogenesis, and mechanisms of disease (particularly studies with potential application to disease prevention and treatment); 2) clinical knowledge, improved diagnosis (including development of new diagnostic methods or devices), natural history of disease, and biomedical informatics; and 3) disease management (including therapeutics aimed at molecular targets), molecular epidemiology, and limited small-scale trials involving novel approaches or interventions that provide evidence for effectiveness of therapy. Large-scale clinical trials, epidemiological studies, and health services research are not eligible. Applicants must have an M.D. or M.D./Ph.D. degree and be tenure-track investigators at the late assistant professor or associate professor level; individuals holding the rank of professor are ineligible. Nominations may come from a wide range of departments, including pharmacology, pediatrics, obstetrics and gynecology, surgery, medicine, neurology, pathology, and psychiatry; applications are especially encouraged in the area of reproductive science. Each institution (including its medical school, graduate schools, and all affiliated hospitals or research institutes) may nominate up to 4 candidates; if the institution nominates more than 2, at least 1 of the candidates must be a woman and at least 1 must be a member of an underrepresented minority group (African American, Hispanic, or Native American). Selection is based on qualifications of the candidate and potential to conduct innovative translational research; demonstration of track record and commitment to mentoring physician-scientist trainees; quality and originality of the proposed research and its potential to advance clinical care; clear and concise plans for translating results into the clinical setting; quality of proposed collaborations; and evidence from the nominating institution that its laboratory and patient facilities are adequate for the proposed research.

**Financial data**  The grant provides $150,000 per year. No more than $100,000 of the award may be used for the awardee's salary support. At least $50,000 of the award must be allocated annually to research expense.

**Duration**  5 years.

**Additional information**  Awardees are required to devote at least 75% of their time to research-related activities.

**Number awarded**  Up to 9 each year.

**Deadline**  August of each year.

## [1087]
## COLLABORATIVE RESEARCH EXPERIENCE FOR UNDERGRADUATES IN COMPUTER SCIENCE AND ENGINEERING

Computing Research Association
1100 17th Street, N.W., Suite 507
Washington, DC 20036-4632
(202) 234-2111                    Fax: (202) 667-1066
Web: www.cra.org/Activities/craw/creu/index.php

**Summary**  To provide funding to undergraduate students, especially minorities and women, who are interested in conducting a research project in computer science or engineering.

**Eligibility**  This program is open to teams of 2 or 3 undergraduates who have completed 2 years of study, including at least 4 courses in computer science or computer engineering, at a college or university in the United States or Canada. Applicants must be interested in conducting a research project directly related to computer science or computer engineering. They must apply jointly with 1 or 2 sponsoring faculty members. Teams consisting of all women or all underrepresented minorities are especially encouraged to apply. Individual teams should be homogeneous with respect to minority status or gender. Selection is based on the following criteria: the scope and goals of the project should be reasonable and realistic, based upon the students' prior education and experience; the plan for the project should be well-defined and should describe a collaborative approach to be taken; the project should warrant background research on the part of the students and should have an active, investigative, and experiential nature by which the students can discover their results; the proposal should be complete and well-written; students should

be actively involved in writing the proposal, with guidance and support of the sponsoring faculty member; the project should further the goal of the program (to increase the numbers of women and minorities who continue on to graduate school in computer science and engineering); the project should enable student empowerment, leadership development, confidence-building, and skill-building in project management; the students should have good potential for doing independent work; the sponsor(s) should have the background necessary to oversee the research and an appropriate strategy for keeping the students on track; and the sponsor(s) and students must have enough time to devote to the research project so that weekly meetings can occur and additional independent work can take place outside of those meetings.

**Financial data**  Each student participant receives a stipend of $1,000. Each project receives an additional grant of $500 to be used for special equipment, travel, supporting materials, or as an honorarium for the faculty member(s).

**Duration**  1 academic year.

**Additional information**  This program is sponsored by the Computing Research Association's Committee on the Status of Women in Computing Research (CRA-W) and the Coalition to Diversify Computing (CDC). Information is also available from Sheila Casteñeda, Clarke College, Computer Science Department, Dubuque, IA 52001, (563) 588-6401, Fax: (563) 588-6789, E-mail: cast@clarke.edu.

**Number awarded**  Varies each year; recently, 11 teams of students received support from this program.

**Deadline**  May of each year.

## [1088]
## COLLABORATIVE RESEARCH GRANTS FOR WOMEN

Association for Women in Mathematics
11240 Waples Mill Road, Suite 200
Fairfax, VA 22030
(703) 934-0163                    Fax: (703) 359-7562
E-mail: awm@math.umd.edu
Web: www.awm-math.org/travelgrants.html

**Summary**  To provide funding to women postdoctorates in mathematics who wish to travel to conduct collaborative research with another mathematician.

**Eligibility**  This program is open to women holding a doctorate or equivalent experience and with a work address in the United States. They must be tenured. The applicant's research may be in any field that is funded by the Division of Mathematical Sciences (DMS) of the National Science Foundation (NSF). The proposed travel must be to an institute or a department to conduct collaborative research with another mathematician.

**Financial data**  These grants provide full or partial support for travel, subsistence, and other required expenses, to a maximum of $2,500.

**Duration**  The proposed visit may last up to 1 month.

**Additional information**  Funding for this program is provided by the Division of Mathematical Sciences of the NSF. For foreign travel, U.S. carriers must be used whenever possible.

**Number awarded**  1 or 2 each year.

**Deadline**  January of each year.

## [1089]
## COMMUNITY ACTION GRANTS

American Association of University Women
Attn: AAUW Educational Foundation
301 ACT Drive, Department 60
P.O. Box 4030
Iowa City, IA 52243-4030
(319) 337-1716                                    Fax: (319) 337-1204
E-mail: aauw@act.org
Web: www.aauw.org

**Summary**   To provide seed money to branches or divisions of the American Association of University Women (AAUW) or to individual women for projects or nondegree research that promote education and equity for women and girls.

**Eligibility**   This program is open to individual women who are U.S. citizens or permanent residents, AAUW branches, AAUW state organizations, and local community-based nonprofit organizations. Applicants must be proposing projects that have direct public impact, are nonpartisan, and take place within the United States or its territories. Grants for 1 year provide seed money for new projects; topic areas are unrestricted but should include a clearly defined activity that promotes education and equity for women and girls. Grants for 2 years provide start-up funds for longer-term programs that address the particular needs of the community and develop girls' sense of efficacy through leadership or advocacy opportunities; funds support planning activities, coalition building, implementation, and evaluation. Special consideration is given to 1) AAUW branch and state projects that seek community partners (e.g., local schools or school districts, businesses, other community-based organizations); 2) AAUW members; and 3) projects focused on K-14 girls' achievement in mathematics, science, and/or technology. Selection is based on relevance of the proposed project to education and equity for women and girls, strength of the project rationale, creativity of the project design, feasibility of the project, strength of the evaluation plan, strength of the dissemination plan, impact of the project, overall quality of the proposal, and potential for and/or commitment of additional funds and involvement from community organizations and/or businesses.

**Financial data**   Grants for 1 year range from $2,000 to $7,000. Grants for 2 years range from $5,000 to $10,000. Funds are to be used for such project-related expenses as office supplies, mailing, photocopying, honoraria, and transportation. Funds cannot cover salaries for project directors or regular, ongoing overhead costs for any organization.

**Duration**   1 or 2 years.

**Additional information**   The filing fee is $25 for AAUW members or $35 for nonmembers.

**Number awarded**   Varies each year. Recently, 21 1-year grants and 9 2-year grants were awarded.

**Deadline**   January of each year.

## [1090]
## CONNECTICUT SPACE GRANT COLLEGE CONSORTIUM GRADUATE STUDENT FELLOWSHIPS

Connecticut Space Grant College Consortium
c/o University of Hartford
UT 219
200 Bloomfield Avenue
West Hartford, CT 06117-1599
(860) 768-4813                                    Fax: (860) 768-5073
E-mail: ctspgrant@hartford.edu
Web: uhaweb.hartford.edu

**Summary**   To provide funding to graduate students especially women, minority, and disabled students) at member institutions of the Connecticut Space Grant College Consortium interested in working on space-related projects under the guidance of a faculty member.

**Eligibility**   This program is open to full-time graduate students at member institutions of the Connecticut Space Grant College Consortium. Applicants must be proposing to conduct research on a topic that is consistent with the mission of the U.S. National Aeronautics and Space Administration (NASA): earth science, space science, human exploration and development of space, and aerospace technology. U.S. citizenship is required. The program actively encourages women, underrepresented minorities, and those with disabilities to apply.

**Financial data**   The grant is $8,000.

**Duration**   1 semester or 1 year.

**Additional information**   Member institutions are the University of Connecticut, University of Hartford, University of New Haven, and Trinity College. This program is funded by NASA.

**Number awarded**   Varies each year; recently, 2 of these grants were awarded.

**Deadline**   February or October of each year.

## [1091]
## CONNECTICUT SPACE GRANT COLLEGE CONSORTIUM STUDENT PROJECT GRANTS

Connecticut Space Grant College Consortium
c/o University of Hartford
UT 219
200 Bloomfield Avenue
West Hartford, CT 06117-1599
(860) 768-4813                                    Fax: (860) 768-5073
E-mail: ctspgrant@hartford.edu
Web: uhaweb.hartford.edu

**Summary**   To provide funding to undergraduate students (especially women, minority, and disabled students) at member institutions of the Connecticut Space Grant College Consortium who need to purchase supplies or equipment for space-related projects.

**Eligibility**   This program is open to undergraduate students at member institutions of the Connecticut Space Grant College Consortium. Applicants must be proposing to conduct a project on a topic that is consistent with the mission of the U.S. National Aeronautics and Space Administration (NASA): earth science, space science, human exploration and development of space, and aerospace technology. U.S. citizenship is required. A faculty member must agree to serve as project advisor. The program actively encourages women, underrepresented minorities, and those with disabilities to apply.

**Financial data** The maximum grant is $500. Funds may be used for supplies and materials only, not for travel, entertainment, entry fees, tuition, salaries, fringe benefits, or indirect costs.

**Duration** 1 semester or 1 year.

**Additional information** Member institutions are the University of Connecticut, University of Hartford, University of New Haven, and Trinity College. This program is funded by NASA.

**Number awarded** Varies each year; recently, 3 of these grants were awarded.

**Deadline** February or October of each year.

## [1092]
## CONNECTICUT SPACE GRANT COLLEGE CONSORTIUM TRAVEL GRANTS

Connecticut Space Grant College Consortium
c/o University of Hartford
UT 219
200 Bloomfield Avenue
West Hartford, CT 06117-1599
(860) 768-4813               Fax: (860) 768-5073
E-mail: ctspgrant@hartford.edu
Web: uhaweb.hartford.edu/CTSPGRANT

**Summary** To provide funding for travel to students and faculty (particularly women, minorities, and persons with disabilities) at member institutions of the Connecticut Space Grant College Consortium.

**Eligibility** This program is open to students and faculty at member institutions of the Connecticut Space Grant College Consortium. Applicants normally must be proposing to collaborate with researchers at the U.S. National Aeronautics and Space Administration (NASA), to present their aerospace-related research at conferences, to use specialized equipment at NASA facilities, or to visit NASA centers to establish research contacts. Travel is normally limited to destinations within the United States. The program actively encourages women, underrepresented minorities, and those with disabilities to apply.

**Financial data** Grants cover expenses up to $1,000 per trip.

**Additional information** Member institutions are the University of Connecticut, University of Hartford, University of New Haven, and Trinity College. This program is funded by NASA.

**Number awarded** Varies each year; recently, a total of $7,500 was available for student travel and $2,600 for faculty travel.

**Deadline** February or October of each year.

## [1093]
## CONNECTICUT SPACE GRANT COLLEGE CONSORTIUM UNDERGRADUATE STUDENT FELLOWSHIPS

Connecticut Space Grant College Consortium
c/o University of Hartford
UT 219
200 Bloomfield Avenue
West Hartford, CT 06117-1599
(860) 768-4813               Fax: (860) 768-5073
E-mail: ctspgrant@hartford.edu
Web: uhaweb.hartford.edu

**Summary** To enable undergraduate students (especially women, minority, and disabled students) at member institutions of the Connecticut Space Grant College Consortium to work on space-related projects under the guidance of a faculty member.

**Eligibility** This program is open to full-time undergraduate students at member institutions of the Connecticut Space Grant College Consortium. Applicants must be proposing to conduct a senior project, honors research, or other educational activity that will assist them in establishing contacts at the U.S. National Aeronautics and Space Administration (NASA) or with local industrial companies in aerospace, space science, or technology-related fields. U.S. citizenship is required. The program actively encourages women, underrepresented minorities, and those with disabilities to apply.

**Financial data** Grants are $4,000.

**Duration** 1 semester or 1 year.

**Additional information** Member institutions are the University of Connecticut, University of Hartford, University of New Haven, and Trinity College. This program is funded by NASA.

**Number awarded** Varies each year; recently, 5 of these grants were awarded.

**Deadline** February or October of each year.

## [1094]
## CONTEMPLATIVE PRACTICE FELLOWSHIPS

American Council of Learned Societies
Attn: Office of Fellowships and Grants
633 Third Avenue, 8C
New York, NY 10017-6795
(212) 697-1505               Fax: (212) 949-8058
E-mail: grants@acls.org
Web: www.acls.org/conprac.htm

**Summary** To provide funding to college faculty members (especially women and minorities) who are interested in conducting research leading to the development of courses and teaching materials that integrate contemplative practices into courses.

**Eligibility** This program is open to full-time faculty members at accredited academic institutions in the arts, humanities, and humanities-related sciences and social sciences. There are no citizenship requirements. Applicants must be interested in conducting individual or collaborative research to advance scholarship in the field of contemplative practices and to encourage innovative pedagogy and course design. Methodologies that include practical and experiential approaches to the subject matter are especially welcome. Proposals of particular interest are those in which classroom contemplative practices are related clearly to the content of the course itself. Applications are particularly invited from women and members of minority groups.

**Financial data**   The maximum grant is $10,000.

**Duration**   1 semester or 1 summer.

**Additional information**   This program is sponsored by the Center for Contemplative Mind in Society and funded by the Fetzer Institute.

**Number awarded**   Approximately 10 each year.

**Deadline**   November of each year.

## [1095]
## COVAD BROADBAND ENTREPRENEUR AWARD

Association for Enterprise Opportunity
1601 North Kent Street, Suite 1101
Arlington, VA 22209
(703) 841-7760                              Fax: (703) 841-7748
E-mail: aeo@assoceo.org
Web: www.microenterpriseworks.org/projects/covad

**Summary**   To provide funding to entrepreneurs (especially women, minorities, and people with disabilities) who are interested in obtaining broadband access to the Internet.

**Eligibility**   This program is open to low- and moderate-income entrepreneurs who have 5 or fewer employees, $35,000 or less cash on hand, and no access to traditional bank loans. Preference is given to entrepreneurs who are women, minorities, or people with disabilities. Applicants must be based in and/or serve clients within the service area of Covad Communications Group, Inc. in the following states: Arizona, California, Colorado, Florida, Georgia, Illinois, Massachusetts, Michigan, New Mexico, Pennsylvania, Tennessee, Texas, or Virginia. They must own or have regular access to a computer and be able to implement installation of broadband within 30 days of the grant award. It is not necessary that entrepreneurs have existing access to the Internet or an e-mail address as long as they intend to use the grant funds to set up Internet and e-mail service. They must submit a cover letter and business plan that demonstrate how broadband access will improve and strengthen their business.

**Financial data**   Grants provide a $500 cash award (which may be used for purchase of a new computer) and free Covad broadband installation and service for 1 year. The total value of the grant is more than $2,500.

**Duration**   These are 1-time grants.

**Additional information**   Covad Communications Group, Inc. established this program in 2003 and selected the Association for Enterprise Opportunity (AEO) to administer it. The association selected 10 local partners to process and forward applications and added another 6 in 2004. Those 16 local organizations are ACCION New Mexico of Albuquerque; Business Investment Growth (BiG) Austin, serving Travis and 13 surrounding counties in Texas; CHARO Community Development Corporation of Los Angeles; Cobb Microenterprise Center of Kennesaw, Georgia; Community Business Network of Boston; Detroit Entrepreneurship Institute, Inc. of Detroit; Enterprise Development Group of Arlington, Virginia; Miami Urban Ministries, serving Miami-Dade and Monroe counties in Florida; Microbusiness Development of Denver, Colorado; Philadelphia Development

Partnership, serving the greater Philadelphia area of Pennsylvania; Renaissance Entrepreneurship Center of San Francisco; Self-Employment Loan Fund of Phoenix; Start Up of East Palo Alto, California; The Abilities Fund of Centerville, Iowa; Women's Opportunities Resource Center of Philadelphia; Women's Self-Employment Project of Chicago; and World Relief of Nashville, Tennessee.

**Number awarded**   Up to 144 each year.

**Deadline**   Each of the 16 local partners sets its own deadline date.

## [1096]
## DARE TO DREAM MINIGRANTS

Ann Bancroft Foundation
207 County Road North
Plymouth, MN 55441
(763) 541-9363                              Fax: (763) 595-8315
Web: www.annbancroftfoundation.org

**Summary**   To provide funding to girls in Minnesota from age 10 to grade 10 who wish to complete an activity of their own design.

**Eligibility**   This program is open to girls in Minnesota who are at least 10 years of age and no higher in school than grade 10. Applicants must describe "a special interest that has sparked their imagination, creativity, or a dream they may not have thought possible." They must describe their dream, what they hope to learn or accomplish, who is helping them achieve this dream, and why financial support from the foundation is important to them. An adult mentor other than a member of their immediate family must explain how the experience will impact the girl and verify her financial need for assistance.

**Financial data**   Grants range from $100 to $500.

**Duration**   These are 1-time grants.

**Additional information**   Past activities these grants have supported include classes, camps or lessons to improve a skill, outdoor adventures or camps, honors programs, travel with approved schools or groups, choir trips, and school activities.

**Number awarded**   Varies each year; recently, 59 of these grants were awarded.

**Deadline**   November of each year.

## [1097]
## DELTA KAPPA GAMMA SCHOLARSHIP PROGRAM

Delta Kappa Gamma Society International
416 West 12th Street
P.O. Box 1589
Austin, TX 78767-1589
(512) 478-5748                              Toll-free: (888) 762-4685
Fax: (512) 478-3961
E-mail: scholarships@deltakappagamma.org
Web: www.deltakappagamma.org

**Summary**   To provide financial assistance to members of Delta Kappa Gamma Society International interested in graduate study or research.

**Eligibility**   Applicants must have been members in good standing of the Delta Kappa Gamma Society International (an honorary society of women educators) for at least 3

years, have completed a master's degree or equivalent, and have been accepted and enrolled in a graduate program at a nationally accredited institution of higher education, preferably working on a doctoral degree. Selection is based on active participation and demonstrated leadership in Delta Kappa Gamma, excellence in scholarship, and service to the community.

**Financial data** The stipend is $5,000.

**Duration** 1 year.

**Additional information** Delta Kappa Gamma Society International has 170,000 members in 13 countries and is the largest organization of its kind. This program includes the following named awards: the Marjorie Jeanne Allen Scholarship, the Mamie Sue Bastian Scholarship, the Annie Webb Blanton Scholarship, the Blanton Centennial Scholarship, the A. Margaret Boyd Scholarship, the Edna McGuire Boyd Scholarship, the Eula Lee Carter Scholarship, the Delta Kappa Gamma Founders Scholarship, the Delta Kappa Gamma Golden Anniversary Scholarship, the Delta Kappa Gamma 60th Anniversary Scholarship, the Delta Kappa Gamma 70th Anniversary Scholarship, the Zora Ellis Scholarship, the Emma Giles Scholarship, the Carolyn Guss Scholarship, the Ola B. Hiller Scholarship, the Eunah Temple Holden Scholarship, the Berneta Minkwitz Scholarship, the Lois and Marguerite Morse Scholarship, the Catherine Nutterville Scholarship, the Alida W. Parker Scholarship, the J. Maria Pierce Scholarship, the Emma Reinhart Scholarship, the Norma Bristow Salter Scholarship, the Mary Katherine Shoup Scholarship, the Maycie K. Southall Scholarship, the M. Margaret Stroh Scholarship, the Letti P. Trefz Scholarship, and the Mary Frances White Scholarship. Recipients must remain active members of Delta Kappa Gamma, work full time on the study or research outlined in their applications, submit reports requested by the society, and acknowledge assistance of the society in any publication that results from data gathered while the award was being used.

**Number awarded** 28 each year.

**Deadline** January of each year.

## [1098]
## DENISE GAUDREAU AWARD FOR EXCELLENCE IN QUATERNARY STUDIES

American Quaternary Association
c/o Eric Grimm, President
Illinois State Museum Research and Collections Center
1011 East Ash Street
Springfield, IL 62703
(217) 785-4846            Fax: (217) 785-2857
E-mail: president@amqua.org
Web: www.amqua.org/about/awards

**Summary** To support the early career development of women graduate students in quaternary studies.

**Eligibility** This program is open to female scientists in any field of quaternary studies who are within 2 years of completing a doctoral degree. Applicants must not have completed their dissertation research. The application should include a curriculum vitae, a summary of research interests, copies of graduate transcripts, and the names of 2 referees. Selection is based on scientific accomplishments, promise, and demonstration of original thinking.

Emphasis is placed on the quality and carefulness of the work, rather than simply on quantity.

**Financial data** The award is $500.

**Duration** The award is presented biennially, in even-numbered years.

**Additional information** This award was established in 1993.

**Number awarded** 1 every other year.

**Deadline** February of even-numbered years.

## [1099]
## DESGC SUMMER SCHOLARSHIPS

Delaware Space Grant Consortium
c/o University of Delaware
Bartol Research Institute
106 Sharp Lab
Newark, DE 19716
(302) 831-1094            Fax: (302) 831-1843
E-mail: desgc@bartol.udel.edu
Web: www.delspace.org

**Summary** To provide funding to undergraduate students in Delaware and Pennsylvania (especially women, minority, and disabled students) for summer research on space-related subjects.

**Eligibility** This program is open to undergraduate students at member or affiliate colleges and universities of the Delaware Space Grant Consortium (DESGC). Applicants must have a proven interest and aptitude for space-related studies and be proposing a summer research project. U.S. citizenship is required. The DESGC is a component of the U.S. National Aeronautics and Space Administration (NASA) Space Grant program, which encourages applications from women, minorities, and persons with disabilities.

**Financial data** A stipend is provided (amount not specified).

**Duration** Summer months.

**Additional information** This program, established in 1994, is funded by NASA. Members of the consortium include Delaware State University (Dover, Delaware), Delaware Technical and Community College (Dover, Georgetown, Newark, and Wilmington, Delaware), Franklin and Marshall College (Lancaster, Pennsylvania), Gettysburg College (Gettysburg, Pennsylvania), Lehigh University (Bethlehem, Pennsylvania), Swarthmore College (Swarthmore, Pennsylvania), University of Delaware (Newark, Delaware), Villanova University (Villanova, Pennsylvania), and Wilmington College (New Castle, Delaware).

**Number awarded** Varies each year; recently, 12 of these scholarships were awarded.

**Deadline** February of each year.

## [1100]
### DIANE H. RUSSELL AWARD
Association for Women in Science
Attn: AWIS Educational Foundation
1200 New York Avenue, N.W., Suite 650
Washington, DC 20005
(202) 326-8940       Toll-free: (866) 657-AWIS
Fax: (202) 326-8960       E-mail: awisedfd@awis.org
Web: www.awis.org/careers/edfoundation.html

**Summary** To provide funding to women conducting doctoral research in biochemistry or pharmacology.

**Eligibility** This program is open to women graduate students in the fields of biochemistry or pharmacology. Applicants must have passed their qualifying exam and be within 2 years of completing their Ph.D. Foreign students are eligible if they are enrolled in a U.S. institution of higher education. Selection is based on academic achievement, the importance of the research question addressed, the quality of the research, and the applicant's potential for future contributions to biochemistry or pharmacology.

**Financial data** The stipend is $1,000. Funds may be used for tuition, books, housing, research, travel and meeting registration, or publication costs.

**Duration** 1 year.

**Additional information** Information is also available from Barbara Filner, President, AWIS Educational Foundation, 7008 Richard Drive, Bethesda, MD 20817-4838.

**Number awarded** 1 each year.

**Deadline** January of each year.

## [1101]
### DIENJE KENYON FELLOWSHIP
Society for American Archaeology
900 Second Street, N.E., Suite 12
Washington, DC 20002-3560
(202) 789-8200       Fax: (202) 789-0284
E-mail: headquarters@saa.org
Web: www.saa.org

**Summary** To provide research funding to women working on a graduate degree in zooarchaeology.

**Eligibility** This program is open to women enrolled in the first 2 years of graduate studies. Applicants must be enrolled in a graduate degree program in archaeology with the intention of conducting research for a master's or Ph.D. degree on a topic related to zooarchaeology. They must submit a 1,500-word statement describing their proposed research related to zooarchaeology, a curriculum vitae, and 2 letters of support (including 1 from their primary advisor). Strong preference is given to students working with faculty members with zooarchaeological expertise.

**Financial data** The grant is $500.

**Additional information** This grant was first awarded in 2000.

**Number awarded** 1 each year.

**Deadline** January of each year.

## [1102]
### DIRECTING WORKSHOP FOR WOMEN
American Film Institute
Attn: Education and Training
2021 North Western Avenue
Los Angeles, CA 90027-1657
(323) 856-7628       Fax: (323) 467-4578
Web: www.afi.com/education/dww/dww.asp

**Summary** To provide funding to women who have no professional credits as a narrative director but are interested in developing a movie or television project.

**Eligibility** This program is open to women who have at least 5 years' experience in the arts but no professional credits as a narrative director. Applicants must submit a narrative script of 15 pages or less for a movie or television project they propose to develop; the script may have been written by anyone. They must be U.S. citizens or permanent residents and must reside and work in the United States during the grant period.

**Financial data** A $5,000 production grant is provided to each participant. Those who reside in Los Angeles are encouraged to raise an additional $20,000 to cover living expenses; those who live outside the area may raise an additional $25,000. The institute provides production equipment and editing facilities.

**Duration** The workshop is conducted over an 8-month period.

**Additional information** Sponsors of this program, which began in 1974, include the Academy of Motion Picture Arts and Sciences, Sony Corporation of America, and the National Endowment for the Arts. Projects are planned for a maximum of 30 minutes, with a shooting schedule of no more than 5 days and an editing time of 3 weeks. Workshop sessions for screening and discussion of projects are held at the American Film Institute throughout the cycle. This is the only workshop of its type offered in the country. Participants should be available in the Los Angeles area during the workshop's 8-month program. There is a non-refundable application fee of $75 for early applications or $100 for final applications.

**Number awarded** 8 participants are chosen each year.

**Deadline** November of each year for early applications; January of each year for final applications.

## [1103]
### DISSERTATION FELLOWSHIPS IN SOUTHEAST EUROPEAN STUDIES
American Council of Learned Societies
Attn: Office of Fellowships and Grants
633 Third Avenue, 8C
New York, NY 10017-6795
(212) 697-1505       Fax: (212) 949-8058
E-mail: grants@acls.org
Web: www.acls.org/seguide.htm

**Summary** To provide funding to doctoral candidates (particularly women and minorities) who are interested in conducting dissertation research in the social sciences and humanities relating to southeastern Europe.

**Eligibility** This program is open to U.S. citizens or permanent residents who are working on a dissertation in the humanities or social sciences as related to southeastern

Europe, including Albania, Bosnia and Herzegovina, Bulgaria, Croatia, Former Yugoslav Republic of Macedonia, Kosovo, Montenegro, Romania, and Serbia. Applicants may be proposing comparative work considering more than 1 country of southeastern Europe or relating southeastern European societies to those of other parts of the world. They may be seeking any of 3 types of support: 1) developmental fellowships, for use at a location in the United States other than the home university in preparation for field research in southeastern Europe, including intensive language training, acquisition of methodological or other specialized skills, or preliminary work in archives located in the United States; 2) research fellowships, for use in southeastern Europe to conduct fieldwork or archival investigations; or 3) writing fellowships, for use in the United States, after all research is complete, to write the dissertation. Selection is based on the scholarly potential of the applicant, the quality and scholarly importance of the proposed work, and its importance to the development of scholarship on southeastern Europe. Applications are particularly invited from women and members of minority groups.

**Financial data**   The maximum stipend is $17,000. Recipients' home universities are required (consistent with their policies and regulations) to provide or to waive normal academic year tuition payments or to provide alternative cost-sharing support.

**Duration**   1 year. The 3 types of support (developmental, research, and writing) are considered sequential; recipients are invited to apply the following year for the next level of support.

**Additional information**   This program is sponsored jointly by the American Council of Learned Societies, (ACLS) and the Social Science Research Council, funded by the U.S. Department of State under the Research and Training for Eastern Europe and the Independent States of the Former Soviet Union Act of 1983 (Title VIII) but administered by ACLS.

**Number awarded**   Varies each year; recently, 7 of these fellowships were awarded.

**Deadline**   November of each year.

## [1104]
## DOCTORAL DISSERTATION IMPROVEMENT GRANTS IN THE DIRECTORATE FOR BIOLOGICAL SCIENCES

National Science Foundation
Directorate for Biological Sciences
Attn: Division of Environmental Biology
4201 Wilson Boulevard
Arlington, VA 22230
(703) 292-8480                    TDD: (800) 281-8749
E-mail: ddig-deb@nsf.gov
Web: www.nsf.gov

**Summary**   To provide partial support for dissertation research in selected areas supported by the National Science Foundation (NSF) Directorate for Biological Sciences (DBS).

**Eligibility**   Applications may be submitted through regular university channels by dissertation advisors on behalf of graduate students who have advanced to candidacy and have begun or are about to begin dissertation research. Students must be enrolled at U.S. institutions but need not be

U.S. citizens. Proposals should focus on the ecology, ecosystems, systematics, or population biology programs in the DBS Division of Environmental Biology, or the animal behavior or ecological and evolutionary physiology programs in the DBS Division of Integrative Organismal Biology. Women, minorities, and persons with disabilities are strongly encouraged to apply.

**Financial data**   Grants range up to $12,000; funds may be used for travel to specialized facilities or field research locations, specialized research equipment, purchase of supplies and services not otherwise available, fees for computerized or other forms of data, and rental of environmental chambers or other research facilities. Funding is not provided for stipends, tuition, textbooks, journals, allowances for dependents, travel to scientific meetings, publication costs, dissertation preparation or reproduction, or indirect costs.

**Duration**   Normally 2 years.

**Additional information**   Information on programs in the Division of Environmental Biology is available at the address and telephone number above; information from the Division of Integrative Organismal Biology is available at (703) 292-8423, E-mail: ddig-iob@nsf.gov.

**Number awarded**   120 each year; approximately $1,300,000 is available for this program each year.

**Deadline**   November of each year.

## [1105]
## DOROTHY WIEGNER AWARD

Vermont Studio Center
80 Pearl Street
P.O. Box 613
Johnson, VT 05656
(802) 635-2727                    Fax: (802) 635-2730
E-mail: info@vermontstudiocenter.org
Web: www.vermontstudiocenter.org

**Summary**   To provide funding to women artists and writers who are cancer survivors and interested in a residency at the Vermont Studio Center in Johnson, Vermont.

**Eligibility**   Eligible to apply for this support are women painters, sculptors, printmakers, photographers, poets, and other writers of fiction and creative nonfiction who are cancer survivors. Applicants must be interested in a residency at the center in Johnson, Vermont. Visual artists must submit up to 20 slides of their work, poets must submit up to 10 pages, and other writers must submit 10 to 15 pages. Selection is based on artistic merit.

**Financial data**   The residency fee of $3,500 covers studio space, room, board, lectures, and studio visits. The award pays all residency fees.

**Duration**   4 weeks.

**Additional information**   This award is sponsored by the Dorothy Wiegner Foundation. The application fee is $25.

**Number awarded**   1 each year.

**Deadline**   June of each year.

## [1106]
### DR. ALEXANDRA KIRKLEY TRAVELING FELLOWSHIPS

Ruth Jackson Orthopaedic Society
6300 North River Road, Suite 727
Rosemont, IL 60018-4226
(847) 698-1637          Fax: (847) 823-0536
E-mail: rjos@aaos.org
Web: www.rjos.org/awards/index.htm

**Summary**  To provide funding to women orthopedic medical students who are interested in traveling to enrich their academic career.

**Eligibility**  This program is open to women medical students who are members of the Ruth Jackson Orthopaedic Society (RJOS). Applicants must be Board Eligible orthopedic surgeons and citizens of the United States or Canada. They must be interested in a program of travel to 1) enrich their academic career or 2) learn new techniques or expand their sub-specialty interests.

**Financial data**  Grants up to $6,000 are available.

**Number awarded**  2 each year: 1 academic grant and 1 practice enrichment grant.

**Deadline**  November of each year.

## [1107]
### EARLY CAREER PATIENT-ORIENTED DIABETES RESEARCH AWARD

Juvenile Diabetes Research Foundation
Attn: Grant Administrator
120 Wall Street, 19th Floor
New York, NY 10005-4001
(212) 479-7572          Toll-free: (800) 533-CURE
Fax: (212) 785-9595          E-mail: info@jdrf.org
Web: www.jdrf.org/index.cfm?page_id=103207

**Summary**  To provide funding to physician scientists (particularly women, minorities, and persons with disabilities) interested in pursuing a program of clinical diabetes-related research training.

**Eligibility**  This program is open to investigators in diabetes-related research who have an M.D. or M.D./Ph.D. degree and a faculty appointment at the late training or assistant professor level. Applicants must be sponsored by an investigator who is affiliated full time with an accredited institution, who pursues patient-oriented clinical research, and who agrees to supervise the applicant's training. There are no citizenship requirements. Applications are encouraged from women, members of minority groups underrepresented in the sciences, and people with disabilities. Areas of relevant research can include: mechanisms of human disease, therapeutic interventions, clinical trials, and the development of new technologies. The proposed research may be conducted at foreign and domestic, for-profit and non-profit, and public and private institutions, including universities, colleges, hospitals, laboratories, units of state and local government, and eligible agencies of the federal government.

**Financial data**  The total award may be up to $150,000 each year, up to $75,000 of which may be requested for research (including a technician, supplies, equipment, and travel). The salary request must be consistent with the established salary structure of the applicant's institution.

Equipment purchases in years other than the first must be strongly justified. Indirect costs may not exceed 10%.

**Duration**  The award is for 5 years.

**Deadline**  January or July of each year.

## [1108]
### EDUCATIONAL TESTING SERVICE POSTDOCTORAL FELLOWSHIP AWARD PROGRAM

Educational Testing Service
Attn: Fellowships
Rosedale Road
MS 09-R
Princeton, NJ 08541-0001
(609) 734-1806          Fax: (609) 734-5410
E-mail: internfellowships@ets.org
Web: www.ets.org

**Summary**  To provide funding to postdoctorates (particularly women and minorities) who wish to conduct independent research at the Educational Testing Service (ETS).

**Eligibility**  Applicants must have a doctorate in a relevant discipline and be able to provide evidence of prior research. They must be interested in conducting research at ETS in 1 of the following areas: computer science, education, learning, literacy, minority issues, psychology, statistics, teaching educational technology, or testing issues (including alternate forms of assessment for special populations and new forms of assessment). Selection is based on the scholarship and importance of the proposed research, the relationship between the objective of the research and ETS goals and priorities, and the ETS affirmative action objectives. An explicit goal of the program is to increase the number of women and underrepresented minority professionals in educational measurement and related fields.

**Financial data**  The stipend is $50,000 per year; fellows and their families also receive limited reimbursement for relocation expenses.

**Duration**  1 year, normally beginning in September.

**Additional information**  Fellows work with senior staff at ETS in Princeton, New Jersey.

**Number awarded**  Up to 3 each year.

**Deadline**  January of each year.

## [1109]
### ELLEN DOUGHERTY ACTIVIST FUND

Open Meadows Foundation
Attn: Project Coordinator
P.O. Box 150-607
Van Brunt Station
Brooklyn, NY 11215-0607
(718) 885-0969          E-mail: openmeadows@igc.org
Web: www.openmeadows.org

**Summary**  To provide funding to teen-aged women who are interested in carrying on a project focused on activism and social change.

**Eligibility**  This program is open to women 19 years of age and younger who are proposing to conduct a project that is focused on activism and social change. Applicants must submit their request through a tax-exempt organization or institution. As part of their application, they must provide a

3-page narrative describing the project, covering such matters as why the project is needed; the main issue that it addresses; the racial/ethnic constituency that it will serve; the person primarily responsible for the project and its implementation; why it needs funding; why funding from Open Meadows will make a difference to the project; the age, national origin, and racial/ethnic background of the project organization; and how the organization's leadership reflects the constituency that it serves.

**Financial data**　Grants range up to $2,000.

**Duration**　1 year.

**Number awarded**　Varies each year; recently, 4 of these grants were awarded.

**Deadline**　February of each year.

## [1110]
## ELOISE GERRY FELLOWSHIPS

Sigma Delta Epsilon-Graduate Women in Science, Inc.
c/o Jennifer Ingram, Fellowships Coordinator
Duke University-Department of Medicine
Box 2641, 275 MSRB, Research Drive
Durham, NC 27710
(919) 668-1439
E-mail: fellowshipsquestions@gwis.org
Web: www.gwis.org/grants/default.htm

**Summary**　To provide funding to women interested in conducting research anywhere in the world in the biological or chemical sciences.

**Eligibility**　This program is open to graduate and postdoctoral women in the biological or chemical sciences who show outstanding ability and promise in scientific research. Applicants may be proposing to conduct research at an institution in the United States or abroad. Along with their application, they must submit a brief description of relevant personal factors, including financial need, that should be considered in the selection process. Appointments are made without regard to race, nationality, creed, national origin, or age. Applicants must either be members of Sigma Delta Epsilon–Graduate Women in Science or include a processing fee of $20 (the cost of a 1-year membership).

**Financial data**　Grants range up to $4,000. The funds must be used for scientific research, including professional travel costs. They may not be used for tuition, child care, travel to professional meetings or to begin a new appointment, administrative overhead or indirect costs, personal computers, living allowances, or equipment for general use.

**Duration**　1 year; may be renewed in unusual circumstances, contingent upon receipt of an annual progress report.

**Additional information**　This fellowship was first awarded in 1975.

**Number awarded**　Varies each year; recently, 4 of these fellowships were awarded.

**Deadline**　January of each year.

## [1111]
## EMILIE DU CHATELET AWARD FOR INDEPENDENT SCHOLARSHIP

American Society for Eighteenth-Century Studies
c/o Wake Forest University
P.O. Box 7867
Winston-Salem, NC 27109
(336) 727-4694　　Fax: (336) 727-4697
E-mail: asecs@wfu.edu
Web: asecs.press.jhu.edu/awards.html

**Summary**　To provide funding to adjunct and independent scholars interested in conducting research on topics that deal with women's issues in the 18th-century.

**Eligibility**　This program is open to independent and adjunct scholars who have research in progress on a topic that deals with women's experiences and/or contributions to 18th-century culture or offers a feminist analysis of any aspect of 18th-century society and/or culture. Applicants must be members of the American Society for Eighteenth-Century Studies (ASECS) who have received a Ph.D. but do not currently have a tenured, tenure-track, or job-secure position in a college or university nor any permanent position that requires or supports the pursuit of research. Faculty emeritae are not eligible. The proposed research project may be a scholarly article, book chapter, or edition.

**Financial data**　The grant is $500.

**Duration**　The grant is offered annually.

**Additional information**　This award is presented by the Women's Caucus of the ASECS. The recipient is asked to submit a brief written report on the progress of the project 1 year after receiving the award and, whenever possible, will serve on the award committee in the following year.

**Number awarded**　1 each year.

**Deadline**　January of each year.

## [1112]
## ENGINEERING DISSERTATION FELLOWSHIPS

American Association of University Women
Attn: AAUW Educational Foundation
301 ACT Drive, Department 60
P.O. Box 4030
Iowa City, IA 52243-4030
(319) 337-1716　　Fax: (319) 337-1204
E-mail: aauw@act.org
Web: www.aauw.org

**Summary**　To provide funding to women who are working on their doctoral dissertation in engineering.

**Eligibility**　This program is open to women who have completed all required course work and passed all preliminary examinations for the doctorate in engineering. Students holding a fellowship for the writing of their dissertation in the prior year are not eligible to apply for this program. Applicants must be U.S. citizens or permanent residents. Special consideration is given to applicants who show professional promise in innovative or neglected areas of research and/or practice in areas of public interest. Selection is based on qualifications of the applicant, including academic record, recommendations, and publications (40%); potential of applicant to make a significant future contribution to the field and to women in the discipline (25%); feasibility of research plan and proposed time scheduled (20%); scope, complexity, and innovation of the project (15%).

**Financial data**   The grant is $20,000. These funds may not be used to cover tuition for additional course work.

**Duration**   1 year, beginning in July.

**Additional information**   The filing fee is $40. Fellows are expected to devote full time to writing their dissertation and to receive their degree at the end of the fellowship year.

**Deadline**   December of each year.

## [1113]
## EPILEPSY FOUNDATION RESEARCH GRANTS PROGRAM

Epilepsy Foundation
Attn: Research Department
8301 Professional Place
Landover, MD 20785-2237
(301) 459-3700           Toll-free: (800) EFA-1000
Fax: (301) 577-2684      TDD: (800) 332-2070
E-mail: grants@efa.org
Web: www.epilepsyfoundation.org

**Summary**   To provide funding to junior investigators (particularly women, minorities, and persons with disabilities) interested in conducting research that will advance the understanding, treatment, and prevention of epilepsy.

**Eligibility**   Applicants must have a doctoral degree and an academic appointment at the level of assistant professor in a university or medical school (or equivalent standing at a research institution or medical center). They must be interested in conducting basic or clinical research in the biological, behavioral, or social sciences related to the causes of epilepsy. Faculty with appointments at the level of associate professor or higher are not eligible. Applications from women, members of minority groups, and people with disabilities are especially encouraged. U.S. citizenship is not required, but the research must be conducted in the United States. Selection is based on the scientific quality of the research plan, the relevance of the proposed research to epilepsy, the applicant's qualifications, and the adequacy of the institution and facility where research will be conducted.

**Financial data**   The maximum grant is $50,000 per year.

**Duration**   Up to 2 years.

**Additional information**   Support for this program is provided by many individuals, families, and corporations, especially the American Epilepsy Society, Abbott Laboratories, Ortho-McNeil Pharmaceutical, and Pfizer Inc.

**Number awarded**   Varies each year; recently, 9 of these grants were awarded.

**Deadline**   August of each year.

## [1114]
## EPILEPSY RESEARCH AWARDS PROGRAM

American Epilepsy Society
342 North Main Street
West Hartford, CT 06117-2507
(860) 586-7505           Fax: (860) 586-7550
Web: www.aesnet.org

**Summary**   To provide funding to investigators (particularly

women and minorities) anywhere in the world who are interested in conducting research related to epilepsy.

**Eligibility**   This program is open to active scientists and clinicians working in any aspect of epilepsy. Candidates must be nominated by their home institution. There are no geographic restrictions; nominations from outside the United States and North America are welcome. Nominations of women and members of minority groups are especially encouraged. Selection is based on pioneering research, originality of research, quality of publications, research productivity, relationship of the candidate's work to problems in epilepsy, training activities, other contributions in epilepsy, and productivity over the next decade; all criteria are weighted equally.

**Financial data**   The grant is $10,000. No institutional overhead is allowed.

**Additional information**   This program, established in 1991, is funded by the Milken Family Foundation.

**Number awarded**   2 each year.

**Deadline**   August of each year.

## [1115]
## EUNICE V. DAVIS GRANT FOR WOMEN STARTING SMALL BUSINESSES

Business and Professional Women of Virginia
Attn: Virginia BPW Foundation
P.O. Box 4842
McLean, VA 22103-4842
Web: www.bpwva.org/financialassist.shtml

**Summary**   To provide funding to women in Virginia who are starting new small businesses.

**Eligibility**   Applicants must be women who are 21 years of age or older, at least a high school graduate, U.S. citizens, residents of Virginia, and members (for at least 1 year) of Business and Professional Women of Virginia (BPW/VA). Applicants must have a defined business plan and financial strategy for establishing a business and be able to demonstrate financial need. They must have started a new business in Virginia in the past 2 years or intend to start a new business in the state in the next year. Selection is based on financial need, personal character and reliability, credit, education, work and business experience, ability to establish and successfully operate a business, availability of a customer or client base, achievement in prior jobs and/or community, and special circumstances. An interview may be required.

**Financial data**   Each grant ranges from $1,000 to $3,000. Funds must be used to cover expenses associated with starting a new business, including purchase of capital equipment and supplies and application fees to obtain professional and business licenses.

**Duration**   These are 1-time grants.

**Number awarded**   1 or more each year.

**Deadline**   March of each year.

**[1116]**
## EVA L. EVANS MATHEMATICS AND SCIENCE FELLOWSHIPS

Alpha Kappa Alpha Sorority, Inc.
Attn: Educational Advancement Foundation
5656 South Stony Island Avenue
Chicago, IL 60637
(773) 947-0026          Toll-free: (800) 653-6528
Fax: (773) 947-0277          E-mail: akaeaf@aol.com
Web: www.akaeaf.org/fellowships.htm

**Summary**  To provide funding to pre- and postdoctoral scholars (especially African American women) engaged in research in mathematics, science, or technology.

**Eligibility**  This program is open to graduate students and more advanced scholars who are interested in conducting research in the area of mathematics, science, or technology. Men and women of all ethnic groups are eligible, but the sponsor is a traditionally African American women's sorority.

**Financial data**  A stipend is awarded (amount not specified).

**Duration**  These fellowships are awarded biennially, in even-numbered years.

**Number awarded**  Varies each biennium; recently, 2 of these fellowships were awarded.

**Deadline**  January of even-numbered years.

**[1117]**
## FACULTY AND STUDENT TEAMS (FAST) PROGRAM

Department of Energy
Attn: Office of Science
1000 Independence Avenue, S.W.
Washington, DC 20585
(202) 586-7174          Toll-free: (800) DIAL-DOE
Fax: (202) 586-0019
E-mail: todd.clark@science.doe.gov
Web: www.scied.science.doe.gov

**Summary**  To provide support to faculty-student teams, especially those from institutions serving women and minorities, interested in conducting summer research at designated laboratories of the Department of Energy.

**Eligibility**  This program is open to teams of faculty and students from colleges, universities with limited prior research capabilities, and those institutions serving populations, women, and minorities underrepresented in the fields of science, engineering, and technology. Faculty applicants must be U.S. citizens or permanent residents. Students must be currently enrolled as undergraduates, have completed at least 1 semester of college work, be U.S. citizens or permanent residents, and have coverage under a health insurance plan. Preference is given to faculty at community colleges; at universities and colleges that are in the 50th percentile or lower of total federal funding; and those associated with 1 of the following programs supported by the National Science Foundation (NSF): Tribal Colleges and Universities Program (TCUP), Historically Black Colleges and Universities Undergraduate Program (HBCU-UP), Louis Stokes Alliances for Minority Participation (LSAMP), Centers of Research Excellence in Science and Technology (CREST), Advanced Technology Education (ATE), Computer

Science, Engineering, and Mathematics Scholarships (CSEMS), Centers for Learning and Teaching (CLT), Gender Diversity in STEM Education (GDSE), Math and Science Partnership (MSP), Collaboratives for Excellence in Teacher Preparation (CETP), Science, Technology, Engineering and Mathematics Teacher Preparation (STEMTP), and Program for People with Disabilities (PPD).

**Financial data**  Students receive a stipend of $4,500, allocated as 10 weekly stipends of $400 each and up to $500 for travel. Faculty members receive a stipend equal to 2/9 of their academic year salary, up to $12,000. Both student and faculty team members receive funding assistance with travel and housing. An additional grant of $1,000 is available as support for unusual travel expenses incurred by people with disabilities.

**Duration**  10 weeks during the summer. Students may participate in only 2 of these projects.

**Additional information**  Teams work on specified projects at the following Department of Energy facilities: Argonne National Laboratory in Argonne, Illinois; Brookhaven National Laboratory in Upton, New York; Lawrence Berkeley National Laboratory in Berkeley, California; Lawrence Livermore National Laboratory in Livermore, California; Oak Ridge National Laboratory in Oak Ridge, Tennessee; or Pacific Northwest National Laboratory in Richland, Washington.

**Number awarded**  Varies each year.

**Deadline**  March of each year.

**[1118]**
## FACULTY AWARDS FOR RESEARCH

American Society for Engineering Education
Attn: Projects Department
1818 N Street, N.W., Suite 600
Washington, DC 20036-2479
(202) 331-3509          Fax: (202) 265-8504
E-mail: nasa@asee.org
Web: www.asee.org

**Summary**  To provide funding for space-related summer research to faculty (particularly women, minorities, and person with disabilities) at recognized minority colleges and universities.

**Eligibility**  This program is open to full-time faculty at 1) an accredited 2-year or 4-year minority college or university with enrollment of a single underrepresented minority group or the combination of underrepresented minority groups that exceeds 50% of the total student enrollment; 2) an accredited 2-year or 4-year Hispanic-Serving Institution (HSI); 3) an accredited 2-year or 4-year Historically Black College or University (HBCU); or 4) a recognized Tribal College or University (TCU). Applicants must be U.S. citizens who have a Ph.D. in an engineering, mathematics, or science discipline applicable to the research and/or technology development needs of the National Aeronautics and Space Administration (NASA). They must be interested in conducting a summer research project at a participating NASA center. Women, underrepresented minorities, and persons with disabilities are strongly encouraged to apply. Selection is based on relevance and merit of the research (40%), qualifications of the faculty applicant (40%), and overall academic benefit to the faculty applicant and his or her institution (20%).

**Financial data** The stipend is $1,200 per week, for a maximum of $12,000. A relocation allowance of $1,500 is available for fellows who live more than 50 miles from their assigned center and reasonable travel expenses for a round-trip are also reimbursed for fellows who receive the relocation allowance. The maximum allowance for relocation and travel is $2,000. To facilitate the participation of individuals with disabilities, NASA provides up to $1,500 in supplemental funding for special assistance and/or equipment necessary to enable the principal investigator to perform the work under the award.

**Duration** 10 weeks during the summer.

**Additional information** This program, established in 1992, is currently managed by the American Society for Engineering Education (ASEE) and the Universities Space Research Association (USRA) with funding from NASA's Minority University Research and Education Programs. Participating NASA centers are Ames Research Center (Moffett Field, California); Hugh L. Dryden Flight Research Facility (Edwards, California); Goddard Space Flight Center (Greenbelt, Maryland) and its Wallops Flight Facility (Wallops Island, Virginia) and Goddard Institute for Space Studies (New York, New York); Jet Propulsion Laboratory (Pasadena, California); Lyndon B. Johnson Space Center (Houston, Texas) and its White Sands Test Facility (Las Cruces, New Mexico); John F. Kennedy Space Center (Cape Canaveral, Florida); Langley Research Center (Hampton, Virginia); Glenn Research Center (Cleveland, Ohio); George C. Marshall Space Flight Center (Huntsville, Alabama); and John C. Stennis Space Center (Stennis Space Center, Mississippi).

**Number awarded** Varies each year.

## [1119]
## FACULTY EARLY CAREER DEVELOPMENT PROGRAM

National Science Foundation
Directorate for Education and Human Resources
Attn: Senior Staff Associate for Cross Directorate
   Programs
4201 Wilson Boulevard, Room 805
Arlington, VA 22230
(703) 292-8600          TDD: (800) 281-8749
Web: www.nsf.gov

**Summary** To provide support for science and engineering research to outstanding new faculty (especially women, minorities, and persons with disabilities) who intend to develop academic careers involving both research and education.

**Eligibility** This program, identified as the CAREER program, is open to faculty members who meet all of the following requirements: 1) be employed in a tenure-track (or equivalent) position at an institution in the United States, its territories or possessions, or the Commonwealth of Puerto Rico that awards degrees in a field supported by the National Science Foundation (NSF) or that is a nonprofit, non-degree granting organization such as a museum, observatory, or research laboratory; 2) have a doctoral degree in a field of science or engineering supported by NSF; 3) not have competed more than 3 times in this program; 4) be untenured; and 5) not be a current or former recipient of a Presidential Early Career Award for Scientists and Engineers (PECASE) or CAREER award. Applicants

must be U.S. citizens, nationals, or permanent residents. They must submit a career development plan that indicates a description of the proposed research project, including preliminary supporting data if appropriate, specific objectives, methods, and procedures to be used, and expected significance of the results; a description of the proposed educational activities, including plans to evaluate their impact; a description of how the research and educational activities are integrated with each other; and results of prior NSF support, if applicable. Proposals from women, underrepresented minorities, and persons with disabilities are especially encouraged.

**Financial data** The total grant is $400,000 (or $500,000 for the Directorate of Biological Sciences) over the full period of the award.

**Duration** 5 years.

**Additional information** This program is operated by various disciplinary divisions within the NSF; for a list of the participating divisions and their telephone numbers, contact the sponsor. Outstanding recipients of these grants are nominated for the NSF component of the PECASE awards, which are awarded to 20 recipients of these grants as an honorary award.

**Number awarded** 300 to 400 each year. Approximately $85 million is budgeted to support this program annually.

**Deadline** July of each year.

## [1120]
## FELLOWSHIPS IN ENVIRONMENTAL REGULATORY IMPLEMENTATION

Resources for the Future
Attn: Coordinator for Academic Programs
1616 P Street, N.W.
Washington, DC 20036-1400
(202) 328-5090        Fax: (202) 939-3460
E-mail: eri-award@rff.org
Web: www.rff.org

**Summary** To provide funding to postdoctoral researchers (particularly women and minorities) who are interested in conducting research that documents the implementation and outcomes of environmental regulation.

**Eligibility** This program is open to scholars from universities and research organizations who have a doctoral or equivalent degree or equivalent professional research experience. Applicants must be interested in conducting research that examines environmental regulations in practice and can be used to inform regulators, industry, and others of assumptions of environmental laws and policies. The proposed research must be documentary in nature, without arguing in favor of any particular policy or result. Funding is not available for studies balancing costs and benefits or conducting other policy analyses of regulations. Interested scholars must first submit a pre-proposal that describes the project and its expected result, schedule, and budget. Women and minority candidates are strongly encouraged to apply. Preference is given to applicants who have sabbatical or other sources of support from their home institution.

**Financial data** Fellows receive an annual stipend commensurate with experience, research support, office facilities and limited support for relocation (if they choose to conduct the project at RFF), and funding for travel and conferences. Fellowships do not provide medical insurance or other RFF fringe benefits.

**Duration** 1 or 2 years.

**Additional information** Fellows may be in residence at RFF or remain at their current institution. They are requested to visit RFF to discuss progress on their research. This program is supported by the Andrew W. Mellon Foundation.

**Number awarded** 1 or 2 each year.

**Deadline** Pre-proposals must be submitted by January of each year. Final proposals are due in February

## [1121]
## FELLOWSHIPS IN SCIENCE AND INTERNATIONAL AFFAIRS

Harvard University
John F. Kennedy School of Government
Belfer Center for Science and International Affairs
Attn: Fellowship Coordinator
79 John F. Kennedy Street
Cambridge, MA 02138
(617) 495-8806        Fax: (617) 495-8963
E-mail: bcsia_fellowships@ksg.harvard.edu
Web: bcsia.ksg.harvard.edu

**Summary** To provide funding to professionals, postdoctorates, and graduate students (particularly women and minorities) who are interested in conducting research in areas of concern to the Belfer Center for Science and International Affairs at Harvard University in Cambridge, Massachusetts.

**Eligibility** The postdoctoral fellowship is open to recent recipients of the Ph.D. or equivalent degree, university faculty members, and employees of government, military, international, humanitarian, and private research institutions who have appropriate professional experience. Applicants for predoctoral fellowships must have passed their general examinations. Lawyers, economists, physical scientists, and others of diverse disciplinary backgrounds are also welcome to apply. The program especially encourages applications from women, minorities, and citizens of all countries. All applicants must be interested in conducting research in 1 of the 4 major program areas of the center: the International Security Program (ISP); the Science, Technology, and Public Policy Program (STPP); the Program on Intrastate Conflict and Conflict Resolution (ICP); and the Dubai initiative. Fellowships may also be available in other specialized areas, such as science, technology, and globalization; managing the atom; and energy technology and innovation.

**Financial data** The stipend is $34,000 for postdoctoral research fellows or $20,000 for predoctoral research fellows. Health insurance is also provided.

**Duration** 10 months.

**Number awarded** A limited number each year.

**Deadline** December of each year.

## [1122]
## FICHTER RESEARCH GRANT COMPETITION

Association for the Sociology of Religion
Attn: Executive Officer
618 S.W. Second Avenue
Galva, IL 61434-1912
(309) 932-2727        Fax: (309) 932-2282
Web: www.sociologyofreligion.com

**Summary** To provide funding to scholars interested in conducting research on women and religion or sociology of the parish.

**Eligibility** This program is open to scholars involved in research on 1) women and religion, gender issues, and feminist perspectives on religion; or 2) sociology of the parish. Dissertation research qualifies for funding. Applicants must be members of the association at the time the application is submitted. The proposal must not be more than 5 double-spaced pages and should outline the rationale and plan of the research, previous research, methodology proposed, timeline, and budget; a curriculum vitae should also be included. Scholars at the beginning of their careers are particularly encouraged to apply. Simultaneous submissions to other grant competitions are permissible if the applicant is explicit about which budget items in the Fichter grant proposal do not overlap items in other submitted proposals.

**Financial data** Each year, a total of $20,000 is available to be awarded.

**Duration** 1 year.

**Additional information** Information is also available from Barbara J. Denison, P.O. Box 211, Mechanicsburg, PA 17055, (717) 477-1257, E-mail: bjeni@ship.edu.

**Number awarded** Varies each year; recently, 6 of these grants were awarded.

**Deadline** February of each year.

## [1123]
## FIELD MUSEUM WOMEN IN SCIENCE GRADUATE FELLOWSHIP

Field Museum of Natural History
Academic Affairs
Attn: Chair, Scholarship Committee
Roosevelt Road at Lake Shore Drive
Chicago, IL 60605-2496
(312) 665-7627        Fax: (312) 665-7641
E-mail: ezeiger@fieldmuseum.org
Web: www.fieldmuseum.org

**Summary** To provide financial assistance to women interested in conducting graduate research in selected scientific areas.

**Eligibility** Eligible to apply are women doctoral candidates who are working on their dissertation in the following areas: anthropology, botany, geology, and zoology. Normally, candidates are expected to have formal involvement with the Field Museum of Natural History (i.e., having a curator serve on the student's academic committee and relying upon the collections and facilities of the museum).

**Financial data** Fellowships provide a stipend and limited tuition support.

**Duration** 1 year. The recipient must be in residence in the Chicago area and is expected to spend a significant portion of her research time at the museum.

**Number awarded** 1 each year.
**Deadline** January of each year.

## [1124]
## FOREIGN POLICY STUDIES PREDOCTORAL FELLOWSHIPS

Brookings Institution
Attn: Foreign Policy Studies
1775 Massachusetts Avenue, N.W.
Washington, DC 20036-2103
(202) 797-6156          Fax: (202) 797-2481
E-mail: akramer@brookings.edu
Web: www.brookings.edu/admin/fellowships.htm

**Summary** To support predoctoral policy-oriented research on U.S. foreign policy and international relations at the Brookings Institution.

**Eligibility** This program is open to doctoral students who have completed their preliminary examinations and have selected a dissertation topic that directly relates to public policy issues and the major research issues of the Brookings Institution. Candidates cannot apply to conduct research at the institution; they must be nominated by their graduate department. They may be at any stage of their dissertation research. Selection is based on 1) relevance of the topic to contemporary U.S. foreign policy and/or post-Cold War international relations, and 2) evidence that the research will be facilitated by access to the institution's resources or to Washington-based organizations. The institution particularly encourages the nomination of women and minority candidates.

**Financial data** Fellows receive a stipend of $22,000 for the academic year, supplementary assistance for copying and other essential research requirements up to $750, reimbursement for transportation, health insurance, reimbursement for research-related travel up to $750, and access to computer/library facilities.

**Duration** 1 year, beginning in September.

**Additional information** Fellows participate in seminars, conferences, and meetings at the institution. Outstanding dissertations may be published by the institution. Fellows are expected to conduct their research at the Brookings Institution.

**Number awarded** A limited number are awarded each year.

**Deadline** Nominations must be submitted by mid-December and applications by mid-February.

## [1125]
## FOUNDATION FOR THE HISTORY OF WOMEN IN MEDICINE FELLOWSHIPS

College of Physicians of Philadelphia
Attn: Francis C. Wood Institute for the History of Medicine
19 South 22nd Street
Philadelphia, PA 19103-3097
(215) 563-3737, ext. 305          Fax: (215) 561-6477
E-mail: mpatton@collphyphil.org
Web: www.collphyphil.org/woodfell.htm

**Summary** To provide funding to students and scholars interested in short-term use of resources in the Philadelphia area to conduct research on the history of women and medicine.

**Eligibility** This program is open to doctoral candidates and other advanced scholars interested in using the historical collections of the Historical Medical Library of the College of Physicians of Philadelphia, the Mütter Museum, or the archives and special collections on women in medicine at the Drexel University College of Medicine. The proposed research must relate to the history of women and medicine. Preference is given to projects that deal specifically with women as physicians or other health workers, but proposals dealing with the history of women's health issues are also considered.

**Financial data** Grants up to $1,000 are available.

**Duration** Grants are available for spring, summer, or fall visits of at least 1 week.

**Number awarded** Up to 2 each year.

**Deadline** February of each year.

## [1126]
## FRANCES C. ALLEN FELLOWSHIPS

Newberry Library
Attn: D'Arcy McNickle Center for American Indian History
60 West Walton Street
Chicago, IL 60610-3305
(312) 255-3564          Fax: (312) 255-3513
E-mail: mcnickle@newberry.org
Web: www.newberry.org/mcnickle/frances.html

**Summary** To provide funding to Native American women graduate students who wish to use the resources of the D'Arcy McNickle Center for the History of the American Indian at the Newberry Library.

**Eligibility** This program is open to women of American Indian heritage who are interested in using the library for a project appropriate to its collections. Applicants must be enrolled in a graduate or pre-professional program, especially in the humanities or social sciences. Recommendations are required; at least 2 must come from academic advisors or instructors who can comment on the significance of the proposed project of an applicant and explain how it will help in the achievement of professional goals.

**Financial data** Grants range from $1,200 to $8,000 in approved expenses, which may include travel expenses.

**Duration** From 1 month to 1 year.

**Additional information** These grants were first awarded in 1983. Fellows must spend a significant portion of their time at the library's D'Arcy McNickle Center.

**Deadline** February of each year.

## [1127]
## FREDERICK BURKHARDT RESIDENTIAL FELLOWSHIPS FOR RECENTLY TENURED SCHOLARS

American Council of Learned Societies
Attn: Office of Fellowships and Grants
633 Third Avenue, 8C
New York, NY 10017-6795
(212) 697-1505              Fax: (212) 949-8058
E-mail: grants@acls.org
Web: www.acls.org/burkguid.htm

**Summary** To provide funding to scholars (especially women and minorities) in all disciplines of the humanities and the humanities-related social sciences who are interested in conducting research at designated residential centers.

**Eligibility** This program is open to citizens and permanent residents of the United States who achieved tenure in a humanities or humanities-related social science discipline at a U.S. institution within the past 4 years. Applicants must be interested in conducting research at 1 of 11 participating residential centers in the United States or abroad. Appropriate fields of specialization include, but are not limited to, anthropology, archaeology, art and architectural history, economic history, film, geography, history, languages and literatures, legal studies, linguistics, musicology, philosophy, political science, psychology, religion, rhetoric and communication, sociology and theater studies. Proposals in those fields of the social sciences are eligible only if they employ predominantly humanistic approaches (e.g., economic history, law and literature, political philosophy). Proposals in interdisciplinary and cross-disciplinary studies are welcome, as are proposals focused on any geographic region or on any cultural or linguistic group. Applications are particularly invited from women and members of minority groups.

**Financial data** The stipend is $75,000. If that stipend exceeds the fellow's normal academic year salary, the excess is available for research and travel expenses.

**Duration** 1 academic year.

**Additional information** This program, which began in 1999, is supported by funding from the Andrew W. Mellon Foundation with additional support from the Rockefeller Foundation. The participating residential research centers are the National Humanities Center (Research Triangle Park, North Carolina), the Center for Advanced Study in the Behavioral Sciences (Stanford, California), the Institute for Advanced Study, Schools of Historical Studies and Social Science (Princeton, New Jersey), the Radcliffe Institute for Advanced Study at Harvard University (Cambridge, Massachusetts), the American Antiquarian Society (Worcester, Massachusetts), the Folger Shakespeare Library (Washington, D.C.), the Newberry Library (Chicago, Illinois), the Huntington Library, Art Collections, and Botanical Gardens (San Marino, California), the American Academy in Rome, Collegium Budapest, and Villa I Tatti (Florence, Italy).

**Number awarded** Up to 11 each year.

**Deadline** September of each year.

## [1128]
## GEIS MEMORIAL AWARD

American Psychological Association
Attn: Division 35 (Psychology of Women)
750 First Street, N.E.
Washington, DC 20002-4242
(202) 336-6000              Fax: (202) 336-5953
E-mail: scistudent@apa.org
Web: www.apa.org/divisions/div35/geis.html

**Summary** To provide funding to psychology doctoral students interested in conducting feminist research.

**Eligibility** This program is open to psychology graduate students interested in conducting dissertation research. The research must be feminist, address a feminist/womanist issue, use social psychology research methods, and make a significant contribution to social psychology theory and practice. Selection is based on suitability, feasibility, merit of the research, and potential of the student to have a career as a feminist researcher in social psychology.

**Financial data** The grant is $15,000.

**Duration** 1 academic year.

**Additional information** Information is also available from Mimi Ormerod, University of Illinois, Department of Psychology, 603 East Daniel Street, (217) 333-4899, Fax: (217) 244-5876, E-mail: aormerod@uiuc.edu.

**Number awarded** 1 each year.

**Deadline** March of each year.

## [1129]
## GEOLOGICAL SOCIETY OF AMERICA GRADUATE STUDENT RESEARCH GRANTS

Geological Society of America
Attn: Program Officer-Grants, Awards and Recognition
3300 Penrose Place
P.O. Box 9140
Boulder, CO 80301-9140
(303) 357-1028      Toll-free: (800) 472-1988, ext. 1028
Fax: (303) 357-1070      E-mail: awards@geosociety.org
Web: www.geosociety.org/grants/gradgrants.htm

**Summary** To provide support to graduate student members of the Geological Society of America (GSA) interested in conducting research at universities in the United States, Canada, Mexico, or Central America.

**Eligibility** This program is open to GSA members working on a master's or doctoral degree at a university in the United States, Canada, Mexico, or Central America. Applicants must be interested in conducting geological research. Minorities, women, and persons with disabilities are strongly encouraged to apply. Selection is based on the scientific merits of the problems, the capability of the investigator, and the reasonableness of the budget.

**Financial data** Grants can be used for the cost of travel, room and board in the field, materials and supplies, and other expenses directly related to the fulfillment of the research contract. Expenses requested for equipment or rental of equipment, film, some supplies, computer time, software, thin sections, and in-house charges for analytical instruments usually provided by a university must be fully justified. Funds cannot be used for the purchase of ordinary field equipment, for maintenance of the families of the grantees and their assistants, as reimbursement for work already accomplished, to attend professional meetings, for thesis preparation, to defray the costs of tuition, or for the employment of persons to conduct research. Recently, grants averaged $1,963.

**Duration** 1 year.

**Additional information** In addition to general grants, GSA awards a number of specialized grants: the Gretchen L. Blechschmidt Award for women (especially in the fields of biostratigraphy and/or paleoceanography); the John T. Dillon Alaska Research Award for earth science problems particular to Alaska; the Robert K. Fahnestock Memorial Award for the field of sediment transport or related aspects of fluvial geomorphology; the Lipman Research Award for volcanology and petrology; the Bruce L. "Biff" Reed Award for studies in the tectonic and magmatic evolution of Alaska; the Alexander Sisson Award for studies in Alaska and the Caribbean; the Harold T. Stearns Fellowship Award for work on the geology of the Pacific Islands and the circum-Pacific region; the Parke D. Snavely, Jr. Cascadia Research Fund Award for studies of the Pacific Northwest convergent margin; the Alexander and Geraldine Wanek Fund Award for studies of coal and petroleum; the Charles A. and June R.P. Ross Research Fund Award for stratigraphy; and the John Montagne Fund Award for research in the field of quaternary geology or geomorphology. Furthermore, 9 of the 14 GSA divisions (geophysics, hydrogeology, sedimentary geology, structural geology and tectonics, archaeological geology, coal geology, planetary geology, quaternary geology and geomorphology, and engineering geology) also offer divisional grants. Some of those awards are named: the Allan V. Cox Award of the Geophysics Division, the Claude C. Albritton, Jr. Scholarship of the Archaeological Geology Division, the Antoinette Lierman Medlin Scholarships of the Coal Geology Division, the J. Hoover Mackin Research Grants and the Arthur D. Howard Research Grants of the Quaternary Geology and Geomorphology Division, and the Roy J. Shlemon Scholarship Awards of the Engineering Geology Division. In addition, 4 of the 6 geographic sections (south-central, north-central, southeastern, and northeastern) offer grants to graduate students at universities within their section.

**Number awarded** Varies each year; recently, the society awarded 224 grants worth more than $400,000 through this and all of its specialized programs.

**Deadline** January of each year.

## [1130]
## GEOLOGICAL SOCIETY OF AMERICA UNDERGRADUATE STUDENT RESEARCH GRANTS

Geological Society of America
Attn: Program Officer-Grants, Awards and Recognition
3300 Penrose Place
P.O. Box 9140
Boulder, CO 80301-9140
(303) 357-1028   Toll-free: (800) 472-1988, ext. 1028
Fax: (303) 357-1070   E-mail: awards@geosociety.org
Web: www.geosociety.org/grants/ugrad.htm

**Summary** To provide support to undergraduate student members of the Geological Society of America (GSA) interested in conducting research at universities in designated sections of the United States.

**Eligibility** This program is open to undergraduate students who are interested in conducting research and are majoring in geology at universities in 4 GSA sections: north-central, northeastern, south-central, and southeastern. Applicants must be student associates of the GSA. Applications from women, minorities, and persons with disabilities are strongly encouraged.

**Financial data** Grant amounts vary.

**Duration** 1 year.

**Additional information** Within the 4 participating sections, information is available from each secretary. For the name and address of the 4 section secretaries, contact the sponsor.

**Number awarded** 1 or more each year in each of the 4 sections.

**Deadline** January of each year.

## [1131]
## GERALDINE R. DODGE RESIDENCY GRANTS

Women's Studio Workshop
722 Binnewater Lane
P.O. Box 489
Rosendale, NY 12472
(845) 658-9133                    Fax: (845) 658-9031
E-mail: info@wsworkshop.org
Web: www.wsworkshop.org

**Summary** To provide a residency and financial support at the Women's Studio Workshop (WSW) to women artists from New Jersey.

**Eligibility** This program is open to artists who are residents of New Jersey. Applicants must be interested in creating a new body of work or editing a bookwork while in residence at the WSW. They must provide a 1-paragraph description of the proposed project, a resume, and 10 slides of their recent work. Eligible art fields include printmaking, papermaking, photography, book arts, and clay arts. Emerging artists are especially encouraged to apply.

**Financial data** The program provides a stipend of $2,000 to $3,000, a $150 travel stipend, a materials budget of $500, unlimited studio use, and housing while in residence.

**Duration** 6 to 8 weeks.

**Additional information** This program is sponsored by the Geraldine R. Dodge Foundation.

**Number awarded** 2 each year.

**Deadline** March of each year.

## [1132]
## GERTRUDE AND MAURICE GOLDHABER DISTINGUISHED FELLOWSHIPS

Brookhaven National Laboratory
Attn: Dr. Leonard Newman
Building 815E
P.O. Box 5000
Upton, NY 11973-5000
(631) 344-4467                    E-mail: newman@bnl.gov
Web: www.bnl.gov/hr/goldhaber.asp

**Summary** To provide funding to postdoctoral scientists (particularly women and minorities) who are interested in conducting research at Brookhaven National Laboratory (BNL).

**Eligibility** This program is open to scholars who are no more than 3 years past receipt of the Ph.D. and are interested in working at BNL. Candidates must be interested in working in close collaboration with a member of the BNL scientific staff and qualifying for a scientific staff position at BNL upon completion of the appointment. The sponsoring scientist must have an opening and be able to support the candidate at the standard starting salary for postdoctoral research associates. The program especially encourages applications from women and minorities.

**Financial data** The program provides additional funds to bring the salary to $72,000 per year.

**Duration** 3 years.

**Additional information** This program is funded by Battelle Memorial Institute and the State University of New York at Stony Brook.

**Number awarded** 1 or 2 each year.

## [1133]
## GILBERT F. WHITE POSTDOCTORAL FELLOWSHIP PROGRAM

Resources for the Future
Attn: Coordinator for Academic Programs
1616 P Street, N.W.
Washington, DC 20036-1400
(202) 328-5090                    Fax: (202) 939-3460
E-mail: white-award@rff.org
Web: www.rff.org

**Summary** To provide funding to postdoctoral researchers (particularly women and minorities) who wish to devote a year to scholarly work at Resources for the Future (RFF) in Washington, D.C.

**Eligibility** This program is open to individuals in any discipline who have completed their doctoral requirements and are interested in conducting scholarly research at RFF in social or policy science areas that relate to natural resources, energy, or the environment. Teaching and/or research experience at the postdoctoral level is preferred though not essential. Individuals holding positions in government as well as at academic institutions are eligible. Women and minority candidates are strongly encouraged to apply.

**Financial data** Fellows receive an annual stipend (based on their academic salary) plus research support, office facilities at RFF, and an allowance of up to $1,000 for moving or living expenses. Fellowships do not provide medical insurance or other RFF fringe benefits.

**Duration** 11 months.

**Additional information** Fellows are assigned to an RFF research division: the Energy and Natural Resources division, the Quality of the Environment division, or the Center for Risk, Resource, and Environmental Management. Fellows are expected to be in residence at Resources for the Future for the duration of the program.

**Number awarded** 1 each year.

**Deadline** February of each year.

## [1134]
## GLOBAL CHANGE GRADUATE RESEARCH ENVIRONMENTAL FELLOWSHIPS (GREF)

Oak Ridge Institute for Science and Education
Attn: Global Change Education Program
120 Badger Avenue, M.S. 36
P.O. Box 117
Oak Ridge, TN 37831-0117
(865) 576-9655            E-mail: mary.kinney@orau.gov
Web: www.atmos.anl.gov/GCEP

**Summary** To provide doctoral students (especially women and minority students) with an opportunity to conduct research on global change.

**Eligibility** This program is open to students who have completed their first year of graduate school, unless they previously participated in the Global Change Summer Undergraduate Research Experience (SURE) or the Significant Opportunities in Atmospheric Research and Science (SOARS) program. Applicants must be proposing to conduct research at a national laboratory in a program area within the Department of Energy's Office of Biological and Environmental Research (DOE-BER): the atmospheric science program, the environmental meteorology program, the atmospheric radiation measurement program, the terrestrial carbon processes effort, the program for ecosystem research, and studies carried out under the direction of the National Institute for Global Environmental Change. They must submit a 5-page description of their proposed project that includes the basic reasons for the research, the methods to be used, the backgrounds and expertise of their 2 mentors (a university thesis advisor and a national laboratory researcher who will guide the thesis research activities), and a statement of career goals with special attention to long-term global change research interests. Minority and female students are particularly encouraged to apply. U.S. citizenship is required.

**Financial data** Participants receive an annual stipend of $19,500 ($1,500 per month plus a $600 research education supplement in March and October); tuition and fees at the college or university they attend; and transportation, per diem, and lodging for summer activities.

**Duration** Up to 3 years.

**Additional information** This program, funded by DOE-BER, began in 1999. Fellows are encouraged to participate in the Summer Undergraduate Research Experience (SURE) orientation and focus sessions at a participating university.

**Number awarded** 10 to 15 each year.

**Deadline** February of each year.

## [1135]
## GLOBAL CHANGE SUMMER UNDERGRADUATE RESEARCH EXPERIENCE (SURE)

Oak Ridge Institute for Science and Education
Attn: Global Change Education Program
120 Badger Avenue, M.S. 36
P.O. Box 117
Oak Ridge, TN 37831-0117
(865) 576-9655            E-mail: mary.kinney@orau.gov
Web: www.atmos.anl.gov/GCEP

**Summary** To provide undergraduate students (particularly women and minority students) with an opportunity to conduct research during the summer on global change.

**Eligibility** This program is open to undergraduates in their sophomore and junior years, although outstanding freshman and senior applicants are also considered. Applicants must be proposing to conduct research in a program area within the Department of Energy's Office of Biological and Environmental Research (DOE-BER): the atmospheric science program, the environmental meteorology program, the atmospheric radiation measurement program, the terrestrial carbon processes effort, the program for ecosystem research, and studies carried out under the direction of the National Institute for Global Environmental Change. Minority and female students are particularly encouraged to apply. U.S. citizenship is required.

**Financial data** Participants receive a weekly stipend of $475 and support for travel and housing.

**Duration** 10 to 12 weeks during the summer. Successful participants are expected to reapply for a second year of research with their mentors.

**Additional information** This program, funded by DOE-BER, began in summer 1999. The first 2 weeks are spent in an orientation and focus session at a participating university. For the remaining 10 weeks, students conduct mentored research at 1 of the national laboratories or universities conducting BER-supported global change research.

**Number awarded** 20 to 30 each year.

**Deadline** February of each year.

## [1136]
## GOVERNANCE STUDIES PREDOCTORAL FELLOWSHIPS

Brookings Institution
Attn: Governmental Studies
1775 Massachusetts Avenue, N.W.
Washington, DC 20036-2188
(202) 797-6090          Fax: (202) 797-6144
E-mail: sbinder@brookings.edu
Web: www.brookings.edu/admin/fellowships.htm

**Summary** To support predoctoral policy-oriented research in governmental studies at the Brookings Institution.

**Eligibility** This program is open to doctoral students who have completed their preliminary examinations and have selected a dissertation topic that directly relates to the study of public policy and political institutions and thus to the major interests of the Brookings Institution. Candidates cannot apply to conduct research at the institution; they must be nominated by their graduate department. The proposed research should benefit from access to the data, opportunities for interviewing, and consultation with senior staff members afforded by the institution and by residence in Washington, D.C. The institution particularly encourages the nomination of women and minority candidates.

**Financial data** Fellows receive a stipend of $22,000 for the academic year, supplementary assistance for copying and other essential research requirements up to $750, reimbursement for research-related travel up to $750, health insurance, reimbursement for transportation, and access to computer/library facilities.

**Duration** 1 year.

**Additional information** Fellows participate in seminars, conferences, and meetings at the institution. Outstanding dissertations may be published by the institution. Fellows are expected to conduct their research at the Brookings Institution.

**Number awarded** A limited number are awarded each year.

**Deadline** Nominations must be submitted by mid-December and applications by mid-February.

## [1137]
## HADASSAH-BRANDEIS INSTITUTE RESEARCH AWARDS

Brandeis University
Hadassah-Brandeis Institute
Attn: Program Manager
Mailstop 079
Waltham, MA 02454-9110
(781) 736-2064          E-mail: hbi@brandeis.edu
Web: www.brandeis.edu/hbi/grants/res_awards.html

**Summary** To provide funding to scholars, graduate students, writers, activists, and artists conducting research in the field of Jewish women's studies.

**Eligibility** This program offers senior grants (for established scholars and professionals) and junior grants (for graduate students and scholars within 3 years of receiving a Ph.D.). All applicants must be interested in conducting interdisciplinary research on Jewish women and gender issues. Graduate students in recognized master's and Ph.D. programs are encouraged to apply. Applications from outside the United States are welcome. Grants are awarded in 7 categories: Jewish women film and video projects, Jewish women's biography, Jewish women's history, Jewish women and social studies, Jewish women and the arts, Jewish women and Judaism, and Jewish women in the Yishuv and Israel. Applications must specify the category and may be for only 1 category. Selection is based on originality, clarity of research design, scholarly importance, feasibility, and benefit to the Jewish community.

**Financial data** Senior grants are $5,000 and junior grants are $2,000.

**Duration** 1 year.

**Additional information** The Hadassah-Brandeis Institute was formerly the Hadassah International Research Institute on Jewish Women at Brandeis University.

**Number awarded** Varies each year; recently, 12 senior and 4 junior grants were awarded.

**Deadline** September of each year.

## [1138]
## HADASSAH-BRANDEIS INSTITUTE SCHOLAR IN RESIDENCE PROGRAM

Brandeis University
Hadassah-Brandeis Institute
Attn: Program Manager
Mailstop 079
Waltham, MA 02454-9110
(781) 736-2064          E-mail: hbi@brandeis.edu
Web: www.brandeis.edu/hbi/grants/res_scholars.html

**Summary** To provide an opportunity for scholars, writers, and communal professionals to conduct research in the field of Jewish women's studies while in residence at the Hadassah-Brandeis Institute of Brandeis University.

**Eligibility** This program is open to scholars, writers, and communal professionals who are working in the area of Jewish women's and gender studies. Applicants must be interested in taking time from their regular institutional duties to work at the institute. Scholars outside the United States and those with an international research focus are especially encouraged to apply.

**Financial data** Scholars receive a stipend of $3,000 per month and office space at the Brandeis University Women's Research Center.

**Duration** 3 months to 1 year.

**Additional information** The Hadassah-Brandeis Institute was formerly the Hadassah International Research Institute on Jewish Women at Brandeis University.

**Number awarded** Varies each year; recently, 4 of these residencies were awarded.

**Deadline** January of each year.

## [1139]
## HEALTH SCIENCES STUDENT FELLOWSHIPS IN EPILEPSY

Epilepsy Foundation
Attn: Research Department
8301 Professional Place
Landover, MD 20785-2237
(301) 459-3700          Toll-free: (800) EFA-1000
Fax: (301) 577-2684          TDD: (800) 332-2070
E-mail: grants@efa.org
Web: www.epilepsyfoundation.org

**Summary** To provide financial assistance to medical and health science graduate students (particularly women, minority, and disabled students) interested in working on an epilepsy project during the summer.

**Eligibility** This program is open to students enrolled, or accepted for enrollment, in a medical school, a doctoral program, or other graduate program. Applicants must have a defined epilepsy-related study or research plan to be carried out under the supervision of a qualified mentor. Because the program is designed as a training opportunity, the quality of the training plans and environment are considered in the selection process. Other selection criteria include the quality of the proposed project, the relevance of the proposed work to epilepsy, the applicant's interest in the field of epilepsy, the applicant's qualifications, and the mentor's qualifications, including his or her commitment to the student and the project. U.S. citizenship is not required, but the project must be conducted in the United

States. Applications from women, members of minority groups, and people with disabilities are especially encouraged. The program is not intended for students working on a dissertation research project.

**Financial data** Stipends are $3,000.

**Duration** 3 months during the summer.

**Additional information** Support for this program is provided by many individuals, families, and corporations, especially the American Epilepsy Society, Abbott Laboratories, Ortho-McNeil Pharmaceutical, and Pfizer Inc.

**Number awarded** Varies each year; recently, 3 of these fellowships were awarded.

**Deadline** February of each year.

## [1140]
## HELEN CROMER COOPER/ROSA PARKS FELLOWSHIPS FOR NON-VIOLENT ALTERNATIVES TO CONFLICT

Alpha Kappa Alpha Sorority, Inc.
Attn: Educational Advancement Foundation
5656 South Stony Island Avenue
Chicago, IL 60637
(773) 947-0026          Toll-free: (800) 653-6528
Fax: (773) 947-0277          E-mail: akaeaf@aol.com
Web: www.akaeaf.org/fellowships.htm

**Summary** To provide funding to academic and other professionals (especially African American women) who are interested in working on a project to find non-violent solutions to human problems.

**Eligibility** This program is open to professionals involved in finding non-violent solutions to human problems. Applicants may be involved in scholarly pursuits, but that is not required.

**Financial data** A stipend is awarded (amount not specified).

**Duration** These fellowships are awarded biennially, in even-numbered years.

**Number awarded** Varies each biennium; recently, 2 of these fellowships were awarded.

**Deadline** January of even-numbered years.

## [1141]
## HENRY LUCE FOUNDATION/ACLS DISSERTATION FELLOWSHIPS IN AMERICAN ART

American Council of Learned Societies
Attn: Office of Fellowships and Grants
633 Third Avenue, 8C
New York, NY 10017-6795
(212) 697-1505          Fax: (212) 949-8058
E-mail: grants@acls.org
Web: www.acls.org/luceguid.htm

**Summary** To provide funding to doctoral students (especially women and minority students) who are interested in conducting dissertation research anywhere in the world on the history of American art.

**Eligibility** This program is open to Ph.D. candidates in departments of art history whose dissertations are focused on the history of the visual arts in the United States and are object-oriented. Applicants must be proposing to conduct research at their home institution, abroad, or at another appropriate site. U.S. citizenship or permanent resident status is required. Students preparing theses for a Master of Fine Arts degree are not eligible. Applications are particularly invited from women and members of minority groups.

**Financial data** The grant is $25,000. Fellowship funds may not be used to pay tuition costs.

**Duration** 1 year; nonrenewable.

**Additional information** This program is funded by the Henry Luce Foundation and administered by the American Council of Learned Societies (ACLS).

**Number awarded** 10 each year.

**Deadline** November of each year.

## [1142]
## HENRY LUCE FOUNDATION/ACLS GRANTS TO INDIVIDUALS FROM THE UNITED STATES AND CANADA IN EAST ASIAN ARCHAEOLOGY AND EARLY HISTORY

American Council of Learned Societies
Attn: Office of Fellowships and Grants
633 Third Avenue, 8C
New York, NY 10017-6795
(212) 697-1505                    Fax: (212) 949-8058
E-mail: grants@acls.org
Web: www.acls.org/eaaeh.htm

**Summary** To provide funding to American and Canadian scholars at all levels interested in conducting research on east Asian archaeology or early history.

**Eligibility** This program is open to residents of the United States and Canada who have their primary professional affiliation at an institution in the region. Applicants must 1) have an advanced degree in a discipline related to east Asian archaeology or early history, including anthropology, archaeology, art history, literature, or history; 2) be near completion of such a degree; or 3) have related experience in scholarship, archives, museums, or field sites. They must have linguistic ability sufficient to conduct the proposed work. Funding is available for 4 forms of assistance: 1) dissertation fellowships, for graduate students at U.S. and Canadian institutions, to conduct research in east Asia or, if research is complete, for writing the dissertation in North America; 2) postdoctoral fellowships, for scholars who have a Ph.D. degree, to be used for research or writing in east Asia, the United States, or Canada; 3) translation grants, for scholars (including Ph.D. candidates), for translation of scholarly works of significant value to the field, from an east Asian language into English, that fill a critical gap in English-language literature; or 4) advanced training grants, for individuals to work at east Asian museums or other artifact or archival collections, or at archaeological sites. Applications are particularly invited from women and members of minority groups.

**Financial data** Maximum grants are $28,000 for dissertation fellowships, $32,000 for postdoctoral fellowships, $20,000 for translation grants, or $22,000 for advanced training grants.

**Duration** 10 months for dissertation fellowships, postdoctoral fellowships, and advanced training grants; 6 months for translation grants.

**Additional information** This program, established in 2005, is funded by the Henry Luce Foundation and administered by the American Council of Learned Societies (ACLS). For purposes of this program, east Asia refers to northeast Asia (China, Hong Kong, Japan, Korea, Macau, Mongolia, and Taiwan) and southeast Asia (Brunei, Burma/Myanmar, Cambodia, Indonesia, Laos, Malaysia, Philippines, Singapore, Thailand, and Vietnam).

**Number awarded** Varies each year; recently, 8 of these fellowships were awarded.

**Deadline** November of each year.

## [1143]
## HERBERT AND BETTY CARNES FUND

American Ornithologists' Union
Attn: Research Awards Committee
1313 Dolley Madison Boulevard, Suite 402
McLean, VA 22101
(703) 790-1745                    Fax: (703) 790-2672
E-mail: aou@aou.org
Web: www.aou.org/student/researchaward.php3

**Summary** To provide funding to female graduate students interested in conducting research in ornithology.

**Eligibility** This program is open to female graduate students who are members of the American Ornithologists' Union and have no access to major funding agencies. Applicants must be interested in conducting research on avian biology. They must be nonsmokers (have not smoked in at least the previous 6 months). Along with their application, they should send a cover letter (about 5 pages) describing their proposed project, a budget, and 1 letter of reference. Selection is based on significance and originality of the research question, clarity of the objectives, feasibility of the plan of research, appropriateness of the budget, and the letter of recommendation.

**Financial data** The maximum award is $1,800 per year.

**Duration** 1 year; recipients may reapply for 1 additional award.

**Additional information** Information is also available from the Committee Chair, Reed Bowman, Archbold Biological Station, Avian Ecology Laboratory, 123 Main Drive, Venus, FL 33960, (863) 465-2571. Recipients must acknowledge their awards in publications resulting from the funded project.

**Number awarded** The sponsor awards a total of 28 to 30 grants each year.

**Deadline** January of each year.

**[1144]**
## HOMELAND SECURITY FELLOWSHIP PROGRAM

Stanford University
Center for International Security and Cooperation
Attn: Fellowship Program Coordinator
Encina Hall, Room E210
616 Serra Street
Stanford, CA 94305-6055
(650) 723-9626                    Fax: (650) 723-0089
E-mail: mgellner@stanford.edu
Web: cisac.stanford.edu

**Summary**  To provide funding to scholars and professionals (particularly women and minorities) who are interested in conducting research on homeland security.

**Eligibility**  This program is open to predoctoral candidates, postdoctoral scholars, scientists, engineers, and professionals (e.g., military officers or civilian members of the U.S. government, members of military or diplomatic services from other countries, and journalists interested in homeland security issues). Applicants must be interested in conducting research that explores ways to facilitate organizational learning to help strengthen U.S. homeland security capability. Suitable topics may include, but are not limited to, historical interactions and competitive learning between state and non-state organizations; causes and prevention of terrorism; military and other exercises and simulations; success and failure in intelligence and forecasting; history, including U.S. civil defense and disaster prevention and response; engineering failures; or operations research, decision analysis, and other analytic tools. Applications from women and minorities are encouraged.

**Financial data**  Stipends are determined on a case-by-case basis commensurate with experience and availability of other funds. Health insurance is provided, and funds are available for travel and other research-related expenses.

**Duration**  9 months.

**Additional information**  This program was established in 2004.

**Number awarded**  Varies each year.

**Deadline**  January of each year.

**[1145]**
## HORIZONS/FRAMELINE FILM AND VIDEO COMPLETION FUND

Frameline
Attn: Completion Fund
145 Ninth Street, Suite 300
San Francisco, CA 94103
(415) 703-8650                    Fax: (415) 861-1404
E-mail: info@frameline.org
Web: www.frameline.org

**Summary**  To provide funding to lesbian, gay, bisexual, and transgender (LGBT) film/video artists.

**Eligibility**  This program is open to LGBT artists who are in the last stages of the production of documentary, educational, narrative, animated, or experimental projects about or of interest to LGBT people and their communities. Applicants may be independent artists, students, producers, or nonprofit corporations. They must be interested in completion work and must have 90% of the production completed; projects in development, script-development, pre-

production, or production are not eligible. Student projects are eligible only if the student maintains artistic and financial control of the project. Women and people of color are especially encouraged to apply. Selection is based on financial need, the contribution the grant will make to completing the project, assurances that the project will be completed, and the statement the project makes about LGBT people and/or issues of concern to them and their communities.

**Financial data**  Grants range from $5,000 to $10,000.

**Number awarded**  Varies each year; recently, 4 of these grants were awarded.

**Deadline**  October of each year.

**[1146]**
## HOWARD HUGHES MEDICAL INSTITUTE RESEARCH TRAINING FELLOWSHIPS FOR MEDICAL STUDENTS

Howard Hughes Medical Institute
Attn: Office of Grants and Special Programs
4000 Jones Bridge Road
Chevy Chase, MD 20815-6789
(301) 215-8889      Toll-free: (800) 448-4882, ext. 8889
Fax: (301) 215-8888          E-mail: fellows@hhmi.org
Web: www.hhmi.org

**Summary**  To provide financial assistance to medical students (particularly women, minority, and disabled students) interested in pursuing research training.

**Eligibility**  Applicants must be enrolled in a medical school in the United States, although they may be citizens of any country. They must describe a proposed research project to be conducted at an academic or nonprofit research institution in the United States, other than a facility of the National Institutes of Health in Bethesda, Maryland. Research proposals should reflect the interests of the Howard Hughes Medical Institute (HHMI), especially in biochemistry, bioinformatics, biomedical engineering, biophysics, biostatistics, cell biology, developmental biology, epidemiology, genetics, immunology, mathematical and computational biology, microbiology, molecular biology, neuroscience, pharmacology, physiology, structural biology, or virology. Applications from women and minorities underrepresented in the sciences (Blacks, Hispanics, American Indians, Native Alaskans, and Native Pacific Islanders) are especially encouraged. Students enrolled in M.D./Ph.D., Ph.D., or Sc.D. programs and those who have completed a Ph.D. or Sc.D. in a laboratory-based science are not eligible. Selection is based on the applicant's ability and promise for a research career as a physician-scientist and the quality of training that will be provided.

**Financial data**  Fellows receive a stipend of $25,000 per year; their institution receives an institutional allowance of $5,500 and a research allowance of $5,500.

**Duration**  1 year.

**Additional information**  This program complements the HHMI-NIH Research Scholars Program; students may not apply to both programs in the same year.

**Number awarded**  Up to 60 each year.

**Deadline**  January of each year.

## [1147]
## HYDE GRADUATE STUDENT RESEARCH GRANTS

American Psychological Association
Attn: Division 35 (Psychology of Women)
750 First Street, N.E.
Washington, DC 20002-4242
(202) 336-6000                    Fax: (202) 336-5953
E-mail: scistudent@apa.org
Web: www.apa.org/divisions/div35/hyde.html

**Summary** To provide funding to psychology graduate students interested in conducting feminist research.

**Eligibility** This program is open to psychology graduate students interested in conducting feminist research. Selection is based on theoretical and methodological soundness, relevance to feminist goals, applicant's training and qualifications to conduct the research, and feasibility of completing the project.

**Financial data** The grant is $500.

**Duration** These are 1-time awards.

**Additional information** This program is supported by Janet Hyde through the royalties from her book, *Half the Human Experience,* (5th edition). Information is also available from Silvia Sara Canetto, Colorado State University, Department of Psychology, Fort Collins, CO 80523-1876, (970) 491-5415, Fax: (970) 491-1032.

**Number awarded** 4 each year.

**Deadline** March of September of each year.

## [1148]
## IDA B. WELLS GRADUATE STUDENT FELLOWSHIP

Coordinating Council for Women in History
211 Marginal Way, Number 733
P.O. Box 9715
Portland, ME 04104-5015
Web: theccwh.org/berkwellsapp.htm

**Summary** To provide funding to women graduate students for completion of their doctoral dissertations on an historical topic.

**Eligibility** This program is open to women graduate students in history departments at U.S. institutions who are members of the Coordinating Council for Women in History (CCWH). Applicants must have passed to A.B.D. status. They may be specializing in any field, but they must be working on an historical project. Preference is given to applicants working in an interdisciplinary area such as women's studies or ethnic studies.

**Financial data** The grant is $500.

**Duration** 1 year.

**Additional information** This program, established in 1999, is administered by the CCWH and the Berkshire Conference of Women Historians. The award is presented at the CCWH luncheon at the annual meeting of the American Historical Association, although the recipient does not need to be present to accept the award. Information is also available from Ann Le Bar, Eastern Washington University, Department of History, Patterson Hall 200, Cheney, WA 99004, (509) 359-6094.

**Number awarded** 1 each year.

**Deadline** August of each year.

## [1149]
## IDAHO SPACE GRANT CONSORTIUM GRADUATE FELLOWSHIPS

Idaho Space Grant Consortium
c/o University of Idaho
College of Engineering
P.O. Box 441011
Moscow, ID 83844-1011
(208) 885-6438                    Fax: (208) 885-1399
E-mail: isgc@uidaho.edu
Web: isgc.uidaho.edu

**Summary** To provide funding for research in space-related fields to graduate students (especially women, minorities, and persons with disabilities) at institutions belonging to the Idaho Space Grant Consortium (ISGC).

**Eligibility** This program is open to graduate students at ISGC member institutions. Applicants may be majoring in engineering, mathematics, science, or science/math education, but they must be interested in conducting research in an area of focus of the National Aeronautics and Space Administration (NASA). An undergraduate and current GPA of 3.5 or higher and U.S. citizenship are required. As a component of the NASA Space Grant program, ISGC encourages participation by women, underrepresented minorities, and persons with disabilities.

**Financial data** The stipend ranges up to $15,000 per year. Funds are to be used to pay for registration fees at colleges in the consortium.

**Duration** 1 year; may be renewed.

**Additional information** Members of the consortium include Albertson College of Idaho, Boise State University, College of Southern Idaho, Idaho State University, Lewis Clark State College, North Idaho College, Northwest Nazarene College, Brigham Young University of Idaho, and the University of Idaho. This program is funded by NASA.

**Number awarded** Varies each year; recently, 6 of these fellowships were awarded.

**Deadline** February of each year.

## [1150]
## INDIANA SPACE GRANT CONSORTIUM GRADUATE FELLOWSHIPS

Indiana Space Grant Consortium
c/o Purdue University
550 Stadium Mall Drive
West Lafayette, IN 47907
(765) 494-5873                    Fax: (765) 494-1299
E-mail: bauermm@purdue.edu
Web: www.insgc.org

**Summary** To provide funding to graduate students (especially women, minority, and disabled students) at member institutions of the Indiana Space Grant Consortium (INSGC) interested in conducting research related to space.

**Eligibility** This program is open to graduate students enrolled full time at institutions that are members of the INSGC. Applicants must be working on a master's degree in space-related science or engineering, a doctoral degree in space-related science or engineering, or a doctoral degree in science education. They must be involved in a research project related to the interests of the U.S. National Aeronautics and Space Administration (NASA) in science, technology, engineering, and mathematics (STEM). U.S. citizenship is required. The program encourages representation of women, underrepresented minorities, and persons with disabilities.

**Financial data**  The maximum grant is $5,000 per year for master's degree students or $10,000 for doctoral students.

**Duration**  1 year; students may not receive an award in consecutive years.

**Additional information**  This program is funded by NASA. The academic member institutions of the INSGC are Purdue University, Ball State University, Indiana University, Indiana University-Purdue University at Indianapolis, Indiana State University, Purdue University at Calumet, Taylor University, University of Evansville, and Valparaiso University.

**Number awarded**  Varies each year.

**Deadline**  December of each year.

## [1151]
## INDIANA SPACE GRANT CONSORTIUM UNDERGRADUATE SCHOLARSHIPS

Indiana Space Grant Consortium
c/o Purdue University
550 Stadium Mall Drive
West Lafayette, IN 47907
(765) 494-5873                    Fax: (765) 494-1299
E-mail: bauermm@purdue.edu
Web: www.insgc.org

**Summary**  To provide funding to undergraduate students (particularly women, minority, and disabled students) at member institutions of the Indiana Space Grant Consortium (INSGC) interested in conducting research related to space.

**Eligibility**  This program is open to undergraduate students enrolled full time at institutions that are members of the INSGC. Applicants must be interested in conducting research related to the interests of the U.S. National Aeronautics and Space Administration (NASA) in science, technology, engineering, and mathematics (STEM). Along with their application, they must submit an essay on either the impact of the space program on their life or the impact of STEM on their life. U.S. citizenship is required. The program encourages representation of women, underrepresented minorities, and persons with disabilities.

**Financial data**  The maximum grant is $1,000 per year.

**Duration**  1 year; may be renewed.

**Additional information**  This program is funded by NASA. The academic member institutions of the INSGC are Purdue University, Ball State University, Indiana University, Indiana University-Purdue University at Indianapolis, Indiana State University, Purdue University at Calumet, Taylor University, University of Evansville, and Valparaiso University.

**Number awarded**  Varies each year.

**Deadline**  December of each year.

## [1152]
## JDRF CENTERS FOR DIABETES RESEARCH GRANTS

Juvenile Diabetes Research Foundation
Attn: Grant Administrator
120 Wall Street, 19th Floor
New York, NY 10005-4001
(212) 479-7572                    Toll-free: (800) 533-CURE
Fax: (212) 785-9595              E-mail: info@jdrf.org
Web: www.jdrf.org/index.cfm?page_id=103207

**Summary**  To provide funding to senior scientists and clinicians (particularly women, minorities, and persons with disabilities) who are interested in becoming the director of a center for diabetes research.

**Eligibility**  This program is open to senior scientists and clinicians who have an M.D., D.M.D., D.O., Ph.D., D.V.M., or equivalent degree and a faculty position at a university, medical school, or other research facility. Applicants must be interested in serving as the director of a diabetes research center that will provide leading scientists and clinicians with the opportunity to bring together, in a collaborative and mission-driven environment, the diverse expertise needed to capture and rapidly translate new and emerging ideas into clinical benefits for people with diabetes. The major focus should be on 1 of the following target areas: human islet transplantation, complications (including hypoglycemia), or autoimmunity and prevention. The center must have a clear clinical mission with defined goals and milestones. The director is expected to provide strong intellectual and scientific leadership and milestone-based management of the center's component projects. There are no citizenship requirements. Applications are encouraged from women, members of minority groups underrepresented in the sciences, and people with disabilities. The proposed center may be located at foreign or domestic, for-profit or nonprofit, or public and private institutions, including universities, colleges, hospitals, laboratories, units of state and local government, and eligible agencies of the federal government.

**Financial data**  The total award may be up to $2,000,000 per year, including indirect costs up to 10%.

**Duration**  Up to 5 years. Support beyond that term will be determined based on a competitive review of the accomplishments and future plans of the center.

**Deadline**  Letters of intent must be submitted by January of each year for centers focusing on autoimmunity and prevention, February of each year for centers focusing on complications, or July of each year for centers focusing on human islet transplantation.

## [1153]
## JDRF CLINICAL INVESTIGATION RESEARCH GRANTS

Juvenile Diabetes Research Foundation
Attn: Grant Administrator
120 Wall Street, 19th Floor
New York, NY 10005-4001
(212) 479-7572                    Toll-free: (800) 533-CURE
Fax: (212) 785-9595              E-mail: info@jdrf.org
Web: www.jdrf.org/index.cfm?page_id=103207

**Summary**  To provide funding to clinicians (especially women, minorities, and persons with disabilities) who are interested in conducting research on diabetes that does not qualify for other support offered by the Juvenile Diabetes Research Foundation (JDRF).

**Eligibility**  This program is open to clinicians who have an M.D., D.M.D., D.O., Ph.D., D.V.M., or equivalent degree and a faculty position at a university, medical school, or other research facility. Applicants must be interested in conducting clinical research that exceeds the fiscal limitations of the JDRF regular grant mechanism and/or does not fit the structure of the Center or Program Project Grant mechanisms. Special consideration is given to translational research proposals that lead to and develop unique and innovative solutions to the clinical problems of people with diabetes. There are no citizenship requirements. Applications are encouraged from women, members of minority groups underrepresented in the sciences, and people with disabilities. The research may be conducted at foreign and domestic, for-profit and nonprofit, and public and private institutions, including universities, colleges, hospitals, laboratories, units of state and local government, and eligible agencies of the federal government.

**Financial data**  The total award, including both direct and indirect costs, may be up to $660,000 per year.

**Duration**  Up to 5 years.

**Deadline**  Letters of intent must be submitted by June or December of each year.

## [1154]
## JDRF PROGRAM PROJECT GRANTS

Juvenile Diabetes Research Foundation
Attn: Grant Administrator
120 Wall Street, 19th Floor
New York, NY 10005-4001
(212) 479-7572                    Toll-free: (800) 533-CURE
Fax: (212) 785-9595              E-mail: info@jdrf.org
Web: www.jdrf.org/index.cfm?page_id=103207

**Summary**  To provide funding to senior scientists and clinicians (particularly women, minorities, and persons with disabilities) who are interested in becoming the manager of a program project devoted to diabetes research.

**Eligibility**  This program is open to senior scientists and clinicians who have an M.D., D.M.D., D.O., Ph.D., D.V.M., or equivalent degree and a faculty position at a university, medical school, or other research facility. Applicants must be interested in serving as the manager of a diabetes research program project composed of 3 to 6 projects and 1 to 3 cores. The component projects must be highly interactive, benefiting from the use of common cores, and having interdependent outcomes. In general, they should focus on basic or preclinical research that seeks to impact the treatment or prevention of Type 1 diabetes and its complications. The manager should serve by mutually agreed-upon leadership and common consent of the individual project principal investigators. There are no citizenship requirements. Applications are encouraged from women, members of minority groups underrepresented in the sciences, and people with disabilities. The proposed program project may be based at foreign or domestic, for-profit or nonprofit, or public or private institutions, including universities, colleges, hospitals, laboratories, units of state and local government, and eligible agencies of the federal government.

**Financial data**  The total award, including both direct and indirect costs, may be up to $660,000 per year.

**Duration**  Up to 3 years.

**Deadline**  Letters of intent must be submitted by June or December of each year.

## [1155]
## JDRF SCHOLAR AWARDS

Juvenile Diabetes Research Foundation
Attn: Grant Administrator
120 Wall Street, 19th Floor
New York, NY 10005-4001
(212) 479-7572                    Toll-free: (800) 533-CURE
Fax: (212) 785-9595              E-mail: info@jdrf.org
Web: www.jdrf.org/index.cfm?page_id=103207

**Summary**  To provide funding to established independent physician scientists (especially women, minorities, and persons with disabilities) who are interested in conducting basic or clinical diabetes-related research.

**Eligibility**  This program is open to established investigators in diabetes-related research who have an M.D., D.M.D., D.O., Ph.D., D.V.M., or equivalent degree and an independent investigator position at a university, health science center, or comparable institution. Normally, applicants should have at least 7 years of relevant experience since receiving their doctoral degree. They must be willing to take risks and attempt new approaches to accelerate Type 1 diabetes research. This program is not intended to expand the funding of scientists already well supported for exploring this concept. There are no citizenship requirements. Applications are encouraged from women, members of minority groups underrepresented in the sciences, and people with disabilities. The proposed research may be conducted at foreign and domestic, for-profit and nonprofit, and public and private institutions, including universities, colleges, hospitals, laboratories, units of state and local government, and eligible agencies of the federal government. Selection is based on relevance on the research to and impact on the mission of the Juvenile Diabetes Research Foundation (JDRF); innovation, creativity, and the potential for future innovation relative to the applicant's career stage; and the applicant's motivation, enthusiasm, and intellectual energy to pursue a challenging problem.

**Financial data**  The total award may be up to $250,000 each year, including indirect costs.

**Duration**  Up to 5 years.

**Number awarded**  Up to 4 each year.

**Deadline**  An intent to submit must be received by August of each year. Completed applications are due in September.

## [1156]
## JEANNE HUMPHREY BLOCK DISSERTATION AWARD PROGRAM

Harvard-MIT Data Center
Attn: Henry A. Murray Research Archive
N318, GIS Knafel Building
1737 Cambridge Street
Cambridge, MA 02138
(617) 495-7841                    Fax: (617) 496-5149
E-mail: mra@help.hmdc.harvard.edu
Web: www.murray.harvard.edu/mra/index.jsp

**Summary**  To provide funding to women graduate students who wish to research girls' or women's psychological development at the Henry A. Murray Research Archive of Harvard University.

**Eligibility**  Candidates must be in a recognized doctoral program and must have completed their course work by the time the award is made. The subject of the proposed research must involve girls' or women's psychological development and focus on the development of sex differences or some other developmental issue of particular concern to girls and women. Priority is given to projects that draw on or contribute to the resources of the Murray Research Archive. Research concerned with the life experiences of racially or ethnically diverse populations within the United States is encouraged. Proposals are evaluated on the basis of their contribution to the literature of the field; the adequacy of the research design; the extent to which the project makes creative use of the center's resources or can contribute to those resources; and the general academic excellence of the candidate.

**Financial data**  The grant is $2,500.

**Duration**  1 year.

**Number awarded**  1 each year.

**Deadline**  March of each year.

## [1157]
## JOHN V. KRUTILLA RESEARCH STIPEND

Resources for the Future
Attn: Coordinator for Academic Programs
1616 P Street, N.W.
Washington, DC 20036-1400
(202) 328-5090                    Fax: (202) 939-3460
E-mail: krutilla-award@rff.org
Web: www.rff.org

**Summary**  To provide funding for research related to environmental and resource economics to young scholars, particularly those who are women or minorities.

**Eligibility**  This program is open to scholars who received their doctoral degree within the past 2 years. Applicants must be interested in conducting research related to environmental and resource economics. They must submit a short description of the proposed research, a curriculum vitae, and a letter of recommendation. Women and minority candidates are strongly encouraged to apply.

**Financial data**  The grant is $9,000.

**Duration**  1 year.

**Additional information**  This award was first presented in 2006.

**Number awarded**  1 each year.

**Deadline**  February of each year.

## [1158]
## JOSEPH L. FISHER DOCTORAL DISSERTATION FELLOWSHIPS

Resources for the Future
Attn: Coordinator for Academic Programs
1616 P Street, N.W.
Washington, DC 20036-1400
(202) 328-5090                    Fax: (202) 939-3460
E-mail: fisher-award@rff.org
Web: www.rff.org

**Summary**  To support doctoral dissertation research in economics on issues related to the environment, natural resources, or energy.

**Eligibility**  This program is open to graduate students in the final year of research on a dissertation related to the environment, natural resources, or energy. Applicants must submit a brief letter of application and a curriculum vitae, a graduate transcript, a 1-page abstract of the dissertation, a technical summary of the dissertation (up to 2,500 words), a letter from the student's department chair, and 2 letters of recommendation from faculty members on the student's dissertation committee. The technical summary should describe clearly the aim of the dissertation, its significance in relation to the existing literature, and the research methods to be used. Women and minority candidates are strongly encouraged to apply.

**Financial data**  The stipend is $12,000 per year.

**Duration**  1 academic year.

**Additional information**  It is expected that recipients will not hold other employment during the fellowship period. Recipients must notify Resources for the Future of any financial assistance they receive from any other source for support of doctoral work.

**Number awarded**  2 or 3 each year.

**Deadline**  February of each year.

## [1159]
## JUVENILE DIABETES RESEARCH FOUNDATION INNOVATIVE GRANTS

Juvenile Diabetes Research Foundation
Attn: Grant Administrator
120 Wall Street, 19th Floor
New York, NY 10005-4001
(212) 479-7572                    Toll-free: (800) 533-CURE
Fax: (212) 785-9595                    E-mail: info@jdrf.org
Web: www.jdrf.org/index.cfm?page_id=103207

**Summary**  To provide funding to scientists (particularly women, minorities, and persons with disabilities) who are interested in conducting innovative diabetes-related research.

**Eligibility**  Applicants must have an M.D., D.M.D., D.V.M., Ph.D., or equivalent degree and have a full-time faculty position or equivalent at a college, university, medical school, or other research facility. They must be seeking "seed" money for investigative work based on a sound hypothesis for which preliminary data are insufficient for a regular research grant but that are likely to lead to important results for the treatment of diabetes and its complications. Applicants must specifically explain how the proposal is innovative. Selection is based on whether 1) the proposed research is innovative; 2) the underlying premise, goal, or hypothesis is plausible; 3) the proposed research can be completed in 1 year; and 4) the proposed research is relevant to the mission of the Juvenile Diabetes Research Foundation and its potential impact. Applications are encouraged from women, members of minority groups underrepresented in the sciences, and people with disabilities. The proposed research may be conducted at foreign and domestic, for-profit and nonprofit, and public and private institutions, including universities, colleges, hospitals, laboratories, units of state and local government, and eligible agencies of the federal government.

**Financial data** Awards are limited to $100,000 plus 10% indirect costs.

**Duration** 1 year.

**Deadline** January or July of each year for grants that include clinical trials; January, March, or August of each year for other grants.

## [1160]
## JUVENILE DIABETES RESEARCH FOUNDATION REGULAR RESEARCH GRANTS

Juvenile Diabetes Research Foundation
Attn: Grant Administrator
120 Wall Street, 19th Floor
New York, NY 10005-4001
(212) 479-7572          Toll-free: (800) 533-CURE
Fax: (212) 785-9595          E-mail: info@jdrf.org
Web: www.jdrf.org/index.cfm?page_id=103207

**Summary** To provide funding to scientists (especially women, minorities, and persons with disabilities) who are interested in conducting research on diabetes and its related complications.

**Eligibility** Applicants must have an M.D., D.M.D., D.V.M., Ph.D., or equivalent degree and have a full-time faculty position or equivalent at a college, university, medical school, or other research facility. They must be interested in conducting research related to the priorities of the Juvenile Diabetes Research Foundation (JDRF), which currently include 1) restoration and maintenance of normal glucose regulation in Type 1 diabetes, including restoration of beta cell function, immunoregulation, and metabolic control; 2) prevention and treatment of complications of diabetes; and 3) prevention of Type 1 diabetes. Applications are encouraged from women, members of minority groups underrepresented in the sciences, and people with disabilities. The proposed research may be conducted at foreign and domestic, for-profit and nonprofit, and public and private institutions, including universities, colleges, hospitals, laboratories, units of state and local government, and eligible agencies of the federal government. Selection is based on potential to generate new approaches to unsolved scientific problems related to Type 1 diabetes; relevance to the objectives of JDRF; scientific, technical, or medical significance of the research proposal; innovativeness; appropriateness and adequacy of the experimental approach and methodology; qualifications and research experience of the principal investigator and collaborators; availability of resources and facilities necessary for the project; and appropriateness of the proposed budget in relation to the proposed research.

**Financial data** Grants up to $165,000 (plus 10% for indirect costs) per year are available.

**Duration** 3 years.

**Deadline** January or July of each year.

## [1161]
## KANSAS SPACE GRANT CONSORTIUM PROGRAM

Kansas Space Grant Consortium
c/o University of Kansas
Learned Hall
1530 West 15th
Lawrence, KS 66045-7609
(785) 864-7401          Fax: (785) 864-3361
E-mail: ksgc@nasainkansas.org
Web: nasainkansas.org

**Summary** To provide funding for space-related activities to students and faculty (particularly women, minorities, and persons with disabilities) at member institutions of the Kansas Space Grant Consortium.

**Eligibility** This program is open to faculty and students at member institutions. Support is provided for undergraduate research scholarships, graduate research assistantships, undergraduate and graduate student participation in activities sponsored by the U.S. National Aeronautics and Space Administration (NASA), faculty participation in NASA research projects, and other activities in fields of interest to NASA. The consortium is a component of NASA's Space Grant program, which encourages participation by women, underrepresented minorities, and persons with disabilities.

**Financial data** Each participating institution determines the amounts of its awards.

**Additional information** The member institutions of the consortium are Emporia State University, Fort Hayes State University, Haskell Indian Nations University, Kansas State University, Pittsburgh State University, University of Kansas, and Wichita State University. Funding for this program is provided by NASA.

**Number awarded** Varies each year.

**Deadline** Each participating institution establishes its own deadlines.

## [1162]
## KENTUCKY SPACE GRANT CONSORTIUM GRADUATE FELLOWSHIPS

Kentucky Space Grant Consortium
c/o Western Kentucky University
Department of Physics and Astronomy, TCCW 246
1906 College Heights Boulevard 11077
Bowling Green, KY 42101-1077
(270) 745-4156          Fax: (270) 745-4255
E-mail: Richard.Hackney@wku.edu
Web: www.wku.edu/KSGC

**Summary** To provide financial assistance for study and research in space-related fields to graduate students in Kentucky, particularly women, minority, and disabled students.

**Eligibility** This program is open to graduate students at member institutions of the Kentucky Space Grant Consortium (KSGC). Applicants must be enrolled in a graduate degree program in a space-related field or teaching specialization. As part of the program, a faculty member must agree to serve as a mentor on a research project. U.S. citizenship is required. Selection is based on the academic qualifications of the applicant, quality of the proposed research program and its relevance to space-related science and technology, and applicant's motivation for a space-related career as expressed in an essay on interests and goals. Applications are especially encouraged from women, members of other underrepresented groups (including minorities and people with disabilities), and students involved in projects of the U.S. National Aeronautics and Space Administration (NASA), such as NASA EPSCoR and SHARP.

**Financial data** The stipend is $16,000 per year, with an additional $2,000 for use in support of the student's mentored research project. Matching grants of at least $12,000 are required. Preference is given to applicants from schools that agree to waive tuition for the fellow as part of the program.

**Duration** 1 year; may be renewed, depending on the quality of the student's research and satisfactory grades, presentation of research results, and evaluation of progress by the mentor.

**Additional information** This program is funded by NASA. The KSGC member institutions are Bellarmine University, Centre College, Eastern Kentucky University, Kentucky State University, Morehead State University, Murray State University, Northern Kentucky University, Thomas More College, Transylvania University, University of Kentucky, University of Louisville, and Western Kentucky University.

**Number awarded** Varies each year.

**Deadline** February of each year.

## [1163]
## KENTUCKY SPACE GRANT CONSORTIUM RESEARCH GRANTS

Kentucky Space Grant Consortium
c/o Western Kentucky University
Department of Physics and Astronomy, TCCW 246
1906 College Heights Boulevard 11077
Bowling Green, KY 42101-1077
(270) 745-4156                    Fax: (270) 745-4255
E-mail: Richard.Hackney@wku.edu
Web: www.wku.edu/KSGC

**Summary** To provide funding to faculty members (particularly women, minorities, and persons with disabilities) at designated institutions in Kentucky who are interested in conducting space-related research.

**Eligibility** This program is open to faculty members at member institutions of the Kentucky Space Grant Consortium (KSGC). Applicants must be interested in conducting research that will include students as researchers, that involves travel to take the students to a center or research installation of the U.S. National Aeronautics and Space Administration (NASA), and that will establish an interaction with NASA researchers. The KSGC is a component of the NASA Space Grant program, which encourages participation by women, underrepresented minorities, and persons with disabilities.

**Financial data** Awards up to $5,000 require a 1:1 institutional match; awards up to $15,000 require a 2:1 match.

**Duration** 1 year; may be renewed.

**Additional information** This program is funded by NASA. The KSGC member institutions are Bellarmine University, Centre College, Eastern Kentucky University, Kentucky State University, Morehead State University, Murray State University, Northern Kentucky University, Thomas More College, Transylvania University, University of Kentucky, University of Louisville, and Western Kentucky University. The institution must provide adequate faculty time and cover any indirect costs.

**Number awarded** Varies each year.

**Deadline** February of each year.

## [1164]
## KENTUCKY SPACE GRANT CONSORTIUM UNDERGRADUATE SCHOLARSHIPS

Kentucky Space Grant Consortium
c/o Western Kentucky University
Department of Physics and Astronomy, TCCW 246
1906 College Heights Boulevard 11077
Bowling Green, KY 42101-1077
(270) 745-4156                    Fax: (270) 745-4255
E-mail: Richard.Hackney@wku.edu
Web: www.wku.edu/KSGC

**Summary** To provide financial assistance to undergraduate students (particularly women, minority, and disabled students) at member institutions of the Kentucky Space Grant Consortium (KSGC) interested in pursuing education and research in space-related fields.

**Eligibility** This program is open to undergraduate students at member institutions of the KSGC. Applicants must be enrolled in a baccalaureate degree program in a space-related field or teaching specialization. As part of the program, a faculty member must agree to serve as a mentor on a research project. U.S. citizenship is required. Selection is based on academic qualifications of the applicant, quality of the proposed research program and its relevance to space-related science and technology, and applicant's motivation for a space-related career as expressed in an essay on interests and goals. Applications are especially encouraged from women, members of other underrepresented groups (including minorities and people with disabilities), and students involved in projects of the U.S. National Aeronautics and Space Administration (NASA), such as NASA EPSCoR and SHARP.

**Financial data** The grant is $5,000, including a stipend of $4,500 and an additional $500 to support the student's mentored research project. Matching grants of at least $4,000 are required. Preference is given to applicants from schools that agree to waive tuition for the scholar as part of the program.

**Duration** 1 year; may be renewed depending on the quality of the student's research and satisfactory performance in the program of study as evidenced by grades, presentation of research results, and evaluation of progress by the mentor.

**Additional information** This program is funded by NASA. The KSGC member institutions are Bellarmine University, Centre College, Eastern Kentucky University, Kentucky State University, Morehead State University, Murray State University, Northern Kentucky University, Thomas More College, Transylvania University, University of Kentucky, University of Louisville, and Western Kentucky University.

**Number awarded** Varies each year.

**Deadline** February of each year.

## [1165]
## LASPACE GRADUATE STUDENT RESEARCH ASSISTANCE PROGRAM

Louisiana Space Consortium
c/o Louisiana State University
Department of Physics and Astronomy
371 Nicholson Hall
Baton Rouge, LA 70803-4001
(225) 578-8697                   Fax: (225) 578-1222
E-mail: laspace@lsu.edu
Web: laspace.lsu.edu/fellowships.html

**Summary** To provide research funding to students (particularly women, minority, and disabled students) who are working on a graduate degree in an aerospace-related discipline at designated colleges and universities belonging to the Louisiana Space Consortium (LaSPACE).

**Eligibility** This program is open to U.S. citizens working on a master's or doctoral degree in a space- or aerospace-related field as a full-time student at a designated LaSPACE member school. Members of groups underrepresented in science, mathematics, and engineering (women, minorities, and persons with disabilities) are strongly encouraged to apply. Students at 4-year schools without graduate programs, smaller regional schools, and Historically Black Colleges and Universities (HBCUs) are also encouraged to apply. Selection is based on space and aerospace relevance of the research, overall utility and relevance to LaSPACE research and human resources development objectives, and applicant's need (particularly post-hurricane related needs).

**Financial data** The grant is $4,000 per year. Students at schools in areas affected by the hurricanes are entitled to an additional $1,000, bringing the total grant to $5,000 per year. The recipient's institution must commit to a 1:1 match with non-federal and non-LaSPACE funds.

**Duration** 1 year; recipients may reapply.

**Additional information** This program began in 2006. Fellows work with an established aerospace researcher at the following LaSPACE institutions: Louisiana State University, Louisiana Tech University, Loyola University, McNeese State University, Nicholls State University, Northwestern State University of Louisiana, Southeastern Louisiana University, Southern University and A&M College, Southern University in New Orleans, Tulane University, University of New Orleans, University of Louisiana at Lafayette, University of Louisiana at Monroe, and Xavier University of Louisiana. Funding for this program is provided by the U.S. National Aeronautics and Space Administration (NASA).

**Number awarded** Approximately 10 each year.

**Deadline** Applications may be submitted at any time.

## [1166]
## LASPACE RESEARCH ENHANCEMENT AWARDS PROGRAM

Louisiana Space Consortium
c/o Louisiana State University
Department of Physics and Astronomy
371 Nicholson Hall
Baton Rouge, LA 70803-4001
(225) 578-8697                   Fax: (225) 578-1222
E-mail: laspace@lsu.edu
Web: laspace.lsu.edu/grantopps.html

**Summary** To provide funding to faculty (particularly women, minorities, and persons with disabilities) at Louisiana Space Consortium (LaSPACE) member institutions for projects that will help to build a research infrastructure in aerospace-related fields.

**Eligibility** This program is open to faculty at LaSPACE member schools. Applicants may be proposing projects in either of 2 subprogram areas: 1) research facilitation/initiation awards, to provide faculty with research support for such aerospace-related activities as pre-proposal travel to a National Aeronautics and Space Administration (NASA) field center, support for a graduate student to join a faculty member at a NASA field center for part of a summer term, support to develop a new research project among scientists at several LaSPACE campuses, summer support at facilities not covered by existing programs, or development of new interdisciplinary areas of research or technology that can contribute to the NASA mission; or 2) visiting researchers, to bring outside researchers to LaSPACE campuses for extended visits to work with faculty and students in developing new research directions. A goal of NASA is to increase diversity in science, technology, engineering, and mathematics (STEM) disciplines. Traditionally, minority groups, women, and people with disabilities have been underrepresented in STEM disciplines; applicants are encouraged to help address the diversity objective. Selection is based on scientific and technical merit of the proposed project; relevance of the proposal to aerospace goals and alignment with the NASA mission; contribution of the proposed project to increasing diversity, particularly underrepresented groups, women, and persons with disabilities; competency of the project personnel with emphasis on the potential degree of enhancement and of the probability for the project to lead to increased competitiveness and subsequently funded work; degree to which new research directions and capabilities are to be developed; and degree to which the project will contribute to workforce development and human capital needs, both locally and nationally.

**Financial data** The amounts of the awards depend on the availability of funds and the nature of the proposal. Historically, research facilitation awards have ranged around $30,000 and visiting researcher awards from $10,000 to $15,000.

**Duration** Depends on the nature of the proposal.

**Additional information** The participating LaSPACE member institutions are Dillard University, Grambling State University, L.S.U. Agricultural Center, Louisiana State University, Louisiana Tech University, Loyola University, McNeese State University, Nicholls State University, Northwestern State University of Louisiana, Southeastern Louisiana University, Southern University and A&M College, Southern University in New Orleans, Tulane University, University of New Orleans, University of Louisiana at Lafayette, University of Louisiana at Monroe, and Xavier University of Louisiana. Funding for this program is provided by NASA.

**Number awarded** Varies each year; recently, a total of approximately $140,000 was available for this program.

**Deadline** October of each year.

## [1167]
## LASPACE RESEARCH INITIATION GRANTS PROGRAM

Louisiana Space Consortium
c/o Louisiana State University
Department of Physics and Astronomy
371 Nicholson Hall
Baton Rouge, LA 70803-4001
(225) 578-8697                    Fax: (225) 578-1222
E-mail: laspace@lsu.edu
Web: laspace.lsu.edu/grantopps.html

**Summary** To provide seed grant funding for research to faculty (particularly women, minorities, and persons with disabilities) at Louisiana Space Consortium (LaSPACE) institutions that are 4-year colleges without major graduate programs or minority-serving institutions, especially Historically Black Colleges and Universities (HBCUs).

**Eligibility** This program is open to faculty at LaSPACE member schools that are 4-year colleges without major graduate programs or HBCUs. Applicants may be proposing projects to provide research support for such aerospace-related activities as pre-proposal travel to a National Aeronautics and Space Administration (NASA) field center, support for a graduate student to join a faculty member at a NASA field center for part of a summer term, support to develop a new research project among scientists at several LaSPACE campuses, or development of new interdisciplinary areas of research or technology that can contribute to the NASA mission. A goal of NASA is to increase diversity in science, technology, engineering, and mathematics (STEM) disciplines. Traditionally, minority groups, women, and people with disabilities have been underrepresented in STEM disciplines; applicants are encouraged to help address the diversity objective. Selection is based on scientific and technical merit of the proposed project; relevance of the proposal to aerospace goals and alignment with the NASA mission; contribution of the proposed project to increasing diversity, particularly underrepresented groups, women, and persons with disabilities; competency of the project personnel with emphasis on the potential degree of enhancement and of the probability for the project to lead to increased competitiveness and subsequently funded work; degree to which new research directions and capabilities are to be developed; and degree to which the project will contribute to workforce development and human capital needs, both locally and nationally.

**Financial data** The maximum grant is $20,000. Funds may be used for summer salary, student support, laboratory supplies, and research travel. A match of 2:1 (i.e., $1 in match for every $2 in LaSPACE funds requested) is required.

**Duration** 1 year or less.

**Additional information** The LaSPACE member institutions eligible for this program are Dillard University, Grambling State University, Loyola University, McNeese State

University, Nicholls State University, Northwestern State University of Louisiana, Southeastern Louisiana University, Southern University and A&M College, Southern University in New Orleans, University of Louisiana at Monroe, and Xavier University of Louisiana. Funding for this program is provided by NASA.

**Number awarded** Varies each year.

**Deadline** Applications are accepted on a first-come, first-served basis.

## [1168]
## LEO GOLDBERG FELLOWSHIPS

National Optical Astronomy Observatories
Attn: Human Resources Manager
P.O. Box 26732
Tucson, AZ 85726
(520) 318-8100                    Fax: (520) 318-8456
E-mail: hrnoao@noao.edu
Web: www.noao.edu/goldberg/fellows.html

**Summary** To provide an opportunity for postdoctorates in astronomy (particularly women and minorities) to conduct research at the facilities of the National Optical Astronomy Observatories (NOAO) in Arizona or Chile.

**Eligibility** This program is open to recent Ph.D. recipients in observational astronomy, astronomical instrumentation, or theoretical astrophysics. Applicants must be interested in conducting a research program of their own choosing or participating in a current NOAO initiative at Kitt Peak National Observatory (KPNO) near Tucson, Arizona or Cerro Tololo Inter-American Observatory (CTIO) in La Serena, Chile. Women and candidates from underrepresented minorities are particularly encouraged to apply. Selection is based on the applicant's promise for an outstanding career in astronomy, their proposed use of KPNO or CTIO facilities, the relationship of their research to a proposed interaction with NOAO programs to plan the next generation of community facilities, and the relationship of their research to programs conducted by NOAO staff.

**Financial data** A competitive salary is paid. Additional support is provided to fellows and their families in Chile.

**Duration** 5 years. The first 4 years are spent either at Kitt Peak or in La Serena; the final year is spent at an U.S. university or astronomical institute willing to host the fellow.

**Additional information** NOAO is supported under a contract between the National Science Foundation and the Association of Universities for Research in Astronomy, Inc. This program was formerly known as the NOAO 5-Year Science Fellowship.

**Number awarded** 1 each year.

**Deadline** November of each year.

## [1169]
## LEONARD R. SUGERMAN SCHOLARSHIP

New Mexico Space Grant Consortium
c/o New Mexico State University
Sugerman Space Grant Building
3050 Knox Street
MSC SG, Box 30001
Las Cruces, NM 88003-0001
(505) 646-6414                    Fax: (505) 646-7791
E-mail: nmsgc@pathfinder.nmsu.edu
Web: spacegrant.nmsu.edu

**Summary**  To provide funding to undergraduate students (particularly women, minority, and disabled students) who are interested in working on research projects in space-related fields at institutions that are members of the New Mexico Space Grant Consortium (NMSGC).

**Eligibility**  This program is open to full-time undergraduate students at NMSGC institutions who are interested in working with faculty on funded research. Applicants must have a declared major in the arts and sciences (astronomy, biology, chemistry, computer science, earth science, mathematics, or physics), engineering (chemical, civil, computer, electrical, industrial, mechanical, surveying, or engineering technology), or agriculture and home economics (agronomy, animal and range sciences, entomology, fishery and wildlife sciences, horticulture, plant pathology, and weed science). They must have a GPA of 3.0 or higher. Along with their application, they must submit a current transcript; a statement of their career and research interests in space and aerospace-related science; any relevant work or co-op experience, academic honors, or awards; any past or present financial aid; a 1-page description of the project, including its relationship to a mission directorate of the U.S. National Aeronautics and Space Administration (NASA); and an indication of how the student will work with a faculty member for the term of the award. The NMSGC is a component of the NASA Space Grant program, which encourages participation by groups underrepresented in science, technology, engineering and mathematics: women, minorities, and persons with disabilities. U.S. citizenship is required.

**Financial data**  The stipend is $2,000.

**Duration**  1 year.

**Additional information**  The NMSGC institutional members are: New Mexico State University, New Mexico Institute of Mining and Technology, University of New Mexico, Doña Ana Branch Community College, and San Juan Community College. This program is funded by NASA.

**Number awarded**  1 each year.

**Deadline**  October of each year.

## [1170]
## LEROY C. MERRITT HUMANITARIAN FUND AWARD

LeRoy C. Merritt Humanitarian Fund
Attn: Secretary
50 East Huron Street
Chicago, IL 60611
(312) 280-4226      Toll-free: (800) 545-2433, ext. 4226
Fax: (312) 280-4227      E-mail: merrittfund@ala.org
Web: www.merrittfund.org

**Summary**  To provide financial support to librarians facing discrimination on the basis of race, sex, or other factors.

**Eligibility**  The fund was established in 1970 to provide direct financial aid for the support, maintenance, medical care, legal fees, and welfare of librarians who are or have been "threatened with loss of employment or discharged because of their stand for the cause of intellectual freedom." In 1975, the scope of the fund was broadened to include librarians who had been discriminated against on the basis of gender, age, race, color, creed, sexual orientation, place of national origin, or defense of intellectual freedom. Applicants should describe their situation, including a brief explanation of its financial ramifications and of the amount of aid requested.

**Financial data**  The amount awarded varies, depending upon the needs of the recipient.

**Duration**  The award is granted annually.

**Number awarded**  Varies each year.

**Deadline**  Applications may be submitted at any time.

## [1171]
## LILLA JEWEL AWARD FOR WOMEN ARTISTS

McKenzie River Gathering Foundation
Attn: Office Manager
2705 East Burnside, Suite 210
Portland, OR 97214
(503) 289-1517                    Toll-free: (800) 489-6743
Fax: (503) 232-1731    E-mail: info@mrgfoundation.org
Web: www.mrgfoundation.org

**Summary**  To provide funding to women artists in Oregon.

**Eligibility**  Eligible to apply for this funding are women artists in Oregon. The artistic category rotates on a quadriennial cycle among visual arts (e.g., conceptual art, installations, still photography, stencils, painting) in 2008; literary arts (e.g., poetry, short stores, novels, scripts, creative nonfiction) in 2009; performing arts (e.g., music, dance, performance art, theater) in 2010; and media arts (e.g., film, video, animation, web) in 2011. Although the award is not based on financial need, the intent is to support a women artist who lacks traditional access to funding. Selection is based on the artistic impact of the work presented for consideration; whether the artist is a member of another traditionally underfunded group, such as women of color or lesbians; the ideas embodied in the work as represented in the written application; how the work challenges the status quo and supports the sponsor's mission of progressive social change; and the potential impact of the award on the artist at this point in her career.

**Financial data**  The maximum grant is $4,000.

**Duration**  1 year.

**Additional information** This is the only funding available to individuals through the McKenzie River Gathering Foundation.

**Number awarded** 1 each year.

**Deadline** April of each year.

## [1172]
## L'OREAL USA FOR WOMEN IN SCIENCE FELLOWSHIP PROGRAM

L'Oréal USA
Attn: Women in Science Fellowship Program
575 Fifth Avenue
New York, NY 10017
(212) 818-1500          E-mail: infoofice@us.loreal.com
Web: www.lorealusa.com/?uid=forwomeninscience

**Summary** To provide research funding to pre- and post-doctoral women scientists.

**Eligibility** This program is open to women who are 1) enrolled in the third or fourth year of a Ph.D. program, or 2) postdoctoral researchers. Applicants must have completed or be working on a degree in the natural sciences (biological and physical), engineering, computer science, or mathematics. They must be U.S. citizens, plan to become citizens by the time the awards are announced, or permanent residents.

**Financial data** The grant is $20,000.

**Duration** 1 year.

**Additional information** This program, established in 2003, is sponsored by L'Oréal USA.

**Number awarded** 5 each year.

**Deadline** October of each year.

## [1173]
## LUISE MEYER-SCHUTZMEISTER AWARD

Association for Women in Science
Attn: AWIS Educational Foundation
1200 New York Avenue, N.W., Suite 650
Washington, DC 20005
(202) 326-8940          Toll-free: (866) 657-AWIS
Fax: (202) 326-8960          E-mail: awisedfd@awis.org
Web: www.awis.org/careers/edfoundation.html

**Summary** To provide funding to women conducting doctoral research in physics.

**Eligibility** This program is open to women graduate students in physics. Applicants must have passed their qualifying exam and be within 2 years of completing their Ph.D. Foreign students are eligible if they are enrolled in a U.S. institution of higher education. Selection is based on academic achievement, the importance of the research question addressed, the quality of the research, and the applicant's potential for future contributions to physics.

**Financial data** The stipend is $1,000. Funds may be used for tuition, books, housing, research, travel and meeting registration, or publication costs.

**Duration** 1 year.

**Additional information** Information is also available from Dr. Gerald Hardie of Western Michigan University, E-mail: gerald.hardie@wmich.edu.

**Number awarded** 1 each year.

**Deadline** January of each year.

## [1174]
## LYNN CAMPBELL MEMORIAL FUND

Astraea Lesbian Foundation for Justice
Attn: Program Director
116 East 16th Street, Seventh Floor
New York, NY 10003
(212) 529-8021          Fax: (212) 982-3321
E-mail: grants@astraeafoundation.org
Web: www.astraeafoundation.org

**Summary** To support women's projects in community organizing.

**Eligibility** This program is open to individuals or organizations interested in developing projects in community organization or serving as a resource for community organization. Candidates must have directly addressed issues related to heterosexism, homophobia, and sexism. Organizations must demonstrate an understanding of the connections among oppressions and be working actively to eliminate all forms of oppression based on sexual orientation, gender, class, race, ethnicity, age, physical and mental ability, national identity, or religious affiliation. Projects must reflect the diversity of the lesbian community in their leadership, membership, constituency, and content of their programs.

**Financial data** The maximum grant is $10,000.

**Duration** 1 year.

**Additional information** Direct applications for these grants are not accepted.

**Number awarded** 1 each year.

## [1175]
## M. HILDRED BLEWETT SCHOLARSHIP

American Physical Society
Attn: Committee on the Status of Women in Physics
One Physics Ellipse, Fourth Floor
College Park, MD 20740-3844
(301) 209-3231          Fax: (301) 209-0865
E-mail: blewett@aps.org
Web: www.aps.org

**Summary** To provide funding to early-career women interested in returning to physics research after have had to interrupt those careers for family reasons.

**Eligibility** This program is open to women who have completed work toward a Ph.D. in physics and currently have an affiliation with a research-active educational institution or national laboratory in Canada or the United States. Applicants must be interested in conducting a research project after interrupting their career for family reasons. They may be from any country and of any nationality, but they must currently reside in the United States or Canada and be legal residents of those countries. No matching contribution from the institution is required, but institutional support is considered as evidence of support for the applicant.

**Financial data** The grant is $45,000. Funds may be used for dependent care (limited to 50% of the award), salary, travel, equipment, and tuition and fees.

**Duration** 1 year.

**Additional information** This program was established in 2005.

**Number awarded** 1 each year.

**Deadline** May of each year.

## [1176]
## M. LOUISE CARPENTER GLOECKNER, M.D. SUMMER RESEARCH FELLOWSHIP

Drexel University College of Medicine
Attn: Director, Archives and Special Collections on Women in Medicine
Hagerty Library
33rd and Market Streets
Philadelphia, PA 19104
(215) 895-6661                    Fax: (215) 895-6660
E-mail: archives@drexelmed.edu
Web: archives.drexelmed.edu/fellowship.php

**Summary** To provide financial assistance to scholars and students interested in conducting research during the summer on the history of medicine at the Archives and Special Collections on Women in Medicine at Drexel University in Philadelphia.

**Eligibility** This program is open to students at all levels, scholars, and general researchers. Applicants must be interested in conducting research utilizing the archives, which emphasize the history of women in medicine, nursing, medical missionaries, the American Medical Women's Association, American Women's Hospital Service, and other women in medicine organizations. Selection is based on research background of the applicant, relevance of the proposed research project to the goals of the applicant, overall quality and clarity of the proposal, appropriateness of the proposal to the holdings of the collection, and commitment of the applicant to the project.

**Financial data** The grant is $4,000.

**Duration** 4 to 6 weeks during the summer.

**Number awarded** 1 each year.

**Deadline** January of each year.

## [1177]
## MAINE SPACE GRANT CONSORTIUM SCHOLARSHIP AND FELLOWSHIP PROGRAM

Maine Space Grant Consortium
Attn: Executive Director
87 Winthrop Street, Suite 200
Augusta, ME 04330
(207) 622-4688       Toll-free: (877) 397-7223, ext. 173
Fax: (207) 622-4548       E-mail: shehata@msgc.org
Web: www.msgc.org/education_students.asp

**Summary** To provide funding to undergraduate and graduate students (especially women, minority, and disabled students) at colleges and universities in Maine who are interested in working on projects related to space.

**Eligibility** This program is open to U.S. citizens who are enrolled on a full-time basis in an undergraduate or graduate program at a 2- or 4-year college or university in Maine, including those not members of the Maine Space Grant Consortium. Applicants must be proposing to conduct a project on a topic of interest to the U.S. National Aeronautics and Space Administration (NASA) in biological, earth,

physical, social, or space science; human exploration and development of space; or other related science, technology, computer, or engineering fields. Undergraduates must have a GPA of 3.0 or higher; graduate students must have a GPA of 3.2 or higher. Proposals may involve conducting research at their home institution, traveling to conduct research and/or to present finished project work at a NASA field center, or facilitating technology transfer from NASA to their institution and industry in Maine. Applications are especially encouraged from women, minorities, and persons with disabilities. Selection is based on the relevance of the project to NASA's mission and its strategic enterprises, collaboration with researchers at NASA space flight centers, qualifications of the student, technical content and quality of the proposal, and recommendation from a faculty member.

**Financial data** Stipends are $2,500 for undergraduates or $5,000 for graduate students.

**Duration** 1 year.

**Additional information** This program is funded by NASA.

**Number awarded** Varies each year.

**Deadline** May or October of each year.

## [1178]
## MARGARET FULLER AWARDS PROGRAM

Unitarian Universalist Association
Attn: UU Women's Federation
25 Beacon Street
Boston, MA 02108-2800
(617) 948-4692                    Fax: (617) 742-2402
E-mail: uuwf@uua.org
Web: www.uuwf.org/awards-about.html

**Summary** To provide funding to Unitarian Universalists working on projects that promote feminist theology.

**Eligibility** This program is open to Unitarian Universalist (UU) women interested in working on a project that relates to any of the thematic strands of UU feminist theology. The project should result in a product that can be used by local congregations or other groups to further an understanding of that subject. Examples of appropriate projects include creative endeavors in the arts, educational materials for congregations, seed money for conferences, or innovative performance events.

**Financial data** Grants range from $500 to $5,000.

**Duration** Proposed projects should take not more than 1 to 2 years to complete.

**Additional information** This program originated as the Feminist Theology Award program in 1989. That program ended in 1997 and was succeeded by this in 2002. Funds are not available for graduate school or to support dissertations. Funding is no longer available for computer hardware.

**Number awarded** 3 each year.

**Deadline** October of each year.

## [1179]
## MARGARET MORSE NICE FUND

American Ornithologists' Union
Attn: Research Awards Committee
1313 Dolley Madison Boulevard, Suite 402
McLean, VA 22101
(703) 790-1745            Fax: (703) 790-2672
E-mail: aou@aou.org
Web: www.aou.org/student/researchaward.php3

**Summary** To provide funding to female graduate students interested in conducting research in ornithology.

**Eligibility** This program is open to female graduate students who are members of the American Ornithologists' Union and have no access to major funding agencies. Applicants must be interested in conducting research in avian biology. They should send a cover letter (about 5 pages) describing their proposed project, a budget, and 1 letter of reference. Selection is based on significance and originality of the research question, clarity of the objectives, feasibility of the plan of research, appropriateness of the budget, and the letter of recommendation.

**Financial data** The maximum award is $1,800 per year.

**Duration** 1 year; recipients may reapply for 1 additional award.

**Additional information** Information is also available from the Committee Chair, Reed Bowman, Archbold Biological Station, Avian Ecology Laboratory, 123 Main Drive, Venus, FL 33960, (863) 465-2571. Recipients must acknowledge their awards in publications resulting from the funded project.

**Number awarded** The sponsor awards a total of 28 to 30 grants each year.

**Deadline** January of each year.

## [1180]
## MARGO HARRIS HAMMERSCHLAG GRANT

National Association of Women Artists, Inc.
80 Fifth Avenue, Suite 1405
New York, NY 10011-8002
(212) 675-1616            Fax: (212) 675-1616
E-mail: nawomena@msn.com
Web: www.nawanet.org/pages/127/37/32

**Summary** To provide funding to women artists whose medium is direct carving.

**Eligibility** This program is open to female U.S. citizens and permanent residents who are artists working in direct carving. Applicants must submit 20 slides of direct carved sculpture or 20 images on CD-R or in JPEG format for PC. Slides or images must depict at least 10 works. At least 75% of the applicant's individual work must have been produced by direct carving.

**Financial data** The grant is $10,000.

**Duration** The grant is awarded biennially.

**Number awarded** 1 every other year.

**Deadline** November of even-numbered years.

## [1181]
## MARY ISABEL SIBLEY FELLOWSHIP FOR FRENCH STUDIES

Phi Beta Kappa Society
Attn: Awards Coordinator
1785 Massachusetts Avenue, N.W., Fourth Floor
Washington, DC 20036
(202) 265-3808            Fax: (202) 986-1601
E-mail: awards@pbk.org
Web: staging.pbk.org

**Summary** To support women involved in advanced research or writing projects dealing with French language or literature.

**Eligibility** Candidates must be unmarried women between 25 and 35 years of age who have demonstrated their ability to conduct original research. They must hold the doctorate or have fulfilled all the requirements for the doctorate except the dissertation, and they must be planning to devote full time to their research during the fellowship year. Eligibility is not restricted to members of Phi Beta Kappa or to U.S. citizens.

**Financial data** The award carries a stipend of $20,000, one half of which will be paid after June 1 following the award and the balance 6 months later.

**Duration** 1 year (the fellowship is offered in even-numbered years only). Periodic progress reports are not required, but they are welcomed. It is the hope of the committee that the results of the year of research will be made available in some form, although no pressure for publication will be put on the recipient.

**Number awarded** 1 every other year.

**Deadline** January of even-numbered years.

## [1182]
## MARY ISABEL SIBLEY FELLOWSHIP FOR GREEK STUDIES

Phi Beta Kappa Society
Attn: Awards Coordinator
1785 Massachusetts Avenue, N.W., Fourth Floor
Washington, DC 20036
(202) 265-3808            Fax: (202) 986-1601
E-mail: awards@pbk.org
Web: staging.pbk.org

**Summary** To support women involved in advanced research or writing projects dealing with Greek language, literature, history, or archaeology.

**Eligibility** Candidates must be unmarried women between 25 and 35 years of age who have demonstrated their ability to conduct original research. They must hold the doctorate or have fulfilled all the requirements for the doctorate except the dissertation, and they must be planning to devote full time to their research during the fellowship year. Eligibility is not restricted to members of Phi Beta Kappa or to U.S. citizens.

**Financial data** The award carries a stipend of $20,000, one half of which will be paid after June 1 following the award and the balance 6 months later.

**Duration** 1 year (the fellowship is offered in odd-numbered years only).

**Additional information** Periodic progress reports are not required, but they are welcomed. It is the hope of the committee that the results of the year of research will be made available in some form, although no pressure for publication will be put on the recipient.

**Number awarded**  1 every other year.

**Deadline**  January of odd-numbered years.

## [1183]
## MARY LILY RESEARCH GRANTS

Duke University
Rare Book, Manuscript, and Special Collections Library
Attn: Sallie Bingham Center for Women's History and
    Culture
P.O. Box 90185
Durham, NC 27708-0185
(919) 660-5828                    Fax: (919) 660-5934
E-mail: cwhc@duke.edu
Web: library.duke.edu

**Summary**  To provide funding to scholars and students who wish to use the Special Collections Library at Duke University to conduct research in women's studies.

**Eligibility**  This program is open to faculty, graduate students, and independent scholars with an interest in women's studies research. The proposed research must involve the use of the Special Collections Library at Duke University and may represent a wide variety of disciplines and approaches to women's studies topics.

**Financial data**  Grants up to $1,000 are available; funds may be used for travel, costs of copying pertinent resources, and living expenses while conducting the research.

**Additional information**  The library's collections are especially strong in feminism and radical feminism in the United States, women's prescriptive literature from the 19th and 20th centuries, girls' literature, artistsÖ books by women, and history and culture of women in the South. A number of prominent women writers have placed their personal and professional papers in the collections.

**Number awarded**  Varies each year; recently, 8 of these grants were awarded.

**Deadline**  January of each year.

## [1184]
## MICHIGAN SPACE GRANT CONSORTIUM FELLOWSHIPS

Michigan Space Grant Consortium
c/o University of Michigan
2106 Space Physics Research Laboratory
2455 Hayward Avenue
Ann Arbor, MI 48109-2143
(734) 764-9508                    Fax: (734) 764-4585
E-mail: blbryant@umich.edu
Web: www.engin.umich.edu/dept/aero/msgc/fellow

**Summary**  To provide funding to students (particularly women, minority, and disabled students) at member institutions of the Michigan Space Grant Consortium who wish to conduct space-related research.

**Eligibility**  This program is open to undergraduate and graduate students at affiliates of the Michigan consortium who are proposing to conduct research in aerospace, space science, earth system science, and other related fields in science, engineering, or mathematics; students working on educational research topics in mathematics, science, or technology are also eligible. Applicants must identify a mentor in the faculty research, education, or public service communities with whom they intend to work and who is available to write a letter of recommendation for the student. U.S. citizenship is required. Women, underrepresented minorities, and persons with disabilities are especially encouraged to apply.

**Financial data**  The maximum grant is $2,500 for undergraduates or $5,000 for graduate students.

**Additional information**  The consortium consists of Eastern Michigan University, Grand Valley State University, Hope College, Michigan State University, Michigan Technological University, Oakland University, Saginaw Valley State University, University of Michigan, Wayne State University, and Western Michigan University. This program is supported by the U.S. National Aeronautics and Space Administration (NASA).

**Number awarded**  Varies each year; recently, 23 undergraduate fellowships and 13 graduate fellowships were awarded.

**Deadline**  November of each year.

## [1185]
## MICHIGAN SPACE GRANT CONSORTIUM PRE-COLLEGE EDUCATION PROGRAM GRANTS

Michigan Space Grant Consortium
c/o University of Michigan
2106 Space Physics Research Laboratory
2455 Hayward Avenue
Ann Arbor, MI 48109-2143
(734) 764-9508                    Fax: (734) 764-4585
E-mail: blbryant@umich.edu
Web: www.engin.umich.edu/dept/aero/msgc/fellow

**Summary**  To provide funding for programs and projects that encourage and enrich the study of mathematics, science, or technology in general space science, aerospace, and aeronautics for K-12 students in Michigan.

**Eligibility**  Teachers in Michigan may apply for these grants to fund projects that encourage and enrich the study of mathematics, science, or technology for K-12 students. Preference is given to projects that focus on earth system science, aerospace, and space science. Programs targeted to women, underrepresented minorities, and persons with disabilities are strongly encouraged. Eligible projects include development, implementation, and/or testing of activities or supplementary resources that meet the national standards for mathematics, science, and technology education as well as state educational requirements. Activities may include both in-classroom work as well as informal programs occurring outside the classroom. Single-event activities receive low priority. Underrepresented minorities, women, and disabled individuals are strongly encouraged to apply.

**Financial data**  Grants up to $5,000 are available. At least 1:1 cost matching (cash contributions or in-kind support) with nonfederal funds is required. Augmented support of an additional $5,000 is available for proposals targeted toward the recruitment of women, underrepresented minorities, and persons with disabilities.

**Additional information** This program is supported by the U.S. National Aeronautics and Space Administration (NASA).

**Number awarded** Varies each year; recently, 11 of these grants were awarded.

**Deadline** November of each year.

## [1186]
## MICHIGAN SPACE GRANT CONSORTIUM RESEARCH SEED GRANTS

Michigan Space Grant Consortium
c/o University of Michigan
2106 Space Physics Research Laboratory
2455 Hayward Avenue
Ann Arbor, MI 48109-2143
(734) 764-9508                    Fax: (734) 764-4585
E-mail: blbryant@umich.edu
Web: www.umich.edu/~msgc

**Summary** To provide funding to faculty (particularly women, minorities, and persons with disabilities) at member institutions of the Michigan Space Grant Consortium (MSGC) who are interested in conducting space-related research.

**Eligibility** This program is open to faculty (research and professorial) at affiliates of the MSGC. Applicants must be interested in conducting a research project in engineering, science, mathematics, life sciences, or related educational areas. Preference is given to projects focusing on aerospace, space, or earth system science, although awards are not strictly limited to those topics. Initiation of a new area of research is preferred over efforts to continue an existing project or study. Women, underrepresented minorities, and persons with disabilities are encouraged to apply.

**Financial data** Grants up to $5,000 are available. At least 1:1 cost matching (cash contributions or in-kind support) with nonfederal funds is required.

**Additional information** The consortium consists of Eastern Michigan University, Grand Valley State University, Hope College, Michigan State University, Michigan Technological University, Oakland University, Saginaw Valley State University, University of Michigan, Wayne State University, and Western Michigan University. This program is supported by the U.S. National Aeronautics and Space Administration (NASA).

**Number awarded** Varies each year; recently, 7 of these grants were awarded.

**Deadline** November of each year.

## [1187]
## MINNESOTA WOMEN AT CROSSROADS GRANTS

Minnesota State Federation of Business and
    Professional Women's Clubs, Inc.
Attn: Minnesota Business and Professional Women's
    Foundation
3432 Denmark Avenue
PMB 167
Eagan, MN 55123
E-mail: MinnesotaBPW_Foundation@hotmail.com
Web: www.bpwmn.org/bpw_mn_foundation.htm

**Summary** To provide funding to women in Minnesota who need assistance for professional development.

**Eligibility** This program is open to female residents of Minnesota who are 25 years of age or older. Applicants must be seeking funding to improve their employment opportunities, for career development, or to obtain economic self-sufficiency. They must be able to demonstrate an immediate (within 3 months) need for assistance and a measurable and long-term impact. Daily living expenses and support for college or general education are not covered.

**Financial data** Grants range from $200 to $500. Funds must be used for such expenses as license fees, start-up equipment, or certification test fees.

**Duration** These are 1-time grants.

**Number awarded** Several each year.

## [1188]
## MINNESOTA WOMEN'S CAMPAIGN FUND AWARDS

Minnesota Women's Campaign Fund
P.O. Box 582944, Suite 106
Minneapolis, MN 55458
(612) 331-2366                    Fax: (612) 331-0073
E-mail: info@mnwcf.org
Web: www.mnwomenscampaignfund.org

**Summary** To provide funds to pro-choice women in Minnesota who are running for public office.

**Eligibility** Eligible to receive funds under this program are women who are supporters of Roe v. Wade and reproductive choice, are advocates of equal rights for women, and are running for office in Minnesota at the federal, state, or local level. The fund is nonpartisan. Recipients may be affiliated with the Republican, Democratic, or Independent parties. Selection is based on willingness and ability to conduct a vigorous, well-organized campaign; interest and knowledge in a broad spectrum of political, economic, and social issues; an enlightened position on women's issues, including equal rights and reproductive choice; a commitment to democratic principles and ethical practices; and evidence of need for financial help.

**Financial data** Since 1982, the fund has contributed more than $1 million.

**Number awarded** Since it was established, the fund has supported more than 825 women candidates.

## [1189]
### MINNIE L. MAFFETT FELLOWSHIPS

Texas Federation of Business and Professional
   Women's Foundation, Inc.
Attn: TFBPW Foundation
803 Forest Ridge Drive, Suite 207
Bedford, TX 76022
(817) 283-0862                 Fax: (817) 283-0872
E-mail: bpwtx@swbell.net
Web: www.bpwtx.org/foundation.asp

**Summary** To provide financial assistance to women in Texas interested in continuing their education or conducting research in a medical field.

**Eligibility** This program is open to 1) women graduates of Texas medical schools interested in postgraduate or research work; 2) women who have been awarded a Ph.D. degree from a Texas university and are doing research in a medical field; 3) women who need financial aid for the first year in establishing a family practice in a rural area of Texas with a population of less than 5,000; and 4) fourth-year women medical students for completion of an M.D. or O.D. degree in an accredited medical school in Texas.

**Financial data** The stipend recently was $1,500.

**Duration** 1 year; nonrenewable.

**Additional information** This program was established in 1948.

**Number awarded** Varies each year; recently, 3 of these fellowships were awarded.

**Deadline** January of each year.

## [1190]
### MISSISSIPPI SPACE GRANT CONSORTIUM SCHOLARSHIPS AND FELLOWSHIPS

Mississippi Space Grant Consortium
c/o University of Mississippi
217 Vardaman Hall
P.O. Box 1848
University, MS 38677-1848
(662) 915-1187                 Fax: (662) 915-3927
E-mail: mschaff@olemiss.edu
Web: www.olemiss.edu/programs/nasa

**Summary** To provide funding to undergraduate and graduate students (particularly women, minority, and disabled students) for space-related activities at colleges and universities that are members of the Mississippi Space Grant Consortium.

**Eligibility** This program is open to undergraduate and graduate students at member institutions of the Mississippi consortium. Each participating college or university establishes its own program and criteria for admission, but all activities are in engineering, mathematics, and science fields of interest to the U.S. National Aeronautics and Space Administration (NASA). U.S. citizenship is required. The consortium is a component of NASA's Space Grant program, which encourages participation by women, underrepresented minorities, and persons with disabilities.

**Financial data** Each participating institution establishes the amounts of the awards. Recently, the average undergraduate award was $1,308 and the average graduate award was $2,975. A total of $96,350 was awarded.

**Additional information** Consortium members include Alcorn State University, Coahoma Community College, Delta State University, Hinds Community College (Utica Campus), Itawamba Community College, Jackson State University, Meridian Community College, Mississippi Delta Community College, Mississippi Gulf Coast Community College, Mississippi State University, Mississippi University for Women, Mississippi Valley State University, Northeast Mississippi Community College, Pearl River Community College, the University of Mississippi, and the University of Southern Mississippi. This program is funded by NASA.

**Number awarded** Varies each year; recently, a total of 47 students received support through this program.

## [1191]
### MISSOURI SPACE GRANT CONSORTIUM UNDERGRADUATE RESEARCH INTERNSHIP PROGRAM

Missouri Space Grant Consortium
c/o University of Missouri at Rolla
226 Mechanical Engineering Building
1870 Miner Circle
Rolla, MO 65409-0050
(573) 341-4887                 Fax: (573) 341-4607
E-mail: spaceg@umr.edu
Web: www.umr.edu/~spaceg

**Summary** To provide research experience to undergraduate students in Missouri (especially women, minority, and disabled students) who are working on a degree in an aerospace field.

**Eligibility** This program is open to undergraduate students studying engineering, physics, astronomy, or planetary sciences at member institutions of the Missouri Space Grant Consortium. Applicants must be proposing a specific research or education project in a research laboratory, a computing facility, or the galleries of the St. Louis Science Center. Selection is based on academic records, letters of recommendation, and reasons for wanting to enter the program. U.S. citizenship is required. The Missouri Space Grant Consortium is a component of the U.S. National Aeronautics and Space Administration (NASA), which encourages participation by women, underrepresented minorities, and people with disabilities.

**Financial data** Awards are approximately $2,000 for the summer or $3,000 for the academic year.

**Duration** Both summer and academic year appointments are available.

**Additional information** The consortium members are Southwest Missouri State University, University of Missouri at Columbia, University of Missouri at Rolla, University of Missouri at St. Louis, and Washington University. This program is funded by NASA.

**Number awarded** Approximately 30 each year.

## [1192]
## MONTANA BPW FOUNDATION GRANTS

Montana Federation of Business and Professional
    Women's Organizations
Attn: Montana BPW Foundation, Inc.
P.O. Box 303
Great Falls, MT 59403
Web: www.montanabpw.org/foundation

**Summary** To provide funding for projects and programs that promote equality, self-sufficiency, professional development, and personal fulfillment for Montana women.

**Eligibility** This program is open to women and organizations in Montana seeking funding for educational workshops, speakers, consultants, on-site training programs, forums, seminars, retreats, publications, and information. Eligible projects or programs are those focused on women's issues in business, politics, education, poverty, the Equal Rights Amendment, pay equity, health and health care, social justice, sexual harassment and/or discrimination, domestic and sexual violence, child care, family relations, and retirement. Funding is not available for purchasing equipment, operating capital, religious purposes, veteran or fraternal organizations, general endowment funds, or fundraising. Applicants must submit a brief narrative that includes their mission statement, goals and objectives, history, and a description of recent programs, activities, and achievements. Organizations must also submit documentation of their nonprofit status.

**Financial data** Grants up to $1,000 are available.

**Additional information** Information is also available from Norma Boetel, P.O. Box 1511, Bozeman, MT 59771, (406) 587-8321, E-mail: normab@imt.net.

**Number awarded** Varies each year.

**Deadline** November of each year.

## [1193]
## MONTANA SPACE GRANT CONSORTIUM RESEARCH INITIATION GRANTS

Montana Space Grant Consortium
c/o Montana State University
261 EPS Building
P.O. Box 173835
Bozeman, MT 59717-3835
(406) 994-4223                    Fax: (406) 994-4452
E-mail: msgc@montana.edu
Web: spacegrant.montana.edu

**Summary** To provide seed money for research related to space sciences and engineering to students and faculty (particularly women, minorities, and persons with disabilities) at institutions that are members of the Montana Space Grant Consortium (MSGC).

**Eligibility** This program is open to students and faculty at MSGC member institutions (most of the awards go to full-time graduate students) who need support to conduct research related to space sciences and/or engineering. This program is part of the U.S. National Aeronautics and Space Administration (NASA) Space Grant program, which encourages participation by women, underrepresented minorities, and persons with disabilities.

**Financial data** These grants provide "seed money" only.

**Duration** 1 year; generally nonrenewable.

**Additional information** The MSGC member institutions are Blackfeet Community College, Carroll College, Chief Dull Knife College, Fort Belknap College, Fort Peck Community College, Little Big Horn College, Montana State University at Billings, Montana State University at Bozeman, Montana State University Northern, Montana Tech, Rocky Mountain College, Salish Kootenai College, Stone Child College, University of Great Falls, University of Montana, and University of Montana Western. Funding for this program is provided by NASA. Awardees are required to submit a follow-on proposal to NASA for regular research funding during the year of the grant.

**Number awarded** Varies each year; recently, 2 of these grants were awarded.

## [1194]
## MONTICELLO COLLEGE FOUNDATION FELLOWSHIP FOR WOMEN

Newberry Library
Attn: Committee on Awards
60 West Walton Street
Chicago, IL 60610-3305
(312) 255-3666                    Fax: (312) 255-3513
E-mail: research@newberry.org
Web: www.newberry.org

**Summary** To provide young women scholars with the opportunity to work in residence at the Newberry Library.

**Eligibility** This program is open to women who have completed their doctorates, are U.S. citizens or permanent residents, and are at an early stage in their professional careers. Their work must give clear promise of scholarly productivity. Preference is given to applicants whose scholarship is particularly concerned with the study of women, but projects may be proposed in any field appropriate to the Newberry's collection.

**Financial data** The stipend is $15,000.

**Duration** 6 months.

**Additional information** Nearly all of the Newberry's 1 million volumes and 5 million manuscripts relate to the history of western Europe and the Americas. Fellows must be in residence at the Newberry Library.

**Number awarded** 1 each year.

**Deadline** January of each year.

## [1195]
## MSGC UNDERGRADUATE AND GRADUATE RESEARCH FELLOWSHIPS

Maine Space Grant Consortium
Attn: Executive Director
87 Winthrop Street, Suite 200
Augusta, ME 04330
(207) 622-4688        Toll-free: (877) 397-7223, ext. 173
Fax: (207) 622-4548        E-mail: shehata@msgc.org
Web: www.msgc.org/education_students.asp

**Summary** To provide funding to undergraduate and graduate students (especially women and minorities) at member institutions of the Maine Space Grant Consortium (MSGC) interested in working on projects related to space.

**Eligibility** This program is open to U.S. citizens who are enrolled on a full-time basis in an undergraduate or graduate program at a MSGC member institution. Applicants must be proposing to conduct a project on a topic of interest to the U.S. National Aeronautics and Space Administration (NASA) in aerospace technology, biological and physical research, space science, earth science, human exploration and development of space, and other related science or engineering fields. They may be proposing to conduct research at their home institution, spend time conducting research at a NASA flight center, facilitate the development of a liaison between researchers at their home institution and a NASA center, or facilitate technology transfer from their home institution to industry. Selection is based on the relevance of the proposed research project to NASA's mission. Applications are especially encouraged from women and minorities.

**Financial data** Stipends vary at participating institutions, ranging from $2,500 to $5,000 per year for undergraduates and from $5,000 to $15,000 per year for graduate students.

**Duration** 1 year; may be renewed.

**Additional information** The member institutions are the University of Maine, the University of Southern Maine, the University of New England, and Maine Maritime Academy. This program is funded by NASA.

**Number awarded** Varies each year.

**Deadline** Each participating institution sets its own deadline.

## [1196]
## MYRNA F. BERNATH FELLOWSHIP AWARD
Society for Historians of American Foreign Relations
c/o Ohio State University
Department of History
106 Dulles Hall
230 West 17th Avenue
Columbus, OH 43210
(614) 292-1951　　　　Fax: (614) 292-2282
E-mail: shafr@osu.edu
Web: www.shafr.org/prizes.htm

**Summary** To provide funding to women who wish to go to another country to conduct research on foreign relations.

**Eligibility** This program is open to American women who wish to conduct historically-based research in another country or to women from other countries who wish to conduct research in the United States. The proposed study should focus on U.S. foreign relations, transnational history, international history, peace studies, cultural interchange, or defense or strategic studies. Preference is given to applications from graduate students and those within 5 years of completion of their Ph.D.s. Applicants must submit a curriculum vitae, a letter of intent, and a detailed research proposal that discusses the sources to be consulted and their value, the funds needed, and the plan for spending those funds.

**Financial data** The grant is $2,500.

**Duration** These awards are presented biennially, in odd-numbered years.

**Additional information** Further information is available from Thomas Borstelmann, University of Nebraska at Lincoln, Department of History, 640 Oldfather Hall, Lincoln, NE 68588.

**Number awarded** 1 each odd-numbered year.

**Deadline** November of each even-numbered year.

## [1197]
## NASA FACULTY FELLOWSHIP PROGRAM
American Society for Engineering Education
Attn: Projects Department
1818 N Street, N.W., Suite 600
Washington, DC 20036-2479
(202) 331-3509　　　　Fax: (202) 265-8504
E-mail: nasa@asee.org
Web: www.asee.org

**Summary** To provide support to faculty members in engineering and science (especially women, minorities, and persons with disabilities) who wish to conduct summer research at facilities of the National Aeronautics and Space Administration (NASA).

**Eligibility** This program is open to tenured or tenure-track faculty at 4-year institutions and full-time faculty at 2-year institutions. Applicants must be U.S. citizens who have a Ph.D. in an engineering, mathematics, or science discipline applicable to the research and/or technology development needs of the National Aeronautics and Space Administration (NASA). They must be interested in conducting a summer research project at a participating NASA center. Faculty who participated in this program within the past 5 years, who have received more than $300,000 in NASA funding within the past 5 years, or who have received a NASA Faculty Awards for Research grant are not eligible. Women, underrepresented minorities, and persons with disabilities are strongly encouraged to apply. Selection is based on relevance and merit of the research (40%), qualifications of the faculty applicant (40%), and overall academic benefit to the faculty applicant and his or her institution (20%).

**Financial data** The stipend is $1,200 per week, for a maximum of $12,000. A relocation allowance of $1,500 is available for fellows who live more than 50 miles from their assigned center and reasonable travel expenses for a round-trip are also reimbursed for fellows who receive the relocation allowance. The maximum allowance for relocation and travel is $2,000. To facilitate the participation of individuals with disabilities, NASA provides up to $1,500 in supplemental funding for special assistance and/or equipment necessary to enable the principal investigator to perform the work under the award.

**Duration** 10 weeks during the summer.

**Additional information** Participating NASA centers are Ames Research Center (Moffett Field, California); Hugh L. Dryden Flight Research Facility (Edwards, California); Goddard Space Flight Center (Greenbelt, Maryland) and its Wallops Flight Facility (Wallops Island, Virginia) and Goddard Institute for Space Studies (New York, New York); Jet Propulsion Laboratory (Pasadena, California); Lyndon B. Johnson Space Center (Houston, Texas) and its White Sands Test Facility (Las Cruces, New Mexico); John F. Kennedy Space Center (Cape Canaveral, Florida); Langley Research Center (Hampton, Virginia); Glenn Research Center (Cleveland, Ohio); George C. Marshall Space Flight Center (Huntsville, Alabama); and John C. Stennis Space Center (Stennis Space Center, Mississippi). This program is funded by NASA and administered by the American Society for Engineering Education (ASEE) and the Universities Space Research Association (USRA).

**Number awarded** Varies each year.

**Deadline** January of each year.

## [1198]
## NASA GRADUATE STUDENT RESEARCHERS PROGRAM

National Aeronautics and Space Administration
Attn: Office of Education
300 E Street, S.W., 1800M-A
Washington, DC 20546-0001
(202) 358-7327          Fax: (202) 606-0122
E-mail: ben.oni@nasa.gov
Web: fellowships.hq.nasa.gov/gsrp/program

**Summary** To provide funding to graduate students (particularly women, minority, or disabled students) who are interested in conducting research in fields of interest to the U.S. National Aeronautics and Space Administration (NASA).

**Eligibility** This program is open to full-time students enrolled or planning to enroll in an accredited graduate program at a U.S. college or university. Applicants must be citizens of the United States, sponsored by a faculty advisor or department chair, and interested in conducting research in space sciences at their home university or at NASA field centers. Selection is based on academic qualifications, quality of the proposed research and its relevance to NASA's program, the student's proposed utilization of center research facilities (except for NASA headquarters), and ability of the student to accomplish the defined research. Individuals from underrepresented groups in science, technology, engineering, and mathematics (STEM) fields (African Americans, Native Americans, Alaskan Natives, Mexican Americans, Puerto Ricans, Native Pacific Islanders, women, and persons with disabilities) are strongly urged to apply.

**Financial data** The program provides a $18,000 student stipend, a $3,000 student expense allowance, and a $3,000 university allowance.

**Duration** 1 year; may be renewed for up to 2 additional years.

**Additional information** This program was established in 1980. Under the reorganized NASA organizational structure, the Exploration Systems Mission Directorate (ESMD) supports research in chemical, electrical, materials, mechanical, and metallurgical engineering, chemistry, physics, biological and life science, environmental science, and other sciences; the Science Mission Directorate, Office of Earth Science Division (SMD-ES) supports research in mechanical engineering, chemistry, physics, physical science, mathematics, computer science, biological science, social science, atmospheric science, geological science, oceanography, and environmental science; the Science Mission Directorate-Office of Space Science (SMD-SS) supports research in astronomy, chemistry, physics, physical science, computer science, biological science, and atmospheric science; the Space Operations Mission Directorate (SOMD) supports research in materials, mechanical, and metallurgical engineering, mathematics, and computer science. Other awards are distributed through NASA field centers, each of which has its own research agenda and facilities. These centers include Ames Research Center (Moffett Field, California), Dryden Flight Research Facility (Edwards, California), Goddard Space Flight Center (Greenbelt, Maryland), Jet Propulsion Laboratory (Pasadena, California), Johnson Space Center (Houston, Texas), Kennedy Space Center (Kennedy Space Center, Florida), Langley Research Center (Hampton, Virginia), Glenn Research Center (Cleveland, Ohio), Marshall Space Flight Center (Huntsville, Alabama), and Stennis Space Center (Stennis Space Center, Mississippi). Fellows spend some period of time in residence at the center, taking advantage of the unique research facilities of the installation and working with center personnel. Travel outside the United States is allowed if it is essential to the research effort and charged to a grant.

**Number awarded** This program supports approximately 300 graduate students each year.

**Deadline** January of each year.

## [1199]
## NATIONAL CENTER FOR ATMOSPHERIC RESEARCH POSTDOCTORAL APPOINTMENTS

National Center for Atmospheric Research
Attn: Advanced Study Program
1850 Table Mesa Drive
P.O. Box 3000
Boulder, CO 80307-3000
(303) 497-1601          Fax: (303) 497-1646
E-mail: paulad@ucar.edu
Web: www.asp.ucar.edu/pdfp/pd_announcement.jsp

**Summary** To provide funding to recent Ph.D.s (particularly women and minorities) who wish to conduct research at the National Center for Atmospheric Research (NCAR) in Boulder, Colorado.

**Eligibility** This program is open to recent Ph.D.s and Sc.D.s in applied mathematics, chemistry, engineering, and physics as well as specialists in atmospheric sciences from such disciplines as biology, economics, geography, geology, and science education. Applicants must be interested in conducting research at the center in atmospheric sciences and global change. Selection is based on the applicant's scientific capability and potential, originality and independence, and the match between their interests and the research opportunities at the center. Applications from women and minorities are encouraged.

**Financial data** The stipend is $48,500 in the first year and $50,500 in the second year. Fellows also receive life and health insurance, a relocation allowance (up to $1,000 for travel within the United States or up to $2,500 for travel from abroad), an allowance of $750 for moving and storing personal belongings, and scientific travel and registration fee reimbursement up to $1,500 per year.

**Duration** 2 years.

**Additional information** NCAR is operated by the University Corporation for Atmospheric Research (a consortium of 70 universities and research institutes) and sponsored by the National Science Foundation.

**Number awarded** Varies; currently, up to 7 each year.

**Deadline** January of each year.

## [1200]
## NATIONAL PHYSICAL SCIENCE CONSORTIUM DISSERTATION SUPPORT PROGRAM

National Physical Science Consortium
c/o University of Southern California
3716 South Hope Street, Suite 348
Los Angeles, CA 90007-4344
(213) 743-2409          Toll-free: (800) 854-NPSC
Fax: (213) 743-2407     E-mail: npschq@npsc.org
Web: www.npsc.org

**Summary** To provide financial assistance to women and underrepresented minorities conducting dissertation research in designated science and engineering fields.

**Eligibility** This program is open to U.S. citizens who are enrolled in a doctoral program and about to begin dissertation research. Eligible fields of study are generally limited to astronomy, chemistry, computer science, geology, materials science, mathematical sciences, physics, their subdisciplines, and related engineering fields (chemical, computer, electrical, environmental, and mechanical). The program welcomes applications from all qualified students and continues to emphasize the recruitment of underrepresented minority (African American, Hispanic, Native American Indian, Eskimo, Aleut, and Pacific Islander) and women physical science and engineering students. Fellowships are provided to students at the 116 universities that are members of the consortium. Selection is based on academic standing (GPA), undergraduate and graduate course work and grades, university and/or industry research experience, letters of recommendation, and GRE scores.

**Financial data** The fellowship pays tuition and fees plus an annual stipend of $16,000.

**Duration** Up to 4 years.

**Number awarded** Varies each year.

**Deadline** November of each year.

## [1201]
## NAVAL RESEARCH LABORATORY BROAD AGENCY ANNOUNCEMENT

Naval Research Laboratory
Attn: Deputy for Small Business
4555 Overlook Avenue, S.W.
Washington, DC 20375-5320
(202) 767-0666                Fax: (202) 767-0494
E-mail: marita.thompson@nrl.navy.mil
Web: www.nrl.navy.mil

**Summary** To provide funding to investigators (particularly women and minorities) who are interested in conducting scientific research of interest to the U.S. Navy.

**Eligibility** This program is open to investigators qualified to perform research in designated scientific and technical areas. Topics cover a wide range of technical and scientific areas; recent programs included radar technology, artificial intelligence technologies, software engineering, surface chemistry sciences, ceramic materials, structural acoustics, and seafloor sciences. The Naval Research Laboratory (NRL) encourages industry, educational institutions, small businesses, small disadvantaged business concerns, women-owned small businesses, veteran-owned small businesses, Historically Black Colleges and Universities, and Minority Institutions to submit proposals. Selection is based on the degree to which new and creative solutions to technical issues important to NRL programs are proposed and the offeror's understanding of the proposed approach and technical objectives; the offeror's ability to implement the proposed approach; the degree to which technical data and/or computer software developed under the proposed contract are to be delivered to the NRL with rights compatible with NRL research and development objectives; proposed cost and cost realism; and the extent to which offerors identify and commit to small business, small disadvantaged business, veteran-owned small business, women-owned small business, Historically Black College and University, or Minority Institution participation in the proposed effort, whether as a joint venture, teaming arrangement, or subcontractor.

**Financial data** The typical range of funding is from $100,000 to $2,000,000.

**Duration** 1 year.

**Additional information** The Naval Research Laboratory conducts most of its research in its own facilities in Washington, D.C., Stennis Space Center, Mississippi, and Monterey, California, but also funds some related research.

**Number awarded** Varies each year.

**Deadline** Each program establishes its own application deadline; for a complete list of all the programs, including their deadlines, contact the address above.

## [1202]
## NELL I. MONDY FELLOWSHIP

Sigma Delta Epsilon-Graduate Women in Science, Inc.
c/o Jennifer Ingram, Fellowships Coordinator
Duke University-Department of Medicine
Box 2641, 275 MSRB, Research Drive
Durham, NC 27710
(919) 668-1439
E-mail: fellowshipsquestions@gwis.org
Web: www.gwis.org/grants/default.htm

**Summary** To provide funding to women interested in conducting research in the United States or abroad in the natural sciences.

**Eligibility** The program is open to women in the United States and Canada who are doing graduate or postdoctoral work in the natural sciences (defined to include anthropology, computer sciences, environmental sciences, life sciences, mathematics, psychology, physical sciences, and statistics). Preference is given to students working in the areas of food science, nutrition, and toxicology. Applicants must give evidence of outstanding ability and promise in scientific research. They may be proposing to conduct research at an institution in the United States or abroad. Along with their application, they must submit a brief description of relevant personal factors, including financial need, that should be considered in the selection process. Applicants must either be members of Sigma Delta Epsilon–Graduate Women in Science or include a processing fee of $20 (the cost of a 1-year membership).

**Financial data** Grants range up to $3,000. The funds must be used for scientific research, including professional travel costs. They may not be used for tuition, child care, travel to professional meetings or to begin a new appointment, administrative overhead or indirect costs, personal computers, living allowances, or equipment of general use.

**Duration** 1 year; may be renewed in unusual circumstances, contingent upon receipt of an annual progress report.

**Additional information** This fellowship was first awarded in 2002.

**Number awarded** 1 each year.

**Deadline** January of each year.

## [1203]
## NEVADA SPACE GRANT CONSORTIUM GRADUATE FELLOWSHIP PROGRAM

Nevada Space Grant Consortium
c/o University of Nevada at Reno
Mackay School of Mines Building, Room 308
MS 168
Reno, NV 89557
(775) 784-6261                    Fax: (775) 327-2235
E-mail: nvsg@mines.unr.edu
Web: www.unr.edu/spacegrant

**Summary** To provide financial assistance for space-related study or research to graduate students (particularly women, minority, and disabled students) at institutions that are members of the University and Community College System of Nevada (UCCSN) and participate in the Nevada Space Grant Consortium (NSGC).

**Eligibility** This program is open to graduate students at UCCSN member institutions. Applicants must be working on a degree in an aerospace-related field (including engineering, mathematics, physical and life sciences, and technology) that will prepare them for a career in aerospace science, technology, and related fields. They must be U.S. citizens, be enrolled full time (or accepted for full-time study), present a proposed study or research plan related to aerospace, include in the research or activity plan an extramural experience at a field center of the U.S. National Aeronautics and Space Administration (NASA), plan to be involved in NSGC outreach activities, not receive other federal funds, and intend to prepare for a career in a field of interest to NASA. Members of underrepresented groups (African Americans, Hispanics, American Indians, Pacific Islanders, people with physical disabilities, and women of all races) who have an interest in aerospace fields are encouraged to apply. Selection is based on the academic qualifications of the applicant, the quality of the proposed research program or plan of study and its relevant to NASA's aerospace science and technology program, the quality of the approach to achieving the objectives of the proposed utilization of a NASA center in carrying out the objectives of the program, the prospects for completion of the project within the allotted time, and the applicant's motivation for an aerospace career.

**Financial data** The grant is $22,500, including $16,000 as a stipend for the student and $6,500 for tuition and a student research and travel allowance.

**Duration** 12 months; may be renewed up to 24 additional months.

**Additional information** Funding for this program is provided by NASA.

**Number awarded** Varies each year; recently, 3 of these awards were granted.

**Deadline** March of each year.

## [1204]
## NEW HAMPSHIRE SPACE GRANT CONSORTIUM PROJECT SUPPORT

New Hampshire Space Grant Consortium
c/o University of New Hampshire
Institute for the Study of Earth, Oceans, and Space
Morse Hall
39 College Road
Durham, NH 03824-3525
(603) 862-0094                    Fax: (603) 862-1915
E-mail: nhspacegrant@unh.edu
Web: www.nhsgc.sr.unh.edu

**Summary** To provide financial assistance to students at member institutions of the New Hampshire Space Grant Consortium (NHSGC) who are interested in participating in space-related activities.

**Eligibility** This program is open to students at member institutions of the NHSGC. Applicants must be studying space physics, astrophysics, astronomy, or aspects of computer science, engineering, earth sciences, ocean sciences, atmospheric sciences, or life sciences that utilize space technology and/or adopt a planetary view of the global environment. U.S. citizenship is required. The New Hampshire Space Grant Consortium is a component of the U.S. National Aeronautics and Space Administration (NASA) Space Grant program, which encourages participation by women, underrepresented minorities, and persons with disabilities.

**Financial data** The amount of the award depends on the nature of the project.

**Duration** From 1 quarter to 1 year.

**Additional information** This program is funded by NASA. Currently, projects operating through this program include space grant fellowships at the University of New Hampshire, Agnes M. Lindsay Trust/NASA Challenge Scholars Initiative at the New Hampshire Community Technical College System, Presidential Scholars Research Assistantships at Dartmouth College, and Women in Science Internships at Dartmouth.

**Number awarded** Varies each year.

**Deadline** Each participating college or university sets its own deadline.

## [1205]
## NEW JERSEY SPACE GRANT CONSORTIUM UNDERGRADUATE SUMMER FELLOWSHIPS

New Jersey Space Grant Consortium
c/o Stevens Institute of Technology
Castle Point on the Hudson
Hoboken, NJ 07030
(201) 216-8964                    Fax: (201) 216-8929
E-mail: sthangam@stevens-tech.edu
Web: www.njsgc.org

**Summary** To provide financial assistance for summer research experiences in space-related fields to college students in New Jersey, particularly women, minority, and disabled students.

**Eligibility** This program is open to undergraduate students who have completed at least 2 years at member institutions of the New Jersey Space Grant Consortium (NJSGC). Applicants must be proposing a program of space-related research in industry or at universities and their affiliated research laboratories. Their field of study may be aerospace engineering, biological science, chemical engineering, computer science and engineering, electrical engineering, material science and engineering, mechanical engineering, natural science, or physical science. U.S. citizenship is required. The New Jersey Space Grant Consortium is a component of the U.S. National Aeronautics and Space Administration (NASA) Space Grant program, which encourages participation by women, underrepresented minorities, and people with disabilities. Selection is based on a biographical sketch, a brief statement of what they hope to accomplish as a space grant fellow, a statement of career goals (including their relationship to aerospace engineering and science), and a description of their plan for the immediate future.

**Financial data** The stipend is $600 per week, with an additional $600 per student available for laboratory supplies.

**Duration** 10 weeks during the summer.

**Additional information** Members of the NJSGC include New Jersey Institute of Technology, Princeton University, Rutgers University, Stevens Institute of Technology, and the University of Medicine and Dentistry of New Jersey. This program is funded by NASA.

**Number awarded** 10 to 12 each year. Approximately 60% of the fellows are placed in industries (or industry sponsored programs) and 40% go to universities and their affiliated research laboratories.

**Deadline** March of each year.

## [1206]
## NEW YORK FOUNDATION FOR THE ARTS ARTISTS' FELLOWSHIPS

New York Foundation for the Arts
155 Avenue of the Americas, Sixth Floor
New York, NY 10013-1507
(212) 366-6900, ext. 217         Fax: (212) 366-1778
E-mail: nyfaafp@nyfa.org
Web: www.nyfa.org/level2.asp?id=1&fid=1

**Summary** To provide funding for career development to creative artists (particularly women and minorities) living and working in the state of New York.

**Eligibility** Artists in New York state who are more than 18 years of age are eligible to apply for this program if they are not currently enrolled in a degree program. Applicants must have lived in the state for at least 2 years at the time of application. They are required to submit, along with the application form, samples of current work. In odd-numbered years, applications are accepted for architecture/environmental structures, choreography, fiction, music composition, painting, photography, playwriting/screenwriting, and video. In even-numbered years, applications are accepted for computer arts, crafts, film, nonfiction literature, performance art/multidisciplinary work, poetry, printmaking/drawing/artists' books, and sculpture. Selection is based on artistic excellence. The program is committed to supporting artists of diverse cultural, sexual, and ethnic backgrounds.

**Financial data** The grant is $7,000.

**Duration** 1 year.

**Additional information** Since this program began in 1985, the sponsor has awarded more than $22 million to more than 3,500 artists. Named awards include the Geri Ashur Screenwriting Award, the Gregory Millard Fellowships (supported by the New York City Department of Cultural Affairs for artists in several categories), and the Homer Avila Memorial Fellowship (for choreographers). Other sponsors include the New York State Council on the Arts, the Lily Auchincloss Foundation, the Milton & Sally Avery Arts Foundation, Deutsche Bank Americas Foundation, and the Harkness Foundation for Dance. Recipients must perform a public service activity coordinated by the Artists and Audiences Exchange.

**Number awarded** Varies each year; recently, 113 of these fellowships, worth $791,000, were awarded.

**Deadline** October of each year.

## [1207]
## NEW YORK PUBLIC LIBRARY FELLOWSHIPS

American Council of Learned Societies
Attn: Office of Fellowships and Grants
633 Third Avenue, 8C
New York, NY 10017-6795
(212) 697-1505         Fax: (212) 949-8058
E-mail: grants@acls.org
Web: www.acls.org/felguide.htm

**Summary** To provide funding to postdoctorates (especially women and minorities) who are interested in conducting research at the Dorothy and Lewis B. Cullman Center for Scholars and Writers of the New York Public Library.

**Eligibility** This program is open to scholars at all stages of their careers who received a Ph.D. degree at least 2 years previously. Established scholars who can demonstrate the equivalent of the Ph.D. in publications and professional experience may also qualify. Applicants must be U.S. citizens or permanent residents who have not had supported leave time for at least 3 years prior to the start of the proposed research. Appropriate fields of specialization include, but are not limited to, anthropology, archaeology, art and architectural history, economic history, film, geography, history, languages and literatures, legal studies, linguistics, musicology, philosophy, political science, psychology, religion, rhetoric and communication, sociology, and theater studies. Proposals in those fields of the social sciences are eligible only if they employ predominantly humanistic approaches (e.g., economic history, law and literature, political philosophy). Proposals in interdisciplinary and cross-disciplinary studies are welcome, as are proposals focused on any geographic region or on any cultural or linguistic group. Applicants must be interested in conducting research at the New York Public Library's Dorothy and Lewis B. Cullman Center for Scholars and Writers. Women and members of minority groups are particularly invited to apply.

**Financial data** The stipend is $60,000 for full professors or $50,000 for assistant and associate professors.

**Duration** 9 months, beginning in September.

**Additional information** This program was first offered for 1999-2000, the inaugural year of the center. Candidates must also submit a separate application that is available from the New York Public Library, Humanities and Social Sciences Library, Dorothy and Lewis B. Cullman Center for

Scholars and Writers, Fifth Avenue and 42nd Street, New York, NY 10018-2788, E-mail: csw@nypl.org. Fellows are required to be in continuous residence at the center and participate in its activities and programs.

**Number awarded** Up to 5 each year.

**Deadline** September of each year.

## [1208]
## NORTH CAROLINA SPACE GRANT CONSORTIUM GENERAL PUBLIC ENGAGEMENT PROGRAM

North Carolina Space Grant Consortium
c/o North Carolina State University
Mechanical and Aerospace Engineering
1009 Capability Drive, Suite 210
Box 7515
Raleigh, NC 27695-7515
(919) 515-4240              Fax: (919) 515-5934
E-mail: proposals@ncspacegrant.org
Web: www.ncspacegrant.org

**Summary** To provide funding to faculty members (particularly women, minorities, and persons with disabilities) at institutions affiliated with the North Carolina Space Grant Consortium (NCSGC) who are interested in developing a space-related program for the general public.

**Eligibility** This program is open to U.S. citizens qualified to serve as principal investigators at institutions affiliated with the NCSGC. Applicants must be interested in developing and implementing activities that will increase the appreciation and knowledge of aerospace-related issues in the general population of North Carolina. They must describe 1) how the activity will increase the general public appreciation and knowledge of the impact of NASA's current mission on their lives; 2) how the program will actively seek and recruit the involvement of women, underrepresented minorities, and persons with disabilities; and 3) any NASA-sponsored or aerospace-related research, teaching, or outreach that is performed by the principal investigator. The NCSGC especially encourages the participation of principal investigators who are female, a member of an underrepresented minority group, or a person with a disability.

**Financial data** The maximum grant is $5,000. A 1:1 cost match with non-federal funds is required.

**Duration** Activities must be completed within 12 months.

**Additional information** The affiliated institutions are North Carolina State University, North Carolina A&T State University, Duke University, North Carolina Central University, the University of North Carolina at Charlotte, the University of North Carolina at Chapel Hill, the University of North Carolina at Pembroke, and Winston-Salem State University. This program is funded by NASA.

**Number awarded** 7 to 12 each year.

**Deadline** Letters of intent must be submitted by January of each year. Completed proposals are due in March.

## [1209]
## NORTH CAROLINA SPACE GRANT CONSORTIUM GRADUATE STUDENT RESEARCH FELLOWSHIPS

North Carolina Space Grant Consortium
c/o North Carolina State University
Mechanical and Aerospace Engineering
1009 Capability Drive, Suite 210
Box 7515
Raleigh, NC 27695-7515
(919) 515-4240              Fax: (919) 515-5934
E-mail: fellowships@ncspacegrant.org
Web: www.ncspacegrant.org

**Summary** To provide funding to graduate students (particularly women, minority, and disabled students) at institutions affiliated with the North Carolina Space Grant Consortium (NCSGC) interested in conducting space-related research.

**Eligibility** This program is open to full-time graduate students who are conducting research projects under the direct supervision of a faculty mentor at institutions affiliated with the NCSGC. Applicants must be working on a degree in science, technology, engineering, or mathematics (STEM) disciplines of interest to the U.S. National Aeronautics and Space Administration (NASA). They must be receiving at least half-time support from their home institution in the form of a teaching assistantship, research assistantship, or fellowship. The research project must be space or aeronautics related or have a space or aeronautics application. Selection is based on the quality of the proposed research project, the student's academic achievement, letter of recommendation from the research mentor, and exhibited leadership qualities. U.S. citizenship is required. A primary goal of this program is the recruitment and retention of underrepresented minorities, women, and persons with disabilities into space-related fields.

**Financial data** The maximum grant is $7,000 for students conducting research at a NASA center or industrial contractor or $5,000 for students conducting research at their home institution.

**Duration** 1 year; may be renewed 1 additional year.

**Additional information** The affiliated institutions are North Carolina State University, North Carolina A&T State University, Duke University, North Carolina Central University, the University of North Carolina at Charlotte, the University of North Carolina at Chapel Hill, the University of North Carolina at Pembroke, and Winston-Salem State University. This program is funded by NASA.

**Number awarded** Varies each year; recently, 10 of these fellowships were awarded.

**Deadline** March of each year.

## [1210]
## NORTH CAROLINA SPACE GRANT CONSORTIUM HIGHER EDUCATION COURSE DEVELOPMENT PROGRAM

North Carolina Space Grant Consortium
c/o North Carolina State University
Mechanical and Aerospace Engineering
1009 Capability Drive, Suite 210
Box 7515
Raleigh, NC 27695-7515
(919) 515-4240                    Fax: (919) 515-5934
E-mail: proposals@ncspacegrant.org
Web: www.ncspacegrant.org

**Summary** To provide funding to faculty members (particularly women, minorities, and persons with disabilities) at institutions affiliated with the North Carolina Space Grant Consortium (NCSGC) who are interested in developing a space-related course.

**Eligibility** This program is open to U.S. citizens qualified to serve as principal investigators at institutions affiliated with the NCSGC. Applicants must be interested in initiating interdisciplinary and/or distance learning courses that focus on equipping the future science, technology engineering, and mathematics (STEM) workforce to gain a better understanding of complex aerospace issues. They must describe 1) how the activity will benefit the local university, other universities, and NCSGC; 2) how the program will actively seek and recruit the involvement of women, underrepresented minorities, and persons with disabilities; and 3) how the program will be sustained after the completion of NCSGC funding. The NCSGC especially encourages the participation of principal investigators who are female, a member of an underrepresented minority group, or a person with a disability.

**Financial data** The maximum grant is $10,000. A 1:1 cost match with non-federal funds is required.

**Duration** Activities must be completed within 24 months.

**Additional information** The affiliated institutions are North Carolina State University, North Carolina A&T State University, Duke University, North Carolina Central University, the University of North Carolina at Charlotte, the University of North Carolina at Chapel Hill, the University of North Carolina at Pembroke, and Winston-Salem State University. This program is funded by NASA.

**Number awarded** 5 to 10 each year.

**Deadline** Letters of intent must be submitted by January of each year. Completed proposals are due in March.

## [1211]
## NORTH CAROLINA SPACE GRANT CONSORTIUM K-12 PROFESSIONAL DEVELOPMENT PROGRAM

North Carolina Space Grant Consortium
c/o North Carolina State University
Mechanical and Aerospace Engineering
1009 Capability Drive, Suite 210
Box 7515
Raleigh, NC 27695-7515
(919) 515-4240                    Fax: (919) 515-5934
E-mail: proposals@ncspacegrant.org
Web: www.ncspacegrant.org

**Summary** To provide funding to faculty members (particularly women, minorities, and persons with disabilities) at institutions affiliated with the North Carolina Space Grant Consortium (NCSGC) who are interested in developing a program for K-12 teachers and administrators.

**Eligibility** This program is open to U.S. citizens qualified to serve as principal investigators at institutions affiliated with the NCSGC. Applicants must be interested in initiating and carrying out professional development and training activities for K-12 teachers and administrators in the state. The proposed program should have the primary goal of better equipping North Carolina educators to inspire the future science, technology, engineering, and mathematics (STEM) workforce to pursue education and careers in aerospace-related fields. They must describe 1) how the activity will engage K-12 educators and/or administrators utilizing aerospace-related content, materials, or personnel; 2) how the program will actively seek and recruit the involvement of women, underrepresented minorities, and persons with disabilities; and 3) any NASA-sponsored or aerospace-related research, teaching, or outreach that is performed by the principal investigator. The NCSGC especially encourages the participation of principal investigators who are female, a member of an underrepresented minority group, or a person with a disability.

**Financial data** The maximum grant is $15,000. A 1:1 cost match with non-federal funds is required.

**Duration** Activities must be completed within 12 months.

**Additional information** The affiliated institutions are North Carolina State University, North Carolina A&T State University, Duke University, North Carolina Central University, the University of North Carolina at Charlotte, the University of North Carolina at Chapel Hill, the University of North Carolina at Pembroke, and Winston-Salem State University. This program is funded by NASA.

**Number awarded** 5 to 10 each year.

**Deadline** Letters of intent must be submitted by January of each year. Completed proposals are due in March.

## [1212]
## NORTH CAROLINA SPACE GRANT CONSORTIUM NEW INVESTIGATIONS PROGRAM GRANTS

North Carolina Space Grant Consortium
c/o North Carolina State University
Mechanical and Aerospace Engineering
1009 Capability Drive, Suite 210
Box 7515
Raleigh, NC 27695-7515
(919) 515-4240                        Fax: (919) 515-5934
E-mail: proposals@ncspacegrant.org
Web: www.ncspacegrant.org

**Summary**  To provide funding for space-related research to faculty members (particularly women, minorities, and persons with disabilities) at institutions affiliated with the North Carolina Space Grant Consortium (NCSGC).

**Eligibility**  This program is open to U.S. citizens and permanent residents qualified to serve as principal investigators at institutions affiliated with the NCSGC. Applicants must 1) have yet to become established researchers, or 2) be pursuing a significant change in research direction. They must be proposing to conduct research that is directly relevant to the priorities of the U.S. National Aeronautics and Space Administration (NASA). The NCSGC especially encourages the participation of principal investigators who are female, a member of an underrepresented minority group, or a person with a disability.

**Financial data**  The maximum grant is $25,000. A 1:1 cost match with non-federal funds is required.

**Duration**  Activities must be completed within 12 to 24 months.

**Additional information**  The affiliated institutions are North Carolina State University, North Carolina A&T State University, Duke University, North Carolina Central University, the University of North Carolina at Charlotte, the University of North Carolina at Chapel Hill, the University of North Carolina at Pembroke, and Winston-Salem State University. This program is funded by NASA.

**Number awarded**  10 to 15 each year.

**Deadline**  Letters of intent must be submitted by January of each year. Completed proposals are due in March.

## [1213]
## NORTH CAROLINA SPACE GRANT CONSORTIUM UNDERGRADUATE RESEARCH SCHOLARSHIPS

North Carolina Space Grant Consortium
c/o North Carolina State University
Mechanical and Aerospace Engineering
1009 Capability Drive, Suite 210
Box 7515
Raleigh, NC 27695-7515
(919) 515-4240                        Fax: (919) 515-5934
E-mail: scholarships@ncspacegrant.org
Web: www.ncspacegrant.org

**Summary**  To provide funding to undergraduate students (particularly women, minority, and disabled students) at institutions affiliated with the North Carolina Space Grant Consortium (NCSGC) who are interested in conducting space-related research.

**Eligibility**  This program is open to full-time undergraduate students at institutions affiliated with the NCSGC who are interested in working on a research project under the direct supervision of a faculty mentor. Applicants must be working on a degree in a science, technology, engineering, or mathematics (STEM) discipline of interest to the U.S. National Aeronautics and Space Administration (NASA). The research project must be space or aeronautics related or have a space or aeronautics application. Selection is based on the quality of the research proposal, the student's academic achievement, a letter of recommendation from the research mentor, and exhibited leadership qualities. U.S. citizenship is required. A primary goal of this program is the recruitment and retention of underrepresented minorities, women, and persons with disabilities into space-related fields.

**Financial data**  The maximum grant is $4,000 for a summer project on campus, $2,000 for an academic year project on campus, or $7,000 for a project at a NASA center or industrial contractor.

**Duration**  1 summer or 1 academic year.

**Additional information**  The affiliated institutions are North Carolina State University, North Carolina A&T State University, Duke University, North Carolina Central University, the University of North Carolina at Charlotte, the University of North Carolina at Chapel Hill, the University of North Carolina at Pembroke, and Winston-Salem State University. This program is funded by NASA.

**Number awarded**  Varies each year; recently, 8 of these scholarships were awarded.

**Deadline**  March of each year.

## [1214]
## NORTH DAKOTA SPACE GRANT PROGRAM FELLOWSHIPS

North Dakota Space Grant Program
c/o University of North Dakota
Department of Space Studies
Clifford Hall, Fifth Floor
P.O. Box 9008
Grand Forks, ND 58202-9008
(701) 777-4856                        Toll-free: (800) 828-4274
Fax: (701) 777-3711                   E-mail: bieri@space.edu
Web: www.space.edu/spacegrant/fellowships.html

**Summary**  To provide funding for space-related research to undergraduate and graduate students (particularly women, minority, and disabled students) at public and tribal academic institutions in North Dakota.

**Eligibility**  This program is open to undergraduate and graduate students at tribal or public 2-year and 4-year institutions of higher education in North Dakota who have a GPA of 3.0 or higher. U.S. citizenship is required. Applicants must be working on a degree in an area of science, technology, engineering, or mathematics (STEM) that is relevant to the interests of the U.S. National Aeronautics and Space Administration (NASA). They are required to conduct a science research project under the supervision of a faculty advisor. Acceptable majors include, but are not limited to, astronomy, atmospheric science, biology, chemistry, engineering, geology, mathematics, nursing, physics, and space studies. A goal of the program is to encourage members of underrepresented groups (women, minorities, and persons with disabilities) to enter STEM fields of study. Selection is based on academic excellence and relevance of the student's disciplines and interests to STEM.

**Financial data** The undergraduate stipend is $2,000 per semester. Graduate students receive a quarter-time appointment as a graduate research assistant (GRA); the GRA appointment must include a tuition waiver as a match.

**Duration** 1 semester; may be renewed for 1 additional semester.

**Additional information** This program is funded by NASA. Recipients are required to submit a 10- to 15-page paper on their research at the end of the semester.

**Number awarded** Varies each year.

**Deadline** September of each year for fall semester; November of each year for spring semester.

## [1215]
## OHIO SPACE GRANT CONSORTIUM SENIOR SCHOLARSHIP

Ohio Space Grant Consortium
c/o Ohio Aerospace Institute
22800 Cedar Point Road
Cleveland, OH 44142
(440) 962-3032          Toll-free: (800) 828-OSGC
Fax: (440) 962-3057          E-mail: osgc@oai.org
Web: www.osgc.org/Scholarship.html

**Summary** To provide funding to students (particularly women, minority, and disabled students) in their senior year at designated universities in Ohio who wish to conduct research while working on a baccalaureate degree in an aerospace-related field.

**Eligibility** This program is open to U.S. citizens who expect to complete the requirements for a bachelor's degree in an aerospace-related discipline (aeronautical engineering, aerospace engineering, astronomy, biology, chemical engineering, chemistry, civil engineering, computer engineering and science, control engineering, electrical engineering, engineering mechanics, geography, geology, industrial engineering, manufacturing engineering, materials science and engineering, mathematics, mechanical engineering, petroleum engineering, physics, and systems engineering) within 1 year. Applicants must be attending a member university of the Ohio Space Grant Consortium (OSGC) or another participating university. They must propose a research project to be conducted in a campus laboratory under the guidance of a faculty member. The project should involve collaboration with the faculty project advisor and/or with graduate students in the laboratory. Women, underrepresented minorities, and persons with disabilities are particularly encouraged to apply.

**Financial data** The grant is $3,000.

**Duration** 1 year.

**Additional information** These scholarships are funded through the National Space Grant College and Fellowship Program administered by the National Aeronautics and Space Administration (NASA), with matching funds provided by the member universities, the Ohio Aerospace Institute, and private industry. The OSGC member universities include the University of Akron, Case Western Reserve University, Central State University, University of Cincinnati, Cleveland State University, University of Dayton, Ohio State University, Ohio University, University of Toledo, Wilber-

force University, and Wright State University. Other participating universities are Cedarville University, Marietta College (petroleum engineering), Miami University (manufacturing engineering), Ohio Northern University (mechanical engineering), and Youngstown State University (mechanical and industrial engineering). Scholars are required to describe their research at an annual spring research symposium sponsored by the consortium.

**Number awarded** Varies each year; recently, 31 of these scholarships were awarded.

**Deadline** February of each year.

## [1216]
## OKUN-MODEL EARLY-CAREER FELLOWSHIP IN ECONOMIC STUDIES

Brookings Institution
Attn: Mellon Fellows Program
1775 Massachusetts Avenue, N.W.
Washington, DC 20036-2188
(202) 797-6104          Fax: (202) 797-6181
E-mail: erobinson@brookings.edu
Web: www.brookings.edu/admin/fellowships.htm

**Summary** To provide funding to economists (particularly women and minorities) who are interested in conducting an independent research project in residence at the Brookings Institution.

**Eligibility** This program is open to economists, especially junior faculty members who have between 2 and 6 years of teaching experience. Applicants should have a Ph.D. or equivalent and a commitment to conducting research on real-world issues in economics and public policy. They must submit a curriculum vitae, a 500-word research proposal, 2 letters of recommendation, and copies of up to 5 significant publications and working papers. The institution particularly encourages applications from women and members of minority groups.

**Financial data** Fellows receive a salary and partial support for staff and research assistance.

**Duration** 1 year.

**Additional information** Fellows participate in workshops and conferences at the institution. Fellows are expected to pursue their research at the Brookings Institution.

**Number awarded** 1 or more each year.

**Deadline** November of each year.

## [1217]
## ORA SCHNEIDER ART WRITER RESIDENCY GRANTS

Women's Studio Workshop
722 Binnewater Lane
P.O. Box 489
Rosendale, NY 12472
(845) 658-9133          Fax: (845) 658-9031
E-mail: info@wsworkshop.org
Web: www.wsworkshop.org

**Summary** To provide financial assistance and a residency at the Women's Studio Workshop (WSW) to women interested in writing an essay on an issue or topic related to contemporary art.

**Eligibility** This residency is open to women writers whose focus is on contemporary art. Applicants must be interested in a residency at WSW to engage in conversation and critical discussion with visual artists who are themselves working in extended residencies at WSW. They must submit a letter of interest, a resume or curriculum vitae, published and/or unpublished writing samples, and names and contact information for 2 references.

**Financial data** The program provides a stipend of $2,000, housing at WSW, and assistance with travel costs.

**Duration** Up to 3 full weeks in residence or a series of shorter visits to WSW.

**Additional information** This grant was first awarded in 2007. The recipient is expected to complete an essay of 1,500 to 2,500 words based on her experiences during the residency. WSW will publish the essay.

**Number awarded** 1 each year.

**Deadline** September of each year.

## [1218]
## OSAGE CHAPTER SCHOLARSHIP

Association for Women Geoscientists
Attn: AWG Foundation
P.O. Box 30645
Lincoln, NE 68503-0645
E-mail: awgscholarship@yahoo.com
Web: www.awg.org/eas/osage-scholarship.html

**Summary** To provide funding to women undergraduate students who are interested in conducting a research project in the geosciences.

**Eligibility** This program is open to undergraduate women conducting independent research in the geosciences (environmental science, hydrogeology, geography, geology, geophysics, geoscience museum studies, or paleontology/evolution). Applicants must submit a 1-page description of their research project, a budget outline, an original letter of support from their research supervisor, and a transcript.

**Financial data** The grant is $500.

**Duration** The project must be completed within 1 year.

**Additional information** This program is sponsored by the Osage chapter of the Association for Women Geoscientists. Information is also available from Jessica Finnearty, University of Kansas, Department of Geology, 1475 Jayhawk Boulevard, Room 120, Lawrence, KS 66045, E-mail: jfinne@ku.edu.

**Number awarded** 1 each year.

**Deadline** March of each year.

## [1219]
## PATSYLU MUSIC FUND

Open Meadows Foundation
Attn: Project Coordinator
P.O. Box 150-607
Van Brunt Station
Brooklyn, NY 11215-0607
(718) 885-0969        E-mail: openmeadows@igc.org
(718) 768-2249
Web: www.openmeadows.org

**Summary** To provide funding to women who are interested in carrying on a music project.

**Eligibility** This program is open to women who are composers, music educators, musicologists, or performers (or in performing groups). Lesbians and women of ethnic, cultural, and racial diversity are especially encouraged to apply. They must submit their request through a tax-exempt organization or institution. As part of their application, they must provide a 3-page narrative describing the project, covering such matters as why the project is needed; the main issue that it addresses; the racial/ethnic constituency that it will serve; the person primarily responsible for the project and its implementation; why it needs funding; why funding from Open Meadows will make a difference to the project; the age, national origin, and racial/ethnic background of the project organization; and how the organization's leadership reflects the constituency that it serves.

**Financial data** Grants range up to $2,000.

**Duration** 1 year.

**Number awarded** Varies each year; recently, 10 of these grants were awarded.

**Deadline** February of each year.

## [1220]
## PEDIATRIC RENAL RESEARCH AWARD

National Kidney Foundation of Massachusetts, Rhode Island, New Hampshire, and Vermont, Inc.
Attn: Medical Advisory Board
85 Astor Avenue, Suite 2
Norwood, MA 02062
(781) 278-0222        Toll-free: (800) 542-4001
Fax: (781) 278-0333    E-mail: sdean@kidneyhealth.org
Web: www.kidneyhealth.org

**Summary** To encourage research in the Northeast that will have significant impact on the understanding and treatment of pediatric kidney and urological diseases.

**Eligibility** This program is open to scientists located in Massachusetts, Rhode Island, New Hampshire, and Vermont who are interested in conducting research related to all areas of pediatric kidney and urological diseases, including developmental abnormalities of the kidney and focal sclerosis. Preference is given to research addressing the pathophysiology and treatment of nephrotic syndrome in children. Both clinical and basic research proposals are considered. Applicants should have a serious commitment to a career in research. They may not currently have a grant from NIH. There is no age limitation, and applications from women and members of underrepresented minority groups are encouraged.

**Financial data** The grant is $35,000.

**Duration** 1 year.

**Number awarded** 1 each year.

**Deadline** January of each year.

## [1221]
## PEMBROKE CENTER POSTDOCTORAL FELLOWSHIPS

Brown University
Attn: Pembroke Center for Teaching and Research on Women
Box 1958
Providence, RI 02912
(401) 863-2643                    Fax: (401) 863-1298
E-mail: Donna_Goodnow@brown.edu
Web: www.pembrokecenter.org/RP-Postdoctoral.asp

**Summary** To provide research support for scholars interested in conducting research at Brown University's Pembroke Center for Teaching and Research on Women on the cross-cultural study of gender.

**Eligibility** Fellowships are open to scholars in the humanities, social sciences, or life sciences who do not have a tenured position at an American college or university. Applicants must be willing to spend a year in residence at the Pembroke Center for Teaching and Research on Women and participate in a research project related to gender. The project focuses on a theme that changes annually (recently: "The Question of Identity in Psychoanalysis"). The center encourages minority and Third World scholars to apply.

**Financial data** The stipend is $35,000. Health insurance is also provided.

**Duration** 1 academic year.

**Additional information** Postdoctoral fellows in residence participate in weekly seminars and present at least 2 public papers during the year, as well as conduct an individual research project. Supplementary funds are available for assistance with travel expenses from abroad. This program includes the following named fellowships: the Nancy L. Buc Postdoctoral Fellowship, the Artemis A.W. and Martha Joukowsky Postdoctoral Fellowship, and the Carol G. Lederer Postdoctoral Fellowship.

**Number awarded** 3 or 4 each year.

**Deadline** December of each year.

## [1222]
## POSTDOCTORAL FELLOWSHIPS IN DIABETES RESEARCH

Juvenile Diabetes Research Foundation
Attn: Grant Administrator
120 Wall Street, 19th Floor
New York, NY 10005-4001
(212) 479-7572                    Toll-free: (800) 533-CURE
Fax: (212) 785-9595            E-mail: info@jdrf.org
Web: www.jdrf.org/index.cfm?page_id=103207

**Summary** To provide research training to scientists (particularly women, minorities, and persons with disabilities) who are beginning their professional careers and are interested in participating in research training on the causes, treatment, prevention, or cure of diabetes or its complications.

**Eligibility** This program is open to postdoctorates who are interested in a career in Type 1 diabetes-relevant research. Applicants must have received their first doctoral (M.D., Ph.D., D.M.D., or D.V.M.) degree within the past 5 years and may not have a faculty appointment. There are no citizenship requirements. Applications are encouraged from women, members of minority groups underrepresented in the sciences, and people with disabilities. The proposed research training may be conducted at foreign and domestic, for-profit and nonprofit, and public and private institutions, including universities, colleges, hospitals, laboratories, units of state and local government, and eligible agencies of the federal government. Applicants must be sponsored by an investigator who is affiliated full time with an accredited institution and who agrees to supervise the applicant's training. Selection is based on the applicant's previous experience and academic record; the caliber of the proposed research; and the quality of the mentor, training program, and environment.

**Financial data** Stipends range from $36,996 to $46,992 (depending upon years of experience). In any case, the award may not exceed the salary the recipient is currently earning. Fellows also receive a research allowance of $5,500 per year.

**Duration** 1 year; may be renewed for up to 1 additional year.

**Additional information** Fellows must devote at least 80% of their effort to the fellowship project.

**Deadline** January or July of each year.

## [1223]
## POSTDOCTORAL FELLOWSHIPS IN SOUTHEAST EUROPEAN STUDIES

American Council of Learned Societies
Attn: Office of Fellowships and Grants
633 Third Avenue, 8C
New York, NY 10017-6795
(212) 697-1505                    Fax: (212) 949-8058
E-mail: grants@acls.org
Web: www.acls.org/seguide.htm

**Summary** To provide funding to postdoctorates (particularly women and minorities) who are interested in conducting original research in the social sciences and humanities relating to southeastern Europe.

**Eligibility** Applicants must be U.S. citizens or permanent residents who hold a Ph.D. degree or equivalent as demonstrated by professional experience and publications. Priority is given to scholars in the early part of their careers, i.e. before tenure. They must be interested in conducting research in the social sciences or humanities relating to Albania, Bosnia and Herzegovina, Bulgaria, Croatia, Former Yugoslav Republic of Macedonia, Kosovo, Montenegro, Romania, or Serbia. Comparative work considering more than 1 country of southeastern Europe or relating southeastern European societies to those of other parts of the world are also supported. Proposals may be for 1) research fellowships, for scholars with area expertise in southeastern Europe interested in research and writing; or 2) developmental fellowships, for scholars with primary area expertise in a region of the world outside southeastern Europe to acquire expertise in southeastern Europe, including language skills, in order to add a southeastern Europe comparative perspective to their current or proposed research. Selection is based on the scholarly merit of the proposal, its importance to the development of eastern European studies, and the scholarly potential and accomplishments of the applicant. Applications are particularly invited from women and members of minority groups.

**Financial data** Up to $25,000 is provided as a stipend. Funds are intended primarily as salary replacement, but they may be used to supplement sabbatical salaries or awards from other sources.

**Duration** 6 to 12 consecutive months.

**Additional information** This program is sponsored jointly by the American Council of Learned Societies, (ACLS) and the Social Science Research Council, funded by the U.S. Department of State under the Research and Training for Eastern Europe and the Independent States of the Former Soviet Union Act of 1983 (Title VIII) but administered by ACLS.

**Number awarded** Varies each year; recently, 3 of these fellowships were awarded.

**Deadline** November of each year.

## [1224]
## POSTDOCTORAL RESEARCH FELLOWSHIPS IN EPILEPSY

Epilepsy Foundation
Attn: Research Department
8301 Professional Place
Landover, MD 20785-2237
(301) 459-3700          Toll-free: (800) EFA-1000
Fax: (301) 577-2684      TDD: (800) 332-2070
E-mail: grants@efa.org
Web: www.epilepsyfoundation.org

**Summary** To provide funding for a program of postdoctoral training to academic physicians and scientists (particularly women, minorities, and persons with disabilities) committed to epilepsy research.

**Eligibility** Applicants must have a doctoral degree (M.D., Ph.D., or equivalent) and be a resident or postdoctoral fellow at a university, medical school, research institution, or medical center. They must be interested in participating in a training experience and research project that has potential significance for understanding the causes, treatment, or consequences of epilepsy. The program is geared toward applicants who will be trained in research in epilepsy rather than those who will use epilepsy as a tool for research in other fields. Equal consideration is given to applicants interested in acquiring experience either in basic laboratory research or in the conduct of human clinical studies. Academic faculty holding the rank of instructor or higher are not eligible, nor are graduate or medical students, medical residents, permanent government employees, or employees of private industry. Applications from women, members of minority groups, and people with disabilities are especially encouraged. Selection is based on scientific quality of the proposed research, a statement regarding its relevance to epilepsy, the applicant's qualifications, the preceptor's qualifications, and the adequacy of facility and related epilepsy programs at the institution.

**Financial data** The grant is $40,000. No indirect costs are provided.

**Duration** 1 year.

**Additional information** Support for this program is provided by many individuals, families, and corporations, especially the American Epilepsy Society, Abbott Laboratories, Ortho-McNeil Pharmaceutical, and Pfizer Inc. The fellowship must be carried out at a facility in the United States where there is an ongoing epilepsy research program.

**Number awarded** Varies each year; recently, 13 of these fellowships were awarded.

**Deadline** August of each year.

## [1225]
## POSTDOCTORAL RESEARCH LEAVE FELLOWSHIPS

American Association of University Women
Attn: AAUW Educational Foundation
301 ACT Drive, Department 60
P.O. Box 4030
Iowa City, IA 52243-4030
(319) 337-1716          Fax: (319) 337-1204
E-mail: aauw@act.org
Web: www.aauw.org

**Summary** To enable American women scholars who have achieved distinction or promise of distinction in their fields of scholarly work to engage in additional research.

**Eligibility** This program is open to women who have a research doctorate (e.g., Ph.D., Ed.D., D.B.A., D.M.) or an M.F.A. degree as of the application deadline. Applicants must be interested in conducting independent research; preference is given to projects that are not simply a revision of a doctoral dissertation. Fields of study include the arts and humanities, social sciences, and natural sciences. Selection is based on scholarly excellence, quality of project design, originality of project, scholarly significance of project to discipline, feasibility of project and proposed schedule, qualifications of applicant, potential of applicant to make a significant contribution to field, applicant's commitment to women's issues in profession and community, applicant's teaching experience, and applicant's mentoring of other women. U.S. citizenship or permanent resident status is required. At least 1 fellowship is designated for a woman from an underrepresented group.

**Financial data** The stipend is $30,000. Funding is not provided for laboratory supplies and equipment, research assistants, publication costs, travel to professional meetings or seminars, tuition for additional course work, repayment of loans or other personal obligations, or tuition for a dependent's education.

**Duration** 1 year, beginning in July.

**Additional information** The filing fee is $45.

**Number awarded** Varies each year; recently, 19 of these fellowships were awarded.

**Deadline** November of each year.

## [1226]
## PREDOCTORAL RESEARCH TRAINING FELLOWSHIPS IN EPILEPSY

Epilepsy Foundation
Attn: Research Department
8301 Professional Place
Landover, MD 20785-2237
(301) 459-3700          Toll-free: (800) EFA-1000
Fax: (301) 577-2684      TDD: (800) 332-2070
E-mail: grants@efa.org
Web: www.epilepsyfoundation.org

**Summary** To provide funding to doctoral candidates (particularly women, minorities, and persons with disabilities) in designated fields for dissertation research on a topic related to epilepsy.

**Eligibility** This program is open to full-time graduate students working on a Ph.D. in biochemistry, genetics, neuroscience, nursing, pharmacology, pharmacy, physiology, or psychology. Applicants must be conducting dissertation research on a topic relevant to epilepsy under the guidance of a mentor with expertise in the area of epilepsy investigation. Applications from women, members of minority groups, and people with disabilities are especially encouraged. Selection is based on the relevance of the proposed work to epilepsy, the applicant's qualifications, the mentor's qualifications, the scientific quality of the proposed dissertation research, the quality of the training environment for research related to epilepsy, and the adequacy of the facility.

**Financial data** The grant is $20,000, consisting of $19,000 for a stipend and $1,000 to support travel to attend the annual meeting of the American Epilepsy Society.

**Duration** 1 year.

**Additional information** Support for this program, which began in 1998, is provided by many individuals, families, and corporations, especially the American Epilepsy Society, Abbott Laboratories, Ortho-McNeil Pharmaceutical, and Pfizer Inc.

**Number awarded** Varies each year; recently, 8 of these fellowships were awarded.

**Deadline** August of each year.

## [1227]
## PRESIDENTIAL EARLY CAREER AWARDS FOR SCIENTISTS AND ENGINEERS

National Science and Technology Council
Executive Office of the President
Attn: Office of Science and Technology Policy
725 17th Street, Room 5228
Washington, DC 20502
(202) 456-0721                    Fax: (202) 456-6021
E-mail: twackler@ostp.eop.gov
Web: www.ostp.gov

**Summary** To recognize and reward the nation's most outstanding young science and engineering faculty members (particularly women, minorities, and persons with disabilities) by providing them with additional research funding.

**Eligibility** Eligible for these awards are U.S. citizens, nationals, and permanent residents who have been selected to receive research grants from other departments of the U.S. government. Recipients of designated research grant programs are automatically considered for these Presidential Early Career Awards for Scientists and Engineers (PECASE). Most of the participating programs encourage applications from racial/ethnic minority individuals, women, and persons with disabilities.

**Financial data** Awards carry a grant of at least $80,000 per year.

**Duration** 5 years.

**Additional information** The departments with research programs that nominate candidates for the PECASE program are: 1) the National Aeronautics and Space Administration, which selects recipients of Early Career Awards based on exceptionally meritorious proposals funded through the traditional research grant process or the unsolicited proposal process; 2) the Department of Veterans Affairs, which nominates the most meritorious recipients of Veterans Health Administration Research Awards in the categories in medical research, rehabilitation research, and health services research; 3) the National Institutes of Health, which nominates the most meritorious investigators funded through its First Independent Research Support and Transition (FIRST) Awards and NIH Individual Research Project Grants (R01) programs; 4) the Department of Energy, which nominates staff members of the national laboratories and the most meritorious recipients of the DOE–Energy Research Young Scientist Awards and DOE–Defense Programs Early Career Scientist and Engineer Awards; 5) the Department of Defense, which nominates outstanding recipients of the Office of Naval Research Young Investigator Program, the Air Force Office of Scientific Research Broad Agency Program, and the Army Research Office Young Investigator Program; 6) the Department of Agriculture, which nominates staff scientists from the Agricultural Research Service, the most meritorious investigators funded through the National Research Initiative Competitive Grants Program (NRICGP) New Investigator Awards, and staff scientists of the Forest Service; 7) the Department of Commerce, which nominates outstanding staff members of the National Oceanic and Atmospheric Administration and the National Institute of Standards and Technology; 8) the Department of Transportation, which nominates the most qualified and innovative researchers in its University Transportation Centers and University Research Institutes programs; and 9) the National Science Foundation, which selects its nominees from the most meritorious investigators funded through the Faculty Early Career Development (CAREER) Program. For a list of the names, addresses, and telephone numbers of contact persons at each of the participating agencies, write to the Office of Science and Technology Policy.

**Number awarded** Varies each year; recently, 56 of these awards were granted.

## [1228]
## R. ROBERT & SALLY D. FUNDERBURG RESEARCH SCHOLAR AWARD IN GASTRIC BIOLOGY RELATED TO CANCER

Foundation for Digestive Health and Nutrition
Attn: Research Awards Program
4930 Del Ray Avenue
Bethesda, MD 20814-2512
(301) 222-4012                    Fax: (301) 652-3890
E-mail: info@fdhn.org
Web: www.fdhn.org/html/awards/elect_app.html

**Summary** To provide funding to established investigators (particularly women and minorities) who are working on research that enhances fundamental understanding of gastric cancer pathobiology.

**Eligibility** This program is open to faculty at accredited North American institutions who have established themselves as independent investigators in the field of gastric biology, pursuing novel approaches to gastric mucosal cell biology, regeneration and regulation of cell growth, inflammation as precancerous lesions, genetics of gastric carcinoma, oncogenes in gastric epithelial malignancies, epidemiology of gastric cancer, etiology of gastric epithelial malignancies, or clinical research in diagnosis or treatment of gastric carcinoma. Applicants must be individual members of the American Gastroenterological Association (AGA). Women and minority investigators are strongly encouraged to apply. Selection is based on the novelty, feasibility, and significance of the proposal; attributes of the candidate; and the likelihood that support will lead to a research career in the field of gastric biology. Preference is given to novel approaches, especially for initiation of projects by young investigators or established investigators new to the field.

**Financial data** The award is $25,000 per year. Funds are to be used for the salary of the investigator. Indirect costs are not allowed.

**Duration** 2 years.

**Additional information** This program is administered by the Foundation for Digestive Health and Nutrition (FDHN) and sponsored by the AGA.

**Number awarded** 1 each year.

**Deadline** September of each year.

## [1229]
## RESEARCH AND TRAINING FELLOWSHIPS IN EPILEPSY FOR CLINICIANS

Epilepsy Foundation
Attn: Research Department
8301 Professional Place
Landover, MD 20785-2237
(301) 459-3700          Toll-free: (800) EFA-1000
Fax: (301) 577-2684      TDD: (800) 332-2070
E-mail: clinical_postdocs@efa.org
Web: www.epilepsyfoundation.org

**Summary** To provide funding to clinically trained professionals (particularly women, minorities, and persons with disabilities) interested in gaining additional training in order to develop an epilepsy research program.

**Eligibility** Applicants must have an M.D., D.O., Ph.D., D.S., or equivalent degree and be a clinical or postdoctoral fellow at a university, medical school, or other appropriate research institution. Holders of other doctoral-level degrees (e.g., Pharm.D., D.S.N.) may also be eligible. Candidates must be interested in a program of research training that may include mechanisms of epilepsy, novel therapeutic approaches, clinical trials, development of new technologies, or behavioral and psychosocial impact of epilepsy. The training program may consist of both didactic training and a supervised research experience that is designed to develop the necessary knowledge and skills in the chosen area of research and foster the career goals of the candidate. Academic faculty holding the rank of instructor or higher are not eligible, nor are graduate or medical students, medical residents, permanent government employees, or employees of private industry. Applications from women, members of minority groups, and people with disabilities are especially encouraged. Selection is based on the quality of the proposed research training program, the applicant's qualifications, the preceptor's qualifications, and the adequacy of clinical training, research facilities, and other epilepsy-related programs at the institution.

**Financial data** The grant is $50,000 per year. No indirect costs are provided.

**Duration** Up to 2 years.

**Additional information** Support for this program is provided by many individuals, families, and corporations, especially the American Epilepsy Society, Abbott Laboratories, Ortho-McNeil Pharmaceutical, and Pfizer Inc. Grantees are expected to dedicate at least 50% of their time to research training and conducting research.

**Number awarded** Varies each year; recently, 5 of these fellowships were awarded.

**Deadline** October of each year.

## [1230]
## RESEARCH ON GENDER IN SCIENCE AND ENGINEERING EXTENSION SERVICES GRANTS

National Science Foundation
Directorate for Education and Human Resources
Attn: Division of Human Resource Development
4201 Wilson Boulevard, Room 815
Arlington, VA 22230
(703) 292-7303          Fax: (703) 292-9018
TDD: (800) 281-8749      E-mail: jjesse@nsf.gov
Web: www.nsf.gov

**Summary** To provide funding to professionals interested in providing consulting services to educators and institutions, to enable them to adopt policies and programs related to the underrepresentation of girls and women in science, technology, engineering, and mathematics (STEM) education.

**Eligibility** This program is open to anyone with professional skills that will enable them to 1) provide consulting services within a certain geographic region or within a community of practice, explaining in simple language the practical meaning and benefits of adopting programs, tools, or approaches that enhance the interest and persistence of female students in STEM studies through the undergraduate level, in those fields where they are underrepresented; 2) show educators how to adapt exemplary projects, research-based learning tools, pedagogical approaches, and service or support programs; 3) communicate back to researchers the problems that practicing educators find most urgent or troublesome in adopting the new methods or tools; 4) integrate various findings about gender in science and engineering into a unified program of change and facilitate the interpretation of research knowledge into practice. The target community may be a mix of teachers, counselors, parents, community leaders, administrators, faculty, and others.

**Financial data** Grants up to $500,000 per year are available.

**Duration** Up to 5 years.

**Additional information** The National Science Foundation (NSF) established this program in 1993 under the name "Program for Women and Girls." That was replaced with the "Program for Gender Equity in Science, Mathematics, Engineering and Technology," and then in the 2003 fiscal year by "Gender Diversity in STEM Education." The current title became effective in the 2007 fiscal year.

**Number awarded** 2 to 3 each year. The Research on Gender in Science and Engineering program plans to award 22 to 27 grants per year for research, outreach and communication, and extension service activities. A total of $5,000,000 is available for the program annually.

**Deadline** Required preliminary proposals must be submitted in January of each year; full proposals are due by the end of March

## [1231]
## RESEARCH ON GENDER IN SCIENCE AND ENGINEERING OUTREACH AND COMMUNICATION GRANTS

National Science Foundation
Directorate for Education and Human Resources
Attn: Division of Human Resource Development
4201 Wilson Boulevard, Room 815
Arlington, VA 22230
(703) 292-7303          Fax: (703) 292-9018
TDD: (800) 281-8749     E-mail: jjesse@nsf.gov
Web: www.nsf.gov

**Summary** To provide funding to scholars interested in conducting activities to make known education program evaluation results and research findings related to the underrepresentation of girls and women in science, technology, engineering, and mathematics (STEM) education.

**Eligibility** This program is open to scholars interested in conducting activities designed to 1) extend to significant audiences awareness and information about research-based and demonstrated strategies and practices to increase the participation of girls and women in STEM education and workforce, in order to inform educational practice; and 2) catalyze new thinking and future action about educational institutions by convening conferences, workshops, or symposia that are not possible at regular meetings of professional societies. Activities should be directed to significant national audiences, especially to the broader education community.

**Financial data** Grants up to a total of $200,000 are available.

**Duration** Up to 2 years.

**Additional information** The National Science Foundation (NSF) established this program in 1993 under the name "Program for Women and Girls." That was replaced with the "Program for Gender Equity in Science, Mathematics, Engineering and Technology," and then in the 2003 fiscal year by "Gender Diversity in STEM Education." The current title became effective in the 2007 fiscal year.

**Number awarded** 10 to 12 each year. The Research on Gender in Science and Engineering program plans to award 22 to 27 grants per year for research, outreach and communication, and extension service activities. A total of $5,000,000 is available for the program annually.

**Deadline** Required preliminary proposals must be submitted in January of each year; full proposals are due by the end of March

## [1232]
## RESEARCH ON GENDER IN SCIENCE AND ENGINEERING RESEARCH GRANTS

National Science Foundation
Directorate for Education and Human Resources
Attn: Division of Human Resource Development
4201 Wilson Boulevard, Room 815
Arlington, VA 22230
(703) 292-7303          Fax: (703) 292-9018
TDD: (800) 281-8749     E-mail: jjesse@nsf.gov
Web: www.nsf.gov

**Summary** To provide funding to investigators interested in conducting research related to the underrepresentation of girls and women in science, technology, engineering, and mathematics (STEM) education.

**Eligibility** This program is open to investigators interested in conducting research designed to 1) discover and describe gender-based differences and preferences in learning science and mathematics in K-16 and factors that affect interest, performance, and choice of STEM study and careers in fields where there are significant gender gaps; 2) discover and describe how experiences and interactions in informal and formal educational settings inhibit or encourage interest and performance of students based on gender; 3) increase the knowledge about organizational models that lead to more equitable and inviting STEM educational environments in K-16; or 4) increase knowledge of the process of institutional change required to achieve more equitable and inviting STEM educational environments in K-16. Behavioral, cognitive, affective, and social differences may be investigated, using methods of sociology, psychology, anthropology, economics, or statistics disciplines.

**Financial data** Grants up to a total of $500,000 are available.

**Duration** Up to 3 years.

**Additional information** The National Science Foundation (NSF) established this program in 1993 under the name "Program for Women and Girls." That was replaced with the "Program for Gender Equity in Science, Mathematics, Engineering and Technology," and then in the 2003 fiscal year by "Gender Diversity in STEM Education." The current title became effective in the 2007 fiscal year.

**Number awarded** 10 to 12 each year. The Research on Gender in Science and Engineering program plans to award 22 to 27 grants per year for research, outreach and communication, and extension service activities. A total of $5,000,000 is available for the program annually.

**Deadline** Required preliminary proposals must be submitted in January of each year; full proposals are due by the end of March

## [1233]
## RESEARCH PROGRAM AT EARTHWATCH

Earthwatch Institute
Attn: Director of Research
3 Clock Tower Place, Suite 100
P.O. Box 75
Maynard, MA 01754-0075
(978) 461-0081             Toll-free: (800) 776-0188
Fax: (978) 461-2332
E-mail: research@earthwatch.org
Web: www.earthwatch.org

**Summary** To support field research anywhere in the world by scientists (particularly women) who are working to investigate and/or preserve our physical, biological, and cultural heritage.

**Eligibility** This program is open to doctoral and postdoctoral researchers and researchers with equivalent scholarship or life experience. Applicants must be interested in conducting field research worldwide in the biological, physical, social, and cultural sciences. They may be of any nationality, covering any geographic region, as long as the research design integrates non-specialist volunteers into the field research agenda. Applicants intending to conduct research in foreign countries are strongly encouraged to include host-country nationals in their research staffs. Early career scientists, women in science, and developing country nationals are especially encouraged to apply.

**Financial data** Grants are awarded on a per capita basis, determined by multiplying the per capita grant by the number of volunteers on the project. Per capita grants average $850; total project grants range from $17,000 to $51,000. Grants cover all expenses for food, accommodations, and in-field transportation for the research team (principal investigator, research staff, and volunteers); principal investigator travel to and from the field; leased or rented field equipment; insurance; support of staff and visiting scientists; and support for associates from the host country. Funds are not normally provided for capital equipment, principal investigator salaries, university overhead or indirect costs, or preparation of results for publication. Volunteers donate time, services, and skills to the research endeavor in the field and pay their own travel expenses to and from the research site.

**Duration** 1 year; may be renewed. Projects typically involve from 30 to 60 total volunteers, with 5 to 12 volunteers each on 4 to 5 sequential teams. Each team normally spends 8 to 15 days in the field.

**Additional information** Earthwatch was established in 1971 to support the efforts of scholars to preserve the world's endangered habitats and species, to explore the vast heritage of its peoples, and to promote world health and international cooperation. Its research program was formerly known as the Center for Field Research. Earthwatch also recruits and screens volunteers; in the past, 20% of these have been students, 20% educators, and 60% nonacademic professionals.

**Number awarded** Varies each year. Recently, 134 of these grants were awarded, including 35 in marine science, 34 in zoology, 4 in plant science, 22 in conservation biology, 3 in earth science, 4 in paleontology, 1 in planetary and atmospheric science, 19 in archaeology, 4 in climate change, 4 in cultural anthropology, 2 in architecture, 1 in public health, and 1 in sustainable development.

**Deadline** January of each year for projects with field seasons starting from July through September; April of each year for projects with field seasons starting from October through December; October of each year for projects with field seasons starting from April through June.

## [1234]
## RESEARCH SCHOLAR AWARD IN PANCREATITIS

Foundation for Digestive Health and Nutrition
Attn: Research Awards Program
4930 Del Ray Avenue
Bethesda, MD 20814-2512
(301) 222-4012             Fax: (301) 652-3890
E-mail: info@fdhn.org
Web: www.fdhn.org/html/awards/elect_app.html

**Summary** To provide funding to young gastroenterology investigators (especially women and minorities) who are interested in preparing for a career in academic research related to understanding, improving treatments, or curing pancreatitis.

**Eligibility** This program is open to members of the American Gastroenterological Association (AGA) who have an M.D., Ph.D., or equivalent degree. Applicants must hold full-time faculty positions at North American universities or professional institutes at the time the award begins. They should be early in their careers (fellows and established investigators are not appropriate candidates). Candidates with an M.D. degree must have completed clinical training within the past 5 years and those with a Ph.D. must have received their degree within the past 5 years. The proposed research must related to pancreatitis. Selection is based on novelty, feasibility and significance of the proposal; attributes of the candidate, including potential for independence; evidence of institutional commitment; and the research environment. Special consideration is given to applicants with a focus in nutrition or geriatrics. Women, minorities, and physician/scientists are encouraged to apply.

**Financial data** The grant is $75,000 per year. Funds are to be used for project costs, including salary, supplies, and equipment but excluding travel. Indirect costs are not allowed.

**Duration** 3 years.

**Additional information** This program is administered by the Foundation for Digestive Health and Nutrition (FDHN) with support from the AGA. Recipients must devote at least 70% of their efforts to research related to pancreatitis. They cannot hold or have held an R01, R29, K121, K08, VA Research Award, or any award with similar objectives from nonfederal sources.

**Number awarded** 1 each year.

**Deadline** September of each year.

## [1235]
## RHODE ISLAND SPACE GRANT GRADUATE FELLOWSHIP PROGRAM

Rhode Island Space Grant
c/o Brown University
Lincoln Field Building
Box 1846
Providence, RI 02912-1846
(401) 863-2889                          Fax: (401) 863-1292
E-mail: RISpaceGrant@brown.edu
Web: www.planetary.brown.edu/RI_Space_Grant

**Summary**  To provide financial assistance to graduate students (particularly women, minority, and disabled students) at institutions that are members of the Rhode Island Space Grant Consortium (RISGC) who wish to pursue studies and space-related research in science, mathematics, or engineering.

**Eligibility**  This program is open to graduate students at RISGC-member universities. Applicants must be studying in science, mathematics, or engineering fields of interest to the National Aeronautics and Space Administration (NASA). U.S. citizenship is required. The sponsor is a component of NASA's Space Grant program, which encourages participation by women, underrepresented minorities, and persons with disabilities.

**Financial data**  The stipend is $19,500 per year, plus payment of tuition and the health services fee.

**Duration**  1 year.

**Additional information**  Members of the RISGC are Bryant College, Community College of Rhode Island, Providence College, Roger Williams University, Rhode Island College, Rhode Island School of Design, Salve Regina University, University of Rhode Island, and Wheaton College. This program is funded by NASA. Fellows are required to devote 75% of their time to their studies and research and 25% of their time to science education outreach activities organized and coordinated by Rhode Island Space Grant.

**Number awarded**  Varies each year; recently, 3 of these fellowships were awarded.

**Deadline**  February of each year.

## [1236]
## RHODE ISLAND SPACE GRANT UNDERGRADUATE SUMMER SCHOLAR PROGRAM

Rhode Island Space Grant
c/o Brown University
Lincoln Field Building
Box 1846
Providence, RI 02912-1846
(401) 863-2889                          Fax: (401) 863-1292
E-mail: RISpaceGrant@brown.edu
Web: www.planetary.brown.edu/RI_Space_Grant

**Summary**  To provide funding for summer research activities to undergraduate students (particularly women, minority, and disabled students) at institutions that are members of the Rhode Island Space Grant Consortium (RISGC) who are interested in a career in a space-related field of science, mathematics, or engineering.

**Eligibility**  This program is open to undergraduate students at RISGC-member universities. Applicants must be

studying in science, mathematics, or engineering fields of interest to the National Aeronautics and Space Administration (NASA). They must be interested in participating in a research project during the summer with an advisor in their own department. U.S. citizenship is required. The sponsor is a component of NASA's Space Grant program, which encourages participation by women, underrepresented minorities, and persons with disabilities.

**Financial data**  The stipend is $4,000.

**Duration**  1 summer.

**Additional information**  Members of the RISGC are Bryant College, Community College of Rhode Island, Providence College, Roger Williams University, Rhode Island College, Rhode Island School of Design, Salve Regina University, University of Rhode Island, and Wheaton College. This program is funded by NASA. Scholars are required to devote 75% of their time to their research and 25% of their time to science education outreach activities organized and coordinated by Rhode Island Space Grant.

**Number awarded**  Varies each year; recently, 3 of these scholarships were awarded.

**Deadline**  February of each year.

## [1237]
## RITA MAE KELLY ENDOWMENT FELLOWSHIP

American Political Science Association
Attn: Centennial Center Visiting Scholars Program
1527 New Hampshire Avenue, N.W.
Washington, DC 20036-1206
(202) 483-2512                          Fax: (202) 483-2657
E-mail: center@apsanet.org
Web: www.apsanet.org/content_14801.cfm

**Summary**  To provide funding to members of the American Political Science Association (APSA) who are interested in conducting research on the intersection of gender, race, ethnicity, and political power at the Centennial Center for Political Science and Public Affairs.

**Eligibility**  This program is open to members of the association who are interested in conducting research on the intersection of gender, race, ethnicity, and political power while in residence at the center. Support is available to pre-dissertation graduate students as well as for an award or public presentation. Nonresident scholars may also be eligible.

**Financial data**  Grants provide supplemental financial support to resident scholars.

**Duration**  2 weeks to 12 months.

**Additional information**  The APSA launched its Centennial Center for Political Science and Public Affairs in 2003 to commemorate the centennial year of the association. This program was established in affiliation with the Women's Caucus for Political Science, the Latina Caucus for Political Science, the Committee for the Status of Latino/Latinas in the Profession, the Women and Politics Research Organized Section, and the Race, Ethnicity and Politics Organized Section.

**Number awarded**  1 or more each year.

**Deadline**  February of each year.

## [1238]
## ROCKY MOUNTAIN NASA SPACE GRANT CONSORTIUM GRADUATE RESEARCH FELLOWSHIPS

Rocky Mountain NASA Space Grant Consortium
c/o Utah State University
EL Building, Room 302
Logan, UT 84322-4140
(435) 797-3666                     Fax: (435) 797-3382
E-mail: spacegrant@cc.usu.edu
Web: spacegrant.usu.edu

**Summary**  To provide financial support for research and study to graduate students (particularly women, minority, and disabled students) at designated universities in Utah or Colorado who are working on a degree in fields of interest to the National Aeronautics and Space Administration (NASA).

**Eligibility**  This program is open to graduate students at member institutions of the Rocky Mountain NASA Space Grant Consortium who are studying engineering, science, medicine, or technology. U.S. citizenship is required. Selection is based on academic performance to date and potential for the future, with emphasis on space-related research interests. This program is part of the NASA Space Grant program, which encourages participation by women, underrepresented minorities, and persons with disabilities.

**Financial data**  Stipends range from $500 to $1,200.

**Duration**  1 year.

**Additional information**  Members of the consortium are Utah State University, the University of Utah, Brigham Young University, Dixie State College, Salt Lake Community College, Shoshone-Bannock School, Snow College, Southern Utah University, the University of Denver, and Weber State University. This program is funded by NASA.

**Number awarded**  Varies each year; recently, 23 of these fellowships, worth $20,000, were awarded.

**Deadline**  June of each year.

## [1239]
## RUTH AND LINCOLN EKSTROM FELLOWSHIP

Brown University
Attn: John Carter Brown Library
P.O. Box 1894
Providence, RI 02912
(401) 863-2725                     Fax: (401) 863-3477
E-mail: JCBL_Fellowships@Brown.edu
Web: www.brown.edu

**Summary**  To support scholars and graduate students interested in conducting research on the history of women at the John Carter Brown Library, which is renowned for its collection of historical sources pertaining to the Americas prior to 1830.

**Eligibility**  This fellowship is open to U.S. and foreign graduate students, scholars, and independent researchers. Graduate students must have passed their preliminary or general examinations. Applicants must be proposing to conduct research on the history of women and the family in the Americas prior to 1825, including the question of cultural influences on gender formation. Selection is based on the applicant's scholarly qualifications, the merits and significance of the project, and the particular need that the

holdings of the John Carter Brown Library will fill in the development of the project.

**Financial data**  The stipend is $1,800 per month.

**Duration**  From 2 to 4 months.

**Additional information**  Fellows are expected to be in regular residence at the library and to participate in the intellectual life of Brown University for the duration of the program.

**Number awarded**  1 or more each year.

**Deadline**  January of each year.

## [1240]
## RUTH I. MICHLER MEMORIAL PRIZE

Association for Women in Mathematics
11240 Waples Mill Road, Suite 200
Fairfax, VA 22030
(703) 934-0163                     Fax: (703) 359-7562
E-mail: awm@math.umd.edu
Web: www.awm-math.org/michlerprize.html

**Summary**  To recognize and reward, with a fellowship at Cornell University, outstanding women mathematicians.

**Eligibility**  This prize is available to women recently promoted to associate professor or equivalent position in the mathematical sciences at an institution of higher learning other than Cornell University. Applicants may be of any nationality and hold a position in any country. They must submit a proposal describing a research or book project to be undertaken during the fellowship period and explaining how the semester in the mathematics department at Cornell University will enhance their project or research career. Selection is based on the excellence of the applicant's research and the potential benefit to her of a semester in the mathematics department at Cornell.

**Financial data**  The prize is $40,000.

**Duration**  The prize is presented annually. The recipient may spend a semester of her choice in residence at Cornell.

**Additional information**  This prize was first presented in 2007.

**Number awarded**  1 each year.

**Deadline**  October of each year.

## [1241]
## RUTH R. AND ALYSON R. MILLER FELLOWSHIPS

Massachusetts Historical Society
Attn: Short-Term Fellowships
1154 Boylston Street
Boston, MA 02215-3695
(617) 646-0513                     Fax: (617) 859-0074
E-mail: fellowships@masshist.org
Web: www.masshist.org/fellowships/short_term.cfm

**Summary**  To fund research visits to the Massachusetts Historical Society for graduate students and other scholars interested in women's history.

**Eligibility**  This program is open to advanced graduate students, postdoctorates, and independent scholars who are conducting research in women's history and need to use the resources of the Massachusetts Historical Society. Applicants must submit a curriculum vitae and a proposal describing the project and indicating collections at the society to be consulted. Graduate students must also arrange for a letter of recommendation from a faculty member familiar with their work and with the project being proposed. Preference is given to candidates who live 50 or more miles from Boston.

**Financial data** The grant is $2,000.

**Duration** 4 weeks.

**Additional information** This fellowship was first awarded in 1998.

**Number awarded** 1 or more each year.

**Deadline** February of each year.

## [1242]
## RUTH SATTER MEMORIAL AWARD

Association for Women in Science
Attn: AWIS Educational Foundation
1200 New York Avenue, N.W., Suite 650
Washington, DC 20005
(202) 326-8940      Toll-free: (866) 657-AWIS
Fax: (202) 326-8960      E-mail: awisedfd@awis.org
Web: www.awis.org/careers/edfoundation.html

**Summary** To provide financial assistance to reentry women interested in working on a doctoral degree in engineering or the sciences.

**Eligibility** Female students enrolled in any life science, physical science, social science, or engineering program leading to a Ph.D. degree are eligible to apply if they have had to interrupt their education for 3 or more years to raise a family. They may apply at any time in their Ph.D. program, including the first year. Foreign students are eligible if they are enrolled in a U.S. institution of higher education. Selection is based on academic achievement, the importance of the research question addressed, the quality of the research, and the applicant's potential for future contributions to science or engineering.

**Financial data** The stipend is $1,000. Funds may be used for tuition, books, housing, research, travel and meeting registration, or publication costs.

**Duration** 1 year.

**Additional information** Information is also available from Barbara Filner, President, AWIS Educational Foundation, 7008 Richard Drive, Bethesda, MD 20817-4838.

**Number awarded** 1 each year.

**Deadline** January of each year.

## [1243]
## SANOFI-AVENTIS WOMEN PHYSICIAN IN ALLERGY JUNIOR FACULTY DEVELOPMENT AWARD

American Academy of Allergy, Asthma & Immunology
555 East Wells Street, Suite 1100
Milwaukee, WI 53202-3823
(414) 272-6071      Fax: (414) 272-6070
E-mail: info@aaaai.org
Web: www.aaaai.org

**Summary** To provide funding to women members of the American Academy of Allergy, Asthma & Immunology (AAAAI) interested in conducting basic and/or clinical research.

**Eligibility** Applicants must be women AAAAI members (or applicants for membership) who are full-time faculty members with an appointment for less than 5 years at the instructor or assistant professor level. They must be interested in conducting basic and/or clinical research in the specialty of allergy, asthma, and immunology. The award is directed at M.D.s and D.O.s.

**Financial data** The grant is $20,000 per year; funds may be used for salary, services, and supplies.

**Duration** 2 years.

**Additional information** Funding for this program is provided by Sanofi-Aventis.

**Number awarded** 1 each year.

**Deadline** November of each year.

## [1244]
## SBE DOCTORAL DISSERTATION RESEARCH IMPROVEMENT GRANTS

National Science Foundation
Attn: Directorate for Social, Behavioral, and Economic Sciences
4201 Wilson Boulevard, Room 905N
Arlington, VA 22230
(703) 292-8700      Fax: (703) 292-9083
TDD: (800) 281-8749
Web: www.nsf.gov

**Summary** To provide partial support to doctoral candidates (especially women, minorities, and persons with disabilities) who are conducting dissertation research in areas of interest to the Directorate for Social, Behavioral, and Economic Sciences (SBE) of the National Science Foundation (NSF).

**Eligibility** Applications may be submitted through regular university channels by dissertation advisors on behalf of graduate students who have advanced to candidacy and have begun or are about to begin dissertation research. Students must be enrolled at U.S. institutions but need not be U.S. citizens. The proposed research must relate to SBE's Division of Behavioral and Cognitive Sciences (archaeology, cultural anthropology, geography and regional science, linguistics, or physical anthropology), Division of Social and Economic Sciences (decision, risk, and management science; economics; law and social science; methodology, measurement, and statistics; political science; sociology; and science and society), or Division of Science Resources Statistics (research on science and technology surveys and statistics). Women, minorities, and persons with disabilities are strongly encouraged to apply.

**Financial data** Grants have the limited purpose of providing funds to enhance the quality of dissertation research. They are to be used exclusively for necessary expenses incurred in the actual conduct of the dissertation research, including (but not limited to) conducting field research in settings away from campus that would not otherwise be possible, data collection and sample survey costs, payments to subjects or informants, specialized research equipment, analysis and services not otherwise available, supplies, travel to archives, travel to specialized facilities or field research locations, and partial living expenses for conducting necessary research away from the student's U.S. academic institution. Funding is not provided for stipends, tuition, textbooks, journals, allowances for dependents, travel to scientific meetings, publication costs, dissertation preparation or reproduction, or indirect costs.

**Duration** Up to 2 years.

**Number awarded** 200 to 300 each year. Approximately $2.5 million is available for this program annually.

**Deadline** Deadline dates for the submission of dissertation improvement grant proposals differ by program within the divisions of the SBE Directorate; applicants should obtain information regarding target dates for proposals from the relevant program.

## [1245]
## SIGMA ALPHA IOTA DOCTORAL STUDY GRANT

Sigma Alpha Iota Philanthropies, Inc.
One Tunnel Road
Asheville, NC 28805
(828) 251-0606                          Fax: (828) 251-0644
E-mail: philonline@sai-national.org
Web: www.sai-national.org/phil/philsch1.html

**Summary** To provide funding for doctoral research in music to members of Sigma Alpha Iota (an organization of women musicians).

**Eligibility** Members of the organization may apply if they are enrolled in program leading to a doctoral degree. They must be conducting doctoral research on music education, music therapy, musicology, ethnomusicology, music theory, psychology of music, or applied research (including performance or pedagogy).

**Financial data** The grant is $2,500 per year.

**Duration** 1 year.

**Additional information** There is a $25 nonrefundable application fee.

**Number awarded** 1 each year.

**Deadline** March of each year.

## [1246]
## SIGMA DELTA EPSILON FELLOWSHIPS

Sigma Delta Epsilon-Graduate Women in Science, Inc.
c/o Jennifer Ingram, Fellowships Coordinator
Duke University-Department of Medicine
Box 2641, 275 MSRB, Research Drive
Durham, NC 27710
(919) 668-1439
E-mail: fellowshipsquestions@gwis.org
Web: www.gwis.org/grants/default.htm

**Summary** To provide funding to women interested in conducting research in the United States or abroad in the natural sciences.

**Eligibility** The program is open to women in the United States and Canada who are doing graduate or postdoctoral work in the natural sciences (defined to include anthropology, computer sciences, environmental sciences, life sciences, mathematics, psychology, physical sciences, and statistics). Applicants must give evidence of outstanding ability and promise in scientific research. They may be proposing to conduct research at an institution in the United States or abroad. Along with their application, they must submit a brief description of relevant personal factors, including financial need, that should be considered in the selection process. Applicants must either be members of

Sigma Delta Epsilon–Graduate Women in Science or include a processing fee of $20 (the cost of a 1-year membership).

**Financial data** Grants recently ranged from $1,250 to $3,000. The funds must be used for scientific research, including professional travel costs. They may not be used for tuition, child care, travel to professional meetings or to begin a new appointment, administrative overhead or indirect costs, personal computers, living allowances, or equipment for general use.

**Duration** 1 year; may be renewed in unusual circumstances, contingent upon receipt of an annual progress report.

**Additional information** The highest scoring applicant receives the Adele Lewis Grant. The second-highest scoring applicant receives the Hartley Fellowship.

**Number awarded** Varies each year. Recently, 5 of these fellowships were awarded: 2 at $3,000, 2 at $2,000, and 1 at $1,250.

**Deadline** January of each year.

## [1247]
## SONIA KOVALEVSKY HIGH SCHOOL MATHEMATICS DAYS GRANTS

Association for Women in Mathematics
11240 Waples Mill Road, Suite 200
Fairfax, VA 22030
(703) 934-0163                          Fax: (703) 359-7562
E-mail: awm@math.umd.edu
Web: www.awm-math.org/kovalevsky.html

**Summary** To provide funds (particularly to staff at Historically Black and women's colleges) for Sonia Kovalevsky High School Mathematics Days.

**Eligibility** Staff at universities and colleges may apply for these grants to support Sonia Kovalevsky High School Mathematics Days; staff at Historically Black institutions and women's colleges are particularly encouraged to apply. Programs targeted towards inner-city or rural high schools are especially welcomed. Applications should not exceed 5 pages and should include the following: tentative plans for activities, qualifications of the persons in charge, plans for recruitment (including securing diversity among participants), budget, local resources in support of the project (if any), and tentative follow-up and evaluation plans.

**Financial data** Grants up to $3,000 are available.

**Duration** The grants are awarded annually.

**Additional information** This program is supported by grants from the National Security Agency and Elizabeth City State University.

**Number awarded** 2 to 5 each year.

**Deadline** August or February of each year.

## [1248]
## SOUTH CAROLINA SPACE GRANT CONSORTIUM CURRICULUM DEVELOPMENT AWARDS

South Carolina Space Grant Consortium
c/o College of Charleston
Department of Geology and Environmental Sciences
66 George Street
Charleston, SC 29424
(843) 953-5463          Fax: (843) 953-5446
E-mail: scozzarot@cofc.edu
Web: www.cofc.edu

**Summary** To provide funding for development of space-related course work to faculty (particularly women, minority and disabled faculty members) at institutional members of the South Carolina Space Grant Consortium (SCSGC).

**Eligibility** This program is open to tenured or tenure-track faculty at SCSGC member institutions. Applicants must be proposing to develop course work or educational materials related to science and engineering fields of interest to the U.S. National Aeronautics and Space Administration (NASA). Selection is based on scientific merit of the proposed project, relevancy to NASA strategic plans, competency of project personnel, and reasonableness of budget. The consortium is a component of the NASA Space Grant program, which encourages the participation of women, underrepresented minorities, and persons with disabilities.

**Financial data** Grants range up to $4,000. Matching on a 1:1 basis with nonfederal funds is required.

**Duration** These are 1-time grants.

**Additional information** Members of the consortium are Benedict College, The Citadel, College of Charleston, Clemson University, Coastal Carolina University, Furman University, University of South Carolina, Wofford College, South Carolina State University, The Medical University of South Carolina, and University of the Virgin Islands. This program is funded by NASA.

**Number awarded** Varies each year.

**Deadline** Letters of intent must be submitted by December each year. Final proposals are due in January.

## [1249]
## SOUTH CAROLINA SPACE GRANT CONSORTIUM RESEARCH FACILITATION/INITIATION AWARDS

South Carolina Space Grant Consortium
c/o College of Charleston
Department of Geology and Environmental Sciences
66 George Street
Charleston, SC 29424
(843) 953-5463          Fax: (843) 953-5446
E-mail: scozzarot@cofc.edu
Web: www.cofc.edu

**Summary** To provide funding for space-related activities to faculty (particularly women, minority, and disabled faculty members) at institutional members of the South Carolina Space Grant Consortium (SCSGC).

**Eligibility** This program is open to tenured or tenure-track faculty at SCSGC member institutions. Applicants must be proposing to engage in aerospace-related activities, including (but not limited to) initiating a research project, enhancing an existing research activity, supporting a graduate student to join a faculty member at a field center for part of a

summer term, developing a new research project among scientists at several SCSGC campuses, or providing faculty summer support at facilities not covered by existing programs. They must be working in science and engineering fields of interest to the U.S. National Aeronautics and Space Administration (NASA). Selection is based on scientific merit of the proposed project, relevancy to NASA strategic plans, competency of project personnel, and reasonableness of budget. The consortium is a component of the NASA Space Grant program, which encourages the participation of women, underrepresented minorities, and persons with disabilities.

**Financial data** Grants range up to $8,000. Matching on a 1:1 basis with nonfederal funds is required.

**Duration** These are 1-time grants.

**Additional information** Members of the consortium are Benedict College, The Citadel, College of Charleston, Clemson University, Coastal Carolina University, Furman University, University of South Carolina, Wofford College, South Carolina State University, The Medical University of South Carolina, and University of the Virgin Islands. This program is funded by NASA.

**Number awarded** Varies each year.

**Deadline** Letters of intent must be submitted by December each year. Final proposals are due in January.

## [1250]
## SOUTH CAROLINA SPACE GRANT CONSORTIUM RESEARCH GRANTS

South Carolina Space Grant Consortium
c/o College of Charleston
Department of Geology and Environmental Sciences
66 George Street
Charleston, SC 29424
(843) 953-5463          Fax: (843) 953-5446
E-mail: scozzarot@cofc.edu
Web: www.cofc.edu

**Summary** To provide funding for space-related research to faculty (particularly women, minority, and disabled faculty members) at institutional members of the South Carolina Space Grant Consortium (SCSGC).

**Eligibility** This program is open to tenured or tenure-track faculty at SCSGC member institutions. Applicants must be proposing to conduct research in earth science, space science, aeronautics, or the human exploration and development of space. Priority is given to researchers who wish to conduct research at a center of the U.S. National Aeronautics and Space Administration (NASA). Selection is based on scientific merit of the proposed project, relevancy to NASA strategic plans, competency of project personnel, and reasonableness of budget. The consortium is a component of the NASA Space Grant program, which encourages the participation of women, underrepresented minorities, and persons with disabilities.

**Financial data** Grants range up to $30,000. Matching on a 1:1 basis with nonfederal funds is required.

**Duration** 1 year; may be renewed 1 additional year.

**Additional information** Members of the consortium are Benedict College, The Citadel, College of Charleston, Clemson University, Coastal Carolina University, Furman University, University of South Carolina, Wofford College, South

Carolina State University, The Medical University of South Carolina, and University of the Virgin Islands. This program is funded by NASA.

**Number awarded** Up to 2 each year.

**Deadline** Letters of intent must be submitted by December each year. Final proposals are due in January.

## [1251]
## SOUTH CAROLINA SPACE GRANT CONSORTIUM TRAVEL AWARDS

South Carolina Space Grant Consortium
c/o College of Charleston
Department of Geology and Environmental Sciences
66 George Street
Charleston, SC 29424
(843) 953-5463　　　　Fax: (843) 953-5446
E-mail: scozzarot@cofc.edu
Web: www.cofc.edu

**Summary** To provide funding for the development of space-related course work to students and faculty (particularly women, minorities, and persons with disabilities) at institutional members of the South Carolina Space Grant Consortium (SCSGC).

**Eligibility** This program is open to students and faculty at SCSGC member institutions. Applicants must be interested in making short trips to federal facilities, especially facilities of the U.S. National Aeronautics and Space Administration (NASA); meeting with international groups or other Space Grant campuses; or (to a lesser extent) presenting results at professional meetings They must demonstrate the need for, and expected benefit from, the proposed travel. Selection is based on scientific merit of the proposed project, relevancy to NASA strategic plans, competency of project personnel, and reasonableness of budget. The consortium is a component of the NASA Space Grant program, which encourages the participation of women, underrepresented minorities, and persons with disabilities.

**Financial data** Grants range up to $2,000. Matching on a 1:1 basis with nonfederal funds is required.

**Duration** These are 1-time grants.

**Additional information** Members of the consortium are Benedict College, The Citadel, College of Charleston, Clemson University, Coastal Carolina University, Furman University, University of South Carolina, Wofford College, South Carolina State University, The Medical University of South Carolina, and University of the Virgin Islands. This program is funded by NASA.

**Number awarded** Varies each year.

**Deadline** Letters of intent must be submitted by December each year. Final proposals are due in January.

## [1252]
## SOUTH CAROLINA SPACE GRANT CONSORTIUM UNDERGRADUATE RESEARCH PROGRAM

South Carolina Space Grant Consortium
c/o College of Charleston
Department of Geology and Environmental Sciences
66 George Street
Charleston, SC 29424
(843) 953-5463　　　　Fax: (843) 953-5446
E-mail: scozzarot@cofc.edu
Web: www.cofc.edu/~scsgrant/scholar/overview.html

**Summary** To provide funding for space-related research to undergraduate students in South Carolina, particularly women, minority, and disabled students.

**Eligibility** This program is open to undergraduate students at member institutions of the South Carolina Space Grant Consortium. Applicants should be rising juniors or seniors interested in aerospace and space-related studies, including the basic sciences, astronomy, science education, planetary science, environmental studies, engineering, fine arts, and journalism. U.S. citizenship is required. Selection is based on academic qualifications of the applicant; 2 letters of recommendation; a description of past activities, current interests, and future plans concerning a space science or aerospace-related field; and faculty sponsorship. Women, minorities, and persons with disabilities are encouraged to apply.

**Financial data** The stipend is $3,000. Up to $500 of the $3,000 will be available for research related expenses, not including any application fees.

**Duration** 1 academic year or 10 weeks during the summer.

**Additional information** Members of the consortium are Benedict College, The Citadel, College of Charleston, Clemson University, Coastal Carolina University, Furman University, University of South Carolina, Wofford College, South Carolina State University, The Medical University of South Carolina, and University of the Virgin Islands. This program is funded by the U.S. National Aeronautics and Space Administration (NASA).

**Number awarded** Varies each year.

**Deadline** January of each year.

## [1253]
## SPECIAL FUND FOR THE STUDY OF WOMEN AND POLITICS

American Political Science Association
Attn: Centennial Center Visiting Scholars Program
1527 New Hampshire Avenue, N.W.
Washington, DC 20036-1206
(202) 483-2512　　　　Fax: (202) 483-2657
E-mail: center@apsanet.org
Web: www.apsanet.org/content_6334.cfm

**Summary** To provide funding to members of the American Political Science Association (APSA) who are interested in conducting research on women and politics at the Centennial Center for Political Science and Public Affairs.

**Eligibility** This program is open to members of the association who are interested in conducting research on women and politics while in residence at the center. Junior faculty members, postdoctoral fellows, and advanced graduate students are strongly encouraged to apply, but scholars at all stages of their careers are eligible. International applicants are also welcome if they have demonstrable command of spoken English. Nonresident scholars may also be eligible.

**Financial data** Grants provide supplemental financial support to resident scholars.

**Duration** 2 weeks to 12 months.

**Additional information** The APSA launched its Centennial Center for Political Science and Public Affairs in 2003 to commemorate the centennial year of the association.

**Number awarded** 1 or more each year.

**Deadline** February of each year.

## [1254]
## SWS FEMINIST LECTURERSHIP AWARD

Sociologists for Women in Society
Attn: Executive Officer
University of Rhode Island
Department of Sociology
Kingston, RI 02881
(401) 874-9510                Fax: (401) 874-2588
E-mail: jessicasherwood@mail.uri.edu
Web: www.socwomen.org

**Summary** To bring major feminist scholars to campuses that might otherwise not be able to afford to do so.

**Eligibility** Feminists scholars (with advanced degrees or the equivalent experience) are eligible to be nominated. They must be interested in delivering a lecture at 2 college campuses that are rural, isolated, or not located in or near major metropolitan centers.

**Financial data** The society pays the recipient $1,000 as an honorarium and provides travel funds (up to $750) to visit each site; the host college pays the remainder of the travel expenses and other direct costs.

**Duration** The award is presented annually.

**Additional information** This program was established in 1985. The lecture may be published in the association's journal, *Gender and Society*. Further information is available from Susan A. Farrell, Kingsborough Community College, Behavioral Sciences, 2001 Oriental Boulevard, Brooklyn, NY 11235, (718) 368-4511.

**Number awarded** 1 lecturer is selected each year; 2 institutions are selected to host her.

**Deadline** Nominations for the lecturer and applications from institutions interested in serving as a host are due by March of each year.

## [1255]
## SYLVIA LANE MENTOR RESEARCH FELLOWSHIP

Committee on Women in Agricultural Economics
c/o Cheryl Doss
YCIAS
P.O. Box 208206
New Haven, CT 06520-8206
(203) 432-9395            E-mail: Charyl.Doss@yale.edu
Web: www.aaea.org/sections/cwae/lane.htm

**Summary** To provide funding to young female scholars who are working on food, agricultural, or resource issues

and interested in relocating in order to conduct research with an established expert at another university, institution, or firm.

**Eligibility** These fellowships are awarded to mentee/mentor pairs of individuals. Mentees must have completed at least 1 year in residence in an accredited American graduate degree program in agricultural economics or a closely-related discipline; women with Ph.D. degrees and advanced graduate students are encouraged to apply. Mentors must have a Ph.D. and established expertise in an area of food, agriculture, or natural resources. The goal is to enable scholars to relocate in order to conduct research with an established expert at another university, institution, or firm, even though they may reside in different parts of the country or the world. Selection is based on the relevance of the research problem, potential for generating output, synergy of the mentor/mentee pairing, and opportunity for advancing the mentee's research skills beyond her graduate studies and current position.

**Financial data** Awards may be used to cover direct research costs, travel, and temporary relocation expenses for the mentee.

**Duration** Several weeks.

**Additional information** This program is sponsored by the American Agricultural Economics Association Foundation and by academic, foundation, and industry donors; it is administered by the Committee on Women in Agricultural Economics.

**Number awarded** 1 each year.

**Deadline** June of each year.

## [1256]
## TAP ENDOWED RESEARCH SCHOLAR AWARD IN ACID-RELATED DISEASES

Foundation for Digestive Health and Nutrition
Attn: Research Awards Program
4930 Del Ray Avenue
Bethesda, MD 20814-2512
(301) 222-4012                Fax: (301) 652-3890
E-mail: info@fdhn.org
Web: www.fdhn.org/html/awards/elect_app.html

**Summary** To provide funding to young gastroenterology investigators (especially women and minorities) who are interested in preparing for a research career in acid-related diseases.

**Eligibility** This program is open to members of the American Gastroenterological Association (AGA) who have an M.D., Ph.D., or equivalent degree. Applicants must hold full-time faculty positions at North American universities or professional institutes at the time the award begins. They should be early in their careers (fellows and established investigators are not appropriate candidates). Candidates with an M.D. degree must have completed clinical training within the past 5 years and those with a Ph.D. must have received their degree within the past 5 years. The proposed research must involve acid-related diseases. Selection is based on novelty, feasibility and significance of the proposal; likelihood of impact on care of patients with acid-related diseases; attributes of the candidate, including potential for independence; evidence of institutional commitment; and the research environment. Women, minorities, and physician/scientist investigators are strongly encouraged to apply.

**Financial data** The grant is $75,000 per year. Funds are to be used for project costs, including salary, supplies, and equipment but excluding travel. Indirect costs are not allowed.

**Duration** 3 years.

**Additional information** This program is administered by the Foundation for Digestive Health and Nutrition (FDHN) with support from TAP Pharmaceuticals, Inc. and the AGA. Recipients must devote at least 70% of their efforts to research involving acid-related diseases. They cannot hold or have held an R01, R29, K121, K08, VA Research Award, or any award with similar objectives from nonfederal sources.

**Number awarded** 1 each year.

**Deadline** September of each year.

## [1257]
## TED SCRIPPS FELLOWSHIPS IN ENVIRONMENTAL JOURNALISM

University of Colorado at Boulder
Attn: Center for Environmental Journalism
1511 University Avenue
Campus Box 478
Boulder, CO 80309-0478
(303) 492-4114                    E-mail: cej@colorado.edu
Web: www.colorado.edu/journalism/cej

**Summary** To provide journalists (particularly women, minorities, and journalists with disabilities) with an opportunity to gain more knowledge about environmental issues at the University of Colorado at Boulder.

**Eligibility** This program is open to full-time U.S. print and broadcast journalists who have at least 5 years' professional experience and have completed an undergraduate degree. Applicants may be general assignment reporters, editors, producers, environmental reporters, or full-time freelancers. Prior experience in covering the environment is not required. Professionals in such related fields as teaching, public relations, or advertising are not eligible. Applicants must be interested in a program at the university that includes classes, weekly seminars, and field trips. They also must engage in independent study expected to lead to a significant piece of journalistic work. Applications are especially encouraged from women, ethnic minorities, disabled persons, and veterans (particularly veterans of the Vietnam era).

**Financial data** The program covers tuition and fees and pays a $44,000 stipend. Employers are strongly encouraged to continue benefits, including health insurance.

**Duration** 9 months.

**Additional information** This program, established in 1992 at the University of Michigan and transferred to the University of Colorado in 1997, is supported by the Scripps Howard Foundation. This is a non-degree program. Fellows must obtain a leave of absence from their regular employment and must return to their job following the fellowship.

**Number awarded** 5 each year.

**Deadline** February of each year.

## [1258]
## TEXAS SPACE GRANT CONSORTIUM K-12 EDUCATION PROGRAMS

Texas Space Grant Consortium
Attn: Program Manager
3925 West Braker Lane, Suite 200
Austin, TX 78759
(512) 471-3583                    Toll-free: (800) 248-8742
Fax: (512) 471-3585
E-mail: proposals@tsgc.utexas.edu
Web: www.tsgc.utexas.edu/epo

**Summary** To provide funding to faculty and staff (especially women, minorities, and persons with disabilities) at institutional members of the Texas Space Grant Consortium (TSGC) who are interested in developing projects to help K-12 teachers learn more about the benefits of space exploration and space-based research.

**Eligibility** This program is open to individuals qualified to serve as principal investigators at TSGC member institutions in good standing. Applicants must be interested in developing a project for the professional development of K-12 teachers in Texas that will assist them to learn more about the benefits of space exploration and space-based research. Principal investigators must be U.S. citizens. The program encourages the participation of principal investigators who are women, underrepresented minorities, or persons with disabilities.

**Financial data** Grants up to $15,000 are available. Funds may be used for salary, wages, and fringe benefits for the principal investigator, staff, graduate students, and undergraduate students; tuition costs for graduate students; domestic travel; and materials and supplies. No funding is provided for overhead or indirect costs.

**Duration** The project must be completed within 2 years.

**Additional information** The participating universities are Baylor University, Lamar University, Prairie View A&M University, Rice University, San Jacinto College, Southern Methodist University, Sul Ross State University, Texas A&M University (including Kingsville and Corpus Christi campuses), Texas Christian University, Texas Southern University, Texas Tech University, Trinity University, University of Houston (including Clear Lake and Downtown campuses), University of Texas at Arlington, University of Texas at Austin, University of Texas at Dallas, University of Texas at El Paso, University of Texas at San Antonio, and University of Texas/Pan American. This program is funded by the National Aeronautics and Space Administration (NASA).

**Number awarded** 4 to 7 each year.

**Deadline** Notices of intent must be submitted by January of each year; completed proposals are due by the end of February.

## [1259]
## UNIVERSITY OF CALIFORNIA PRESIDENT'S POSTDOCTORAL FELLOWSHIP PROGRAM

University of California
Attn: Office of the President
1111 Franklin Street, 11th Floor
Oakland, CA 94607-5200
(510) 987-9503                     Fax: (510) 587-6077
E-mail: kim.adkinson@ucop.edu
Web: www.ucop.edu/acadadv/ppfp

**Summary** To provide recent postdoctorates (particularly women and minorities) who are committed to careers in university teaching and research with an opportunity to conduct research at 1 of the 10 University of California campuses.

**Eligibility** This program is open to U.S. citizens or permanent residents who have a Ph.D. from an accredited university. Applicants must be proposing to conduct research at a branch of the university under the mentorship of a faculty or laboratory sponsor. For the humanities, arts, social sciences, and professions, preference is given to candidates whose research emphasizes such issues as diversity, multiculturalism, and communities underserved by traditional academic research. The program is particularly interested in research that considers such issues as race, ethnicity, and/or gender as they relate to traditional academic fields. That includes research in such areas as community development, social justice, educational reform, economic development, public health and safety, and the dynamics of multicultural communities. For the life sciences, physical sciences, mathematics, and engineering, preference is given to candidates who have participated in teaching, mentoring, or outreach programs that promote educational opportunities for underrepresented students in higher education. In all fields, special consideration is given to applicants who have demonstrated significant academic achievement by overcoming such barriers as economic, social, or educational disadvantage. The program is particularly interested in applicants whose family members may have experienced barriers in participation in higher education, who are bilingual or bicultural, or who have participated in teaching, mentoring, or outreach programs (e.g., MESA, Puente) that are designed to foster the participation of underrepresented students in higher education.

**Financial data** The stipend is $33,800 to $35,300 for fields except mathematics, engineering, and the physical sciences; in those fields, stipends range from $35,300 to $44,000, depending upon experience. The program also offers health benefits and up to $4,000 for supplemental and research-related expenses.

**Duration** Appointments are for 1 academic year, with possible renewal for a second year.

**Additional information** Research may be conducted on any of the University of California's 10 campuses (Berkeley, Davis, Irvine, Los Angeles, Merced, Riverside, San Diego, San Francisco, Santa Barbara, or Santa Cruz). The program provides mentoring and guidance in preparing for an academic career.

**Number awarded** 15 to 20 each year.

**Deadline** November of each year.

## [1260]
## UNIVERSITY SCHOLAR-IN-RESIDENCE AWARD

American Association of University Women
Attn: AAUW Educational Foundation
1111 16th Street, N.W.
Washington, DC 20036-4873
(202) 728-7602                Toll-free: (800) 326-AAUW
Fax: (202) 872-1425          TDD: (202) 785-7777
E-mail: foundation@aauw.org
Web: www.aauw.org

**Summary** To provide funding to support women scholars who wish to conduct research on gender equity.

**Eligibility** This program is open to women scholars interested in undertaking and disseminating research on gender equity in education and/or economic security. Scholars must be selected by a college or university, which then submits an application to the American Association of University Women (AAUW). Selection is based on quality of scholarship (the proposed scholar's demonstrated expertise in research and the originality of the proposed research project); impact (the relevance of the research topic to the AAUW mission and current research agenda, clarity of stated outcomes, and potential for research to affect lasting change on a local and national level); cost sharing and budget (the feasibility of costs and timeline, evidence of institutional support, and planning for efficient use of the grant); and dissemination (potential for local and national visibility and collaboration with AAUW national or branch activities).

**Financial data** The grant is $100,000.

**Duration** 2 years.

**Additional information** This program began in 1999.

**Number awarded** 1 each year.

**Deadline** Letters of intent must be submitted by November of each year; completed proposals are due by January of each year.

## [1261]
## VERNA ROSS ORNDORFF CAREER PERFORMANCE GRANT

Sigma Alpha Iota Philanthropies, Inc.
One Tunnel Road
Asheville, NC 28805
(828) 251-0606                     Fax: (828) 251-0644
E-mail: philonline@sai-national.org
Web: www.sai-national.org/phil/philsch1.html

**Summary** To provide funding for advanced study, coaching, or other activities directly related to the development of a musical career to members of Sigma Alpha Iota (an organization of women musicians).

**Eligibility** This program is open to members of the organization who are preparing for a concert career. Singers may not be older than 35 years of age and instrumentalists may not be older than 32. Applicants may not have professional management, but they must have had considerable performing experience outside the academic environment.

**Financial data** The grant is $5,000; funds must be used for advanced study, coaching, or other purposes directly related to the development of a professional performing career.

**Duration** 1 year.

**Additional information** The area supported rotates annually among piano, harpsichord, organ, and percussion (2008); and voice (2009); and strings, woodwinds, and brass (2010) There is a $35 nonrefundable application fee.

**Number awarded** 1 each year.

**Deadline** October of each year.

## [1262]
## VESSA NOTCHEV FELLOWSHIPS

Sigma Delta Epsilon-Graduate Women in Science, Inc.
c/o Jennifer Ingram, Fellowships Coordinator
Duke University-Department of Medicine
Box 2641, 275 MSRB, Research Drive
Durham, NC 27710
(919) 668-1439
E-mail: fellowshipsquestions@gwis.org
Web: www.gwis.org/grants/default.htm

**Summary** To provide funding to members of Sigma Delta Epsilon–Graduate Women in Science who are interested in conducting research in the United States or abroad in the natural sciences.

**Eligibility** The program is open to women in the United States and Canada who are doing graduate or postdoctoral work in the natural sciences (defined as anthropology, computer sciences, environmental sciences, life sciences, mathematics, psychology, physical sciences, and statistics). Applicants must give evidence of outstanding ability and promise in scientific research. They may be proposing to conduct research at any institution in the United States or abroad. Along with their application, they must submit a brief description of relevant personal factors, including financial need, that should be considered in the selection process. Applicants must either be members of Sigma Delta Epsilon–Graduate Women in Science or include a processing fee of $20 (the cost of a 1-year membership).

**Financial data** Grants range up to $1,000. The funds must be used for scientific research, including professional travel costs. They may not be used for tuition, child care, travel to professional meetings or to begin a new appointment, administrative overhead or indirect costs, personal computers, living allowances, or equipment for general use.

**Duration** 1 year; may be renewed in unusual circumstances, contingent upon receipt of an annual progress report.

**Additional information** This program was established in 1994.

**Number awarded** Varies each year; recently, 2 of these fellowships were awarded.

**Deadline** January of each year.

## [1263]
## VIRGINIA SPACE GRANT AEROSPACE GRADUATE RESEARCH FELLOWSHIPS

Virginia Space Grant Consortium
Attn: Fellowship Coordinator
Old Dominion University Peninsula Center
600 Butler Farm Road
Hampton, VA 23666
(757) 766-5210　　　　　　　　Fax: (757) 766-5205
E-mail: vsgc@odu.edu
Web: www.vsgc.odu.edu/Menu3_1_1.htm

**Summary** To provide funding for research in space-related fields to graduate students in Virginia, particularly women, minority, and disabled students.

**Eligibility** This program is open to graduate students who will be enrolled in a program of full-time study in an aerospace-related discipline at 1 of the Virginia Space Grant Consortium (VSGC) Colleges. Applicants must be U.S. citizens with a GPA of 3.0 or higher. They must submit a research proposal with a plan of study that includes its key elements, what the applicant intends to accomplish, and the aerospace application of the proposed research activity. Eligibility is not limited to science and engineering majors; students in any field of study that includes course work related to an understanding of or interest in aerospace may apply. Selection is based on the applicants' academic qualifications, the quality of their proposed research plan, and its relevance to this program. Since an important purpose of this program is to increase the participation of underrepresented minorities, females, and persons with disabilities in aerospace-related careers, the VSGC especially encourages applications from those students.

**Financial data** The grant is $5,000. Funds are add-on awards, designed to supplement and enhance such basic graduate research support as research assistantships, teaching assistantships, and nonfederal scholarships and fellowships.

**Duration** 1 year; may be renewed up to 2 additional years.

**Additional information** The VSGC colleges are College of William and Mary, Hampton University, Old Dominion University, the University of Virginia, and Virginia Polytechnic Institute and State University. This program is funded by the U.S. National Aeronautics and Space Administration (NASA). Awardees are required to certify through their academic department that basic research support of at least $5,000 is being provided before receipt of Space Grant funds.

**Number awarded** At least 5 each year.

**Deadline** February of each year.

## [1264]
## VIRGINIA SPACE GRANT AEROSPACE UNDERGRADUATE RESEARCH SCHOLARSHIPS

Virginia Space Grant Consortium
Attn: Fellowship Coordinator
Old Dominion University Peninsula Center
600 Butler Farm Road
Hampton, VA 23666
(757) 766-5210                    Fax: (757) 766-5205
E-mail: vsgc@odu.edu
Web: www.vsgc.odu.edu/Menu3_1_1.htm

**Summary** To provide funding for research in space-related fields to undergraduate students in Virginia, particularly women, minority, and disabled students.

**Eligibility** This program is open to undergraduate students who will be enrolled in a program of full-time study in an aerospace-related discipline at 1 of the Virginia Space Grant Consortium (VSGC) Colleges. Applicants must be U.S. citizens who have completed at least 2 years of an undergraduate program with a GPA of 3.0 or higher. They must be proposing to participate in an active, identified research activity that has aerospace applications. The research must be supervised by a faculty mentor and may be conducted on the home campus or at an industrial or government facility. It should be continuous and may be conducted any time during the academic year, summer, or both. Since an important purpose of this program is to increase the participation of underrepresented minorities, females, and persons with disabilities in aerospace-related careers, the VSGC especially encourages applications from those students.

**Financial data** Grants provide a student stipend of $3,000 during the academic year and a $3,500 stipend during the summer (either before or after the academic year). Recipients may request an additional $1,000 research allocation for materials and travel to support research activities conducted during the academic year and/or a $1,000 research allocation during the summer. The maximum award per year cannot exceed $8,500.

**Duration** 1 year; renewable.

**Additional information** The VSGC colleges are College of William and Mary, Hampton University, Old Dominion University, the University of Virginia, and Virginia Polytechnic Institute and State University. This program is funded by the U.S. National Aeronautics and Space Administration (NASA). Awardees are required to participate in the VSGC annual student research conference in late March or early April.

**Number awarded** Varies each year.

**Deadline** February of each year.

## [1265]
## W. NEWTON LONG AWARD

American College of Nurse-Midwives
Attn: ACNM Foundation, Inc.
8403 Coleville Road, Suite 1550
Silver Spring, MD 20915
(240) 485-1850                    Fax: (240) 485-1818
Web: www.midwife.org

**Summary** To provide funding to midwives who are interested in conducting a research or other project in the United States or abroad.

**Eligibility** This program is open to midwives, including certified nurse midwives (CNMs) and certified midwives (CMs). Applicants must be seeking funding for a project that relates to 1 or more of the following areas: advancement of nurse-midwifery clinical skills; advancement of nurse-midwifery through research; dissemination of nurse-midwifery research; promotion of professional nurse-midwifery; presentations by nurse midwives at medical or midwifery conferences; establishment of new nurse-midwifery practice or service; or study of different aspects of nurse-midwifery practice in the United States and abroad.

**Financial data** The maximum grant is $1,500.

**Duration** The grants are presented annually.

**Additional information** Information is also available from Elaine M. Moore, Chair, W. Newton Long Fund Committee, 9307 Cheviot Drive, Brentwood, TN 37027.

**Number awarded** 1 or 2 each year.

**Deadline** March of each year.

## [1266]
## WASHINGTON NASA SPACE GRANT CONSORTIUM SEED GRANTS FOR FACULTY

Washington NASA Space Grant Consortium
c/o University of Washington
Johnson Hall, Room 141
Box 351310
Seattle, WA 98195-1310
(206) 543-1943                    Toll-free: (800) 659-1943
Fax: (206) 543-0179   E-mail: nasa@u.washington.edu
Web: www.waspacegrant.org/faculty.html

**Summary** To provide funding to faculty (particularly women, minorities, and persons with disabilities) at member institutions of the Washington NASA Space Grant Consortium who are interested in conducting space-related research.

**Eligibility** This program is open to faculty members at institutions that are members of the consortium. Applicants must be interested in initiating research efforts in disciplines relevant to the missions of the U.S. National Aeronautics and Space Administration (NASA) on earth and in space. The program values diversity and strongly encourages women and minorities to apply.

**Financial data** Grants range from $10,000 to $20,000. Matching funds must be provided.

**Duration** 1 year.

**Additional information** This program is funded by NASA. Members of the consortium include Heritage College, Northwest Indian College, North Seattle Community College, Seattle Central Community College, University of Washington, University of Puget Sound, Washington State University, Western Washington University, and Whitman College.

**Number awarded** 1 each year.

## [1267]
## WASHINGTON NASA SPACE GRANT CONSORTIUM UNDERGRADUATE RESEARCH AWARDS

Washington NASA Space Grant Consortium
c/o University of Washington
Johnson Hall, Room 141
Box 351310
Seattle, WA 98195-1310
(206) 543-1943                    Toll-free: (800) 659-1943
Fax: (206) 543-0179    E-mail: nasa@u.washington.edu
Web: www.waspacegrant.org/ura.html

**Summary**  To provide funding to undergraduate students in Washington (particularly women, minority, and disabled students) who are interested in conducting a science or engineering research project on a topic of interest to the U.S. National Aeronautics and Space Administration (NASA).

**Eligibility**  This program is open to full-time undergraduate students at colleges and universities that are members of the Washington NASA Space Grant Consortium. Applicants must be interested in conducting a research project, under the guidance of a faculty mentor, in a NASA-related field of science and engineering, including science education. U.S. citizenship is required. The program is part of the NASA National Space Grant program, which encourages participation by members of underrepresented groups (women, minorities, and persons with disabilities).

**Financial data**  The grant is $3,000.

**Duration**  Grantees may elect to receive their award for full-time research during the summer or for part-time research during 2 academic quarters or semesters.

**Additional information**  This program is funded by NASA. Members of the consortium include Heritage College, Northwest Indian College, North Seattle Community College, Seattle Central Community College, University of Washington, University of Puget Sound, Washington State University, Western Washington University, and Whitman College.

**Number awarded**  Varies each year; recently, 9 of these awards were granted.

**Deadline**  February of each year.

## [1268]
## WAWH FOUNDERS DISSERTATION FELLOWSHIP

Western Association of Women Historians
c/o Alexandra M. Nickliss
City College of San Francisco
Department of History
50 Phelan Avenue
San Francisco, CA 94112
(415) 239-3283
Web: wawh.org/awardsandprizes.html

**Summary**  To provide dissertation funding to graduate students who are members of the Western Association of Women Historians (WAWH).

**Eligibility**  This program is open to graduate students who are members of WAWH, have advanced to candidacy, are writing their dissertation at the time of application, and are expecting to receive their Ph.D. no earlier than December of the calendar year in which the award is made. Selection is based on scholarly potential of the student, significance of the dissertation project for historical scholarship, and progress already made towards completing necessary research.

**Financial data**  The grant is $1,000. Funds may be used for any expenses related to the dissertation.

**Duration**  1 year.

**Additional information**  This fellowship was first awarded in 1986.

**Number awarded**  1 each year.

**Deadline**  January of each year.

## [1269]
## WEST VIRGINIA SPACE GRANT CONSORTIUM GRADUATE FELLOWSHIP PROGRAM

West Virginia Space Grant Consortium
c/o West Virginia University
College of Engineering and Mineral Resources
G-68 Engineering Sciences Building
P.O. Box 6070
Morgantown, WV 26506-6070
(304) 293-4099, ext. 3737          Fax: (304) 293-4970
E-mail: nasa@cemr.wvu.edu
Web: www.nasa.wvu.edu/scholarships.html

**Summary**  To provide funding to graduate students (especially women, minorities, and disabled students) at designated academic institutions affiliated with the West Virginia Space Grant Consortium who wish to conduct research on space-related science or engineering topics.

**Eligibility**  This program is open to graduate students in space-related mathematics, science, and engineering disciplines at participating member institutions of the consortium. Applicants must be interested in working on a research project with a faculty member who agrees to serve as a mentor and research advisor. U.S. citizenship is required. The consortium is a component of the Space Grant program of the U.S. National Aeronautics and Space Administration (NASA), which strongly encourages participation by members of underrepresented groups (minorities, women, and persons with disabilities).

**Financial data**  The grant is $12,000. The recipient's home institution must supplement the grant with a 1:1 cost share; graduate tuition waiver by the college or university and documented time spent by the faculty to supervise and mentor the student may be counted toward fulfillment of the cost-share requirement.

**Duration**  1 year.

**Additional information**  Funding for this program is provided by NASA. The participating consortium members are Marshall University, West Virginia Institute of Technology, West Virginia University, and Wheeling-Jesuit University.

**Number awarded**  Varies each year.

**Deadline**  March of each year.

## [1270]
## WEST VIRGINIA SPACE GRANT CONSORTIUM RESEARCH INITIATION GRANTS

West Virginia Space Grant Consortium
c/o West Virginia University
College of Engineering and Mineral Resources
G-68 Engineering Sciences Building
P.O. Box 6070
Morgantown, WV 26506-6070
(304) 293-4099, ext. 3737          Fax: (304) 293-4970
E-mail: nasa@cemr.wvu.edu
Web: www.nasa.wvu.edu/research.html

**Summary** To provide funding for space-related research to faculty (particularly women, minorities, and persons with disabilities) at academic institutions affiliated with the West Virginia Space Grant Consortium.

**Eligibility** This program is open to faculty members at colleges and universities that are members of the West Virginia Space Grant Consortium. Applicants must be seeking to pursue research in areas of interest to the U.S. National Aeronautics and Space Administration (NASA) and to establish long-term relationships with NASA researchers. U.S. citizenship is required. Selection is based on technical and scientific merit (30 points), potential for future funding and long-term impact (20 points), soundness of approach (20 points), relevance to NASA mission and West Virginia's priorities in science and technology (20 points), and budget (10 points). The consortium is a component of NASA's Space Grant program, which strongly encourages participation by members of underrepresented groups (minorities, women, and persons with disabilities).

**Financial data** Grants range from $5,000 to $20,000. The consortium provides two-thirds of the total budget and the researcher's institution must agree to provide the remainder on a cost-sharing basis. At least 35% of the award must be allocated for a graduate student research assistant.

**Duration** 1 year.

**Additional information** Funding for this program is provided by NASA. The consortium includes Bethany College, Bluefield College, Fairmont State College, Marshall University, Shepherd College, West Liberty State College, West Virginia Institute of Technology, West Virginia State College, West Virginia University, West Virginia Wesleyan College, and Wheeling-Jesuit University.

**Number awarded** Varies each year; recently, 7 of these grants were awarded.

**Deadline** March of each year.

## [1271]
## WEST VIRGINIA SPACE GRANT CONSORTIUM UNDERGRADUATE RESEARCH FELLOWSHIP PROGRAM

West Virginia Space Grant Consortium
c/o West Virginia University
College of Engineering and Mineral Resources
G-68 Engineering Sciences Building
P.O. Box 6070
Morgantown, WV 26506-6070
(304) 293-4099, ext. 3737          Fax: (304) 293-4970
E-mail: nasa@cemr.wvu.edu
Web: www.nasa.wvu.edu/scholarships.html

**Summary** To provide funding to undergraduate students (particularly women, minority, and disabled students) at academic institutions affiliated with the West Virginia Space Grant Consortium who wish to conduct a space-related science or engineering research project.

**Eligibility** This program is open to full-time undergraduates enrolled in mathematics, science, or engineering programs at member institutions of the consortium. Applicants must be interested in conducting a space-related research project with a faculty member from their department who agrees to serve as a mentor and research advisor. Selection is based on soundness and technical merit of the proposed research (50 points), student's academic and extracurricular achievements (30 points), and budget and plans for dissemination and publicizing of the results (20 points). The consortium is a component of the Space Grant program of the U.S. National Aeronautics and Space Administration (NASA), which strongly encourages participation by members of underrepresented groups (minorities, women, and persons with disabilities).

**Financial data** Grants range from $1,000 to $5,000.

**Duration** 1 academic year or summer.

**Additional information** Funding for this program is provided by NASA. The consortium includes Bethany College, Bluefield College, Fairmont State College, Marshall University, Shepherd College, West Liberty State College, West Virginia Institute of Technology, West Virginia State College, West Virginia University, West Virginia Wesleyan College, and Wheeling-Jesuit University.

**Number awarded** Varies each year.

**Deadline** March of each year.

## [1272]
## WISCONSIN SPACE GRANT CONSORTIUM GRADUATE FELLOWSHIPS

Wisconsin Space Grant Consortium
c/o University of Wisconsin at Green Bay
Department of Natural and Applied Sciences
2420 Nicolet Drive
Green Bay, WI 54311-7001
(920) 465-2108          Fax: (920) 465-2376
E-mail: wsgc@uwgb.edu
Web: www.uwgb.edu/wsgc/students/gf.asp

**Summary** To provide funding to graduate students (especially women, minority, and disabled students) at member institutions of the Wisconsin Space Grant Consortium (WSGC) who are interested in conducting aerospace, space science, or other interdisciplinary aerospace-related research.

**Eligibility** This program is open to graduate students enrolled at colleges and universities participating in the WSGC. Applicants must be U.S. citizens; be enrolled full time in a master's or Ph.D. program related to space science aerospace, or interdisciplinary aerospace studies (including, but not limited to, engineering, the sciences, architecture, law, business, nursing and medicine); have a GPA of 3.0 or higher; and be interested in conducting space-related research. The consortium especially encourages applications from underrepresented minorities, women, persons with disabilities, and those pursuing interdisciplinary aerospace studies. Selection is based on academic performance, space-related promise, and the proposal.

**Financial data** Grants up to $5,000 per year are provided.

**Duration** 1 academic year or summer.

**Additional information** Funding for this program is provided by the U.S. National Aeronautics and Space Administration (NASA). The schools participating in the consortium include the University of Wisconsin campuses at Fox Valley, Green Bay, La Crosse, Madison, Milwaukee, Oshkosh, Parkside, Superior, and Whitewater; Alverno College; Marquette University; College of the Menominee Nation; Carroll College; Lawrence University; Milwaukee School of Engineering; Ripon College; Medical College of Wisconsin; Western Wisconsin Technical College; and Wisconsin Lutheran College.

**Number awarded** Varies each year; recently, 15 of these fellowships were awarded.

**Deadline** February of each year.

## [1273]
## WISCONSIN SPACE GRANT CONSORTIUM RESEARCH INFRASTRUCTURE PROGRAM

Wisconsin Space Grant Consortium
c/o University of Wisconsin at Madison
Space Science and Engineering Center
1225 West Dayton Street, Room 251
Madison, WI 53706-1280
(608) 263-4206                    Fax: (608) 263-5974
E-mail: tom.achtor@ssec.wisc.edu
Web: www.uwgb.edu/wsgc/research/ri.asp

**Summary** To provide funding to staff (particularly women, minorities, and persons with disabilities) at academic and industrial affiliates of the Wisconsin Space Grant Consortium (WSGC) who are interested in developing space-related research infrastructure.

**Eligibility** This program is open to faculty and research staff at the WSGC universities and colleges and staff at WSGC industrial affiliates. Applicants must be interested in establishing a space-related research program. Faculty and staff on university/industry teams in all areas of research are considered, but research initiatives must focus on activities related to the mission of the U.S. National Aeronautics and Space Administration (NASA). Those activities include earth and atmospheric sciences, astronautics, aeronautics, space sciences, and other space-related fields (e.g., agriculture, business, law, medicine, nursing, social and behavioral sciences, and space architecture). Grants are made in 2 categories: 1) faculty research seed grants and/or faculty pro-

posal writing grants; and 2) other research initiatives, such as seminars, workshops, and/or travel to NASA centers. Preference is given to applications that emphasize new lines of space-related research, establishing collaborations among faculty from liberal arts colleges with faculty from research-intensive doctoral universities, linking academic and industrial affiliates, coordinated efforts with other NASA programs, increasing research capability, building research infrastructure, establishing research collaborations, and initiating research opportunities in line with the NASA Strategic Enterprises, especially by women, underrepresented minorities, and persons with disabilities. Selection is based on the proposal topic, quality, credentials of the investigator(s), and probability of success in developing space-related research infrastructure.

**Financial data** For faculty research seed grants and proposal writing grants, most awards range up to $5,000, although 1 grant of $10,000 is available. For other research initiatives, the maximum grant is $1,000.

**Duration** 1 year. Proposals for 2-year projects may be considered if they include a 2-year budget and justification of why the project requires a 2-year effort.

**Additional information** Funding for this program is provided by NASA. Academic members of WSGC include the University of Wisconsin campuses at Fox Valley, Green Bay, La Crosse, Madison, Milwaukee, Oshkosh, Parkside, Superior, and Whitewater; Alverno College; Marquette University; College of the Menominee Nation; Carroll College; Lawrence University; Milwaukee School of Engineering; Ripon College; Medical College of Wisconsin; Western Wisconsin Technical College; and Wisconsin Lutheran College. Industrial affiliates include Aerogel Technologies, Astronautics Corporation of America, KT Engineering, Orbital Technologies Corporation, Promega Corporation, Space Explorers, Inc., Wisconsin Association of CESA Administrators, Wisconsin Department of Public Instruction, Wisconsin Department of Transportation, and Wisconsin Space Business Roundtable.

**Number awarded** Varies each year; recently, 7 of these grants were awarded.

**Deadline** February of each year.

## [1274]
## WISCONSIN SPACE GRANT CONSORTIUM UNDERGRADUATE RESEARCH AWARDS

Wisconsin Space Grant Consortium
c/o University of Wisconsin at Madison
Space Science and Engineering Center
1225 West Dayton Street, Room 251
Madison, WI 53706-1280
(608) 263-4206                    Fax: (608) 263-5974
E-mail: tom.achtor@ssec.wisc.edu
Web: www.uwgb.edu/wsgc/research/ur.asp

**Summary** To provide funding to undergraduate students (particular women, minority, and disabled students) at colleges and universities participating in the Wisconsin Space Grant Consortium (WSGC) who are interested in conducting space-related research.

**Eligibility** This program is open to undergraduate students enrolled at an institution participating in the WSGC. Applicants must be U.S. citizens; be enrolled full time in an undergraduate program related to space science, aerospace, or interdisciplinary space studies; and have a GPA of 3.0 or higher. They must be proposing to create and implement a small research project of their own design as academic year, summer, or part-time employment that is directly related to their interests and career objectives in space science, aerospace, or space-related studies. Students must request a faculty or research staff member on their campus to act as an advisor; the consortium locates a scientist or engineer from 1 of the research-intensive universities to serve as a second mentor for successful applicants. The consortium especially encourages applications from students pursuing interdisciplinary space studies (e.g., engineering, the sciences, architecture, law, business, nursing, and medicine), students from small colleges and universities, students from departments with newly developing space research infrastructure, underrepresented minorities, women, and persons with disabilities. Selection is based on academic performance and space-related promise.

**Financial data** Stipends up to $3,500 per year or summer session are available. An additional $500 may be awarded for exceptional expenses, such as high travel costs.

**Duration** 1 academic year or summer.

**Additional information** Funding for this program is provided by the U.S. National Aeronautics and Space Administration (NASA). The schools participating in the consortium include the University of Wisconsin campuses at Fox Valley, Green Bay, La Crosse, Madison, Milwaukee, Oshkosh, Parkside, Superior, and Whitewater; Alverno College; Marquette University; College of the Menominee Nation; Carroll College; Lawrence University; Milwaukee School of Engineering; Ripon College; Medical College of Wisconsin; Western Wisconsin Technical College; and Wisconsin Lutheran College.

**Number awarded** Varies each year; recently, 9 of these grants were awarded.

**Deadline** February of each year.

## [1275]
## WOMEN'S LAW AND PUBLIC POLICY FELLOWSHIP PROGRAM

Georgetown University Law Center
Attn: Women's Law and Public Policy Fellowship
Program
600 New Jersey Avenue, N.W., Suite 334
Washington, DC 20001
(202) 662-9650                    Fax: (202) 662-9539
E-mail: mail@wlppfp.org
Web: www.wlppfp.org

**Summary** To provide an opportunity for recently-graduated lawyers in the Washington D.C. area to work on women's rights issues.

**Eligibility** This program is open to recent graduates of law schools accredited by the American Bar Association. Applicants must be interested in working on women's rights issues in the Washington, D.C. area.

**Financial data** The stipend is $37,500 per year.

**Duration** 1 year.

**Additional information** Participants are placed with different entities in the Washington, D.C. area, including women's rights organizations, civil rights groups, Congressional offices, government agencies, and Georgetown Uni-

versity Law Center clinics working on women's issues. This program includes 2 named fellowships: the Rita Charmatz Davidson Fellowship (to work on issues primarily affecting poor women) and the Harriet R. Burg Fellowship (to work primarily on issues affecting women with disabilities). Fellows are supervised by attorneys at the participating organizations.

**Number awarded** Varies each year.

**Deadline** October of each year.

## [1276]
## WOMEN'S STUDIES IN RELIGION PROGRAM

Harvard Divinity School
Attn: Director of Women's Studies in Religion Program
45 Francis Avenue
Cambridge, MA 02138
(617) 495-5705                    Fax: (617) 495-8564
E-mail: wsrp@hds.harvard.edu
Web: www.hds.harvard.edu/wsrp

**Summary** To encourage and support research on the relationship between religion, gender, and culture.

**Eligibility** This program is open to scholars who have a Ph.D. in the field of religion. Candidates with primary competence in other humanities, social sciences, and public policy fields who have a serious interest in religion and religious professionals with equivalent achievements are also eligible. Applicants should be proposing to conduct research projects at Harvard Divinity School's Women's Studies in Religion Program (WSRP) on topics related to the history and function of gender in religious traditions, the institutionalization of roles in religious communities, or the interaction between religion and the personal, social, and cultural situations of women. Appropriate topics include feminist theology, biblical studies, ethics, women's history, and interdisciplinary scholarship on women in world religions. Selection is based on the quality of the applicant's research prospectus, outlining objectives and methods; its fit with the program's research priorities; the significance of the contribution of the proposed research to the study of religion, gender, and culture, and to its field; and agreement to produce a publishable piece of work by the end of the appointment.

**Financial data** Research associates/visiting lecturers in the WSRP receive a stipend of $40,000 and benefits for a full-time appointment.

**Duration** 1 academic year, from September to June.

**Additional information** This program was founded in 1973. Fellows at the WSRP devote the majority of their appointments to individual research projects in preparation for publication, meeting together regularly for discussion of research in process. They also design and teach new courses related to their research projects and offer a series of lectures in the spring. Recipients are required to be in full-time residence at the school while carrying out their research project.

**Number awarded** 5 each year. The group each year usually includes at least 1 international scholar, 1 scholar working on a non-western tradition, 1 scholar of Judaism, and 1 minority scholar.

**Deadline** October of each year.

## [1277]
## WOMEN'S STUDIES PROGRAM DISSERTATION SCHOLARS

University of California at Santa Barbara
Women's Studies Program
Attn: Fellowship Selection Committee
4631 South Hall
Santa Barbara, CA 93106-7110
(805) 893-4330　　　　　　Fax: (805) 893-8676
E-mail: wmst@womst.ucsb.edu
Web: www.womst.ucsb.edu

**Summary** To provide funding to doctoral candidates working on dissertations in women's studies.

**Eligibility** This program is open to graduate students at any university in the United States who are U.S. citizens, have advanced to candidacy in the humanities or social sciences, demonstrate strong research and teaching interests, expect completion of their dissertation within a year, and would benefit from a residency at the University of California at Santa Barbara. Applicants should be working on a dissertation in women's studies that reflects the intersections of race, class, gender, sexuality, and cultural difference. They should send a curriculum vitae, a brief description of the dissertation project, a writing sample (up to 25 pages), and 3 letters of reference. The program is particularly interested in candidates who can contribute to the diversity and excellence of the academic community through research, teaching, and service.

**Financial data** The stipend is approximately $20,000.

**Duration** 9 months.

**Additional information** Recipients teach 1 undergraduate course and present 1 colloquium while in residence. Scholars are expected to be in residence during the residency and complete their dissertation.

**Number awarded** 2 each year.

**Deadline** January of each year.

## [1278]
## WOMEN'S STUDIO WORKSHOP STUDIO RESIDENCIES

Women's Studio Workshop
722 Binnewater Lane
P.O. Box 489
Rosendale, NY 12472
(845) 658-9133　　　　　　Fax: (845) 658-9031
E-mail: info@wsworkshop.org
Web: www.wsworkshop.org

**Summary** To provide a residency and financial support at the Women's Studio Workshop (WSW) to women artists.

**Eligibility** This program is open to artists in all stages of their careers and working in printmaking, papermaking, photography, book arts, or ceramics. Applicants must be interested in creating a new body of work while in residence at the WSW. They must provide a 1-paragraph description of the proposed project, a resume, and 10 slides of their recent work. International artists are especially encouraged to apply.

**Financial data** The program provides a stipend of $2,000 to $3,000, a $500 materials grant, a travel stipend, unlimited studio use, and housing while in residence.

**Duration** 6 to 8 weeks.

**Number awarded** Varies each year.

**Deadline** March of each year.

## [1279]
## WOODROW WILSON DISSERTATION FELLOWSHIPS IN WOMEN'S STUDIES

Woodrow Wilson National Fellowship Foundation
5 Vaughn Drive, Suite 300
P.O. Box 5281
Princeton, NJ 08543-5281
(609) 452-7007　　　　　　Fax: (609) 452-0066
E-mail: charlotte@woodrow.org
Web: www.woodrow.org/womens-studies

**Summary** To provide funding to doctoral candidates in women's studies.

**Eligibility** Students in doctoral programs who have completed all pre-dissertation requirements in any field of study at graduate schools in the United States are eligible. They must be conducting research on women that crosses disciplinary, regional, and cultural boundaries. Applications must include graduate school transcripts, letters of reference, a dissertation prospectus, a selected bibliography, a statement of interest in women's studies, and a timetable for completion of the dissertation. Selection is based on originality and significance to women's studies, scholarly validity, applicant's academic preparation and ability to accomplish the work, and probability that the dissertation will be completed within a reasonable time period.

**Financial data** Winners receive grants of $3,000 to be used for research expenses connected with the dissertation (travel, books, microfilming, photocopying, taping, and computer services).

**Additional information** Support for the program is provided by the Ford Foundation, Philip Morris Companies, and others.

**Number awarded** 10 each year.

**Deadline** November of each year.

## [1280]
## WYOMING SPACE GRANT CONSORTIUM UNDERGRADUATE RESEARCH FELLOWSHIPS

Wyoming Space Grant Consortium
c/o University of Wyoming
Physical Sciences Building, Room 210
1000 East University Avenue
P.O. Box 3905
Laramie, WY 82071-3905
(307) 766-2862　　　　　　Fax: (307) 766-2652
E-mail: wy.spacegrant@uwyo.edu
Web: wyomingspacegrant.uwyo.edu/UGFellInfo.asp

**Summary** To provide funding for space-related research to undergraduate students in Wyoming, particularly women, minority and disabled students.

**Eligibility** This program is currently open to undergraduate students at the University of Wyoming and all community colleges in Wyoming. Applicants must be U.S. citizens who are interested in conducting a space-related research project under the mentorship of a faculty member. A major in science or engineering is not required, because the program assumes that even non-science majors broaden their educations with a research experience. The faculty mentor must have active status and/or plan to be on-site and readily available to the student. Selection is based on the scientific merit of the proposed project, the pedagogical benefits to the student as a result of the overall research experience, and the quality of the proposal and recommendations. Wyoming Space Grant is a component of the Space Grant program of the U.S. National Aeronautics and Space Administration (NASA), which encourages participation by women, underrepresented minorities, and persons with disabilities.

**Financial data** Grants range up to $5,000. Funds may be used only for undergraduate salary support, at the rate of $7.75 per hour. Tuition is not provided for the student's home institution, special institutes, or off-campus programs. Other expenditures not usually supported include travel, page charges, equipment, and supplies; applicants are encouraged to seek matching funds to cover those expenditures, and proposals that include matching by non-federal funds are given priority.

**Duration** Research may be conducted during the academic year or summer.

**Additional information** This program is funded by NASA. Recipients are expected to keep the program informed of their progress, submit a final report in a timely manner, participate in publications of research results, and present a colloquium on their research.

**Number awarded** Varies each year; recently, 8 of these fellowships were awarded.

**Deadline** February of each year.

# Awards

Described in this section are 147 competitions, prizes, and honoraria granted to women in recognition or support of their personal accomplishments, professional contributions, or public service. If you are looking for a particular program and don't find it in this section, be sure to check the Program Title Index to see if it is covered elsewhere in the *Directory*.

## [1281]
## AAUW ACHIEVEMENT AWARD

American Association of University Women
Attn: AAUW Educational Foundation
1111 16th Street, N.W.
Washington, DC 20036-4873
(202) 785-7713                     Toll-free: (800) 326-AAUW
Fax: (202) 872-1425               TDD: (202) 785-7777
E-mail: foundation@aauw.org
Web: www.aauw.org/fga/awards/achieve.cfm

**Summary** To recognize and reward mature women for outstanding achievement in an academic or professional field.

**Eligibility** This program is open to women whose work in an academic or professional field is judged to be outstanding. There are no restrictions on age or field of the nominee, but the award is usually given to a mature woman whose accomplishments have spanned 10 years or more. The work must agree with the mission of the American Association of University Women (AAUW), the nominee must have national or international prominence, and she is expected to make further contributions to the lives of women.

**Financial data** The award is $10,000.

**Duration** The award is presented biennially.

**Additional information** The Northwest Central Region of the American Association of University Women (AAUW) established this award in 1943 and transferred it to the AAUW Educational Foundation in 1972. Since 1991, it has been presented every 2 years during Foundation Night at the AAUW convention.

**Number awarded** 1 each odd-numbered year.

**Deadline** Nominations must be submitted by March of each even-numbered year.

## [1282]
## AETNA SUSAN B. ANTHONY AWARD FOR EXCELLENCE IN RESEARCH ON OLDER WOMEN AND PUBLIC HEALTH.

American Public Health Association
Attn: Gerontological Health Section
800 I Street, N.W.
Washington, DC 20001-3710
(202) 777-APHA                    Fax: (202) 777-2534
E-mail: comments@apha.org
Web: www.apha.org

**Summary** To recognize and reward authors of outstanding papers on aging and women presented at the annual meeting of the American Public Health Association (APHA).

**Eligibility** This award is presented to the author of a paper that 1) frames a research question addressing an issue of importance to older women and public health; and 2) includes explicit recommendations for furthering research and practice of relevance to older women. Applicants must submit an abstract of a paper for presentation at the APHA annual meeting. Selection is based on the importance of the topic; rigor of the design, analysis, and conclusions; quality of writing; and potential benefit to the field.

**Financial data** The award is at least $500.

**Duration** The award is presented annually.

**Additional information** This award, first presented in 2000, is sponsored by Aetna Inc.

**Number awarded** 1 each year.

**Deadline** Abstracts must be submitted by February of each year.

## [1283]
## AGNES FAY MORGAN RESEARCH AWARD

Iota Sigma Pi
c/o National Director for Professional Awards
Dr. Sara Paisner
GE Global Research
One Research Circle, K1-4D17
Niskayuna, NY 12309
(518) 387-4599         E-mail: paisners@research.ge.com
Web: www.iotasigmapi.info

**Summary** To recognize and reward young women chemists and biochemists for their outstanding research achievements.

**Eligibility** Nominees must be women chemists or biochemists under 40 years of age. They may be, but need not be, members of Iota Sigma Pi (a national honor society for women in chemistry). Selection is based on the significance of their accomplishments in chemistry or biochemistry. Nominations may be made by active chapters, members, or groups of members of Iota Sigma Pi. The dossier submitted for each nominee must include a biography; a description of research achievement, indicating the specific research for which the candidate is being nominated and the significance of the research; letters of recommendation from the nominator and the seconder; and a list of publications.

**Financial data** The award consists of $500, a certificate, and a 1-year waiver of Iota Sigma Pi dues.

**Duration** The award is presented every 3 years at the triennial convention of Iota Sigma Pi, or in non-convention years at a local Iota Sigma Pi Chapter meeting, at a local American Chemical Society meeting, or at a suitable time arranged by the chair of the research award committee.

**Additional information** This award was first presented in 1951.

**Number awarded** 1 each year.

**Deadline** January of each year.

## [1284]
## AIRCRAFT TECHNICAL PUBLISHERS MAINTENANCE TECHNICIAN OF THE YEAR AWARD

Women in Aviation, International
Attn: Scholarships
Morningstar Airport
3647 State Route 503 South
West Alexandria, OH 45381
(937) 558-7655                    Fax: (937) 839-4645
E-mail: scholarships@wai.org
Web: www.wai.org/education/scholarships.cfm

**Summary** To recognize and reward members of Women in Aviation, International (WAI) who have made outstanding contributions to the maintenance field.

**Eligibility** Eligible for this award are WAI members who are licensed A&Ps or IAs and have at least 3 years of experience in an aviation maintenance field. Nominations (which should be submitted without knowledge of the nominee) must include a 500-word essay describing achievements, attitude toward self and others, dedication to career, and demonstrations of professionalism.

**Financial data**   The award is $1,000.

**Additional information**   WAI is a nonprofit professional organization dedicated to encouraging women to consider an aviation career, providing educational outreach activities, and providing networking opportunities to women active in the industry. This program is sponsored by Aircraft Technical Publishers (ATP).

**Number awarded**   1 each year.

**Deadline**   November of each year.

## [1285]
## ALEXANDRA SYMONDS AWARD

American Psychiatric Association
Attn: Committee on Women
1000 Wilson Boulevard, Suite 1825
Arlington, VA 22209-3901
(703) 907-7300          Toll-free: (888) 35-PSYCH
Fax: (703) 907-1085     E-mail: women@psych.org
Web: www.psych.org

**Summary**   To recognize and reward women who are members of the American Psychiatric Association (APA) and have contributed to the promotion of women's health.

**Eligibility**   This award is presented to a women APA member who has demonstrated sustained, high-level contributions and significant leadership in promoting women's health and the advancement of women.

**Financial data**   The award provides a $500 honorarium and a plaque.

**Duration**   The award is presented annually.

**Additional information**   This program was established in 1997. It is co-sponsored by the Association of Women Psychiatrists and supported by Wyeth-Ayerst Laboratories.

**Number awarded**   1 each year.

**Deadline**   Nominations must be submitted by June of each year.

## [1286]
## ALICE ABEL NATIONAL ARTS AWARDS

American Mothers, Inc.
Attn: Cultural and Creative Arts Program
1940 Duke Street, Suite 200
Alexandria, VA 22314
(703) 486-5760          Toll-free: (877) 242-4AMI
Fax: (703) 486-5761
E-mail: info@americanmothers.org
Web: www.americanmothers.org

**Summary**   To recognize and reward outstanding art created by members of American Mothers, Inc.

**Eligibility**   This competition is open to mothers who are artists at any level of accomplishment. Women first enter state competitions, in which they are not required to be members of American Mothers, Inc. (AMI). State winners are then entered into the national competition, for which they are required to be or become AMI members. Entries are limited to 1 per state in each of 8 categories: sculpture (modeled, carved, cast, constructed, assembled); painting (oil, acrylic); water color (water color, gouache, casein, tempera on paper); pastels (on canvas, board, paper, or any flat surface); crafts (ceramics, jewelry and metal work, textile and fabric design, quilts, porcelain dolls, stained glass); photography (black and white, color, experimental); computer graphics; and mixed media (collages, drawings, printmaking, etching, silk screen, woodcuts). All entries must adhere to the national theme: the sentiment of home, family, mothers, or motherhood.

**Financial data**   Prizes are $500.

**Duration**   The competition is held annually.

**Additional information**   The entry fee is $20 per entry. Entries must be transported personally to the national convention. Transportation costs and insurance required, if any, are the responsibility of the applicant. American Mothers, Inc. assumes no financial responsibility or liability for loss or damage to works in transit.

**Number awarded**   8 each year: 1 in each of the categories.

**Deadline**   Applications from state winners must be submitted for the national competition by February of each year.

## [1287]
## ALICE ABEL NATIONAL INSTRUMENTAL AWARD

American Mothers, Inc.
Attn: Cultural and Creative Arts Program
1940 Duke Street, Suite 200
Alexandria, VA 22314
(703) 486-5760          Toll-free: (877) 242-4AMI
Fax: (703) 486-5761
E-mail: info@americanmothers.org
Web: www.americanmothers.org

**Summary**   To recognize and reward outstanding piano or violin performances by members of American Mothers, Inc.

**Eligibility**   This competition is open to all mothers who are members of American Mothers, Inc. or who join the association when entering the competition. Applicants may not have entered into an instrumental performance contractual agreement exceeding $5,000 for 12 months prior to the application deadline. They must submit 1) a recording of their instrumental performance within the past year; 2) a 1-page biography describing musical education, performance experience, and upcoming engagements; 3) a statement describing how they instill a love of music in their family, how they balance family and musical endeavors, and how they have used their musical talents to serve their community; 4) a photograph; and 5) a $20 entry fee. Entries representing each state must have been selected for the national contest by a juried competition held in that state.

**Financial data**   The prize is $1,000.

**Duration**   The competition is held annually.

**Additional information**   The competition was started in 1984.

**Number awarded**   2 each year: 1 for piano and 1 for violin.

**Deadline**   Applications from state winners must be submitted for the national competition by February of each year.

## [1288]
### ALICE T. SCHAFER MATHEMATICS PRIZE

Association for Women in Mathematics
11240 Waples Mill Road, Suite 200
Fairfax, VA 22030
(703) 934-0163                    Fax: (703) 359-7562
E-mail: awm@math.umd.edu
Web: www.awm-math.org/schaferprize.html

**Summary** To recognize and reward undergraduate women who have demonstrated excellence in mathematics.

**Eligibility** Women may not apply for this award; they must be nominated by a member of the mathematical community. The nominee may be at any level in her undergraduate career. Selection is based on the quality of the student's performance in advanced mathematics courses and special programs, evidence of a real interest in mathematics, an ability to work independently, and performance in local and national mathematics competitions.

**Financial data** The prize is $1,000.

**Duration** The prize is presented annually.

**Additional information** This prize was first presented in 1990.

**Number awarded** 1 each year.

**Deadline** Nominations must be submitted by September of each year.

## [1289]
### AMERICAN MOTHERS VOCAL COMPETITION

American Mothers, Inc.
Attn: Cultural and Creative Arts Program
1940 Duke Street, Suite 200
Alexandria, VA 22314
(703) 486-5760                    Toll-free: (877) 242-4AMI
Fax: (703) 486-5761
E-mail: info@americanmothers.org
Web: www.americanmothers.org

**Summary** To recognize and reward outstanding vocal performances by members of American Mothers, Inc.

**Eligibility** This competition is open to all mothers who are members of American Mothers, Inc. or who join the association when entering the competition. Applicants may not have entered into an instrumental performance contractual agreement exceeding $5,000 for 12 months prior to the application deadline. They must submit 1) a tape or CD with 3 selections: a classical song or aria written before 1900, a 20th-century song or musical theater work, and a lullaby of any kind; 2) a 1-page biography describing musical education, performance experience, and upcoming engagements; 3) a statement describing how they instill a love of music in their family, how they balance family and musical endeavors, and how they have used their musical talents to serve their community; 4) a photograph; and 5) a $20 entry fee. Entries representing each state must have been selected for the national contest by a juried competition held in that state.

**Financial data** The prize is $1,000.

**Duration** The competition is held annually.

**Number awarded** 1 each year.

**Deadline** Applications from state winners must be submitted for the national competition by February of each year.

## [1290]
### AMERICAN WOMAN'S SOCIETY OF CERTIFIED PUBLIC ACCOUNTANTS PAPER AWARDS

American Woman's Society of Certified Public
   Accountants
Attn: Executive Director
136 South Keowee Street
Dayton, OH 45402
(937) 222-1872                    Toll-free: (800) AWSCPA-1
Fax: (937) 222-5794                E-mail: info@awscpa.org
Web: www.awscpa.org/frameset.php?cf=awards.htm

**Summary** To recognize and reward outstanding papers on the impact of gender on professional issues in accounting.

**Eligibility** Eligible to be considered are papers on the effects of gender on accounting, auditing, and the accounting profession. Applicants should submit papers from 8 to 10 pages in length that are directed to practitioners, not academics.

**Financial data** The awards are $500.

**Duration** Awards are presented annually.

**Additional information** Winning papers may be presented at regional or annual meetings of the American Woman's Society of Certified Public Accountants (AWSCPA) and/or published in AWSCPA publications with the author's permission.

**Number awarded** Up to 3 each year.

**Deadline** June of each year.

## [1291]
### AMERICA'S JUNIOR MISS SCHOLARSHIPS

America's Junior Miss
Attn: Foundation Administrator
751 Government Street
P.O. Box 2786
Mobile, AL 36652
(251) 438-3621                    Fax: (251) 431-0063
TDD: (800) 256-5435               E-mail: foundation@ajm.org
Web: www.ajm.org

**Summary** To recognize and reward, with college scholarships, female high school seniors who enter the America's Junior Miss competition.

**Eligibility** This competition is open to girls who are seniors in high school. Contestants first enter local competitions, from which winners advance to the state level. The winner in each state is invited to the national competition, held in Mobile, Alabama in June of each year. Prior to the contestants' arrival for the national competition, the judges evaluate their high school academic records for the scholastics score (20% of the overall score). At the competition, girls are given scores on the basis of their personality, maturity, and ability to express themselves in an interview (25% of overall score); their performing arts talent presented on stage in front of an audience (25% of overall score); their fitness as demonstrated during a choreographed aerobic routine (15% of overall score); and their self-expression, demeanor, sense of style, and speaking ability (15% of overall score). The girls with the highest scores in the categories of talent, scholastics, fitness, and self-expression receive awards. Overall scores are used for selection of 8 finalists, from whom the winner and 2 runners-up are selected. Girls also submit a scrapbook, a daily journal, and essays on their community service, "Be Your Best Self," and "My Town." All of those are also evaluated for selection of awardees.

**Financial data** In a recent national competition, the winner received a $50,000 scholarship, first runner-up $15,000, second runner-up $10,000, and each other finalist $3,500. Other awards included $1,500 for the Community Service Essay Award and $1,000 each for the Spirit of Junior Miss Award, talent awards, scholastic awards, fitness awards, self-expression awards, "Be Your Best Self" Essay Awards, Scrapbook Awards, Daily Journal Award, and "My Town" Award. A total of $121,000 was awarded. Other scholarships are presented in state and local competitions.

**Duration** The competition is held annually.

**Additional information** This program was established in 1958 and closed in 2005. In 2006, it was reopened. National sponsors include Tyson Foods, SeaWorld, Busch Gardens, the Mitchell Company, the City of Mobile (Alabama), and Mobile County.

**Number awarded** Recently, awards included 1 winner, 1 first runner-up, 1 second runner up, 5 other finalists, 1 Community Service Essay Award, 1 Spirit of Junior Miss Award, 5 talent awards, 5 scholastic awards, 5 fitness awards, 5 self-expressions awards, 3 "Be Your Best Self" Essay Awards, 1 Scrapbook Award, 1 Daily Journal Award, and 1 "My Town" Award. Because each competitor could receive multiple awards, a total of 21 girls received awards.

**Deadline** Deadlines vary in different parts of the country.

## [1292]
## AMERICA'S NATIONAL TEEN-AGER SCHOLARSHIP PROGRAM

National Teen-Ager Scholarship Foundation
Attn: Cheryl Snow
808 Deer Crossing Court
Nashville, TN 37220
(615) 370-4338          Toll-free: (866) NAT-TEEN
Fax: (615) 377-0223     E-mail: telwar@comcast.net
Web: www.nationalteen.com

**Summary** To recognize (locally and nationally) the scholastic and leadership achievements of America's teenage girls and to provide cash, tuition scholarships, and awards to the participants.

**Eligibility** Girls who are 12 to 15 years of age are eligible to enter the Miss Junior National Teenager competition and girls who are 16 to 18 may enter the Miss National Teenager competition. Entrants must have no children and never have been married. Selection is based on academic excellence (15%), school and community involvement (15%), social and conversational skills in an interview (30%), poise and personality in an evening gown (15%), personal expression (15%), and response to an on-stage question (10%). There is no swimsuit competition.

**Financial data** Miss National Teenager receives approximately $40,000 in cash, trips, and prizes, including a $10,000 college scholarship. Miss Junior National Teenager receives approximately $35,000 in cash, trips, and prizes, including a $5,000 college scholarship. In addition, a number of academic institutions offer scholarships to state or national winners.

**Duration** The contest is held annually.

**Additional information** The contest began in 1971, to recognize the leadership achievements of America's teenagers and to provide travel, entertainment, and scholarships for their college education. The application fee is $25.

**Deadline** Deadline dates vary. Check with the sponsors of your local and state pageant.

## [1293]
## ANN AND GORDON GETTY AWARDS

National Federation of Music Clubs
1336 North Delaware Street
Indianapolis, IN 46202-2481
(317) 638-4003          Fax: (317) 638-0503
E-mail: info@nfmc-music.org
Web: www.nfmc-music.org

**Summary** To recognize and reward outstanding singers who participate in the Biennial Young Artist Awards competition of the National Federation of Music Clubs (NFMC).

**Eligibility** Voice entrants must be between 25 and 37 years of age. Separate competitions are held for men and women. Membership in the federation and U.S. citizenship are required. Candidates for the NFMC Biennial Young Artist Awards competition are automatically considered for these awards; no separate application is necessary.

**Financial data** Each award is $500.

**Duration** The competition is held biennially, in odd-numbered years.

**Additional information** Applications and further information are available from Mrs. Nannette Hanslowe, 296 Medford Leas, Medford, NJ 08055; information on all federation scholarships and awards is available from Chair, Competitions and Awards Board, Dr. George R. Keck, 421 Cherry Street, Arkadelphia, AR 71923-5116, E-mail: keckg@obu.edu. There is a $40 entry fee.

**Number awarded** 2 every other year: 1 for a man and 1 for a woman.

**Deadline** February of odd-numbered years.

## [1294]
## ANNA LOUISE HOFFMAN AWARD FOR OUTSTANDING ACHIEVEMENT IN GRADUATE RESEARCH

Iota Sigma Pi
c/o National Director for Student Awards, Kathryn A. Thomasson
University of North Dakota, Department of Chemistry
P.O. Box 9024
Grand Forks, ND 58202-9024
(701) 777-3199          Fax: (701) 777-2331
E-mail: kthomasson@chem.und.edu
Web: www.iotasigmapi.info

**Summary** To recognize and reward outstanding research proposals in chemistry by women graduate students.

**Eligibility** Nominated women must be full-time (as defined by their institution) graduate students in chemistry at an accredited institution. Nomination for the award must be made by members of the institution's graduate faculty. Only 1 nomination may be submitted by each chemistry department. Nominees may be, but need not be, members of Iota Sigma Pi. The research proposed by the candidate must be original research that can be described by 1 of the main chemical divisions (e.g., analytical, biochemical, inorganic, organic, physical, and/or ancillary divisions of chemistry). The nomination dossier must contain the candidate's permanent and school addresses, an academic history, 2 recommendations, and a brief description of the candidate's research (no more than 1,000 words and prepared by the candidate).

**Financial data** The award is $500 and a certificate.

**Duration** The award is offered annually.

**Additional information** This award was first presented in 1979.

**Number awarded** 1 each year.

**Deadline** February of each year.

## [1295]
## ANNE C. CARTER STUDENT LEADERSHIP AWARD

American Medical Women's Association Foundation
Attn: AMWA Foundation
211 North Union Street, Suite 100
Alexandria, VA 22314
(703) 838-0500                    Fax: (703) 549-3864
E-mail: foundation@amwa-doc.org
Web: www.amwa-doc.org

**Summary** To recognize and reward student members of the American Medical Women's Association (AMWA) who have demonstrated exceptional leadership skills.

**Eligibility** This program is open to student members of the association who are nominated by their chapter. Nominees must have demonstrated exceptional leadership skills through vision, inspiration, innovation, and coordination of local projects that further the mission of AMWA by improving women's health and/or supporting women in medicine.

**Financial data** The award is $750. The nominating chapter also receives an award of $750 to be used at its discretion.

**Duration** The award is presented annually.

**Number awarded** 1 each year.

**Deadline** October of each year.

## [1296]
## ANNIE JUMP CANNON AWARD IN ASTRONOMY

American Astronomical Society
Attn: Annie J. Cannon Award Committee
2000 Florida Avenue, N.W., Suite 400
Washington, DC 20009-1231
(202) 328-2010                    Fax: (202) 234-2560
E-mail: aassec@aas.org
Web: www.aas.org/grants/awards.html

**Summary** To recognize and reward women postdoctoral scholars for significant research in astronomy.

**Eligibility** This award is available to North American female astronomers who are within 5 years of completing their Ph.D. Self nominations are allowed. Selection is based on completed research and promise for future research.

**Financial data** The award is $1,500.

**Duration** The award is presented annually.

**Additional information** This award was established in 1934 by the American Astronomical Society (AAS). From 1974 through 2004, it was awarded by the American Association of University Women (AAUW) Educational Foundation with the advice of the AAS. Effective in 2005, the AAS resumed administration of the award.

**Number awarded** 1 each year.

**Deadline** September of each year.

## [1297]
## AQHA NATIONAL FEMALE EQUESTRIAN AWARD

Women's Sports Foundation
Attn: Award and Grant Programs Manager
Eisenhower Park
1899 Hempstead Turnpike, Suite 400
East Meadow, NY 11554-1000
(516) 542-4700                    Toll-free: (800) 227-3988
Fax: (516) 542-4716
E-mail: info@womenssportsfoundation.org
Web: www.womenssportsfoundation.org

**Summary** To recognize and reward outstanding female equestrians.

**Eligibility** This award is presented to a female equestrian with national ranking who demonstrates leadership, sportsmanship, and commitment to the sport and its athletes. Applicants must exhibit national or international ranking or the potential for such ranking in sanctioned events and/or competing with a registered horse, serve as a role model for female equestrians, practice exemplary communication skills with the media and public, aspire to benefit the horse industry, and explain how they plan to contribute to the sponsoring organization and women's sports.

**Financial data** The award is $2,000. The recipient must use the funds for pursuit of her equestrian career.

**Duration** The award is presented annually.

**Additional information** This award is presented in collaboration with the American Quarter Horse Association (AQHA).

**Number awarded** 1 each year.

**Deadline** June of each year.

## [1298]
## ART SCHOLARSHIPS FOR MATURE WOMEN

National League of American Pen Women
1300 17th Street, N.W.
Washington, DC 20036-1973
(202) 785-1997                    Fax: (202) 452-8868
E-mail: nlapw1@verizon.net
Web: www.americanpenwomen.org

**Summary** To provide financial assistance for education to mature women artists.

**Eligibility** Women artists or photographers who are 35 years of age or older are eligible to apply if neither they nor members of their immediate family are members of the league. They must submit 3 color prints (4 by 6 inches or larger) of any media (oil, water color, original works on paper, acrylic, or sculpture) or 3 color or black-and-white prints (8 by 10 inches) of photographic works.

**Financial data** The award is $1,000. Funds are to be used for education.

**Duration** The award is granted biennially.

**Additional information** This award is offered in memory of Helen Trueheart Cox. An entry fee of $8 and a self-addressed stamped envelope must accompany each application.

**Number awarded** 1 each even-numbered year.

**Deadline** January of even-numbered years.

## [1299]
## BARBARA PENNY KANNER AWARD

Western Association of Women Historians
c/o MariaElena Raymond
17400 Amethyst Drive
Fort Bragg, CA 95437
Web: wawh.org/awardsandprizes.html

**Summary** To recognize and reward outstanding scholarly bibliographical and historical guides to research focused on women's or gender history.

**Eligibility** This award is presented in alternate years to 1) bibliomethodologies that reflect the critical tools of the historian's craft as they have been developed to provide research guides (not library catalogues), and 2) autobiographies in historical context that reflect the craft of history as developed and interpreted in individual lives. Book-length submissions are preferred, but substantial guides in other forms (articles or book chapters) may also be considered. Applicants must be members of the Western Association of Women Historians at the time of application. Their project must relate to women's or gender history.

**Financial data** The award is $500.

**Duration** The competition is held annually.

**Additional information** This award was established in 1994.

**Number awarded** 1 each year.

**Deadline** January of each year.

## [1300]
## BARNARD WOMEN POETS PRIZE

Barnard College
Attn: Department of English
417 Barnard Hall
3009 Broadway
New York, NY 10027-6598
(212) 854-2116        Fax: (212) 854-9498
E-mail: english@barnard.edu
Web: www.barnard.edu/english/wpprize.html

**Summary** To recognize and reward outstanding unpublished poetry written by American women.

**Eligibility** This program is open to women writers who have already published 1 book of poetry and are seeking a publisher for a second collection. Manuscripts that are under option to another publisher are not eligible. Interested applicants should submit 2 copies of a book-length manuscript (the page limit is not specified).

**Financial data** The prize is $1,500 and publication of the manuscript.

**Duration** The competition is held annually.

**Additional information** Winning submissions are published by W.W. Norton & Co. The entry fee is $20.

**Number awarded** 1 each year.

**Deadline** October of each year.

## [1301]
## BARNUM FESTIVAL FOUNDATION/JENNY LIND COMPETITION FOR SOPRANOS

Barnum Festival Foundation
Attn: Director
1070 Main Street
Bridgeport, CT 06604
(203) 367-8495        Toll-free: (866) 867-8495
E-mail: office@barnumfestival.com
Web: www.barnumfestival.com

**Summary** To recognize and reward (with scholarships and a concert trip to Sweden) outstanding young female singers who have not yet reached professional status.

**Eligibility** Applicants must be sopranos between the ages of 20 and 30 who have not yet attained professional status and who are residents and citizens of the United States. Past finalists may reapply, but former first-place winners and mezzo-sopranos are not eligible. The preliminary audition for 16 contestants chosen on the basis of audio tapes is held at the Barnum Festival in Bridgeport, Connecticut every April. From this audition, 6 finalists are chosen. Final selection of the winner is based on technique, musicianship, diction, interpretation, and stage presence.

**Financial data** The winner of the competition is presented with a $2,000 scholarship award to further her musical education at a recognized voice training school, academy, or college or with a recognized voice teacher or coach. She is featured in a concert in June with the Swedish Jenny Lind at a locale in Connecticut, and is sent to Sweden with her Swedish counterpart to perform in concerts for 2 weeks in July and August. The runner-up receives a $500 scholarship.

**Duration** The competition is held annually.

**Additional information** The winner of this competition serves as the American Jenny Lind, a 20th-century counterpart of the Swedish Nightingale brought to the United States for a successful concert tour in 1850 by P.T. Barnum. There is a $35 application fee.

**Number awarded** 2 each year: 1 winner and 1 runner-up.

**Deadline** March of each year.

## [1302]
## BERKSHIRE CONFERENCE ARTICLE PRIZE

Berkshire Conference of Women Historians
c/o Annelise Orleck
Dartmouth College, Department of History
6107 Carson Hall, Room 402
Hanover, NH 03755
(603) 646-3283        Fax: (603) 646-3353
E-mail: annelise.orleck@dartmouth.edu
Web: www.berksconference.org

**Summary** To recognize and reward women who have written outstanding historical articles.

**Eligibility** This prize is awarded for the best article on any historical subject written by a woman normally resident in North America during the preceding year. Articles may be nominated by the author herself, by colleagues, or by journal editors.

**Financial data** The prize $500.

**Duration** The prize is awarded annually.

**Number awarded** 1 each year.

**Deadline** January of each year.

## [1303]
## BERKSHIRE CONFERENCE FIRST BOOK PRIZE

Berkshire Conference of Women Historians
c/o Kathryn Norberg
UCLA, Department of History
5248 Bunche Hall
Los Angeles, CA 90095-1473
(310) 825-7317          E-mail: knorberg@ucla.edu
Web: www.berksconference.org

**Summary** To recognize and reward women who have written outstanding first books in history.

**Eligibility** This prize is awarded for the best first book on any historical subject written by a woman normally resident in North America during the preceding year. Books need not focus on women's history. Textbooks, juveniles, collections of essays, and documentary collections are not eligible.

**Financial data** The prize $1,000.

**Duration** The prize is awarded annually.

**Number awarded** 1 each year.

**Deadline** January of each year.

## [1304]
## BILL WHITEHEAD AWARD FOR LIFETIME ACHIEVEMENT

Publishing Triangle
332 Bleecker Street, D36
New York, NY 10014
E-mail: awards@publishingtriangle.org
Web: www.publishingtriangle.org/awards.asp

**Summary** To recognize and reward writers who have dealt openly with gay or lesbian issues.

**Eligibility** This is a lifetime achievement award. It is presented to writers whose body of work makes a significant contribution to gay and lesbian literature. The award alternates between women (in even-numbered years) and men (in odd-numbered years). Only members of the Publishing Triangle may nominate candidates for the award.

**Financial data** The award is $3,000.

**Duration** The award is presented annually.

**Additional information** The Publishing Triangle is an association of lesbians and gay men in publishing. This award was first presented in 1989. Current Publishing Triangle members may submit a nomination for free, but others must include a $25 fee.

**Number awarded** 1 each year.

**Deadline** November of each year.

## [1305]
## CALGON TAKE ME AWAY TO COLLEGE SCHOLARSHIPS

Coty US LLC
One Park Avenue, Fifth Floor
New York, NY 10016
(212) 479-4300          Fax: (212) 479-4399
Web: www.takemeaway.com

**Summary** To recognize and reward, with college scholarships, women who are graduating high school seniors or already enrolled in college and provide excellent answers to online essay questions.

**Eligibility** This competition is open to women residents of the United States who are 18 years of age or older. Applicants must be enrolled or planning to enroll as a full-time undergraduate student at a 4-year U.S. college or university and have a GPA of 3.0 or higher. They must submit online answers (up to 900 characters) to questions that change annually; recently, applicants were invited to write on 1) how stepping outside their comfort zone to try something new has taken them on an unexpected path and changed their life; and 2) a childhood event that they feel has most shaped who they are and what they believe in. Those short answers are judged on the basis of originality, quality of expression, and accordance with standard rules of English grammar, mechanics, and spelling. Financial need is not considered. The 35 finalists are then invited to submit a short essay on a specified topic, transcripts, a list of extracurricular activities, and other documents as part of an application packet to be provided. Scholarship America ranks the finalists on the basis of merit, exclusive of the essays. Maddenmedia selects the winner on the basis of that ranking and the essays.

**Financial data** First place is a $5,000 scholarship, second a $2,000 scholarship, third a $1,000 scholarship, and runners-up $500 scholarships.

**Duration** The competition is held annually.

**Additional information** This annual competition began in 1999. Information is also available from Scholarship America, One Scholarship Way, P.O. Box 297, St. Peter, MN 56082, (507) 931-1682, (800) 537-4180, Fax: (507) 931-9168, E-mail: smsinfo@csfa.org, and from Maddenmedia, 1650 East Fort Lowell Road, Suite 100, Tucson, AZ 85719.

**Number awarded** 9 each year: 1 first place, 1 second, 1 third, and 6 runners-up.

**Deadline** February of each year.

## [1306]
## C.A.R. COACH OF THE YEAR AWARD

Women's Sports Foundation
Attn: Award and Grant Programs Manager
Eisenhower Park
1899 Hempstead Turnpike, Suite 400
East Meadow, NY 11554-1000
(516) 542-4700          Toll-free: (800) 227-3988
Fax: (516) 542-4716
E-mail: info@womenssportsfoundation.org
Web: www.womenssportsfoundation.org

**Summary** To recognize and reward women coaches working with community youth, schools, and college athletes.

**Eligibility** These awards are presented to women who are coaching at the community, school, junior college, and NCAA Division III levels.

**Financial data** Winners receive national recognition and a $500 grant to the girls sports program of their choice.

**Duration** The awards are presented annually.

**Additional information** These awards, originally established in 1986, are part of the Coaches Advisory Roundtable (C.A.R.) program.

**Number awarded** Up to 4 each year.

**Deadline** January of each year.

## [1307]
## CARRIE CHAPMAN CATT PRIZE FOR RESEARCH ON WOMEN AND POLITICS

Iowa State University
Attn: Carrie Chapman Catt Center for Women and
    Politics
309 Carrie Chapman Catt Hall
Ames, IA 50011-1305
(515) 294-3181                    Fax: (515) 294-3741
E-mail: cattcntr@iastate.edu
Web: www.iastate.edu/~cccatt

**Summary** To recognize and reward outstanding research in the area of women and politics.

**Eligibility** This competition is open to scholars at all levels, including graduate students and junior faculty, who are planning to conduct research in the area of women and politics. Applicants must submit a detailed description of their research project, including 1) its purpose and content; 2) a discussion of relevant theory, contributions to literature in the field, and methodology; 3) a statement on how this prize will contribute to the research project; and 4) a timetable for completion of the project. They also must submit a 1-page biographical statement, highlighting their research interests, significant publications and/or presentations, and professional interests and experiences. Research projects can address the annual conference theme or any other topic related to women and politics.

**Financial data** Prizes are $1,000 for winners or $500 for honorable mention. All prize-winners may also receive travel expenses to Des Moines, Iowa where awards are presented at the annual conference of the Carrie Chapman Catt Center for Women and Politics.

**Duration** The prizes are awarded annually.

**Number awarded** Up to 4 winners and up to 2 honorable mentions are selected each year.

**Deadline** September of each year.

## [1308]
## CARROLL L. BIRCH STUDENT RESEARCH AWARD

American Medical Women's Association Foundation
Attn: AMWA Foundation
211 North Union Street, Suite 100
Alexandria, VA 22314
(703) 838-0500                    Fax: (703) 549-3864
E-mail: foundation@amwa-doc.org
Web: www.amwa-doc.org

**Summary** To recognize and reward the most outstanding paper written by a student member of the American Medical Women's Association (AMWA).

**Eligibility** This competition is open to national AMWA medical student members who attend an accredited U.S. allopathic or osteopathic medical school. Applicants must submit an original research paper (and a 250-word abstract) that has not been previously published.

**Financial data** The prize is $1,000 and publication in the *Journal of the American Medical Women's Association*.

**Duration** The award is presented annually.

**Additional information** This award is sponsored by the association's Chicago Branch. It has been presented since 1965.

**Number awarded** 1 each year.

**Deadline** June of each year.

## [1309]
## COLGATE-PALMOLIVE RESEARCH SCHOLARSHIP AWARD

American Association of Women Dentists
216 West Jackson Boulevard, Suite 625
Chicago, IL 60606
Toll-free: (800) 920-AAWD          Fax: (312) 750-1203
E-mail: info@aawd.org
Web: www.aawd.org

**Summary** To recognize and reward members of the American Association of Women Dentists (AAWD) who have shown academic distinction and excellence in research.

**Eligibility** This program is open to AAWD members who are junior or senior dental students. Along with their applications, students must submit a curriculum vitae, transcripts, and letters of recommendation. Selection is based on academic distinction and demonstration of excellence in research.

**Financial data** The award is $500.

**Duration** The awards are presented annually.

**Additional information** This program, which began in 1980, is funded by the Colgate-Palmolive Company.

**Number awarded** 10 each year.

**Deadline** February of each year.

## [1310]
## COURAGE IN JOURNALISM AWARDS

International Women's Media Foundation
Attn: Project Manager
1625 K Street, N.W., Suite 1275
Washington, DC 20006-1680
(202) 496-1992          Fax: (202) 496-1977
E-mail: courage@iwmf.org
Web: www.iwmf.org/courage

**Summary** To recognize and reward women journalists from any country who have demonstrated extraordinary strength of character in pursuing their craft under difficult or dangerous circumstances.

**Eligibility** Eligible to be nominated are women journalists (full-time, part-time, or freelance) working in print, broadcast, or online media from any country. Nominees must have demonstrated extraordinary strength of character, bravery, and perseverance in reporting the news; have a strong commitment to press freedom; and be well-respected journalists. They must have pursued their craft under difficult or dangerous circumstances: physical danger, official secrecy or oppression, political pressure, or any other professionally-intimidating obstacle. Letters of nomination should include a brief biography highlighting the nominee's work history as it relates to the award, the nominee's resume or curriculum vitae, samples of the nominee's work, and 2 letters of support from professional associates.

**Financial data** The prize is $5,000 and a crystal sculpture symbolizing freedom and courage.

**Duration** The prize is awarded annually.

**Additional information** This award was established in 1990. Nomination materials are not returned.

**Number awarded** 3 each year.

**Deadline** March of each year.

## [1311]
## CRA UNDERGRADUATE AWARDS

Computing Research Association
1100 17th Street, N.W., Suite 507
Washington, DC 20036-4632
(202) 234-2111          Fax: (202) 667-1066
E-mail: awards@cra.org
Web: www.cra.org

**Summary** To recognize and reward undergraduate students who show exceptional promise in an area of importance to computing research.

**Eligibility** Eligible to be nominated by their department chairs for this award are undergraduate students in the United States or Canada who are majoring in computer science, computer engineering, or an equivalent program. A department may nominate more than 1 candidate. The nomination package must include a completed nomination form, the nominee's resume (up to 2 pages), the nominee's transcript, a verification statement signed by the department chair, 2 letters of support, and a 1-page description of the student's research or other achievements. Out of the pool of candidates, the most outstanding woman and the most outstanding man are selected on the basis of academic record and computing research contributions.

**Financial data** The award is $1,000.

**Duration** The competition is held annually.

**Additional information** This award is sponsored by Microsoft Corporation (in odd-numbered years) and Mitsubishi Electric Research Labs (in even-numbered years). The 2 first-prize winners also receive financial assistance to attend a major computing research conference, where the prizes are awarded.

**Number awarded** 2 cash prizes (1 to a woman and 1 to a man) and a number of certificates of honorable mention.

**Deadline** October of each year.

## [1312]
## CYNOSURE SCREENWRITING AWARDS

BroadMind Entertainment
3699 Wilshire Boulevard, Suite 850
Los Angeles, CA 90010
(310) 855-8730   E-mail: cynosure@broadmindent.com
Web: www.broadmindent.com

**Summary** To recognize and reward outstanding unpublished screenplays with 1) a female protagonist or 2) a minority protagonist.

**Eligibility** Writers in any country are eligible to submit unpublished feature-length scripts (90-130 pages) with either a female protagonist or with a minority protagonist (either male or female). Scripts may be submitted under 1 category only. Scripts by multiple authors are acceptable. More than 1 script may be submitted, provided the signed entry/release form and an application fee accompany each submission. Scripts must be registered with the WGA or with the U.S. Copyright Office. Screenplays must be in English and may be of any genre.

**Financial data** The prize is $2,500.

**Duration** The competition is held annually.

**Additional information** This competition began in 1999. The fee is $45 for early entries, $50 for regular entries, or $55 for late entries.

**Number awarded** 2 each year: 1 for scripts with female protagonists and 1 for scripts with a minority protagonist.

**Deadline** Deadlines are March of each year for early, April of each year for regular, or June of each year for late entries.

## [1313]
## DENISE GAUDREAU AWARD FOR EXCELLENCE IN QUATERNARY STUDIES

American Quaternary Association
c/o Eric Grimm, President
Illinois State Museum Research and Collections Center
1011 East Ash Street
Springfield, IL 62703
(217) 785-4846          Fax: (217) 785-2857
E-mail: president@amqua.org
Web: www.amqua.org/about/awards

**Summary** To support the early career development of women graduate students in quaternary studies.

**Eligibility** This program is open to female scientists in any field of quaternary studies who are within 2 years of completing a doctoral degree. Applicants must not have completed their dissertation research. The application should include a curriculum vitae, a summary of research interests, copies of graduate transcripts, and the names of 2 referees. Selection is based on scientific accomplishments, promise, and demonstration of original thinking. Emphasis is placed on the quality and carefulness of the work, rather than simply on quantity.

**Financial data** The award is $500.

**Duration** The award is presented biennially, in even-numbered years.

**Additional information** This award was established in 1993.

**Number awarded** 1 every other year.

**Deadline** February of even-numbered years.

## [1314]
## DOLORES E. FISHER AWARD

Mel Fisher Maritime Heritage Society and Museum
Attn: Curator, Department of Education
200 Greene Street
Key West, FL 33040
(305) 294-2633                Fax: (305) 294-5671
Web: www.melfisher.org/deoaward.htm

**Summary** To recognize and reward, with funding for college or graduate school, women who submit outstanding essays on the oceans.

**Eligibility** This competition is open to women between 16 and 30 years of age. Candidates must submit a 1,000-word essay on how they hope to make a difference in the world through their passion for the oceans, their career goals, and how this award will help them achieve those goals. They must also include 3 letters of recommendation and a brief statement on the personality characteristic they value most in themselves and why. If they are currently enrolled in school, they must identify their program, but school enrollment is not required.

**Financial data** The award is $1,000.

**Duration** The award is presented annually.

**Number awarded** 1 each year.

**Deadline** March of each year.

## [1315]
## DOROTHEA M. LANG PIONEER AWARD

American College of Nurse-Midwives
Attn: ACNM Foundation, Inc.
8403 Coleville Road, Suite 1550
Silver Spring, MD 20915
(240) 485-1850                Fax: (240) 485-1818
Web: www.midwife.org

**Summary** To recognize and reward members of the American College of Nurse-Midwives (ACNM) who have made outstanding contributions to the profession of midwifery.

**Eligibility** Nominees for this award must have been ACNM members for at least 10 years. They must have demonstrated vision and leadership in 1 of the following categories: pioneering midwives who, after 1958, demonstrated what midwifery care could and should be on the health team; pioneering efforts to integrate midwives and midwifery into the health care system of the United States or internationally; unsung heroes who initiated, rescued, enhanced, or save midwifery services or educational programs or are working to accomplish those goals; visionaries who encouraged or created open-minded pathways in edu-

cation for professional midwives or are working to accomplish that goal; energetic anticipants who have furthered or are furthering the legislative agenda for certified midwives; or have contributed other pioneering activities.

**Financial data** The award includes a cash honorarium and a necklace.

**Duration** The award is presented annually.

**Additional information** This program was established in 2002.

**Number awarded** Varies each year; recently, 3 of these awards were presented.

**Deadline** January of each year.

## [1316]
## DOTTIE LAMM AWARD

Women's Foundation of Colorado
1580 Logan Street, Suite 500
Denver, CO 80203
(303) 832-8800, ext. 25          Fax: (303) 832-8362
E-mail: wfco@wfco.org
Web: www.wfco.org/dottielamm.asp

**Summary** To recognize and reward outstanding high school women students in Colorado.

**Eligibility** Women in Colorado who are currently sophomores in high school may be nominated for this award. Selection is based on service to the community, especially on matters that affect women.

**Financial data** The award is $1,500.

**Duration** The award is presented annually.

**Additional information** This program was established in 1988 to honor Colorado's former first lady, a founder and the first president of the Women's Foundation of Colorado.

**Number awarded** 2 each year.

**Deadline** April of each year.

## [1317]
## EDITH M. WORTMAN ANNUAL MATRIX
## FOUNDATION PUBLIC SPEAKING COMPETITION

Association for Women in Communications
Attn: Matrix Foundation
3337 Duke Street
Alexandria, VA 22314
(703) 370-7436                Fax: (703) 370-7437
E-mail: mail@matrixfoundation.us
Web: www.matrixfoundation.us

**Summary** To recognize and reward women who present outstanding public speeches on the First Amendment.

**Eligibility** This competition is open to women who present on videotape a speech that relates to First Amendment issues. Tapes, in English and no longer than 10 minutes, must first be presented to a participating local chapter of the Association for Women in Communications (AWC). Each submission must include the complete written text of the speech, verification of its originality, and a release to allow the sponsor to use the speech for fundraising and educational purposes.

**Financial data** Awards are $500 for first place, $300 for second, and $100 for third.

**Duration** The competition is held annually.

**Additional information** This competition was established in 2003. The prizes are designated the Helen Duhamel Achievement Awards. Information is also available from Mary Kay Switzer, Matrix Foundation Secretary/Treasurer, 4133 West Wilson, Number 171, Banning, CA 92220-1302. The entry fee is $10 for AWC members or $15 for nonmembers.

**Number awarded** 3 each year.

**Deadline** The recommended local deadline is April of each year.

## [1318]
## EDUCATOR'S AWARD

Delta Kappa Gamma Society International
416 West 12th Street
P.O. Box 1589
Austin, TX 78767-1589
(512) 478-5748                    Toll-free: (888) 762-4685
Fax: (512) 478-3961
E-mail: educatorsaward@deltakappagamma.org
Web: www.deltakappagamma.org

**Summary** To recognize women's contributions to education that may influence future directions in the profession; these contributions may be in research, philosophy, or any other area of learning that is stimulating and creative.

**Eligibility** Any published book in research, philosophy, or another area of learning that stimulates the intellect and imagination may be submitted for consideration if it is written by 1 or 2 women in Canada, Costa Rica, El Salvador, Finland, Germany, Guatemala, Iceland, Mexico, the Netherlands, Norway, Puerto Rico, Sweden, the United Kingdom, or the United States and copyrighted (in its first edition or the first English translation) during the preceding calendar year. Contributions should possess excellence in style, be well-edited and attractive in format, and be of more than local interest. Ineligible are methods books, skill books, textbooks, and unpublished manuscripts.

**Financial data** The award is $1,500. In the case of dual authorship, the prize is divided in the same manner as royalties are divided by the awardees' publisher.

**Duration** The award is granted annually.

**Additional information** This award was first presented in 1946.

**Number awarded** 1 each year.

**Deadline** February of each year.

## [1319]
## ELEANOR ROOSEVELT FUND AWARD

American Association of University Women
Attn: AAUW Educational Foundation
1111 16th Street, N.W.
Washington, DC 20036-4873
(202) 785-7602                    Toll-free: (800) 326-AAUW
Fax: (202) 872-1425               TDD: (202) 785-7777
E-mail: foundation@aauw.org
Web: www.aauw.org/fga/awards/erf.cfm

**Summary** To recognize and reward individuals, organizations, institutions, or projects that provide an equitable school environment for women and girls.

**Eligibility** Nominations for this award are not solicited from the general public. The goals of the Eleanor Roosevelt Fund are to 1) remove barriers to women's and girls' participation in education; 2) promote the value of diversity and cross-cultural communication; and 3) develop greater understanding of the ways women learn, think, work, and play. Individuals, organizations, institutions, or projects that work for those goals are eligible to be nominated for this award. Their activities may include classroom teaching, educational and research contributions, and legal and legislative work that contribute to equity for women and girls. Although the award focuses on education, the nominee need not be an educator.

**Financial data** The award is $5,000.

**Duration** The award is presented biennially.

**Additional information** This award was established in 1989.

**Number awarded** 1 each odd-numbered year.

**Deadline** Nominations must be submitted by November of even-numbered years.

## [1320]
## ELIZABETH LOWELL PUTNAM PRIZE

Mathematical Association of America
1529 18th Street, N.W.
Washington, DC 20036-1358
(202) 387-5200                    Toll-free: (800) 741-9415
Fax: (202) 265-2384               E-mail: maahq@maa.org
Web: www.maa.org/Awards/putnam.html

**Summary** To recognize and reward outstanding women participants in a mathematics competition.

**Eligibility** This program is open to women at colleges and universities in Canada and the United States. Entrants participate in an examination containing mathematics problems designed to test originality as well as technical competence. The woman with the highest score receives this prize.

**Financial data** The prize is $1,000.

**Duration** The competition is held annually.

**Additional information** This program was established in 1992.

**Number awarded** 1 each year.

## [1321]
## EQUALITY AWARD

American Library Association
Attn: Governance Office, Awards Program
50 East Huron Street
Chicago, IL 60611-2795
(312) 280-3247      Toll-free: (800) 545-2433, ext. 3247
Fax: (312) 280-3256               TDD: (312) 944-7298
TDD: (888) 814-7692               E-mail: awards@ala.org
Web: www.ala.org

**Summary** To recognize and reward the person or group that best promotes equality in librarianship.

**Eligibility** This program is open to librarians and other people who work in a library, are a trustee, work in a library-related institution, work in an organization, work in an association, or work in a subdivision of any of those. Nominees must have contributed significantly to promoting equality in the library profession, either through a sustained contribution or a single outstanding accomplishment. The award may be given for an activist or scholarly contribution in such areas as pay equity, affirmative action, legislative work, or non-sexist education.

**Financial data**  The award is $500 and a citation.

**Duration**  The award is presented annually.

**Additional information**  The award, first presented in 1984, is funded by Scarecrow Press and administered by the American Library Association.

**Number awarded**  1 each year.

**Deadline**  November of each year.

## [1322]
## EUDORA WELTY PRIZE

Mississippi University for Women
Attn: Department of Languages, Literature, and
  Philosophy
Painter Hall, Room 111
W-Box 1634
Columbus, MS 39701
(662) 329-7386                    Fax: (662) 329-7387
E-mail: info@humanities.muw.edu
Web: www.muw.edu/welty

**Summary**  To recognize and reward original works of interpretive scholarship from disciplines within the humanities and related to women's studies, Southern studies, or modern letters.

**Eligibility**  Eligible to be submitted are unpublished book-length manuscripts (80,000 to 100,000 words) complete at the time of submission and not under consideration by any other press. Submissions must be original works of interpretive scholarship and from disciplines within the humanities related to women's studies, Southern studies, or modern literature. Collections of essays, bibliographies, translations, and unrevised theses or dissertations are not eligible.

**Financial data**  The prize consists of a cash award of $1,500 and publication of the winning manuscript by the University Press of Mississippi.

**Duration**  The competition is held annually.

**Additional information**  This prize, established in 1989, is jointly sponsored by Mississippi University for Women and the University Press of Mississippi.

**Number awarded**  1 each year.

**Deadline**  April of each year.

## [1323]
## FASEB EXCELLENCE IN SCIENCE AWARD

Federation of American Societies for Experimental
  Biology
Attn: Excellence in Science Award
9650 Rockville Pike
Bethesda, MD 20814-3998
(301) 634-7090                    Fax: (301) 634-7049
E-mail: rwoodson@faseb.org
Web: www.faseb.org/excellenceinscience

**Summary**  To recognize and reward women whose research in experimental biology has contributed significantly to our understanding of their discipline.

**Eligibility**  Nominations for this award may be submitted by members of the component societies of the Federation

of American Societies for Experimental Biology (FASEB). Nominees must be women who are also members of 1 or more of the societies of FASEB. Letters of nomination should identify the nominee's contributions to the field that represents her outstanding achievement in science, leadership and mentorship, evidence of national recognition, and honors and awards. Self-nominations are not accepted.

**Financial data**  The award consists of a $10,000 unrestricted research grant, travel expenses to the annual meeting, complimentary registration at the meeting, and a plaque.

**Duration**  This award is presented annually.

**Additional information**  Funding for this award, first presented in 1989, is provided by Eli Lilly and Company. Member societies of FASEB include the American Physiological Society (APS), American Society for Biochemistry and Molecular Biology (ASBMB), American Society for Pharmacology and Experimental Therapeutics (ASPET), American Society for Investigative Pathology, American Society for Nutritional Sciences (ASNS), American Association of Immunologists (AAI), The Biophysical Society, American Association of Anatomists, The Protein Society, American Society for Bone and Mineral Research, American Society for Clinical Investigation, The Endocrine Society, American Society of Human Genetics, and the Society for Developmental Biology.

**Number awarded**  1 each year.

**Deadline**  Nominations must be submitted by February of each year.

## [1324]
## FEMINIST ACTIVISM AWARD

Sociologists for Women in Society
Attn: Executive Officer
University of Rhode Island
Department of Sociology
Kingston, RI 02881
(401) 874-9510                    Fax: (401) 874-2588
E-mail: jessicasherwood@mail.uri.edu
Web: www.socwomen.org

**Summary**  To recognize and reward members of Sociologists for Women in Society (SWS) who have used sociology to improve conditions for women in society.

**Eligibility**  This program is open to SWS members who have notably and consistently used sociology to improve conditions for women in society. The award honors outstanding feminist advocacy efforts that embody the goal of service to women and that have identifiably improved women's lives. Selection is based on activist contributions, rather than occupational and academic achievements.

**Financial data**  The award includes an honorarium of $1,000 and a travel budget of $1,500 for presentations (lectures, workshops, or training sessions) related to the recipient's field of activism at 2 selected campus sites.

**Duration**  The award is presented annually.

**Additional information**  This award was first presented in 1995. Further information is available from Shirley Hill, Kansas University, Department of Sociology, 1415 Jayhawk Boulevard, Room 716, Lawrence, KS 66045-7556, (785) 864-4111, Fax: (785) 864-5280.

**Number awarded**  1 each year.

**Deadline** Nominations must be submitted by February of each year.

## [1325]
## FERRO-GRUMLEY AWARDS

Publishing Triangle
332 Bleecker Street, D36
New York, NY 10014
E-mail: awards@publishingtriangle.org
Web: www.publishingtriangle.org/awards.asp

**Summary** To recognize and reward outstanding fiction by lesbian and gay authors.

**Eligibility** Nominations for this award may be made by members of the Publishing Triangle or by anyone else. Eligible to be nominated are works of fiction by lesbian and gay authors that were published during the past calendar year. Lesbians and gay men compete separately. Books of short stories are eligible, but books of poetry are not. There is no application process.

**Financial data** The prize is $1,000.

**Duration** The prize is awarded annually.

**Additional information** Publishing Triangle is an organization for lesbians and gays in the publishing industry. These awards were first presented in 1990. Current Publishing Triangle members may submit a nomination for free, but others must include a $25 fee.

**Number awarded** 2 each year: 1 to a lesbian author and 1 to a gay man author.

**Deadline** November of each year.

## [1326]
## FLORENCE NIGHTINGALE DAVID AWARD

Committee of Presidents of Statistical Societies
c/o Linda J. Young, Chair
University of Florida
Department of Statistics, College of Medicine
P.O. Box 100212
Gainesville, FL 32610
(352) 392-8446                                   Fax: (352) 392-4168
E-mail: lyoung@ufl.edu
Web: www.niss.org/copss/committees.htm

**Summary** To recognize and reward women statisticians who have made notable contributions to the field.

**Eligibility** This program is open to women statisticians who have demonstrated excellence in any of the following areas: role model to women, statistical research, leadership of multidisciplinary collaborative groups, statistics education, or service to the profession. Nominees may be of any age, race, sexual orientation, nationality, or citizenship, but they must be living at the time of their nomination.

**Financial data** The award consists of a plaque, a citation, and a cash honorarium.

**Duration** The award is presented biennially, in odd-numbered years.

**Additional information** The award was established in 2001.

**Number awarded** 1 every other year.

**Deadline** January of odd-numbered years.

## [1327]
## FOUNDERS DISTINGUISHED SENIOR SCHOLAR AWARD

American Association of University Women
Attn: AAUW Educational Foundation
1111 16th Street, N.W.
Washington, DC 20036-4873
(202) 785-7602                        Toll-free: (800) 326-AAUW
Fax: (202) 463-7169                   TDD: (202) 785-7777
E-mail: foundation@aauw.org
Web: www.aauw.org/fga/awards/fdss.cfm

**Summary** To recognize and reward American women for a lifetime of scholarly excellence.

**Eligibility** Eligible for nomination are women scholars who can demonstrate a lifetime of outstanding research, college or university teaching, publications, and positive impact upon women in their profession and community. U.S. citizenship or permanent resident status is required. Selection is based on lifetime commitment to women's issues in the profession or in the community, significance and impact of the nominee's scholarship upon her field, demonstrated excellence in and commitment to teaching and mentoring female college students, and total impact upon her profession and the community. The sponsor strongly encourages nomination of women from underrepresented groups.

**Financial data** The award is $10,000.

**Duration** The award is presented annually.

**Additional information** The award includes a trip to the annual AAUW convention (where the award is presented).

**Number awarded** 1 each year.

**Deadline** February of each year.

## [1328]
## FRANCIS P. GARVAN-JOHN M. OLIN MEDAL

American Chemical Society
Attn: Office of the Awards Program
1155 16th Street, N.W.
Washington, DC 20036-4800
(202) 452-2109                          Fax: (202) 776-8211
E-mail: awards@acs.org
Web: www.chemistry.org

**Summary** To recognize and reward distinguished service to chemistry by women chemists.

**Eligibility** Nominees must be women citizens of the United States who have performed distinguished service to the field of chemistry.

**Financial data** The award consists of $5,000, a medallion, a certificate, and reimbursement of reasonable travel expenses to the meeting at which the award is presented.

**Duration** The award is presented annually.

**Additional information** This award was established in 1936 through a donation from Francis P. Garvan and has been supported by a fund set up at that time. The Olin Corporation currently sponsors the award.

**Number awarded** 1 each year.

**Deadline** Nominations must be submitted by the end of October of each year.

## [1329]
## FRANK NELSON DOUBLEDAY MEMORIAL AWARD

Wyoming Arts Council
2320 Capitol Avenue
Cheyenne, WY 82002
(307) 777-7742                    Fax: (307) 777-5499
TDD: (307) 777-5964          E-mail: mshay@state.wy.us
Web: wyoarts.state.wy.us/Literature.html

**Summary**  To recognize and reward outstanding women writers (in any genre) who live in Wyoming.

**Eligibility**  This program is open to women writers in Wyoming, over 18 years of age, who are not full-time students or faculty members. Writers are eligible if they have never published a book; if they have published only 1 full-length book of fiction, poetry, or nonfiction; of if they have published no more than 1 book of poetry, 1 of fiction, and 1 of nonfiction. They are invited to submit manuscripts of poetry (up to 10 printed pages with no more than 1 poem per page), fiction or creative nonfiction (up to 25 pages), or drama and screenplays (up to 25 pages).

**Financial data**  The award is $1,000.

**Duration**  The award is presented annually.

**Additional information**  Recipients must agree to remain a Wyoming resident for a year and to remain within the state's borders for at least 10 months of the year.

**Number awarded**  1 each year.

**Deadline**  August of each year.

## [1330]
## GIRLS GOING PLACES ENTREPRENEURSHIP AWARDS

Guardian Life Insurance Company of America
Attn: Girls Going Places
7 Hanover Square, 26-J
New York, NY 10004-2616
(212) 598-7881                    Toll-free: (888) 600-4667
Fax: (212) 919-2586  E-mail: diana_acevedo@glic.com
Web: www.guardianlife.com

**Summary**  To recognize and reward outstanding girls between 12 and 18 years of age who demonstrate "budding entrepreneurship."

**Eligibility**  Eligible to be nominated are girls between the ages of 12 and 18 who are U.S. citizens or legal residents and enrolled in middle school, high school, or a home-school program; students enrolled at a college or university are ineligible. Nominators must submit a 750-word recommendation letter in which they explain how their nominee makes a difference in her school, her community, or people's lives; how she has demonstrated budding entrepreneurship or financial acumen; and how she has taken the first steps toward financial independence. Nominees must submit 250-word personal statements on such topics as entrepreneurship, business leadership, financial independence, or making a difference in the community through entrepreneurship. Selection is based on the nominee's demonstration of budding entrepreneurship; nominee's first steps toward financial independence; nominee's ability to make a difference in her school and community; nominee's initiative to start a new business or service; significance of the nominee's entrepreneurial achievements and contribu-

tions; originality and proficiency of the nominee's approach to entrepreneurship; originality and clarity of the personal statement; originality and clarity of the recommendation letter; and presentation of the application.

**Financial data**  First prize is $10,000, second $5,000, and third $3,000; 12 other finalists receive $1,000.

**Duration**  The competition is held annually.

**Number awarded**  15 each year.

**Deadline**  February of each year.

## [1331]
## GLAMOUR'S TOP TEN COLLEGE WOMEN COMPETITION

Glamour
4 Times Square
New York, NY 10036-6593
Toll-free: (800) 244-GLAM          Fax: (212) 286-6922
E-mail: TTCW@glamour.com
Web: www.glamour.com

**Summary**  To recognize and reward outstanding college women.

**Eligibility**  This competition is open to women enrolled full time in their junior year at accredited colleges and universities in the United States and Canada. Applications must be approved and signed by the appropriate members of the school's faculty and administration (i.e., faculty advisor, the director of public relations, the director of student activities, or the dean of students). There is no limit on the number of applicants from any 1 school. Applicants must write an essay (of 500 to 700 words) describing their most meaningful achievements and how those relate to their field of study and future goals. Selection is based on the essay, leadership experience, personal involvement in campus and community affairs, and academic excellence.

**Financial data**  Each winner receives national recognition for herself and her college, a $2,000 cash prize, and a trip to New York City. Along with a photograph, a synopsis of the winner's accomplishments is featured in the October issue of *Glamour* magazine.

**Duration**  The competition is held annually.

**Additional information**  The first competition was held in 1990.

**Number awarded**  10 each year.

**Deadline**  February of each year.

## [1332]
## GLASGOW-RUBIN ESSAY AWARD

American Medical Women's Association Foundation
Attn: AMWA Foundation
211 North Union Street, Suite 100
Alexandria, VA 22314
(703) 838-0500                    Fax: (703) 549-3864
E-mail: foundation@amwa-doc.org
Web: www.amwa-doc.org

**Summary**  To recognize and reward outstanding papers written by women medical students.

**Eligibility**  This award is presented for the best essay (approximately 1,000 words) identifying a woman physician who has been a significant mentor and role model. Applicants must be student members of the American Medical

Women's Association (AMWA) attending an accredited U.S. allopathic or osteopathic medical school.

**Financial data** The award consists of $1,000 and a plaque.

**Duration** The award is presented annually.

**Additional information** The winning paper may be published in AMWA's journal. This award was formerly known as the Janet M. Glasgow Essay Award.

**Number awarded** 1 monetary award each year.

**Deadline** May of each year.

## [1333]
## HATTIE HEMSCHEMEYER AWARD

American College of Nurse-Midwives
Attn: Associate Director
8403 Coleville Road, Suite 1550
Silver Spring, MD 20915
(240) 485-1800                    Fax: (240) 485-1818
Web: www.midwife.org

**Summary** To recognize and reward long-time members of the American College of Nurse-Midwives (ACNM) who have made outstanding contributions to midwifery.

**Eligibility** Nominees for this award must be ACNM members who have been certified nurse midwives (CNMs) or certified midwives (CMs) for at least 10 years. They must have demonstrated 1) continuous outstanding contributions or distinguished service to midwifery and/or MCH, or 2) contributions of historical significance to the development and advancement of midwifery, ACNM, or MCH.

**Financial data** A monetary award is presented.

**Duration** The award is presented annually.

**Additional information** This award was first presented in 1977.

**Number awarded** 1 each year.

**Deadline** January of each year.

## [1334]
## HAZEL HEFFNER BECCHINA AWARD

National Federation of Music Clubs
1336 North Delaware Street
Indianapolis, IN 46202-2481
(317) 638-4003                    Fax: (317) 638-0503
E-mail: info@nfmc-music.org
Web: www.nfmc-music.org

**Summary** To recognize and reward outstanding young singers who are members of the National Federation of Music Clubs (NFMC).

**Eligibility** This award is presented to singers between 18 and 26 years of age. Men and women are judged separately. Membership in the federation and U.S. citizenship are required. Candidates for the NFMC Biennial Student Audition Awards competition are automatically considered for this award; no separate application is necessary.

**Financial data** The prize is $1,500. Funds must be used for continued study.

**Duration** The competition is held biennially, in odd-numbered years.

**Additional information** Applications and further information on these awards are available from Mrs. Robert Car-

roll, 17583 North 1090 East Road, Pontiac, IL 61764-9801, E-mail: scarroll@frontiernet.net; information on all federation scholarships and awards is available from Chair, Competitions and Awards Board, Dr. George R. Keck, 421 Cherry Street, Arkadelphia, AR 71923-5116, E-mail: keckg@obu.edu. The entry fee is $30.

**Number awarded** 2 every other year: 1 to a woman and 1 to a man.

**Deadline** January of odd-numbered years.

## [1335]
## HELENE CECIL LEADERSHIP AWARD

Poultry Science Association
1111 North Dunlap Avenue
Savoy, IL 61874
(217) 356-5285                    Fax: (217) 398-4119
Web: www.poultryscience.org/awarddesc.htm

**Summary** To recognize and reward women who have contributed to activities of the Poultry Science Association (PSA).

**Eligibility** This award is presented to a women who is a PSA member in good standing. Nominees must have demonstrated recent significant or sustained scientific contributions in the field of poultry science or a recent significant leadership role in the promotional and developmental opportunities for women in the area of poultry science.

**Financial data** The award is $3,000.

**Duration** The award is presented annually.

**Number awarded** 1 each year.

**Deadline** Nominations must be submitted by February of each year.

## [1336]
## INDIANA AMERICAN LEGION AMERICANISM AND GOVERNMENT TEST

American Legion
Attn: Department of Indiana
777 North Meridian Street
Indianapolis, IN 46204
(317) 630-1200                    Fax: (317) 630-1277
Web: www.indlegion.org

**Summary** To recognize and reward high school students in Indiana who score highest on a test on Americanism.

**Eligibility** All Indiana students in grades 10-12 are eligible to take a written test on Americanism and government. Scholarships are awarded to the students with the highest scores. Girls and boys compete separately.

**Financial data** The award is $500.

**Number awarded** 6 each year: 3 are set aside for girls in grades 10, 11, and 12 respectively and 3 to a boy in each of the participating grades.

**Deadline** The test is given during National Education Week in November of each year. Schools that wish to have their students participate must order the tests by October of each year.

## [1337]
## INTERNATIONAL WOMEN'S FILM FESTIVAL PRIZES

Festival International de Films de Femmes
c/o Maison des Arts de Créteil
Place Salvador Allende
94000 Créteil
France
33 1 49 80 38 98          Fax: 33 1 43 99 04 10
E-mail: filmsfemmes@wanadoo.fr
Web: www.filmsdefemmes.com

**Summary**  To recognize and reward outstanding films directed by women at a competition in France.

**Eligibility**  Recent films directed by women from any country may be considered for this competition. There are 3 sections: full-length films, full-length documentaries, and short-length fiction and documentary films. Entries must be submitted in 16mm, 35mm, or video. They must have been completed within the previous 21 months and not yet shown or broadcast in France. Entries in the full-length film section compete for the Jury Prize and the Public Prize. Full-length documentaries compete for the Public Prize and the AFJ (Association of Women Journalists) Prize. Short-length fiction and documentary films compete for the Public Prize, the Paris XII Jury Prize, the Graine de Cinéphage Prize, and the Beaumarchais Prize.

**Financial data**  The prizes vary each year. Recently, the Jury Prize was 3,811 Euros, the Public Prizes were 3,048 Euros, the AFJ Prize was 1,525 Euros, the Paris XII Jury Prize was 1,525 Euros, the Graine de Cinéphage Prize was 3,048 Euros, and the Beaumarchais Prize provided an honorarium of 1,525 Euros and a writing scholarship of 1,525 to 3,048 Euros.

**Duration**  The prizes are awarded annually.

**Additional information**  The competition, which began in 1978, is held at the Festival in Créteil, a suburb in the south of Paris. A registration fee of $15 is required to cover shipping and handling.

**Number awarded**  The number of prizes varies each year.

**Deadline**  November of each year.

## [1338]
## IOTA SIGMA PI CENTENNIAL AWARD FOR EXCELLENCE IN UNDERGRADUATE TEACHING

Iota Sigma Pi
c/o National Director for Professional Awards
Dr. Sara Paisner
GE Global Research
One Research Circle, K1-4D17
Niskayuna, NY 12309
(518) 387-4599      E-mail: paisners@research.ge.com
Web: www.iotasigmapi.info

**Summary**  To recognize and reward outstanding women chemistry teachers.

**Eligibility**  This award is presented to women chemists or biochemists who demonstrate excellence in teaching chemistry, biochemistry, or a chemistry-related field at an undergraduate institution that does not offer a graduate program in that field. The nominee may be, but need not be, a member of Iota Sigma Pi. Each active chapter is entitled to make only 1 nomination, but individual members, individual chem-

ists, or groups of chemists may make independent nominations if properly documented.

**Financial data**  The award consists of $500, a certificate, and a 1-year waiver of Iota Sigma Pi dues.

**Duration**  The award is granted triennially.

**Additional information**  This award was first presented in 2003.

**Number awarded**  1 every 3 years.

**Deadline**  January of the year of the award (the next award is in 2008).

## [1339]
## IOTA SIGMA PI NATIONAL HONORARY MEMBER

Iota Sigma Pi
c/o National Director for Professional Awards
Dr. Sara Paisner
GE Global Research
One Research Circle, K1-4D17
Niskayuna, NY 12309
(518) 387-4599      E-mail: paisners@research.ge.com
Web: www.iotasigmapi.info

**Summary**  To recognize exceptional and significant achievement by women working in chemistry or allied fields.

**Eligibility**  Nominees for the award must be outstanding women chemists. They may be from any country and need not be members of Iota Sigma Pi. Each active chapter is entitled to make only 1 nomination, but individual members, individual chemists, or groups of chemists may make independent nominations if properly documented. The nomination dossier must contain the candidate's name and address, educational and professional background, membership in professional societies, area of specialization or research, honors, awards, citations, publications, and letters of recommendation.

**Financial data**  The award consists of $1,000, a certificate, and a lifetime waiver of Iota Sigma Pi dues.

**Duration**  The award is granted triennially.

**Additional information**  This award was first presented in 1921.

**Number awarded**  1 every 3 years.

**Deadline**  Nominations must be submitted by January of the year of award (the next award is in 2008).

## [1340]
## IRENE S. MUIR AWARD

National Federation of Music Clubs
1336 North Delaware Street
Indianapolis, IN 46202-2481
(317) 638-4003          Fax: (317) 638-0503
E-mail: info@nfmc-music.org
Web: www.nfmc-music.org

**Summary**  To recognize and reward outstanding young singers who are members of the National Federation of Music Clubs (NFMC).

**Eligibility**  This award is presented to singers between 18 and 26 years of age. Men and women are judged separately. Membership in the federation and U.S. citizenship are required. Candidates for the NFMC Biennial Student Audition Awards competition are automatically considered for this award; no separate application is necessary.

**Financial data** The prize is $1,000. Funds must be used for continued study.

**Duration** The competition is held biennially, in odd-numbered years.

**Additional information** Applications and further information on these awards are available from Mrs. Robert Carroll, 17583 North 1090 East Road, Pontiac, IL 61764-9801, E-mail: scarroll@frontiernet.net; information on all federation scholarships and awards is available from Chair, Competitions and Awards Board, Dr. George R. Keck, 421 Cherry Street, Arkadelphia, AR 71923-5116, E-mail: keckg@obu.edu. The entry fee is $30.

**Number awarded** 2 every other year: 1 to a woman and 1 to a man.

**Deadline** January of odd-numbered years.

## [1341]
## JACQUELIN PERRY, MD RESIDENT RESEARCH AWARD

Ruth Jackson Orthopaedic Society
6300 North River Road, Suite 727
Rosemont, IL 60018-4226
(847) 698-1637　　　　　　Fax: (847) 823-0536
E-mail: rjos@aaos.org
Web: www.rjos.org/awards/index.htm

**Summary** To recognize and reward women orthopedic residents who submit outstanding abstracts of papers for presentation at the annual meeting of the American Academy of Orthopaedic Surgeons (AAOS).

**Eligibility** This program is open to women residents in accredited orthopedic surgical residency programs. Applicants must be the primary investigator for a research project. They must submit an abstract of the project for presentation at the annual meeting of the AAOS.

**Financial data** The award is $2,000.

**Duration** The award is presented annually.

**Number awarded** 1 each year.

**Deadline** September of each year.

## [1342]
## JANE CHAMBERS PLAYWRITING AWARD

Association for Theatre in Higher Education
Attn: Women and Theatre Program
P.O. Box 1290
Boulder, CO 80306-1290
(303) 530-2167　　　　　Toll-free: (888) 284-3737
Fax: (303) 530-2168　　　　E-mail: wtp@athe.org
Web: www.athe.org/wtp/html/chambers.html

**Summary** To recognize and reward outstanding plays and performance texts that were created by women and have a majority of parts for women performers.

**Eligibility** Women are invited to submit plays and performance texts that reflect a feminist perspective and contain significant opportunities for women performers. Scripts may be produced or unproduced. There is no limitation on length, style, or subject. Current undergraduate and graduate students may enter the student category of the competition.

**Financial data** The general award consists of $1,000, free registration to attend the Women and Theatre Conference

(late July), and a rehearsed reading of the winning piece at that conference. The student award is $250 and a reading at the conference.

**Duration** The competition is held annually.

**Additional information** Information is also available from Maya Roth, Georgetown University, 108 Davis Center, Box 571063, Washington, DC 20057-1063. The processing fee is $35 for general applicants, $15 for low-income applicants, or $10 for students.

**Number awarded** 1 general award and 1 student award are presented each year.

**Deadline** February of each year.

## [1343]
## JERARD FUND AWARD

PEN American Center
Attn: Literary Awards Coordinator
588 Broadway, Suite 303
New York, NY 10012
(212) 334-1660, ext. 101　　　　Fax: (212) 334-2181
E-mail: awards@pen.org
Web: www.pen.org

**Summary** To recognize and reward American women who are emerging nonfiction writers.

**Eligibility** Applicants must be women and residents of the United States. The minimum requirement is the publication of at least 1 magazine article in a national publication or in a major literary magazine. Applicants must not have published more than 1 book of any kind. They must submit 5 copies of no more than 50 pages of their English language book-length nonfiction work-in-progress (accompanied by her list of publications) to be considered for this award. Although there are no restrictions on the content of the work, the emphasis is on the quality of writing rather than the subject. The award is not intended to focus exclusively on women's studies or personal memoirs; all serious literary subjects are welcome. However, such manuscripts as how-to manuals, inspirational tracts, cookery or craft books, fashion guides, and celebrity biographies are not considered.

**Financial data** The award is $5,500.

**Duration** The award is granted biennially, in odd-numbered years.

**Additional information** This is the first award of its kind established for American women writers of nonfiction. It is the outgrowth of the Elise Jerard Environmental and Humanitarian Trust, administered by the New York Community Trust, which became effective in 1979 in order "to foster the talents and human purposes to which Elise Jerard had devoted her time and energy for many years."

**Number awarded** 1 every other year.

**Deadline** January of odd-numbered years.

## [1344]
## JESSIE BERNARD AWARD

American Sociological Association
Attn: Governance Office
1307 New York Avenue, N.W., Suite 700
Washington, DC 20005-4701
(202) 383-9005, ext. 327          Fax: (202) 638-0882
TDD: (202) 872-0486   E-mail: governance@asanet.org
Web: www.asanet.org

**Summary**  To recognize and reward scholarly works in sociology that relate to the role of women in society.

**Eligibility**  Works may be nominated only by members of the American Sociological Association. The nominated work may be empirical research, in theory or in methodology. It may be an exceptional single work, several pieces of work, or significant cumulative work done throughout a professional career. Nominations must include a 1- or 2-page statement explaining the importance of the work. The award is not restricted to works by sociologists, but only members of the American Sociological Association may submit nominations. The work need not have been published recently, but it must have been published by the date of nomination.

**Financial data**  The award is $500.

**Duration**  The award is presented annually at the American Sociological Association convention.

**Number awarded**  1 each year.

**Deadline**  Nominations must be submitted by December of each year.

## [1345]
## JOAN KELLY MEMORIAL PRIZE IN WOMEN'S HISTORY

American Historical Association
Attn: Book Prize Administrator
400 A Street, S.E.
Washington, DC 20003-3889
(202) 544-2422                    Fax: (202) 544-8307
E-mail: info@historians.org
Web: www.historians.org/prizes/index.cfm

**Summary**  To recognize and reward outstanding works in women's history and/or feminist theory that were published during the previous year.

**Eligibility**  The prize is open to works in any chronological period, any geographical location, or any area of feminist theory that incorporate an historical perspective. Preference is given to books that demonstrate originality of research, creativity of insight, graceful stylistic presentation, analytical skills, and recognition of the important role of sex and gender in the historical process.

**Financial data**  The prize is $1,000.

**Duration**  The award is granted annually.

**Additional information**  This prize was established in 1984 by the Coordinating Committee on Women in the Historical Profession and the Conference Group on Women's History (now the Coordinating Council for Women in History) and is administered by the American Historical Association.

**Number awarded**  1 each year.

**Deadline**  May of each year.

## [1346]
## JUDY GRAHN AWARD FOR LESBIAN NONFICTION

Publishing Triangle
332 Bleecker Street, D36
New York, NY 10014
E-mail: awards@publishingtriangle.org
Web: www.publishingtriangle.org/awards.asp

**Summary**  To recognize and reward outstanding lesbian nonfiction writers or writings.

**Eligibility**  This award is presented to authors of books that have had significant influence on lesbians. For the purposes of this award, "lesbian nonfiction" is defined as nonfiction affecting lesbian lives. The book may be by a lesbian, for example, or about lesbians or lesbian culture, or both. Anthologies of nonfiction are eligible. The book must have been published in the United States or Canada.

**Financial data**  The award is $1,000.

**Duration**  The award is presented annually.

**Additional information**  The Publishing Triangle is an association of lesbians and gay men in publishing. This award was first presented in 1997. Current members of the Publishing Triangle may nominate authors for free; all others must enclose a check for $25 per playwright nominated.

**Number awarded**  1 each year.

**Deadline**  November of each year.

## [1347]
## JULIA CHERRY SPRUILL PUBLICATION PRIZE IN SOUTHERN WOMEN'S HISTORY

Southern Association for Women Historians
c/o Megan Taylor Shockley
Clemson University
Department of History
Clemson, SC 29634
(864) 656-4427                    E-mail: mshockl@clemson.edu
Web: www2.h-net.msu.edu/~sawh/prizes.html

**Summary**  To recognize and reward outstanding books on the history of southern women.

**Eligibility**  Eligible for consideration are books about the history of southern women published during the year preceding the award. The manuscripts must be written in English, but the competition is not restricted to publications printed in the United States. Anthologies, edited works, and all other types of historical publications are eligible.

**Financial data**  The award consists of $750 and a plaque.

**Duration**  The award is granted annually.

**Number awarded**  1 each year.

**Deadline**  March of each year.

## [1348]
### KALLIOPE SHORT FICTION CONTEST

Kalliope Women Writers' Collective
c/o Florida Community College at Jacksonville
11901 Beach Boulevard, Room N-123
Jacksonville, FL 32246
(904) 646-2081          E-mail: opencampus@fccj.edu
Web: opencampus.fccj.org/kalliope/k-shortstory.html

**Summary**  To recognize and reward outstanding short fiction written by women.

**Eligibility**  Fiction in any style and on any subject may be submitted if it does not exceed 3000 words each and is written by a woman. Short fiction that has been previously published or received monetary awards is not eligible.

**Financial data**  The prize is $1,000.

**Duration**  The competition is held annually.

**Additional information**  This prize was first awarded in 2007. The winning story is published in *Kalliope: a journal of women's literature & art*. The entry fee is $15.

**Number awarded**  1 each year.

**Deadline**  October of each year.

## [1349]
### KITTY ERNST AWARD

American College of Nurse-Midwives
Attn: Associate Director
8403 Coleville Road, Suite 1550
Silver Spring, MD 20915
(240) 485-1800          Fax: (240) 485-1818
Web: www.midwife.org

**Summary**  To recognize and reward recent members of the American College of Nurse-Midwives (ACNM) who have made outstanding contributions to midwifery.

**Eligibility**  Nominees for this award must be ACNM members who have been certified nurse midwives (CNMs) or certified midwives (CMs) for less than 10 years. They must have demonstrated innovative, creative endeavors in midwifery and/or women's health clinical practice, education, administration, or research.

**Financial data**  A monetary award is presented.

**Duration**  The award is presented annually.

**Additional information**  This award was first presented in 1998.

**Number awarded**  1 each year.

**Deadline**  January of each year.

## [1350]
### KPMG BEST PAPER AWARD GENDER SECTION

American Accounting Association
Attn: Gender Issues and Worklife Balance Section
5717 Bessie Drive
Sarasota, FL 34233-2399
(941) 921-7747          Fax: (941) 923-4093
E-mail: office@aaahq.org
Web: aaahq.org/awards/GenderIssuesAwards.htm

**Summary**  To recognize and reward outstanding papers on gender issues presented at the annual meeting of the American Accounting Association (AAA).

**Eligibility**  This competition is open to authors of papers presented at the AAA annual meeting. At least 1 of the authors must be a member of the Gender Issues and Worklife Balance section.

**Financial data**  The award is $1,000.

**Duration**  The award is presented annually.

**Additional information**  This award is supported by the KPMG Foundation.

**Number awarded**  1 each year.

## [1351]
### KPMG OUTSTANDING DISSERTATION AWARD GENDER SECTION

American Accounting Association
Attn: Gender Issues and Worklife Balance Section
5717 Bessie Drive
Sarasota, FL 34233-2399
(941) 921-7747          Fax: (941) 923-4093
E-mail: office@aaahq.org
Web: aaahq.org/awards/GenderIssuesAwards.htm

**Summary**  To recognize and reward outstanding dissertations on gender issues in accounting.

**Eligibility**  This competition is open to authors of dissertations completed in the prior calendar year. Manuscripts need not be focused solely on gender issues and worklife balance, but they must include some consideration of those topics.

**Financial data**  The award is $1,000.

**Duration**  The award is presented annually.

**Additional information**  This award is supported by the KPMG Foundation.

**Number awarded**  1 each year.

**Deadline**  February of each year.

## [1352]
### KPMG OUTSTANDING PUBLISHED MANUSCRIPT AWARD GENDER SECTION

American Accounting Association
Attn: Gender Issues and Worklife Balance Section
5717 Bessie Drive
Sarasota, FL 34233-2399
(941) 921-7747          Fax: (941) 923-4093
E-mail: office@aaahq.org
Web: aaahq.org/awards/GenderIssuesAwards.htm

**Summary**  To recognize and reward outstanding research publications on gender issues in accounting.

**Eligibility**  This competition is open to authors of articles published in the prior calendar year. Manuscripts need not be focused solely on gender issues and worklife balance, but they must include some consideration of those topics. At least 1 of the authors must be a member of the Gender Issues and Worklife Balance section of the American Accounting Association.

**Financial data**  The award is $1,000.

**Duration**  The award is presented annually.

**Additional information**  This award is supported by the KPMG Foundation.

**Number awarded**  1 each year.

**Deadline**  March of each year.

## [1353]
## LERNER-SCOTT DISSERTATION PRIZE

Organization of American Historians
Attn: Award and Prize Coordinator
112 North Bryan Street
P.O. Box 5457
Bloomington, IN 47408-5457
(812) 855-9852                  Fax: (812) 855-0696
E-mail: oahawards@oah.org
Web: www.oah.org

**Summary**  To recognize and reward outstanding doctoral dissertations written during the previous academic year on U.S. women's history.

**Eligibility**  This competition is open to doctoral dissertations completed during the previous year that relate to U.S. women's history. Each application must contain a letter of support from a faculty member at the degree-granting institution, along with an abstract, table of contents, and a sample chapter from the dissertation. Finalists will be asked to submit a complete copy of the dissertation to each committee member at a later date.

**Financial data**  The prize is $1,000 and a certificate.

**Duration**  The prize is awarded annually.

**Additional information**  This prize was established in 1991 and is named for Gerda Lerner and Anne Firor Scott, both pioneers in women's history and past presidents of the Organization of American Historians.

**Number awarded**  1 each year.

**Deadline**  September of each year.

## [1354]
## LESBIAN VISUAL ARTS AWARDS

Astraea Lesbian Foundation for Justice
Attn: Program Director
116 East 16th Street, Seventh Floor
New York, NY 10003
(212) 529-8021                  Fax: (212) 982-3321
E-mail: grants@astraeafoundation.org
Web: www.astraeafoundation.org

**Summary**  To recognize and reward the work of lesbian artists.

**Eligibility**  This program is open to U.S. residents who agree to be acknowledged publicly as lesbian artists in the following categories: sculpture, painting in any medium, print, drawing, work on paper, and mixed media (traditional or non-traditional materials). Students currently enrolled in an arts degree-granting program or its equivalent are not eligible. Applicants must submit slides of their original works of art, a current resume, and a 250-word statement responding to the goal of the fund.

**Financial data**  The award is $2,500.

**Duration**  The awards are presented annually.

**Additional information**  This program was established in 2002. An application fee of $5 must be included.

**Number awarded**  3 each year.

**Deadline**  February of each year.

## [1355]
## LESBIAN WRITERS FUND AWARDS

Astraea Lesbian Foundation for Justice
Attn: Program Director
116 East 16th Street, Seventh Floor
New York, NY 10003
(212) 529-8021                  Fax: (212) 982-3321
E-mail: grants@astraeafoundation.org
Web: www.astraeafoundation.org

**Summary**  To recognize and reward lesbian writers.

**Eligibility**  These awards are presented to emerging lesbian writers of poetry and fiction who reside in the United States. Applicants must have published at least 1 piece of their writing (in any genre) in a newspaper, magazine, journal, or anthology, but no more than 1 book. Their work must include some lesbian content. Submissions may consist of up to 20 pages of fiction (a novel or collection of short stories) or at least 10 but no more than 15 pages of poetry.

**Financial data**  Awards are either $10,000 or $1,500; honorable mentions are $100.

**Additional information**  This fund was established in 1991. It includes the *Claire of the Moon* Award for Fiction, the Loving Lesbians Award for Fiction, and the Loving Lesbians Award for Poetry. Requests for applications must be accompanied by a self-addressed stamped envelope.

**Number awarded**  Varies each year. Recently, 12 of these grants were awarded: 2 at $10,000 (1 for fiction and 1 for poetry), 4 at $1,500 (2 for fiction and 2 for poetry), and 6 honorable mentions (3 for fiction and 3 for poetry).

**Deadline**  June of each year.

## [1356]
## M. CAREY THOMAS AWARD

Alumnae Association of Bryn Mawr College
Wyndham Alumnae House
101 North Merion Avenue
Bryn Mawr, PA 19010-2899
(610) 526-5227                  Toll-free: (800) BMC-ALUM
Fax: (610) 526-5228  E-mail: bmcalum@brynmawr.edu
Web: www.brynmawr.edu/alumnae

**Summary**  To recognize and reward unusual achievement on the part of distinguished American women.

**Eligibility**  Applications are not accepted. Recipients are chosen by a special committee that is formed several months prior to the presentation of the award. Selection is based on eminent and outstanding achievement.

**Financial data**  The award is $10,000.

**Duration**  The award is granted every 5 years (2007, 2012).

**Additional information**  Past recipients have included Martha Graham and Georgia O'Keefe.

## [1357]
## MAKING A DIFFERENCE AWARD

Epilepsy Foundation
Attn: Women and Epilepsy Initiative
8301 Professional Place
Landover, MD 20785-2237
(301) 459-3700          Toll-free: (800) EFA-1000
Fax: (301) 577-2684      TDD: (800) 332-2070
Web: www.epilepsyfoundation.org

**Summary** To recognize and reward women with epilepsy who have inspired and changed the lives of others.

**Eligibility** This program is open to women from all backgrounds who are at least 18 years of age and have epilepsy. Nominees should have contributed in a significant way to support and advance the quality of life for women with epilepsy, inspire people with epilepsy and those with other chronic disabilities, or enhance public understanding of epilepsy and its impact on women. Nominations are accepted from all parties, including the nominee herself. Selection is based on the significant or positive differences already made in the lives of others (70%) and any ongoing activities designed to achieve positive change (30%).

**Financial data** The award consists of $1,500 plus travel and expenses to attend the awards presentation ceremonies during the Epilepsy Foundation's annual national conference.

**Duration** The awards are presented annually.

**Additional information** This award, first presented in 2001, is sponsored by GlaxoSmithKline.

**Number awarded** 1 each year.

**Deadline** June of each year.

## [1358]
## MARCIA FEINBERG AWARD

Association of Jewish Women Publishers
3160 Wedgewood Court
Reno, NV 89509-7103

**Summary** To recognize and reward Jewish women who have made outstanding contributions to careers in library science and publishing.

**Eligibility** This award is presented to Jewish women who received a library science doctoral degree from a university in the upper Midwest (Montana, South Dakota, North Dakota, or Minnesota). Nominees must have spent a portion of their career working as a librarian, and then changed careers to enter the field of publishing. They may currently reside in any state except Nebraska or Rhode Island. Selection is based on service to the library profession, awards received for librarianship, innovativeness, and loyalty to colleagues.

**Financial data** The award includes an honorarium of $10,000 and a gold engraved plaque.

**Duration** The award is presented annually.

**Additional information** This award, named in honor of a well-known 19th-century Jewish woman librarian and publisher, has been presented annually since 1923. Self-nominations are not accepted. Only professional colleagues may nominate a candidate.

**Number awarded** 1 each year.

**Deadline** August of each year.

## [1359]
## MARGARET OAKLEY DAYHOFF AWARD

Biophysical Society
Attn: Awards Committee
9650 Rockville Pike, Room L-0512
Bethesda, MD 20814-3998
(301) 634-7114          Fax: (301) 634-7133
E-mail: society@biophysics.org
Web: www.biophysics.org

**Summary** To recognize and reward outstanding junior women scientists in fields of interest to the Biophysical Society.

**Eligibility** This program is open to junior women scientists whose writings have made substantial contributions to scientific fields within the range of interest of the society but who have not yet attained university tenure. Candidates who have a Ph.D. or equivalent degree remain eligible until they have completed 10 years of full-time work following the degree. Candidates with a baccalaureate degree but without a Ph.D. have 12 years of eligibility. Time taken off for child rearing is not counted. Candidates who work in non-academic environments are eligible if their work is published and meets academic standards, and if they do not have tenure equivalency. U.S. citizenship or permanent resident status is required. Nominations may be submitted by any member of the society in good standing, but self-nominations are not accepted.

**Financial data** The award is $2,000.

**Duration** The award is presented annually.

**Additional information** This award was established in 1984.

**Number awarded** 1 each year.

**Deadline** March of each year.

## [1360]
## MARGARET W. ROSSITER HISTORY OF WOMEN IN SCIENCE PRIZE

History of Science Society
Attn: Nominations
University of Florida
3310 Turlington Hall
P.O. Box 117360
Gainesville, FL 32611-7360
(352) 392-1677          Fax: (352) 392-2795
E-mail: info@hssonline.org
Web: www.hssonline.org

**Summary** To recognize and reward scholars who publish outstanding work in the specialty field of women in the history of science.

**Eligibility** Books and articles published during the last 4 years are eligible for consideration, provided they deal with a topic related to women in science, including discussions of women's activities in science, analyses of past scientific practices that deal explicitly with gender, and investigations regarding women as viewed by scientists. Entries may take a biographical, institutional, theoretical, or other approach to the topic. They may relate to medicine, technology, and the social sciences as well as the natural sciences.

**Financial data** The prize is $1,000.

**Duration** This is an annual award, presented in alternate years to the most outstanding article (even-numbered years) and the most outstanding book (odd-numbered years).

**Additional information** This award was established in 1987 and given its current name in 2004.

**Number awarded** 1 each year.

**Deadline** March of each year.

## [1361]
## MARIA GOEPPERT-MAYER AWARD

American Physical Society
Attn: Honors Program
One Physics Ellipse
College Park, MD 20740-3844
(301) 209-3268            Fax: (301) 209-0865
E-mail: honors@aps.org
Web: www.aps.org

**Summary** To recognize the achievements of outstanding women physicists and to offer them an opportunity to share these achievements by delivering public lectures.

**Eligibility** This award is available to female U.S. citizens and permanent residents who are working in a field of physics and are in the early stages of their careers. They must have received their doctorates no more than 10 years ago.

**Financial data** The award is $2,500 plus a $4,000 travel allowance to cover the costs of providing lectures at 4 institutions of the recipient's choice.

**Duration** The lectures must be given within 2 years after the award is presented.

**Additional information** The lectures may be given at 4 institutions of the recipient's choice within the United States or its possessions, and at the meeting of the American Physical Society at which the award is presented. The award was established by the General Electric Foundation (now the GE Fund) in 1985.

**Number awarded** 1 each year.

**Deadline** June of each year.

## [1362]
## MARY JANE OESTMANN PROFESSIONAL WOMEN'S ACHIEVEMENT AWARD

American Nuclear Society
Attn: Honors and Awards
555 North Kensington Avenue
La Grange Park, IL 60526-5592
(708) 352-6611            Fax: (708) 579-8295
E-mail: honors@ans.org
Web: www.ans.org/honors/va-untermyer

**Summary** To recognize and reward women who have made outstanding contributions to the field of nuclear science.

**Eligibility** This award is presented to women who have contributed outstanding personal dedication and technical achievement in the fields of nuclear science, engineering, research, or education. Nominees need not be a member of the American Nuclear Society (ANS), but they should be affiliated with the nuclear community in some manner. The award may be given for lifetime achievement or for a singular outstanding contribution to the technical community.

**Financial data** The award consists of a monetary award and an engraved plaque.

**Duration** The award is presented annually.

**Additional information** This award was first presented in 1991.

**Number awarded** 1 each year.

**Deadline** June of each year.

## [1363]
## MEDTRONIC PRIZE FOR SCIENTIFIC CONTRIBUTIONS TO WOMEN'S HEALTH DEVELOPMENT IN WOMEN'S HEALTH

Society for Women's Health Research
1025 Connecticut Avenue, N.W., Suite 701
Washington, DC 20036
(202) 223-8224            Fax: (202) 833-3472
E-mail: info@womenshealthresearch.org
Web: www.womenshealthresearch.org

**Summary** To recognize and reward women scientists and engineers who have made outstanding contributions to women's health.

**Eligibility** This award is available to women scientists and engineers in midcareer whose work has led or will lead directly to the improvement of women's health. Nominees should have devoted a significant part of their careers to the area of women's health, especially to work on sex differences. Priority is given to nominees whose commitment to women's health has been passed on to their collaborators and students, both as a role model and as a mentor.

**Financial data** The award is $75,000.

**Duration** The award is presented annually.

**Additional information** This award, first presented in 2006, is sponsored by Medtronic.

**Number awarded** 1 each year.

## [1364]
## MEERSBURGER DROSTE-PREIS

Kulturamt der Stadt Meersburg
Postfach 1140
D-88701 Meersburg
Germany
49 7532 440 260            Fax: 49 7532 440 264
E-mail: kulturamt@meersburg.de

**Summary** To recognize and reward women poets writing in the German language.

**Eligibility** The competition is open to women poets of any nationality writing in German. Self-nominations are not accepted.

**Financial data** The prize is 6,000 Euros.

**Duration** The competition is held every 3 years (2009, 2012, etc.).

**Additional information** This prize was first awarded in 1957.

**Number awarded** 1 every 3 years.

## [1365]
## MERLE MONTGOMERY OPERA AWARDS

National Federation of Music Clubs
1336 North Delaware Street
Indianapolis, IN 46202-2481
(317) 638-4003          Fax: (317) 638-0503
E-mail: info@nfmc-music.org
Web: www.nfmc-music.org

**Summary** To recognize and reward outstanding opera singers who participate in the Biennial Young Artist Awards competition of the National Federation of Music Clubs (NFMC).

**Eligibility** Opera voice entrants must be between 25 and 37 years of age. Separate competitions are held for men and women. Membership in the federation and U.S. citizenship are required. Candidates for the NFMC Biennial Young Artist Awards competition are automatically considered for this award; no separate application is necessary.

**Financial data** Each award is $1,000.

**Duration** The competition is held biennially, in odd-numbered years.

**Additional information** Applications and further information are available from Mrs. Nannette Hanslowe, 296 Medford Leas, Medford, NJ 08055, E-mail: nannettehans-lowe@yahoo.com; information on all federation scholarships and awards is available from Chair, Competitions and Awards Board, Dr. George R. Keck, 421 Cherry Street, Arkadelphia, AR 71923-5116. There is a $40 entry fee.

**Number awarded** 2 every other year: 1 for a man and 1 for a woman.

**Deadline** February of odd-numbered years.

## [1366]
## MINISTRY TO WOMEN AWARD

Unitarian Universalist Association
Attn: UU Women's Federation
25 Beacon Street
Boston, MA 02108-2800
(617) 948-4692          Fax: (617) 742-2402
E-mail: uuwf@uua.org
Web: www.uuwf.org

**Summary** To recognize and reward significant actions that have improved the lot of women.

**Eligibility** Individuals or organizations that have ministered to women in an outstanding manner are considered for this award. In past years, only non-Unitarian Universalists were eligible.

**Financial data** The prize is a $1,000 honorarium, a citation, and travel expenses to the awards presentation.

**Duration** The award is presented annually.

**Additional information** This award was established in 1974.

**Number awarded** 1 each year.

## [1367]
## MISS AMERICA COMPETITION AWARDS

Miss America Pageant
Attn: Scholarship Department
Two Miss America Way, Suite 1000
Atlantic City, NJ 08401
(609) 345-7571, ext. 27          Toll-free: (800) 282-MISS
Fax: (609) 347-6079          E-mail: info@missamerica.org
Web: www.missamerica.org

**Summary** To provide educational scholarships to participants in the Miss America Pageant on local, state, and national levels.

**Eligibility** To enter an official Miss America Preliminary Pageant, candidates must meet certain basic requirements and agree to abide by all the rules of the local, state, and national Miss America Pageants. Among the qualifications required are that the applicant be female, between the ages of 17 and 24, a resident of the town or state in which they first compete, in good health, of good moral character, and a citizen of the United States. A complete list of all eligibility requirements is available from each local and state pageant. In addition to the general scholarship awards, participants are also considered for a number of special awards: the Bernie Wayne Performing Arts Award is presented to the contestant with the highest talent score among those women with performing arts as a stated ambition; the Charles and Theresa Brown Scholarships are presented to Miss America, the 4 runners-up, Miss Alaska, Miss Hawaii, Miss Illinois, and Miss Ohio; and the Quality of Life Awards are presented to the 3 contestants who demonstrate the most outstanding commitment to enhancing the quality of life for others through volunteerism and community service.

**Financial data** More than $45 million in cash and tuition assistance is awarded annually at the local, state, and national Miss America Pageants. At the national level, a total of $455,000 is awarded: Miss America receives $30,000 in scholarship money, the first runner-up $20,000, second runner-up $15,000, third runner-up $10,000, fourth runner-up $8,000, finalists $7,000 each, and national contestants $3,000 each. Other awards include those for the preliminary talent winners at $2,000 each, the preliminary lifestyle and fitness in swimsuit winners at $1,000 each, and the non-finalist talent winners at $1,000 each. Of the special awards presented to national contestants, the Bernie Wayne Performing Arts Award is $2,500; the Charles and Theresa Brown Scholarships are $2,500 each; and the Quality of Life Awards are $3,000 for the winner, $3,000 for first runner-up, and $1,000 for second runner-up.

**Duration** The pageants are held every year.

**Additional information** The Miss America Pageant has been awarding scholarships since 1945. Scholarships are to be used for tuition, room, board, supplies, and other college expenses. Use of the scholarships must begin within 4 years from the date of the award (5 years if the recipient is Miss America), unless a reasonable extension is requested and granted. Training under the scholarship should be continuous and completed within 10 years from the date the scholarship is activated; otherwise, the balance of the scholarship may be canceled without further notice.

**Number awarded** At the national level, 52 contestants (1 from each state, the District of Columbia, and the Virgin Islands) share the awards.

**Deadline** Varies, depending upon the date of local pageants leading to the state and national finals.

## [1368]
## MISS AMERICAN COED PAGEANT

American Coed Pageants
4120 Piedmont Road
Pensacola, FL 32503
(850) 438-2078          E-mail: nationals@gocoed.com
Web: www.americancoed.com

**Summary** To recognize and reward girls who could become "tomorrow's leaders".

**Eligibility** This pageant is open to girls in 5 age divisions: princess for girls from 3 to 6 years of age, sweetheart for girls from 7 to 9, pre-teen for girls from 10 to 12, junior teen for girls from 13 to 15, and teen for girls from 16 to 18. Selection is based on poise and appearance in formal wear, personality during an interview, and presentation and appearance in the interview outfit. Girls may also enter several additional optional contests: talent, photogenic, Miss Model, and sportswear. Other optional contests (speech, academic achievement, and volunteer service) are only open to girls in the junior teen and teen divisions.

**Financial data** In each division, state winners receive up to $300 in travel expenses to participate in the national competition; a $1,000 cash award; a $200 VIP Day in Walt Disney World for 2; the official state crown, banner, and trophy; and a free weekend at next year's pageant to crown their successor. Prizes in the optional contests include $250 for talent, $250 for photogenic, $100 for Miss Model, $250 for sportswear, $150 for speech, $150 for academic achievement, and $150 for volunteer service. In the national competition, more than $20,000 in cash, trophies, and prizes are awarded each year.

**Duration** The competition is held annually.

**Additional information** The total entry fee is $405 (a $20 registration fee and a $385 sponsor fee). The sponsor fees are used to pay all the contestants' prizes and cash awards, as well as trophies, flowers, entertainment, judges, chaperones, pageant staff expenses, cost of vacation for state winners, and the other costs associated with producing the state pageant. The optional contests for talent, photogenic, and sportswear have an additional entry fee of $50.

**Number awarded** Varies on the state and national level.

**Deadline** State deadlines vary; check with your state pageant director to determine the deadline in your area.

## [1369]
## MISS BLACK AMERICA

Miss Black America Pageant
P.O. Box 25668
Philadelphia, PA 19144
(215) 844-8872
Web: www.missblackamerica.com

**Summary** To recognize and reward beautiful and talented Black American women.

**Eligibility** All African American women between 17 and 29 years of age, including married contestants and contestants with children, are eligible. Finalists who compete in the national pageant are selected after competitions on the local and state levels. The winner at the national pageant is chosen by a panel of judges on the basis of beauty, talent, and personality.

**Financial data** Miss Black America receives a cash award and an array of prizes.

**Duration** The competition is held annually.

**Additional information** This competition began in 1968. There is a $100 application fee and a $750 sponsorship fee.

**Number awarded** 1 each year.

**Deadline** December of each year.

## [1370]
## MISS CHEERLEADER OF AMERICA
## SCHOLARSHIPS

Miss Cheerleader of America
Attn: Program Director
P.O. Box 667
Taylor, MI 48180
(734) 946-1200                          Fax: (734) 946-1204
E-mail: misscheerleaderofamerica@yahoo.com
Web: www.misscheerleaderofamerica.com

**Summary** To recognize and reward, with college scholarships, women who are high school cheerleaders.

**Eligibility** This program is open to female high school cheerleaders in grades 9 through 12. Girls who are interested apply to participate in a pageant in their home state. Based on their applications, finalists are invited to their state pageant, where they participate in an evening gown demonstration and an interview. The program is not a beauty, bathing suit, cheer skill, or talent competition. Judges attempt to select "the all-American girl, who normally would not even think about being in a pageant."

**Financial data** Prizes are generally scholarships of $1,000 for first place, $750 for second, and $500 for third.

**Duration** The competition is held annually.

**Number awarded** Varies each year; normally, 3 prizes are awarded in each state in which a pageant is held.

## [1371]
## MISS DEAF AMERICA PAGEANT AWARDS

National Association of the Deaf
814 Thayer Avenue
Silver Spring, MD 20910-4500
(301) 587-1788                          Fax: (301) 587-1791
TTY: (301) 587-1789                     E-mail: mda@nad.org
Web: www.nad.org/mda

**Summary** To recognize and reward outstanding young deaf women.

**Eligibility** This is a 2-tiered competition. Young deaf women between the ages of 18 and 28 compete first on the state level; winners take part in the national pageant. Winners are selected on the basis of talent, community service, academics, current events, deaf culture, and more.

**Financial data** The amounts awarded vary. For example, state winners receive an all-expense paid trip to the national competition and a cash award (generally in the $200 range). The national winner and runners-up receive larger cash awards.

**Duration** The competition is held biennially during the summer of even-numbered years, in conjunction with the National Association of the Deaf conventions.

**Deadline** The deadline dates of the state competitions vary; check with the sponsor in your area.

## [1372]
## MISS INDIAN USA SCHOLARSHIP PROGRAM

American Indian Heritage Foundation
P.O. Box 6301
Falls Church, VA 22040
(703) 532-1921      E-mail: MissIndianUSA@indians.org
Web: www.indians.org

**Summary** To recognize and reward the most beautiful and talented Indian women.

**Eligibility** American Indian women between the ages of 18 and 26 are eligible to enter this national contest if they are high school graduates and have never been married, cohabited with the opposite sex, been pregnant, or had children. U.S. citizenship is required. Selection is based on public appearance (20%), a traditional interview (15%), a contemporary interview (15%), beauty of spirit (15%), a cultural presentation (10%), scholastic achievement (10%), a platform question (10%), and a finalist question (5%).

**Financial data** Miss Indian USA receives an academic scholarship of $4,000 plus a cash grant of $6,500, a wardrobe allowance of $2,000, appearance fees of $3,000, a professional photo shoot worth $500, gifts worth more than $4,000, honoring gifts worth more than $2,000, promotional materials worth more than $2,000, and travel to Washington, D.C. with a value of approximately $2,000; the total value of the prize is more than $26,000. Members of her court receive scholarships of $2,000 for the first runner-up, $1,500 for the second runner-up, $1,000 for the third runner-up, and $500 for the fourth runner-up.

**Duration** This competition is held annually.

**Additional information** The program involves a week-long competition in the Washington, D.C. metropolitan area that includes seminars, interviews, cultural presentations, and many public appearances. The application fee is $100 if submitted prior to mid-April or $200 if submitted later. In addition, a candidate fee of $750 is required.

**Number awarded** 1 winner and 4 runners-up are selected each year.

**Deadline** May of each year.

## [1373]
## MISS LATINA WORLD

Dawn Rochele Productions
6150 West El Dorado Parkway, Suite 160-120
McKinney, TX 75070
(206) 666-DAWN      E-mail: info@misslatina.com
Web: www.misslatina.com

**Summary** To recognize and reward young Latina women, with college scholarships and other funds, who compete in a national beauty pageant.

**Eligibility** This program is open to women between 18 and 35 years of age who are at least 25% Hispanic. Applicants may be single, married, or divorced, and they may have children. They appear in a nationally-televised pageant where selection is based one third on an interview, one third on swimsuit appearances, and one third on evening gown appearances. Height and weight are not factors, but contestants should be proportionate. Pageant experience and fluency in Spanish are not required.

**Financial data** Each year, prizes include scholarships, gifts, a cruise to the Bahamas, a trip to Las Vegas, a modeling contract, and use of an apartment in Miami. The total value is more than $25,000.

**Duration** The pageant is held annually.

**Number awarded** 1 winner and 4 runners-up are selected each year.

## [1374]
## MISS STATE SCHOLAR AWARDS

Miss America Pageant
Attn: Scholarship Department
Two Miss America Way, Suite 1000
Atlantic City, NJ 08401
(609) 345-7571, ext. 27      Toll-free: (800) 282-MISS
Fax: (609) 347-6079      E-mail: info@missamerica.org
Web: www.missamerica.org

**Summary** To recognize and reward, with college scholarships, women who participate in the Miss America Pageant at the state level and demonstrate academic excellence.

**Eligibility** This competition is open to women who compete at the state level of the Miss America Pageant. Selection is based on academic excellence (grades, course content, and academic standing of the institution).

**Financial data** The stipend is $1,000.

**Duration** 1 year.

**Additional information** This program, established in 1998, is administered by Scholarship America, One Scholarship Way, P.O. Box 297, St. Peter, MN 56082, (507) 931-1682, (800) 537-4180, Fax: (507) 931-9168.

**Number awarded** Up to 52 each year: 1 for each of the states, the District of Columbia, and the Virgin Islands.

**Deadline** Varies, depending upon the date of local pageants leading to the state finals.

## [1375]
## MISS TEEN AMERICA

Continental Miss Teen America Scholarship Program, Inc.
Attn: CEO/President
P.O. Box 330
Middletown, CT 06457
(860) 346-2200      Fax: (860) 346-2201
E-mail: rfenmore@missteenamerica.com
Web: www.missteenamerica.com

**Summary** To recognize and reward, with college scholarships and other prizes, teen-aged women who participate in a talent and beauty competition.

**Eligibility** This competition is open to women between 14 and 18 years of age who have never been to college, been married, or given birth to a child. Applicants must first apply for state or metropolitan area competitions by submitting a 1-page essay on why they want to represent their state. At the national level, winners participate in talent, modeling, and photogenic competitions. Selection is based on a personal interview with judges (20%), talent or spokesmodel presentation (20%), physical fitness, in recommended swimsuit (20%). a formal eveningwear presentation (10%), a 30-second commercial or public service announcement about their state (10%), the photogenic competition (10%), and modeling (10%).

**Financial data**  Cash scholarships, for use at an accredited college or university, are $5,000 for Miss Teen America, $2,500 for the first alternate, $2,000 for the second alternate, $1,500 for the third alternate, and $1,000 for the fourth alternate. All winners, including those at the state level, receive scholarships for use at Nova Southeastern University and many other prizes and awards.

**Duration**  The competition is held annually.

**Additional information**  All participants are required to pay a total sponsorship fee of $1,050, including a deposit of $75 to accompany the application. They are also required to sell $400 worth of ads for the national program.

**Number awarded**  5 winners receive national scholarships each year.

## [1376]
## MISS TEEN USA

Miss Universe Organization
1370 Avenue of the Americas, 16th Floor
New York, NY 10019
(212) 373-4999                    Fax: (212) 315-5378
E-mail: MissUPR@missuniverse.com
Web: www.missteenusa.com

**Summary**  To recognize and reward beautiful and talented women between 15 and 19 years of age in the United States.

**Eligibility**  Some cities and all states have preliminary pageants. The winner of the city pageant goes on to compete in the state pageant for her home city. A delegate may also enter a state pageant without having won a city title. One delegate from each of the 50 states and the District of Columbia is selected to compete in the pageant. Participants must be between 15 and 19 years of age. They must never have been married or pregnant. Selection is based on beauty, intelligence, and ability to handle an interview.

**Financial data**  Miss Teen USA receives cash and prizes worth more than $150,000. Recently, that included a $45,000 scholarship to the School for Film and Television, a Preciosa trophy worth $3,500, a crystal chandelier from Preciosa worth $5,000, a $2,500 pre-paid VISA BUXX card, a $2,000 cash prize and complimentary UV-Free Tanning for the year of her reign from Mystic Tan, a pearl tiara worth $12,000 from Mikimoto, a fashion footwear wardrobe from Nina Footwear, a swimwear wardrobe from Pink Sands Swim, a 5-day/4 night trip for 2 anywhere American Airlines flies in the continental United States or Caribbean, a pajama wardrobe by Jamatex worth $500, a 1-year salary, a luxury apartment while in New York City, a personal appearance wardrobe, a modeling portfolio, and other services and training. Other prizes included $3,000 for first runner-up, $2,000 for second runner-up, $1,000 for third and fourth runners-up, and $500 for semifinalists. In addition, the delegate selected by the television audience as Miss Photogenic and the delegate selected by her peers as Miss Congeniality each received $1,000 cash prizes and a commemorative Preciosa crystal trophy worth $3,500.

**Duration**  The national pageant is held annually, usually at the end of the summer.

**Additional information**  The competition began in 1983.

**Number awarded**  1 national winner each year.

**Deadline**  June of each year.

## [1377]
## MISS USA

Miss Universe Organization
1370 Avenue of the Americas, 16th Floor
New York, NY 10019
(212) 373-4999                    Fax: (212) 315-5378
E-mail: MissUPR@missuniverse.com
Web: www.missusa.com

**Summary**  To identify and reward the most beautiful women selected in a competition among women from each state.

**Eligibility**  This program is open to women between 18 and 27 years of age who have never been married or pregnant. Entrants are first selected in state competitions, and then 51 women (1 from each state and the District of Columbia) compete in the Miss USA Pageant. Selection of the winner is based on interviews by pageant judges (on successes, talents, goals, and ambitions), a swimsuit competition (with swimsuit styles provided by the pageant), and an evening gown competition (with gowns chosen by the competitors). The Photogenic Award is presented to the delegate voted on and selected by the television audience, and the Congeniality Award is presented to the delegate selected by her sister delegates as the most charismatic and inspirational.

**Financial data**  Miss USA receives cash and prizes that recently included a 2-year scholarship valued at $60,000 from The School for Film and Television, a pearl tiara worth $17,500 from Mikimoto, a cash prize of $3,000 and a shoe wardrobe from Steve Madden, a cash prize of $5,000 and a year supply of Covergirl cosmetics, a 1-year salary, a luxury apartment while in New York City, a personal appearance wardrobe from Tadashi Fashions, a modeling portfolio, and other services and training. Other prizes included $3,000 for first runner-up, $2,000 for second runner-up, $1,000 for third and fourth runners-up, and $500 for semifinalists. In addition, the delegate selected by the television audience as Miss Photogenic and the delegate selected by her peers as Miss Congeniality each received $1,000 cash prizes.

**Duration**  The national pageant is held annually, in February or March.

**Additional information**  This pageant began in 1952. Miss USA competes for additional prizes in the Miss Universe Pageant.

**Number awarded**  1 each year.

**Deadline**  January of each year.

**[1378]**
## MOTHERWELL PRIZE

Fence Books
Attn: Alberta Prize
303 East Eighth Street, B1
New York, NY 10009
E-mail: fence@angel.net
Web: www.fencemag.com/contest/motherwell.html

**Summary** To recognize and reward outstanding unpublished first or second books of poetry by American women.

**Eligibility** Interested women poets are invited to submit an unpublished manuscript (48 to 80 pages). They may not have published more than 1 book of poetry previously. Unpublished poets are also eligible. Translations are not accepted.

**Financial data** The prize is $1,000 and publication of the winning manuscript by Fence Books.

**Duration** The competition is held annually.

**Additional information** This prize was formerly known as the Alberta Prize. There is a $25 entry fee.

**Number awarded** 1 each year.

**Deadline** December of each year.


**[1379]**
## MS. AMERICA

Ms. America, Inc.
Attn: CEO/President
P.O. Box 330
Middletown, CT 06457
(860) 346-2200          Fax: (860) 346-2201
E-mail: rfenmore@missteenamerica.com
Web: www.ms-america.org

**Summary** To recognize and reward women who participate in a talent and beauty competition.

**Eligibility** This competition is open to women 23 years of age and older. Applicants may be single, married, or divorced. They must first apply for state or metropolitan area competitions. Selection is based on an evening wear presentation (25%), a swimwear presentation (25%), a 30-second spokesmodel presentation (25%), and personal expression in an outfit of the applicant's choice. No talent or interview presentations are included; all activities are on stage.

**Financial data** The winner receives $1,000 in cash and other gifts and awards.

**Duration** The competition is held annually.

**Number awarded** 1 each year.


**[1380]**
## MUSIC SCHOLARSHIPS FOR MATURE WOMEN

National League of American Pen Women
1300 17th Street, N.W.
Washington, DC 20036-1973
(202) 785-1997          Fax: (202) 452-8868
E-mail: nlapw1@verizon.net
Web: www.americanpenwomen.org

**Summary** To provide financial assistance for education to mature women composers.

**Eligibility** Women composers who are 35 years of age or older are eligible to apply if they (or their immediate family) are not affiliated with the sponsor. They must submit 2 compositions that have not been publicly performed as part of their application. At least 1 of the scores should have been written in the past 5 years. The performance time for the scores must range between 10 and 25 minutes.

**Financial data** The award is $1,000. Funds are to be used for education.

**Duration** The award is granted biennially.

**Additional information** These awards are presented in honor of Grace Powers Hudson. An entry fee of $8 and a self-addressed stamped envelope must accompany each application.

**Number awarded** 1 each even-numbered year.

**Deadline** January of even-numbered years.


**[1381]**
## MYRNA F. BERNATH BOOK AWARD

Society for Historians of American Foreign Relations
c/o Ohio State University
Department of History
106 Dulles Hall
230 West 17th Avenue
Columbus, OH 43210
(614) 292-1951          Fax: (614) 292-2282
E-mail: shafr@osu.edu
Web: www.shafr.org/prizes.htm

**Summary** To recognize and reward outstanding books written by women on U.S. foreign relations.

**Eligibility** Eligible to be considered for this award are books written by women on U.S. foreign relations, transnational history, international history, peace studies, cultural interchange, and defense or strategic studies that were published during the previous 2 years. Authors or publishers should submit 5 copies of books that meet these requirements. Selection is based on the book's contribution to scholarship.

**Financial data** The prize is $2,500.

**Duration** The prize is offered biennially.

**Additional information** Further information is available from Thomas Borstelmann, University of Nebraska at Lincoln, Department of History, 640 Oldfather Hall, Lincoln, NE 68588.

**Number awarded** 1 each even-numbered year.

**Deadline** November of each odd-numbered year.


**[1382]**
## NATIONAL ASSOCIATION OF WOMEN ARTISTS ANNUAL EXHIBITION AWARDS

National Association of Women Artists, Inc.
80 Fifth Avenue, Suite 1405
New York, NY 10011-8002
(212) 675-1616          Fax: (212) 675-1616
E-mail: nawomena@msn.com
Web: www.nawanet.org/pages/37/32/0

**Summary** To recognize and reward outstanding paintings, sculptures, and prints created by women artists.

**Eligibility** Members of the National Association of Women Artists are eligible to enter the competition. Only oil paintings, sculptures, watercolors, photographs/computer-generated art, and prints are considered.

**Financial data** Awards range from $100 to $1,000.

**Duration** The competition is held annually.

**Additional information** This program includes the following named awards: in the category of works on canvas, the Elizabeth Stanton Blake Memorial Award and N.A.W.A. Medal of Honor ($1,000), the Solveig Stromsoe Palmer Memorial Award ($350) for a conservative portrait, the Audrey Hope Shirk Memorial Award ($350) for an outstanding figure painting, the S. Magnet Knapp Award ($225) for work in acrylic, the Florence B. Andresen Memorial Award ($200), the Beatrice Jackson Memorial Award ($100), the France Lieber Memorial Award ($175), the Molly M. Canaday Memorial Award ($150), the Doris Kreindler Memorial Award ($150) for oil painting, the Mariam E. Halpern Memorial Award ($150), the Susan Kahn Award ($150) for objective figurative painting, the Hazel Witte Memorial Award ($125), the Jared Phillip Apple Memorial Award ($125), the April Z. Newhouse Memorial Award ($100), and the Bertha Pessel Greenblatt Memorial Award ($100) for an abstract painting; in the printmaking category, the Elizabeth Morse Genius Foundation Award and N.A.W.A. Medal of Honor ($1,000), the Ernst and Cecile Holzinger Memorial Award ($325), the Stelly Sterling Memorial Award ($300), the Esther K. Gayner Memorial Award ($125), the Ada Whedon Memorial Award ($225), the Hortense Ferne Memorial Award ($150), the Martha Reed Memorial Award ($150), and the Irwin Zlowe Memorial Award ($100); in the works on paper category, the Elizabeth Stanton Blake Memorial Award and N.A.W.A. Medal of Honor ($1,000), the D. Wu and Elsie Ject-Key Memorial Award ($300), the Miriam E. Halpern Memorial Award ($150), the Mary K. Karasick Memorial Award ($125), the Dorothy Tabak Memorial Award ($500) for a collage, the Belle Cramer Memorial Award ($300) for abstract painting, the Eve Helman Award ($125), the Elizabeth Erlanger Memorial Award ($125), the Miriam Shorr Memorial Award ($200), the Dr. Irving H. Silver Award ($175) for an innovative collage, the Gene Alden Walker Memorial Award ($125) for a conservative watercolor, the Myra Biggerstaff Award ($150), the Sara Winston Memorial Award ($100), the Jeffrey Childs Willis Memorial Award ($100), the Miriam Russo Enders Award ($250), and the Clara Shainess Memorial Award ($175); in the sculpture category, the Margo Liebes Harris Memorial Award and N.A.W.A. Medal of Honor ($1,000), the Margo Liebes Harris Memorial Award ($400), the Amelia Peabody Memorial Award ($500), the Cleo Hartwig Memorial Award ($175), the Beatrice G. Epstein Memorial Award ($150), and the Gretchen Richardson Memorial Award ($150); in the photography/computer art category, the Gladys S. Blum Memorial Award ($250), and the Marion de Sola Mendes Memorial Award ($150).

**Number awarded** A total of 47 awards are currently available each year, although an entry may win more than 1 award.

## [1383]
## NATIONAL COMMUNITY SERVICE SCHOLARSHIP

Miss America Pageant
Attn: Scholarship Department
Two Miss America Way, Suite 1000
Atlantic City, NJ 08401
(609) 345-7571, ext. 27      Toll-free: (800) 282-MISS
Fax: (609) 347-6079      E-mail: info@missamerica.org
Web: www.missamerica.org

**Summary** To recognize and reward, with college scholarships, women who participate in the Miss America Pageant at the state level and demonstrate outstanding community service.

**Eligibility** This program is open to women who compete at the state level of the Miss America Pageant but do not win their state title. Selection is based on excellence of community service.

**Financial data** The stipend is $5,000.

**Duration** 1 year.

**Additional information** This program was established in 1994.

**Number awarded** 1 each year.

**Deadline** Varies, depending upon the date of local pageants leading to the state finals.

## [1384]
## NFMC BIENNIAL STUDENT AUDITION AWARDS

National Federation of Music Clubs
1336 North Delaware Street
Indianapolis, IN 46202-2481
(317) 638-4003      Fax: (317) 638-0503
E-mail: info@nfmc-music.org
Web: www.nfmc-music.org

**Summary** To recognize and reward outstanding young musicians who are members of the National Federation of Music Clubs (NFMC).

**Eligibility** Instrumentalists must be between 16 and 26 years of age; vocalists must be between 18 and 26. All applicants must be U.S. citizens and either student or junior division members of the federation. Competition categories include: women's voice, men's voice, piano, organ, harp, classical guitar, violin, viola, cello, double bass, orchestral woodwinds, orchestral brass, and percussion. Awards are presented at the national level after auditions at the state and district levels.

**Financial data** The winner in each category is awarded $1,500.

**Duration** The competition is held biennially, in odd-numbered years.

**Additional information** Applications and further information on these awards are available from Mrs. Robert Carroll, 17583 North 1090 East Road, Pontiac, IL 61764-9801, E-mail: scarroll@frontiernet.net; information on all federation scholarships and awards is available from Chair, Competitions and Awards Board, Dr. George R. Keck, 421 Cherry Street, Arkadelphia, AR 71923-5116. Students who enter this competition are also automatically considered for the following awards the Annie Lou Ellis Piano Award, the Dr. Barbara Irish Violin Award, the Dr. Barbara M. Irish Award, the Hazel Heffner Becchina Award, the Irene S. Muir Award, the Janice Clarkson Cleworth Award, the Josef Kaspar Awards, the Josephine Trott Strings Award, the Lawrence Foster Violoncello Award, the Louise L. Henderson Violoncello Award, the Louise Oberne Strings Awards, the Marie Morrisey Keith Awards, the Ruby Simmonds Vought Organ Award, the Thor Johnson Strings Awards, the Lucille Heimrich Awards, and the Virginia Peace Mackey-Althouse Voice Award. The entry fee is $30 for each category.

**Deadline** January of odd-numbered years.

## [1385]
## NFMC BIENNIAL YOUNG ARTIST AWARDS

National Federation of Music Clubs
1336 North Delaware Street
Indianapolis, IN 46202-2481
(317) 638-4003          Fax: (317) 638-0503
E-mail: info@nfmc-music.org
Web: www.nfmc-music.org

**Summary** To recognize and reward outstanding young musicians who are members of the National Federation of Music Clubs (NFMC).

**Eligibility** Vocalists must be between 25 and 37 years of age; instrumentalists must be at least 18. Competitions are held in 4 categories: women's voice, men's voice, piano, and strings. Membership in the federation and U.S. citizenship are required.

**Financial data** Awards are $10,000; in addition, applicants are automatically considered for a number of supplemental awards.

**Duration** The competition is held biennially, in odd-numbered years.

**Additional information** Applications and further information are available from Mrs. Nannette Hanslowe, 296 Medford Leas, Medford, NJ 08055, E-mail: nannettehanslowe@yahoo.com; information on all federation scholarships and awards is available from Chair, Competitions and Awards Board, Dr. George R. Keck, 421 Cherry Street, Arkadelphia, AR 71923-5116. There is a $40 entry fee for each category.

**Number awarded** 4 every other year: 1 in each of the 4 categories.

**Deadline** February of odd-numbered years.

## [1386]
## OPTIMIST INTERNATIONAL ORATORICAL CONTEST

Optimist International
Attn: Programs Department
4494 Lindell Boulevard
St. Louis, MO 63108
(314) 371-6000     Toll-free: (800) 500-8130, ext. 235
Fax: (314) 371-6009     E-mail: programs@optimist.org
Web: www.optimist.org

**Summary** To recognize and reward outstanding orators at the high school or younger level.

**Eligibility** All students in public, private, or parochial elementary, junior high, and senior high schools in the United States, Canada, or the Caribbean who are under 16 years of age may enter. All contestants must prepare their own orations of 4 to 5 minutes, but they may receive advice and

make minor changes or improvements in the oration at any time. Each year a different subject is selected for the orations; a recent topic was "My Future is Bright because..." The orations may be delivered in a language other than English if that language is an official language of the country in which the sponsoring club is located. Selection is based on poise (20 points), content of speech (35 points), delivery and presentation (35 points), and overall effectiveness (10 points). Competition is first conducted at the level of individual clubs, with winners advancing to zone and then district competitions. At the discretion of the district, boys may compete against boys and girls against girls in separate contests.

**Financial data** Each district awards either 2 scholarships of $1,500 (1 for a boy and 1 for a girl) or (if the district chooses to have a combined gender contest) a first-place scholarship of $1,500, a second-place scholarship of $1,000, and a third-place scholarship of $500.

**Duration** The competition is held annually.

**Additional information** This competition was first held in 1928. Nearly 2,000 Optimist International local clubs participate in the program each year. Entry information is available only from local Optimist Clubs.

**Number awarded** Each year, more than $150,000 is awarded in scholarships.

**Deadline** Each local club sets its own deadline. The district deadline is the end of June.

## [1387]
## ORANGE PRIZE FOR FICTION

Book Trust
45 East Hill
London SW18 2QZ
England
44 20 8516 2072     E-mail: tarryn@booktrust.org.uk
Web: www.orangeprize.co.uk

**Summary** To recognize and reward novels by women written in English and published in the United Kingdom.

**Eligibility** Eligible to be considered for this prize are novels written by women in English and published in the United Kingdom during the 12 months prior to March 31 of the year of the award. Submissions may also have been published in other countries, including the United States, as long as its first U.K. publication was within the prescribed time period. Ineligible works include books of short stories, novellas (stories between 12,000 and 30,000 words), and translations of books originally written in other languages.

**Financial data** The prize is 30,000 pounds and a bronze figurine known as the "Bessie".

**Duration** The prize is awarded annually.

**Additional information** This prize, first awarded in 1996, is the United Kingdom's largest annual literary award for a single novel. It is administered by Book Trust and sponsored by Orange UK, the national digital wireless telephone service.

**Number awarded** 1 each year.

## [1388]
## OUTSTANDING WOMAN GEOLOGIST AWARD

Association for Women Geoscientists
Attn: AWG Foundation
P.O. Box 30645
Lincoln, NE 68503-0645
E-mail: awgscholarship@yahoo.com
Web: www.awg.org/eas/owga.html

**Summary** To recognize and reward women undergraduates at colleges and universities in Utah and Idaho who demonstrate outstanding achievement in geology.

**Eligibility** This award is available to undergraduate women with a declared major in geology at colleges and universities in Utah and Idaho. Nominees must exhibit outstanding achievement in geology courses, good academic achievement in other course work, and a strong interest in or passion for geology. Nominations must be submitted by a geology professor.

**Financial data** The award is $500.

**Duration** The award is presented annually.

**Additional information** This program is sponsored by the Salt Lake chapter of the Association for Women Geoscientists. Information is also available from Janae Wallace Boyer, P.O. Box 58691, Salt Lake City, UT 84158-0691, (801) 537-3387, E-mail: janaewallace@utah.gov.

**Number awarded** 1 each year.

**Deadline** March of each year.


## [1389]
## PALLAS ATHENE AWARD

Women's Army Corps Veterans' Association
P.O. Box 5577
Fort McClellan, AL 36205-5577
E-mail: info@armywomen.org
Web: www.armywomen.org/award.shtml

**Summary** To recognize and reward outstanding college and university women who are Army ROTC cadets.

**Eligibility** College and university military science departments are invited to nominate outstanding Army Senior ROTC Program women cadets. Nominees must be graduating within the academic school year, be in the top 50% of their military science and academic class, and have successfully completed the ROTC Advanced Camp or Nursing Advanced Camp. A board of Army officers in each of the 3 ROTC regions selects the winning student.

**Financial data** The award consists of a medallion, a $500 cash prize, and a 3-year membership in the Women's Army Corps Veterans' Association.

**Duration** The award is presented annually.

**Additional information** This award was first presented in 1983.

**Number awarded** 3 each year (1 in each of the ROTC regions).


## [1390]
## PEPSI USBC YOUTH BOWLING CHAMPIONSHIPS

United States Bowling Congress
Attn: Pepsi-Cola Youth Bowling Event Manager
5301 South 76th Street
Greendale, WI 53129-1192
(414) 423-3442   Toll-free: (800) 514-BOWL, ext. 3442
Fax: (414) 421-3014
E-mail: maureen.vicena@bowl.com
Web: www.bowl.com

**Summary** To recognize and reward (with college scholarships) members of the United States Bowling Congress (USBC) who achieve high scores in an international competition.

**Eligibility** This competition is open to USBC members in the United States, Puerto Rico, U.S. military zones, and Canada. Applicants enter in 1 of 6 categories: 11 and under boys' handicap, 12 and above boys' handicap, 12 and above boys' scratch, 11 and under girls' handicap, 12 and above girls' handicap, and 12 and above girls' scratch. Based on their bowling scores in state and zone competitions, the top bowlers in the 12 and above boys' and girls' handicap categories advance to the international finals. Also advancing to the international finals are the state and zone winners in the 12 and above boys' and girls' scratch categories who are also USBC Junior Gold members (boys must have an average of 175 or above, girls must have an average of 165 or above). All selected finalists (more than 200 qualify each year), are then assigned to Division I or Division II for the international competition, held annually at a site in the United States; assignment is based on their adjusted score from year-end averages and state and zone competitions. Bowlers whose scores are in the top half are assigned to Division I and bowlers whose scores are in the bottom half are assigned to Division II. Scholarships are awarded solely on the basis of bowling performance in the international finals.

**Financial data** At the international finals, the top finishers in each division receive scholarships of $2,000, $1,500, $1,000, and $500, respectively.

**Duration** The competition is held annually.

**Additional information** This competition is sponsored by the Pepsi-Cola Company and conducted by the USBC. More than $300,000 is scholarships is awarded at state and zone competitions for all 6 categories. USBC also awards a $400 stipend to each competitor at the international finals (Canadian athletes are not eligible for the stipend and competitors from U.S. military bases must pay for their own transportation to the United States); the stipend is intended to assist with the cost of travel, meals, and housing.

**Number awarded** Each year, 16 scholarships are awarded: 8 are set aside for girls (4 in each division) and 8 for boys (4 in each division).

**Deadline** Qualifying tournaments are held in bowling centers from October through February of each year. Center and section qualifying takes place in March and April. State and zone competitions take place through the end of May. The national finals are held in July.

## [1391]
## PETER B. WAGNER MEMORIAL AWARD FOR WOMEN IN ATMOSPHERIC SCIENCES

Desert Research Institute
Attn: Vanda Grubisic
2215 Raggio Parkway
Reno, NV 89512-1095
(702) 673-7031                          Fax: (702) 673-7421
E-mail: Vanda.Grubisic@dri.edu
Web: ia.dri.edu/Wagner

**Summary** To recognize and reward outstanding research papers written by women graduate students on atmospheric sciences.

**Eligibility** Women working on a master's or doctoral degree in atmospheric sciences or a related field are invited to submit a research paper for consideration. The applicants may be enrolled at a university anywhere in the United States. They must submit a paper, up to 15 pages in length, based on original research directly related to the identification, clarification, and/or resolution of an atmospheric/climatic problem. Selection is based on the originality of ideas expressed, presentation of concept, how well the subject matter relates to real-world atmospheric/climatic problems or their resolution, and how well the research is defined by the introduction, methods, results, and conclusions of the manuscript.

**Financial data** The award is $1,500.

**Duration** The competition is held annually.

**Additional information** This award was first presented in 1998.

**Number awarded** 1 each year.

**Deadline** April of each year.

## [1392]
## RECOGNITION AWARD FOR EMERGING SCHOLARS

American Association of University Women
Attn: AAUW Educational Foundation
1111 16th Street, N.W.
Washington, DC 20036-4873
(202) 785-7609                Toll-free: (800) 326-AAUW
Fax: (202) 463-7169           TDD: (202) 785-7777
E-mail: foundation@aauw.org
Web: www.aauw.org/fga/awards/raes.cfm

**Summary** To recognize and reward young women who show promise of future academic distinction.

**Eligibility** Eligible for nomination are nontenured women faculty members who earned a Ph.D. or equivalent within the past 5 years. They must be U.S. citizens or permanent residents. Selection is based on demonstrated excellence in teaching and commitment to women students, a documented and active research record, potential to make a significant contribution to her field, and commitment to women's issues in the profession or in the community. The sponsor strongly encourages nomination of women from underrepresented groups.

**Financial data** The award is $10,000.

**Duration** The award is presented annually.

**Additional information** The award includes a trip to the annual AAUW convention (where the award is presented).

**Number awarded** 1 each year.

**Deadline** Nominations must be submitted by February of each year.

## [1393]
## ROBERT CHESLEY AWARD FOR LESBIAN AND GAY PLAYWRITING

Publishing Triangle
332 Bleecker Street, D36
New York, NY 10014
E-mail: awards@publishingtriangle.org
Web: www.publishingtriangle.org/awards.asp

**Summary** To recognize and reward playwrights who have dealt openly with gay and lesbian issues.

**Eligibility** Eligible to be nominated for this award are gay or lesbian playwrights whose work contains significant gay and lesbian content. The award alternates between a woman (in odd-numbered years) and a man (in even-numbered years). Neither aspiring writers nor those with unpublished manuscripts are eligible.

**Financial data** The award is $1,000.

**Duration** The award is presented annually.

**Additional information** The Publishing Triangle is an association of lesbians and gay men in publishing. This award was first presented in 1994. Information is also available from Victor Bumbalo, 828 North Laurel Avenue, Los Angeles, CA 90046. Current members of the Publishing Triangle may nominate playwrights for free; all others must enclose a check for $25 per playwright nominated.

**Number awarded** 1 each year.

**Deadline** November of each year.

## [1394]
## ROSE MARY CRAWSHAY PRIZES

British Academy
Attn: Assistant Secretary Lectures and Symposia
10 Carlton House Terrace
London SW1Y 5AH
England
44 20 7969 5264                    Fax: 44 20 7969 5414
E-mail: a.pusey@britac.ac.uk
Web: www.britac.ac.uk

**Summary** To recognize and reward women who have written or published outstanding historical or critical works on any subject connected with English literature.

**Eligibility** Women of any nationality are eligible to be nominated if within the preceding 3 years they have written an historical or critical work on any subject connected with English literature. Preference is given to works on Byron, Shelley, or Keats. Submissions are invited from publishing houses only.

**Financial data** The prize is 500 pounds.

**Duration** The prize is awarded each year.

**Additional information** The prize was established by Rose Mary Crawshay in 1888.

**Number awarded** 2 each year.

**Deadline** December of each year.

## [1395]
## RUTH I. MICHLER MEMORIAL PRIZE

Association for Women in Mathematics
11240 Waples Mill Road, Suite 200
Fairfax, VA 22030
(703) 934-0163       Fax: (703) 359-7562
E-mail: awm@math.umd.edu
Web: www.awm-math.org/michlerprize.html

**Summary** To recognize and reward, with a fellowship at Cornell University, outstanding women mathematicians.

**Eligibility** This prize is available to women recently promoted to associate professor or equivalent position in the mathematical sciences at an institution of higher learning other than Cornell University. Applicants may be of any nationality and hold a position in any country. They must submit a proposal describing a research or book project to be undertaken during the fellowship period and explaining how the semester in the mathematics department at Cornell University will enhance their project or research career. Selection is based on the excellence of the applicant's research and the potential benefit to her of a semester in the mathematics department at Cornell.

**Financial data** The prize is $40,000.

**Duration** The prize is presented annually. The recipient may spend a semester of her choice in residence at Cornell.

**Additional information** This prize was first presented in 2007.

**Number awarded** 1 each year.

**Deadline** October of each year.

## [1396]
## RUTH LYTTLE SATTER PRIZE IN MATHEMATICS

American Mathematical Society
Attn: Membership and Programs Department
201 Charles Street
P.O. Box 6248
Providence, RI 02940-6248
(401) 455-4107      Toll-free: (800) 321-4AMS
Fax: (401) 331-3842     E-mail: prof-serv@ams.org
Web: www.ams.org/prizes/satter-prize.html

**Summary** To recognize and reward women who have made outstanding contributions to mathematics.

**Eligibility** This program is open to female mathematicians who have made outstanding contributions to research in the field. The work must have been completed over the past 6 years.

**Financial data** The prize is $5,000.

**Duration** The prize is awarded biennially, in odd-numbered years.

**Additional information** This prize was first awarded in 1991.

**Number awarded** 1 every other year.

**Deadline** June of each even-numbered year.

## [1397]
## SANOFI-AVENTIS WOMEN PHYSICIAN IN ALLERGY GRANT AWARDS

American Academy of Allergy, Asthma & Immunology
555 East Wells Street, Suite 1100
Milwaukee, WI 53202-3823
(414) 272-6071      Fax: (414) 272-6070
E-mail: info@aaaai.org
Web: www.aaaai.org

**Summary** To recognize and reward women members of the American Academy of Allergy, Asthma & Immunology (AAAAI) who have made outstanding contributions to the field of allergy, asthma, and immunology research.

**Eligibility** Applicants must be women AAAAI members who are physicians residing in the United States involved in the field of allergy, asthma, and immunology. They must have made creative, impactful, and/or permanent contributions in 1 or more of the following fields: education (either professional or public), research (either basic or clinical), or service (to a community, institution, or organization). Only self-nominations are accepted.

**Financial data** The award is $20,000; funds are to be used to enable the awardees to continue their award-winning work.

**Duration** Awards are presented annually.

**Additional information** Funding for this program is provided by Sanofi-Aventis.

**Number awarded** 2 each year.

**Deadline** November of each year.

## [1398]
## SELMA MOIDEL SMITH LAW STUDENT WRITING COMPETITION

National Association of Women Lawyers
American Bar Center, MS 15.2
321 North Clark Street
Chicago, IL 60610
Fax: (312) 988-5491     E-mail: nawl@nawl.org
Web: www.abanet.org

**Summary** To recognize and reward original law student writing on issues concerning women and the law.

**Eligibility** Currently-enrolled law students are invited to submit original and unpublished essays (up to 15 pages) on a topic related to women and the law. Essays are judged on content, quality of research, originality, writing style, and timeliness.

**Financial data** The author of the first-place essay receives $500 and an expense-paid trip to the sponsor's meeting. The winning essay is published in *Women Lawyers Journal*.

**Duration** This is an annual competition.

**Additional information** The first competition was held in 2006.

**Number awarded** 1 each year.

**Deadline** February of each year.

## [1399]
## SHARON KEILLOR AWARD FOR WOMEN IN ENGINEERING EDUCATION

American Society for Engineering Education
Attn: Manager, Administrative Services
1818 N Street, N.W., Suite 600
Washington, DC 20036-2479
(202) 331-3500        Fax: (202) 265-8504
Web: www.asee.org

**Summary** To recognize and reward outstanding women engineering educators.

**Eligibility** This award is presented to a woman engineering educator who has an outstanding record in teaching engineering students and reasonable performance histories of research and service within an engineering school. Nominees must have an earned doctoral degree in an engineering discipline and have at least 5 years of teaching experience in an engineering school.

**Financial data** The award consists of a $2,000 honorarium and an inscribed plaque.

**Duration** The award is granted annually.

**Number awarded** 1 each year.

**Deadline** January of each year.

## [1400]
## SIGMA ALPHA IOTA GRADUATE PERFORMANCE AWARDS

Sigma Alpha Iota Philanthropies, Inc.
One Tunnel Road
Asheville, NC 28805
(828) 251-0606        Fax: (828) 251-0644
E-mail: philonline@sai-national.org
Web: www.sai-national.org/phil/philsch3.html

**Summary** To recognize and reward outstanding performances in vocal and instrumental categories by graduate student members of Sigma Alpha Iota (an organization of women musicians).

**Eligibility** This program is open to college and alumna members of the organization who are working on a graduate degree in the field of performance. Competitions are held in 4 categories: voice, piano and percussion, strings, and winds and brass.

**Financial data** Awards are $2,000 for first place or $1,500 for second place. Funds must be used for graduate study in the field of performance.

**Duration** The competition is held triennially.

**Additional information** The awards for piano and percussion and for woodwinds and brass are designated as the Mary Ann Starring Memorial Awards. The awards for strings are designated as the Dorothy E. Morris Memorial Awards. For vocalists, the award for first place is designated the Glad Robinson Youse Memorial Award and the award for second place is designated the Lucille Malish Memorial Award. There is a $25 nonrefundable application fee.

**Number awarded** 8 every 3 years: 1 first place and 1 second place in each of the 4 categories.

**Deadline** March of the year of the awards (2009, 2012, etc.).

## [1401]
## SIGMA ALPHA IOTA SCHOLARSHIPS FOR UNDERGRADUATE PERFORMANCE

Sigma Alpha Iota Philanthropies, Inc.
One Tunnel Road
Asheville, NC 28805
(828) 251-0606        Fax: (828) 251-0644
E-mail: philonline@sai-national.org
Web: www.sai-national.org/phil/philsch3.html

**Summary** To recognize and reward outstanding performances in vocal and instrumental categories by undergraduate members of Sigma Alpha Iota (an organization of women musicians).

**Eligibility** Undergraduate student members of the organization may enter this competition if they are vocalists or instrumentalists. Entrants must be younger than 25 years of age. Selection is based on taped auditions in 4 categories: voice, keyboard and percussion, strings, and winds and brass.

**Financial data** The stipend is $1,500.

**Duration** The competition is held triennially.

**Additional information** This program consists of the following named awards: the Blanche Z. Hoffman Memorial Award for Voice, the Mary Ann Starring Memorial Award for Piano, the Dorothy E. Morris Memorial Award for Strings or Harp, and the Mary Ann Starring Memorial Award for Woodwinds or Brass. There is a $25 nonrefundable application fee.

**Number awarded** 4 every 3 years: 1 in each of the 4 categories.

**Deadline** March of the year of the awards (2009, 2012, etc.).

## [1402]
## SO TO SPEAK ANNUAL POETRY AND FICTION CONTESTS

George Mason University
Attn: So to Speak: A Feminist Journal of Language and Art
4400 University Drive
MSN 2D6
Fairfax, VA 22030-4444
E-mail: sts@gmu.edu
Web: www.gmu.edu/org/sts/contests.htm

**Summary** To recognize and reward outstanding unpublished short stories and poetry of interest to feminist readers.

**Eligibility** This competition is sponsored by a feminist journal. Fiction entries may include up to 3 short stories, each up to 1,500 words in length. Nonfiction entries (nonacademic), including memoirs and vignettes, may be up to 4,000 words. Poetry entries may include 2 to 5 poems, no more than 5 pages total. All submissions must be previously unpublished.

**Financial data** First prize is $500 and publication in the journal, *So to Speak*.

**Duration** The competition is held annually.

**Additional information** All entrants receive a copy of the issue with the winning works. The entry fee is $15.

**Number awarded** 3 each year: 1 each for fiction, nonfiction, and poetry.

**Deadline**  March of each year for fiction; October of each year for nonfiction and poetry.

## [1403]
## SPEAKING OUT FOR JUSTICE AWARD

American Association of University Women
Attn: Legal Advocacy Fund
1111 16th Street, N.W.
Washington, DC 20036-4873
(202) 785-7750    Toll-free: (800) 326-AAUW, ext. 145
Fax: (202) 785-8754        TDD: (202) 785-7777
E-mail: laf@aauw.org
Web: www.aauw.org/laf/speaking_out.cfm

**Summary**  To recognize and reward women who have contributed to the mission of the American Association of University Women (AAUW).

**Eligibility**  Nominees for this award must be nationally prominent individuals who have advocated for change on behalf of women and girls. They must have raised national attention and awareness on issues that reflect the mission and work of the AAUW. Selection is based on the significance of the nominee's contribution to the betterment and well-being of women, the nominee's leadership and commitment to equity and to issues facing women and girls, and the national prominence of the nominee's work.

**Financial data**  The award is $5,000.

**Duration**  The award is presented biennially, in odd-numbered years.

**Number awarded**  1 every other year.

**Deadline**  March of even-numbered years.

## [1404]
## STATE BAR OF CALIFORNIA COMMITTEE ON WOMEN IN THE LAW ESSAY CONTEST

State Bar of California
Attn: Committee on Women in the Law
180 Howard Street
San Francisco, CA 94105-1639
(415) 538-2141    E-mail: Kate.Oconnor@calbar.ca.gov
Web: www.calbar.ca.gov

**Summary**  To recognize and reward law students and recent graduates who submit essays on a topic related to women in the law.

**Eligibility**  This competition is open to currently-enrolled law students and people who have graduated from law school within the past year. Essays must be on a topic that changes annually but relates to women in the law. Recently, the topic was, "Are there issues of special relevance to women law students that those who recruit and hire lawyers should be aware of?" Essays must be between 1,200 and 1,500 words, specifically prepared for this contest, and previously unpublished.

**Financial data**  First prize is $1,000, second $500, and third $250.

**Duration**  The competition is held annually.

**Additional information**  The winning essay is submitted to a major legal publication.

**Number awarded**  3 each year.

**Deadline**  April of each year.

## [1405]
## STATE COMMUNITY SERVICE SCHOLARSHIPS

Miss America Pageant
Attn: Scholarship Department
Two Miss America Way, Suite 1000
Atlantic City, NJ 08401
(609) 345-7571, ext. 27    Toll-free: (800) 282-MISS
Fax: (609) 347-6079    E-mail: info@missamerica.org
Web: www.missamerica.org

**Summary**  To recognize and reward, with college scholarships, women who participate in the Miss America Pageant at the state level and demonstrate outstanding community service.

**Eligibility**  This competition is open to women who compete at the state level of the Miss America Pageant. Applicants must demonstrate that they have fulfilled a legitimate need in their community through the creation, development, and/or participation in a community service project. Selection is based on excellence of community service.

**Financial data**  The stipend is $1,000.

**Duration**  1 year.

**Additional information**  This program, established in 1998, is administered by Scholarship America, One Scholarship Way, P.O. Box 297, St. Peter, MN 56082, (507) 931-1682, (800) 537-4180, Fax: (507) 931-9168.

**Number awarded**  Up to 52 each year: 1 for each of the states, the District of Columbia, and the Virgin Islands.

**Deadline**  Varies, depending upon the date of local pageants leading to the state finals.

## [1406]
## SUBARU OUTSTANDING WOMAN IN SCIENCE AWARD

Geological Society of America
Attn: Program Officer-Grants, Awards and Recognition
3300 Penrose Place
P.O. Box 9140
Boulder, CO 80301-9140
(303) 357-1028    Toll-free: (800) 472-1988, ext. 1028
Fax: (303) 357-1070    E-mail: awards@geosociety.org
Web: www.geosociety.org/aboutus/awards

**Summary**  To recognize and reward women who have exerted a major impact on the field of geosciences through their Ph.D. research.

**Eligibility**  This program is open to women geoscientists who are within 3 years of completion of their Ph.D. degree. Nominations should include a letter that describes how the Ph.D. research has impacted geosciences in a major way, a short summary of the research, a short resume with a list of publications, and a copy of the dissertation abstract, published abstracts, and/or reprints as available.

**Financial data**  The award is $2,500.

**Duration**  The award is presented annually.

**Additional information**  This award, first presented in 2001, is sponsored by Subaru of America, Inc. It was formerly named the Doris M. Curtis Memorial Fund for Women in Science Award.

**Number awarded**  1 each year.

**Deadline**  January of each year.

## [1407]
## SUE SANIEL ELKIND POETRY CONTEST

Kalliope Women Writers' Collective
c/o Florida Community College at Jacksonville
11901 Beach Boulevard, Room N-123
Jacksonville, FL 32246
(904) 646-2081          E-mail: opencampus@fccj.edu
Web: opencampus.fccj.org/kalliope/k-contst.html

**Summary**  To recognize and reward outstanding poetry written by women.

**Eligibility**  Poems in any style and on any subject may be submitted if they do not exceed 50 lines each and are written by a woman. Any number may be submitted. Poems that have been previously published, have received monetary awards, or are under consideration elsewhere are not eligible.

**Financial data**  The prize is $1,000.

**Duration**  The competition is held annually.

**Additional information**  This prize was first awarded in 1993. The winning poem is published in *Kalliope: a journal of women's literature & art*. The entry fee is $5 per poem (or $12 for 3 poems).

**Number awarded**  1 each year.

**Deadline**  October of each year.

## [1408]
## SUSIE PRYOR AWARD IN ARKANSAS WOMEN'S HISTORY

Arkansas Historical Association
Attn: Arkansas Women's History Institute
University of Arkansas
Department of History, Old Main 416
Fayetteville, AR 72701
(479) 575-5884          E-mail: dludlow@uark.edu
Web: www.uark.edu/depts/arkhist/home/awards.html

**Summary**  To recognize and reward the best unpublished essay or article on topics related to Arkansas women's history.

**Eligibility**  Manuscripts should be no longer than 35 pages. They are judged on the basis of 1) their contribution to knowledge of women in Arkansas history; 2) use of primary and secondary materials; 3) creative interpretation and originality; and 4) stylistic excellence.

**Financial data**  The prize is $1,000.

**Duration**  The prize is awarded annually.

**Additional information**  The winning paper may be published by the institute. This prize was first awarded in 1986 as a feature of Arkansas' sesquicentennial celebration. All entries, including illustrations, become the property of the Arkansas Women's History Institute and will not be returned. They will be placed in archival collections that receive contributions from the institute.

**Number awarded**  1 each year.

**Deadline**  February of each year.

## [1409]
## SWEET 16 MAGAZINE SCHOLARSHIP CONTEST

Guideposts
Attn: Sweet 16 Magazine Scholarship Contest
16 East 34th Street
New York, NY 10016
(212) 251-8100          Toll-free: (800) 932-2145
Fax: (212) 684-0679
E-mail: scholarship@sweet16mag.com
Web: www.guidepostsmag.com

**Summary**  To recognize and reward, with college scholarships, middle and high school girls who submit outstanding spiritual stories.

**Eligibility**  This competition is open to girls between 13 and 18 years of age. Applicants must submit a true, first-person story about a memorable or life-changing experience they have had. Manuscripts must be written in English and be no more than 1,200 words.

**Financial data**  Prizes, in the form of scholarships to accredited 4-year colleges or universities of the recipients' choice, are $16,000 for first, $10,000 for second, $5,000 for third, and $2,500 for fourth. Honorable mentions are cash prizes of $500.

**Duration**  The competition is held annually. Scholarships must be used within 5 years of high school graduation.

**Additional information**  This competition was formerly known as the Guideposts Young Writers Contest. Manuscripts will not be returned unless accompanied by a self-addressed stamped envelope.

**Number awarded**  16 each year: 4 scholarships and 12 honorable mentions.

**Deadline**  October of each year.

## [1410]
## SYLVIA FORMAN PRIZE COMPETITION

American Anthropological Association
Attn: Association for Feminist Anthropology
2200 Wilson Boulevard, Suite 600
Arlington, VA 22201-3357
(703) 528-1902          Fax: (703) 528-3546
Web: sscl.berkeley.edu/~afaweb/forman.html

**Summary**  To recognize and reward the best student essays in feminist anthropology.

**Eligibility**  Both graduate and undergraduate students may compete. They are invited to submit essays (up to 35 pages) in any subfield of anthropology that focus on topics including (but not limited to) feminist analysis of women's work, reproduction, sexuality, religion, language and expressive culture, family and kin relations, economic development, gender and material culture, gender and biology, women and development, globalization, or race and class. Essays that have been submitted for publication but have not yet been accepted may be eligible as entries. Already accepted or published articles may not be submitted. Only 1 submission per student is accepted. Selection is based on the use of feminist theory to analyze a particular issue; organization, quality, and clarity of writing; effective use of both theory and data; significance to feminist scholarship; timeliness and relevance of the topic; and originality of work.

**Financial data** The prize is $500 for a graduate student or $300 for an undergraduate.

**Duration** The competition is held annually.

**Additional information** The winning essays are published in the association's *Anthropology Newsletter*. This competition began in 1995. Information is also available from Cheryl Rodriguez, University of South Florida, Africana Studies Department, FAO 270, Tampa, FL 33620, E-mail: crodrigu@chuma1.cas.usf.edu.

**Number awarded** At least 2 each year: 1 for an undergraduate and 1 for a graduate student.

**Deadline** May of each year.

## [1411]
## TEEN LATINA WORLD

Dawn Rochele Productions
6150 West El Dorado Parkway, Suite 160-120
McKinney, TX 75070
(206) 666-DAWN     E-mail: info@misslatina.com
Web: www.misslatina.com

**Summary** To recognize and reward teen-aged Latina women, with college scholarships and other awards, who compete in a national beauty pageant.

**Eligibility** This program is open to women between 13 and 17 years of age who are at least 25% Hispanic. Applicants must be single and they may not have children. They appear in a nationally-televised pageant where selection is based one third on an interview, one third on swimsuit appearances, and one third on evening gown appearances. Height and weight are not factors, but contestants should be proportionate. Pageant experience and fluency in Spanish are not required.

**Financial data** Each year, prizes include scholarships, gifts, a cruise to the Bahamas, a trip to Las Vegas, a modeling contract, and use of an apartment in Miami. The total value is more than $25,000.

**Duration** The pageant is held annually.

**Number awarded** 1 winner and 4 runners-up are selected each year.

## [1412]
## TWINING HUMBER AWARD FOR LIFETIME ARTISTIC ACHIEVEMENT

Artist Trust
Attn: Director of Grant Programs
1835 12th Avenue
Seattle, WA 98122-2437
(206) 467-8734     Toll-free: (866) 21-TRUST
Fax: (206) 467-9633     E-mail: info@artisttrust.org
Web: www.artisttrust.org/grants/THA

**Summary** To recognize and reward the artistic achievements of older women artists in Washington.

**Eligibility** Eligible to be nominated for this award are women visual artists over 60 years of age from Washington state. Nominees must have devoted at least 25 years of their lives to creating art. Selection is based on creative excellence, professional accomplishment, and dedication to the visual arts.

**Financial data** The award is $10,000.

**Duration** The award is presented annually.

**Number awarded** At least 1 each year.

**Deadline** January of each year.

## [1413]
## UNDERGRADUATE AWARD FOR EXCELLENCE IN CHEMISTRY

Iota Sigma Pi
c/o National Director for Student Awards, Kathryn A. Thomasson
University of North Dakota, Department of Chemistry
P.O. Box 9024
Grand Forks, ND 58202-9024
(701) 777-3199     Fax: (701) 777-2331
E-mail: kthomasson@chem.und.edu
Web: www.iotasigmapi.info

**Summary** To recognize and reward excellence in chemistry on the part of female undergraduate students.

**Eligibility** Nominees must be women who are seniors at an accredited 4-year college or university and majoring in chemistry. They may be, but need not be, members of Iota Sigma Pi. Only 1 nomination may be forwarded by any chemistry department each year. The nomination dossier must contain the candidate's addresses, a transcript, a list of the student's activities while in college, a statement of plans after graduation, and 2 or more faculty recommendations.

**Financial data** The award of $500 and a certificate are presented at Honors Day on the recipient's campus, at a nearby local meeting of Iota Sigma Pi or the American Chemical Society, or at a suitable time arranged with the department chair of the awardee.

**Duration** The award is presented annually.

**Additional information** This award was first presented in 1975.

**Number awarded** 1 each year.

**Deadline** February of each year.

## [1414]
## USBC JUNIOR GOLD CHAMPIONSHIPS

United States Bowling Congress
Attn: Junior Gold Program
5301 South 76th Street
Greendale, WI 53129-1192
(414) 423-3171     Toll-free: (800) 514-BOWL, ext. 3171
Fax: (414) 421-3014
E-mail: USBCjuniorgold@bowl.com
Web: www.bowl.com/bowl/yaba

**Summary** To recognize and reward, with college scholarships, United States Bowling Congress (USBC) Junior Gold program members who achieve high scores in a national competition.

**Eligibility** This program is open to USBC members who qualify for the Junior Gold program by maintaining a bowling average score of 165 for girls or 175 for boys, based on at least 21 games. Competitions for Junior Gold members are held throughout the season at bowling centers and in bowling leagues in the United States. Each approved competition may enter its top 10% of scorers in the Junior Gold Championships, held annually at a site in the United States. In addition, USBC Junior Gold members who participate in the Pepsi USBC Youth Bowling Championship in the girls' and boys' 12 and over scratch categories and achieve high scores in state and zone competitions are eligible to advance to the national tournament of this program. They compete in separate divisions for boys and girls. Scholarships are awarded solely on the basis of bowling performance in the national tournament.

**Financial data** Scholarships depend on the availability of funding provided by sponsors. Recently, more than $50,000 in scholarships was awarded. Another $15,000 in scholarships was awarded to Junior Gold participants who qualified for the national tournament through the Pepsi competition. That includes $3,000 for first, $2,000 for second, $1,500 for third, and $1,000 for fourth for boys and girls.

**Duration** The competition is held annually.

**Additional information** This competition was first held in 1998. The sponsoring league or center must pay a fee of $150 for each participant who advances to the national tournament.

**Number awarded** Varies each year. Recently, a total of 1,458 spots were available at the national tournament and scholarships were provided to approximately 10% of the competitors. For bowlers from the Pepsi competition, 4 girls and 4 boys win scholarships.

**Deadline** Applications must by submitted by May of each year. The national finals are held in July.

## [1415]
## USBC YOUTH LEADERS OF THE YEAR AWARDS

United States Bowling Congress
Attn: SMART Program
5301 South 76th Street
Greendale, WI 53129-1192
(414) 423-3223  Toll-free: (800) 514-BOWL, ext. 3223
Fax: (414) 421-3014  E-mail: smart@bowl.com
Web: www.bowl.com/scholarships/main.aspx

**Summary** To recognize and reward, with college scholarships, outstanding young bowlers.

**Eligibility** These awards are presented to participants in the Youth Leader program of the United States Bowling Congress (USBC) who are 18 years of age or older. Males and females are considered in separate competitions. Selection is based on exemplary Youth Leader activities and contributions to the sport of bowling.

**Financial data** The awards consist of $1,500 college scholarships.

**Duration** The awards are presented annually.

**Additional information** Awardees also serve for 2 years on the USBC Board of Directors.

**Number awarded** 2 each year: 1 for a female and 1 for a male.

**Deadline** Nominations must be submitted by January of each year.

## [1416]
## VICTORIA FISHER MEMORIAL PRIZE ESSAY

University of Leicester
Attn: Faculty of Law
Leicester
LE1 7RH
United Kingdom
0116 252 2363  E-mail: l.henfrey@leicester.ac.uk
Web: www.le.ac.uk/la/news/fisher.html

**Summary** To recognize and reward outstanding essays on topics related to women and the law.

**Eligibility** Entries are encouraged from people regardless of age, experience, qualifications, or place of residence, as long as they have never had work published in a learned journal or as a nonfiction book. Essays may be on any topic relating to women and the law, up to 10,000 words in length in English.

**Financial data** The prize is 250 pounds.

**Duration** The competition is held annually.

**Number awarded** 1 each year.

**Deadline** September of each year.

## [1417]
## VICTORIA SCHUCK AWARD

American Political Science Association
1527 New Hampshire Avenue, N.W.
Washington, DC 20036-1206
(202) 483-2512  Fax: (202) 483-2657
E-mail: apsa@apsanet.org
Web: www.apsanet.org/section_283.cfm

**Summary** To recognize and reward outstanding scholarly books on women and politics.

**Eligibility** Eligible to be nominated (by publishers or individuals) are scholarly political science books issued the previous year on women and politics.

**Financial data** The award is $500.

**Duration** The award is presented annually.

**Additional information** This award was first presented in 1988.

**Number awarded** 1 each year.

**Deadline** February of each year.

## [1418]
## VIOLET AND LOUIS LANG AWARD

National Federation of Music Clubs
1336 North Delaware Street
Indianapolis, IN 46202-2481
(317) 638-4003  Fax: (317) 638-0503
E-mail: info@nfmc-music.org
Web: www.nfmc-music.org

**Summary** To recognize and reward outstanding singers who participate in the Biennial Young Artist Awards competition of the National Federation of Music Clubs (NFMC).

**Eligibility** Voice entrants must be between 23 and 35 years of age. Separate competitions are held for men and women. Membership in the federation and U.S. citizenship are required. Candidates for the NFMC Biennial Young Artist Awards competition are automatically considered for these awards; no separate application is necessary.

**Financial data** Each award is $750.

**Duration** The competition is held biennially, in odd-numbered years.

**Additional information** Applications and further information are available from Mrs. Nannette Hanslowe, 296 Medford Leas, Medford, NJ 08055, E-mail: nannettehanslowe@yahoo.com; information on all federation scholarships and awards is available from Chair, Competitions and Awards Board, Dr. George R. Keck, 421 Cherry Street, Arkadelphia, AR 71923-5116, E-mail: keckg@obu.edu. There is a $40 entry fee.

**Number awarded** 2 every other year: 1 for a man and 1 for a woman.

**Deadline** February of odd-numbered years.

## [1419]
## VIOLET DILLER PROFESSIONAL EXCELLENCE AWARD

Iota Sigma Pi
c/o National Director for Professional Awards
Dr. Sara Paisner
GE Global Research
One Research Circle, K1-4D17
Niskayuna, NY 12309
(518) 387-4599     E-mail: paisners@research.ge.com
Web: www.iotasigmapi.info

**Summary** To recognize exceptional and significant achievement by women working in chemistry or allied fields.

**Eligibility** Nominees for the award must be women chemists who have made significant contributions to academic, governmental, or industrial chemistry; in education; in administration; or in a combination of those areas. They may be from any country and need not be members of Iota Sigma Pi. Each active chapter is entitled to make only 1 nomination, but individual members, individual chemists, or groups of chemists may make independent nominations if properly documented. Contributions may include innovation design, development, application, or promotion of a principle or practice that has widespread significance to the scientific community or society on a national level.

**Financial data** The award consists of $1,000, a certificate, and a lifetime waiver of Iota Sigma Pi dues.

**Duration** The award is granted triennially.

**Additional information** This award was first presented in 1984.

**Number awarded** 1 every 3 years.

**Deadline** Nominations must be submitted by January of the year of award (the next award is in 2008).

## [1420]
## WEC MINI BAJA CHALLENGE FOR WOMEN TEAM LEADERS

Society of Automotive Engineers
Attn: Award Program Staff
400 Commonwealth Drive
Warrendale, PA 15096-0001
(724) 772-4009                    Fax: (724) 776-1830
E-mail: awards@sae.org
Web: www.sae.org/awards/wecminibaja.htm

**Summary** To recognize and reward student teams with women leaders and predominantly women members who enter the Society of Automotive Engineers (SAE) Mini Baja Competition.

**Eligibility** The SAE Mini Baja is open to teams of student members of the society who design and build a prototype of a rugged, single seat, off-road recreational vehicle. For 3 competitions held in North America, all team members must be 1) enrolled as degree-seeking undergraduate or graduate students (team members who have graduated during the 7-month period prior to the competition remain eligible to participate) and 2) SAE members. This award is presented to the team with a women leader and/or predominantly women members submitting the outstanding project proposal prior to the deadline.

**Financial data** The award is $1,000. Funds may be used to help the winning team complete its vehicle and travel to the event.

**Duration** The award is presented annually.

**Additional information** This award is presented by the SAE Women Engineers Committee (WEC).

**Number awarded** 1 each year.

**Deadline** Proposals must be submitted by October of each year.

## [1421]
## WEIZMANN WOMEN AND SCIENCE AWARD

American Committee for the Weizmann Institute of
   Science
Attn: Vice President of National Programs
633 Third Avenue
New York, NY 10017
(212) 895-7900                    Fax: (212) 895-7999
E-mail: info@acwis.org
Web: www.acwis.org

**Summary** To recognize and reward outstanding women scientists in the United States.

**Eligibility** Eligible to be considered for this award are women in the United States who have made a significant contribution to science, engineering, or technology. The candidate can be engaged in basic or applied science, research, education, or policy making in the United States.

**Financial data** The recipient is given a $25,000 research grant to support the project of her choice. In addition, she is awarded a trip to visit the Weizmann Institute of Science in Rehovot, Israel.

**Duration** The award is presented biennially, in even-numbered years.

**Additional information** This award was first presented in 1994.

**Number awarded** 1 each even-numbered year.

## [1422]
## WILLIE LEE ROSE PUBLICATION PRIZE IN SOUTHERN HISTORY

Southern Association for Women Historians
c/o Megan Taylor Shockley
Clemson University
Department of History
Clemson, SC 29634
(864) 656-4427    E-mail: mshockl@clemson.edu
Web: www2.h-net.msu.edu/~sawh/prizes.html

**Summary** To recognize and reward outstanding books written about southern history by women.

**Eligibility** Eligible for consideration are books on southern history that were written by women during the preceding year. Authors, publishers, and third parties may submit manuscripts. To be eligible, manuscripts must be written in English, but the competition is not restricted to publications printed in the United States. Anthologies, edited works, and all other types of historical publications are eligible.

**Financial data** The award consists of $750 and a plaque.

**Duration** The award is granted annually.

**Number awarded** 1 each year.

**Deadline** March of each year.

## [1423]
## WRITING SCHOLARSHIPS FOR MATURE WOMEN

National League of American Pen Women
1300 17th Street, N.W.
Washington, DC 20036-1973
(202) 785-1997    Fax: (202) 452-8868
E-mail: nlapw1@verizon.net
Web: www.americanpenwomen.org

**Summary** To provide financial assistance for education to mature women writers.

**Eligibility** Women writers who are 35 years of age or older are eligible to apply if they (or their immediate family) are not affiliated with the league. They must submit an article, short story (up to 4,000 words), editorial, drama, TV script, 3 poems, or first chapter of novel and 10-page outline.

**Financial data** The award is $1,000. Funds are to be used for education.

**Duration** The award is granted biennially.

**Additional information** These scholarships are presented in memory of Dr. Adeline Hoffman. An entry fee of $8 and a self-addressed stamped envelope must accompany each application.

**Number awarded** 1 each even-numbered year.

**Deadline** January of even-numbered years.

## [1424]
## WSS AWARD FOR CAREER ACHIEVEMENT IN WOMEN'S STUDIES LIBRARIANSHIP

American Library Association
Attn: Association of College and Research Libraries
50 East Huron Street
Chicago, IL 60611-2795
(312) 280-2514    Toll-free: (800) 545-2433, ext. 2514
Fax: (312) 280-2520    TDD: (312) 944-7298
TDD: (888) 814-7692    E-mail: acrl@ala.org
Web: www.ala.org

**Summary** To recognize and reward academic librarians who have made outstanding career contributions to women's studies.

**Eligibility** Nominees should have made a contribution in 1 or more of the following areas: 1) service to the organized profession through the Women's Studies Section (WSS) of the Association of College and Research Libraries and/or related organizations; 2) academic or research library service in the area of women's studies; 3) research and publication in areas of academic or research library services in women's studies; or 4) planning and implementation of academic/research library programs in women's studies disciplines of such exemplary quality that they could serve as a model for others.

**Financial data** The award is $1,000 and a citation.

**Duration** The award is presented annually.

**Additional information** Funds for this award, first presented in 2000, are donated by Greenwood Publishing.

**Number awarded** 1 each year.

**Deadline** November of each year.

## [1425]
## WSS AWARD FOR SIGNIFICANT ACHIEVEMENT IN WOMEN'S STUDIES LIBRARIANSHIP

American Library Association
Attn: Association of College and Research Libraries
50 East Huron Street
Chicago, IL 60611-2795
(312) 280-2514    Toll-free: (800) 545-2433, ext. 2514
Fax: (312) 280-2520    TDD: (312) 944-7298
TDD: (888) 814-7692    E-mail: acrl@ala.org
Web: www.ala.org

**Summary** To recognize and reward academic librarians who have made outstanding contributions to women's studies.

**Eligibility** Nominees should have demonstrated an achievement during the year of the award in an area of academic women's studies librarianship, including 1) publication of a monograph, journal article, media project, or web site; 2) presentation or talk at a nationally-recognized conference; 3) innovations in women's studies librarianship, including (but not limited to) instruction; 4) development of an exemplary program, collection, digitization project, or access tool to serve women's studies faculty and/or students; or 5) significant creative and innovative contribution to the work of the Women's Studies Section (WSS) of the Association of College and Research Libraries.

**Financial data** The award is $1,000 and a citation.

**Duration** The award is presented annually.

**Additional information** Funds for this award, first presented in 2000, are donated by Routledge Press.

**Number awarded** 1 each year.

**Deadline** November of each year.

## [1426]
## ZOE CAVALARIS OUTSTANDING FEMALE ATHLETE AWARD

Daughters of Penelope
1909 Q Street, N.W., Suite 500
Washington, DC 20009-1007
(202) 234-9741          Fax: (202) 483-6983
E-mail: daughters@ahepa.org
Web: www.ahepa.org

**Summary** To recognize and reward, with a college scholarship, women of Greek descent who demonstrate excellence in high school or college athletics.

**Eligibility** This award is presented to a young women of Hellenic descent who has unusually high quality athletic ability and a record of accomplishment in any sport or any series of sports. Nominees must be outstanding high school or college amateur female athletes recognized for their accomplishments during their high school and/or college years. Along with a letter of nomination from a sponsoring chapter of Daughters of Penelope, they must submit documentation of their current overall GPA, academic honors, other honors, extracurricular activities (other than sports), church and/or community activities, and special achievements (other than sports).

**Financial data** The award includes a $500 college scholarship, an engraved plaque, and public recognition through Daughters of Penelope events and publications.

**Duration** The award is presented annually.

**Additional information** Information is also available from Kiki Sekles, Athletics Chair, 2035 Streamwood Lane, Sterling Heights, MI 48310-7816, (586) 979-8359, E-mail: ksekles@wowway.com.

**Number awarded** 1 each year.

**Deadline** May of each year.

## [1427]
## ZONTA INTERNATIONAL YOUNG WOMEN IN PUBLIC AFFAIRS AWARDS

Zonta International
Attn: Foundation
557 West Randolph Street
Chicago, IL 60661-2202
(312) 930-5848          Fax: (312) 930-0951
E-mail: Zontafdtn@Zonta.org
Web: www.zonta.org

**Summary** To recognize and reward women in secondary schools who are interested in a career in public policy, government, or volunteer organizations.

**Eligibility** This program is open to young women, 16 to 20 years of age, who are currently enrolled in a secondary school anywhere in the world. Applicants must submit essays on their student activities (200 to 300 words), their community service activities (200 to 300 words), their efforts to understand other countries (150 to 200 words), the status of women in their country (300 to 500 words), and the status of women worldwide (300 to 500 words). Selection is based on those essays (20 points for the essay on student activities, 20 points for the essay on community service activities, 10 points for the essay on international awareness, 30 points for the essay on the status of women in their country, and 20 points for the essay on the status of women worldwide). Winners are selected at the club level and forwarded for a district competition; district winners are entered in the international competition.

**Financial data** District awardees receive $500 and international awardees receive $1,000.

**Duration** The competition is held annually.

**Additional information** This program was established in 1990.

**Number awarded** Several U.S. district winners and 5 international winners are selected each year.

**Deadline** Clubs set their own deadlines but must submit their winners to the district governor by March of each year.

# Internships

Described here are 84 work experience programs available to women undergraduates, graduate students, and recent graduates. Only salaried positions are covered. If you are looking for a particular program and don't find it here, be sure to check the Program Title Index to see if it is covered elsewhere in the *Directory*.

## [1428]
## AAPG SEMESTER INTERNSHIPS IN GEOSCIENCE PUBLIC POLICY

American Geological Institute
Attn: Government Affairs Program
4220 King Street
Alexandria, VA 22302-1502
(703) 379-2480                     Fax: (703) 379-7563
E-mail: govt@agiweb.org
Web: www.agiweb.org/gap/interns/internse.html

**Summary** To provide work experience to geoscience students (especially women and minority students) who have a strong interest in federal science policy.

**Eligibility** This program is open to geoscience students who are interested in working with Congress and federal agencies to promote sound public policy in areas that affect geoscientists, including water, energy, and mineral resources; geologic hazards; environmental protection, and federal funding for geoscience research and education. Applicants must submit official copies of college transcripts, a resume with the names and contact information for 2 references, and a statement of their science and policy interests and what they feel they can contribute to the program. Women and minorities are especially encouraged to apply.

**Financial data** The stipend is $4,500.

**Duration** 14 weeks, during the fall or spring semester.

**Additional information** This program is jointly funded by the American Geological Institute (AGI) and the American Association of Petroleum Geologists (AAPG). Activities for the interns include monitoring and analyzing geoscience-related legislation in Congress, updating legislative and policy information on AGI's web site, attending House and Senate hearings and preparing summaries, responding to information requests from AGI's member societies, and attending meetings with policy-level staff members in Congress, federal agencies, and non-governmental organizations.

**Number awarded** 2 each semester.

**Deadline** April of each year for fall internships; October of each year for spring internships.

## [1429]
## ACT SUMMER INTERNSHIP PROGRAM

American College Testing
Attn: Human Resources Department
500 ACT Drive
P.O. Box 168
Iowa City, IA 52243-0168
(319) 337-1763               E-mail: working@act.org
Web: www.act.org/humanresources/jobs/intern.html

**Summary** To provide work experience during the summer to doctoral students (particularly women and minorities) interested in careers in assessment and educational studies.

**Eligibility** This program is open to doctoral students enrolled in such fields as educational psychology, measurement, program evaluation, counseling psychology, educational policy, mathematical and applied statistics, industrial or organizational psychology, and counselor education. Applicants must be interested in working at American College Testing (ACT) in 1 of the following categories: 1) psy-

chometrics and statistics; 2) education and workforce research services; 3) industrial-organizational psychology; or 4) career and vocational psychology. Along with their application, they must submit a description of their interests and experiences. They must be able to demonstrate the ability to function both independently and as a team member in a professional work environment and must possess excellent written and oral communication skills. The program is also intended to assist in increasing the number of women and minority professionals in measurement and related fields.

**Financial data** Interns receive a stipend of $5,000 and round-trip transportation between their graduate institution and Iowa City. A supplemental living allowance of $400 is provided if a spouse and/or children accompany the intern.

**Duration** 8 weeks during the summer.

**Number awarded** Varies each year.

**Deadline** February of each year.

## [1430]
## AIPG SUMMER INTERNSHIPS IN GEOSCIENCE PUBLIC POLICY

American Geological Institute
Attn: Government Affairs Program
4220 King Street
Alexandria, VA 22302-1502
(703) 379-2480, ext 212          Fax: (703) 379-7563
E-mail: govt@agiweb.org
Web: www.agiweb.org/gap/interns/internsu.html

**Summary** To provide summer work experience to geoscience students (particularly women and minority students) who have a strong interest in federal science policy.

**Eligibility** This program is open to geoscience students who are interested in working with Congress and federal agencies to promote sound public policy in areas that affect geoscientists, including water, energy, and mineral resources; geologic hazards; environmental protection, and federal funding for geoscience research and education. Applicants must submit official copies of college transcripts, a resume with the names and contact information for 2 references, and a statement of their science and policy interests and what they feel they can contribute to the program. Women and minorities are especially encouraged to apply.

**Financial data** The stipend is $4,000.

**Duration** 12 weeks during the summer.

**Additional information** This program is jointly funded by the American Geological Institute (AGI) and the American Institute of Professional Geologists (AIPG). Activities for the interns include monitoring and analyzing geoscience-related legislation in Congress, updating legislative and policy information on AGI's web site, attending House and Senate hearings and preparing summaries, responding to information requests from AGI's member societies, and attending meetings with policy-level staff members in Congress, federal agencies, and non-governmental organizations.

**Number awarded** 3 each summer.

**Deadline** March of each year.

## [1431]
## ALASKA SPACE GRANT PROGRAM FELLOWSHIPS

Alaska Space Grant Program
c/o University of Alaska at Fairbanks
Duckering Hall, Room 269
P.O. Box 755919
Fairbanks, AK 99775-5919
(907) 474-6833                     Fax: (907) 474-5135
E-mail: fyspace@uaf.edu
Web: www.uaf.edu/asgp

**Summary** To provide undergraduate and graduate students (especially women, minority, and disabled students) at member institutions of the Alaska Space Grant Program (ASGP) with an opportunity to work on aerospace-related projects.

**Eligibility** This program is open to undergraduate and graduate students at the lead institution and academic affiliates of the ASGP. Applicants must be interested in assisting on projects that provide a professional development opportunity for the student but also develop aerospace capabilities within Alaska. The ASGP is a component of the Space Grant program of the U.S. National Aeronautics and Space Administration (NASA), which encourages participation by women, underrepresented minorities, and persons with disabilities.

**Financial data** The amount of each award depends on the scope of the project and the level of responsibility assumed by the recipient. Most awards are less than $5,000.

**Additional information** The ASGP lead institution is the University of Alaska at Fairbanks; academic affiliates include the University of Alaska Southeast, the University of Alaska at Anchorage, and Alaska Pacific University. Funding for this program is provided by NASA.

**Number awarded** Varies each year.

## [1432]
## AMERICAN HEART ASSOCIATION UNDERGRADUATE STUDENT RESEARCH PROGRAM

American Heart Association-Western States Affiliate
Attn: Research Department
1710 Gilbreth Road
Burlingame, CA 94010-1317
(650) 259-6725                     Fax: (650) 259-6891
E-mail: research@heart.org
Web: www.americanheart.org

**Summary** To provide students from California, Nevada, and Utah (particularly women and minority students) with an opportunity to work on a cardiovascular research project during the summer.

**Eligibility** This program is open to college students who are enrolled full time at an accredited academic institution at the junior or senior level and are interested in a career in heart or stroke research. Applicants must be residents of California, Nevada, or Utah (or attending a college or university in 1 of those states) and interested in a summer internship at a cardiovascular research laboratory in those states. They must have completed the following (or equivalent) courses: 4 semesters (or 6 quarters) of biological sciences,

physics, or chemistry; and 1 quarter of calculus, statistics, computational methods, or computer science. Selection is based on an assessment of the student's application, academic record (preference is given to students with superior academic standing), and faculty recommendations. Women and minorities are particularly encouraged to apply.

**Financial data** Participants receive a $4,000 stipend.

**Duration** 10 weeks during the summer.

**Additional information** Participants are assigned to laboratories in California, Nevada, or Utah to work under the direction and supervision of experienced scientists.

**Deadline** January of each year.

## [1433]
## ARIZONA SPACE GRANT CONSORTIUM UNDERGRADUATE RESEARCH INTERNSHIPS

Arizona Space Grant Consortium
c/o University of Arizona
Gerard P. Kuiper Space Sciences Building, Room 345
1629 East University Boulevard
Tucson, AZ 85721-0092
(520) 621-8556                     Fax: (520) 621-4933
E-mail: sbrew@lpl.arizona.edu
Web: spacegrant.arizona.edu

**Summary** To provide an opportunity for undergraduate students (particularly women and minority students) at member and affiliate institutions of the Arizona Space Grant Consortium to participate as interns in scientific research activities on campus.

**Eligibility** This program is open to full-time undergraduate students at member institutions (University of Arizona, Northern Arizona University, and Arizona State University) and affiliate institutions (Pima Community College) of the consortium. Applicants must be at least sophomores and U.S. citizens, but they do not need to be science or engineering majors. Applications are especially encouraged from members of underrepresented minority groups and women.

**Financial data** Interns are paid at the rate of $8 per hour.

**Duration** 1 academic year.

**Additional information** Interns work with faculty members and graduate students on space-related science projects. Funding for this program is provided by the U.S. National Aeronautics and Space Administration (NASA).

**Number awarded** Varies; recently, the program provided for 43 interns at the University of Arizona, 8 at Northern Arizona University, 30 at Arizona State University, and 1 at Pima Community College.

**Deadline** June of each year.

## [1434]
## ARKANSAS SPACE GRANT CONSORTIUM SCHOLARSHIPS AND FELLOWSHIPS

Arkansas Space Grant Consortium
c/o University of Arkansas at Little Rock
Graduate Institute of Technology
2801 South University Avenue
Little Rock, AR 72204
(501) 569-8212                    Fax: (501) 569-8039
E-mail: asgc@ualr.edu
Web: asgc.ualr.edu/spacegrant

**Summary** To provide funding to students (especially women, minority, and disabled students) at designated universities in Arkansas who are interested in working on a space-related research project.

**Eligibility** This program is open to undergraduate and graduate students at colleges and universities that participate in the Arkansas Space Grant Consortium (ASGC). Applicants must be interested in working with a faculty mentor on a specific research project. Fields of study include astronomy, biochemistry, biology, chemistry, computer science, earth science, engineering, engineering technology, instrumentation, materials science, mathematics, physics, psychology, and space medicine. Students must be U.S. citizens. The consortium is a component of NASA's Space Grant program, which encourages participation by underrepresented minorities, women, and persons with disabilities.

**Financial data** The funding depends on the nature of the proposal.

**Additional information** ASGC member institutions are Arkansas State University, Arkansas Tech University, Harding University, Henderson State University, Hendrix College, Lyon College, Ouachita Baptist University, University of Central Arkansas, University of Arkansas at Fayetteville, University of Arkansas at Little Rock, University of Arkansas at Montecito, University of Arkansas at Pine Bluff, University of Arkansas for Medical Sciences, and University of the Ozarks. This program is funded by NASA.

**Number awarded** Varies each year; since this program began in 1990, it has awarded nearly 400 undergraduate scholarships and 100 graduate fellowships.

## [1435]
## ARMY JUDGE ADVOCATE GENERAL'S CORPS SUMMER INTERN PROGRAM

U.S. Army
Attn: Judge Advocate Recruiting Office
1777 North Kent Street, Suite 5200
Rosslyn, VA 22209-2194
(703) 696-2822                    Toll-free: (866) ARMY-JAG
Fax: (703) 588-0100
Web: www.jagcnet.army.mil

**Summary** To provide law students (especially women and minority students) with an opportunity to gain work experience during the summer in Army legal offices throughout the United States and overseas.

**Eligibility** This program is open to full-time students enrolled in law schools accredited by the American Bar Association. Applications are accepted both from students who are completing the first year of law school and those completing the second year. Students must be interested in a summer internship with the Army Judge Advocate General's Corps (JAGC). U.S. citizenship is required. The program actively seeks applications from women and minority group members. Selection is based on academic ability and demonstrated leadership potential.

**Financial data** Interns who have completed the first year of law school are paid at the GS-5 scale, starting at $474 per week. Interns who have completed the second year of law school are paid at the GS-7 scale, starting at $588 per week.

**Duration** Approximately 60 days, beginning in May or June.

**Additional information** Interns work under the supervision of an attorney and perform legal research, write briefs and opinions, conduct investigations, interview witnesses, and otherwise assist in preparing civil or criminal cases. Positions are available at Department of the Army legal offices in Washington, D.C. and at Army installations throughout the United States and overseas. These are not military positions. No military obligation is incurred by participating in the summer intern program.

**Number awarded** 100 per year: 25 first-year students and 75 second-year students.

**Deadline** February of each year for first-year students; October of each year for second-year students.

## [1436]
## ARTTABLE MENTORED INTERNSHIPS

ArtTable Inc.
116 John Street, Suite 822
New York, NY 10038
(212) 343-1735, ext. 22                    Fax: (212) 343-1430
E-mail: women@arttable.org
Web: www.arttable.org/mentoring.html

**Summary** To provide an opportunity for women art students who are from diverse backgrounds to gain mentored work experience during the summer.

**Eligibility** This program is open to women undergraduates, recent graduates, and graduate students interested in preparing for a career in arts administration. Applicants must be a member of an ethnic, racial, cultural, or financial group that is underrepresented in the field. They must be interested in working during the summer with a mentor at an art museum or similar facility in New York City Tri-State region, Washington D.C. metropolitan area, San Francisco Bay area, or Los Angeles are. U.S. citizenship or permanent resident status is required.

**Financial data** The stipend is $2,400. The hosting institution or mentor receives $500 for administrative and other costs.

**Duration** 8 weeks during the summer.

**Additional information** This program began in 2000.

**Number awarded** 4 each year: 1 in each of the participating locations.

**Deadline** February of each year.

## [1437]
## ASPET INDIVIDUAL SUMMER UNDERGRADUATE RESEARCH FELLOWSHIPS

American Society for Pharmacology and Experimental
   Therapeutics
9650 Rockville Pike
Bethesda, MD 20814-3995
(301) 634-7060         Fax: (301) 634-7061
E-mail: info@aspet.org
Web: www.aspet.org/public/surf/surf.htm

**Summary** To provide funding to undergraduate students who are interested in participating in a summer research project at a laboratory affiliated with the American Society for Pharmacology and Experimental Therapeutics (ASPET).

**Eligibility** This program is open to undergraduate students interested in working during the summer in the laboratory of a society member who must agree to act as a sponsor. Applications must be submitted jointly by the student and the sponsor, and they must include 1) a letter from the sponsor with a brief description of the proposed research, a statement of the qualifications of the student, the degree of independence the student will have, a description of complementary activities available to the student, and a description of how the student will report on the research results; 2) a letter from the student indicating the nature of his or her interest in the project and a description of future plans; 3) a copy of the sponsor's updated curriculum vitae; and 4) copies of all the student's undergraduate transcripts. Selection is based on the nature of the research opportunities provided, student and sponsor qualifications, and the likelihood the student will prepare for a career in pharmacology. Applications from women and underrepresented minorities are particularly encouraged.

**Financial data** The stipend is $2,500. Funds are paid directly to the institution but may be used only for student stipends.

**Duration** 10 weeks during the summer.

**Additional information** Some of these awards are funded through the Glenn E. Ullyot Fund; those recipients are designated as the Ullyot Fellows.

**Number awarded** Varies each year; recently, 4 of these fellowships were awarded.

**Deadline** February of each year.

## [1438]
## ASSOCIATION FOR WOMEN IN SCIENCE INTERNSHIPS

Association for Women in Science
Attn: Internship Coordinator
1200 New York Avenue, N.W., Suite 650
Washington, DC 20005
(202) 326-8940        Toll-free: (866) 657-AWIS
Fax: (202) 326-8960       E-mail: awis@awis.org
Web: www.awis.org/careers/internship.html

**Summary** To provide an opportunity to gain work experience at the offices of the Association for Women in Science (AWIS) in Washington, D.C.

**Eligibility** Students and others interested in the work of the association may apply for these internships if they are interested in contributing to the organization's goal of achieving equity and full participation for women in science

and technology. Interns work closely with a staff member, who could be the executive director, the financial manager, the membership manager, or the publications manager. The association deals with women in any life, physical, behavioral, or social science, or engineering and looks for applicants with a background in those areas.

**Financial data** These are paid internships.

**Duration** 2 to 4 months.

**Number awarded** Varies each year.

**Deadline** Applications may be submitted at any time.

## [1439]
## ASSOCIATION FOR WOMEN IN SPORTS MEDIA SCHOLARSHIP/INTERNSHIP PROGRAM

Association for Women in Sports Media
c/o Rachel Cohen, Scholarship Coordinator
Dallas Morning News
P.O. Box 655237
Dallas, TX 75265
(979) 450-0146       E-mail: rcohen@dallasnews.com
Web: www.awsmonline.org/scholarship.htm

**Summary** To provide financial assistance and work experience to women undergraduate and graduate students who are interested in preparing for a career in sportswriting.

**Eligibility** This program is open to women who are enrolled in college or graduate school full time and plan to prepare for a career in sportswriting, sports copy editing, sports broadcasting, or sports public relations. Applicants must submit a 1-page essay describing their most memorable experience in sports or sports media, a 1-page resume highlighting their journalism experience, 2 letters of recommendation, up to 5 samples of their work, and a $15 application fee.

**Financial data** Awardees receive a paid summer internship, a $1,000 scholarship for the next year of college or graduate school, $300 toward travel expenses to attend the annual convention of the Association for Women in Sports Media, waived convention fees, and free lodging at the host hotel. Copy editing interns receive an additional $1,000 scholarship from the Associated Press Sports Editors.

**Duration** 1 year; nonrenewable.

**Additional information** Organizations that have hosted interns in the past include *Arizona Republic, Cleveland Plain Dealer, Colorado Springs Gazette, Detroit News,* ESPN, *Fort Worth Star-Telegram, Miami Herald, Newark Star-Ledger, Newsday,* Nike, *Sports Illustrated, St. Petersburg Times,* United States Olympic Committee, and USA Track & Field.

**Number awarded** Varies each year.

**Deadline** October of each year.

## [1440]
## AT&T LABORATORIES FELLOWSHIP PROGRAM
AT&T Laboratories
Attn: Fellowship Administrator
180 Park Avenue, Room C103
P.O. Box 971
Florham Park, NJ 07932-0971
(973) 360-8109               Fax: (973) 360-8881
E-mail: recruiting@research.att.com
Web: www.research.att.com/academic/alfp.html

**Summary**  To provide financial assistance and work experience to underrepresented minority and women students who are working on a doctoral degree in computer and communications-related fields.

**Eligibility**  This program is open to minorities underrepresented in the sciences (Blacks, Hispanics, and Native Americans) and to women. Applicants must be U.S. citizens or permanent residents beginning full-time Ph.D. study in disciplines relevant to the business of AT&T; currently, those include communications, computer science, electrical engineering, human computer interaction, industrial engineering, information science, mathematics, operations research, and statistics. Along with their application, they must submit a personal statement on why they are enrolled in their present academic program and how they intend to use their technical training, official transcripts, 3 academic references, and GRE scores. Selection is based on potential for success in scientific research.

**Financial data**  This program covers all educational expenses during the school year, including tuition, books, fees, and approved travel expenses; educational expenses for summer study or university research; a stipend for living expenses of $2,380 per month (paid for 10 months of the year); and support for attending approved scientific conferences.

**Duration**  1 year; may be renewed for up to 2 additional years, as long as the fellow continues making satisfactory progress toward the Ph.D.

**Additional information**  The AT&T Laboratories Fellowship Program (ALFP) provides a mentor who is a staff member at AT&T Labs as well as a summer research internship within AT&T Laboratories during the first summer. The ALFP replaces the Graduate Research Program for Women (GRPW) and the Cooperative Research Fellowship Program (CRFP) run by the former AT&T Bell Laboratories. If recipients accept other support, the tuition payment and stipend received from that fellowship will replace that provided by this program. The other provisions of this fellowship will remain in force and the stipend will be replaced by an annual grant of $2,000.

**Number awarded**  Approximately 8 each year.

**Deadline**  January of each year.

## [1441]
## BETTY F. JAYNES INTERNSHIP
Women's Basketball Coaches Association
Attn: Executive Assistant
4646 Lawrenceville Highway
Lilburn, GA 30047-3620
(770) 279-8027, ext 122        Fax: (770) 279-8473
E-mail: wbca@wbca.org
Web: www.wbca.org/BettyInternship.asp

**Summary**  To provide work experience to undergraduate or graduate students who are interested in preparing for a career in women's sports.

**Eligibility**  This program is open to undergraduate and graduate students who are interested in women's basketball, have excellent computer and communication skills, and intend to prepare for a career in sports administration. Applicants must submit a resume, cover letter, a list of references, and an original writing sample on their choice of topics related to basketball, the internship program, sports, or a person who has influenced their life.

**Financial data**  The stipend is $1,200 per month.

**Duration**  4 or 6 months.

**Additional information**  Interns work in event operations (convention logistics, convention banquets, high school All-America game and All-Star Challenge), marketing and sales, and communications and awards in the national office in Lilburn, Georgia, a suburb of Atlanta.

**Number awarded**  Approximately 6 each year.

**Deadline**  March of each year.

## [1442]
## BROOKHAVEN NATIONAL LABORATORY SCIENCE AND ENGINEERING PROGRAMS FOR WOMEN AND MINORITIES
Brookhaven National Laboratory
Attn: Diversity Office, Human Resources Division
Building 185A
P.O. Box 5000
Upton, New York 11973-5000
(631) 344-2703                Fax: (631) 344-5305
E-mail: rpalmore@bnl.gov
Web: www.bnl.gov/diversity/programs.asp

**Summary**  To provide on-the-job training in scientific areas at Brookhaven National Laboratory (BNL) during the summer to underrepresented minority and women students.

**Eligibility**  This program at BNL is open to women and underrepresented minority (African American/Black, Hispanic, Native American, or Pacific Islander) students who have completed their freshman, sophomore, or junior year of college. Applicants must be U.S. citizens or permanent residents, at least 18 years of age, and majoring in applied mathematics, biology, chemistry, computer science, engineering, high and low energy particle accelerators, nuclear medicine, physics, or scientific writing. Since no transportation or housing allowance is provided, preference is given to students who reside in the BNL area.

**Financial data**  Participants receive a competitive stipend.

**Duration**  10 to 12 weeks during the summer.

**Additional information**  Students work with members of the scientific, technical, and professional staff of BNL in an educational training program developed to give research experience.

**Deadline** April of each year.

## [1443]
## CALIFORNIA SPACE GRANT CONSORTIUM STUDENT-MENTOR AEROSPACE WORKFORCE DEVELOPMENT SCHOLARSHIPS

California Space Grant Consortium
c/o University of California at San Diego
Chemistry Research Building, Room 319
9500 Gilman Drive, Department 0524
La Jolla, CA 92093-0524
(858) 822-1597                         Fax: (858) 534-7840
E-mail: spacegrant@ucsd.edu
Web: calspace.ucsd.edu/casgc/sm_scholarships.html

**Summary** To provide assistance to undergraduate and graduate students (particularly women, minority, and disabled students) at affiliate institutions of the California Space Grant Consortium (CaSGC) who are interested in working on space-related projects.

**Eligibility** This program is open to teams of science, engineering, and management students at K-12, undergraduate, and graduate levels. Applicants must be interested in participating in aerospace workforce student-mentor development efforts at CaSGC affiliates under the guidance of mentors from the industrial, academic, and government sectors. The program is sponsored by the U.S. National Aeronautics and Space Administration (NASA) Space Grant program, which encourages participation by underrepresented minorities, women, and persons with disabilities.

**Financial data** Scholarships and training grants are provided by each project.

**Duration** 1 semester, summer, or year.

**Additional information** CaSGC affiliate members include the University of California campuses at Berkeley, Davis, Irvine, Los Angeles, Riverside, San Diego, Santa Barbara, and Santa Cruz; the California State University campuses at Long Beach, Los Angeles, Sacramento, San Bernardino, San Diego, and San Luis Obispo; Santa Clara University; Stanford University; the University of Southern California; and the Grossmont-Cuyamaca Community College District. Associate members, whose students may participate on a project-by-project basis, include California State Polytechnic University at Pomona, California State University at Fresno, San Jose State University, California Institute of Technology, Pomona College, San Francisco Art Institute, and the University of San Diego.

**Number awarded** Varies each year.

**Deadline** Each of the participating institutions sets its own deadline.

## [1444]
## CAROLYN WEATHERFORD SCHOLARSHIP FUND

Woman's Missionary Union
Attn: WMU Foundation
100 Missionary Ridge
P.O. Box 11346
Birmingham, AL 35202-1346
(205) 408-5525                    Toll-free: (877) 482-4483
Fax: (205) 408-5508
E-mail: wmufoundation@wmu.org
Web: www.wmufoundation.com/scholar_scholar.asp

**Summary** To provide an opportunity for women to prepare for service to the Woman's Missionary Union (WMU).

**Eligibility** This program is open to women who are members of the Baptist Church and are interested in 1) field work experience as interns or in women's missionary work in the United States; or 2) service in women's missionary work in the United States). Applicants must arrange for 3 letters of endorsement, from a recent professor, a state or associational WMU official, and a recent pastor. Selection is based on current active involvement in WMU, previous activity in WMU, plans for long-term involvement in WMU and/or home missions, academic strength, leadership skills, and personal and professional characteristics.

**Financial data** A stipend is awarded (amount not specified).

**Duration** 1 year.

**Additional information** This fund was begun by Woman's Mission Union, Auxiliary to Southern Baptist Convention, in appreciation for the executive director of WMU during its centennial year. Recipients must attend a Southern Baptist seminary or divinity school.

**Number awarded** 1 or more each year.

**Deadline** February of each year.

## [1445]
## CENTER ON BUDGET AND POLICY PRIORITIES INTERNSHIPS

Center on Budget and Policy Priorities
Attn: Internship Coordinator
820 First Street, N.E., Suite 510
Washington, DC 20002
(202) 408-1080                       Fax: (202) 408-1056
E-mail: internship@center.cbpp.org
Web: www.cbpp.org/internship.html

**Summary** To provide work experience at the Center on Budget and Policy Priorities (CBPP) in Washington, D.C. to undergraduates, graduate students, and recent college graduates, especially women and minority students.

**Eligibility** This program is open to undergraduates, graduate students, and recent college graduates who are interested in public policy issues affecting low-income families and individuals. Applicants must be interested in working at CBPP in the following areas: media, federal legislation, health policy, housing policy, international budget project, Food Stamps, national budget and tax policy, outreach campaigns, state budget and tax policy, welfare reform, and income support. They should have research, fact-gathering, writing, analytic, and computer skills and a willingness to do administrative as well as substantive tasks. Women and minorities are encouraged to apply.

**Financial data** Hourly stipends are $7.50 for undergraduates, $8.00 for interns with a bachelor's degree, $9.00 for graduate students, $10.00 for interns with a master's or law degree, and $10.00 to $15.00 for doctoral students (depending on progress towards completion of degree requirements, relevant course work, and research).

**Duration** 1 semester; may be renewed.

**Additional information** The center specializes in research and analysis oriented toward practical policy decisions and produces analytic reports that are accessible to public officials at national, state, and local levels, to non-profit organizations, and to the media.

**Number awarded** Varies each semester; recently, 5 interns were appointed for a fall semester.

**Deadline** February of each year for summer internships; July of each year for fall internships; November of each year for spring internships.

## [1446]
## CHESTERFIELD SMITH INTERNSHIPS

National Women's Law Center
Attn: Human Resources Department
11 Dupont Circle, N.W., Suite 800
Washington, DC 20036
(202) 588-5180                    Fax: (202) 588-5185
E-mail: humanresources@nwlc.org
Web: www.nwlc.org

**Summary** To provide law students with work experience at the National Women's Law Center.

**Eligibility** This program is open to second- and third-year law students who are interested in working for a nonprofit legal advocacy organization is committed to advancing the rights of women, particularly the rights of low-income women and girls. Applicants must submit a current resume, a cover letter that indicates the dates they are available for work, a transcript or list of law school grades, a recent writing sample, and the names of 3 references. They must be available to work in Washington, D.C. for 20 hours per week.

**Financial data** The stipend is $200 per week.

**Duration** 12 weeks.

**Additional information** The work assignments vary, including drafting court pleadings and briefs, writing articles and fact sheets, commenting on proposed federal agency regulations, preparing Congressional testimony, researching legislative history, and attending court, executive branch, and/or Congressional proceedings and meetings.

**Number awarded** 1 each year.

**Deadline** January of each year for spring semester; May of each year for fall semester.

## [1447]
## COCA-COLA ENDOWED INTERNSHIP PROGRAM

National Museum of Women in the Arts
Attn: Manager of Volunteer and Visitor Services
1250 New York Avenue, N.W.
Washington, DC 20005-3920
(202) 783-7982                    Fax: (202) 393-3235
Web: www.nmwa.org

**Summary** To provide work experience at the National Museum of Women in the Arts (NMWA) to undergraduate and graduate students interested in a career in museums.

**Eligibility** This program is open to undergraduates who have completed at least their sophomore year, graduate students, and recent graduates. Applicants must be interested in preparing for a museum career. They must have at least a 3.25 GPA and be interested in interning at the NMWA. Along with their application, they must submit a letter of purpose describing their interest in the internship, the top 3 or 4 departments in which they would prefer to work, how this internship will further personal and professional goals, and how they learned about the program.

**Financial data** The stipend is $1,500.

**Duration** 12 weeks, in summer, fall, or spring.

**Additional information** This program is sponsored by Coca-Cola USA. Internships are offered in the following departments at the museum: accounting, administration, development, curatorial, education, exhibition design and production, library and research center, membership, national programs, publications, public relations, registrar, retail operations, and special events. The internship program includes field trips to other museums and the opportunity to meet and discuss career options with professionals at the NMWA and other arts organizations.

**Number awarded** 1 each term (fall, spring, and summer).

**Deadline** March of each year for summer; June of each year for fall; October of each year for spring.

## [1448]
## COLORADO SPACE GRANT RESEARCH SUPPORT

Colorado Space Grant Consortium
c/o University of Colorado at Boulder
Discovery Learning Center, 270
Campus Box 520
Boulder, CO 80309-0520
(303) 492-4750                    Fax: (303) 492-5456
E-mail: koehler@colorado.edu
Web: spacegrant.colorado.edu

**Summary** To provide an opportunity to participate in space-related research to undergraduate and graduate students (particularly women, minority, and disabled students) at member institutions of the Colorado Space Grant Consortium (CoSGC).

**Eligibility** This program is open to undergraduate and graduate students at the 13 colleges and universities affiliated with the consortium. Applicants must be interested in participating in designing, flying, building, operating, and analyzing real space engineering and science experiments. The sponsored research activities are part of the Space Grant program of the U.S. National Aeronautics and Space Administration (NASA), which encourages participation by women, underrepresented minorities, and people with disabilities.

**Financial data** Stipends are provided.

**Additional information** The members of CoSGC include the University of Colorado at Boulder, the University of Colorado at Colorado Springs, Colorado State University at Fort Collins, Colorado State University at Pueblo, Pikes Peak Community College, Mesa State College, the University of Northern Colorado, Western State College, Adams

State College, Colorado School of Mines, Fort Lewis College, Metro State College, and Front Range Community College. This program is funded by NASA.

**Number awarded** Varies each year.

## [1449]
## COMMUNICATION INTERNSHIPS AT LEGAL MOMENTUM

Legal Momentum
Attn: Vice President Communications
395 Hudson Street, Fifth Floor
New York, NY 10014-3684
(212) 925-6635          Fax: (212) 226-1066
E-mail: mmcfadden@legalmomentum.org
Web: www.legalmomentum.org

**Summary** To provide summer work experience to undergraduate and graduate students interested in working in the communications department of Legal Momentum in New York City.

**Eligibility** The internship is open to undergraduate and graduate students interested in a communications internship at Legal Momentum. Applicants must be accomplished in reporting and editing, and they must be able to present samples of their writing. A background in journalism is preferred.

**Financial data** Interns receive a stipend of $230 per week.

**Duration** Summer interns work at least 35 hours per week for 10 weeks.

**Additional information** Legal Momentum was formerly known as the NOW Legal Defense and Education Fund. The communications department is responsible for public relations and media outreach.

**Number awarded** Varies each year.

## [1450]
## COMMUNITY INTERNSHIPS OF THE WOMEN'S SPORTS FOUNDATION

Women's Sports Foundation
Attn: Award and Grant Programs Manager
Eisenhower Park
1899 Hempstead Turnpike, Suite 400
East Meadow, NY 11554-1000
(516) 542-4700        Toll-free: (800) 227-3988
Fax: (516) 542-4716
E-mail: info@womenssportsfoundation.org
Web: www.womenssportsfoundation.org

**Summary** To provide work experience to individuals interested in promoting women's and girls' sports at programs in Atlanta, Chicago, or San Antonio.

**Eligibility** This program is open to undergraduate and graduate students interested in preparing for a sports-related career. Job hunters, senior citizens, retirees, and persons reentering the job market or changing career goals may also be eligible. Applicants must be interested in working at the foundation offices in Atlanta, Chicago, or San Antonio on the local GoGirlGo! community projects. They must submit a personal statement that includes the skills, experiences, language abilities, and computer knowledge that they feel are important resources for the foundation.

**Financial data** The stipend ranges from $800 to $900 per month.

**Duration** 6 months, either from January through June or July through December.

**Additional information** Assignments include assisting with the coordination of special events, the distribution of GoGirlGo! educational materials to girl-serving programs, developing and maintaining contact with local target agencies and/or organizations, helping execute Internet fundraising and activism campaign plans, data entry, forms management, and responding to miscellaneous information requests and correspondence.

**Number awarded** Varies each year.

**Deadline** Applications should be submitted no later than 120 days prior to the desired internship start date.

## [1451]
## COMPUTATIONAL CHEMISTRY AND MATERIALS SCIENCE SUMMER INSTITUTE

Lawrence Livermore National Laboratory
Chemistry and Materials Science
Attn: Computational Chemistry and Materials Science
    Summer Institute
P.O. Box 808, L-090
Livermore, CA 94551-0808
(925) 422-8285        Fax: (925) 422-6594
E-mail: hutcheon3@llnl.gov
Web: www-cms.llnl.gov/ccms_summer_inst

**Summary** To provide entering graduate students (especially women and minority students) with an opportunity to participate in a summer research project in computational materials science and chemistry at Lawrence Livermore National Laboratory (LLNL).

**Eligibility** This program is open to graduate students in their first few years of work in computational materials sciences, computational chemistry, or other research areas of computational science. Applicants must be interested in becoming the guest of an LLNL host scientist working on a computational project in the host's area of expertise. Selection is based on academic achievements, prior experience, technical interest, and number of positions available. Women and minorities are encouraged to apply.

**Financial data** Participants are paid a competitive salary and travel expenses.

**Duration** 10 weeks, beginning in mid-June.

**Additional information** Students also take short courses presented by LLNL professors and scientists, covering state-of-the-art and emerging computational methods, while focusing on the practical aspects of their numerical implementation.

**Number awarded** 10 each year.

**Deadline** January of each year.

## [1452]
## CONGRESSIONAL FELLOWSHIPS ON WOMEN AND PUBLIC POLICY

Women's Research and Education Institute
Attn: Education and Training Programs
3300 North Fairfax Drive, Suite 218
Arlington, VA 22201
(703) 812-7990          Fax: (703) 812-0687
E-mail: wrei@wrei.org
Web: www.wrei.org

**Summary** To provide tuition assistance and an opportunity to work as a legislative aide on policy issues affecting women to female graduate students and young professionals.

**Eligibility** This program is open to women who are currently enrolled in a master's or doctoral program at an accredited institution in the United States or who have completed such a program within the past 18 months. Students should have completed at least 9 hours of graduate course work or the equivalent and have a demonstrated interest in research or political activity relating to women's social and political status. Applicants of diverse age, race, religions, sexual orientation, experience, and academic field are encouraged to apply. They must be articulate and adaptable and have strong writing skills; they may come from diverse traditional or nontraditional academic backgrounds. Selection is based on academic competence, as well as demonstrated interest and skills in the public policy process. Interviews are required of semifinalists.

**Financial data** Fellows receive a stipend of $1,300 per month, $500 for health insurance, and up to $1,500 for reimbursement of 3 hours of tuition at their home institutions.

**Duration** 8 months, from January through August; nonrenewable.

**Additional information** Fellows are assigned to Congressional or committee offices to work for at least 30 hours per week as a legislative assistant monitoring, researching, and providing information on policy issues affecting women.

**Number awarded** 6 to 10 each year.

**Deadline** May of each year.

## [1453]
## DAVID FOSTER MARKETING INTERNSHIPS

Women's Sports Foundation
Attn: Award and Grant Programs Manager
Eisenhower Park
1899 Hempstead Turnpike, Suite 400
East Meadow, NY 11554-1000
(516) 542-4700          Toll-free: (800) 227-3988
Fax: (516) 542-4716
E-mail: info@womenssportsfoundation.org
Web: www.womenssportsfoundation.org

**Summary** To provide work experience to individuals interested in sports marketing activities at the Women's Sports Foundation.

**Eligibility** This program is open to undergraduate and graduate students interested in preparing for a sports-related career. Job hunters, senior citizens, retirees, and persons reentering the job market or changing career goals may also be eligible. Applicants must be interested in working in the marketing/corporate relations department at the foundation offices on Long Island, New York. Along with their application, they must submit a personal statement that includes the skills, experiences, language abilities, and computer knowledge that they feel are important resources for the foundation. An interview is required.

**Financial data** The stipend ranges from $800 to $900 per month.

**Duration** 6 months, either from January through June or July through December.

**Additional information** Interns assist in managing, maintaining, and helping corporate sponsors in marketing and leveraging their relationship with the foundation through grants, educational materials, grassroots programs, trade entertainment, and product promotions. They may receive academic credit for their work.

**Number awarded** Up to 2 each year (1 for each session).

**Deadline** Applications should be submitted no later than 120 days prior to the desired internship start date.

## [1454]
## DEPARTMENT OF STATE STUDENT INTERN PROGRAM

Department of State
Attn: Foreign Service Specialists
Student Program
2401 E Street, N.W., Room H-518
Washington, DC 20522-0108
(202) 261-8888          Toll-free: (800) JOB-OVERSEAS
Fax: (301) 562-8968
E-mail: StudentPrograms@state.gov
Web: www.careers.state.gov

**Summary** To provide a work/study opportunity to undergraduate and graduate students, especially women and minority students, who are interested in foreign service.

**Eligibility** This program is open to full- and part-time continuing college and university juniors, seniors, and graduate students. Applications are encouraged from students with a broad range of majors, such as business or public administration, social work, economics, information management, journalism, and the biological, engineering, and physical sciences, as well as those majors more traditionally identified with international affairs. U.S. citizenship is required. The State Department particularly encourages eligible women and minority students with an interest in foreign affairs to apply.

**Financial data** Most internships are unpaid. A few paid internships are granted to applicants who can demonstrate financial need. If they qualify for a paid internship, college juniors are placed at the GS-4 level with an annual salary of $22,056; college seniors and first-year graduate students are placed at the GS-5 level with an annual salary of $24,667; second-year graduate students are placed at the GS-7 level with an annual salary of $30,567. Interns placed abroad may also receive housing, medical insurance, a travel allowance, and a dependents' allowance.

**Duration** Paid internships are available only for 10 weeks during the summer. Unpaid internships are available for 1 semester or quarter during the academic year, or for 10 weeks during the summer.

**Additional information** About half of all internships are in Washington, D.C., or occasionally in other large cities in the United States. The remaining internships are at embassies and consulates abroad. Depending upon the needs of the department, interns are assigned junior-level professional duties, which may include research, preparing reports, drafting replies to correspondence, working in computer science, analyzing international issues, financial management, intelligence, security, or assisting in cases related to domestic and international law. Interns must agree to return to their schooling immediately upon completion of their internship.

**Number awarded** Approximately 800 internships are offered each year, but only about 5% of those are paid positions.

**Deadline** February of each year for fall internships; June of each year for spring internships; October of each year for a summer internships.

## [1455]
## DOROTHY ANDREWS KABIS INTERNSHIPS

National Federation of Republican Women
Attn: Scholarships and Internships
124 North Alfred Street
Alexandria, VA 22314-3011
(703) 548-9688                  Fax: (703) 548-9836
E-mail: mail@nfrw.org
Web: www.nfrw.org/programs/internships.htm

**Summary** To provide summer work experience to undergraduate women interested in working at the headquarters of the National Federation of Republican Women.

**Eligibility** This program is open to women who are at least juniors in college but have not graduated. Applicants should have a general knowledge of government and a keen interest in politics, including campaign experience and clerical office skills. Along with their application, they must submit 3 letters of recommendation, an official transcript, a 1-page essay on their interest in the internship, and a 1-page description of a particular political, extracurricular, or community activity in which they have been involved, including an account of their personal contribution to the activity. Optionally, a photograph may be supplied. Applications must be submitted to the federation president in the applicant's state. Each president chooses 1 application from her state to submit for scholarship consideration. U.S. citizenship is required.

**Financial data** Interns receive housing in the Washington, D.C. metropolitan area, round-trip airfare, and a small stipend.

**Duration** 6 weeks during the summer.

**Number awarded** 3 each year.

**Deadline** February of each year.

## [1456]
## EDUCATIONAL TESTING SERVICE SUMMER PROGRAM IN RESEARCH FOR GRADUATE STUDENTS

Educational Testing Service
Attn: Fellowships
Rosedale Road
MS 09-R
Princeton, NJ 08541-0001
(609) 734-5543                  Fax: (609) 734-5410
E-mail: internfellowships@ets.org
Web: www.ets.org

**Summary** To provide an opportunity for doctoral students, particularly women and minority students, to conduct summer research under guidance of senior staff at the Educational Testing Service (ETS).

**Eligibility** This program is open to doctoral students interested in working on a research project at ETS in 1 of the following areas: education, learning, linguistics, literacy, minority issues, new constructs, policy research, psychology, psychometrics, statistics, teaching educational technology, or testing issues (including alternate forms of assessment for special populations and new forms of assessment). Applicants must have completed at least 2 years of full-time graduate study. Selection is based on the scholarship of the applicant, match of applicant interests with participating ETS researchers, and the ETS affirmative action objectives. An explicit goal of the program is to increase the number of women and underrepresented minority professionals in educational measurement and related fields.

**Financial data** The award includes a stipend of $5,000, limited round-trip travel reimbursement, and a $1,000 housing allowance for interns residing outside a 50-mile radius of the ETS campus.

**Duration** 8 weeks in the summer.

**Additional information** Fellows work with senior staff at ETS in Princeton, New Jersey.

**Number awarded** Up to 16 each year.

**Deadline** January of each year.

## [1457]
## FAMILY INITIATIVE INTERNSHIPS AT LEGAL MOMENTUM

Legal Momentum
Attn: Family Initiative
1522 K Street, N.W., Suite 550
Washington, DC 20005
(202) 326-0040                  Fax: (202) 589-0511
E-mail: dcinternships@legalmomentum.org
Web: www.legalmomentum.org

**Summary** To provide work experience to undergraduate and graduate students interested in working on the family initiative of Legal Momentum in Washington, D.C.

**Eligibility** The internship is open to students and recent graduates interested in a family initiative internship at Legal Momentum. Applicants must be interested in working on a range of tasks, including compiling research from agencies, newspapers, and fact sheets; researching, tracking, and analyzing legislation; writing grants; attending briefings and coalition meetings; placing relevant phone calls and writing fact sheets, alerts, and memos; and sharing in answering the general office phone line. Interns should be a recent graduate, graduate student, or undergraduate with a strong interest in women's legal rights. A love of feminist issues, politics, and hard work is useful and a working knowledge of the American political process and/or early education and child care is recommended. Bilingual individuals are especially encouraged to apply.

**Financial data** These are paid internships (stipend not specified).

**Duration** Interns are encouraged to work from 15 to 35 hours per week for 10 to 12 weeks. Positions are available in the fall, spring, or summer.

**Additional information** Legal Momentum was formerly known as the NOW Legal Defense and Education Fund.

**Number awarded** Varies each year.

**Deadline** February of each year for summer; June of each year for fall; November of each year for spring.

## [1458]
## FELLOWSHIP ON WOMEN AND PUBLIC POLICY

University at Albany
Center for Women in Government and Civil Society
Attn: Fellowship Program Coordinator
135 Western Avenue, Draper 302
Albany, NY 12222
(518) 442-3900                     Fax: (518) 442-3877
E-mail: cwig@csc.albany.edu
Web: www.cwig.albany.edu/fellowprogram.htm

**Summary** To provide an opportunity for women graduate students in New York to contribute to the improvement of the status of women and underrepresented populations through work experience and course work.

**Eligibility** This program is open to women graduate students at all accredited colleges and universities within New York state who have completed 12 graduate credit hours. Applicant must have demonstrated an interest in studies, research, employment, or voluntary activities designed to improve the status of women and underrepresented populations. They must be available to accept an assignment to a policy-making office, such as the legislature, a state agency, or a nonprofit organization, while earning graduate credits from the Rockefeller College of Public Affairs and Policy at the University at Albany, SUNY. Along with their application, they must submit a 1,500-word essay on why they are interested in becoming a fellow.

**Financial data** Fellows receive a $9,000 stipend plus free tuition for 9 graduate credits of related academic work.

**Duration** 7 months.

**Additional information** This program was initiated in 1983. Fellows work 30 hours a week at their assignment and complete 3 courses: Topics in Public Policy Advocacy, New York State Public Policy Process, and an independent study and research course.

**Number awarded** Varies each year; recently, 11 of these fellows were appointed.

**Deadline** May of each year.

## [1459]
## HAYWOOD BURNS MEMORIAL FELLOWSHIPS FOR SOCIAL AND ECONOMIC JUSTICE

National Lawyers Guild
132 Nassau Street, Suite 922
New York, NY 10038
(212) 679-5100                     Fax: (212) 679-2811
E-mail: nlgno@nlg.org
Web: www.nlg.org

**Summary** To provide law students and professionals (particularly women and minorities) with summer work experience in progressive legal work.

**Eligibility** This program is open to law students, legal workers, and lawyers interested in working with civil rights and poverty law groups. Applicants must submit essays on their legal, political, educational, and work experience; their reasons for applying; what they expect to gain from the fellowship; the types of legal and political work they hope to do in the future; how this internship will help them in their goals; the kind of work structure with which they are most comfortable; and how they plan to share their summer experience and skills with others. Women and ethnic minorities are particularly encouraged to apply.

**Financial data** Interns receive a $2,000 stipend. Recipients are encouraged to seek other funding sources, including law school work-study and fellowship programs.

**Duration** 10 weeks during the summer; renewable the following year.

**Additional information** Recently, fellowships were available at the following organizations: the Asian Law Caucus (San Francisco, California), Cleveland Works, Inc. (Cleveland, Ohio), Camden Regional Legal Services, Farmworker Division (Bridgeton, New Jersey), Defender Association of Philadelphia (Philadelphia, Pennsylvania), East Bay Community Law Center (Berkeley, California), Florence Immigrant and Refugee Rights Project, Inc. (Florence, Arizona), Georgia Resource Center (Atlanta, Georgia), Harm Reduction Law Project (New York, New York), Lesbian and Gay Community Services Center (New York, New York), Massachusetts Correctional Legal Services (Boston, Massachusetts), Maurice and Jane Sugar Law Center for Economic and Social Justice (Detroit, Michigan), Meiklejohn Civil Liberties Institute (Berkeley, California), National Housing Law Project (Oakland, California), National Whistleblower Center (Washington, D.C.), Northwest Immigrant Rights Project (Seattle, Washington), Protection and Advocacy, Inc. (Oakland, California), and Southern Arizona People's Law Center (Tucson, Arizona).

**Number awarded** Approximately 25 each year.

**Deadline** January of each year.

## [1460]
## IMMIGRANT WOMEN PROGRAM INTERNSHIPS AT LEGAL MOMENTUM

Legal Momentum
Attn: Immigrant Women Program
1522 K Street, N.W., Suite 550
Washington, DC 20005
(202) 326-0040                     Fax: (202) 589-0511
E-mail: dcinternships@legalmomentum.org
Web: www.legalmomentum.org

**Summary**  To provide work experience to undergraduate and graduate students interested in working on the immigrant women program of Legal Momentum in Washington, D.C.

**Eligibility**  The internship is open to students and recent graduates interested in an immigrant women internship at Legal Momentum. Applicants must be interested in working on a range of tasks, including researching and analyzing legislation; drafting letters, fact sheets, and articles; attending briefings and coalition meetings; answering requests for technical assistance; assisting with administrative tasks as needed; and coordinating the work of coalitions dealing with violence against women, welfare reform, child care, and immigrant women's rights. Non-legal interns should be a recent graduate, graduate student, or undergraduate with a strong interest in women's legal rights. Legal interns should be a law student or attorney with a strong interest in gender equality, women's legal rights, and immigrant women's rights. A love of feminist issues, politics, and hard work is useful and a working knowledge of the American political process is recommended. Bilingual individuals are especially encouraged to apply.

**Financial data**  These are paid internships (stipend not specified).

**Duration**  Interns are encouraged to work from 15 to 35 hours per week for 10 to 12 weeks. Positions are available in the fall, spring, or summer.

**Additional information**  Legal Momentum was formerly known as the NOW Legal Defense and Education Fund.

**Number awarded**  Varies each year.

**Deadline**  February of each year for summer; June of each year for fall; November of each year for spring.

## [1461]
## IWPR SUMMER INTERNSHIPS

Institute for Women's Policy Research
Attn: Internship Coordinator
1707 L Street, N.W., Suite 750
Washington, DC 20036
(202) 785-5100                     Fax: (202) 833-4362
E-mail: iwpr@iwpr.org
Web: www.iwpr.org/About/employment.htm

**Summary**  To provide work experience opportunities during the summer at the Institute for Women's Policy Research (IWPR) to students interested in women's policy issues.

**Eligibility**  This program is open to college students, graduate students, and recent graduates who are interested in economic justice for women. Applicants must have good computer skills, excellent writing and communication skills, and an interest in women's issues. Prior office experience is desirable and a background in the social sciences and/or statistics is preferred. People of all ethnic, cultural, economic, and sexual orientations are encouraged to apply.

**Financial data**  Interns receive a stipend of $100 per week and a local transportation subsidy.

**Duration**  At least 10 weeks; some flexibility can be arranged for starting and ending dates.

**Additional information**  Interns work in Washington D.C. for IWPR, a nonprofit research organization that works primarily on issues related to equal opportunity and economic and social justice for women. They work in 1 of 3 departments: research (reviewing literature, collecting data and resources, gathering information from public officials and organization representatives, and preparing reports and summaries), communications and outreach (handling special requests for public information materials, planning special events, editing and proofreading, and assisting in the maintenance of web activities), or development (grant-writing, nonprofit fundraising, and direct mail programs). The institute gives special emphasis to issues of race, ethnicity, and class in its projects.

**Number awarded**  Varies each year.

**Deadline**  February of each year.

## [1462]
## JAMES H. DUNN, JR. MEMORIAL FELLOWSHIP PROGRAM

Office of the Governor
Attn: Department of Central Management Services
505 William G. Stratton Building
Springfield, IL 62706
(217) 524-1381                     Fax: (217) 785-7702
TDD: (217) 785-3979
Web: www.illinois.gov/gov/intopportunities.cfm

**Summary**  To provide recent college graduates (especially women, minorities, and persons with disabilities) with work experience in the Illinois Governor's office.

**Eligibility**  Applicants to this program may be residents of any state who have completed a bachelor's degree and are interested in working in the Illinois Governor's office or in various agencies under the Governor's jurisdiction. They may have majored in any field, but they must be able to demonstrate a substantial commitment to excellence as evidenced by academic honors, leadership ability, extracurricular activities, and involvement in community or public service. Along with their application, they must submit 1) a 500-word personal statement on the qualities or attributes they will bring to the program, their career goals or plans, how their selection for this program would assist them in achieving those goals, and what they expect to gain from the program; and 2) a 1,000-word essay in which they identify and analyze a public issue that they feel has great impact on state government. A particular goal of the program is to achieve affirmative action through the nomination of qualified minorities, women, and persons with disabilities.

**Financial data**  The stipend is $29,028 per year.

**Duration**  1 year, beginning in August.

**Additional information**  Assignments are in Springfield and, to a limited extent, in Chicago or Washington, D.C.

**Number awarded**  Varies each year.

**Deadline**  January of each year.

## [1463]
## JIM ATKIN ADVOCACY INTERNSHIPS

Women's Sports Foundation
Attn: Award and Grant Programs Manager
Eisenhower Park
1899 Hempstead Turnpike, Suite 400
East Meadow, NY 11554-1000
(516) 542-4700               Toll-free: (800) 227-3988
Fax: (516) 542-4716
E-mail: info@womenssportsfoundation.org
Web: www.womenssportsfoundation.org

**Summary** To provide work experience to individuals interested in dealing with gender equity issues in sports at the Women's Sports Foundation.

**Eligibility** This program is open to undergraduate and graduate students interested in preparing for a sports-related career. Job hunters, senior citizens, retirees, and persons reentering the job market or changing career goals may also be eligible. Applicants must be familiar with gender equity educational resources. They must be interested in working at the foundation offices on Long Island, New York. Along with their application, they must submit a personal statement that includes their skills, experiences, language abilities, and computer knowledge that they feel would be important resources for the foundation. An interview is required.

**Financial data** The stipend ranges from $800 to $900 per month.

**Duration** 6 months, either from January through June or July through December.

**Additional information** Interns respond to all telephone, mail, and e-mail requests for information related to Title IX, the Amateur Sports Act, and other gender equity situations in women's sports. They may receive academic credit for their work.

**Number awarded** Up to 2 each year (1 for each session).

**Deadline** Applications should be submitted no later than 120 days prior to the desired internship start date.

## [1464]
## JPMORGAN INVESTMENT BANK HONORS PROGRAM

JPMorganChase
Campus Recruiting
Attn: Honors Program
277 Park Avenue, Second Floor
New York, NY 10172
(212) 270-6000
Web: newhire.jpmorganchase.com

**Summary** To provide work experience at JPMorgan in New York during the summer to minorities, women, and students with disabilities who are entering their sophomore or junior year of college.

**Eligibility** This program is open to students at U.S. colleges and universities who are completing their freshman or sophomore year. Applicants must be students of color (Asian American, African American, or Latino), women, or persons with a disability and interested in working at JPMorgan in New York in the corporate finance, sales and trading, or research divisions. Applicants must have strong quantitative, analytical, and technical skills and be able to

thrive in a demanding, team-oriented environment. Course work in finance or economics is recommended and a GPA of 3.5 or higher is required.

**Financial data** Competitive stipends are paid.

**Duration** 10 to 12 weeks during the summer.

**Additional information** A goal of the program is to enable the intern to prepare for possible work as a senior intern during the summer following their junior year in college.

**Number awarded** Varies each year.

**Deadline** January of each year.

## [1465]
## LASPACE UNDERGRADUATE RESEARCH ASSISTANTSHIPS

Louisiana Space Consortium
c/o Louisiana State University
Department of Physics and Astronomy
371 Nicholson Hall
Baton Rouge, LA 70803-4001
(225) 578-8697               Fax: (225) 578-1222
E-mail: laspace@lsu.edu
Web: laspace.lsu.edu/scholarships.html

**Summary** To provide undergraduate science and engineering students in Louisiana (especially women, minority, and disabled students) with a mentored research experience in the space sciences.

**Eligibility** This program is open to U.S. citizens who are high school seniors, recent high school graduates, and students currently enrolled at 1 of the Louisiana Space Consortium (LaSPACE) member schools. The consortium is a component of the U.S. National Aeronautics and Space Administration (NASA) Space Grant program, which encourages participation by members of groups underrepresented in mathematics, science, and engineering (women, African Americans, Native Americans, Native Pacific Islanders, Mexican Americans, Puerto Ricans, Alaska Natives, and persons with disabilities). Applicants must be studying or planning to study a space- or aerospace-related field or program at an LaSPACE institution full time. They must coordinate with a faculty member at the institution who will file a joint application with the student and agree to serve as a mentor on a proposed research project. Selection is based on scholastic accomplishments, pertinent science experiences and accomplishments, leadership and recognitions, intellectual abilities, character, and relevance of the proposed research project to a future career in space or aerospace fields.

**Financial data** Grants are provided in blocks of $5,000. Funding may support 1 or 2 assistants. Funds may be used for wage support for the student(s), travel for a student research presentation, or research supplies.

**Duration** 12 months.

**Additional information** The participating LaSPACE member institutions are Dillard University, Grambling State University, Louisiana State University, Louisiana Tech University, Loyola University, McNeese State University, Nicholls State University, Northwestern State University of Louisiana, Southeastern Louisiana University, Southern University and A&M College, Southern University in New Orleans, Southern University at Shreveport, Tulane University, University of New Orleans, University of Louisiana at Lafayette, University of Louisiana at Monroe, and Xavier University of Louisiana. This program was established in 2000 as a replacement for the LaSPACE Undergraduate Scholars Program. Funding is provided by NASA.

**Number awarded** 5 each year.

**Deadline** March of each year.

## [1466]
## LAWRENCE LIVERMORE NATIONAL LABORATORY UNDERGRADUATE SUMMER INSTITUTES IN APPLIED SCIENCE

Lawrence Livermore National Laboratory
Chemistry and Materials Science
Attn: Computational Chemistry and Materials Science
   Summer Institute
P.O. Box 808, L-090
Livermore, CA 94551-0808
(925) 422-4108                    Fax: (925) 422-6594
E-mail: hutcheon3@llnl.gov
Web: www-cms.llnl.gov/usi

**Summary** To provide undergraduate students, especially women and minority students, with an opportunity to participate in a summer research project in various fields of science at Lawrence Livermore National Laboratory (LLNL).

**Eligibility** This program is open to full-time undergraduate students entering their senior year of a recognized program in physics, chemistry, biology, materials science, or engineering. Applicants must be interested in working under the guidance of an LLNL scientist on a project in such areas of applied science as laser and magnetic fusion, free-electron lasers, laboratory x-ray lasers, computational modeling, surface and intersurface science, solid state chemistry and physics, biomedical sciences, metallurgy, materials, precision engineering, neural networks, or selected topics on national security. Selection is based on academic record, aptitude, research interests, and the recommendations of instructors. Strong preference is given to students with truly exceptional academic records and potential for making outstanding contributions to applied science. Women and minorities are encouraged to apply.

**Financial data** Participants are paid a competitive salary and travel expenses.

**Duration** 8 weeks, beginning in mid-June.

**Additional information** This program began in 1985.

**Number awarded** 20 each year.

**Deadline** January of each year.

## [1467]
## LEGAL INTERNSHIPS AT LEGAL MOMENTUM

Legal Momentum
Attn: Senior Staff Attorney
395 Hudson Street, Fifth Floor
New York, NY 10014-3684
(212) 925-6635                    Fax: (212) 226-1066
E-mail: legalinternhiring@legalmomentum.org
Web: www.legalmomentum.org

**Summary** To provide law students with the opportunity to perform a broad range of legal and educational services at Legal Momentum during the summer or school year in support of women's efforts to eliminate sex-based discrimination and secure equal rights.

**Eligibility** Summer internships are open to first- and second-year law students. Fall and spring internships are open to second- and third-year law students. All applicants must be interested in participating in litigation and other projects, performing such duties as researching and drafting legal memoranda and briefs, preparing Congressional testimony, drafting model legislation, screening potential cases for Legal Momentum involvement, and drafting information pamphlets on legal topics. Interns should expect most of their work to involve legal research and writing.

**Financial data** Stipends are $420 per week during the summer or $12 per hour during fall and spring semesters.

**Duration** Summer interns are expected to work full time. Fall and spring interns are expected to work at least 10 hours per week.

**Additional information** Legal Momentum was formerly known as the NOW Legal Defense and Education Fund.

**Number awarded** Varies each year.

**Deadline** For summer internships, first-year students must apply by January of each year and second-year students must apply by November of each year. Applications for fall and spring internships are accepted on a rolling basis.

## [1468]
## LIBRARY OF CONGRESS JUNIOR FELLOWS PROGRAM

Library of Congress
Library Services
Attn: Junior Fellows Program Coordinator
101 Independence Avenue, S.E., Room LM-642
Washington, DC 20540-4600
(202) 707-0901                    Fax: (202) 707-6269
E-mail: jrfell@loc.gov
Web: www.loc.gov/rr/jrfell

**Summary** To provide summer work experience at the Library of Congress (LC) to upper-division and graduate students, particularly women, minority, and disabled students.

**Eligibility** This program at LC is open to applicants with subject expertise in the following areas: American history and literature; cataloging; history of graphic arts, architecture, design, and engineering; history of photography; film, television and radio; sound recordings; music; rare books and book arts; librarianship; and preservation. Applicants must 1) be juniors or seniors at an accredited college or university, 2) be at the graduate school level, or 3) have completed their degree in the past year. Applications from women, minorities, and persons with disabilities are particularly encouraged. Applications must include the following materials: cover letter, Application for Federal Employment (SF 171) or a resume, letter of recommendation, and official transcript. Telephone interviews are conducted with the most promising applicants.

**Financial data** Fellows are paid a taxable stipend of $300 per week.

**Duration** 3 months, beginning in either May or June. Fellows work a 40-hour week.

**Additional information** Fellows work with primary source materials and assist selected divisions at the Library of Congress in the organization and documentation of archival collections, production of finding aids and bibliographic records, preparation of materials for preservation and service, completion of bibliographical research, and digitization of LC's historical collections.

**Number awarded** Varies each year; recently, 6 of these internships were awarded.

**Deadline** March of each year.

## [1469]
## LILY SAFRA INTERNSHIP PROGRAM

Brandeis University
Hadassah-Brandeis Institute
Attn: Program Manager
Mailstop 079
Waltham, MA 02454-9110
(781) 736-2064                    E-mail: hbi@brandeis.edu
Web: www.brandeis.edu

**Summary** To provide summer work experience to undergraduates in the field of Jewish women's studies at the Hadassah-Brandeis Institute of Brandeis University.

**Eligibility** This program is open to undergraduate students attending universities in the United States and abroad. Applicants must have a demonstrated interest in women's studies, Jewish women's studies, or issues relating to Jewish women around the world. They must be interested in working at the institute with Brandeis staff and scholars on new and established research projects.

**Financial data** Interns receive a stipend of $350 per week and partially subsidized housing on the Brandeis campus.

**Duration** Summer months.

**Additional information** The Hadassah-Brandeis Institute was formerly the Hadassah International Research Institute on Jewish Women at Brandeis University. This program is funded by the Edmond J. Safra Philanthropic Foundation. Interns also produce an original piece of scholarly or creative work about Jewish women and gender issues under staff supervision, learn about the daily operations of an academic research institute by occasionally assisting with administrative tasks, visit local institutions and organizations of Jewish interest, meet local community activists, and travel to the Hadassah national convention.

**Number awarded** 6 each year.

**Deadline** March of each year.

## [1470]
## MARIAM K. CHAMBERLAIN FELLOWSHIPS

Institute for Women's Policy Research
Attn: Internship Coordinator
1707 L Street, N.W., Suite 750
Washington, DC 20036
(202) 785-5100                    Fax: (202) 833-4362
E-mail: iwpr@iwpr.org
Web: www.iwpr.org/About/employment.htm

**Summary** To provide work experience at the Institute for Women's Policy Research (IWPR) to college graduates and graduate students who are interested in economic justice for women.

**Eligibility** Applicants for this internship should have at least a bachelor's degree in social science, statistics, or women's studies. Graduate work is desirable but not required. They should have strong quantitative and library research skills and knowledge of women's issues. Familiarity with Microsoft Word and Excel is required; knowledge of STATA, SPSS, SAS, and graphics software is a plus. People of color are especially encouraged to apply.

**Financial data** The stipend is $1,750 per month and includes health insurance and a public transportation stipend.

**Duration** 9 months, beginning in September.

**Additional information** The institute is a nonprofit, scientific research organization that works primarily on issues related to equal opportunity and economic and social justice for women. Recent research topics for the fellows included women's wages, political participation, access to health care, and other indicators of the status of women on a state-by-state basis; the work and welfare experiences of low-income women on the state and national levels; reforming such income support policies for women as unemployment insurance, family leave, and Social Security; strategies for improving child care access, affordability, and quality; older women's economic issues; and women's civic engagement and public vision.

**Number awarded** 1 each year.

**Deadline** February of each year.

## [1471]
## MARY MORGAN WOMEN'S FELLOWSHIP

Pride Law Fund
Attn: Fellowship Program
P.O. Box 2602
San Francisco, CA 94126-2602
E-mail: info@pridelawfund.org
Web: www.pridelawfund.org

**Summary** To provide funding to law students who are interested in a summer internship project dealing with legal issues of concern to lesbians and bisexual women.

**Eligibility** This program is open to students at law schools in the United States. Applicants must be interested in gaining work experience in the area of legal issues of concern to lesbians and bisexual women. They must be proposing a project on which they may work independently or with an organization, but they must work under the supervision of a sponsoring attorney at a tax-exempt nonprofit organization in the United States. Preference is given to students who indicate that the sponsoring organization or attorney has expressed a specific interest in assisting them with their particular project. Preference is also given to applicants who have shown a commitment to the lesbian, gay, bisexual, and transgendered community (through leadership positions, volunteer activities, etc.) and to those with a demonstrated financial need.

**Financial data** The funds can be used to supplement other summer fellowships or income, as long as total funding does not exceed $5,000.

**Duration** The fellowship must be no shorter than 8 weeks during the summer. Preference is given to projects that are at least 10 weeks.

**Additional information** Since this program was established in 1984, fellowships have funded students to work in the areas of sexual orientation discrimination, individual rights litigation, direct legal services for people with HIV/AIDS, and other legal concerns of the lesbian, gay, bisexual, and transgendered community. The program is funded in part through the support of Bay Area Lawyers for Individual Freedom. Information is also available from David A. Lowe, c/o Rudy, Exelrod & Zieff, LLP, 351 California Street, Suite 700, San Francisco, CA 94104, (415) 434-9800, Fax: (415) 434-0513, E-mail: dal@reztlaw.com. Fellows must agree to maintain contact with the sponsor, mention the sponsor in any publication produced during the project, draft a short summary for the sponsor's newsletter, and attend sponsor events.

**Number awarded**   1 or more each year.

**Deadline**   March of each year.

## [1472]
## MICROSOFT NATIONAL SCHOLARSHIPS

Microsoft Corporation
Attn: National Minority Technical Scholarship
One Microsoft Way
Redmond, WA 98052-8303
(425) 882-8080                          TTY: (800) 892-9811
E-mail: scholars@microsoft.com
Web: www.microsoft.com/college/ss_overview.mspx

**Summary**   To provide financial assistance and summer work experience to undergraduate students, especially members of underrepresented groups, interested in preparing for a career in computer science or other related technical fields.

**Eligibility**   This program is open to students who are enrolled full time and making satisfactory progress toward an undergraduate degree in computer science, computer engineering, or a related technical discipline (such as electrical engineering, mathematics, or physics) with a demonstrated interest in computer science. Applicants must be enrolled at a 4-year college or university in the United States, Canada, or Mexico. They must have a GPA of 3.0 or higher. Although all students who meet the eligibility criteria may apply, a large majority of scholarships are awarded to women, underrepresented minorities (African Americans, Hispanics, and Native Americans), and students with disabilities. Along with their application, students must submit an essay that describes the following 4 items: 1) how they demonstrate their passion for technology outside the classroom; 2) the toughest technical problem they have worked on, how they addressed the problem, their role in reaching the outcome if it was team-based, and the final outcome; 3) a situation that demonstrates initiative and their willingness to go above and beyond; and 4) how they are currently funding their college education.

**Financial data**   Scholarships cover 100% of the tuition as posted by the financial aid office of the university or college the recipient designates. Scholarships are made through that school and are not transferable to other academic institutions. Funds may be used for tuition only and may not be used for other costs on the recipient's bursar bill, such as room and board.

**Duration**   1 year.

**Additional information**   Selected recipients are offered a paid summer internship where they will have a chance to develop Microsoft products.

**Number awarded**   Varies; a total of $540,000 is available for this program each year.

**Deadline**   January of each year.

## [1473]
## MISSOURI SPACE GRANT CONSORTIUM SUMMER HIGH SCHOOL INTERNSHIPS

Missouri Space Grant Consortium
c/o University of Missouri at Rolla
226 Mechanical Engineering Building
1870 Miner Circle
Rolla, MO 65409-0050
(573) 341-4887                          Fax: (573) 341-4607
E-mail: spaceg@umr.edu
Web: www.umr.edu/~spaceg

**Summary**   To provide work experience during the summer to high school students in Missouri, particularly women, minority, and disabled students, who are interested in a career in an aerospace field.

**Eligibility**   This program is open to Missouri high school students who have just completed their junior or senior year. Applicants must be proposing a specific research or education project at a nearby university or the St. Louis Science Center. Selection is based on academic records, letters of recommendation, and reasons for wanting to enter the program. U.S. citizenship is required. The Missouri Space Grant Consortium is a component of the U.S. National Aeronautics and Space Administration (NASA), which encourages participation by women, underrepresented minorities, and people with disabilities.

**Financial data**   The maximum award is $2,000.

**Duration**   Summer months.

**Additional information**   This program is funded by NASA.

**Number awarded**   Approximately 5 each year.

## [1474]
## MISSOURI SPACE GRANT CONSORTIUM UNDERGRADUATE RESEARCH INTERNSHIP PROGRAM

Missouri Space Grant Consortium
c/o University of Missouri at Rolla
226 Mechanical Engineering Building
1870 Miner Circle
Rolla, MO 65409-0050
(573) 341-4887                          Fax: (573) 341-4607
E-mail: spaceg@umr.edu
Web: www.umr.edu/~spaceg

**Summary**   To provide research experience to undergraduate students in Missouri (especially women, minority, and disabled students) who are working on a degree in an aerospace field.

**Eligibility**   This program is open to undergraduate students studying engineering, physics, astronomy, or planetary sciences at member institutions of the Missouri Space Grant Consortium. Applicants must be proposing a specific research or education project in a research laboratory, a computing facility, or the galleries of the St. Louis Science Center. Selection is based on academic records, letters of recommendation, and reasons for wanting to enter the program. U.S. citizenship is required. The Missouri Space Grant Consortium is a component of the U.S. National Aeronautics and Space Administration (NASA), which encourages participation by women, underrepresented minorities, and people with disabilities.

**Financial data** Awards are approximately $2,000 for the summer or $3,000 for the academic year.

**Duration** Both summer and academic year appointments are available.

**Additional information** The consortium members are Southwest Missouri State University, University of Missouri at Columbia, University of Missouri at Rolla, University of Missouri at St. Louis, and Washington University. This program is funded by NASA.

**Number awarded** Approximately 30 each year.

## [1475]
## MODINE MANUFACTURING COLLEGE-TO-WORK PROGRAM

Wisconsin Foundation for Independent Colleges, Inc.
Attn: College-to-Work Program
735 North Water Street, Suite 600
Milwaukee, WI 53202-4100
(414) 273-5980                    Fax: (414) 273-5995
E-mail: wfic@wficweb.org
Web: www.wficweb.org/work.html

**Summary** To provide financial assistance and work experience to students (particularly women and minorities) who are majoring in fields related to business at member institutions of the Wisconsin Foundation for Independent Colleges (WFIC).

**Eligibility** This program is open to full-time juniors and seniors at WFIC member colleges or universities. Women and minorities are especially encouraged to apply. Applicants must be preparing for or considering a career in business, finance, or marketing and have a GPA of 3.0 or higher. They must be interested in an internship at Modine Manufacturing Company in Racine, Wisconsin. Along with their application, they must submit a 1-page essay that includes why they are applying for the internship, why they have selected their major and what interests them about it, why they are attending their chosen college or university, and their future career objectives.

**Financial data** The stipend is $1,500 for the scholarship; the internship is paid hourly.

**Duration** 1 year for the scholarship; 10 weeks for the internship.

**Additional information** The WFIC member schools are Alverno College, Beloit College, Cardinal Stritch University, Carroll College, Carthage College, Concordia University of Wisconsin, Edgewood College, Lakeland College, Lawrence University, Marian College, Marquette University, Milwaukee Institute of Art & Design, Milwaukee School of Engineering, Mount Mary College, Northland College, Ripon College, St. Norbert College, Silver Lake College, Viterbo University, and Wisconsin Lutheran College. This program is sponsored by Modine Manufacturing Company.

**Number awarded** 1 each year.

**Deadline** February of each year.

## [1476]
## MURF FELLOWSHIPS PROGRAM

California Institute of Technology
Attn: Minority Undergraduate Research Fellowship
    Program
Student-Faculty Programs Office
Mail Code 139-74
Pasadena, CA 91125
(626) 395-2887                    Fax: (626) 449-9649
E-mail: murf@its.caltech.edu
Web: www.its.caltech.edu/~murf

**Summary** To provide an opportunity for underrepresented college juniors to work in a research laboratory at California Institute of Technology (Caltech) or the Jet Propulsion Laboratory (JPL) during the summer under the guidance of scientists and engineers.

**Eligibility** This program is open to African Americans, Hispanics, Native Americans, Puerto Ricans, and other students whose gender is underrepresented in a discipline. Applications are also encouraged from first generation college students and those attending an institution that presents challenges for success at an elite research university. Applicants must be undergraduate juniors or nongraduating seniors with a GPA of 3.0 or higher and majoring in astronomy, biology, chemistry and chemical engineering, engineering and applied science, geological and planetary sciences, mathematics, or physics. They must be interested in a program at either Caltech or JPL working on a research project under the supervision of a faculty member and a postdoctoral fellow and/or advanced graduate student. U.S. citizenship or permanent resident status is required.

**Financial data** Students receive a fellowship stipend of $4,000 for the 8-week program, $4,500 for the 9-week program, or $5,000 for the 10-week program. Housing and travel allowances are also provided. Meals and other expenses are not covered.

**Duration** 8 to 10 weeks during the summer, beginning in June.

**Additional information** Support for this program is provided by the NSF Center for Science and Engineering Materials and the Howard Hughes Medical Institute.

**Number awarded** Up to 15 in biology and chemistry; up to 6 in astronomy, earth and space sciences, engineering, mathematics, and physics.

**Deadline** December of each year.

## [1477]
## NARAL PRO-CHOICE AMERICA ORGANIZING INTERNSHIP

NARAL Pro-Choice America
Attn: Shalini Batra
1156 15th Street, N.W., Suite 700
Washington, DC 20005
(202) 973-2016                    Fax: (202) 973-3096
E-mail: sbatra@prochoiceamerica.org
Web: www.prochoiceamerica.org

**Summary** To offer opportunities to work as an intern in the organizing department of NARAL Pro-Choice America.

**Eligibility** This program is open to college students interested in working in the organizing department of NARAL Pro-Choice America. Applicants must have at least 6 months effective grassroots organizing or activism experience; knowledge of and strong commitment to reproductive rights issues and NARAL Pro-Choice America's mission and goals; strong organizational skills; excellent attention to detail; good academic standing; ability to work at least 15 to 20 hours per week; ability to prioritize and handle a variety of projects simultaneously; ability to produce concrete results with minimal supervision; excellent written and verbal communications skills; and ability to work effectively both individually and in a team.

**Financial data** The stipend is $7 per hour.

**Duration** Start and end dates are based on the intern's academic schedule.

**Additional information** Interns may receive college credit for their work with the organization. NARAL Pro-Choice America (formerly the National Abortion and Reproduction Rights Action League) is a 750,000 member political organization working to keep abortion legal.

**Number awarded** 2 each year.

**Deadline** December of each year.

## [1478]
## NARAL PRO-CHOICE MONTANA LEGISLATIVE INTERNSHIP

NARAL Pro-Choice Montana Foundation
Attn: Internship Program
P.O. Box 226
Helena, MT 59624
(406) 442-8193                    Fax: (406) 442-4801
E-mail: prochoice@mt.net
Web: www.prochoicemontana.org

**Summary** To provide an opportunity for students to work as legislative interns for NARAL Pro-Choice Montana.

**Eligibility** This program is open to students interested in working as a legislative intern for NARAL Pro-Choice Montana. Applicants must be able to demonstrate strong communication and interpersonal skills as well as the ability to work independently.

**Financial data** Interns receive a living stipend of $500 per month.

**Duration** 4 months, including summer.

**Additional information** The sponsor will assist the intern to receive academic credit, if available.

**Number awarded** 1 each year.

**Deadline** December of each year.

## [1479]
## NASA ACADEMIES

National Aeronautics and Space Administration
Goddard Space Flight Center
Attn: Office of Higher Education
Building 28, Room N159
Greenbelt, MD 20771
(301) 286-0904                    Fax: (301) 286-1610
E-mail: David.J.Rosage@nasa.gov
Web: www.nasa-academy.nasa.gov

**Summary** To provide opportunities to selected students (especially women and minority students) to work during the summer on research projects at specified field centers of the National Aeronautics and Space Administration (NASA).

**Eligibility** Applicants for this program must 1) be enrolled as juniors, seniors, or first- or second-year graduate students; 2) maintain a minimum GPA of 3.0; 3) major in engineering, science, mathematics, computer science, or other area of interest to the space program; 4) be U.S. citizens or permanent residents; and 5) be interested in a program in which they work at a NASA field center under the direction of NASA scientists and engineers. NASA is strongly committed to increasing cultural diversity among its pool of future leaders; underrepresented minority and female students are encouraged to apply.

**Financial data** Stipends range from $3,000 to $4,000; round-trip travel to the center, housing, meals, and local transportation are also provided.

**Duration** 10 weeks during the summer.

**Additional information** This program, which began in 1993, currently operates at 4 NASA centers: Goddard Space Flight Center in Greenbelt, Maryland; Glenn Research Center in Cleveland, Ohio; Marshall Space Flight Center in Huntsville, Alabama; and Ames Research Center in Moffett Field, California. Applications are also available from the Space Grant Consortium office in each state; for a list of those, contact the Office of University Programs.

**Number awarded** Up to 20 students are selected for each of the participating NASA field centers.

**Deadline** January of each year.

## [1480]
## NATIONAL MUSEUM OF NATURAL HISTORY RESEARCH TRAINING PROGRAM

National Museum of Natural History
Attn: RTP Program Coordinator
NHB, MRC 106, Room 59A
P.O. Box 37012
Washington, DC 20013-7012
(202) 633-4548                    Fax: (202) 786-0153
E-mail: sangreym@si.edu
Web: www.nmnh.si.edu/rtp

**Summary** To provide undergraduate students (particularly women, minority, and disabled students) with a summer research training internship at the Smithsonian Institution's National Museum of Natural History in Washington, D.C.

**Eligibility** This program is open to currently-enrolled undergraduate students interested in preparing for a career in anthropology, botany, entomology, invertebrate zoology, mineral sciences and geology, paleobiology, or vertebrate zoology. Although foreign students may apply, all applicants must be proficient in reading and understanding English. Applications are especially encouraged from women, international and minority students, and persons with disabilities.

**Financial data** Interns receive a stipend of approximately $3,000, housing, an allowance for transportation to Washington, D.C. (generally $500), and a research allowance (up to $1,000).

**Duration** 10 weeks during the summer.

**Additional information** The heart of the program is a research project, designed by the intern in collaboration with a museum staff advisor. In addition, students participate in a laboratory experience and collection workshop;

lectures, discussions, tours, and field trips; and other regular museum activities, such as seminars and special lectures. This program receives support from a number of funds within the Smithsonian and from the National Science Foundation through its Research Experiences for Undergraduates (REU) Program and Louis Stokes Alliances for Minority Participation Program.

**Number awarded** 10 to 24 each year.

**Deadline** January of each year.

## [1481]
## NATIONAL PHYSICAL SCIENCE CONSORTIUM GRADUATE FELLOWSHIPS

National Physical Science Consortium
c/o University of Southern California
3716 South Hope Street, Suite 348
Los Angeles, CA 90007-4344
(213) 743-2409          Toll-free: (800) 854-NPSC
Fax: (213) 743-2407      E-mail: npschq@npsc.org
Web: www.npsc.org

**Summary** To provide financial assistance and summer work experience to women and underrepresented minorities interested in working on a Ph.D. in designated science and engineering fields.

**Eligibility** This program is open to U.S. citizens who are seniors graduating from college with a GPA of 3.0 or higher, enrolled in the first year of a doctoral program, completing a terminal master's degree, or returning from the work force and holding no more than a master's degree. Students currently in the third or subsequent year of a Ph.D. program or who already have a doctoral degree in any field (Ph.D., M.D., J.D., Ed.D.) are ineligible. Applicants must be interested in working on a Ph.D. in the physical sciences or related fields of science or engineering. The program welcomes applications from all qualified students and continues to emphasize the recruitment of underrepresented minority (African American, Hispanic, Native American Indian, Eskimo, Aleut, and Pacific Islander) and women physical science and engineering students. Fellowships are provided to students at the 116 universities that are members of the consortium. Selection is based on academic standing (GPA), course work taken in preparation for graduate school, university and/or industry research experience, letters of recommendation, and GRE scores.

**Financial data** The fellowship pays tuition and fees plus an annual stipend of $16,000. It also provides on-site paid summer employment to enhance technical experience. The exact value of the fellowship depends on academic standing, summer employment, and graduate school attended; the total amount awarded generally exceeds $200,000.

**Duration** Support is initially provided for 2 or 3 years, depending on the employer-sponsor. If the fellow makes satisfactory progress and continues to meet the conditions of the award, support may continue for a total of up to 6 years or completion of the Ph.D., whichever comes first.

**Additional information** This program began in 1989. Tuition and fees are provided by the participating universities. Stipends and summer internships are provided by sponsoring organizations. Students must submit separate applications for internships, which may have additional eligibility requirements. Internships are currently available at Lawrence Livermore National Laboratory in Livermore, California (astronomy, chemistry, computer science, geology, materials science, mathematics, and physics); Los Alamos National Laboratory in Los Alamos, New Mexico (computer science, engineering, mathematics, and physics); National Security Agency in Fort Meade, Maryland (astronomy, chemistry, computer science, geology, materials science, mathematics, and physics); Sandia National Laboratory in Livermore, California (biology, chemistry, computer science, environmental science, geology, materials science, mathematics, and physics); and Sandia National Laboratory in Albuquerque, New Mexico (chemical engineering, chemistry, computer science, materials science, mathematics, mechanical engineering, and physics). Fellows must submit a separate application for dissertation support in the year prior to the beginning of their dissertation research program, but not until they can describe their intended research in general terms.

**Number awarded** Varies each year; recently, 11 of these fellowships were awarded.

**Deadline** November of each year.

## [1482]
## NATIONAL SECURITY INTERNSHIP PROGRAM

Pacific Northwest National Laboratory
Attn: Science Education Programs
902 Battelle Boulevard
P.O. Box 999, MS K8-15
Richland, WA 99352
(509) 375-2569          Toll-free: (888) 375-PNNL
E-mail: nsip@pnl.gov
Web: www.pnl.gov/nsd/nsip/index.stm

**Summary** To provide undergraduate and graduate students (especially women and minority students) with an opportunity to work on a national security-related science research project at Pacific Northwest National Laboratory (PNNL) during the summer.

**Eligibility** This program is open to undergraduate and graduate students who have a GPA of 3.0 or higher (preferably 3.4 or higher). Applicants should be majoring in chemistry, computer science, electrical engineering, nuclear science, nuclear engineering, or physics. They must be interested in working at PNNL on a summer science project related to national security. Women and minorities are encouraged to apply. Selection is based on academic achievement, prior experience, and technical interest.

**Financial data** Interns receive a stipend (amount not specified).

**Duration** 8 to 12 weeks during the summer; may be extended up to 1 year of part-time work during the academic year.

**Additional information** Tuition reimbursement is available to interns who agree to work as full-time employees at PNNL for a set period of time following graduation. Interns who accept tuition reimbursement and then fail to complete full-time employment for the specified period of time must repay a prorated portion of the educational expenses.

**Number awarded** Up to 20 each year.

**Deadline** January of each year.

## [1483]
## NATIVE AMERICAN WOMEN'S HEALTH EDUCATION RESOURCE CENTER INTERNSHIPS

Native American Women's Health Education Resource
   Center
Attn: Internship Coordinator
P.O. Box 572
Lake Andes, SD 57356-0572
(605) 487-7072                    Fax: (605) 487-7964
E-mail: colleenfasthorse@yahoo.com
Web: www.nativeshop.org/internships.html

**Summary** To provide work experience to students and recent graduates interested in Native American womenÖs rights and health issues.

**Eligibility** This program is open to college students, graduate students, and recent graduates. Applicants must have a background of work in Native American rights and health issues to promote civil rights, women's rights, and a healthy environment. They must be interested in working at the Native American Women's Health Education Resource Center and its Domestic Violence Shelter.

**Financial data** Interns receive a stipend of $500 per month, free room at the shelter, and partial board from the resource center's food pantry.

**Duration** 3 months to 1 year; priority is given for internships of 6 months or longer.

**Additional information** The Native American Women's Health Education Resource Center is a project of the Native American Community Board. It is located in Lake Andes, South Dakota in a rural area of the Yankton Sioux Reservation. The Domestic Violence Shelter is 4 blocks away. Past intern projects have included domestic violence advocacy at the shelter, counseling on the youth crisis hotline, environmental activism, Native women's reproductive health and rights, indigenous people's rights projects, web site development, organizing the annual community health fair, producing a Dakota language CD-ROM, and AIDS education.

**Number awarded** Varies each year.

## [1484]
## NCAA ETHNIC MINORITY AND WOMEN'S INTERNSHIP GRANT PROGRAM

National Collegiate Athletic Association
Attn: Office for Diversity and Inclusion
700 West Washington Avenue
P.O. Box 6222
Indianapolis, IN 46206-6222
(317) 917-6222                    Fax: (317) 917-6888
E-mail: kford@ncaa.org
Web: www.ncaa.org

**Summary** To provide work experience at Division III institutions of the National Collegiate Athletic Association (NCAA) to women or minority college graduates.

**Eligibility** This program is open to women and ethnic minorities who have completed the requirements for an undergraduate degree. Applicants must have demonstrated a commitment to preparing for a career in intercollegiate athletics and the ability to succeed in such a career. They must be selected by an NCAA Division III college or university to work full time in athletics administration.

**Financial data** Grants provide $19,110 per year as stipend for the intern and $3,000 to cover the cost of attendance at professional development activities.

**Duration** 2 years.

**Number awarded** Up to 15 each year.

**Deadline** February of each year.

## [1485]
## NEW JERSEY SPACE GRANT CONSORTIUM UNDERGRADUATE SUMMER FELLOWSHIPS

New Jersey Space Grant Consortium
c/o Stevens Institute of Technology
Castle Point on the Hudson
Hoboken, NJ 07030
(201) 216-8964                    Fax: (201) 216-8929
E-mail: sthangam@stevens-tech.edu
Web: www.njsgc.org

**Summary** To provide financial assistance for summer research experiences in space-related fields to college students in New Jersey, particularly women, minority, and disabled students.

**Eligibility** This program is open to undergraduate students who have completed at least 2 years at member institutions of the New Jersey Space Grant Consortium (NJSGC). Applicants must be proposing a program of space-related research in industry or at universities and their affiliated research laboratories. Their field of study may be aerospace engineering, biological science, chemical engineering, computer science and engineering, electrical engineering, material science and engineering, mechanical engineering, natural science, or physical science. U.S. citizenship is required. The New Jersey Space Grant Consortium is a component of the U.S. National Aeronautics and Space Administration (NASA) Space Grant program, which encourages participation by women, underrepresented minorities, and people with disabilities. Selection is based on a biographical sketch, a brief statement of what they hope to accomplish as a space grant fellow, a statement of career goals (including their relationship to aerospace engineering and science), and a description of their plan for the immediate future.

**Financial data** The stipend is $600 per week, with an additional $600 per student available for laboratory supplies.

**Duration** 10 weeks during the summer.

**Additional information** Members of the NJSGC include New Jersey Institute of Technology, Princeton University, Rutgers University, Stevens Institute of Technology, and the University of Medicine and Dentistry of New Jersey. This program is funded by NASA.

**Number awarded** 10 to 12 each year. Approximately 60% of the fellows are placed in industries (or industry sponsored programs) and 40% go to universities and their affiliated research laboratories.

**Deadline** March of each year.

## [1486]
## NSBE/SHPE/SWE MEMBERS SCHOLARSHIP

Morgan Stanley
c/o Joyce Arencibia, IT College Recruiting
750 Seventh Avenue, 30th Floor
New York, NY 10019
(212) 762-4000
E-mail: diversityrecruiting@morganstanley.com
Web: www.morganstanley.com

**Summary** To provide financial assistance and work experience to members of the National Society of Black Engineers (NSBE), Society of Hispanic Professional Engineers (SHPE), and Society of Women Engineers (SWE) who are working on an undergraduate degree in computer science or engineering.

**Eligibility** This program is open to active members of NSBE, SHPE, and SWE who are enrolled in their sophomore or junior year of college (or the third or fourth year of a 5-year program). Applicants must be enrolled full time and have a GPA of 3.0 or higher. They must be willing to commit to a paid summer internship in the Morgan Stanley Information Technology Division. All majors and disciplines are eligible, but preference is given to students preparing for a career in computer science or engineering. Along with their application, they must submit 1-page essays on 1) why they are applying for this scholarship and why they should be selected as a recipient; 2) a technical project on which they worked, either through a university course or previous work experience, their role in the project, and how they contributed to the end result; and 3) a software, hardware, or new innovative application of existing technology that they would create if they could and the impact it would have. Financial need is not considered in the selection process.

**Financial data** Students who receive a scholarship as juniors (or fourth-year students in a 5-year program) receive $10,000 for their final year of college. Students who receive a scholarship as sophomores (or third-year students in a 5-year program) receive $5,000 for their junior year (or fourth year of a 5-year program).

**Duration** 1 year; may be renewed for the final year for students who receive a scholarship as sophomores (or third-year students in a 5-year program).

**Additional information** The program includes a paid summer internship in the Morgan Stanley Information Technology Division during the summer following the time of application.

**Number awarded** 1 or more each year.

**Deadline** February of each year.

## [1487]
## PEDRO ZAMORA PUBLIC POLICY FELLOWSHIP

AIDS Action
Attn: Fellowship Program
1906 Sunderland Place, N.W.
Washington, DC 20036
(202) 530-8030          Fax: (202) 530-8031
E-mail: Zamora@aidsaction.org
Web: www.aidsaction.org/fellowship_new.htm

**Summary** To provide work experience at AIDS Action to undergraduate and graduate students (particularly women) interested in public policy.

**Eligibility** This program is open to undergraduates, graduate students, and young professionals who can demonstrate strong research, writing, and organizational skills and experience working in a professional office. Familiarity with HIV-related issues and the legislative process is preferred. Applicants must 1) describe their participation in school or extracurricular activities related to HIV and AIDS (e.g., peer prevention programs, volunteer activities); 2) describe their participation in any school, work, or extracurricular activities related to advocacy (e.g., lobbying, political campaigns); 3) explain why they would be the best candidate for this fellowship; and 4) explain how they would use the skills they acquire from the fellowship. People of color, women, gay, lesbian, bisexual, transgender, and HIV-positive individuals are encouraged to apply.

**Financial data** A stipend is provided (amount not specified).

**Duration** From 8 to 26 weeks.

**Additional information** Responsibilities include assisting in researching a variety of public health and civil rights issues related to HIV prevention, treatment, and care; attending Congressional hearings and coalition meetings; monitoring voting records; reviewing the Federal Register and Congressional Record; and preparing correspondence, mailings, and briefing materials. Fellows must commit to a minimum of 30 hours per week at AIDS Action in Washington, D.C.

**Number awarded** Varies each year.

**Deadline** March of each year for summer; July of each year for fall; October of each year for spring.

## [1488]
## PROFESSIONAL ASSOCIATES PROGRAM FOR WOMEN AND MINORITIES AT BROOKHAVEN NATIONAL LABORATORY

Brookhaven National Laboratory
Attn: Diversity Office, Human Resources Division
Building 185A
P.O. Box 5000
Upton, New York 11973-5000
(631) 344-2703          Fax: (631) 344-5305
E-mail: rpalmore@bnl.gov
Web: www.bnl.gov/diversity/programs.asp

**Summary** To provide professional experience in scientific areas at Brookhaven National Laboratory (BNL) to members of underrepresented groups.

**Eligibility** This program is open to underrepresented minorities (African Americans, Hispanics, Native Americans, or Pacific Islanders), people with disabilities, and women. Applicants must have earned at least a bachelor's degree and be seeking professional experience in such fields as biology, chemistry, computer science, engineering, health physics, medical research, or physics. They must plan to attend a graduate or professional school and express an interest in long-term employment at BNL.

**Financial data** Participants receive a competitive salary.

**Duration** 1 year.

**Additional information** Interns work in a goal-oriented on-the-job training program under the supervision of employees who are experienced in their areas of interest.

**Number awarded** Varies each year.

**Deadline**  Applications may be submitted at any time.

## [1489]
## PUBLIC EDUCATION AND OUTREACH INTERNSHIPS AT LEGAL MOMENTUM

Legal Momentum
Attn: Public Education and Outreach Department
395 Hudson Street, Fifth Floor
New York, NY 10014-3684
(212) 925-6635                    Fax: (212) 226-1066
E-mail: mhalperin-robinson@legalmomentum.org
Web: www.legalmomentum.org

**Summary**  To provide graduate students with the opportunity to work in the public education and outreach department of Legal Momentum.

**Eligibility**  This program is open to graduate students interested in working on the national helpline maintained by Legal Momentum to provide information, resources, and referrals to women with concerns ranging from domestic violence and child custody to employment discrimination. Applicants must be able to communicate effectively orally and in writing, have a commitment to women's rights issues, and have excellent interpersonal skills. Proficiency in word processing and proven office skills are required. Knowledge of women's rights issues and public interest organizations is helpful. Proficiency in Spanish is also strongly preferred.

**Financial data**  Stipends are $12 per hour for at least 15 hours per week.

**Duration**  Fall semester.

**Additional information**  Legal Momentum was formerly known as the NOW Legal Defense and Education Fund.

**Number awarded**  1 each year.

**Deadline**  August of each year.

## [1490]
## PUBLIC INTEREST INTERNSHIP PROGRAM

Center for Science in the Public Interest
Attn: Human Resources Department
1875 Connecticut Avenue, N.W., Suite 300
Washington, DC 20009-5728
(202) 332-9110                    Fax: (202) 265-4954
E-mail: cspi@cspinet.org
Web: www.cspinet.org/about/jobs.html

**Summary**  To provide work experience to undergraduate and graduate students at the Center for Science in the Public Interest, especially women, minority, and disabled students.

**Eligibility**  This program is open to students currently enrolled in undergraduate, graduate, law, and medical schools. Applicants should be interested in working on programs of the center, focusing on health and nutrition issues, deceptive marketing practices, dangerous food additives or contaminants, and flawed science propagated by profits. Minorities, women, and persons with disabilities are particularly encouraged to apply.

**Financial data**  The stipend is $6 per hour for undergraduate or $7 per hour for graduate students.

**Duration**  10 weeks, during the school year.

**Additional information**  Fellows work in the center's Washington office in 1 of the following programs: nutrition and public policy, legal affairs, alcohol and public policy, grassroots advocacy, food safety, marketing, technology, fundraising, communications, biotechnology, integrity in science, food and agriculture, or the litigation project.

**Number awarded**  Varies each year.

**Deadline**  Applications may be submitted at any time.

## [1491]
## PUBLIC POLICY INTERNSHIPS AT LEGAL MOMENTUM

Legal Momentum
Attn: Public Policy Department
1522 K Street, N.W., Suite 550
Washington, DC 20005
(202) 326-0040                    Fax: (202) 589-0511
E-mail: dcinternships@legalmomentum.org
Web: www.legalmomentum.org

**Summary**  To provide work experience to undergraduate and graduate students interested in working in the public policy department of Legal Momentum in Washington, D.C.

**Eligibility**  The internship is open to students and recent graduates interested in a public policy internship at Legal Momentum. Applicants must be interested in working on a range of tasks, including researching and analyzing legislation; drafting letters, fact sheets, and articles; attending briefings and coalition meetings; assisting with administrative tasks as needed; and coordinating the work of coalitions dealing with violence against women, welfare reform, child care, and immigrant women's rights. Non-legal interns should be a recent graduate, graduate student, or undergraduate with a strong interest in women's legal rights. Legal interns should be a law student or attorney with a strong interest in gender equality, women's legal rights, and/or immigrant rights. A love of feminist issues, politics, and hard work is useful and a working knowledge of the American political process is recommended. Bilingual individuals are especially encouraged to apply.

**Financial data**  These are paid internships (stipend not specified).

**Duration**  Interns are encouraged to work from 15 to 35 hours per week for 10 to 12 weeks. Positions are available in the fall, spring, or summer.

**Additional information**  Legal Momentum was formerly known as the NOW Legal Defense and Education Fund.

**Number awarded**  Varies each year.

**Deadline**  February of each year for summer; June of each year for fall; November of each year for spring.

## [1492]
### RESOURCES FOR THE FUTURE SUMMER INTERNSHIPS
Resources for the Future
Attn: Coordinator for Academic Programs
1616 P Street, N.W.
Washington, DC 20036-1400
(202) 328-5060                Fax: (202) 939-3460
E-mail: summerintern@rff.org
Web: www.rff.org

**Summary** To provide internships to undergraduate and graduate students (particularly women and minority students) who are interested in working on research projects in public policy during the summer.

**Eligibility** This program is open to undergraduate and graduate students (with priority to graduate students) interested in an internship at Resources for the Future (RFF). Applicants must be working on a degree in the social and natural sciences and have training in economics and quantitative methods or an interest in public policy. They should display strong writing skills and a desire to analyze complex environmental policy problems amenable to interdisciplinary methods. The ability to work without supervision in a careful and conscientious manner is essential. Women and minority candidates are strongly encouraged to apply. Both U.S. and non-U.S. citizens are eligible, if the latter have proper work and residency documentation.

**Financial data** The stipend is $375 per week for graduate students or $350 per week for undergraduates. Housing assistance is not provided.

**Duration** 10 weeks during the summer; beginning and ending dates can be adjusted to meet particular student needs.

**Deadline** February of each year.

## [1493]
### RUTH CHANCE LAW FELLOWSHIP
Equal Rights Advocates, Inc.
Attn: Human Resources Manager
1663 Mission Street, Suite 250
San Francisco, CA 94103
(415) 621-0672                Fax: (415) 621-6744
E-mail: sgershenson@equalrights.org
Web: www.equalrights.org/about/jobs.asp

**Summary** To provide work experience at Equal Rights Advocates (ERA) to recent law school graduates who are interested in working for the equal rights of women and minorities.

**Eligibility** This program is open to recent law school graduates who are licensed to practice law in California. Applicants must be able to demonstrate knowledge of and commitment to women's rights and legal issues affecting women; skill in legal research, analysis, and writing; knowledge of and commitment to civil rights and legal issues affecting people of color and other disadvantaged populations; knowledge of and/or experience in employment law and employment discrimination; ability to complete assignments and responsibilities accurately and in a timely manner; proficiency in computer applications; commitment to and involvement with community concerns; verbal and written communication skills; and ability to interact professionally and effectively with co-workers, board members, volun-

teers, outside counsel, court personnel, organization donors, and guests. Preference is given to applicants who are bilingual in English and Spanish, Cantonese, or Mandarin.

**Financial data** The annual salary ranges up to $40,000; benefits are also provided.

**Duration** 1 year, beginning in September.

**Additional information** Equal Rights Advocates is a nonprofit, public interest law firm that is dedicated to combating the disenfranchisement of women, particularly low-income and minority women. The responsibilities of the fellow include overseeing and coordinating an advice and counseling program, assisting staff attorneys with ongoing litigation, and participating in the firm's public policy and education activities.

**Number awarded** 1 each year.

**Deadline** January of each year.

## [1494]
### SCIENCE AND ENGINEERING APPRENTICE PROGRAM
George Washington University
Attn: Office of Science and Engineering Apprentice
   Program
1776 G Street, N.W., Suite 171
Washington, DC 20052
(202) 994-2234                E-mail: seap@gwu.edu
Web: www.gwseap.net

**Summary** To provide an opportunity for high school students (especially women, African Americans, and Hispanics) to work during the summer on research projects at selected Department of Defense laboratories.

**Eligibility** This program is open to high school students interested in careers in science and engineering. A goal of the program is to encourage women, African Americans, and Hispanics to expand their interest in science and engineering careers. Applicants must submit a 1-page statement on their personal goals and why they want to participate in a research project at a Department of Defense laboratory, 1 or 2 letters of recommendation, and a transcript. Most laboratories require U.S. citizenship, although some accept permanent residents. In a few laboratories, security clearance is required. Selection is based on grades, science and mathematics courses taken, scores on national standardized tests, areas of interest, teacher recommendations, and the personal statement.

**Financial data** The stipend is at least $1,500. Students are responsible for transportation to and from the laboratory site.

**Duration** 8 weeks during the summer.

**Additional information** Funding for this program is provided by the U.S. Department of Defense. Participating laboratories include the Armed Forces Institute of Pathology (Washington, D.C.); Army Engineer Research and Development Center, Topographic Engineering Center (Alexandria, Virginia); Army Medical Research Institute of Chemical Defense (Edgewood, Maryland); Army Research Laboratory (Aberdeen Providing Ground, Maryland and Adelphi, Maryland); Army Research, Development and Engineering Command (Aberdeen Proving Ground, Maryland); Center for Health Promotion and Preventive Medicine (Aberdeen Proving Ground, Maryland); Defense Threat Reduction Agency (Fort Belvoir, Virginia); Night Vision and Electronic Sensors Directorate (Fort Belvoir, Virginia); Walter Reed Army Institute of Research (Silver Spring, Maryland); Aviation and Missile Command (Redstone Arsenal, Alabama); Army Communications-Electronics Command (Fort Monmouth, New Jersey); Army Forces Command (Fort McPherson, Georgia); Army Soldier and Biological Chemical Command (Natick, Massachusetts and Rock Island Arsenal, Illinois); and Anser Corporation (Arlington, Virginia).

**Number awarded** Varies each year.

**Deadline** February of each year.

## [1495]
## SCOTTS COMPANY SCHOLARS PROGRAM

Golf Course Superintendents Association of America
Attn: Environmental Institute for Golf
1421 Research Park Drive
Lawrence, KS 66049-3859
(785) 832-4424      Toll-free: (800) 472-7878, ext. 4424
Fax: (785) 832-3673      E-mail: ahoward@gcsaa.org
Web: www.gcsaa.org

**Summary** To provide financial assistance and summer work experience to high school seniors and college students, particularly those from diverse backgrounds, who are preparing for a career in golf management.

**Eligibility** This program is open to high school seniors and college students (freshmen, sophomores, and juniors) who are interested in preparing for a career in golf management (the "green industry"). Applicants should come from diverse ethnic, cultural, and socioeconomic backgrounds, defined to include women, minorities, and people with disabilities. Selection is based on cultural diversity, academic achievement, extracurricular activities, leadership, employment potential, essay responses, and letters of recommendation. Financial need is not considered. Finalists are selected for summer internships and then compete for scholarships.

**Financial data** The finalists receive a $500 award to supplement their summer internship income. Scholarship stipends are $2,500.

**Duration** 1 year.

**Additional information** The program is funded by a permanent endowment established by Scotts Company. Finalists are responsible for securing their own internships.

**Number awarded** 5 finalists, of whom 2 receive scholarships, are selected each year.

**Deadline** February of each year.

## [1496]
## SIGMA ALPHA IOTA/KENNEDY CENTER INTERNSHIP

Sigma Alpha Iota Philanthropies, Inc.
One Tunnel Road
Asheville, NC 28805
(828) 251-0606      Fax: (828) 251-0644
E-mail: philonline@sai-national.org
Web: www.sai-national.org/phil/kcenter.html

**Summary** To provide summer internships at the Kennedy

Center to members of Sigma Alpha Iota (an organization of women musicians).

**Eligibility** Student members of the organization may apply if they are interested in a summer internship at the John F. Kennedy Center for the Performing Arts in Washington, D.C. Applicants must be juniors, seniors, graduate students, or graduates out of school for less than 2 years.

**Financial data** The stipend is $800 per month.

**Duration** 3 months during the summer.

**Additional information** Assignments are full time, with possible college credit available.

**Number awarded** 1 or more each year.

**Deadline** January of each year.

## [1497]
## SOUTH DAKOTA SPACE GRANT CONSORTIUM GRADUATE FELLOWSHIPS AND UNDERGRADUATE SCHOLARSHIPS

South Dakota Space Grant Consortium
Attn: Deputy Director and Outreach Coordinator
South Dakota School of Mines and Technology
Mineral Industries Building, Room 228
501 East St. Joseph Street
Rapid City, SD 57701-3995
(605) 394-1975      Fax: (605) 394-5360
E-mail: Thomas.Durkin@sdsmt.edu
Web: www.sdsmt.edu/space

**Summary** To provide funding to undergraduate and graduate students (particularly women, minority, and disabled students) for space-related activities in South Dakota.

**Eligibility** This program is open to undergraduate and graduate students at member and affiliated institutions of the South Dakota Space Grant Consortium. Applicants must be interested in 1) earth- and space-science related educational and research projects in fields relevant to the goals of the U.S. National Aeronautics and Space Administration (NASA); or 2) eventual employment with NASA or in a NASA-related career field in science, technology, engineering, and mathematics (STEM) education. Activities may include student research and educational efforts in remote sensing, GIS, global and regional geoscience, environmental science, and K-12 educational outreach; exposure to NASA-relevant projects; and internship experiences at various NASA centers and the Earth Resources Observation and Science (EROS) Center in Sioux Falls. U.S. citizenship is required. Women, members of underrepresented groups (African Americans, Hispanics, Pacific Islanders, Asian Americans, Native Americans, and persons with disabilities), and Tribal College students are specifically encouraged to apply. Selection is based on academic qualifications of the application (preference is given to students with a GPA of 3.0 or higher), quality of the application and its career goal statement, and assessment of the applicant's motivation toward an earth science, aerospace, or engineering career or research.

**Financial data** Stipends range from $1,000 to $7,500.

**Duration** 1 academic year, semester, or summer.

**Additional information** Member institutions include South Dakota School of Mines and Technology, South Dakota State University, and Augustana College. Educational affiliates include Black Hills State University, the University of South Dakota, Dakota State University, Lower Brule Community College, Oglala Lakota College, Sinte Gleska University, and Lake Area Technical Institute.

**Number awarded** Varies each year. Approximately $70,000 is available for this program annually.

**Deadline** January of each year.

## [1498]
## SOUTHERN CALIFORNIA COUNCIL INTERNSHIP PROGRAM

National Museum of Women in the Arts
Attn: Manager of Volunteer and Visitor Services
1250 New York Avenue, N.W.
Washington, DC 20005-3920
(202) 783-7982                    Fax: (202) 393-3235
Web: www.nmwa.org

**Summary** To provide summer work experience at the National Museum of Women in the Arts (NMWA) to undergraduate and graduate students from Los Angeles County, California who are interested in a career in museums.

**Eligibility** This program is open to undergraduate and graduate students who are residents of Los Angeles County and have completed at least the second year at a college, university, or college-level design or art school in that area. Applicants must be interested in preparing for a museum career or employment in a closely-related field. They must have at least a 3.25 GPA and be interested in interning during the summer at the NMWA. Along with their application, they must submit a letter of purpose describing their interest in the internship, their personal and professional goals, how this internship will assist them in reaching their goals, and their 3 preferred choices for placement in a department.

**Financial data** The stipend is $2,000.

**Duration** 12 weeks during the summer.

**Additional information** This program is sponsored by the Southern California Council of the NMWA. Internships are offered in the following departments at the museum: accounting, administration, development, curatorial, education, exhibition design and production, library and research center, membership, national programs, publications, public relations, registrar, retail operations, and special events. The internship program includes field trips to other museums and the opportunity to meet and discuss career options with professionals at the NMWA and other arts organizations.

**Number awarded** 1 each summer.

**Deadline** March of each year.

## [1499]
## SUMMER TRANSPORTATION INTERNSHIP PROGRAM FOR DIVERSE GROUPS

Department of Transportation
Federal Highway Administration
Attn: Office of Human Resources
HAHR-40, Room 4323
400 Seventh Street, S.W.
Washington, DC 20590
(202) 366-1159
Web: www.fhwa.dot.gov/education/stipdg.htm

**Summary** To enable students from diverse groups to gain work experience during the summer at facilities of the U.S. Department of Transportation (DOT).

**Eligibility** This program is open to women, persons with disabilities, and members of diverse social and ethnic groups. Applicants must be U.S. citizens currently enrolled in a degree-granting program of study at an accredited institution of higher learning at the undergraduate (community or junior college, university, college, or Tribal College) or graduate level. Undergraduates must be entering their junior or senior year (students attending a Tribal College must have completed their "first year" of school). Students who will graduate during the spring or summer are not eligible unless they have been accepted for enrollment in graduate school. Major fields of study include, but are not limited to, aviation, business, criminal justice, economics, engineering, environmental studies, hazardous materials, law (second or third year), management information systems, marketing, planning, public administration, or transportation management. Applicants must be interested in a summer work experience at various DOT facilities. They must have a GPA of 3.0 or higher. Law students must be entering their second or third year and must be in the upper 30% of their class. Selection is based on an expressed interest in pursuing a transportation-related career, GPA or class standing, a reference from a professor or advisor, the endorsement of the department chair, an essay on transportation interests, areas of interest outside of school, and completeness of application package.

**Financial data** A stipend is paid (amount not specified).

**Duration** 10 weeks during the summer.

**Additional information** Assignments are at the DOT headquarters in Washington, D.C., a selected modal administration, or selected field offices around the country.

**Number awarded** Varies each year; recently, 17 interns participated in this program.

**Deadline** February of each year.

## [1500]
## TRANSPORTATION FELLOWSHIP PROGRAM

North Central Texas Council of Governments
Attn: Transportation Department
616 Six Flags Drive, Centerpoint Two
P.O. Box 5888
Arlington, TX 76005-5888
(817) 695-9242                    Fax: (817) 640-7806
Web: www.nctcog.org/trans/admin/fellowship

**Summary** To provide financial assistance to ethnic minorities, women, and economically disadvantaged persons who are interested in obtaining an undergraduate or graduate degree and work experience in a transportation-related field in Texas.

**Eligibility** This program is open to ethnic minorities (African Americans, Hispanics, American Indians, Alaskan Natives, Asians, and Pacific Islanders), women, and those who are economically disadvantaged. Only U.S. citizens or permanent residents may apply. They must attend or be willing to attend a college or university within the 16-county north central Texas region as an undergraduate or graduate student. Applicants must have a GPA of 2.5 or higher. They may be enrolled full or part time, but they must be majoring in a designated transportation-related field: transportation planning, transportation or civil engineering, urban and regional planning, transportation/environmental sciences, transportation law, urban or spatial geography, logistics, geographic information systems, or transportation management. Selection is based on financial need, interest in a professional career in transportation, and ability to complete the program.

**Financial data** The stipend is $2,000.

**Duration** 1 year; may be renewed if the recipient maintains a GPA of 3.0 or higher.

**Additional information** These fellowships are financed by the Federal Highway Administration, Federal Transit Administration, and Texas Department of Transportation, in conjunction with local governments in north central Texas. An important part of the fellowship is an internship with a local agency (city or county), school, or transportation agency.

**Deadline** March of each year.

## [1501]
## UNION SUMMER INTERNSHIPS

AFL-CIO
Attn: Union Summer
815 16th Street, N.W.
Washington, DC 20006
(202) 639-6220          Toll-free: (800) 952-2550
Fax: (202) 639-6230   E-mail: unionsummer@aflcio.org
Web: www.aflcio.org/aboutus/unionsummer

**Summary** To provide college juniors and seniors (especially women and minorities) with a summer opportunity to learn more about social justice through workplace and community organizing.

**Eligibility** This program is open to college students currently enrolled as juniors or seniors. Applicants must be interested in participating in a summer activity to learn more about organizing unions to work for social justice. Desirable qualifications include "strong commitments to social and economic justice, as well as an openness to work with people of a different race, ethnicity, religion or sexual orientation." Applicants should be "people oriented, enthusiastic, energetic, flexible and willing to work long hours on an unpredictable schedule." Previous union experience is not required. Women and people of color are especially encouraged to apply.

**Financial data** The stipend is $300 per week. Transportation to the site and housing are also provided.

**Duration** 2 sessions are held each summer, each lasting 5 weeks; the first session begins in June and the second in July. Interns are assigned to 1 of those sessions.

**Additional information** Internships are conducted at selected sites throughout the country.

**Number awarded** Varies each year; since this program began in 1996, more than 2,500 students and other activists have participated.

**Deadline** April of each year.

## [1502]
## URBAN FELLOWSHIP PROGRAM

North Central Texas Council of Governments
Attn: Transportation Department
616 Six Flags Drive, Centerpoint Two
P.O. Box 5888
Arlington, TX 76005-5888
(817) 695-9103                    Fax: (817) 640-7806
Web: www.nctcog.org/edo/ufp.asp

**Summary** To provide financial assistance and work experience to ethnic minorities, women, and economically disadvantaged persons who are interested in obtaining a master's degree in Texas in preparation for a career in public management and/or planning.

**Eligibility** This program is open to ethnic minorities (African Americans, Hispanics, American Indians, Alaskan Natives, Asians, and Pacific Islanders), women, and those who are economically disadvantaged. Only U.S. citizens or permanent residents may apply. Applicants must be interested in obtaining a master's degree at a participating university in Texas as preparation for a career in public management and/or planning. Full-time enrollment is required. Selection is based on 1) financial need; 2) interest in, and commitment to, a professional career in urban management and/or planning; and 3) the ability to complete the academic and work placement responsibilities of the program.

**Financial data** The program provides up to $30,000 for tuition, books, professional memberships, and conferences, and a 20 hour-a-week internship.

**Duration** 1 year; may be renewed if the recipient maintains a GPA of 3.0 or higher.

**Additional information** This program was established in 1970. The fellowships are financed by the U.S. Department of Housing and Urban Development in conjunction with local governments in north central Texas (the Dallas/Fort Worth metropolitan area). Fellows are assigned to an internship in a local government unit in that area. Universities currently participating in the program are the University of North Texas, the University of Texas at Arlington, and the University of Texas at Dallas. Fellows are required to agree to make a good-faith effort to obtain employment in community-building fields for at least 2 consecutive years after graduation.

**Deadline** July of each year.

## [1503]
### VITO MARZULLO INTERNSHIP PROGRAM
Office of the Governor
Attn: Department of Central Management Services
505 William G. Stratton Building
Springfield, IL 62706
(217) 524-1381          Fax: (217) 785-7702
TDD: (217) 785-3979
Web: www.illinois.gov/gov/intopportunities.cfm

**Summary** To provide recent college graduates (especially women, minorities, and persons with disabilities) with work experience in the Illinois Governor's office.

**Eligibility** Applicants must be residents of Illinois who have completed a bachelor's degree and are interested in working in the Illinois Governor's office or in various agencies under the Governor's jurisdiction. They may have majored in any field, but they must be able to demonstrate a substantial commitment to excellence as evidenced by academic honors, leadership ability, extracurricular activities, and involvement in community or public service. Along with their application, they must submit 1) a 500-word personal statement on the qualities or attributes they will bring to the program, their career goals or plans, how their selection for this program would assist them in achieving those goals, and what they expect to gain from the program; and 2) a 1,000-word essay in which they identify and analyze a public issue that they feel has great impact on state government. A particular goal of the program is to achieve affirmative action through the nomination of qualified minorities, women, and persons with disabilities.

**Financial data** The stipend is $29,028 per year.

**Duration** 1 year, beginning in August.

**Additional information** Assignments are in Springfield and, to a limited extent, in Chicago or Washington, D.C.

**Number awarded** Varies each year.

**Deadline** January of each year.

## [1504]
### WALTER O. SPOFFORD, JR. MEMORIAL INTERNSHIP
Resources for the Future
Attn: Coordinator for Academic Programs
1616 P Street, N.W.
Washington, DC 20036-1400
(202) 328-5090          Fax: (202) 939-3460
E-mail: spofford-award@rff.org
Web: www.rff.org

**Summary** To provide summer internships to graduate students (particularly women and minority students) interested in working on Chinese environmental issues at Resources for the Future (RFF).

**Eligibility** This program is open to first- or second-year graduate students in the social or natural sciences. Applicants must have a special interest in Chinese environmental issues and outstanding policy analysis and writing skills. They must be interested in an internship in Washington, D.C. at RFF. Women and minority candidates are strongly encouraged to apply. Both U.S. and non-U.S. citizens (especially Chinese students) are eligible, if the latter have proper work and residency documentation.

**Financial data** The stipend is $375 per week. Housing assistance is not provided.

**Duration** The duration of the internship depends on the intern's situation.

**Number awarded** 1 each year.

**Deadline** February of each year.

## [1505]
### WASHINGTON NASA SPACE GRANT CONSORTIUM PRIVATE INDUSTRY INTERNSHIPS
Washington NASA Space Grant Consortium
c/o University of Washington
Johnson Hall, Room 141
Box 351310
Seattle, WA 98195-1310
(206) 543-1943          Toll-free: (800) 659-1943
Fax: (206) 543-0179    E-mail: nasa@u.washington.edu
Web: www.waspacegrant.org/pvtindinterns.html

**Summary** To provide an opportunity for upper-division students in Washington (particularly women, minority, and disabled students) who are interested in gaining summer work experience in a science or engineering field of interest to the U.S. National Aeronautics and Space Administration (NASA).

**Eligibility** This program is open to full-time juniors and seniors at colleges and universities that are members of the Washington NASA Space Grant Consortium. Applicants must be interested in a summer internship with a private firm in a NASA-related field of science and engineering. U.S. citizenship is required. The program is part of the NASA National Space Grant program, which encourages participation by members of underrepresented groups (women, minorities, and persons with disabilities).

**Financial data** The stipend is at least $3,400, half of which is paid by NASA and half by the industry partner.

**Duration** Summer months.

**Additional information** Members of the consortium include Heritage College, Northwest Indian College, North Seattle Community College, Seattle Central Community College, University of Washington, University of Puget Sound, Washington State University, Western Washington University, and Whitman College.

**Number awarded** Varies each year; recently, 4 of these internships were awarded.

**Deadline** April of each year.

## [1506]
### WOMEN ART INTERNSHIPS
Women's Studio Workshop
722 Binnewater Lane
P.O. Box 489
Rosendale, NY 12472
(845) 658-9133          Fax: (845) 658-9031
E-mail: info@wsworkshop.org
Web: www.wsworkshop.org/_art_opp/internships.htm

**Summary** To provide internship opportunities in the arts at the Women's Studio Workshop (WSW) in Rosendale, New York.

**Eligibility** All people interested in internships at the studio are eligible, although the program is especially interested in young women art students and recent college graduates. Applicants should send a resume, 10 to 20 slides, 3 letters of reference, and a letter of interest. They should have studio experience, be hard-working, and have a desire and ability to live in a close-knit female space. A college degree is helpful but not necessary. International students are especially encouraged to apply.

**Financial data** Interns receive off-site housing and a stipend of $150 per month.

**Duration** Session I internships are from January through July. Session II internships run from August through December. Summer internships are for 8 weeks.

**Additional information** Tasks include (but are not limited to) preparing studios for Summer Arts Institute workshops; assisting artists-in-residence in production of book works; preparing studios for and assisting artist/teachers with young people in an Art-in-Education program; designing, printing, and distributing catalogs, brochures, and posters; assisting in all aspects of exhibition program; preparing studios and on-site apartments for visiting artists; preparing and helping at various WSW fundraisers; and ongoing administrative and maintenance tasks.

**Number awarded** 7 each year: 3 for Session I, 3 for Session II, and 1 for the summer.

**Deadline** October of each year for Session I; March of each year for Session II and for the summer.

## [1507]
## WOMEN IN TECHNOLOGY SCHOLARSHIP

Morgan Stanley
c/o Joyce Arencibia, IT College Recruiting
750 Seventh Avenue, 30th Floor
New York, NY 10019
(212) 762-4000
E-mail: diversityrecruiting@morganstanley.com
Web: www.morganstanley.com

**Summary** To provide financial assistance and work experience to women who are working on an undergraduate degree in computer science or engineering.

**Eligibility** This program is open to women who are enrolled in their sophomore or junior year of college (or the third or fourth year of a 5-year program). Applicants must be enrolled full time and have a GPA of 3.0 or higher. They must be willing to commit to a paid summer internship in the Morgan Stanley Information Technology Division. All majors and disciplines are eligible, but preference is given to students preparing for a career in computer science or engineering. Along with their application, they must submit 1-page essays on 1) why they are applying for this scholarship and why they should be selected as a recipient; 2) a technical project on which they worked, either through a university course or previous work experience, their role in the project, and how they contributed to the end result; and 3) a software, hardware, or new innovative application of existing technology that they would create if they could and the impact it would have. Financial need is not considered in the selection process.

**Financial data** Students who receive a scholarship as juniors (or fourth-year students in a 5-year program) receive $10,000 for their final year of college. Students who receive

a scholarship as sophomores (or third-year students in a 5-year program) receive $5,000 for their junior year (or fourth year of a 5-year program).

**Duration** 1 year; may be renewed for the final year for students who receive a scholarship as sophomores (or third-year students in a 5-year program).

**Additional information** The program includes a paid summer internship in the Morgan Stanley Information Technology Division in the summer following the time of application.

**Number awarded** 1 or more each year.

**Deadline** February of each year.

## [1508]
## WOMEN'S LAW AND PUBLIC POLICY FELLOWSHIP PROGRAM

Georgetown University Law Center
Attn: Women's Law and Public Policy Fellowship
   Program
600 New Jersey Avenue, N.W., Suite 334
Washington, DC 20001
(202) 662-9650                    Fax: (202) 662-9539
E-mail: mail@wlppfp.org
Web: www.wlppfp.org

**Summary** To provide an opportunity for recently-graduated lawyers in the Washington D.C. area to work on women's rights issues.

**Eligibility** This program is open to recent graduates of law schools accredited by the American Bar Association. Applicants must be interested in working on women's rights issues in the Washington, D.C. area.

**Financial data** The stipend is $37,500 per year.

**Duration** 1 year.

**Additional information** Participants are placed with different entities in the Washington, D.C. area, including women's rights organizations, civil rights groups, Congressional offices, government agencies, and Georgetown University Law Center clinics working on women's issues. This program includes 2 named fellowships: the Rita Charmatz Davidson Fellowship (to work on issues primarily affecting poor women) and the Harriet R. Burg Fellowship (to work primarily on issues affecting women with disabilities). Fellows are supervised by attorneys at the participating organizations.

**Number awarded** Varies each year.

**Deadline** October of each year.

## [1509]
## WOMEN'S SPORTS FOUNDATION INTERNSHIPS

Women's Sports Foundation
Attn: Award and Grant Programs Manager
Eisenhower Park
1899 Hempstead Turnpike, Suite 400
East Meadow, NY 11554-1000
(516) 542-4700                    Toll-free: (800) 227-3988
Fax: (516) 542-4716
E-mail: info@womenssportsfoundation.org
Web: www.womenssportsfoundation.org

**Summary** To provide work experience to individuals interested in promoting women's and girls' sports.

**Eligibility** This program is open to undergraduate and graduate students interested in preparing for a sports-related career. Job hunters, senior citizens, retirees, and persons reentering the job market or changing career goals may also be eligible. Applicants must be interested in working at the foundation offices on Long Island, New York. They must submit a personal statement that includes their skills, experiences, language abilities, and computer knowledge that they feel would be important resources for the foundation. Applicants for online media, public relations, and publications internships should also submit 2 writing samples.

**Financial data** The stipend ranges from $800 to $900 per month.

**Duration** 6 months, either from January through June or July through December.

**Additional information** Assignments are available in athlete marketing and promotions, education programs, fundraising and external relations, information technology, online media, program management, public relations, publications, and special events.

**Number awarded** Varies each year. To date, more than 250 people have served as interns.

**Deadline** Applications should be submitted no later than 120 days prior to the desired internship start date.

## [1510]
## WOMEN'S STUDIO WORKSHOP ARTS ADMINISTRATION INTERNSHIP

Women's Studio Workshop
722 Binnewater Lane
P.O. Box 489
Rosendale, NY 12472
(845) 658-9133 Fax: (845) 658-9031
E-mail: info@wsworkshop.org
Web: www.wsworkshop.org

**Summary** To provide work experience at the Women's Studio Workshop (WSW) in Rosendale, New York to people interested in preparing for a career in arts administration.

**Eligibility** This program is open to people considering a career in arts administration. Applicants must be interested in working with administrative staff at WSW attending to details that keep an arts organization functioning smoothly. Graphic design and web skills are a plus. Experience with Filemaker Pro, Dreamweaver, InDesign, and Photoshop are beneficial but not required. Communication skills and phone poise are a must. Along with their application, they must submit a resume, 3 letters of reference, 3 work samples, and a letter of interest explaining why an internship at WSW is important to them and the type of experiences they would bring to WSW.

**Financial data** Interns receive a $12,000 compensation package, including a stipend of $300 per month, a private room in a shared house, and health care benefits.

**Duration** 1 year, beginning in July.

**Additional information** Projects include database management, membership systems, donor and grant research, event planning assistance, writing and distributing press releases, archiving WSW documents, and sending out E-communications.

**Number awarded** 1 each year.

**Deadline** April of each year.

## [1511]
## WOMEN'S STUDIO WORKSHOP CERAMICS INTERNSHIPS

Women's Studio Workshop
722 Binnewater Lane
P.O. Box 489
Rosendale, NY 12472
(845) 658-9133 Fax: (845) 658-9031
E-mail: info@wsworkshop.org
Web: www.wsworkshop.org/_art_opp/intern_clay.htm

**Summary** To provide internship opportunities in ceramics at the Women's Studio Workshop (WSW) in Rosendale, New York.

**Eligibility** This program is open to young women interested in working on ceramics at WSW. Applicants must have wheel-throwing experience. Along with their application, they must submit a resume, 10 to 20 slides, 3 letters of reference, and a letter of interest.

**Financial data** Interns receive off-site housing and a stipend of $150 per month.

**Duration** 8 weeks between January and March.

**Additional information** Responsibilities include wheel throwing and glazing both bowls and tumblers for the annual WSW Chili Bowl Fiesta; helping community members throw, handbuild, and glaze bowls; loading and firing electric kilns, and maintaining ceramics studio and equipment.

**Number awarded** 2 each year.

**Deadline** October of each year.

# Indexes

# Program Title Index

If you know the name of a particular funding program and want to find out where it is covered in the directory, use the Program Title Index. Here, program titles are arranged alphabetically, word by word. To assist you in your search, every program is listed by all its known names or abbreviations. In addition, we've used an alphabetical code (within parentheses) to help you determine if the program falls within your scope of interest: S = Scholarships; F = Fellowships; L = Loans; G = Grants; A = Awards; and I = Internships. Here's how the code works: if a program is followed (S) 241, the program is described in entry 241 in the Scholarships section. If the same program title is followed by another entry number—for example, (L) 680—the program is also described in entry 680 in the Loans section. Remember: the numbers cited here refer to program entry numbers, not to page numbers in the book.

---

S–Scholarships          F–Fellowships          L–Loans          G–Grants          A–Awards          I–Internships

485

Amelia Earhart Memorial Scholarships, (S) 29, (F) 684

Amelia Earhart Research Scholar Grant, (G) 1051

Amelia Peabody Memorial Award. *See* National Association of Women Artists Annual Exhibition Awards, entry (A) 1382

American Association of Japanese University Women Scholarship Program, (S) 30, (F) 685

American Association of Obstetricians and Gynecologists Foundation Scholarships, (F) 686, (G) 1052

American Association of Obstetricians and Gynecologists Foundation Scholarships. *See* American Association of Obstetricians and Gynecologists Foundation Scholarships, entries (F) 686, (G) 1052

American Association of Petroleum Geologists Semester Internships in Geoscience Public Policy. *See* AAPG Semester Internships in Geoscience Public Policy, entry (I) 1428

American Association of University Women Achievement Award. *See* AAUW Achievement Award, entry (A) 1281

American Association of University Women Career Development Academic Grants. *See* AAUW Career Development Grants, entry (F) 660

American Association of University Women Dissertation Fellowships, (G) 1053

American Association of University Women Legal Advocacy Fund Support for Sex Discrimination Lawsuits. *See* AAUW Legal Advocacy Fund Support for Sex Discrimination Lawsuits, entry (G) 1033

American Association of University Women Summer/Short–Term Research Publication Grants. *See* AAUW Summer/Short–Term Research Publication Grants, entry (G) 1034

American Business Women's Association President's Scholarship. *See* ABWA President's Scholarship, entry (F) 661

American College of Nurse–Midwives Foundation Fellowship for Graduate Education. *See* ACNM Foundation Fellowship for Graduate Education, entry (F) 662

American College of Nurse–Midwives Foundation Memorial Scholarship. *See* Basic Midwifery Scholarships, entries (S) 73, (F) 704

American College Testing Summer Internship Program. *See* ACT Summer Internship Program, entry (I) 1429

American Council of Learned Societies Digital Innovation Fellowships. *See* ACLS Digital Innovation Fellowships, entry (G) 1036

American Council of Learned Societies Dissertation Completion Fellowships. *See* Andrew W. Mellon Foundation/ACLS Dissertation Completion Fellowships, entry (G) 1056

American Council of Learned Societies Dissertation Fellowships in American Art. *See* Henry Luce Foundation/ACLS Dissertation Fellowships in American Art, entry (G) 1141

American Council of Learned Societies Fellowships. *See* ACLS Fellowships, entry (G) 1037

American Council of Learned Societies Grants to Individuals from the United States and Canada in East Asian Archaeology and Early History. *See* Henry Luce Foundation/ACLS Grants to Individuals from the United States and Canada in East Asian Archaeology and Early History, entry (G) 1142

American Council of Learned Societies/SSRC/NEH International and Area Studies Fellowships. *See* ACLS/SSRC/NEH International and Area Studies Fellowships, entry (G) 1038

American Gastroenterological Association Fellowship/Faculty Transition Awards. *See* AGA Fellowship/Faculty Transition Awards, entries (F) 666, (G) 1041

American Gastroenterological Association Foundation Outcomes Research Awards. *See* AGA Foundation Outcomes Research Awards, entry (G) 1042

American Gastroenterological Association Research Scholar Awards. *See* AGA Research Scholar Awards, entry (G) 1044

American Gastroenterological Association Student Research Fellowship Awards. *See* AGA Student Research Fellowship Awards, entry (G) 1045

American Gastroenterology Association Pilot Research Awards. *See* AGA Pilot Research Awards, entry (G) 1043

American Heart Association Undergraduate Student Research Program, (I) 1432

American Institute of Professional Geologists Summer Internships in Geoscience Public Policy. *See* AIPG Summer Internships in Geoscience Public Policy, entry (I) 1430

American Legion Auxiliary Emergency Fund, (S) 31

American Legion Auxiliary Spirit of Youth Scholarship for Junior Members. *See* Spirit of Youth Scholarship for Junior Members, entry (S) 550

American Meteorological Society Freshman Undergraduate Scholarships. *See* AMS Freshman Undergraduate Scholarships, entry (S) 40

American Meteorological Society Graduate Fellowship in the History of Science, (G) 1054

American Meteorological Society Undergraduate Scholarships, (S) 32

American Meteorological Society 75th Anniversary Endowed Scholarship. *See* American Meteorological Society Undergraduate Scholarships, entry (S) 32

American Military Spouse Education Foundation Scholarships, (S) 33

American Mothers Vocal Competition, (A) 1289

American News Women's Club Scholarships, (S) 34, (F) 687

American Polish Engineering Scholarship, (S) 35

American Quarter Horse Association National Female Equestrian Award. *See* AQHA National Female Equestrian Award, entry (A) 1297

American Society for Eighteenth–Century Studies Women's Caucus Editing and Translation Fellowship. *See* ASECS Women's Caucus Editing and Translation Fellowship, entry (G) 1067

American Society for Pharmacology and Experimental Therapeutics Individual Summer Undergraduate Research Fellowships. *See* ASPET Individual Summer Undergraduate Research Fellowships, entries (G) 1068, (I) 1437

American Society of Civil Engineers Maine Section Scholarship. *See* ASCE Maine Section Scholarship, entry (S) 59

American Society of Mechanical Engineers Graduate Teaching Fellowship. *See* ASME Graduate Teaching Fellowship, entry (F) 698

American Society of Women Accountants Undergraduate Scholarships, (S) 36

American Society of Women Accountants 2–Year College Scholarships, (S) 37

---

Blum Memorial Award. *See* National Association of Women Artists Annual Exhibition Awards, entry (A) 1382

Bob Glahn Scholarship in Statistical Meteorology, (S) 87

Bobbi McCallum Memorial Scholarship, (S) 88

Bobby Sox High School Senior Scholarship Program, (S) 89

Boeing Company Career Enhancement Scholarship, (S) 90, (F) 713

Boney Memorial Scholarships. *See* New Mexico Elks Association Charitable and Benevolent Trust Scholarships, entry (S) 435

Bonnie Seymour Memorial Scholarship. *See* Amelia Earhart Memorial Scholarships, entries (S) 29, (F) 684

Borg Scholarships. *See* Anita Borg Scholarships, entries (S) 43, (F) 689

Boston Affiliate AWSCPA Scholarship, (S) 91, (F) 714

Bowers Scholarship. *See* Pi Beta Phi Undergraduate Scholarships, entry (S) 486

Bowfin Memorial Continuing Education Scholarships, (S) 92

Boyd Graduate Scholarship. *See* Winifred Hill Boyd Graduate Scholarship, entry (F) 972

Boyd Scholarship. *See* Delta Kappa Gamma Scholarship Program, entries (F) 743, (G) 1097

BPW/Maine Career Advancement Scholarship, (S) 93

BPW/Maine Continuing Education Scholarship, (S) 94

BPW/NC Foundation Scholarship, (S) 95, (F) 715

Bradford Grant-in-Aid, (S) 96

Bradham Social Work Fellowship. *See* Mildred Cater Bradham Social Work Fellowship, entry (F) 858

Brant Memorial Scholarship. *See* Kappa Alpha Theta Founders' Memorial Scholarships, entry (S) 291

Brian Pearson Memorial Scholarships, (S) 97

Brick Scholarship. *See* Amelia Earhart Memorial Scholarships, entries (S) 29, (F) 684

Bridge Scholarship. *See* William Bridge Scholarship, entry (S) 614

Brookhaven National Laboratory Science and Engineering Programs for Women and Minorities, (I) 1442

Brown Scholarship. *See* Erma Metz Brown Scholarship, entry (S) 184

Brown Scholarships. *See* Miss America Competition Awards, entries (S) 385, (A) 1367

Brown–NM7N Memorial Scholarship. *See* Young Ladies' Radio League Scholarship, entries (S) 653, (F) 988

Bruce L. "Biff" Reed Award. *See* Geological Society of America Graduate Student Research Grants, entry (G) 1129

Buc Postdoctoral Fellowship. *See* Pembroke Center Postdoctoral Fellowships, entry (G) 1221

Buck Fellowship. *See* Dorothea Buck Fellowship, entry (F) 748

Buena M. Chesshir Memorial Women's Educational Scholarship, (S) 98, (F) 716

Bufton Jr. Scholarship. *See* Hilary A. Bufton Jr. Scholarship, entry (F) 799

Bufton Memorial Education Fund Grants. *See* Stephen Bufton Memorial Education Fund Grants, entries (S) 554, (F) 947

Bufton Scholarship. *See* Ruth H. Bufton Scholarship, entry (F) 927

Burg Fellowship. *See* Women's Law and Public Policy Fellowship Program, entries (G) 1275, (I) 1508

Burkhardt Residential Fellowships for Recently Tenured Scholars. *See* Frederick Burkhardt Residential Fellowships for Recently Tenured Scholars, entry (G) 1127

Burns Memorial Fellowships for Social and Economic Justice. *See* Haywood Burns Memorial Fellowships for Social and Economic Justice, entry (I) 1459

Business and Professional Women of Iowa Foundation Educational Scholarship, (S) 99

Business and Professional Women's Foundation of Maryland Scholarship, (S) 100

Butcher Scholar Award, (G) 1076

Butler Career Development Awards. *See* Mildred A. Butler Career Development Awards, entry (S) 372

Byers Postgraduate Scholarship Program. *See* Walter Byers Postgraduate Scholarship Program, entry (F) 963

Byrd Fellowship Program, (G) 1077

C. Dan Keffer Award. *See* Virginia Golf Foundation Scholarship Program, entry (S) 597

CAA Professional Development Fellowships, (F) 717

Cady McDonnell Memorial Scholarship, (S) 101

Calder Summer Undergraduate Research Program, (G) 1078

Calgon Take Me Away to College Scholarships, (S) 102, (A) 1305

Calhoun Scholarships. *See* Hermione Grant Calhoun Scholarships, entries (S) 240, (F) 798

California Fee Waiver Program for Dependents of Totally Disabled Veterans, (S) 103

California Interscholastic Federation Scholar–Athlete of the Year, (S) 104

California Job's Daughters Educational Loan Fund, (L) 998

California Job's Daughters Scholarships, (S) 105

California Legion Auxiliary Past Department President's Junior Scholarship, (S) 106

California P.E.O. Scholarships, (S) 107, (F) 718

California Real Estate Endowment Fund Scholarship Program, (S) 108

California Space Grant Consortium Graduate Research Fellowships, (F) 719, (G) 1079

California Space Grant Consortium Student–Mentor Aerospace Workforce Development Scholarships, (I) 1443

California Spirit of Youth Scholarship for Junior Members, (S) 109

Callahan Scholar Athlete. *See* Lindy Callahan Scholar Athlete, entry (S) 317

CalVet Home Improvement Loan Program, (L) 999

Campbell Memorial Fund. *See* Lynn Campbell Memorial Fund, entry (G) 1174

Campbell Memorial Scholarship. *See* Dorothy Campbell Memorial Scholarship, entry (S) 159

Campbell Memorial Scholarships. *See* Eloise Campbell Memorial Scholarships, entry (S) 182

Canaday Memorial Award. *See* National Association of Women Artists Annual Exhibition Awards, entry (A) 1382

Candon Scholarship. *See* Sister Elizabeth Candon Scholarship, entry (S) 538

Cannon Award in Astronomy. *See* Annie Jump Cannon Award in Astronomy, entry (A) 1296

C.A.R. Coach of the Year Award, (A) 1306

Career Advancement Scholarships, (S) 110, (F) 720

Career Awards at the Scientific Interface, (F) 721, (G) 1080

Career Awards for Medical Scientists, (G) 1081

Career Awards in the Biomedical Sciences. *See* Career Awards for Medical Scientists, entry (G) 1081

Career Development Academic Grants. *See* AAUW Career Development Grants, entry (F) 660

Career Development Awards in Diabetes Research, (G) 1082

Career Start Scholarships. *See* AMVETS Ladies Auxiliary Career Start Scholarships, entry (S) 41

Carl W. Kreitzberg Endowed Scholarship. *See* American Meteorological Society Undergraduate Scholarships, entry (S) 32

Carmen Schipper Memorial Award. *See* Hanscom Officers' Spouses' Club Scholarships, entry (S) 233

Carnes Fund. *See* Herbert and Betty Carnes Fund, entry (G) 1143

Carol G. Lederer Postdoctoral Fellowship. *See* Pembroke Center Postdoctoral Fellowships, entry (G) 1221

Carol Inge Warren Scholarship. *See* Pi Beta Phi Undergraduate Scholarships, entry (S) 486

Carolyn Guss Scholarship. *See* Delta Kappa Gamma Scholarship Program, entries (F) 743, (G) 1097

Carolyn Weatherford Scholarship Fund, (S) 111, (F) 722, (I) 1444

Carrie Chapman Catt Prize for Research on Women and Politics, (A) 1307

Carroll L. Birch Student Research Award, (A) 1308

Carter Scholarship. *See* Delta Kappa Gamma Scholarship Program, entries (F) 743, (G) 1097

Carter Student Leadership Award. *See* Anne C. Carter Student Leadership Award, entry (A) 1295

Caterpillar Scholarships, (S) 112, (F) 723

Catherine Nutterville Scholarship. *See* Delta Kappa Gamma Scholarship Program, entries (F) 743, (G) 1097

Catherine Prelinger Award, (G) 1083

Catt Prize for Research on Women and Politics. *See* Carrie Chapman Catt Prize for Research on Women and Politics, entry (A) 1307

Cavalaris Outstanding Female Athlete Award. *See* Zoe Cavalaris Outstanding Female Athlete Award, entries (S) 659, (A) 1426

Cecil Leadership Award. *See* Helene Cecil Leadership Award, entry (A) 1335

Cecile Holzinger Memorial Award. *See* National Association of Women Artists Annual Exhibition Awards, entry (A) 1382

Celia M. Howard Fellowship, (F) 724

Center on Budget and Policy Priorities Internships, (I) 1445

Central New Mexico Section SWE Pioneer Scholarships, (S) 113

Chamberlain Art Scholarship. *See* Pi Beta Phi Undergraduate Scholarships, entry (S) 486

Chamberlain Fellowships. *See* Mariam K. Chamberlain Fellowships, entry (I) 1470

Chamberlin Loan Fund, (L) 1000

Chambers Playwriting Award. *See* Jane Chambers Playwriting Award, entry (A) 1342

Chance Law Fellowship. *See* Ruth Chance Law Fellowship, entry (I) 1493

Chancellor Endowment. *See* Arizona BPW Foundation Annual Scholarships, entry (S) 51

Chao Scholarship. *See* Ruth Mu–Lan Chu and James S.C. Chao Scholarship, entry (S) 520

Chappie Hall Memorial Scholarship Program, (S) 114

Charles A. and June R.P. Ross Research Fund Award. *See* Geological Society of America Graduate Student Research Grants, entry (G) 1129

Charles A. Ryskamp Research Fellowships, (G) 1084

Charles and Theresa Brown Scholarships. *See* Miss America Competition Awards, entries (S) 385, (A) 1367

Charles Mahr Memorial Scholarship. *See* New Mexico Elks Association Charitable and Benevolent Trust Scholarships, entry (S) 435

Charles P. Greco Graduate Fellowships. *See* Bishop Charles P. Greco Graduate Fellowships, entry (F) 710

Charles T. Stoner Law Scholarship Award, (F) 725

Chase Scholarship. *See* Kappa Delta Sorority Undergraduate Scholarships, entry (S) 294

Cheryl A. Ruggiero Scholarship, (S) 115

Cheryl Hennesy Scholarship, (S) 116

Chesley Award for Lesbian and Gay Playwriting. *See* Robert Chesley Award for Lesbian and Gay Playwriting, entry (A) 1393

Chesshir Memorial Women's Educational Scholarship. *See* Buena M. Chesshir Memorial Women's Educational Scholarship, entries (S) 98, (F) 716

Chesterfield Smith Internships, (I) 1446

Chevron Corporation Scholarships, (S) 117

Chi Omega Foundation Alumnae Educational Grants, (F) 726

Chicago Alumnae Panhellenic Scholarship, (S) 118

Chicago Network of Executive Women in Hospitality Scholarship Awards, (S) 119, (F) 727

Chief Justice Mary Ann G. McMorrow Scholarship. *See* WBF Scholarship Awards, entry (F) 967

Chief of Staff Award. *See* Hanscom Officers' Spouses' Club Scholarships, entry (S) 233

Chief Petty Officer Scholarship Fund. *See* CPO Scholarship Fund, entry (S) 130

Christensen National Scholarship. *See* Olga Christensen National Scholarship, entry (S) 458

Chrysalis Scholarship, (G) 1085

Chu and James S.C. Chao Scholarship. *See* Ruth Mu–Lan Chu and James S.C. Chao Scholarship, entry (S) 520

Circle Key Grants of the Rose McGill Fund, (F) 728

Citrus District 2 Scholarships, (S) 120, (F) 729

Claire of the Moon Award for Fiction. *See* Lesbian Writers Fund Awards, entry (A) 1355

Clara Shainess Memorial Award. *See* National Association of Women Artists Annual Exhibition Awards, entry (A) 1382

Clare Boothe Luce Program Scholarship, (F) 730

Clark Memorial Graduate Fellowship. *See* Dr. Laurel Salton Clark Memorial Graduate Fellowship, entry (F) 753

Claude C. Albritton, Jr. Scholarship. *See* Geological Society of America Graduate Student Research Grants, entry (G) 1129

Claudia Steele Baker Graduate Fellowships, (F) 731

Cleo Hartwig Memorial Award. *See* National Association of Women Artists Annual Exhibition Awards, entry (A) 1382

Cleworth Award. *See* NFMC Biennial Student Audition Awards, entry (A) 1384

Clinical Scientist Awards in Translational Research, (G) 1086

Coaches Advisory Roundtable Coach of the Year Award. *See* C.A.R. Coach of the Year Award, entry (A) 1306

Coale, M.D. Scholarships. *See* Edith SeVille Coale Scholarships, entry (F) 760

Coast Guard Enlisted Dependent Spouse Scholarship. *See* Navy/Marine Corps/Coast Guard Enlisted Dependent Spouse Scholarship, entries (S) 417, (F) 874

Coca–Cola Endowed Internship Program, (I) 1447

Coddington Memorial Scholarship. *See* Kittredge Coddington Memorial Scholarship, entry (S) 303

Cohen Scholarship. *See* Alpha Epsilon Phi Foundation Scholarships, entries (S) 21, (F) 677

Coleman Aviation Scholarship. *See* Tweet Coleman Aviation Scholarship, entry (S) 579

Colgate–Palmolive Research Scholarship Award, (A) 1309

Collaborative Research Experience for Undergraduates in Computer Science and Engineering, (G) 1087

Collaborative Research Grants for Women, (G) 1088

Colleen Conley Memorial Scholarship, (S) 121

Collins Memorial Scholarship. *See* Mary Love Collins Memorial Scholarship, entry (F) 849

Collins Scholarship. *See* Eloise Collins Scholarship, entry (F) 767

Colonel Harold M. Beardslee Memorial Scholarship Awards, (S) 122

Colonel Hayden W. Wagner Memorial Fund. *See* Society of Daughters of the United States Army Scholarships, entry (S) 542

Colorado BPW Education Foundation Scholarships, (S) 123

Colorado Legion Auxiliary Department President's Scholarship for Junior Auxiliary Members, (S) 124

Colorado Legion Auxiliary Past President's Parley Nurse's Scholarship, (S) 125

Colorado Space Grant Research Support, (I) 1448

Colson and Isabelle Saalwaechter Fitzpatrick Memorial Scholarship. *See* Thaddeus Colson and Isabelle Saalwaechter Fitzpatrick Memorial Scholarship, entry (S) 573

Columbia Crew Memorial Undergraduate Scholarships, (S) 126, (F) 732

Columbia Memorial Scholarship, (S) 127, (F) 733

Comly Scholarship. *See* Pi Beta Phi Undergraduate Scholarships, entry (S) 486

Communication Internships at Legal Momentum, (I) 1449

Community Action Grants, (G) 1089

Community Internships of the Women's Sports Foundation, (I) 1450

Computational Chemistry and Materials Science Summer Institute, (I) 1451

Computing Research Association Undergraduate Awards. *See* CRA Undergraduate Awards, entry (A) 1311

Conducting Scholarship for Graduate Students, (F) 734

Congressional Fellowships on Women and Public Policy, (F) 735, (I) 1452

Conley Memorial Scholarship. *See* Colleen Conley Memorial Scholarship, entry (S) 121

Connecticut Federation of Business and Professional Women's Clubs Education Scholarships, (S) 128

Connecticut Space Grant College Consortium Graduate Student Fellowships, (G) 1090

Connecticut Space Grant College Consortium Student Project Grants, (G) 1091

Connecticut Space Grant College Consortium Travel Grants, (G) 1092

Connecticut Space Grant College Consortium Undergraduate Student Fellowships, (G) 1093

Connolly Scholar–Athlete Award. *See* Hal Connolly Scholar–Athlete Award, entry (S) 231

Constance Bauman Abraham Scholarship. *See* Alpha Epsilon Phi Foundation Scholarships, entries (S) 21, (F) 677

Constance L. Lloyd Scholarship, (S) 129, (F) 736

Contemplative Practice Fellowships, (G) 1094

Cook Recruitment Grants. *See* Florence A. Cook Recruitment Grants, entry (S) 197

Cooley Scholarship. *See* E. Wayne Cooley Scholarship Award, entry (S) 172

Cooper Scholarship. *See* Judge William F. Cooper Scholarship, entry (S) 283

Cooper/Rosa Parks Fellowships for Non–Violent Alternatives to Conflict. *See* Helen Cromer Cooper/Rosa Parks Fellowships for Non–Violent Alternatives to Conflict, entry (G) 1140

Copeland Scholarship for Females. *See* Helen Copeland Scholarship for Females, entries (S) 237, (F) 795

Corey Scholarship. *See* Hanscom Officers' Spouses' Club Scholarships, entry (S) 233

Cornell Scholarship. *See* Holly A. Cornell Scholarship, entry (F) 800

Corrine Hammond Gray Graduate Fellowship. *See* Pi Beta Phi Graduate Fellowships, entry (F) 906

Count–Me–In Loans, (L) 1001

Courage in Journalism Awards, (A) 1310

Covad Broadband Entrepreneur Award, (G) 1095

Cox Award. *See* Geological Society of America Graduate Student Research Grants, entry (G) 1129

Cox Scholarship in Statistics. *See* Gertrude M. Cox Scholarship in Statistics, entry (F) 784

CPO Scholarship Fund, (S) 130

CRA Undergraduate Awards, (A) 1311

Craig Scholarship for Women in Transition. *See* Mary Craig Scholarship for Women in Transition, entry (S) 345

Craig Scholarship Fund. *See* Mary Craig Scholarship Fund, entries (S) 346, (F) 846

Cramer Memorial Award. *See* National Association of Women Artists Annual Exhibition Awards, entry (A) 1382

Crawford Personal Development Scholarship. *See* Mara Crawford Personal Development Scholarship, entry (S) 336

Crawshay Prizes. *See* Rose Mary Crawshay Prizes, entry (A) 1394

Creed Scholarship. *See* Patricia Creed Scholarship, entry (S) 470

Crow Memorial Scholarship. *See* Loren W. Crow Memorial Scholarship, entry (S) 324

Crowe Star of Tomorrow Award. *See* Alberta E. Crowe Star of Tomorrow Award, entry (S) 19

Crowell Endowment. *See* Arizona BPW Foundation Annual Scholarships, entry (S) 51

Curtis Memorial Fund for Women in Science Award. *See* Subaru Outstanding Woman in Science Award, entry (A) 1406

Cushing Scholarships. *See* Ellen Cushing Scholarships, entry (F) 766

Cynosure Screenwriting Awards, (A) 1312

Cynthia Hunt–Lines Scholarship, (S) 131, (F) 737

C200 Scholar Awards, (F) 738

Gloeckner, M.D. Summer Research Fellowship. *See* M. Louise Carpenter Gloeckner, M.D. Summer Research Fellowship, entry (G) 1176

Gloria Hoegh Memorial Scholarship for the Education of Rural Librarians, (F) 788

Gloria Pennington Scholarship. *See* Reed and Gloria Pennington Scholarship, entry (S) 502

Glorine Tuohey Memorial Scholarship, (F) 789

Goeppert–Mayer Award. *See* Maria Goeppert–Mayer Award, entry (A) 1361

Gold Fund. *See* Delta Phi Epsilon Scholarships, entries (S) 151, (F) 744

Goldberg Fellowships. *See* Leo Goldberg Fellowships, entry (G) 1168

Goldfeder Memorial Scholarship. *See* Alpha Epsilon Phi Foundation Scholarships, entries (S) 21, (F) 677

Goldhaber Distinguished Fellowships. *See* Gertrude and Maurice Goldhaber Distinguished Fellowships, entry (G) 1132

Goldman Education Awards. *See* Rhode Island Commission on Women/Freda H. Goldman Education Awards, entry (S) 503

Goldman, Sachs Scholarships, (S) 223

Golf Association of Michigan Scholarships, (S) 224

Gonzalez Memorial Scholarships. *See* Millie Gonzalez Memorial Scholarships, entry (S) 376

Gordon Getty Awards. *See* Ann and Gordon Getty Awards, entry (A) 1293

Gordon Scholarships. *See* Kappa Delta Sorority Undergraduate Scholarships, entry (S) 294

Governance Studies Predoctoral Fellowships, (G) 1136

Grace Follmer Scholarship. *See* Kappa Delta Sorority Undergraduate Scholarships, entry (S) 294

Grace Harrington Wilson Scholarship, (S) 225, (F) 790

Grace LeGendre Fellowship for Advanced Graduate Study, (F) 791

Grahn Award for Lesbian and Gay Nonfiction. *See* Judy Grahn Award for Lesbian Nonfiction, entry (A) 1346

Grand Guardian Council of Pennsylvania Scholarships, (S) 226

Grandma Moses Scholarship, (S) 227

Gratiot Scholarship. *See* California P.E.O. Scholarships, entries (S) 107, (F) 718

Grau Undergraduate Scholarship. *See* American Meteorological Society Undergraduate Scholarships, entry (S) 32

Gray Graduate Fellowship. *See* Pi Beta Phi Graduate Fellowships, entry (F) 906

Grayce Chase Scholarship. *See* Kappa Delta Sorority Undergraduate Scholarships, entry (S) 294

Greater New York Network of Executive Women in Hospitality Scholarship Awards, (S) 228

Greco Graduate Fellowships. *See* Bishop Charles P. Greco Graduate Fellowships, entry (F) 710

Green Scholarship. *See* Non Commissioned Officers Association Scholarship Fund, entry (S) 437

Greenblatt Memorial Award. *See* National Association of Women Artists Annual Exhibition Awards, entry (A) 1382

Greene Memorial Scholarship. *See* Delta Phi Epsilon Scholarships, entries (S) 151, (F) 744

Greenwood Scholarship. *See* William Rucker Greenwood Scholarship, entries (S) 616, (F) 970

Gregory Millard Fellowships. *See* New York Foundation for the Arts Artists' Fellowships, entry (G) 1206

Gretchen L. Blechschmidt Award. *See* Geological Society of America Graduate Student Research Grants, entry (G) 1129

Gretchen Richardson Memorial Award. *See* National Association of Women Artists Annual Exhibition Awards, entry (A) 1382

Griswold Scholarships. *See* Janet H. Griswold Scholarships, entries (S) 269, (F) 813

Grotto/Job's Daughters Scholarship, (S) 229, (F) 792

Grumley Awards. *See* Ferro–Grumley Awards, entry (A) 1325

Guaranteed Loans for Socially Disadvantaged Farmers and Ranchers, (L) 1009

Guidant Foundation Scholarships, (S) 230

Guideposts Young Writers Contest. *See* Sweet 16 Magazine Scholarship Contest, entries (S) 564, (A) 1409

Guillermo Salazar Rodriguez Scholarship. *See* American Meteorological Society Undergraduate Scholarships, entry (S) 32

Guss Scholarship. *See* Delta Kappa Gamma Scholarship Program, entries (F) 743, (G) 1097

Hadassah–Brandeis Institute Research Awards, (G) 1137

Hadassah–Brandeis Institute Scholar in Residence Program, (G) 1138

Haemer Scholarship. *See* Kappa Delta Sorority Undergraduate Scholarships, entry (S) 294

Hafter Fellowship. *See* Delta Delta Delta Unrestricted Graduate Scholarships, entry (F) 741

Hagan Memorial Scholarship. *See* Amelia Earhart Memorial Scholarships, entries (S) 29, (F) 684

Hagemeyer Scholarship. *See* American Meteorological Society Undergraduate Scholarships, entry (S) 32

Hal Connolly Scholar–Athlete Award, (S) 231

Hall Memorial Scholarship Program. *See* Chappie Hall Memorial Scholarship Program, entry (S) 114

Hall Memorial Scholarship. *See* Phi Chi Theta Scholarships, entries (S) 481, (F) 904

Hall Scholarship. *See* Alpha Kappa/Jean Hall Scholarship, entry (S) 25

Halpern Memorial Award. *See* National Association of Women Artists Annual Exhibition Awards, entry (A) 1382

Halse–Hanf Scholarship. *See* Delaware BPW Foundation Scholarships, entry (S) 142

Hamilton Memorial Scholarship. *See* Kappa Alpha Theta Founders' Memorial Scholarships, entry (S) 291

Hammerschlag Grant. *See* Margo Harris Hammerschlag Grant, entry (G) 1180

Hammond Memorial Scholarship. *See* Amelia Earhart Memorial Scholarships, entries (S) 29, (F) 684

Hancock Award. *See* Indiana Extension Homemakers Association Career Advancement Scholarships, entry (S) 257

Hanks, Jr. Scholarship in Meteorology. *See* American Meteorological Society Undergraduate Scholarships, entry (S) 32

Hannah Fitch Shaw Memorial Scholarship. *See* Kappa Alpha Theta Founders' Memorial Scholarships, entry (S) 291

Hannah Keenan Scholarships, (S) 232

Hannah Mervine Miles Scholarship. *See* Pi Beta Phi Undergraduate Scholarships, entry (S) 486

Hanscom Officers' Spouses' Club Scholarships, (S) 233

Hansen Continuing Education Grants. *See* Betty Hansen Continuing Education Grants, entry (S) 81

Hansen National Scholarships. *See* Betty Hansen National Scholarships, entries (S) 82, (F) 708

Hanshaw Scholarship. *See* Penelope Hanshaw Scholarship, entries (S) 471, (F) 901

Harold Aggesen Grand Bethel Memorial Scholarship. *See* California Job's Daughters Scholarships, entry (S) 105

Harold M. Beardslee Memorial Scholarship Awards. *See* Colonel Harold M. Beardslee Memorial Scholarship Awards, entry (S) 122

Harold T. Stearns Fellowship Award. *See* Geological Society of America Graduate Student Research Grants, entry (G) 1129

Harriet Hass Scholarship. *See* Wisconsin Legion Auxiliary Merit and Memorial Scholarships, entry (S) 622

Harriet R. Burg Fellowship. *See* Women's Law and Public Policy Fellowship Program, entries (G) 1275, (I) 1508

Harriet Rutherford Johnstone Scholarship. *See* Pi Beta Phi Undergraduate Scholarships, entry (S) 486

Harriett G. Jenkins Predoctoral Fellowship Program, (F) 793

Harris Endowed Scholarship. *See* Dorothy Harris Endowed Scholarship, entry (F) 750

Harris Memorial Award. *See* National Association of Women Artists Annual Exhibition Awards, entry (A) 1382

Harrod Scholarships. *See* B.J. Harrod Scholarships, entry (S) 85

Hartley Fellowship. *See* Sigma Delta Epsilon Fellowships, entry (G) 1246

Hartwig Memorial Award. *See* National Association of Women Artists Annual Exhibition Awards, entry (A) 1382

Harvin Award. *See* Rachel Royston Permanent Scholarship, entry (F) 915

Hass Scholarship. *See* Wisconsin Legion Auxiliary Merit and Memorial Scholarships, entry (S) 622

Hattie Hemschemeyer Award, (A) 1333

Hayden Memorial Fund Loan Program. *See* Gillette Hayden Memorial Fund Loan Program, entry (L) 1008

Hayden W. Wagner Memorial Fund. *See* Society of Daughters of the United States Army Scholarships, entry (S) 542

Haywood Burns Memorial Fellowships for Social and Economic Justice, (I) 1459

Hazel E. Ritchey Loans, (L) 1010

Hazel Heffner Becchina Award, (S) 234, (A) 1334

Hazel Heffner Becchina Award. *See* NFMC Biennial Student Audition Awards, entry (A) 1384

Hazel Palmer General Scholarship. *See* Judge Hazel Palmer General Scholarship, entry (S) 282

Hazel Witte Memorial Award. *See* National Association of Women Artists Annual Exhibition Awards, entry (A) 1382

Health Research and Educational Trust Scholarships, (S) 235, (F) 794

Health Sciences Student Fellowships in Epilepsy, (G) 1139

Heflin Scholarship. *See* Linly Heflin Scholarship, entry (S) 318

Heghinian Scholarship. *See* Lavonne Heghinian Scholarship, entry (S) 309

Heimrich Awards. *See* NFMC Biennial Student Audition Awards, entry (A) 1384

Helen A. Snyder Scholarship. *See* Kappa Delta Sorority Graduate Scholarships, entry (F) 826

Helen and Arnold Barben Scholarship, (S) 236

Helen Copeland Scholarship for Females, (S) 237, (F) 795

Helen Cromer Cooper/Rosa Parks Fellowships for Non–Violent Alternatives to Conflict, (G) 1140

Helen D. Snow Memorial Scholarship. *See* Phi Chi Theta Scholarships, entries (S) 481, (F) 904

Helen D. Thompson Memorial Scholarship. *See* California P.E.O. Scholarships, entries (S) 107, (F) 718

Helen Davies Award. *See* Association for Women in Science College Scholarships, entry (S) 62

Helen Duhamel Achievement Awards. *See* Edith M. Wortman Annual Matrix Foundation Public Speaking Competition, entry (A) 1317

Helen Hagemeyer Scholarship. *See* American Meteorological Society Undergraduate Scholarships, entry (S) 32

Helene Cecil Leadership Award, (A) 1335

Helene M. Overly Memorial Graduate Scholarship, (F) 796

Helman Award. *See* National Association of Women Artists Annual Exhibition Awards, entry (A) 1382

Helping Hands of WSC Endowment Scholarship, (S) 238

Hemschemeyer Award. *See* Hattie Hemschemeyer Award, entry (A) 1333

Henderson Violoncello Award. *See* NFMC Biennial Student Audition Awards, entry (A) 1384

Hennesy Scholarship. *See* Cheryl Hennesy Scholarship, entry (S) 116

Henry H. Arnold Education Grant Program. *See* General Henry H. Arnold Education Grant Program, entry (S) 211

Henry Luce Foundation/ACLS Dissertation Fellowships in American Art, (G) 1141

Henry Luce Foundation/ACLS Grants to Individuals from the United States and Canada in East Asian Archaeology and Early History, (G) 1142

Henry Scholarship. *See* California P.E.O. Scholarships, entries (S) 107, (F) 718

Henry Scholarship. *See* Virginia D. Henry Scholarship, entry (S) 596

Hentges Scholarship. *See* Mary Lou Hentges Scholarship, entries (S) 348, (F) 847

Herbert and Betty Carnes Fund, (G) 1143

Herff Jones Graduate Scholarship. *See* Kappa Delta Sorority Graduate Scholarships, entry (F) 826

Herman Scholarship. *See* Women's Jewelry Association Scholarship, entry (S) 643

Hermine Dalkowitz Tobolowsky Scholarship, (S) 239, (F) 797

Hermione Grant Calhoun Scholarships, (S) 240, (F) 798

High Volume Transaction Output Woman of Distinction Award. *See* HVTO Woman of Distinction Award, entries (S) 249, (F) 806

Hilary A. Bufton Jr. Scholarship, (F) 799

Hiller Scholarship. *See* Delta Kappa Gamma Scholarship Program, entries (F) 743, (G) 1097

History of Women in Science Prize. *See* Margaret W. Rossiter History of Women in Science Prize, entry (A) 1360

Hodge Scholarship. *See* New Jersey Schoolwomen's Club Scholarships, entry (S) 432

Hodo Scholarship. *See* Women's Alabama Golf Association Scholarships, entry (S) 638

Hoegh Memorial Scholarship for the Education of Rural Librarians. *See* Gloria Hoegh Memorial Scholarship for the Education of Rural Librarians, entry (F) 788

Hofacre Scholarship. *See* Pi Beta Phi Undergraduate Scholarships, entry (S) 486

---

Hoffman Award for Outstanding Achievement in Graduate Research. *See* Anna Louise Hoffman Award for Outstanding Achievement in Graduate Research, entry (A) 1294

Hoffman Memorial Award for Voice. *See* Sigma Alpha Iota Scholarships for Undergraduate Performance, entry (A) 1401

Hoffman Scholarships. *See* Dorothy M. & Earl S. Hoffman Scholarships, entry (S) 164

Holden Scholarship. *See* Delta Kappa Gamma Scholarship Program, entries (F) 743, (G) 1097

Holiday Scholarship. *See* Pi Beta Phi Undergraduate Scholarships, entry (S) 486

Holland Missionary Scholarship. *See* Ida V. Holland Missionary Scholarship, entries (S) 252, (F) 809

Holly A. Cornell Scholarship, (F) 800

Holmes Memorial Scholarship. *See* Susie Holmes Memorial Scholarship, entry (S) 561

Hologgitas, Ph.D. Scholarship. *See* Daughters of Penelope Undergraduate Scholarships, entry (S) 138

Holzinger Memorial Award. *See* National Association of Women Artists Annual Exhibition Awards, entry (A) 1382

Homeland Security Fellowship Program, (G) 1144

Homer Avila Memorial Fellowship. *See* New York Foundation for the Arts Artists' Fellowships, entry (G) 1206

Honeywell International Scholarships, (S) 241

Honolulu Alumnae Panhellenic Association Collegiate Scholarships, (S) 242

Honolulu Alumnae Panhellenic Association High School Scholarships, (S) 243

Honorable Harrison W. Ewing Fellowships, (F) 801

Hope Endowed Scholarship in Atmospheric Science. *See* American Meteorological Society Undergraduate Scholarships, entry (S) 32

Hopgood Future Teachers Scholarship. *See* Rollie Hopgood Future Teachers Scholarship, entry (S) 514

Hopkins Grant. *See* Anne Peel Hopkins Grant, entries (S) 47, (F) 691

Hopper Memorial Scholarships, (S) 244

Horizons/Frameline Film and Video Completion Fund, (G) 1145

Horn Award for Legal Studies. *See* Leonard C. Horn Award for Legal Studies, entry (F) 834

Horn Memorial Softball Scholarship. *See* Jaime Horn Memorial Softball Scholarship, entry (S) 265

Hortense Ferne Memorial Award. *See* National Association of Women Artists Annual Exhibition Awards, entry (A) 1382

Houston Network of Executive Women in Hospitality Scholarship Awards, (S) 245

Howard Fellowship. *See* Celia M. Howard Fellowship, entry (F) 724

Howard H. Hanks, Jr. Scholarship in Meteorology. *See* American Meteorological Society Undergraduate Scholarships, entry (S) 32

Howard & Howard Award, (F) 802

Howard Hughes Medical Institute Research Training Fellowships for Medical Students, (F) 803, (G) 1146

Howard Medlin Memorial Scholarship. *See* New Mexico Elks Association Charitable and Benevolent Trust Scholarships, entry (S) 435

Howard Research Grants. *See* Geological Society of America Graduate Student Research Grants, entry (G) 1129

Howard Scholarship. *See* Oliver and Esther R. Howard Scholarship, entry (S) 461

Howard T. Orville Endowed Scholarship in Meteorology. *See* American Meteorological Society Undergraduate Scholarships, entry (S) 32

Howarth Scholarships. *See* Dorothy Lemke Howarth Scholarships, entry (S) 163

H.S. and Angeline Lewis Scholarships, (S) 246, (F) 804

Hughes Medical Institute Research Training Fellowships for Medical Students. *See* Howard Hughes Medical Institute Research Training Fellowships for Medical Students, entries (F) 803, (G) 1146

Humber Award for Lifetime Artistic Achievement. *See* Twining Humber Award for Lifetime Artistic Achievement, entry (A) 1412

Humble Artesian Chapter Outright Grants, (S) 247

Huneycutt Scholarship. *See* Sarah E. Huneycutt Scholarship, entry (S) 523

Hunt–Lines Scholarship. *See* Cynthia Hunt–Lines Scholarship, entries (S) 131, (F) 737

Huntsville Chapter ASWA Scholarships, (S) 248, (F) 805

HVTO Woman of Distinction Award, (S) 249, (F) 806

Hyde Graduate Student Research Grants, (G) 1147

IADES Fellowship Award, (F) 807

IBM Corporation SWE Scholarships, (S) 250

Ida B. Wells Graduate Student Fellowship, (G) 1148

Ida M. Pope Memorial Trust Scholarships, (S) 251, (F) 808

Ida V. Holland Missionary Scholarship, (S) 252, (F) 809

Idaho Space Grant Consortium Graduate Fellowships, (G) 1149

Idaho Space Grant Consortium Scholarship Program, (S) 253

Illinois MIA/POW Scholarship, (S) 254

Immigrant Women Program Internships at Legal Momentum, (I) 1460

Indiana American Legion Americanism and Government Test, (A) 1336

Indiana BPW Women in Transition Scholarship, (S) 255

Indiana BPW Working Woman Scholarship, (S) 256

Indiana Extension Homemakers Association Career Advancement Scholarships, (S) 257

Indiana Legion Auxiliary Past Presidents Parley Nursing Scholarship, (S) 258

Indiana Space Grant Consortium Graduate Fellowships, (G) 1150

Indiana Space Grant Consortium Undergraduate Scholarships, (G) 1151

Industry/Government Graduate Fellowships, (F) 810

Institute for Women's Policy Research Summer Internships. *See* IWPR Summer Internships, entry (I) 1461

International Alumnae of Delta Epsilon Sorority Fellowship Award. *See* IADES Fellowship Award, entry (F) 807

International Communications Industries Foundation AV Scholarships, (S) 259

International Women's Film Festival Prizes, (A) 1337

Iota Sigma Pi Centennial Award for Excellence in Undergraduate Teaching, (A) 1338

Iota Sigma Pi National Honorary Member, (A) 1339

Iowa Pork Queen Contest, (S) 260

Iowa Space Grant Scholarship Program, (S) 261

Irene and Daisy MacGregor Memorial Scholarship, (F) 811

Irene Meyer Memorial Scholarship. *See* Phi Chi Theta Scholarships, entries (S) 481, (F) 904

Johnson Scholarship. *See* Ruth M. Johnson Scholarship, entry (F) 928

Johnson Strings Awards. *See* NFMC Biennial Student Audition Awards, entry (A) 1384

Johnstone Scholarship. *See* Pi Beta Phi Undergraduate Scholarships, entry (S) 486

Johnstone Scholarships. *See* Kappa Delta Sorority Undergraduate Scholarships, entry (S) 294

Jones Memorial Fine Arts Scholarship. *See* California P.E.O. Scholarships, entries (S) 107, (F) 718

Jones Scholarship. *See* NPC Foundation Regional Scholarships, entry (S) 447

Josef Kaspar Awards. *See* NFMC Biennial Student Audition Awards, entry (A) 1384

Joseph L. Fisher Doctoral Dissertation Fellowships, (G) 1158

Joseph R. Baranski Emeritus Scholarship, (F) 820

Josephine Trott Strings Award. *See* NFMC Biennial Student Audition Awards, entry (A) 1384

Joukowsky Postdoctoral Fellowship. *See* Pembroke Center Postdoctoral Fellowships, entry (G) 1221

Joyce Wherritt Bowers Scholarship. *See* Pi Beta Phi Undergraduate Scholarships, entry (S) 486

JPMorgan Investment Bank Honors Program, (I) 1464

Judge Hazel Palmer General Scholarship, (S) 282

Judge Judy M. West Scholarship, (F) 821

Judge William F. Cooper Scholarship, (S) 283

Judith McManus Price Scholarships, (S) 284, (F) 822

Judith Resnik Memorial Scholarship, (S) 285

Judith Resnik Memorial Scholarship. *See* Alpha Epsilon Phi Foundation Scholarships, entries (S) 21, (F) 677

Judy Boucher Chamberlain Art Scholarship. *See* Pi Beta Phi Undergraduate Scholarships, entry (S) 486

Judy Grahn Award for Lesbian Nonfiction, (A) 1346

Judy M. West Scholarship. *See* Judge Judy M. West Scholarship, entry (F) 821

Julia Cherry Spruill Publication Prize in Southern Women's History, (A) 1347

Julia H. Dodds Junior Girl's Award, (S) 286

Julianne Malveaux Scholarship. *See* Dr. Julianne Malveaux Scholarship, entry (S) 168

Julie P. Microutsicos Scholarship.. *See* Citrus District 2 Scholarships, entries (S) 120, (F) 729

June Herman Scholarship. *See* Women's Jewelry Association Scholarship, entry (S) 643

June R.P. Ross Research Fund Award. *See* Geological Society of America Graduate Student Research Grants, entry (G) 1129

Junior Girls Scholarships, (S) 287

Juvenile Diabetes Research Foundation Centers for Diabetes Research Grants. *See* JDRF Centers for Diabetes Research Grants, entry (G) 1152

Juvenile Diabetes Research Foundation Clinical Investigation Research Grants. *See* JDRF Clinical Investigation Research Grants, entry (G) 1153

Juvenile Diabetes Research Foundation Innovative Grants, (G) 1159

Juvenile Diabetes Research Foundation Program Project Grants. *See* JDRF Program Project Grants, entry (G) 1154

Juvenile Diabetes Research Foundation Regular Research Grants, (G) 1160

Juvenile Diabetes Research Foundation Scholar Awards. *See* JDRF Scholar Awards, entry (G) 1155

Kabanica Scholarships. *See* Mike Kabanica Scholarships, entry (S) 368

Kahn Award. *See* National Association of Women Artists Annual Exhibition Awards, entry (A) 1382

Kahn Scholarship. *See* Alpha Epsilon Phi Foundation Scholarships, entries (S) 21, (F) 677

Kailash, Mona, and Anila Jain Scholarship, (F) 823

Ka'iulani Home for Girls Trust Scholarship, (S) 288

Kalliope Short Fiction Contest, (A) 1348

Kammer Memorial Fellowship Fund. *See* Ann E. Kammer Memorial Fellowship Fund, entry (G) 1057

Kanner Award. *See* Barbara Penny Kanner Award, entry (A) 1299

Kansas African American Legislative Caucus Scholarships, (S) 289

Kansas Alpha Scholarship. *See* Pi Beta Phi Undergraduate Scholarships, entry (S) 486

Kansas Alpha 4.0 Awards. *See* Pi Beta Phi Undergraduate Scholarships, entry (S) 486

Kansas Space Grant Consortium Program, (S) 290, (F) 824, (G) 1161

Kappa Alpha Theta Alumnae Scholarships, (F) 825

Kappa Alpha Theta Founders' Memorial Scholarships, (S) 291

Kappa Alpha Theta Student Loans, (L) 1011

Kappa Alpha Theta Undergraduate Scholarships, (S) 292

Kappa Delta Founders' Scholarships. *See* Kappa Delta Sorority Undergraduate Scholarships, entry (S) 294

Kappa Delta Magazine Agency Scholarship, (S) 293

Kappa Delta Sorority Graduate Scholarships, (F) 826

Kappa Delta Sorority Undergraduate Scholarships, (S) 294

Kappa Kappa Gamma Graduate Fellowship Awards, (F) 827

Kappa Kappa Gamma Undergraduate Scholarships, (S) 295

Karasick Memorial Award. *See* National Association of Women Artists Annual Exhibition Awards, entry (A) 1382

Karen B. Lewis Career Education Scholarship, (S) 296

Karen Tucker Centennial Scholarship, (S) 297, (F) 828

Kaspar Awards. *See* NFMC Biennial Student Audition Awards, entry (A) 1384

Katherine A. Menges Brick Scholarship. *See* Amelia Earhart Memorial Scholarships, entries (S) 29, (F) 684

Katherine J. Schutze Memorial Scholarship, (F) 829

Kathryn M. Daugherty Scholarship for Education Majors, (S) 298

Kathy Loudat Music Scholarship, (S) 299

Kaufman Women's Scholarships. *See* Lucile B. Kaufman Women's Scholarships, entry (S) 328

Keck Scholarship. *See* California P.E.O. Scholarships, entries (S) 107, (F) 718

Keenan Scholarships. *See* Hannah Keenan Scholarships, entry (S) 232

Keffer Award. *See* Virginia Golf Foundation Scholarship Program, entry (S) 597

Keillor Award for Women in Engineering Education. *See* Sharon Keillor Award for Women in Engineering Education, entry (A) 1399

Keith Awards. *See* NFMC Biennial Student Audition Awards, entry (A) 1384

Kelley Memorial Scholarship of the Aeons. *See* Amelia Earhart Memorial Scholarships, entries (S) 29, (F) 684

Kelly Endowment Fellowship. *See* Rita Mae Kelly Endowment Fellowship, entry (G) 1237

Kelly Memorial Prize in Women's History. *See* Joan Kelly
    Memorial Prize in Women's History, entry (A) 1345
Kelly Memorial Scholarship. *See* Amelia Earhart Memorial
    Scholarships, entries (S) 29, (F) 684
Kentucky High School Athletic Association Sweet 16
    Scholarships. *See* National City/KHSAA Sweet 16
    Scholarships, entry (S) 412
Kentucky Space Grant Consortium Graduate Fellowships, (F)
    830, (G) 1162
Kentucky Space Grant Consortium Research Grants, (G) 1163
Kentucky Space Grant Consortium Undergraduate
    Scholarships, (S) 300, (G) 1164
Kentucky Veterans Tuition Waiver Program, (S) 301
Kenyon Fellowship. *See* Dienje Kenyon Fellowship, entry (G)
    1101
Key Graduate Scholarship. *See* Delta Delta Delta Unrestricted
    Graduate Scholarships, entry (F) 741
Key Scholarship. *See* Delta Delta Delta Unrestricted
    Undergraduate Scholarships, entry (S) 149
KHSAA Sweet 16 Scholarships. *See* National City/KHSAA
    Sweet 16 Scholarships, entry (S) 412
Kim Bates Memorial Fund. *See* Delta Phi Epsilon Scholarships,
    entries (S) 151, (F) 744
King Merit Award. *See* Virginia Golf Foundation Scholarship
    Program, entry (S) 597
Kirkley Traveling Fellowships. *See* Dr. Alexandra Kirkley
    Traveling Fellowships, entry (G) 1106
Kirsten R. Lorentzen Award, (S) 302
Kittredge Coddington Memorial Scholarship, (S) 303
Kitty Ernst Award, (A) 1349
Klausman Women in Business Scholarships. *See* Jane M.
    Klausman Women in Business Scholarships, entry (S) 267
Knapp Award. *See* National Association of Women Artists
    Annual Exhibition Awards, entry (A) 1382
Kornblutt Scholarship Fund. *See* Dr. Dorothy Weitzner
    Kornblutt Scholarship Fund, entry (S) 167
Kottis Family Scholarship. *See* Daughters of Penelope
    Undergraduate Scholarships, entry (S) 138
Kovalevsky High School Mathematics Days Grants. *See* Sonia
    Kovalevsky High School Mathematics Days Grants, entry (G)
    1247
KPMG Best Paper Award Gender Section, (A) 1350
KPMG Outstanding Dissertation Award Gender Section, (A)
    1351
KPMG Outstanding Published Manuscript Award Gender
    Section, (A) 1352
Kraft Education and College Scholarships. *See* Eve Kraft
    Education and College Scholarships, entry (S) 188
Kranig Scholarship. *See* Wisconsin Legion Auxiliary Merit and
    Memorial Scholarships, entry (S) 622
Krause Corporation Scholarships, (S) 304
Kreindler Memorial Award. *See* National Association of Women
    Artists Annual Exhibition Awards, entry (A) 1382
Kreitzberg Endowed Scholarship. *See* American Meteorological
    Society Undergraduate Scholarships, entry (S) 32
Krenzer Reentry Scholarship. *See* B.K. Krenzer Reentry
    Scholarship, entries (S) 86, (F) 712
Krutilla Research Stipend. *See* John V. Krutilla Research
    Stipend, entry (G) 1157

LA FRA Scholarship, (S) 305
Ladies Auxiliary of the Fleet Reserve Association Scholarship.
    *See* LA FRA Scholarship, entry (S) 305
Lambert Graduate Scholarships. *See* Kappa Alpha Theta
    Alumnae Scholarships, entry (F) 825
Lamm Award. *See* Dottie Lamm Award, entry (A) 1316
Lamme Memorial Scholarship. *See* Bertha Lamme Memorial
    Scholarship, entry (S) 77
Lane Mentor Research Fellowship. *See* Sylvia Lane Mentor
    Research Fellowship, entry (G) 1255
Lang Award. *See* Violet and Louis Lang Award, entry (A) 1418
Lang Pioneer Award. *See* Dorothea M. Lang Pioneer Award,
    entry (A) 1315
Las Vegas Network of Executive Women in Hospitality
    Scholarship Awards, (S) 306, (F) 831
LaSPACE Graduate Fellowships, (F) 832
LaSPACE Graduate Student Research Assistance Program, (G)
    1165
LaSPACE Minority Research Scholars Program, (S) 307
LaSPACE Research Enhancement Awards Program, (G) 1166
LaSPACE Research Initiation Grants Program, (G) 1167
LaSPACE Undergraduate Research Assistantships, (I) 1465
Latina Leadership Network Student Scholarships, (S) 308
Laurel Salton Clark Memorial Graduate Fellowship. *See* Dr.
    Laurel Salton Clark Memorial Graduate Fellowship, entry (F)
    753
Laurels Fund Scholarships, (F) 833
Lavonne Heghinian Scholarship, (S) 309
Lawrence Foster Violoncello Award. *See* NFMC Biennial
    Student Audition Awards, entry (A) 1384
Lawrence Livermore National Laboratory Undergraduate
    Summer Institutes in Applied Science, (I) 1466
Lederer Postdoctoral Fellowship. *See* Pembroke Center
    Postdoctoral Fellowships, entry (G) 1221
Legal Advocacy Fund Case Support. *See* AAUW Legal
    Advocacy Fund Support for Sex Discrimination Lawsuits,
    entry (G) 1033
Legal Internships at Legal Momentum, (I) 1467
LeGendre Fellowship for Advanced Graduate Study. *See*
    Grace LeGendre Fellowship for Advanced Graduate Study,
    entry (F) 791
Lela Murphy Scholarship, (S) 310
Lemieux Youth Scholarship. *See* Rachel E. Lemieux Youth
    Scholarship, entry (S) 496 497
Leo Goldberg Fellowships, (G) 1168
Leonard C. Horn Award for Legal Studies, (F) 834
Leonard R. Sugerman Scholarship, (G) 1169
Lerner–Scott Dissertation Prize, (A) 1353
LeRoy C. Merritt Humanitarian Fund Award, (G) 1170
Leroy Callendar Awards, (S) 311
Lesbian Visual Arts Awards, (A) 1354
Lesbian Writers Fund Awards, (A) 1355
Leslie Wickfield Scholarship, (S) 312
Lester F. Richardson Memorial Scholarship. *See* Phi Chi Theta
    Scholarships, entries (S) 481, (F) 904
Leta Andrews Scholarship, (S) 313
Letti P. Trefz Scholarship. *See* Delta Kappa Gamma
    Scholarship Program, entries (F) 743, (G) 1097
Levine Memorial Scholarship. *See* Rita Levine Memorial
    Scholarship, entries (S) 507, (F) 921
Lewis Career Education Scholarship. *See* Karen B. Lewis
    Career Education Scholarship, entry (S) 296

Lewis Grant. *See* Sigma Delta Epsilon Fellowships, entry (G) 1246

Lewis, Jr. Memorial Fund Scholarship. *See* First Lieutenant Michael L. Lewis, Jr. Memorial Fund Scholarship, entry (S) 194

Lewis Memorial Scholarship in Medical Health Sciences. *See* S. Evelyn Lewis Memorial Scholarship in Medical Health Sciences, entries (S) 521, (F) 930

Lewis Scholarships. *See* H.S. and Angeline Lewis Scholarships, entries (S) 246, (F) 804

Library of Congress Junior Fellows Program, (I) 1468

Lieber Memorial Award. *See* National Association of Women Artists Annual Exhibition Awards, entry (A) 1382

Lilla Jewel Award for Women Artists, (G) 1171

Lillian Halse–Hanf Scholarship. *See* Delaware BPW Foundation Scholarships, entry (S) 142

Lillian Moller Gilbreth Scholarship, (S) 314

Lillie Lois Ford Scholarships, (S) 315

Lilly Scholarship. *See* Pi Beta Phi Undergraduate Scholarships, entry (S) 486

Lily Research Grants. *See* Mary Lily Research Grants, entry (G) 1183

Lily Safra Internship Program, (I) 1469

Lincoln Community Foundation Medical Research Scholarship, (S) 316, (F) 835

Lincoln Ekstrom Fellowship. *See* Ruth and Lincoln Ekstrom Fellowship, entry (G) 1239

Lind Competition for Sopranos. *See* Barnum Festival Foundation/Jenny Lind Competition for Sopranos, entries (S) 71, (A) 1301

Linda J. Murphy Scholarships, (F) 836

Linda Jones Memorial Fine Arts Scholarship. *See* California P.E.O. Scholarships, entries (S) 107, (F) 718

Lindsey Memorial Scholarship. *See* Kappa Alpha Theta Founders' Memorial Scholarships, entry (S) 291

Lindy Callahan Scholar Athlete, (S) 317

Linly Heflin Scholarship, (S) 318

Lipman Research Award. *See* Geological Society of America Graduate Student Research Grants, entry (G) 1129

Lisa Marie Whalen Memorial Scholarship, (S) 319

Lisa Sechrist Memorial Foundation Scholarship, (S) 320

Lloyd Scholarship. *See* Constance L. Lloyd Scholarship, entries (S) 129, (F) 736

Lockheed Martin Aeronautics Company Scholarships, (S) 321

Lockheed Martin Foundation Scholarships, (S) 322

Loftis Scholarship for Acteens. *See* Jessica Powell Loftis Scholarship for Acteens, entry (S) 276

Lofton Scholarships. *See* Pi Beta Phi Undergraduate Scholarships, entry (S) 486

Lois and Marguerite Morse Scholarship. *See* Delta Kappa Gamma Scholarship Program, entries (F) 743, (G) 1097

Lois Shafer Scholarship, (F) 837

Long Award. *See* W. Newton Long Award, entry (G) 1265

Lonn Educational Fund Grants. *See* Florence Staiger Lonn Educational Fund Grants, entries (S) 199, (F) 776

L'Oréal USA for Women in Science Fellowship Program, (G) 1172

L'Oréal/Family Circle Cup "Personal Best" Scholarship, (S) 323

Loren W. Crow Memorial Scholarship, (S) 324

Lorentzen Award. *See* Kirsten R. Lorentzen Award, entry (S) 302

Lothrop–Ely Endowment. *See* Arizona BPW Foundation Annual Scholarships, entry (S) 51

Loudat Music Scholarship. *See* Kathy Loudat Music Scholarship, entry (S) 299

Louis Lang Award. *See* Violet and Louis Lang Award, entry (A) 1418

Louise L. Henderson Violoncello Award. *See* NFMC Biennial Student Audition Awards, entry (A) 1384

Louise Moritz Molitoris Leadership Award, (S) 325

Louise Oberne Strings Awards. *See* NFMC Biennial Student Audition Awards, entry (A) 1384

Louisiana Alpha Triple M Scholarship. *See* Pi Beta Phi Undergraduate Scholarships, entry (S) 486

Louisiana Space Consortium Graduate Fellowships. *See* LaSPACE Graduate Fellowships, entry (F) 832

Louisiana Space Consortium Graduate Student Research Assistance Program. *See* LaSPACE Graduate Student Research Assistance Program, entry (G) 1165

Louisiana Space Consortium Minority Research Scholars Program. *See* LaSPACE Minority Research Scholars Program, entry (S) 307

Louisiana Space Consortium Research Enhancement Awards Program. *See* LaSPACE Research Enhancement Awards Program, entry (G) 1166

Louisiana Space Consortium Research Initiation Grants Program. *See* LaSPACE Research Initiation Grants Program, entry (G) 1167

Louisiana Space Consortium Undergraduate Research Assistantships. *See* LaSPACE Undergraduate Research Assistantships, entry (I) 1465

Louisiana State Farm Scholarship Program, (S) 326

Louisiana Veterans State Aid Program, (S) 327

Loving Lesbians Award for Fiction. *See* Lesbian Writers Fund Awards, entry (A) 1355

Loving Lesbians Award for Poetry. *See* Lesbian Writers Fund Awards, entry (A) 1355

Lowther Scholarship. *See* Zeta State Scholarship, entry (F) 991

Luce Foundation/ACLS Dissertation Fellowship Program in American Art. *See* Henry Luce Foundation/ACLS Dissertation Fellowships in American Art, entry (G) 1141

Luce Foundation/ACLS Grants to Individuals from the United States and Canada in East Asian Archaeology and Early History. *See* Henry Luce Foundation/ACLS Grants to Individuals from the United States and Canada in East Asian Archaeology and Early History, entry (G) 1142

Luce Program Scholarship. *See* Clare Boothe Luce Program Scholarship, entry (F) 730

Lucile B. Kaufman Women's Scholarships, (S) 328

Lucille Heimrich Awards. *See* NFMC Biennial Student Audition Awards, entry (A) 1384

Lucille Malish Memorial Award. *See* Sigma Alpha Iota Graduate Performance Awards, entries (F) 938, (A) 1400

Luella Akins Key Graduate Scholarship. *See* Delta Delta Delta Unrestricted Graduate Scholarships, entry (F) 741

Luella Atkins Key Scholarship. *See* Delta Delta Delta Unrestricted Undergraduate Scholarships, entry (S) 149

Luise Meyer–Schutzmeister Award, (G) 1173

Lydia I. Pickup Memorial Scholarship, (S) 329, (F) 838

Lydiellen M. Hagan Memorial Scholarship. *See* Amelia Earhart Memorial Scholarships, entries (S) 29, (F) 684

Lynda Crowell Endowment. *See* Arizona BPW Foundation Annual Scholarships, entry (S) 51

Lynn Campbell Memorial Fund, (G) 1174

M. Amanda Gordon Scholarships. *See* Kappa Delta Sorority Undergraduate Scholarships, entry (S) 294

M. Carey Thomas Award, (A) 1356

M. Hildred Blewett Scholarship, (G) 1175

M. Josephine O'Neal Arts Award, (S) 330

M. Louise Carpenter Gloeckner, M.D. Summer Research Fellowship, (G) 1176

M. Margaret Stroh Scholarship. *See* Delta Kappa Gamma Scholarship Program, entries (F) 743, (G) 1097

M.A. Cartland Shackford Medical Fellowship, (F) 839

Mabel Biever Music Education Scholarship for Graduate Students, (F) 840

Macauley Scholarship. *See* Wisconsin Legion Auxiliary Merit and Memorial Scholarships, entry (S) 622

MacGregor Memorial Scholarship. *See* Irene and Daisy MacGregor Memorial Scholarship, entry (F) 811

Mackey Scholarship. *See* California P.E.O. Scholarships, entries (S) 107, (F) 718

Mackey–Althouse Voice Award. *See* NFMC Biennial Student Audition Awards, entry (A) 1384

Mackin Research Grants. *See* Geological Society of America Graduate Student Research Grants, entry (G) 1129

Maffett Fellowships. *See* Minnie L. Maffett Fellowships, entries (F) 863, (G) 1189

Mahr Memorial Scholarship. *See* New Mexico Elks Association Charitable and Benevolent Trust Scholarships, entry (S) 435

Maids of Athena Scholarships, (S) 331, (F) 841

Maine BPW Continuing Education Scholarship, (S) 332

Maine Media Women Scholarship, (S) 333, (F) 842

Maine Space Grant Consortium Scholarship and Fellowship Program, (G) 1177

Maine Space Grant Consortium Undergraduate and Graduate Research Fellowships. *See* MSGC Undergraduate and Graduate Research Fellowships, entry (G) 1195

Maine Veterans Dependents Educational Benefits, (S) 334, (F) 843

Making a Difference Award, (A) 1357

Making a Difference Scholarship, (S) 335

Malish Memorial Award. *See* Sigma Alpha Iota Graduate Performance Awards, entries (F) 938, (A) 1400

Malveaux Scholarship. *See* Dr. Julianne Malveaux Scholarship, entry (S) 168

Mamie Sue Bastian Scholarship. *See* Delta Kappa Gamma Scholarship Program, entries (F) 743, (G) 1097

Mara Crawford Personal Development Scholarship, (S) 336

Marcia Feinberg Award, (A) 1358

Marcia Hart Foster/D.C. Alpha Scholarship. *See* Pi Beta Phi Undergraduate Scholarships, entry (S) 486

Margaret Budd Haemer Scholarship. *See* Kappa Delta Sorority Undergraduate Scholarships, entry (S) 294

Margaret Edmundson Scholarship. *See* Basic Midwifery Scholarships, entries (S) 73, (F) 704

Margaret Fuller Awards Program, (G) 1178

Margaret L. Harvin Award. *See* Rachel Royston Permanent Scholarship, entry (F) 915

Margaret M. Prickett Scholarship Fund. *See* Society of Daughters of the United States Army Scholarships, entry (S) 542

Margaret Morse Nice Fund, (G) 1179

Margaret Oakley Dayhoff Award, (A) 1359

Margaret Stafford Memorial Scholarship. *See* Delta Delta Delta Unrestricted Graduate Scholarships, entry (F) 741

Margaret W. Rossiter History of Women in Science Prize, (A) 1360

Margo Harris Hammerschlag Grant, (G) 1180

Margo Liebes Harris Memorial Award. *See* National Association of Women Artists Annual Exhibition Awards, entry (A) 1382

Marguerite Morse Scholarship. *See* Delta Kappa Gamma Scholarship Program, entries (F) 743, (G) 1097

Maria Goeppert–Mayer Award, (A) 1361

Mariam E. Halpern Memorial Award. *See* National Association of Women Artists Annual Exhibition Awards, entry (A) 1382

Mariam K. Chamberlain Fellowships, (I) 1470

Marian J. Wettrick Charitable Foundation Medical Scholarships, (F) 844

Marian McKee Smith–Rosalie McKinney Jackson Scholarships, (S) 337

Mariani–Bigler Continuing Education Grant. *See* Mary Frances Guilbert Mariani–Bigler Continuing Education Grant, entry (S) 347

Marie E. Zakrzewski Medical Scholarship. *See* Dr. Marie E. Zakrzewski Medical Scholarship, entry (F) 754

Marie Morrisey Keith Awards. *See* NFMC Biennial Student Audition Awards, entry (A) 1384

Marilyn Mock Scholarship. *See* Kappa Delta Sorority Undergraduate Scholarships, entry (S) 294

Marilynn Smith Scholarship, (S) 338

Marilynne Graboys Wool Scholarship, (F) 845

Marine Corps Counterintelligence Association Scholarships, (S) 339

Marine Corps/Coast Guard Enlisted Dependent Spouse Scholarship. *See* Navy/Marine Corps/Coast Guard Enlisted Dependent Spouse Scholarship, entries (S) 417, (F) 874

Marion Barnick Memorial Scholarship. *See* Amelia Earhart Memorial Scholarships, entries (S) 29, (F) 684

Marion Day Mullins Scholarship, (S) 340

Marion de Sola Mendes Memorial Award. *See* National Association of Women Artists Annual Exhibition Awards, entry (A) 1382

Marjorie Jeanne Allen Scholarship. *See* Delta Kappa Gamma Scholarship Program, entries (F) 743, (G) 1097

Marjorie M. McDonald P.E.O. Scholarship. *See* California P.E.O. Scholarships, entries (S) 107, (F) 718

Mark J. Schroeder Endowed Scholarship in Meteorology, (S) 341

Marks Scholarship for Teacher Education. *See* Albert A. Marks Scholarship for Teacher Education, entries (S) 18, (F) 674

Marshall Graduate Scholarship. *See* Delta Delta Delta Unrestricted Graduate Scholarships, entry (F) 741

Marshall Scholarship. *See* Delta Delta Delta Unrestricted Undergraduate Scholarships, entry (S) 149

Marshall Scholarship. *See* Mary Barrett Marshall Scholarship, entry (S) 344

Marshall Student Loan Fund. *See* Mary Barrett Marshall Student Loan Fund, entry (L) 1012

Marshall–Martha Belle Scholarships. *See* Bernadine Johnson Marshall–Martha Belle Scholarships, entry (F) 706

Martha and Don Romeo Scholarships, (S) 342

Missouri Vietnam Veterans Survivor Grant Program, (S) 396

Missouri Women's Golf Education Association Scholarships, (S) 397

Miszkowicz Memorial Scholarship. *See* Susan Miszkowicz Memorial Scholarship, entry (S) 560

Mock Scholarship. *See* Kappa Delta Sorority Undergraduate Scholarships, entry (S) 294

Modine Manufacturing College–to–Work Program, (S) 398, (I) 1475

Moldovan Memorial Award. *See* Peppy Moldovan Memorial Award, entry (S) 479

Molitoris Leadership Award. *See* Louise Moritz Molitoris Leadership Award, entry (S) 325

Molly M. Canaday Memorial Award. *See* National Association of Women Artists Annual Exhibition Awards, entry (A) 1382

Mona and Anila Jain Scholarship. *See* Kailash, Mona, and Anila Jain Scholarship, entry (F) 823

Mondy Fellowship. *See* Nell I. Mondy Fellowship, entry (G) 1202

Montagne Fund Award. *See* Geological Society of America Graduate Student Research Grants, entry (G) 1129

Montana BPW Foundation Grants, (G) 1192

Montana Dependents of Prisoners of War Fee Waiver, (S) 399

Montana Space Grant Consortium Graduate Fellowships, (F) 866

Montana Space Grant Consortium Research Initiation Grants, (G) 1193

Montana Space Grant Consortium Undergraduate Scholarships, (S) 400

Montana State Women's Golf Association Scholarships, (S) 401

Montgomery Opera Awards. *See* Merle Montgomery Opera Awards, entry (A) 1365

Monticello College Foundation Fellowship for Women, (G) 1194

Moore Endowment Scholarship. *See* Norma L. Moore Endowment Scholarship, entry (S) 438

Morgan Research Award. *See* Agnes Fay Morgan Research Award, entry (A) 1283

Morgan Women's Fellowship. *See* Mary Morgan Women's Fellowship, entry (I) 1471

Morris Education Scholarship. *See* Agnes Morris Education Scholarship, entry (S) 9

Morris Memorial Award for Strings or Harp. *See* Sigma Alpha Iota Scholarships for Undergraduate Performance, entry (A) 1401

Morris Memorial Awards. *See* Sigma Alpha Iota Graduate Performance Awards, entries (F) 938, (A) 1400

Morris Scholarship. *See* Dorothy P. Morris Scholarship, entry (S) 165

Morse Scholarship. *See* Delta Kappa Gamma Scholarship Program, entries (F) 743, (G) 1097

Mosley Scholarships. *See* Dwight Mosley Scholarships, entry (S) 170

Motherwell Prize, (A) 1378

Mower Memorial Scholarship. *See* Barbara Alice Mower Memorial Scholarship, entries (S) 69, (F) 702

Ms. America, (A) 1379

MSCPA Women in Accounting Scholarship, (S) 402

MSGC Undergraduate and Graduate Research Fellowships, (G) 1195

Mueller Scholarships. *See* Elizabeth Banta Mueller Scholarships, entry (S) 176

Muir Award. *See* Irene S. Muir Award, entries (S) 262, (A) 1340

Muir Award. *See* NFMC Biennial Student Audition Awards, entry (A) 1384

Mullins Courageous Achievement Award. *See* Farm Bureau Insurance–VHSL Achievement Awards, entry (S) 191

Mullins Scholarship. *See* Marion Day Mullins Scholarship, entry (S) 340

Mullis Scholarship. *See* Pi Beta Phi Undergraduate Scholarships, entry (S) 486

Munger Memorial Scholarship. *See* Mary V. Munger Memorial Scholarship, entry (S) 352

MURF Fellowships Program, (I) 1476

Muriel Johnstone Scholarship. *See* Kappa Delta Sorority Graduate Scholarships, entry (F) 826

Muriel Johnstone Scholarships. *See* Kappa Delta Sorority Undergraduate Scholarships, entry (S) 294

Muriel Lothrop–Ely Endowment. *See* Arizona BPW Foundation Annual Scholarships, entry (S) 51

Murphy Endowed Memorial Scholarship. *See* Ethan and Allan Murphy Endowed Memorial Scholarship, entry (S) 185

Murphy Graduate Scholarship. *See* Mary Murphy Graduate Scholarship, entry (F) 851

Murphy Scholarship for Women in Ministry. *See* Bishop Frank Murphy Scholarship for Women in Ministry, entry (F) 711

Murphy Scholarship. *See* Lela Murphy Scholarship, entry (S) 310

Murphy Scholarships. *See* Linda J. Murphy Scholarships, entry (F) 836

Murray Scholarship. *See* Bernice Murray Scholarship, entry (S) 76

Murray Scholarships. *See* Gilda Murray Scholarships, entries (S) 218, (F) 785

Musemeche Scholarship Program, (S) 403

Music Business/Technology Scholarship. *See* Dorothy Cooke Whinery Music Business/Technology Scholarship, entry (S) 160

Music Education Scholarship for Graduate Students. *See* Mabel Biever Music Education Scholarship for Graduate Students, entry (F) 840

Music Scholarships for Mature Women, (F) 867, (A) 1380

Music Therapy Scholarship, (S) 404, (F) 868

Myra Biggerstaff Award. *See* National Association of Women Artists Annual Exhibition Awards, entry (A) 1382

Myrna F. Bernath Book Award, (A) 1381

Myrna F. Bernath Fellowship Award, (G) 1196

NAHB Women's Council Strategies for Success Scholarship, (S) 405

Nancy B. Woolridge McGee Graduate Fellowship, (F) 869

Nancy L. Buc Postdoctoral Fellowship. *See* Pembroke Center Postdoctoral Fellowships, entry (G) 1221

Nancy Reagan Pathfinder Scholarships, (S) 406, (F) 870

Nannie W. Norfleet Scholarship, (S) 407

Naomi Berber Memorial Scholarship, (S) 408

Naomi L. Satterfield Scholarship. *See* Phi Chi Theta Scholarships, entries (S) 481, (F) 904

NARAL Pro–Choice America Organizing Internship, (I) 1477

NARAL Pro–Choice Montana Legislative Internship, (I) 1478

NASA Academies, (I) 1479

NASA Faculty Fellowship Program, (G) 1197

Oklahoma Beta Scholarship. See Pi Beta Phi Undergraduate Scholarships, entry (S) 486

Oklahoma NASA Space Grant Consortium Fellowships, (F) 894

Oklahoma NASA Space Grant Consortium Scholarships, (S) 457

Okun–Model Early–Career Fellowship in Economic Studies, (G) 1216

Ola B. Hiller Scholarship. See Delta Kappa Gamma Scholarship Program, entries (F) 743, (G) 1097

Olga Christensen National Scholarship, (S) 458

Olin Medal. See Francis P. Garvan–John M. Olin Medal, entry (A) 1328

Olive Lynn Salembier Scholarship, (S) 459, (F) 895

Olive Whitman Memorial Scholarship, (S) 460

Oliver and Esther R. Howard Scholarship, (S) 461

Om and Saraswati (Sara) Bahethi Scholarship. See American Meteorological Society Undergraduate Scholarships, entry (S) 32

O'Neal Arts Award. See M. Josephine O'Neal Arts Award, entry (S) 330

Operating Engineers Local 3 Academic Scholarships, (S) 462

Opportunity Scholarships for Lutheran Laywomen, (S) 463, (F) 896

Optimist International Oratorical Contest, (S) 464, (A) 1386

Ora Keck Scholarship. See California P.E.O. Scholarships, entries (S) 107, (F) 718

Ora Schneider Art Writer Residency Grants, (G) 1217

Orange Prize for Fiction, (A) 1387

Order of the Amaranth in Pennsylvania Scholarship Program, (S) 465

Oregon Legion Auxiliary Department Nurses Scholarship, (S) 466

Oregon Legion Auxiliary Department Scholarships, (S) 467

Oregon Legion Auxiliary Department Spirit of Youth Scholarship, (S) 468

Oregon Space Grant Graduate Fellowship Program, (F) 897

Oregon Space Grant Undergraduate Scholarship Program, (S) 469

Oregon Veterans Home Loan Program, (L) 1019

Organic Chemistry Graduate Student Fellowships, (F) 898

Orman Memorial Scholarship. See Elizabeth Carmichael Orman Memorial Scholarship, entry (S) 177

Orman, '25, Fellowship. See Doris B. Orman, '25, Fellowship, entry (F) 747

Orndorff Career Performance Grant. See Verna Ross Orndorff Career Performance Grant, entries (F) 960, (G) 1261

Orville Endowed Scholarship in Meteorology. See American Meteorological Society Undergraduate Scholarships, entry (S) 32

Osage Chapter Scholarship, (G) 1218

Outstanding Woman Geologist Award, (A) 1388

Overly Memorial Graduate Scholarship. See Helene M. Overly Memorial Graduate Scholarship, entry (F) 796

Paige Scholarships. See General Emmett Paige Scholarships, entry (S) 210

Pallas Athene Award, (A) 1389

Palmer General Scholarship. See Judge Hazel Palmer General Scholarship, entry (S) 282

Palmer Memorial Award. See National Association of Women Artists Annual Exhibition Awards, entry (A) 1382

Pam Barton Staples Scholarship. See Kappa Delta Sorority Undergraduate Scholarships, entry (S) 294

Pandolfo Scholarship. See Dominique Lisa Pandolfo Scholarship, entry (S) 158

Paolozzi Member's Scholarship. See Mary Paolozzi Member's Scholarship, entries (S) 350, (F) 852

Parke D. Snaveley, Jr. Cascadia Research Fund Award. See Geological Society of America Graduate Student Research Grants, entry (G) 1129

Parker Memorial Scholarship. See Ivy M. Parker Memorial Scholarship, entry (S) 264

Parker Scholarship. See Delta Kappa Gamma Scholarship Program, entries (F) 743, (G) 1097

Parks Fellowships for Non–Violent Alternatives to Conflict. See Helen Cromer Cooper/Rosa Parks Fellowships for Non–Violent Alternatives to Conflict, entry (G) 1140

Paros–Digiquartz Scholarship. See American Meteorological Society Undergraduate Scholarships, entry (S) 32

Past District Governors/Julie P. Microutsicos Scholarship.. See Citrus District 2 Scholarships, entries (S) 120, (F) 729

Past Grand Presidents Memorial Graduate Fellowship. See Pi Beta Phi Graduate Fellowships, entry (F) 906

Patricia Barber Scholarship. See New Jersey Schoolwomen's Club Scholarships, entry (S) 432

Patricia Creed Scholarship, (S) 470

PatsyLu Music Fund, (G) 1219

Paula de Merieux Rheumatology Fellowship Award, (F) 899

Paula J. Alexander Memorial Scholarship. See Daughters of Penelope Undergraduate Scholarships, entry (S) 138

Payne Grant. See Jessie Fanyo Payne Grant, entries (S) 277, (F) 816

Peabody Memorial Award. See National Association of Women Artists Annual Exhibition Awards, entry (A) 1382

Pearl Behrend Scholarship. See Wisconsin Legion Auxiliary Merit and Memorial Scholarships, entry (S) 622

Pearl Prime Scholarship. See California P.E.O. Scholarships, entries (S) 107, (F) 718

Pearson Memorial Scholarships. See Brian Pearson Memorial Scholarships, entry (S) 97

Pediatric Renal Research Award, (G) 1220

Pedro Grau Undergraduate Scholarship. See American Meteorological Society Undergraduate Scholarships, entry (S) 32

Pedro Zamora Public Policy Fellowship, (I) 1487

Peggy Vatter Memorial Scholarships, (F) 900

Pembroke Center Postdoctoral Fellowships, (G) 1221

Penelope Hanshaw Scholarship, (S) 471, (F) 901

Pennington Scholarship. See Reed and Gloria Pennington Scholarship, entry (S) 502

Pennsylvania Business and Professional Women Scholarship, (S) 472

Pennsylvania Rainbow Nursing Scholarship, (S) 473

Pennsylvania Rainbow Scholarship, (S) 474

Pennsylvania Space Grant Consortium Fellowships, (F) 902

Pennsylvania Space Grant Consortium Scholarships, (S) 475

Pennsylvania State Council of Auxiliaries Grant, (S) 476

Pentagon Assistance Fund, (S) 477

P.E.O. Educational Loan Fund, (L) 1020

P.E.O. Program for Continuing Education, (S) 478

P.E.O. Scholar Awards, (F) 903

Peppy Moldovan Memorial Award, (S) 479

Pepsi USBC Youth Bowling Championships, (S) 480, (A) 1390

Perrin Scholarship. See Delta Delta Delta Unrestricted Undergraduate Scholarships, entry (S) 149

Perry, MD Resident Research Award. See Jacquelin Perry, MD Resident Research Award, entry (A) 1341

Peter B. Wagner Memorial Award for Women in Atmospheric Sciences, (A) 1391

Phelps Scholar–Athlete Program. See Richard J. Phelps Scholar–Athlete Program, entry (S) 506

Phi Chi Theta Scholarships, (S) 481, (F) 904

Phi Lambda–Kim Bates Memorial Fund. See Delta Phi Epsilon Scholarships, entries (S) 151, (F) 744

Phipps Memorial Scholarship, (S) 482, (F) 905

Phoenix Section Scholarship, (S) 483

Phy Scholarship. See Pi Beta Phi Undergraduate Scholarships, entry (S) 486

Phyllis J. Van Deventer Scholarship. See California P.E.O. Scholarships, entries (S) 107, (F) 718

Phyllis Sanders Scholarship, (S) 484

Pi Beta Phi Graduate Fellowships, (F) 906

Pi Beta Phi Holiday Scholarships, (S) 485

Pi Beta Phi Undergraduate Scholarships, (S) 486

Pi State Native American Grants–in–Aid, (S) 487, (F) 907

Pickup Memorial Scholarship. See Lydia I. Pickup Memorial Scholarship, entries (S) 329, (F) 838

Pierce Scholarship. See Delta Kappa Gamma Scholarship Program, entries (F) 743, (G) 1097

Pistilli Scholarships. See P.O. Pistilli Scholarships, entry (S) 488

P.O. Pistilli Scholarships, (S) 488

Polissino Memorial Scholarship. See William J. Polissino Memorial Scholarship, entry (S) 615

Pollack Scholarship. See Delta Phi Epsilon Scholarships, entries (S) 151, (F) 744

Polly Thompson Memorial Music Scholarship. See California P.E.O. Scholarships, entries (S) 107, (F) 718

Portland Women's Club Scholarship, (S) 489

Possible Woman Foundation International Scholarship, (S) 490, (F) 908

Postdoctoral Fellowships in Diabetes Research, (F) 909, (G) 1222

Postdoctoral Fellowships in Southeast European Studies, (G) 1223

Postdoctoral Research Fellowships in Epilepsy, (F) 910, (G) 1224

Postdoctoral Research Leave Fellowships, (G) 1225

Predoctoral Research Training Fellowships in Epilepsy, (G) 1226

Prelinger Award. See Catherine Prelinger Award, entry (G) 1083

Prentice Gautt Postgraduate Scholarships. See Dr. Prentice Gautt Postgraduate Scholarships, entry (F) 755

Presidential Early Career Awards for Scientists and Engineers, (G) 1227

Pressman Scholarship. See Ada I. Pressman Scholarship, entries (S) 2, (F) 663

Price Memorial Scholarship. See Nathalie A. Price Memorial Scholarship, entry (S) 410

Price Scholarships. See Judith McManus Price Scholarships, entries (S) 284, (F) 822

Prickett Scholarship Fund. See Society of Daughters of the United States Army Scholarships, entry (S) 542

Prime Scholarship. See California P.E.O. Scholarships, entries (S) 107, (F) 718

Priscilla Maxwell Endicott Scholarships, (S) 491

Procter & Gamble Scholarship, (F) 911

Professional Associates Program for Women and Minorities at Brookhaven National Laboratory, (I) 1488

Professional Golf Management Diversity Scholarship, (S) 492

Project Red Flag Academic Scholarship for Women with Bleeding Disorders, (S) 493, (F) 912

Pryor Award in Arkansas Women's History. See Susie Pryor Award in Arkansas Women's History, entry (A) 1408

Public Education and Outreach Internships at Legal Momentum, (I) 1489

Public Interest Internship Program, (I) 1490

Public Policy Internships at Legal Momentum, (I) 1491

Puget Sound Chapter Helene M. Overly Memorial Scholarship, (F) 913

Puget Sound Chapter Louise Moritz Molitoris Leadership Award for Undergraduates, (S) 494

Putnam Prize. See Elizabeth Lowell Putnam Prize, entry (A) 1320

Pyle Scholarship. See Schuyler S. Pyle Scholarship, entries (S) 525, (F) 933

Pyramid Award for Marketing and Public Relations, (S) 495, (F) 914

Quality of Life Awards. See Miss America Competition Awards, entries (S) 385, (A) 1367

Quick/Gamma Phi Beta Scholarship. See Elizabeth Ahlemeyer Quick/Gamma Phi Beta Scholarship, entry (S) 175

R. Robert & Sally D. Funderburg Research Scholar Award in Gastric Biology Related to Cancer, (G) 1228

Rachel E. Lemieux Youth Scholarship, (S) 496–497

Rachel Royston Permanent Scholarship, (F) 915

Rainer Fellowships. See John Rainer Fellowships, entry (F) 819

Ralph W. Shrader Diversity Scholarships, (F) 916

Ramage Scholarship. See Kappa Delta Sorority Undergraduate Scholarships, entry (S) 294

Rankin Award. See Jeannette Rankin Award, entry (S) 275

Read Scholarship. See Pi Beta Phi Undergraduate Scholarships, entry (S) 486

Reagan Pathfinder Scholarship. See Nancy Reagan Pathfinder Scholarships, entries (S) 406, (F) 870

Ream's Food Stores Scholarships, (S) 498

Rechel Award. See Amy Lutz Rechel Award, entry (G) 1055

Recognition Award for Emerging Scholars, (A) 1392

Recognition Scholarships, (S) 499

Red River Valley Fighter Pilots Association Scholarship Grant Program, (S) 500, (F) 917

Red Speigle Award. See Virginia Golf Foundation Scholarship Program, entry (S) 597

Redd Student Award in Women's History. See Annaley Naegle Redd Student Award in Women's History, entry (G) 1058

Redi–Tag Corporation Scholarship, (S) 501, (F) 918

Reed and Gloria Pennington Scholarship, (S) 502

Roy J. Shlemon Scholarship Awards. *See* Geological Society of America Graduate Student Research Grants, entry (G) 1129

Royston Permanent Scholarship. *See* Rachel Royston Permanent Scholarship, entry (F) 915

Rubin Scholarship Fund. *See* Mary Rubin and Benjamin M. Rubin Scholarship Fund, entry (S) 351

Ruby Simmonds Vought Organ Award. *See* NFMC Biennial Student Audition Awards, entry (A) 1384

Ruby W. Henry Scholarship. *See* California P.E.O. Scholarships, entries (S) 107, (F) 718

Rudloff Scholarship Program. *See* Vanessa Rudloff Scholarship Program, entry (S) 590

Ruggiero Scholarship. *See* Cheryl A. Ruggiero Scholarship, entry (S) 115

Ruhnke Memorial Flight Instructor Scholarship. *See* Amelia Earhart Memorial Scholarships, entries (S) 29, (F) 684

Rural Mutual Insurance Company Scholarships, (S) 517

Russell Award. *See* Diane H. Russell Award, entry (G) 1100

Ruth and Lincoln Ekstrom Fellowship, (G) 1239

Ruth Barrett Smith Scholarship. *See* Pi Beta Phi Undergraduate Scholarships, entry (S) 486

Ruth Billow Memorial Education Fund, (S) 518, (F) 925

Ruth Chance Law Fellowship, (I) 1493

Ruth E. Black Scholarship Fund, (S) 519

Ruth G. White P.E.O. Scholarship, (F) 926

Ruth H. Bufton Scholarship, (F) 927

Ruth I. Michler Memorial Prize, (G) 1240, (A) 1395

Ruth Lyttle Satter Prize in Mathematics, (A) 1396

Ruth M. Johnson Scholarship, (F) 928

Ruth Mu–Lan Chu and James S.C. Chao Scholarship, (S) 520

Ruth R. and Alyson R. Miller Fellowships, (G) 1241

Ruth Rosenbaum Goldfeder Memorial Scholarship. *See* Alpha Epsilon Phi Foundation Scholarships, entries (S) 21, (F) 677

Ruth Satter Memorial Award, (F) 929, (G) 1242

Ruth Trinkle Read Scholarship. *See* Pi Beta Phi Undergraduate Scholarships, entry (S) 486

Ryskamp Research Fellowships. *See* Charles A. Ryskamp Research Fellowships, entry (G) 1084

S. Evelyn Lewis Memorial Scholarship in Medical Health Sciences, (S) 521, (F) 930

S. Magnet Knapp Award. *See* National Association of Women Artists Annual Exhibition Awards, entry (A) 1382

Safra Internship Program. *See* Lily Safra Internship Program, entry (I) 1469

Salembier Scholarship. *See* Olive Lynn Salembier Scholarship, entries (S) 459, (F) 895

Sally D. Funderburg Research Scholar Award in Gastric Biology Related to Cancer. *See* R. Robert & Sally D. Funderburg Research Scholar Award in Gastric Biology Related to Cancer, entry (G) 1228

Sally Tompkins Nursing and Applied Health Sciences Scholarship, (S) 522

Salter Scholarship. *See* Delta Kappa Gamma Scholarship Program, entries (F) 743, (G) 1097

San Francisco Bay Area Alumnae Scholarship. *See* Delta Phi Epsilon Scholarships, entries (S) 151, (F) 744

Sanders Scholarship. *See* Phyllis Sanders Scholarship, entry (S) 484

Sanofi–Aventis Women Physician in Allergy Grant Awards, (A) 1397

Sanofi–Aventis Women Physician in Allergy Junior Faculty Development Award, (G) 1243

Sara Winston Memorial Award. *See* National Association of Women Artists Annual Exhibition Awards, entry (A) 1382

Sarah Bradley Tyson Memorial Fellowship for Advanced Study in Agriculture or Horticulture, (F) 931

Sarah E. Huneycutt Scholarship, (S) 523

Sarah Ruth Mullis Scholarship. *See* Pi Beta Phi Undergraduate Scholarships, entry (S) 486

Sarah Shinn Marshall Graduate Scholarship. *See* Delta Delta Delta Unrestricted Graduate Scholarships, entry (F) 741

Sarah Shinn Marshall Scholarship. *See* Delta Delta Delta Unrestricted Undergraduate Scholarships, entry (S) 149

Saraswati (Sara) Bahethi Scholarship. *See* American Meteorological Society Undergraduate Scholarships, entry (S) 32

Satter Memorial Award. *See* Ruth Satter Memorial Award, entries (F) 929, (G) 1242

Satterfield Scholarship. *See* Phi Chi Theta Scholarships, entries (S) 481, (F) 904

SBE Doctoral Dissertation Research Improvement Grants, (G) 1244

Schafer Mathematics Prize. *See* Alice T. Schafer Mathematics Prize, entry (A) 1288

Schimke Scholarship. *See* Mary McEwen Schimke Scholarship, entry (F) 850

Schipper Memorial Award. *See* Hanscom Officers' Spouses' Club Scholarships, entry (S) 233

Schneider Art Writer Residency Grants. *See* Ora Schneider Art Writer Residency Grants, entry (G) 1217

Schoelzel Memorial Scholarship. *See* Dorothy E. Schoelzel Memorial Scholarship, entries (S) 161, (F) 749

Scholarship in Statistics. *See* Gertrude M. Cox Scholarship in Statistics, entry (F) 784

Scholarships for Women Residents of the State of Delaware, (S) 524, (F) 932

Schroeder Endowed Scholarship in Meteorology. *See* Mark J. Schroeder Endowed Scholarship in Meteorology, entry (S) 341

Schuck Award. *See* Victoria Schuck Award, entry (A) 1417

Schutze Memorial Scholarship. *See* Katherine J. Schutze Memorial Scholarship, entry (F) 829

Schuyler S. Pyle Scholarship, (S) 525, (F) 933

Science and Engineering Apprentice Program, (I) 1494

Science and Technology Group Fellowships, (F) 934

Scott Corey Scholarship. *See* Hanscom Officers' Spouses' Club Scholarships, entry (S) 233

Scott Prize. *See* Lerner–Scott Dissertation Prize, entry (A) 1353

Scotts Company Scholars Program, (S) 526, (I) 1495

Scripps Fellowships in Environmental Journalism. *See* Ted Scripps Fellowships in Environmental Journalism, entries (F) 951, (G) 1257

Seattle Chapter ASWA Scholarships, (S) 527, (F) 935

Sechrist Memorial Foundation Scholarship. *See* Lisa Sechrist Memorial Foundation Scholarship, entry (S) 320

Second Century Graduate Scholarship. *See* Delta Delta Delta Unrestricted Graduate Scholarships, entry (F) 741

Second Wind Scholarship Program, (S) 528

Sehar Saleha Ahmad and Abrahim Ekramullah Zafar Foundation Scholarship, (S) 529

Selma Moidel Smith Law Student Writing Competition, (A) 1398

Semiconductor Research Corporation Master's Scholarship Program, (F) 936

Shackford Medical Fellowship. See M.A. Cartland Shackford Medical Fellowship, entry (F) 839

Shafer Scholarship. See Lois Shafer Scholarship, entry (F) 837

Shainess Memorial Award. See National Association of Women Artists Annual Exhibition Awards, entry (A) 1382

Sharon D. Banks Memorial Undergraduate Scholarship, (S) 530

Sharon D. Banks/Puget Sound Chapter Memorial Undergraduate Scholarship, (S) 531

Sharon Keillor Award for Women in Engineering Education, (A) 1399

Shaw Memorial Scholarship. See Kappa Alpha Theta Founders' Memorial Scholarships, entry (S) 291

Shawn Margaret Donnelley Scholarship, (S) 532, (F) 937

Shinn Distinguished Member of the Year Awards. See Mike Shinn Distinguished Member of the Year Awards, entries (S) 370, (F) 857

Shirk Memorial Award. See National Association of Women Artists Annual Exhibition Awards, entry (A) 1382

Shlemon Scholarship Awards. See Geological Society of America Graduate Student Research Grants, entry (G) 1129

Shonnette Meyer Kahn Scholarship. See Alpha Epsilon Phi Foundation Scholarships, entries (S) 21, (F) 677

Shore Scholarship. See Dinah Shore Scholarship, entry (S) 156

Shorr Memorial Award. See National Association of Women Artists Annual Exhibition Awards, entry (A) 1382

Shoup Scholarship. See Delta Kappa Gamma Scholarship Program, entries (F) 743, (G) 1097

SHPE/SWE Members Scholarship. See NSBE/SHPE/SWE Members Scholarship, entries (S) 448, (I) 1486

Shrader Diversity Scholarships. See Ralph W. Shrader Diversity Scholarships, entry (F) 916

Sibley Fellowship for French Studies. See Mary Isabel Sibley Fellowship for French Studies, entry (G) 1181

Sibley Fellowship for Greek Studies. See Mary Isabel Sibley Fellowship for Greek Studies, entry (G) 1182

Siemens Corporation Scholarships, (S) 533

Sigma Alpha Iota Doctoral Study Grant, (G) 1245

Sigma Alpha Iota Founders Loan Fund, (L) 1021

Sigma Alpha Iota Graduate Performance Awards, (F) 938, (A) 1400

Sigma Alpha Iota Regional Summer Music Scholarships, (S) 534, (F) 939

Sigma Alpha Iota Scholarships for Undergraduate Performance, (A) 1401

Sigma Alpha Iota Special Needs Scholarship, (S) 535, (F) 940

Sigma Alpha Iota Undergraduate Scholarships, (S) 536

Sigma Alpha Iota/Kennedy Center Internship, (I) 1496

Sigma Delta Epsilon Fellowships, (G) 1246

Sign of the Arrow Melissa Scholarship, (S) 537

Silver Award. See National Association of Women Artists Annual Exhibition Awards, entry (A) 1382

Simpson Scholarship Fund. See Society of Daughters of the United States Army Scholarships, entry (S) 542

Sisson Award. See Geological Society of America Graduate Student Research Grants, entry (G) 1129

Sister Elizabeth Candon Scholarship, (S) 538

Sister Thomas More Bertels Scholarship, (S) 539

Slovenian Women's Union of America Continuing Education Awards, (S) 540

Slovenian Women's Union of America Scholarships, (S) 541

Smiley Scholarship. See Robert Smiley Scholarship, entry (S) 509

Smith Internships. See Chesterfield Smith Internships, entry (I) 1446

Smith Law Student Writing Competition. See Selma Moidel Smith Law Student Writing Competition, entry (A) 1398

Smith Scholarship Program. See Walter Reed Smith Scholarship Program, entry (S) 605

Smith Scholarship. See Marilynn Smith Scholarship, entry (S) 486

Smith Scholarship. See Pi Beta Phi Undergraduate Scholarships, entry (S) 338

Smith Scholarship. See Wisconsin Legion Auxiliary Merit and Memorial Scholarships, entry (S) 622

Smith–K4LMB Memorial Scholarship. See Young Ladies' Radio League Scholarship, entries (S) 653, (F) 988

Smith–Rosalie McKinney Jackson Scholarships. See Marian McKee Smith–Rosalie McKinney Jackson Scholarships, entry (S) 337

Snaveley, Jr. Cascadia Research Fund Award. See Geological Society of America Graduate Student Research Grants, entry (G) 1129

Snow Memorial Scholarship. See Phi Chi Theta Scholarships, entries (S) 481, (F) 904

So to Speak Annual Poetry and Fiction Contests, (A) 1402

Social, Behavioral, and Economic Sciences Doctoral Dissertation Research Improvement Grants. See SBE Doctoral Dissertation Research Improvement Grants, entry (G) 1244

Social Science Research Council/NEH International and Area Studies Fellowships. See ACLS/SSRC/NEH International and Area Studies Fellowships, entry (G) 1038

Society of Daughters of the United States Army Scholarships, (S) 542

Society of Hispanic Professional Engineers/SWE Members Scholarship. See NSBE/SHPE/SWE Members Scholarship, entries (S) 448, (I) 1486

Society of Women Engineers Members Scholarship. See NSBE/SHPE/SWE Members Scholarship, entries (S) 448, (I) 1486

Society of Women Engineers New Jersey Scholarship. See New Jersey Scholarship, entry (S) 431

Society of Women Engineers Past Presidents Scholarships. See SWE Past Presidents Scholarships, entries (S) 562, (F) 949

Society of Women Engineers Phoenix Section Scholarship. See Phoenix Section Scholarship, entry (S) 483

Sociologists for Women in Society Feminist Lecturership Award. See SWS Feminist Lecturership Award, entry (G) 1254

Solveig Stromsoe Palmer Memorial Award. See National Association of Women Artists Annual Exhibition Awards, entry (A) 1382

Sonenfeld Scholarship. See Alexandra Apostolides Sonenfeld Scholarship, entry (S) 20

Sonia Kovalevsky High School Mathematics Days Grants, (G) 1247

Sonja Stefanadis Graduate Student Fellowship, (F) 941

Sorensen National Scholarship. *See* Mildred Sorensen National Scholarship, entry (S) 373

South Carolina Legion Auxiliary Gift Scholarships, (S) 543

South Carolina Space Grant Consortium Curriculum Development Awards, (G) 1248

South Carolina Space Grant Consortium Graduate Student Research Program Fellowships, (F) 942

South Carolina Space Grant Consortium Pre–Service Teacher Scholarships, (S) 544, (F) 943

South Carolina Space Grant Consortium Research Facilitation/Initiation Awards, (G) 1249

South Carolina Space Grant Consortium Research Grants, (G) 1250

South Carolina Space Grant Consortium Travel Awards, (G) 1251

South Carolina Space Grant Consortium Undergraduate Research Program, (G) 1252

South Dakota Emergency Loan Fund for Veterans and Their Dependents, (L) 1022

South Dakota Free Tuition for Dependents of Prisoners or Missing in Action, (S) 545

South Dakota Space Grant Consortium Graduate Fellowships and Undergraduate Scholarships, (S) 546, (F) 944, (I) 1497

South Florida Network of Executive Women in Hospitality Scholarship Awards, (S) 547

Southall Scholarship. *See* Delta Kappa Gamma Scholarship Program, entries (F) 743, (G) 1097

Southeast European Language Grants to Individuals for Summer Study, (F) 945

Southeastern Panhellenic Conference Scholarship. *See* NPC Foundation Regional Scholarships, entry (S) 447

Southern California Chapter Scholarship, (S) 548, (F) 946

Southern California Council Internship Program, (I) 1498

Southern Counties Network of Executive Women in Hospitality Scholarship Awards, (S) 549

Speaking Out for Justice Award, (A) 1403

Special Fund for the Study of Women and Politics, (G) 1253

Speigle Award. *See* Virginia Golf Foundation Scholarship Program, entry (S) 597

Spencer–Wilkinson Award. *See* Virginia Golf Foundation Scholarship Program, entry (S) 597

Spirit of Youth Scholarship for Junior Members, (S) 550

Spofford, Jr. Memorial Internship. *See* Walter O. Spofford, Jr. Memorial Internship, entry (I) 1504

SportQuest All–American Scholarships for Females, (S) 551

Sportsmanship Recognition Program Scholarship, (S) 552

Spruill Publication Prize in Southern Women's History. *See* Julia Cherry Spruill Publication Prize in Southern Women's History, entry (A) 1347

SSRC/NEH International and Area Studies Fellowships. *See* ACLS/SSRC/NEH International and Area Studies Fellowships, entry (G) 1038

Stafford Memorial Scholarship. *See* Delta Delta Delta Unrestricted Graduate Scholarships, entry (F) 741

Staples Scholarship. *See* Kappa Delta Sorority Undergraduate Scholarships, entry (S) 294

Starring Memorial Award for Piano. *See* Sigma Alpha Iota Scholarships for Undergraduate Performance, entry (A) 1401

Starring Memorial Award for Woodwinds or Brass. *See* Sigma Alpha Iota Scholarships for Undergraduate Performance, entry (A) 1401

Starring Memorial Awards. *See* Sigma Alpha Iota Graduate Performance Awards, entries (F) 938, (A) 1400

State Bar of California Committee on Women in the Law Essay Contest, (A) 1404

State Community Service Scholarships, (S) 553, (A) 1405

Stearns Fellowship Award. *See* Geological Society of America Graduate Student Research Grants, entry (G) 1129

Stefanadis Graduate Student Fellowship. *See* Sonja Stefanadis Graduate Student Fellowship, entry (F) 941

Stein Memorial Space Grant Scholarship. *See* Pennsylvania Space Grant Consortium Scholarships, entry (S) 475

Stella May Nau Scholarship. *See* California P.E.O. Scholarships, entries (S) 107, (F) 718

Stelly Sterling Memorial Award. *See* National Association of Women Artists Annual Exhibition Awards, entry (A) 1382

Stephen Bufton Memorial Education Fund Grants, (S) 554, (F) 947

Sterling Memorial Award. *See* National Association of Women Artists Annual Exhibition Awards, entry (A) 1382

Stickland Scholarship. *See* Martha Stickland Scholarship, entry (S) 343

Stone Hodo Scholarship. *See* Women's Alabama Golf Association Scholarships, entry (S) 638

Stoner Law Scholarship Award. *See* Charles T. Stoner Law Scholarship Award, entry (F) 725

Stradley Scholarship. *See* Jean Tucker Stradley Scholarship, entry (S) 274

Strategies for Success Scholarship. *See* NAHB Women's Council Strategies for Success Scholarship, entry (S) 405

Stratton/Tipton Scholarship for Adult Returning Students, (S) 555

Stratton/Tipton Scholarship for High School Seniors, (S) 556

Stroh Scholarship. *See* Delta Kappa Gamma Scholarship Program, entries (F) 743, (G) 1097

Subaru Outstanding Woman in Science Award, (A) 1406

Sue Ring–Jarvi Girls'/Women's Hockey Scholarship. *See* Jane Ring/Sue Ring–Jarvi Girls'/Women's Hockey Scholarship, entry (S) 268

Sue Saniel Elkind Poetry Contest, (A) 1407

Sugerman Scholarship. *See* Leonard R. Sugerman Scholarship, entry (G) 1169

Summer Transportation Internship Program for Diverse Groups, (I) 1499

Sunshine Chapter Network of Executive Women in Hospitality Scholarship Awards, (S) 557

Survivors' and Dependents' Educational Assistance Program, (S) 558, (F) 948

Susan B. Anthony Award for Excellence in Research on Older Women and Public Health.. *See* Aetna Susan B. Anthony Award for Excellence in Research on Older Women and Public Health., entry (A) 1282

Susan E. Shepherd Memorial Scholarship. *See* Missouri Women's Golf Education Association Scholarships, entry (S) 397

Susan Ekdale Memorial Scholarship, (S) 559

Susan Kahn Award. *See* National Association of Women Artists Annual Exhibition Awards, entry (A) 1382

Susan Miszkowicz Memorial Scholarship, (S) 560

Susie Holmes Memorial Scholarship, (S) 561

Susie Pryor Award in Arkansas Women's History, (A) 1408

SWE Members Scholarship. *See* NSBE/SHPE/SWE Members Scholarship, entries (S) 448, (I) 1486

---

S–Scholarships    F–Fellowships    L–Loans    G–Grants    A–Awards    I–Internships

SWE Past Presidents Scholarships, (S) 562, (F) 949

SWE/ADC Communications and Foundation Scholarship, (S) 563

Sweet 16 Magazine Scholarship Contest, (S) 564, (A) 1409

SWS Feminist Lecturership Award, (G) 1254

Sylvia Forman Prize Competition, (A) 1410

Sylvia Lane Mentor Research Fellowship, (G) 1255

Sylvia Stein Memorial Space Grant Scholarship. *See* Pennsylvania Space Grant Consortium Scholarships, entry (S) 475

Synod Women's Advocacy Network Theological Education Scholarship, (F) 950

Tabak Memorial Award. *See* National Association of Women Artists Annual Exhibition Awards, entry (A) 1382

Talbots Women's Scholarship Fund, (S) 565

TAP Endowed Research Scholar Award in Acid–Related Diseases, (G) 1256

Taylor Memorial Scholarship. *See* Mildred Richards Taylor Memorial Scholarship, entry (F) 859

Teacher Education Scholarship Program of the Alabama Space Grant Consortium, (S) 566

Ted Scripps Fellowships in Environmental Journalism, (F) 951, (G) 1257

Teen Latina World, (S) 567, (A) 1411

TESA Scholarship Program, (S) 568

Texas Elks State Association Scholarship Program. *See* TESA Scholarship Program, entry (S) 568

Texas Rural Electric Women's Association Scholarship. *See* TREWA Scholarships, entry (S) 577

Texas Space Grant Consortium Graduate Fellowships, (F) 952

Texas Space Grant Consortium K–12 Education Programs, (G) 1258

Texas Space Grant Consortium Undergraduate Scholarships. *See* Columbia Crew Memorial Undergraduate Scholarships, entries (S) 126, (F) 732

Texas State Fire Fighters College Scholarship Fund, (S) 569

Texas Veterans Home Improvement Program, (L) 1023

Texas Veterans Housing Assistance Program, (L) 1024

Texas Veterans Land Program, (L) 1025

Texas Waivers of Nonresident Tuition for Military Personnel and Their Dependents, (S) 570, (F) 953

Texas Waivers of Nonresident Tuition for Military Survivors, (S) 571

Texas Waivers of Nonresident Tuition for Veterans and Their Dependents, (S) 572

Texas Young Lawyers Association Minority Scholarship Program, (F) 954

Thaddeus Colson and Isabelle Saalwaechter Fitzpatrick Memorial Scholarship, (S) 573

Theodore and Mary Jane Rich Memorial Scholarships, (S) 574, (F) 955

Theresa Brown Scholarships. *See* Miss America Competition Awards, entries (S) 385, (A) 1367

Thomas Award. *See* M. Carey Thomas Award, entry (A) 1356

Thomas More Bertels Scholarship. *See* Sister Thomas More Bertels Scholarship, entry (S) 539

Thompson Memorial Music Scholarship. *See* California P.E.O. Scholarships, entries (S) 107, (F) 718

Thompson Memorial Scholarship. *See* California P.E.O. Scholarships, entries (S) 107, (F) 718

Thompson Scholarship for Women in Safety, (F) 956

Thoms Memorial Scholarships. *See* Meridith Thoms Memorial Scholarships, entry (S) 360

Thor Johnson Strings Awards. *See* NFMC Biennial Student Audition Awards, entry (A) 1384

Thornberg Undergraduate Scholarship. *See* Geneva Thornberg Undergraduate Scholarship, entry (S) 213

Tietjen Scholarship. *See* Jill S. Tietjen Scholarship, entries (S) 278, (F) 817

Tobolowsky Scholarship. *See* Hermine Dalkowitz Tobolowsky Scholarship, entries (S) 239, (F) 797

Tompkins Nursing and Applied Health Sciences Scholarship. *See* Sally Tompkins Nursing and Applied Health Sciences Scholarship, entry (S) 522

Trampoline and Tumbling Scholarship Program, (S) 575

Transportation Fellowship Program, (S) 576, (F) 957, (I) 1500

Travers Loan Program. *See* Vice Admiral E.P. Travers Loan Program, entry (L) 1027

Travers Scholarship. *See* Vice Admiral E.P. Travers Scholarship, entry (S) 593

Trefz Scholarship. *See* Delta Kappa Gamma Scholarship Program, entries (F) 743, (G) 1097

TREWA Scholarships, (S) 577

Trott Strings Award. *See* NFMC Biennial Student Audition Awards, entry (A) 1384

Troyansky Fellowship. *See* Organic Chemistry Graduate Student Fellowships, entry (F) 898

Tucker Centennial Scholarship. *See* Karen Tucker Centennial Scholarship, entries (S) 297, (F) 828

Tulsa Area Council Endowment Scholarship, (S) 578

TUMS Calcium for Life Scholarship. *See* Basic Midwifery Scholarships, entries (S) 73, (F) 704

Tuohey Memorial Scholarship. *See* Glorine Tuohey Memorial Scholarship, entry (F) 789

Tweet Coleman Aviation Scholarship, (S) 579

Twining Humber Award for Lifetime Artistic Achievement, (A) 1412

Tyson Memorial Fellowship for Advanced Study in Agriculture or Horticulture. *See* Sarah Bradley Tyson Memorial Fellowship for Advanced Study in Agriculture or Horticulture, entry (F) 931

Ullyot Fellows. *See* ASPET Individual Summer Undergraduate Research Fellowships, entries (G) 1068, (I) 1437

Undergraduate Award for Excellence in Chemistry, (A) 1413

Undergraduate Scholarship Program of the Alabama Space Grant Consortium, (S) 580

Union Summer Internships, (I) 1501

United Parcel Service Scholarship for Female Students, (S) 581

United States Bowling Congress Junior Gold Championships. *See* USBC Junior Gold Championships, entries (S) 582, (A) 1414

United States Bowling Congress Youth Leaders of the Year Awards. *See* USBC Youth Leaders of the Year Awards, entries (S) 583, (A) 1415

United States Department of State Student Intern Program. *See* Department of State Student Intern Program, entry (I) 1454

University of California President's Postdoctoral Fellowship Program, (G) 1259

University Scholar–in–Residence Award, (G) 1260

Upchurch Scholarship. *See* Women's Alabama Golf Association Scholarships, entry (S) 638

Urban Fellowship Program, (F) 958, (I) 1502

U.S. Department of State Student Intern Program. *See* Department of State Student Intern Program, entry (I) 1454

USBC Junior Gold Championships, (S) 582, (A) 1414

USBC Youth Leaders of the Year Awards, (S) 583, (A) 1415

USO Desert Storm Education Fund, (S) 584

USS Lake Champlain (CG–57) Scholarship Fund, (S) 585

USS Stark Memorial Scholarship Fund, (S) 586

Utah Affiliate AWSCPA Scholarship, (S) 587

Utah Elks Association Scholarship Program, (S) 588


VA Home Loan Guaranty Benefits, (L) 1026

VADM Robert L. Walters Scholarship, (S) 589, (F) 959

Van Deuren Memorial Scholarships. *See* Della Van Deuren Memorial Scholarships, entry (S) 145

Van Deventer Scholarship. *See* California P.E.O. Scholarships, entries (S) 107, (F) 718

Vanessa Rudloff Scholarship Program, (S) 590

Vatter Memorial Scholarships. *See* Peggy Vatter Memorial Scholarships, entry (F) 900

Verges Scholarship. *See* Daughters of Penelope Undergraduate Scholarships, entry (S) 138

Vermont Armed Services Scholarships, (S) 591

Vermont Space Grant Undergraduate Scholarships, (S) 592

Verna Ross Orndorff Career Performance Grant, (F) 960, (G) 1261

Vessa Notchev Fellowships, (G) 1262

Vice Admiral E.P. Travers Loan Program, (L) 1027

Vice Admiral E.P. Travers Scholarship, (S) 593

Victoria Fisher Memorial Prize Essay, (A) 1416

Victoria Schuck Award, (A) 1417

VII Corps Desert Storm Veterans Association Scholarship, (S) 594

Violet and Louis Lang Award, (A) 1418

Violet Diller Professional Excellence Award, (A) 1419

Virginia A. Pomeroy Scholarships, (F) 961

Virginia Army/Air National Guard Enlisted Association Scholarship, (S) 595

Virginia D. Henry Scholarship, (S) 596

Virginia Golf Foundation Scholarship Program, (S) 597

Virginia Network of Executive Women in Hospitality Scholarship Awards, (S) 598

Virginia Nurse Practitioner/Nurse Midwife Scholarship Program, (L) 1028

Virginia Peace Mackey–Althouse Voice Award. *See* NFMC Biennial Student Audition Awards, entry (A) 1384

Virginia S. Richardson Memorial Scholarship. *See* Amelia Earhart Memorial Scholarships, entries (S) 29, (F) 684

Virginia Space Grant Aerospace Graduate Research Fellowships, (G) 1263

Virginia Space Grant Aerospace Undergraduate Research Scholarships, (G) 1264

Virginia Space Grant Community College Scholarship Program, (S) 599

Virginia Space Grant Teacher Education Scholarship Program, (S) 600, (F) 962

Vito Marzullo Internship Program, (I) 1503

Vocational and Technical Training Student Loan Program, (L) 1029

Vought Organ Award. *See* NFMC Biennial Student Audition Awards, entry (A) 1384


W. Newton Long Award, (G) 1265

Wachovia Citizenship Awards, (S) 601

Wagner Memorial Award for Women in Atmospheric Sciences. *See* Peter B. Wagner Memorial Award for Women in Atmospheric Sciences, entry (A) 1391

Wagner Memorial Fund. *See* Society of Daughters of the United States Army Scholarships, entry (S) 542

Waivers of Nonresident Tuition for Dependents of Military Personnel Moving to Texas, (S) 602

Waivers of Nonresident Tuition for Dependents of Military Personnel Who Previously Lived in Texas, (S) 603

Waldo and Alice Ayer Music Scholarship, (S) 604

Walker Memorial Award. *See* National Association of Women Artists Annual Exhibition Awards, entry (A) 1382

Walter Byers Postgraduate Scholarship Program, (F) 963

Walter O. Spofford, Jr. Memorial Internship, (I) 1504

Walter Reed Smith Scholarship Program, (S) 605

Walter Scholarship Program. *See* Norma Ross Walter Scholarship Program, entry (S) 439

Walters Scholarship. *See* VADM Robert L. Walters Scholarship, entries (S) 589, (F) 959

Wanek Fund Award. *See* Geological Society of America Graduate Student Research Grants, entry (G) 1129

Ware Scholarship. *See* Elizabeth Ware Scholarship, entry (S) 180

Warmack Scholarship. *See* Pi Beta Phi Undergraduate Scholarships, entry (S) 486

Warren Scholarship. *See* Pi Beta Phi Undergraduate Scholarships, entry (S) 486

Warter College Scholarship. *See* Mike Warter College Scholarship, entry (S) 371

Washington Business and Professional Women's Foundation Educational Scholarship, (S) 606, (F) 964

Washington DC Area Chapter Scholarship, (S) 607

Washington DC Metropolitan Network of Executive Women in Hospitality Scholarship Awards, (S) 608

Washington Episcopal Church Women Memorial Scholarship Fund, (F) 965

Washington NASA Space Grant Consortium Private Industry Internships, (I) 1505

Washington NASA Space Grant Consortium Seed Grants for Faculty, (G) 1266

Washington NASA Space Grant Consortium Undergraduate Research Awards, (G) 1267

Washington NASA Space Grant Consortium Undergraduate Scholarships, (S) 609

Washington State Chapter WAI Scholarship, (S) 610

Washington Women in Need Educational Grants, (S) 611

Washington Zonta Club Scholarships, (S) 612

Watson Midwives of Color Scholarship, (F) 966

# Sponsoring Organization Index

The Sponsoring Organization Index makes it easy to identify agencies that offer financial aid primarily or exclusively to women. In this index, sponsoring organizations are listed alphabetically, word by word. In addition, we've used an alphabetical code (within parentheses) to help you identify which programs sponsored by these organizations fall within your scope of interest: S = Scholarships; F = Fellowships; L = Loans; G = Grants; A = Awards; and I = Internships. Here's how the code works: if the name of a sponsoring organization is followed by (S) 241, a program sponsored by that organization is described in the Scholarships section in entry 241. If the same sponsoring organization's name is followed by another entry number—for example, (L) 680—the same or a different program sponsored by that organization is described in the Loans chapter in entry 680. Remember: the numbers cited here refer to program entry numbers, not to page numbers in the book.

American Baptist Churches USA, (F) 766

American Baptist Women of New Jersey, (S) 141

American Board of Obstetrics and Gynecology, (F) 686, (G) 1052

American Business Women's Association, (S) 554, (F) 661, 789, 799, 927, 947

American Business Women's Association. Flaming Arrow Chapter, (S) 195

American Business Women's Association. Humble Artesian Chapter, (S) 247

American Business Women's Association. New Hampshire Charter Chapter, (S) 427

American Chemical Society, (A) 1328

American Chemical Society. Division of Organic Chemistry, (F) 898

American Coed Pageants, (A) 1368

American College of Medical Practice Executives, (S) 129, (F) 736

American College of Nurse–Midwives, (S) 73, (F) 662, 704, 966, (G) 1265, (A) 1315, 1333, 1349

American College of Rheumatology, (F) 899

American College Testing, (I) 1429

American Committee for the Weizmann Institute of Science, (A) 1421

American Congress on Surveying and Mapping, (S) 101, 449

American Council of Learned Societies, (F) 945, (G) 1036–1038, 1056, 1084, 1094, 1103, 1127, 1141–1142, 1207, 1223

American Epilepsy Society, (F) 910, 919, (G) 1074, 1113–1114, 1139, 1224, 1226, 1229

American Film Institute, (G) 1102

American Fisheries Society, (F) 812

American Foundation for the Blind, (S) 221, 508, (F) 786

American Gastroenterological Association, (F) 666, (G) 1041–1045, 1228, 1234, 1256

American Geological Institute, (I) 1428, 1430

American Health Information Management Association, (S) 501, (F) 918

American Heart Association. Western States Affiliate, (I) 1432

American Historical Association, (A) 1345

American Indian Graduate Center, (F) 764, 819

American Indian Heritage Foundation, (S) 387, (A) 1372

American Institute of Professional Geologists, (I) 1430

American Legion Auxiliary, (S) 31, 219, 550

American Legion. California Auxiliary, (S) 106, 109

American Legion. Colorado Auxiliary, (S) 124–125

American Legion. Florida Auxiliary, (S) 201

American Legion. Georgia Auxiliary, (S) 215

American Legion. Indiana Auxiliary, (S) 258

American Legion. Indiana Department, (A) 1336

American Legion. Kentucky Auxiliary, (S) 344, (L) 1012

American Legion. Maryland Auxiliary, (S) 353–354

American Legion. Michigan Auxiliary, (S) 364–365

American Legion. Minnesota Auxiliary, (S) 380

American Legion. Missouri Auxiliary, (S) 310

American Legion. Missouri Department, (S) 315

American Legion. New York Auxiliary, (S) 194

American Legion. North Carolina Auxiliary, (S) 407

American Legion. Ohio Auxiliary, (S) 452

American Legion. Ohio Department, (S) 453

American Legion. Oregon Auxiliary, (S) 466–468

American Legion Press Club of New Jersey, (S) 58

American Legion. South Carolina Auxiliary, (S) 543

American Legion. Virginia Auxiliary, (S) 45

American Legion. Wisconsin Auxiliary, (S) 145, 246, 621–624, (F) 804, 975

American Library Association. Association of College and Research Libraries, (A) 1424–1425

American Library Association. Governance Office, (A) 1321

American Mathematical Society, (A) 1396

American Medical Women's Association Foundation, (F) 969, (L) 1013, (A) 1295, 1308, 1332

American Mensa Education and Research Foundation, (S) 225, 507, (F) 790, 921

American Meteorological Society, (S) 32, 40, 87, 185, 324, 341, (F) 810, (G) 1054

American Military Spouse Education Foundation, (S) 33

American Mothers, Inc., (A) 1286–1287, 1289

American News Women's Club, (S) 34, (F) 687

American Nuclear Society, (S) 143, (F) 740, (A) 1362

American Occupational Therapy Association, (L) 1007

American Ornithologists' Union, (G) 1143, 1179

American Physical Society, (G) 1175, (A) 1361

American Planning Association, (S) 284, (F) 822

American Polish Engineering Association, (S) 35

American Political Science Association, (G) 1237, 1253, (A) 1417

American Psychiatric Association, (A) 1285

American Psychological Association. Division 35, (G) 1128, 1147

American Public Health Association, (A) 1282

American Quarter Horse Association, (A) 1297

American Quaternary Association, (F) 745, (G) 1098, (A) 1313

American Society for Eighteenth–Century Studies, (G) 1067, 1111

American Society for Engineering Education, (F) 872, (G) 1118, 1197, (A) 1399

American Society for Pharmacology and Experimental Therapeutics, (G) 1068, (I) 1437

American Society of Civil Engineers. Maine Section, (S) 59

American Society of Safety Engineers, (S) 203, (F) 779, 956

American Society of Women Accountants, (S) 36–37

American Society of Women Accountants. Billings Big Sky Chapter, (S) 345–346, (F) 846

American Society of Women Accountants. Denver Chapter, (S) 154

American Society of Women Accountants. Huntsville Chapter, (S) 248, (F) 805

American Society of Women Accountants. Seattle Chapter, (S) 527, (F) 935

American Society of Women Accountants. Wichita Chapter, (S) 613, (F) 968

American Sociological Association, (A) 1344

American Statistical Association, (F) 784, (G) 1066

American Vacuum Society, (F) 878

American Water Works Association, (F) 800

American Woman's Society of Certified Public Accountants, (F) 688, (A) 1290

American Woman's Society of Certified Public Accountants. Boston Affiliate, (S) 91, (F) 714

American Woman's Society of Certified Public Accountants. Georgia Affiliate, (S) 214

American Woman's Society of Certified Public Accountants. South Florida Affiliate, (S) 171

American Woman's Society of Certified Public Accountants. Utah Affiliate, (S) 587

AMVETS Ladies Auxiliary, (S) 41–42

Andrew W. Mellon Foundation, (G) 1036–1037, 1056, 1084, 1120, 1127

Ann Bancroft Foundation, (G) 1096

Appraisal Institute, (S) 49

Arizona Business and Professional Women's Foundation, (S) 51, 53, 636, (F) 693

Arizona Space Grant Consortium, (I) 1433

Arkansas Activities Association, (S) 55

Arkansas Business and Professional Women, (S) 180, (F) 971

Arkansas Department of Higher Education, (S) 54, (F) 694

Arkansas Historical Association, (A) 1408

Arkansas Space Grant Consortium, (G) 1059–1061, (I) 1434

Armed Forces Communications and Electronics Association, (S) 210, 233, (F) 916

Armenian International Women's Association, (S) 8, 655, (F) 667, 989

Army Aviation Association of America, (L) 996

Army Aviation Association of America Scholarship Foundation, (S) 57, (F) 695

Army Emergency Relief, (L) 997

Army Engineer Association, (S) 122

Army Officers' Wives' Club of the Greater Washington Area, (S) 48

Artist Trust, (A) 1412

ArtTable Inc., (I) 1436

ASME International, (F) 698

Associated Press Sports Editors, (S) 63, (F) 699, (I) 1439

Associates of Vietnam Veterans of America, (S) 80

Association for Computing Machinery, (S) 488

Association for Enterprise Opportunity, (G) 1095

Association for Iron & Steel Technology. Midwest Chapter, (S) 83

Association for the Sociology of Religion, (G) 1122

Association for Theatre in Higher Education, (A) 1342

Association for Women Geoscientists, (S) 60, 471, 559, 616, (F) 901, 970, (G) 1085, 1218, (A) 1388

Association for Women in Architecture, (S) 61

Association for Women in Communications, (A) 1317

Association for Women in Communications. Washington DC Area Chapter, (S) 607

Association for Women in Computing. Ann Arbor Chapter, (S) 44

Association for Women in Mathematics, (G) 1069, 1088, 1240, 1247, (A) 1288, 1395

Association for Women in Science, (S) 62, 302, (F) 929, (G) 1055, 1100, 1172–1173, 1242, (I) 1438

Association for Women in Sports Media, (S) 63, (F) 699, (I) 1439

Association for Women Journalists, (S) 64

Association for Women Lawyers, (F) 961

Association of Black Women Lawyers of New Jersey, Inc., (F) 706

Association of Independent Colleges and Universities of Pennsylvania, (S) 12, 363

Association of Jewish Women Publishers, (A) 1358

Association of Old Crows, (S) 233

Association of Universities for Research in Astronomy, Inc., (G) 1168

Association of Women Psychiatrists, (A) 1285

Association of Women's Health, Obstetric and Neonatal Nurses, (G) 1071

Association on American Indian Affairs, Inc., (S) 1

Astraea Lesbian Foundation for Justice, (G) 1174, (A) 1354–1355

AstraZeneca Pharmaceuticals, L.P., (G) 1044

Athletes of Good News, (S) 551

AT&T Laboratories, (F) 700, (I) 1440

Autry National Center, (G) 1076

Aviation Boatswain's Mates Association, (S) 263

Babe Ruth League, Inc., (S) 265

Baptist Convention of New Mexico, (S) 75, (F) 707

Baptist General Convention of Texas, (F) 771

Baptist Women in Ministry of North Carolina, (F) 701

Barbara Alice Mower Memorial Scholarship Committee, (S) 69, (F) 702

Barnard College. Department of English, (A) 1300

Barnum Festival Foundation, (S) 71, (A) 1301

BASF Agricultural Products, (S) 72

Battelle Memorial Institute, (G) 1132

Bay Area Lawyers for Individual Freedom, (I) 1471

Bechtel Foundation, (S) 74

Berkshire Conference of Women Historians, (G) 1075, 1148, (A) 1302–1303

Best Friends Foundation, (S) 78

Big 12 Conference, (F) 755

Biophysical Society, (A) 1359

Bobby Sox Softball, (S) 89

Boeing Company, (S) 233

Book Trust, (A) 1387

Boston Globe, (S) 506

BPW/Maine Futurama Foundation, (S) 93–94, 496

Brandeis University. Hadassah–Brandeis Institute, (G) 1137–1138, (I) 1469

Brigham Young University. Charles Redd Center for Western Studies, (G) 1058

British Academy, (A) 1394

BroadMind Entertainment, (A) 1312

Brookhaven National Laboratory, (G) 1132, (I) 1442, 1488

Brookings Institution, (G) 1124, 1136, 1216

Brown University. John Carter Brown Library, (G) 1239

Brown University. Pembroke Center for Teaching and Research on Women, (G) 1221

Bryn Mawr College. Alumnae Association, (A) 1356

Burroughs Wellcome Fund, (F) 721, (G) 1080–1081, 1086

Busch Gardens, (S) 38, (A) 1291

Business and Professional Women of Iowa Foundation, (S) 99

Business and Professional Women of Virginia, (S) 98, 296, 631, (F) 716, 979, (G) 1115

Business and Professional Women/New Jersey, (S) 372

Business and Professional Women's Clubs of New York State, (F) 791

Business and Professional Women's Foundation, (S) 110, (F) 720

Business and Professional Women's Foundation of Delaware, Inc., (S) 142

Business Investment Growth (BiG) Austin, (G) 1095

---

**S–Scholarships**     **F–Fellowships**     **L–Loans**     **G–Grants**     **A–Awards**     **I–Internships**

Electronics for Imaging, Inc., (S) 173, (F) 763
Eli Lilly and Company, (A) 1323
Elizabeth City State University, (G) 1247
Elks National Foundation, (S) 181
Elsevier Science Ltd., (G) 1043
Epilepsy Foundation, (F) 705, 910, 919, (G) 1073–1074, 1113, 1139, 1224, 1226, 1229, (A) 1357
Episcopal Diocese of Washington, (F) 965
Epsilon Sigma Alpha, (S) 25, 79, 238, 343, 438, 513, 578, (F) 767, 854
Equal Rights Advocates, Inc., (I) 1493
Ethel Louise Armstrong Foundation, (F) 761
Exelon Corporation, (S) 189
ExxonMobil Foundation, (S) 60

Factor Support Network Pharmacy, (S) 376
Family Circle Cup, (S) 323
Fargo–Moorhead Area Foundation, (S) 637
Farm Bureau Insurance, (S) 191, 361
Federal Executives' Association, (S) 76
Federation of American Societies for Experimental Biology, (A) 1323
Fence Books, (A) 1378
Festival International de Films de Femmes, (A) 1337
Fetzer Institute, (G) 1094
Field Museum of Natural History, (G) 1123
First Command Educational Foundation, (S) 48, 233
First Corbin Financial Corporation, (S) 552
Fleet Reserve Association, (S) 196, 461, 525, (F) 775, 787, 820, 922, 933
Florida Board of Accountancy, (S) 200
Florida High School Athletic Association, (S) 192
Florida Space Grant Consortium, (F) 777
Florida Women's State Golf Association, (S) 523
Folger Shakespeare Library, (G) 1127
Force Recon Association, (S) 202
Ford Family Foundation, (S) 205
Ford Foundation, (G) 1037, 1279
Ford Motor Company, (S) 203–204, (F) 779
Fordham University. Louis Calder Center Biological Field Station, (G) 1078
Foundation for Amateur Radio, Inc., (S) 653, (F) 988
Foundation for Digestive Health and Nutrition, (F) 666, (G) 1041–1045, 1228, 1234, 1256
Frameline, (G) 1145
Franklin Pierce Law Center, (F) 911
Freedom Forum, (S) 15

Gallaudet University Alumni Association, (F) 747
GAT Airline Ground Support, (S) 207
GE Foundation, (S) 208
GE Fund, (A) 1361
General Electric Company. Women's Network, (S) 209
General Federation of Women's Clubs of Connecticut, (S) 161, 482, (F) 749, 905
General Federation of Women's Clubs of Massachusetts, (F) 855
General Motors Foundation, (S) 212, (F) 780

Geological Society of America, (G) 1129–1130, (A) 1406
George Mason University. So to Speak: A Feminist Journal of Language and Art, (A) 1402
George Washington University. Office of Science and Engineering Apprentice Program, (I) 1494
Georgetown University. Law Center, (G) 1275, (I) 1508
Georgia Association for Women Lawyers, (F) 782
Georgia Space Grant Consortium, (S) 216, (F) 783
Geraldine R. Dodge Foundation, (G) 1131
Glamour, (A) 1331
GlaxoSmithKline, (S) 73, (F) 704, (A) 1357
Goldman, Sachs & Company, (S) 223
Golf Association of Michigan, (S) 224
Golf Course Superintendents Association of America, (S) 526, (I) 1495
Google Inc., (S) 43, (F) 689
Greenwood Publishing Group, (A) 1424
Guardian Life Insurance Company of America, (A) 1330
Guidant Foundation, (S) 230
Guideposts, (S) 564, (A) 1409

Hanscom Officers' Spouses' Club, (S) 233
Harkness Foundation for Dance, (G) 1206
Harvard University. Divinity School, (G) 1276
Harvard University. Harvard–MIT Data Center. Henry A. Murray Research Archive, (G) 1156
Harvard University. John F. Kennedy School of Government, (G) 1121
Hawai'i Community Foundation, (S) 193, 251, 273, 288, (F) 774, 808
Henry Luce Foundation, (G) 1141–1142
History of Science Society, (A) 1360
Honeywell International Inc., (S) 241
Honolulu Alumnae Panhellenic Association, (S) 242–243
Howard Hughes Medical Institute, (F) 803, (G) 1146, (I) 1476
Huntington Library, Art Collections, and Botanical Gardens, (G) 1127

IBM Corporation, (S) 250
Idaho Space Grant Consortium, (S) 253, (G) 1149
Illinois CPA Society, (S) 4
Illinois Department of Veterans' Affairs, (S) 254
Illinois Federation of Business and Professional Women's Clubs, (F) 724
Illinois. Office of the Governor, (I) 1462, 1503
Illinois Society of Professional Engineers, (S) 479
Illinois Women's Golf Association, (S) 286
Independent Colleges of Indiana, (S) 528
Indiana Business and Professional Women's Foundation, Inc., (S) 166, 255–256
Indiana Extension Homemakers Association, (S) 257
Indiana Space Grant Consortium, (G) 1150–1151
InfoComm International, (S) 259
Institute for Women's Policy Research, (I) 1461, 1470
Institute of Electrical and Electronics Engineers. Circuits and Systems Society, (S) 488
Institute of Industrial Engineers, (S) 581
International Alumnae of Delta Epsilon Sorority, (F) 807

International Order of Job's Daughters, (S) 229, 279, 561, (F) 792, 818

International Order of Job's Daughters. Grand Guardian Council of California, (S) 105, (L) 998

International Union of Operating Engineers, Local 3, (S) 462

International Women's Media Foundation, (A) 1310

Iota Sigma Pi, (S) 220, (A) 1283, 1294, 1338–1339, 1413, 1419

Iowa Girls' High School Athletic Union, (S) 172, 509

Iowa Pork Producers Association, (S) 260

Iowa Space Grant Consortium, (S) 261

Iowa Sports Foundation, (S) 97

Iowa State University. Carrie Chapman Catt Center for Women and Politics, (A) 1307

Jamatex, (S) 392, (A) 1376

Janssen Pharmaceutica Products, L.P., (G) 1044

January, (G) 1197

Jeannette Rankin Foundation, Inc., (S) 275

Jewish Community Federation of Baltimore, (S) 351

Johnson & Johnson/Merck Consumer Pharmaceuticals, (G) 1044

JPMorganChase, (I) 1464

Juvenile Diabetes Research Foundation, (F) 664, 758, 909, (G) 1039, 1082, 1107, 1152–1155, 1159–1160, 1222

Kalliope Women Writers' Collective, (A) 1348, 1407

Kansas African American Legislative Caucus, (S) 289

Kansas Federation of Business & Professional Women's Clubs, Inc., (S) 336

Kansas Space Grant Consortium, (S) 290, (F) 824, (G) 1161

Kansas Women's Golf Association, (S) 409

Kappa Alpha Theta, (S) 291–292, (F) 825, (L) 1011

Kappa Delta Sorority, (S) 176, 184, 274, 293–294, 340, 502, (F) 823, 826, 972

Kappa Kappa Gamma Foundation, (S) 295, 515, (F) 728, 827

Kentucky Association of Vocational Education Special Needs Personnel, (S) 555–556

Kentucky Department of Veterans Affairs, (S) 190, 301, (F) 772

Kentucky Foundation for Women, (G) 1062, 1064

Kentucky High School Athletic Association, (S) 412, 552

Kentucky Space Grant Consortium, (S) 300, (F) 830, (G) 1162–1164

Kentucky Woman's Missionary Union, (S) 270, (F) 814

Knights of Columbus, (S) 281, (F) 710

Kosciuszko Foundation, (F) 754

KPMG Foundation, (A) 1350–1352

Krause Corporation, (S) 304

Kulturamt der Stadt Meersburg, (A) 1364

Ladies Auxiliary of the Fleet Reserve Association, (S) 305

Ladies Professional Golf Association, (S) 156, 338

Latina Leadership Network, (S) 308

Lawrence Livermore National Laboratory, (F) 873, (G) 1200, (I) 1451, 1466, 1481

Legal Momentum, (I) 1449, 1457, 1460, 1467, 1489, 1491

LeRoy C. Merritt Humanitarian Fund, (G) 1170

Lily Auchincloss Foundation, (G) 1206

Lincoln Community Foundation, (S) 316, 421, (F) 835

Linly Heflin Unit, (S) 318

Lisa Sechrist Memorial Foundation, (S) 320

Lockheed Martin Aeronautics Company, (S) 321

Lockheed Martin Foundation, (S) 322

L'Oréal USA., (G) 1172

Los Alamos National Laboratory, (F) 873, (G) 1200, (I) 1481

Louisiana Department of Veterans Affairs, (S) 327

Louisiana Federation of Business and Professional Women's Clubs, Inc., (S) 9

Louisiana High School Athletic Association, (S) 326, 403

Louisiana Space Consortium, (S) 307, (F) 832, (G) 1165–1167, (I) 1465

Maddenmedia, (S) 102, (A) 1305

Maids of Athena, (S) 331, (F) 841

Maine. Bureau of Veterans' Services, (S) 334, (F) 843

Maine Federation of Business and Professional Women, (S) 206, 332, 497

Maine Media Women, (S) 333, (F) 842

Maine Space Grant Consortium, (G) 1177, 1195

Marian J. Wettrick Charitable Foundation, (F) 844

Marine Corps Counterintelligence Association, (S) 339

Maryland Federation of Business and Professional Women's Clubs, Inc., (S) 100, 298

Maryland Space Grant Consortium, (S) 355

Mass Youth Soccer, (S) 357

Massachusetts Democratic Party, (S) 280

Massachusetts Federation of Business and Professional Women's Clubs, Inc., (S) 356

Massachusetts Federation of Polish Women's Clubs, (F) 754

Massachusetts Historical Society, (G) 1241

Massachusetts Society of Certified Public Accountants, (S) 402

Massachusetts Space Grant Consortium, (F) 853

Mathematical Association of America, (A) 1320

McKenzie River Gathering Foundation, (G) 1171

Medtronic, Inc., (A) 1363

Mel Fisher Maritime Heritage Society and Museum, (S) 157, (F) 746, (A) 1314

Miami Urban Ministries, (G) 1095

Michael Baker Corporation, (S) 363

Michigan High School Athletic Association, (S) 361

Michigan Space Grant Consortium, (G) 1184–1186

Microbusiness Development, (G) 1095

Microsoft Corporation, (S) 366–367, (F) 856, (A) 1311, (I) 1472

Mikimoto, (S) 392–393, (A) 1376–1377

Military Order of the Purple Heart, (S) 374, (F) 860

Milken Family Foundation, (G) 1114

Milton & Sally Avery Arts Foundation, (G) 1206

Minnesota Broadcasters Association, (S) 266

Minnesota Higher Education Services Office, (S) 379, 383

Minnesota Nurses Association, (S) 131, (F) 737

Minnesota Space Grant Consortium, (S) 381, (F) 862

Minnesota State Federation of Business and Professional Women's Clubs, Inc., (S) 377, (G) 1187

Minnesota State High School League, (S) 382

Minnesota Women's Campaign Fund, (G) 1188

Minnesota Women's Golf Association, (S) 384

Minnesota Youth Soccer Association, (S) 371

Miss America Pageant, (S) 18, 187, 385, 390, 413, 495, 553, (F) 674, 752, 770, 834, 914, (A) 1367, 1374, 1383, 1405

Miss Black America Pageant, (A) 1369

Miss Cheerleader of America, (S) 386, (A) 1370

Miss Universe Organization, (S) 392–393, (A) 1376–1377

Mississippi High School Activities Association, (S) 317

Mississippi Space Grant Consortium, (S) 394, (F) 864, (G) 1190

Mississippi University for Women. Department of Languages, Literature, and Philosophy, (A) 1322

Mississippi Veterans' Home Purchase Board, (L) 1014

Missouri Business and Professional Women's Foundation, Inc., (S) 282, 395, 484

Missouri Department of Higher Education, (S) 396

Missouri Space Grant Consortium, (F) 865, (G) 1191, (I) 1473–1474

Missouri Women's Golf Association, (S) 397

Mitchell Company, (S) 38, (A) 1291

Mitsubishi Electric Research Lab, (A) 1311

Modine Manufacturing Company, (S) 398, (I) 1475

Montana Federation of Business and Professional Women's Organizations, (G) 1192

Montana Guaranteed Student Loan Program, (S) 399

Montana Space Grant Consortium, (S) 400, (F) 866, (G) 1070, 1193

Montana State Women's Golf Association, (S) 401

Morgan Stanley, (S) 448, 633, (I) 1486, 1507

Ms. America, Inc., (A) 1379

Musemeche Photography, (S) 403

Mystic Tan, (S) 392, (A) 1376

NARAL Pro–Choice America, (I) 1477

NARAL Pro–Choice Montana Foundation, (I) 1478

National Association of Negro Business and Professional Women's Clubs, (S) 168

National Association of the Deaf, (A) 1371

National Association of Women Artists, Inc., (G) 1180, (A) 1382

National Association of Women Lawyers, (A) 1398

National Center for Atmospheric Research, (G) 1199

National City Bank, (S) 412

National Collegiate Athletic Association, (F) 875–876, 963, (I) 1484

National Commission for Cooperative Education, (S) 419

National Federation of Music Clubs, (S) 234, 262, (A) 1293, 1334, 1340, 1365, 1384–1385, 1418

National Federation of Republican Women, (S) 84, 406, (F) 870, (I) 1455

National Federation of the Blind, (S) 240, (F) 798

National Federation of the Blind of Missouri, (S) 348, (F) 847

National FFA Organization, (S) 72, 116, 304

National Hemophilia Foundation, (S) 493, (F) 912

National Housing Endowment, (S) 405

National Humanities Center, (G) 1127

National Kidney Foundation of Massachusetts, Rhode Island, New Hampshire, and Vermont, Inc., (G) 1220

National Latina Alliance, (S) 414

National Lawyers Guild, (I) 1459

National League of American Pen Women, (F) 697, 867, 986, (A) 1298, 1380, 1423

National Museum of Women in the Arts, (I) 1447, 1498

National Optical Astronomy Observatories, (G) 1168

National Panhellenic Conference, (S) 118, 175, 447

National Physical Science Consortium, (F) 873, (G) 1200, (I) 1481

National Science Foundation, (G) 1066, 1168, 1199, (I) 1476, 1480

National Science Foundation. Directorate for Biological Sciences, (G) 1104

National Science Foundation. Directorate for Education and Human Resources, (F) 773, 889, (G) 1119, 1230–1232

National Science Foundation. Directorate for Mathematical and Physical Sciences, (G) 1069, 1088

National Science Foundation. Directorate for Social, Behavioral, and Economic Sciences, (G) 1244

National Society Daughters of the American Revolution, (F) 811

National Society of Black Engineers, (S) 311, 370, (F) 857

National Society of Professional Engineers, (S) 67, 596

National Society of Professional Surveyors, (S) 449

National Sorority of Phi Delta Kappa, Inc., (S) 415

National Strength and Conditioning Association, (F) 888

National Teen–Ager Scholarship Foundation, (S) 39, (A) 1292

National Women's Law Center, (I) 1446

Native American Community Board. Native American Women's Health Education Resource Center, (S) 416, (I) 1483

Navy Wives Club of America, (S) 350, 417, (F) 852, 874

Navy–Marine Corps Relief Society, (S) 477, 586, 593, (L) 1027

Nebraska Association of Fair Managers, (S) 342

Nebraska. Department of Veterans' Affairs, (S) 423

Nebraska Elks Association, (S) 420

Nebraska Rural Community Schools Association, (S) 421

Nebraska Space Grant Consortium, (S) 127, 422, (F) 733, 877

Nesbitt Medical Student Foundation, (F) 879

Network of Executive Women, (S) 424, (F) 880

Network of Executive Women in Hospitality. Arizona Chapter, (S) 52

Network of Executive Women in Hospitality. Atlanta Chapter, (S) 66

Network of Executive Women in Hospitality. Chicago Chapter, (S) 119, (F) 727

Network of Executive Women in Hospitality. Dallas Chapter, (S) 134

Network of Executive Women in Hospitality. Greater New York Chapter, (S) 228

Network of Executive Women in Hospitality. Houston Chapter, (S) 245

Network of Executive Women in Hospitality. Las Vegas Chapter, (S) 306, (F) 831

Network of Executive Women in Hospitality. North Central Chapter, (S) 441

Network of Executive Women in Hospitality. Northwest Chapter, (S) 445

Network of Executive Women in Hospitality. Rocky Mountain Chapter, (S) 512

Network of Executive Women in Hospitality. South Florida Chapter, (S) 547

Network of Executive Women in Hospitality. Southern Counties Chapter, (S) 549

Network of Executive Women in Hospitality. Sunshine Chapter, (S) 557

Network of Executive Women in Hospitality. Virginia Chapter, (S) 598

S–Scholarships          F–Fellowships          L–Loans          G–Grants          A–Awards          I–Internships

# Residency Index

Some programs listed in this book are restricted to residents of a particular city, county, state, or region. Others are open to applicants wherever they may live. The Residency Index will help you pinpoint programs available only to residents in your area as well as programs that have no residency restrictions at all (these are listed under the term "United States"). To use this index, look up the geographic areas that apply to you (always check the listings under "United States"), jot down the entry numbers listed after the program types that interest you (scholarships, fellowships, etc.), and use those numbers to find the program descriptions in the directory. To help you in your search, we've provided some "see also" references in each index entry. Remember: the numbers cited here refer to program entry numbers, not to page numbers in the book.

Alabama: **Scholarships,** 16, 112, 318, 566, 580, 638, 647; **Fellowships,** 671–673, 723; **Grants,** 1050. *See also* United States; names of specific cities and counties

Alaska: **Scholarships,** 17, 101, 238; **Fellowships,** 887; **Loans,** 995; **Internships,** 1431. *See also* United States; names of specific cities

Alexandria, Virginia: **Scholarships,** 48. *See also* Virginia

American Samoa: **Scholarships,** 110; **Fellowships,** 720. *See also* United States

Argentina: **Scholarships,** 644. *See also* Foreign countries; South America

Arizona: **Scholarships,** 51, 53, 101, 238, 483, 636; **Fellowships,** 693; **Loans,** 1016; **Grants,** 1095; **Internships,** 1433. *See also* United States; Western states; names of specific cities and counties

Arkansas: **Scholarships,** 54–55, 112, 180, 647; **Fellowships,** 694, 723, 971; **Grants,** 1059–1061; **Internships,** 1434. *See also* United States; names of specific cities and counties

Arlington, Virginia: **Scholarships,** 48. *See also* Virginia

Australia: **Scholarships,** 238. *See also* Foreign countries

Bahamas: **Scholarships,** 120; **Fellowships,** 729. *See also* Caribbean; Foreign countries

Benewah County, Idaho: **Fellowships,** 887. *See also* Idaho

Bexar County, Texas: **Scholarships,** 252; **Fellowships,** 809. *See also* Texas

Bolivia: **Scholarships,** 644. *See also* Foreign countries; South America

Bonner County, Idaho: **Fellowships,** 887. *See also* Idaho

Boundary County, Idaho: **Fellowships,** 887. *See also* Idaho

Bowie County, Texas: **Scholarships,** 182. *See also* Texas

Brazil: **Scholarships,** 644. *See also* Foreign countries; South America

Britain. *See* United Kingdom

California: **Scholarships,** 61, 101, 103–109, 162, 186, 231, 238, 269, 308; **Fellowships,** 718, 751, 769, 813, 926; **Loans,** 998–999; **Grants,** 1095; **Internships,** 1432. *See also* United States; Western states; names of specific cities and counties

California, northern: **Scholarships,** 462. *See also* California

California, southern: **Scholarships,** 309; **Fellowships,** 950. *See also* California

Calvert County, Maryland: **Scholarships,** 48. *See also* Maryland

Canada: **Scholarships,** 20, 137–138, 150, 291–292, 319, 328, 367, 464, 478, 480, 485–486, 518, 581, 617, 644; **Fellowships,** 666, 686, 709, 721, 742, 762, 784, 825, 878, 903, 911, 925, 941, 980; **Loans,** 1002–1003, 1011, 1020; **Grants,** 1041–1045, 1052, 1080–1081, 1086–1087, 1106, 1129, 1142, 1175, 1202, 1228, 1234, 1246, 1256, 1262; **Awards,** 1296, 1302–1303, 1311, 1318, 1320, 1331, 1386, 1390; **Internships,** 1472. *See also* Foreign countries

Caribbean: **Scholarships,** 464; **Awards,** 1386. *See also* Foreign countries; names of specific countries

Central America: **Fellowships,** 748; **Grants,** 1129. *See also* Foreign countries; names of specific countries

Charles County, Maryland: **Scholarships,** 48. *See also* Maryland

Charlotte, North Carolina: **Scholarships,** 78. *See also* North Carolina

Chatham County, Georgia: **Scholarships,** 283. *See also* Georgia

Chile: **Scholarships,** 644. *See also* Foreign countries; South America

China. *See* Taiwan

Clark County, Indiana: **Scholarships,** 646. *See also* Indiana

Clearwater County, Idaho: **Fellowships,** 887. *See also* Idaho

Colorado: **Scholarships,** 21, 101, 112, 123–125, 153, 511; **Fellowships,** 677, 723, 755, 924; **Grants,** 1095, 1238; **Awards,** 1316; **Internships,** 1448. *See also* United States; Western states; names of specific cities and counties

# Tenability Index

Some programs listed in this book can be used only in specific cities, counties, states, or regions. Others may be used anywhere in the United States (or even abroad). The Tenability Index will help you locate funding that is restricted to a specific area as well as funding that has no tenability restrictions (these are listed under the term "United States"). To use this index, look up the geographic areas where you'd like to go (always check the listings under "United States"), jot down the entry numbers listed after the program types (scholarships, fellowships, etc.) that interest you, and use those numbers to find the program descriptions in the directory. To help you in your search, we've provided some "see also" references in each index entry. Remember: the numbers cited here refer to program entry numbers, not to page numbers in the book.

# Subject Index

There are more than 500 different subject areas indexed in this directory. You can use the Subject Index to identify both the subject focus and the type (scholarships, fellowships, etc.) of available funding programs. To help you pinpoint your search, we've included hundreds of "see" and "see also" references. In addition to looking for terms that represent your specific subject interest, be sure to check the "General programs" entry; hundreds of funding opportunities are listed there that can be used to support study, research, or other activities in *any* subject area (although the programs may be restricted in other ways). Remember: the numbers cited in this index refer to program entry numbers, not to page numbers in the book.

History, Asian: **Grants,** 1142. *See also* General programs; History

History, Greek: **Grants,** 1182. *See also* General programs; History

History, Jewish: **Grants,** 1137. *See also* General programs; History; Jewish studies

History, Latin American: **Grants,** 1194, 1239. *See also* General programs; History; Latin American studies

History, natural: **Internships,** 1480. *See also* Sciences; specific aspects of natural history

History, nursing. *See* Nurses and nursing, history

History, science: **Grants,** 1054, 1125; **Awards,** 1360. *See also* General programs; History; Sciences

History, South American. *See* History, Latin American

Home economics: **Scholarships,** 605. *See also* Family and consumer studies; General programs

Homeland security. *See* Security, national

Homosexuality: **Grants,** 1145; **Awards,** 1304, 1325, 1346, 1355, 1393; **Internships,** 1471. *See also* General programs

Horticulture: **Scholarships,** 573; **Fellowships,** 931. *See also* Agriculture and agricultural sciences; General programs; Landscape architecture; Sciences

Hospitality industry. *See* Hotel and motel industry

Hospitals. *See* Health and health care

Hotel and motel industry: **Scholarships,** 52, 66, 119, 134, 228, 245, 306, 441, 445, 512, 547, 549, 557, 598, 608, 640; **Fellowships,** 727, 831, 983. *See also* General programs

Housing: **Loans,** 995, 999, 1004, 1009, 1014, 1019, 1023–1026, 1030, 1032. *See also* General programs

Human rights. *See* Civil rights

Human services. *See* Social services

Humanities: **Fellowships,** 747; **Grants,** 1036–1038, 1040, 1056, 1084, 1094, 1103, 1126–1127, 1207, 1221, 1223, 1277; **Awards,** 1322. *See also* General programs; names of specific humanities

Hydrology: **Scholarships,** 32, 40, 60, 87, 185, 324, 341; **Fellowships,** 810; **Grants,** 1054. *See also* Earth sciences; General programs

Illustrators and illustrations: **Scholarships,** 61. *See also* Art; General programs; Graphic arts

Immigration law: **Internships,** 1460, 1491. *See also* General programs; Law, general

Immunology: **Fellowships,** 803; **Grants,** 1146, 1243; **Awards,** 1397. *See also* General programs; Medical sciences

Industrial engineering. *See* Engineering, industrial

Industrial hygiene: **Scholarships,** 203; **Fellowships,** 779, 956. *See also* General programs; Health and health care

Information science: **Scholarships,** 249, 259, 501; **Fellowships,** 700, 806, 889, 916, 918, 934; **Internships,** 1440, 1454. *See also* Computer sciences; General programs; Libraries and librarianship

Insurance. *See* Actuarial sciences

Intellectual property law: **Fellowships,** 911. *See also* General programs; Law, general

Interior design: **Scholarships,** 61. *See also* Architecture; Design; General programs; Home economics

International affairs: **Scholarships,** 580; **Fellowships,** 672, 724, 748; **Grants,** 1050, 1121, 1124, 1196; **Awards,** 1381; **Internships,** 1454. *See also* General programs; Political science and politics

International relations. *See* International affairs

Internet design and development: **Grants,** 1095. *See also* General programs; Graphic arts; Technology

Internet journalism. *See* Journalism, online

Jazz. *See* Music, jazz

Jewelry: **Scholarships,** 643; **Awards,** 1286. *See also* Arts and crafts; General programs

Jewish history. *See* History, Jewish

Jewish studies: **Grants,** 1137–1138; **Internships,** 1469. *See also* General programs; Middle Eastern studies; Near Eastern studies; Religion and religious activities

Journalism: **Scholarships,** 15, 34, 58, 64, 88, 168, 225, 259, 277, 450, 502, 607; **Fellowships,** 687, 790, 816, 890, 951; **Grants,** 1252, 1257; **Awards,** 1310; **Internships,** 1449, 1454. *See also* Broadcasting; Communications; General programs; Writers and writing; names of specific types of journalism

Journalism, broadcast: **Scholarships,** 64, 266; **Awards,** 1310. *See also* Communications; General programs; Radio; Television

Journalism, medical. *See* Science reporting

Journalism, online: **Awards,** 1310. *See also* General programs; Journalism

Journalism, science. *See* Science reporting

Journalism, sports. *See* Sports reporting

Jurisprudence. *See* Law, general

Kidney disease: **Grants,** 1220. *See also* Disabilities; General programs; Health and health care; Medical sciences

Labor law. *See* Employment law

Labor unions and members: **Internships,** 1501. *See also* General programs

Landscape architecture: **Scholarships,** 61. *See also* Botany; General programs; Horticulture

Language, Albanian: **Fellowships,** 945. *See also* General programs; Language and linguistics

Language and linguistics: **Grants,** 1037, 1056, 1084, 1127, 1207, 1244; **Internships,** 1456. *See also* General programs; Humanities; names of specific languages

Language, Brazilian. *See* Language, Portuguese

Language, Bulgarian: **Fellowships,** 945. *See also* General programs; Language and linguistics

Language, Danish: **Scholarships,** 81. *See also* General programs; Language and linguistics

Language, English: **Scholarships,** 439, 529. *See also* General programs; Language and linguistics

Language, French: **Grants,** 1181. *See also* General programs; Language and linguistics

Language, Greek: **Grants,** 1182. *See also* General programs; Language and linguistics

Language, Macedonian: **Fellowships,** 945. *See also* General programs; Language and linguistics

Language, Portuguese: **Fellowships,** 748. *See also* General programs; Language and linguistics

Language, Romanian: **Fellowships,** 945. *See also* General programs; Language and linguistics

Language, Serbo–Croatian: **Fellowships,** 945. *See also* General programs; Language and linguistics

Language, Spanish: **Fellowships,** 748. *See also* General programs; Language and linguistics

Language, Yugoslavian. *See* Language, Macedonian; Language, Serbo–Croatian

Latin American history. *See* History, Latin American

Latin American studies: **Grants,** 1038. *See also* General programs; Humanities

Law enforcement. *See* Criminal justice

Law, general: **Scholarships,** 98, 162, 239, 580, 625; **Fellowships,** 672, 706, 709, 716, 724–725, 748, 751, 756, 778, 782, 797, 801–802, 821, 834, 845, 954, 961, 967, 976; **Grants,** 1033, 1037, 1050, 1056, 1084, 1127, 1207, 1244, 1273–1275; **Awards,** 1398, 1404, 1416; **Internships,** 1435, 1446, 1467, 1471, 1493, 1508. *See also* Criminal justice; General programs; Social sciences; names of legal specialties

Lawyers. *See* Law, general

Leadership: **Scholarships,** 136, 539; **Fellowships,** 747. *See also* General programs; Management

Legal assistants. *See* Paralegal studies

Legal studies and services. *See* Law, general

Lesbianism. *See* Homosexuality

Librarians. *See* Libraries and librarianship

Libraries and librarianship: **Fellowships,** 781, 788; **Grants,** 1170; **Awards,** 1321, 1358, 1424–1425; **Internships,** 1468. *See also* General programs; Information science; Social sciences

Libraries and librarianship, school: **Scholarships,** 421. *See also* General programs; Libraries and librarianship

Life insurance. *See* Actuarial sciences

Life sciences. *See* Biological sciences

Linguistics. *See* Language and linguistics

Literature: **Scholarships,** 330, 439, 508; **Fellowships,** 764, 850; **Grants,** 1037, 1056, 1084, 1127, 1171, 1207; **Awards,** 1322. *See also* General programs; Humanities; Writers and writing; specific types of literature

Literature, American: **Awards,** 1344, 1347, 1422; **Internships,** 1468. *See also* American studies; General programs; Literature

Literature, Asian: **Grants,** 1142. *See also* Asian studies; General programs; Literature

Literature, Danish: **Scholarships,** 81. *See also* General programs; Literature

Literature, English: **Scholarships,** 529; **Awards,** 1394. *See also* General programs; Literature

Literature, French: **Grants,** 1181. *See also* General programs; Literature

Literature, German: **Awards,** 1364. *See also* General programs; Literature

Literature, Greek: **Grants,** 1182. *See also* General programs; Literature

Logistics: **Scholarships,** 325, 378, 494, 530–531, 651; **Fellowships,** 796, 861, 913, 987. *See also* General programs; Transportation


Macedonian language. *See* Language, Macedonian

Magazines. *See* Journalism; Literature

Management: **Scholarships,** 90, 129, 147, 160, 207, 501, 576, 629; **Fellowships,** 696, 713, 736, 750, 876, 918, 957, 977–978; **Grants,** 1244; **Internships,** 1484, 1499–1500. *See also* General programs; Social sciences

Manufacturing engineering. *See* Engineering, manufacturing

Marine sciences: **Scholarships,** 157; **Fellowships,** 746, 871; **Grants,** 1233; **Awards,** 1314. *See also* General programs; Sciences; names of specific marine sciences

Marketing: **Scholarships,** 72, 160, 293, 340, 398, 450, 495, 607, 643; **Fellowships,** 890, 914; **Internships,** 1453, 1475, 1499. *See also* General programs; Public relations; Sales

Marriage. *See* Family relations

Mass communications. *See* Communications

Materials engineering. *See* Engineering, materials

Materials sciences: **Scholarships,** 381, 456; **Fellowships,** 793, 862, 871–873, 892–893, 952; **Grants,** 1059–1061, 1200, 1205, 1215; **Internships,** 1434, 1451, 1466, 1481, 1485. *See also* General programs; Physical sciences

Mathematics: **Scholarships,** 62, 126, 210, 216, 253, 261, 307, 355, 367, 381, 394, 419, 425, 436, 440, 443, 455–457, 469, 504, 528, 546, 566, 592, 600, 609, 631; **Fellowships,** 700, 721, 730, 732, 783, 793, 862, 864, 866, 872–873, 881, 884, 886, 889, 892–894, 916, 920, 934, 942, 944, 962, 972, 979; **Loans,** 1017; **Grants,** 1059–1061, 1069, 1080, 1088, 1116–1118, 1149–1151, 1169, 1172, 1184–1186, 1190, 1197–1200, 1202–1203, 1209, 1213–1215, 1227, 1230–1232, 1235–1236, 1240, 1246–1247, 1262, 1269, 1271; **Awards,** 1288, 1320, 1395–1396; **Internships,** 1429, 1434, 1440, 1442, 1472, 1476, 1479, 1481, 1497. *See also* Computer sciences; General programs; Physical sciences; Statistics

Measurement. *See* Testing

Mechanical engineering. *See* Engineering, mechanical

Media. *See* Broadcasting; Communications; names of specific media

Media specialists. *See* Libraries and librarianship; Libraries and librarianship, school

Medical journalism. *See* Science reporting

Medical sciences: **Scholarships,** 98, 136, 166, 178, 257, 316, 353, 381, 452, 511, 521, 539, 574, 625, 631; **Fellowships,** 666, 676, 709, 716, 752, 754, 759–760, 765, 767, 777–778, 803, 811, 835, 839, 844, 862–863, 879, 888, 924, 926, 928, 930, 941, 952, 955, 969, 979; **Loans,** 1013; **Grants,** 1041–1045, 1059–1061, 1086, 1125, 1139, 1146, 1176, 1189, 1228, 1234, 1238, 1256, 1272–1274; **Awards,** 1295, 1308, 1332, 1360, 1363; **Internships,** 1434, 1442, 1488, 1490. *See also* General programs; Health and health care; Sciences; names of specific diseases; names of medical specialties

Medical technology: **Scholarships,** 380. *See also* General programs; Medical sciences; Technology

Mental health nurses and nursing. *See* Nurses and nursing, psychiatry/mental health

Merchandising. *See* Sales

Metallurgical engineering. *See* Engineering, metallurgical

Metallurgy: **Scholarships,** 643; **Internships,** 1466. *See also* Engineering, metallurgical; General programs; Sciences

Meteorology: **Scholarships,** 32, 60, 87, 185, 324, 341, 381, 436, 548, 610; **Fellowships,** 793, 810, 862, 886, 946; **Grants,** 1054. *See also* Atmospheric sciences; General programs

Microcomputers. *See* Computer sciences

Microscopy. *See* Medical technology

Middle Eastern studies: **Grants,** 1038, 1121. *See also* General programs; Humanities

Midwifery. *See* Nurses and nursing, midwifery

Military affairs: **Grants,** 1196; **Awards,** 1381, 1389. *See also* General programs

Military law: **Internships,** 1435. *See also* General programs; Law, general

Mining engineering. *See* Engineering, mining

# Calendar Index

Since most funding programs have specific deadline dates, some may have already closed by the time you begin to look for money. You can use the Calendar Index to identify which programs are still open. To do that, go to the type of program (scholarships, fellowships, etc.) that interests you, think about when you'll be able to complete your application forms, go to the appropriate months, jot down the entry numbers listed there, and use those numbers to find the program descriptions in the directory. Keep in mind that the numbers cited here refer to program entry numbers, not to page numbers in the book. Note: not all sponsoring organizations supplied deadline information to us, so not all programs are listed in this index.

## Scholarships:

*January:* 2–3, 7, 9, 22–25, 43, 59, 62, 70, 74, 79, 81, 86, 112, 117, 123, 133, 143–144, 163, 165, 169, 173, 175–176, 179, 181, 184, 197, 204, 209, 212, 222–223, 225, 230–231, 234, 236, 238, 241, 250, 262, 264, 270, 274, 278, 282, 285, 291–295, 302, 311, 314, 318, 321, 328–330, 340, 343, 352, 358, 360, 366–367, 370, 382, 393, 395, 415, 420, 438–439, 443, 447, 450–451, 460, 469, 473–474, 479, 484–486, 488, 502, 507, 510, 513, 521, 537, 544, 546, 560, 562–563, 578, 583, 588–589, 594, 614–615, 640–641, 650, 654, 656

*February:* 10, 26–27, 32, 36–37, 40, 51, 53, 56, 68, 72, 82, 87, 92, 96, 102, 104, 107, 111, 116, 132, 141, 149–150, 155, 159, 161–162, 166, 170, 177–178, 185–186, 188, 193, 205, 210, 213, 219–220, 242–243, 251, 253, 255–256, 269, 273, 275–276, 281, 288, 297, 300, 304, 308–309, 317, 319, 323–324, 341, 345–346, 348, 351, 359, 368, 373, 398, 408, 412, 419, 421, 424, 426, 432, 446, 448, 456, 458, 463, 480, 482, 489–490, 504, 519–520, 524, 526, 529, 540–542, 548, 566, 573, 580, 586, 593, 595, 597, 599–600, 613, 617, 619, 625, 633, 636, 645–646, 649

*March:* 35, 44–45, 47–48, 64, 66, 71, 73, 88, 98–99, 105, 108–109, 115, 118, 121, 124, 126, 128, 130, 134, 139, 145, 152–153, 157, 160, 171, 180, 182, 191, 194, 198, 206, 217–218, 227–228, 232–233, 240, 246, 248, 257–258, 261, 271–272, 277, 283, 287, 289, 296, 306, 310, 312, 320, 332–333, 337, 344, 349, 357, 364–365, 372, 374, 380–381, 384, 400–401, 404–405, 407–409, 411, 414, 416, 425, 427, 434–435, 437, 440, 462, 467–468, 497–499, 509, 523, 532, 534–536, 547, 549–550, 552, 555–556, 559, 568, 574, 576, 590, 601, 605–608, 621–624, 631, 637–638, 657–658

*April:* 6, 8, 11–12, 21, 49–50, 52, 54–55, 57, 61, 65, 69, 75, 89, 93–95, 106, 110, 122, 125, 127, 129, 142, 151, 158, 168, 174, 183, 196, 211, 221, 226, 229, 239, 247, 259, 268, 279–280, 284, 286, 299, 303, 305, 315, 353–354, 362–363, 371, 376, 388, 402–403, 422, 433, 445, 453, 461, 470–471, 476, 481, 491, 496, 501, 506, 508, 512, 514, 525, 527, 543, 561, 569, 577, 592, 616, 627, 630, 632, 634, 643, 653, 655

*May:* 20, 41–42, 46, 60, 76–77, 80, 83–85, 97, 113–114, 120, 131, 136–138, 140, 164, 189, 200, 208, 215, 241, 244, 249, 263, 266–267, 313, 316, 322, 326, 350, 387, 406, 417, 431, 444, 452, 459, 466, 483, 493, 500, 505, 517, 522, 533, 539, 554, 575, 582, 585, 604, 626, 642, 647, 659

*June:* 18, 54, 58, 100, 154, 156, 167, 187, 265, 298, 338–339, 369, 392, 410, 418, 464–465, 472, 495, 503, 511, 516, 528, 538

*July:* 1, 54, 224, 235, 428, 640

*August:* 81, 123, 237, 355

*September:* 19, 91, 119, 579, 598

*October:* 15, 30, 63, 101, 252, 449, 455, 472, 494, 531, 564, 651

*November:* 4, 13–14, 29, 54, 67, 90, 135, 146–148, 203, 207, 260, 325, 342, 361, 378, 530, 551, 581, 596, 610, 628–629, 635, 644, 648

*December:* 172, 201, 335–336, 429, 457, 516, 565, 612

*Any time:* 16, 28, 31, 33, 199, 307, 347, 477–478, 515, 518, 558, 620, 652

## Fellowships:

*January:* 663–664, 668, 678–679, 689, 697, 700, 703, 711–712, 717, 723, 726, 730, 740, 743, 754, 758, 763, 767, 777–778, 780, 790, 793, 800, 803, 814, 817, 823, 825–827, 838–839, 850, 854, 856–858, 863, 867, 869, 872, 876, 887, 890–891, 906, 909, 916, 921, 929–930, 934, 942–945, 949, 959, 963, 972, 983–984, 986, 990–991

*February:* 669, 672, 680–681, 693, 696, 705–706, 708, 718, 722, 741, 745, 749, 751, 757, 759, 762, 765, 769, 771, 774, 781–782, 791, 808, 810, 813, 828, 830, 846–847, 849, 855, 871, 875, 880, 882, 892–893, 896, 902, 905, 908, 920, 926, 928, 932, 936, 946, 951–952, 962, 968, 973

*March:* 662, 688, 691, 704, 716, 731–732, 734, 742, 746, 748, 753, 784–785, 798, 801, 804–805, 812, 815–816, 829, 831, 836, 840, 842, 851, 859–860, 862, 866, 868, 878, 881, 888, 897, 937–940, 955, 957, 964, 966, 971, 975, 979–980, 992–993

*April:* 667, 670, 673, 676–677, 690, 692, 694–695, 702, 707, 710, 715, 720–721, 733, 736, 744, 747, 768, 775, 786–787, 792, 797, 811, 818, 820, 822, 833, 877, 879, 900–901, 904, 911, 918, 922, 931, 933, 935, 969–970, 988–989

## Loans:

## Grants:

## Awards:

## Internships: